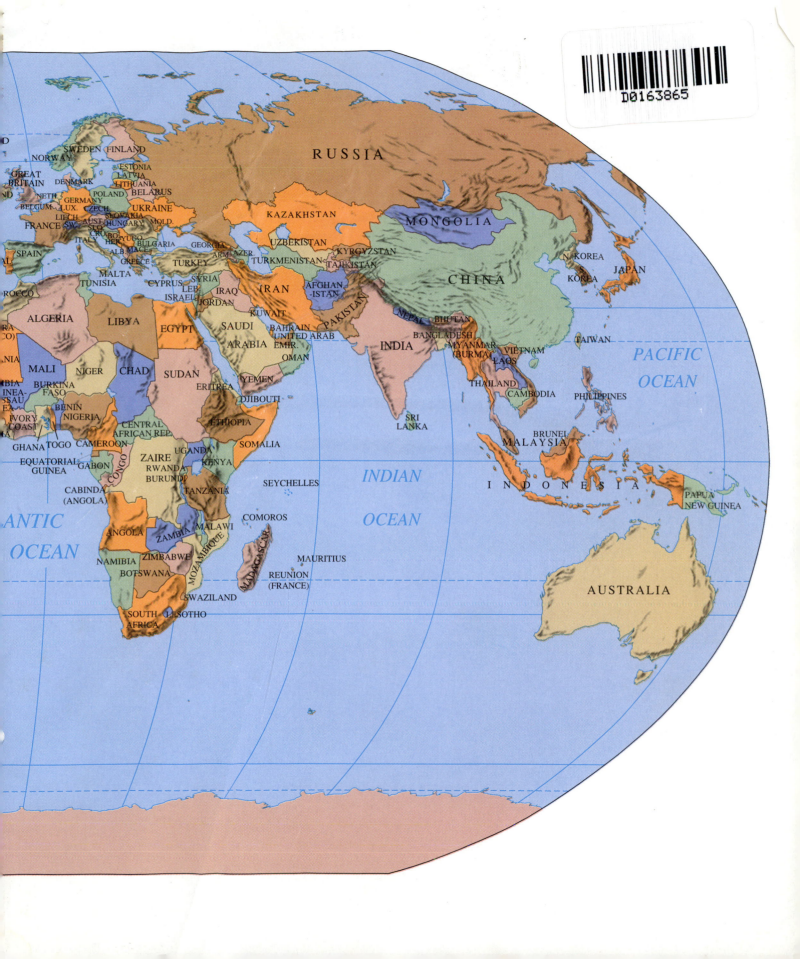

SECOND EDITION

WORLD HISTORY

VOLUME II: SINCE 1500

WILLIAM J. DUIKER

The Pennsylvania State University

JACKSON J. SPIELVOGEL

The Pennsylvania State University

WEST/WADSWORTH
I(T)P® an International Thomson Publishing company

Belmont, CA • Albany, NY • Bonn • Boston • Cincinnati • Detroit • Johannesburg • London • Los Angeles • Madrid
Melbourne • Mexico City • New York • Paris • Singapore • Tokyo • Toronto • Washington

History Editor   Clark Baxter
Senior Developmental Editor   Sharon Adams Poore
Editorial Assistant   Amy Guastello
Print Buyer   Barbara Britton
Marketing Manager   Jay Hu
Production Management   Heather Stratton/GTS Graphics
Composition and Color Separation   GTS Graphics
Maps   GeoSystems Global Corporation
Copy Editor   Patricia Lewis
Art and Photograph Research   Sarah Evertson/Image Quest
Text and Document Permissions Management   Lynn Reichel
Interior and Cover Design   Diane Beasley
Cover Art   The Ginza in downtown Tokyo (see Chapter 23).
Printer   World Color, Taunton

Art, Photograph, Document, and Map credits appear in the rear of the book.

Printed in the United States of America
2 3 4 5 6 7 8 9 10

For more information contact Wadsworth Publishing Company, 10 Davis Drive, Belmont, CA 94002, or
electronically at http://www.thomson.com/wadsworth.html

International Thomson Publishing Europe
Berkshire House 168-173
High Holborn
London, WC1V 7AA, England

International Thomson Editores
Campos Eliseos 385, Piso 7
Col. Polanco
11560 México D.F. México

Thomas Nelson Australia
102 Dodds Street
South Melbourne 3205
Victoria, Australia

International Thomson Publishing Asia
221 Henderson Road
#05-10 Henderson Building
Singapore 0315

Nelson Canada
1120 Birchmount Road
Scarborough, Ontario
Canada M1K 5G4

International Thomson Publishing Japan
Hirakawacho Kyowa Building, 3F
2-2-1 Hirakawacho
Chiyoda-ku, Tokyo 102, Japan

International Thomson Publishing GmbH
Königswinterer Strasse 118
53227 Bonn, Germany

International Thomson Publishing Africa
Building 19, Constantia Park
240 Old Pretoria Road
Halfway House, 1685 South Africa

ISBN 0-534-53119-9

About the Authors

William J. Duiker is Liberal Arts Professor Emeritus of East Asian studies at The Pennsylvania State University. A former U.S. diplomat with service in Taiwan, South Vietnam, and Washington, D.C., he received his doctorate in Far Eastern history from Georgetown University in 1968, where his dissertation dealt with the Chinese educator and reformer Cai Yuanpei. At Penn State, he has written widely on the history of Vietnam and modern China, including the widely acclaimed The Communist Road to Power in Vietnam *(revised edition, Westview Press, 1996), which was selected for a Choice Outstanding Academic Book Award in 1982–1983 and 1996–1997. Other recent books are* China and Vietnam: The Roots of Conflict *(Berkeley, 1987) and* Sacred War: Nationalism and Revolution in a Divided Vietnam *(McGraw-Hill, 1995). He is currently at work on a biography of the Vietnamese revolutionary Ho Chi Minh. While his research specialization is in the field of nationalism and Asian revolutions, his intellectual interests are considerably more diverse. He has traveled widely and has taught courses on the History of Communism and non-Western civilizations at Penn State. He is currently planning his fourth voyage around the world with the Semester at Sea Program.*

Jackson J. Spielvogel is associate professor of history at The Pennsylvania State University. He received his Ph.D. from The Ohio State University, where he specialized in Reformation history under Harold J. Grimm. His articles and reviews have appeared in such journals as Moreana, Journal of General Education, Catholic Historical Review, Archiv für Reformationsgeschichte, *and* American Historical Review. *He has also contributed chapters or articles to* The Social History of the Reformation, The Holy Roman Empire: A Dictionary Handbook, Simon Wiesenthal Center Annual of Holocaust Studies, *and* Utopian Studies. *His work has been supported by fellowships from the Fullbright Foundation and the Foundation for Reformation Research. At Penn State, he helped inaugurate the Western civilization courses as well as a popular course on Nazi Germany. His book* Hitler and Nazi Germany *was published in 1987 (third edition, 1996). He is the author of* Western Civilization, *published in 1991 (third edition, 1997). Professor Spielvogel has won five major university-wide teaching awards. During the year 1988–1989, he held the Penn State Teaching Fellowship, the university's most prestigious teaching award. In 1996, he won the Dean Arthur Ray Warnock Award for Outstanding Faculty Member, and in 1997, he became the first recipient of the Schreyer Institute's Student Choice Award for innovative and inspiring teaching.*

Contents

PART IV

Modern Patterns of World History (1800–1945)   727

CHAPTER 20

The Beginnings of Modernization: Industrialization and Nationalism, 1800–1870   732

CHAPTER 21

The Emergence of Mass Society in the Western World   776

CHAPTER 22

The High Tide of Imperialism   818

PART V

❖❖❖❖❖❖❖❖❖❖❖❖❖❖❖

Toward a Global Civilization? The World since 1945 989

CHAPTER 27

❖❖❖❖❖❖❖❖❖❖❖❖❖❖❖❖

In the Grip of the Cold War: The Breakdown of the Yalta System 992

CHAPTER 28

❖❖❖❖❖❖❖❖❖❖❖❖❖❖❖❖

Brave New World: Communism 1024

CHAPTER 29

❖❖❖❖❖❖❖❖❖❖❖❖❖❖❖❖

Europe and the Western Hemisphere since 1945 1066

CHAPTER 30

Challenges of Nation Building in Africa and the Middle East   1106

CHAPTER 31

Nationalism Triumphant: The Emergence of Independent States in South and Southeast Asia   1148

CHAPTER 32

Toward the Pacific Century: Japan and the Little Tigers   1186

Maps

Chronologies

Preface

For several million years after primates first appeared on the surface of the earth, human beings lived in small communities, seeking to survive by hunting, fishing, and foraging in a frequently hostile environment. Then suddenly, in the space of a few thousand years, there was an abrupt change of direction as human beings in a few widely scattered areas of the globe began to master the art of cultivating food crops. As food production increased, the population in those areas rose correspondingly, and people began to congregate in larger communities. Governments were formed to provide protection and other needed services to the local population. Cities appeared and became the focal point of cultural and religious development. Historians refer to this process as the beginnings of civilization.

For generations, historians in Europe and the United States have pointed to the rise of such civilizations as marking the origins of the modern world. Courses on Western civilization conventionally begin with a chapter or two on the emergence of advanced societies in Egypt and Mesopotamia and then proceed to ancient Greece and the Roman Empire. From Greece and Rome, the road leads directly to the rise of modern civilization in the West.

There is nothing inherently wrong with this approach. Important aspects of our world today can indeed be traced back to these early civilizations, and all human beings the world over owe a considerable debt to their achievements. But all too often this interpretation has been used to imply that the course of civilization has been linear in nature, leading directly from the emergence of agricultural societies in ancient Mesopotamia to the rise of advanced industrial societies in Europe and North America. Until recently, most courses on world history taught in the United States routinely focused almost exclusively on the rise of the West, with only a passing glance at other parts of the world, such as Africa, India, and East Asia. The contributions made by those societies to the culture and technology of our own time were often passed over in silence.

Several reasons have been advanced to justify this approach. Some have argued that students simply are not interested in what is unfamiliar to them. Others have said that it is more important that young minds understand the roots of their own heritage than that of peoples elsewhere in the world. In many cases, however, the motivation for this Eurocentric approach has been the belief that since the time of Socrates and Aristotle Western civilization has been the sole driving force in the evolution of human society.

Such an interpretation, however, represents a serious distortion of the process. During most of the course of human history, the most advanced civilizations have been not in the West, but in East Asia or the Middle East. A relatively brief period of European dominance culminated with the era of imperialism in the late nineteenth century, when the political, military, and economic power of the advanced nations of the West spanned the globe. During recent generations, however, that dominance has gradually eroded, partly as the result of changes taking place within Western societies and partly because new centers of development are emerging elsewhere on the globe—notably in East Asia, where the growing economic strength of Japan and many of its neighbors has led to the now familiar prediction that the twenty-first century will be known as the Pacific Century.

World history, then, is not simply a chronicle of the rise of the West to global dominance, nor is it a celebration of the superiority of the civilization of Europe and the United States over other parts of the world. The history of the world has been a complex process in which many branches of the human community have taken an active part, and the dominance of any one area of the world has been a temporary rather than a permanent phenomenon. It will be our purpose in this book to present a balanced picture of this story, with all respect for the richness and diversity of the tapestry of the human experience. Due attention must be paid to the rise of the West, of course, since that has been the most dominant aspect of world history in recent centuries. But the contributions made by other peoples must be given adequate consideration as well, not only in the period prior to 1500 when the major centers of civilization were located in Asia, but also in our own day, where a multipolar picture of development is clearly beginning to emerge.

Anyone who wishes to teach or write about world history must decide whether to present the topic as an integrated whole or as a collection of different cultures. The world that we live in today, of course, is in many respects an interdependent one in terms of economics as well as culture and communications, a reality that is often expressed by the phrase "global village." The convergence of peoples across the surface of the earth into an integrated world system began in early times and intensified after the rise of capitalism in the early modern era. In growing recognition of this trend, historians trained in global history, as well as instructors in the growing number of world history courses, have now begun to speak and write of a "global approach" that turns attention away from the study of individual civilizations and focuses instead on the "big picture" or, as the world historian Fernand Braudel termed it, interpreting world history as a river with no banks.

On the whole, this development is to be welcomed as a means of bringing the common elements of the evolution of human society to our attention. But there is a risk involved in this approach. For the vast majority of their time on earth, human beings have lived in partial or virtually total isolation from each other. Differences in climate, location, and geographical features have created human societies very different from each other in culture and historical experience. Only in relatively recent times—the commonly accepted date has long been the beginning of the age of European exploration at the end of the fifteenth century, but some would now push it back to the era of the Mongol empire or even further—have cultural interchanges begun to create a common "world system," in which events taking place in one part of the world are rapidly transmitted throughout the globe, often with momentous consequences. In recent generations, of course, the process of global interdependence has been proceeding even more rapidly. Nevertheless, even now the process is by no means complete, as ethnic and regional differences continue to exist and to shape the course of world history. The tenacity of these differences and sensitivities is reflected not only in the rise of internecine conflicts in such divergent areas as Africa, India, and Eastern Europe, but also in the emergence in recent years of such regional organizations as the Organization of African Unity, the Association for the Southeast Asian Nations, and the European Economic Community. Polit-

ical leaders in various parts of the world speak routinely of "Arab unity," the "African road to socialism," and the "Confucian path to economic development."

The second problem is a practical one. College students today are all too often not well informed about the distinctive character of civilizations such as China and India and, without sufficient exposure to the historical evolution of such societies, will assume all too readily that the peoples in these countries have had historical experiences similar to ours and will respond to various stimuli in a similar fashion to those living in Western Europe or the United States. If it is a mistake to ignore those forces that link us together, it is equally a mistake to underestimate those factors that continue to divide us and to differentiate us into a world of diverse peoples.

Our response to this challenge has been to adopt a global approach to world history while at the same time attempting to do justice to the distinctive character and development of individual civilizations and regions of the world. The presentation of individual cultures will be especially important in Parts I and II, which cover a time when it is generally agreed that the process of global integration was not yet far advanced. Later chapters will begin to adopt a more comparative and thematic approach, in deference to the greater number of connections that have been established among the world's peoples since the fifteenth and sixteenth centuries. Part V will consist of a series of chapters that will center on individual regions of the world while at the same time focusing on common problems related to the Cold War and the rise of global problems such as overproduction and environmental pollution. Moreover, sections entitled "Reflections" at the close of the five major parts of the book will attempt to link events together in a broad comparative and global framework.

We have sought balance in another way as well. Many textbooks tend to simplify the content of history courses by emphasizing an intellectual or political perspective or, most recently, a social perspective, often at the expense of sufficient details in a chronological framework. This approach is confusing to students whose high school social studies programs have often neglected a systematic study of world history. We have attempted to write a well-balanced work in which political, economic, social, religious, intellectual, cultural, and military history have been integrated into a chronologically ordered synthesis.

To enliven the past and let readers see for themselves the materials that historians use to create their pictures of the past, we have included primary sources (boxed documents) in each chapter that are keyed to the discussion in the text. The documents include examples of the religious, artistic, intellectual, social, economic, and political aspects of life in different societies and reveal in a vivid fashion what civilization meant to the individual men and women who shaped it by their actions.

Each chapter has a lengthy introduction and conclusion to help maintain the continuity of the narrative and to provide a synthesis of important themes. Time lines enable students to see the major developments of an era at a glance, while the more detailed chronologies reinforce the events discussed in the text. An annotated bibliography at the end of each chapter reviews the most recent literature on each period and also gives references to some of the older, "classic" works in each field. Extensive maps and illustrations serve to deepen the reader's understanding of the text. To facilitate comprehension of cultural movements, illustrations of artistic works discussed in the text are placed next to the discussions.

As preparation for revision of *World History*, we reexamined the entire book and analyzed the comments and reviews of many colleagues who have found the book to be a useful instrument for introducing their students to world history. In making revisions for the second edition, we sought to build upon the strengths of the first edition and, above all, to maintain the balance, synthesis, and narrative qualities that characterized the first edition. To keep up with the ever-growing body of historical scholarship, new or revised material has been added throughout the book. Throughout the revising process, we also worked to craft a book that we hope students will continue to find very readable. Headings and subheadings in every chapter were revised to give students a more vivid introduction to the content of the chapters. Moreover, we added anecdotes to the introductions in order to convey more dramatically the major theme or themes of each chapter.

To provide a more logical arrangement of the material, we also made some major revisions of the book. The material in the Prologue was incorporated into a revised Chapter 1. Part II was extensively reordered and revised. The chapter on "The New World" was moved to the beginning of Part II, while the material in Chapters 10, 12, and 13 was reorganized into two new chapters (Chapter 9, "The Expansion of Civilization in Southern Asia," and Chapter 11, "The East Asian Rimlands: Early Japan, Korea, and Vietnam"). Moreover, the two chapters on European civilization in the Middle Ages (8 and 9) have been condensed and reorganized to form a new Chapter 12, "The Making of Europe and the World of the Byzantine Empire, 500–1300." In Part IV, a new chapter, Chapter 25: "Nationalism, Revolution, and Dictatorship: Africa, Asia, and Latin America from 1919 to 1939," has been

added. In Part V, Chapters 28 and 30 were reorganized and rewritten to form two new thematic chapters: Chapter 27, "In the Grip of the Cold War: The Breakdown of the Yalta System," and Chapter 28, "Brave New World: Communism." Moreover, all "Suggestions for Further Reading" at the end of each chapter were updated, and new illustrations were added to every chapter.

The enthusiastic response to the primary sources (boxed documents) led us to evaluate the content of each document carefully and add a number of new documents throughout the text. For the second edition, the maps have been revised where needed and, as in the first edition, are carefully keyed to all text references. New maps have also been added.

Because courses in world history at American and Canadian colleges and universities follow different chronological divisions, a one-volume comprehensive edition and a two-volume edition of this text are being made available to fit the needs of instructors. Teaching and learning ancillaries include:

Instructor's Manual/Test Bank. Contains chapter outlines, suggestions for lecture topics, essay and identification questions, discussion questions for the primary documents, and suggested films and musical selections. The textbook contains approximately 2,000 test questions.

Instructor's Manual on Disk. Contains the Instructor's Manual portion of the IM/TB Windows.

ESA Computerized Testing. The test bank in a computerized format is available in both Windows and Macintosh formats.

Full Color Transparency Acetates. Contains all the maps in the text as well as commentary on each map. The commentary, by James Harrison of Siena College, includes not only the text caption, but also additional points of interest about the map, what it shows, and its relevance to the study of world history. Possible discussion questions for student involvement are included. Available to qualified adopters.

Study Guide. Contains key terms, critical thinking questions, multiple choice questions, questions to help analyze primary documents, and chapter summaries.

Study Tips for World History. New to this edition, chapter outlines, study questions, and key terms and their pronunciations.

Document Exercise Workbooks. Prepared by Donna Van Raaphorst of Cuyahoga Community College. It provide a collection of exercises based on primary sources in history. Available in two volumes.

Map Exercise Workbooks. Prepared by Cynthia Kosso of Northern Arizona University, these feature approximately thirty map exercises in each volume. Designed to help students feel comfortable with maps by having them work with different kinds of maps and identify places.

World History Reader. New to this edition. Contains additional documents not found in the text and longer excerpts of documents that are included in the text.

Slide Set. A set of 200 slides, including 100 maps from the text and 100 images from the text.

PowerPoint. Acetate map images from the text in the PowerPoint format. Available in both Windows and Macintosh formats.

World History Videodiscs. Short, focused video clips, photos, artwork, animations, music, and dramatic readings are used to bring life to historical topics and events that are most difficult for students to appreciate from a textbook alone. For example, students will experience the grandeur of Versailles and the defeat felt by a German soldier at Stalingrad.

Video Library.

World History CD-ROM. For Windows. Eighteen interactive journeys.

Internet Guide for History. Prepared by Daniel Kurland and John Soares. Section One introduces students to the Internet, including tips for searching on the Web. Section Two introduces students to how history research can be done and lists URL sites by topic.

Web Page.

Acknowledgments

Both authors gratefully acknowledge that without the generosity of many others, this project could not have been completed. William Duiker would like to thank Kumkum Chatterjee and On-cho Ng for their helpful comments about unfamiliar issues related to the history of India and premodern China. His longtime colleague Cyril Griffith, now deceased, was a cherished friend and a constant source of information about modern Africa. Art Goldschmidt has been of invaluable assistance in reading several chapters of the manuscript, as well as in unravelling many of the mysteries of Middle Eastern civilization. Finally, he remains profoundly grateful to his wife, Yvonne V. Duiker, Ph.D. She has not only given her usual measure of love and support when this appeared to be an insuperable task, but she has also contributed her own time and expertise to enrich the sections on art and literature, thereby adding life and sparkle

to this, as well as the first, edition of the book. To her, and to his daughters Laura and Claire, he will be forever thankful for bringing joy to his life.

Jackson Spielvogel would like to thank Art Goldschmidt, David Redles, and Christine Colin for their time and ideas and, above all, his family for their support. The gifts of love, laughter, and patience from his daughters, Jennifer and Kathryn, his sons, Eric and Christian, and his daughters-in-law, Liz and Michele, were invaluable. Diane, his wife and best friend, provided him with editorial assistance, wise counsel, and the loving support that made a project of this magnitude possible.

Thanks to West/Wadsworth's comprehensive review process, many historians were asked to evaluate our manuscript. We are grateful to the following for the innumerable suggestions that have greatly improved our work:

Charles F. Ames, Jr.
Salem State College

Nancy Anderson
Loyola University

Gloria M. Aronson
Normandale College

Charlotte Beahan
Murray State University

Doris Bergen
University of Vermont

Martin Berger
Youngstown State University

Deborah Biffton
University of Wisconsin/LaCrosse

Patricia J. Bradley
Auburn University at Montgomery

Dewey Browder
Austin Peay State University

Antonio Calabria
University of Texas at San Antonio

Alice-Catherine Carls
University of Tennessee-Martin

Yuan Ling Chao
Middle Tennessee State University

Mark W. Chavalas
University of Wisconsin

Hugh Clark
Ursinus College

Joan Coffey
Sam Houston State University

John Davis
Radford University

Ross Dunn
San Diego State University

Lane Earn
University of Wisconsin-Oshkosh

Edward L. Farmer
University of Minnesota

William W. Farris
University of Tennessee

Ronald Fritze
Lamar University

Joe Fuhrmann
Murray State University

Robert Gerlich
Loyola University

Marc J. Gilbert
North Georgia College

William J. Gilmore-Lehne
Richard Stockton College of New Jersey

Richard M. Golden
University of North Texas

Joseph M. Gowaskie
Rider College

Don Gustafson
Augsburg College

Deanna Haney
Lansing Community College

Ed Haynes
Winthrop College

Linda Kerr
University of Alberta at Edmonton

Zoltan Kramar
Central Washington University

Craig A. Lockard
University of Wisconsin-Green Bay

George Longenecker
Norwich University

Robert Luczak
Vincennes University

Patrick Manning
Northeastern University

Dolores Nason McBroome
Humboldt State University

John McDonald
Northern Essex Community College

Andrea McElderry
University of Louisville

Jeff McEwen
Chattanooga State Technical Community College

John A. Mears
Southern Methodist University

Marc A. Meyer
Berry College

Stephen S. Michot
Mississippi County Community College

John Ashby Morton
Benedict College

William H. Mulligan
Murray State University

Henry A. Myers
James Madison University

Sandy Norman
Florida Atlantic University

Patrick M. O'Neill
Broome Community College

Norman G. Raiford
Greenville Technical College

Jane Rausch
University of Massachusetts-Amherst

Dianna K. Rhyan
Columbus State Community College

Merle Rife
Indiana University of Pennsylvania

Patrice C. Ross
Columbus State Coimmunity College

John Rossi
LaSalle University

Keith Sandiford
University of Manitoba

Elizabeth Sarkinnen
Mt. Hood Community College

Bill Schell
Murray State University

Robert M. Seltzer
Hunter College

David Shriver
Cuyahoga Community College

Amos E. Simpson
University of Southwestern Louisiana

Wendy Singer
Kenyon College

Marvin Slind
Washington State University

Paul Smith
Washington State University

John Snetsinger
California Polytechnic State University

George Stow
LaSalle University

Patrick Tabor
Chemeketa Community College

Tom Taylor
Seattle University

John G. Tuthill
University of Guam

Joanne Van Horn
Fairmont State College

Pat Weber
University of Texas-El Paso

Douglas L. Wheeler
University of New Hampshire

David L. White
Appalachian State University

Elmira B. Wicker
Southern University-Baton Rouge

Glee Wilson
Kent State University

Harry Zee
Cumberland County College

The authors are truly grateful to the people who have helped us to produce this book. We especially want to thank Clark Baxter, whose faith in our ability to do this project was inspiring. Hal Humphrey, Production Services Coordinator at West/Wadsworth, was both patient and thoughtful as he guided us through the process of revision for the second edition of our book. Heather Stratton of GTS Graphics was as cooperative and cheerful as she was competent in matters of production. As usual, Pat Lewis was an outstanding copy editor. Lynn Reichel and Sarah Evertson provided valuable assistance in obtaining permissions for the boxed documents and illustrations.

A Note to Students about Languages and the Dating of Time

One of the most difficult challenges in studying world history is coming to grips with the multitude of names, words, and phrases in unfamiliar languages. Unfortunately, this problem has no easy solution. We have tried to alleviate the difficulty, where possible, by providing an English-language translation of foreign words or phrases. The issue is especially complicated in the case of Chinese, since two separate systems are commonly used to transliterate the spoken Chinese language into the Roman alphabet. The Wade-Giles system, invented in the nineteenth century, was the most frequently used until recent years, when the pinyin system was adopted by the People's Republic of China as its own official form of transliteration. We have opted to use the latter, since it appears to be gaining acceptance in the United States, but the initial use of a Chinese word is accompanied by its Wade-Giles equivalent in parentheses for the benefit of those who may encounter the term in their outside reading.

In our examination of world history, we need also to be aware of the dating of time. In recording the past, historians try to determine the exact time when events occurred. World War II in Europe, for example, began on September 1, 1939, when Adolf Hitler sent German troops into Poland, and ended on May 7, 1945, when Germany surrendered. By using dates, historians can place events in order and try to determine the development of patterns over periods of time.

If someone asked you when you were born, you would reply with a number, such as 1979. In the United States, we would all accept that number without question, because it is part of the dating system followed in the Western world (Europe and the Western Hemisphere). In this system, events are dated by counting backward or forward from the birth of Christ (assumed to be the year 1). An event that took place 400 years before the birth of Christ would most commonly be dated 400 B.C. (before Christ). Dates after the birth of Christ are labeled as A.D. These letters stand for the Latin words *anno domini,* which mean "in the year of the Lord" (or the year of the birth of Christ). Thus an event that took place 250 years after the birth of Christ is written A.D. 250, or in the year of the Lord 250. It can also be written as 250, just as you would not give your birth year as A.D. 1979, but simply 1979.

Some historians now prefer to use the abbreviations B.C.E. ("before the common era") and C.E. ("common era") instead of B.C. and A.D. This is especially true of world historians who prefer to use symbols that are not so Western or Christian oriented. The dates, of course, remain the same. Thus, 1950 B.C.E. and 1950 B.C. would be the same year, as would A.D. 40 and 40 C.E. In keeping with the current usage by many world historians, this book will use the terms B.C.E. and C.E.

Historians also make use of other terms to refer to time. A decade is 10 years; a century is 100 years; and a millennium is 1,000 years. The phrase fourth century B.C.E. refers to the fourth period of 100 years counting backward from 1, the assumed date of the birth of Christ. Since the first century B.C.E. would be the years 100 B.C.E. to 1 B.C.E., the fourth century B.C.E. would be the years 400 B.C.E. to 301 B.C.E. We could say, then, that an event in 350 B.C.E. took place in the fourth century B.C.E.

The phrase fourth century C.E. refers to the fourth period of 100 years after the birth of Christ. Since the first period of 100 years would be the years 1 to 100, the fourth period or fourth century would be the years 301 to 400. We could say, then, for example, that an event in 350 took place in the fourth century. Likewise, the first millennium B.C.E. refers to the years 1000 B.C.E. to 1 B.C.E.; the second millennium C.E. refers to the years 1001 to 2000.

The dating of events can also vary from people to people. Most people in the Western world use the Western calendar, also known as the Gregorian calendar after Pope Gregory XIII who refined it in 1582. The Hebrew calendar, on the other hand, uses a different system in which the year one is the equivalent of the Western year 3760 B.C.E., considered by Jews to be the date of the creation of the world. Thus, the Western year 2000 will be the year 5760 on the Jewish calendar. The Islamic calendar begins year 1 on the day Muhammad fled Mecca, which is the year 622 on the Western calendar.

WORLD HISTORY

PART

III

The Emergence of New World
Patterns (1500–1800)

*I*n the centuries that followed the fall of the classical empires at the beginning of the common era, a number of forces were at work in human society. In India and China, new civilizations began to emerge on the ruins of the old. In the Middle East, the rise of Islam led to a sudden burst of energy in the region and the spread of Arab power into North Africa and the Indian subcontinent. A few centuries later, a similar explosion took place in Central Asia, leading to a steady exodus of nomadic peoples to neighboring areas and culminating in the Mongol conquests of the thirteenth century.

In the meantime, organized communities were beginning to emerge in new areas of the world—in Japan, in Southeast Asia, and in sub-Saharan Africa. In some cases, such civilizations appeared as the result of a diffusion of ideas and technology brought by trade or conquest. In other instances, these civilizations developed independently, as in the Americas. Even where cultural ideas were introduced from the outside, they were reshaped and redefined in their new surroundings, as emerging societies assimilated useful elements from older cultures while domesticating them for use in a different environment.

Beginning in the late fifteenth century, a new force entered the world scene in the form of a revived Europe. Western civilization, of course, had a long pedigree, tracing back to the rise of ancient Greek culture in the eastern Mediterranean in the second millennium B.C.E., but it had declined as an influential force after the fall of Rome in the fifth century C.E., except for the Byzantine Empire based in Constantinople. After the tenth century, however, new forces were at work under the seemingly placid surface of medieval society that led gradually to the emergence of a dynamic new European culture by the end of the fifteenth century.

European history in the early modern era (1500–1800) was marked

AFRICA

First Portuguese sugar planation at São Tomé

First boatload of African slaves to the New World

INDIA AND THE MIDDLE EAST

Vasco da Gama
arrives at Calicut

Babur seizes Delhi

Reign of Akbar

Reign of Suleyman the Magnificent

EAST AND SOUTHEAST ASIA

Portuguese seize Malacca

Tokugawa
Ieyasu seizes
power in Japan

Dutch
establish port
at Batavia

Founding of
Qing dynasty

EUROPE AND THE WESTERN HEMISPHERE

Protestant and Catholic Reformations

Wars of Religion

by an explosion of scientific knowledge and the appearance of a new secular ideology that emphasized the power of human beings to dominate nature and improve their material surroundings. The scientific and technological revolution that unfolded in the sixteenth and seventeenth centuries laid the basis for the Industrial Revolution at the end of the eighteenth century. After the breakdown of Christian unity in the Reformation era, Europeans engaged in a vigorous period of state building that resulted in the creation of independent monarchies in western and central Europe that formed the basis for a new European state system. At the end of the eighteenth century, a revolution in one of these states—France—resulted in the creation of a new form of loyalty—of citizens to their nation rather than their monarch—that laid the foundations for the nation-state system that exists in Europe today. It is not without reason that the period from 1500 to 1800 is identified as the seedbed of modern Europe.

The rise of early modern Europe had an immediate as well as a long-term impact on the rest of the world. The first stage began with the discovery of the Americas by Christopher Columbus in 1492 and the equally important voyages of Vasco da Gama and Ferdinand Magellan into the Indian and Pacific Oceans. These voyages and those that followed—collectively known as the Age of Discovery or Age of Exploration—not only injected European seapower into new areas of the world, but also vastly extended the maritime trade network until for

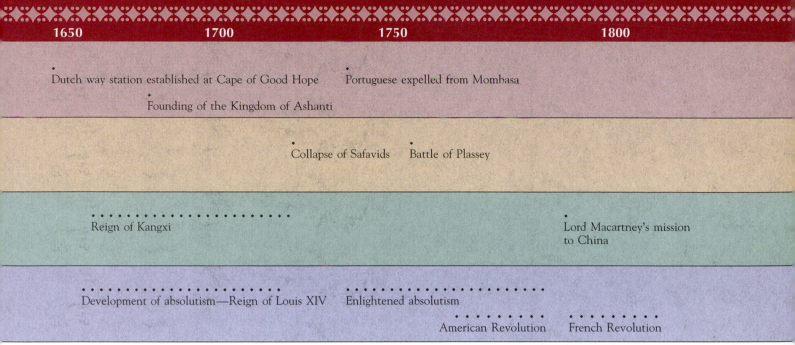

Dutch way station established at Cape of Good Hope   Portuguese expelled from Mombasa

Founding of the Kingdom of Ashanti

Collapse of Safavids   Battle of Plassey

Reign of Kangxi   Lord Macartney's mission to China

Development of absolutism—Reign of Louis XIV   Enlightened absolutism

American Revolution   French Revolution

the first time it literally encircled the globe.

The voyages of Columbus, Magellan, and Vasco da Gama were only the beginning. Soon several other European nations joined the hunt, and by the eighteenth century it was the British, the French, and the Dutch, not the Portuguese and the Spanish, who dominated the sea-lanes of the world. Indian and Arab trading ships still roamed the seas, but the scope of their activities had been significantly restricted. Some historians have labeled the period the beginning of an era of European dominance.

The Age of Exploration led to a vast expansion of world trade. Spices and other tropical products, formerly carried in Arab ships, now traveled in European ships to the markets of the Mediterranean and the Atlantic. In return, European manufactures and textile goods flowed back to the ports of Africa and Asia. In the meantime, new patterns of trade developed across the Atlantic and Pacific Oceans, as European manufactured goods and slaves were shipped to the Americas in return for sugar and other food products, as well as precious metals from the mines of Mexico and Peru. New crops from the Americas, such as corn, potatoes, sweet potatoes, and manioc, entered the world market and changed eating habits and social patterns as far away as China. Tobacco from the New World and coffee and tea from the Orient became the new craze in affluent circles in Europe and the Middle East.

But the impact of this commercial revolution was by no means universally beneficial to those involved. The subjugation of the Americas by the Spanish and the Portuguese, a direct product of the voyages of Hernán Cortés and Francisco Pizarro in the early sixteenth century, led to the destruction of sophisticated civilizations heretofore isolated from the rest of the world. The expansion of the African slave trade brought untold hardship to millions of victims and severely reduced the population in certain areas of Africa. New diseases, such as smallpox, measles, yellow fever, and malaria, were carried by ships from Africa and Europe to the Americas and decimated the populations there.

In general, the consequences of this commercial revolution operated to the advantage of the European countries. Profits from the spice trade, along with gold and silver from the Americas, flowed into state treasuries and the pockets of private traders in London, Paris, and Amsterdam. The wealth and power of Europe in general increased rapidly during this period. But the prevailing philosophy of mercantilism, based on the desire to maintain a favorable balance of trade by importing precious metals in exchange for the export of manufactured goods, brought its own problems in the form of price inflation. First to suffer was Spain, but price increases soon led to vast economic inequalities and widespread hardship in countries throughout Europe, while the massive importation of Mexican silver had similar effects in China and the Ottoman Empire.

Significant as it was, however, the emergence of Europe as a major player on the world stage was by no means the only important feature of this period. Although the introduction of European power and influence into the Indian Ocean had a visible impact on the major civilizations of the Middle East and southern Asia (especially in the Indian Ocean where the scope of Arab shipping in the spice trade was significantly restricted), the effects were less evident on the caravan routes through the Sahara and Central Asia, where patterns of trade were affected more by local conditions than by competitive activities elsewhere. Even in the Indian Ocean routes, Muslim shippers were often able to evade their better-armed European rivals and prevent them from taking over the trade route into the Red Sea.

More important, perhaps, an excessive emphasis on the expanding European civilization tends to overlook the fact that other areas of the world were realizing impressive achievements of their own. Two great new Islamic empires, the Ottomans in Turkey and the Safavids in Persia, arose in the Middle East, while a third—the Mughals—unified the Indian subcontinent for the first time in nearly two thousand years. The religion of Islam was now firmly established in Africa south of the Sahara and as far east as the Indonesian archipelago.

Another area of the world where the level of achievement was little affected by the European revival was East Asia. Portuguese merchants reached the coast of China in the early sixteenth century and landed on the islands of Japan a generation later. Merchants and missionaries from various European nations were active in both countries by the end of the century. But the ruling authorities in Peking and Kyoto, like their counterparts in the mainland states in Southeast Asia, became increasingly wary of the impact of European activities on their own societies, and by the eighteenth century, the Western presence in the region had markedly declined.

The first thrust of European expansion, then, significantly changed the shape of the world, but it did not firmly establish European dominance. China remained, in the eyes of many, the most advanced and sophisticated civilization on the face of the earth, and its achievements were imitated by its neighbors and admired by philosophers in far-off Europe. The era of Muslim dominance over the seas had come to an end, but Islam was still a force to be reckoned with. The bulk of Africa remained essentially outside the purview of European influence.

CHAPTER
14

New Encounters: The Creation of a World Market

When a local official asked the Portuguese explorer Vasco da Gama why he had come all the way to India from his homeland in Europe, the latter replied simply, "Christians and spices." Da Gama might have been more accurate if he had reversed the order of his objectives. As it turned out, God was probably much less important than gold and glory to Europeans like himself who participated in the age of exploration that was already underway. Still, da Gama's comments at Calicut were an accurate forecast of the future, for his voyage inaugurated an extended period of European expansion into Asia, led by merchant adventurers and missionaries, that lasted for several hundred years and had effects that are still felt today. Eventually, it resulted in a Western takeover of existing trade routes in the Indian Ocean and the establishment of colonies throughout Asia, Africa, and Latin America. So complete did Western dominance seem that some historians assumed that the peoples of the non-Western world were mere passive recipients in this process, absorbing and assimilating the advanced knowledge of the West and offering nothing in return. Historians writing about the period after 1500 often talked metaphorically about the "impact of the West" and the "response" of non-Western peoples.

That image of impact and response, however, is not an entirely accurate description of what took place between the end of the fifteenth and the end of the eighteenth century. Although European rule was firmly established in Latin America and the island regions of Southeast

1450	1500	1550	1600	1650	1700	1750

Bartolomeo Dias
sails around
southern tip of Africa

First boatload of slaves
to the New World

Ashanti kingdom
established in
West Africa

Portuguese
expelled from
Mombasa

Vasco da Gama arrives at Calicut in India

Dutch establish port
at Batavia

Battle at Plassey

Portuguese seize Malacca

Voyages of Columbus
to the Americas

Spanish conquest of Mexico

Pizarro's conquest
of the Incas

Plantation system develops in Brazil

Asia, traditional governments and institutions elsewhere remained largely intact and, in some areas, notably southern Asia and the Middle East, displayed considerable vitality. Moreover, although da Gama and his contemporaries are deservedly famous for their contribution to a new era of maritime commerce that circled the globe, they were not alone in extending the world trade network and transporting goods and ideas from one end of the earth to the other. Islam, too, was on the march, blazing new trails into Southeast Asia and across the Sahara to the civilizations that flourished along the banks of the Niger River. In this chapter we shall turn our attention to the stunning expansion in the scope and volume of commercial and cultural contacts that took place in the generations preceding and following da Gama's historic voyage to India, as well as to the factors that brought it about.

An Age of Exploration and Expansion

The voyage of Vasco da Gama has customarily been seen as a crucial step in the opening up of trade routes to the East. In the sense that the voyage was a harbinger of future European participation in the spice trade, this view undoubtedly has merit. In fact, however, as has been pointed out in earlier chapters, the Indian Ocean had been a busy thoroughfare for centuries. Ships from as far away as China had crossed it, sailing from the Indonesian islands to the coast of Africa in search of profit. The spice trade had been carried on by sea in the region since the days of the legendary Queen of Sheba, and Chinese junks had sailed to the area in search of cloves and nutmeg since the Tang dynasty.

Islam and the Spice Trade

By the fourteenth century, a growing percentage of the spice trade was being transported in Muslim ships sailing from ports in India or the Middle East. Muslims, either Arabs or Indian converts, had taken part in the Indian Ocean trade for centuries, and by the thirteenth century, Islam had established a presence in seaports on the islands of Sumatra and Java and was gradually moving inland.

The Venetian traveler Marco Polo was an early observer of this process, remarking in 1292 that Muslims were already engaging in missionary activity in the northern parts of the island of Sumatra. "This kingdom," he said, "is so much frequented by the Saracen merchants that they have converted the natives to the Law of Mahomet—I mean the towns-people only, for the hill people live for all the world like beasts, and eat human flesh, as well as other kinds of flesh, clean or unclean."[1]

But the major impact of Islam came in the early fifteenth century with the rise of the new sultanate at Malacca. Malacca owed its new prominence to its strategic location astride the strait of the same name as well as to the rapid growth of the spice trade itself (see the box on p. 498 for some comments on the strategic importance of

Malacca). Within a few years, Malacca had surpassed the old Hindu state of Majapahit on the island of Java and become the leading power in the region. Shortly thereafter, Majapahit itself was replaced by a new Islamic state called Mataram, and the remnants of the Hindu nobility retreated eastward to the island of Bali, which today is the only remaining preserve of Indian culture in the Indonesian archipelago (see Chapter 9).

The new state of Malacca maintained an element of continuity with Majapahit, for the founder of Malacca was married to a princess from Majapahit. Having established himself at Malacca, he converted to Islam and declared his allegiance to China in order to protect himself from the Thai, who were moving southward along the Malay peninsula. The sultan also faced rivals elsewhere, notably at Acheh, at the northern tip of Sumatra, and on the island of Java, where a number of small Muslim trading states had emerged in the wreckage of the collapsing Majapahit empire.

Unfortunately for these Muslim traders who had come to Southeast Asia for the spice trade, others would also covet that trade. Southeast Asia was on the verge of a new era in which outside forces would compete aggressively to exploit the region's vast riches.

A New Player Enters the Game

For almost a millennium, Catholic Europe had been confined to one area. Its one major attempt to expand beyond those frontiers, the crusades, had largely failed. Of course, Europe had never completely lost contact with the outside world: the goods of Asia and Africa made their way into medieval castles; the works of Muslim philosophers were read in medieval universities; and the Vikings in the ninth and tenth centuries had even made their way to the eastern fringes of North America. Nevertheless, Europe's contacts with non-European civilizations remained limited until the end of the fifteenth century, when Europeans embarked on a remarkable series of overseas journeys. What caused European seafarers to undertake such dangerous voyages to the ends of the earth?

Europeans had long been attracted to the East. In the Middle Ages, myths and legends of an exotic land of great riches and magic were widespread. Although Muslim control of Central Asia cut Europe off from the countries further east, the Mongol conquests in the thirteenth century had reopened the doors. The most famous medieval travelers to the East were the Polos of Venice. In 1271, Nicolò and Maffeo, merchants from Venice, accompanied by Nicolò's son Marco, undertook the lengthy journey to the court of the great Mongol ruler Khubilai Khan (see Chapter 10). As one of the great Khan's ambassadors, Marco traveled to Japan as well and did not return to Italy until 1295. An account of his experiences, the *Travels*, proved to be the most informative of all the descriptions of Asia by medieval European travelers. Others, like the Franciscan friar John Plano Carpini, had preceded the Polos, but in the fourteenth century the conquests of the Ottoman Turks and then the breakup of the Mongol Empire reduced Western traffic to the East. With the closing of the overland routes, a number of people in Europe became interested in the possibility of reaching Asia by sea to gain access to the spices and other precious items of the region. Christopher Columbus had a copy of Marco Polo's *Travels* in his possession when he began to envision his epoch-making voyage across the Atlantic Ocean.

An economic motive thus looms large in Renaissance European expansion. The rise of capitalism in Europe was undoubtedly a powerful spur to the process. Merchants, adventurers, and government officials had high hopes of finding precious metals and expanding the areas of trade, especially for the spices of the East. The latter continued to be transported to Europe via Arab middlemen but were outrageously expensive. Adventurous Europeans did not hesitate to express their desire to share in the wealth. As one Spanish conquistador explained, he and his kind went to the New World to "serve God and His Majesty, to give light to those who were in darkness, and to grow rich, as all men desire to do."[2]

This statement expresses another major reason for the overseas voyages—religious zeal. A crusading mentality was particularly strong in Portugal and Spain where the Muslims had largely been driven out in the Middle Ages. Contemporaries of Prince Henry the Navigator of Portugal (see the next section) said that he was motivated by "his great desire to make increase in the faith of our Lord Jesus Christ and to bring him all the souls that should be saved." The naval academy established by the prince to promote overseas exploration was subsidized in part by a militantly anti-Muslim Christian brotherhood. Although most scholars believe that the religious motive was secondary to economic considerations, it would be foolish to overlook the genuine desire on the part of both explorers and conquistadors, let alone missionaries, to convert the heathen to Christianity. Hernán Cortés, the conqueror of Mexico, asked his Spanish rulers if it was not their duty to ensure that the native Mexicans "are introduced into and instructed in the holy Catholic faith," and predicted that if "the devotion, trust and hope which they now have in their idols turned so as to repose with the divine power of the true God . . . they would work many miracles."[3] Spiritual and secular affairs were closely intertwined in the sixteenth century. No doubt, grandeur and glory as well as plain intellectual curiosity and a spirit of adventure also played some role in European expansion.

If "God, glory, and gold" were the primary motives, what made the voyages possible? First of all, the expansion of Europe was tied to the growth of centralized monarchies during the Renaissance. Although the degree of that centralization is still debated by historians, the reality is that Renaissance expansion was a state enterprise. By the second half of the fifteenth century, European monarchies had increased both their authority and their resources and were in a position to turn their energies beyond their borders. That meant the invasion of Italy for France, but for Portugal, a state not strong enough to pursue power in Europe, it meant going abroad. The Spanish scene was more complex, since the Spanish monarchy was strong enough by the sixteenth century to pursue power on both the continent and beyond.

At the same time, by the end of the fifteenth century, European states had a level of knowledge and technology that enabled them to achieve a regular series of voyages beyond Europe. Although the highly schematic and symbolic medieval maps were of little help to sailors, the *portolani,* or detailed charts made by medieval navigators and mathematicians in the thirteenth and fourteenth centuries, were more useful. With details on coastal contours, distances between ports, and compass readings, they proved of great value for voyages in European waters. But because the *portolani* were drawn on a flat scale and took no account of the curvature of the earth, they were of little use for longer overseas voyages. Only when seafarers began to venture beyond the coasts of Europe did they begin to accumulate information about the actual shape of the earth. By the end of the fifteenth century, cartography had developed to the point that Europeans possessed fairly accurate maps of the known world.

In addition, Europeans had developed remarkably seaworthy ships as well as new navigational techniques. European shipmakers had mastered the use of the axial rudder (an import from China) and had learned how to combine the use of lateen sails with a square rig. With these innovations, they could construct ships mobile enough to sail against the wind and engage in naval warfare and also large enough to mount heavy cannon and carry a substantial amount of goods over long distances. Previously, sailors had used a quadrant and their knowledge of the position of the Pole Star to ascertain their latitude. Below the equator, however, this technique was useless. Only with the assistance of new navigational aids

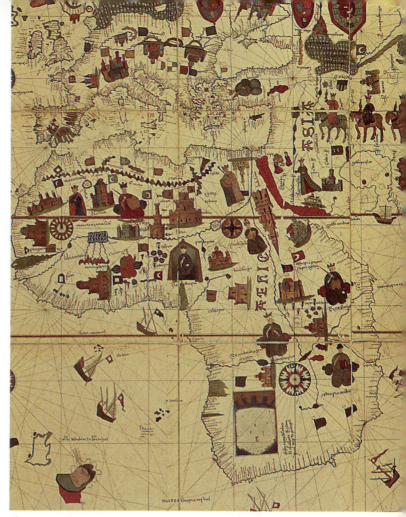

♦ **A Sixteenth-Century Map of Africa.** Advances in mapmaking also contributed to the European Age of Exploration. Here a section of a world map by the early sixteenth-century Spanish cartographer Juan de la Cosa shows the continent of Africa. Note the drawing of the legendary Prester John at the right.

such as the compass and the astrolabe were they able to explore the high seas with confidence.

A final spur to exploration was the growing knowledge of the wind patterns in the Atlantic Ocean. The first European fleets sailing southward along the coast of West Africa had found their efforts to return hindered by the strong winds that blew steadily from the north along the coast. By the late fifteenth century, however, sailors had learned to tack out into the ocean, where they were able to catch westerly winds in the vicinity of the Azores islands that brought them back to the coast of western Europe. Christopher Columbus used this technique in his voyages to the Americas while others relied on their new knowledge of the winds to round the continent of Africa in search of the Spice Islands.

The Development of a Portuguese Maritime Empire

Portugal took the lead in exploration when it began exploring the coast of Africa under the sponsorship of Prince Henry the Navigator (1394–1460). Prince Henry's motives were a blend of seeking a Christian kingdom as an ally against the Muslims, acquiring new trade opportunities for Portugal, and extending Christianity. In 1419, he founded a school for navigators on the southwestern coast of Portugal. Shortly thereafter, Portuguese fleets began probing southward along the western coast of Africa in search of gold, which had for centuries been carried northward from south of the Atlas Mountains in central Morocco. In 1441, Portuguese ships reached the Senegal River, just north of Cape Verde, and brought home a cargo of black Africans, most of whom were sold as slaves to wealthy buyers elsewhere in Europe. Within a few years, an estimated thousand slaves were shipped annually from the area back to Lisbon. Inadvertently, the Portuguese had found a way to circumvent the traditional trans-Sahara slave route from central Africa to the Mediterranean.

Having discovered how to return home from West Africa by tacking out into midocean to take advantage of the mid-Atlantic wind patterns, the Portuguese continued their progress southward. In 1471, they discovered a new source of gold along the southern coast of the hump of West Africa (an area that would henceforth be known to Europeans as the Gold Coast). A few years later, they established contact with the state of Bakongo, near the mouth of the Zaire (Congo) River in central Africa, and with the inland state of Benin, north of the Gold Coast. To facilitate trade in gold, ivory, and slaves (some of the latter were brought back to Lisbon and others were bartered to local merchants for gold), the Portuguese leased land from local rulers and built stone forts along the coast.

Hearing reports of a route to India around the southern tip of Africa, Portuguese sea captains continued their probing. In 1487, Bartolomeu Dias took advantage of westerly winds in the South Atlantic to round the Cape of Good Hope, but he feared a mutiny from his crew and returned home without continuing onward. Ten years later, a fleet under the command of Vasco da Gama rounded the cape and stopped at several ports controlled by Muslim merchants along the coast of East Africa, including Sofala, Kilwa, and Mombasa. Then, having located a Muslim navigator who was familiar with seafaring

◆ **Catching the Wind.** For centuries, seafarers in the Indian Ocean have used the triangular lateen sail as a means of catching the steady monsoon winds that blow alternatively from east and west in the winter and summer seasons. That type of rigging is still common for ships in the area, as this small craft in the waters off the East African island of Zanzibar demonstrates.

in the region, da Gama's fleet crossed the Arabian Sea and arrived off the port of Calicut on the southwestern coast of India, on May 18, 1498. The Portuguese crown had sponsored da Gama's voyage with the clear objective of destroying the Muslim monopoly over the spice trade, a monopoly that had been intensified by the Ottoman conquest of Constantinople in 1453 (see Chapter 16). Calicut was a major entrepôt on the long route from the Spice Islands to the Mediterranean Sea, but the ill-informed Europeans believed it was the source of the spices themselves. They had also heard there was a Christian community in the area, supposedly established by the apostle Thomas in the first century C.E.

On arriving in Calicut, da Gama announced to his surprised hosts that he had arrived in search of "Christians and spices." He did not find the first—although there is some evidence that Saint Thomas did proselytize in the area—but he did find the second. Although he lost two ships en route, da Gama's remaining vessels returned to Europe with their holds filled with ginger and cinnamon, a cargo that earned the investors a profit of several thousand percent. Such returns demonstrated how Muslim middlemen had profited from the spice trade. It is hardly surprising that da Gama's voyage was only the first of many.

For the next several years, Portuguese fleets returned annually to the area to destroy Arabic shipping and establish a monopoly in the spice trade. In 1509, a Portuguese armada defeated a combined fleet of Turkish and Indian ships off the coast of India and began to impose a blockade on the entrance to the Red Sea to cut off the flow of spices to Muslim rulers in Egypt and the Ottoman Empire. The following year, seeing the need for a land base in the area, Admiral Afonso de Albuquerque set up port facilities at Goa, on the western coast of India south of present-day Bombay. Goa henceforth became the headquarters for Portuguese operations throughout the entire area. Although Indian merchants were permitted to continue their maritime trading activities after purchasing naval passes (*cartaze*) from the Portuguese, raiding operations against Arab shippers continued, provoking the following brief report from an Arab source: "In this year the vessels of the Frank [the Portuguese] appeared at sea en route for India, Hurmuz [Hormuz], and those parts. They took about seven vessels, killing those on board and making some prisoner. This was their first action, may God curse them."[4]

The Portuguese now began to range more widely in search of the source of the spice trade. In 1511, Albuquerque sailed into the harbor of Malacca. Today a small, sleepy provincial market town and tourist center on the banks of a small muddy river, Malacca had been trans-

THE CARAVEL SANTA MARIA, IN WHICH COLUMBUS FIRST SAILED ACROSS THE ATLANTIC.

◆ **The Caravel, Workhorse of the Age of Exploration.**
Prior to the fifteenth century, most European ships were either small craft with lateen sails used in the Mediterranean, or slow, unwieldly square-rigged vessels operating in the North Atlantic. By the sixteenth century, European naval architects began to build ships that combined the maneuverability and speed offered by lateen sails with the carrying capacity and seaworthiness of the square-riggers. Shown here is a representation of Christopher Columbus' flagship *Santa Maria*, which took part in the first Spanish voyage across the Atlantic Ocean.

formed by its Muslim rulers into a major stopping point for the spice trade and the capital of the most important state in the region. In the early sixteenth century, a Portuguese observer had described its crucial position:

> Men cannot estimate the worth of Malacca, on account of its greatness and profit. Malacca is a city that was made for merchandise, fitter than any other in the world; the end of monsoons and the beginning of others. Malacca is surrounded and lies in the middle, and the trade and commerce between the different nations for a thousand leagues on every hand must come to Malacca.[5]

The Portuguese Conquest of Malacca

In 1511, a Portuguese fleet led by Afonso de Albuquerque attacked the Muslim sultanate at Malacca, on the west coast of the Malay peninsula. Occupation of the port gave the Portuguese control over the strategic Strait of Malacca and the route to the Spice Islands. In this passage, Albuquerque tells his men the reasons for the attack. Note that he sees control of Malacca as a way to reduce the power of the Muslim world. The relevance of economic wealth to military power continues to underlie conflicts among nations today.

The Commentaries of the Great Afonso de Albuquerque, Second Viceroy of India

Sirs, you will have no difficulty in remembering that when we decided upon attacking this city, it was with the determination of building a fortress within it, for so it appeared to all to be necessary, and after having captured it I was unwilling to let slip the possession of it, yet, because you all advised me to do so, I left it, and withdrew; but being ready, as you see, to put my hands upon it again once more, I learned that you had already changed your opinion. . . . Although there be many reasons which I could allege in favor of our taking this city and building a fortress therein to maintain possession of it, two only will I mention to you, on this occasion, as tending to point out wherefore you ought not to turn back from what you have agreed upon.

The first is the great service which we shall perform to Our Lord in casting the Moors out of this country. . . . If we can only achieve the task before us, it will result

in the Moors resigning India altogether to our rule, for the greater part of them—or perhaps all of them—live upon the trade of this country and are become great and rich, and lords of extensive treasures. . . . Our Lord is blinding his judgment and hardening his heart, and desires the completion of this affair of Malaca: for when we were committing ourselves to the business of cruising in the Straits (of the Red Sea) where the King of Portugal had often ordered me to go (for it was there that His Highness considered we could cut down the commerce which the Moors of Cairo, of Meca, and of Juda, carry on with these parts), Our Lord for his service thought right to lead us hither, for when Malaca is taken the places on the Straits must be shut up, and they will never more be able to introduce their spiceries into those places.

And the other reason is the additional service which we shall render to the King D. Manuel in taking this city, because it is the headquarters of all the spiceries and drugs which the Moors carry every year hence to the Straits without our being able to prevent them from so doing; but if we deprive them of this their ancient market there, there does not remain for them a single port, nor a single situation, so commodious in the whole of these parts, where they can carry on their trade in these things. . . . I hold it as very certain that if we take this trade of Malaca away out of their hands, Cairo and Meca are entirely ruined, and to Venice will no spiceries be conveyed except that which her merchants go and buy in Portugal.

Whoever is lord of Malacca, he concluded, has his hand on the throat of Venice.

For Albuquerque, control of Malacca would serve two purposes. It could help to destroy the Arab spice trade network by blocking passage through the strategically located Strait of Malacca, and it could also provide the Portuguese with a way station en route to the Spice Islands and other points east (see the box above). After a short but bloody battle, the Portuguese seized the city and put the local Arab population to the sword. They then proceeded to erect the normal accoutrements of the day—a fort, a factory (a common term at the time for a warehouse), and a church. The sultan of Malacca was able to escape and fled with his remaining supporters to

the island of Bintang, at the tip of the Malay peninsula, where he tried to recuperate from his defeat.

From Malacca, the Portuguese launched expeditions further east, to China and the Moluccas, then known as the Spice Islands. There they signed a treaty with a local sultan for the purchase and export of cloves to the European market. Within a few years, they had managed to seize control of the spice trade from Muslim traders and had garnered substantial profits for the Portuguese monarchy.

Why were the Portuguese so successful? Basically, their success was a matter of guns and seamanship. The first Portuguese fleet to arrive in Indian waters was relatively modest in size. It consisted of three ships and twenty guns, a force sufficient for self-defense and intimidation, but not for serious military operations. Later Portuguese fleets, which began to arrive with regularity early in the sixteenth century, were more heavily armed and were able not only to intimidate but also to inflict severe defeats if necessary on local naval and land forces. The Portuguese by no means possessed a monopoly on the use of firearms and explosives, but their effective use of naval technology, the heavy guns that could be mounted in the hulls of their sturdy vessels, and their tactics gave them a military superiority over lightly armed rivals that they were able to exploit until the arrival of other European forces several decades later.

The historian Arnold Pacey has compared the Portuguese to the Mongols in their ability to use technology to their advantage against more powerful adversaries. Whereas the Mongols utilized the mobility on land provided by the use of stirrups and compound bows to avoid danger and seek out the weakness of their rivals, the Portuguese used the maneuverability of their light ships to maintain their distance while bombarding the enemy with their powerful cannon. By contrast, local merchantmen, though possessing guns, tended to apply the now outdated tactics of trying to ram and board enemy vessels.

The arrival of the Portuguese, then, changed the dynamics of trade in the Indian Ocean. Single-minded in their pursuit of a monopoly, willing and able to use force to achieve their ends, the Europeans injected a new element into trade patterns that had heretofore been marked primarily by peaceful competition.

Voyages to the "New World"

While the Portuguese sought access to the spice trade of the Indies by sailing eastward through the Indian Ocean, the Spanish attempted to reach the same destination by sailing westward across the Atlantic. Although the Spanish came to overseas discovery and exploration after the initial efforts of Henry the Navigator, their greater resources enabled them to establish a far grander overseas empire of a quite different nature than the Portuguese empire.

An important figure in the history of Spanish exploration was an Italian from Genoa, Christopher Columbus (1451–1506). Knowledgeable Europeans were aware that the world was round, but had little understanding of its circumference or the extent of the continent of Asia. Convinced that the circumference of the earth was less than contemporaries believed and that Asia was larger than people thought, Columbus felt that Asia could be reached by sailing west instead of east around Africa. After being rejected by the Portuguese, he persuaded Queen Isabella of Spain to finance his exploratory expedition, which reached the Americas in October 1492 and explored the coastline of Cuba and the northern shores of

♦ **Columbus Lands in the New World.**   In the log that he wrote during his first voyage to the Americas, Christopher Columbus noted that the peoples of the New World were intelligent and friendly, and relations between them and the Spanish were amicable at first. Later, however, the conquistadors began to mistreat the local people. Here is a somewhat imaginative painting of the first encounter from a European perspective.

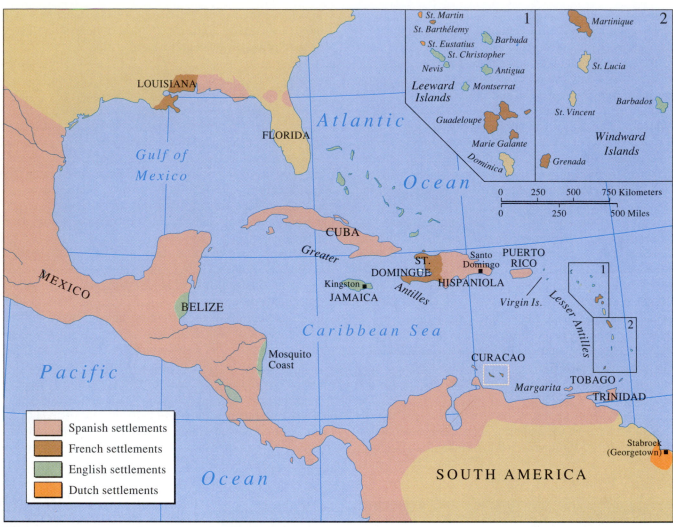

Map 14.1   European Possessions in the West Indies.

Haiti (Hispaniola). Columbus believed that he had reached Asia and in three subsequent voyages (1493, 1498, and 1502) sought in vain to find a route through the outer islands to the Asian mainland. In his four voyages, Columbus reached all the major islands of the Caribbean and Honduras in Central America, which he called the Indies.

Although Columbus clung to his belief till his death, other explorers soon realized that he had discovered a new frontier altogether. State-sponsored explorers joined the race to the New World. A Venetian seaman, John Cabot, explored the New England coastline of the Americas under a license from King Henry VII of England. The continent of South America was discovered accidentally by the Portuguese sea captain Pedro Cabral in 1500. Amerigo Vespucci, a Florentine, accompanied several

voyages and wrote a series of letters describing the geography of the New World. The publication of these letters led to the use of the name "America" (after Amerigo) for the new lands.

The newly discovered territories were called the New World, although they possessed flourishing civilizations populated by millions of people when the Europeans arrived. The Americas were, of course, new to the Europeans who quickly saw opportunities for conquest and exploitation. The Spanish, in particular, were interested because in 1494 the Treaty of Tordesillas had divided up the newly discovered world into separate Portuguese and Spanish spheres of influence. Hereafter the route east around the Cape of Good Hope was to be reserved for the Portuguese while the route across the Atlantic (except for the eastern hump of South America) was assigned to

Spain. The Spanish conquistadors were a hardy lot of mostly upper-class individuals motivated by a typical sixteenth-century blend of glory, greed, and religious crusading zeal. Although sanctioned by the Castilian crown, these groups were financed and outfitted privately, not by the government.

Their superior weapons, organizational skills, and determination brought the conquistadors incredible success. Beginning in 1519 with a small band of men, Hernán Cortés took three years to overthrow the mighty Aztec empire in central Mexico, led by the chieftain Moctezuma (see Chapter 6). Between 1531 and 1550, the Spanish gained control of northern Mexico. Between 1531 and 1536, another expedition led by a hardened and somewhat corrupt soldier, Francisco Pizarro (1470–1541), took control of the Inca empire high in the Peruvian Andes. The Spanish conquests were undoubtedly facilitated by the previous arrival of European diseases, which had decimated the local population. Although it took another three decades before the western part of Latin America was brought under Spanish control (the Portuguese took over Brazil), already by 1535, the Spanish had created a system of colonial administration that made the New World an extension of the old—at least in European eyes.

THE ADMINISTRATION OF THE SPANISH EMPIRE IN THE NEW WORLD

Spanish policy toward the Indians of the New World was a combination of confusion, misguided paternalism, and cruel exploitation. Confusion arose over the nature of the Indians. Unsure whether these strange creatures were "full men" or not, Spanish doctors of law debated how to fit them into currently existing European legal patterns. While the conquistadors made decisions based on expediency and their own interests, Queen Isabella declared the Indians (literally, "Indios") to be subjects of Castile and instituted the Spanish *encomienda*, a system that permitted the conquering Spaniards to collect tribute from the natives and use them as laborers. In return, the holders of an *encomienda* were supposed to protect the Indians and supervise their spiritual and material needs. In practice, this meant that the settlers were free to implement the paternalistic system of the government as they pleased. Three thousand miles from Spain, Spanish settlers largely ignored their government and brutally used the Indians to pursue their own economic interests. Indians were put to work on sugar plantations and in the lucrative gold and silver mines. Forced labor, starvation, and especially disease took a fearful toll of Indian lives.

With little or no natural resistance to European diseases, the Indians of America were ravaged by smallpox, measles, and typhus. These "killers" came with the explorers and the conquistadors. Although scholarly estimates of native populations vary drastically, a reasonable guess is that at least half of the natives died of European diseases. On Hispaniola (Haiti) alone, out of an initial population of 100,000 natives when Columbus arrived in 1493, only 300 Indians survived by 1570. In 1542, largely in response to the publications of Bartolomé de Las Casas, a Dominican monk who championed the Indians (see the box on p. 502), the government abolished the *encomienda* system and provided more protection for the natives.

The Spanish created a formal administrative system for their new empire. While a board of trade known as the *Casa de Contratactión* supervised all economic matters related to the New World, the Council of the Indies became the chief organ of colonial administration. The

♦ **Seat of Argentine Independence.** The Argentine city of Buenos Aires was founded in 1536 by the Spanish explorer Pedro de Mendoza. In 1580 a town council was erected on the city's main square, the Plaza de Mayo. In 1751 it was replaced with a new building, shown below. It was here that Argentine patriots planned their struggle for independence from Spain in 1810.

➤ Las Casas and the Spanish Treatment of the American Natives ◄

Bartolomé de Las Casas (1474–1566) was a Dominican monk who participated in the conquest of Cuba and received land and Indians in return for his efforts. But in 1514 he underwent a radical transformation that led him to believe that the Indians had been cruelly mistreated by his fellow Spaniards. He spent the remaining years of his life (he lived to the age of ninety-two) fighting for the Indians. This section is taken from his most influential work, Brevísima Relación de la Destrucción de las Indias, known to English readers as The Tears of the Indians. This work was largely responsible for the legend of the Spanish as inherently "cruel and murderous fanatics." Many scholars today feel that Las Casas may have exaggerated his account to shock his contemporaries into action.

Bartolomé de Las Casas, The Tears of the Indians

There is nothing more detestable or more cruel, than the tyranny which the Spaniards use toward the Indians for the getting of pearl. Surely the infernal torments cannot much exceed the anguish that they endure, by reason of that way of cruelty; for they put them under water some four or five ells deep, where they are forced without any liberty of respiration, to gather up the shells wherein the Pearls are; sometimes they come up again with nets full of shells to take breath, but if they stay any while to rest themselves, immediately comes a hangman row'd in a little boat, who as soon as he hath well beaten them, drags them again to their labor. Their food is nothing but filth, and the very same that contains the Pearl, with small portion of that bread which that Country affords; in the first whereof there is little nourishment; and as for the latter, it is made with great difficulty, besides that they have not enough of that neither for sustenance; they lie upon the ground in fetters, lest they should run away; and many times they are drown'd in this labor, and are never seen again till they swim upon the top of the waves; oftentimes they also are devoured by certain sea monsters, that are frequent in those seas. Consider whether this hard usage of the poor creatures be consistent with the precepts which God commands concerning charity to our neighbor, by those that cast them so undeservedly into the dangers of a cruel death, causing them to perish without any remorse or pity, or allowing them the benefit of the Sacraments, or the knowledge of Religion; it being impossible for them to live any time under the water; and this death is so much the more painful, by reason that by the coarctation of the breast, while the lungs strive to do their office, the vital parts are so afflicted that they die vomiting the blood out of their mouths. Their hair also, which is by nature black, is hereby changed and made of the same color with that of the sea Wolves; their bodies are also so besprinkled with the froth of the sea, that they appear rather like monsters than men.

---

council nominated colonial officials, oversaw their New World activities, and kept an eye on ecclesiastical affairs in the colonies.

In the New World, the Spanish developed an administrative system based on viceroys. Spanish possessions were initially divided into two major administrative units: New Spain (Mexico, Central America, and the Caribbean islands) with its center in Mexico City, and Peru (western South America), governed by a viceroy in Lima. Each viceroy served as the king's chief civil and military officer and was aided by advisory groups called *audiencias*, which also functioned as supreme judicial bodies.

By papal agreement, the Catholic monarchs of Spain were given extensive rights over ecclesiastical affairs in the New World. They could nominate church officials, build churches, collect fees, and supervise the affairs of the various religious orders who sought to Christianize the heathen. Catholic monks had remarkable success in converting and baptizing hundreds of thousands of Indians in the early years of the conquest. Soon after the missionaries came the establishment of dioceses, parishes, schools, and hospitals—all the trappings of a European society.

The Impact of European Expansion

The arrival of the Europeans had an enormous impact on both the conquerors and the conquered. The native American civilizations, which had their own unique qualities and a degree of sophistication rarely appreciated by the conquerors, were virtually destroyed, while the native populations were ravaged by diseases inadvertently introduced by the Europeans. Ancient social and political structures were ripped up and replaced by European institutions, religion, language, and culture (see the box on p. 503).

An Aztec's Lament

In a previous chapter, we observed the Spanish conquest of Mexico from the point of view of the invaders. Here we present an Aztec account. Aztec memoirs of the battle were collected by the Spanish a few years after the seizure of Tenochtitlán and were later translated from the original Nahuatl language into Spanish or other European languages. In this passage, an Aztec observer describes the enormous sense of sorrow he felt at the tragedy that had befallen his compatriots. Note that the writer concludes that the defeat was ordained by the "Giver of Life" because of his displeasure with the Aztec people.

Flowers and Songs of Sorrow

*Nothing but flowers and songs of sorrow
are left in Mexico and Tlatelolco,
where once we saw warriors and wise men.*

*We know it is true
that we must perish,*

*for we are mortal men.
You, the Giver of Life,
you have ordained it.*

*We wander here and there
in our desolate poverty.
We are mortal men.
We have seen bloodshed and pain
where once we saw beauty and valor.*

*We are crushed to the ground;
we lie in ruins.
There is nothing but grief and suffering
in Mexico and Tlatelolco,
where once we saw beauty and valor.*

*Have you grown weary of your servants?
Are you angry with your servants,
O Giver of Life?*

European expansion also affected the conquerors, perhaps most notably in the economic arena. Wherever they went in the Americas, Europeans sought to find sources of gold and silver. One Aztec observer commented that the Spanish conquerors "longed and lusted for gold. Their bodies swelled with greed, and their hunger was ravenous; they hungered like pigs for that gold."[6] Rich silver deposits were found and exploited in Mexico and southern Peru (modern Bolivia). When the mines at Potosí in Peru were opened in 1545, the value of precious metals imported into Europe quadrupled. It has been estimated that between 1503 and 1650 sixteen million kilograms of silver and 185,000 kilograms of gold entered the port of Seville and helped to create a price revolution that affected the Spanish economy.

But gold and silver were only two of the products sent to Europe from the New World. Into Seville flowed sugar, dyes, cotton, vanilla, and hides from livestock raised on the South American pampas. New agricultural products native to the Americas such as potatoes, coffee, corn, manioc, and tobacco were also imported. Because of its trading posts in Asia, Portugal soon challenged the Italian states as the chief entry point of the eastern trade in spices, jewels, silk, carpets, ivory, leather, and perfumes, although the Venetians clung tenaciously to a portion of the spice trade until they lost out to the Dutch in the seventeenth century. Economic historians believe that the increase in the volume and area of European trade and the rise in fluid capital due to this expansion were crucial factors in producing a new era of commercial capitalism that represented the first step toward the world economy that has characterized the modern historical era.

European expansion, which was in part a product of European rivalries, also deepened those rivalries and increased the tensions among European states. Bitter conflicts arose over the cargoes coming from the New World and Asia. Although the Spanish and Portuguese were first in the competition, by the end of the sixteenth century, new competitors were entering the scene and beginning to challenge the dominance of the Iberian powers. The first to arrive were the English and the Dutch.

New Rivals Enter the Scene

Portugal's efforts to dominate the trade of the Indian Ocean were never totally successful. The Portuguese lacked both the numbers and the wealth to overcome

CHRONOLOGY

◆◆◆◆◆◆◆◆◆◆◆◆◆◆◆◆◆◆◆◆◆◆

Spanish Activities in the Americas

Christopher Columbus's first voyage to the Americas	1492
Last voyages of Columbus	1502–1504
Spanish conquest of Mexico	1519–1522
Francisco Pizarro's conquest of the Incas	1531–1536

points in the Mediterranean. At the other end of the Indian Ocean, Portuguese control over the port of Malacca alarmed other states in the region, and the city was attacked on several occasions by naval forces from the Muslim state of Acheh, itself a major supplier of Sumatran pepper to foreign traders. The Portuguese were able to fend off the assaults and signed a peace treaty with Acheh in 1587. But they had run into similar problems in the Spice Islands, where their success encouraged the Spanish to contest Lisbon's monopoly over the clove trade.

The Spanish had established themselves in the area in the early 1520s, when Ferdinand Magellan, seeking a western route to the Spice Islands across the Pacific Ocean, had landed on the island of Cebu in the Philippine Islands. Although Magellan and some forty of his crew were killed in a skirmish with the local population, one of the two remaining ships, now under the command of the Spanish navigator Sebastian del Cano, sailed on to Tidor, in the Moluccas, and thence around the world via the Cape of Good Hope. In the words of a contemporary historian, they arrived in Cádiz "with precious cargo and fifteen men surviving out of a fleet of five sail."[7]

As it turned out, the Spanish could not follow up on Magellan's accomplishment, and in 1529 they sold their rights in Tidor to the Portuguese. But Magellan's voyage was not a total loss. In the absence of concerted resistance from the local population, the Spanish managed to consolidate their control over the Philippines, which

local resistance and colonize the Asian regions. Moreover, their massive investments in ships and manpower for their empire (hundreds of ships and hundreds of thousands of workers in shipyards and overseas bases) proved very costly. Only half of the ships involved in the India trade survived for a second journey. Disease, shipwreck, and battles took a heavy toll of life. The empire was simply too large and Portugal too small to maintain it, and by the end of the century, the Portuguese were being severely challenged by rivals.

The first threat to Portuguese control over the spice trade came from within the region. Their blockade of the Red Sea at the narrow Bab al Mandab, for example, was effectively evaded by Arabic shippers, who continued to transport products from the east to Cairo and other

◆ **Passage to the Unknown.** During its historic first voyage around the world in the early sixteenth century, Ferdinand Magellan's fleet passed through this passage near the southern tip of South America. Now known as the Strait of Magellan, this narrow body of water between the mainland and the nearby island of Tierra del Fuego remains one of the most terrifying in the world, with 100-mile winds gusting regularly through this passage between the Pacific and the Atlantic Oceans.

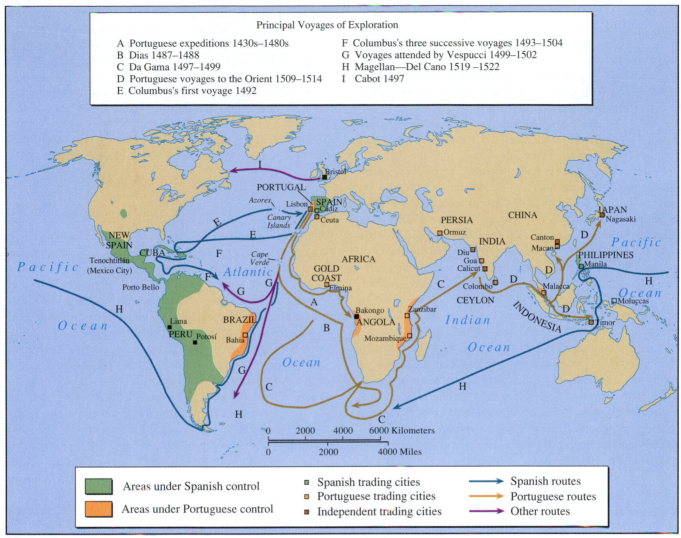

Principal Voyages of Exploration

A Portuguese expeditions 1430s–1480s
B Dias 1487–1488
C Da Gama 1497–1499
D Portuguese voyages to the Orient 1509–1514
E Columbus's first voyage 1492

F Columbus's three successive voyages 1493–1504
G Voyages attended by Vespucci 1499–1502
H Magellan—Del Cano 1519–1522
I Cabot 1497

Areas under Spanish control
Areas under Portuguese control

■ Spanish trading cities
■ Portuguese trading cities
■ Independent trading cities

→ Spanish routes
→ Portuguese routes
→ Other routes

Map 14.2   European Voyages and Possessions in the Sixteenth and Seventeenth Centuries.

eventually became a major Spanish base in the carrying trade across the Pacific. Spanish galleons carried silk and other luxury goods to Acapulco in exchange for silver from the mines of Mexico.

The primary threat to the Portuguese toehold in Southeast Asia, however, came neither from local rivals nor from the Spanish, but from the English and the Dutch, both of whom were now strongly influenced by mercantilist theory. The English had been frustrated by their abortive efforts to find an alternative northern route to Asia, and Sir Francis Drake had followed Magellan's route to the Spice Islands in the 1580s. But when war broke out with Spain in the 1580s, the English decided to ignore papal restrictions on the use of the route

around the Cape of Good Hope to the East. In 1591, the first English expedition to the Indies through the Indian Ocean arrived in London with a cargo of pepper. Nine years later, a private joint-stock company, the East India Company, was founded to provide a stable source of capital for future voyages. In 1608, an English fleet landed at Surat, on the northwestern coast of India. Their request to open trade relations was rejected by Indian authorities, but eventually a commercial treaty was signed, and a permanent English representative was assigned to the Mughal imperial court. Trade with Southeast Asia soon followed (see The Arrival of the West later in this chapter).

The Dutch were quick to follow suit. Dutch sailors had managed to obtain Portuguese maps of the Indian coast, and the first Dutch fleet arrived in India in 1595. In 1602, the Dutch East India Company (the Vereenigde Oost-Indische Compagnie, or VOC) was established under government sponsorship and soon was actively competing with the English and the Portuguese in the region (see The Arrival of the West later in this chapter).

The Dutch and the English also began to make inroads on Spanish and Portuguese possessions in the Americas. War and steady pressure from their Dutch and English rivals eroded Portuguese trade in both the west and east, although Portugal continued to profit from its large colonial empire in Brazil. A formal administration system had been instituted in Brazil in 1549, and Portuguese migrants had established massive plantations there to produce sugar for export to the Old World. The Spanish also maintained an enormous South American empire, but Spain's importance as a commercial power declined rapidly in the seventeenth century because of a drop in the output of the silver mines, the poverty of the Spanish monarchy, and the stifling hand of the Spanish aristocracy as well as the pressure of its English rival.

The Dutch formed their own Dutch West India Company in 1621 to compete with Spanish and Portuguese interests in the Americas. But although it made some inroads in Portuguese Brazil and the Caribbean, the company's profits were never large enough to compensate for the expenditures. Dutch settlements were also established on the North American continent. The mainland colony of New Netherlands stretched from the mouth of the Hudson River as far north as Albany, New York. Present-day names such as Staten Island, Harlem, and the Catskills remind us that it was the Dutch who initially settled the Hudson River valley.

In the second half of the seventeenth century, however, rivalry and years of warfare with the English and the French (who had also become active in North America) brought the decline of the Dutch commercial empire in the New World. In 1664, the English seized the colony of New Netherlands and renamed it New York while the Dutch West India Company soon went bankrupt. In 1663, Canada became the property of the French crown and was administered like a French province. But the French failed to provide adequate men or money, allowing their continental wars to take precedence over the conquest of the North American continent. By the early eighteenth century, the French began to cede some of their American possessions to their English rival.

The English meanwhile had proceeded to create a colonial empire in the New World along the Atlantic seaboard of North America. The failure of the Virginia Company made it evident that colonizing American lands was not necessarily conducive to quick profits. But the desire to escape from religious oppression combined with economic interests did make successful colonialization possible, as the Massachusetts Bay Company demonstrated. The Massachusetts colony had only 4,000 settlers in its early years, but by 1660 their number had swelled to 40,000. Although the English had established control over most of the eastern seaboard by the end of the seventeenth century, the North American colonies still remained of minor significance to the English economy.

Africa in an Era of Transition

Although the primary objective of the Portuguese in rounding the Cape of Good Hope was to find a sea route to the Spice Islands, they soon discovered that profits were to be made en route, along the eastern coast of Africa. In the early sixteenth century, a Portuguese fleet commanded by Francisco de Almeida seized a number of East African port cities, including Kilwa, Sofala, and Mombasa, and built forts along the coast in an effort to control the trade in the area. Above all, the Portuguese wanted to monopolize the trade in gold, which was mined by Bantu workers in the hills along the upper Zambezi River and then shipped to Swahili traders at Sofala on the coast (see Chapter 8). For centuries, the gold trade had been monopolized by local Shona peoples at Zimbabwe. In the fifteenth century, it had come under the control of a Shona dynasty known as the Mwene Metapa (known to Europeans as Monomotapa). The Mwene Metapa had originally controlled the region south of the Zambezi River and may have been the builders of the impressive city known today as Great Zimbabwe, but sometime in the fifteenth century, they moved northeastward to the valley of the Zambezi. Here they encountered the arriving Portuguese who had begun to move inland to gain access to the lucrative gold trade and had established ports at Tete and Sena on the Zambezi River. The Portuguese opened treaty relations with the Mwene Metapa, and Jesuit priests were eventually posted to the court in 1561. At first the Mwene Metapa found the Europeans useful as an ally against local rivals, but when the Portuguese attempted to seize the gold mines for themselves, the former struck back and tried unsuccessfully to drive the Portuguese out. The victorious Portuguese transformed the kingdom of the Mwene Metapa into a protectorate and forced the local ruler to grant title to large tracts of land to Portuguese officials and private individuals living in the area. Eventually, those lands would be integrated into the colony of

Mozambique. The Portuguese, however, lacked the personnel, the capital, and the expertise to dominate the trade in the area (one historian notes that in the late sixteenth century, ninety years after da Gama's fateful voyage, there were only about fifty Portuguese officials in residence throughout the entire area of East Africa. In the late seventeenth century, a vassal of the Mwene Metapa succeeded in driving the Portuguese from the plateau; his descendants maintained control of the area for the next two hundred years.

North of the Zambezi River, Bantu peoples were coming under pressure not only from the Portuguese, but also from pastoralists migrating southward from the southern Sudan. The latter were frequently aggressive and began to occupy the rift valley and parts of the lake district that had previously been controlled by Bantu speakers, most of whom were farmers. In some cases, the conflict between farmers and pastoralists was fairly clear-cut. In Rwanda and Burundi, immediately west of Lake Victoria, farming Hutu peoples (Bantu speakers) defended their hilltop communities against roving Tutsi pastoralists occupying the surrounding lowlands.

Although most of the Bantu communities remained decentralized under the rule of the traditional "big men," a transition to statehood began to take place in the lake region, where the growing population and a mixed pastoral-agricultural economy created increasingly complex societies. By the late sixteenth and seventeenth centuries, powerful kingdoms such as Buganda had begun to extend their control over neighboring regions, transforming chieftains into vassals and their communities into tributary states.

Beyond the valley of the Limpopo River in southern Africa, however, decentralized communities continued to predominate until the emergence of the Zulu kingdom in the early nineteenth century. This condition created a political vacuum eventually filled by Europeans.

The first Europeans to settle in southern Africa were the Dutch. After an unsuccessful attempt to seize the Portuguese settlement on the island of Mozambique off the East African coast, the Dutch set up a way station at the Cape of Good Hope in 1652. Sailing ships had stopped at the cape for years to obtain food supplies from the local tribal peoples in the area. Now the Dutch East India Company planned to establish a more permanent settlement that would serve as a base for Dutch fleets en route to Batavia in the East Indies. At first, the new settlement was meant simply to provide food and other provisions to Dutch ships en route to the Spice Islands, but eventually it developed into a permanent colony. Dutch farmers, known as Boers and speaking a Dutch dialect that evolved into Afrikaans, began to settle in the sparsely occupied areas outside the city of Capetown. The temperate climate and the absence of tropical diseases made the territory near the cape almost the only land south of the Sahara that the Europeans had found suitable for habitation.

In West Africa, contacts with the outside world were well underway when the first Portuguese ships began to stop along the coast on their push southward toward the Cape of Good Hope. The area had been penetrated from across the Sahara since ancient times, and contact undoubtedly increased after the establishment of Muslim control over the Mediterranean coastal regions. Muslim traders crossed the desert carrying Islamic values, political culture, and legal traditions along with their goods. In so doing, they undoubtedly contributed to the process of state building that had been underway since the first millennium. This early stage of state formation had culminated with the kingdom of Mali, symbolized by the renowned Mansa Musa, whose pilgrimage to Mecca in the fourteenth century had left an indelible impression on observers.

After Mali's decline, it was succeeded in the east by the kingdom of Songhai. Under King Askia Mohammed (1493–1528), the leader of a pro-Islamic faction who had seized power from members of the original founding family, the state increasingly relied on Islamic institutions and ideology to strengthen national unity and centralize authority (see the box on p. 508). Askia Mohammed himself embarked on a pilgrimage to Mecca and was recognized by the caliph of Cairo as the Muslim ruler of the Niger River valley. On his return from Mecca, he tried to revive Timbuktu as a major center of Islamic learning, but had little success in converting his subjects to the new religion. He did preside over a significant increase in trans-Saharan trade, which provided a steady source of income to Songhai and other kingdoms in the region. Most of the trade goods were carried across the desert on camels by Berber nomadic peoples, however, and then transported by donkeys or river barges to further destinations.

Despite the efforts of Askia Mohammed and his successors, centrifugal forces within Songhai eventually led to its breakup after his death. Most administrative authority in the region was little more than a thin political veneer over relatively autonomous villages united in local alliances (known as *kafu*), and when succession struggles weakened the power of the central government, decentralizing forces often seized the advantage.

The period of Songhai's decline was also a time of increased contact with Europeans. The English, the French,

The *Epic of Askia Mohammed is an oral history passed down through generations of West Africans. It relates the heroic deeds of the famous monarch who led the kingdom of Songhai to the zenith of its power in the early sixteenth century. In the epic, the young hero, called Mamar Kassaye, becomes chieftain by killing his evil uncle Si (Sonni Ali Ber, who ruled Songhai from 1463 to 1492). Once in power, Mamar consolidated the expanding Songhai kingdom and ruled it until his death in 1528. He was revered for his piety, his patronage of scholarship at Timbuktu, and his celebrated pilgrimage to Mecca. The following passage describes his assumption of power and the means he used to convert his subjects to Islam.*

The Epic of Askia Mohammed

His father gave him a white stallion, really white, really, really, really, really, really, really, really white like, like percale.
He gave him all the things necessary.
He gave him two lances.
He gave him a saber, which he wore.
He gave him a shield.
He bid him good-bye.
…
The horse gallops swiftly, swiftly, swiftly, swiftly, swiftly, swiftly he is approaching.
He comes into view suddenly, leaning forward on his mount.
Until, until, until, until, until, until, until he touches the prayer skin of his uncle, then he reins his horse there.
…
As he approaches the prayer skin of his uncle,
He reins his horse.
He unslung his lance, and pierced his uncle with it until the lance touched the prayer skin.

Until the spear went all the way to the prayer skin.
…
They took away the body, and Mamar came to sit down on the prayer skin of his uncle.
They prayed.
They took away the body to bury it.
That is how Mamar took the chieftaincy.
…
He ruled then, he ruled, he ruled, he ruled, he converted.
Throughout Mamar's reign, what he did was to convert people.
Any village that he hears is trying to resist,
That is not going to submit,
He gets up and destroys the village.
If the village accepts, he makes them pray.
If they resist, he conquers the village, he burns the village.
Mamar made them convert, Mamar made them convert, Mamar made them convert.
Until, until, until, until, until, until he got up and said he would go to Mecca.
…
They build a mosque before his arrival.
When he arrives, he and his people,
He teaches the villagers prayers from the Koran.
He makes them pray.
They—they learn how to pray.
After that, in the morning, he continues on.
Every village that follows his orders, that accepts his wishes,
He conquers them, he moves on.
Every village that refuses his demand,
He conquers it, he burns it, he moves on.
Until the day—Mamar did that until, until, until, until the day he arrived at the Red Sea.

and the Dutch all became active in the West African trade in the mid-sixteenth century. The Dutch, in particular, encroached on the Portuguese spheres of influence. During the mid-seventeenth century, the Dutch seized a number of Portuguese forts along the West African coast, while at the same time taking over the bulk of the Portuguese trade across the Indian Ocean.

The Slave Trade

The European exploration of the African coastline had little apparent significance for most peoples living in the interior of the continent, except for a few who engaged in direct or indirect trade with the foreigners. But for peoples living on or near the coast, the impact was often

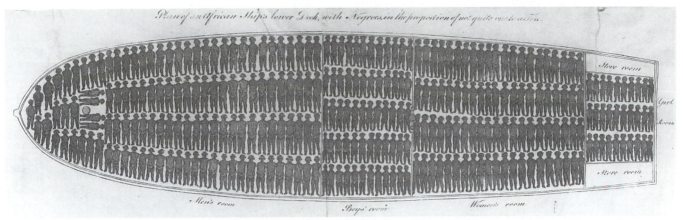

Plan of an African Ship's lower Deck, with Negroes in the proportion of not quite one to a Ton.

Store room

Girls' room

Store room

Men's room

Boys' room

Women's room

♦ **A Slave Ship.** Beginning in the sixteenth century, European traders began to ship native Africans to the Americas to be used as slave labor on the plantations. During the first shipments, up to one-third of the human cargo died of disease. Later merchants became more efficient and reduced losses to about 10 percent. As this sketch shows, the victims were still crammed together in an inhuman manner.

great indeed. As the trade in slaves increased during the sixteenth through the eighteenth centuries, thousands, and then millions, were removed from their homes and forcibly exported to plantations in the New World.

Traffic in slaves had existed for centuries before the arrival of Portuguese fleets along African shores. West African states like the kingdoms of Mali and Songhai routinely used slaves (mostly captured in battles with neighboring rivals) as agricultural laborers. In East Africa and the upper Nile valley, slavery had been practiced since ancient times and continued at a fairly steady level during the fifteenth century, with the major trade routes snaking across the Sahara and up the Nile River. The primary market for African slaves was the Middle East, where most were used as domestic servants. Slavery also existed in many European countries, where a few slaves from Africa or war captives from the regions north of the Black Sea were used for domestic purposes or as agricultural workers in the lands adjacent to the Mediterranean.

At first, the Portuguese simply replaced European slaves with African ones. During the last half of the fifteenth century, about a thousand slaves were taken to Portugal each year; the vast majority were apparently destined to serve as domestic servants for affluent families throughout Europe. But the discovery of the New World in the 1490s and the subsequent planting of sugarcane in South America and the islands of the Caribbean changed the situation. Cane sugar was native to Indonesia and had first been introduced to Europeans from the Middle East during the crusades. By the fifteenth century, it was grown (often by slaves from Africa or the region of the

Black Sea) in modest amounts on Cyprus, Sicily, and southern regions of the Iberian peninsula. In 1490, the Portuguese established sugar plantations worked by African laborers at São Tomé, an island in the Bay of Biafra off the central coast of Africa. Demand increased as sugar gradually replaced honey as a sweetener, especially in northern Europe.

But the primary impetus to the sugar industry came from the colonization of the Americas. During the sixteenth century, plantations were established along the eastern coast of Brazil and on several islands in the Caribbean. Because the cultivation of cane sugar is an arduous process demanding both skill and large quantities of labor, the new plantations required more workers than could be provided by the small and inexperienced American Indian population in the New World, many of whom had in any case died of diseases imported from the Old World. Since the climate and soil of much of West Africa were not especially conducive to the cultivation of sugar, African slaves began to be shipped to Brazil and the Caribbean to work on the plantations. The first were sent from Portugal, but in 1518 a Spanish ship carried the first boatload of African slaves directly from Africa to the New World.

During the next two centuries, the trade in slaves increased by massive proportions. An estimated 275,000 enslaved Africans were exported to other countries during the sixteenth century, with 2,000 going annually to the Americas alone. During the next century, the total climbed to over a million and jumped to six million in the eighteenth century, when the trade spread from West

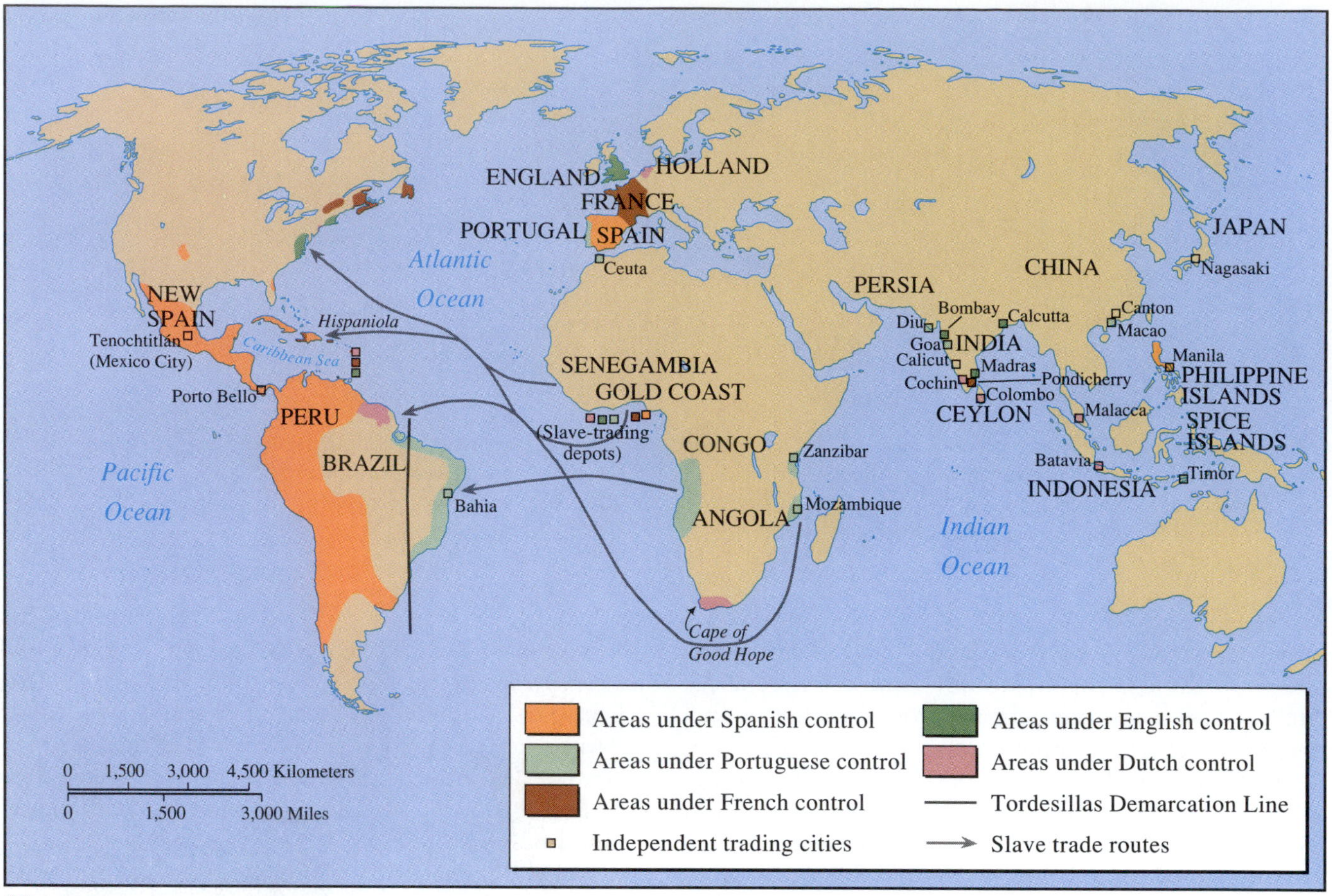

Map 14.3 The Slave Trade.

and central Africa to East Africa. Even during the nineteenth century, when Great Britain and a number of other European countries attempted to end the slave trade, nearly two million were exported. It has been estimated that altogether as many as ten million African slaves were transported to the Americas between the early sixteenth and the late nineteenth century. As many as two million were exported to other areas during the same period.

One reason for these astonishing numbers, of course, was the tragically high death rate. While figures on the number of slaves who died on the journey are almost entirely speculative, a high proportion undoubtedly died on the voyage before arriving at their destination. According to one source, mortality rates among crew members were as high as one in four. Later, mortality rates among slaves were apparently reduced to an average of about 5 percent per voyage, still a figure of epidemic proportions. Mortality rates for Europeans in the West Indies were ten to twenty times higher on average than in Europe, and a European arriving in the West Indies had a life expectancy of five to ten years (in Africa, where yellow fever was prevalent, the average life expectancy for an arriving European was only about one year). Ironically, African slaves fared somewhat better if they survived the brutal voyage. Death rates for newly arrived Europeans in the West Indies averaged over 125 per 1,000 annually, but the figure for Africans was only about 30 per 1,000.

The reason for these staggering death rates was clearly more than maltreatment, although that was certainly a factor. As we have seen, the transmission of diseases from one continent to another brought high death rates among those lacking immunity. African slaves were somewhat less susceptible to European diseases than the American Indian populations. Indeed, they seem to have possessed a degree of immunity, perhaps because their ancestors had developed antibodies to "white people's diseases" owing to the trans-Saharan trade. The Africans would not have had immunity to native American diseases, however.

The mortality rates, of course, were higher for immigrants than for those born in the New World, who as children gradually developed at least a partial immunity to many of the more fatal diseases. Death rates for native-born slaves tended to be significantly lower than for recent arrivals, which raises the question of why the slave population did not begin to rise after the initial impact of settlement had worn off. The answer appears to be a matter of economics. In the first place, only half as many women were enslaved as men, and birth rates for women living in slavery were low, while infant mortality was high. In the second place, as long as the price of slaves was low, many slave owners in the West Indies apparently believed that purchasing a new slave was less expensive than raising a child from birth to working age at adolescence. After the price of slaves began to rise during the eighteenth century, plantation owners started to devote more efforts to replenishing the supply of workers by natural means.

Slaves were obtained by traditional means. Before the coming of the Europeans in the fifteenth century, most slaves in Africa were prisoners or war captives or had inherited their status. Many served as domestic servants or as wageless workers for the local ruler, and some were permitted to purchase their freedom under certain conditions. When Europeans first began to take part in the slave trade, they would normally purchase slaves from local African merchants at the infamous "slave markets" in exchange for gold, guns, or other European manufactured goods such as textiles or copper or iron utensils (see the box on p. 512). At first, local slave traders obtained their supply from immediately surrounding regions, but as demand increased, they had to move further inland to locate their victims. In a few cases, local rulers became concerned about the impact of the slave trade on the political and social well-being of their societies. In a letter to the king of Portugal in 1526, King Affonso of Congo (Bakongo) complained that "so great, Sire, is the corruption and licentiousness that our country is being completely depopulated. . . ."[8] As a general rule, however, local monarchs viewed the slave trade as a source of income, and many launched forays against defenseless villages in search of unsuspecting victims.

Historians once thought that Europeans controlled the terms of the slave trade and were able to obtain victims at bargain prices. Recently, however, it has become clear that African middlemen—whether private merchants, local elites, or trading state monopolies—were very active in the process and were often able to dictate the price, volume, and availability of slaves to European purchasers. The majority of the slaves sold to European buyers were males, while females, who were in great demand in Africa and on the trans-Saharan trade, tended to be reserved for those markets. The slave merchants were often paid in various types of imported goods, including East Asian textiles (highly desired for their bright colors and durability), furniture, and other manufactured products. Until the end of the seventeenth century, the Portuguese preferred gold to slaves and would sometimes pay for the gold by selling slaves to African kingdoms that were short of labor.

The effects of the slave trade varied from area to area. It might be assumed that, apart from the tragic effects on the lives of individual victims and their families, the practice would have led to the depopulation of vast areas of the continent. This did occur in some areas, notably in modern-day Angola, south of the Zaire River basin, and in thinly populated areas in East Africa, but it was less true in West Africa. There high birth rates were often able to counterbalance the loss of able-bodied adults, and the introduction of new crops from the New World, such as maize, peanuts, and manioc, led to an increase in food production that made it possible to support a larger population. One of the many cruel ironies of history is that while the institution of slavery was a tragedy for many, it resulted in benefits for others.

Still, there is no denying the reality that from a moral point of view, the slave trade represented a tragic loss for millions of Africans, not only for the individual victims, but also for their families. One of the more poignant aspects of the trade is that as many as 20 percent of those sold to European slavers were children, a statistic that may be partly explained by the fact that many European countries had enacted regulations that permitted more children than adults to be transported aboard the ships.

Political and Social Structures in a Changing Continent

Of course, the Western economic penetration of Africa had other dislocating effects. As in other parts of the non-Western world, the importation of inexpensive manufactured goods from Europe undermined the foundations of local cottage industry and impoverished countless families. Both the demand for slaves and the introduction of firearms intensified political instability and civil strife. The diversion of trade from the interior to the sea routes weakened inland societies in favor of coastal states in the western Sahara. In addition, the abortive Portuguese attempt to take over the Indian Ocean trade in the sixteenth century led to the decline of

❧ A Slave Market in Africa ❧

Traffic in slaves had been carried on in Africa since the kingdom of the pharaohs in ancient Egypt. But the slave trade increased dramatically after the arrival of European ships off the coast of West Africa. The following passage by a Dutch observer describes a slave market in Africa and the conditions on the ships that carried the slaves to the New World. Note the difference in tone between this account and the far more critical views expressed in Chapter 22.

Slavery in Africa: A Firsthand Report

Not a few in our country fondly imagine that parents here sell their children, men their wives, and one brother the other. But those who think so deceive themselves, for this never happens on any other account but that of necessity, or some great crime; most of the slaves that are offered to us are prisoners of war, who are sold by the victors as their booty.

When these slaves come to Fida, they are put in prison all together; and when we treat concerning buying them, they are brought out into a large plain. There, by our surgeons, whose province it is, they are thoroughly examined, even to the smallest member, and that naked too, both men and women, without the least distinction or modesty. Those that are approved as good are set on one side; and the lame or faulty are set by as invalids, which are here called *mackrons*. These are such as are above five and thirty years old, or are maimed in the arms, legs, hands or feet, have lost a tooth, are gray-haired, or have films over their eyes; as well as all those which are affected with any venereal distemper or several other diseases.

The invalids and the maimed being thrown out, as I have told you, the remainder are numbered, and it is entered who delivered them. In the meanwhile, a burning iron, with the arms or name of the companies, lies in the fire, with which ours are marked on the breast. This is done that we may distinguish them from the slaves of the English, French, or others (which are also marked with their mark), and to prevent the Negroes exchanging them for worse, at which they have a good hand.

I doubt not but this trade seems very barbarous to you, but since it is followed by mere necessity, it must go on; but we take all possible care that they are not burned too hard, especially the women, who are more tender than the men.

When we have agreed with the owners of the slaves, they are returned to their prison. There from that time forward they are kept at our charge, costing us two pence a day a slave; which serves to subsist them, like our criminals, on bread and water. To save charges, we send them on board our ships at the very first opportunity, before which their masters strip them of all they have on their backs so that they come aboard stark naked, women as well as men. In this condition they are obliged to continue, if the master of the ship is not so charitable (which he commonly is) as to bestow something on them to cover their nakedness.

You would really wonder to see how these slaves live on board, for though their number sometimes amounts to six or seven hundred, yet by the careful management of our masters of ships, they are so regulated that it seems incredible. And in this particular our nation exceeds all other Europeans, for the French, Portuguese and English slave ships are always foul and stinking; on the contrary, ours are for the most part clean and neat.

The slaves are fed three times a day with indifferent good victuals, and much better than they eat in their own country. Their lodging place is divided into two parts, one of which is appointed for the men, the other for the women, each sex being kept apart. Here they lie as close together as it is possible for them to be crowded.

We are sometimes sufficiently plagued with a parcel of slaves which come from a far inland country who very innocently persuade one another that we buy them only to fatten and afterward eat them as a delicacy. When we are so unhappy as to be pestered with many of this sort, they resolve and agree together (and bring over the rest to their party) to run away from the ship, kill the Europeans, and set the vessel ashore, by which means they design to free themselves from being our food.

I have twice met with this misfortune; and the first time proved very unlucky to me, I not in the least suspecting it, but the uproar was quashed by the master of the ship and myself by causing the abettor to be shot through the head, after which all was quiet.

the interregional trade in that part of the world, and the destruction of the traditional commercial entrepôts along the coast of East Africa brought hardship to the population in that area.

Such changes in the economic picture often had political consequences. At the insistence of African rulers and merchants, European influence generally did not penetrate beyond the coastal regions. Nevertheless, inland areas were often affected by events taking place elsewhere. In the western Sahara, for example, the diversion of trade routes toward the coast led to the irreparable weakening of the old Songhai trading empire and its eventual conquest by a vigorous new Moroccan dynasty in the late sixteenth century. Morocco had long hoped to expand its influence into the Sahara in order to seize control over the commerce in gold and salt, and in 1590 Moroccan forces defeated Songhai's army at Gao, on the Niger River, and then occupied the great caravan center of Timbuktu (see the box on p. 515). The Moroccans were unable to exploit their victory, however, and after revolts broke out throughout the region, they turned over authority to a local *pasha* who was only nominally responsible to the Moroccan government in Marrakech. But even after the departure of the invaders, Songhai was beyond recovery, and the next two centuries were marked by civil disorder among diverse tribal groups and intense competition between Muslims in the cities and towns and adherents of traditional African religions in rural areas.

European influence had a more direct impact along the coast of West Africa, especially in the vicinity of European forts and factories such as Dakar and Sierra Leone, but no European colonies were established there before 1800. Nor did the coming of the Europeans result in a massive disruption of the trans-Saharan caravan trade, which was effectively protected from European competition by geographical obstacles and the prevalence of disease, which prevented Europeans from penetrating far into the interior. In fact, not until the beginning of the eighteenth century did slaves surpass gold and ivory as the continent's leading exports.

Most of the numerous African states in the area from Cape Verde to the delta of the Niger River were sufficiently strong to resist Western encroachments, and they often allied with each other to force European purchasers to respect their monopoly on trading operations. At the same time, they occasionally relied on the support of European powers against inland rivals. Some, like the powerful Ashanti kingdom, established in 1680 on the Gold Coast, profited substantially from their favorable position to take advantage of the rise in seaborne commerce.

CHRONOLOGY

The Penetration of Africa

Life of Prince Henry the Navigator	1394–1460
Portuguese ships reach the Senegal River	1441
Bartolomeo Dias sails around the tip of Africa	1487
First Portuguese sugar plantation at São Tomé	1490
First boatload of slaves to the Americas	1518
Jesuit priests reside at the court of the Mwene Metapa	1561
Dutch way station established at Cape of Good Hope	1652
Ashanti kingdom established in West Africa	1680
Portuguese expelled from Mombasa	1728

Some states, particularly along the so-called Slave Coast, in what is now Dahomey and Togo, or in the densely populated Niger River delta, took an active part in the slave trade. The demands of slavery and the temptations of economic profit, however, also contributed to the increase in conflict among the states in the area.

This was especially true in the region of the Zaire River, where Portuguese activities eventually led to the splintering of the Congo Empire and two centuries of rivalry and internal strife among the successor states in the area. A similar pattern developed in East Africa, where Portuguese activities led to the decline and eventual collapse of the Mwene Metapa. Northward along the coast, in present-day Kenya and Tanzania, African rulers, assisted by Arab forces from Oman and Muscat in the Arabian peninsula, expelled the Portuguese from Fort Jesus in Mombasa in 1728. Swahili culture, continually enriched by elements from the African mainland as well as from the Muslim world, now regained some of the dynamism it had possessed before the arrival of Vasco da Gama and his successors. But with much of the shipping now diverted southward to the route around the Cape of Good Hope, the commerce of the area never completely recovered and was increasingly dependent upon the export of slaves and ivory obtained through contacts with African states in the interior.

◆ **The Great Gate at Marrakech.**   The Moroccan city of Marrakech was a major northern terminus of the trans-Saharan trade and one of the chief commercial centers in all Africa. Widely praised by such famous travelers as Ibn Battuta, the city was an architectural marvel in that all its major public buildings were constructed in red sandstone. Shown here is the Great Gate to the city, through which camel caravans passed en route to or from the vast desert.

The overall impact of the growing foreign presence in Africa, then, was mixed. Clearly, it was greater along the coast than in the interior, but some historians feel that the influence of the slave trade on the evolution of African societies should not be exaggerated. Only in a few isolated areas, such as South Africa and what would become the modern state of Mozambique, were there signs that a permanent European presence was being established. Along the eastern coast, Swahili culture remained far stronger.

The effect of this foreign presence on African institutions and society, then, must be considered on a case-by-case basis. In a political sense, the foreign penetration had relatively little effect, and in general, traditional African political systems continued to maintain their vitality. By now, monarchy had become a common form of political institution throughout much of the continent. Some states, like the kingdom of Benin in West Africa, were highly centralized, and the person of the king was imbued with a mystical quality that bespoke his semi-divine status. An example of the awesome authority of some African rulers was the Yoruba custom whereby members of the king's family and entourage were immolated or expected to commit suicide at his death.

Other states more closely resembled a collection of decentralized principalities knit together by ties of kinship or other loyalties. The state of Ashanti in the Gold Coast was a case in point. The kingdom consisted of a number of previously independent microstates linked together by kinship ties and subordinated to the king, who served as a sort of *primus inter pares* (first among equals) and the representative of the unity of the entire state. To provide visible evidence of this unity, each local ruler was assigned a ceremonial stool of office to serve as a symbol of the kinship ties linking the rulers together, while the king possessed a "golden stool" to symbolize the unity of the entire state. Some historians believe that the decision to integrate the various decentralized principalities into a larger state was made in response to the growing challenge of European power.

The Great City of Timbuktu

After its founding in the twelfth century, Timbuktu became a great center of Islamic learning and a fabled city of mysteries and riches to Europeans. In the sixteenth century, Timbuktu was still a major commercial center on the trade route through the Sahara. This description of the city was written in 1526 by Leo Africanus, a Muslim from the Islamic state of Granada and one of the great travelers of his time.

Leo Africanus, History and Description of Africa

Here are many shops of artificers and merchants, and especially of such as weave linen and cotton cloth. And hither do the Barbary merchants bring cloth of Europe. All the women of this region, except the maid-servants, go with their faces covered, and sell all necessary victuals. The inhabitants, and especially strangers there residing, are exceeding rich, insomuch that the king that now is, married both his daughters to rich merchants. Here are many wells containing sweet water; and so often as the river Niger overflows, they convey the water thereof by certain sluices into the town. Corn, cattle, milk, and butter this region yields in great abundance: but salt is very scarce here; for it is brought hither by land from Taghaza which is 500 miles distant. When I myself was here, I saw one camel's load of salt sold for 80 ducats. The rich king of Timbuktu has many plates and scepters of gold, some whereof weigh 1300 pounds: and he keeps a magnificent and well-furnished court. When he travels any whither he rides upon a camel which is led by some of his noblemen; and so he does likewise when he goes forth to warfare, and all his soldiers ride upon horses. Whoever will speak unto this king must first fall down before his feet, and then taking up earth must first sprinkle it upon his own head and shoulders: which custom is ordinarily observed by . . . ambassadors from other princes. He has always 3000 horsemen, and a number of footmen that shoot poisoned arrows, attending upon him. They have often skirmishes with those that refuse to pay tribute, and so many as they take, they sell unto the merchants of Timbuktu. Here are very few horses bred, and the merchants and courtiers keep certain little nags which they use to travel upon: but their best horses are brought out of Barbary. . . . Here are great store of doctors, judges, priests, and other learned men, that are bountifully maintained at the king's cost and charges, and hither are brought divers manuscripts or written books out of Barbary, which are sold for more money than any other merchandise. The coin of Timbuktu is of gold without any stamp or superscription: but in matters of small value they use certain shells brought hither out of the kingdom of Persia, 400 of which are worth a ducat: and 6-2/3 pieces of their gold coin weigh an ounce. The inhabitants are people of gentle and cheerful disposition, and spend a great part of the night singing and dancing through all the streets of the city. . . .

Many Africans, however, continued to live in decentralized political units where authority rested in a village or tribal chief or among the heads of local kinship groups. The Ibo peoples of eastern Nigeria were an example. Ibo society, based on semi-independent villages linked together by convenience, was highly individualistic and egalitarian and lacked the hierarchical quality of many other societies within the region. The Ibo were active traders, and the area produced more slaves than practically any other on the continent.

Although foreign influence hardly affected African political institutions, it certainly made inroads in other areas. The steady growth of interregional contacts stimulated trade and manufacturing although, as we have seen, the importation of Western manufactured goods undermined a number of local handicraft industries, and Portuguese activities along the east coast virtually destroyed the traditional Indian Ocean trade network. The introduction of new crops from the Americas, such as corn and manioc, led to an increase in population and in some cases to changes in social patterns. Manioc, for example, was cultivated primarily by women, thus freeing men from agricultural activities to take part in commercial pursuits. The impact of European commercial activities was particularly strong in West Africa, and some historians have interpreted the activities of merchants and rulers in this region as a form of early capitalism. Still, the vast majority of Africans continued to live on the land as farmers, herders, fishermen, or food gatherers.

A final area where foreign influence had an impact was the realm of religious beliefs. This was particularly the case in North Africa, where the imprint of Islam steadily grew more visible. Islam had made its first appearance in North Africa shortly after the death of Muhammad, when Arab warriors swept across the northern edge of the continent toward the Strait of Gibraltar. In later centuries, Islam became dominant along the northern coast and gradually spread southward into the Sahara in the baggage of merchants, where it coexisted uneasily with the traditional religions practiced by nomadic peoples in the vast wastes beyond the towns.

Like other "great tradition" religions (such as Buddhism, Christianity, and Hinduism) that spread beyond their natural habitat, Islam survived and prospered in its new environment in part because it was able to adapt to local beliefs and practices. As in Southeast Asia (see "Daily Life" below), as time went on, the original Muslim doctrine absorbed a number of local practices to enhance its appeal to the peoples of West Africa and the Sahara. One example of this process is Sufism (based on the Arabic word for "wool"; many early adherents of Sufist beliefs wore woolen garments similar to those worn by Western monks at the time). Sufism was a mystical form of Islam that was based on the desire to establish a more intimate and emotional relationship with God than was provided by the more strict forms of classical Islam practiced by its first adherents on the Arabian peninsula (see Chapter 7). Sufi mystics also believed that some of their leaders possessed special powers (known as *baraka*, or holiness) and formed brotherhoods around such individuals to engage in ritual practices that enabled adherents to achieve a mystical communion with God.

For a time, such concepts received serious and favorable consideration from Muslim scholars throughout the Islamic world. In the seventeenth and eighteenth centuries, however, when Islam was forced to retreat before the concerted offensive launched by Christendom, some Muslim thinkers became convinced that their losses were due to the corruption of Muhammad's teachings by heretical doctrines and practices. In the mid-eighteenth century, a reformist movement to purify Islam began in the Arabian peninsula under the leadership of a legal scholar named Muhammad ibn Abd al-Wahhab. His doctrine, called Wahhabism, was one of several efforts at the time to cleanse Islam of its encrusted impurities and return to the basic elements in the doctrine: God, Muhammad, and the Koran. Supported by Ibn Saud, a local tribal chief and an ancestor of the first king of the modern state of Saudi Arabia, Wahhabism began to influence Muslim beliefs and practices throughout the Islamic world.

The spread of Wahhabi reformism created problems for ruling groups in West Africa and the Sahara. Islam had provided these societies with a number of benefits, including a written language, literature, and ethics and a system of law. But a strict interpretation of Islamic doctrine undoubtedly alienated some elements in the local population whose commitment to the Muslim religion was tempered by remnants of traditional beliefs and practices. Often, local rulers whose religious convictions obviously had strong political connotations compromised on the issue, a stance that aroused the disapproval of orthodox elements within the merchant community and occasionally resulted in a takeover of the local government by reformist clerics. In all regions, the struggle between purity and accommodation created new tensions within the world of Islam.

The growing European presence led to the first appearance of Christianity in sub-Saharan Africa. Certainly, a key element in the European voyages of exploration was an effort to destroy the Arab monopoly of the trade with the East. But the missionary impulse was by no means absent. During their early years in Africa, the Portuguese had engaged in some missionary activity, notably in the kingdom of the Mwene Metapa and in the region of the Zaire River, where the local king of the state of Bakongo was converted to Christianity (see the box on p. 517). But when Portuguese authority declined, the small Christian community virtually disappeared, and Portugal's European successors, the English, the Dutch, and the French, made little effort to combine their commercial activities with the message of the Gospel. Except for the tiny European foothold in South Africa and the isolated kingdom of Ethiopia, Christianity provided little obstacle to the spread of Islam in Africa.

Southeast Asia in the Era of the Spice Trade

In Southeast Asia, the encounter with the West that began with the arrival of Portuguese fleets in the Indian Ocean at the end of the fifteenth century eventually resulted in the breakdown of traditional societies and the advent of colonial rule. In general, however, the process was a gradual one. It began in 1511, when the Portuguese conquered the Islamic sultanate of Malacca, on the west coast of the Malay peninsula. During the next several decades, the Portuguese and the Spanish vied for control of the spice trade between the Indonesian archipelago and the Mediterranean Sea. Spain established its own base of operations in the Philippine Islands, while Portugal remained dominant in the Spice Islands further to the south.

≋ Christianity in the Congo ≋

The kingdom of the Congo (Bakongo) was one of the first states in West Africa to be introduced to Christianity. The following passage, written by a Portuguese slave merchant named Duarte Lopez, describes the effect that conversion to Christianity had on the dress of the local elite and the dining habits of the king.

Duarte Lopez at the Court of the King of the Congo

In ancient times the king and his courtiers dressed themselves in cloths made from palms, as we have previously described. With these they covered the lower part of the body, securing them with a belt woven from the same material, and finely worked. In front they used to suspend, like aprons, pretty and delicate little skins of animals, such as baby tigers, civet cats, sables, and martens, always with the head left on.

The poor and common people dressed from the waist down in the way described, but using coarser cloth. The upper part of the body was naked.

The women cover the lower part of the body with three cloths, one long and coming down to the heels, the second shorter, and the third shorter still and edged with its own fringe. Each of them are draped on the cross and open in front. They cover the breast with a bodice that comes down to the waist. The cloths are made from the same palm fibers, as are also the capes they wear on their shoulders. They go about with the face uncovered, and wearing similar little caps to the men.

Middle class women also dress in this fashion, but using coarser material. The slaves and lower class women only cover the body from the waist down, the rest being naked.

But after the kingdom had received the Christian faith, the grandees of the court began to dress like the Portuguese, wearing mantles, capes, and cloaks of scarlet silk, each according to his means. They began to wear hats, and bonnets, and velvet and leather sandals, and Portuguese style bootees, and to carry large swords at the side.

The common people who cannot afford to dress in the Portuguese fashion continue to wear the traditional costume.

The women also dress like the Portuguese, except that they do not wear the cloak. They cover their heads with a veil, and place under it a cap of black velvet ornamented with jewels, and they wear several gold chains round the neck. Only the ladies of the court adorn themselves in this fashion. The poor retain the old costumes.

When the king was converted to Christianity, he reformed the court to a certain extent in imitation of that of the king of Portugal, beginning with the service of his table. When he eats in public, they erect a three-tiered dais covered with Indian carpets. On it they place the table with a seat of crimson velvet studded with gold nails. The king always eats there alone, as no one may sit at table with him. The princes remain covered. He has table plate of gold and silver, which does credit to his food and drink.

At the opening of the seventeenth century, new competitors entered the field. The English, the Dutch, and the French began to take part in the scramble for trading rights in the region. A European presence was established on the Southeast Asian mainland, as several European states set up factories (stations run by merchants) in Burma, Vietnam, and Thailand, as well as in the Malay states to the south. The effects of this first maritime encounter between Europeans and the peoples of Southeast Asia varied from one area to another. By 1700, most of the European factories on the mainland had been abandoned. Only in the Indonesian archipelago, where the Dutch emerged triumphant from a bloody competition with the English, did a European power begin to undermine indigenous states. Here the Dutch would succeed in taking over virtually the entire region by the end of the eighteenth century. Elsewhere, states in the region maintained their independence and vitality.

Building Stable Political Systems on the Mainland

In 1500, Southeast Asia was becoming a relatively stable region, at least by comparison with past eras. The last of the great migrations into the area, that of the Thai and the Lao peoples, had taken place two centuries earlier. Throughout mainland Southeast Asia, from Burma in the west to Vietnam in the east, a series of kingdoms with distinctive ethnic, linguistic, and cultural characteristics were in the process of formation.

Nevertheless, periodic interregional conflicts did erupt among the emerging states on the Southeast Asian mainland. After their arrival in the area, the Thai peoples destroyed the remnants of the Angkor kingdom, forcing the surviving rulers of that once-powerful state to establish a new Khmer capital further to the southeast at Phnom Penh. The Thai then secured their control over the lower Chao Phraya River valley, with their capital at Ayuthaya. To the northwest, the Burmese kingdom of Ava in Upper Burma conquered the Mons state in the Irrawaddy delta and then turned its attention to Ayuthaya. Bitter and almost incessant conflict between the Thai and the Burmese culminated in the sack of Ayuthaya by a Burmese army in 1767. The Thai then moved their capital further to the south, finally settling at the end of the century at Bangkok on the Chao Phraya River a few miles upstream from the Gulf of Thailand.

Across the Annamite Mountains to the east, the Vietnamese had already begun their "March to the South" from their ancient homeland in the Red River valley in the thirteenth and fourteenth centuries. By the 1470s, the rival state of Champa on the central coast had been subdued, and the Vietnamese then gradually seized the Mekong delta from the Khmer. By the beginning of the nineteenth century, the Khmer monarchy (the successor of the old Angkor kingdom) had virtually disappeared,

◆ **The Thai Capital at Ayuthaya.**   The longest lasting Thai capital was at Ayuthaya, which was one of the finest cities in Asia from the fifteenth to the eighteenth century. After the Burmese invasion in 1767, most of Ayuthaya's inhabitants were killed, and all official Thai records were destroyed. Here the remains of some Buddhist stupas, erected in a ceremonial precinct in the center of the city, remind us of the greatness of Thai civilization.

surviving only as a joint protectorate of the Thai and the Vietnamese.

The Arrival of the West

In this context, the appearance of the small Portuguese fleet at Malacca in 1511 could not have seemed all that important. As we have seen, the Portuguese seized Malacca and soon occupied the Moluccas, the primary source of the cloves and nutmeg that had attracted them to the Indian Ocean. But the Portuguese lacked the military and financial resources to impose their authority in other areas and limited themselves to the occupation of small enclaves along the coast, which they used as trading posts or as way stations en route to the Spice Islands.

The situation changed with the arrival of new European powers on the scene. As the result of the formation of the East India Company and the VOC, the English and the Dutch were better financed than were the Portuguese. They moved aggressively to take advantage of the traditional trading patterns in the Indian Ocean and began to participate in the regional carrying trade, transporting Indian cotton goods to Southeast Asia for spices and precious metals to India from Japan and the Middle East.

The shift in power began in the early seventeenth century, when the Dutch seized the Portuguese fort at Amboina in the Moluccas. Taking advantage of their greater resources and superior seamanship, the Dutch then gradually squeezed the Portuguese out of the spice trade. During the next half century, the Dutch occupied most of the Portuguese coastal ports along the trade routes through the Indian Ocean, including the island of Ceylon (today's Sri Lanka, then valuable for its cinnamon) and Malacca. The Portuguese managed to retain their base at Goa, but a Dutch blockade bottled up Portuguese ships in the harbor for several years, rendering the fort useless for defending Lisbon's interests in the region. The aggressive and well-financed Dutch (the VOC possessed ten times the capital of the rival East India Company) drove the English traders out of the spice market as well, eventually reducing the English to a single port at Bencoolen on the southern coast of Sumatra. The Dutch also used force against Asian shippers to extend their role in the regional trade network. In 1622, a Dutch fleet attacked and sank a number of Chinese ships in an abortive effort to obtain access to the China market. A few years later, they established a fort on the island of Taiwan.

Having elbowed their rivals out of the lucrative spice trade, the Dutch now proceeded to select a new route to

CHRONOLOGY

The Spice Trade

Vasco da Gama lands at Calicut in southwestern India	1498
Portuguese seize Malacca	1511
Portuguese ships land in southern China	1514
Magellan's voyage around the world	1519–1522
East India Company established	1600
Vereenigde Oost-Indische Compagnie (VOC) established	1602
Dutch arrive at Bantam in Java	1605
English arrive at Surat in northwestern India	1608
Dutch fort established at Batavia	1619
Dutch seize Malacca from the Portuguese	1641
Burmese sack of Ayuthaya	1767
British seize Malacca from the Dutch	1795

the source of their profits. Rather than heading northeast from the Cape of Good Hope to India and thence through the Strait of Malacca to the Indies, Dutch fleets began to sail directly eastward from the cape on the strong westerly winds at that latitude. Then they caught the trade winds, which carried them northward through the Sunda Strait into the South China Sea. Although a ship occasionally failed to catch the southerly winds south of Java and ran aground on the west coast of Australia, the Dutch considered the new route worth the risk. By skirting the old trade route, they avoided the need to share their profits with the middlemen. Since they could no longer carry goods from the countries of the Indian Ocean to exchange for spices, the Dutch began to ship manufactured goods directly from Holland.

The Dutch also began to consolidate their political and military control over the entire area. They attempted to monopolize the clove trade by limiting cultivation of the crop to one island and forcing others to stop growing and trading the product. Then the Dutch turned their attention to the island of Java, where Governor General Jan Pieterszoon Coen had established a fort at Batavia (today's Jakarta) in 1619 to protect Dutch possessions in

⚜ An Exchange of Royal Correspondence ⚜

In 1681, King Louis XIV of France wrote a letter to the "king of Tonkin" (the Trinh family head, then acting as viceroy to the Vietnamese ruler) requesting permission for Christian missionaries to proselytize in Vietnam. The latter politely declined the request on the grounds that such activity was prohibited by ancient custom. In fact, Christian missionaries had been active in Vietnam for years, and their intervention in local politics had aroused the anger of the court in Hanoi.

A Letter to the King of Tonkin from Louis XIV

Most high, most excellent, most mighty and most magnanimous Prince, our very dear and good friend, may it please God to increase your greatness with a happy end!

We hear from our subjects who were in your Realm what protection you accorded them. We appreciate this all the more since we have for you all the esteem that one can have for a prince as illustrious through his military valor as he is commendable for the justice which he exercises in his Realm. We have even been informed that you have not been satisfied to extend this general protection to our subjects but, in particular, that you gave effective proofs of it to Messrs. Deydier and de Bourges. We would have wished that they

might have been able to recognize all the favors they received from you by having presents worthy of you offered you; but since the war which we have had for several years, in which all of Europe had banded together against us, prevented our vessels from going to the Indies, at the present time, when we are at peace after having gained many victories and expanded our Realm through the conquest of several important places, we have immediately given orders to the Royal Company to establish itself in your kingdom as soon as possible, and have commanded Messrs. Deydier and de Bourges to remain with you in order to maintain a good relationship between our subjects and yours, also to warn us on occasions that might present themselves when we might be able to give you proofs of our esteem and of our wish to concur with your satisfaction as well as with your best interests.

By way of initial proof, we have given orders to have brought to you some presents which we believe might be agreeable to you. But the one thing in the world which we desire most, both for you and for your Realm, would be to obtain for your subjects who have already embraced the law of the only true God of heaven and earth, the freedom to profess it, since this law is the highest, the noblest, the most sacred and especially

---

the East. At first, the VOC was forced to pay tribute to the inland state of Mataram, which had succeeded Majapahit as the major power on the island. But eventually, like the British in India (see Chapter 16), the Dutch were compelled to bring inland areas under their control in order to protect their position. Gradually, they stripped Mataram of its coastal possessions until it became a virtual protectorate of the VOC. The Dutch did not initially establish a formal colony, however; instead, as the British would do later in India, they tried to rule as much as possible through the local landed aristocracy. In Java and the neighboring island of Sumatra, they established pepper plantations, which soon became the source of massive profits for Dutch merchants in Amsterdam.

The arrival of the Europeans had somewhat less impact on mainland Southeast Asia, where cohesive monarchies in Burma, Thailand, and Vietnam resisted foreign encroachment. The Portuguese established limited trade relations with several mainland states, including Ayuthaya, Burma, Vietnam, and the remnants of the

old Angkor kingdom in Cambodia. By the early seventeenth century, other nations had followed and had begun to compete actively for trade and missionary privileges. As was the case elsewhere, the Europeans soon became involved in local factional disputes as a means of obtaining political and economic advantages. In Burma, the English and the French supported rival groups in the internal struggles of the monarchy at Ava until a new dynasty emerged and threw the foreigners out. A similar process took place at Ayuthaya. The French were especially active in both Ava and Ayuthaya and established an organization called the Society for Foreign Missions to promote missionary activities in Southeast Asia. At Ayuthaya, however, the French managed to arouse the suspicion of both the Thai monarchy and the English and were forced to evacuate the area in the late seventeenth century.

In Vietnam, the arrival of Western merchants and missionaries coincided with a period of internal conflict among ruling groups in the country. By the seventeenth

the most suitable to have kings reign absolutely over the people.

We are even quite convinced that, if you knew the truths and the maxims which it teaches, you would give first of all to your subjects the glorious example of embracing it. We wish you this incomparable blessing together with a long and happy reign, and we pray God that it may please Him to augment your greatness with the happiest of endings.

Written at Saint-Germain-en-Laye, the 10th day of January, 1681,
Your very dear and good friend,
Louis

Answer from the King of Tonkin to Louis XIV

The King of Tonkin sends to the King of France a letter to express to him his best sentiments, saying that he was happy to learn that fidelity is a durable good of man and that justice is the most important of things. Consequently practicing of fidelity and justice cannot but yield good results. Indeed, though France and our Kingdom differ as to mountains, rivers, and boundaries, if fidelity and justice reign among our villages, our conduct will express all of our good feelings and contain precious gifts. Your communication, which comes from a country which is a thousand leagues away, and which proceeds from the heart as a testimony of your sincerity, merits repeated consideration and infinite praise. Politeness toward strangers is nothing unusual in our country. There is not a stranger who is not well received by us. How then could we refuse a man from France, which is the most celebrated among the kingdoms of the world and which for love of us wishes to frequent us and bring us merchandise? These feelings of fidelity and justice are truly worthy to be applauded. As regards your wish that we should cooperate in propagating your religion, we do not dare to permit it, for there is an ancient custom, introduced by edicts, which formally forbids it. Now, edicts are promulgated only to be carried out faithfully; without fidelity nothing is stable. How could we disdain a well-established custom to satisfy a private friendship? . . .

We beg you to understand well that this is our communication concerning our mutual acquaintance. This then is my letter. We send you herewith a modest gift which we offer you with a glad heart.

This letter was written at the beginning of winter and on a beautiful day.

century, the Vietnamese "March to the South" had resulted in the final destruction of the Champa protectorate and the seizure of the Mekong delta from the Khmer state. But expansion brought internal problems in the form of a civil war that temporarily divided the country into two separate states, one in the north and the other in the south. After their arrival in the mid-seventeenth century, the European powers characteristically began to intervene in local politics, with the Portuguese and the Dutch supporting rival factions. By the end of the century, when it became clear that economic opportunities were limited, most European states abandoned their factories in the area. French missionaries attempted to remain, but their efforts were hampered by the local authorities, who viewed the Catholic insistence that converts give their primary loyalty to the pope as a threat to the legal status and prestige of the Vietnamese emperor (see the box on p. 520).

Why were the mainland states better able to resist the European challenge than their counterparts in the Malay world? One factor may have been their relatively cohesive character. Divided from each other by clear-cut ethnic and cultural differences, the mainland states in Burma, Thailand, and Vietnam had begun to define themselves as distinct political entities—if not nations—in a highly competitive environment. In the Indies, the relative absence of recognizable ethnic and religious differences made for a more fluid political situation even in the absence of Western pressure and made it more difficult for local authorities to resist the Europeans when they appeared.

Ironically, the Malay states may also have been victimized by their resources and strategic location. The huge profits to be made from the spice trade intensified the determination of European merchants and their rulers to gain control of the source of the spices. The mainland states, lacking the geographical and climatic conditions necessary to produce key spices such as cloves and pepper, did not have to face that challenge. As we shall see, their reprieve was only temporary.

State and Society in Precolonial Southeast Asia

Between 1500 and 1800, Southeast Asia experienced the last flowering of traditional culture before the advent of European colonial rule in the nineteenth century. Although the coming of the Europeans had an immediate and direct impact in some areas, notably the Philippines and parts of the Malay world, in most areas Western influence was still relatively limited. Europeans occasionally dabbled in local politics and modified regional trade patterns, but they generally were not a decisive factor in the evolution of local political or social systems.

Nevertheless, Southeast Asian societies were changing in several subtle ways—in their trade patterns, their means of livelihood, and their religious beliefs. In some ways, these changes accentuated the differences between individual states in the region. Yet beneath these differences was an underlying commonality of life for most people. Despite the diversity of cultures and religious beliefs in the area, in most respects, Southeast Asians were closer to each other than they were to peoples outside the region. For the most part, the states and peoples of Southeast Asia were still in control of their own destiny.

GOVERNMENT AND POLITICS

The early modern era in Southeast Asia witnessed the development of increasingly sophisticated states. As the political systems began to mature, they evolved into four main types: Buddhist kings, Javanese kings, Islamic sultans, and Vietnamese emperors (for the case of Vietnam, which was strongly influenced by China, see Chapter 11). Significantly, all of them drew their original inspiration from foreign models. In every case, institutions and concepts imported from abroad were adapted to local circumstances.

The Buddhist style of kingship took shape between the eleventh and the fifteenth century, as Theravada Buddhism spread throughout the area in the wake of the collapse of the Hinduized empires of the past. It became the predominant form of political system in the Buddhist states of mainland Southeast Asia—Burma, Ayuthaya, Laos, and Cambodia.

Perhaps the dominant feature of the Buddhist model was the godlike character of the monarch. The king, by virtue of his *karma*, was considered to be innately superior to other human beings and, in fact, served as a link between human society and the cosmos. Court rituals stressed the sacred character of the monarch, and even the palace was modeled after the symbolic design of the Hindu universe. In its center was an architectural rendering of sacred Mount Meru, the legendary home of the gods.

Beyond the capital, the authority of the king rested essentially on his personal relationship with the provincial and district officials. The court appointed most high officials outside the capital, and the majority were nobles or members of the royal family. In general, these officials ruled their territories as miniature kingdoms, and the influence of the court over the provinces declined as the distance from the capital increased. At the far extremities of the kingdom were usually tribal peoples living in the mountains and only loosely assimilated into the state.

The Javanese style of kingship, which was also rooted in Indian political traditions, shared many of the characteristics of the mainland Buddhist system. Like their Buddhist counterparts, Javanese monarchs possessed a sacred quality (known in Malay as *wahyu*, or "divine light") and maintained the balance between the sacred and the material world. The royal palace, known as the *kraton*, was designed in the Hindu fashion to represent the center of the universe; from there rays radiated outward to the far corners of the realm.

But the Javanese and Buddhist models also differed in some key respects. In the first place, the Javanese kings generally did not appoint members of the royal family to serve as officials outside the capital. They relied instead on local officials called *priyayi*; although technically servants of the king rather than members of a local nobility, these officials often possessed considerable authority in their administrative territories and established elaborate rituals to maintain their status and prestige.

A second distinction between the Javanese and Buddhist models stemmed from the Islamic penetration of the Indonesian islands in the fifteenth and sixteenth centuries. At first, Muslim influence was felt mainly along the Malay peninsula and the northern coast of Java and Sumatra, but eventually it penetrated into the interior when the ruler of the inland Javanese state of Mataram converted to Islam. As a result, Javanese monarchs began to lose the semidivine quality that they had inherited from the earlier Hindu style of kingship.

The Javanese model was thus a blend of Buddhist and Islamic political traditions. The latter was found mainly on the Malay peninsula and in the small coastal states of the Indonesian archipelago. In the Islamic pattern, the head of state was a sultan, who was viewed as a mortal, although he still possessed some magical qualities. The sultan served as a defender of the faith and staffed his bureaucracy mainly with aristocrats, but he also frequently

The Timely End of Sultan Zainal-'Abidin

Acheh, on the northern tip of the island of Sumatra, was one of the first areas in Southeast Asia to be converted to Islam. This passage from the History of Acheh *describes the cruel habits of Sultan Zainal-'Abidin, who ruled in the early seventeenth century. Note the understated way in which the author describes his deposition.*

The History of Acheh

Then Sultan Seri'Alam was deposed and Sultan Zainal was installed.

The former had occupied the throne for one year before passing away. He passed away in the year 995 (A.H.) [A.D. 1617]. . . .

After the kingdom of Acheh Dar as-Salam and all its subject territories had been handed over to Sultan Zainal-'Abidin, he would always go out on to the arena and would have rutting elephants as well as ones which were not rutting charge each other, and as a result several people were gored to death by them, and the Bunga Setangkai palace was rammed and then collapsed in ruins together with its annexes. He pitted very small elephants against each other, and had buffaloes and bullocks fight, as well as rams. When he had the buffaloes fight a number of people were either killed, had bones broken, or were crippled or blinded. He would order men to beat each other and to duel with staves and shields, and would order Achehnese champion fencers to compete with Indian ones, so that several of the Achehnese and Indian fencers were killed and some were wounded. . . . He would order men from Pigu to do war-dances, and some had their faces smashed and

their cheeks blown out. He would order men from Tiku and men from Periman to fight with the long *kris* [Indonesian dagger], and some of them were injured. . . .

If the Sultan were holding audience in a certain place all the chiefs were instructed to sit in homage in the hot sun or in the rain without distinction between the good or the evil.

If the Sultan should spur on his horse when setting out and the chiefs could not keep up with it and were left behind, then they too would incur his wrath.

When the chiefs noticed these habits of the Sultan, and observed that they were growing worse day by day, they said to each other, "What should we do about our lord, for if his oppression of us is like this while he is still young, what will it be like when he is older? According to us, if he continues to be ruler everything will certainly fall in ruins about our ears." Then Sharif al-Muluk Maharaja Lela said, "If that is how it is, it would be best for us to depose our lord the Sultan."

After the chiefs had reached agreement on this matter, one evening the Sultan summoned persons to recite texts in praise of God, and the chiefs were summoned along with them. On that occasion they were reciting texts in the Friday annex. The Sultan was then put on an elephant and was taken to Makota 'Alam. When he arrived at Makota 'Alam . . . [where he was done to death] . . . the Sultan had occupied the throne for two years when he passed away. He passed away in the year 997 (A.H.) [A.D. 1619]. In that same year Sultan 'Ala ad-Din Ri'ayat Shah Marhum Sayyid al-Mukkamil was installed.

---

relied on the Muslim community of scholars—the *ulama*—and was expected, at least in theory, to rule according to the *Shari'ah* (see the box above).

In reality, Muslim traditions were slow to penetrate into the inland villages of Java and Sumatra, where the local population ignored the new doctrine or integrated it into their traditional forms of spirit worship. Such at least had been Marco Polo's observation when he visited Sumatra in the thirteenth century; he remarked that the hill people "worship this, that, and the other thing; for in fact the first thing that they see on rising in the morning, that they do worship for the rest of the day."[9] Muslim in-

stitutions and values had a greater impact along the coast, where urban merchants encountered their Muslim counterparts from foreign lands on a regular basis and found the new egalitarian creed more conducive to their lifestyle. This division between devout Muslims in the cities and the still essentially animist peasants in the rural villages created a bifurcation in Indonesian society that persists to this day.

At the bottom of the administrative hierarchy in all Southeast Asian societies were the villages, which were as diverse as the styles of kingship. In some areas, such as the Malay peninsula, the headman inherited his position and was considered a minor noble and the direct representative of the king. In the Philippines, the position of the village chief was also hereditary, but in the absence of any central authority, his position was not buttressed by royal power. In the Indonesian states, village life was relatively egalitarian with little sense of private property. Here the chief played a role similar to that of an orchestra conductor, attempting to harmonize the views of the villagers on issues of common concern.

THE ECONOMY

During the early period of European penetration, the economy of virtually all Southeast Asian societies continued to be based on agriculture, as it had been for thousands of years. Probably 90 percent of the total population throughout the region engaged in some form of farming, mostly the cultivation of wet rice or, in upland regions, of dry crops by the slash-and-burn method. Still,

by the sixteenth century, commerce was beginning to affect the daily lives of many Southeast Asians, especially in the cities that were beginning to proliferate along the coasts or on navigable rivers. In part, this was because agriculture itself was becoming more commercialized to a limited degree, as cash crops like sugar and spices replaced subsistence farming in rice or other cereals in some areas.

By the early modern era, trade was taking place at the local, regional, and interregional levels. At the local level, trade consisted primarily of the exchange of goods made by local artisans and other consumer products such as cloth, iron, and salt. For the most part, this local trade was still conducted through barter rather than money, although coins had come into general use in urban areas by about 1500. Sometimes, individual villages would specialize in various products and exchange them for needed commodities from other communities. Much of this commerce was carried by boat on the rivers or canals, since

✳ Map 14.4 The Pattern of World Trade.

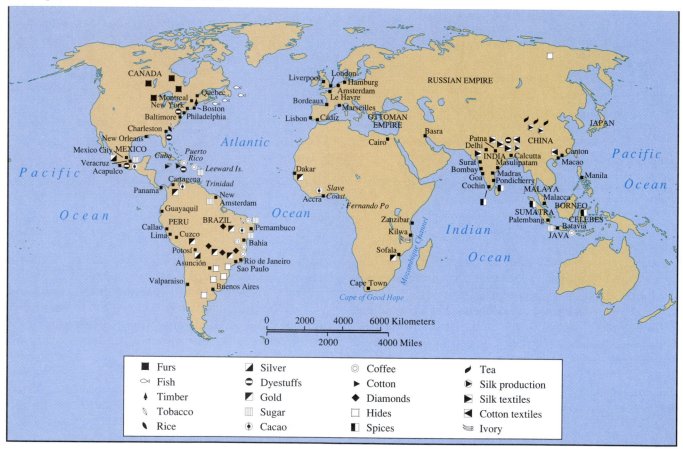

◆ **Bringing Lumber to Java.**   Long before the Europeans arrived, a brisk trade was taking place throughout the Indonesian islands and the South China Sea. Many of the goods that were transported through the area were carried on sturdy boats—called pinisi—that were manned by the Bugi people, who lived mainly in the eastern islands. This trade continues today, as these cargo ships in the harbor of Jakarta attest.

few countries in Southeast Asia had a road network until the colonial period.

Regional and interregional trade were already expanding before the coming of the Europeans. The growing importance of handicrafts contributed to the increase in regional trade, while the central geographical location of Southeast Asia enabled it to become a focal point in an interregional trading network. The spices, of course, were the mainstay of the interregional trade, but Southeast Asia exchanged other products as well. The region exported tin (mined in Malaya since the tenth century), copper, gold, tropical fruits and other agricultural products, cloth, gems, and luxury goods in exchange for manufactured goods, ceramics including Chinese porcelain, and high-quality textiles such as silk from China. Although Southeast Asia on balance was an importer of manufactured goods, the region produced some high-quality goods of its own. The ceramics of Vietnam and Thailand, though not made with the high-firing techniques used in China, were still of good quality. The Portuguese traveler Duarte Barbosa observed that the Javanese were skilled cabinetmakers, weapons manufacturers, shipbuilders, and locksmiths. The royal courts were both the main producers and the primary consumers of luxury goods, most of which were produced by highly skilled slaves in the employ of the court.

Sometimes the courts monopolized foreign trade as well; the sultan of Malacca and the Thai monarch are examples. Nevertheless, private merchants carried much of the long-distance trade. In the absence of social prejudices against commercial activities throughout much of the area (except Vietnam), aristocrats often engaged in trade. In addition, the Chinese, the Arabs, and the Bugis and Sulus from the Celebes and the Philippines, both Malayo-Polynesian–speaking peoples, all specialized in seaborne commerce. Chinese merchants from southern China set up a trade network in the major cities of Southeast Asia that still exists. The Ming and Qing dynasties tried to regulate this trade, but with little success.

Whether life had improved for the average villager in this period is difficult to say, but some comparisons with life in other regions are possible. In the first place, Southeast Asians probably enjoyed a somewhat higher living standard than most of their contemporaries elsewhere in Asia. Although most of the population was poor by modern Western standards, starvation and even widespread hunger were probably fairly rare. One Portuguese traveler noted that Java was "famed to be the most fruitful island in the world; therein is abundance of good rice; fresh meat in great plenty; sheep, cows, hens, goats, swine of great size both tame and wild, all in great numbers."[10]

Several factors help explain this relative prosperity. In the first place, most of Southeast Asia has been blessed by a salubrious climate. Climatic disasters such as typhoons are rare, while the uniformly high temperatures and the abundant rainfall and numerous rivers and streams enable as many as two or even three crops to be grown each year. Secondly, although the soil in some areas is poor, the alluvial deltas on the mainland are fertile, and the volcanoes of Indonesia periodically spew forth rich volcanic ash that renews the mineral resources of the soil of Sumatra and Java. Bananas, mangoes, papaya, citrus fruits, and other tropical products thrive throughout the region. Finally, with some exceptions, most of Southeast Asia was relatively thinly populated. According to one estimate, the population of the entire region in 1600 was about 20 million, or about 5.5 persons per square kilometer, well below levels elsewhere in Asia. Only in a few areas such as the Red River delta in northern Vietnam was overpopulation a serious problem—undoubtedly, one reason for Vietnam's "March to the South."

DAILY LIFE

For most people in Southeast Asia, daily life in the early period of European penetration was not a great deal different from what it had been for hundreds of years. The vast majority of the population still lived as rice farmers, small traders, hunters, or fishermen in the villages that dotted the landscape of rice paddies like blotches on a huge mirror. Their houses were simple, consisting of a main room, a few smaller ones, and a veranda. Because of the warm climate, the windows had neither panes nor shutters. The houses were constructed of wood, mainly palm trees or bamboo, and thatch (other building materials such as stone were scarce—in some countries, the rulers even put restrictions on the use of stone). Generally, houses were raised on stilts, which prevented them from flooding during the monsoon season, provided a storage area for garbage and domestic animals, and protected the family from wild animals. The interiors were also simple. Only royalty and the aristocracy who lived in separate walled compounds in urban areas would have furniture or rugs. Meals consisted of rice, fruit, and vegetables, with occasionally a little meat or fish. Southeast Asians used no dinner utensils and ate on palm leaves.

Like the domestic architecture, social institutions tended to be fairly homogeneous throughout Southeast Asia. Compared with China and India, there was little social stratification, and the nuclear family predominated. In general, women fared better in Southeast Asia than anywhere else in Asia. Although they were usually restricted to specialized work, such as making ceramics, weaving, or transplanting the rice seedlings into the main paddy fields, and rarely possessed legal rights equal to those of men, they enjoyed a comparatively high degree of freedom and status in most societies in the region. Daughters often had the same inheritance rights as sons, while family property was held jointly between husband and wife. Wives were often permitted to divorce their husbands, and monogamy was the rule rather than the exception. In some cases, the family of the groom provided the dowry in marriage, and married couples often went to live in the wife's village.

Religious beliefs were changing during this period, particularly in the Malay world and the Philippines, where Islam and Christianity were beginning to attract converts. Buddhism was advancing on the mainland, where it became dominant, at least in lowland areas, from Burma to Vietnam. These world religions brought other changes in their train—temple education and *pesantran* schools for Islamic scholars, new religious and moral restrictions on human behavior such as sexual practices and eating meat, and often lower status for women, who normally did not receive as much religious training as males. Significantly, however, many of these strictures were ignored in Southeast Asia, where traditional social practices and popular religious beliefs con-

◆ **Your Ancestors are Watching You!** The Toraja people live in the central mountains of the island of Sulawesi (once known as Celebes). Long isolated from peoples living elsewhere in the area, Toraja society was characterized by a number of unique customs, such as burial practices. At first, the remains of the dead were placed in a coffin suspended from a cliff. Later, the coffin was imbedded in the cliff face, while representations of the dead looked out at their descendants in the valley below.

tinued to survive. Buddhists in Burma and Thailand and Muslims in the Indonesian islands continued to believe in the existence of nature spirits even while professing adherence to their new religions. One change did occur in Muslim and Christian communities, however; because the new religions discouraged the traditional tattooing of the body, people turned to the technique of decorating textiles called *batik*.

In general, Islam was more successful than Christianity in much of the area, perhaps because Muslims were more tolerant of local customs. Some foreign Muslims did complain, however, that local converts married infidels, ate dog or pork, or drank wine.

The growing foreign penetration also tended to accentuate the distinctions between elite and popular culture, although the differences were not as clear-cut as in China and India. In general, in Southeast Asia foreign cultural influence blended and intermingled with traditional forms of creative expression. Written literature was still in its infancy (until the sixteenth century, when paper was introduced from abroad, all writing was done on bamboo strips or palm leaves), but theater, accompanied by music and dancing, was popular. In most Southeast Asian societies, theater was strongly influenced by Indian forms and drew its themes from the Ramayana, the Mahabharata, and the Buddhist *jataka* stories. The advent of

Islam did not bring an end to Indian influence, but the Muslim strictures against depicting the human figure may have encouraged the development of the specialized form of Indonesian theater known as *wayang kulit,* or the shadow play.

Conclusion

At the end of the fifteenth century, Europeans burst upon the world scene. Beginning with the seemingly modest ventures of the Portuguese ships that sailed southward along the West African coast in the mid-fifteenth century, the process accelerated with the epoch-making voyages of Christopher Columbus to the Americas and Vasco da Gama to the Indian Ocean in the 1490s. Soon a number of other European states had entered the scene, and by the end of the eighteenth century, they had created a global trade network dominated by Western ships and Western power.

In less than three hundred years, the European age of exploration changed the shape of the world. In some areas, such as the Americas and the Spice Islands, it led to the destruction of indigenous civilizations and the establishment of European colonies. In others, as in Africa, South Asia, and mainland Southeast Asia, it left native regimes intact but had a strong impact on local societies and regional trade patterns.

At the time, many European observers viewed the process in a favorable light. It not only expanded world trade and encouraged economic development, but it also introduced "heathen peoples" to the message of Jesus Christ. Some modern historians have been much more critical, concluding that European activities during the sixteenth and seventeenth centuries had already created a "tributary mode of production" based on European profits from unequal terms of trade that foreshadowed the highly exploitative relationship characteristic of the later colonial period. Some recent scholars have questioned that contention, however, and argue that although Western commercial operations had a significant impact on global trade patterns, they did not—at least before the eighteenth century—freeze out non-European participants. Muslim merchants, for example, were long able to evade European efforts to eliminate them from the spice trade, while the trans-Saharan caravan trade was relatively unaffected by European merchant shipping along the West African coast. In some cases, the European presence may even have encouraged new economic activity, as in the Indian subcontinent (see Chapter 16). If there was an "age of Western dominance," then, it did not take shape before the end of the period under consideration here.

CHAPTER NOTES

1. Harry J. Benda and John A. Larkin, eds., *The World of Southeast Asia: Selected Historical Readings* (New York, 1967), p. 13.
2. Quoted in J. H. Parry, *The Age of Reconnaissance: Discovery, Exploration and Settlement, 1450 to 1650* (New York, 1963), p. 33.
3. Quoted in Richard B. Reed, "The Expansion of Europe," in Richard DeMolen, ed., *The Meaning of the Renaissance and Reformation* (Boston, 1974), p. 308.
4. K. N. Chaudhuri, *Trade and Civilization in the Indian Ocean: An Economic History from the Rise of Islam to 1750* (Cambridge, 1985), p. 65.
5. J. H. Parry, *The European Reconnaissance: Selected Documents* (New York, 1968), p. 113, quoting from Armando Cortesao, *The Summa Oriental of Tome Pires* (London, 1944), 2:283–87.
6. Miguel Leon-Portilla, ed., *The Broken Spears: The Aztec Account of the Conquest of Mexico* (Boston, 1969), p. 51.
7. Quoted in Parry, *The Age of Reconnaissance*, pp. 176–77.
8. Quoted in Basil Davidson, *Africa in History: Themes and Outlines* (London, 1968), p. 137.
9. Benda and Larkin, *The World of Southeast Asia*, p. 13.
10. *The Book of Duarte Barbosa* (Nedeln, 1967), 2:191.

SUGGESTED READINGS

Classic works on the period of European expansion include J. H. Parry, *The Age of Reconnaissance: Discovery, Exploration and Settlement, 1450 to 1650* (New York, 1963); B. Penrose, *Travel and Discovery in the Renaissance, 1420–1620* (New York, 1962); and the brief work by J. H. Parry, *The Establishment of European Hegemony, 1415–1715* (New York, 1961). Also, see K. M. Panikkar, *Asia and Western Dominance* (London, 1959) and H. Furber, *Rival Empires of Trade in the Orient, 1600–1800* (Minneapolis, 1976). For a more critical interpretation, see E. Wolf, *Europe and the People without History* (Berkeley, Calif., 1982) and A. G. Frank, *World Accumulation, 1492–1789* (New York, 1978).

On the technological aspects, see C. M. Cipolla, *Guns, Sails, and Empires: Technological Innovation and the Early Phases of European Expansion, 1400–1700* (New York, 1965); F. Fernandez-Armesto, ed., *The Times Atlas of World Exploration* (New York, 1991); R. C. Smith, *Vanguard of Empire: Ships of Exploration in the Age of Columbus* (Oxford, 1993); and D. Boorstin, *The Discoverers* (New York, 1983). For an overview on the impact of European expansion in the Indian Ocean, see K. N. Chaudhuri, *Trade and Civilization in the Indian Ocean: An Economic History from the Rise of Islam to 1750* (Cambridge, 1985). For a series of stimulating essays reflecting recent scholarship, see J. D. Tracy, *The Rise of Merchant Empires: Long-Distance Trade in the Early Modern World, 1350–1750* (Cambridge, 1990).

On European expansion in the Americas, see S. E. Morison, *The European Discovery of America: The Southern Voyages, A.D. 1492–1616* (New York, 1974). On Columbus, see the brief biography by J. S. Collis, *Christopher Columbus* (London, 1976). For a fundamental work on Spanish colonization, see J. H. Parry, *The Spanish Seaborne Empire* (New York, 1966). The standard work on the conquistadors is F. A. Kirkpatrick, *The Spanish Conquistadores* (Cleveland, 1968). See also the richly illustrated H. Innes, *The Conquistadors* (New York, 1969). The human effects of the interaction of New World and Old World cultures are examined thoughtfully in A. W. Crosby, *The Columbia Exchange: Biological and Cultural Consequences of 1492* (Westport, Conn., 1972).

On Portuguese expansion, the fundamental work is C. R. Boxer, *The Portuguese Seaborne Empire, 1415–1825* (New York, 1969). For a more recent interpretation, see W. B. Diffie and G. D. Winius, *Foundations of the Portuguese Empire, 1415–1580* (Minneapolis, 1979). On the Dutch, see J. I. Israel, *Dutch Primacy in World Trade, 1585–1740* (Oxford, 1989). The effects of European trade in Southeast Asia are discussed in A. Reid, *Southeast Asia in the Age of Commerce, 1450–1680* (New Haven, Conn., 1989).

On the African slave trade, the standard work is P. Curtin, *The African Slave Trade: A Census* (Madison, 1969). For more recent treatments, see H. S. Klein, *The Middle Passage: Comparative Studies in the Atlantic Slave Trade* (Princeton, N. J., 1978); P. Lovejoy, *Transformations in Slavery: A History of Slavery in Africa* (1983); and P. Manning, *Slavery and African Life* (1990). Also, see C. Palmer, *Human Cargoes: The British Slave Trade to Spanish America, 1700–1739* (Urbana, Ill., 1981) and K. F. Kiple, *The Caribbean Slave: A Biological History* (Cambridge, 1984).

CHAPTER

15

Religious Reform and State Building in Europe

On April 18, 1520, a lowly monk stood before the emperor and princes of Germany in the city of Worms. He had been called before this august gathering to answer charges of heresy, charges that could threaten his very life. The monk was confronted with a pile of his books and asked if he wished to defend them all or reject a part. Courageously, Martin Luther defended them all and asked to be shown where any part was in error on the basis of "Scripture and plain reason." The emperor was outraged by Luther's response and made his own position clear the next day: "Not only I, but you of this noble German nation, would be forever disgraced if by our negligence not only heresy but the very suspicion of heresy were to survive. After having heard yesterday the obstinate defense of Luther, I regret that I have so long delayed in proceeding against him and his false teaching. I will have no more to do with him." Luther's appearance at Worms set the stage for a serious challenge to the authority of the Catholic church. It was by no means the first in the church's fifteen-hundred-year history, but its consequences were more far-reaching than anyone at Worms in 1520 could have imagined. The unity of Christendom was shattered by the Protestant Reformation initiated by Martin Luther.

Although the Protestant and Catholic Reformations of the sixteenth century made religion a central focus of people's lives, by the middle of the sixteenth century this renewal of religious passion had been accomplished at a great cost— the breakup of the religious unity of medieval

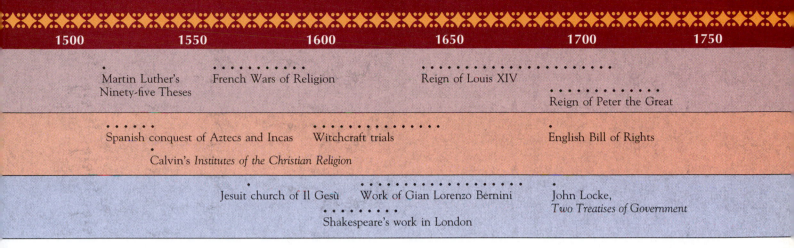

Martin Luther's Ninety-five Theses   French Wars of Religion   Reign of Louis XIV

Reign of Peter the Great

Spanish conquest of Aztecs and Incas   Witchcraft trials   English Bill of Rights

Calvin's *Institutes of the Christian Religion*

Jesuit church of Il Gesù   Work of Gian Lorenzo Bernini   John Locke, *Two Treatises of Government*

Shakespeare's work in London

Europe. This religious division (Catholics versus Protestants) was instrumental in beginning a series of wars that dominated much of European history from 1560 to 1650 and, in turn, exacerbated the economic and social crises that were besetting Europe. Wars, revolutions and constitutional crises, economic depression, social disintegration, the witchcraft craze, and demographic crisis all afflicted Europe and have led some historians to speak of the almost hundred years from 1560 to 1650 as an age of crisis in European life.

One of the responses to these crises was a search for order and harmony. As the internal social and political rebellions and revolts died down, it became apparent that the privileged classes of society—the aristocrats—remained in control, although the various states exhibited important differences in political forms. The most general trend was an extension of monarchical power as a stabilizing force. This development, which historians have called absolutism or absolute monarchy, was most evident in France during the flamboyant reign of Louis XIV. But other states, such as England, responded differ-ently to domestic crisis, and another very different system emerged where monarchs were limited by the power of their representative assemblies. Absolute and limited monarchy were the two poles of seventeenth-century state building.

The Protestant Reformation

The Protestant Reformation had its beginning in a typical medieval question—what must I do to be saved? Martin Luther, a deeply religious man, found an answer that did not fit within the traditional teachings of the late medieval church. Ultimately he split with that church, destroying the religious unity of western Christendom. That other people were concerned with the same question is evident in the rapid spread of the Reformation. But religion was so entangled in the social, economic, and political forces of the period that the hope of the Protestant reformers to transform the church quickly proved illusory.

Prelude to Reformation

Martin Luther's reform movement was not the first in sixteenth-century Europe. Christian or northern Renaissance humanism, which evolved as Italian Renaissance humanism spread to northern Europe, had as one of its major goals the reform of Christendom. The new classical learning of the Italian Renaissance did not spread to the European countries north of the Alps until the second half of the fifteenth century. Gradually, intellectuals and artists from the cities north of the Alps flocked to

Italy and returned home enthusiastic about the new education and the recovery of ancient thought and literature that we associate with Italian Renaissance humanism.

The most important characteristic of northern Renaissance humanism was its reform program. With their belief in the ability of human beings to reason and improve themselves, the northern humanists thought that through education in the sources of classical, and especially Christian, antiquity, they could instill a true inner piety or an inward religious feeling that would bring about a reform of the church and society. For this reason, Christian humanists supported schools, brought out new editions of the classics, and prepared new editions of the Bible and writings of the church fathers. In the preface to his edition of the Greek New Testament, the famous humanist Desiderius Erasmus wrote:

> Indeed, I disagree very much with those who are unwilling that Holy Scripture, translated into the vulgar tongue, be read by the uneducated, as if Christ taught such intricate doctrines that they could scarcely be understood by very few theologians, or as if the strength of the Christian religion consisted in men's ignorance of it . . . I would that even the lowliest women read the Gospels and the Pauline Epistles. And I would that they were translated into all languages so that they could be read and understood not only by Scots and Irish but also by Turks and Saracens. . . . Would that, as a result, the farmer sing some portion of them at the plow, the weaver hum some parts of them to the movement of his shuttle, the traveler lighten the weariness of the journey with stories of this kind![1]

This belief in the power of education would remain an important characteristic of European civilization. Like later intellectuals, Christian humanists believed that to change society they must first change the human beings who compose it.

The most influential of all the Christian humanists was Erasmus (1466–1536), who formulated and popularized the reform program of Christian humanism. After withdrawing from a monastery, he wandered to France, England, Italy, Germany, and Switzerland, conversing everywhere in the classical Latin that might be called his mother tongue. The *Handbook of the Christian Knight*, published in 1503, reflected his preoccupation with religion. He called his conception of religion "the philosophy of Christ," by which he meant that Christianity should be a guiding philosophy for the direction of daily life rather than the system of dogmatic beliefs and practices that the medieval church seemed to stress. In other words, he emphasized inner piety and ethics while deemphasizing the external forms of religion (such as the sacraments, pilgrimages, fasts, veneration of saints, and relics).

To Erasmus, the reform of the church meant spreading an understanding of the philosophy of Christ, providing enlightened education in the sources of early Christianity, and making commonsense criticism of the abuses in the church. The latter is especially evident in his work, *The Praise of Folly*, written in 1511, in which Erasmus undertook a humorous, yet effective criticism of the most corrupt practices of his own society. He was especially harsh on the abuses in the church.

Erasmus's reform program, however, was not destined to effect the reform of the church that he so desired. His moderation and his emphasis on education were quickly overwhelmed by the violence unleashed by the passions of the Reformation. Undoubtedly, his work helped to prepare the way for the Reformation; as contemporaries proclaimed, "Erasmus laid the egg that Luther hatched." Yet Erasmus eventually disapproved of Luther and the Protestant reformers. He had no intention of destroying the unity of the medieval Christian church; instead, his whole program was based on reform within the church.

Church and Religion on the Eve of the Reformation

The institutional problems of the Catholic church in the fourteenth and fifteenth centuries, especially the failure of the Renaissance popes to provide spiritual leadership, were bound to affect the spiritual life of all Christendom. The general impression of the tenor of religious life on the eve of the Reformation is one of much deterioration, coupled with abundant evidence of a continuing desire for valid religious experience from millions of devout lay people.

The economic changes of the fourteenth and fifteenth centuries and the continuing preoccupation of the papal court with finances had an especially strong impact upon the clergy. The highest positions of the clergy were increasingly held by either the nobility or wealthier members of the bourgeoisie. At the same time, to enhance their revenues, high church officials accumulated church offices in ever-larger numbers. This practice of pluralism (the holding of many church offices) led, in turn, to the problem of absenteeism, as church officeholders neglected their episcopal duties and delegated the entire administration of their dioceses to underlings, who were often underpaid and little interested in performing their duties. No wonder that the fifteenth century was rife with complaints about the ignorance and incapacity of parish priests.

At the same time, the atmosphere of the fourteenth and fifteenth centuries, with its uncertainty of life and immediacy of death, brought a craving for meaningful religious expression and certainty of salvation. This impulse, especially strong in Germany, expressed itself in two ways that often seemed contradictory.

One manifestation of religious piety in the fifteenth century was the almost mechanical view of the process of salvation. Collections of relics grew as more and more people sought certainty of salvation through their veneration. By 1509, Frederick the Wise, elector of Saxony and Martin Luther's prince, had amassed over five thousand relics to which were attached indulgences (a remission of the penalties due to sin) that could officially reduce one's time in purgatory by 1,443 years. Despite the physical dangers, increasing numbers of Christians made pilgrimages to such holy centers as Rome and Jerusalem to gain spiritual benefits.

Another form of religious piety, the quest for a tranquil spirituality, was evident in the popular mystical movement known as the Modern Devotion. The Modern Devotion featured a disregard for religious dogma and an emphasis on following a life of inner piety based on the precepts of Christ. In the great mystical classic of the Modern Devotion, *The Imitation of Christ*, Thomas à Kempis (1380–1471) wrote that "Truly, at the day of judgment we shall not be examined by what we have read, but what we have done; not how well we have spoken, but how religiously we have lived."

What is striking about the revival of religious piety in the fifteenth century—whether expressed through such external forces as the veneration of relics and the buying of indulgences or the mystical path—was its adherence to the orthodox beliefs and practices of the Catholic church. The agitation for certainty of salvation and spiritual peace was done within the framework of the "holy mother Church." But disillusionment grew as the devout experienced the clergy's inability to live up to their expectations. The deepening of religious life, especially in the second half of the fifteenth century, found little echo among the worldly-wise clergy, and it is this divergence that helps to explain the tremendous and immediate impact of Luther's ideas.

Martin Luther and the Reformation in Germany

Martin Luther was born in Germany on November 10, 1483. His father wanted him to become a lawyer, so Luther enrolled at the University of Erfurt. In 1505, after becoming a master in the liberal arts, the young Martin began to study law. But Luther was not content with the study of law and all along had shown religious inclinations. In the summer of 1505, en route back to Erfurt after a brief visit home, he was caught in a ferocious thunderstorm and vowed that if he were spared, he would become a monk. He then entered the monastic order of the Augustinian Hermits in Erfurt. Later, he studied theology at the University of Wittenberg, where he received

◆ **Woodcut: Luther versus the Pope.** In the 1520s, after Luther's return to Wittenberg, his teachings began to spread rapidly, ending ultimately in a reform movement supported by state authorities. Pamphlets containing picturesque woodcuts were important in the spread of Luther's ideas. In the woodcut shown here, the crucified Jesus attends Luther's service on the left, while on the right the pope is at a table selling indulgences.

his doctorate in 1512 and then became a professor in the theological faculty, lecturing on the Bible. Probably sometime between 1513 and 1516, through his study of the Bible, he arrived at an answer to a problem—the assurance of salvation—that had disturbed him since his entry into the monastery.

Catholic doctrine had emphasized that both faith and good works were required of a Christian to achieve personal salvation. In Luther's eyes, human beings, weak and powerless in the sight of an almighty God, could never do enough good works to merit salvation. Through his study of the Bible, Luther rediscovered another way of viewing this problem. To Luther, humans are not saved through their good works, but through faith in the promises of God, made possible by the sacrifice of Christ on the cross. The doctrine of salvation or justification by grace through faith alone became the primary doctrine of the Protestant Reformation. Because Luther had arrived at this doctrine from his study of the Bible, the Bible became for him, as it would be for all other Protestants, the chief guide to religious truth. Justification by faith and the Bible as the sole authority in religious affairs were the twin pillars of the Protestant Reformation.

Luther did not see himself as either an innovator or a heretic, but his involvement in the indulgence controversy propelled him into an open confrontation with church officials and forced him to see the theological implications of justification by faith alone. Luther was greatly distressed by the widespread hawking of indulgences; he was certain that people were guaranteeing their eternal damnation by relying on these pieces of paper to assure themselves of salvation. In response, he issued his Ninety-Five Theses, which were a stunning indictment of the abuses in the sale of indulgences (see the box on p. 535). Luther never intended to break with the church over the issue of indulgences. If the pope had clarified the use of indulgences as Luther wished, he would probably have been satisfied and the controversy closed. But the Renaissance pope Leo X did not take the issue seriously and is even reported to have said that Luther was simply "some drunken German who will amend his ways when he sobers up." Thousands of copies of a German translation of the Ninety-Five Theses were quickly printed and received sympathetically in a Germany that had a long tradition of dissatisfaction with papal policies and power.

In three pamphlets published in 1520, Luther moved toward a more definite break with the Catholic church. The *Address to the Nobility of the German Nation* was a political tract written in German in which Luther called upon the German princes to overthrow the papacy in Germany and establish a reformed German church. *The Babylonian Captivity of the Church* attacked the sacramental system as the means by which the pope and church had held the real meaning of the Gospel in captivity for a thousand years. Here Luther called for the reform of monasticism and for the clergy to marry. *On the Freedom of a Christian Man* was a short treatise on the doctrine of salvation. It is faith alone, not good works, which justifies, frees, and brings salvation through Christ. Being saved and freed by his faith in Christ, however, does not free the Christian from doing good works. Rather he performs good works out of gratitude to God: "Good works do not make a good man, but a good man does good works."[2]

Unable to accept Luther's forcefully worded dissent from traditional Catholic teachings, the church excommunicated him in January 1521. He was also summoned to appear before the imperial diet or Reichstag of the Holy Roman Empire, convened by the newly elected emperor Charles V (1519–1556). Expected to recant the heretical doctrines he had espoused, Luther refused and made the famous reply that became the battle cry of the Reformation:

> Since then Your Majesty and your lordships desire a simple reply, I will answer without horns and without teeth. Unless I am convicted by Scripture and plain reason—I do not accept the authority of popes and councils, for they have contradicted each other—my conscience is captive to the Word of God. I cannot and I will not recant anything, for to go against conscience is neither right nor safe. Here I stand, I cannot do otherwise. God help me. Amen.[3]

The young emperor Charles was outraged at Luther's audacity and gave his opinion that "a single friar who goes counter to all Christianity for a thousand years must be wrong." By the Edict of Worms, Martin Luther was made an outlaw within the empire. His works were to be burned and Luther himself captured and delivered to the emperor.

Between 1521 and 1525, Luther's religious movement became a revolution. Luther was able to gain the support of his prince, the elector of Saxony, as well as other German rulers among the three hundred–odd states that made up the Holy Roman Empire. These rulers were instrumental in instituting new state-dominated churches in their territories. The Lutheran churches in Germany (and later in Scandinavia) quickly became territorial or state churches in which the state supervised and disciplined church members. As part of the development of these state-dominated churches, Luther also instituted new religious services to replace the mass. These featured

Luther and the Ninety-Five Theses

To most historians, the publication of Luther's Ninety-Five Theses marks the beginning of the Reformation. To Luther, they were simply a response to what he considered to be the blatant abuses committed by sellers of indulgences. Although written in Latin, the theses were soon translated into German and disseminated widely across Germany. They made an immense impression on Germans already dissatisfied with the ecclesiastical and financial policies of the papacy.

Martin Luther, Selections from the Ninety-Five Theses

5. The Pope has neither the will nor the power to remit any penalties beyond those he has imposed either at his own discretion or by canon law.

20. Therefore the Pope, by his plenary remission of all penalties, does not mean "all" in the absolute sense, but only those imposed by himself.

21. Hence those preachers of Indulgences are wrong when they say that a man is absolved and saved from every penalty by the Pope's Indulgences.

27. It is mere human talk to preach that the soul flies out [of purgatory] immediately the money clinks in the collection-box.

28. It is certainly possible that when the money clinks in the collection-box greed and avarice can increase; but the intercession of the Church depends on the will of God alone.

45. Christians should be taught that he who sees a needy person and passes him by, although he gives money for pardons, wins for himself not Papal Indulgences but the wrath of God.

50. Christians should be taught that, if the Pope knew the exactions of the preachers of Indulgences, he would rather have the basilica of St. Peter reduced to ashes than built with the skin, flesh and bones of his sheep [the indulgences that so distressed Luther were being sold to raise money for the construction of the new St. Peter's Basilica in Rome].

81. This wanton preaching of pardons makes it difficult even for learned men to redeem respect due to the Pope from the slanders or at least the shrewd questionings of the laity.

82. For example: "Why does not the Pope empty purgatory for the sake of most holy love and the supreme need of souls? This would be the most righteous of reasons, if he can redeem innumerable souls for sordid money with which to build a basilica, the most trivial of reasons."

86. Again: "Since the Pope's wealth is larger than that of the crassest Crassi of our time, why does he not build this one basilica of St. Peter with his own money, rather than with that of the faithful poor?"

88. Again: "What greater good would be done to the Church if the Pope were to bestow these remissions and dispensations, not once, as now, but a hundred times a day, on any believer whatever?"

90. To suppress these most conscientious questionings of the laity by authority only, instead of refuting them by reason, is to expose the Church and the Pope to the ridicule of their enemies, and to make Christian people unhappy.

91. If, therefore, pardons were preached in accordance with the spirit and mind of the Pope, all these difficulties would be easily overcome, or rather would never have arisen.

94. Christians should be exhorted to seek earnestly to follow Christ, their Head, through penalties, deaths, and hells.

95. And let them thus be more confident of entering heaven through many tribulations rather than through a false assurance of peace.

a worship service consisting of a German liturgy that focused on Bible reading, preaching of the word of God, and song. Following his own denunciation of clerical celibacy, Luther married a former nun, Katherina von Bora, in 1525. His union provided a model of married and family life for the new Protestant minister.

A series of crises in the mid-1520s made it apparent, however, that spreading the word of God was not as easy as Luther had originally envisioned, the usual plight of most reformers. Luther experienced dissent within his own ranks in Wittenberg as well as defection from many Christian humanists who feared that Luther's movement threatened the unity of Christendom. The Peasants' War constituted Luther's greatest challenge, however. In June 1524, peasants in Germany rose in revolt against their lords and looked to Luther for support. But Luther, who

◆ Charles V. Charles V sought to maintain religious unity throughout his vast empire by keeping all his subjects within the bounds of the Catholic church. Due to his conflict with Francis I as well as difficulties with the Turks, the papacy, and the German princes, Charles was never able to check the spread of Lutheranism. This is a portrait of Charles V by the Venetian painter Titian.

knew how much his reformation of the church depended upon the full support of the German princes and magistrates, supported the rulers. To Luther, God had ordained the state and its rulers and given them the authority to maintain the peace and order necessary for the spread of the Gospel. It was the duty of princes to suppress all revolts. By May 1525, the German princes had ruthlessly suppressed the peasant hordes. By this time, Luther found himself ever more dependent on state authorities for the growth and maintenance of his reformed church.

From its very beginning, the fate of Luther's movement had been closely tied to political affairs. In 1519, Charles I, king of Spain and the grandson of the Emperor Maximilian, had been elected Holy Roman emperor as Charles V (1519–1556). Charles V ruled over an immense empire, consisting of Spain and its overseas possessions, the traditional Austrian Habsburg lands, Bohemia, Hungary, the Low Countries, and the kingdom of Naples in southern Italy. Politically, Charles wanted to maintain his dynasty's control over his enormous empire; religiously, he hoped to preserve the unity of his empire in the Catholic faith. Despite his strengths, Charles spent a lifetime in futile pursuit of his goals. Four major problems—the French, the papacy, the Turks, and Germany's internal situation—kept him preoccupied and cost him both his dream and his health. At the same time, these four factors contributed to the survival of Lutheranism by giving the Lutherans time to organize before having to face the concerted onslaught of the Catholic forces.

Between 1521 and 1544, Charles fought a series of wars with his chief rival, the French king Francis I (1515–1547). At the same time, Charles faced opposition from Pope Clement VII (1523–1534), who, guided by political considerations, joined the side of Francis I. The advance of the Ottoman Turks (see Chapter 16) into the eastern part of Charles's empire forced the emperor to divert forces there as well.

Finally, the internal political situation in the Holy Roman Empire was also not in Charles's favor. Germany was a land of several hundred territorial states: princely states, ecclesiastical principalities, and free imperial cities. While all owed loyalty to the emperor, Germany's medieval development had enabled these states to become quite independent of imperial authority. They had no desire to have a strong emperor. By the time Charles V was able to bring military forces to Germany—in 1546—Lutheranism had become well established and the Lutheran princes well organized. Unable to impose his will on Germany, Charles was forced to negotiate a truce. An end to religious warfare in Germany came in 1555 with the Peace of Augsburg, which marks an important turning point in the history of the Reformation. The division of Christianity was formally acknowledged when Lutheranism was granted the same legal rights as Catholicism. Moreover, the peace settlement accepted the right of each German ruler to determine the religion of his subjects.

The Peace of Augsburg was a victory for the German princes. The independence of the numerous German territorial states guaranteed the weakness of the Holy Roman Empire and the continued decentralization of Germany. Charles's hope for a united empire had been completely dashed. At the same time, what had at first been merely feared was now confirmed: the ideal of medieval Christian unity was irretrievably lost. The rapid proliferation of new Protestant groups served to underscore the new reality.

The Spread of the Protestant Reformation

Switzerland was home to two major Reformation movements, Zwinglianism and Calvinism. Ulrich Zwingli (1484–1531) was ordained a priest in 1506 and accepted an appointment as a cathedral priest in the Great Minster of Zürich in 1518. Zwingli's preaching of the Gospel caused such unrest that in 1523 the city council held a public disputation or debate in the town hall. Zwingli's party was accorded the victory, and the council declared that "Mayor, Council and Great Council of Zürich, in order to do away with disturbance and discord, have upon due deliberation and consultation decided and resolved that Master Zwingli should continue as heretofore to proclaim the Gospel and the pure sacred Scriptures."[4] Over the next two years, evangelical reforms were promulgated in Zürich by a city council strongly influenced by Zwingli. Relics and images were abolished; all paintings and decorations were removed from the churches and replaced by whitewashed walls. The mass was replaced by a new liturgy consisting of Scripture reading, prayer, and sermons. Monasticism, pilgrimages, the veneration of saints, clerical celibacy, and the pope's authority were all abolished as remnants of papal Christianity.

As his movement began to spread to other cities in Switzerland, Zwingli sought an alliance with Martin Luther and the German reformers. Although both the German and the Swiss reformers realized the need for unity to defend against the opposition of the Catholic authorities, they were unable to agree on the interpretation of the Lord's Supper (see the box on p. 538). Zwingli believed that the scriptural words "This is my Body, This is my blood" should be taken figuratively, not literally, and refused to accept Luther's insistence on the real presence of the body and blood of Christ "in, with, and under the bread and wine." In October 1531, war erupted between the Swiss Protestant and Catholic states. Zürich's army was routed, and Zwingli was found wounded on the battlefield. His enemies killed him, cut up his body, and burned the pieces, scattering the ashes. The leadership of Swiss Protestantism now passed to John Calvin (1509–1564), the systematic theologian and organizer of the Protestant movement.

John Calvin was educated in his native France, but after his conversion to Protestantism, he was forced to flee France for the safety of Switzerland. In 1536, he published the first edition of the *Institutes of the Christian Religion*, a masterful synthesis of Protestant thought, a manual for ecclesiastical organization, and a work that immediately secured his reputation as one of the new leaders of Protestantism.

On most important doctrines, Calvin stood very close to Luther. He adhered to the doctrine of justification by faith alone to explain how humans achieved salvation. But Calvin also placed much emphasis on the absolute

◆ **John Calvin.** After a conversion experience, John Calvin abandoned his life as a humanist and became a reformer. In 1536, Calvin began working to reform the city of Geneva, where he remained until his death in 1564. This sixteenth-century portrait of Calvin pictures him near the end of his life.

A Reformation Debate: The Marburg Colloquy

Debates played a crucial role in the Reformation period. They were a primary instrument in introducing the Reformation into innumerable cities as well as a means of resolving differences among like-minded Protestant groups. This selection contains an excerpt from Luther's and Zwingli's vivacious and often brutal debate over the sacrament of the Lord's Supper at Marburg in 1529. The two protagonists failed to reach agreement.

The Marburg Colloquy, 1529

THE HESSIAN CHANCELLOR FEIGE: My gracious prince and lord [Landgrave Philip of Hesse] has summoned you for the express and urgent purpose of settling the dispute over the sacrament of the Lord's Supper. . . . And let everyone on both sides present his arguments in a spirit of moderation, as becomes such matters. . . . Now then, Doctor Luther, you may proceed.

LUTHER: Noble prince, gracious lord! Undoubtedly the colloquy is well intentioned. . . . Although I have no intention of changing my mind, which is firmly made up, I will nevertheless present the grounds of my belief and show where the others are in error. . . . Your basic contentions are these: In the last analysis you wish to prove that a body cannot be in two places at once, and you produce arguments about the unlimited body which are based on natural reason. I do not question how Christ can be God and man and how the two natures can be joined. For God is more powerful than all our ideas, and we must submit to his word.

Prove that Christ's body is not there where the Scripture says, "This is my body!" Rational proofs I will not listen to. . . . God is beyond all mathematics and the words of God are to be revered and carried out in awe. It is God who commands, "Take, eat, this is my body." I request, therefore, valid scriptural proof to the contrary.

Luther writes on the table in chalk, "This is my body," and covers the words with a velvet cloth.

OECOLAMPADIUS [leader of the reform movement in Basel and a Zwinglian partisan]: The sixth chapter of John clarifies the other scriptural passages. Christ is not speaking there about a local presence. "The flesh is of no avail," he says [John 6:63]. It is not my intention to employ rational, or geometrical, arguments—neither am I denying the power of God—but as long as I have the complete faith I will speak from that. For Christ is risen; he sits at the right hand of God; and so he cannot be present in the bread. Our view is neither new nor sacrilegious, but is based on faith and Scripture. . . .

ZWINGLI: I insist that the words of the Lord's Supper must be figurative. This is ever apparent, and even required by the article of faith: "taken up into heaven, seated at the right hand of the Father." Otherwise, it would be absurd to look for him in the Lord's Supper at the same time that Christ is telling us that he is in heaven. One and the same body cannot possibly be in different places. . . .

LUTHER: I call upon you as before: your basic contentions are shaky. Give way, and give glory to God!

ZWINGLI: And we call upon you to give glory to God and to quit begging the question! The issue at stake is this: Where is the proof of your position? I am willing to consider your words carefully—no harm meant! You're trying to outwit me. I stand by this passage in the sixth chapter of John, verse 63 and shall not be shaken from it. You'll have to sing another tune.

LUTHER: You're being obnoxious.

ZWINGLI (*excitedly*): Don't you believe that Christ was attempting in John 6 to help those who did not understand?

LUTHER: You're trying to dominate things! You insist on passing judgment! Leave that to someone else! . . . It is your point that must be proved, not mine. But let us stop this sort of thing. It serves no purpose.

ZWINGLI: It certainly does! It is for you to prove that the passage in John 6 speaks of a physical repast.

LUTHER: You express yourself poorly and make about as much progress as a cane standing in a corner. You're going nowhere.

ZWINGLI: No, no, no! This is the passage that will break your neck!

LUTHER: Don't be so sure of yourself. Necks don't break this way. You're in Hesse, not Switzerland. . . .

sovereignty of God or the "power, grace, and glory of God." Thus, "God asserts his possession of omnipotence, and claims our acknowledgment of this attribute; not such as is imagined by sophists, vain, idle, and almost asleep, but vigilant, efficacious, operative and engaged in continual action."[5]

One of the ideas derived from his emphasis on the absolute sovereignty of God—predestination—gave a unique cast to Calvin's teachings. Although it was but one aspect of his doctrine of salvation, predestination became the central focus of succeeding generations of Calvinists. This "eternal decree," as Calvin called it, meant that God had predestined some people to be saved (the elect) and others to be damned (the reprobate). According to Calvin, "He has once for all determined, both whom he would admit to salvation, and whom he would condemn to destruction."[6] Calvin identified three tests to assure his followers of their possible salvation: an open profession of faith, a "decent and godly life," and participation in the sacraments of baptism and communion. Although Calvin stressed that there could be no absolute certainty of salvation, his followers did not always make this distinction. The practical psychological effect of predestination was to give later Calvinists an unshakable conviction that they were doing God's work on earth. Thus, Calvinism became a dynamic and activist faith. It is no accident that Calvinism became the militant international form of Protestantism.

In 1536, Calvin began working to reform the city of Geneva. He was able to fashion a tightly organized church order that employed both clergy and laymen in the service of the church. The Consistory, a special body for enforcing moral discipline, was also created and functioned as a court to oversee the moral life, daily behavior, and doctrinal orthodoxy of Genevans and to admonish and correct deviants. As its power increased, the Consistory went from "fraternal corrections" to the use of public penance and excommunication. More serious cases could be turned over to the city councils for punishments greater than excommunication. Calvin separated church and state and expected the church, as a divine institution, to function largely independently of state power.

Calvin's success in Geneva enabled the city to become a vibrant center of Protestantism. John Knox, the Calvinist reformer of Scotland, called Geneva "the most perfect school of Christ on earth." Following Calvin's lead, missionaries trained in Geneva were sent to all parts of Europe. Calvinism became established in France, the Netherlands, Scotland, and central and eastern Europe. By the mid-sixteenth century, Calvinism had replaced Lutheranism as the militant international form of Protestantism while Calvin's Geneva stood as the fortress of the Reformation.

CHRONOLOGY

Key Events of the Reformation Era

Luther's Ninety-Five Theses	1517
Excommunication of Luther	1521
Beginning of Zwingli's reformation in Switzerland	1523
Peasants' War in Germany	1524–1525
Act of Supremacy in England	1534
Pontificate of Paul III	1534–1549
John Calvin's *Institutes of the Christian Religion*	1536
Jesuits recognized as religious order	1540
Council of Trent	1545–1563
Peace of Augsburg	1555

While Calvin was forging his militant brand of Protestantism in Switzerland, the English Reformation had been initiated by an act of state. King Henry VIII (1509–1547) had a strong desire to divorce his first wife Catherine of Aragon, who had failed to produce a male heir. Normally, church authorities might have been willing to grant the king an annulment of his marriage, but Pope Clement VII was dependent upon the Holy Roman emperor Charles V, who happened to be the nephew of Queen Catherine. Impatient with the pope's inaction, Henry sought to obtain an annulment of his marriage in England's own ecclesiastical courts. As archbishop of Canterbury and head of the highest ecclesiastical court in England, Thomas Cranmer held official hearings on the king's case and ruled in May 1533 that the king's marriage to Catherine was "null and absolutely void." In 1534, upon Henry's request, Parliament moved to finalize the break of the Church of England with Rome. An Act of Supremacy of 1534 declared that the king was "taken, accepted, and reputed the only supreme head on earth of the Church of England," a position that gave him control of doctrine, clerical appointments, and church discipline. Using his new powers, Henry dissolved the monasteries. About four hundred religious houses were closed in 1536, and their land and possessions confiscated by the king. Many were sold to nobles, gentry, and some merchants. The king not only received a great boost to his treasury but created a group of supporters who now had a stake in the new Tudor order.

Although Henry VIII had broken with the papacy, little change occurred in matters of doctrine, theology, and ceremony. Some of his supporters, such as Archbishop Thomas Cranmer, wished to have a religious reformation as well as an administrative one, but Henry was unyielding. But he died in 1547 and was succeeded by his son, the underage and sickly Edward VI (1547–1553). During Edward's reign, Archbishop Cranmer and others inclined toward Protestant doctrines were able to move the Church of England (or Anglican church) in more of a Protestant direction. New acts of Parliament instituted the right of the clergy to marry, the elimination of images, and the creation of a revised Protestant liturgy that was elaborated in a new prayer book and liturgical guide known as the Book of Common Prayer. These rapid changes in doctrine and liturgy aroused much opposition and prepared the way for the reaction that occurred when Mary, Henry's first daughter by Catherine of Aragon, came to the throne.

There was no doubt that Mary (1553–1558) was a Catholic who intended to return England to Roman Catholicism. But her restoration of Catholicism aroused much opposition. There was widespread antipathy to Mary's unfortunate marriage to Philip II, the son of Charles V and future king of Spain. Philip was strongly disliked in England, and Mary's foreign policy based on alliance with Spain aroused further hostility. The burning of over three hundred Protestant heretics roused further ire against "bloody Mary." As a result of her policies, Mary managed to achieve the opposite of what she had intended: England was more Protestant by the end of her reign than it had been at the beginning.

Although many reformers were ready to allow the state to play an important, if not dominant, role in church affairs, some people rejected this kind of magisterial reformation and favored a far more radical reform movement. Collectively called the Anabaptists, these radicals actually formed a large variety of different groups who, nevertheless, shared some common characteristics. Anabaptism was especially attractive to those peasants, weavers, miners, and artisans who had been adversely affected by the economic changes of the age.

Anabaptists everywhere shared some common ideas. To them, the true Christian church was a voluntary association of believers who had undergone spiritual rebirth and had then been baptized into the church. Anabaptists advocated adult rather than infant baptism. They also took literally a return to the practices and spirit of early Christianity. Adhering to the accounts of early Christian communities in the New Testament, they followed a strict sort of democracy in which all believers were considered equal. Each church chose its own minister, who might be any member of the community because all Christians were considered priests (though women were often excluded). Those chosen as ministers led the services, which were very simple and contained nothing not found in the early church. Anabaptists rejected theological speculation in favor of simple Christian living according to what they believed was the pure word of God. The Lord's Supper was interpreted as a remembrance, a meal of fellowship celebrated in the evening in private houses according to Christ's example. Finally, unlike the Catholics and other Protestants, most Anabaptists believed in the complete separation of church and state. Not only was government to be excluded from the realm of religion, it was not even supposed to exercise political jurisdiction over real Christians. Anabaptists refused to hold political office or bear arms because many took literally the commandment "Thou shall not kill," although some Anabaptist groups did become quite violent. Their political beliefs as much as their religious beliefs caused the Anabaptists to be regarded as dangerous radicals who threatened the very fabric of sixteenth-century society. Indeed, the chief thing Protestants and Catholics could agree on was the need to persecute Anabaptists.

The Social Impact of the Protestant Reformation

Christianity was such an integral part of European life that it was inevitable that the Reformation would have an impact on the family and popular religious practices.

THE FAMILY

For centuries, Catholicism had praised the family and sanctified its existence by making marriage a sacrament. But the Catholic church's high regard for abstinence from sex as the surest way to holiness made the celibate state of the clergy preferable to marriage. Nevertheless, since not all men could remain chaste, marriage offered the best means to control sexual intercourse and give it a purpose, the procreation of children. To some extent, this attitude persisted among the Protestant reformers; Luther, for example, argued that sex in marriage allowed one to "make use of this sex in order to avoid sin," and Calvin advised that every man should "abstain from marriage only so long as he is fit to observe celibacy." If "his power to tame lust fails him," then he must marry.

But the Reformation did bring some change to the conception of the family. Both Catholic and Protestant

➤ A Protestant Woman ➤

In the initial zeal of the Protestant Reformation, women were frequently allowed to play unusual roles. Catherine Zell of Germany (c. 1497–1562) first preached beside her husband in 1527. After the death of her two children, she devoted the rest of her life to helping her husband and their Anabaptist faith. This selection is taken from one of her letters to a young Lutheran minister who had criticized her activities.

Catherine Zell to Ludwig Rabus of Memmingen

I, Catherine Zell, wife of the late lamented Mathew Zell, who served in Strasburg, where I was born and reared and still live, wish you peace and enhancement in God's grace. . . .

From my earliest years I turned to the Lord, who taught and guided me, and I have at all times, in accordance with my understanding and His grace, embraced the interests of His church and earnestly sought Jesus. Even in youth this brought me the regard and affection of clergymen and others much concerned with the church, which is why the pious Mathew Zell wanted me as a companion in marriage; and I, in turn, to serve the glory of Christ, gave devotion and help to my husband, both in his ministry and in keeping his house. . . . Ever since I was ten years old I have been a student and a sort of church mother, much given to attending sermons. I have loved and frequented the company of learned men, and I conversed much with them, not about dancing, masquerades, and worldly pleasures but about the kingdom of God. . . .

Consider the poor Anabaptists, who are so furiously and ferociously persecuted. Must the authorities everywhere be incited against them, as the hunter drives his dog against wild animals? Against those who acknowledge Christ the Lord in very much the same way we do and over which we broke with the papacy? Just because they cannot agree with us on lesser things, is this any reason to persecute them and in them Christ, in whom they fervently believe and have often professed in misery, in prison, and under the torments of fire and water?

Governments may punish criminals, but they should not force and govern belief, which is a matter for the heart and conscience not for temporal authorities. . . . When the authorities pursue one, they soon bring forth tears, and towns and villages are emptied.

---

clergy preached sermons emphasizing a more positive side to family relationships. The Protestants were especially important in developing this new view of the family. Because Protestantism had eliminated any idea of special holiness for celibacy, abolishing both monasticism and a celibate clergy, the family could be placed at the center of human life, and a new stress on "mutual love between man and wife" could be extolled. But were doctrine and reality the same? For more radical religious groups, at times they were (see the box above). One Anabaptist wrote to his wife before his execution: "My faithful helper, my loyal friend. I praise God that he gave you to me, you who have sustained me in all my trial."[7] But more often reality reflected the traditional roles of husband as the ruler and wife as the obedient servant whose chief duty was to please her husband. Luther stated it clearly:

The rule remains with the husband, and the wife is compelled to obey him by God's command. He rules the home and the state, wages war, defends his possessions, tills the soil, builds, plants, etc. The woman on the other hand is like a nail driven into the wall . . . so the wife should stay at home and look after the affairs of the household, as one who has been deprived of the ability of administering those affairs that are outside and that concern the state. She does not go beyond her most personal duties.[8]

Obedience to her husband was not a wife's only role; her other important duty was to bear children. To Calvin and Luther, this function of women was part of the divine plan. God punishes women for the sins of Eve by the burdens of procreation and feeding and nurturing their children, but "it is a gladsome punishment if you consider the hope of eternal life and the honor of motherhood which had been left to her."[9] Although Protestantism sanctified this role of woman as mother and wife, viewing it as a holy vocation, it also left few alternatives for women. Because monasticism had been destroyed, that career avenue was no longer available; for most Protestant women, family life was their only destiny. At the same time, by emphasizing the father as "ruler" and hence the center of household religion, Protestantism even removed the woman from her traditional role as controller of religion in the home. Overall, the Protestant Reformation did not noticeably transform women's subordinate place in society.

RELIGIOUS PRACTICES AND POPULAR CULTURE

Although Protestant reformers were conservative in their political and social attitudes, their attacks on the Catholic church led to radical changes in religious practices. The Protestant Reformation abolished or severely curtailed such customary practices as indulgences, the veneration of relics and saints, pilgrimages, monasticism, and clerical celibacy. The elimination of saints put an

end to the numerous celebrations of religious holy days and changed a community's sense of time. Thus, in Protestant communities, religious ceremonies and imagery, such as processions and statues, tended to be replaced with individual private prayer, family worship, and collective prayer and worship at the same time each week on Sunday.

Many popular religious practices that had played an important role in popular culture were criticized by Protestant reformers as superstitious or remnants of pagan culture. In addition to abolishing saints' days and religious carnivals, some Protestant reformers even tried to eliminate customary forms of entertainment. English

Map 15.1 Catholics and Protestants in Europe by 1560.

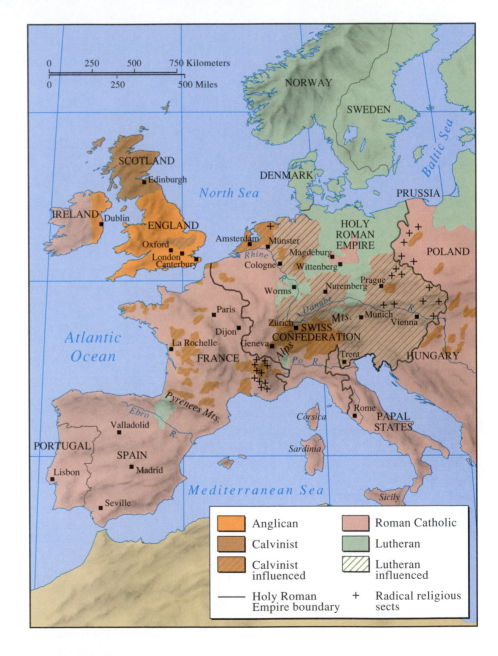

Puritans (as English Calvinists were called), for example, attempted to ban drinking in taverns, dramatic performances, and dancing. Dutch Calvinists denounced the tradition of giving small presents to children on the feast of Saint Nicholas, near Christmas. Many of these Protestant attacks on popular culture were unsuccessful, however. The importance of taverns in English social life made it impossible to eradicate them, while celebrating at Christmastime persisted in the Dutch Netherlands.

The Catholic Reformation

By the mid-sixteenth century, Lutheranism had become established in Germany and Scandinavia and Calvinism in Switzerland, France, the Netherlands, and eastern Europe. In England, the split from Rome had resulted in the creation of a national church. The situation in Europe did not look particularly favorable to the Roman Catholic church. But even at the beginning of the sixteenth century, constructive, positive forces were at work for reform within the Catholic church, and by the mid-sixteenth century, they came to be directed by a revived and reformed papacy, giving the Catholic church new strength. We call the story of the revival of Roman Catholicism the Catholic Reformation, although some historians prefer to use the term Counter-Reformation,

especially for those elements of the Catholic Reformation that were directly aimed at stopping the spread of the Protestant Reformation. Historians focus on three chief pillars of the Catholic Reformation: the development of the Jesuits, the emergence of a reformed and revived papacy, and the Council of Trent.

The Society of Jesus, known as the Jesuits, was founded by a Spanish nobleman, Ignatius of Loyola (1491–1556). Loyola gathered together a small group of individuals who were recognized as a religious order by a papal bull in 1540. The new order was grounded on the principles of absolute obedience to the papacy, a strict hierarchical order for the society, the use of education to achieve its goals, and a dedication to engage in "conflict for God." Jesuit organization came to resemble the structure of a military command. Executive leadership was put in the hands of a general, who nominated all important positions in the order and was to be revered as its absolute head. Loyola served as the first general of the order until his death in 1556. A special vow of absolute obedience to the pope made the Jesuits an important instrument for papal policy. Jesuit missionaries proved singularly successful in restoring Catholicism to parts of Germany and eastern Europe.

A reformed papacy was another important factor in the development of the Catholic Reformation. The involvement of the Renaissance papacy in dubious finances

◆ **Ignatius Loyola.** The Jesuits became the most important new religious order of the Catholic Reformation. Shown here in a sixteenth-century painting by an unknown artist is Ignatius Loyola, founder of the Society of Jesus. Loyola is seen kneeling before Pope Paul III, who officially recognized the Jesuits in 1540.

and Italian political and military affairs had created numerous sources of corruption. It took the jolt of the Protestant Reformation to bring about serious reform. The pontificate of Pope Paul III (1534–1549) proved to be a turning point. He perceived the need for change and expressed it decisively. Advocates of reform were made cardinals. In 1535, Paul took the audacious step of appointing a Reform Commission to ascertain the church's ills. The commission's report in 1537 blamed the church's problems on the corrupt policies of popes and cardinals. It was also Paul III who formally recognized the Jesuits and initiated the Council of Trent.

A decisive change in the direction of the Catholic Reformation and the nature of papal reform came in the 1540s, when the Catholic moderates, who favored concessions to Protestants in the hope of restoring Christian unity, were overshadowed by hard-liners who regarded all compromise with Protestant innovations as heresy. It soon became apparent that the conservative reformers were in the ascendancy when Cardinal Caraffa, one of the hard-liners, was able to convince Paul III to establish a Roman Inquisition or Holy Office in 1542 to ferret out doctrinal errors. When Cardinal Caraffa was chosen pope as Paul IV (1555–1559), he so increased the power of the Inquisition that even liberal cardinals were silenced. This "first true pope of the Catholic Counter-Reformation," as he has been called, also created an Index of Forbidden Books, a list of books that Catholics were not allowed to read. It included all the works of Protestant theologians as well as authors considered "unwholesome." Any hope of restoring Christian unity by compromise was fast fading. The activities of the Council of Trent, the third major pillar of the Catholic Reformation, made compromise virtually impossible.

In March 1545, a group of cardinals, archbishops, bishops, abbots, and theologians met in the city of Trent on the border between Germany and Italy and initiated the Council of Trent, which met intermittently from 1545 to 1563 in three major sessions. Moderate Catholic reformers hoped that compromises would be made in formulating doctrinal definitions that would encourage Protestants to return to the church. Conservatives, however, favored an uncompromising restatement of Catholic doctrines in strict opposition to Protestant positions. The latter group won. The final doctrinal decrees of the Council of Trent reaffirmed traditional Catholic teachings in opposition to Protestant beliefs. Scripture and tradition were affirmed as equal authorities in religious matters; only the church could interpret Scripture. Both faith and good works were declared necessary for salvation. The seven sacraments, the Catholic doctrine

of transubstantiation, and clerical celibacy were all upheld. Belief in purgatory and in the efficacy of indulgences was strengthened, although hawking of indulgences was prohibited.

After the Council of Trent, the Roman Catholic church possessed a clear body of doctrine and a unified church under the acknowledged supremacy of the popes who had triumphed over bishops and councils. The Roman Catholic church had become one Christian denomination among many with an organizational framework and doctrinal pattern that would not be significantly altered until Vatican Council II four hundred years later. With a new spirit of confidence, the Catholic church entered a militant phase, as well prepared as the Calvinists to do battle for the Lord. An era of religious warfare was about to unfold.

Europe in Crisis: War, Revolution, and Social Disintegration, 1560–1650

Between 1560 and 1650, Europe experienced religious wars, revolutions and constitutional crises, economic and social disintegration, and a witchcraft craze. It was truly an age of crisis.

Politics and the Wars of Religion in the Sixteenth Century

The so-called wars of religion were a product of Reformation ideologies that allowed little room for compromise or toleration of differing opinions. By the middle of the sixteenth century, Calvinism and Catholicism had become highly militant religions dedicated to spreading the word of God as they interpreted it. While their struggle for the minds and hearts of Europeans was at the heart of the religious wars of the sixteenth century, economic, social, and political forces also played an important role in these conflicts. Of the sixteenth-century religious wars, none was more momentous nor shattering than the French civil wars known as the French Wars of Religion.

THE FRENCH WARS OF RELIGION (1562–1598)

Religion was at the heart of the French civil wars of the sixteenth century. The growth of Calvinism had led to persecution by the French kings, but the latter did little to stop the spread of Calvinism. Huguenots (as the French Calvinists were called) came from all layers of society: artisans and shopkeepers hurt by rising prices and a rigid guild system, merchants and lawyers in provincial towns whose local privileges were tenuous, and members of the nobility. Possibly 40 to 50 percent of the French nobility became Huguenots, including the house of Bourbon, which stood next to the Valois in the royal line of succession and ruled the southern French kingdom of Navarre. The conversion of so many nobles made the Huguenots a potentially dangerous political threat to monarchical power. Although the Calvinists constituted only about 7 percent of the population, they were a dedicated, determined, and well-organized minority.

The Calvinist minority was greatly outnumbered by the Catholic majority. The Valois monarchy was staunchly Catholic, and its control of the Catholic church gave it little incentive to look favorably upon Protestantism. At the same time, an extreme Catholic party—known as the ultra-Catholics—favored strict opposition to the Huguenots. Possessing the loyalty of Paris and large sections of northern and northwestern France, the ultra-Catholics could recruit and pay for large armies and received support abroad from the papacy and Jesuits who favored their noncompromising Catholic position.

The religious issue was not the only factor that contributed to the French civil wars. Towns and provinces, which had long resisted the growing power of monarchical centralization, were only too willing to join a revolt against the monarchy. This was also true of the nobility, and the fact that so many of them were Calvinists created an important base of opposition to the crown. The French Wars of Religion, then, constituted a major constitutional crisis for France and temporarily halted the development of the French centralized territorial state. The claim of the ruling dynasty to a person's loyalties was temporarily superseded by loyalty to one's religious belief. For thirty years, battles raged in France between Catholic and Calvinist parties, who obviously considered the unity of France less important than religious truth. But there also emerged in France a group of *politiques* who placed politics before religion and believed that no religious truth was worth the ravages of civil war. The *politiques* ultimately prevailed, but not until both sides were exhausted by bloodshed.

Finally, in 1589, Henry of Navarre, the political leader of the Huguenots and a member of the Bourbon dynasty, succeeded to the throne as Henry IV (1589–1610). Realizing, however, that he would never be accepted by Catholic France, Henry took the logical way out and converted to Catholicism. With his coronation in 1594, the wars of religion finally came to an end. The Edict of Nantes in 1598 solved the religious problem by acknowledging Catholicism as the official religion of France while guaranteeing the Huguenots the right to worship and to enjoy all political privileges, including the holding of public offices.

PHILIP II AND THE CAUSE OF MILITANT CATHOLICISM

The greatest advocate of militant Catholicism in the second half of the sixteenth century was King Philip II of Spain (1556–1598), the son and heir of Charles V. Philip's reign ushered in an age of Spanish greatness, both politically and culturally. His first major goal was to consolidate and secure the lands he had inherited from his father. These included Spain, the Netherlands, and possessions in Italy and the New World. For Philip consolidation meant maintaining a strict conformity to Catholicism, enforced by aggressive use of the Spanish Inquisition, and establishing strong, monarchical authority. The latter was not an easy task because Philip had inherited a structure of government in which each of the various states and territories of his empire stood in an individual relationship to the king. Even in Spain, there was no really deep sense of nationhood. Philip did manage, however, to expand royal power by making the monarchy less dependent on the traditional landed aristocracy, especially in the higher echelons of government.

Crucial to an understanding of Philip II is the importance of Catholicism to the Spanish people and their ruler. Driven by a heritage of crusading fervor, the Spanish had little difficulty seeing themselves as a nation of people divinely chosen to save Catholic Christianity from the Protestant heretics. Philip II, the "Most Catholic King," became the champion of Catholicism throughout Europe, a role that led to spectacular victories and equally spectacular defeats for the Spanish king. Spain's leadership of a Holy League against Turkish encroachments in the Mediterranean resulted in a stunning victory over the Turkish fleet in the Battle of Lepanto in 1571. But Philip's attempt to crush the revolt in the Netherlands and his tortured policy with the English Queen Elizabeth led to his greatest misfortunes.

One of the richest parts of Philip's empire, the Spanish Netherlands was of great importance to the "Most Catholic King." Philip's attempt to strengthen his control in the Netherlands, which consisted of seventeen provinces (modern Netherlands, Belgium, and Luxembourg), soon led to a revolt. The nobles, who stood to lose the most politically if their jealously guarded privileges and freedoms were weakened, strongly opposed Philip's efforts. Resentment against Philip was also aroused by the collection of taxes when the residents of the Netherlands realized that these revenues were being used for Spanish interests. Finally, religion became a major catalyst for rebellion when Philip attempted to crush Calvinism. Violence erupted in 1566, when Calvinists—especially nobles—began to destroy statues and stained glass windows in Catholic churches. Philip responded by sending 10,000 veteran Spanish and Italian troops to crush the rebellion.

But the revolt became organized, especially in the northern provinces where the Dutch, under the leadership of William of Nassau, the prince of Orange, offered growing resistance. The struggle dragged on for decades until 1609, when a twelve-year truce ended the war, virtually recognizing the independence of the northern provinces. These seven northern provinces, which began to call themselves the United Provinces of the Netherlands in 1581, became the core of the modern Dutch state. The new state was officially recognized by the Peace of Westphalia in 1648. The seventeenth century has often been called the "golden age" of the Dutch Republic as the United Provinces held center stage as one of Europe's great powers. Like France and England, the United Provinces was an Atlantic power, underlining the importance of the shift of political and economic power in the seventeenth century from the Mediterranean Sea to the countries on the Atlantic seaboard.

At the beginning of the seventeenth century, Spain possessed the most populous empire in the world, controlling almost all of South America and a number of settlements in Asia and Africa. To most Europeans, Spain still seemed the greatest power of the age, but the reality was quite different. The treasury was empty; Philip II went bankrupt in 1596 from excessive expenditures on war while his successor did the same in 1607 by spending a fortune on his court. The armed forces were out-of-date; the government was inefficient; and the commercial class was weak in the midst of a suppressed peasantry, a luxury-loving nobility, and an oversupply of priests and monks. Spain continued to play the role of a great power, but appearances were deceiving.

THE ENGLAND OF ELIZABETH

When Elizabeth Tudor, the younger daughter of Henry VIII, ascended the throne in 1558, the population of England numbered fewer than four million people. During her reign, England rose to prominence as the relatively small island kingdom became the leader of the Protestant nations of Europe and laid the foundations for a world empire.

Shrewd, calculating, cautious, and self-confident, Elizabeth moved quickly to solve the difficult religious problem she had inherited from her half-sister, Queen Mary. Elizabeth's religious policy was based on moderation and compromise. The Catholic legislation of Mary's reign was repealed, and a new Act of Supremacy designated Elizabeth as "the only supreme governor of this realm, as well in all spiritual or ecclesiastical things or causes, as temporal." An Act of Uniformity restored the church service of the Book of Common Prayer from the reign of Edward VI with some revisions to make it more acceptable to Catholics. Elizabeth's religious settlement was basically Protestant but a moderate Protestantism that avoided subtle distinctions and extremes. The new religious settlement worked, at least to the extent that it smothered religious differences in England in the second half of the sixteenth century.

Elizabeth's foreign policy was also dictated by caution, moderation, and expediency. Fearful of other countries' motives, Elizabeth realized that war could be disastrous for her island kingdom and her own rule. While encouraging English piracy and providing clandestine aid to French Huguenots and Dutch Calvinists to weaken France and Spain, she pretended complete aloofness and avoided alliances that would force her into war with any major power. Gradually, however, Elizabeth was drawn into conflict with Spain. After resisting for years the idea of invading England as too impractical, Philip II of Spain was finally persuaded to do so by advisers who assured him that the people of England would rise against their queen when the Spaniards arrived. Moreover, Philip was easily convinced that the revolt in the Netherlands would never be crushed as long as England provided support for it. In any case, a successful invasion of England would mean the overthrow of heresy and the return of England to Catholicism, surely an act in accordance with the will of God. Accordingly Philip ordered preparations for an Armada to spearhead the invasion of England.

The Armada proved to be a disaster. The Spanish fleet that finally set sail had neither the ships nor the manpower that Philip had planned to send. Battered by a number of encounters with the English, the Spanish fleet sailed back to Spain by a northerly route around Scotland and Ireland where it was further pounded by storms. Although the English and Spanish would continue their war for another sixteen years, the defeat of the Armada guaranteed for the time being that England would remain a Protestant country. Although Spain made up for its losses within a year and a half, the defeat was a psychological blow to the Spaniards.

Economic and Social Crises: The Witchcraft Craze

The period of European history from 1560 to 1650 witnessed severe economic and social crises as well as political upheaval. The inflation-fueled prosperity of the sixteenth century showed signs of slackening by the beginning of the seventeenth century. Economic contraction began to be evident in some parts of Europe by the 1620s. In the 1630s and 1640s, as imports of silver from the Americas declined, economic recession intensified, especially in the Mediterranean area. Italy, the industrial and financial center of Europe in the age of the Renaissance, was now becoming an economic backwater. Spain's economy was also encountering serious problems by the decade of the 1640s.

Population trends of the sixteenth and seventeenth centuries also reveal Europe's worsening conditions. The sixteenth century was a period of expanding population, possibly related to a warmer climate and increased food supplies. It has been estimated that the population of Europe increased from 60 million in 1500 to 85 million by 1600, the first major recovery of the European population since the devastation of the Black Death in the mid-fourteenth century. However, records also indicate a leveling off of the population by 1620 and even a decline by 1650, especially in central and southern Europe. Only the Dutch, English, and, to a lesser degree, the French grew in number in the first half of the seventeenth century. Europe's longtime adversaries, war, famine, and plague, continued to affect population levels. Furthermore, the onset of another "little ice age" after the middle of the sixteenth century, when average temperatures fell and glaciers engulfed small Alpine villages, affected harvests and gave rise to famines. These economic problems created social tensions that manifested themselves in various ways including the witchcraft craze.

Hysteria over witchcraft affected the lives of many Europeans in the sixteenth and seventeenth centuries. Witchcraft trials were prevalent in England, Scotland, Switzerland, Germany, some parts of France and the Low Countries, and even New England in America.

Witchcraft was not a new phenomenon in the sixteenth and seventeenth centuries. Although its practice had been part of traditional village culture for centuries, the medieval church made witchcraft both sinister and dangerous by connecting witches to the activities of the Devil, thereby transforming witchcraft into a heresy that had to be extirpated. By the thirteenth century, after the creation of the Inquisition, people were being accused of a variety of witchcraft practices and, following the biblical injunction "Thou shalt not suffer a witch to live," were turned over to secular authorities for burning at the stake or hanging (in England).

What distinguished witchcraft in the sixteenth and seventeenth centuries from these previous developments

◆ **The Persecution of Witches.** Hysteria over witchcraft affected the daily lives of many Europeans in the sixteenth and seventeenth centuries. This picture by Frans Francken the Young, painted in 1607, shows a number of activities commonly attributed to witches. In the center, several witches are casting spells with their magic books and instruments while at the top, a witch on a post prepares to fly off on her broomstick.

was the high level of hysteria at which neighbors accused neighbors of witchcraft, leading to widespread trials of witches. Perhaps more than 100,000 people were prosecuted throughout Europe on charges of witchcraft. As more and more people were brought to trial, the fear of witches as well as the fear of being accused of witchcraft escalated to frightening proportions. Although larger cities were affected first, the trials also spread to smaller towns and rural areas as the hysteria persisted well into the seventeenth century (see the box on p. 549).

Although even city officeholders were not immune to persecution, women of the lower classes were more likely to be accused of witchcraft. Indeed, where lists are given, those mentioned most often are milkmaids, peasant women, and servant girls. In the witchcraft trials of the sixteenth and seventeenth centuries, more than 75 percent of those accused were women, most of them single or widowed and many over fifty years old. Moreover, almost all victims belonged to the lower classes, the poor and propertyless.

The accused witches usually confessed to a number of practices. Many of their confessions were extracted by torture, which greatly added to the number and intensity of activities mentioned. Many said that they had sworn allegiance to the devil and attended sabbats or nocturnal gatherings where they feasted, danced, and even copulated with the devil in sexual orgies. More common, however, were admissions of using evil incantations and special ointments and powders to wreak havoc on neighbors by killing their livestock, injuring their children, or raising storms to destroy their crops.

A number of contributing factors have been suggested to explain why the witchcraft craze became so widespread in the sixteenth and seventeenth centuries. Religious uncertainties clearly played some part. Many witchcraft trials occurred in areas where Protestantism had been recently victorious or in regions, such as southwestern Germany, where Protestant-Catholic controversies still raged. As religious passions became inflamed, accusations of being in league with the devil became common on both sides. Recently, however, historians have emphasized the importance of social conditions, especially the problems of a society in turmoil, in explaining the witchcraft hysteria. At a time when the old communal values that stressed working together for the good of the community were disintegrating, property owners became more fearful of the growing numbers of poor among them and transformed them psychologically into agents of the devil. Old women were particularly susceptible to suspicion. Many of them, no longer the recipients of the local charity found in traditional society, may even

have tried to survive by selling herbs, potions, or secret remedies for healing. When problems arose, and there were many in this crisis-laden period, these same women were the most likely scapegoats at hand.

That women should be the chief victims of witchcraft trials was hardly accidental. Nicholas Rémy, a witchcraft judge in France in the 1590s, found it "not unreasonable that this scum of humanity, i.e., witches, should be drawn chiefly from the feminine sex." To another judge, it came as no surprise that witches would confess to sexual experiences with Satan: "The Devil uses them so, because he knows that women love carnal pleasures, and he means to bind them to his allegiance by such agreeable provocations."[10] Of course, witch hunters were not the only ones to hold such low estimates of women. Most theologians, lawyers, and philosophers in early modern Europe maintained a belief in the natural inferiority of women, making it plausible to them that women would be more susceptible to witchcraft.

By the mid-seventeenth century, the witchcraft hysteria began to subside. The destruction of the religious wars had at least forced people to accept a grudging toleration that allowed religious passions to subside. Moreover, as governments began to stabilize after the period of crisis, fewer magistrates were willing to accept the unsettling and divisive conditions generated by the trials of witches. Finally, by the end of the seventeenth century and the beginning of the eighteenth, more and more people were questioning their old attitudes toward religion altogether and found it especially contrary to reason to believe in a world haunted by evil spirits.

Seventeenth-Century Crises: Revolution and War

Although many Europeans responded to the upheavals of the second half of the sixteenth century with a desire for peace and order, the first fifty years of the seventeenth century continued to be a period of crisis. A series of rebellions and civil wars stemming from the discontent of both nobles and commoners rocked the domestic stability of many European governments. To strengthen their power, monarchs attempted to extend their authority at the expense of traditional powerful elements who resisted their rulers' efforts. At the same time, to pay for armies to fight their battles, governments increased taxes and created such hardships that common people also rose in opposition. The resulting widespread revolts of subjects against their ruling princes have caused some historians to speak of a general crisis of authority in the first half of the seventeenth century. By far the most famous and

A Witchcraft Trial in France

Persecutions for witchcraft reached their high point in the sixteenth and seventeenth centuries when tens of thousands of people were brought to trial. In this excerpt from the minutes of a trial in France in 1652, we can see why the accused witch stood little chance of exonerating herself.

The Trial of Suzanne Gaudry

28 May, 1652. . . . Interrogation of Suzanne Gaudry, prisoner at the court of Rieux. . . . [During interrogations on May 28 and May 29, the prisoner confessed to a number of activities involving the devil.]

Deliberation of the Court—June 3, 1652

The undersigned advocates of the Court have seen these interrogations and answers. They say that the aforementioned Suzanne Gaudry confesses that she is a witch, that she had given herself to the devil, that she had renounced God, Lent, and baptism, that she has been marked on the shoulder, that she has cohabited with the devil and that she has been to the dances, confessing only to have cast a spell upon and caused to die a beast of Philippe Cornié. . . .

Third Interrogation, June 27

This prisoner being led into the chamber, she was examined to know if things were not as she had said and confessed at the beginning of her imprisonment.

—Answers no, and that what she has said was done so by force.

Pressed to say the truth, that otherwise she would be subjected to torture, having pointed out to her that her aunt was burned for this same subject.

—Answers that she is not a witch. . . .

She was placed in the hands of the officer in charge of torture, throwing herself on her knees, struggling to cry, uttering several exclamations, without being able, nevertheless, to shed a tear. Saying at every moment that she is not a witch.

The Torture

On this same day, being at the place of torture.

This prisoner, before being strapped down, was admonished to maintain herself in her first confessions and to renounce her lover.

—Says that she denies everything she has said, and that she has no lover. Feeling herself being strapped down, says that she is not a witch, while struggling to cry . . . and upon being asked why she confessed to being one, said that she was forced to say it.

Told that she was not forced, that on the contrary she declared herself to be a witch without any threat.

—Says that she confessed it and that she is not a witch, and being a little stretched [on the rack] screams ceaselessly that she is not a witch.

Asked if she did not confess that she had been a witch for twenty-six years.

—Says that she said it, that she retracts it, crying that she is not a witch.

Asked if she did not make Philippe Cornié's horse die, as she confessed.

—Answers no, crying Jesus-Maria, that she is not a witch.

The mark having been probed by the officer, in the presence of Doctor Bouchain, it was adjudged by the aforesaid doctor and officer truly to be the mark of the devil.

Being more tightly stretched upon the torture-rack, urged to maintain her confessions.

—Said that it was true that she is a witch and that she would maintain what she had said.

Asked how long she has been in subjugation to the devil.

—Answers that it was twenty years ago that the devil appeared to her, being in her lodgings in the form of a man dressed in a little cow-hide and black breeches. . . .

Verdict

July 9, 1652. In the light of the interrogations, answers and investigations made into the charge against Suzanne Gaudry, . . . seeing by her own confessions that she is said to have made a pact with the devil, received the mark from him, . . . and that following this, she had renounced God, Lent, and baptism and had let herself be known carnally by him, in which she received satisfaction. Also, seeing that she is said to have been a part of nocturnal carols and dances.

For expiation of which the advice of the undersigned is that the office of Rieux can legitimately condemn the aforesaid Suzanne Gaudry to death, tying her to a gallows, and strangling her to death, then burning her body and burying it here in the environs of the woods.

Europe in Crisis, 1560–1650:
Key Events

Reign of Philip II	1556–1598
The French Wars of Religion	1562–1598
Outbreak of revolt in the Netherlands	1566
The Spanish Armada	1588
Edict of Nantes	1598
Twelve-year truce (Spain and the Netherlands)	1609
The Thirty Years' War	1618–1648
Peace of Westphalia	1648
Independence of the United Provinces	1648

wide-ranging struggle was the civil war and rebellion in England, commonly known as the English Revolution (see Limited Monarchy: England and the Emergence of Constitutional Monarchy later in this chapter). A devastating war that affected much of Europe also added to the sense of crisis.

THE THIRTY YEARS' WAR (1618–1648)

Religion, especially the struggle between a militant Catholicism and a militant Calvinism, certainly played an important role in the outbreak of the Thirty Years' War, often called the "last of the religious wars." As the war progressed, however, it became increasingly clear that secular, dynastic-nationalist considerations were far more important.

The Thirty Years' War began in 1618 in the Germanic lands of the Holy Roman Empire as a struggle between Catholic forces, led by the Habsburg Holy Roman emperors, and Protestant—primarily Calvinist—nobles in Bohemia who rebelled against Habsburg authority. What began as a struggle over religious issues soon became a wider conflict perpetuated by political considerations as both minor and major European powers—Denmark, Sweden, France, and Spain—entered the war. The rivalry between the Bourbon dynasty of France and the Habsburg dynasties of Spain and the Holy Roman Empire for European leadership was an especially important

factor. Nevertheless, most of the battles were fought on German soil, with devastating results for the German people.

The war in Germany was officially ended by the Peace of Westphalia in 1648. What were the results of this "basically meaningless conflict," as one historian has called it? The Peace of Westphalia ensured that all German states, including the Calvinist ones, were free to determine their own religion. The major combatants gained new territories, and one of them, France, emerged as the dominant nation in Europe. The more than three hundred states that made up the Holy Roman Empire were virtually recognized as independent, since each received the power to conduct its own foreign policy; this brought an end to the Holy Roman Empire as a political entity and ensured German disunity for another two hundred years. The Peace of Westphalia made it clear that religion and politics were now separate worlds. Political motives became the guiding forces in public affairs as religion was in the process of becoming primarily a matter of personal conviction and individual choice.

Germany suffered the most from the Thirty Years' War. Some areas of the country were completely devastated. Many people in Germany would have agreed with this comment by Otto von Guericke, a councillor in the city of Magdeburg, which was sacked ten times:

> Then there was nothing but beating and burning, plundering, torture, and murder. Most especially was every one of the enemy bent on securing much booty. . . . In this frenzied rage, the great and splendid city . . . was now . . . given over to the flames, and thousands of innocent men, women and children, in the midst of a horrible din of heartrending shrieks and cries, were tortured and put to death in so cruel and shameful a manner that no words would suffice to describe. . . . Thus in a single day this noble and famous city, the pride of the whole country, went up in fire and smoke.[11]

The Thirty Years' War was undoubtedly the most destructive conflict Europeans had yet experienced. Unfortunately, it was not the last.

Response to Crisis: The Practice of Absolutism

Many people responded to the crises of the seventeenth century by searching for order and harmony. An increase in monarchical power became an obvious means of achieving stability. The result was what historians have called absolutism or absolute monarchy. Absolute monarchy or absolutism meant that the sovereign power or ultimate authority in the state rested in the hands of a king or queen who claimed to rule by divine right—the idea that rulers received their power from God and were responsible to no one (including parliaments) except God. But what did sovereignty mean? Late sixteenth-century political theorists believed that sovereign power consisted of the authority to make laws, tax, administer justice, control the state's administrative system, and determine foreign policy. These powers made a ruler sovereign.

The Practice of Absolutism: France under Louis XIV

France during the reign of Louis XIV (1643–1715) has traditionally been regarded as the best example of the practice of absolute monarchy in the seventeenth century. French culture, language, and manners reached into all levels of European society. French diplomacy and wars overwhelmed the political affairs of western and central Europe. The court of Louis XIV seemed to be imitated everywhere in Europe. Of course, the stability of Louis's reign was magnified by the instability that had preceded it.

⊠ Map 15.2   Europe in the Seventeenth Century.

◆ **Louis XIV.** Louis XIV was determined to be the sole ruler of France. Louis eliminated the threat of the high nobility by removing them from the royal council and replacing them with relatively new aristocrats whom he could dominate. This portrait by Hyacinth Rigaud captures the king's sense of royal dignity and grandeur.

The history of France before the reign of Louis XIV was hardly a story of steady, unbroken progress toward an ideal of absolute monarchy. The fifty or so years before Louis were a period of struggle by royal and ministerial governments to avoid the breakdown of the state. The line between order and anarchy was often a narrow one. The situation was especially complicated by the fact that in both 1610 and 1643, when Louis XIII and Louis XIV, respectively, succeeded to the throne, they were only boys, leaving the government dependent upon royal ministers. Two especially competent ministers played crucial roles in maintaining monarchical authority.

Cardinal Richelieu, Louis XIII's chief minister from 1624 to 1642, initiated policies that eventually strengthened the power of the monarchy. By eliminating the political and military rights of the Huguenots while preserving their religious ones, Richelieu transformed the Huguenots into more reliable subjects. Richelieu acted more cautiously in "humbling the pride of the great men," the important French nobility. He understood the influential role played by the nobles in the French state. The dangerous ones were those who asserted their territorial independence when they were excluded from participating in the central government. Proceeding slowly but determinedly, Richelieu developed an efficient network of spies to uncover noble plots and then crushed the conspiracies and executed the conspirators.

When Louis XIV succeeded to the throne in 1643 at the age of four, Cardinal Mazarin, the trained successor of Cardinal Richelieu, came to dominate the government. The most important event during Mazarin's rule was the Fronde, a revolt led primarily by nobles who wished to curb the centralized administrative power being built up at the expense of the provincial nobility. The Fronde was crushed by 1652, and with its end, a vast number of Frenchmen concluded that the best hope for stability in France lay in the crown. When Mazarin died in 1661, the greatest of the seventeenth-century monarchs, Louis XIV, took over supreme power. The day after Cardinal Mazarin's death, the new king, at the age of twenty-three, expressed his determination to be a real king and the sole ruler of France:

> Up to this moment I have been pleased to entrust the government of my affairs to the late Cardinal. It is now time that I govern them myself. You [secretaries and ministers of state] will assist me with your counsels when I ask for them. I request and order you to seal no orders except by my command, . . . I order you not to sign anything, not even a passport . . . without my command; to render account to me personally each day and to favor no one.[12]

Louis proved willing to pay the price of being a strong ruler.

Although Louis may have believed in the theory of absolute monarchy and consciously fostered the myth of himself as the Sun King, the source of light for all of his people, historians are quick to point out that the realities fell far short of the aspirations. Despite the centralizing efforts of Cardinals Richelieu and Mazarin, France still possessed a bewildering system of overlapping authorities in the seventeenth century. Provinces had their own regional courts, their own local Estates, their own sets of laws. Members of the high nobility with their huge estates and clients among the lesser nobility still exercised much authority. Both towns and provinces possessed privileges and powers seemingly from time immemorial that they would not easily relinquish. Much of Louis's success rested less on the modernization of administrative machinery, as is frequently claimed, than on his clever and adroit manipulation of the traditional priorities and values of French society.

One of the keys to Louis's power was that he was able to restructure the central policy-making machinery of government because it was part of his own court and household. The royal court located at Versailles was an elaborate structure that served three purposes simultaneously: it was the personal household of the king, the location of central governmental machinery, and the place where powerful subjects came to find favors and offices for themselves and their clients, as well as the main arena where rival aristocratic factions jostled for power. The greatest danger to Louis's personal rule came from the very high nobles and princes of the blood (the royal princes) who considered it their natural function to assert the policy-making role of royal ministers. Louis eliminated this threat by removing them from the royal council, the chief administrative body of the king and overseer of the central machinery of government, and enticing them to his court where he could keep them preoccupied with court life and out of politics. Instead of the high nobility and royal princes, Louis relied for his ministers on nobles who came from relatively new aristocratic families. His ministers were expected to be subservient; said Louis, "I had no intention of sharing my authority with them."

Louis's domination of his ministers and secretaries gave him control of the central policy-making machinery of government and thus authority over the traditional areas of monarchical power: the formulation of foreign policy, the making of war and peace, the assertion of the secular power of the crown against any religious authority, and the ability to levy taxes to fulfill these functions. However, Louis had considerably less success with the internal administration of the kingdom. The traditional groups and institutions of French society—the nobles, officials, town councils, guilds, and representative Estates in some provinces—were simply too powerful for the king to have direct control over the lives of his subjects. As a result, the control of the central government over the provinces and the people was carried out largely by carefully bribing the important people to ensure that the king's policies were executed.

The maintenance of religious harmony had long been considered an area of monarchical power. The desire to keep it led Louis to pursue an anti-Protestant policy, aimed at converting the Huguenots to Catholicism. In October 1685, Louis revoked the Edict of Nantes and ordered the destruction of Huguenot churches and the closing of their schools. Although they were forbidden to leave France, an estimated 200,000 Huguenots left for shelter in England, the United Provinces, and the German states.

The cost of building palaces, maintaining his court, and pursuing his wars made finances a crucial issue for Louis XIV. He was most fortunate in having the services of Jean-Baptiste Colbert (1619–1683) as controller-general of finances. Colbert sought to increase the wealth and power of France by general adherence to mercantilism, a name historians use to identify a set of economic principles that dominated economic thought in the seventeenth century. According to the mercantilists, the prosperity of a nation depended upon a plentiful supply of bullion or gold and silver. For this reason, it was desirable to achieve a favorable balance of trade in which exported goods were of greater value than those imported, promoting an influx of gold and silver payments that would increase the quantity of bullion. To encourage exports, governments should stimulate and protect export industries and trade by granting trade monopolies, encouraging investment in new industries through subsidies, and

♦ **Palace of Versailles.**   Louis XIV spent untold sums of money in the construction of a new royal residence at Versailles. The enormous palace of Versailles also housed the members of the king's government and served as home for thousands of French nobles. As the largest royal residence in Europe, Versailles impressed foreigners and became a source of envy for other rulers.

improving transportation systems by building roads, bridges, and canals. By imposing high tariffs on foreign goods, they could be kept out of the country and prevented from competing with the products of domestic industries. Colonies were also deemed valuable as sources of raw materials and markets for finished goods. As a system of economic principles, mercantilism focused on the role of the state, believing that state intervention in some aspects of the economy was desirable for the sake of the national good.

Colbert was an avid practitioner of mercantilism. To decrease the need for imports and increase exports, he founded new luxury industries; drew up instructions regulating the quality of goods produced; oversaw the training of the workers; and granted special privileges, including tax exemptions, loans, and subsidies to those who established new industries. To improve communications and the transportation of goods internally, he built roads and canals. To decrease imports directly, Colbert raised tariffs on foreign manufactured goods and created a merchant marine to facilitate the conveyance of French goods.

The increase in royal power that Louis pursued as well as his desire for military glory led the king to develop a professional army numbering 100,000 men in peacetime and 400,000 in time of war. Louis made war an almost incessant activity of his reign. To achieve the prestige and military glory befitting a Sun King as well as to ensure the domination of his Bourbon dynasty over European affairs, Louis waged four wars between 1667 and 1713. His ambitions roused much of Europe to form coalitions aimed at preventing a Bourbon hegemony that would mean the certain destruction of the European balance of power. Although Louis added some territory to France's northeastern frontier and established a member of his own Bourbon dynasty on the throne of Spain, he also left France impoverished and surrounded by enemies.

Absolutism in Central and Eastern Europe

During the seventeenth century, a development of great importance for the modern Western world took place in central and eastern Europe, the appearance of three new powers: Prussia, Austria, and Russia.

The Peace of Westphalia, which officially ended the Thirty Years' War in 1648, left each of the three hundred or more German states comprising the Holy Roman Empire virtually autonomous and sovereign. Properly speaking, there was no German state, but rather over three hundred "Germanies." Of these states, two emerged in the seventeenth and eighteenth centuries as great European powers.

The development of Brandenburg as a state was largely the story of the Hohenzollern dynasty. By the seventeenth century, the dominions of the house of Hohenzollern, now called Brandenburg-Prussia, consisted of three disconnected masses in western, central, and eastern Germany. Each had its own privileges, customs, and loyalties; only the person of the Hohenzollern ruler connected them. Brandenburg-Prussia was an artificial creation, highly vulnerable and dependent upon its ruling dynasty to create a state where one simply did not exist.

Frederick William the Great Elector (1640–1688) laid the foundation for the Prussian state. Realizing that Brandenburg-Prussia was a small, open territory with no natural frontiers for defense, Frederick William built a competent and efficient standing army. By 1678, he possessed a force of 40,000 men, making the Prussian army the fourth largest in Europe. To sustain the army and his own power, Frederick William established the General War Commissariat to levy taxes for the army and oversee its growth and training. The Commissariat soon evolved into an agency for civil government as well. Directly responsible to the elector, the new bureaucratic machine became his chief instrument for governing the state. Many of its officials were members of the Prussian landed aristocracy, the Junkers, who also served as officers in the all-important army.

Frederick William the Great Elector established the foundations for the Prussian state. In 1701, his son Frederick officially gained the title of king. Elector Frederick III was transformed into King Frederick I, and Brandenburg-Prussia became simply Prussia. In the eighteenth century, Prussia emerged as a great power on the European stage.

The Austrian Habsburgs had long played a significant role in European politics as Holy Roman emperors. By the end of the Thirty Years' War, the Habsburg hopes of creating an empire in Germany had been dashed. In the seventeenth century, the house of Austria made a difficult transition; the German empire was lost, but a new empire was created in eastern and southeastern Europe.

The nucleus of the new Austrian Empire remained the traditional Austrian hereditary possessions: Lower and Upper Austria, Carinthia, Carniola, Styria, and Tyrol. To these had been added the kingdom of Bohemia and parts of northwestern Hungary. After the defeat of the Turks in 1687 (see Chapter 18), Austria took control of all of Hungary, Transylvania, Croatia, and Slovenia, thus establishing an Austrian Empire in southeastern Europe. By the beginning of the eighteenth century, the house of Austria had acquired a new empire of considerable size.

The Austrian monarchy, however, never became a highly centralized, absolutist state, primarily because it contained so many different national groups. The Austrian Empire remained a collection of territories held together by a personal union. The Habsburg emperor was archduke of Austria, king of Bohemia, and king of Hungary. Each of these areas, however, had its own laws, Estates-General, and political life. There was no common sentiment to tie the regions together; only the ideal of service to the house of Habsburg, whether as military officers or government bureaucrats, provided a common bond that linked the landed aristocracies throughout the empire. Nevertheless, by the beginning of the eighteenth century, Austria was a populous empire in central Europe of great potential military strength.

FROM MUSCOVY TO RUSSIA

A new Russian state had emerged in the fifteenth century under the leadership of the principality of Muscovy and its grand dukes. In the sixteenth century, Ivan IV the Terrible (1533–1584), who was the first ruler to take the title of tsar, expanded the territories of Russia eastward, after finding westward expansion blocked by the powerful Swedish and Polish states. Ivan also extended the autocracy of the tsar by crushing the power of the Russian nobility known as the boyars. Ivan's dynasty came to an end in 1598 and was followed by a resurgence of aristocratic power in a period of anarchy known as the Time of Troubles. It did not end until the Zemsky Sobor or national assembly chose Michael Romanov as the new tsar, establishing a dynasty that lasted until 1917.

In the seventeenth century, Muscovite society was highly stratified. At the top was the tsar, who claimed to be a divinely ordained autocratic ruler, assisted by two consultative bodies, a Duma or council of boyars and the Zemsky Sobor, a parliamentary body of sorts begun in 1550 by Ivan IV to facilitate support for his programs. Russian society was dominated by an upper class of landed aristocrats who, in the course of the seventeenth century, managed to bind their peasants to the land. An abundance of land and a shortage of peasants made serfdom desirable to the landowners, who sustained a highly oppressive system. Townspeople were also stratified and controlled. Artisans were sharply separated from merchants, and many of the latter were not allowed to move from their cities without government permission or to sell their businesses to anyone outside their class. In the seventeenth century, merchant and peasant revolts as well as a schism in the Russian Orthodox church created very unsettled conditions. In the midst of these political and religious upheavals, seventeenth-century Muscovy was experiencing more frequent contacts with the West while Western ideas also began to penetrate a few Russian circles. At the end of the seventeenth century, Peter the Great noticeably accelerated this westernizing process.

Peter the Great (1689–1725) was an unusual character. A strong, towering man at six feet, nine inches tall, Peter was coarse in his tastes and rude in his behavior. He enjoyed a low kind of humor—belching contests and crude jokes—and vicious punishments including flogging, impalings, and roastings (see the box on p. 556). Peter obtained a firsthand view of the West when he made a trip there in 1697–1698 and returned to Russia with a firm determination to westernize Russia. Perhaps too much has been made of Peter's desire to westernize a "backward country." Peter's policy was largely technical. He admired Western technology and gadgets and wanted to transplant them to Russia. Only this kind of modernization could give him the army and navy he needed to make Russia a great power.

As could be expected, one of his first priorities was the reorganization of the army and the creation of a navy. Employing both Russians and Europeans as officers, he conscripted peasants for twenty-five-year stints of service to build a standing army of 210,000 men. Peter has also been given credit for forming the first Russian navy.

Peter reorganized the central government, partly along Western lines. What remained of the consultative bodies disappeared; neither the Duma of boyars nor the Zemsky Sobor was ever summoned. In 1711, Peter created a Senate to supervise the administrative machinery of state while he away on military campaigns. In time the Senate became something like a ruling council, but its ineffectiveness caused Peter to borrow the Western institution of "colleges," or boards of administrators entrusted with specific functions, such as foreign affairs, war, and justice. To impose the rule of the central government more effectively throughout the land, Peter divided Russia into eight provinces and later, in 1719, into fifty. Although he hoped to create a "police state," by which he meant a well-ordered community governed in accordance with law, few of his bureaucrats shared his concept of honest service and duty to the state. Peter hoped for a sense of civic duty, but his own forceful personality created an atmosphere of fear that prevented it.

To satisfy his insatiable need of money for an army and navy that absorbed as much as four-fifths of the state revenue, Peter adopted Western mercantilistic policies to stimulate economic growth. He tried to increase exports and develop new industries while exploiting domestic

❧ *Peter the Great Deals with a Rebellion* ❧

During his first visit to the West in 1697–1698, Peter received word that the Streltsy, an elite military unit stationed in Moscow, had revolted against his authority. Peter hurried home and crushed the revolt in a very savage fashion. This selection is taken from an Austrian account of how Peter dealt with the rebels.

Peter and the Streltsy

How sharp was the pain, how great the indignation, to which the tsar's Majesty was mightily moved, when he knew of the rebellion of the Streltsy, betraying openly a mind panting for vengeance! He was still tarrying at Vienna, quite full of the desire of setting out for Italy; but, fervid as was his curiosity of rambling abroad, it was, nevertheless, speedily extinguished on the announcement of the troubles that had broken out in the bowels of his realm. Going immediately to Lefort . . . , he thus indignantly broke out: "Tell me, Francis, how I can reach Moscow by the shortest way, in a brief space, so that I may wreak vengeance on this great perfidy of my people, with punishments worthy of their abominable crime. Not one of them shall escape with impunity. Around my royal city, which, with their impious efforts, they planned to destroy, I will have gibbets and gallows set upon the walls and ramparts, and each and every one of them will I put to a direful death." Nor did he long delay the plan for his justly excited wrath; he took the quick post, as his ambassador suggested,

and in four weeks' time he had got over about three hundred miles without accident, and arrived the 4th of September, 1698—a monarch for the well disposed, but an avenger for the wicked.

His first anxiety after his arrival was about the rebellion—in what it consisted, what the insurgents meant, who dared to instigate such a crime. And as nobody could answer accurately upon all points, and some pleaded their own ignorance, others the obstinacy of the Streltsy, he began to have suspicions of everybody's loyalty. . . . No day, holy or profane, were the inquisitors idle; every day was deemed fit and lawful for torturing. There were as many scourges as there were accused, and every inquisitor was a butcher. . . . The whole month of October was spent in lacerating the backs of culprits with the knout and with flames; no day were those that were left alive exempt from scourging or scorching; or else they were broken upon the wheel, or driven to the gibbet, or slain with the ax. . . .

To prove to all people how holy and inviolable are those walls of the city which the Streltsy rashly meditated scaling in a sudden assault, beams were run out from all the embrasures in the walls near the gates, in each of which two rebels were hanged. This day beheld about two hundred and fifty die that death. There are few cities fortified with as many palisades as Moscow has given gibbets to her guardian Streltsy.

resources like the iron mines in the Urals. But his military needs were endless, and he came to rely on the old expedient of simply raising taxes, placing additional burdens upon hapless peasants whose position in Peter's Russia grew ever more oppressed.

Peter also sought to gain state control of the Russian Orthodox church. In 1721, he abolished the position of patriarch and created a body called the Holy Synod to make decisions for the church. At its head stood a procurator, a layman who represented the interests of the tsar and assured Peter of effective domination of the church.

Already after his first trip to the West in 1697–1698, Peter had begun to introduce Western customs, practices, and manners into Russia. He ordered the preparation of the first Russian book of etiquette to teach Western manners. Among other things, it pointed out that it was not polite to spit on the floor or scratch oneself at dinner.

Since westerners did not wear beards or the traditional long-skirted coat, Russian beards had to be shaved and coats shortened, a reform Peter personally enforced at court by shaving off his nobles' beards and cutting their coats at the knees with his own hands. Outside the court, the edicts were enforced by barbers and tailors planted at town gates with orders to cut the beards and cloaks of those who entered or left. One group of Russians benefited greatly from Peter's cultural reforms—women. Having watched women mixing freely with men in Western courts, Peter shattered the seclusion of upper-class Russian women and demanded that they remove the traditional veils that covered their faces. Peter also encouraged gatherings in which both sexes could mix for conversation and dancing, which Peter had learned in the West. The tsar also now insisted that women could marry of their own free will.

The object of Peter's domestic reforms was to make Russia into a great state and military power. His primary goal was to "open a window to the west," meaning an ice-free port easily accessible to Europe. This could only be achieved on the Baltic, but at that time the Baltic coast was controlled by Sweden, the most important power in northern Europe. A long and hard-fought war with Sweden enabled Peter to acquire the lands he sought. Already in 1703, in these northern lands on the Baltic, Peter had begun the construction of a new city, St. Petersburg, his window on the west and a symbol that Russia was looking westward to Europe. Built on marshland, St. Petersburg cost the lives of thousands of peasants during its construction. Nevertheless, the city was finished during Peter's lifetime and remained the Russian capital until 1917.

Peter modernized and westernized Russia to the extent that it became a great military power, and by his death in 1725, it was an important member of the European state system. But his policies were also detrimental to Russia. Westernization was a bit of a sham, since Western culture reached only the upper classes while the real object of the reforms, the creation of a strong military, only added more burdens to the masses of the Russian people. The forceful way in which Peter the Great brought westernization led many Russians to distrust Europe and Western civilization.

Limited Monarchy: England and the Emergence of Constitutional Monarchy

One of the most prominent examples of resistance to absolute monarchy came in seventeenth-century England where king and Parliament struggled to determine the roles each should play in governing England. But the struggle over this political issue was complicated by a deep and profound religious controversy. With the victory of Parliament, the foundation for constitutional monarchy was laid by the end of the seventeenth century.

Revolution and Civil War

With the death of Queen Elizabeth I in 1603, the Tudor dynasty became extinct, and the Stuart line of rulers was inaugurated with the accession to the throne of Elizabeth's cousin, King James VI of Scotland, who became James I (1603–1625) of England. Although used to royal power as king of Scotland, James understood little about the laws, institutions, and customs of the English. He espoused the divine right of kings, the belief that kings re-

◆ **Peter the Great.** Peter the Great wished to westernize Russia, especially in the realm of technical skills. His foremost goal was the creation of a strong army and navy in order to make Russia a great power. A Dutch artist painted this portrait of the armored tsar during his visit to the West in 1697.

ceive their power directly from God and are responsible to no one except God. This viewpoint alienated Parliament, which had grown accustomed under the Tudors to act on the premise that monarch and Parliament together ruled England as a "balanced polity." Then, too, the Puritans—those Protestants within the Anglican church who, inspired by Calvinist theology, wished to eliminate any trace of popery from the Church of England—were alienated by the king's strong defense of the Anglican church. Many of England's lesser landed nobility, the gentry, had become Puritans, and these Puritan gentry not only formed an important and substantial part of the House of Commons, the lower house of Parliament, but also held important positions locally as justices of the peace and sheriffs. It was not wise to alienate them.

The conflict that had begun during the reign of James came to a head during the reign of his son Charles I

(1625–1649). Charles believed as strongly in divine-right monarchy as his father had, and from the first stormy session of Parliament, it became apparent that the constitutional issues between this king and Parliament would not be easily resolved. In 1628, Parliament passed a Petition of Right that the king was supposed to accept before being granted any taxes. This petition prohibited taxes without Parliament's consent, arbitrary imprisonment, the quartering of soldiers in private houses, and the declaration of martial law in peacetime. Although he initially accepted it, Charles later reneged on the agreement because of its limitations on royal power.

Religious differences also added to the hostility between Charles I and Parliament. The king's attempt to impose more ritual on the Anglican church struck the Puritans as a return to Catholic "popery." Charles's efforts to force them to conform to his religious policies infuriated the Puritans, thousands of whom went to the "howling wildernesses" of America rather than be forced to conform their consciences to the king's supposed pro-popery nonsense.

Grievances mounted until England finally slipped into a civil war (1642–1648) that was won by the parliamentary forces. Most important to Parliament's success was the creation of the New Model Army by Oliver Cromwell, the only real military genius of the war. The New Model Army was composed primarily of more extreme Puritans known as the Independents, who, in typical Calvinist fashion, believed they were doing battle for the Lord.

Between 1648 and 1660, England faced a trying situation. After the execution of Charles I on January 30, 1649, Parliament abolished the monarchy and the House of Lords and proclaimed England a republic or Commonwealth. But Cromwell and his army, unable to work effectively with Parliament, dispersed it by force and established a military dictatorship. Unable to find a constitutional basis for a working government, Cromwell had resorted to military force to maintain the rule of the Independents, ironically using even more arbitrary policies than those of Charles I.

Oliver Cromwell died in 1658. After floundering for eighteen months, the military establishment decided that arbitrary rule by the army was no longer feasible and reestablished the monarchy in the person of Charles II (1660–1685), the son of Charles I. The restoration of the Stuart monarchy ended England's time of troubles, but it would not be long before England would experience yet another constitutional crisis.

Restoration and a Glorious Revolution

The restoration of the monarchy did not mean that the work of the English Revolution was undone. Parliament kept much of the power it had won: arbitrary courts were still abolished; Parliament's role in government was acknowledged; and the necessity for its consent to taxation was accepted. Yet Charles II continued to push his own ideas, some of which were clearly out of step with many of the English people.

Charles was sympathetic to and perhaps even inclined toward Catholicism. Moreover, Charles's brother James, heir to the throne, did not hide the fact that he was a Catholic. Parliament's suspicions were therefore aroused

◆ **Execution of Charles I.** When Charles I attempted to arrest radical members of Parliament, a civil war erupted that eventually led to the rise of Oliver Cromwell and the execution of the king. This contemporary painting of the execution of Charles I shows a woman fainting at the bottom while the executioner holds the king's head aloft at the top. At the top left is a portrait of Charles I.

in 1672 when Charles took the audacious step of issuing a Declaration of Indulgence that suspended the laws that Parliament had passed against Catholics and Puritans after the restoration of the monarchy. Parliament would have none of it and induced the king to suspend the declaration. Propelled by a strong anti-Catholic sentiment, Parliament then passed a Test Act in 1673, specifying that only Anglicans could hold military and civil offices.

The accession of James II (1685–1688) to the crown virtually guaranteed a new constitutional crisis for England. An open and devout Catholic, his attempt to further Catholic interests made religion once more a primary cause of conflict between king and Parliament. Contrary to the Test Act, James named Catholics to high positions in the government, army, navy, and universities. In 1687, he issued a Declaration of Indulgence, which suspended all laws excluding Catholics and Puritans from office. Parliamentary outcries against James's policies stopped short of rebellion because members knew that he was an old man and his successors were his Protestant daughters Mary and Anne, born to his first wife. But on June 10, 1688, a son was born to James's second wife, also a Catholic. Suddenly, the specter of a Catholic hereditary monarchy loomed large. A group of prominent English noblemen invited the Dutch chief executive, William of Orange, husband of James's daughter Mary, to invade England. William and Mary raised an army and invaded England while James, his wife, and infant son fled to France. With almost no bloodshed, England had undergone a "Glorious Revolution," not over the issue of whether there would be a monarchy, but rather over who would be the monarch.

The events of late 1688 constituted only the initial stage of the Glorious Revolution. In January 1689, Parliament offered the throne to William and Mary, who accepted it along with the provisions of a Bill of Rights (see the box on p. 560). The Bill of Rights affirmed Parliament's right to make laws and levy taxes and made it impossible for kings to oppose or do without Parliament by stipulating that standing armies could be raised only with the consent of Parliament. The rights of citizens to petition the sovereign, keep arms, have a jury trial, and not be subject to excessive bail were also confirmed. The Bill of Rights helped to fashion a system of government based on the rule of law and a freely elected Parliament, thus laying the foundation for a constitutional monarchy.

The Bill of Rights did not settle the religious questions that had played such a large role in England's troubles in the seventeenth century. The Toleration Act of 1689 granted Puritan Dissenters the right of free public worship (Catholics were still excluded). Although the Toler-

Absolute and Limited Monarchy

France		
Louis XIII	1610–1643	
Cardinal Richelieu as chief minister	1624–1642	
Ministry of Cardinal Mazarin	1642–1661	
Louis XIV	1643–1715	
Revocation of Edict of Nantes	1685	
Brandenburg-Prussia		
Frederick William the Great Elector	1640–1688	
Elector Frederick III (King Frederick I)	1688–1713	
Russia		
Ivan IV the Terrible	1533–1584	
Time of Troubles	1598–1613	
Peter the Great	1689–1725	
First trip to the West	1697–1698	
Construction of St. Petersburg begins	1703	
Holy Synod	1721	
England		
Civil wars	1642–1648	
Commonwealth	1649–1653	
Charles II	1660–1685	
Declaration of Indulgence	1672	
Test Act	1673	
James II	1685–1688	
Declaration of Indulgence	1687	
Glorious Revolution	1688	
Bill of Rights	1689	

ation Act did not mean complete religious freedom and equality, it marked a departure in English history since few people would ever again be persecuted for religious reasons.

Many historians have viewed the Glorious Revolution as the end of the seventeenth-century struggle between

❧ The Bill of Rights ❧

In 1688, the English experienced yet another revolution, a rather bloodless one in which the Stuart king James II was replaced by Mary, James's daughter, and her husband, William of Orange. After William and Mary had assumed power, Parliament passed a Bill of Rights that specified the rights of Parliament and laid the foundation for a constitutional monarchy.

The Bill of Rights

Whereas the said late King James II having abdicated the government, and the throne being thereby vacant, his Highness the prince of Orange (whom it hath pleased Almighty God to make the glorious instrument of delivering this kingdom from popery and arbitrary power) did (by the device of the lords spiritual and temporal, and diverse principal persons of the Commons) cause letters to be written to the lords spiritual and temporal, being Protestants, and other letters to the several counties, cities, universities, boroughs, and Cinque Ports, for the choosing of such persons to represent them, as were of right to be sent to parliament, to meet and sit at Westminster upon the two and twentieth day of January, in this year 1689, in order to such an establishment as that their religion, laws, and liberties might not again be in danger of being subverted; upon which letters elections have been accordingly made.

And thereupon the said lords spiritual and temporal and Commons, pursuant to their respective letters and elections, being now assembled in a full and free representation of this nation, taking into their most serious consideration the best means for attaining the ends aforesaid, do in the first place (as their ancestors in like case have usually done), for the vindication and assertion of their ancient rights and liberties, declare:

1. That the pretended power of suspending laws, or the execution of laws, by regal authority, without consent of parliament is illegal.

2. That the pretended power of dispensing with the laws, or the execution of law by regal authority, as it hath been assumed and exercised of late, is illegal.

3. That the commission for erecting the late court of commissioners for ecclesiastical causes, and all other commissions and courts of like nature, are illegal and pernicious.

4. That levying money for or to the use of the crown by pretense of prerogative, without grant of parliament, for longer time or in other manner than the same is or shall be granted, is illegal.

5. That it is the right of the subjects to petition the king, and all commitments and prosecutions for such petitioning are illegal.

6. That the raising or keeping a standing army within the kingdom in time of peace, unless it be with consent of parliament, is against law.

7. That the subjects which are Protestants may have arms for their defense suitable to their conditions, and as allowed by law.

8. That election of members of parliament ought to be free.

9. That the freedom of speech, and debates or proceedings in parliament, ought not to be impeached or questioned in any court or place out of parliament.

10. That excessive bail ought not to be required, nor excessive fines imposed, nor cruel and unusual punishments inflicted.

11. That jurors ought to be duly impaneled and returned, and jurors which pass upon men in trials for high treason ought to be freeholders.

12. That all grants and promises of fines and forfeitures of particular persons before conviction are illegal and void.

13. And that for redress of all grievances, and for the amending, strengthening, and preserving of the laws, parliament ought to be held frequently.

king and Parliament. By deposing one king and establishing another, Parliament had destroyed the divine-right theory of kingship (William was, after all, king by grace of Parliament, not God) and confirmed its right to participate in the government. Parliament did not have complete control of the government, but it now had an unquestioned right to participate in affairs of state. Over the next century, it would gradually prove to be the real authority in the English system of constitutional monarchy.

Responses to Revolution

The English revolutions of the seventeenth century prompted very different responses from two English political thinkers—Thomas Hobbes and John Locke. Thomas Hobbes (1588–1679), who lived during the English civil wars, was alarmed by the revolutionary upheavals in his contemporary England. Hobbes's name has since been associated with the state's claim to absolute authority over its subjects, which he elaborated in his major treatise on political thought known as the *Leviathan*, published in 1651.

Hobbes viewed human nature in materialistic terms. He claimed that in the state of nature, before society was organized, human life was "solitary, poor, nasty, brutish, and short." Humans were guided not by reason and moral ideals, but by animalistic instincts and a ruthless struggle for self-preservation. To save themselves from destroying each other, people contracted to form a commonwealth, which Hobbes called "that great Leviathan (or rather, to speak more reverently, that mortal god) to which we owe our peace and defense." This commonwealth placed its collective power into the hands of a sovereign authority, preferably a single ruler, who served as executor, legislator, and judge. This absolute ruler possessed unlimited power. Subjects may not rebel; if they do, they must be suppressed.

John Locke (1632–1704) viewed the exercise of political power quite differently from Hobbes and argued against the absolute rule of one man. Locke's experience of English politics during the Glorious Revolution was transformed into a political work called *Two Treatises of Government*. Like Hobbes, Locke began with the state of nature before human existence became organized socially. But, unlike Hobbes, Locke believed humans lived then in a state of equality and freedom rather than a state of war. In this state of nature, humans had certain inalienable natural rights—to life, liberty, and property. Like Hobbes, Locke did not believe all was well in the state of nature. Because there was no impartial judge in the state of nature, people found it difficult to protect these natural rights. So they mutually agreed to establish a government to ensure the protection of their rights. This agreement established mutual obligations: government would protect the people's rights while the people would act reasonably toward government. But if a government broke this agreement—if a monarch, for example, failed to live up to his obligation to protect the natural rights or claimed absolute authority and made laws without the consent of the community—the people might form a new government. For Locke, however, the community of people meant primarily the landholding aristocracy who were represented in Parliament, not the landless masses. Locke was hardly an advocate of political democracy, but his ideas proved important to both Americans and French in the eighteenth century and were used to support demands for constitutional government, the rule of law, and the protection of rights.

The World of European Culture

In the sixteenth and seventeenth centuries, art and literature passed through several major stylistic stages. These changes were closely linked to the religious, political, and intellectual developments of the period.

Art

The artistic Renaissance came to an end when a new movement called Mannerism emerged in Italy in the decades of the 1520s and 1530s. The age of the Reformation had brought a revival of religious values accompanied by much political turmoil. Especially in Italy, the worldly enthusiasm of the Renaissance gave way to anxiety, uncertainty, suffering, and a yearning for spiritual experience. Mannerism reflected this environment in its deliberate attempt to break down the High Renaissance principles of balance, harmony, and moderation. Italian Mannerist painters deliberately distorted the rules of proportion by portraying elongated figures that conveyed a sense of suffering and a strong emotional atmosphere filled with anxiety and confusion.

Mannerism spread from Italy to other parts of Europe and perhaps reached its apogee in the work of El Greco (1541–1614). Doménikos Theotocópoulos (called "the Greek"—El Greco) was from Crete, but after studying in Venice and Rome, in the 1570s he moved to Spain where he became a church painter in Toledo. El Greco's use of elongated and contorted figures, portrayed in unusual shades of yellow and green against an eerie background of turbulent grays, reflect well the unresolved tensions created by the religious upheavals of the Counter-Reformation.

Mannerism was eventually replaced by a new movement—the Baroque—that dominated the artistic world for another century and a half. The Baroque originated in Italy in the last quarter of the sixteenth century and spread to the rest of Europe. Baroque artists sought to harmonize the classical traditions of Renaissance art with the spiritual dimensions of the sixteenth-century religious revival in a new search for order and harmony. The Baroque first appeared in Rome in the Jesuit church of Il Gesù, whose facade was completed in 1575. Although Protestants were also influenced, it was the Catholic reform movement that most wholeheartedly adopted the Baroque, as is evident at Catholic courts, especially those of the Habsburgs in Madrid, Prague, Vienna, and Brussels. Eventually, the Baroque style spread to all of Europe and Latin America.

In large part, Baroque art and architecture reflected

◆ **El Greco,** *Laocöon.* Mannerism reached one of its highest expressions in the work of El Greco. Born in Crete, trained in Venice and Rome, and settling finally in Spain, El Greco worked as a church painter in Toledo. Pictured here is his version of the *Laocöon,* a famous piece of Hellenistic sculpture that had been discovered in Rome in 1506. The elongated, contorted bodies project a world of suffering while the somber background scene of the city of Toledo adds a sense of terror and doom.

the search for power that was characteristic of much of the seventeenth century. Baroque churches and palaces featured richly ornamented facades, sweeping staircases, and an overall splendor that were meant to impress people. Kings and princes wanted other kings and princes as well as their subjects to be in awe of their power.

The Baroque painting style was known for its use of dramatic effects to heighten emotional intensity, especially evident in the works of Peter Paul Rubens (1577–1640), a prolific artist and an important figure in the spread of the Baroque from Italy to other parts of Europe. In his artistic masterpieces, bodies in violent motion, heavily fleshed nudes, a dramatic use of light and shadow, and rich sensuous pigments converge to show intense emotions. The restless forms and constant movement blend together into a dynamic harmony.

Perhaps the greatest figure of the Baroque was the Italian architect and sculptor Gian Lorenzo Bernini (1598–1680), who completed Saint Peter's Basilica and designed the vast colonnade enclosing the piazza in front of it. Action, exuberance, profusion, and dramatic effects mark Bernini's work in the interior of Saint Peter's, where his *Throne of St. Peter* hovers in mid-air, held by the hands of the four great doctors of the Catholic church. Above the chair, rays of heavenly light drive a mass of clouds and angels toward the spectator.

In the second half of the seventeenth century, France replaced Italy as the cultural leader of Europe. Rejecting the Baroque style as overly showy and passionate, the French remained committed to the classical values of the High Renaissance. French late classicism, with its emphasis on clarity, simplicity, balance, and harmony of design was, however, a rather "frigid" version of the High Renaissance style. Its triumph reflected the shift in seventeenth-century French society from chaos to order. While French classicism rejected the emotionalism and high drama of the Baroque, the latter's conception of grandeur was still evident in the portrayal of noble subjects, especially those from classical antiquity. The paintings of Nicholas Poussin (1594–1665) exemplified these principles. His choice of scenes from classical mythology, the serenity of his vistas, his figures in postures copied from the sculptures of antiquity, and his use of brown tones all reflect the classical principles of the French Academy.

A Golden Age of Literature: England and Spain

Periods of crisis often produce great writing, and this period, which was characterized by a golden age of theater, was no exception. In both England and Spain, writing for

◆ Peter Paul Rubens, *The Landing of Marie de' Medici at Marseilles.*   Peter Paul Rubens played a key role in spreading the Baroque style from Italy to other parts of Europe. In *The Landing of Marie de' Medici at Marseilles*, Rubens made a dramatic use of light and color, bodies in motion, and luxurious nudes to heighten the emotional intensity of the scene. This was one of a cycle of twenty-one paintings dedicated to the queen mother of France.

the stage reached new heights between 1580 and 1640. The golden age of English literature is often called the Elizabethan Era because much of the English cultural flowering of the late sixteenth and early seventeenth centuries occurred during her reign. Elizabethan literature exhibits the exuberance and pride associated with English exploits under Queen Elizabeth (see the box on p. 565). Of all the forms of Elizabethan literature, none expressed the energy and intellectual versatility of the era better than drama. Of all the dramatists, none is more famous than William Shakespeare (1564–1614).

Shakespeare was the son of a prosperous glovemaker from Stratford-upon-Avon. When he appeared in London in 1592, Elizabethans were already addicted to the stage. By 1576, two professional theaters run by actors' companies were in existence. Elizabethan theater became a tremendously successful business. Soon at least four to six theaters were open six afternoons a week in or near London. They ranged from the Globe, which was a circular unroofed structure holding 3,000, to the Blackfriars, which was roofed and held only 500. In the former, an admission charge of one or two pennies enabled even the lower classes to attend, while the higher prices in the latter ensured an audience of the well-to-do. Elizabethan audiences varied greatly, putting pressure on playwrights to write works that pleased nobles, lawyers, merchants, and even vagabonds.

William Shakespeare was a "complete man of the theater." Although best known for writing plays, he was also an actor and shareholder in the chief company of the time, the Lord Chamberlains' Company, which played in theaters as diverse as the Globe and the Blackfriars. Shakespeare has long been recognized as a universal genius. A master of the English language, he was instrumental in transforming a language that was still in a period of transition. His technical proficiency, however, was matched by an incredible insight into human psychology. Whether in his tragedies or comedies, Shakespeare exhibited a remarkable understanding of the human condition.

The theater was one of the most creative forms of expression during Spain's golden century. The first professional theaters established in Seville and Madrid in the 1570s were run by actors' companies as in England. Soon, every large town had a public playhouse, including Mexico City in the New World. Touring companies brought the latest Spanish plays to all parts of the Spanish empire. Beginning in the 1580s, the agenda for playwrights was set by Lope de Vega (1562–1635). Like Shakespeare, he was from a middle-class background. He was an incredibly prolific writer; almost 500 of his 1,500 plays survive. They have been characterized as witty, charming, action-packed, and realistic. Lope de Vega made no apologies for the fact that he wrote his plays to please his audiences. In a treatise on drama written in 1609, he stated that the foremost duty of the playwright was to satisfy public demand. He remarked that if anyone thought he had written his plays for fame, "undeceive him and tell him that I wrote them for money."

One of the crowning achievements of the golden age of Spanish literature was the work of Miguel de Cervantes (1547–1616), whose *Don Quixote* has been acclaimed as one of the greatest literary works of all time. While satirizing medieval chivalric literature, Cervantes also perfected the chivalric novel and reconciled it with literary realism. In the two main figures of his famous

◆ **Nicholas Poussin, *Landscape with the Burial of Phocian.*** France became the new cultural leader of Europe in the second half of the seventeenth century. French classicism upheld the values of High Renaissance style, but in a more static version. In Nicholas Poussin's work, we see the emphasis of French classicism on the use of scenes from classical sources and the creation of a sense of grandeur and noble strength in both human figures and landscape.

William Shakespeare: In Praise of England

William Shakespeare is one of the most famous playwrights in the Western world. He was a universal genius, outclassing all others in his psychological insights, depth of characterization, imaginative skills, and versatility. His historical plays reflected the patriotic enthusiasm of the English in the Elizabethan Era, as this excerpt from *Richard II* illustrates.

William Shakespeare, *Richard II*

This royal throne of kings, this sceptered isle,
This earth of majesty, this seat of Mars,
This other Eden, demi-Paradise,
This fortress built by Nature for herself
Against infection and the hand of war,
This happy breed of men, this little world,
This precious stone set in the silver sea,
Which serves it in the office of a wall
Or as a moat defensive to a house
Against the envy of less happier lands—
This blessed plot, this earth, this realm, this England,

This nurse, this teeming womb of royal kings,
Feared by their breed and famous by their birth,
Renowned for their deeds as far from home,
For Christian service and true chivalry,
As is the sepulcher in stubborn Jewry [the Holy Sepulcher
   in Jerusalem]
Of the world's ransom, blessed Mary's Son—
This land of such dear souls, this dear dear land,
Dear for her reputation through the world,
Is now leased out, I die pronouncing it,
Like a tenement or pelting farm.
England, bound in with the triumphant sea,
Whose rocky shore beats back the envious siege
Of watery Neptune, is now bound in with shame,
With inky blots and rotten parchment bonds.
That England, that was wont to conquer others,
Hath made a shameful conquest of itself.
Ah, would the scandal vanish with my life,
How happy then were my ensuing death!

work, Cervantes presented the dual nature of Spanish character. The knight Don Quixote from La Mancha is the visionary who is so involved in his lofty ideals that he is oblivious to the hard realities around him. To him, for example, windmills appear as four-armed giants. In contrast, the knight's fat and earthy squire, Sancho Panza, is the realist who cannot get his master to see the realities in front of him. But after adventures that took them to all parts of Spain, each came to see the value of the other's perspective. We are left with Cervantes's conviction that idealism and realism, visionary dreams and the hard work of reality, are both necessary to the human condition.

The Theater: The Triumph of French Neoclassicism

As the great age of theater in England and Spain was drawing to a close around 1630, a new dramatic era began to dawn in France that lasted into the 1680s. Unlike Shakespeare in England and Lope de Vega in Spain, French playwrights wrote for a more elite audience and were forced to depend upon royal patronage. Louis XIV used theater as he did art and architecture—to attract attention to his monarchy.

French dramatists cultivated a classical style that closely followed the Aristotelian rules for dramatic composition, observing the three unities of time, place, and action. French neoclassicism emphasized the clever, polished, and correct over the emotional and imaginative. Many of the French works of this period derived both their themes and their plots from Greek and Roman sources.

Jean-Baptiste Molière (1622–1673) enjoyed the favor of the French court and benefited from the patronage of the Sun King. He wrote, produced, and acted in a series of comedies that often satirized the religious and social world of his time (see the box on p. 566). In *The Misanthrope*, he mocked the corruption of court society, while

French Comedy: *The Would-Be Gentleman*

*T*he comedy writer Jean-Baptiste Molière has long been regarded as one of the best playwrights of the age of Louis XIV. Molière's comedy, The Would-Be Gentleman, *focuses on Monsieur Jourdain, a vain and pretentious Parisian merchant who aspires to become a gentleman (at that time, a term for a member of the nobility who possessed, among other things, a title, fine clothes, and good taste). Jourdain foolishly believes that he can buy these things and hires a number of teachers to instruct him. In this scene from Act II, Jourdain learns from his philosophy teacher that he has been speaking prose all his life.*

Jean-Baptiste Molière, *The Would-Be Gentleman*

PHILOSOPHY MASTER: I will explain to you all these curiosities to the bottom.

M. JOURDAIN: Pray do. But now, I must commit a secret to you. I'm in love with a person of great quality, and I should be glad you would help me to write something to her in a short *billet-doux* [love letter], which I'll drop at her feet.

PHILOSOPHY MASTER: Very well.

M. JOURDAIN: That will be very gallant, won't it?

PHILOSOPHY MASTER: Without doubt. Is it verse that you would write to her?

M. JOURDAIN: No, no, none of your verse.

PHILOSOPHY MASTER: You would only have prose?

M. JOURDAIN: No, I would neither have verse nor prose.

PHILOSOPHY MASTER: It must be one or the other.

M. JOURDAIN: Why so?

PHILOSOPHY MASTER: Because, sir, there's nothing to express one's self by, but prose, or verse.

M. JOURDAIN: Is there nothing then but prose, or verse?

PHILOSOPHY MASTER: No, sir, whatever is not prose, is verse; and whatever is not verse, is prose.

M. JOURDAIN: And when one talks, what may that be then?

PHILOSOPHY MASTER: Prose.

M. JOURDAIN: How? When I say, Nicole, bring me my slippers, and give me my nightcap, is that prose?

PHILOSOPHY MASTER: Yes, sir.

M. JOURDAIN: On my conscience, I have spoken prose above these forty years without knowing anything of the matter; and I have all the obligations in the world to you for informing me of this. I would therefore put into a letter to her: Beautiful marchioness, your fair eyes make me die with love; but I would have this placed in a gallant manner; and have a gentle turn.

PHILOSOPHY MASTER: Why, add that the fire of her eyes has reduced your heart to ashes: that you suffer for her night and day all the torments—

M. JOURDAIN: No, no, no, I won't have all that—I'll have nothing but what I told you. Beautiful marchioness, your fair eyes make me die with love.

PHILOSOPHY MASTER: You must by all means lengthen the thing out a little.

M. JOURDAIN: No, I tell you, I'll have none but those very words in the letter: but turned in a modish way, ranged handsomely as they should be. I desire you'd show me a little, that I may see the different manners in which one may place them.

PHILOSOPHY MASTER: One may place them first of all as you said: Beautiful marchioness, your fair eyes make me die for love. Or suppose: For love die me make, beautiful marchioness, your fair eyes. Or perhaps: Your eyes fair, for love me make, beautiful marchioness, die. Or suppose: Die your fair eyes, beautiful marchioness, for love me make. Or however: Me make your eyes fair die, beautiful marchioness, for love.

M. JOURDAIN: But of all these ways, which is the best?

PHILOSOPHY MASTER: That which you said: Beautiful marchioness, your fair eyes make me die for love.

M. JOURDAIN: Yet at the same time, I never studied it, and I made the whole of it at the first touch. I thank you with all my heart, and desire you would come in good time tomorrow.

PHILOSOPHY MASTER: I shall not fail.

in *Tartuffe*, he ridiculed the bigotry of the clergy. Molière's satires, however, sometimes got him into trouble. The Paris clergy did not find *Tartuffe* funny and had it banned for five years. Only the protection of Louis XIV saved Molière from more severe harassment.

Conclusion

The movement begun by Martin Luther when he challenged the church's hawking of indulgences quickly spread across Europe. Within a short time, new forms of religious practices, doctrines, and organizations attracted adherents all over Europe. Although seemingly helpless to stop the new Protestant churches, the Catholic church also underwent a religious renaissance and managed to revive its fortunes. By the mid-sixteenth century, this religious division became a crucial factor in precipitating an age of religious warfare. It took a hundred years of religious warfare complicated by serious political, economic, and social issues—the worst series of wars and civil wars since the collapse of the Roman Empire in the west—before Europeans finally admitted that they would have to tolerate different ways to worship God. That men who were disciples of the Apostle of Peace would kill each other—often in brutal and painful fashion—aroused skepticism about Christianity itself. It is surely no accident that the search for a stable, secular order of politics became so important during the seventeenth century.

To many historians, the seventeenth century has assumed extraordinary proportions. The concept of a united Christendom, held as an ideal since the Middle Ages, had been irrevocably destroyed by the religious wars, enabling a system of nation-states to emerge in which power politics took on increasing significance. The growth of political thought focusing on the secular origins of state power reflected the changes that were going on in seventeenth-century society. Within those states slowly emerged some of the machinery that made possible a growing centralization of power. In those states called absolutist, strong monarchs with the assistance of their aristocracies took the lead in providing the leadership for greater centralization. In all the major European states, a growing concern for power and dynastic expansion led to larger armies and greater conflict. Similar developments were taking place in a series of Muslim empires in the Middle East and India.

CHAPTER NOTES

1. Erasmus, *The Paraclesis*, in John Olin, ed., *Christian Humanism and the Reformation: Selected Writings of Erasmus*, 3d ed. (New York, 1987), p. 101.
2. *On the Freedom of a Christian Man*, quoted in E. G. Rupp and Benjamin Drewery, eds., *Martin Luther* (New York, 1970), p. 50.
3. Quoted in Roland Bainton, *Here I Stand: A Life of Martin Luther* (New York, 1950), p. 144.
4. Quoted in De Lamar Jensen, *Reformation Europe* (Lexington, Mass., 1981), p. 83.
5. John Calvin, *Institutes of the Christian Religion*, trans. John Allen (Philadelphia, 1936), 1:220.
6. Ibid., 1:228; 2:181.
7. Quoted in Roland Bainton, *Women of the Reformation in Germany and Italy* (Boston, 1971), p. 154.
8. Quoted in Bonnie S. Anderson and Judith P. Zinsser, *A History of Their Own: Women in Europe from Prehistory to the Present* (New York, 1988), 1:259.
9. Quoted in John A. Phillips, *Eve: The History of an Idea* (New York, 1984), p. 105.
10. Quoted in Joseph Klaits, *Servants of Satan: The Age of the Witch Hunts* (Bloomington, Ind., 1985), p. 68.
11. Quoted in James Harvey Robinson, *Readings in European History* (Boston, 1934), 2:211–12.
12. Quoted in John B. Wolf, *Louis XIV* (New York, 1968), p. 134.

SUGGESTED READINGS

Basic surveys of the Reformation period include H. J. Grimm, *The Reformation Era, 1500–1650,* 2d ed. (New York, 1973); D. L. Jensen, *Reformation Europe,* 2d ed. (Lexington, Mass., 1990); G. R. Elton, *Reformation Europe, 1517–1559* (Cleveland, 1963); and E. Cameron, *The European Reformation* (New York, 1991). L. W. Spitz, *The Protestant Reformation, 1517–1559* (New York, 1985) is a sound and up-to-date history. Also see the interesting and useful book by S. Ozment, *Protestants: The Birth of a Revolution* (New York: 1992). The best general biography of Erasmus is still R. Bainton, *Erasmus of Christendom* (New York, 1969), although the shorter works by J. K. Sowards, *Desiderius Erasmus* (Boston, 1975) and J. McConica, *Erasmus* (Oxford, 1991) are also good. On religious conditions in Europe on the eve of the Reformation, see T. N. Tentler, *Sin and Confession on the Eve of the Reformation* (Princeton, N.J., 1977).

The classic account of Martin Luther's life is R. Bainton, *Here I Stand: A Life of Martin Luther* (New York and Nashville, 1950). More recent works include J. M. Kittelson, *Luther the Reformer: The Story of the Man and His Career* (Minneapolis, Minn., 1986) and H. A. Oberman, *Luther: Man between God and the Devil* (New York, 1992). The best account of Ulrich Zwingli is G. R. Potter, *Zwingli* (Cambridge, 1976). The most comprehensive account of the various groups and individuals who are called Anabaptist is G. H. Williams, *The Radical Reformation* (Philadelphia, 1962). Two worthwhile surveys of the English Reformation are A. G. Dickens, *The English Reformation* (New York, 1964) and G. R. Elton, *Reform and Reformation: England, 1509–1558* (Cambridge, Mass., 1977). For a good biography of Calvin, see the work by W. J. Bouwsma, *John Calvin* (New York, 1988).

The best overall account of the impact of the Reformation on the family is S. Ozment, *When Fathers Ruled: Family Life in Reformation Europe* (Cambridge, Mass., 1983). M. E. Wiesner's *Working Women in Renaissance Germany* (New Brunswick, N.J., 1986) covers primarily the sixteenth century. A good introduction to the Catholic Reformation can be found in M. R. O'Connell, *The Counter Reformation, 1559–1610* (New York, 1974).

General works on the sixteenth and seventeenth centuries include C. Wilson, *The Transformation of Europe, 1558–1648* (Berkeley, 1976); D. H. Pennington, *Europe in the Seventeenth Century,* 2d ed. (London and New York, 1989); and R. S. Dunn, *The Age of Religious Wars, 1559–1715,* 2d ed. (New York, 1979).

Two works by J. H. M. Salmon provide the best studies on the French Wars of Religion. They are *Society in Crisis: France in the Sixteenth Century* (New York, 1975) and *French Government and Society in the Wars of Religion* (St. Louis, 1976). The best biographies of Philip II are P. Pierson, *Philip II of Spain* (London, 1975) and G. Parker, *Philip II* (Boston and London, 1978). Elizabeth's reign can be examined in J. Ridley, *Elizabeth I* (New York, 1988). On the Thirty Years' War, see G. Parker, *The Thirty Years War* (London, 1984). A good general work on the period of the English Revolution is G. E. Aylmer, *Rebellion or Revolution? England, 1640–1660* (New York, 1986). On Oliver Cromwell, see R. Howell, Jr., *Cromwell* (Boston, 1977) and the beautifully written popular account by A. Fraser, *Cromwell: The Lord Protector* (New York, 1974).

The story of the witchcraft craze can be examined in two recent works, J. B. Russell, *A History of Witchcraft* (London, 1980) and B. P. Levack, *The Witch-Hunt in Early Modern Europe* (London, 1987).

For a brief account of seventeenth-century French history, see R. Briggs, *Early Modern France, 1560–1715* (Oxford, 1977). A solid and very readable biography of Louis XIV is J. B. Wolf, *Louis XIV* (New York, 1968). A now classic work on life in Louis XIV's France is W. H. Lewis, *The Splendid Century* (Garden City, N.Y., 1953). Well-presented summaries of revisionist views on Louis's monarchical power are R. Mettam, *Power and Faction in Louis XIV's France* (Oxford, 1988) and W. Beik, *Absolutism and Society in Seventeenth-Century France* (Cambridge, 1985). On the creation of an Austrian state, see R. J. W. Evans, *The Making of the Habsburg Monarchy, 1550–1700* (Oxford, 1979). The older work by F. L. Carsten, *The Origins of Prussia* (Oxford, 1954), remains an outstanding study of early Prussian history. Works on Peter the Great include M. S. Anderson, *Peter the Great* (London, 1978); B. H. Sumner, *Peter the Great and the Emergence of Russia* (New York, 1962); and the massive popular biography by R. K. Massie, *Peter the Great* (New York, 1980). On England, see also J. P. Kenyon, *Stuart England* (London, 1978). A more specialized study is J. R. Jones, *The Revolution of 1688 in England* (London, 1972).

For a brief, readable guide to Mannerism, see L. Murray, *The Late Renaissance and Mannerism* (New York, 1967). For a general survey of Baroque culture, see J. S. Held, *Seventeenth and Eighteenth Century Art: Baroque Painting, Sculpture, Architecture* (New York, 1971). On the Spanish golden century of literature, see R. O. Jones, *The Golden Age: Prose and Poetry*, which is volume 2 of *The Literary History of Spain* (London, 1971). The literature on Shakespeare is enormous. For a biography, see A. L. Rowse, *The Life of Shakespeare* (New York, 1963). French theater and literature are examined in A. Adam, *Grandeur and Illusion: French Literature and Society, 1600–1715*, trans. J. Tint (New York, 1972).

CHAPTER

16

The Muslim Empires

One of the European states' primary objectives in seeking a route to the Spice Islands was to lessen the political and economic power of Islam by reducing the Muslims' strong position in the global trade network. As we saw in Chapter 14, Portuguese fleets, followed by those of the Spanish, the English, and the Dutch, had some success in wresting control over the spice trade from Muslim shippers, although the latter were never totally driven out of the business. By the eighteenth century, the Indian Ocean had ceased to be an Arab preserve and had become, in some respects, a European lake.

Thus, the European dream of controlling global trade markets had become a reality. But in the broader scheme of things, the goal of crippling the power of Islam was not entirely realized, for Europe's success had not been achieved by the collapse of its great Muslim rival. To the contrary, the Muslim world, which appeared to have entered a period of decline with the collapse of the Abbasid caliphate during the era of the Mongols, managed to revive in the shadow of Europe's age of exploration, a period that also saw the rise of three great Muslim empires. Known as the Ottomans, the Safavids, and the Mughals, these three powerful Muslim states dominated the Middle East and the South Asia subcontinent and brought stability to a region that had been in turmoil for centuries.

This stability lasted for about two hundred years. By the end of the eighteenth century, much of India and the Middle East had come under severe European pressure and had

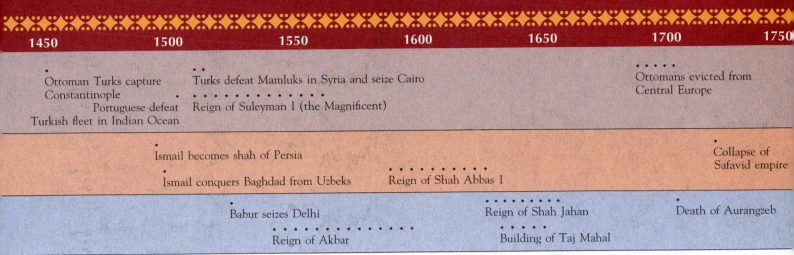

1450	1500	1550	1600	1650	1700	1750

Ottoman Turks capture
Constantinople

Turks defeat Mamluks in Syria and seize Cairo

Ottomans evicted from
Central Europe

Portuguese defeat
Turkish fleet in Indian Ocean

Reign of Suleyman I (the Magnificent)

Ismail becomes shah of Persia

Collapse of
Safavid empire

Ismail conquers Baghdad from Uzbeks

Reign of Shah Abbas 1

Babur seizes Delhi

Reign of Shah Jahan

Death of Aurangzeb

Reign of Akbar

Building of Taj Mahal

returned to a state of anarchy, while the Ottoman Empire had entered a period of gradual decline. But that decline was due more to internal factors than to the challenge posed by a resurgent Europe.

The Ottoman Empire

The Ottoman Turks were among the various Turkic-speaking peoples who had spread westward from Central Asia in the ninth to the eleventh centuries C.E. The first to dominate were the Seljuk Turks, who initially attempted to revive the declining Abbasid caliphate in Baghdad. Later they consolidated their power in the Anatolian peninsula at the expense of the Byzantine Empire. Turkish tribal peoples settled the area, while their leaders served as warriors or administrators. The peasants who tilled the farmland were mainly Greek. In the thirteenth century, the advancing Mongols managed to seize and destroy the Seljuk capital at Konya, south of modern-day Ankara, but then they withdrew, leaving the Turks in control of the area.

In the late thirteenth century, a new group of Turks under the tribal leader Osman (1280–1326) began to consolidate their power in the northwestern corner of the Anatolian peninsula. That land had been given to them by the Seljuk rulers as a reward for helping to drive out the Mongols in the late thirteenth century. At first, the Osman Turks were relatively peaceful and engaged in pastoral pursuits, but as the Seljuk empire began to disintegrate in the early fourteenth century, they began to expand and in 1326 seized Bursa, which they turned into

their capital. They now founded the Osmanli (later to be known as Ottoman) dynasty.

A key advantage for the Ottomans was their location in the northwestern corner of the peninsula. From there they were able to expand westward and eventually control the Bosporus and the Dardanelles, two bodies of water separated by the Sea of Marmara that mark the passage between the Mediterranean and the Black Sea. The Byzantine Empire, of course, had controlled the area for centuries, serving as a buffer between the Muslim Middle East and the Latin West. The Byzantines, however, had been severely weakened by the sack of Constantinople in the fourth crusade of 1204 and the Western occupation of much of the empire for the next half century. In 1345, Ottoman forces under their leader Orkhan I (1326–1360) crossed the Bosporus for the first time to support a usurper against the Byzantine emperor Paleologus in Constantinople. Setting up their first European base at Gallipoli at the Mediterranean entrance to the Dardanelles, Turkish forces expanded gradually into the Balkans and allied with fractious Serbian and Bulgar forces against the Byzantines. In 1355, the Ottomans briefly supported the Serbian leader Stephen Dusan in an attack on Constantinople, but the campaign failed and Dusan's Serbian empire collapsed. In these unstable conditions, the Ottomans gradually established permanent settlements throughout the area, where Turkish beys (provincial governors in the Ottoman Empire; from the Turkish *beg*, "knight") drove out the previous landlords and collected taxes from the local Slavic peasants. The Ottoman leader now began to claim the title of sultan.

In 1360, Orkhan was succeeded by his son Murad I, who consolidated Ottoman power in the Balkans, set up a capital at Edirne (today Adrianople), and gradually

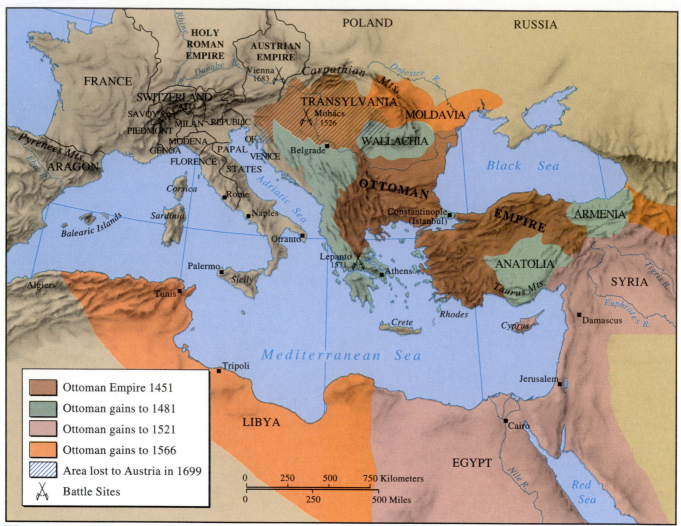

❋ Map 16.1   The Ottoman Empire.

reduced the Byzantine emperor to a vassal. Murad did not initially attempt to conquer Constantinople, because his forces were composed mostly of the traditional Turkish cavalry and lacked the ability to breach the strong walls of the city. Instead, he began to build up a strong military administration based on the recruitment of Christians into an elite guard. Called Janissaries (from the Turkish *Yeni Cheri,* "new troops"), they were recruited from the local Christian population in the Balkans and then converted to Islam and trained as foot-soldiers or administrators. One of the major advantages of the Janissaries was that they were directly subordinated to the sultanate and therefore owed their loyalty to the person of the sultan. Other military forces were organized by the beys and were thus loyal to their local tribal leaders.

The new Janissary corps was also important because it represented a response to changes in warfare. As the knowledge of firearms spread in the late fourteenth century, the Turks began to master the new technology, including siege cannons and muskets. The traditional nomadic cavalry charge was now outmoded and was superseded by infantry forces armed with muskets. Thus, the Janissaries provided a well-armed infantry who served both as an elite guard to protect the palace and also as a means of extending Turkish control in the Balkans. With his new forces, Murad defeated the Serbs at the famous Battle of Kossovo in 1389 and ended Serbian hegemony in the area.

Under Murad's successor Bayazid I (1389–1402), the Ottomans advanced northward and annexed Bulgaria.

Bayazid's leadership was bold and ambitious; his forces slaughtered the flower of French cavalry at a major battle on the Danube. Following that victory, he planned to attack Constantinople and seize the remnants of the Byzantine Empire, but his base in Anatolia was suddenly faced with a new threat from the forces of the Mongol warrior Tamerlane (see Chapter 9).

Tamerlane had seized Baghdad in 1393 and Syria in 1400. In 1402, he moved into Turkey, defeated the Turkish forces at Ankara, and seized Bayazid, who died in captivity. But Tamerlane left for the east in 1403 and died two years later, thereby ending the threat from the Mongols. The respite provided an opportunity for the Ottomans to revive under Bayazid's successors, who consolidated Turkish rule in western Anatolia and the lower Balkans. When Mehmet II (1451–1481) succeeded to the throne, he was determined to capture Constantinople. Already in control of the Dardanelles, he ordered the construction of a major fortress on the Bosporus just north of the city, which put the Turks in a position to strangle the Byzantines.

The last Byzantine emperor desperately called for help from the Europeans, but only the Genoese came to his defense. With 80,000 troops ranged against only 7,000 defenders, Mehmet laid siege to Constantinople in 1453. In their attack on the city, the Turks made use of massive cannons with twenty-six-foot barrels that could launch stone balls weighing up to 1,200 pounds each. The Byzantines stretched heavy chains across the Golden Horn to prevent a naval attack from the north and prepared to make their final stand behind the thirteen-mile-long wall along the western edge of the city. But Mehmet's forces seized Galata, at the tip of the peninsula north of the Golden Horn, and then dragged Turkish ships overland across the peninsula from the Bosporus and put them into the water behind the chains. Finally, the walls were breached; the Byzantine emperor died in the final battle (see the box on p. 574). Mehmet II, standing before the palace of the emperor, paused to reflect on the passing nature of human glory. But it was not long before he and the Ottomans were again on the march.

Expansion of the Empire

With their new capital at Constantinople, now renamed Istanbul, the Ottoman Turks were now a dominant force in the Balkans and the Anatolian peninsula. Ottoman expansion to the east began at the end of the fifteenth century, when a conflict broke out with the Shi'ite kingdom of the Safavids in Persia (see The Safavids later in

CHRONOLOGY

The Ottoman Empire

Reign of Osman I	1280–1326
Ottoman Turks first cross the Bosporus	1345
Attack on Constantinople by the Ottomans and Serbs	1355
Murad I consolidates Turkish power in the Balkans	1360
Ottomans defeat Serbian Army at Kossovo	1389
Tamerlane defeats Ottoman army at Ankara	1402
Rule of Mehmet II (the Conqueror)	1451–1481
Turkish conquest of Constantinople	1453
Portuguese defeat the Turkish fleet in the Indian Ocean	1509
Turks defeat Mamluks in Syria and seize Cairo	1516–1517
Reign of Suleyman I (the Magnificent)	1520–1566
Defeat of Hungarians at Battle of Mohács	1526
Defeat of Turks at Vienna	1529
Battle of Lepanto	1571
Sinan era in Ottoman architecture	Sixteenth century

this chapter), which had been promoting rebellion among the Anatolian tribal population and disrupting Turkish trade through the Middle East. After defeating the Safavids at a major battle in 1514, Emperor Selim I (1512–1520) consolidated Turkish control over Mesopotamia and then turned his attention to the Mamluks in Egypt, who had failed to support the Ottomans in their struggle against the Safavids. The Mamluks were defeated in Syria in 1516; Cairo fell a year later. Now controlling several of the holy cities of Islam, including Jerusalem, Mecca, and Medina, Selim declared himself to be the new caliph, or successor to Muhammad. During the next few years, Turkish armies and fleets advanced westward along the African coast, occupying Tripoli, Tunis, and Algeria and eventually penetrating almost to the

The Fall of Constantinople

Few events in the history of the Ottoman Empire are more dramatic than the conquest of Constantinople in 1453. In this excerpt, the conquest is described by Kritovoulos, a Greek who later served in the Ottoman administration. Although the author did not witness the conquest itself, he was apparently well informed about the event and provides us with a vivid description.

Kritovoulos, *Life of Mehmed the Conqueror*

So saying, he [the Sultan] led them himself. And they, with a shout on the run and with a fearsome yell, went on ahead of the Sultan, pressing on up to the palisade. After a long and bitter struggle they hurled back the Romans [Byzantines] from there and climbed by force up the palisade. They dashed some of their foe down into the ditch between the great wall and the palisade, which was deep and hard to get out of, and they killed them there. The rest they drove back to the gate.

He had opened this gate in the great wall, so as to go easily over to the palisade. Now there was a great struggle there and great slaughter among those stationed there, for they were attacked by the heavy infantry and not a few others in irregular formation, who had been attracted from many points by the shouting. There the Emperor Constantine [Constantine XIII Paleologus], with all who were with him, fell in gallant combat.

The heavy infantry were already streaming through the little gate into the City, and others had rushed in through the breach in the great wall. Then all the rest of the army, with a rush and a roar, poured in brilliantly and scattered all over the City. And the Sultan stood before the great wall, where the standard also was and the ensigns, and watched the proceedings. The day was already breaking. . . .

The soldiers fell on them [the citizens] with anger and great wrath. For one thing, they were actuated by the hardships of the siege. For another, some foolish people had hurled taunts and curses at them from the battlements all through the siege. Now, in general they killed so as to frighten all the City, and to terrorize and enslave all by the slaughter.

When they had had enough of murder, and the City was reduced to slavery, some of the troops turned to the mansions of the mighty, by bands and companies and divisions, for plunder and spoil. Others went to the robbing of churches, and others dispersed to the simple homes of the common people, stealing, robbing, plundering, killing, insulting, taking and enslaving men, women, and children, old and young, priests, monks—in short, every age and class. . . .

They say that many of the maidens, even at the mere unaccustomed sight and sound of these men, were terror-stricken and came near losing their very lives. And there were also honorable old men who were dragged by their white hair, and some of them beaten unmercifully. And well-born and beautiful young boys were carried off. . . .

After this the Sultan entered the City and looked about to see its great size, its situation, its grandeur and beauty, its teeming population, its loveliness, and the costliness of its churches and public buildings and of the private houses and community houses and those of the officials. . . . When he saw what a large number had been killed, and the ruin of the buildings, and the wholesale ruin and destruction of the City, he was filled with compassion and repented not a little at the destruction and plundering. Tears fell from his eyes as he groaned deeply and passionately: "What a city we have given over to plunder and destruction."

Thus he suffered in spirit. And indeed this was a great blow to us, in this one city, a disaster the like of which had occurred in no one of the great renowned cities of history, whether one speaks of the size of the captured City or of the bitterness and harshness of the deed. And no less did it astound all others than it did those who went through it and suffered, through the unreasonable and unusual character of the event and through the overwhelming and unheard-of horror of it.

As for the great City of Constantine, raised to a great height of glory and dominion and wealth in its own times, overshadowing to an infinite degree all the cities around it, renowned for its glory, wealth, authority, power, and greatness, and all its other qualities, it thus came to its end.

Strait of Gibraltar. In their advance, the invaders had taken advantage of the progressive disintegration of the Nasrid dynasty in Morocco, which had been in decline for decades and had lost its last foothold on the European continent when Granada fell to the rising power of Spain in 1492.

The impact of Turkish rule on the peoples of North Africa was relatively light. Like their predecessors, the Turks were Muslims, and they preferred where possible to administer their conquered regions through local rulers. Central government direction was achieved through appointed *pashas* who collected taxes (and then paid a fixed percentage as tribute to the central government), maintained law and order, and were directly responsible to Istanbul. The Turks ruled from coastal cities like Algiers, Tripoli, and Tunis and made no attempt to control the interior beyond maintaining the trade routes through the Sahara to the trading centers along the Niger River. Meanwhile local pirates along the Barbary Coast competed with their Christian rivals in raiding the shipping that passed through the Mediterranean.

The Turks did make a halfhearted effort to extend their control up the Nile River, but were never able to establish their authority beyond Nubia, leaving the area to the south under the independent kingdom of Funj. The Turks also attempted to extend their influence into the Indian Ocean in order to take part in the lucrative trade with the east, but after a major naval defeat by the Portuguese in 1509, their authority was restricted to the Red Sea (see Chapter 14). This state of affairs continued after the penetration of the Indian Ocean by the English and the Dutch. The rise of Turkish power in the region may have been a factor in the accelerated efforts by local Muslim states to subdue the Christian kingdom in mountainous Ethiopia. For a time, the attacks were fairly successful, but eventually, with some assistance from the Portuguese, who had sent an ambassadorial mission to the Ethiopian court in 1520 and considered Ethiopia the home of the legendary "Prester John," the kingdom was able to survive in its isolated grandeur.

By the seventeenth century, the links between the imperial court in Istanbul and its appointed representatives in the Turkish regencies in North Africa had begun to decline. Some of the *pashas* were dethroned by local elites while others, such as the bey of Tunis, became hereditary rulers. Even Egypt, whose agricultural wealth and control over the route to the Red Sea made it the most important country in the area to the Turks, gradually became autonomous under a new official class of Janissaries. Many of them became wealthy landowners by

◆ **The Turkish Conquest of Constantinople.** Mehmet II put a stranglehold on the Byzantine capital of Constantinople with a surprise attack by Turkish ships, which were dragged overland and placed in the water behind the enemy's defense lines. In addition, the Turks made use of massive cannons that could launch stone balls weighing up to 1,200 pounds each. Notice the fanciful Gothic interpretation of the city in this contemporary French miniature of the siege of Constantinople.

exploiting their official function to collect tax revenues far in excess of what they had to remit to Istanbul. In the early eighteenth century, the Mamluks returned to power, although the Turkish government managed to retain some control by means of a viceroy appointed from Istanbul.

A Portrait of Suleyman the Magnificent

Suleyman the Magnificent was perhaps the greatest of all Ottoman sultans. This description of him was written by Ghislain de Busbecq, the Habsburg ambassador to Constantinople. Busbecq observed Suleyman at first hand and, as this excerpt indicates, was highly impressed by the Turkish ruler.

Ghislain de Busbecq, *The Turkish Letters*

The Sultan was seated on a rather low sofa, no more than a foot from the ground and spread with many costly coverlets and cushions embroidered with exquisite work. Near him were his bow and arrows. His expression, as I have said, is anything but smiling, and has a sternness which, though sad, is full of majesty. On our arrival we were introduced into his presence by his chamberlains, who held our arms—a practice which has always been observed since a Croatian sought an interview and murdered the Sultan Amurath in a revenge for the slaughter of his master, Marcus the Despot of Serbia. After going through the pretence of kissing his hand, we were led to the wall facing him backwards, so as not to turn our backs or any part of them toward him. He then listened to the recital of my message, but, as it did not correspond with his expectations (for the demands of my imperial master [the Habsburg emperor Ferdinand I] were full of dignity and independence, and, therefore, far from acceptable to one who thought that his slightest wishes ought to be obeyed) he assumed an expression of disdain, and merely answered "Giusel, Giusel," that is, "Well, Well." We were then dismissed to our lodging. . . .

You will probably wish me to describe the impression which Suleyman made upon me. He is beginning to feel the weight of years, but his dignity of demeanor and his general physical appearance are worthy of the ruler of so vast an empire. He has always been frugal and temperate, and was so even in his youth, when he might have erred without incurring blame in the eyes of the Turks. Even in his earlier years he did not indulge in wine or in those unnatural vices to which the Turks are often addicted. Even his bitterest critics can find nothing more serious to allege against him than his undue submission to his wife and its result in his somewhat precipitate action in putting Mustapha [his firstborn son, by another wife] to death, which is generally imputed to her employment of love-potions and incantations. It is generally agreed that, ever since he promoted her to the rank of his lawful wife, he has possessed no concubines, although there is no law to prevent his doing so. He is a strict guardian of his religion and its ceremonies, being not less desirous of upholding his faith than of extending his dominions. For his age—he has almost reached his sixtieth year—he enjoys quite good health, though his bad complexion may be due to some hidden malady; and indeed it is generally believed that he has an incurable ulcer or gangrene on his leg. This defect of complexion he remedies by painting his face with a coating of red powder, when he wishes departing ambassadors to take with them a strong impression of his good health; for he fancies that it contributes to inspire greater fear in foreign potentates if they think that he is well and strong. I noticed a clear indication of this practice on the present occasion; for his appearance when he received me in the final audience was very different from that which he presented when he gave me an interview on my arrival.

TURKISH EXPANSION IN EUROPE

After their conquest of Constantinople in 1453, the Ottoman Turks tried to complete their conquest of the Balkans, where they had been established since the fourteenth century. Although they were successful in taking the Romanian territory of Wallachia in 1476, the resistance of the Hungarians initially kept the Turks from advancing up the Danube valley. From 1480 to 1520, internal problems and the need to consolidate their eastern frontiers kept the Turks from any further attacks on Europe.

Suleyman I the Magnificent (1520–1566), the greatest of the Ottoman sultans (see the box above), however, brought the Turks back to Europe's attention. Advancing up the Danube, the Turks seized Belgrade in 1521 and won a major victory over the Hungarians at the Battle of Mohács on the Danube in 1526. Subsequently, the Turks overran most of Hungary, moved into Austria, and advanced as far as Vienna, where they were finally repulsed in 1529. At the same time, the Turks extended their power into the western Mediterranean and threatened to turn it into a Turkish lake until a large Turkish fleet was destroyed by the Spanish at Lepanto in 1571. Despite the defeat, the Turks continued to hold nominal suzerainty over the southern shores of the Mediterranean.

Although Europeans frequently called for new Christian crusades against the "infidel" Turks, by the beginning of the seventeenth century the Ottoman Empire was being treated like any other European power by European rulers seeking alliances and trade concessions. During the first half of the seventeenth century, the Ottoman Empire was a "sleeping giant." Involved in domestic bloodletting and heavily threatened by a challenge from Persia, the Ottomans were content with the status quo in eastern Europe. But under a new line of grand vezirs in the second half of the seventeenth century, the Ottoman Empire again took the offensive. By mid-1683, the Ottomans had marched through the Hungarian plain and laid siege to Vienna. Repulsed by a mixed army of Austrians, Poles, Bavarians, and Saxons, the Turks retreated and were pushed out of Hungary by a new European coalition. Although they retained the core of their empire, the Ottoman Turks would never again be a threat to Europe. Although the Turkish empire held together for the rest of the seventeenth and the eighteenth centuries, it would be faced with new challenges from the ever-growing Austrian Empire in southeastern Europe and the new Russian giant to the north.

The Nature of Turkish Rule

Like other Muslim empires in Persia and India, the Ottoman political system was the result of the evolution of tribal institutions into a sedentary empire. The three states are often called "gunpowder empires" because to a considerable extent they owed their success to their mastery of the technology of firearms. At the apex of the Ottoman system was the sultan, who was the supreme authority in both a political and a military sense. The origins of this system can be traced back to the bey, who was only a tribal leader, a first among equals, who could claim loyalty from his chiefs so long as he could provide booty and grazing lands for his subordinates. Disputes were settled by tribal law, while Muslim laws (the *Sheriat*, or *Shari'ah*) were secondary. Tribal leaders collected taxes—or booty—from areas under their control and

sent one-fifth on to the bey. Both administrative and military power were centralized under the bey, and the capital was wherever the bey and his administration happened to be.

But the rise of empire brought about changes and an adaptation to Byzantine traditions of rule. The status and prestige of the sultan now increased relative to the subordinate tribal leaders, and the position took on the trappings of imperial rule. Court rituals were inherited from the Byzantines and Persians, and a centralized administrative system was adopted that increasingly isolated the sultan in his palace. The position of the sultan was hereditary, with a son, although not necessarily the eldest, always succeeding the father. This practice led to chronic

♦ **Mehmet II, Conqueror of Constantinople.** Identified with the seizure of Constantinople from the Byzantine Empire in 1453, Mehmet II was one of the most illustrious Ottoman sultans. This Turkish miniature portrays Mehmet II with his handkerchief, a symbol of the supreme power of the Ottoman ruler. He is also smelling a rose, representing his cultural interests, especially as patron of the arts.

succession struggles upon the death of individual sultans, and the losers were often executed (strangled with a silk bowstring) or later imprisoned. Heirs to the throne were assigned as provincial governors to provide them with experience.

The heart of the sultan's power was in the Topkapi (meaning "cannon gate") Palace in the center of Istanbul. Topkapi was constructed in 1459 by Mehmet II and served as an administrative center as well as the private residence of the sultan and his family. Eventually, it had a staff of 20,000 employees. The private domain of the sultan was called the harem (sacred place). Here he resided with his concubines. Normally, a sultan did not marry, but chose several concubines as his favorites; they were accorded this status after they gave birth to sons. When a son became a sultan, his mother became known as the queen mother and served as adviser to the throne. This tradition, initiated by the influential wife of Suleyman the Magnificent, often resulted in considerable authority for the queen mother in the affairs of state.

Members of the harem, like the Janissaries, were often of slave origins and formed an elite element in Ottoman society. Some concubines were prisoners selected for the position, while others were purchased or offered to the sultan as a gift. They were then trained and educated like the Janissaries in a system called *devshirme* (collection). The *devshirme* had originated in the practice of requiring local clan leaders to provide prisoners to the sultan as part of their tax obligation. Talented males were given special training for eventual placement in military or administrative positions, while their female counterparts were trained for service in the harem. They were ranked according to their status, and some were permitted to leave the harem to marry officials. If they were later divorced, they were sometimes allowed to return to the harem.

The sultan ruled through an imperial council that met four days a week and was chaired by the chief minister known as the grand vezir (*wazir*, sometimes known in English as vizier). The sultan often attended from behind a screen, whence he could privately indicate his desires to the grand vezir. The latter presided over the imperial bureaucracy. Like the palace guard, the bureaucrats were not an exclusive group, but were chosen at least partly by merit from a palace school for training officials. Most officials were Muslims by birth, but some talented Janissaries became senior members of the bureaucracy, and almost all the later grand vezirs came from the *devshirme* system.

Local administration during the imperial period was a product of Turkish tribal tradition and was similar in some respects to the feudal system in Europe. The empire was divided into provinces and districts governed by officials who, like their tribal predecessors, combined both civil and military functions in their persons. They were assisted by bureaucrats trained in the palace school in Istanbul.

Senior officials were assigned land in fief by the sultan and were then responsible for collecting taxes and supplying armies to the empire. These lands were then farmed out to the local cavalry elite called the *sipahis*, who exacted a tax from all peasants in their fiefdoms for their salary. These local officials were not hereditary aristocrats, but sons often inherited their father's landholdings, and the vast majority were descendants of the tribal beys who had served as a tribal elite during the pre-imperial period.

Religion and Society in the Ottoman World

Like most Turkic-speaking peoples in the Anatolian peninsula and throughout the Middle East, the Ottoman ruling elites were Sunni Muslims. Ottoman sultans had claimed the title of caliph (defender of the faith) since the early sixteenth century and thus theoretically were responsible for guiding the flock and maintaining Islamic law, the *Shari'ah*. In practice, the sultan assigned these duties to a supreme religious authority who administered the law and maintained a system of schools for educating Muslims.

Islamic law and customs were applied to all Muslims in the empire. Like their rulers, most Turkic-speaking people were Sunni Muslims, but some communities were attracted to Sufism (see Chapter 7) or other heterodox doctrines. The government tolerated such activities so long as their practitioners remained loyal to the empire, but it was unrest among these groups—some of whom converted to the Shi'ite version of Islamic doctrine—that outraged the conservative *ulama* and eventually led to the war against the Safavids in the early sixteenth century (see The Safavids later in this chapter).

Non-Muslims—mostly Orthodox Christians (Greeks and Slavs), Jews, and Armenian Christians—formed a significant minority within the empire, which treated them with relative tolerance. Non-Muslims were compelled to pay a head tax (because of their exemption from military service), but they were permitted to practice their religion or convert to Islam, although Muslims were prohibited from adopting another faith. Most of the population in European areas of the empire remained Christian, but in some places, such as the territory now called Bosnia, substantial numbers converted to Islam.

Each religious group within the empire was organized as an administrative unit called a *millet* (nation or community). Each group, including the Muslims themselves, had its own patriarch or grand rabbi who dealt as an intermediary with the government and administered the community according to its own laws. The leaders of the individual nations were responsible to the sultan and his officials for the behavior of the subjects under their care and collected taxes for transmission to the government. Each nation not only established its own system of justice, but also set its own educational policies and provided welfare for the needy.

The subjects of the Ottoman Empire were also divided by occupation and place of residence. In addition to the ruling class, there were four main occupational groups: peasants, artisans, merchants, and pastoral peoples. The first three were classified as "urban" residents. Peasants tilled land that was leased to them by the state (ultimate ownership of all land resided with the sultan), but the land was deeded to them, so they were able to pass it along to their heirs. They were not allowed to sell the land and thus in practice were forced to remain on the soil. Taxes were based on the amount of land the peasants possessed and were paid to the local *sipahis*, who held the district in fief.

Artisans were organized according to craft guilds. Each guild, headed by a council of elders, was responsible not only for dealing with the governmental authorities, but also for providing financial services, social security, and training for its members. Outside the ruling elite, merchants were the most privileged class in Ottoman society. They were largely exempt from government regulations and taxes and were therefore able in many cases to amass large fortunes. Charging interest was technically illegal under Islamic law, but the rules were often ignored in practice. In the absence of regulations, merchants often established monopolies and charged high prices, which caused them to be bitterly resented by other subjects of the empire.

Nomadic peoples were placed in a separate "nation" and were subject to their own regulations and laws. They were divided into the traditional nomadic classifications of tribes, clans, and "tents" (individual families) and were governed by their hereditary chiefs, the beys. As we have seen, the beys were responsible for administration and for collecting taxes for the state.

Technically, women in the Ottoman Empire were subject to the same disabilities that afflicted their counterparts in other Muslim societies, but their position was ameliorated to some degree by various factors. In the first place, non-Muslims were subject to the laws and customs of their own religions; thus, Orthodox Christian, Jewish, and Armenian Christian women were spared some of the restrictions applied to their Muslim sisters. In the second place, Islamic laws as applied in the Ottoman Empire defined the legal position of women comparatively tolerantly. Women were permitted to own and inherit property, including their dowries. They could not be forced into marriage and in certain cases were permitted to seek a divorce. As we have seen, women often exercised considerable influence in the palace and in a few instances even served as senior officials, such as governors of provinces. The relatively tolerant attitude toward women in Ottoman-held territories has been ascribed by some to Turkish tribal traditions, which took a more egalitarian view of sex roles than did the sedentary societies of the region.

The Ottomans in Decline

The Ottoman Empire reached its zenith under Suleyman the Magnificent, often known as Suleyman Kanuni, or "the lawgiver." It was he who had launched the conquest of Hungary and ordered the construction of the famous Suleymaniye mosque on the pattern of Hagia Sophia, which had been turned into a mosque by Mehmet II. But it was also Suleyman who probably initiated what Western historians often describe as a period of decline. Suleyman executed his two most able sons on suspicion of factionalism and was succeeded by Selim II (the Sot, or "the drunken sultan"). He was the only surviving son; another had fled to the Safavids and was later executed for treason.

Although some historians maintain that the decline of the Ottoman Empire did not begin until 1699 with the first loss of imperial territory at the Battle of Carlowitz, signs of internal rot had already appeared by the seventeenth century. Apparently, a number of factors were involved. In the first place, the system inherited from the tribal period and used during the early empire was replaced by one more reminiscent of imperial practice elsewhere. While the *devshirme* system of training officials continued to function, it lost some of its previous effectiveness, as senior positions were increasingly assigned to sons or daughters of aristocrats.

Ironically, officials trained by the system continued to be prominent within the bureaucracy and even increased in number relative to members of the traditional ruling class. But unlike in the past, *devshirme* graduates were now permitted to marry and inherit property and to enroll their sons in the palace corps. The training of officials declined, and they were gradually transformed from a meritocratic administrative elite into a privileged and often degenerate hereditary caste susceptible, like all

◆ **The Blue Mosque, Istanbul.**   The magnificent mosques built under the partonage of Suleyman the Magnificent are a great legacy of the Ottoman Empire. Towering under a central dome, they seem to defy gravity, and, like European Gothic catherdrals, convey to the viewer a sense of weightlessness. The Blue Mosque, so called for the blue tiles in its interior, is one of the most impressive and graceful in Istanbul.

others, to dreams of wealth and power. Local administrators were corrupted and taxes rose as the central bureaucracy lost its links with rural areas. The imperial treasure was depleted by constant wars, and transport and communications were neglected. Combined with the increasing influence of the imperial family within the harem, these developments led to an increase in corruption and palace intrigue.

Another sign of change within the empire was the increasing degree of material affluence and the impact of Western ideas and customs. Sophisticated officials and merchants began to ape the habits and lifestyles of their European counterparts, dressing in the European fashion, purchasing Western furniture and art objects, and ignoring Muslim strictures against the consumption of alcohol and sexual activities outside marriage. During the sixteenth and early seventeenth centuries, coffee and to-bacco were introduced into polite Ottoman society, and cafés for the consumption of both began to appear in the major cities (see the box on p. 581). Some sultans and high officials attempted to counter these trends. One sultan in the early seventeenth century issued a decree prohibiting the consumption of both coffee and tobacco, arguing (correctly, no doubt) that many cafés were nests of antigovernment intrigue. He even began to wander incognito through the streets of Istanbul at night. Any of his subjects detected in immoral or illegal acts were summarily executed and their bodies left on the streets as an example to others.

There were also signs of a decline in competence within the ruling family. Whereas the first sultans reigned twenty-seven years on average, later ones averaged only thirteen years. The throne now went to the oldest surviving male, while his rivals were kept secluded in a lat-

A Turkish Discourse on Coffee

Coffee was first introduced to Turkey from the Arabian peninsula in the mid-sixteenth century. The following account was written by Katib Chelebi, a seventeenth-century Turkish author who, among other things, compiled an extensive encyclopedia and bibliography. Here, in The Balance of Truth, *he describes how coffee entered the empire and the problems it caused for public morality. Chelebi died in Istanbul in 1657, allegedly while drinking a cup of coffee.*

Katib Chelebi, *The Balance of Truth*

This matter too was much disputed in the old days. It originated in Yemen and has spread, like tobacco, over the world. Certain sheikhs, who lived with their dervishes in the mountains of Yemen, used to crush and eat the berries . . . of a certain tree. Some would roast them and drink their water. Coffee is a cold dry food, suited to the ascetic life and sedative of lust. The people of Yemen learned of it from one another, and sheikhs, Sufis, and others used it.

It came to Asia Minor by sea, about 1543, and met with a hostile reception, fetwas [decrees] being delivered against it. For they said, Apart from its being roasted, the fact that it is drunk in gatherings, passed from hand to hand, is suggestive of loose living. It is related of Abul-Suud Efendi that he had holes bored in the ships that brought it, plunging their cargoes of coffee into the sea. But these strictures and prohibitions availed nothing. The fetwas, the talk, made no impression on the people. One coffeehouse was opened after another, and men would gather together, with great eagerness and enthusiasm, to drink. Drug addicts in particular, finding it a life-giving thing, which increased their pleasure, were willing to die for a cup.

Since then, muftis pronounced it permissible. . . . Thus coffeehouses experienced varying fortunes for several years, now banned, now permitted. After the year 1591–1592, they ceased to be prohibited. They were opened everywhere, freely: on every street corner a coffeehouse appeared.

Storytellers and musicians diverted the people from their employments, and working for one's living fell into disfavor. Moreover the people, from prince to beggar, amused themselves with knifing one another. Toward the end of 1633, the late Ghazi Gultan Murad, becoming aware of the situation, promulgated an edict, out of regard and compassion for the people, to this effect: Coffeehouses throughout the Guarded Domains shall be dismantled and not opened hereafter. Since then, the coffeehouses of the capital have been as desolate as the heart of the ignorant. In the hope that they might be reopened, their proprietors did not dismantle them, for a while, but merely closed them. Later the majority, if not all of them, were dismantled and turned into other kinds of shops. But in cities and towns outside Istanbul, they are opened just as before. As has been said above, such things do not admit of a perpetual ban.

Now let us come to the description of coffee itself. . . . To those of dry temperament, especially to the man of melancholic temperament, large quantities are unsuitable, and may be repugnant. Taken in excess, it causes insomnia and melancholic anxiety. If drunk at all, it should be drunk with sugar.

To those of moist temperament, and especially to women, it is highly suited. They should drink a great deal of strong coffee. Excess of it will do them no harm, so long as they are not melancholic.

ticed cage and thus had no governmental experience if they succeeded to rule. Later sultans also became less involved in government, and more power flowed to the office of the grand vezir (called the *Sublime Porte*) or to eunuchs and members of the harem.

In addition, the empire was increasingly beset by economic difficulties, caused by the diversion of trade routes away from the eastern Mediterranean and the price inflation brought about by the influx of cheap American silver. The growing influence of conservative *ulama,* who were often suspicious of commercial interests, also contributed to the economic problems.

Ottoman Art

The Ottoman sultans were enthusiastic patrons of the arts and maintained large ateliers of artisans and artists, primarily at the Topkapi Palace in Istanbul but also in other important cities of the vast empire, including Bursa, Edirne, and even Baghdad, Damascus, and Cairo.

The period from Mehmet II in the fifteenth century to the early eighteenth century witnessed the flourishing of pottery, rugs, silk and other textiles, jewelry, arms and armor, and calligraphy. All adorned the palaces of the new rulers, testifying to their opulence and exquisite taste. The artists came from all parts of the realm and beyond. Besides Turks, there were Persians, Greeks, Armenians, Hungarians, and Italians, all vying for the esteem and generous rewards of the sultans and fearing that losing favor might mean losing their heads! In the second half of the sixteenth century, Istanbul alone listed over 150 craft guilds, ample proof of the artistic activity of the era.

By far the greatest contribution of the Ottoman Empire to world art was its architecture, especially the magnificent mosques of the last half of the sixteenth century. Traditionally, prayer halls in mosques were subdivided by numerous pillars that supported small individual domes, creating a private forestlike atmosphere. The Turks, how-

◆ **Inside a Turkish Mosque.** Originally, mosques were impromptu open-air courtyards in the desert. Often no more than a ditch with water for ablutions and palm trees to provide shelter against the sun and sand, they provided the faithful with the necessary coolness and quiet for devotion. Although mosques have evolved architecturally over time, they still remain oases for rest, prayer, and reflection.

ever, modeled their new mosques on the open floor plan of the Byzantine church of Hagia Sophia (completed in 537) and began as early as 1500 to push the pillars toward the outer wall to create a prayer hall with an uninterrupted central area under one large dome. With this plan, large numbers of believers could worship in unison in accordance with Muslim preference. By the mid-sixteenth century, the greatest of all Ottoman architects, Sinan, began erecting the first of his eighty-one mosques with an uncluttered prayer area. Each was topped by an imposing dome, and often, as at Edirne, the entire building was framed with four towering narrow minarets. By emphasizing its vertical lines, the minarets camouflaged the massive stone bulk of the structure and gave it a feeling of incredible lightness. These four graceful minarets would find new expression sixty years later in India's white marble Taj Mahal (see Mughal Culture later in this chapter).

The lightness of the exterior was reinforced in the mosque's interior by the soaring height of the dome and the numerous windows. Added to this were delicate plasterwork and tile decoration that transformed the mosque into a monumental oasis of spirituality, opulence, and power. Sinan's masterpieces, such as the Suleymaniye and the Blue Mosque of Istanbul, were always part of a large socioreligious compound that included a library, school, hospital, mausolea, and even bazaars, all of equally magnificent construction. A far cry from the seventh-century desert mosques of palm trunks, the Ottoman mosques stand as one of the architectural wonders of the world.

Earlier the thirteenth-century Seljuk Turks of Anatolia had created beautiful tile decorations with two-color mosaics. Now Ottoman artists invented a new glazed tile art with painted flowers and geometrical designs in brilliant blue, green, yellow, and their own secret "tomato red." Entire walls, both interior and exterior, were covered with the painted tiles, which adorned palaces as well as mosques. Produced at Iznik (the old Nicaea), the distinctive tiles and pottery were in great demand; the city's ateliers boasted more than three hundred artisans in the late sixteenth century.

The Iznik pottery appeared in the form of vases, bowls, plates, jugs, and especially lamps for reading the Koran. Also of note are the small egg-shaped objects that were attached to the cords suspending the reading lamps or candelabra to prevent mice from reaching the fixtures to drink the oil or eat the candles. Moreover, once Jerusalem had been incorporated into the Ottoman Empire, the sultans restored the seventh-century Dome of the Rock with Iznik reading lamps and decorative tile work on the outside.

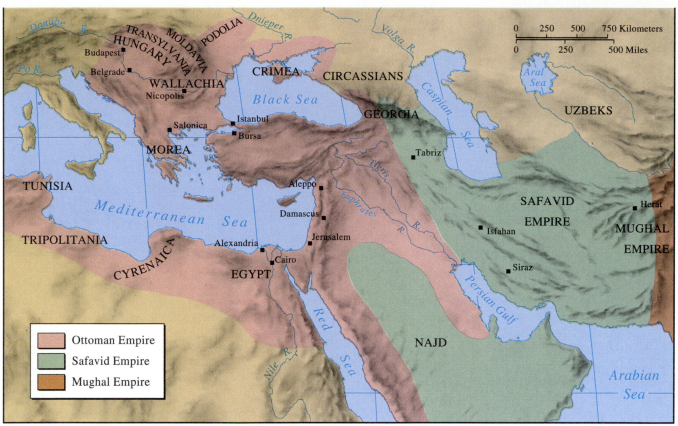

🜲 **Map 16.2**   The Ottoman and Safavid Empires, ca. 1683.

The sixteenth century also witnessed the flourishing of textiles and rugs. The Byzantine emperor Justinian had introduced the cultivation of silkworms to the West in the sixth century, and the silk industry resurfaced under the Ottomans. Its capital was at Bursa, where factories produced silks for wall hangings, soft covers, and especially court costumes. Many are on display in the Palace Museum in Istanbul, looking as radiant and opulent as when they adorned the court of the sultans four hundred years ago.

Perhaps even more famous than Turkish silk are the rugs. But whereas silks were produced under the patronage of the sultans, rugs were a peasant industry. Each village boasted its own distinctive design and color scheme for the rugs it produced. Common to all the rugs, however, was the use of the knot from the Gordes region—hence the term "Gordian knot."

Ottoman painting was very different from the romantic, almost dreamlike, paintings of the Persian school. Emphasizing realistic scenes of the sultans, the court, and military exploits, it was a virile, action-filled art packed with detail. Of special interest are the illustrations for the *Lives of Sultans* and the *Books of Festivals* that depict daily life in Istanbul from the sixteenth to the early eighteenth century. These colorful and energetic paintings bring the magnificence of the Ottoman Empire to life.

The Safavids

After the collapse of the empire of Tamerlane in the early fifteenth century, the area extending from Persia into Central Asia lapsed into anarchy. The Uzbeks, Turkic-speaking peoples from Central Asia, were the chief political and military force in the area. From their capital at Bokhara, they maintained a semblance of control over the highly fluid tribal alignments until the emergence of the Safavid dynasty in Persia at the beginning of the sixteenth century.

The Safavid dynasty was founded by Shah Ismail, the descendant of a sheikh called Safi al-Din (thus the name Safavid), who traced his origins to Ali, the fourth imam of the Muslim faith. In the early fourteenth century, Safi had been the leader of a community of Turkic-speaking tribesmen in Azerbaijan, near the Caspian Sea. Safi's community was only one of many Sufi mystical religious groups throughout the area. Their activities, including mystical rituals practiced in secret, were tolerated by the local ruling Sunni governments, and in time the doctrine spread among nomadic groups throughout the Middle East and was transformed into the more activist Shi'i heresy. Its adherents were known as "red heads" because of their distinctive red cap with twelve folds meant to symbolize allegiance to the twelve imams of the Shi'i faith.

In 1501, Ismail's forces seized much of Iran and Iraq, and he called himself the shah of a new Persian state. Baghdad was subdued in 1508 and the Uzbeks in Bokhara shortly thereafter. Ismail (1487–1524) now sent Shi'ite preachers into Anatolia to proselytize among Turkish tribal peoples in the Ottoman Empire. Although the Ottoman sultan Bayazid tried to negotiate with him, Ismail persisted and ordered the massacre of Sunni Muslims when Baghdad was conquered in 1508. One of Ismail's followers invaded southern Anatolia and promoted revolt among the local tribesmen. He was killed by the Ottomans in 1511, and the revolt collapsed. The new Ottoman sultan Selim I advanced against the Safavids in Iran and won a major battle near Tabriz in 1514. But Selim could not maintain control of the area, and Ismail regained Tabriz a few years later.

During the next decades, the Safavids attempted to consolidate their rule throughout Persia and in areas to the west. Faced with the problem of integrating unruly Turkic-speaking tribal peoples with the sedentary Persian-speaking population of the urban areas, they used the Shi'ite faith as an unifying force. The shah himself acquired an almost divine quality and claimed to be the spiritual leader of all Islam (see the box on p. 585).

The Safavid claim of supremacy and orthodoxy caused continuing problems with the Ottomans, who returned to the attack in the 1580s; they placed Azerbaijan under Turkish rule, controlled the Caspian Sea with their fleet, and allied with the Uzbeks. The new Safavid shah, Abbas I (1587–1629), was forced to sign a punitive peace in which much territory was lost. The capital was subsequently moved from Tabriz in the northwest to Isfahan in the south. Abbas also promised to stop proselytizing among the nomads in Turkey, a move that tempered his subjects' religious zeal. Still, it was under Shah Abbas that the Safavids reached the zenith of their glory. He established a system similar to the Janissaries in Turkey to train administrators to replace the traditional warrior elite. He also used the period of peace to strengthen his army, now armed with modern weapons, and in the early seventeenth century he moved against both the Uzbeks and the Turks to regain the lost territories. In this effort, Abbas was assisted by some European states, whose leaders viewed the Safavids as useful allies against their primary adversaries in Istanbul. The Safavids had some initial success and managed to regain Azerbaijan under a treaty of 1612, but they could not hold their other territorial gains against the organized force of the Ottoman armies. War resumed in the 1620s, and a lasting peace was not achieved until 1638.

Abbas the Great had managed to strengthen the dynasty significantly, and for a time after his death in 1629, it remained stable and vigorous. But succession conflicts—always a problem undermining the power of the state—continued to plague the dynasty, while attempts to suppress the religious beliefs of minorities led to increased popular unrest. In the early eighteenth century, during the reign of Shah Hussein (1694–1723), Afghan tribesmen took advantage of local revolts to seize the capital of Isfahan, forcing the remnants of the Safavid ruling family to retreat to Azerbaijan, their original homeland. The Ottomans took advantage of the situation to seize territories along the western border. Eventually, order was restored by the military adventurer Nadir Shah Afshar, who launched an extended series of campaigns that restored the country's borders and even occupied the Mughal capital of Delhi (see Twilight of the Mughals later in this chapter). After his death, the Zand dynasty ruled until the end of the eighteenth century.

The Religious Zeal of Shah Abbas the Great

Shah Abbas I, probably the greatest of the Safavid rulers, expanded the borders of his empire into areas of the southern Caucasus inhabited by Christians and other non-Muslim peoples. After Persian control was assured, he instructed that the local population be urged to convert to Islam for their own protection and the glory of God. In this passage, his biographer, the Persian historian Eskander Beg Monshi, recounts the story of that effort.

The Conversion of a Number of Christians to Islam

This year the Shah decreed that those Armenians and other Christians who had been settled in [the southern Caucasus] and had been given agricultural land there, should be invited to become Muslims. Life in this world is fraught with vicissitudes, and the Shah was concerned lest, in a period when the authority of the central government was weak, these Christians, . . . might be subjected to attack by the neighboring Lor tribes (who are naturally given to causing injury and mischief), and their women and children carried off into captivity. In the areas in which these Christian groups resided, it was the Shah's purpose that the places of worship which they had built should become mosques, and the muezzin's call should be heard in them, so that these Christians might assume the guise of Muslims, and their future status accordingly be assured.

[An emir] was entrusted with the task of ensuring their conversion; his family had been servants of the Safavid house for generations, and he himself had grown up from infancy under the Shah's tutelage, and was distinguished among his peers by his closeness to the Shah and the degree of trust the Shah placed in him. Some of the Christians, guided by God's grace, embraced Islam voluntarily; others found it difficult to abandon their Christian faith and felt revulsion at the idea. They were encouraged by their monks and priests to remain steadfast in their faith. After a little pressure had been applied to the monks and priests, however, they desisted, and these Christians saw no alternative but to embrace Islam, though they did so with reluctance. The women and children embraced Islam with great enthusiasm, vying with one another in their eagerness to abandon their Christian faith and declare their belief in the unity of God. Some five thousand people embraced Islam. As each group made the Muslim declaration of faith, it received instruction in the Koran and the principles of the religious law of Islam, and all bibles and other Christian devotional material were collected and taken away from the priests.

In the same way, all the Armenian Christians who had been moved to [the area] were also forcibly converted to Islam. . . . Most people embraced Islam with sincerity, but some felt an aversion to making the Muslim profession of faith. True knowledge lies with God! May God reward the Shah for his action with long life and prosperity!

Safavid Politics and Society

Like the Ottoman Empire, Iran under the Safavids was a mixed society. The Safavids had come to power with the support of nomadic Turkic-speaking tribal groups, and leading elements from those groups retained considerable influence within the empire. But the majority of the population were Iranian; most of them were farmers or townspeople, with attitudes inherited from the relatively sophisticated and urbanized culture of pre-Safavid Iran. Virtually all aspects of Safavid society, from its political institutions to its social customs, reflected that diversity.

The Safavid political system was pyramidal in shape like most traditional empires of the time; the shah was at the top, the bureaucracy and landed classes in the middle, and the common people at the bottom. Influenced perhaps by Iranian tradition, the monarchy possessed a semi-divine character, a belief that was eagerly embraced by militant Shi'ites, who traced the founder of the empire to the direct succession from the Prophet Muhammad. In return, the Safavids declared Shi'ism to be the state religion. Contemporary visitors reported that the shahs were more accessible than rulers elsewhere despite their semi-divine nature. "They show great familiarity to strangers," remarked one, "and even to their own subjects, eating and drinking with them pretty freely."[1]

In a manner somewhat reminiscent of the situation in the Ottoman Empire, the armed forces were organized under the command of tribal leaders connected to the "red head" groups that had supported the founders of the dynasty. Known as *amirs*, these leaders received fiefs from the court from which they could extract taxes as income. In return, the *amir* forwarded a fixed sum to the central government and maintained troops that could be placed under royal command in case of need.

Although there was a landed aristocracy, aristocratic power and influence were firmly controlled by strong-minded shahs who confiscated aristocratic estates when possible and brought them under the control of the crown. Appointment to senior positions in the bureaucracy was by merit rather than birth. To avoid encouraging competition between Turkish and non-Turkish elements, Shah Abbas I hired a number of foreigners from neighboring countries for positions in his government.

The Safavid shahs took a direct interest in the economy and actively engaged in commercial and manufacturing activities, although there was also a large and affluent urban bourgeoisie. Like the Ottoman sultan, one shah regularly traveled the city streets incognito to check on the honesty of his subjects. When he discovered that a baker and butcher were overcharging for their products, he had the baker cooked in his own oven and the butcher roasted on a spit. The road system was reportedly quite poor, but most goods traveled by caravan. They included the brocades, carpets, and leather goods of Iran that were prized throughout the world. The government provided accommodations for weary travelers and, at least in times of strong rulers, kept the roads relatively clear of thieves and bandits.

At its height, Safavid Iran was a worthy successor of the great Persian empires of the past, although it was probably not as wealthy as its neighbors to the east and west—the Mughals and the Ottomans. Hemmed in by the sea power of the Europeans to the south and by the land power of the Ottomans to the west, the early Safavids had no navy and were forced to divert overland trade with Europe through southern Russia to avoid an Ottoman blockade. In the early seventeenth century, the situation improved when Iranian forces, in cooperation with the British, seized the island of Hormuz from Portugal and established a new seaport on the southern coast at Bandar Abbas. As a consequence, commercial ties with Europe began to increase.

After the death of Shah Abbas I in 1629, most of his successors lacked his talent and political acumen. The power of the more militant Shi'ites began to increase at court and in Safavid society at large. The intellectual freedom that had characterized the empire at its height was curtailed under the pressure of religious orthodoxy,

while Iranian women, who had enjoyed considerable freedom and influence during the early empire, were forced to withdraw into seclusion and to the veil.

Safavid Art and Literature

Persia witnessed an extraordinary flowering of the arts during the reign of Shah Abbas I. His new capital of Isfahan was a grandiose planned city with wide visual perspectives and a sense of order almost unique in the region. Shah Abbas ordered his architects to position his palaces, mosques, and bazaars around the Maydan-i-Shah, a massive rectangular polo ground. Much of the original city is still in good condition and remains the gem of modern-day Iran. The immense mosques are richly decorated with elaborate blue tiles. The palaces are delicate structures with unusual slender wooden columns. These architectural wonders of Isfahan epitomize the grandeur, delicacy, and color that defined the Safavid golden age. To adorn the splendid buildings, Safavid artisans created imaginative metalwork, tile decorations, and original and delicate glass vessels. The ceramics of the period, imitating Chinese prototypes of celadon or blue and white Ming design, largely ignored traditional Persian designs.

The greatest area of productivity, however, was in textiles. Silk weaving based on new techniques became a national industry. The silks depicted birds, animals, and flowers in a brilliant mass of color with silver and gold threads. Above all, carpet weaving flourished, stimulated by the great demand for Persian carpets in the West. Made primarily of wool with some cotton, Persian carpets varied in size from small to very large and depicted a variety of motifs called "garden," "floral," "animal," "vase," and "medallion." Still highly prized all over the world, these seventeenth-century carpets reflect the grandeur and artistry of the Safavid dynasty.

The long tradition of Persian painting continued in the Safavid era, but changed from paintings to line drawings and from landscape scenes to portraits, mostly of young ladies, boys, lovers, or dervishes. Although some Persian artists studied in Rome, Safavid art was little influenced by the West. Riza-i-Abassi, the most famous artist of this period, created exquisite works on simple naturalistic subjects, such as an ox plowing, hunters, or lovers. Soft colors, delicacy, and flowing movement were the dominant characteristics of the painting of this era.

Although the artistic excellence of the period is clear, Safavid literature lacked a similar luster. A large amount of poetry was written, but its lack of quality testified to the decline of Persian poetry. Notwithstanding the fact

◆ **The Royal Academy of Isfahan.**   Along with institutions such as libraries and hospitals, theological schools were often included in the mosque compound. One of the most sumptuous was the Royal Academy of Isfahan, built by the shah of Iran in the early eighteenth century. This view shows the large courtyard surrounded by arcades of student rooms, reminiscent of the arrangement of monks' cells in European cloisters.

that many Safavid poets were enticed to India to write for the Mughal emperors, the literature of this era is not significant. Why Safavid creativity expressed itself in art but not in literature remains a puzzle. We should also note, though, that a school of philosophy that sought truth in a fusion of rationalist and intuitive methods flourished in the sixteenth and seventeenth centuries, while Safavid science, medicine, and mathematics were the equal of other societies in the region.

The Grandeur of the Mughals

In retrospect, the period from the sixteenth to the eighteenth century can be viewed both as a high point of tra-ditional culture in India and as the first stage of perhaps its greatest challenge. The era began with the creation of one of the subcontinent's greatest empires—that of the Mughals. Mughal rulers, although foreigners and Muslims like many of their immediate predecessors, nevertheless brought India to a peak of political power and cultural achievement. For the first time since the age of the Mauryan dynasty, the entire subcontinent was united under a single government with a common culture that inspired admiration and envy throughout the entire region.

The Mughal Empire reached the peak of its greatness under the famed Emperor Akbar and then maintained its vitality under a series of strong rulers for another century. Then the dynasty began to weaken, a process that was undoubtedly hastened by the increasingly insistent challenge of the foreigners arriving by sea. The Portuguese, whose first fleet arrived on the southwestern coast of the subcontinent in 1498, were little more than an irritant. Two centuries later, however, Europeans began to seize control of regional trade routes and to meddle in the internal politics of the subcontinent. By the end of the eighteenth century, nothing remained of the empire but a shell.

But some historians see the seeds of decay less in the challenge from abroad than in internal weakness—in the very nature of the dynasty itself, which was always more a heterogeneous collection of semiautonomous political forces than a centralized empire in the style of neighboring China. At its height, the dynasty was fully capable of fending off the demands of the Europeans. But after two centuries of expansion and consolidation, it began to lose its vitality, and by the end of the eighteenth century, it had lapsed into a mere shadow of its former self. Into the vacuum left by its final decrepitude stepped the British,

who used a combination of firepower and guile to consolidate their power over the subcontinent.

The Mughal Dynasty: A "Gunpowder Empire"?

When the Portuguese fleet led by Vasco da Gama arrived at the port of Calicut in the spring of 1498, the Indian subcontinent was still divided into a number of Hindu and Muslim kingdoms. But it was on the verge of a new era of unity that would be brought about by a foreign dynasty called the Mughals. Like so many recent rulers of North India, the founders of the Mughal Empire were not natives of India, but came from the mountainous region north of the Ganges River. The founder of the dynasty, known to history as Babur (1483–1530), had an illustrious pedigree. His father was descended from the great Asian conqueror Tamerlane, his mother from the Mongol conqueror Genghis Khan.

Map 16.3   The Mughal Empire.

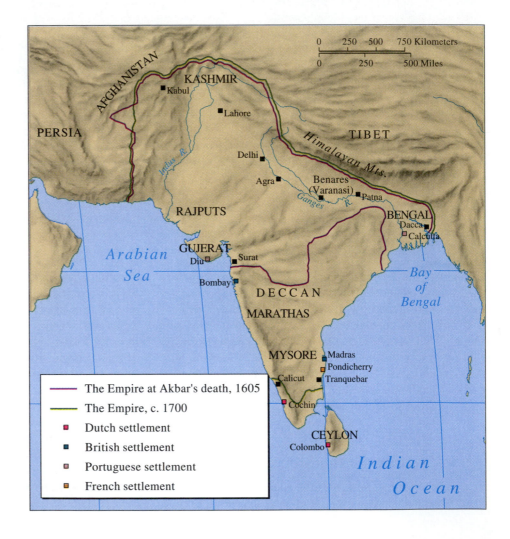

Babur had inherited a fragment of Tamerlane's empire in an upland valley of the Syr Darya River. As a youth, he mobilized warriors loyal to him in an unsuccessful campaign to conquer Samarkand. Driven south by the rising power of the Uzbeks and then the Safavid dynasty in Persia, Babur and his warriors seized Kabul in 1504 and then, thirteen years later, crossed the Khyber pass to India.

Following a classical pattern that we have seen before, Babur began his rise to power by offering to help an ailing dynasty against its opponents. Although his own forces were far smaller than those of his adversaries, he possessed advanced weapons, including artillery, and used them to great affect. His use of mobile cavalry tactics was particularly successful against the massed forces, supplemented by mounted elephants, of his enemy. In 1526, with only 12,000 troops against an enemy force nearly ten times that size, Babur captured Delhi and established his power in the plains of northern India (see the box on p. 590). Over the next several years, he continued his conquests in northern India until his early death in 1530 at the age of forty-seven.

Babur's success was due in part to his vigor and his charismatic personality, which earned him the undying loyalty of his followers. His son and successor Humayun (1530–1556) was, in the words of one British historian, "intelligent but lazy." Whether or not this is a fair characterization, Humayun clearly lacked the will to consolidate his father's conquests and the personality to inspire personal loyalty among his subjects. Inheriting an empire already composed of most of northern India, Humayun was unable to subdue his fractious rivals, and in 1540 he fled westward into Persia, where he lived in exile for sixteen years. Finally, with the aid of the Safavid shah of Persia, he retook Kandahar in 1545. Taking advantage of divisions in the enemy camp, he reconquered Delhi in 1555, but died the following year in a household accident, reportedly from injuries suffered from a fall after smoking a pipeful of opium.

Humayun was succeeded by his son Akbar (1556–1605). Born while his father was living in exile, Akbar was only fourteen when he mounted the throne. Illiterate but highly intelligent and industrious, Akbar set out to extend his domain, then limited to Punjab and the upper Ganges River valley. By the end of his life, he had brought Mughal rule to most of the subcontinent, from the Himalaya Mountains to the Godavari River in central India and from Kashmir to the mouths of the Brahmaputra and the Ganges. Akbar had created the greatest Indian empire since the Mauryan dynasty nearly two thousand years before. In so doing, he followed the illustrious tradition of Indian statecraft. "A monarch," he

◆ **Two Lovers.** Safavid painting continued Persian tradition, but shifted from landscapes to portraits, mostly of young ladies, boys, lovers, or dervishes. This delicate painting of a couple embracing was produced in the early seventeenth century by Riza-i-Abassi, the most famous artist of Isfahan. It conveys passion with refined elegance.

remarked, "should be ever intent on conquest, otherwise his neighbors rise in arms against him. The army should be exercised in warfare, lest from want of training they become self-indulgent."[2]

Akbar's ability to bring almost the entire subcontinent of India under his rule, thus re-creating the universal empire of Asoka, has provoked interest among scholars. One explanation for his success might be called the "gunpowder empire" thesis. This theory holds that having mastered the use of heavy artillery, Akbar's armies were able to besiege and subdue the traditional stone fortresses of their rivals and conquer all of the subcontinent. This view has been challenged by the historian Douglas Streusand, who argues that the Mughals used the "carrot and

Babur, the founder of the great Mughal dynasty, began his career by allying with one Indian prince against another and then turned on his ally to put himself in power, a tactic that had been used by the Ottomans and the Mongols before him. In this excerpt from his memoirs, Babur describes his triumph over the powerful army of his Indian enemy, the Sultan Ibrâhim.

Babur, *Memoirs*

They made one or two very poor charges on our right and left divisions. My troops making use of their bows, plied them with arrows, and drove them in upon their center. The troops on the right and the left of their center, being huddled together in one place, such confusion ensued, that the enemy, while totally unable to advance, found also no road by which they could flee. The sun had mounted spear-high when the onset of battle began, and the combat lasted till midday, when the enemy were completely broken and routed, and my friends victorious and exulting. By the grace and mercy of Almighty God, this arduous undertaking was rendered easy for me, and this mighty army, in the space of half a day, laid in the dust. Five or six thousand men were discovered lying slain, in one spot, near Ibrâhim. We reckoned that the number lying slain, in different parts of this field of battle, amounted to fifteen or sixteen thousand men. On reaching Agra, we found, from the accounts of the natives of Hindustân, that forty or fifty thousand men had fallen in this field. After routing the enemy, we continued the pursuit, slaughtering, and making them prisoners. Those who were ahead, began to bring in the Amîrs and Afghâns as prisoners. They brought in a very great number of elephants with their drivers, and offered them to me as peshkesh. Having pursued the enemy to some distance, and supposing that Ibrâhim had escaped from the battle, I appointed Kismâi Mirza, Bâba Chihreh, and Bujkeh, with a party of my immediate adherents, to follow him in close pursuit down as far as Afra. Having passed through the middle of Ibrâhim's camp, and visited his pavilions and accommodations, we encamped on the banks of the Siâh-ab.

It was now afternoon prayers when Tahir Taberi, the younger brother of Khalîfeh, having found Ibrâhim lying dead amidst a number of slain, cut off his head, and brought it in. . . .

Yet, under such circumstances, and in spite of this power, placing my trust in God, and leaving behind me my old and inveterate enemy the Uzbeks, who had an army of a hundred thousand men, I advanced to meet so powerful a prince as Sultan Ibrâhim, the lord of numerous armies, and emperor of extensive territories. In consideration of my confidence in Divine aid, the Most High God did not suffer the distress and hardships that I had undergone to be thrown away, but defeated my formidable enemy, and made me the conqueror of the noble country of Hindustân. This success I do not ascribe to my own strength, nor did this good fortune flow from my own efforts, but from the fountain of the favor and mercy of God.

---

the stick" to extend their authority, relying not just on heavy artillery, but also on other forms of siege warfare and the offer of negotiations. The end result was an empire that appeared highly centralized from the outside, but was actually a collection of semiautonomous principalities ruled by provincial elites and linked together by the overarching majesty of the Mughal emperor.

Akbar and Indo-Muslim Civilization

Although Akbar was probably the greatest of the conquering Mughal monarchs, like his famous predecessor Asoka, he is best known for the humane character of his rule. Although born a Muslim like all Mughal rulers, Akbar accepted the diversity of Indian society and adopted a policy of religious tolerance. He patronized classical Indian arts and architecture and abolished many of the disabilities faced by Hindus in a Muslim-dominated society. Akbar also permitted Hindus to serve at court, although most of the high positions were reserved for Muslims.

Akbar's cosmopolitanism showed above all in his approach to religion. Though he was apparently raised an orthodox Muslim, he had been exposed to other beliefs during his childhood and had little patience with the pedantic views of Muslim scholars at court. As emperor, he displayed a keen interest in other religions, not only tolerating Hindu practices in his own domains, but also welcoming the expression of Christian views by his Jesuit advisers. Akbar put his policy of religious tolerance into practice by taking a Hindu princess as one of his wives, and the success of this marriage may well have had an effect on his religious convictions.

During his later years, Akbar became steadily more hostile to Islam. To the dismay of many Muslims at court, he sponsored a new form of worship called the "Divine Faith" (*Din-i-Ilahi*), which combined characteristics of several religions with a central belief in the infallibility of all decisions reached by the emperor. Some historians have maintained that Akbar totally abandoned Islam and adopted a Persian model of imperial divinity. But others have pointed out that the emperor was not claiming divine status, only divine guidance, and that the new

ideology was designed to cement the loyalty of officials and provincial authorities to the person of the monarch. Whatever the case, the new faith aroused deep hostility in Muslim circles and rapidly vanished after his death.

Akbar also extended his innovations to the area of administration. While the upper ranks of the government hierarchy continued to be dominated by nonnative Muslims, all of them technically holding a military rank, a substantial proportion of lower-ranking officials were Hindus, and a few Hindus were appointed to positions of importance. At first, most officials were paid salaries, but later they were ordinarily assigned sections of agricultural land for their temporary use; they kept a portion of the taxes paid by the local peasants in lieu of a salary. These

◆ **Akbar Restrains an Elephant.** Akbar was probably the greatest of the conquering Mughal monarchs. In this contemporary Indian miniature, the young Akbar is seen mounted on a fierce elephant, leading an attack. The

pontoon bridge is sinking under the heavy weight, while on the shore, before the towers of the royal palace at the Red Fort of Agra, his chief minister is begging Akbar to cease his reckless behavior.

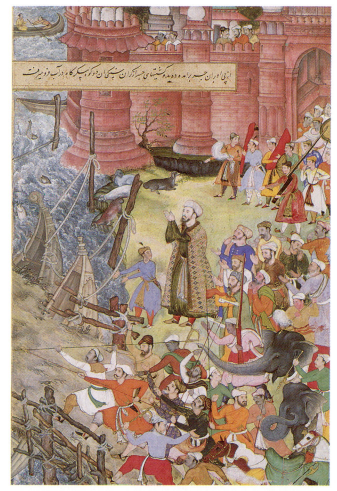

local officials, known as *zamindars*, were expected to forward the rest of the taxes from the lands under their control to the central government. *Zamindars* often recruited a number of military and civilian retainers and accumulated considerable power in their localities.

The same tolerance that marked Akbar's attitude toward religion and administration extended to the Mughal legal system. While Muslims were subject to the Islamic codes (the *Shari'ah*), Hindu law (the *Dharmashastra*) applied to areas settled by Hindus, who after 1579 were no longer required to pay the hated *jizya*, or poll tax on non-Muslims. Punishments for crime were relatively mild, at least by the standards of the day, and justice was administered in a relatively impartial and efficient manner.

Overall, the Akbar era was relatively benign, at least by contemporary standards. Although all Indian peasants were required to pay about one-third of their annual harvest to the state through the *zamindars*, the system was applied fairly, and when drought struck in the 1590s, the taxes were reduced or even suspended altogether. Thanks to a long period of relative peace and political stability, commerce and manufacturing flourished. Foreign trade, in particular, thrived as Indian goods, notably textiles, tropical food products, spices, and precious stones, were exported in exchange for gold and silver. Tariffs on imports were low. Much of the foreign commerce was handled by Arab traders, since the Indians, like their Mughal rulers, did not care for travel by sea. Internal trade, however, was dominated by large merchant castes, who also were active in banking and handicrafts.

Twilight of the Mughals

Akbar died in 1605 and was succeeded by his son Jahangir (1605–1628). Able and ambitious, the latter had launched an unsuccessful rebellion against his father during the final days of Akbar's rule, and during the early years of his reign, he continued to strengthen central control over the vast empire. Eventually, however, Jahangir's grip began to weaken (according to his memoirs, he "only wanted a bottle of wine and a piece of meat to make merry"), and the court fell under the influence of one of his wives, the Persian-born Nur Jahan. The empress took advantage of her position to enrich her own family and arranged for her niece Mumtaz Mahal to marry her husband's third son and ultimate successor Shah Jahan. When Shah Jahan succeeded to the throne in 1628, he quickly demonstrated the single-minded quality of his grandfather (albeit in a much more brutal manner), ordering the assassination of all of his rivals in order to secure his own position.

During a reign of three decades, Shah Jahan maintained the system established by his predecessors while expanding the boundaries of the empire by successful campaigns in the Deccan Plateau and against Samarkand, north of the Hindu Kush. But Shah Jahan's rule was marred by his failure to deal with the growing domestic problems. He had inherited a nearly empty treasury because of Empress Nur Jahan's penchant for luxury and ambitious charity projects. While the majority of his subjects lived in grinding poverty, Shah Jahan's frequent military campaigns and expensive building projects put a heavy strain on the imperial finances and compelled him to raise taxes (see the box on p. 593). At the same time, the government did little to improve rural conditions. In a country where transport was primitive (it often took three months to travel from Patna, in the middle of the Ganges River valley, to Delhi, a distance of a little more than six hundred miles) and drought conditions frequent, the dynasty made few efforts to increase agricultural efficiency or to improve the roads or the irrigation network. A pathetic description of famine conditions in the mid-seventeenth century has been provided by a Dutch merchant in Gujarat:

> As the famine increased, men abandoned towns and villages and wandered helplessly. It was easy to recognize their condition: eyes sunk deep in head, lips pale and covered with slime, the skin hard, with the bones showing through, the belly nothing but a pouch hanging down empty, knuckles and knee-caps showing prominently. One would cry and howl for hunger, while another lay stretched on the ground dying in misery; wherever you went, you saw nothing but corpses.[3]

It is a scene with which our own century is all too familiar.

In 1648, Shah Jahan moved his capital from Agra to Delhi and built the famous Red Fort in his new capital city. But he is best known for the Taj Mahal in Agra, widely considered to be the most beautiful building in India, if not in the entire world. The story is a romantic one—that the Taj was built by the emperor in memory of his wife Mumtaz Mahal, who had died giving birth to her thirteenth child at the age of thirty-nine. But the story has a less attractive side: the expense of the building, which employed 20,000 masons over twenty years, forced the government to raise agricultural taxes, further impoverishing many Indian peasants.

Succession struggles returned to haunt the dynasty in the mid-1650s when Shah Jahan's illness led to a struggle for power between his sons Dara Shikoh and Aurangzeb. Dara Shikoh was described by his contemporaries as progressive and humane, although possessed of a violent

An Elephant Fight for the King's Entertainment

François Bernier was a well-traveled Frenchman who visited India during the mid-seventeenth century. In this excerpt from his account of the visit, he describes a festival held just outside the Red Fort at Delhi for the amusement of the emperor. The account is indicative of the wealth and majesty of the Mughal Empire at its height.

François Bernier, *Travels in the Mogul Empire*

The festivals generally conclude with an amusement unknown in Europe—a combat between two elephants; which takes place in the presence of all the people on the sandy space near the river: the King, the principal ladies of the court, and the *Omrahs* viewing the spectacle from different apartments in the fortress.

A wall of earth is raised three or four feet wide and five or six high. The two ponderous beasts meet one another face to face, on opposite sides of the wall, each having a couple of riders, that the place of the man who sits on the shoulders, for the purpose of guiding the elephant with a large iron hook, may immediately be supplied if he should be thrown down. The riders animate the elephants either by soothing words, or by chiding them as cowards, and urge them on with their heels, until the poor creatures approach the wall and are brought to the attack. The shock is tremendous, and it appears surprising that they ever survive the dreadful wounds and blows inflicted with their teeth, their heads, and their trunks. There are frequent pauses during the fight; it is suspended and renewed; and the mud wall being at length thrown down, the stronger or more courageous elephant passes on and attacks his opponent, and, putting him to flight, pursues and fastens upon him with so much obstinacy, that the animals can be separated only by means of *cherkys*, or fireworks, which are made to explode between them; for they are naturally timid, and have a particular dread of fire, which is the reason why elephants have been used with so very little advantage in armies since the use of firearms. The boldest come from Ceylon, but none are employed in war which have not been regularly trained, and accustomed for years to the discharge of muskets close to their heads, and the bursting of crackers between their legs.

The fight of these noble creatures is attended with much cruelty. It frequently happens that some of the riders are trodden underfoot, and killed on the spot, the elephant having always cunning enough to feel the importance of dismounting the rider of his adversary, whom he therefore endeavors to strike down with his trunk. So imminent is the danger considered, that on the day of combat the unhappy men take the same formal leave of their wives and children as if condemned to death. They are somewhat consoled by the reflection that if their lives should be preserved, and the King be pleased with their conduct, not only will their pay be augmented, but a sack of *Peyssas* (equal to fifty francs) will be presented to them the moment they alight from the elephant. . . . The mischief with which this amusement is attended does not always terminate with the death of the rider: it often happens that some of the spectators are knocked down and trampled upon by the elephants, or by the crowd; for the rush is terrible when, to avoid the infuriated combatants, men and horses in confusion take to flight. The second time I witnessed this exhibition I owed my safety entirely to the goodness of my horse and the exertions of my two servants.

---

temper and a strong sense of mysticism. But he apparently lacked political acumen and was outmaneuvered by his brother, who had Dara Shikoh put to death and then imprisoned his father in the fort at Agra. Aurangzeb had himself crowned emperor in 1658.

Aurangzeb is one of the most controversial individuals in the history of India. A man of high principle, he attempted to eliminate many of what he considered to be India's social evils, prohibiting the immolation of widows on their husband's funeral pyre (*sati*), the castration of eu-nuchs, and the exaction of illegal taxes. With less success, he tried to forbid gambling, drinking, and prostitution. But Aurangzeb, a devout and somewhat doctrinaire Muslim, also adopted a number of measures that reversed the policies of religious tolerance established by his predecessors. The building of new Hindu temples was prohibited and the Hindu poll tax was restored. Forced conversions to Islam were resumed and non-Muslims were driven from the court. The emperor's actions were fervently praised by a later historian, clearly a fellow believer:

CHRONOLOGY

The Mughal Era

Arrival of Vasco da Gama at Calicut	1498
Babur seizes Delhi	1526
Death of Babur	1530
Humayun recovers throne in Delhi	1555
Death of Humayun and accession of Akbar	1556
First Jesuit Mission to Agra	1580
Death of Akbar and accession of Jahangir	1605
Arrival of English at Surat	1608
Reign of Emperor Shah Jahan	1628–1657
Foundation of English fort at Madras	1639
Aurangzeb succeeds to the throne	1658
Bombay ceded to England	1661
Death of Aurangzeb	1707
French capture Madras	1746
Battle of Plassey	1757

Glory be to God who has given us the faith of Islam, that in the reign of the destroyer of false gods, an undertaking so difficult of accomplishment has been brought to a successful termination! The vigorous support given to the true faith was a severe blow to the arrogance of the rajas, and like idols they turned their faces awe-struck to the wall. The richly-jeweled idols taken from the pagan temples were transferred to Agra, and there placed beneath the steps leading to the Nawab Begam Sahib's mosque, in order that they might ever be pressed under foot by true believers.[4]

Aurangzeb's heavy-handed religious policies led to considerable domestic unrest and to a revival of Hindu fervor during the last years of his reign. A number of revolts also broke out against imperial authority. The most serious threat came from the area along the western coast, where the warrior Shivaji rebelled against Mughal rule and created a new Hindu state in Maharashtra. Shivaji was eventually captured, but internal conflict continued until Aurangzeb's death in 1707. During the eighteenth century, Mughal power was threatened both from within and without. Fueled by the growing power and autonomy of local gentry and merchant elements, rebellious groups in provinces throughout the empire, from the Deccan to the Punjab, began to reassert local authority and reduce the power of the Mughal emperor to that of a "tinsel sovereign." Increasingly divided, India was vulnerable to attack from abroad. In 1739, Delhi was sacked by the Persians, who left it in ashes and carried off its splendid Peacock Throne (see The Safavids earlier in this chapter).

The reasons for the virtual collapse of the Mughal Empire have aroused considerable interest among modern historians. A number of obvious factors were at work, including the draining of the imperial treasury and the decline in competence of Mughal rulers. But recent scholarship suggests that the distinction between the empire at its height and in its final state of weakness is less clear-cut than meets the eye. From the outset, Akbar's empire was a loosely knit collection of heterogeneous principalities held together by the authority of the throne, which tried to combine Persian concepts of kingship with the Indian tradition of decentralized power. Decline set in when centrifugal forces gradually began to predominate over centripetal ones.

Ironically, one element in this process was the very success of the system, which led to the rapid expansion of wealth and autonomous power at the local level. As local elites increased their wealth and influence, they became less willing to accept the authority and financial demands from Delhi. The reassertion of Muslim orthodoxy under Aurangzeb and his successors simply exacerbated the problem. Finally, this process was undoubtedly hastened by the growing European military and economic presence along the periphery of the empire. It is to that factor that we now turn.

The Impact of Western Power in India

As we have seen, the first to arrive were the Portuguese. Lisbon's determination to create a virtual Portuguese monopoly of regional trade in the Indian Ocean undoubtedly had an impact on the commercial activities of maritime Indian states. Nevertheless, Portugal did not aggressively seek to penetrate the interior of the subcontinent, although Lisbon did assign representatives to the court of the Mughals to protect Portuguese interests. The situation changed at the end of the sixteenth century, when two new claimants, the English and the Dutch, entered the scene. Soon both powers were in active competition with Portugal, and with each other, for trading privileges in the region.

Penetration of the new market was not easy. When the first English fleet arrived at Surat (a thriving port along the northwestern coast of India) in 1608, their request for trading privileges was rejected by Emperor Jahangir, who acted at the suggestion of the Portuguese advisers already in residence at the imperial court. Stimulated by the need to find a lightweight Indian cloth to trade for spices in the East Indies, the English persisted, and in 1616 they were finally permitted to install their own ambassador at the imperial court in Agra. That representative signed a commercial treaty between the two countries. Three years later the first English factory was established at Surat.

During the next several decades, the English presence in India steadily increased while Mughal power gradually waned. By mid-century additional English factories had been established at Fort William (now the great city of Calcutta) on the River Hoogly near the Bay of Bengal and at Madras on the southeastern coast. From there English ships carried Indian-made cotton goods to the East Indies where they were bartered for spices, which were in turn shipped back to England. Tensions between local authorities and the English over the payment of taxes led to a short war in 1686. The English were briefly expelled, but after differences were patched up, Aurangzeb permitted them to return.

English success in India attracted rivals, including the Dutch, the Danes, and the French. The Dutch abandoned their interests to concentrate on the spice trade in the middle of the seventeenth century, but the French were more persistent and established their own factory on the east coast at Pondicherry, about one hundred miles south of Madras, as well as at Surat and in the Bay of Bengal. For a brief period, under the aggressive sponsorship of the ambitious empire builder Joseph François Dupleix, the French competed successfully with the British. Dupleix even captured the British fort of St. George at Madras in 1748. But the British were saved by the military genius of Sir Robert Clive, an aggressive British administrator and empire builder who eventually became the chief representative of the East India Company in the subcontinent. The British were aided as well by the refusal of the French government to provide financial support for Dupleix's efforts in far-off India. Dupleix was recalled to France, and eventually the French were restricted to the fort at Pondicherry and a handful of small territories on the southeastern coast.

In the meantime, Clive began to consolidate British control in Bengal, where the local ruler had attacked Fort William and imprisoned the local British population in the infamous "Black Hole of Calcutta" (an underground prison for holding the prisoners, many of whom died in captivity). In 1757, a small British force numbering about 3,000 defeated a Mughal-led army over ten times that size in the Battle of Plassey. As part of the spoils of victory, the British East India Company exacted from the now-decrepit Mughal court the authority to collect taxes from extensive lands in the area surrounding Calcutta. Less than ten years later, British forces seized the reigning Mughal emperor in a skirmish at Buxar, and the British began to consolidate their economic and administrative control over Indian territory through the surrogate power of the now-powerless Mughal court.

To officials of the East India Company, the expansion of their authority into the interior of the subcontinent probably seemed like a simple commercial decision, a move designed to seek guaranteed revenues to pay for the increasingly expensive military operations in India. To historians, it marks a major step in the gradual transfer of all of the Indian subcontinent to the British East India Company and later, in 1858, to the British crown. The process was more haphazard than deliberate. Under a new governor general, Warren Hastings, the British attempted to consolidate areas under their control and defeat such rivals as the rising Hindu Marathas, who exploited the decline of the Mughals to expand their own empire in Maharashtra.

Britain's rise to power in India was not a chronicle of constant success. Officials of the East India Company, from the governor general on down, often combined arrogance and corruption with incompetence, alienating both their indigenous princely allies and the local population, who were taxed heavily to meet growing company expenses. Astute Indian commanders avoided pitched battles with the well-armed British troops, but harassed and ambushed them in the manner of guerrillas in our time. Said Haidar Ali, one of Britain's primary rivals for control in southern India:

> You will in time understand my mode of warfare. Shall I risk my cavalry which cost a thousand rupees each horse, against your cannon ball which cost two pice? No! I will march your troops until their legs swell to the size of their bodies. You shall not have a blade of grass, nor a drop of water. I will hear of you every time your drum beats, but you shall not know where I am once a month. I will give your army battle, but it must be when I please, and not when you choose.[5]

Unfortunately for India, not all its commanders were as astute as Haidar Ali. In the last years of the eighteenth century, when the East India Company's authority came into the capable hands of Lord Cornwallis and his successor Lord Mornington, the future marquess of Wellesley, the stage was set for the final consolidation of British rule over the subcontinent.

The immediate impact of these developments was felt mainly along the coast, where Europeans began to establish forts and trading centers to serve their needs in the region. The land around the future city of Madras was leased to the British in 1639, and a major metropolis came to surround the original settlement at Fort St. George. A similar process took place at Fort William (the future Calcutta) in the Bay of Bengal and at Bombay on the west coast. Bombay had been ceded to England by the Portuguese in 1662 as a dowry for the marriage of Princess Catherine of Braganza to King Charles II of England, who then leased the land to the East India Company for the nominal sum of ten pounds a year.

During the eighteenth century, the pattern began to change, as the British moved inland from the great coastal cities. Their original motivation was to obtain access to tax revenues from the land to pay for the company's military and administrative expenses, but British expansion greatly enriched individual merchants and British officials, who were able to squeeze money from local rulers by selling trade privileges.

The company's takeover of vast landholdings, notably in the eastern Indian states of Orissa and Bengal, may have been a windfall for enterprising British officials, but it was a disaster for the Indian economy. In the first place, it resulted in the transfer of capital from the hands of the local Indian aristocracy to company officials, most of whom sent their profits back to Britain. Second, it hastened the destruction of once-healthy local industries, because British goods such as machine-made textiles were imported duty-free into India to compete against local products.

Finally, British expansion hurt the peasants. As the British took over the administration of the land tax, they also applied British law, according to which the lands of those unable to pay the tax could be confiscated. As a

Map 16.4 India in 1805.

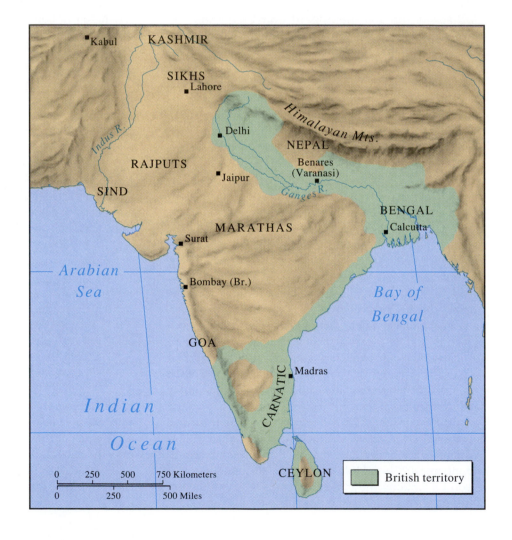

result, many peasants were impoverished, particularly in cases where local cottage industries had also been destroyed by British imports. In the 1770s, a series of massive famines led to the death of an estimated one-third of the population in the areas under company administration. The British government attempted to resolve the problem by assigning tax lands to the local revenue collectors (*zamindars*) in the hope of transforming them into English-style rural gentry, but many collectors themselves fell into bankruptcy and sold their lands to absentee bankers while the now-landless peasants remained in abject poverty. It was hardly an auspicious beginning to "civilized" British rule.

Society and Culture under the Mughals

The Mughals were the last of the great traditional Indian dynasties. Like so many of their predecessors since the fall of the Guptas nearly a thousand years before, the Mughals were Muslims. But to their credit, the best Mughal rulers did not simply impose Islamic institutions and beliefs on a predominantly Hindu population, but combined Muslim with Hindu and even Persian concepts and cultural values in a unique social and cultural synthesis that still today seems to epitomize the greatness of Indian civilization.

DAILY LIFE

Whether Mughal rule had much effect on the lives of ordinary Indians seems somewhat problematic. The treatment of women is a good example. Women had traditionally played an active role in Mongol tribal society—many actually fought on the battlefield alongside the men—and Babur and his successors often relied on the women in their families for political advice. Women from aristocratic families were often awarded honorific titles, received salaries, and were permitted to own land and engage in business. Women at court sometimes received an education, and Emperor Akbar reportedly established a girls' school at Fatehpur Sikri to provide teachers for his own daughters. Aristocratic women often expressed their creative talents by writing poetry, painting, or playing music.

To a certain degree, these Mughal attitudes toward women may have had an impact on Indian society. Women were allowed to inherit land, and some even possessed *zamindar* rights. Women from mercantile castes sometimes took an active role in business activities. At the same time, however, as Muslims, the Mughals subjected women to certain disabilities under Islamic law.

On the whole, these Mughal practices coincided with and even accentuated existing tendencies in Indian society. The Muslim practice of isolating women and preventing them from associating with men outside the home (*purdah*) was adopted by many upper-class Hindus as a means of enhancing their status or protecting their women from unwelcome advances by Muslims in positions of authority. In other ways, Hindu practices continued unabated. The custom of *sati* continued to be practiced despite efforts by the Mughals to abolish it, and child marriage (most women were betrothed before the age of ten) remained common. Women were still instructed to obey their husbands without question and to remain chaste. Maratha rulers attempted to discourage the rural tradition of arranging expensive wedding ceremonies and tried to extend the legal rights of widows, but such efforts had little effect in the countryside.

Then again, Hindus sometimes attempted to defend themselves and their religious practices against the efforts of some Mughal monarchs to impose the Islamic religion and Islamic mores on the indigenous population.

♦ **The Palace of the Winds at Jaipur.** Built by the maharaja of Jaipur in 1799, this imposing building, part of a palace complex, is today actually only a facade. Behind the intricate pink sandstone window screens, the women of the palace were able to observe city life while at the same time remaining invisible to prying eyes.

➤ A Description of Hindustan ➤

Although the founding Mughal emperor Babur spent much of his life conquering North India, he was evidently not much impressed by the land and its people. Here, in a short excerpt from his Memoirs, *he expresses contempt for the people of Hindustan and waxes nostalgic about the land of his birth in the mountains far to the north.*

Babur, *Memoirs*

Hindustân is a country which has few pleasures to recommend it. The people are not handsome. They have no idea of the charms of friendly society, of frankly mixing together, or familiar intercourse. They have no genius, no comprehension of mind, no politeness of manner, no kindness or fellow-feeling, no ingenuity or mechanical invention in planning or executing their handicraft works, no skill or knowledge in design or architecture; they have no horses, no good flesh, no grapes or muskmelons, no good fruits, no ice or cold water, no good food or bread in their bazaars, no baths or colleges, no candles, no torches, not a candlestick. . . . Beside their rivers and standing waters, they have some running water in their ravines and hollows; they have no aqueducts nor canals in their gardens or palaces. In their buildings they study neither elegance nor climate, appearance nor regularity. . . . The chief excellency of Hindustân is, that it is a large country and has abundance of gold and silver. The climate during the rains is very pleasant. On some days it rains ten, fifteen, and even twenty times. During the rainy season inundations come pouring down all at once, and form rivers, even in places where at other times there is no water. While the rains continue on the ground, the air is singularly delightful, insomuch that nothing can surpass its soft and agreeable temperature. Its defect is, that the air is rather moist and damp. During the rainy season you cannot shoot even with the bow of our country and it becomes quite useless. Nor is it the bow alone that becomes useless: the coats of mail, books, clothes and furniture all feel the bad effects of the moisture. Their houses too, suffer from not being substantially built. There is pleasant enough weather in the winter and summer, as well as in the rainy season; but then the north wind always blows, and there is an excessive quantity of earth and dust flying about. When the rains are at hand, this wind blows five or six times with excessive violence, and such a quantity of dust flies about that you cannot see one another. They call this an *andhi* [storm or tempest]. It gets warm during Taurus and Gemini, but not so warm as to become intolerable. The heat cannot be compared to the heats of Balkh and Kandahar. It is not half so warm as in these places. Another convenience of Hindustân is that the workmen of every profession and trade are innumerable and without end. For any work, or any employment, there is always a set ready, to whom the same employment and trade have descended from father to son for ages.

In some cases, despite official prohibitions Hindu men forcibly married Muslim women and then converted them to the native faith, while converts to Islam normally lost all of their inheritance rights within the Indian family. Government orders to destroy Hindu temples were often ignored by local officials, sometimes as the result of bribery or intimidation. Sometimes Indian practices had an influence on the Mughal elites. Although Babur had expressed contempt for the society that he had conquered (see the box above), his successors clearly did not agree. Many Mughal chieftains married Indian women and adopted Indian forms of dress.

Long-term stability led to increasing commercialization and the spread of wealth to new groups within Indian society. The Mughal era saw the emergence of an affluent landed gentry and a prosperous merchant class.

Members of prestigious castes from the pre-Mughal period reaped many of the benefits of the increasing wealth, but there is evidence that some of these changes transcended caste boundaries and led to the emergence of new groups who achieved status and wealth on the basis of economic achievement rather than traditional kinship ties. During the late eighteenth century, this economic prosperity was shaken by the decline of the Mughal Empire and the increasing European presence. But many prominent Indians reacted by establishing commercial relationships with the foreigners. For a time, that relationship often worked to the Indians' benefit. Later, as we shall see, they would have cause to regret the arrangement.

Because so little about the daily lives of ordinary Indians is recorded in official documents, most of what we know comes from the observations of foreign visitors (see the box on p. 600). Normally, however, foreigners were more familiar with city life than with rural conditions and generally had little contact with the common people. Life in the villages, therefore, has been left largely unrecorded except for observations such as the following, which might still describe much of rural India today:

> Their houses are built of mud with thatched roofs. Furniture there is little or none except some earthenware pots to hold water and for cooking and two beds, one for the man, the other for his wife; their bed cloths are scanty, merely a sheet or perhaps two, serving as under- and over-sheet. This is sufficient for the hot weather, but the bitter cold nights are miserable indeed, and they try to keep warm over little cow-dung fires.[6]

MUGHAL CULTURE

The era of the Mughals was one of synthesis in culture as well as in politics and religion. The Mughals combined Islamic themes with Persian and indigenous motifs to produce a unique style that enriched and embellished Indian art and culture.

Undoubtedly, their most visible achievement was in architecture. Here the Mughals integrated Persian and Indian styles in a new and sometimes breathtakingly beautiful form best symbolized by the Taj Mahal, built by the emperor Shah Jahan in the mid-seventeenth century. Although the human and economic cost of the Taj tar-nishes the romantic legend of its construction, there is no denying the beauty of the building. It had evolved from a style that originated several decades earlier with the tomb of Humayun, which was built by his widow in Agra in 1565 during the reign of Akbar.

Humayun's mausoleum had combined Persian and Islamic motifs in a square building finished in red sandstone and topped with a dome. The style was repeated in a number of other buildings erected throughout the empire, but the Taj brought the style to perfection. Working with a model created by his Persian architect, Shah Jahan raised the dome and replaced the red sandstone with brilliant white marble. The entire exterior and interior surface is decorated with cut stone geometrical patterns, delicate black stone tracery, or intricate inlay of colored precious stones in floral and Koranic arabesques. The technique of creating dazzling floral mosaics of lapis lazuli, malachite, carnelian, turquoise, and mother of pearl may have been introduced by Italian artists at the Mughal court. The effect is one of monumental size, near blinding brilliance, and delicate lightness. Shah Jahan had intended to erect a similar building in black marble across the river for his own remains, but the plans were abandoned after he was deposed by his son Aurangzeb. Shah Jahan spent his last years imprisoned in a room in the Red Fort at Agra; from his windows, he could see the beautiful memorial to his beloved wife.

The Taj was by no means the only magnificent building erected during the Mughal era. Akbar, who, in the

◆ **The Taj Mahal.** The Taj Mahal was completed in 1653 by Emperor Shah Jahan as a tomb to glorify his beloved wife's memory. Raised on a marble platform above the Jumna River, the Taj is dramatically framed by contrasting twin red sandstone mosques, magnificent gardens, and a long reflecting pool that mirrors and magnifies its beauty. The effect is one of monumental size, near blinding brilliance, and delicate lightness.

❧ The Uses of the Coconut ❧

The Portuguese traveler Duarte Barbosa was one of the most astute observers of the lands that he visited as an official of the Portuguese crown in the early sixteenth century. Here, in a section devoted to the lands of Malabar, on the southwestern coast of India, he writes of the many uses that the local population made of the coconut palm. Many peoples of Asia still use the coconut in similar ways in our own day.

Duarte Barbosa, *The Book of Duarte Barbosa*

This land, or rather the whole land of Malabar, is covered along the strand with palm-trees as high as lofty cypresses, the trunk whereof is extremely clean and smooth, and on the top a crown of branches among which grows a great fruit which they call *cocos*, it is a fruit of which they make great profit, and whereof they load many cargoes yearly. They bear their fruit every year without fail, never either more or less. All the folk of Malabar have these palms, and by their means they are free from any dearth, even though other food be lacking, for they produce ten or twelve things all very needful for the service of man, by which they help and profit themselves greatly, and everything is produced in every month of the year.

In the first place they produce these cocos, a very sweet and grateful fruit when green; from them is drawn milk like that of almonds, and each one when green, has within it a pint of a fresh and pleasant water, better than that from a spring. When they are dry this same water thickens within them into a white fruit as large as an apple which also is very sweet and dainty. The coco itself after being dried is eaten, and from it they get much oil by pressing it, as we do. And from the shell which they have close to the kernel is made charcoal for the goldsmiths who work with no other kind. And from the outer husk which throws out certain threads, they make all the cord which they use, a great article of trade in many parts. And from the sap of the tree itself they extract a *must*, from which they make wine, or properly speaking a strong water, and that in such abundance that many shops are laden with it, for export. From this same *must* they make very good vinegar, and also a sugar of extreme sweetness which is much sought after in India. From the leaf of the tree they make many things, in accordance with the size of the branch. They thatch the houses with them, for as I have said above, no house is roofed with tiles, save the temples or the palaces; all others are thatched with palm-leaves. From the same tree they get timber for their houses and firewood as well, and all this in such abundance that ships take in cargoes thereof for export.

Other palm-trees there are of a lower kind whence they get the leaves on which the Heathen write; it serves as paper. There are other very slender palms the trunks of which are of extreme height and smoothness; these bear a fruit as large as walnuts which they call Areca, which they eat with betel. Among them it is held in high esteem. It is very ugly and disagreeable in taste.

words of a contemporary, "dresses the work of his mind and heart in the garment of stone and clay," was the first of the great Mughal builders. His first palace at Agra, known as the Red Fort, was begun in 1565, and its enclosed buildings of various styles sat inside massive walls of red sandstone. A few years later, he ordered the construction of a new palace at Fatehpur Sikri, twenty-six miles west of Agra. The new palace was built in honor of a Sufi mystic who had correctly forecast the birth of a son to the emperor. In gratitude, Akbar decided to build a new capital city and palace on the site of the mystic's home in the village of Sikri. Over a period of fifteen years, from 1571 to 1586, a magnificent new city in red sandstone was constructed. Unfortunately, it was soon discovered that water resources in the area were inadequate, and shortly before completion the city was abandoned and now stands almost untouched, although it is a popular destination for tourists and pilgrims.

The other major artistic achievement of the Mughal period was painting. Painting had never been one of the great attainments of Indian culture due in part to a technological difficulty. Paper was not introduced to India from Persia until the latter part of the fourteenth century, so traditionally painting had been done on palm leaves, which had severely hampered artistic creativity. By the fifteenth century, Indian painting had made the transition from palm leaf to paper, and the new medium eventually stimulated a burst of creativity, particularly in

◆ **Fatehpur Sikri.** In gratitude to a Sufi mystic who had correctly forecast the birth of his son, Akbar chose the mystic's village of Sikri as the site for his new palace and capital city. Completed at great speed in 1586, the splendid city, which was built of red sandstone and measured two miles long and one mile wide, was soon abandoned because of an inadequate water supply. Its elaborate palaces, mosque, reflecting pools and courtyards, harems, and impressive Gate of Victory all symbolize the elegance and greatness of Akbar's reign.

the genre of miniatures, or book illustrations.

As in so many other areas of endeavor, painting in Mughal India resulted from the blending of two cultures. While living in exile, Emperor Humayun had learned to admire Persian miniatures. On his return to India in 1555, he invited two Persian masters to live in his palace and introduce the technique to his adopted land. His successor Akbar appreciated the new style and popularized it with his patronage. He established a state workshop at Fatehpur Sikri for two hundred artists, mostly Hindus, who worked under the guidance of the Persian masters to create the Mughal school of painting.

The "Akbar style" combined Persian with Indian motifs, such as the use of extended space and the portrayal of physical human action, characteristics not usually seen in Persian art. Akbar also apparently encouraged the imitation of European art forms, including the portrayal of Christian subjects, the use of perspective, lifelike portraits, and the shading of colors in the Renaissance style. The depiction of the human figure in Mughal painting outraged orthodox Muslims at court, but Akbar argued that the painter, "in sketching anything that has life . . . must come to feel that he cannot bestow individuality upon his work, and is thus forced to think of God, the Giver of Life, and will thus increase in knowledge."[7]

Essentially, painting during Akbar's reign followed the trend toward realism and historical narrative that had developed in Ottoman Turkey. For example, Akbar had the illustrated *Book of Akbar* made to record his military exploits and court activities. Many of these paintings of Akbar's life portray him in action in his real world. After his death, his son and grandson continued the patronage of the arts. Jahangir continued to promote the chronicle of the times in painting and also favored a new emphasis on portraiture. Shah Jahan also favored portraiture but concentrated on architecture. After he reduced the size of the state workshop, many of the painters found employment at minor courts.

The Mughal emperors were zealous patrons of the arts and made India the Mecca for painters, poets, and artisans from as far away as the Mediterranean. Apparently, the generosity of the Mughals made it difficult to refuse a trip to India for fame and fortune. It is said that they would reward a poet with his weight in gold.

The development of literature was held back by the absence of printing, which was not introduced until the end of the Mughal era. Literary works were inscribed by calligraphers, and one historian has estimated that the library of Agra contained more than 24,000 volumes. Poetry, in particular, flourished under the Mughals, who established poet laureates at court. Poems were written in the Persian style and in the Persian language. In fact, Persian became the official language of the court until the sack of Delhi in 1739. At the time, the Indians' anger at their conquerors led them to adopt Urdu as the new language for the court and for poetry. By that time, Indian verse on the Persian model had already lost its original vitality and simplicity and had become more artificial in the manner of court literature everywhere.

Another aspect of the long Mughal reign was a Hindu revival of devotional literature, much of it dedicated to Krishna and Rama. Devotional literature expressed itself in the cult of Rama and Sita. The retelling of the Ramayana in the vernacular, beginning in the southern Tamil languages in the eleventh century and spreading slowly northward, culminated in the sixteenth-century Hindi version by the great poet Tulsidas (1532–1623). His *Ramcaritmanas* presents the devotional story with a deified Rama and Sita. No longer a human with divine attributes, Rama is now a god. Sita also is divine, remaining pure as Rama's necessary female component even while she is held captive by the villainous Ravana.

Tulsidas's genius was in combining the conflicting cults of Vishnu and Siva into a unified and overwhelming love for the divine, which he expressed in some of the most moving of all Indian poetry. His language was majestic and innovative; he borrowed from Sanskrit as well as from Persian and Arabic and grounded the whole in everyday village speech. The *Ramcaritmanas*, called by Mahatma Gandhi India's "greatest book in all devotional literature," has eclipsed its 2,000-year-old Sanskrit ancestor in popularity and even became the basis of an Indian television series in the late 1980s. Tulsidas's poetry continues to be performed at festivals and temples and in private homes, another testament to its enduring popularity.

The ecstatic Krishna cult found artistic expression in the school of Rajasthani painting that developed with the weakening of the Mughal hold on the arts. During Aurangzeb's reign, court painting was virtually abolished as many Muslims denounced any interpretation of the human form as idolatry. Artists fled Delhi to the numerous small Hindu courts, especially in the foothills of the Himalayas. There, until the domination of the British, these Rajasthani artists created idealized and romantic paintings of Krishna filled with Hindu symbolism. Whereas Mughal art had expressed realism and action, these Rajasthani paintings presented a dreamy and static escapism. Often they were accompanied by poetry and music in a combined effort to express one of the thirty-six fundamental *ragas*, or modes of North Indian art. These modes normally portrayed one aspect of a love relationship such as unrequited love, despair from separation, or anticipation of reunion.

Conclusion

The three empires that we have discussed in this chapter exhibit a number of striking similarities. First of all, they were, of course, Muslim in their religious affiliation, although the Safavids were Shi'ite rather than Sunni in persuasion, a distinction that, as we have seen, often led to mutual tensions and conflict. More importantly, perhaps, they were all nomadic in origin, and the political and social institutions that they adopted carried the imprint of their pre-imperial past. Once they achieved imperial power, however, all three ruling dynasties displayed an impressive capacity to administer a large empire and brought a degree of stability to peoples who had all too often lived in conditions of internal division and war.

Another similarity that many historians have pointed out is that in all three cases, the mastery of the techniques of modern warfare, including the use of firearms, played a central role in the empires' ability to overcome their rivals and rise to regional hegemony. Some scholars, following historian Marshall Hodgson, have therefore labeled them "gunpowder empires" in the belief that technical prowess in the art of warfare was a key element in their success. While that is undoubtedly true, we should not forget that other factors, such as dynamic leadership, political acumen, and the possession of an ardent following motivated by religious zeal, were equally if not more important in their drive to power and ability to retain it. Weapons by themselves do not an empire make.

The rise of these powerful Muslim states coincided with the opening period of European expansion at the end of the fifteenth and the beginning of the sixteenth century. The military and political talents of these empires helped to protect much of the Muslim world from the resurgent forces of Christianity—Islam's bitter enemy. To the contrary, the Ottoman Turks carried their empire into the heart of Christian Europe and briefly reached the gates of the great city of Vienna. By the end of the eighteenth century, however, the Safavid dynasty had collapsed while the powerful Mughal Empire was in a state of virtual collapse. Only the Ottoman Empire was still a functioning enterprise. Yet it too had lost much of its early expansionistic vigor and was showing signs of internal decay.

The reasons for the decline of these empires have inspired considerable debate among historians. One factor was undoubtedly the expansion of European power into the Indian Ocean and the Middle East. But internal causes were probably more important in the long run. All three empires experienced growing factionalism within the ruling elite, incompetence within the palace, and the emergence of divisive forces in the empire at large—factors that have marked the passing of traditional empires since early times. Climatic change (the region was reportedly hotter and drier after the beginning of the seventeenth century) may have been a hidden reason. Paradoxically, one of the greatest strengths of these empires—their mastery of gunpowder—may have simultaneously been a serious weakness in that it allowed them to develop a complacent sense of security. With little incentive to turn their attention to new developments in science and technology, they were increasingly vulnerable to attack by the advanced nations of the West. The weakening of the "gunpowder empires" created a political vacuum into which the dynamic and competitive forces of European capitalism were quick to enter.

The gunpowder empires, however, were not the only states in the Old World that were able to resist the first outward thrust of European expansion. Further to the east, the mature civilizations in China and Japan successfully faced a similar challenge from Western merchants and missionaries. Unlike their counterparts in South Asia and the Middle East, as the nineteenth century dawned, they continued to thrive.

CHAPTER NOTES

1. Quoted in Roger Savory, *Iran under the Safavids* (Cambridge, 1980), p. 179.
2. Vincent A. Smith, *The Oxford History of India* (Oxford, 1967), p. 341.
3. Quoted in Michael Edwardes, *A History of India: From the Earliest Times to the Present Day* (London, 1961), p. 188.
4. Quoted in Smith, *The Oxford History of India*, p. 416.
5. Quoted in Edwardes, *A History of India*, p. 220.
6. Ibid., p. 187.
7. Quoted in Roy C. Craven, *Indian Art: A Concise History* (New York, 1976), p. 205.

SUGGESTED READINGS

The most complete general survey of the Ottoman Empire is S. J. Shaw, *History of the Ottoman Empire and Modern Turkey* (Cambridge, 1976). Volume 2 of the two-volume set deals with the period up to the beginning of the nineteenth century. Shaw is difficult reading, but informative on administrative matters. A more readable, if less definitive account is Lord Kinross, *The Ottoman Centuries: The Rise and Fall of the Ottoman Empire* (New York, 1977), which is larded with human interest stories. Also of interest is B. Lewis, *Istanbul and the Civilization of the Ottoman Empire* (Norman, Okla., 1963), written by a veteran Arabist.

For a dramatic account of the conquest of Constantinople in 1453, see S. Runciman, *The Fall of Constantinople, 1453* (Cambridge, 1965). The life of Mehmet II is chronicled in F. Babinger, *Mehmed the Conqueror and His Time*, trans. R. Manheim (Princeton, N.J., 1979). On Suleyman the Magnificent, see R. Merriman, *Suleiman the Magnificent, 1520–1566* (Cambridge, 1944). On the Safavids, see R. M. Savory, *Iran under the Safavids* (Cambridge, 1980) and E. B. Monshi, *History of Shah Abbas the Great*, 2 vols. (Boulder, Colo., 1978).

For a concise introduction to Ottoman art, consult D. T. Rice, *Islamic Art* (London, 1975) and E. J. Grube, *The World of Islam* (New York, 1967). For Ottoman architecture, see G. Michell, ed., *Architecture of the Islamic World* (London, 1978). For an interesting discussion of the minor military arts of the Ottomans, see Z. Zygulski, Jr., *Ottoman Art in the Service of the Empire* (New York, 1992).

For an overview of the Mughal era, see such standard works as S. Wolpert, *New History of India* (New York, 1989) and the more detailed V. A. Smith, *The Oxford History of India* (Oxford, 1967). A more dramatic account for the general reader is W. Hansen, *The Peacock Throne: The Drama of Mogul India* (New York, 1972).

There are a number of specialized works on various aspects of the period. For a treatment of the Mughal era in the context of Islamic rule in India, see S. M. Ikram, *Muslim Civilization in India* (New York, 1964). The concept of "gunpowder empires" is persuasively analyzed in D. E. Streusand, *The Formation of the Mughal Empire* (Delhi, 1989). Economic issues predominate in much of the recent scholarship. For example, S. Subrahmanyan, *The Political Economy of Commerce: Southern India, 1500–1650* (Cambridge, 1990) focuses on the interaction between internal and external trade in South India during the early stages of the period. For a persuasive view of the relationship between economic changes and the extension of British rule, see C. A. Bayly, *Indian Society and the Making of the British Empire* (Cambridge, 1988). Finally, K. N. Chaudhuri, *Trade and Civilization in the Indian Ocean: An Economic History from the Rise of Islam to 1750* (Cambridge, 1985) views Indian commerce in the perspective of the regional trade network throughout the Indian Ocean.

Personal accounts of the period are numerous, although most are by European visitors. For some examples, see R. C. Temple, ed., *The Travels of Peter Mundy, in Europe and Asia, 1608–1667* (Cambridge,

1907–1936); J. B. Tavernier, *Travels in India* (London, 1925); T. Roe, *The Embassy of Sir Thomas Roe, 1615–1619* (London, 1926); and F. Bernier, *Travels in the Mogul Empire, A.D. 1656–1668* (London, 1968). For an inside look, see J. Leyden and W. Erskine, trans., *Memoirs of Zehir-ed-Din Muhammad Babur* (London, 1921). Excerpts from this and other works cited here can be found in M. Edwardes, *A History of India: From the Earliest Times to the Present Day* (London, 1961); J. Kritzeck, *Anthology of Islamic Literature* (New York, 1964); and J. H. Parry, ed., *The European Reconnaissance: Selected Documents* (New York, 1968).

Standard works on Mughal art and culture include A. L. Basham, *A Cultural History of India* (Oxford, 1975); E. C. Dimock, *The Literature of India: An Introduction* (Chicago, 1974); and R. C. Craven, *Indian Art: A Concise History* (New York, 1976).

For treatments of all three Muslim empires in a comparative context, see J. J. Kissling et al., *The Last Great Muslim Empires* (Princeton, N.J., 1996) and M. G. S. Hodgson, *Rethinking World History: Essays on Europe, Islam, and World History* (Cambridge, 1993).

CHAPTER

17

The East Asian World

In December 1717, the emperor Kangxi returned from a hunting trip north of the Great Wall and began to suffer from dizzy spells. Conscious of his approaching date with mortality—he was now nearly seventy years of age—the emperor called together his sons and leading government officials in the imperial palace and issued the following edict:

> The rulers of the past all took reverence for Heaven's laws and reverence for their ancestors as the fundamental way in ruling the country. To be sincere in reverence for Heaven and ancestors entails the following: Be kind to men from afar and keep the able ones near, nourish the people, think of the profit of all as being the real profit and the mind of the whole country as being the real mind, be considerate to officials and act as the father to the people, protect the state before danger comes and govern well before there is any disturbance, be always diligent and always careful, and maintain the balance between leniency and strictness, between principle and expediency, so that long-range plans can be made for the country: That's all there is to it.[1]

As a primer for political leadership, the emperor's edict reflects the genius of Confucian philosophy at its best and has a timeless quality that applies to our age as well as to the Golden Age of the Qing dynasty.

Kangxi reigned during one of the most glorious eras in the long history of China. Under the Ming (1369–1644) and the early Qing (1644–1911) dynasties, the empire expanded its borders to a degree not seen since the Han and the Tang. Chinese culture was the envy of its neighbors and earned the admiration of many European visitors, including Jesuit priests and Enlightenment philosophes.

On the surface, China appeared to be an unchanging society patterned after the Confucian

Phonetic alphabet for
Korean language devised

Manchus seize China

Reign of Qianlong

Reign of Kangxi

White Lotus Rebellion

Rule of Oda Nobunaga   Rule of Tokugawa Ieyasu

European post es-
tablished in Korea

Rule of Toyotomi Hideyoshi   Christian uprising suppressed

Portuguese
arrive in
South China

Portuguese sailors
land in Japan

Christian missionaries
expelled from Japan

First English trading
post at Canton

vision of a "Golden Age" in the remote past. This indeed was the image presented by China's rulers, who referred constantly to tradition as a model for imperial institutions and cultural values. In actuality, however, China was changing—and rather rapidly. Although few observers could have been aware of it at the time, Confucian precepts were increasingly irrelevant in a society that was becoming ever more complex.

A similar process was underway in neighboring Japan. A vigorous new shogunate called the Tokugawa rose to power in the early seventeenth century and managed to revitalize the traditional system in a somewhat more centralized form that enabled it to survive for another two hundred and fifty years. But major structural changes were taking place in Japanese society, and by the nineteenth century, tensions were growing as the gap between theory and reality widened.

One of the many factors involved in the quickening pace of change in both countries was contact with the West, which began with the arrival of Portuguese ships in Chinese and Japanese ports in the first half of the sixteenth century.

The Ming and the Tokugawa initially opened their doors to European trade and missionary activity. Later, however, Chinese and Japanese rulers became concerned at the corrosive effects of Western ideas and practices and attempted to protect their traditional societies from external intrusion. But neither could forever resist the importunities of Western trading nations, nor could they arrest the pace of change taking place within. When the doors to the West were finally reopened in the mid-nineteenth century, both societies were ripe for radical change.

China at Its Apex

In 1514, a Portuguese fleet dropped anchor off the coast of China, just south of the Pearl River estuary and the former British crown colony of Hong Kong. It was the first direct contact between the Chinese Empire and the West since the voyages of Marco Polo two centuries earlier, and it opened an era that would eventually change the face of China and, indeed, all of Asia.

At the time, however, the Chinese would have thought it preposterous that the arrival of a small handful of Portuguese sailing ships could have great historical significance. Whereas Portugal was merely one of a number of small European nations on the western edge of the Eurasian continent, an area only recently removed from the Middle Ages, China appeared to be at the zenith of

The Tribute System in Action

In 1793, the British emissary Lord Macartney visited the Qing Empire to request the opening of formal diplomatic and trading relations between his country and China. Emperor Qianlong's reply, addressed to King George III of England, illustrates how the imperial court in Beijing viewed the world. King George could not have been pleased. The document provides a good example of the complacency with which the Celestial Empire viewed the world beyond its borders.

A Decree of Emperor Qianlong

An Imperial Edict to the King of England: You, O King, are so inclined toward our civilization that you have sent a special envoy across the seas to bring to our Court your memorial of congratulations on the occasion of my birthday and to present your native products as an expression of your thoughtfulness. On perusing your memorial, so simply worded and sincerely conceived, I am impressed by your genuine respectfulness and friendliness and greatly pleased.

As to the request made in your memorial, O King, to send one of your nationals to stay at the Celestial Court to take care of your country's trade with China, this is not in harmony with the state system of our dynasty and will definitely not be permitted. Traditionally people of the European nations who wished to render some service under the Celestial Court have been permitted to come to the capital. But after their arrival they are obliged to wear Chinese court costumes, are placed in a certain residence and are never allowed to return to their own countries. This is the established rule of the Celestial Dynasty with which presumably you, O King, are familiar. Now you, O King, wish to send one of your nationals to live in the capital, but he is not like the Europeans, who come to Peking as Chinese employees, live there and never return home again, nor can he be allowed to go and come and maintain any correspondence. This is indeed a useless undertaking.

Moreover the territory under the control of the Celestial Court is very large and wide. There are well-established regulations governing tributary envoys from the outer states to Peking, giving them provisions (of food and traveling expenses) by our post-houses and limiting their going and coming. There has never been a precedent for letting them do whatever they like. Now if you, O King, wish to have a representative in Peking, his language will be unintelligible and his dress different from the regulations; there is no place to accommodate him. . . .

The Celestial Court has pacified and possessed the territory within the four seas. Its sole aim is to do its utmost to achieve good government and to manage political affairs, attaching no value to strange jewels and precious objects. The various articles presented by you, O King, this time are accepted by my special order to the office in charge of such functions in consideration of the offerings having come from a long distance with sincere good wishes. As a matter of fact, the virtue and prestige of the Celestial Dynasty having spread far and wide, the kings of the myriad nations come by land and sea with all sorts of precious things. Consequently there is nothing we lack, as your principal envoy and others have themselves observed. We have never set much store on strange or ingenious objects, nor do we need any more of your country's manufactures. . . .

---

its development as the most magnificent and culturally advanced civilization on the face of the earth. An empire that stretched from the steppes of Central Asia to the China Sea, from the Gobi Desert to the tropical rain forests of Southeast Asia, China dominated all of the eastern rim of the Eurasian landmass and already had a history as an organized society that stretched back well over three thousand years to the first emergence of organized states during the Shang dynasty. From the lofty perspective of the imperial throne in Beijing (also written Peking), the Europeans could only have seemed like an unusually exotic form of barbarian to be placed within the familiar framework of the tributary system, the hierarchical arrangement that defined the rulers of all other countries as "younger brothers" of the Son of Heaven (see the box above).

From the Ming to the Qing

The magnificence of China had originally been reported to Europe by the Venetian adventurer Marco Polo, who visited Beijing during the reign of Khubilai Khan, the great Mongol ruler. By the time the Portuguese fleet arrived off the coast of China, of course, the Mongol Empire had long since disappeared. It had gradually weakened after the death of Khubilai Khan and was finally overthrown in 1368 by a massive peasant rebellion under the leadership of Zhu Yuanzhang who had declared himself the founding emperor of a new Ming (Bright) dynasty (see Chapter 10). The Ming inaugurated a new era of greatness in Chinese history. Under a series of strong rulers, China extended its rule into Mongolia and Central Asia. The Ming even briefly reconquered Vietnam, which, after a thousand years of Chinese rule, had reclaimed its independence following the collapse of the Tang dynasty in the tenth century. Along the northern frontier, the Emperor Yongle (Yung Lo) strengthened the Great Wall and pacified the nomadic tribesmen who had troubled China in previous centuries. A tributary relationship was established with the Yi dynasty in Korea, which attempted to reorganize Korean society along the Confucian model, complete with Chinese administrative techniques and the civil service examinations.

The internal achievements of the Ming were equally impressive. When the Ming dynasty replaced the Mongols in the fourteenth century, its rulers turned to traditional Confucian institutions as a means of ruling their vast empire. These included the six ministries at the apex of the bureaucracy, the use of the civil service examinations to select members of the bureaucracy, and the division of the empire into provinces, districts, and counties. As before, Chinese villages were relatively autonomous, and local councils of elders continued to be responsible for adjudicating disputes, initiating local construction and irrigation projects, mustering a militia, and assessing and collecting taxes.

In some cases, the Ming institutionalized principles that had existed in various stages of development for centuries. For example, they formalized the civil service examination system, providing for three levels of examinations for entrance into the bureaucracy. During the late Ming, each year about two hundred candidates on average were successful in these imperial examinations and became eligible for high positions in the central or local administration.

The Ming also sought to broaden the social base of the bureaucracy by establishing a system of government-supported schools at the county level and offering scholarships to young and deserving candidates. In some cases, graduates from these schools entered the bureaucracy directly, but most official positions were filled by successful candidates in the civil service examinations.

The society that was governed by this vast hierarchy

◆ **World Class China Ware.** Ming porcelain was noted throughout the world for its delicate blue and white floral decorations. The blue coloring was produced with cobalt that had originally been brought from the Middle East along the Silk Route. In the early seventeenth century, the first Ming ware arrived in Holland, where it was called "kraak" because it had been loaded on two Portuguese carracks seized by the Dutch fleet. It took Dutch artisans over a century to learn how to produce a porcelain as fine as the examples brought from China.

of officials was a far cry from the predominantly agrarian society that had been ruled by the Han and the Tang. In the burgeoning cities near the coast and along the rich Yangtze River valley, factories and workshops were vastly increasing the variety and output of their manufactured goods. The population had doubled, and new crops had been introduced, greatly expanding the agricultural economy of the empire.

In the early fifteenth century, a fleet of Chinese trading ships, at that time the largest vessels afloat, sailed through the Strait of Malacca and out into the Indian

◆ **The Potala Palace in Tibet.** Tibet was among the most distant appendages of the Qing Empire. Long an independent state, Tibet was peopled by a distant ethnic group who practiced a distinct form of Buddhism. The leading figure in Tibetan Buddhism was the Dalai Lama, who lived in this building, constructed in the seventeenth century in the capital of Lhasa.

Ocean; there they traveled as far west as the eastern coast of Africa, stopping on the way at ports in South Asia. Although China seemed about to become a direct and active participant in the vast trade network that extended from its shores to the Mediterranean Sea and the European coasts of the Atlantic Ocean, China's emergence as a major commercial and maritime power ceased almost as abruptly as it had begun. Bureaucratic infighting at court undermined the influence of those who favored the project, and in 1433 the policy was reversed. Although Chinese junks would continue to ply the South China Sea, they were privately owned and operated and would no longer sail into the open sea. An early European visitor reported that "no one sails the sea from north to south; it is prohibited by the king, in order that the country may not become known."[2]

Trade with the Middle East and the Mediterranean Sea via the Silk Road also began to decline during this period. Some scholars have attributed the decay of the caravan trade to the growth of maritime traffic brought about by the arrival of Westerners along the Chinese coast. But others ascribe it to growing political instability in Central Asia. After the fall of the empire of Tamerlane in the early fifteenth century, Kazakh and Uzbek warriors periodically raided caravans passing through the area and increased the cost of the goods being transported. Some commerce in horses, camels, porcelain, and textiles continued to take place, but increasingly goods moved by sea.

FIRST CONTACTS WITH THE WEST

It was in these circumstances that China's early acquaintance with the West began. The beginnings were seemingly innocuous. After their arrival in 1514, the Portuguese outraged Chinese officials with their bellicose and uncultured behavior and were eventually expelled from Canton. After further negotiations, however, the Portuguese were finally permitted to occupy the tiny territory of Macao, just south of the Pearl River estuary, as a base of operations, a foothold they would retain until the end of the twentieth century.

Initially, the arrival of the Portuguese did not have much impact on Chinese society. Direct trade between Europe and China was limited, and Portuguese ships became involved in the regional trade network, carrying silk to Japan in return for Japanese silver. Eventually, the Spanish also began to participate, using their possession in the Philippines as an anchor in the galleon trade between China and the great silver mines in the Americas.

More influential than trade, perhaps, were ideas. Accompanying European merchant ships on the long voyage to China were Christian missionaries. The Jesuits were among the most active and the most effective. Many of the early Jesuit missionaries to China were highly educated men who were familiar with European philosophical and scientific developments. Inventions such as the clock, the prism, and various astronomical and musical instruments impressed court officials, hitherto deeply imbued with a sense of the superiority of Chinese civilization, and helped Western ideas win acceptance at court. The Jesuits attempted to use this acceptance in their primary mission of inducing Chinese officials to promote Christianity. Recognizing the Chinese pride in their own culture, the Jesuits attempted to draw parallels between Christian and Confucian concepts (for example, they identified the Western concept of God with the Chinese character for Heaven) and to show the similarities between Christian morality and Confucian ethics. The Italian priest Matteo Ricci (1552–1610), who impressed Chinese officials with his scientific knowledge, described the Jesuit approach:

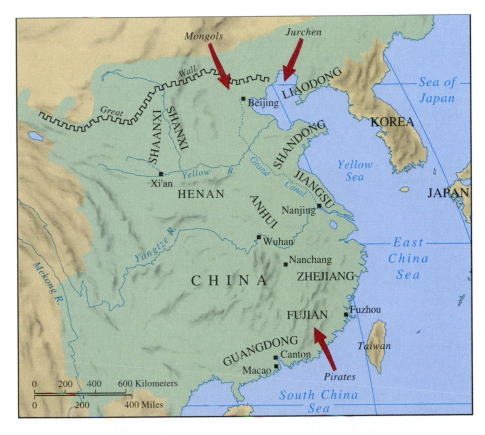

✕ **Map 17.1**   China and Its Enemies during the Late Ming Era.

In order that the appearance of a new religion might not arouse suspicion among the Chinese people, the Fathers did not speak openly about religious matters when they began to appear in public. What time was left to them, after paying their respects and civil compliments and courteously receiving their visitors, was spent in studying the language of the country, the methods of writing and the customs of the people. They did, however, endeavor to teach this pagan people in a more direct way, namely, by virtue of their example and by the sanctity of their lives. In this way they attempted to win the good will of the people and little by little, without affectation, to dispose their minds to receive what they could not be persuaded to accept by word of mouth, without endangering what had been thus far accomplished. . . . From the time of their entrance they wore the ordinary Chinese outer garment, which was somewhat similar to their own religious habits; a long robe reaching down to the heels and with very ample sleeves, which are much in favor with the Chinese.[3]

Both sides derived benefits from this exchange of cultural influence. An elderly Chinese scholar expressed his wonder at the miracle of eyeglasses in this following passage:

White glass from across the Western Seas
Is imported through Macao:
Fashioned into lenses big as coins,
They encompass the eyes in a double frame.
I put them on—it suddenly becomes clear;
I can see the very tips of things!
And read fineprint by the dim-lit window
Just like in my youth.[4]

For their part, Christian missionaries to the imperial court were very much impressed with many aspects of Chinese civilization, and reports of their experiences heightened European curiosity about this great society on the other side of the world (see the box on p. 613).

THE MING BROUGHT TO EARTH

The Ming, however, were not immune to the great cyclical pattern of Chinese history in which great dynasties experienced a period of prosperity and growth, but then gradually lost their internal vitality and declined. During the late sixteenth century, a series of weak rulers led to an era of corruption, concentration of land ownership, and ultimately to peasant rebellions and tribal unrest along the northern frontier. The inflow of vast amounts of foreign silver led to an alarming increase in inflation. Then the arrival of the English and the Dutch disrupted the silver trade; silver imports plummeted, severely straining the Chinese economy by raising the value of the metal relative to that of copper. Crop yields declined due to harsh weather—linked to the "Little Ice Age" of the early seventeenth century—and the resulting scarcity reduced the ability of the government to provide food in times of imminent starvation. High taxes, provoked in part by increased official corruption, led to peasant unrest and worker violence in urban areas. In the words of a folk song of the period, addressed to the "Lord of Heaven," the Ming dynasty was about to be brought down to earth:

Old skymaster,
You're getting on, your ears are deaf, your eyes are gone.
Can't see people, can't hear words.
Glory for those who kill and burn;
For those who fast and read the scriptures,
Starvation.
Fall down, old master sky, how can you be so high?
How can you be so high? Come down to earth.[5]

As always, internal problems were accompanied by unrest along the northern frontier. Following long precedent, the Ming had attempted to pacify the frontier tribes by forging alliances with them, arranging marriages between them and the local aristocracy, and granting trade privileges. One of the alliances was with the Manchus (also known as the Jurchen), the descendants of peoples who had briefly established a kingdom in North China during the early thirteenth century. The Manchus, a mixed agricultural and hunting people, lived northeast of the Great Wall in the area known today as Manchuria.

At first the Manchus were satisfied with consolidating their territory and made little effort to extend their rule south of the Great Wall. But during the first decades of the seventeenth century, the problems of the Ming dynasty began to come to a head. A major epidemic decimated the population in many areas of the country. According to an observer writing in the summer of 1643, in one major city "there were few signs of human life in the streets and all that was heard was the buzzing of flies."[6] The suffering brought on by the epidemic helped spark a vast peasant revolt led by Li Zicheng (Li Tzu-ch'eng, 1604–1651). Li was a postal worker in central China who had been dismissed from his job as part of a cost-saving measure by the imperial court, now increasingly preoccupied by tribal attacks along the frontier. In the 1630s, Li managed to extend the revolt throughout the country and finally occupied the capital of Beijing in 1644. The last Ming emperor committed suicide by hanging himself from a tree in the palace gardens.

The Art of Printing

Europeans obtained much of their early information about China from the Jesuits who served at the Ming court in the sixteenth and seventeenth centuries. Clerics such as Matteo Ricci found much to admire in Chinese civilization. Here Ricci expresses a keen interest in Chinese printing methods, which at that time were well in advance of the techniques used in the West.

Matteo Ricci, *The Diary of Matthew Ricci*

The art of printing was practiced in China at a date somewhat earlier than that assigned to the beginning of printing in Europe, which was about 1405. It is quite certain that the Chinese knew the art of printing at least five centuries ago, and some of them assert that printing was known to their people before the beginning of the Christian era, about 50 B.C. Their method of printing differs widely from that employed in Europe, and our method would be quite impracticable for them because of the exceedingly large number of Chinese characters and symbols. At present they cut their characters in a reverse position and in a simplified form, on a comparatively small tablet made for the most part from the wood of the pear tree or the apple tree, although at times the wood of the jujube tree is also used for this purpose.

Their method of making printed books is quite ingenious. The text is written in ink, with a brush made of very fine hair, on a sheet of paper which is inverted and pasted on a wooden tablet. When the paper has become thoroughly dry, its surface is scraped off quickly and with great skill, until nothing but a fine tissue bearing the characters remains on the wooden tablet. Then, with a steel graver, the workman cuts away the surface following the outlines of the characters until these alone stand out in low relief. From such a block a skilled printer can make copies with incredible speed, turning out as many as fifteen hundred copies in a single day. Chinese printers are so skilled in engraving these blocks, that no more time is consumed in making one of them than would be required by one of our printers in setting up a form of type and making the necessary corrections. This scheme of engraving wooden blocks is well adapted for the large and complex nature of the Chinese characters, but I do not think it would lend itself very aptly to our European type which could hardly be engraved upon wood because of its small dimensions.

Their method of printing has one decided advantage, namely, that once these tablets are made, they can be preserved and used for making changes in the text as often as one wishes. Additions and subtractions can also be made as the tablets can be readily patched. Again, with this method, the printer and the author are not obliged to produce here and now an excessively large edition of a book, but are able to print a book in smaller or larger lots sufficient to meet the demand at the time. We have derived great benefit from this method of Chinese printing, as we employ the domestic help in our homes to strike off copies of the books on religious and scientific subjects which we translate into Chinese from the languages in which they were written originally. In truth, the whole method is so simple that one is tempted to try it for himself after once having watched the process. The simplicity of Chinese printing is what accounts for the exceedingly large numbers of books in circulation here and the ridiculously low prices at which they are sold. Such facts as these would scarcely be believed by one who had not witnessed them.

They have another odd method of reproducing reliefs which have been cut into marble or wood. An epitaph, for example, or a picture set out in low relief on marble or on wood, is covered with a piece of moist paper which in turn is overlayed with several pieces of cloth. Then the entire surface is beaten with a small mallet until all the lineaments of the relief are impressed upon the paper. When the paper dries, ink or some other coloring substance is applied with a light touch, after which only the impression of the relief stands out on the original whiteness of the paper. This method cannot be employed when the relief is shallow or made in delicate lines.

China During the Early Modern Era

Portuguese arrive in South China	1514
Matteo Ricci arrives in China	1601
Dutch occupy Zeelandia on island of Taiwan	1624
Li Zicheng occupies Beijing	1644
Manchus seize China	1644
Reign of Kangxi	1661–1722
Koxinga expels Dutch from Taiwan	1662
Qing dynasty seizes Taiwan	1683
Treaty of Nerchinsk	1689
First English trading post at Canton	1699
Reign of Qianlong	1736–1795
Lord Macartney's mission to China	1793
White Lotus Rebellion	1796–1804

But Li was unable to hold his conquest. The overthrow of the Ming dynasty presented a great temptation to the Manchus. With the assistance of many military commanders who had deserted from the Ming, they conquered Beijing on their own. Li Zicheng's army disintegrated, and the Manchus declared the creation of a new dynasty with the reign title of the Qing (Ch'ing, or Pure). Once again, China was under foreign rule.

The Greatness of the Qing

The accession of the Manchus to power in Beijing was not universally applauded. Their ruthless policies and insensitivity to Chinese customs soon provoked resistance. Some Ming loyalists fled to Southeast Asia, while others continued their resistance to the new rulers from inside the country. The most famous rebel was the general Zheng Chenggong, better known in the West by his popular name of Koxinga. He first set up headquarters on the island of Amoy (today known as Xiamen) on the south China coast. Driven from the mainland by the pressure of advancing Manchu armies, he then seized a Dutch fort on the island of Taiwan, ninety miles off the coast, and settled the area with some of his followers from the mainland. Koxinga died shortly thereafter, and the island was eventually conquered by the Manchus and integrated

into the Qing Empire. In preparation for its attack on Koxinga, the government evacuated the entire coastline across from the island of Taiwan. To make it easier to identify the rebels, the government also ordered all Chinese to adopt Manchu dress and hairstyles. All Chinese males were to shave their foreheads and braid their hair into a queue; those who refused were to be executed. As a popular saying put it, "lose your hair or lose your head."[7]

But the Manchus eventually proved themselves to be more adept at adapting to Chinese conditions than their predecessors, the Mongols. Unlike the latter, who had tried to impose their own methods of ruling, the Manchus adopted the Chinese political system (although, as we shall see, they retained their distinct position within it) and were gradually accepted by most Chinese as the legitimate rulers of the country.

Like all of China's great dynasties, the Qing was blessed with a series of strong early rulers who pacified the country, rectified many of the most obvious social and economic inequities, and restored peace and prosperity. For the Ming dynasty, these strong emperors had been Hongwu and Yongle; under the Qing, they would be Kangxi (K'ang Hsi) and Qianlong (Ch'ien Lung). The two Qing monarchs ruled China for well over a century, from the middle of the seventeenth century to the end of the eighteenth, and were responsible for much of the greatness of Manchu China.

Kangxi (1661–1722) was arguably the greatest ruler in Chinese history. Ascending to the throne at the age of seven, he was blessed with diligence, political astuteness, and a strong character and began to take charge of Qing administration while still in his adolescence. During his long reign of six decades, Kangxi not only stabilized imperial rule by pacifying the restive peoples along the northern and western frontiers, but he also managed to make the dynasty acceptable to the general population. As an active patron of arts and letters, he cultivated the support of scholars through a number of major projects that, among other things, contributed to the revival of Confucian scholarship and a sense of orthodoxy in the interpretation of history.

During Kangxi's reign, the activities of the Western missionaries, Dominicans and Franciscans as well as Jesuits, reached their height. The emperor was quite tolerant of the Christians, and several Jesuit missionaries became influential at court. Several hundred court officials converted to Christianity, as did an estimated 300,000 ordinary Chinese. But ultimately the Christian effort was undermined by squabbling among the Western religious orders over the Jesuit policy of accommodating local beliefs and practices in order to facilitate conversion. The Jesuits had acquiesced to the emperor's insistence that traditional Confucian rituals such as ancestor worship were civil ceremonies and thus could be undertaken by Christian converts. Jealous Dominicans and Franciscans complained to the pope, who issued an edict ordering all missionaries and converts to conform to the official orthodoxy set forth in Europe. At first Kangxi attempted to resolve the problem by appealing directly to the Vatican, but the pope was uncompromising. After Kangxi's death, his successor began to suppress Christian activities throughout China.

Kangxi's achievements were carried on by his successors, Yongzheng (Yung Cheng, 1722–1736) and Qianlong (1736–1795). Like Kangxi, Qianlong was known for his diligence, tolerance, and intellectual curiosity, and he too combined vigorous military action against the unruly tribes along the frontier with active efforts to promote economic prosperity, administrative efficiency, and scholarship and artistic excellence. The result was continued growth for the Manchu Empire throughout much of the eighteenth century.

QING POLITICS

Certainly, one reason for the success of the Manchus was their ability to adapt to their new environment. They retained the Ming political system with relatively few changes. The most obvious difference, of course, was that the Manchus, like the Mongols, were ethnically, linguistically, and culturally distinct from their subject population. The Qing attempted to cope with this reality by adopting a two-pronged strategy. On the one hand, the Manchus, representing less than 2 percent of the entire population, were legally defined as distinct from everyone else in China. The Manchu nobles retained their aristocratic privileges, while their economic base was protected by extensive landholdings and revenues provided from the state treasury. Other Manchus were assigned farmland and organized into military units, called banners, which were stationed as separate units in various strategic positions throughout China. These "bannermen" were the primary fighting force of the empire, although a Chinese "green standard" army served as a local police force. Ethnic Chinese were prohibited from settling in Manchuria and were still compelled to wear their hair in a queue as a sign of submission to the ruling dynasty.

But while the Qing attempted to protect their distinct identity within an alien society, they also recognized the need to bring ethnic Chinese into the top ranks of imperial administration. Their solution was to create a system, known as dyarchy, in which all important administrative positions were shared equally by Chinese and Manchus. Of the six members of the grand secretariat, three were Manchu and three were Chinese. Each of the six ministries had an equal number of Chinese and Manchu members, while Manchus and Chinese also shared responsibilities at the provincial level. While provincial governors were usually Chinese, two provinces were often linked under a governor-general, or viceroy, who was normally a Manchu. Below the provinces, Chinese were dominant. Although the system did not work perfectly, the Manchus' willingness to share power did win over the allegiance of many Chinese. Meanwhile the Manchus themselves, despite official efforts to preserve their separate language and culture, were increasingly assimilated into Chinese civilization.

The Qing did make some additional changes in the administration system. When the grand secretariat became increasingly mired in administrative detail, the government created a new high-level organ, the grand council, to serve the emperor as an advisory body.

The new rulers also tinkered with the civil service examination system. In an effort to make it more equitable, quotas were established for each major ethnic group and each province to prevent the positions from being monopolized by candidates from certain provinces in central China that had traditionally produced large numbers of officials. In practice, however, the examination system probably became less equitable during the Manchu era, because increasingly positions were assigned to candidates who had purchased their degree rather than competing through the system. Positions were becoming harder to obtain because their number did not rise fast enough to match the unprecedented increase in population under Qing rule.

Members of the Qing dynasty tried to establish their legitimacy as China's rightful rulers by stressing their devotion to the principles of Confucianism. Emperor Kangxi ostentatiously studied the sacred Confucian classics and issued a "Sacred Edict" that proclaimed to the entire empire the importance of the moral values established by the master (see the box on p. 617). Nevertheless, many scholars opposed the new dynasty on principle and sought to find reasons for the fall of the native Ming. Some found the answer in Wang Yangming's "School of the Mind," which sought truth in introspection and emphasized internal self-searching rather than investigation of the outside world. Such convictions led to the rise of a new school of "Textual Criticism" that attempted to move from introspection to an intensive study of the classics in an effort to search for facts. These scholars hoped that a more accurate understanding of ancient Confucian texts would provide them with clues on how to deal more effectively with the contemporary world.

CHINA ON THE EVE OF THE WESTERN ONSLAUGHT

In some ways, China was at the height of its power and glory in the mid-eighteenth century. But it was also under Qianlong that the first signs of the internal decay of the Manchu dynasty began to appear. The clues were familiar ones. Qing military campaigns along the frontier were expensive and placed heavy demands on the imperial treasury. As the emperor aged, he became less astute in selecting his subordinates and fell under the influence of corrupt elements at court, including the notorious Manchu official Heshen (Ho Shen). Funds officially destined for military or other official use were increasingly si-

phoned off to Heshen or his favorites, arousing resentment among military and civilian officials.

Corruption at the center led inevitably to unrest in rural areas, where higher taxes, bureaucratic venality, and rising pressure on the land because of the growing population had produced economic hardship and rising discontent. The heart of the unrest was located in central China, where discontented peasants who had recently been settled on infertile land launched a revolt known as the White Lotus Rebellion (1796–1804). The revolt was eventually suppressed but at great expense, and it forewarned that the glory years of the Manchus were ending.

Unfortunately for China, the decline of the Qing dynasty occurred just as China's modest relationship with the West was about to give way to a new era of military confrontation and increased pressure for trade. The first signs had come from the north, where Russian traders seeking skins and furs began to penetrate the region of the Amur River, which forms the present-day boundary between Siberian Russia and Manchuria. Earlier the Ming dynasty had attempted to deal with the Russians by the traditional method of placing them in a tributary

◆ **Sweating Out Exam Results.**   Success in the civil service examination was the key to a prestigious life as an official or scholar in traditional China. The students worked for years, learning the Confucian classics by rote. A few attempted to cheat by sewing copies of texts inside the linings of their robes. Here students of the Qing dynasty anxiously await the examination results.

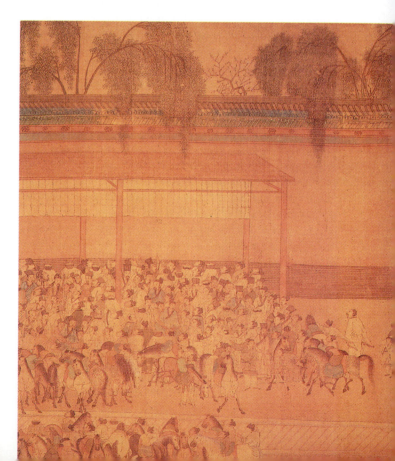

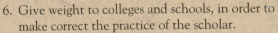

A Confucian Sixteen Commandments

Although the Qing dynasty was of foreign origin, its rulers found Confucian maxims convenient for maintaining the social order. In 1670, the great emperor Kangxi issued the Sacred Edict to popularize Confucian values among the common people. The edict was read publicly at periodic intervals in every village in the country and set the standard for behavior throughout the empire. Note the similarities and differences with the Japanese decree on p. 636 later in this chapter.

Kangxi's Sacred Edict

1. Esteem most highly filial piety and brotherly submission, in order to give due importance to the social relations.
2. Behave with generosity toward your kindred, in order to illustrate harmony and benignity.
3. Cultivate peace and concord in your neighborhoods, in order to prevent quarrels and litigations.
4. Recognize the importance of husbandry and the culture of the mulberry tree, in order to ensure a sufficiency of clothing and food.
5. Show that you prize moderation and economy, in order to prevent the lavish waste of your means.
6. Give weight to colleges and schools, in order to make correct the practice of the scholar.
7. Extirpate strange principles, in order to exalt the correct doctrine.
8. Lecture on the laws, in order to warn the ignorant and obstinate.
9. Elucidate propriety and yielding courtesy, in order to make manners and customs good.
10. Labor diligently at your proper callings, in order to stabilize the will of the people.
11. Instruct sons and younger brothers, in order to prevent them from doing what is wrong.
12. Put a stop to false accusations, in order to preserve the honest and good.
13. Warn against sheltering deserters, in order to avoid being involved in their punishment.
14. Fully remit your taxes, in order to avoid being pressed for payment.
15. Unite in hundreds and tithing, in order to put an end to thefts and robbery.
16. Remove enmity and anger, in order to show the importance due to the person and life.

relationship and playing them off against other non-Chinese groups in the area. But the tsar refused to play by Chinese rules. His envoys to Beijing ignored the tribute system and refused to perform the kowtow (literally "strike the head"; the ritual of prostration and knocking the head on the ground performed by foreign emissaries before the emperor), the classical symbol of fealty demanded of all foreign ambassadors to the Chinese court. Formal diplomatic relations were finally established in 1689, when the Treaty of Nerchinsk (negotiated with the aid of Jesuit missionaries resident at the Qing court) settled the boundary dispute along the Amur River and provided for regular trade between the two countries. A second treaty signed at Kiakhta forty years later completed the boundary settlement by confirming Chinese rule over all of Mongolia in return for formal trading rights and permanent residence for Russian merchants and missionaries in Beijing. Through such arrangements, the Manchus were able not only to pacify the northern frontier but also to extend their rule over Xinjiang and Tibet to the west and southwest. In the meantime, tributary relations were established with such neighboring countries as Korea, Burma, Vietnam, and Ayuthaya.

Dealing with the foreigners who arrived by sea was more difficult. By the end of the seventeenth century, the English had replaced the Portuguese as the dominant force in European trade. Operating through the East India Company, which served as both a trading unit and the administrator of English territories in Asia, the English established their first trading post at Canton in 1699. Over the next decades, trade with China, notably the export of tea and silk to England, increased rapidly.

At first, the imperial court attempted to deal with the Europeans in the traditional manner of granting trade privileges in exchange for periodic tribute missions to Beijing. Eventually, however, the Qing rulers abandoned this practice for a system they already used to administer the activities of their own merchants. They licensed Chinese trading firms at Canton (known to Europeans as Co hong, or "officially authorized merchants") as the

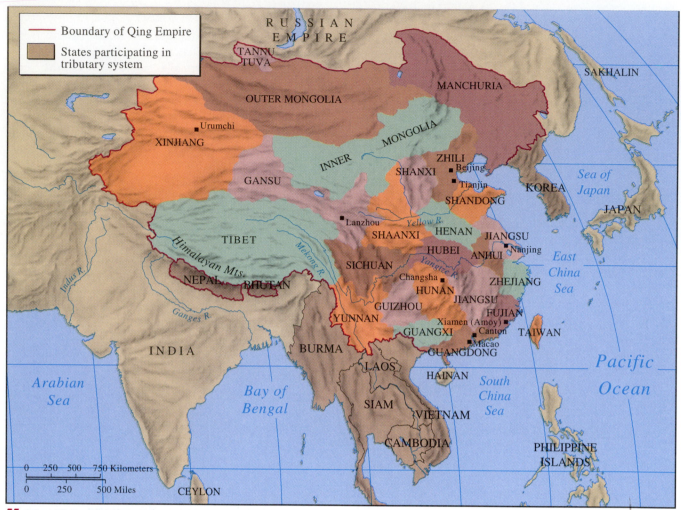

Map 17.2   The Qing Empire in the Eighteenth Century.

exclusive conduit for trade with the West. To limit contacts between Europeans and Chinese, the Qing eventually confined the Europeans to the small island of Shamian on the Pearl River just outside the city walls and permitted them to reside there only from October through March.

For a while, the British tolerated this system, which brought considerable profit to the East India Company and its shareholders. But by the end of the eighteenth century, some British traders had begun to demand access to other cities along the Chinese coast, while the government in London was under increasing pressure from merchants to open China to British manufactured goods. The British government and traders alike were restive at the uneven balance of trade between the two countries, which forced the British to ship vast amounts of silver bullion to China in exchange for its silks, porcelains, and

teas. In 1793, a mission under Lord Macartney visited Beijing to press for liberalization of trade restrictions. A compromise was reached on the kowtow (Macartney was permitted to bend on one knee as was the British custom), but Qianlong expressed no interest in British manufactured products. As the emperor noted in his letter to King George III, China received many "precious things" from tribute missions from nations the world over. Consequently, he said, "there is nothing we lack, as your principal envoy and others have themselves observed. We have never set much store on strange or ingenious objects, nor do we need more of your country's manufactures" (see the box on p. 608). An exasperated Macartney compared the Chinese Empire to "an old, crazy, first-rate man-of-war" that had once awed its neighbors "merely by her bulk and appearance" but was now destined under incompetent leadership to be "dashed to pieces on the shore."[8] With his contemptuous dismissal of the British request, the emperor had inadvertently sowed the seeds for a century of humiliation.

Changing China

An earlier chapter discussed the evolution of Chinese history in terms of a society that was gradually changing, but within the general framework of a strong set of traditional institutions and principles. That sense of change within continuity seems particularly applicable to the period of the Ming and Qing dynasties. Whereas historians once assumed that China was an essentially static society when it came into contact with the West, many scholars today argue that during the late Ming and Qing periods, Chinese society was actually in a state of rapid transition. Some have even contended that China was about to embark on a road that would lead to a cultural renaissance and industrial revolution as in the West. If so, European influence cannot be solely responsible for the changes taking place in China in our day. At the most, the West has helped to shape and hasten, and perhaps to distort, the process. Thus, an important question in considering the late Ming and Qing periods is whether China was still firmly within the bounds of Confucian principles elucidated centuries earlier or whether it was on the verge of major changes that would lead to a new form of society based on principles and institutions analogous to those of the modern West.

Nowhere was change more evident than in the economic sector. During the early modern period, China remained a predominantly agricultural society, as it had been throughout recorded history. Nearly 85 percent of the population were farmers. In the south, the main crop was rice; in the north, it was wheat or other dry crops. As always, most Chinese were small farmers, although there were a few large landowners who hired out their land to tenants. But although China was still a country of villages with a few scattered urban centers, the economy was changing during the late Ming and Qing and was by no means the same as it had been under the Tang and the Song or even the Yuan.

THE POPULATION EXPLOSION

In the first place, the center of gravity was continuing to shift steadily from the north to the south. In the early centuries of Chinese civilization, the bulk of the population had been located along the Yellow River from the capital of Chang'an (near present-day Xian) downriver to the Gulf of Bohai. Smaller settlements were located

◆ **Emperor Qianlong Meets Lord Macartney.** In 1793, Lord Macartney was dispatched to China to press for the liberalization of trade restrictions. Although he offered gifts of Western scientific instruments and texts, the Chinese, who believed their nation had been the cultural center of the world for the last two thousand years, were not impressed. Lord Macartney won little Chinese sympathy for his refusal to kowtow to the emperor. Here the two prepare to meet.

along the Yangtze and in the mountainous regions of the south, but the administrative and economic center of gravity was clearly in the north. By the Song period, however, that emphasis had already begun to shift drastically as a result of climatic changes, deforestation, and continuing pressure from nomads in the Gobi Desert. This process continued in later centuries, and by the late Ming and early Qing, the economic breadbasket of China, if not the administrative headquarters, was located along the Yangtze River or in the mountains to the south. One concrete indication of this process occurred during the Ming dynasty, when Emperor Yongle ordered the renovation of the Grand Canal to facilitate the shipment of rice, usually requisitioned in the form of taxes, from the Yangtze delta to the food-starved north.

Moreover, the population was beginning to increase rapidly. For centuries, China's population had remained within a range of 50 to 100 million. It was higher in times of peace and prosperity and lower in periods of foreign invasion and internal anarchy. In general, the population rose whenever a new dynasty was becoming stronger and fell during periods of dynastic decay and the interludes of chaos that usually followed a dynasty's collapse. During the late Ming and the early Qing, however, the population increased from an estimated 70 to 80 million in 1390 to over 300 million at the end of the eighteenth century. There were probably several reasons for this population increase: the relatively long period of peace and stability under the early Qing; the introduction of new crops from the Americas, including peanuts, sweet potatoes, and maize; and the planting of a new species of rice from Southeast Asia, known as Champa rice, whose harvest cycle was much shorter than that of existing varieties.

Of course, this population increase meant much greater population pressure on the land, smaller farms, and a razor-thin margin of safety in case of climatic disaster. The imperial court attempted to deal with the problem by a variety of means, most notably by preventing the concentration of land in the hands of wealthy landowners. Nevertheless, by the eighteenth century, almost all the land that could be irrigated was already under cultivation, and the problems of rural hunger and landlessness became increasingly serious. Not surprisingly, economic hardship was quickly translated into rural unrest.

SEEDS OF INDUSTRIALIZATION

Another change that took place during the early modern period in China was the steady growth of manufacturing and commerce. Trade and manufacturing had existed in China since early times, of course, but they had been limited by a number of factors, including social prejudice, official restrictions, and state monopolies on mining and on the production of such commodities as alcohol and salt. Now, taking advantage of the long era of peace and prosperity, merchants and manufacturers began to expand their operations beyond their immediate provinces. Commercial networks began to operate on a regional and sometimes even a national basis, as trade in silk, metal and wood products, porcelain, cotton goods, and cash crops like cotton and tobacco developed rapidly. A Portuguese visitor in the sixteenth century viewed the process from the environs of Canton:

> This country of China is great, and its commerce is between certain provinces of it and others. Cantao [Canton] has iron, which there is not in the whole of the rest of the country of China, according to what I am informed. From here it goes inland to the other side of the mountain range; and the rest lies in the vicinity of this city of Cantao. From this they manufacture pots, nails, Chinese trade of goods from the provinces to Cantao and from Cantao arms and everything else of iron. They have also cordage, thread and silk, and cotton cloths. By reason of trade all goods come here, because this is the port whither foreigners come for this trade of goods from the provinces to Cantao and from Cantao to the interior, and the people are more numerous than in the other provinces.[9]

With the expansion of trade came an extension of commercial contacts and guild organizations on a nationwide basis. Merchant guilds began to be established in cities and market towns throughout the country to provide legal protection, an opportunity to do business, and food and lodging for merchants from particular provinces. Foreign trade also expanded, as Chinese merchants, mainly from the coastal provinces of the south, set up extensive contacts with countries in Southeast Asia. In many instances, the contacts in Southeast Asia were themselves Chinese who had settled in the area during the seventeenth and eighteenth centuries.

Some historians believe that this rise in industrial and commercial activity would have led under other circumstances to an indigenous industrial revolution and the emergence of a capitalist society such as that already taking shape in Europe. By this reasoning, the arrival of Western imperialism in the nineteenth century not only failed to hasten economic change, but may actually have hindered it.

But the significance of these changes should not be exaggerated. In fact, there were some key differences between China and Western Europe that would have hindered the emergence of capitalism in China. In the first place, the bourgeoisie in China were not as independent as their European counterparts. Free cities such as had long existed in the West had not emerged in China, and trade and manufacturing remained under the firm control of the state. In addition, political and social prejudices against commercial activity remained strong at court and in society at large. Reflecting an ancient preference for agriculture over manufacturing and trade, the state levied heavy taxes on manufacturing and commerce while attempting to keep agricultural taxes low. Such attitudes were still shared by key groups in the population. Although much money could be made in commerce, most gentry resisted the temptation, and many merchants who accumulated wealth used it to buy their way into the ranks of the gentry.

One of the consequences of these differences was a growing technological gap between China and Europe. The Chinese reaction to European clock-making techniques provides an example. In the eleventh century, a Chinese civil servant named Su Sung had invented a massive, water-driven clock five stories high to be used by the emperor in ritual appearances, especially those connected to the harvest cycle. Eventually, however, the device fell victim to court intrigue and was dismantled and virtually forgotten.

In the early seventeenth century, the Jesuit Matteo Ricci introduced the Ming emperor Wan Li to advanced European clocks driven by weights or springs. The emperor was fascinated and found the clocks more reliable than Chinese methods of keeping time. Over the next decades, European timepieces became a popular novelty at court, but the Chinese expressed relatively little curiosity about the technology involved, provoking one European to remark that playthings like cuckoo clocks "will be received here with much greater interest than scientific instruments or *objets d'art.*"[10]

Considering that rapid advances in technology were a crucial factor in Europe's rise to prominence in the early modern world, China's lack of interest in scientific theory can be seen as a serious hindrance in its effort to comprehend the fundamental laws of the universe. The most that can really be said, then, is that during the late Ming and Qing dynasties, China was beginning to undergo major economic and social changes that might have led, in due time, to the emergence of an industrialized society.

Daily Life in Qing China

For the most part, daily life in China under the Ming and early Qing dynasties was not much different than it had been in early periods. Chinese visitors from the Tang dynasty magically transported to the eighteenth century would have recognized much of what they saw. Certainly, the eating and living habits would have been familiar, even though they seemed strange to travelers arriving from Europe.

THE FAMILY

As in earlier periods, Chinese society under the Qing dynasty was organized around the family. The family not only provided room and board, but it was also the primary source of moral and civic education for the young, support for unmarried daughters, and care for the elderly; it was even a focus for religious belief and ritual. At the same time, all family members were expected to sacrifice their individual desires for the benefit of the family as a whole.

The hierarchical nature of the family was embodied in the famous Confucian concept of the "five relationships." Children were expected to obey their parents, just as all subjects were expected to obey their ruler. Wives were expected to obey their husbands, younger children to obey their older siblings, and friends to obey the wishes of older friends. Within the family, the oldest male was king, and his wishes theoretically had to be obeyed by all family members. These values were reiterated in Emperor Kangxi's Sacred Edict, which listed filial piety and loyalty to the family as its first two maxims (see the box on p. 617).

For many Chinese, the effects of these values were most apparent in the choice of a marriage partner. Marriages were normally arranged for the benefit of the family, often by a go-between, and the groom and bride were usually not consulted. Frequently, they did not meet until the marriage ceremony. Under such conditions, love was clearly a secondary consideration. In fact, it was often viewed as detrimental, since it inevitably distracted the attention of the husband and wife from their primary responsibility to the larger family unit.

Although this emphasis on filial piety might seem to represent a blatant disregard for individual rights, the obligations were not all on the side of the children. The father was expected to provide support for his wife and children and, like the ruler, was supposed to treat those in his care with respect and compassion. All too often, however, the male head of the family was able to exact his privileges without performing his responsibilities in return.

In many cases, the head of the family would be responsible for more than just his own wife and children.

As in earlier times, the ideal family unit in Qing China was the joint family, in which as many as three or even four generations lived under the same roof. When sons married, they brought their wives to live with them in the family homestead. Prosperous families would add a separate section to the house to accommodate the new family unit. Unmarried daughters would also remain in the house, while those who wed departed to live with their husbands. Aging parents and grandparents remained under the same roof until they died and were cared for by younger members of the household. This ideal did not always correspond to reality, however, since many families did not possess sufficient amounts of land to support a large household. One historian has estimated that only about 40 percent of Chinese families actually lived in joint families.

The family continued to be important in early Qing China for much the same reasons as in earlier times. As a labor-intensive society based primarily on the cultivation of rice, the Chinese needed large families not only to help with the harvest, but also to provide security for the parents when they were too old to work in the fields. Sons were particularly prized, not only because they had strong backs, but also because they would raise their own families under the parental roof. The joint family offered the children benefits as well. In a densely populated country where the land available for cultivation was limited, children had few opportunities for employment outside the family, so sons had little choice but to remain with their parents and help on the land. A prosperous family would manage to purchase additional lands, while a poorer one would be forced to survive on its existing fields.

Similarly, prosperous families would live in larger houses. According to a sixteenth-century Spanish visitor, the houses of the wealthy were often "very large and they occupy a great space, for they have courtyards and more courtyards, and great halls and many chambers and kitchen-gardens." One mansion had "a very fine pond all paved with flagstones, and with arbors and paths above the water, and very fine tables made from single slabs of stone."[11] The houses of the well-to-do might be raised above the ground on stone foundations and feature brick floors and tiled ceilings. Each corner was supported by a sturdy wooden pillar, while the space in between was covered with wood or plaster. The houses of ordinary Chinese were much smaller, consisting of two rooms with a courtyard in between. In urban areas, the front of the house that abutted on the street might be used as a store.

Beyond the joint family was the clan. Sometimes called a lineage, a clan was an extended kinship unit consisting of dozens or even hundreds of joint and nuclear families linked together by a clan council of elders and a variety of other common social and religious functions. The clan served a number of useful purposes. In a society where welfare and unemployment benefits did not exist, individual families had to survive on their own. In bad times family members could go hungry or even starve. When it worked effectively, the clan system could help to alleviate such problems. Some clans possessed corporate lands that could be rented out to poorer families or exploited in other ways. Richer families within the clan could provide land for the poor. Since there was no general state-supported educational system, the clan also provided talented and ambitious young men with the opportunity for education. In such cases, sons of poor families might be invited to study in a school established in the home of a more prosperous relative. This system not only provided the young man with the possibility of upward mobility, but potentially benefited the richer family as well. If the young man succeeded in becoming an official, he would be expected to provide favors and prestige for the clan as a whole.

Like joint families, clans were not universal, and millions of Chinese had none. The clans apparently originated in the great landed families of the Tang period and managed to survive despite periodic efforts to weaken and destroy them by the imperial court. In many cases, clan solidarity was weakened by intralineage conflicts or differing levels of status and economic achievement. Nevertheless, in the early modern period, they were still an influential force at the local level and were particularly prevalent in the south.

THE ROLE OF WOMEN

In traditional China, the role of women had always been inferior to that of men. A sixteenth-century Spanish visitor to South China observed that Chinese women were "very secluded and virtuous, and it was a very rare thing for us to see a woman in the cities and large towns, unless it was an old crone." Women were more visible, he said, in rural areas, where they frequently could be seen working in the fields.[12]

The concept of female inferiority had deep roots in Chinese history. This view was embodied in the belief that only a male would carry on sacred family rituals and that only males had the talent to govern others. Only males could aspire to a career in government or scholarship. Within the family system, the wife was clearly subordinated to the husband. Legally, she could not divorce her husband or inherit property. The husband, on the other hand, could divorce his wife if she did not produce male heirs, or he could take a second wife as well as a concubine for his pleasure. Although technically China was a monogamous society, secondary wives or concubines were not rare in well-to-do families.

The subordinate position of women within the family also affected the children. Female children were less desirable because of their limited physical strength and because their parents would be required to pay a dowry to the parents of their future husband. Female children normally did not receive an education, and in times of scarcity when food was in short supply, daughters might even be put to death.

Though women were clearly inferior to men in theory, this was not always the case in practice. Attitudes toward the relationships between the sexes had apparently been relatively relaxed during the early imperial period, but became more strict during the Ming, at a time when Confucian orthodoxy became dominant at court and among the elite. Even then, capable women often compensated for their legal inferiority by playing a strong role within the family. Women were often in charge of educating the children and handled the family budget. Some women also received training in the Confucian classics, although their schooling was generally for a shorter time than that of their male counterparts and did not focus on preparation for an official career. The tradition of the fierce mother-in-law, a common theme in popular literature, justifiably alarmed many a bride-to-be and the henpecked husband was as much a subject of laughter and ridicule in traditional China as he is in the United States today.

All in all, however, life for women in traditional China was undoubtedly difficult. In Chinese novels like *The Dream of the Red Chamber*, *The Scholars*, and *The Golden Lotus*, women were treated as scullery maids or as love objects. They were frequently under the domination of both their husband and their mother-in-law, and in some cases the bullying was so brutal that suicide appeared to be the only way out. A particularly vivid and painful symbol of women's subordination was the tradition of foot-binding. Because small feet were highly prized as sexually attractive in traditional China, the feet of female infants were often deliberately deformed by a binding process that not only was exceedingly painful but also distorted the bones and hindered walking for life. The custom began during the Tang dynasty, but became increasingly popular during the late imperial period, when an estimated one-half to two-thirds of the female population were subjected to the practice. Although the custom was legally prohibited after the establishment of the first Chinese republic, even today it is not unusual in mainland China to see older women still carrying with them the consequences of this practice.

Cultural Developments

During the late Ming and the early Qing dynasties, traditional culture in China reached new heights of achievement. With the rise of a wealthy urban class, the demand for art, porcelain, textiles, and literature was at a premium.

THE RISE OF THE CHINESE NOVEL

Until the fourteenth century, prose literature was dominated by classical styles and was written by and for the educated audience. As in Europe, popular literature consisted primarily of oral traditions, folktales, folk songs, and village theater. During the Ming dynasty, however, a new form of literature arose that eventually evolved into the modern Chinese novel. Although still considered less respectable than poetry and nonfiction prose, these ground-breaking works (often written anonymously or under pseudonyms) were enormously popular, especially among well-to-do urban dwellers.

Written in a colloquial style, the new fiction was characterized by a new realism that resulted in vivid portraits of Chinese society. Many of the stories sympathized with society's downtrodden, often helpless maidens, and dealt with such crucial issues as love, money, marriage, and power. Adding to the realism were sexually explicit passages that depicted the private side of Chinese life. Readers delighted in sensuous tales that, no matter how pornographic, always professed a moral lesson; the villains were punished and the virtuous rewarded. During the more puritanical Qing era, a number of the more erotic works were censored or banned and found refuge in Japan, where several have recently been rediscovered by scholars.

Three works stand out as classical examples of the traditional Chinese novel. Unfortunately, little is known about their authors, who were apparently not deemed worthy of recognition. *Journey to the West*, known to English-speaking audiences as *Monkey*, originated as an oral tradition and was published in its final version in 1592. It relates the supernatural tale of the hero Tripitaka's quest to obtain the Buddhist sutras in the Western heaven. With the help of a number of Buddhist and Daoist deities, including the animal spirit Monkey, Tripitaka reaches his goal and becomes a Buddhist saint. Filled with gripping adventures and eternal humor, *Monkey* has remained popular with generations of Chinese down to present times.

In addition to supernatural tales like *Monkey*, the late Ming era also witnessed the emergence of realistic and satirical novels featuring sharp social commentary. *Gold Vase Plum*, known in English translation as *The Golden Lotus*, presents a cutting exposé of the decadent aspects of late Ming society. Considered by many the first realistic social novel—preceding its European counterparts by two centuries—*The Golden Lotus* depicts the depraved life of the wealthy landlord Hsi-men Ch'ing, who cruelly manipulates those around him for sex, money, and power. In the process, the novel describes the daily lives of an extended Chinese family, including the patriarch, his six wives, and numerous concubines and servants, in an overindulgent age gone awry. In a rare exception in Chinese fiction, the villain is not punished for his evil ways; justice is served instead by the misfortunes that befall his descendants. The explicit pornographic detail (translated into Latin in the first English-language versions) prevented the novel from winning general acceptance. Nevertheless, it remains one of the greatest Chinese novels ever written.

Even today *The Dream of the Red Chamber* is generally considered to be China's most distinguished popular novel. Published in 1791, 150 years after *The Golden Lotus*, it tells of the tragic love between two young people caught in the financial and moral disintegration of a powerful Chinese clan. Set against the background of daily life in an affluent eighteenth-century family with its elaborate housing compound, Confucian tradition, intrigues, and regimented hierarchy, the novel weaves together the stories of thirty main characters from a cast of over four hundred. The main characters, trapped in their precipitous fall from greatness, are seen up close with all their strengths and flaws. The hero and the heroine, both sensitive and spoiled, represent the inevitable decline of the Chia family and come to an equally inevitable tragic end, she in death and he in an unhappy marriage to another. Although the novel is set in a different time, their humanity still speaks directly to us today (see the box on p. 625).

THEATER AND POPULAR DRAMA

Chinese drama resurfaced during the Ming era in a new refined form produced for the elite. The most famous Ming play, entitled *The Peony Pavilion*, relates the tribulations of a young student and the daughter of a high official. In a manner reminiscent of Daoist writings during the post-Han period, harassed urban Chinese escape from the bustle of the city to find peace in nature and in the delicacy of exquisite works of art.

Meanwhile folk drama had by no means totally disappeared. Theater had always been a popular form of entertainment for the rural population, the majority of whom were unable to read and write. During the late Ming and Qing, this form of cultural expression underwent considerable development, sparked by the growth in wealth, social mobility, and education. Plays were presented in the cities, market towns, villages, and even clan ancestral halls as a means of creating group unity and promoting acceptable social norms. Like popular literature, popular theater often drew upon the same themes as classical drama, but developed them differently for a different audience. The language was more colloquial, the emotions expressed were less refined, and often the didactic element characteristic of officially supported works was replaced by a focus on adventure, romance, and even the supernatural.

THE ART OF THE MING AND THE QING

During the Ming and the early Qing, China produced its last outpouring of traditional artistic brilliance. Although most of the creative work was modeled on past examples, the art of this period is impressive for its technical perfection and breathtaking quantity.

In architecture, the most outstanding example is the Imperial City in Beijing. Building on the remnants of the palace of the Yuan dynasty, the third Ming emperor ordered renovations when he returned the capital to Beijing in 1421. Succeeding emperors continued to add to the palace, but the basic design has not changed since the Ming era. Surrounded by six and one-half miles of walls, the immense enclosed compound is divided into a maze of private apartments and offices and an imposing ceremonial quadrangle with a series of stately halls for imperial audiences and banquets. The grandiose scale, richly carved marble, spacious gardens, and graceful upturned roofs also contribute to the splendor of the "Forbidden City."

In the late Ming period, wealthy urban elites throughout the country dedicated their wealth to the arts, constructing grand estates with artificial hills, rock gardens, pools, and elaborate interiors, as well as amassing fine collections of books and paintings. Separate schools of painting were established to imitate various styles from previous dynasties, while court artists were kept busy decorating the numerous rooms in the imperial palace. Court painters fared better than in the fourteenth century, when the founding Ming emperor Hongwu executed four artists because he disliked their works. Wood-

The Art of Using Chopsticks

This passage from The Dream of the Red Chamber is characteristic of the historical detail of the novel. It describes a country cousin's visit to the elegant mansion of her city relatives and the comic scene that she provokes by her naïveté. Such writing brings to life the wealth and luxury of the Qing dynasty and shows that Europeans were not the only people who had trouble with chopsticks.

The Dream of the Red Chamber

As soon as Old Dame Liu was seated, she picked up the chopsticks which were uncannily heavy and hard to manage. It was because Phoenix and Mandarin Duck had previously plotted to give her a pair of old-fashioned, angular-shaped ivory chopsticks gilded with gold. Looking at them, Old Dame Liu remarked: "These fork-like things are even heavier than our iron prongs. How can one hold them up?" Everyone laughed. By this time a woman servant had brought in a tiny food box and, as she stood there, another maid came forward to lift the lid. Inside were two bowls of food. Li Huan (Pao-yu's elder brother's widow) took one bowl and placed it on the Matriarch's table as Phoenix picked up a bowl of pigeon eggs to place it on Old Dame Liu's table.

Just as the Matriarch had finished saying, "Please eat," Old Dame Liu rose from her seat and said aloud:

Old Liu, Old Liu, her appetite as big as a cow!
She eats like an old sow without lifting her head.

Having said her piece, with her cheeks puffed out she looked straight ahead without uttering another word. At first, all those present were astonished, but upon a moment's reflection, all burst out laughing at the same time. Unable to restrain herself, River Cloud (Matriarch's grandniece) spluttered out a mouthful of tea; Black Jade was choked with laughter and leaning on the table, could only cry and groan, "Ai-ya!" Pao-yu rolled down into the Matriarch's lap; joyously she hugged him and cried out, "Oh, my heart! my liver!"

Madame Wang (Pao-yu's mother) also laughed, then pointed her finger at Phoenix, but could not utter one word. Aunt Hsueh (Precious Clasp's mother), unable to control herself, spurted out her mouthful of tea on the skirt of Quest Spring (she and the other "Spring" girls were all Pao-yu's cousins and sisters), whose teacup fell on the body of Greeting Spring. Compassion Spring left her seat and pulling the wet nurse to her, asked her to rub her belly. None among the servants did not twist her waist or bend her back as they giggled. Some slipped out to have a good laugh while squatting down and others, having stopped laughing by now, came forward to change the dresses for the girls. Only Phoenix and Mandarin Duck controlled themselves and kept urging Old Dame Liu to eat.

Old Dame Liu lifted up the chopsticks but they were hardly manageable. Looking at the bowl in front of her, she remarked: "Well, well, even your hens are smarter than ours! They lay such tiny delicate eggs, very dainty indeed. Let me try one!" All the people had just stopped laughing but they burst out again upon hearing these words. The Matriarch laughed so much that tears dropped down; she just couldn't stop them and Amber (Matriarch's maidservant) had to pound her back to relieve her. The Matriarch said: "This must have been the work of that sly, impish Phoenix. Don't listen to her."

Old Dame Liu was still exclaiming about how tiny and dainty the eggs were when Phoenix said jocularly to her: "They cost an ounce of silver apiece. You had better hurry up and taste one before they get cold." Old Dame Liu then stretched out her chopsticks to seize the eggs with both ends, but how could she pick them up? After having chased them all over the bowl, she finally captured one with no little effort and was about to crane her neck to eat it when lo! it slipped off and fell on the floor. She was going to pick it up herself when a woman servant got it and took it out. Old Dame Liu sighed: "An ounce of silver! How it disappears without even making a noise!"

block prints became popular in the seventeenth century and later spread to Japan.

The decorative arts flourished in this period, especially the intricately carved lacquerware and the boldly shaped and colored cloisonné. Silk production reached its zenith, and the best-quality silks were highly prized in Europe, where chinoiserie, as Chinese art of all kinds was called, was in vogue. Perhaps the most famous of all the

◆ **The Imperial City in Beijing.** During the fifteenth century, the Ming dynasty erected an immense Imperial City on the remnants of the palace of Khubilai Khan in Beijing. Surrounded by six and one-half miles of walls, the enclosed compound is divided into a maze of private apartments and offices; it also includes an imposing ceremonial quadrangle with stately halls for imperial audiences and banquets. Because it was off-limits to commoners, the compound was known as the "Forbidden City."

achievements of the Ming era was the blue-and-white porcelain, which is still prized by collectors throughout the world. Different styles would be produced during the reign of each emperor. One variety (called *kraak* because the Dutch seized a shipment from a Portuguese carrack) caused a sensation in Holland and led to the manufacture of blue-and-white porcelain at the Dutch porcelain factory at Delft.

During the Qing dynasty, artists produced great quantities of paintings, mostly for home consumption. The wealthy city of Yangzhou on the Grand Canal emerged as an active artistic center. Inside the Forbidden City in Beijing, court painters worked alongside Jesuit artists and experimented with Western techniques. European art, however, did not greatly influence Chinese painting at this time; some dismissed it as mere "craftsmanship." Scholarly painters and the literati totally rejected foreign techniques and became obsessed with traditional Chinese styles. As a result, Qing painting became progressively more repetitive and stale. Ironically, the Qing dynasty thus represents the apogee of traditional Chinese art and the beginning of its decline.

Tokugawa Japan

At the end of the fifteenth century, the traditional Japanese system was at a point of near anarchy. With the decline in the authority of the Ashikaga shogunate at Kyoto, clan rivalries had exploded into an era of "warring states" similar to the period of the same name in Zhou dynasty China. Even at the local level, power was frequently diffuse. The typical daimyo domain had often become little more than a coalition of fiefholders held together by a loose allegiance to the manor lord. Prince Shotoku's dream of a united Japan appeared to be only a distant memory (see Chapter 11). In actuality, Japan was on the verge of an extended era of national unification and peace under the rule of its greatest shogunate—the Tokugawa.

The Three Great Unifiers

The process began in the mid-sixteenth century with the emergence of three very powerful political figures,

Oda Nobunaga (1568–1582), Toyotomi Hideyoshi (1582–1598), and Tokugawa Ieyasu (1598–1616). In 1568, Oda Nobunaga, the son of a samurai and a military commander under the Ashikaga shogunate, seized the imperial capital of Kyoto and placed the reigning shogun under his domination. During the next few years, the brutal and ambitious Nobunaga attempted to consolidate his rule throughout the central plains by defeating his rivals and suppressing the power of the Buddhist estates, but he was killed by one of his generals in 1582 before the process was complete. He was succeeded by Toyotomi Hideyoshi, a farmer's son who had worked his way up within the ranks to become a military commander. Orig-

inally lacking a family name of his own, he eventually adopted the name Toyotomi ("abundant provider") to embellish his reputation for improving the material standards of his domain. Hideyoshi located his capital at Osaka, where he built a castle to accommodate his headquarters, and gradually extended the base of his own power outward to the southern islands of Shikoku and Kyushu. By 1590, he had persuaded most of the daimyo on the Japanese islands to accept his authority and created a national currency. Then he invaded Korea in an abortive effort to export his rule to the Asian mainland.

The invasion of Korea had been provoked by Hideyoshi's imperial ambitions to attack China. He had

◆ **The Siege on Osaka Castle.** After the death of Toyotomi Hideyoshi in 1598, titular authority in Japan passed on to his infant son Hideyori, whose supporters located their headquarters at Osaka Castle in Central Japan. In 1615, the powerful warlord

Tokugawa Ieyasu seized the castle, scattered Hideyori's supporters, and declared himself shogun. The family's control over Japan lasted nearly 250 years.

invited the ruler of the Korean Yi dynasty to join with him in the attack, but the latter had refused. Since their rise to power over Koguryo in 1392, Yi rulers had accepted tributary status to the Ming dynasty and had faithfully attempted to implement the Confucian model in Korea. In revenge, Hideyoshi invaded the peninsula with 160,000 troops armed with modern firearms and soon occupied the capital of Seoul. But the defenders responded with guerrilla attacks and eventually forced the Japanese to negotiate. When Hideyoshi died in 1598, the Japanese troops withdrew, and good relations were restored.

The unification of Japan during the era of Oda Nobunaga and Toyotomi Hideyoshi is reminiscent of the rise of centralized monarchies in Europe during the sixteenth century, but there were some clear differences. Neither Nobunaga nor Hideyoshi was able to eliminate the power of the local daimyo. Both were compelled to form alliances with some daimyo in order to destroy other more powerful rivals. At the conclusion of his conquests in 1590, Toyotomi Hideyoshi could claim to be the supreme proprietor of all registered lands in areas under his authority. But he then reassigned those lands as fiefs to the local daimyo, who declared their allegiance to him. The daimyo in turn began to pacify the countryside, carrying out extensive "sword hunts" to disarm the population and attracting samurai to serve the interests of their lord at his headquarters in the castle town. The Japanese tradition of decentralized rule had not been overcome.

After Hideyoshi's death in 1598, Tokugawa Ieyasu, the powerful daimyo of Edo (modern-day Tokyo) moved to fill the vacuum. Neither Hideyoshi nor Oda Nobunaga had claimed the title of shogun, but Ieyasu, after forcing his predecessor's heir to take refuge in the castle at Osaka, named himself shogun in 1603, initiating the most powerful and long-lasting of all Japanese shogunates. The Tokugawa rulers completed the restoration of central authority begun by Nobunaga and Hideyoshi and remained in power at their capital at Edo until 1868, when a war dismantled the entire system. As a contemporary phrased it, "Oda pounds the national rice cake, Hideyoshi kneads it, and in the end Ieyasu sits down and eats it."[13]

Opening to the West

The unification of Japan under the three great commanders took place almost simultaneously with the arrival of the first Europeans. Portuguese traders sailing in a Chinese junk that had possibly been blown off course by a typhoon had landed on the islands in 1543, about thirty years after their countrymen had arrived in China. In a few years, Portuguese ships began stopping at Japanese ports on a regular basis to take part in the regional trade between Japan, China, and Southeast Asia. The first Jesuit missionary, Francis Xavier, arrived in 1549 and had some success in converting the local population to Christianity. As he noted in a letter to Jesuit colleagues at Goa:

> One thing I tell you, for which you may give many thanks to God Our Lord, that this land of Japan is very fit for our holy faith greatly to increase therein; and if we knew how to speak the language, I have no doubt whatsoever that we would make many Christians. May it please our Lord that we may learn it soon, for already we begin to appreciate it, and we learned to repeat the ten commandments in the space of forty days, which we applied ourselves thereto.[14]

Initially, the visitors were welcomed. The curious Japanese (the Japanese were "very desirous of knowledge," said Francis Xavier) were fascinated by tobacco, clocks, spectacles, and other European goods, while local daimyo were interested in purchasing all types of European weapons and armaments (see the box on p. 629). Oda Nobunaga and Toyotomi Hideyoshi found the new firearms helpful in defeating their enemies and unifying the islands. The effect on Japanese military architecture was particularly striking, as local lords began to erect castles on the European model. Many of these castles, such as Himeji and Hideyoshi's castle at Osaka, still exist today.

As Francis Xavier had hoped, the missionaries also had some success. Assisted by misleading translations of sacred concepts in both cultures (Francis Xavier was notoriously poor at learning foreign languages), they converted a number of local daimyo, some of whom may have been motivated in part by the desire for commercial profits. By the end of the sixteenth century, thousands of Japanese in the southernmost islands of Kyushu and Shikoku had become Christians. One converted daimyo ceded the superb natural harbor of the modern-day city of Nagasaki to the Society of Jesus, which proceeded to use the new settlement for both missionary and trading purposes. But papal claims to the loyalty of all Japanese Christians and the European habit of intervening in local politics soon began to arouse suspicion in official circles. Missionaries added to the problem by deliberately destroying local idols and shrines and turning some temples into Christian schools or churches.

Inevitably, the local authorities reacted. In 1587, having extended his rule over the southern islands, Toyotomi Hideyoshi issued an edict prohibiting further Christian activities within his domains. Japan, he declared, was

☙ A Present for Lord Tokitaka ☙

The Portuguese introduced firearms to Japan in the six-teenth century. In this passage, the daimyo of a small island off the southern tip of Japan receives an explanation of how to use the new weapons and is fascinated by the re-sults. Note how Lord Tokitaka attempts to understand the procedures in terms of traditional Daoist beliefs.

The Japanese Discover Firearms

"There are two leaders among the traders, the one called Murashusa, and the other Christian Mota. In their hands they carried something two or three feet long, straight on the outside with a passage inside, and made of a heavy substance. The inner passage runs through it although it is closed at the end. At its side there is an aperture which is the passageway for fire. Its shape defies comparison with anything I know. To use it, fill it with powder and small lead pellets. Set up a small . . . target on a bank. Grip the object in your hand, compose your body, and closing one eye, apply fire to the aperture. Then the pellet hits the target squarely. The explosion is like lightning and the report like thunder. Bystanders must cover their ears. . . . This thing with one blow can smash a mountain of silver and a wall of iron. If one sought to do mischief in an-other man's domain and he was touched by it, he would lose his life instantly. Needless to say this is also true for the deer and stag that ravage the plants in the fields."

Lord Tokitaka saw it and thought it was the wonder of wonders. He did not know its name at first nor the details of its use. Then someone called it "iron-arms," although it was not known whether the Chinese called it so, or whether it was so called only on our island. Thus, one day, Tokitaka spoke to the two alien leaders through an interpreter: "Incapable though I am, I should like to learn about it." Whereupon, the chiefs answered, also through an interpreter: "If you wish to learn about it, we shall teach you its mysteries." Toki-taka then asked, "What is its secret?" The chief replied: "The secret is to put your mind aright and close one eye." Tokitaka said: "The ancient sages have often taught how to set one's mind aright, and I have learned something of it. If the mind is not set aright, there will be no logic for what we say or do. Thus, I understand what you say about setting our minds aright. However, will it not impair our vision for objects at a distance if we close an eye? Why should we close an eye?" To which the chiefs replied: "That is because concentra-tion is important in everything. When one concen-trates, a broad vision is not necessary. To close an eye is not to dim one's eyesight but rather to project one's concentration farther. You should know this." De-lighted, Tokitaka said: "That corresponds to what Lao Tzu has said, 'Good sight means seeing what is very small.'"

That year the festival day of the Ninth Month fell on the day of the Metal and the Boar. Thus, one fine morning the weapon was filled with powder and lead pellets, a target was set up more than a hundred paces away, and fire was applied to the weapon. At first the people were astonished; then they became frightened. But in the end they all said in unison: "We should like to learn!" Disregarding the high price of the arms, To-kitaka purchased from the aliens two pieces of the firearms for his family treasure. As for the art of grind-ing, sifting, and mixing of the powder, Tokitaka let his retainer, Shinokawa Shoshiro, learn it. Tokitaka occu-pied himself, morning and night, and without rest in handling the arms. As a result, he was able to convert the misses of his early experiments into hits—a hun-dred hits in a hundred attempts. . . .

"the land of the Gods" and the destruction of shrines by the foreigners was "something unheard of in previous ages." To "corrupt and stir up the lower classes" to com-mit such sacrileges, he declared, was "outrageous."[15] Those responsible (the Jesuits) were ordered to leave the country within twenty days. Hideyoshi was careful to dis-tinguish missionary from trading activities, however, and merchants were permitted to continue their operations (see the box on p. 631).

The Jesuits protested the expulsion, and eventually Hideyoshi relented, permitting them to continue prose-lytizing so long as they were discreet. But he refused to re-peal the edicts, and when the aggressive activities of newly arrived Spanish Franciscans aroused his ire, he or-dered the execution of nine missionaries and a number of their Japanese converts. When the missionaries contin-ued to interfere in local politics (some even tried to in-cite the daimyo in the southern islands against the

◆ The Portuguese Arrive at Nagasaki. Portuguese traders landed in Japan by accident in 1543. In a few years, they arrived regularly, taking part in a regional trade network between Japan, China, and Southeast Asia. Here we see a late sixteenth-century Japanese interpretation of the first Portuguese landing at Nagasaki.

shogunate government in Edo), Tokugawa Ieyasu completed the process by ordering the eviction of all missionaries in 1612. The persecution of Japanese Christians intensified, leading to an abortive revolt by Christian peasants on the island of Kyushu in 1637, which was bloodily suppressed.

At first, Japanese authorities hoped to maintain commercial relations with European countries even while suppressing the Western religion, but eventually they decided to prohibit foreign trade altogether and closed the two major foreign factories on the island of Hirado and at Nagasaki. The sole remaining opening to the West was at Deshima Island in Nagasaki harbor, where a small Dutch community that had been expelled from Hirado was permitted to engage in limited trade with Japan (the Dutch, unlike the Portuguese and the Spanish, had not allowed missionary activities to interfere with their commercial interests). A small amount of commerce took place with China, but Japanese subjects of the shogunate were forbidden to leave the country on penalty of death. Strict conditions were imposed on the Dutch for retaining their presence in Japan. Dutch ships were permitted to dock at

Nagasaki harbor once a year and, after close inspection, were allowed to remain for two or three months. Conditions on the island of Deshima itself were quite confining, as the Dutch physician Engelbert Kaempfer indignantly reported in 1692:

> . . . in the year 1641, soon after the total expulsion of the Portuguese, orders were sent us to quit our old factory at Firando [Hirado], to exchange the protection of a good and indulgent Prince, for the severe and strict government of Nagasaki, and under a very narrow inspection to confine our selves within that small Island, I should rather say, Prison, which was built for the Portuguese. So great was the covetousness of the Dutch, and so great the alluring power of the Japanese gold, that rather than to quit the prospect of a trade, indeed most advantageous, they willingly underwent an almost perpetual imprisonment, for such in fact is our stay at Desima, and chose to suffer many hardships in a foreign and heathen country . . . , to leave off praying and singing of psalms in publick . . . , and lastly, patiently and submissively to bear the abusiveness and injurious behavior of these proud infidels towards us, than which nothing can be offer'd more shocking to a generous and noble mind.[16]

❧ Toyotomi Hideyoshi Expels the Missionaries ❧

When Christian missionaries in sixteenth-century Japan began to interfere in local politics and criticize traditional religious practices, Toyotomi Hideyoshi issued an edict calling for their expulsion. In this letter to the Portuguese viceroy in Asia, Hideyoshi explains his decision. Note his conviction that Buddhists, Confucianists, and followers of Shinto all believe in the same God and his criticism of Christianity for rejecting all other faiths. Hideyoshi's dream of conquering China was aborted when he died in 1598.

Toyotomi Hideyoshi, Letter to the Viceroy of the Indies

Reading your message from afar, I can appreciate the immense expanse of water which separates us. As you have noted in your letter, my country, which is comprised of sixty-odd provinces, has known for many years more days of disorder than days of peace; rowdies have been given to fomenting intrigue, and bands of warriors have formed cliques to defy the court's orders. Ever since my youth, I have been constantly concerned over this deplorable situation. I studied the art of self-cultivation and the secret of governing the country. Through profound planning and forethought, and according to the three principles of benevolence, wisdom, and courage, I cared for the warriors on the one hand and looked after the common people on the other; while administering justice, I was able to establish security. Thus, before many years had passed, the unity of the nation was set on a firm foundation, and now foreign nations, far and near, without exception, bring tribute to us. Everyone, everywhere, seeks to obey my orders. . . . Though our own country is now safe and secure, I nevertheless entertain hopes of ruling the great Ming nation. I can reach the Middle Kingdom aboard my palace-ship within a short time. It will be as easy as pointing to the palm of my hand. I shall then use the occasion to visit your country regardless of the distance or the differences between us.

Ours is the land of the Gods, and God is mind. Everything in nature comes into existence because of mind. Without God there can be no spirituality. Without God there can be no way. God rules in times of prosperity as in times of decline. God is positive and negative and unfathomable. Thus, God is the root and source of all existence. This God is spoken of by Buddhism in India, Confucianism in China, and Shinto in Japan. To know Shinto is to know Buddhism as well as Confucianism.

As long as man lives in this world, Humanity will be a basic principle. Were it not for Humanity and Righteousness, the sovereign would not be a sovereign, nor a minister of a state a minister. It is through the practice of Humanity and Righteousness that the foundations of our relationships between sovereign and minister, parent and child, and husband and wife are established. If you are interested in the profound philosophy of God and Buddha, request an explanation and it will be given to you. In your land one doctrine is taught to the exclusion of others, and you are not yet informed of the [Confucian] philosophy of Humanity and Righteousness. Thus there is no respect for God and Buddha and no distinction between sovereign and ministers. Through heresies you intend to destroy the righteous law. Hereafter, do not expound, in ignorance of right and wrong, unreasonable and wanton doctrines. A few years ago the so-called Fathers came to my country seeking to bewitch our men and women, both of the laity and clergy. At that time punishment was administered to them, and it will be repeated if they should return to our domain to propagate their faith. It will not matter what sect or denomination they represent— they shall be destroyed. It will then be too late to repent. If you entertain any desire of establishing amity with this land, the seas have been rid of the pirate menace, and merchants are permitted to come and go. Remember this.

The Tokugawa "Great Peace"

Once in power, the Tokugawa attempted to strengthen the system that had governed Japan for over three hundred years. They followed precedent in ruling through the *bakufu*, composed now of a coalition of daimyo, and a council of elders. But the system was more centralized than it had been previously. Now the shogunate government played a dual role. It set national policy on behalf of the emperor in Kyoto, while simultaneously governing the shogun's own domain which included about one-quarter of the national territory as well as the three great cities of Edo, Kyoto, and Osaka. As before, the state was divided into separate territories, called domains (*han*), which were ruled by a total of about 250 individual daimyo lords. The daimyo were themselves divided into two types: the *fudai* (inside) daimyo, who were mostly small daimyo directly subordinate to the shogunate, and the *tozama* (outside) daimyo, who were larger and more independent lords usually more distant from the center of shogunate power in Edo.

In theory, the daimyo were essentially autonomous, since they were able to support themselves from taxes on their lands (the shogunate received its own revenues from its extensive landholdings). In actuality, the shogunate was able to guarantee daimyo loyalties by what has sometimes been called a "hostage system." Under this system, daimyo lords were compelled to maintain two residences, one in their own domains and the other at Edo. This not only placed the daimyo in hostage to the shogun, since daimyo families were forced to reside in Edo during the absence of the lord himself, but it also placed the Japanese nobility in a difficult economic position, since many of them felt compelled to keep up appearances in both residences. Some were able to defray the high costs by concentrating on cash crops such as sugar, fish, and forestry products, but most were rice producers, and their revenues remained roughly the same throughout the period. The daimyo were also able to protect their economic interests by depriving their samurai retainers of their proprietary rights over the land and transforming them into salaried officials. The fief thus became a stipend, and the personal relationship between the daimyo and his retainers gradually gave way to a bureaucratic authority.

The Tokugawa also tinkered with the social system by limiting the size of the samurai class and reclassifying samurai who supported themselves by tilling the land as commoners. In fact, with the long period of peace brought about by Tokugawa rule, the samurai gradually ceased to be a warrior class and were required to live in the castle towns. As a gesture to their glorious past, samurai were still permitted to wear their two swords, and a rigid separation was maintained between persons of samurai status and the nonaristocratic segment of the population. The rigid class distinctions within Japanese society were noticed by the Jesuit missionary Francis Xavier, who observed that "on no account would a poverty-stricken gentleman marry with someone outside the gentry, even if he were given great sums to do so," since he would lose honor by marrying into the lower class.

SEEDS OF CAPITALISM

The major change that took place in Japanese society under the Tokugawa was not a deliberate act of the shogunate, but a process that undermined the Tokugawa feudal structure and ultimately helped to bring it to an end. Since the fourteenth century, some trade and industry had been carried on in Japan and eventually had become centered around the daimyo castle towns. As in China, commerce and industry had always suffered under the dual weight of official restrictions and social prejudice, but under the Tokugawa they began to flourish as never before. By the nineteenth century, trade and manufacturing had become a significant part of the Japanese economy.

The reasons for this commercial expansion have been a matter of debate; some scholars view the Tokugawa era as the first stage in the rise of an indigenous form of capitalism. Certainly, Japanese merchants benefited from the long period of peace that followed the centuries of almost constant civil war. They also benefited from low taxes and the patronage of the upper classes. Although Tokugawa shoguns exhibited the same disdain for commercial activity as their predecessors, they relied primarily on agricultural taxes for their revenue. Moreover, the hostage system also spurred the growth of manufacturing and trade. The daimyo, compelled to maintain a residence at the shogun's court as well as in their own domains, promoted the sale of local goods, such as textiles, forestry products, sugar, and *sake* (a Japanese rice wine), in order to pay their heavy expenses.

Most of this expansion took place in the major cities and the castle towns, where the merchants and artisans lived along with the samurai, who were clustered in neighborhoods surrounding the daimyo's castle. Because the peasants, who comprised about 80 percent of the population, were restricted to villages and prohibited from all but the most menial forms of production, the urban areas now became the focus for manufacturing, distribution, and consumption for the entire country. As the standard of living rose—driven in part by technological advances in agriculture and an expansion of arable land—a new consumer culture began to permeate the cities and towns.

Eventually, the increased pace of industrial activity spread beyond the cities into rural areas. As in Great Britain, cotton was a major factor. Cotton had been introduced to China during the Song dynasty and spread to Korea shortly thereafter. Small amounts were exported to Japan, but cotton cloth was too expensive for the common people, who had traditionally worn clothing made

♦ **A Japanese Castle.** The Japanese perfected a new type of fortress-palace in the early seventeenth century. Strategically placed high on a hilltop, constructed of heavy stone with tiny windows and fortified by numerous watchtowers and massive walls, these strongholds were impregnable to arrows and cata- pults. They served as a residence for the local *daimyo*, while the castle compound also housed his army and contained the seat of the local government. Himeji castle, shown here, is one of the most beautiful in Japan.

of hemp. Imports increased during the sixteenth century, however, when cotton cloth began to be used for uniforms, matchlock fuses, and sails. Eventually, technological advances made the process cheaper, and merchant houses began to enter the business of purchasing and distributing the cloth. Specialized communities for manufacturing cotton cloth began to appear in the countryside and were gradually transformed into towns. By the eighteenth century, cotton had firmly replaced hemp as the clothing of choice for most Japanese.

These developments, along with rising living standards and the voracious appetite of the aristocrats, provided the impetus for a dramatic rise in commerce and manufacturing under the Tokugawa, notably in the growing cities of Edo, Kyoto, and Osaka. By the mid-eigh-

teenth century, Edo had a population of over one million and was one of the largest cities in the world. With growth came increasing sophistication. Banking flourished and paper money became the normal medium of exchange in commercial transactions. Merchants formed guilds not only to control market conditions but also to facilitate government control, and the collection of taxes. Under the benign if somewhat contemptuous supervision of Japan's noble rulers, a Japanese merchant class gradually began to emerge from the shadows to play a significant role in the life of the Japanese nation.

One class that was hard hit by the economic changes of the seventeenth and eighteenth centuries was the samurai. Barred by tradition and prejudice from commercial activities, the samurai were unable to benefit from

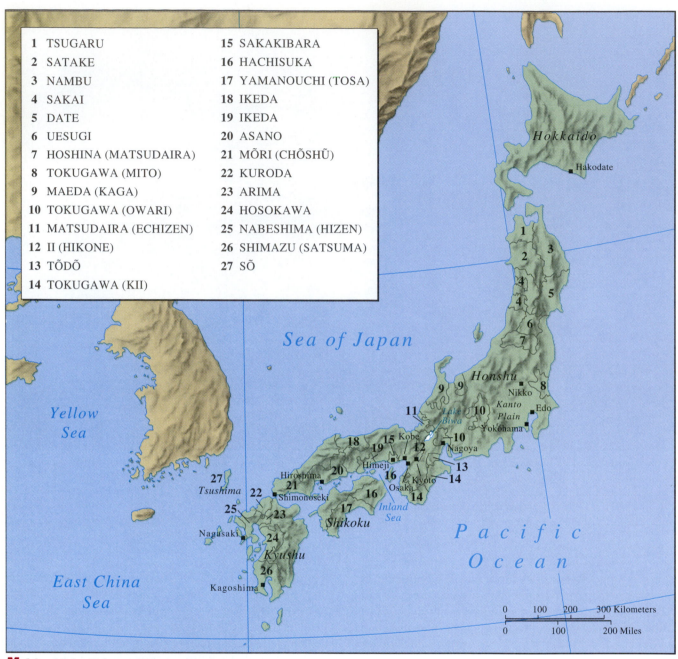

1 TSUGARU	15 SAKAKIBARA
2 SATAKE	16 HACHISUKA
3 NAMBU	17 YAMANOUCHI (TOSA)
4 SAKAI	18 IKEDA
5 DATE	19 IKEDA
6 UESUGI	20 ASANO
7 HOSHINA (MATSUDAIRA)	21 MŌRI (CHŌSHŪ)
8 TOKUGAWA (MITO)	22 KURODA
9 MAEDA (KAGA)	23 ARIMA
10 TOKUGAWA (OWARI)	24 HOSOKAWA
11 MATSUDAIRA (ECHIZEN)	25 NABESHIMA (HIZEN)
12 II (HIKONE)	26 SHIMAZU (SATSUMA)
13 TŌDŌ	27 SŌ
14 TOKUGAWA (KII)	

Map 17.3 Tokugawa Japan.

the rising tempo of economic activity under the Tokugawa. Although some profited from their transformation into a managerial class on the daimyo domains, most still relied for their incomes on revenues from rice lands and thus often failed to cover their rising expenses and fell heavily into debt. Others were released from servitude to their lord and became "masterless samurai," thereby creating an explosive situation reminiscent of the problems of unemployed intellectuals in many developing societies in our own day. Occasionally, these unemployed warriors (known as *ronin*, or "wave men") revolted or plotted against the local authorities. In one episode, made famous in song and story as the "Forty-seven Ronin," the masterless samurai of a local lord who had been forced to commit suicide by a shogunate official later assassinated the official in revenge. Although their act received wide popular acclaim, the *ronin* were later forced to take their own lives.

The effects of economic developments on the rural population during the Tokugawa era are harder to estimate. Some farm families benefited by exploiting the growing demand for cash crops. But not all prospered. Most peasants continued to rely on rice cultivation and were whipsawed between declining profits and rising costs and taxes (as daimyo expenses increased, land taxes often took up to 50 percent of the annual harvest). Many were forced to become tenants or to work as wage laborers on the farms of wealthy neighbors or in village industries. When rural conditions in some areas became desperate, peasant revolts erupted. One scholar has estimated that nearly seven thousand disturbances took place during the Tokugawa era.

Some Japanese historians, influenced by a Marxist view of history, have interpreted such evidence as an indication that the Tokugawa economic system was highly exploitative, with feudal aristocrats oppressing powerless peasants. Recent scholars, however, have tended to adopt a more balanced view, maintaining that agriculture as well as manufacturing and commerce experienced extensive growth. Some point out that although the population doubled in the seventeenth century, a relatively low rate for the time period, so did the amount of cultivable land, while agriculture technology made significant advances.

Recent evidence has shown that the primary reasons for the relatively low rate of population growth were late marriage, abortion, and infanticide. Some historians have interpreted these practices as rational decisions by peasants attempting to increase their standard of living. But Honda Toshiaki, a late eighteenth-century demographer, believed they were often motivated by economic hardship:

> Whenever there has been a period of continued peace, husbands and wives are fearful lest it become increasingly difficult for them to earn a living. Aware that if they have many children they will not have any property to leave them, they confer and decide that rather than rear children who in later years will have great difficulty in making a decent living, it is better to take precautions before they are born and not add another mouth to feed. If they do have a child, they secretly destroy it, calling the process by the euphemism of "thinning out."[17]

In general, then, the rise in rural unrest during the Tokugawa era was probably motivated less by a decline in the standard of living than by local factors and a new sense of peasant assertiveness that was itself a product of the disappearance of the *shoen* system during the pre-Tokugawa period (see Chapter 11). Recent studies suggest that peasant disturbances were becoming a more or less routine means of protesting against rising taxes and official corruption or of demanding "benevolence" from the manor lord in times of climatic disaster. As such, they reflected a desire to return to a more satisfactory status quo rather than an attempt to overthrow the existing order and establish a utopian future.

Following the Straight and Narrow in Tokugawa Japan

Like the Qing dynasty in China, the Tokugawa shoguns attempted to keep their subjects in line with decrees that carefully prescribed all kinds of behavior. As this decree, which was circulated in all Japanese villages, shows, the bakufu sought to be the moral instructor as well as the guardian and protector of the Japanese people. Compare and contrast this decree with Emperor Kangxi's Sacred Edict in the box earlier in this chapter.

Maxims for Peasant Behavior

1. Young people are forbidden to congregate in great numbers.

2. Entertainments unsuited to peasants, such as playing the samisen or reciting ballad dramas, are forbidden.

3. Staging sumo matches is forbidden for the next five years.

4. The edict on frugality issued by the *han* at the end of last year must be observed.

5. Social relations in the village must be conducted harmoniously.

6. If a person has to leave the village for business or pleasure, that person must return by ten at night.

7. Father and son are forbidden to stay overnight at another person's house. An exception is to be made if it is to nurse a sick person.

8. Corvée assigned by the *han* must be performed faithfully.

9. Children who practice filial piety must be rewarded.

10. One must never get drunk and cause trouble for others.

11. Peasants who farm especially diligently must be rewarded.

12. Peasants who neglect farm work and cultivate their paddies and upland fields in a slovenly and careless fashion must be punished.

13. The boundary lines of paddy and upland fields must not be changed arbitrarily.

14. Recognition must be accorded to peasants who contribute greatly to village political affairs.

15. Fights and quarrels are forbidden in the village.

16. The deteriorating customs and morals of the village must be rectified.

17. Peasants who are suffering from poverty must be identified and helped.

18. This village has a proud history compared to other villages, but in recent years bad times have come upon us. Everyone must rise at six in the morning, cut grass, and work hard to revitalize the village.

19. The punishments to be meted out to violators of the village code and gifts to be awarded the deserving are to be decided during the last assembly meeting of the year.

Life in the Village

The changes that took place during the Tokugawa era had a major impact on the lives of ordinary Japanese. In some respects, the result was an increase in the power of the central government at the village level. The shogunate increasingly relied on Confucian maxims advocating obedience and hierarchy to enhance its authority with the general population. Decrees from the *bakufu* instructed the peasants on all aspects of their lives, including their eating habits and their behavior (see the box above). At the same time, the increased power of the government led to more autonomy from the local daimyo for the peasants. Villages now had more control over their local affairs and were responsible to the central government as much as to the nearby manor lord, although land taxes were still paid to the daimyo.

At the same time, the Tokugawa era saw the emergence of the nuclear family (*ie*) as the basic unit in Japanese society. In previous times, Japanese peasants had had few legal rights. Most were too poor to keep their conjugal family unit intact or to pass property on to their children. Many lived at the manorial residence or worked as servants in the households of more affluent villagers. Now, with farm income on the rise, the nuclear family took on the same form as in China, although without the joint family concept. The Japanese system of inheritance was based on the concept of primogeniture. Family property was passed on to the eldest son, although younger sons often received land from their parents to set up their own families after marriage.

Another result of the changes under the Tokugawa was that the role of women became somewhat more restricted than it had been in the previous era. The rights of females were especially restricted in the samurai class, where Confucian values were highly influential. Male heads of households had broad authority over property, marriage, and divorce, while wives were expected to obey their husbands on pain of death. Males often took concubines or homosexual partners, while females were expected to remain chaste. The male offspring of samurai parents studied the Confucian classics in schools established by the daimyo, while females were reared at home, where only the fortunate might receive a rudimentary training in Chinese characters.

Women were similarly at a disadvantage among the common people. Marriages were arranged, and as in China, wives were expected to move in with the family of their husband. A wife who did not meet the expectations of her spouse or his family was likely to be divorced. Still, sexual relations were more egalitarian than among the nobility. Women were generally valued as childbearers and homemakers, and both sexes worked in the fields although men performed the heavier labor. Coeducational schools were established in villages and market towns, and about one-quarter of the students were female. Poor families, however, often put infant daughters to death or sold them into prostitution and the "floating world" of entertainment (see The Literature of the New Middle Class later in this chapter).

Such attitudes toward women operated within the context of the increasingly rigid stratification of Japanese society. Deeply conservative in their social policies, the Tokugawa rulers established strict legal distinctions between the four main classes in Japan (warriors, artisans, peasants, and merchants). Intermarriage between classes was forbidden in theory, although sometimes the prohibitions were ignored in practice. Below these classes were Japan's outcastes, the *eta*. Formerly, they were permitted to escape their status, at least in theory. The Tokugawa made their status hereditary and enacted severe discriminatory laws against them, regulating their place of residence, their dress, and even their hairstyles.

Tokugawa Culture

Under the Tokugawa, the tensions between the old society and the emerging new one were starkly reflected in the arena of culture. On the one hand, the classical culture, influenced by Confucian themes, Buddhist quietism, and the samurai warrior tradition, continued to flourish under the patronage of the shogunate. On the other, a vital new set of cultural values was beginning to appear, especially in the cities. This innovative era witnessed the rise of popular literature written by and for the townspeople. After centuries of periodic strife, the stability of the Tokugawa era allowed ordinary Japanese to enjoy entertainment aimed at them in both the theater and in books. With the development of woodblock printing in the early seventeenth century, literature became available to the common people, literacy levels rose, and lending libraries increased the accessibility of the printed word. In contrast to the previous mood of doom and gloom, the new prose was cheerful and even frivolous, its primary aim being to divert and amuse.

THE LITERATURE OF THE NEW MIDDLE CLASS

The best examples of this new urban fiction are the works of Saikaku (1642–1693), considered to be one of Japan's greatest novelists. Beginning his career as a poet, Saikaku switched early in life to prose and created a new genre with his first novel, which relates the amorous and financial adventures of its hero, who was the prototype of the new self-made merchant. The novel, which was the first to proclaim the energy and optimism of the new era, was enormously popular and sold over a thousand copies in its first printing.

Saikaku's greatest novel, *Five Women Who Loved Love*, relates the amorous exploits of five women of the merchant class. Based partly on real-life experiences, it broke from the Confucian ethic of wifely fidelity to her husband and portrayed women who were willing to die for love—and all but one eventually did. Despite the tragic circumstances, the tone of the novel is upbeat and sometimes comic, as the author's wry comments prevent the reader from becoming emotionally involved with the heroines' misfortunes. After all, they are experiencing a unique passionate love, and death is but a small price to pay for ecstasy. As one of the heroines approaches the moment of death, the novel dwells not on her agony, but rather on the image of her "beautiful figure, clothed in the pale orange slip which she wore to her execution."[18]

Obviously, money was of great interest to the merchant class, and Saikaku also wrote about how to make money and how to keep it in a work entitled *The Millionaire's Gospel, Revised Version*. In addition to heterosexual novels for the merchant class, Saikaku wrote of homosexual liaisons among the samurai. As a keen observer of

◆ **The Floating World of Edo.** In eighteenth-century Japan, the self-confidence of the newly affluent bourgeoisie expressed itself in the woodblock print. Many prints portrayed "the floating world," as the pleasure district in Edo was called. Seen here are courtesans, storytellers, jesters, and various other entertainers.

human frailties and a superb storyteller as well, Saikaku was immensely popular in his day. His works greatly influenced later Japanese novelists and reinstated prose fiction as a dynamic art form after four hundred years of neglect.

In the theater, the rise of *kabuki* threatened the long dominance of the *no* play, replacing the somewhat restrained and elegant thematic and stylistic approach of the classical drama with a new emphasis on violence, music, and dramatic gestures. Significantly, the new drama emerged not from the rarefied world of the court but from the new world of entertainment and amusement. Its very commercial success, however, led to difficulties with the government, which periodically attempted to restrict or even suppress it. Early *kabuki* was often performed by prostitutes and depicted the increasingly popular "floating world" of brothels, teahouses, and

dance halls that began to proliferate in the growing cities. Shogunate officials feared that such activities could have a corrupting effect on the nation's morals and prohibited women from appearing on the stage; at the same time, they attempted to create a new professional class of male actors to impersonate female characters on stage. The decree had a mixed effect, however, because it encouraged homosexual activities that had been popular among the samurai and in Buddhist monasteries since medieval times. Yet the use of male actors also promoted a greater emphasis on physical activities such as acrobatics and swordplay and furthered the evolution of *kabuki* into a mature dramatic art.

Whereas *kabuki* is essentially a showcase for the virtuosity of the actor, *bunraku*, or puppet theater, is a theatrical performance of a literary text. Both were popular in the Tokugawa era, but by the late seventeenth century, *bunraku* actually eclipsed *kabuki* in popularity due to the genius of Chikamatsu, one of the greatest Japanese dramatists. Reportedly, he wrote for the puppet theater rather than *kabuki* to protect his texts, because *kabuki* actors were known for modifying the scripts to aggrandize their own parts. Chikamatsu's puppet plays told of the loves of shop clerks and prostitutes, favorite themes of the townspeople, but were written in beautiful poetic language.

In contrast to the popular literature of the Tokugawa period, poetry persevered in its more serious tradition. Although linked verse, so popular in the fourteenth and fifteenth centuries, found a more lighthearted expression in the sixteenth century, the most exquisite poetry was produced in the seventeenth century by the greatest of all Japanese poets, Basho (1644–1694). He was concerned with the search for the meaning of existence and the poetic expression of his experience. His preferred poetic form was the *hokku*, or 5–7–5 syllable, three-line verse, which is followed by a 7–7 syllable two-line accompanying verse. In his hands, the *hokku* could either serve as the opening component in a linked verse or stand independently as a complete poem by itself. Not until the nineteenth century did Japanese poets write the independent 5–7–5 verse, called *haiku*, with the specific intention that it be a complete entity and not linked to additional verse. The brevity of *hokku* leads to ambiguity, hinting at the mysteries of life without intellectual discourse. Basho's genius lies in his sudden juxtaposition of a general or eternal condition with an immediate perception, an electrical spark that instantly reveals a moment of truth. With his love of Daoism and Zen Buddhism, Basho found answers to his quest for the meaning of life in nature, and his poems are grounded in seasonal imagery.

Basho was highly admired in his own lifetime, especially in the latter part of his life, and had many disciples who recorded his aesthetic theories and details of his life. In the late eighteenth century, both the Shinto hierarchy and the imperial court regarded him as a saint. Today Basho is revered but no longer sanctified. More has been written about him than about any other Japanese poet, and his work has justly earned world acclaim. The following are perhaps his most famous poems:

The ancient pond
A frog leaps in
The sound of the water.

On the withered branch
A crow has alighted—
The end of autumn.

Such stillness—
The cries of the cicadas
Sink into the rocks.

The sea darkens,
The cries of the seagulls
Are faintly white.

His last poem, dictated to a disciple only three days prior to his death, succinctly expressed his frustration with the unfinished business of life:

On a journey, ailing—
my dreams roam about
on a withered moor.

Like all great artists, Basho made his poems appear effortless and simple. He speaks directly to everyone, everywhere.

TOKUGAWA ART

Art also reflected the dynamism and changes in Japanese culture under the Tokugawa regime. The shogun's order that all daimyo and their families live every other year in Edo set off a burst of building as provincial rulers competed to erect the most magnificent mansion. Furthermore, the shoguns themselves constructed splendid castles adorned with sumptuous, almost ostentatious decor and furnishings. Lastly, the prosperity of the newly rising merchant class added fuel to the fire. Japanese paintings, architecture, textiles, and ceramics all flourished during this affluent era.

Court painters filled magnificent multipaneled screens with gold foil, which was also used to cover walls and even ceilings. This lavish use of gold foil mirrored the grandeur of the new Japanese rulers but also served a practical purpose: it reflected light in the dark castle rooms, where windows were kept small for defensive purposes. In contrast to the almost gaudy splendors of court painting, however, some Japanese artists of the late sixteenth century returned to the tradition of black inkwash. No longer copying the Chinese, these masterpieces expressed Japanese themes and techniques. In the *Pine Forest* by Tohaku, a pair of six-panel screens depicting pine trees, 85 percent of the paper is left blank, suggesting mist and the quiet of an autumn dawn. In the early seventeenth century, the nobility and upper-class merchants established an artist colony that produced a variety of crafts and paintings of a quality not seen since the Heian era.

Although Japan was isolated from the Western world during much of the Tokugawa era, Japanese art was enriched by ideas from other cultures. Japanese pottery makers borrowed both techniques and designs from Korea to produce the handsome ceramics of Bizen, Iga, and Nabeshima. The passion for "Dutch learning" inspired Japanese to study Western medicine, astronomy, and languages and also led to experimentation with oil painting and Western ideas of perspective and the interplay of light and dark. Some painters depicted the "southern barbarians," with their strange ships and costumes, large noses, and plumed hats. Europeans desired Japanese lacquerware and metalwork, inlay with ivory and mother-of-pearl, and especially the ceramics, which were now as highly prized as those of the Chinese.

Perhaps the most famous of all Japanese art of the Tokugawa era is the woodblock print. Genre painting, or representations of daily life, began in the sixteenth century and found its new mass-produced form in the eighteenth-century woodblock print. The now-literate mercantile class was eager for illustrated texts of the amusing and bawdy tales that had circulated in oral tradition. At first, these prints were done in black and white, but later they included vibrant colors. The self-confidence of the age is dramatically captured in these prints, which represent a collective self-portrait of the late Tokugawa urban classes. Some prints depict entire city blocks filled with people, trades, and festivals, while others show the interiors of houses; thus, they provide us with excellent visual documentation of the times. Others portray the "floating world" of the entertainment quarter with scenes of carefree revelers enjoying the pleasures of life.

One of the most renowned of the numerous blockprint

artists was Utamaro (1754–1806), who painted erotic and sardonic women in everyday poses, such as walking down the steet, cooking, or drying their bodies after a bath. Sharaku's exaggerated and satirical prints of *kabuki* actors still amuse viewers today, but they so offended the actors that his publisher dropped the portraits after only ten months. Hokusai (1760–1849) was famous for the *Thirty-six Views of Mount Fuji*, which created a new and bold interpretation of the Japanese landscape. Finally, Hiroshige (1797–1858) developed the genre of the travelogue print in his *Fifty-three Stages of the Tokaido Highway*, which presented ordinary scenes of daily life, both in the country and the cities, all enveloped in a lyrical, quiet mood. These colorful prints were the most innovative and distinctive art form of the era and are highly prized the world over.

Why did a new popular culture begin to appear in Tokugawa Japan, while traditional values continued to prevail in neighboring China? Certainly, one factor was the rapid growth of the cities as the main point of convergence for all the dynamic forces taking place in Japanese society. But other factors may have been at work as well. Despite the patent efforts of the Tokugawa rulers to promote traditional Confucian values as a code of behavior and an ideological worldview for their subjects, Confucian doctrine had historically occupied a relatively weak position in Japanese society. In China the scholar gentry class served as the traditional defenders and propagators of traditional orthodoxy, but the samurai, who were steeped in warrior values and had little exposure to Confucian learning, did not play a similar role in Japan. Tokugawa policies only exacerbated the problem. While the scholar gentry in Qing China continued to reside in the villages, serving as members of the local village council or as instructors of the young in local schools, the samurai class in Japan was deliberately isolated by government fiat and class privilege from the remainder of the population. The result was an ideological and cultural vacuum that would eventually be filled by the growing population of merchants and artisans in the major cities.

Korea: The Hermit Kingdom

While Japan was gradually moving away from its agrarian origins, the Yi dynasty in Korea was attempting to pattern its own society on the Chinese model. The dynasty had been founded by the military commander Yi Song Gye in the late fourteenth century and immediately set out to establish close political and cultural relations with the Ming dynasty. From their new capital at Seoul, located on the Han River in the center of the peninsula, the Yi rulers accepted a tributary relationship with their powerful neighbor and engaged in the wholesale adoption of Chinese institutions and values (see the box on p. 641). As in China, the civil service examinations tested candidates on their knowledge of the Confucian classics, and success was viewed as an essential step toward upward mobility.

There were differences, however. As in Japan, the dynasty continued to restrict entry into the bureaucracy to members of the aristocratic class, known in Korea as the *yangban* (or "two groups," the civilian and military). At the same time, the peasantry remained in virtually serf-like conditions, working on government estates or on the manor holdings of the landed elite. A class of slaves (*chonmin*) labored on government plantations or served in certain occupations, such as butchers and entertainers, considered beneath the dignity of other groups in the population.

Eventually, Korean society began to show signs of independence from Chinese orthodoxy. In the fifteenth century, a phonetic alphabet for writing the Korean spoken language (*hangul*) was devised. Although it was initially held in contempt by the elites and used primarily as a teaching device, eventually it became the medium for private correspondence and the publishing of fictional stories for a popular audience. At the same time, changes were taking place in the economy, where rising agricultural production contributed to a population increase and the appearance of a small urban industrial and commercial sector, and in society, where the long domination of the *yangban* class began to weaken. As their numbers increased and their power and influence declined, some *yangban* became merchants or even moved into the ranks of the peasantry, thus further blurring the distinction between the aristocratic class and the common people.

In general, Korean rulers tried to keep the country isolated from the outside world, but they were not always successful. The Japanese invasion under Toyotomi Hideyoshi in the late sixteenth century had a disastrous impact on Korean society, as did the rise of the Qing dynasty in China a few generations later. A Manchu invasion force entered northern Korea in the 1630s and eventually compelled the Yi dynasty to grant allegiance to the new imperial government in Beijing. Korea was relatively untouched by the arrival of European merchants and missionaries, although information about Christianity was brought to the peninsula by Koreans returning from tribute missions to China, and a small Catholic community was established there in the late eighteenth century.

Waste Not, Want Not: A Korean Prescription for Prosperity

Concern about high levels of government spending is not an attitude exclusive to the twentieth century. In this passage from the sixteenth-century treatise Essentials of the Sages' Learning, *the Neo-Confucianist philosopher Yi I (Yulgok, 1536–1584) advised the Korean monarch to avoid extravagant expenses so as to avoid setting a bad example to his subjects and causing hardship to the common people. Note the obligatory reference to China's Golden Age and the legendary Emperor Yao, "who lived in a house thatched with reeds and used earthen steps."*

Yi I, *Essentials of the Sages' Learning*

Economy in my humble opinion means showing respect for virtue, whereas extravagance is a great evil. . . . There is nothing in the state's treasury that is not produced by the toil and sweat of the people. How dare one carelessly indulge himself in extravagance and dissipate this precious wealth, causing distress among the people and bringing ruin to the achievements of our forefathers?

The former kings of this country ruled the state by means of economy for many generations and their expenditures were always based on revenues; therefore, the country was affluent and the storehouses were full of surplus. But since the time of Yŏnsangun [1494–1506], the expenditures in the palace have increased extravagantly, disregarding the practices of former rulers. Since then, the court has followed undesirable customs and has so far failed to reform itself. Therefore, the state's expenditures have increased daily. There are at present no unusual luxurious customs being practiced in the palace and no unessential public work projects being carried out within the country; yet the annual revenues cannot support the annual expenditures and the savings accrued under many for-

mer kings will be exhausted in the future. If a famine strikes or a war breaks out, we will be utterly helpless. Is this not truly deplorable?

The costumes being used in the palace now, which were reformed at the beginning of the dynasty, no longer demonstrate economy. Thus, the ordinary people too have developed a luxurious lifestyle; they dress themselves in colorful costumes, indulge in rich viands and sumptuous fare, and try to outdo each other in luxury. Even the bedding of the lowly actors and singing girls is all made of silk. As there is no regulation governing the relationship between the upper and the lower people and as waste abounds, people's morality has become lax and their livelihood progressively more difficult. If there is no reform from above, the state will lose its reason for existence. The way to correct this cannot be found in the ordinary rules. Instead, the reform must come from above, with the heart of Emperor Yao, who lived in a house thatched with reeds and used earthen steps. The queen and the court ladies must emulate the Empress Ma of Later Han, who always dressed herself in costumes made of coarse cloth, and must economize by reducing the palace expenditures. If the economizing starts in the palace and the families of scholar-officials become impressed by these practices and accept them, economizing will then spread to the people. Only then can we expect the old detrimental practices to be reformed, the precious wealth to be saved, and people's wealth to grow. As Wu-chu in the Spring and Autumn era said: "If selfish interest prevails and flourishes, it is difficult for virtue and righteousness to grow. If virtue and righteousness are not practiced, the people nearby will rise against the government, and the people in the distance will further be alienated." I humbly beseech Your Majesty to ponder this matter seriously.

Conclusion

When Christopher Columbus sailed from southern Spain in his three ships in August of 1492, he was seeking a route to China and Japan. He did not find it, but others soon did. In 1514, Portuguese ships arrived on the coast of South China. Thirty years later, a small contingent of Portuguese merchants became the first Europeans to set foot on the islands of Japan.

At first the new arrivals were welcomed, if only as curiosities. Eventually, several European nations established trade relations with China and Japan, and Christian missionaries of various religious orders were active in both countries, and in Korea as well. But their success was short-lived. Europeans eventually began to appear as a detriment to law and order, and during the seventeenth century, the majority of the foreign merchants and missionaries were evicted from all three countries. From that time until the middle of the nineteenth century, China, Japan, and Korea were relatively little affected by events taking place beyond their borders.

For long, that fact has deluded many observers into the assumption that the societies of East Asia were essentially stagnant, characterized by agrarian institutions and values reminiscent of those of the feudal era in Europe. As we have seen, however, that picture is misleading, for all three countries were changing and by the early nineteenth century were quite different from what they had been three centuries earlier.

Ironically, these changes were especially marked in Tokugawa Japan, an allegedly "closed country," where traditional classes and institutions were under increasing strain, not only from the emergence of a new merchant class, but also from the centralizing tendencies of the powerful Tokugawa shogunate. Some historians have seen strong parallels between Tokugawa Japan and early modern Europe, which gave birth to centralized empires and a strong merchant class during the same period. The image of the monarchy is reflected in a song sung at the shrine of Toyotomi Hideyoshi in Kyoto:

◆ **Seoul Palace Pagoda.** When the Yi dynasty came into power in the late fourteenth century, it established its capital at Seoul on the Han River. There it constructed a new palace. Korean public architecture was highly influenced by the Chinese classical model, as the multi-tiered pagoda on the palace grounds attest.

Who's that
Holding over four hundred provinces
In the palm of his hand
And entertaining at a tea-party?
It's His Highness
So mighty, so impressive![19]

By the beginning of the nineteenth century, then, powerful tensions, reflecting a growing gap between ideal and reality, were at work in both Chinese and Japanese society. Under these conditions, both countries were soon forced to face a new challenge from the aggressive power of an industrializing Europe.

CHAPTER NOTES

1. From Jonathan D. Spence, *Emperor of China: Self-Portrait of K'ang Hsi* (New York, 1974), pp. 143–44.

2. Quoted in J. H. Parry, ed., *The European Reconnaissance: Selected Documents* (New York, 1968), p. 129.

3. Louis J. Gallagher, ed. and trans., *China in the Sixteenth Century: The Journals of Matthew Ricci* (New York, 1953), p. 154.

4. Richard Strassberg, *The World of K'ang Shang-jen: A Man of Letters in Early Ch'ing China* (New York, 1983), p. 275.

5. Quoted in Frederick Wakeman, Jr., *The Great Enterprise* (Berkeley, Calif., 1985), p. 16.

6. Quoted in Jonathan D. Spence, *The Search for Modern China* (New York, 1990), p. 23.

7. Lynn Struve, *The Southern Ming, 1644–1662* (New Haven, Conn., 1984), p. 61.

8. Spence, *The Search for Modern China*, p. 123, citing J. L. Cranmer-Byng, *An Embassy to China: Lord MacArtney's Journal, 1793–1794* (London, 1912), p. 340.

9. Quoted in Parry, *The European Reconnaissance*, pp. 135–36.

10. Daniel J. Boorstin, *The Discoverers: A History of Man's Search to Know His World and Himself* (New York, 1983), p. 63.

11. Parry, *The European Reconnaissance*, p. 273, citing C. R. Boxer, ed., *South China in the Sixteenth Century* (London, 1953).

12. Ibid., p. 265.

13. Chie Nakane and Sinzaburo Oishi, eds., *Tokugawa Japan* (Tokyo, 1990), p. 14.

14. Parry, *The European Reconnaissance*, p. 146.

15. Quoted in Jurgis Elisonas, "Christianity and the daimyo," in John Whitney Hall, ed., *The Cambridge History of Japan*, vol. 4 (Cambridge, 1991), p. 360.

16. Engelbert Kaempfer, *The History of Japan: Together with a Description of the Kingdom of Siam, 1690–1692*, vol. 2 (Glasgow, 1906), pp. 173–74.

17. Quoted in Donald Keene, *The Japanese Discovery of Europe, 1720–1830*, revised ed. (Stanford, Calif., 1969), p. 114.

18. Quoted in Donald Keene, *Anthology of Japanese Literature* (New York, 1955), p. 353.

19. Quoted in Ryusaku Tsunoda et al., *Sources of Japanese Tradition* (New York, 1964), p. 313.

SUGGESTED READINGS

For a general overview of this period in East Asian history, see J. K. Fairbank, E. O. Reischauer, and A. Craig, *East Asia: Tradition and Transformation* (Boston, 1973) and C. Shirokauer, *A Brief History of Chinese and Japanese Civilizations*, 2d ed. (San Diego, 1989). A more detailed treatment of specific issues can be found in volumes 8 and 9 of F. W. Mote and D. Twitchett, eds., *The Cambridge History of China* (Cambridge, 1976) and J. W. Hall, ed., *The Cambridge History of Japan*, vol. 4 (Cambridge, 1991).

The best documentary surveys are W. T. de Bary, *Sources of Chinese Tradition* (New York, 1964) and R. Tsunoda, W. T. de Bary, and D. Keene, *Sources of Japanese Tradition* (New York, 1958). Also, see F. Schurmann and O. Schell, *The China Reader*, vol. 1 (New York, 1967). Early documents on European activities can be found in J. H. Parry, *The European Reconnaissance: Selected Documents* (New York, 1968).

On the late Ming, see J. D. Spence, *The Search for Modern China* (New York, 1990) and L. Struve, *The Southern Ming, 1644–1662* (New Haven, Conn., 1984). On the rise of the Qing, see F. Wakeman, Jr., *The Great Enterprise: The Manchu Reconstruction of Imperial Order in Seventeenth Century China* (Berkeley, Calif., 1985). On Kangxi, see J. D. Spence, *Emperor of China: Self-Portrait of K'ang Hsi* (New York, 1974). Social issues are discussed in S. Naquin and E. Rawski, *Chinese Society in the Eighteenth Century* (New Haven, Conn., 1987). Also, see J. D. Spence and J. Wills, eds., *From Ming to Ch'ing* (New Haven, Conn., 1979). For a very interesting account of Jesuit missionary experiences in China, see L. J. Gallagher, ed. and trans., *China in the Sixteenth Century: The Journals of Matthew Ricci, 1583–1616* (New York, 1953). For brief biographies of Ming-Qing luminaries such as Wang Yangming, Zheng Chenggong, and the Emperor Qianlong, see J. E. Wills, Jr., *Mountains of Fame: Portraits in Chinese History* (Princeton, N.J., 1994).

For an excellent introduction to the Chinese literature of this period, consult the classic *An Introduction to Chinese Literature* by Liu Wu-chi (Indiana, 1966). For the best translation of *The Dream of the Red Chamber*, see Chi-chen Wang, revised ed. (New York, 1958). For a concise discussion of the novel, see *The Dream of the Red Chamber: A Critical Study*, by J. Knoerle, S.P. (Bloom-

ington, Ind., 1972). To explore Chinese history through its art, see the beautifully illustrated *China: A History in Art* by B. Smith and W. Weng, revised ed. (New York, 1979). For a concise and comprehensive introduction to the Chinese art of this period, see M. Sullivan, *The Arts of China*, 3d ed. (Berkeley, 1984). For a beautifully illustrated text on Chinese imperial art, see *Son of Heaven: Imperial Arts of China* by R. L. Thorp (Seattle, 1988). For the best introduction to the painting of this era, see J. Cahill, *Chinese Painting* (New York, 1977).

On Japan before the rise of the Tokugawa, see J. W. Hall, et al., eds., *Japan before Tokugawa: Political Consolidation and Economic Growth* (Princeton, N.J., 1981) and G. Elison and B. L. Smith, eds., *Warlords, Artists, and Commoners: Japan in the Sixteenth Century* (Honolulu, 1981). See also M. E. Berry, *Hideyoshi* (Cambridge, Mass., 1982), the first biography of this fascinating figure in Japanese history. On the first Christian activities, see G. Elison, *Deus Destroyed: The Image of Christianity in Early Modern Japan* (Cambridge, Mass., 1973) and C. R. Boxer, *The Christian Century in Japan, 1549–1650* (Berkeley, 1951). Buddhism is dealt with in N. McMullin, *Buddhism and the State in Sixteenth Century Japan* (Princeton, N.J., 1984).

On the Tokugawa, see H. Bolitho, *Treasures among Men: The Fudai Daimyo in Tokugawa Japan* (New Haven, Conn., 1974) and R. B. Toby, *State and Diplomacy in Early Modern Japan: Asia in the Development of the Tokugawa Bakufu* (Princeton, N.J., 1984). See also R. N. Bellah, *Tokugawa Religion: The Values of Pre-Industrial Japan* (New York, 1957). For a provocative interpretation of this period, see J. W. Dower, ed., *The Origins of the Meiji State: Selected Writings of E. H. Norman* (New York, 1975). See also C. I. Mulhern, ed., *Heroic with Grace: Legendary Women of Japan* (Armonk, N.Y., 1991). Three other recent studies are S. Vlastos, *Peasant Protests and Uprisings in Tokugawa Japan* (Berkeley, 1986); H. Ooms, *Tokugawa Ideology: Early Constructs, 1570–1680* (Princeton, N.J., 1985); and C. Nakane, ed., *Tokugawa Japan: The Social and Economic Antecedents of Modern Japan* (Tokyo, 1990).

Of specific interest to Japanese literature of the Tokugawa era are D. Keene, *World within Walls: Japanese Literature of the Pre-Modern Era, 1600–1867* (New York, 1976) and N. Yukihiko, "Modern Period A.D. 1600 to

1868," in E. Putzar, *Japanese Literature: A Historical Outline* (Arizona, 1973) pp. 105–69. Of special value for the college student are D. Keene's *Anthology of Japanese Literature* (New York, 1955), *The Pleasures of Japanese Literature* (New York, 1988), and *Japanese Literature: An Introduction for Western Readers* (London, 1953). For an introduction to Basho's life, poems, and criticism, consult the stimulating *Basho and His Interpreters: Selected Hokku with Commentary* (Stanford, Calif., 1991) by M. Ueda.

For the most comprehensive and accessible overview of Japanese art, see P. Mason, *Japanese Art* (New York, 1993). For a concise introduction to Japanese art of the Tokugawa era, see J. Stanley-Baker, *Japanese Art* (London, 1984). For magnificent photographs and stimulating interpretation, consult D. and V. Elisseeff, *Art of Japan* (New York, 1985) and J. E. Kidder, Jr., *The Art of Japan* (London, 1985).

CHAPTER

18

Toward a New Heaven and a New Earth: An Intellectual Revolution in the West

In addition to the political, economic, social, and international crises of the seventeenth century, we need to add an intellectual one. The Scientific Revolution questioned and ultimately challenged conceptions and beliefs about the nature of the external world and reality that had been held by Europeans for centuries. The Scientific Revolution brought to Europeans a new way of viewing the universe and their place in it. The shift from an earth-centered to a sun-centered cosmos had an emotional as well as an intellectual effect upon those who understood it.

The transition to a new worldview, however, was not an easy one. The Italian scientist Galileo, an outspoken advocate of the new worldview in the seventeenth century, found his ideas challenged by the authorities of the Catholic church. Galileo was clear on his position: "I hold the sun to be situated motionless in the center of the revolution of the celestial bodies, while the earth rotates on its axis and revolves about the sun." Moreover, "nothing physical that sense-experience sets before our eyes . . . ought to be called in question (much less condemned) upon the testimony of Biblical passages." But the church had a different view, and in 1633, Galileo, now sixty-eight and in ill health, was called before the dreaded inquisition in Rome. He was kept waiting for two months before being tried and found guilty of heresy and disobedience. Completely shattered by the experience, he denounced his errors: "With a sincere heart and unfeigned faith I curse and detest the said errors

Copernicus,
*On the Revolutions
of the Heavenly Spheres*

Descartes, *Discourse on Method*

Newton, *Principia*

Rousseau,
The Social Contract

Kepler's laws

French Royal Academy
of Sciences

Diderot, *Encyclopedia*

Voltaire, *Candide*

Bach, Mass in B Minor

Handel, *Messiah*

Mozart, *The Marriage of Figaro*

Haydn, *The Creation*

and heresies contrary to the Holy Church, and I swear that I will nevermore in future say or assert anything that may give rise to a similar suspicion of me." Legend holds that when he left the trial room, Galileo muttered to himself: "And yet it does move!" In any case, Galileo had been silenced, but his writings remained, and they began to spread through Europe. The Inquisition had failed to stop the spread of the new ideas of the Scientific Revolution.

The earth-shattering work of the "natural philosophers" in the Scientific Revolution affected only a relatively small number of Europe's educated elite. But in the eighteenth century, this changed dramatically as a group of intellectuals known as the philosophes popularized the ideas of the Scientific Revolution and used them to undertake a dramatic reexamination of all aspects of life. The widespread impact of the philosophes' ideas on their society has caused historians ever since to call the eighteenth century in Europe the Age of Enlightenment.

For most of the philosophes, "enlightenment" included the rejection of traditional Christianity.

The religious wars and intolerance of the sixteenth and seventeenth centuries had created an environment in which intellectuals had become so disgusted with religious fanaticism that they were open to the new ideas of the Scientific Revolution. Whereas the great scientists of the seventeenth century believed that their work exalted God, the intellectuals of the eighteenth century read their conclusions a different way and increasingly turned their backs on their Christian heritage. Consequently, European intellectual life in the eighteenth century was marked by a revolutionary transition to the largely secular, rational, and materialistic perspective that has defined the modern Western mentality since its full acceptance in the nineteenth and twentieth centuries.

The Scientific Revolution

In one sense, the Scientific Revolution was not a revolution. It was not characterized by the explosive change and rapid overthrow of traditional authority that we normally associate with the word *revolution*. The Scientific Revolution did overturn centuries of authority, but only in a gradual and piecemeal fashion.

Background to the Scientific Revolution

To say that the Scientific Revolution brought about a dissolution of the medieval worldview is not to say that the Middle Ages was a period of scientific ignorance. Many educated Europeans took an intense interest in the world around them because it was, after all, "God's handiwork" and therefore an appropriate subject for study. Late medieval scholastic philosophers had advanced mathematical and physical thinking in many ways, but the subjection of these thinkers to a strict theological framework and their unquestioning reliance on a few ancient authorities, especially Aristotle and Galen, limited where they could go. Many "natural philosophers," as medieval scientists were called, preferred refined logical analysis to systematic observations of the natural world. A number of changes and advances in the fifteenth and sixteenth centuries may have played a major role in helping "natural philosophers" abandon their old views and develop new ones.

The Renaissance humanists mastered Greek as well as Latin and made available new works of Galen, Ptolemy, and Archimedes as well as Plato and the pre-Socratics. These writings made it apparent that even the unquestioned authorities of the Middle Ages, Aristotle and Galen, had been contradicted by other thinkers. The desire to discover which school of thought was correct stimulated new scientific work that sometimes led to a complete rejection of the classical authorities.

Renaissance artists have also been credited with having an impact on scientific study. Their desire to imitate nature led them to rely upon a close observation of nature. Their accurate renderings of rocks, plants, animals, and human anatomy established new standards for the study of natural phenomena. At the same time, the "scientific" study of the problems of perspective and correct anatomical proportions led to new insights. "No painter," one Renaissance artist declared, "can paint well without a thorough knowledge of geometry."[1]

Technical problems, such as calculating the tonnage of ships accurately, also stimulated scientific activity because they required careful observation and precise measurements. Then, too, the invention of new instruments and machines, such as the telescope and microscope, often made fresh scientific discoveries possible. Above all, the printing press played a crucial role in spreading innovative ideas quickly and easily.

Mathematics, which played such a fundamental role in the scientific achievements of the sixteenth and seventeenth centuries, was promoted in the Renaissance by the rediscovery of the works of ancient mathematicians and the influence of Plato, who had emphasized the importance of mathematics in explaining the universe. During the Renaissance, mathematics was not only applauded as the key to navigation, military science, and geography, but was also widely believed to be the key to understanding the nature of things. According to Leonardo da Vinci, God eternally geometrizes, so nature is inherently mathematical: "Proportion is not only found in numbers and measurements but also in sounds, weights, times, positions, and in whatsoever power there may."[2] Copernicus, Kepler, Galileo, and Newton were all great mathematicians who believed that the secrets of nature were written in the language of mathematics.

Another possible contributor to the origins of the Scientific Revolution was magic. Renaissance magic was the preserve of an intellectual elite from all of Europe. By the end of the sixteenth century, Hermetic magic had fused with alchemical thought to form a single intellectual framework. According to this tradition, the world was a living embodiment of divinity. Humans, who were also thought to have that spark of divinity within, could use magic, especially mathematical magic, to understand and dominate the world of nature or employ the powers of nature for beneficial purposes. Was it Hermeticism, then, that inaugurated the shift in consciousness that made the Scientific Revolution possible, since the desire to control and dominate the natural world was a crucial motivating force in the Scientific Revolution? Scholars debate the issue, but histories of the Scientific Revolution frequently overlook the fact that the great names we associate with the revolution in cosmology—Copernicus, Kepler, Galileo, and Newton—all had a serious interest in Hermetic ideas and the fields of astrology and alchemy. The mention of these names also reminds us of one final consideration in the origins of the Scientific Revolution: it largely resulted from the work of a handful of great intellectuals.

Toward a New Heaven: A Revolution in Astronomy

The greatest achievements in the Scientific Revolution of the sixteenth and seventeenth centuries came in those fields most dominated by the ideas of the Greeks—astronomy, mechanics, and medicine. The cosmological views of the Late Middle Ages had been built upon a synthesis of the ideas of Aristotle, Claudius Ptolemy (the greatest astronomer of antiquity who lived in the second century C.E.), and Christian theology. In the resulting Ptolemaic or geocentric conception, the universe was

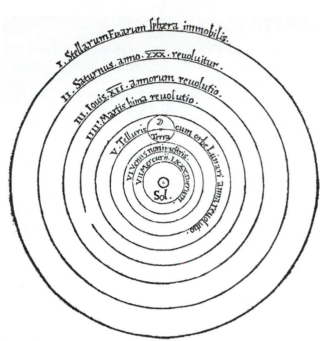

◆ **Medieval Conception of the Universe.** As this sixteenth-century illustration shows, the medieval cosmological view placed the earth at the center of the universe, surrounded by a series of concentric spheres. The earth was imperfect and constantly changing while the heavenly bodies that surrounded it were perfect and incorruptible. Beyond the tenth and final sphere was heaven where God and all the saved souls were located.

◆ **The Copernican System.** The Copernican system was presented in *On the Revolutions of the Heavenly Spheres*, published shortly before Copernicus's death. As shown in this illustration from the first edition of the book, Copernicus maintained that the sun was the center of the universe while the planets, including the earth, revolved around it. Moreover, the earth rotated daily on its axis.

seen as a series of concentric spheres with a fixed or motionless earth at its center. Composed of material substance, the earth was imperfect and constantly changing. The spheres that surrounded the earth were made of a crystalline, transparent substance and moved in circular orbits around the earth. Circular movement, according to Aristotle, was the most "perfect" kind of motion and hence appropriate for the "perfect" heavenly bodies, which were thought to consist of a nonmaterial, incorruptible "quintessence." These heavenly bodies, pure orbs of light, were embedded in the moving, concentric spheres and in 1500 numbered ten. Working outward from the earth, the first eight spheres contained the moon, Mercury, Venus, the sun, Mars, Jupiter, Saturn, and the fixed stars. The ninth sphere imparted to the eighth sphere of the fixed stars its diurnal motion while the tenth sphere was frequently described as the prime mover that moved itself and imparted motion to the other spheres. Beyond the tenth sphere was the Empyrean Heaven—the location of God and all the saved souls. This Christianized Ptolemaic universe, then,

was a finite one. It had a fixed end in harmony with Christian thought and expectations. God and the saved souls were at one end of the universe while humans were at the center. They had been given power over the earth, but their real purpose was to achieve salvation.

In May 1543, shortly before his death, Nicolaus Copernicus (1473–1543), who had studied mathematics and astronomy first at Cracow in his native Poland and later at the Italian universities of Bologna and Padua, published his famous book, *On the Revolutions of the Heavenly Spheres*. Copernicus was not an accomplished observational astronomer and relied for his data on the records of his predecessors. But he was a mathematician who felt that Ptolemy's geocentric system was too complicated and failed to accord with the observed motions of the heavenly bodies (see the box on p. 650). Copernicus hoped that his heliocentric or sun-centered conception would offer a more accurate explanation.

Copernicus argued that the universe consisted of eight spheres with the sun motionless at the center and the sphere of the fixed stars at rest in the eighth sphere. The

≋ On the Revolutions of the Heavenly Spheres ≋

Nicolaus Copernicus began a revolution in astronomy when he argued that the sun, not the earth, was at the center of the universe. Expecting controversy and scorn, Copernicus hesitated to publish the work in which he put forth his heliocentric theory. He finally relented, however, and managed to see a copy of it just before he died.

Nicolaus Copernicus, *On the Revolutions of the Heavenly Spheres*

For a long time, then, I reflected on this confusion in the astronomical traditions concerning the derivation of the motions of the universe's spheres. I began to be annoyed that the movements of the world machine, created for our sake by the best and most systematic Artisan of all, were not understood with greater certainty by the philosophers, who otherwise examined so precisely the most insignificant trifles of this world. For this reason I undertook the task of rereading the works of all the philosophers which I could obtain to learn whether anyone had ever proposed other motions of the universe's spheres than those expounded by the teachers of astronomy in the schools. And in fact first I found in Cicero that Hicetas supposed the earth to move. Later I also discovered in Plutarch that certain others were of this opinion. I have decided to set his words down here, so that they may be available to everybody:

> Some think that the earth remains at rest. But Philolaus the Pythagorean believes that, like the sun and moon, it revolves around the fire in an oblique circle. Heraclides of Pontus and Ecphantus the Pythagorean make the earth move, not in a progressive motion, but like a wheel in a rotation from the west to east about its own center.

Therefore, having obtained the opportunity from these sources, I too began to consider the mobility of the earth. And even though the idea seemed absurd, nevertheless I knew that others before me had been granted the freedom to imagine any circles whatever for the purpose of explaining the heavenly phenomena. Hence I thought that I too would be readily permitted to ascertain whether explanations sounder than those of my predecessors could be found for the revolution of the celestial spheres on the assumption of some motion of the earth.

Having thus assumed the motions which I ascribe to the earth later on in the volume, by long and intense study I finally found that if the motions of the other planets are correlated with the orbiting of the earth, and are computed for the revolution of each planet, not only do their phenomena follow therefrom but also the order and size of all the planets and spheres, and heaven itself is so linked together that in no portion of it can anything be shifted without disrupting the remaining parts and the universe as a whole. . . .

Hence I feel no shame in asserting that this whole region engirdled by the moon, and the center of the earth, traverse this grand circle amid the rest of the planets in an annual revolution around the sun. Near the sun is the center of the universe. Moreover, since the sun remains stationary, whatever appears as a motion of the sun is really due rather to the motion of the earth.

planets revolved around the sun in the order of Mercury, Venus, the earth, Mars, Jupiter, and Saturn. The moon, however, revolved around the earth. Moreover, according to Copernicus, what appeared to be the movement of the sun and the fixed stars around the earth was really explained by the daily rotation of the earth on its axis and the journey of the earth around the sun each year. Copernicus, however, was basically conservative. He did not reject Aristotle's principle of the existence of heavenly spheres moving in circular orbits.

The immediate response to Copernicus was muted—no revolution occurred overnight. Nevertheless, although most people were not yet ready to accept his theory, there were growing doubts about the Ptolemaic system. The next step in destroying the geocentric conception and supporting the Copernican system was taken by Johannes Kepler (1571–1630).

Kepler's work illustrates well the narrow line that often separated magic and science in the early Scientific Revolution. An avid astrologer, Kepler possessed a keen interest in Hermetic thought and mathematical magic. In a book written in 1596, he elaborated upon his theory that the universe was constructed on the basis of geometric figures, such as the pyramid and the cube. Believing that the harmony of the human soul (a divine attribute) was mirrored in the numerical relationships existing between the planets, he focused much of his attention upon discovering the "music of the spheres." Kepler was also a brilliant mathematician and astronomer who took a post as imperial mathematician to Emperor Rudolf II. Using the detailed astronomical data compiled by his predecessor, the astronomer Tycho Brahe, Kepler arrived at his laws of planetary motion that confirmed Copernicus's heliocentric theory. In his first law, however, he contradicted Copernicus by showing that the orbits of the planets around the sun were not circular but elliptical in shape with the sun at one focus of the ellipse rather than at the center.

Kepler's work effectively eliminated the idea of uniform circular motion as well as the idea of crystalline spheres revolving in circular orbits. The basic structure of the traditional Ptolemaic system had been destroyed, and people had been freed to think in new terms of the actual paths of planets revolving around the sun in elliptical orbits. By the end of Kepler's life, the Ptolemaic system was rapidly losing ground to the new ideas. Important questions remained unanswered, however. What were the planets made of? And how could motion in the universe be explained? It was an Italian scientist who achieved the next important breakthrough to a new cosmology by answering the first question.

Galileo Galilei (1564–1642) taught mathematics, first at Pisa and later at Padua, one of the most prestigious universities in Europe. Galileo was the first European to make systematic observations of the heavens by means of a telescope, thereby inaugurating a new age in astronomy. He had heard of a Flemish lens grinder who had created a "spyglass" that magnified objects seen at a distance and soon constructed his own after reading about it. Instead of peering at terrestrial objects, Galileo turned his telescope to the skies and made a remarkable series of discoveries: mountains on the moon, four moons revolving around Jupiter, the phases of Venus, and sun spots. Galileo's observations seemed to destroy yet another aspect of the traditional cosmology in that the universe seemed to be composed of material substance similar to that of the earth rather than ethereal or perfect and unchanging substance.

Galileo's revelations, published in the *The Starry Messenger* in 1610, stunned his contemporaries and probably did more to make Europeans aware of the new picture of the universe than did the mathematical theories of Copernicus and Kepler (see the box on p. 652). But even in the midst of his newfound acclaim, Galileo found himself increasingly suspect by the authorities of the

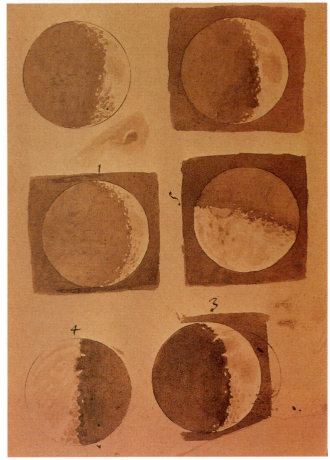

♦ **Galileo's Sketch of the Phases of the Moon.** Galileo Galilei was the first European scientist to use a telescope in making systematic observations of the heavens. Galileo discovered mountains on the moon, sunspots, and the phases of Venus. Shown here are drawings of the moon from Galileo's notes for one of his books.

Catholic church. The Roman Inquisition (or Holy Office) of the Catholic church condemned Copernicanism and ordered Galileo to abandon the Copernican thesis. The report of the Inquisition ran: "That the doctrine that the sun was the center of the world and immovable was false and absurd, formally heretical and contrary to Scripture, whereas the doctrine that the earth was not the center of the world but moved, and has further a daily motion, was philosophically false and absurd and theologically at least erroneous."[3] It is apparent from the Inquisition's response that the church attacked the Copernican system because it threatened not only Scripture, but also an entire conception of the universe. The heavens were no longer a spiritual world, but a world of matter. Humans were no longer at the center and God

❧ The Starry Messenger ❧

The Italian Galileo Galilei was the first European to use a telescope to make systematic observations of the heavens. His observations, as reported in The Starry Messenger in 1610, stunned European intellectuals by revealing that the celestial bodies were not perfect and immutable, as had been believed, but were apparently composed of material substance similar to the earth. In this selection, Galileo describes how he devised a telescope and what he saw with it.

Galileo Galilei, *The Starry Messenger*

About ten months ago a report reached my ears that a certain Fleming had constructed a spyglass by means of which visible objects, though very distant from the eye of the observer, were distinctly seen as if nearby. Of this truly remarkable effect several experiences were related, to which some persons gave credence while others denied them. A few days later the report was confirmed to me in a letter from a noble Frenchman at Paris, Jacques Badovere, which caused me to apply myself wholeheartedly to inquire into the means by which I might arrive at the invention of a similar instrument. This I did shortly afterwards, my basis being the theory of refraction. First I prepared a tube of lead, at the ends of which I fitted two glass lenses, both plane on one side while on the other side one was spherically convex and the other concave. Then placing my eye near the concave lens I perceived objects satisfactorily large and near, for they appeared three times closer and nine times larger than when seen with the naked eye alone. Next I constructed another one, more accurate, which represented objects as enlarged more than sixty times. Finally, sparing neither labor nor expense, I suc-

ceeded in constructing for myself so excellent an instrument that objects seen by means of it appeared nearly one thousand times larger and over thirty times closer than when regarded with our natural vision.

It would be superfluous to enumerate the number and importance of the advantages of such an instrument at sea as well as on land. But forsaking terrestrial observations, I turned to celestial ones, and first I saw the moon from as near at hand as if it were scarcely two terrestrial radii. After that I observed often with wondering delight both the planets and the fixed stars, and since I saw these latter to be very crowded, I began to seek (and eventually found) a method by which I might measure their distances apart. . . .

Now let us review the observations made during the past two months, once more inviting the attention of all who are eager for true philosophy to the first steps of such important contemplations. Let us speak first of that surface of the moon which faces us. For greater clarity I distinguish two parts of this surface, a lighter and a darker; the lighter part seems to surround and to pervade the whole hemisphere, while the darker part discolors the moon's surface like a kind of cloud, and makes it appear covered with spots. . . . From observation of these spots repeated many times I have been led to the opinion and conviction that the surface of the moon is not smooth, uniform, and precisely spherical as a great number of philosophers believe it (and the other heavenly bodies) to be, but is uneven, rough, and full of cavities and prominences, being not unlike the face of the earth, relieved by chains of mountains and deep valleys.

was no longer in a specific place. The new system raised such uncertainties that it seemed prudent simply to condemn it. In 1633, Galileo was found guilty of teaching the condemned Copernican system and was forced to recant his errors. Placed under house arrest on his estate near Florence, he spent the remaining eight years of his life studying mechanics, a field in which he made significant contributions.

The condemnation of Galileo by the Inquisition seriously hampered further scientific work in Italy, which had been at the forefront of scientific innovation. Leadership in science now passed to the northern countries, especially England, France, and the Dutch Netherlands. By the 1630s and 1640s, no reasonable astronomer could overlook that Galileo's discoveries combined with Kepler's mathematical laws had made nonsense of the Ptolemaic-Aristotelian world system and clearly established the reasonableness of the Copernican model. Nevertheless, the problem of explaining motion in the universe and tying together the ideas of Copernicus, Galileo, and Kepler had not yet been solved. This would be the work of an Englishman who has long been considered the greatest genius of the Scientific Revolution.

Born in the little English village of Woolsthorpe in 1642, the young Isaac Newton showed little brilliance until he attended Cambridge University. In 1669, he accepted a chair of mathematics at the university. During an intense period of creativity from 1684 to 1686, he wrote his major work, *Mathematical Principles of Natural Philosophy,* known simply as the *Principia* by the first word of its Latin title. In this work, Newton set out the mathematical proofs demonstrating his universal law of gravitation. Newton's work was the culmination of the theories of Copernicus, Kepler, and Galileo. Although each had undermined some part of the Ptolemaic-Aristotelian cosmology, no one until Newton had pieced together a coherent synthesis for a new cosmology.

In the first book of the *Principia,* Newton defined the basic concepts of mechanics by elaborating the three laws of motion: the law of inertia that every object continues in a state of rest or uniform motion in a straight line unless deflected by a force; the rate of change of motion of an object is proportional to the force acting upon it; and to every action there is always an equal and opposite reaction. In Book Three, Newton applied his theories of mechanics to the problems of astronomy by demonstrating that these three laws of motion govern the planetary bodies as well as terrestrial objects. Integral to his whole argument was the use of the universal law of gravitation to explain why the planetary bodies did not go off in straight lines but continued in elliptical orbits about the sun. In mathematical terms, Newton explained that every object in the universe was attracted to every other object with a force (that is, gravity) that is directly proportional to the product of their masses and inversely proportional to the square of the distance between them.

The implications of Newton's universal law of gravitation were enormous, although it took another century before they were widely recognized. Newton had demonstrated that one universal law mathematically proved could explain all motion in the universe. The secrets of the natural world could be known by human investigations. At the same time, the Newtonian synthesis created a new cosmology in which the world was seen largely in mechanistic terms. The universe was one huge, regulated, and uniform machine that operated according to natural laws in absolute time, space, and motion. Although Newton believed that God was "everywhere present" and acted as the force that moved all bodies on the basis of the laws he had discovered, later generations dropped his spiritual assumptions. Newton's world-machine, conceived as operating absolutely in space, time, and motion, dominated the modern worldview until the twentieth century, when the Einsteinian revolution based on a concept of relativity superseded the Newtonian mechanistic concept.

Newton's ideas were soon accepted in England, possibly out of national pride and conviction, or, as has been argued recently, for political reasons. Natural philosophers on the Continent resisted Newton's ideas, and it took much of the eighteenth century before they were generally accepted everywhere in Europe. They were also reinforced by developments in other fields, especially medicine.

The Breakthrough in Medicine

Although the Scientific Revolution of the sixteenth and seventeenth centuries is associated primarily with the dramatic changes in astronomy and mechanics that precipitated a new perception of the universe, a third field that had been dominated by Greek thought in the Late Middle Ages, that of medicine, also experienced a transformation. Late medieval medicine was dominated by the teachings of the Greek physician Galen who had lived in the second century C.E.

Galen's impact on the medieval medical world's view of anatomy, physiology, and disease had been pervasive. Even when Europeans began to practice human dissection in the Late Middle Ages, instruction in anatomy still relied on Galen. While a professor read a text of Galen, an assistant dissected a cadaver for illustrative purposes. Galen had relied on animal, rather than human, dissection to arrive at a picture of human anatomy that was quite inaccurate in many instances. Yet physiology or the functioning of the body was also dominated by Galenic hypotheses, including the belief that there were two separate blood systems. One controlled muscular activities and contained bright red blood moving upward and downward through the arteries; the other governed the digestive functions and contained dark red blood that ebbed and flowed in the veins.

Two major figures are associated with the changes in medicine in the sixteenth and seventeenth centuries: Andreas Vesalius and William Harvey. The new anatomy of the sixteenth century was the work of Andreas Vesalius (1514–1564), who studied medicine at Paris including the works of Galen. Especially important to him was a recently discovered text of Galen, *On Anatomical Procedures,* that led Vesalius to emphasize practical research as the principal avenue for understanding human anatomy. After receiving a doctorate in medicine at the University of Padua in 1536, he accepted a position there as professor of surgery. In 1543, he published his masterpiece, *On the Fabric of the Human Body.*

This book was based on his Paduan lectures, in which he deviated from traditional practice by personally dissecting a body to illustrate what he was discussing. Vesalius's anatomical treatise presented a careful examination of the individual organs and general structure of the human body. The book would not have been feasible without both the artistic advances of the Renaissance and the technical developments in the art of printing. Together, they made possible the creation of illustrations superior to any hitherto produced.

Vesalius's "hands-on" approach to teaching anatomy enabled him to overthrow some of Galen's most glaring errors. He did not hesitate, for example, to correct Galen's assertion that the great blood vessels originated at the liver because his own observations made it apparent that they came from the heart. Nevertheless, Vesalius still clung to a number of Galen's erroneous assertions, including the Greek physician's ideas on the ebb and flow of two kinds of blood in the veins and arteries. It was not until William Harvey's work on the circulation of the blood that this Galenic misperception was corrected.

William Harvey (1578–1657) attended Cambridge University and later Padua where he received a doctorate of medicine in 1602. His reputation rests upon his book, On the Motion of the Heart and Blood, published in 1628. Although questions had been raised in the sixteenth century about Galen's physiological principles, no major break from his system had occurred. Harvey's work, which was based upon meticulous observations and experiments, led him to demolish the ancient Greek's work.

Harvey demonstrated that the heart and not the liver was the beginning point of the circulation of blood in the body, that the same blood flows in both veins and arteries, and, most importantly, that the blood makes a complete circuit as it passes through the body. Although Galen's ideas had received a severe blow, Harvey's work did not begin to achieve general recognition until the 1660s, when the capillaries, which explained how the body's blood passed from the arteries to the veins, were discovered. Harvey's theory of the circulation of the blood laid the foundation for modern physiology.

Women in the Origins of Modern Science

During the Middle Ages, except for members of religious orders, women who sought a life of learning were severely hampered by the traditional attitude that a woman's proper role was to be a daughter, wife, and mother. But in the late fourteenth and early fifteenth centuries, new opportunities for elite women emerged as enthusiasm for the new secular learning called humanism led Europe's privileged and learned men to encourage women to read and study classical and Christian texts. The ideal of a humanist education for some of the daughters of Europe's elite persisted into the seventeenth century.

In the same fashion as they were drawn to humanism, women were also attracted to the Scientific Revolution. Unlike females educated formally in humanist schools, women attracted to science had to obtain a largely informal education. European nobles had the leisure and resources that gave them easy access to the world of learning. This door was also open to noblewomen who could participate in the informal scientific networks of their fathers and brothers. One of the most prominent female scientists of the seventeenth century, Margaret Cavendish (1623–1673), came from an aristocratic background. Cavendish was not a popularizer of science for women but a participant in the crucial scientific debates of her time. Despite her achievements, however, she was excluded from membership in the Royal Society (see The Spread of Scientific Knowledge later in this chapter), although she was once allowed to attend a meeting. She wrote a number of works on scientific matters including Observations upon Experimental Philosophy and Grounds of Natural Philosophy. In these works she did not hesitate to attack what she considered the defects of the rationalist and empiricist approaches to scientific knowledge and was especially critical of the growing belief that through science humans could master nature: "We have no power at all over natural causes and effects. . . . for man is but a small part, . . . his powers are but particular actions of Nature, and he cannot have a supreme and absolute power."[4]

As an aristocrat, the duchess of Cavendish was a good example of the women in France and England who worked in science. Women interested in science who lived in Germany came from a different background. There the tradition of female participation in crafts enabled some women to become involved in observational science, especially astronomy. Between 1650 and 1710, women constituted 14 percent of all German astronomers.

The most famous of the female astronomers in Germany was Maria Winkelmann (1670–1720). She was educated by her father and uncle and received advanced training in astronomy from a nearby self-taught astronomer. Her opportunity to be a practicing astronomer came when she married Gottfried Kirch, Germany's foremost astronomer. She became his assistant at the astronomical observatory operated in Berlin by the Academy of Science. She made some original contributions, including a hitherto undiscovered comet, as her husband related:

> Early in the morning (about 2:00 A.M.) the sky was clear and starry. Some nights before, I had observed a variable star, and my wife (as I slept) wanted to find and see it for herself. In so doing, she found a comet in the sky. At which time she woke me, and I found that it was indeed a comet . . . I was surprised that I had not seen it the night before.[5]

When her husband died in 1710, Winkelmann submitted herself as a candidate for a position as assistant astronomer for which she was highly qualified. As a woman—with no university degree—she was denied the post by the Berlin Academy, which feared that it would establish a precedent by hiring a woman ("mouths would gape").

Winkelmann's difficulties with the Berlin Academy reflect the obstacles women faced in being accepted in scientific work, which was considered a male preserve. Although no formal statutes excluded women from membership in the new scientific societies, no woman was invited to join either the Royal Society of England or the French Academy of Sciences until the twentieth century. All of these women scientists were exceptional women because a life devoted to any kind of scholarship was still viewed as at odds with the domestic duties women were expected to perform.

The nature and value of women had been the subject of an ongoing, centuries-long debate. Male opinions in the debate were largely a carryover from medieval times and were not favorable. Women were portrayed as inherently base, prone to vice, easily swayed, and "sexually insatiable." Hence, men needed to control them. Learned women were viewed as having overcome female liabilities to become like men. One man praised a woman scholar by remarking that her writings were so good that you "would hardly believe they were done by a woman at all."

In the seventeenth century, women joined this debate by arguing against the distorted images of women held by men. They argued that women also had rational minds and could grow from education. Further, since most women were pious, chaste, and temperate, there was no need for male authority over them. These female defenders of women emphasized education as the key to women's ability to move into the world. How, then, did the Scientific Revolution affect this debate over the nature of women? Since it was an era of intellectual revolution in which traditional authorities were being overthrown, we might expect significant change in men's views of women. But by and large, instead of becoming an instrument for liberation, science was used to find new support for the old, traditional views about a woman's true place in the scheme of things. New views on anatomy appeared, for example, but interestingly enough were used to perpetuate old stereotypes about women.

An important project in the new anatomy of the sixteenth and seventeenth centuries was the attempt to illustrate the human body and skeleton. For Vesalius, the portrayal of physical differences between males and females was limited to external bodily form (the outlines of the body) and the sexual organs. Vesalius saw no difference in skeletons and portrayed them as the same for men and women. It was not until the eighteenth century, in fact, that a new anatomy finally prevailed. Drawings of female skeletons between 1730 and 1790 varied, but females tended to have a larger pelvic area, and, in some instances, female skulls were portrayed as smaller than those of males. Eighteenth-century studies on the anatomy and physiology of sexual differences provided "scientific evidence" to reaffirm the traditional inferiority of women. The larger pelvic area "proved" that women were meant to be childbearers while the larger skull "demonstrated" the superiority of the male mind. Male-dominated science had been used to "prove" male social dominance.

Overall the Scientific Revolution reaffirmed traditional ideas about women's nature. Male scientists used the new science to spread the view that women were inferior by nature, subordinate to men, and suited by nature to play a domestic role as nurturing mothers. The widespread distribution of books ensured the continuation of these ideas. Jean de La Bruyère, the seventeenth-century French moralist, was typical when he remarked that an educated woman was like a gun that was a collector's item "which one shows to the curious, but which has no use at all, any more than a carousel horse."[6]

Toward a New Earth: Descartes, Rationalism, and a New View of Humankind

The fundamentally new conception of the universe contained in the cosmological revolution of the sixteenth and seventeenth centuries inevitably had an impact on the Western view of humankind. Nowhere is this more evident than in the work of René Descartes (1596–1650). Descartes began by reflecting the doubt and uncertainty that seemed pervasive in the confusion of the seventeenth century and ended with a philosophy that dominated Western thought until the twentieth century.

The starting point for Descartes's new system was doubt, as he explained at the beginning of his most famous work, *Discourse on Method*, written in 1637:

From my childhood I have been familiar with letters; and as I was given to believe that by their means a clear and assured knowledge can be acquired of all that is useful in life, I was extremely eager for instruction in them. As soon, however, as I had completed the course of study, at the close of which it is customary to be admitted into the order of the learned, I entirely changed my opinion. For I found myself entangled in so many doubts and errors that, as it seemed to me, the endeavor to instruct myself had served only to disclose to me more and more of my ignorance.[7]

Descartes decided to set aside all that he had learned and begin again. One fact seemed to Descartes beyond doubt—his own existence:

But I immediately became aware that while I was thus disposed to think that all was false, it was absolutely necessary that I who thus thought should be something; and noting that this truth *I think, therefore I am*, was so steadfast and so assured that the suppositions of the skeptics, to whatever extreme they might all be carried, could not avail to shake it, I concluded that I might without scruple accept it as being the first principle of the philosophy I was seeking.[8]

With this emphasis on the mind, Descartes asserted that he would accept only those things that his reason said were true.

◆ **Descartes with Queen Christina of Sweden.** René Descartes was one of the primary figures in the Scientific Revolution. Claiming to use reason as his sole guide to truth, Descartes posited a sharp distinction between mind and matter. He is shown here, standing to the right of Queen Christina of Sweden. The queen had a deep interest in philosophy and invited Descartes to her court.

The Father of Modern Rationalism

René Descartes has long been viewed as the founder of modern rationalism and modern philosophy because he believed that human beings could understand the world—itself a mechanical system—by the same rational principles inherent in mathematical thinking. In his Discourse on Method, he elaborated upon his approach to discovering truth.

René Descartes, *Discourse on Method*

In place of the numerous precepts which have gone to constitute logic, I came to believe that the four following rules would be found sufficient, always provided I took the firm and unswerving resolve never in a single instance to fail in observing them.

The first was to accept nothing as true which I did not evidently know to be such, that is to say, scrupulously to avoid precipitance and prejudice, and in the judgments I passed to include nothing additional to what had presented itself to my mind so clearly and so distinctly that I could have no occasion for doubting it.

The second, to divide each of the difficulties I examined into as many parts as may be required for its adequate solution.

The third, to arrange my thoughts in order, beginning with things the simplest and easiest to know, so that I may then ascend little by little, as it were step by step, to the knowledge of the more complex, and in doing so, to assign an order of thought even to those objects which are not of themselves in any such order of precedence.

And the last, in all cases to make enumerations so complete, and reviews so general, that I should be assured of omitting nothing.

Those long chains of reasonings, each step simple and easy, which geometers are wont to employ in arriving even at the most difficult of their demonstrations, have led me to surmise that all the things we human beings are competent to know are interconnected in the same manner, and that none are so remote as to be beyond our reach or so hidden that we cannot discover them—that is, provided we abstain from accepting as true what is not thus related, i.e., keep always to the order required for their deduction one from another. And I had no great difficulty in determining what the objects are with which I should begin, for that I already knew, namely, that it was with the simplest and easiest. Bearing in mind, too, that of all those who in time past have sought for truth in the sciences, the mathematicians alone have been able to find any demonstrations, that is to say, any reasons which are certain and evident, I had no doubt that it must have been by a procedure of this kind that they had obtained them.

From his first postulate, Descartes deduced an additional principle, the separation of mind and matter. Descartes argued that since "the mind cannot be doubted but the body and material world can, the two must be radically different." From this came an absolute dualism between mind and matter, or what has also been called Cartesian dualism. Using mind or human reason, the path to certain knowledge, and its best instrument, mathematics, humans can understand the material world because it is pure mechanism, a machine that is governed by its own physical laws because it was created by God—the great geometrician.

Descartes's conclusions about the nature of the universe and human beings had important implications. His separation of mind and matter allowed scientists to view matter as dead or inert, as something that was totally separate from themselves and could be investigated independently by reason. The split between mind and body led Westerners to equate their identity with mind and reason rather than with the whole organism. Descartes has rightly been called the father of modern rationalism (see the box above). His books were placed on the papal Index of Forbidden Books and condemned by many Protestant theologians. The radical Cartesian split between mind and matter, and between mind and body, had devastating implications not only for traditional religious views of the universe, but for how Westerners viewed themselves; the perspective it provided would not be seriously questioned or challenged until the twentieth century.

Science and Religion in the Seventeenth Century

In Galileo's struggle with the inquisitorial Holy Office of the Catholic church, we see the beginning of the conflict between science and religion that has marked the history of modern civilization. Since time immemorial, theology had seemed to be the queen of the sciences. It was natural that the churches would continue to believe that religion was the final measure of everything. To the emerging scientists, however, it often seemed that theologians knew not of what they spoke. These "natural philosophers" then tried to draw lines between the knowledge of religion and the knowledge of "natural philosophy" or nature. Galileo had clearly felt that it was unnecessary to pit science against religion:

> In discussions of physical problems we ought to begin not from the authority of scriptural passages, but from sense-experiences and necessary demonstrations; for the Holy Bible and the phenomena of nature proceed alike from the divine word, the former as the dictate of the Holy Ghost and the latter as the observant executrix of God's commands. It is necessary for the Bible, in order to be accommodated to the understanding of every man, to speak many things which appear to differ from the absolute truth so far as the bare meaning of the words is concerned. But Nature, on the other hand, is inexorable and immutable; she never transgresses the laws imposed upon her, or cares a whit whether her abstruse reasons and methods of operation are understandable to men.[9]

To Galileo it made little sense for the church to determine the nature of physical reality on the basis of biblical texts that were subject to radically divergent interpretations. The church, however, decided otherwise in Galileo's case and lent its great authority to one scientific theory, the Ptolemaic-Aristotelian cosmology, no doubt because it fit so well with its own philosophical views of reality. But the church's decision had tremendous consequences, just as the rejection of Darwin's ideas would have in the nineteenth century. For educated individuals, it established a dichotomy between scientific investigations and religious beliefs. As the scientific beliefs triumphed, it became almost inevitable that religious beliefs would suffer, leading to a growing secularization in European intellectual life, precisely what the church had hoped to combat by opposing Copernicanism. Many seventeenth-century intellectuals were both religious and scientific and believed that this split would have tragic implications. Some believed that the split was largely unnecessary while others felt the need to combine God, humans, and a mechanistic universe into a new philosophical synthesis. Blaise Pascal illustrates how one European intellectual responded to the implications of the cosmological revolution of the seventeenth century.

Blaise Pascal (1623–1662) sought to keep science and religion united. Pascal had a brief, but checkered career.

He was an accomplished scientist and brilliant mathematician, who was at home with both the practical and the abstract; in the former area, he invented a calculating machine, while in the latter he devised a theory of chance or probability and worked on conic sections. After a profound mystical vision on the night of November 23, 1654, which assured him that God cared for the human soul, he devoted the rest of his life to religious matters. He planned to write an "Apology for the Christian Religion" but died before he could do so. He did leave a set of notes for the larger work, however, which in published form became known as *Pensées* or *The Thoughts*.

In the *Pensées*, Pascal tried to convert rationalists to Christianity by appealing to both their reason and their emotions. Humans, he argued, were frail creatures, often deceived by their senses, misled by reason, and battered by their emotions. And yet they were beings whose very nature involved thinking: "Man is but a reed, the weakest in nature; but he is a thinking reed. . . . Our whole dignity consists, therefore, in thought. By thought we must raise ourselves. . . . Let us endeavor, then, to think well; this is the beginning of morality."[10]

Pascal was determined to show that the Christian religion was not contrary to reason: "If we violate the principles of reason, our religion will be absurd, and it will be laughed at." Christianity, he felt, was the only religion that recognized people's true state of being as both vulnerable and great. To a Christian, a human being was both fallen and at the same time God's special creation. But it was not necessary to emphasize one at the expense of the other—to view humans as only rational or only hopeless. Thus, "Knowledge of God without knowledge of man's wretchedness leads to pride. Knowledge of man's wretchedness without knowledge of God leads to despair. Knowledge of Jesus Christ is the middle course, because by it we discover both God and our wretched state." Pascal even had an answer for skeptics in his famous wager. God is a reasonable bet; it is worthwhile to assume that God exists. If he does, then we win all; if he does not, we lose nothing.

Despite his own background as a scientist and mathematician, Pascal refused to rely on the scientist's world of order and rationality to attract people to God: "If we submit everything to reason, there will be no mystery and no supernatural element in our religion." In the new cosmology of the seventeenth century, "finite man," Pascal believed, was lost in the new infinite world, a realization that frightened him: "The eternal silence of those infinite spaces strikes me with terror." The world of nature, then, could never reveal God: "Because they have failed to contemplate these infinities, men have rashly plunged into the examination of nature, as though they bore some proportion to her. . . . Their assumption is as infinite as their object." A Christian could only rely on a God who through Jesus cared for human beings. In the final analysis, after providing reasonable arguments for Christianity, Pascal came to rest on faith. Reason, he believed, could take people only so far: "The heart has its reasons of which the reason knows nothing." As a Christian, faith was the final step: "The heart feels God, not the reason. This is what constitutes faith: God experienced by the heart, not by the reason."[11]

In retrospect, it is obvious that Pascal failed to achieve his goal. Increasingly, the gap between science and traditional religion grew wider as Europe continued along its path of secularization. Of course, traditional religions were not eliminated, nor is there any evidence that churches had yet lost their numbers. That would happen later. Nevertheless, more and more of the intellectual, social, and political elites began to act on the basis of secular rather than religious assumptions.

The Spread of Scientific Knowledge

In the course of the seventeenth century, scientific learning and investigation began to increase dramatically. Major European universities established new chairs of science, especially in medicine. Royal and princely patronage of individual scientists became an international phenomenon. Of particular importance to the work of science were the creation of a scientific method and the emergence of new learned societies that enabled the new scientists to communicate their ideas to each other and to disseminate them to a wider, literate public.

In the course of the Scientific Revolution, attention was paid to the problem of establishing the proper means for examining and understanding the physical realm. This creation of a scientific method was crucial to the evolution of science in the modern world. Curiously enough, it was an Englishman with few scientific credentials who attempted to put forth a new method of acquiring knowledge that made an impact on English scientists in the seventeenth century and other European scientists in the eighteenth century. Francis Bacon (1561–1626), a lawyer and lord chancellor, rejected Copernicus and Kepler and misunderstood Galileo. And yet in his unfinished work, *The Great Instauration* (*The Great Restoration*), he called for his contemporaries "to commence a total reconstruction of sciences, arts, and all human knowledge, raised upon the proper foundations." Bacon did not doubt humans' ability to know the natural world,

but believed that they had proceeded incorrectly: "The entire fabric of human reason which we employ in the inquisition of nature is badly put together and built up, and like some magnificent structure without foundation."

Bacon's new foundation—a correct scientific method—was to be built upon inductive principles. Rather than beginning with assumed first principles from which logical conclusions could be deduced, he urged scientists to proceed from the particular to the general. Carefully organized experiments and systematic, thorough observations would lead to the development of correct generalizations. Bacon was clear about what he believed his method could accomplish. His concern was more for practical than for pure science. He stated that "the true and lawful goal of the sciences is none other than this: that human life be endowed with new discoveries and power." He wanted science to contribute to the "mechanical arts" by creating devices that would benefit industry, agriculture, and trade. Bacon was prophetic when he said that "I am laboring to lay the foundation, not of any sect or doctrine, but of human utility and power." And how would this "human power" be used? To "conquer nature in action."[12] The control and domination of nature became a central proposition of modern science and the technology that accompanied it. Only in the twentieth century have some scientists wondered whether this assumption might not be at the heart of the twentieth-century ecological crisis.

The first of the scientific societies appeared in Italy but those of England and France were ultimately of more significance. The English Royal Society evolved out of informal gatherings of scientists at London and Oxford in the 1640s, although it did not receive a formal charter from King Charles II until 1662. The French Royal Academy of Sciences also arose out of informal scientific meetings in Paris during the 1650s. In 1666, Louis XIV formally recognized the group. The French Academy received abundant state support and remained under government control; its members were appointed and paid salaries by the state. In contrast, the Royal Society of England received little government encouragement, and its fellows simply co-opted new members.

Early on, both the English and French scientific societies formally emphasized the practical value of scientific research. The Royal Society appointed a committee to investigate technological improvements for industry while the French Academy collected tools and machines. This concern with the practical benefits of science proved short-lived, however, as both societies came to focus their attention on theoretical work in mechanics and astronomy. The construction of observatories at Paris in

1667 and at Greenwich, England, in 1675 greatly facilitated research in astronomy by both groups. Although both the English and French societies made useful contributions to scientific knowledge in the second half of the seventeenth century, their true significance arose from their example that science should proceed along the lines of a cooperative venture.

The importance of science in the history of modern civilization is usually taken for granted. But how did science become such an integral part of Western culture in the seventeenth and early eighteenth centuries? Recent research has stressed that one cannot simply assert that people perceived that science was a rationally superior system. An important social factor, however, might help to explain the relatively rapid acceptance of the new science.

It has been argued that the literate mercantile and propertied elites of Europe were soon attracted to a new science that offered new ways to exploit resources for profit. Some of the early scientists made it easier for these groups to accept the new ideas when they showed how these ideas could be applied directly to specific industrial and technological needs. Galileo, for example, consciously sought an alliance between science and the material interests of the educated elite when he assured his listeners that the science of mechanics would be quite useful "when it becomes necessary to build bridges or other structures over water, something occurring mainly in affairs of great importance." At the same time, Galileo stressed that science was fit for the "minds of the wise" and not for "the shallow minds of the common people." This made science part of the high culture of Europe's wealthy elites at a time when that culture was being increasingly separated from the popular culture of the lower classes.

The Enlightenment

In 1784, the German philosopher Immanuel Kant defined the Enlightenment as "man's leaving his self-caused immaturity." Whereas earlier periods had been handicapped by the inability to "use one's intelligence without the guidance of another," Kant proclaimed as the motto of the Enlightenment: "Dare to Know!: Have the courage to use your own intelligence!" The eighteenth-century Enlightenment was a movement of intellectuals who dared to know. They were greatly impressed with the accomplishments of the Scientific Revolution, and when they used the word *reason*—one of their favorite words—they were advocating the application of the scientific method to the understanding of all life. All institutions and all systems of thought were subject to the rational, scientific way of thinking if people would only free themselves from the shackles of past, worthless traditions, especially religious ones. If Isaac Newton could discover

◆ **Louis XIV and Colbert Visit the Academy of Sciences.** In the seventeenth century, individual scientists received royal and princely patronage, and a number of learned societies were established. In France, Louis XIV, urged on by his minister Colbert, gave formal recognition to the French Academy in 1666. In this painting by Henri Testelin, Louis XIV is shown seated, surrounded by Colbert and members of the French Royal Academy of Sciences.

the natural laws regulating the world of nature, they too by using reason could find the laws that governed human society. This belief in turn led them to hope that they could make progress toward a better society than the one they had inherited. Reason, natural law, hope, progress—these were common words in the heady atmosphere of the eighteenth century.

The Paths to Enlightenment

The Enlightenment did not arrive full-blown in the eighteenth century, but was the culmination of four intellectual developments that had begun in the seventeenth century: the popularization of science, skepticism about religion, the growth of travel literature, and the work of Isaac Newton and John Locke.

Although the intellectuals of the eighteenth century were much influenced by the scientific ideas of the seventeenth century, they did not always acquire this knowledge directly from the original sources. After all, Newton's *Principia* was not an easy book to read or comprehend. The spread of scientific ideas to ever-widening circles of educated Europeans was accomplished not so much by the scientists themselves as by popularizers. Especially important as a direct link between the Scientific Revolution of the seventeenth century and the intellectuals of the eighteenth was Bernard de Fontenelle (1657–1757). In his *Plurality of Worlds*, he used the form of an intimate conversation between a lady aristocrat and her lover to present a detailed account of the new mechanistic universe. Scores of the educated elite of Europe learned the new cosmology in this light-hearted fashion.

Thanks to Fontenelle, science was no longer the monopoly of experts, but part of literature. He was especially fond of downplaying the religious backgrounds of the seventeenth-century scientists. Himself a skeptic, Fontenelle portrayed the churches as enemies of scientific progress, adding to the growing skepticism about religion at the end of the seventeenth century.

Although religion had once again become the central focus of people's lives during the Reformation, it was perhaps inevitable that the dogmatic controversies, religious intolerance, and religious warfare engendered by it would open the door to the questioning of religious truths and values. The overthrow of medieval cosmology and the advent of scientific ideas and rational explanations in the seventeenth century likewise affected the belief of educated men and women in the traditional teachings of Christianity. Skepticism about religion and a growing secularization of thought were important factors in the emergence of the Enlightenment.

Skepticism about Christianity as well as about European culture itself was nourished by travel reports. In the course of the seventeenth century, traders, missionaries, physicians, and navigators began to publish an increasing number of travel books that gave accounts of many different cultures. By the end of the seventeenth century, this travel literature had begun to make an impact on the minds of educated Europeans. The discovery of highly developed civilizations with different customs such as the civilizations of Asia forced Europeans to evaluate their own civilization relative to others. What had seemed to be practices grounded in reason now appeared to be matters of custom. This development of cultural relativism was a healthy antidote to European parochialism.

A final source of inspiration for the Enlightenment came primarily from two Englishmen, Isaac Newton and John Locke. Enchanted by the grand design of the Newtonian world-machine, the intellectuals of the Enlightenment were convinced that by following Newton's rules of reasoning they could discover the natural laws that governed politics, economics, justice, religion, and the arts. They regarded the world and everything in it as a giant machine.

John Locke's theory of knowledge made a great impact on eighteenth-century intellectuals. In his *Essay Concerning Human Understanding*, written in 1690, Locke denied Descartes's belief in innate ideas. Instead, argued Locke, every person was born with a *tabula rasa*, a blank mind:

> Let us then suppose the mind to be, as we say, white paper, void of all characters, without any ideas. How comes it to be furnished? Whence comes it by that vast store which the busy and boundless fancy of man has painted on it with an almost endless variety? Whence has it all the materials of reason and knowledge? To this I answer, in one word, from experience. . . . Our observation, employed either about external sensible objects or about the internal operations of our minds perceived and reflected on by ourselves, is that which supplies our understanding with all the materials of thinking.[13]

Our knowledge, then, is derived from our environment, not from heredity; from reason, not from faith. By denying innate ideas, Locke's philosophy implied that people were molded by their environment, by the experiences that they received through their senses from their surrounding world. By changing the environment and subjecting people to proper influences, they could be changed and a new society created. Evil was not innate in human beings, but a product of bad education, rotten institutions, and inherited prejudices. And how should the environment be changed? Newton had already paved the way by showing

♦ **Voltaire.** François-Marie Arouet, better known as Voltaire, achieved his first success as a playwright. A philosophe, Voltaire was well known for his criticism of traditional religion and his support of religious toleration.

how reason enabled enlightened people to discover the natural laws to which all institutions should conform. No wonder the philosophes were enamored of Newton and Locke. Taken together, their ideas seemed to offer the hope of a "brave new world" built on reason.

The Philosophes and Their Ideas

The intellectuals of the Enlightenment were known by the French name of *philosophes* although they were not all French and few were philosophers in the strict sense of the term. They were literary people, professors, journalists, statesmen, economists, political scientists, and, above all, social reformers. They came from both the nobility and the middle class, and a few even stemmed from lower-middle-class origins. Although it was a truly international and cosmopolitan movement, the Enlighten-

ment also enhanced the dominant role being played by French culture; Paris was its recognized capital, and most of its leaders were French. The French philosophes, in turn, affected intellectuals elsewhere and created a movement that touched the entire Western world, including the British and Spanish colonies in America.

Although the philosophes faced different political circumstances depending upon the country in which they lived, they shared common bonds as part of a truly international movement. Although they were called philosophers, philosophy to them meant only effective criticism. The role of philosophy was to change the world, not just discuss it. As one writer said, the philosophe is one who "applies himself to the study of society with the purpose of making his kind better and happier." To the philosophes, rationalism did not mean the creation of a grandiose system of thought to explain all things. Reason was scientific method, and it meant an appeal to facts, to experience, to reasonableness. A spirit of rational criticism was to be applied to everything, including religion and politics. The philosophes aggressively pursued a secular view of life because their focus was not on an afterlife, but on this world and how it could be improved and enjoyed.

Although the philosophes constituted a kind of "family circle" bound together by common intellectual bonds, they often disagreed as well. Spanning almost an entire century, the Enlightenment evolved over time with each succeeding generation becoming more radical as it built upon the contributions of its predecessors. A few people, however, dominated the landscape completely, and we might best begin our survey of the ideas of the philosophes by looking at the three French giants— Montesquieu, Voltaire, and Diderot.

Charles de Secondat, the baron de Montesquieu (1689–1755), came from the French nobility. He received a classical education and then studied law. His first work, the *Persian Letters*, published in 1721, is supposedly written by two Persians traveling in Western Europe and sending their impressions back home. This device enabled Montesquieu to criticize French institutions, especially the Catholic church and the French monarchy. Much of the program of the French Enlightenment is contained in this work: the attack on traditional religion, the advocacy of religious toleration, the denunciation of slavery, and the use of reason to liberate human beings from their prejudices.

His most famous work, *The Spirit of the Laws*, was published in 1748. This treatise was a comparative study of governments in which Montesquieu attempted to apply the scientific method to the social and political arena to ascertain the "natural laws" governing the social relationships of human beings. Montesquieu distinguished three basic kinds of governments: republics, suitable for small states and based on citizen involvement; monarchy, appropriate for middle-sized states and grounded in the ruling class's adherence to law; and despotism, apt for large empires and dependent on fear to inspire obedience. Montesquieu used England as an example of monarchy, and it was his praise and analysis of England's constitution that led to his most far-reaching and lasting contribution to political thought—the importance of checks and balances created by means of a separation of powers. He believed that England's system, with its separate executive, legislature, and judiciary that served to limit and control each other, provided the greatest freedom and security for a state. His work was translated into English two years after publication and was read by American philosophes who incorporated its principles into the American constitution.

The greatest figure of the Enlightenment was François-Marie Arouet, known simply as Voltaire (1694–1778). Son of a prosperous middle-class family from Paris, Voltaire received a classical education typical of Jesuit schools. Although he studied law, he wished to be a writer and achieved his first success as a playwright. Voltaire was a prolific author and wrote an almost endless stream of pamphlets, novels, plays, letters, philosophical essays, and histories. His writings brought him both fame and wealth.

Although he touched on all of the themes of importance to the philosophes, he was especially well known for his criticism of traditional religion and his strong attachment to the ideal of religious toleration (see the box on p. 664). He lent his prestige and skills as a polemicist to fight cases of intolerance in France. In 1763, he penned his *Treatise on Toleration* in which he argued that religious toleration had created no problems for England and Holland and reminded governments that "all men are brothers under God." As he grew older, Voltaire's denunciations became ever more strident. "Crush the infamous thing," he thundered repeatedly—the infamous thing being religious fanaticism, intolerance, and superstition.

Throughout his life, Voltaire championed not only religious tolerance, but also deism, a religious outlook shared by most other philosophes. Deism was built upon the Newtonian world-machine, which implied the existence of a mechanic (God) who had created the universe. To Voltaire and most other philosophes, God had no direct involvement in the world he had created and allowed it to run according to its own natural laws. Jesus might be a "good fellow," as Voltaire called him, but he was not divine as Christianity claimed. Deism proved to be a halfway house between belief in religion and disbelief and satisfied most philosophes. Voltaire feared athe-

ism, however, feeling that it posed a threat to social stability among the masses.

Denis Diderot (1713–1784) was the son of a skilled craftsman from eastern France. He received a Jesuit education and went on to the University of Paris to fulfill his father's hopes that he would be a lawyer or pursue a career in the church. Diderot did neither. Instead he became a freelance writer so that he could be free to study and read in many subjects and languages. For the rest of his life, Diderot remained dedicated to his independence and was always in love with new ideas.

Diderot wrote numerous essays that reflected typical Enlightened interests. One of his favorite topics was Christianity, which he condemned as fanatical and unreasonable. As he grew older, his literary attacks on Christianity grew more vicious. Of all religions, he averred, Christianity was the worst, "the most absurd and the most atrocious in its dogma" (see the box on p. 665). This progression reflected his own transformation from deism to atheism, ending with a basic materialistic conception of life: "This world is only a mass of molecules."

Diderot's most famous contribution to the Enlightenment was the *Encyclopedia, or Classified Dictionary of the Sciences, Arts, and Trades*, a twenty-eight-volume compendium of knowledge that he edited and referred to as the "great work of his life." Its purpose, according to Diderot, was to "change the general way of thinking." It did precisely that, becoming a major weapon of the philosophes' crusade against the old French society. The contributors included many philosophes who expressed their major concerns. They attacked religious superstition and advocated toleration as well as a program for social, legal, and political improvements that would lead to a society that was more cosmopolitan, more tolerant, more humane, and more reasonable. In later editions, the price of the *Encyclopedia* was drastically reduced, dramatically increasing its sales and making it available to doctors, clergymen, teachers, lawyers, and even military officers, thus furthering the spread of the ideas of the Enlightenment.

TOWARD A NEW "SCIENCE OF MAN"

The Enlightenment belief that Newton's scientific methods could be used to discover the natural laws underlying all areas of human life led to the emergence in the eighteenth century of what the philosophes called a "science of man" or what we would call the social sciences. In a number of areas, such as economics, philosophes arrived at natural laws that they believed governed human actions. If these "natural laws" seem less than universal to

⇒ The Attack on Religious Intolerance ⇐

Although Voltaire's ideas on religion were in no way original, his lucid prose, biting satire, and clever wit caused his attacks to be widely read and all the more influential. These two selections present different sides of Voltaire's attack on religious intolerance. The first is from his straightforward treatise, The Ignorant Philosopher, while the second is from his only real literary masterpiece, the novel Candide, where he uses humor to make the same fundamental point about religious intolerance.

Voltaire, *The Ignorant Philosopher*

The contagion of fanaticism then still subsists. . . . The author of the Treatise upon Toleration has not mentioned the shocking executions wherein so many unhappy victims perished in the valleys of Piedmont. He has passed over in silence the massacre of six hundred inhabitants of Valtelina, men, women, and children, who were murdered by the Catholics in the month of September, 1620. I will not say it was with the consent and assistance of the archbishop of Milan, Charles Borome, who was made a saint. Some passionate writers have averred this fact, which I am very far from believing; but I say, there is scarce any city or borough in Europe, where blood has not been spilt for religious quarrels; I say, that the human species has been perceptibly diminished, because women and girls were massacred as well as men; I say, that Europe would have had a third larger population, if there had been no theological disputes. In fine, I say, that so far from forgetting these abominable times, we should frequently take a view of them, to inspire an eternal horror for them; and that it is for our age to make reparation by toleration, for this long collection of crimes, which has taken place through the want of toleration, during sixteen barbarous centuries.

Let it not then be said, that there are no traces left of that shocking fanaticism, of the want of toleration; they are still everywhere to be met with, even in those countries that are esteemed the most humane. The Lutheran and Calvinist preachers, were they masters, would, perhaps, be as little inclined to pity, as obdurate, as insolent as they upbraid their antagonists with being.

Voltaire, *Candide*

At last he [Candide] approached a man who had just been addressing a big audience for a whole hour on the subject of charity. The orator peered at him and said:

"What is your business here? Do you support the Good Old Cause?"

"There is no effect without a cause," replied Candide modestly. "All things are necessarily connected and arranged for the best. It was my fate to be driven from Lady Cunégonde's presence and made to run the gauntlet, and now I have to beg my bread until I can earn it. Things could not have happened otherwise."

"Do you believe that the Pope is Antichrist, my friend?" said the minister.

"I have never heard anyone say so," replied Candide; "but whether he is or he isn't, I want some food."

"You don't deserve to eat," said the other. "Be off with you, you villain, you wretch! Don't come near me again or you'll suffer for it."

The minister's wife looked out of the window at that moment, and seeing a man who was not sure that the Pope was Antichrist, emptied over his head a pot full of urine, which shows to what lengths ladies are driven by religious zeal.

us, it reminds us how much the philosophes were people of their times reacting to the conditions they faced. Nevertheless, their efforts did result in establishing their disciplines on a rational basis and at least laying the foundations for the modern social sciences.

The Physiocrats and Adam Smith have been viewed as the founders of the modern discipline of economics. The leader of the Physiocrats was François Quesnay (1694–1774), a highly successful French court physician. Quesnay and the Physiocrats claimed they would discover the natural economic laws that governed human society. Their major "natural law" of economics represented a repudiation of mercantilism, specifically, its emphasis on controlling the economy for the benefit of the state. Instead the Physiocrats stressed that the existence of the natural economic forces of supply and demand made it imperative that individuals be left free to pursue their own economic self-interest. All society would ultimately benefit from the actions of these individuals. Consequently, the Physiocrats argued that the state

⇒ Diderot Questions Christian Sexual Standards ⇐

enis Diderot was one of the bolder thinkers of the Enlightenment. He moved from outspoken criticism of the Christian religion to outright atheism. Although best remembered for the Encyclopedia, *he wrote many other works that he considered too advanced and withheld from publication. In his* Supplement to the Voyage of Bougainville, *he constructed a dialogue between Orou, a Tahitian, who symbolizes the wisdom of a* philosophe, *and a chaplain who defends Christian sexual mores. The dialogue gave Diderot the opportunity to criticize the practice of sexual chastity and monogamy.*

Denis Diderot, Supplement to the Voyage of Bougainville

[Orou] "You are young and healthy [speaking to the chaplain] and you have just had a good supper. He who sleeps alone, sleeps badly; at night a man needs a woman at his side. Here is my wife and here are my daughters. Choose whichever one pleases you most, but if you would like to do me a favor, you will give your preference to my youngest girl, who has not yet had any children. . . ."

The chaplain replied that his religion, his holy orders, his moral standards and his sense of decency all prevented him from accepting Orou's invitation.

Orou answered: "I don't know what this thing is that you call religion, but I can only have a low opinion of it because it forbids you to partake of an innocent pleasure to which Nature, the sovereign mistress of us all, invites everybody. It seems to prevent you from bringing one of your fellow creatures into the world, from doing a favor asked of by a father, a mother and their children, from repaying the kindness of a host, and from enriching a nation by giving it an additional citizen. . . . Look at the distress you have caused to appear on the faces of these four women—they are afraid

you have noticed some defect in them that arouses your distaste. . . ."

The Chaplain: "You don't understand—it's not that. They are all four of them equally beautiful. But there is my religion! My holy orders! . . . [God] spoke to our ancestors and gave them laws; he prescribed to them the way in which he wishes to be honored; he ordained that certain actions are good and others he forbade them to do as being evil."

Orou: "I see. And one of these evil actions which he has forbidden is that of a man who goes to bed with a woman or girl. But in that case, why did he make two sexes?"

The Chaplain: "In order that they might come together—but only when certain conditions are satisfied and only after certain initial ceremonies have been performed. By virtue of these ceremonies one man belongs to one woman and only to her; one woman belongs to one man and only to him."

Orou: "For their whole lives?"

The Chaplain: "For their whole lives. . . ."

Orou: "I find these strange precepts contrary to nature, and contrary to reason. . . . Furthermore, your laws seem to me to be contrary to the general order of things. For in truth is there anything so senseless as a precept that forbids us to heed the changing impulses that are inherent in our being, or commands that require a degree of constancy which is not possible, that violate the liberty of both male and female by chaining them perpetually to one another? . . . I don't know what your great workman [God] is, but I am very happy that he never spoke to our forefathers, and I hope that he never speaks to our children, for if he does, he may tell them the same foolishness, and they may be foolish enough to believe it. . . ."

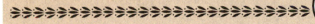

should in no way interrupt the free play of natural economic forces by imposing government regulations on the economy, but should leave it alone, a doctrine that subsequently became known by its French name, *laissez-faire* (to let alone).

The best statement of *laissez-faire* was made in 1776 by a Scottish philosopher, Adam Smith (1723–1790), in his famous work, *Inquiry into the Nature and Causes of the Wealth of Nations,* known simply as *The Wealth of Na-*

tions. Like the Physiocrats, Smith believed that the state should not interfere in economic matters; indeed, he gave to government only three basic functions: it should protect society from invasion (army); defend individuals from injustice and oppression (police); and keep up certain public works, such as roads and canals that private individuals could not afford. Thus, in Smith's view the state should be a kind of "passive policeman" that remains out of the lives of individuals. In emphasizing the economic liberty of the individual, the Physiocrats and Adam Smith laid the foundation for what became known in the nineteenth century as economic liberalism.

THE LATER ENLIGHTENMENT

By the late 1760s, a new generation of philosophes who had grown up with the worldview of the Enlightenment began to move beyond their predecessors' beliefs. The most famous of these later philosophes was Jean-Jacques Rousseau (1712–1778). He was born in the city of Geneva, the son of a watchmaker. Almost entirely self-educated, he wandered about as a youth holding various jobs in France and Italy. Eventually, he made his way to Paris where he became a friend of Diderot and was introduced into the circles of the philosophes. He never really liked the social life of the cities, however, and frequently withdrew into long periods of solitude.

Rousseau's political beliefs were presented in two major works. In his *Discourse on the Origins of the Inequality of Mankind*, Rousseau argued that people had adopted laws and governors in order to preserve their private property. In the process, they had become enslaved by government. In his celebrated treatise *The Social Contract*, published in 1762, Rousseau tried to harmonize individual liberty with governmental authority. The social contract was basically an agreement on the part of an entire society to be governed by its general will. If any individual wished to follow his own self-interest, then he should be compelled to abide by the general will. "This means nothing less than that he will be forced to be free," said Rousseau, because the general will represented a community's highest aspirations, that which was best for the entire community. Thus, liberty was achieved by being forced to follow what was best for each individual. To Rousseau, because everybody was responsible for framing the general will, the creation of laws could never be delegated to a parliamentary institution:

> Thus the people's deputies are not and could not be its representatives; they are merely its agents; and they cannot decide anything finally. Any law which the people has not ratified in person is void; it is not law at all. The English people believes itself to be free; it is gravely mistaken; it is free only during the election of Members of Parliament; as soon as the Members are elected, the people is enslaved; it is nothing.[14]

This is an extreme, idealistic statement, but it is the ultimate statement of participatory democracy.

Another influential treatise by Rousseau also appeared in 1762. Entitled *Emile*, it is one of the Enlightenment's most important works on education. Written in the form of a novel, the work was really a general treatise "on the education of the natural man." Rousseau's fundamental concern was that education should foster rather than restrict children's natural instincts. Life's experiences had shown Rousseau the importance of the promptings of the heart, and what he sought was a balance between heart and mind, between sentiment and reason. This emphasis on heart and sentiment made him a precursor of the intellectual movement called Romanticism that dominated Europe at the beginning of the nineteenth century.

But Rousseau did not necessarily practice what he preached. His own children were sent to foundling homes, where many children died at a young age. Rousseau also viewed women as "naturally" different from men: "to fulfill [a woman's] functions, an appropriate physical constitution is necessary to her . . . she needs a soft sedentary life to suckle her babies. How much care and tenderness does she need to hold her family together." In Rousseau's *Emile*, Sophie, who was Emile's intended wife, was educated for her role as wife and mother by learning obedience and the nurturing skills that would enable her to provide loving care for her husband and children. Not everyone in the eighteenth century agreed with Rousseau, however, making ideas of gender an important issue in the Enlightenment.

THE "WOMAN'S QUESTION" IN THE ENLIGHTENMENT

For centuries, men had dominated the debate about the nature and value of women. In general, many male intellectuals had argued that the base nature of women made them inferior to men and male domination of women

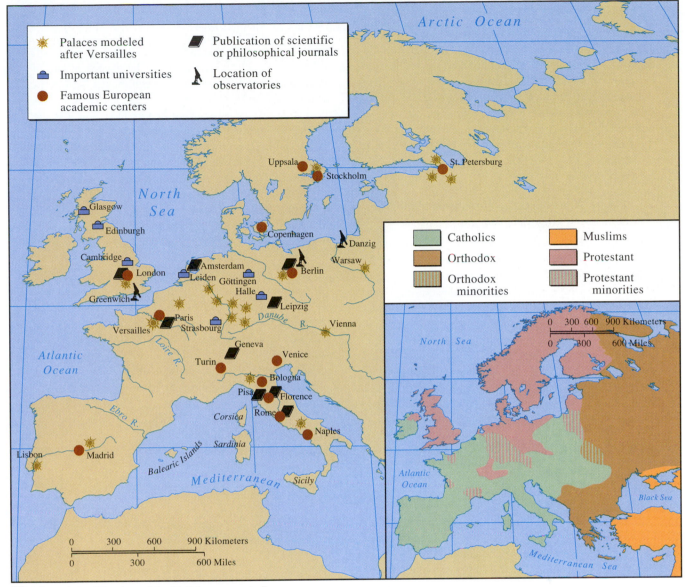

Map 18.1 The Age of the Enlightenment in Europe.

necessary. In the seventeenth and eighteenth centuries, many male thinkers reinforced this view by arguing that it was based on "natural" biological differences between men and women. Like Rousseau, they argued that the female constitution made women mothers. Male writers, in particular, were critical of the attempts of some women in the Enlightenment to write on intellectual issues and insisted that women by nature were intellectually inferior to men. Nevertheless, some Enlightenment thinkers offered more positive views of women. Diderot, for exam-

ple, maintained that men and women were not all that different while Voltaire asserted that "women are capable of all that men are" in intellectual affairs.

It was women thinkers, however, who added new perspectives to the "woman question" by making specific suggestions for improving the condition of women. Mary Astell (1666–1731), daughter of a wealthy English coal merchant, argued in 1697 in *A Serious Proposal to the Ladies* that women needed to become better educated. Men, she believed, would resent her proposal, "but they

➤ The Rights of Women ➤

Mary Wollstonecraft responded to an unhappy childhood in a large family by seeking to lead an independent life. Few occupations were available for middle-class women in her day, but she survived by working as a teacher, chaperone, and governess to aristocratic children. All the while, she wrote and developed her ideas on the rights of women. This excerpt was taken from her Vindication of the Rights of Woman, *written in 1792. This work led to her reputation as the foremost British feminist thinker of the eighteenth century.*

Mary Wollstonecraft, *Vindication of the Rights of Woman*

It is a melancholy truth—yet such is the blessed effect of civilization—the most respectable women are the most oppressed; and, unless they have understandings far superior to the common run of understandings, taking in both sexes, they must, from being treated like contemptible beings, become contemptible. How many women thus waste life away the prey of discontent, who might have practiced as physicians, regulated a farm, managed a shop, and stood erect, supported by their own industry, instead of hanging their heads surcharged with the dew of sensibility, that consumes the beauty to which it at first gave luster. . . .

Proud of their weakness, however, [women] must always be protected, guarded from care, and all the rough toils that dignify the mind. If this be the fiat of fate, if they will make themselves insignificant and contemptible, sweetly to waste 'life away,' let them not expect to be valued when their beauty fades, for it is the fate of the fairest flowers to be admired and pulled to pieces by the careless hand that plucked them. In how many ways do I wish, from the purest benevolence, to impress this truth on my sex; yet I fear that they will not listen to a truth that dear-bought experience has brought home to many an agitated bosom, nor willingly resign the privileges of rank and sex for the privileges of humanity, to which those have no claim who do not discharge its duties. . . .

Would men but generously snap our chains, and be content with rational fellowship instead of slavish obedience, they would find us more observant daughters, more affectionate sisters, more faithful wives, and more reasonable mothers—in a word, better citizens. We should then love them with true affection, because we should learn to respect ourselves; and the peace of mind of a worthy man would not be interrupted by the idle vanity of his wife. . . .

must excuse me, if I be as partial to my own sex as they are to theirs, and think women as capable of learning as men are, and that it becomes them as well."[15]

The strongest statement for the rights of women in the eighteenth century was advanced by the English writer Mary Wollstonecraft (1759–1797), viewed by many as the founder of modern European feminism. In *Vindication of the Rights of Woman*, written in 1792, Wollstonecraft pointed out two contradictions in the views of women held by such Enlightenment thinkers as Rousseau. To argue that women must obey men, she said, was contrary to the beliefs of the same individuals that a system based on the arbitrary power of monarchs over their subjects or slave owners over their slaves was wrong. The subjection of women to men was equally wrong. In addition, she argued that the Enlightenment was based on an ideal of reason innate in all human beings. If women have reason, then they too are entitled to the same rights that men have. Women, Wollstonecraft declared, should have equal rights with men in education and in economic and political life as well (see the box above).

The Social Environment of the Philosophes

The social background of the philosophes varied considerably, from the aristocratic Montesquieu to the lower-middle-class Diderot and Rousseau. The Enlightenment was not the preserve of any one class, although it obviously had its greatest appeal to the aristocracy and upper middle classes of the major cities. The common people, especially the peasants, were little affected by the Enlightenment.

Of great importance to the Enlightenment was the spread of its ideas to the literate elite of European society. While the publication and sale of books and treatises were important to this process, equally important was the salon. Salons came into being in the seventeenth century but rose to new heights in the eighteenth. The salons were the elegant drawing rooms of the wealthy class's great urban houses where invited philosophes and guests gathered together and engaged in witty, sparkling conversations often centered on the new ideas of the philosophes. In France's rigid hierarchical society, the salons were important in bringing writers and artists together with aristocrats, government officials, and wealthy bourgeoisie.

In Paris, the cultural capital of Europe, women took the lead in bringing together groups of men and women to discuss the new ideas of the philosophes. At her fashionable home in the Rue St.-Honoré, Marie-Thérèse de Geoffrin (1699–1777), wife of a wealthy merchant, held sway over gatherings that became the talk of France and even Europe. Distinguished foreigners, including a future king of Sweden and a future king of Poland, competed to receive invitations. When Madame Geoffrin made a visit to Vienna, she was so well received that she exclaimed, "I am better known here than a couple of yards from my own house." Madame Geoffrin was an amiable but firm hostess who allowed wide-ranging discussions as long as they remained in good taste. When she found that artists and philosophers did not mix particularly well (the artists were high-strung and the philosophers talked too much), she set up separate meetings. Artists were only invited on Mondays; philosophers on Wednesdays. These gatherings were but one of many avenues for the spread of the ideas of the philosophes.

Other means of spreading Enlightenment ideas were also available. Coffeehouses, cafés, reading clubs, and public lending libraries created by the state were gathering places to exchange ideas. Learned societies spread to cities throughout Europe and America. At such gatherings as the Select Society of Edinburgh in Scotland and the American Philosophical Society in Philadelphia, lawyers, doctors, and local officials gathered to discuss Enlightened ideas. Secret societies were also formed. The most famous was the Freemasons, established in London in 1717, France and Italy in 1726, and Prussia in 1744. It was no secret that the Freemasons were sympathetic to the ideas of the philosophes.

Culture and Society in an Age of Enlightenment

The intellectual adventure fostered by the philosophes was accompanied by both traditional practices and important changes in the eighteenth-century world of culture and daily life.

Innovations in Art, Music, and Literature

Although the Baroque and neoclassical styles that had dominated the seventeenth century continued into the eighteenth century, by the 1730s, a new style of decoration and architecture known as Rococo had spread all over Europe. Though a French invention and enormously popular in Germany, Rococo became a truly international style.

Unlike the Baroque, which stressed majesty, power, and movement, Rococo emphasized grace and gentle action. Rococo rejected strict geometrical patterns and had a fondness for curves; it liked to follow the wandering lines of natural objects, such as seashells and flowers. It made much use of interlaced designs colored in gold with delicate contours and graceful curves. Highly secular, its lightness and charm spoke of the pursuit of pleasure, happiness, and love.

Some of Rococo's appeal is evident already in the painting of Antoine Watteau (1684–1721), whose lyrical views of aristocratic life—refined, sensual, civilized, with gentlemen and ladies in elegant dress—revealed a world of upper-class pleasure and joy. Underneath that exterior, however, was an element of sadness as the artist revealed the fragility and transitory nature of pleasure, love, and life.

Another aspect of Rococo was the sense of enchantment and exuberance, especially evident in the work of Giovanni Battista Tiepolo (1696–1770). Much of Tiepolo's painting came to adorn the walls and ceilings of churches and palaces. His masterpiece is the ceiling of

◆ **The Salon of Madame Geoffrin.** An important factor in the development of the Enlightenment was the spread of new ideas to the literate elites of European society. Salons were an important part of this process. Madame Geoffrin, who presided over one of the best-known Parisian salons, is shown here, the third figure from the right in the front row.

the Bishop's Palace at Würzburg, a massive scene representing the four continents. Tiepolo's work reminds us that Rococo decorative work could easily be used with Baroque architecture.

The palace of Versailles had made an enormous impact on Europe. "Keeping up with the Bourbons" became important as the Austrian emperor, the Swedish king, German princes and prince-bishops, Italian princes, and even a Russian tsar built grandiose palaces. While imitating Versailles's size, they drew less upon its French classical style than upon the seventeenth-century Italian Baroque, as modified by a series of brilliant German and Austrian sculptor-architects. This Baroque-Rococo architectural style of the eighteenth century was conceived of as a total work of art in which building, sculptural figures, and wall and ceiling paintings were blended into a harmonious whole. This style was used in both palaces and ecclesiastical buildings, and often the same architects did both. This is evident in the work of the one of the greatest architects of the eighteenth century, Balthasar Neumann (1687–1753).

Neumann's two masterpieces are the pilgrimage church of the Vierzehnheiligen (The Fourteen Saints) in southern Germany and the Bishop's Palace known as the Residenz, the residential palace of the Schönborn prince-bishop of Würzburg. Secular and spiritual become easily interchangeable as lavish and fanciful ornaments, light, bright colors, and an elaborate and rich detail greet us in both buildings.

The eighteenth century was one of the greatest in the history of European music. In the first half of the eighteenth century, two composers—Handel and Bach—stand out as musical geniuses. Johann Sebastian Bach (1685–1750) came from a family of musicians. Bach held the post of organist and music director at a number of small German courts before becoming director of church music at the church of St. Thomas in Leipzig in 1723. There Bach composed his Mass in B Minor, his St. Matthew Passion, and the cantatas and motets that have established his reputation as one of the greatest composers of all time. Above all, for Bach music was a means of worshiping God; in his own words, his task in life was to make "well-ordered music in the honor of God."

The other great musical giant of the early eighteenth century, George Frederick Handel (1685–1759) was, like Bach, born in Saxony in Germany and in the same year. Unlike Bach, however, he was profoundly secular in temperament. He began his career by writing operas in the Italian manner and thereafter remained faithful to the Italian Baroque style. In 1712, he moved to England and remained there the rest of his life. Although he found patrons at the English royal court, Handel wrote music for large public audiences and was not averse to writing huge, unusual-sounding pieces. The orchestra for his *Fireworks Music*, for example, was supposed to be accompanied by 101 cannons. Although he wrote much secular music, ironically the worldly Handel is probably best known for his religious music. He had no problem moving from Italian operas to religious oratorios when they proved to be in greater demand by his English public. An oratorio was an extended musical composition on a religious subject, usually taken from a biblical story. Handel's oratorio known as the *Messiah* has been called "one of

◆ Antoine Watteau, *The Pilgrimage to Cythera.* Antoine Watteau was one of the most gifted painters in eighteenth-century France. His portrayal of aristocratic life reveals a world of elegance, wealth, and pleasure. In this painting, Watteau depicts a group of aristocratic pilgrims about to depart the island of Cythera, where they have paid homage to Venus, the goddess of love.

those rare works that appeal immediately to everyone, and yet is indisputably a masterpiece of the highest order."[16]

Bach and Handel perfected the Baroque musical style with its monumental and elaborate musical structures. Two geniuses of the second half of the eighteenth century—Haydn and Mozart—were innovators who wrote music called Classical rather than Baroque. Their renown caused the musical center of Europe to shift from Italy to the Austrian Empire.

Franz Joseph Haydn (1732–1809) spent most of his adult life as musical director for the wealthy Hungarian princes, the Esterhazy brothers. Haydn was incredibly prolific, composing 104 symphonies in addition to string quartets, concerti, songs, oratorios, and masses. His visits to England in 1790 and 1794 introduced him to another world where musicians wrote for public concerts rather than princely patrons. This "liberty," as he called it, induced him to write his two great oratorios, *The Creation* and *The Seasons,* both of which were dedicated to the common people.

Wolfgang Amadeus Mozart (1756–1791) was truly a child prodigy who gave his first harpsichord concert at six and wrote his first opera at twelve. He, too, sought a patron, but his discontent with the overly demanding archbishop of Salzburg forced him to move to Vienna where his failure to achieve a permanent patron made his life miserable. Nevertheless, he wrote music prolifically and passionately: string quartets, sonatas, symphonies, concerti, and operas. *The Marriage of Figaro, The Magic Flute,* and *Don Giovanni* are three of the world's greatest operas. Mozart composed with an ease of melody and a blend of grace, precision, and emotion that arguably no one has ever excelled. Haydn remarked to Mozart's father that "your son is the greatest composer known to me either in person or by reputation."

The eighteenth century was also decisive in the development of the novel. The novel was not a completely new literary genre but grew out of the medieval romances and the picaresque stories of the sixteenth century. The English are credited with establishing the "modern novel as the chief vehicle" for fiction writing. With no established rules, the novel was open to much experimentation. It also proved especially attractive to women readers and women writers.

Samuel Richardson (1689–1761) was a printer by trade who did not turn to writing until his fifties. His first novel, *Pamela: or, Virtue Rewarded* focused on a servant girl's resistance to numerous seduction attempts by her master. Finally, by reading the girl's letters describing her feelings about his efforts, the master realizes that her mind is as impressive as her body and marries her. Virtue

◆ **Vierzehnheiligen, Exterior View.**   Balthasar Neumann, one of the most prominent architects of the eighteenth century, used the Baroque-Rococo style of architecture to design some of the most beautiful buildings of the century. Pictured here is the exterior of his pilgrimage church of the Vierzehnheiligen (The Fourteen Saints), located in southern Germany.

is rewarded. *Pamela* won Richardson a large audience as he appealed to the eighteenth century's growing cult of sensibility—the taste for the sentimental and emotional.

Reacting against the moral seriousness of Richardson, Henry Fielding (1707–1754) wrote novels about people without scruples who survived by their wits. His best work was *The History of Tom Jones, a Foundling,* a lengthy novel about the numerous adventures of a young scoundrel. Fielding presented scenes of English life from the hovels of London to the country houses of the English aristocracy. In a number of hilarious episodes, he described characters akin to real types in English society. Although he emphasized action rather than inner feeling, Fielding did his own moralizing by attacking the hypocrisy of his age.

High Culture

Historians and cultural anthropologists have grown accustomed to distinguishing between a civilization's high and popular culture. By high culture is usually meant the literary and artistic culture of the educated and wealthy ruling classes; by popular culture is meant the written and unwritten culture of the masses, most of which is passed down orally. By the eighteenth century, European high culture consisted of a learned culture of theologians, scientists, philosophers, intellectuals, poets, and dramatists, for whom Latin remained a truly international language. Their work was supported by a wealthy and literate lay group, the most important of whom were the landed aristocracy and the wealthier upper classes in the cities. European high culture was noticeably cosmopolitan. In addition to Latin, French had become an international language of the cultural elites. This high culture of Europe's elite was institutionally expressed in the salons, universities, and academies.

Especially noticeable in the eighteenth century was the expansion of both publishing and the reading public. A recent study of French publishing, for example, reveals that the number of titles issued annually by French publishers rose from 300 titles in 1750 to about 1,600 in the 1780s. Although many of these titles were still geared for small groups of the educated elite, many were also directed to the new reading public of the middle classes, which included women and even urban artisans. The growth of publishing houses made it possible for authors to make money from their works and be less dependent on wealthy patrons.

An important aspect of the growth of publishing and reading in the eighteenth century was the development of magazines for the general public. Great Britain, an important center for the new magazines, saw 25 periodicals published in 1700, 103 in 1760, and 158 in 1780. Along with magazines came daily newspapers. The first was printed in London in 1702, but by 1780, thirty-seven other English towns had their own newspapers. Filled with news and special features, they were relatively cheap and were available free in coffeehouses.

Popular Culture

Popular culture refers to the often unwritten and unofficial culture passed down orally that was fundamental to the lives of most people. The distinguishing characteristic of popular culture is its collective and public nature. Group activity was especially common in the festival, a broad name used to cover a variety of celebrations: family festivals, such as weddings; community festivals in Catholic Europe that celebrated the feastday of the local patron saint; annual festivals, such as Christmas and Easter that go back to medieval Christianity; and Carnival, the most spectacular form of festival, which was celebrated in the Mediterranean world of Spain, Italy, and France as well as in Germany and Austria. All of these festivals shared common characteristics. While having a spiritual function, they were celebrated in a secular fashion. They were special occasions on which people ate, drank, and celebrated to excess. In traditional societies, festival was a time of play because much of the rest of the year was a time of unrelieved work. As the poet Thomas Gray said of Carnival in Turin in 1739: "This Carnival lasts only from Christmas to Lent; one half of the remaining part of the year is passed in remembering the last, the other in expecting the future Carnival."[17]

"The example par excellence of the festival" was Carnival, which started in January and lasted until the beginning of Lent, traditionally the forty-day period of fasting and purification leading up to Easter. Carnival was a time of great indulgence, just the reverse of Lent when people were expected to abstain from meat, sex, and most recreations. A heavy consumption of food, especially meat and other delicacies, and heavy drinking were the norm. Carnival was a time of intense sexual activity as well. Songs with double meanings could be sung publicly at this time of year whereas otherwise they would be considered offensive to the community. A float of Florentine "key-makers," for example, sang this ditty to the ladies: "Our tools are fine, new and useful; We always carry them with us; They are good for anything; If you want to touch them, you can." Finally, Carnival was a time of aggression, a time to release pent-up feelings. Most often this took the form of verbal aggression because people could openly insult other people and were even allowed to criticize their social superiors and authorities. But other acts of violence were also permitted. People pelted each other with apples, eggs, flour, and pigs' bladders filled with water. This limited and sanctioned violence also led to unplanned violence. All contemporaries observed that the incidence of murder increased dramatically during Carnival.

The same sense of community evident in festival was also present in the chief gathering places of the common people, the local taverns or cabarets. Taverns functioned as a regular gathering place for neighborhood men to talk, play games, conduct small business matters, and, of course, to drink. In some countries, the favorite drinks of

The Punishment of Crime

Torture and capital punishment remained common features of European judicial systems well into the eighteenth century. Public spectacles were especially gruesome as this excerpt from the Nocturnal Spectator *of Restif de la Bretonne demonstrates.*

Restif de la Bretonne, Nocturnal Spectator: The Broken Man

I went home by way of rue Saint-Antoine and the Place de Grève. Three murderers had been broken on the wheel there, the day before. I had not expected to see any such spectacle, one that I had never dared to witness. But as I crossed the square I caught sight of a poor wretch, pale, half dead, wracked by the pains of the interrogation inflicted on him twenty hours earlier; he was stumbling down from the Hôtel de Ville sup-

ported by the executioner and the confessor. These two men, so completely different, inspired an inexpressible emotion in me! I watched the latter embrace a miserable man consumed by fever, filthy as the dungeons he came from, swarming with vermin! And I said to myself, "O Religion, here is your greatest glory! . . ."

I saw a horrible sight, even though the torture had been mitigated. . . . The wretch had revealed his accomplices. He was garroted before he was put to the wheel. A winch set under the scaffold tightened a noose around the victim's neck and he was strangled; for a long while the confessor and the hangman felt his heart to see whether the artery still pulsed, and the hideous blows were dealt only after it beat no longer. . . . I left, with my hair standing on end in horror.

the poor, such as gin in England and vodka in Russia, proved devastating as poor people regularly drank themselves into oblivion. Gin was cheap; the classic sign in English taverns, "Drunk for a penny, dead drunk for two pence," was literally true. In England, the consumption of gin rose from two to five million gallons between 1714 and 1733 and only declined when complaints finally led to strict laws to restrict sales in the 1750s.

In the eighteenth century, the separation between elite and poor grew ever wider. In 1500, popular culture was for everyone; a second culture for the elite, it was the only culture for the rest of society. But between 1500 and 1800, the nobility, clergy, and bourgeoisie had abandoned popular culture to the lower classes. This was, of course, a gradual process, and in abandoning the popular festivals, the upper classes were also abandoning the popular worldview as well. The new scientific outlook had brought a new mental world for the upper classes, and they now viewed such things as witchcraft, faith healing, fortune telling, and prophecy as the beliefs of "such as are of the weakest judgment and reason, as women, children, and ignorant and superstitious persons."

Crime and Punishment

By the eighteenth century, most European states had developed a hierarchy of courts to deal with civil and criminal cases. With the exception of England, they continued to use judicial torture as an important means of

obtaining evidence before trial until almost the end of the century. Courts used the rack, thumbscrews, and other instruments to obtain confessions in criminal cases. Seventeenth-century legal reforms, however, led to the gradual demise of judicial torture. It persisted longer in France than in other European states but was finally abolished there in 1780.

Most crimes in the eighteenth century fell into four broad categories: violent crimes such as murder; crimes against property; crimes against the government, such as smuggling; and begging or public vagrancy. The eighteenth century seems to have witnessed a decline in crimes of violence although there was a noticeable increase in theft and other crimes against property, especially in the cities. Particularly in rural areas, the unplanned violence of desperate people that had been a prominent feature of the seventeenth century was replaced by "semi-professional vagabonds" who were primarily interested in theft.

Punishments for crimes were often cruel and even spectacular. Public spectacle was a basic part of traditional punishment because it was believed to deter potential offenders in an age when the state's police arm was too weak to assure the capture of criminals. Although nobles were executed by simple beheading, lower-class criminals condemned to death were tortured, broken on the wheel, or drawn and quartered (see the box above). The death penalty was still commonly used in property as well as criminal cases. By 1800, the English listed over two hundred crimes that were subject to the death penalty. In addition to executions, European states resorted to forced labor in mines, forts, and navies. England also sent criminals as indentured servants to colonies in the New World and, after the American Revolution, to Australia.

Religion and the Churches

The music of Bach and the pilgrimage and monastic churches of southern Germany and Austria make us cognizant of a curious fact. While much of the great art and music of the time was religious, the thought of the time was antireligious as life became increasingly secularized and men of reason attacked the established churches. And yet most Europeans were still Christians. Except for governments, churches remained the most important institutions in people's lives. Even many of those most critical of the churches accepted that society could not function without religious faith.

In the eighteenth century, the established Catholic and Protestant churches were basically conservative institutions that upheld society's hierarchical structure, privileged classes, and traditions. Although churches experienced change because of new state policies, they did not sustain any dramatic internal changes. Whether in Catholic or Protestant countries, the parish church run by priest or pastor remained the center of religious practice. In addition to providing religious services, the parish church kept records of births, deaths, and marriages, provided charity for the poor, supervised whatever primary education there was, and cared for orphans.

Toleration and Religious Minorities

One of the chief battle cries of the philosophes had been a call for religious toleration. Out of political necessity, a certain level of tolerance of different creeds had occurred in the seventeenth century in such places as Germany after the Thirty Years' War and France after the divisive religious wars. But many rulers still found it difficult to accept. Louis XIV had turned back the clock in France at the end of the seventeenth century, insisting on religious uniformity and suppressing the rights of the Huguenots. Devout rulers continued to believe that there was only one path to salvation; it was the true duty of a ruler not to allow subjects to be condemned to hell by being heretics. Catholic minorities in Protestant countries and Protestant minorities in Catholic countries did not enjoy full civil or political rights. Persecution of heretics continued; the last burning of a heretic took place in 1781.

The Jews remained the despised religious minority of Europe. The largest population of Jews (known as the Ashkenazic Jews) lived in eastern Europe. Except in relatively tolerant Poland, Jews were restricted in their movements, forbidden to own land or hold many jobs, forced to pay burdensome special taxes, and also subject to periodic outbursts of popular wrath. The resulting pogroms in which Jewish communities were looted and massacred made Jewish existence precarious and dependent upon the favor of their territorial rulers.

Another major group was the Sephardic Jews who had been expelled from Spain in the fifteenth century. Although many had migrated to Turkish lands, some of them had settled in cities, such as Amsterdam, Venice, London, and Frankfurt, where they were relatively free to participate in the banking and commercial activities that Jews had practiced since the Middle Ages. The highly successful ones came to provide valuable services to rulers, especially in central Europe where they were known as the court Jews. But even these Jews were insecure because their religion set them apart from the Christian majority and served as a catalyst to social resentment.

Some Enlightenment thinkers in the eighteenth century favored a new acceptance of Jews. They argued that Jews and Muslims were all human and deserved the full rights of citizenship despite their religion. Many philosophes denounced persecution of the Jews but made no attempt to hide their hostility and ridiculed Jewish customs. Diderot, for example, said that the Jews had "all the defects peculiar to an ignorant and superstitious nation." Many Christians favored the assimilation of the Jews into the mainstream of society as the basic solution to the "Jewish problem," but only by the conversion of the Jews to Christianity. This, of course, was not acceptable to most Jews.

The Austrian emperor Joseph II (1780–1790) attempted to adopt a new policy toward the Jews, although it too was limited. It freed Jews from nuisance taxes and allowed them more freedom of movement and job opportunities, but they were still restricted from owning land and worshiping in public. At the same time, Joseph II encouraged Jews to learn German and work toward greater assimilation into Austrian society.

Popular Religion in the Eighteenth Century

Despite the rise of skepticism and the intellectuals' belief in deism and natural religion, it would appear that religious devotion remained strong in the eighteenth century. Catholic popular piety continued to be strong while within Protestantism the desire for more direct spiritual experience actually led to religious revivalism, especially in England.

It is difficult to assess precisely the religiosity of Europe's Catholics. The Catholic parish church remained an important center of life for the entire community. How many people went to church regularly cannot be known exactly, but it has been established that 90 to 95 percent of Catholic populations did go to mass on Easter Sunday, one of the church's most special celebrations. Confraternities, which were organizations of lay people dedicated to good works and acts of piety, were especially popular with townspeople. Each confraternity was consecrated to a patron saint, who was honored by holy processions in which members proudly wore their special robes.

After the initial religious fervor that created Protestantism in the sixteenth century, Protestant churches in the seventeenth century had settled down into well-established patterns controlled by state authorities and served by a well-educated clergy. In time, these churches became bureaucratized and bereft of religious enthusiasm. In Germany and England, where rationalism and deism had become influential and moved some theologians to a more "rational" Christianity, the desire of ordinary Protestant churchgoers for greater depths of religious experience led to new and dynamic religious movements.

One of the most famous movements—Methodism—was the work of John Wesley (1703–1791). An ordained Anglican minister, John Wesley took religion very seriously, experienced a deep spiritual crisis, and underwent a mystical experience: "I felt I did trust in Christ alone for salvation; and an assurance was given me, that He had taken away my sins, even mine, and saved me from the law of sin and death. I felt my heart strangely warmed." To Wesley, "the gift of God's grace" assured him of salvation and led him to become a missionary to the English people, to bring the "glad tidings" of salvation to all people, despite opposition from the Anglican church, which criticized this emotional mysticism or religious enthusiasm as superstitious nonsense. To Wesley, all could be saved by experiencing God and opening the doors to his grace.

In taking the Gospel to the people, Wesley preached to the masses in open fields, appealing especially to the lower classes neglected by the socially elitist Anglican church. He tried, he said, "to lower religion to the level of the lowest people's capacities." Wesley's charismatic

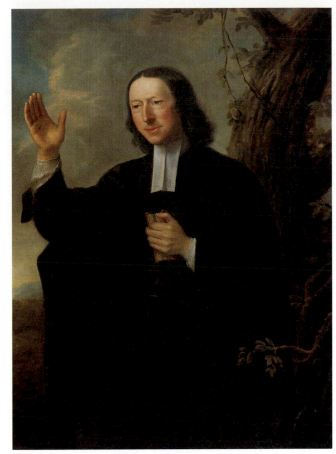

◆ **John Wesley.** In leading a deep spiritual revival in Britain, John Wesley founded a religious movement that came to be known as Methodism. He loved to preach to the masses, and this 1766 portrait by Nathaniel Hope shows him as he might have appeared before a crowd of people.

preaching often provoked highly charged and even violent conversion experiences (see the box on p. 676). Afterward, converts were organized into so-called Methodist societies or chapels in which they could aid each other in doing the good works that Wesley considered a component of salvation. A Central Methodist Conference supervised new lay preachers from Methodist circles. Controlled by Wesley, it enabled him to dominate the evangelical movement he had created. Although Wesley sought to keep Methodism within the Anglican church, after his death it became a separate and independent sect. Methodism represents an important revival of Christianity and proved that the need for spiritual experience had not been expunged by the eighteenth-century search for reason.

The Conversion Experience in Wesley's Methodism

After his own conversion experience, John Wesley traveled extensively to bring the "glad tidings" of Christ to other people. It has been estimated that he preached over 40,000 sermons, some of them to audiences numbering 20,000 listeners. Wesley gave his message wherever people gathered—in the streets, hospitals, private houses, and even pubs. In this selection from his journal, Wesley describes how emotional and even violent conversion experiences could be.

The Works of the Reverend John Wesley

Sunday, May 20 [1759], being with Mr. B--ll at Everton, I was much fatigued, and did not rise: but Mr. B. did, and observed several fainting and crying out, while Mr. Berridge was preaching: afterwards at Church, I heard many cry out, especially children, whose agonies were amazing: one of the eldest, a girl of ten or twelve years old, was full in my view, in violent contortions of body, and weeping aloud, I think incessantly, during the whole service. . . . The Church was equally crowded in the afternoon, the windows being filled within and without, and even the outside of the pulpit to the very top; so that Mr. B. seemed almost stifled by their breath; yet feeble and sickly as he is, he was continually strengthened, and his voice, for the most part, distinguishable, in the midst of all the outcries. I believe there were present three times more men than women, a great part of whom came from far; thirty of them having set out at two in the morning, from a place thirteen miles off. The text was, *Having a form of godliness, but denying the power thereof.* When the power of religion began to be spoken of, the presence of God really filled the place: and while poor sinners felt the sentence of death in their souls, what sounds of distress did I hear! The greatest number of them who cried or fell, were men: but some women, and several children, felt the power of the same almighty Spirit, and seemed just sinking into hell. This occasioned a mixture of several sounds; some shrieking, some roaring aloud. The most general was a loud breathing, like that of people half strangled and gasping for life: and indeed almost all the cries were like those of human creatures, dying in bitter anguish. Great numbers wept without any noise: others fell down as death: some sinking in silence; some with extreme noise and violent agitation. I stood on the pew-seat, as did a young man in the opposite pew, an able-bodied, fresh, healthy countryman: but in a moment, while he seemed to think of nothing less, down he dropped with a violence inconceivable. The adjoining pews seemed to shake with his fall: I heard afterwards the stamping of his feet; ready to break the boards, as he lay in strong convulsions, at the bottom of the pew. Among several that were struck down in the next pew, was a girl, who was as violently seized as he. . . . Among the children who felt the arrows of the Almighty, I saw a sturdy boy, about eight years old, who roared above his fellows, and seemed in his agony to struggle with the strength of a grown man. His face was as red as scarlet: and almost all on whom God laid his hand, turned either very red or almost black. . . .

The violent struggling of many in the above-mentioned churches, has broken several pews and benches. Yet it is common for people to remain unaffected there, and afterwards to drop down in their way home. Some have been found lying as dead on the road: others, in Mr. B.'s garden; not being able to walk from the Church to his house, though it is not two hundred yards. . . .

Conclusion

The Scientific Revolution represents a major turning point in modern civilization. In the Scientific Revolution, the Western world overthrew the medieval, Ptolemaic-Aristotelian worldview and arrived at a new conception of the universe: the sun at the center, the planets as material bodies revolving around the sun in elliptical orbits, and an infinite rather than a finite world. With the changes in the conception of "heaven" came changes in the conception of "earth." The work of Bacon and Descartes left Europeans with the separation of mind and matter and the belief that by using only reason they could, in fact, understand and dominate the world of nature. The development of a scientific method furthered the work of scientists while the new scientific societies and learned journals spread their results. Although traditional churches stubbornly resisted the new ideas and a few intellectuals pointed to some inherent flaws, nothing was able to halt the replacement of the traditional ways of thinking by new ways of thinking that created a more fundamental break with the past than that represented by the breakup of Christian unity in the Reformation.

Highly influenced by the new worldview created by the Scientific Revolution, the philosophes of the eighteenth century hoped that they could create a new society by using reason to discover the natural laws that governed it. They believed that education could produce better human beings and a better human society. They attacked traditional religion as the enemy and developed the new "sciences of man" in economics, politics, and education. Together, the Scientific Revolution of the seventeenth century and the Enlightenment of the eighteenth century constituted an intellectual revolution that laid the foundations for a modern worldview based on rationalism and secularism.

But this was also an age of tradition. While secular thought and rational ideas began to pervade the mental world of the ruling elites, most people in eighteenth-century Europe still lived by seemingly eternal verities and practices—God, religious worship, and farming. The most brilliant architecture and music of the age were religious. And yet, the forces of secularization were too strong to stop. As we shall see in the next chapter, in the midst of intellectual change, economic, political, and social transformations of great purport were taking shape that by the end of the eighteenth century were to lead to both political and industrial revolutions.

CHAPTER NOTES

1. Quoted in Alan G. R. Smith, *Science and Society in the Sixteenth and Seventeenth Centuries* (London, 1972), p. 59.
2. Edward MacCurdy, *The Notebooks of Leonardo da Vinci* (London, 1948), 1:634.
3. Quoted in John H. Randall, *The Making of the Modern Mind* (Boston, 1926), p. 234.
4. Quoted in Londa Schiebinger, *The Mind Has No Sex? Women in the Origins of Modern Science* (Cambridge, Mass., 1989), pp. 52–53.
5. Ibid., p. 85.
6. Quoted in Phyllis Stock, *Better Than Rubies: A History of Women's Education* (New York, 1978), p. 16.
7. René Descartes, *Philosophical Writings*, ed. and trans. Norman K. Smith (New York, 1958), p. 95.
8. Ibid., pp. 118–19.
9. Stillman Drake, ed. and trans., *Discoveries and Opinions of Galileo* (New York, 1957), p. 182.
10. Blaise Pascal, *The Pensées*, trans. J. M. Cohen (Harmondsworth, 1961), p. 100.
11. Ibid., pp. (in order of appearance) 31, 45, 31, 52–53, 164, 165.
12. Francis Bacon, *The Great Instauration*, trans. Jerry Weinberger (Arlington Heights, Ill., 1989), pp. (in order of appearance) 2, 8, 2, 16, 21.
13. John Locke, *An Essay Concerning Human Understanding* (New York, 1964), pp. 89–90.
14. Jean-Jacques Rousseau, *The Social Contract*, trans. Maurice Cranston (Harmondsworth, 1968), p. 141.
15. *A Serious Proposal to the Ladies*, in Moira Ferguson, ed., *First Feminists: British Women Writers, 1578–1799* (Bloomington, Ind., 1985), p. 190.
16. Kenneth Clark, *Civilisation* (New York, 1969), p. 231.
17. Quoted in Peter Burke, *Popular Culture in Early Modern Europe* (New York, 1978), p. 179.

SUGGESTED READINGS

Two general surveys of the entire Scientific Revolution are A. G. R. Smith, *Science and Society in the Sixteenth and Seventeenth Centuries* (London, 1972) and H. Butterfield, *The Origins of Modern Science* (New York, 1962). A more detailed and technical introduction can be found in A. R. Hall, *The Revolution in Science, 1500–1750* (London, 1983). Also of much value is A. G. Debus, *Man and Nature in the Renaissance* (Cambridge, 1978), which covers the period from the mid-fifteenth through the mid-seventeenth centuries. On the relationship of magic to the beginnings of the Scientific Revolution, see the pioneering works by F. Yates, *Giordano Bruno and the Hermetic Tradition* (New York, 1969) and *The Rosicrucian Enlightenment* (London, 1975). An important book on magic in the early modern period is K. Thomas, *Religion and the Decline of Magic* (London, 1971).

On the important figures of the revolution in astronomy, see E. Rosen, *Copernicus and the Scientific Revolution* (New York, 1984); M. Sharratt, *Galileo: Decisive Innovator* (Oxford, 1994); S. Drake, *Galileo* (New York, 1980); M. Casper, *Johannes Kepler*, trans. C. D. Hellman (London, 1959), the standard biography; and R. S. Westfall, *The Life of Isaac Newton* (New York, 1993). On Newton's relationship to alchemy, see the invaluable study by B. J. Dobbs, *The Foundations of Newton's Alchemy* (Cambridge, 1975).

The standard biography of Vesalius is C. D. O'Malley, *Andreas Vesalius of Brussels, 1514–1564* (Berkeley, Calif., 1964). Harvey's work is discussed in G. Whitteridge, *William Harvey and the Circulation of the Blood* (London, 1971). The importance of Francis Bacon in the early development of science is underscored in P. Rossi, *Francis Bacon: From Magic to Science* (Chicago, 1968) and C. Webster, *The Great Instauration: Science, Medicine, and Reform, 1620–1660* (London, 1975). A good introduction to the work of Descartes can be found in A. Kenny, *Descartes* (New York, 1968).

On the subject of women and early modern science, see the comprehensive and highly informative work by L. Schiebinger, *The Mind Has No Sex? Women in the Origins of Modern Science* (Cambridge, Mass., 1989).

The social and political context for the triumph of science in the seventeenth and eighteenth centuries is examined in M. Jacobs, *The Cultural Meaning of the Scientific Revolution* (New York, 1988) and *The Newtonians and the English Revolution, 1689–1720* (Ithaca, N.Y., 1976).

Two sound, comprehensive surveys of eighteenth-century Europe are I. Woloch, *Eighteenth-Century Europe* (New York, 1982) and M. S. Anderson, *Europe in the Eighteenth Century* (London, 1987).

A good, brief introduction to the Enlightenment can be found in N. Hampson, *A Cultural History of the Enlightenment* (New York, 1968) and D. Outram, *The Enlightenment* (Cambridge, 1995). A more detailed synthesis can be found in the two volumes by P. Gay, *The Enlightenment: An Interpretation*, 2 vols. (New York, 1966–1969). For a short, popular survey on the French philosophes, see F. Artz, *The Enlightenment in France* (Kent, Ohio, 1968). Studies on the major Enlightenment intellectuals include R. Shackleton, *Montesquieu, A Critical Biography* (London, 1961); H. T. Mason, *Voltaire: A Biography* (Baltimore, 1981); A. Wilson, *Diderot* (New York, 1972); and R. Grimsley, *Jean-Jacques Rousseau* (Cardiff, 1961). Specialized studies on various aspects of the Enlightenment include M. C. Jacob, *The Radical Enlightenment: Pantheists, Freemasons and Republicans* (London, 1981) and R. Darnton, *The Business of Enlightenment: A Publishing History of the Encyclopédie, 1775–1800* (Cambridge, Mass., 1979). On women in the eighteenth century, see N. Z. Davis and A. Farge, eds., *A History of Women: Renaissance and Enlightenment Paradoxes* (Cambridge, Mass., 1993); P. Quennell, ed., *Affairs of the Mind: The Salon in Europe and America from the 18th to the 20th Century* (Washington, D.C., 1980); and B. S. Anderson and J. P. Zinsser, *A History of Their Own*, vol. 2 (New York, 1988).

Two readable general surveys on the arts and literature are M. Levy, *Rococo to Revolution* (London, 1966) and H. Honour, *Neo-classicism* (Harmondsworth, 1968). Different facets of crime and punishment are examined in the important work by M. Foucault, *Discipline and Punish: The Birth of the Prison* (New York, 1977). Important studies on popular culture include P. Burke, *Popular Culture in Early Modern Europe* (New York, 1978) and R. Darnton, *The Great Cat Massacre and Other Episodes in French Cultural History* (New York, 1984).

A good introduction to the religious history of the eighteenth century can be found in G. R. Cragg, *The Church and the Age of Reason, 1648–1789* (London, 1966). The problem of religious toleration is examined in A. Hertzberg, *The French Enlightenment and the Jews* (New York, 1968).

CHAPTER
19

Europe on the Eve of a New World Order

Historians have often portrayed the eighteenth century as the final phase of Europe's old order before the violent upheaval and reordering of society associated with the French Revolution. The old order, still largely agrarian, dominated by kings and landed aristocrats, and grounded in privileges for nobles, clergy, towns, and provinces, seemed to continue a basic pattern that had prevailed in Europe since medieval times. Recent scholarship, however, has tended to undermine the idea of uniformity in the eighteenth century. Just as a new intellectual order based on rationalism and secularism was emerging in Europe from the intellectual revolution of the Scientific Revolution and Enlightenment, demographic, economic, social, and political patterns were beginning to change in ways that reflect the emergence of a new modern order.

A key factor in the emergence of a new world order was the French Revolution. On the morning of July 14, 1789, a Parisian mob of some eight thousand men and women in search of weapons streamed toward the Bastille, a royal armory filled with arms and ammunition. The Bastille was also a state prison, and although it now held only seven prisoners, in the eyes of these angry Parisians, it was a glaring symbol of the government's despotic policies. It was defended by the Marquis de Launay and a small garrison of 114 men. The attack on the Bastille began in earnest in the early afternoon, and after three hours of fighting, de Launay and the garrison surrendered. Angered by the loss of ninety-

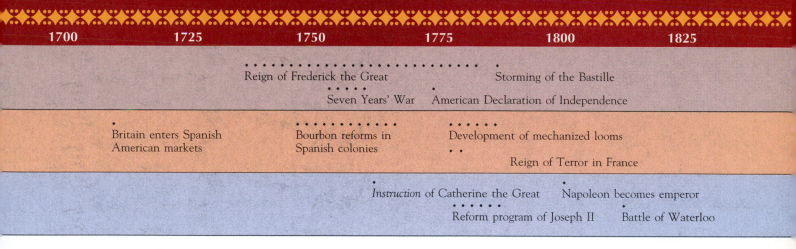

1700	1725	1750	1775	1800	1825

Reign of Frederick the Great   Storming of the Bastille

Seven Years' War   American Declaration of Independence

Britain enters Spanish   Bourbon reforms in   Development of mechanized looms
American markets   Spanish colonies

                                                        Reign of Terror in France

Instruction of Catherine the Great   Napoleon becomes emperor

Reform program of Joseph II   Battle of Waterloo

eight of their members, the victors beat de Launay to death, cut off his head, and carried it aloft in triumph through the streets of Paris. When King Louis XVI was told the news of the fall of the Bastille by the Duc de La Rochefoucauld-Liancourt, he exclaimed, "Why, this is a revolt." "No, Sire," replied the duke. "It is a revolution."

The French Revolution has been portrayed as a major turning point in European political and social history, as a time when the institutions of the "old regime" were destroyed and a new order was created based on individual rights, representative institutions, and a concept of loyalty to the nation rather than the monarch. The revolutionary upheaval of the era, especially in France, did create new liberal and national political ideals, summarized in the French revolutionary slogan, "Liberty, Equality, and Fraternity," that transformed France and then spread to other European countries and the rest of the world. Nevertheless, it would be a mistake to assume that all of the decadent privileges that characterized the old European regime were destroyed in 1789.

Economic Changes and the Persistence of a Traditional Social Order

The eighteenth century witnessed the beginning of economic changes in Europe that ultimately had a strong impact on the rest of the world. Rapid population growth, an agricultural revolution, the beginnings of an industrial revolution, and an increase in worldwide trade characterized the economic patterns of the eighteenth century. Yet these economic changes were taking place within a society that still clung to many of the social patterns established centuries earlier in the Middle Ages. The resulting tensions between the new economic patterns and the old social institutions would contribute to the revolutionary upheavals at the end of the eighteenth century.

Population, Food, and Industry

Despite regional variations, Europe's population began to grow around 1750 and continued a slow upward movement. It has been estimated that the total European population was around 120 million in 1700, expanded to 140 million by 1750, and then grew to 190 million by 1790; thus, the growth rate in the second half of the century was double that of the first half. These increases occurred during the same period that several million Europeans were going abroad as colonists. A falling death rate was perhaps the most important cause of population growth. But why did the death rate decline? More plentiful food and better transportation of available food supplies led to some improvement in diet and relief from devastating famines. Also of great significance in lowering death rates was the disappearance of bubonic plague.

Food became more abundant due in part to improvements in agricultural practices and methods in the eighteenth century, especially in Britain, parts of France, and the Low Countries. The increases in food production can be attributed to four interrelated factors: more land under cultivation, increased yields per acre, healthier and more abundant livestock, and an improved climate. Climatologists believe that the "little ice age" of the seventeenth century declined in the eighteenth, especially evident in the moderate summers that provided more ideal growing conditions. Important to the increased yields was the spread of new vegetables, including two important American crops, the potato and maize (Indian corn). Both had been brought to Europe from America in the sixteenth century although they were not grown in quantity until after 1700. The potato became a staple in Germany, the Low Countries, and especially Ireland, where repression by British landlords forced large numbers of poor peasants to survive on small plots of marginal land. The potato took relatively little effort to produce in large quantities. High in carbohydrates and calories, rich in vitamins A and C, it could be easily stored for winter use.

In the eighteenth century, it was primarily the British who adopted the new techniques that have been characterized as an agricultural revolution. This early modernization of British agriculture with its noticeable increase in productivity made possible the feeding of an expanding population about to enter a new world of industrialization and urbanization.

The most important product of European industry in the eighteenth century was textiles, most of which were still produced by traditional methods. In cities that were textile centers, master artisans used timeworn methods to produce finished goods in their guild workshops. But, by the eighteenth century, textile production had begun to shift to the countryside in some parts of Europe. Textiles were produced in the countryside by the "putting-out" or "domestic" system in which a merchant-capitalist entrepreneur bought the raw materials, mostly wool and flax, and "put them out" to rural workers who spun the raw material into yarn and then wove it into cloth on simple looms. Capitalist-entrepreneurs sold the finished products, made a profit, and used it to manufacture more. This system also was called "cottage industry," because spinners and weavers did their work on spinning wheels and looms in their own cottages. Cottage industry was truly a family enterprise because women and children could spin while men wove on the looms, enabling rural people to earn incomes that supplemented their pitiful wages as agricultural laborers.

The cottage system with its traditional methods of manufacturing was established in many rural areas of Europe during the eighteenth century. But, in the second half of the century, significant changes in industrial production began to occur, pushed along by the introduction of cotton, originally imported from India. The importation of raw cotton from slave plantations encouraged the production of cotton cloth in Europe where a profitable market had developed for lightweight cotton clothes that were less expensive than linens and woolens. But the traditional methods of the cottage industry proved incapable of keeping up with the growing demand, leading British cloth entrepreneurs to develop new methods and new machines. The flying shuttle sped up the process of weaving on a loom, thereby increasing the need for large quantities of yarn. In response, Richard Arkwright (1732–1792) invented a "water frame," powered by horse or water, that turned out yarn much faster than cottage spinning wheels. This abundance of yarn, in turn, led to the development of mechanized looms, invented in the 1780s but not widely adopted until the early nineteenth century. By that time Britain was in the throes of an industrial revolution, but already at the end of the eighteenth century, rural workers, perceiving that the new machines threatened their traditional livelihood, had begun to call for the machines' destruction (see the box on p. 683).

Worldwide Trade

Although bankers and industrialists would come to dominate the nineteenth century economically, in the eighteenth century merchants and traders still reigned supreme. Intra-European trade still dominated total trade figures as wheat, timber, and naval stores from the Baltic, wines from France, wool and fruit from Spain, and silk from Italy were exchanged along with a host of other products. But the eighteenth century witnessed only a slight increase in this trade while overseas trade boomed. Between 1716 and 1789, total French exports quadrupled, but intra-European trade, which constituted 75 percent of these exports in 1716, constituted only 50 percent of the total in 1789. This increase in overseas trade has led some historians to speak of the emergence of a truly global economy in the eighteenth century.

To justify the term *global economy*, historians have usually pointed to the patterns of trade that interlocked Europe, Africa, the Far East, and the American continents. One such pattern involved the influx of gold and silver into Spain from its colonial American empire. Much of this gold and silver made its way to Britain, France, and

The Beginnings of Mechanized Industry: The Attack on New Machines

Already by the end of the eighteenth century, mechanization was beginning to bring changes to the traditional cottage industry of textile manufacturing. Rural workers who depended on the extra wages made in their own homes often reacted by attacking the machinery that threatened their livelihoods. This selection is a petition that English cloth workers published in their local newspapers asking that machines no longer be used to prepare wool for spring.

The Yorkshire Cloth Workers' Petition (1786)

To the Merchants, Clothiers and all such as wish well to the Staple Manufactory of this Nation.

The Humble ADDRESS and PETITION of Thousands, who labour in the Cloth Manufactory.

SHEWETH, That the Scribbling-Machines have thrown thousands of your petitioners out of employ, whereby they are brought into great distress, and are not able to procure a maintenance for their families, and deprived them of the opportunity of bringing up their children to labour: We have therefore to request, that prejudice and self-interest may be laid aside, and that you may pay that attention to the following facts, which the nature of the case requires.

The number of Scribbling-Machines extending about seventeen miles south-west of LEEDS, exceed all belief, being no less than *one hundred and seventy!* and as each machine will do as much work in twelve hours, as ten men can in that time do by hand, (speaking within bounds) and they working night and day, one machine will do as much work in one day as would otherwise employ twenty men.

As we do not mean to assert any thing but what we can prove to be true, we allow four men to be employed at each machine twelve hours, working night and day, will take eight men in twenty-four hours; so that, upon a moderate computation twelve men are thrown out of employ for every single machine used in scribbling;

and as it may be supposed the number of machines in all the other quarters together, nearly equal those in the South-West, full four thousand men are left to shift for a living how they can, and must of course fall to the Parish, if not timely relieved. Allowing one boy to be bound apprentice from each family out of work, eight thousand hands are deprived of the opportunity of getting a livelihood.

We therefore hope, that the feelings of humanity will lead those who have it in their power to prevent the use of those machines, to give every discouragement they can to what has a tendency so prejudicial to their fellow-creatures. . . .

We wish to propose a few queries to those who would plead for the further continuance of these machines:

How are those men, thus thrown out of employ to provide for their families; and what are they to put their children apprentice to, that the rising generation may have something to keep them at work, in order that they may not be like vagabonds strolling about in idleness? Some say, Begin and learn some other business— Suppose we do, who will maintain our families, whilst we undertake the arduous task; and when we have learned it, how do we know we shall be any better for all our pains; for by the time we have served our second apprenticeship, another machine may arise, which may take away that business also. . . .

But what are our children to do; are they to be brought up in idleness? Indeed as things are, it is no wonder to hear of so many executions; for our parts, though we may be thought illiterate men, our conceptions are, that bringing children up to industry, and keeping them employed, is the way to keep them from falling into those crimes, which an idle habit naturally leads to.

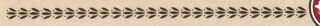

the Netherlands in return for manufactured goods. British, Dutch, and French merchants in turn used their profits to buy tea, spices, silk, and cotton goods from China and India to sell in Europe. Another important source of trading activity came from the plantations of the Western Hemisphere. Plantations, extending from the southern colonies of North America through the West Indies and into Brazil, were worked by African slaves and produced tobacco, cotton, coffee, and sugar, all products in demand by Europeans. A third pattern of trade involved British merchant ships, which carried British manufactured goods to Africa where they were traded for a cargo of slaves, which were then shipped to Virginia and paid for with tobacco, which in turn was shipped back to Britain where it was processed and then sold in Germany for cash. Of all the goods traded in the eighteenth century, perhaps the most profitable and certainly the most infamous were African slaves (see Chapter 14).

Overseas trade created enormous prosperity for some European countries. By the beginning of the eighteenth century, Spain, Portugal, and the Dutch Republic, which had earlier monopolized overseas trade, found themselves increasingly overshadowed by France and Britain, which built enormously profitable colonial empires in the course of the eighteenth century. After 1763, however, when France lost the Seven Years' War and much of its overseas empire, Britain emerged as the world's strongest overseas trading nation, and London became the world's greatest port.

Society in the Eighteenth Century

The pattern of Europe's social organization, first established in the Middle Ages, continued well into the eighteenth century. Social status was still largely determined not by wealth and economic standing but by the division into the traditional "orders" or "estates" determined by heredity and quality. This divinely sanctioned division of society into traditional orders was supported by Christian teaching, which emphasized the need to fulfill the responsibilities of one's estate. Although Enlightenment intellectuals attacked these traditional distinctions, they did not die easily. In the Prussian law code of 1794, marriage between noble males and middle-class females was forbidden without a government dispensation. Even without government regulation, however, different social groups could be easily distinguished everywhere in Europe by the distinctive, traditional clothes they wore.

Nevertheless, some forces of change were at work in this traditional society. The ideas of the Enlightenment made headway as reformers argued that the concept of an unchanging social order based on privilege was hostile to the progress of society. Moreover, especially in some cities, the old structures were becoming difficult to maintain as new economic patterns, especially the emergence of larger industries, brought new social contrasts that destroyed the old order. Despite these forces of change, however, it would take the revolutionary upheavals at the end of the eighteenth century before the old order would finally begin to disintegrate.

Since society was still mostly rural in the eighteenth century, the peasantry constituted the largest social group, making up as much as 85 percent of Europe's population. There were rather wide differences, however, between peasants from area to area. The most important distinction—at least legally—was between the free peasant and the serf. Peasants in Britain, northern Italy, the Low Countries, Spain, most of France, and some areas of western Germany shared freedom despite numerous regional and local differences. Legally free peasants, however, were not exempt from burdens. Some free peasants in Andalusia in Spain, southern Italy, Sicily, and Portugal lived in a poverty more desperate than that of many serfs in Russia and eastern Germany. In France, 40 percent of free peasants owned little or no land whatever by 1789.

◆ **French Port of Dieppe.**
Seen here is the port of Dieppe, typical of several ports along the French coast from which a regular trade was carried on with French colonies in the New World. Rebuilt after it had been bombarded during the War of the League of Augsburg in 1694, Dieppe was a modern town in the eighteenth century.

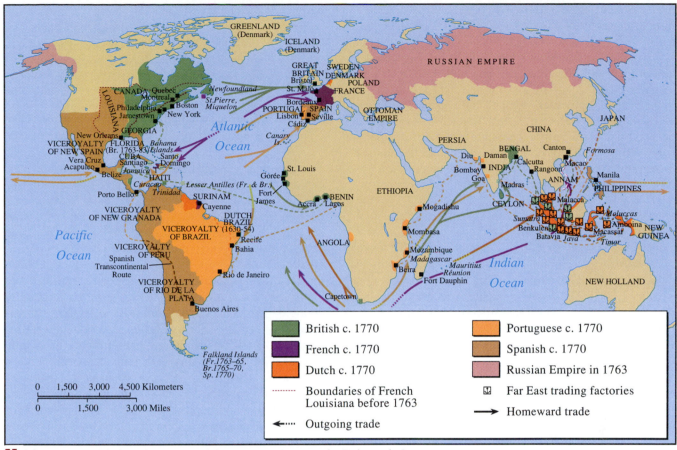

![Map legend]

British c. 1770   Portuguese c. 1770
French c. 1770   Spanish c. 1770
Dutch c. 1770   Russian Empire in 1763
- - - Boundaries of French Louisiana before 1763   Far East trading factories
←···· Outgoing trade   → Homeward trade

Map 19.1　Global Trade Patterns of the European States in the Eighteenth Century.

Small peasant proprietors or tenant farmers in western Europe were also not free from compulsory services. Most owed tithes, often one-third of their crops. Although tithes were intended for parish priests, in France only 10 percent of the priests received them. Instead they wound up in the hands of towns and aristocratic landowners. Moreover, peasants could still owe a variety of dues and fees. Local aristocrats claimed hunting rights on peasant land and had monopolies over the flour mills, community ovens, and wine and oil presses needed by the peasants. Hunting rights, dues, fees, and tithes were all deeply resented.

The local villages in which they dwelt remained the centers of peasants' social lives. Villages, especially in western Europe, maintained public order; provided poor relief, a village church, and sometimes a schoolmaster; collected taxes for the central government; maintained roads and bridges; and established common procedures for sowing, plowing, and harvesting crops. But villages were often dominated by richer peasants and proved highly resistant to innovations, such as new crops and agricultural practices.

The nobles, who constituted about 2 or 3 percent of the European population, played a dominating role in society. Being born a noble automatically guaranteed a place at the top of the social order with all of its attendant special privileges and rights. The legal privileges of the nobility included judgment by their peers, immunity from severe punishment, exemption from many forms of taxation, and rights of jurisdiction. Especially in central and eastern Europe, the rights of landlords over their serfs were overwhelming.

Nobles also played important roles in military and government affairs. Since medieval times, landed aristocrats had functioned as military officers. Although monarchs found it impossible to exclude commoners from the ranks of officers, the tradition remained that nobles made the most natural and hence the best officers. Moreover, the eighteenth-century nobility played a significant role in the administrative machinery of state. In some countries, such as Prussia, the entire bureaucracy reflected aristocratic values. Moreover, in most of Europe, the landholding nobility controlled much of the life of their local districts.

Although the nobles clung to their privileged status and struggled to keep others out, almost everywhere the possession of money made it possible to enter the ranks of the nobility. Rights of nobility were frequently attached to certain lands, so purchasing the lands made one a noble; the acquisition of government offices also often conferred noble status.

Townspeople were still a distinct minority of the total population except in the Dutch Republic, Britain, and parts of Italy. At the end of the eighteenth century, about one-sixth of the French population lived in towns of 2,000 or more. The biggest city in Europe was London with its 1,000,000 inhabitants while Paris numbered between 550,000 and 600,000. Altogether, at least twenty European cities in twelve countries had populations over 100,000, including Naples, Lisbon, Moscow, St. Petersburg, Vienna, Amsterdam, Berlin, Rome, and Madrid.

Although urban dwellers were vastly outnumbered by rural inhabitants, towns played an important role in Western culture. The contrasts between a large city with its education, culture, and material consumption and the surrounding, often poverty-stricken countryside were striking, as is evident in this British traveler's account of Russia's St. Petersburg in 1741:

> The country about Petersburg has full as wild and desert a look as any in the Indies; you need not go above 200 paces out of the town to find yourself in a wild wood of firs, and such a low, marshy, boggy country that you would think God when he created the rest of the world for the use of mankind had created this for an inaccessible retreat for all sorts of wild beasts.[1]

Peasants often resented the prosperity of towns and their exploitation of the countryside to serve urban interests. Palermo in Sicily used one-third of the island's food production while paying only one-tenth of the taxes. Towns lived off the countryside not by buying, but by using tithes, rents, and feudal dues to acquire peasant produce.

Many cities in western and even central Europe had a long tradition of patrician oligarchies that continued to control their communities by dominating town and city councils. Despite their domination, patricians constituted only a small minority of the urban population. Just below the patricians stood an upper crust of the middle classes: nonnoble officeholders, financiers and bankers, merchants, wealthy rentiers who lived off their investments, and important professionals, including lawyers. Another large urban group was the petty bourgeoisie or lower middle class made up of master artisans, shopkeepers, and small traders. Below them were the laborers or working classes. Much urban industry was still done in

◆ **A Market in Turin.**   Below the wealthy patrician elites who dominated the towns and cities were a number of social groups with a wide range of incomes and occupations. This remarkable diversity is evident in this view of a market square in the Italian city of Turin.

⇒ Poverty in France ⇐

*P*overty was a highly visible problem in the eighteenth century. Unlike the British, who had a system of public-supported poor relief, the French responded to poverty with ad hoc policies when conditions became acute. This selection is taken from an intendant's report to the controller-general at Paris describing his suggestions for a program to relieve the grain shortages expected for the winter months.

M. de la Bourdonnaye, Intendant of Bordeaux, to the Controller-General, September 30, 1708

Having searched for the means of helping the people of Agen in this cruel situation and having conferred with His Eminence, the Bishop, it seems to us that three things are absolutely necessary if the people are not to starve during the winter.

Most of the inhabitants do not have seed to plant their fields. However, we decided that we would be going too far if we furnished it, because those who have seed would also apply [for more]. Moreover, we are persuaded that all the inhabitants will make strenuous efforts to find some seed, since they have every reason to expect prices to remain high next year. . . .

But this project will come to nothing if the collectors of the taille continue to be as strict in the exercise of their functions as they have been of late and continue to employ troops [to force collection]. Those inhabitants who have seed grain would sell it to be freed from an oppressive garrison, while those who must buy seed, since they had none left from their harvest and have scraped together a little money for this purchase, would prefer to give up that money [for taxes] when put under police constraint. To avoid this, I feel it is absolutely necessary that you order the receivers-general to reduce their operations during this winter, at least with respect to the poor. . . .

We are planning to import wheat for this region from Languedoc and Quercy, and we are confident

that there will be enough. But there are two things to be feared: one is the greed of the merchants. When they see that general misery has put them in control of prices, they will raise them to the point where the calamity is almost as great as if there were no provisions at all. The other fear is that the artisans and the lowest classes, when they find themselves at the mercy of the merchants, will cause disorders and riots. As a protective measure, it would seem wise to establish two small storehouses. . . . Ten thousand ecus [30,000 livres] would be sufficient for each. . . .

A third point demanding our attention is the support of beggars among the poor, as well as of those who have no other resources than their wages. Since there will be very little work, these people will soon be reduced to starvation. We should establish public workshops to provide work as was done in 1693 and 1694. I should choose the most useful kind of work, located where there are the greatest number of poor. In this manner, we should rid ourselves of those who do not want to work and assure the others of a moderate subsistence. For these workshops, we would need about 40,000 livres, or altogether 100,000 livres. The receiver-general of the taille of Agen could advance this sum. The 60,000 livres for the storehouses he would get back very soon. I shall await your orders on all of the above.

Marginal Comments by the Controller-General

Operations for the collection of the taille are to be suspended. The two storehouses are to be established; great care must be taken to put them to good use. The interest on the advances will be paid by the king. His Majesty has agreed to the establishment of the public workshops for the able-bodied poor and is willing to spend up to 40,000 livres on them this winter.

small guild workshops by masters, journeymen, and apprentices. Urban communities also had a large group of unskilled workers who served as servants, maids, and cooks at pitifully low wages.

Despite an end to the ravages of plague, eighteenth-century cities still experienced high death rates, especially among children, because of unsanitary living conditions, polluted water, and a lack of sewerage facilities.

One observer compared the stench of Hamburg to an open sewer that could be smelled for miles around. Overcrowding also exacerbated urban problems as cities continued to grow from an influx of rural immigrants. But cities proved no paradise for them as unskilled workers found few employment opportunities. The result was a serious problem of poverty in the eighteenth century (see the box above).

Changing Patterns of War: Global Confrontation

Despite the philosophes' denunciations of war as a foolish waste of life and resources in stupid quarrels of no value to humankind, the rivalry among states that led to costly struggles remained unchanged in the European world of the eighteenth century. Although the European state system emerged in the seventeenth century, its implications were more fully realized in the eighteenth century. This system of self-governing, individual states was grounded largely in the amoral and potentially anarchic principle of self-interest. Because international relations were based upon considerations of power, the eighteenth-century concept of a "balance of power" was predicated on how to counterbalance the power of one state by another in order to prevent any one power from dominating the others. This balance of power, however, did not imply a desire for peace. Large armies created to defend a state's security were often used for offensive purposes as well. As Frederick the Great of Prussia remarked, "the fundamental rule of governments is the principle of extending their territories." Nevertheless, there were limits to the use of force in eighteenth-century Europe. The ideological fury that had made the religious wars of the sixteenth and seventeenth centuries so destructive was gone, and its absence made compromises easier and the use of diplomacy more regular.

The diplomacy of the eighteenth century still focused primarily on dynastic interests or the desire of ruling families to provide for their dependents and extend their dynastic holdings. But the eighteenth century also saw the emergence of the concept of "reason of state," on the basis of which rulers looked beyond dynastic interests to the long-term future of their states.

International rivalry and the continuing centralization of the European states were closely related. The need for taxes to support large armies and navies created its own imperative for more efficient and effective control of power in the hands of bureaucrats who could collect taxes and organize states for the task of winning wars. At the same time, the development of large standing armies ensured that political disputes would periodically be resolved by armed conflict rather than diplomacy.

Between 1715 and 1740, however, it seemed that Europeans preferred peace. But in 1740, a major conflict erupted over the succession to the Austrian throne. After the death of the Habsburg emperor Charles VI (1711–1740), King Frederick II of Prussia (1740–1786) took advantage of the succession of a woman, Maria Theresa (1740–1780), to the throne of Austria by invading Austrian Silesia. The vulnerability of Maria Theresa encouraged France to enter the war against its traditional enemy Austria; in turn, Maria Theresa made an alliance with the British who feared French hegemony over continental affairs. All too quickly, the Austrian succession had produced a worldwide conflagration. The war was fought not only in Europe where Prussia seized Silesia, and France occupied the Austrian Netherlands, but in the Far East where France took Madras in India from the British and in North America where the British captured the French fortress of Louisbourg at the entrance to the St. Lawrence River. By 1748, all parties were exhausted and agreed to stop. The peace treaty guaranteed the return of all occupied territories to their original owners except for Silesia. Prussia's refusal to return Silesia guaranteed another war, at least between the two hostile central European powers of Prussia and Austria.

The Seven Years' War (1756–1763): A Global War

Maria Theresa refused to accept the loss of Silesia and prepared for its return by rebuilding her army while working diplomatically to separate Prussia from its chief ally, France. In 1756, Austria achieved what was soon labeled a diplomatic revolution. French-Austrian rivalry had been a fact of European diplomacy since the late sixteenth century. But two new rivalries made this old one seem superfluous: Britain and France over colonial empires, and Austria and Prussia over Silesia. France now abandoned Prussia and allied with Austria. Russia, which saw Prussia as a major hindrance to Russian goals in central Europe, joined the new alliance. In turn, Great Britain allied with Prussia. This diplomatic revolution of 1756 now led to another worldwide war.

There were three major areas of conflict: Europe, India, and North America. Europe witnessed the clash of the two major alliances: the British and Prussians against the Austrians, Russians, and French. With his superb army and military prowess, Frederick the Great of Prussia was able for some time to defeat the Austrian, French, and Russian armies. Under attack from three different directions, however, Frederick's forces were gradually worn down and faced utter defeat until a new Russian tsar, Peter III (1762), withdrew Russian troops from the conflict and from the Prussian lands that the Russians had occupied. His withdrawal guaranteed a stalemate and led the parties to negotiate a peace. The European conflict ended in 1763. All occupied territories were returned while Austria officially recognized Prussia's permanent control of Silesia.

The Anglo-French struggle in the rest of the world had more decisive results. Known as the Great War for Empire, it was fought in India and North America. The French had returned Madras to Britain after the War of the Austrian Succession, but jockeying for power continued as both the French and the British claimed the support of opposing native Indian princes. The British under Robert Clive (1725–1774) ultimately won out, not because they had better forces but because they were more persistent. By the Treaty of Paris in 1763, the French withdrew and left India to the British (see Chapter 16).

By far, the greatest conflicts of the Seven Years' War took place in North America (where the war was known as the French and Indian War). Both the French and British colonial empires in the New World consisted of large parts of the West Indies and the North American continent. In the former, the British held Barbados, Jamaica, and Bermuda while the French possessed Saint Dominique, Martinique, and Guadeloupe. On these tropical islands, both the British and the French had developed plantation economies, worked by African slaves, which produced tobacco, cotton, coffee, and sugar.

On the North American continent, the French and British colonies were structured in different ways. French North America (Canada and Louisiana) was run autocratically as a vast trading area, valuable for the acquisition of fur, leather, fish, and timber. However, the inability of the French state to get its people to emigrate to these North American possessions left them thinly populated.

British North America had come to consist of thirteen colonies on the eastern coast of the present United States. They were well populated, containing about 1.5 million people by 1750, and were also prosperous. Supposedly run by the British Board of Trade, the Royal Council, and Parliament, these thirteen colonies had legislatures that tended to act independently. Merchants in such port cities as Boston, Philadelphia, New York, and Charleston resented and resisted regulation from the British government.

Both the North American and West Indian colonies of Britain and France were assigned roles in keeping with

✳ Map 19.2   The Seven Years' War.

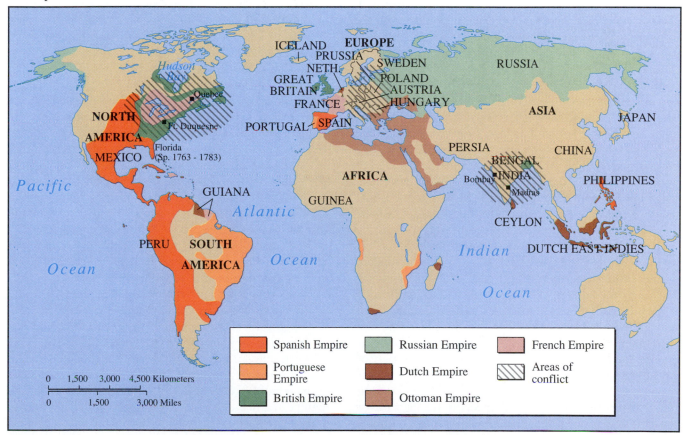

◆ **The Death of Wolfe.** The great powers of Europe fought the Seven Years' War in Europe, India, and North America. Despite initial French successes in North America, the British went on to win the war. This painting by Benjamin West presents a heroic rendering of the death of General Wolfe, the British commander who defeated the French forces at the Battle of Quebec.

mercantilist theory. They provided raw materials for the mother country while buying the latter's manufactured goods. Navigation acts regulated what could be taken from and sold to the colonies. Theoretically, the system was supposed to provide a balance of trade favorable to the mother country.

British and French rivalry in North America led to two primary areas of contention. One consisted of the waterways of the Gulf of St. Lawrence, guarded by the fortress of Louisbourg and by forts near the Great Lakes and Lake Champlain that protected French Quebec and French traders. The other was the unsettled Ohio River valley. The French began to move down from the Great Lakes and up from their forts on the Mississippi to establish forts from the Appalachians to the Mississippi River. To British settlers in the thirteen colonies, French activity threatened to cut off this vast area from exploitation by the settlers. The French were able to gain the support of the Indians; as traders and not settlers, they were viewed by the natives with less hostility than the British.

Despite initial French successes, British fortunes were revived by the efforts of William Pitt the Elder who was convinced that the destruction of the French colonial empire was a necessary prerequisite for the creation of Britain's own colonial empire. Pitt's policy focused on making a minimal effort in Europe while concentrating resources on the colonial war, especially through use of the British navy. Although the French troops outnum-

bered the British, the ability of the French to use their troops in the New World was contingent upon naval support. The defeat of French fleets in major naval battles in 1759 gave the British an advantage because the French could no longer easily reinforce their garrisons. A series of British victories soon followed. In 1759, British forces under General James Wolfe defeated the French under General Louis-Joseph Montcalm on the Plains of Abraham outside Quebec. Both generals died in the battle. The British went on to seize Montreal, the Great Lakes area, and the Ohio valley. The French were forced to make peace. By the Treaty of Paris, they ceded Canada and the lands east of the Mississippi to Britain. Their ally Spain transferred Spanish Florida to British control; in return, the French gave their Louisiana territory to the Spanish. By 1763, Great Britain had become the world's greatest colonial power.

European Armies and Warfare in the Eighteenth Century

The professional standing army, initiated in the seventeenth century, became a standard feature of eighteenth-century Europe. Especially noticeable was the increase in the size of armies, which paralleled the development of absolutist states. From 1740 to 1780, the French army grew from 190,000 to 300,000 men; the Prussian from 83,000 to 200,000; the Austrian from 108,000 to 282,000; and the Russian from 130,000 to 290,000.

The composition of these armies reflected the hierarchical structure of European society and the great chasm that separated the upper and lower classes. Officers were primarily from the landed aristocracy, which had for centuries regarded military activity as one of its major functions. Middle-class individuals were largely kept out of the higher ranks of the officer corps while being admitted to the middle ranks. A prejudice against commoners in the officer corps remained a regular feature of military life in the eighteenth century.

Rank-and-file soldiers came mostly from the lower classes of society. Some states, such as Prussia and Russia, conscripted able-bodied peasants. But many states realized that this was counterproductive because they could not afford to waste agricultural manpower. For that reason, eighteenth-century armies were partially composed of foreign troops, many from Switzerland or the petty German states. Of the great powers, Britain alone had no regular standing army and relied on mercenaries, evident in its use of German troops in America. Most troops in European armies, especially the French and the Austrian, were natives who enlisted voluntarily for six-year terms.

Some were not exactly volunteers; often vagabonds and the unemployed were pressed into service. Most, however, came from the lower classes—peasants and also artisans from the cities—who saw the military as an opportunity to escape from hard times or personal problems.

The maritime powers, such as Britain and the Dutch Republic, regarded navies as more important than armies. In the second half of the eighteenth century, the British possessed 174 warships manned by 80,000 sailors. Conditions on these ships were often poor. Diseases such as scurvy and yellow fever were rampant, and crews were frequently gang pressed into duty.

Colonial Empires and Revolution

As we have seen, the colonial empires in the Western Hemisphere were an integral part of the European economy in the eighteenth century and became entangled in the conflicts of the European states. Despite these close ties with Europe, the colonies of Latin America and British North America were developing along lines that sometimes differed significantly from those of their European mother country. In the case of the thirteen British colonies along the eastern seaboard of North America, these differences led eventually to rebellion and the formation of a new government.

The Society of Latin America

In the sixteenth century, Portugal came to dominate Brazil while Spain established an enormous colonial empire in the New World that included Central America, most of South America, and parts of North America. Within the lands of Central and South America, a new civilization arose that we have come to call Latin America. It was a multiracial society. Iberian (Spanish and Portuguese) settlers who arrived in the Western Hemisphere were small in number compared to the native Indians; many of the newcomers, especially in the early decades of colonization, were males who not only used female natives for their sexual pleasure, but married them as well. Already by 1501, Spanish rulers had authorized intermarriage between Europeans and native American Indians. As a result, a new people—the mestizos—appeared. Europeans also used native Indians to do their work for them. So many Indians succumbed to European diseases (see Chapter 14), however, that another group of people was brought to Latin America—the Africans.

African slaves were first imported to the Western Hemisphere in 1502. Over a period of three centuries, possibly as many as eight million slaves were brought to Spanish and Portuguese America. In Brazil and the Caribbean, where the cultivation of cane sugar by the plantation system demanded much human labor, Africans constituted almost the entire labor force. Because plantation owners preferred males as field hands, two out of every three Africans were male. Although female slaves also worked in the fields, many were used as domestic servants, prostitutes, and mistresses. Over a period of time, Africans were also brought to the cities where they worked as artisans, servants, small tradesmen, and miners. Although Africans made enormous contributions to the economic life of Spanish America and Portuguese Brazil, they were usually treated with contempt and badly abused. But in many ways—music, dance, folklore, diet, language, religion—African influence remained a permanent part of Latin American culture.

Africans also contributed to Latin America's multiracial character. Mulattoes—the offspring of Africans and whites—joined mestizos and descendants of whites, Africans, and native Indians to produce a unique society in Latin America (see the box on p. 692). Unlike Europe, and unlike British North America, which remained a largely white offshoot of Europe, Latin America developed a multiracial society with less rigid attitudes about race. In other ways as well, colonial Latin America developed distinctive features that differed from those found in the North American colonies or in Europe.

THE ECONOMIC FOUNDATIONS

After realizing that the Americas were not Asia, both the Portuguese and the Spanish sought ways to benefit economically from their discoveries. The search for precious metals became a major objective. The Spaniards were especially successful, finding supplies of gold in the Caribbean and New Granada (Colombia) and silver in Mexico and the viceroyalty of Peru. The silver mine of Potosí in Upper Peru (Bolivia) was one of the world's richest. Overall, mines in the viceroyalty of New Spain (largely Mexico) produced half of the precious metals found in the New World. Most of the gold and silver was sent to Europe, and little remained in the New World to benefit those whose labor had produced it.

Although the pursuit of gold and silver offered prospects of fantastic financial rewards, agriculture proved to be a more long-lasting and rewarding source of prosperity for Latin America. Early on, the Spanish had instituted the *encomienda* system that enabled individual Spaniards to collect tribute from the natives and use

≈ Class and Caste in Colonial Latin America ≈

The mixture of white Iberians, African slaves, and native Indians created a multiracial society in Latin America. Gradually, a caste system emerged in which individuals' social status was often determined by their racial background. These excerpts, which are taken from an account by two Spanish travelers, describe this complex class and caste system in the Caribbean port of Cartagena, Colombia, and Lima, Peru.

George Juan and Antonio de Ulloa, *Voyage to South America*

The inhabitants may be divided into different castes or tribes, who derive their origin from a coalition of Whites, Negroes, and Indians. Of each of these we shall treat particularly.

The Whites may be divided into two classes, the Europeans and Creoles, or Whites born in the country. The former are commonly called Peninsulars, but are not numerous; most of them either return into Spain after acquiring a competent fortune, or remove up into inland provinces in order to increase it. Those who are settled at Cartagena, carry on the whole trade of that place, and live in opulence; whilst the other inhabitants are indigent, and reduced to have recourse to mean and hard labor for subsistence. The families of the White Creoles compose the landed interest; some of them have large estates, and are highly respected, because their ancestors came into the country invested with honorable posts, bringing their families with them when they settled here. . . .

Among the other tribes which are derived from an intermarriage of the Whites with the Negroes, the first are the Mulattoes. Next to these the *Tercerones*, produced from a White and a Mulatto. . . . After these follow the *Quarterones*, proceeding from a White and a *Terceron*. The last are the *Quinterones*, who owe their origin to a White and a *Quarteron*. This is the last gradation, there being no visible difference between them and the Whites, either in color or features. . . . Every

person is so jealous of the order of their tribe or caste, that if, through inadvertence, you call them by a degree lower than what they actually are, they are highly offended. . . . These castes, from the Mulattoes, . . . are the mechanics of the city; the Whites, whether Creoles or Peninsulars, disdaining such a mean occupation follow nothing below merchandise. . . .

The inhabitants of Lima are composed of whites, or Spaniards, Negroes, Indians, Mestizos, and other castes, proceeding from the mixture of all three.

The Spanish families are very numerous. . . . Among these are reckoned a third or fourth part of the most distinguished nobility of Peru. . . . All these families live in a manner becoming their rank, having estates equal to their generous dispositions, keeping a great number of slaves and other domestics, and those who affect making the greatest figure, have coaches, while others content themselves with chaises, which are here so common, that no family of any substance is without one. . . . The funds to support these expenses, which in other parts would ruin families, are their large estates and plantations, civil and military employments or commerce, which is here accounted no derogation to families of the greatest distinction; but by this commerce is not to be understood the buying and selling by retail or in shops, every one trading proportional to his character and substance. . . .

The Negroes, Mulattoes, and their descendants, form the greater number of the inhabitants; and of these are the greatest part of the mechanics. . . . The third, and last class of inhabitants are the Indians and Mestizos, but these are very small in proportion to the largeness of the city, and the multitudes of the second class. They are employed in agriculture, in making earthen ware, and bringing all kinds of provisions to market, domestic services being performed by Negroes and Mulattoes, either slaves or free, though generally by the former.

them as laborers. Protests from Catholic missionaries, who were appalled at the mistreatment of Indians and the rapid decline in their numbers, forced the Spanish government to change its policy. Beginning in 1542, the monarchy abolished the *encomienda* and replaced it with the *repartimento*, a new system for Indian labor under

which landowners were permitted to use Indian laborers only on a temporary basis and only with the permission of the royal officials. Royal officials, it was thought, would be more responsible for the welfare of the Indians.

By the seventeenth century, the decline in the number of Indians led to a new system in which the owners of large estates paid wages to their Indian agricultural workers. By making loans to the Indians that the Indians could not repay in their lifetimes because of their low wages, the large landowners created a class of peons—native peasants permanently dependent upon the landowners.

This creation of an oppressed class of wage laborers reminds us of another noticeable feature of Latin American agriculture—the dominating role of the large landowners. Both Spanish and Portuguese landowners amassed immense estates, leaving the Indians to work either as peons on the estates or as poor farmers on marginal lands. This system of large landowners and dependent peasants has remained one of the persistent features of Latin American society. Haciendas (as the estates were called in Spanish America) and fazendas (in Portuguese Brazil) could reach enormous sizes. Some haciendas in Mexico, for example, included over a million acres. Initially, the haciendas of Spanish America grew produce for local markets while the Brazilian fazendas concentrated on sugar or other cash crops that could be sold abroad on the international market. By the eighteenth century, both Spanish haciendas and Brazilian fazendas were producing for sale abroad.

Trade was another avenue for the economic exploitation of the American colonies. Colonies, according to classic mercantilist theory, were intended to be sources of raw materials. The American colonies were certainly that for both Spain and Portugal as gold, silver, sugar, tobacco, diamonds, animal hides, and a number of other natural products made their way to Europe. The decline of Spain and Portugal had led these two states to depend even more on resources from their colonies, and they imposed strict mercantilist rules on them to keep others out. Spain, in particular, closely regulated the trade of its American colonies. Only two Spanish ports, Cádiz and Seville, were permitted to trade with the American colonies. Each year two fleets sailed from these ports to Vera Cruz and Portobelo, the only officially recognized ports in Spanish America for the transshipment of Latin American goods in the New World. From these two ports, the products of the immense colonial empire were shipped to Spain.

The British and French, however, proved too powerful to be excluded from this lucrative Latin American market. The British cajoled the Portuguese into allowing them into their Brazilian trade. The French were the first to break into the Spanish Latin American market when the French Bourbons became kings of Spain. The British entered the Spanish American markets in 1713, when Britain was granted the privilege, known as the *asiento*, of transporting 4,500 slaves a year to Spanish Latin America.

In accordance with mercantilist theory, both Spain and Portugal tried to limit the role of their colonies to providing raw materials while the mother countries supplied their colonists with manufactured goods. Decrees aimed at prohibiting manufacturing in the New World tended to be ignored, however. By the eighteenth century, Latin America was producing cotton cloth, pottery, shoes, and furniture for local markets.

THE STATE AND THE CHURCH IN COLONIAL LATIN AMERICA

Portuguese Brazil and Spanish America were colonial empires that lasted over three hundred years. Although the organization of these empires varied considerably, they shared some fundamental similarities. The difficulties of communication and travel between the New World and Europe made it virtually impossible for the Spanish and Portuguese monarchs to maintain close regulation of their empires. Consequently, colonial officials in Latin America had much autonomy in implementing imperial policies, although the Iberians tried to keep the most important posts of colonial government in the hands of Europeans.

In the early sixteenth century, Portugal's control of its vast Brazilian empire was fairly loose, but beginning in the mid-sixteenth century, the Portuguese monarchy began to assert its control over Brazil by establishing the position of governor-general. The governor-general (later called a viceroy) developed a bureaucracy, but had at best a loose control over the captains-general who were responsible for governing the districts into which Brazil was divided. In the course of the eighteenth century, the Portuguese monarchy attempted to strengthen its control over Brazil by weakening the power of the captains-general and municipal governments. By 1800, the king and his viceroy were more powerful in Brazil than they had ever been.

The king of Spain administered his American empire with the help of the *Casa de Contratación* and the Council of the Indies (see Chapter 14). To rule the empire, the king appointed a viceroy, the first of which was established for New Spain (Mexico) in 1535. Another viceroy was appointed for Peru in 1543. Not until the eighteenth century were two additional viceroyalties—New Granada and La Plata—added. Viceroyalties in turn were subdivided into *presidencias* and captaincies-general, administered by presidents and captains-general who were theoretically subordinate to the viceroys. *Audiencias* or royal courts provided advice and even laws to assist the viceroys in governing. All of these major government positions were held by Spaniards. For creoles—American-born whites—the chief opportunity to hold a government post was the *cabildo* or city council.

In the eighteenth century, a new monarchical dynasty in Spain—the Bourbons—brought some noticeable changes to Spanish America. The powers of the *Casa de Contratación* and the Council of the Indies were curtailed as the king's ministers, especially the minister of the interior, assumed many of their former responsibilities. Moreover, new royal officials called intendants were sent out

to oversee financial and administrative affairs; they gave the monarchy more direct control of colonial Latin America—especially over the finances. The Spanish Bourbon kings also liberalized economic policies by eliminating the old monopolistic trading practices.

From the beginning of their conquest of the New World, Iberian monarchs were determined to Christianize the native peoples. This policy meant that the Catholic church would play an important role in the New World, and one that added considerably to church power. It was also a role that facilitated the goals of the state. Conversion to Christianity meant conversion to

✳ Map 19.3 Latin America in the Eighteenth Century.

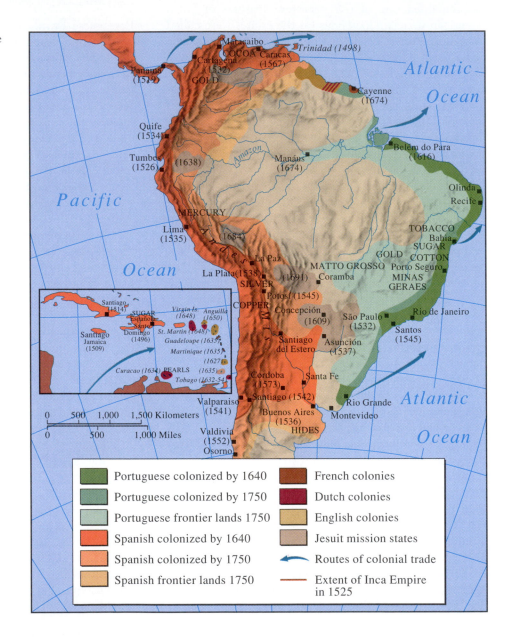

⇒ The Mission ⇐

In 1609, two Jesuit priests embarked upon a missionary calling with the Guarani Indians in eastern Paraguay. Eventually, the Jesuits established more than thirty missions in the region. Well organized and zealous, the Jesuits transformed their missions into profitable business activities. This description of a Jesuit mission in Paraguay was written by Félix de Azara, a Spanish soldier and scientist.

Félix de Azara, *Description and History of Paraguay and Rio de la Plata*

Having spoken of the towns founded by the Jesuit fathers, and of the manner in which they were founded, I shall discuss the government which they established in them. . . . In each town resided two priests, a curate and a sub-curate, who had certain assigned functions. The sub-curate was charged with all the spiritual tasks, and the curate with every kind of temporal responsibility. . . .

The curate allowed no one to work for personal gain; he compelled everyone, without distinction of age or sex, to work for the community, and he himself saw to it that all were equally fed and dressed. For this purpose the curates placed in storehouses all the fruits of agriculture and the products of industry, selling in the Spanish towns their surplus of cotton, cloth, tobacco, vegetables, skins, and wood, transporting them in their own boats down the nearest rivers, and returning with implements and whatever else was required.

From the foregoing one may infer that the curate disposed of the surplus funds of the Indian towns, and that no Indian could aspire to own private property. This deprived them of any incentive to use reason or talent, since the most industrious, able, and worthy person had the same food, clothing, and pleasures as the most wicked, dull, and indolent. It also follows that although this form of government was well designed to enrich the communities it also caused the Indian to work at a languid pace, since the wealth of his community was of no concern to him.

It must be said that although the Jesuit fathers were supreme in all respects, they employed their authority with a mildness and a restraint that command admiration. They supplied everyone with abundant food and clothing. They compelled the men to work only half a day, and did not drive them to produce more. Even their labor was given a festive air, for they went in procession to the fields, to the sound of music . . . and the music did not cease until they had returned in the same way they had set out. They gave them many holidays, dances, and tournaments, dressing the actors and the members of the municipal councils in gold or silver tissue and the most costly European garments, but they permitted the women to act only as spectators.

They likewise forbade the women to sew; this occupation was restricted to the musicians, sacristans, and acolytes. But they made them spin cotton; and the cloth that the Indians wove, after satisfying their own needs, they sold together with the surplus cotton in the Spanish towns, as they did with the tobacco, vegetables, wood, and skins. The curate and his companion, or sub-curate, had their own plain dwellings, and they never left them except to take the air in the great enclosed yard of their college. They never walked through the streets of the town or entered the house of any Indian or let themselves be seen by any woman—or indeed, by any man, except for those indispensable few through whom they issued their orders. . . .

European cultural patterns, and from the monarch's point of view, that meant a more stable empire. Church and state were closely interlinked in colonial Latin America.

Catholic missionaries—especially the Dominicans, Franciscans, and Jesuits—fanned out to different parts of the Spanish empire (see the box above). To facilitate their efforts, the missionaries brought Indians together into villages where the natives could be converted, taught trades, and encouraged to grow crops. A German tourist in the eighteenth century commented, "The road leads through plantations of sugar, indigo, cotton, and coffee. The regularity which we observed in the construction of the villages reminded us that they all owe their origin to monks and missions. The streets are straight and parallel; they cross each other at right angles; and the church is erected in the great square situated in the center."[2] These missions enabled the missionaries to control the lives of the Indians and helped ensure that they would remain docile members of the empire. In such frontier districts as California and Texas, missions served as military barriers to foreign encroachment.

The mass conversion of the Indians brought the organizational structures of Catholicism to the New World. By 1800, Spanish America possessed ten archbishoprics and thirty-eight bishoprics; Portuguese Brazil had one archbishopric and seven bishoprics. The Catholic church constructed hospitals and orphanages and accepted responsibility for educating native Americans. Monastic schools instructed Indian students in the basic rudiments of reading, writing, and arithmetic. Catholic clergy held most of the professorships at the University of Mexico, founded in 1551, as well as at the other twelve Spanish American universities. The Catholic church also provided outlets for women other than marriage. Nunneries

◆ **Sor Juana Inés de la Cruz.** Nunneries in colonial Latin America gave women—especially upper-class women—some opportunity for intellectual activity. As a woman, Juana Inés de la Cruz was denied admission to the University of Mexico. Consequently, she entered a convent where she wrote poetry and plays until her superiors forced her to focus on less worldly activities.

were places of prayer and quiet contemplation, but women in religious orders, many of them of aristocratic background, often lived well and operated outside their establishments by running schools and hospitals. Indeed, one of these nuns, Sor Juana Inés de la Cruz (1651–1695), was one of seventeenth-century Latin America's best-known literary figures. She wrote poetry and prose and urged that women be educated.

The legacies bequeathed to the church by the rich enabled the Catholic church to build the magnificent cathedrals that adorn the cities of Latin America. Even today, their architectural splendor reminds us of the wealth and power that the Catholic church exercised in the Iberian colonial empires of the New World.

British North America

In the eighteenth century, Spanish power in the New World was increasingly challenged by the growing presence of the British. The eighteenth-century British political system was characterized by a sharing of power between king and Parliament, with Parliament gradually gaining the upper hand. (The United Kingdom of Great Britain had come into existence in 1707 when the governments of England and Scotland were united; the term *British* came into use to refer to both English and Scots.) The king chose ministers responsible to himself who set policy and guided Parliament; Parliament had the power to make laws, levy taxes, pass the budget, and indirectly influence the king's ministers. The eighteenth-century British Parliament was dominated by a landed aristocracy that historians usually divide into two groups: an upper aristocracy, or the peers who sat for life in the House of Lords, and the landed gentry, lesser nobles who were elected to the House of Commons. The two groups had much in common; both were landowners with similar economic interests, and they frequently intermarried. In the Parliament of 1761, for example, over 50 percent of the members of the House of Commons were related to the upper aristocracy. The deputies to the House of Commons were chosen from the boroughs and counties but not by popular voting and hardly in any equitable fashion. The number of persons eligible to vote in the boroughs varied wildly and was often quite small, enabling wealthy landed aristocrats to gain support by patronage and bribery. Although deputies from the counties were elected by holders of property worth at least forty shillings a year, members of the leading landed gentry families were elected over and over again.

In 1714, a new dynasty—the Hanoverians—was established when the last Stuart ruler, Queen Anne

(1702–1714), died without an heir. The crown was offered to the Protestant rulers of the German state of Hanover. Since the first Hanoverian king (George I) did not speak English and neither the first nor the second George had much familiarity with the British system, their chief ministers were allowed to handle Parliament. Robert Walpole served as prime minister from 1721 to 1742 and pursued a peaceful foreign policy to avoid new land taxes. But new forces were emerging in eighteenth-century Britain as growing trade and industry led an ever-increasing middle class to favor expansion of trade and world empire. The exponents of empire found a spokesman in William Pitt the Elder, who became prime minister in 1757 and furthered imperial ambitions by acquiring Canada and India in the Seven Years' War.

THE AMERICAN REVOLUTION AND THE BIRTH OF A NEW NATION

At the end of the Seven Years' War in 1763, Great Britain had become the world's greatest colonial power. In North America, Britain now controlled Canada and the lands east of the Mississippi. A change in Britain's imperial policies after the war, however, soon led to a confrontation with its American colonists and the emergence of a new nation. After the Seven Years' War, British policymakers sought to obtain new revenues from the colonies to pay the expenses the British army incurred in defending the colonists. An attempt to levy new taxes by the Stamp Act in 1765 led to riots and the statute's quick repeal. The immediate crisis had ended, but the fundamental cause of the dispute had not been resolved. In the course of the eighteenth century, significant differences had arisen between the American and British political worlds. Both peoples shared the same property requirement for voting—voters had to possess property that could be rented for at least forty shillings a year—but it resulted in a disparity in the number of voters in the two countries. In Britain fewer than one in five adult males had the right to vote. In the colonies, where a radically different economic structure led to an enormous group of independent farmers, the property requirement allowed over 50 percent of adult males to vote.

While both the British and the Americans had representative governments, different systems had evolved. Representation in Britain was indirect; the members of Parliament did not speak for local interests but for the entire kingdom. In the colonies, direct representation meant that representatives should reside in and own property in the communities electing them; hence, they should represent the interests of their local districts.

This divergence in political systems was paralleled by conflicting conceptions of empire. The British envisioned a single empire with Parliament as the supreme authority throughout; as one parliamentarian argued, "in sovereignty there are no gradations." All the people in the empire, including the American colonists, were consequently represented indirectly by members of Parliament, whether they were from the colonies or not. Colonial assemblies in the British perspective were only committees that made "temporary by-laws"; the real authority to make laws for the empire resided in London.

The Americans had developed their own peculiar view of the British Empire. To them, the British Empire was composed of self-regulating parts. Although they conceded that as British subjects they owed allegiance to the king and that Parliament had the right to make laws for the peace and prosperity of the whole realm, they argued, nevertheless, that neither king nor Parliament had any right to interfere in the internal affairs of the colonies because they had their own representative assemblies. American colonists were especially defensive about property and believed strongly that no tax could be levied without the consent of an assembly whose members directly represented the people.

By the 1760s, the American colonists had developed a sense of a common national identity. It was not unusual for American travelers to Britain in the eighteenth century to find British society old and decadent compared to the youthfulness and vitality of their own. This sense of superiority made Americans resentful of British actions that seemed to treat them like children. Resentment eventually led to a desire for independence.

Crisis followed crisis in the 1770s. The colonies' desire to take collective action against what was perceived as Britain's repressive actions led to the First Continental Congress, which met at Philadelphia in September 1774. The more militant members refused to compromise and urged the colonists to "take up arms and organize militias." When a British army attempted to stop rebel mobilization in Massachusetts, fighting erupted at Lexington and Concord between colonists and redcoats in April 1775.

Despite the outbreak of hostilities, the colonists did not rush headlong into rebellion and war. It was more than a year after Lexington and Concord before the decision was made to declare their independence from the British Empire. On July 4, 1776, the Second Continental Congress approved a Declaration of Independence written by Thomas Jefferson. A stirring political document, the Declaration of Independence affirmed the Enlightenment's natural rights of "life, liberty, and the pursuit of happiness" and declared the colonies to be "free and independent states absolved from all allegiance to the British crown." The war for American independence had formally begun.

The war against Great Britain was a great gamble. Britain was a strong European military power with enormous financial resources; by 1778, Britain had sent 50,000 regular British troops and 30,000 German mercenaries to America. The Second Continental Congress had authorized the formation of a Continental Army under George Washington as commander-in-chief. As a southerner, Washington added balance to an effort that up to now had been led by New Englanders. Nevertheless, compared to the British forces, the Continental Army consisted of undisciplined amateurs whose terms of service were usually very brief. The colonies also had militia units, but they likewise tended to be unreliable. Although 400,000 men served in the Continental Army and the militias during the course of the war, Washington never had more than 20,000 troops available for any single battle.

Of great importance to the colonies' cause was the support they received from foreign countries that were eager to gain revenge for their defeats in earlier wars at the hands of the British. The French were particularly generous in supplying arms and money to the rebels from the beginning of the war. French officers and soldiers also served in Washington's army. The defeat of the British at Saratoga in October 1777 finally led the French to grant diplomatic recognition to the American state. When Spain in 1779 and the Dutch Republic in 1780 entered the war against Great Britain, and Russia formed the League of Armed Neutrality in 1780 to protect neutral shipping from British attacks, the British were faced with war against much of Europe as well as the Americans. Despite having won most of the battles, the British were in danger of losing the war. When the army of General Cornwallis was forced to surrender to a combined American and French army and French fleet under Washington at Yorktown in 1781, the British decided to call it quits. After extensive negotiations, the Treaty of Paris was signed in 1783. It recognized the independence of the American colonies and surprisingly granted the Americans control of the western territory from the Appalachians to the Mississippi River. The Americans were off to a good start but soon showed signs of political disintegration.

Although the thirteen American colonies agreed to "hang together" to gain their independence from the British, a fear of concentrated power and concern for their own interests caused them to have little enthusiasm for establishing a united nation with a strong central government. The Articles of Confederation, ratified in 1781, did little to provide for a strong central government. A series of economic, political, and international problems soon led to a movement for a different form of national government. In the summer of 1787, fifty-five delegates met in a convention in Philadelphia that was authorized by the Confederation Congress "for the sole and express purpose of revising the Articles of Confederation." The

◆ **The Declaration of Independence.** John Trumbull's famous painting, *The Signing of the Declaration*, shows members of the committee responsible for the Declaration of Independence (from left to right, John Adams, Roger Sherman, Robert Livingston, Thomas Jefferson, and Benjamin Franklin) standing before John Hancock, president of the Second Continental Congress.

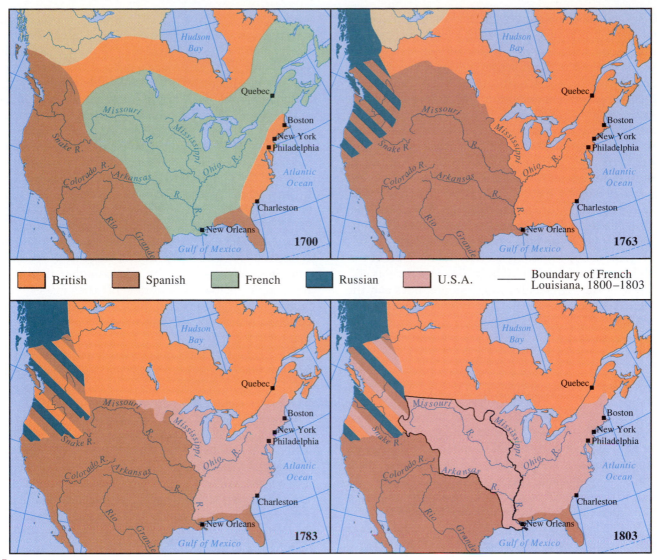

�֍ **Map 19.4**   North America, 1700–1803.

convention's delegates—wealthy, politically experienced, well-educated, and nationalistically inclined—rejected revision and decided to devise a new constitution.

The proposed Constitution created a central government distinct from and superior to the governments of the individual states. The national government was given the power to levy taxes, raise a national army, regulate domestic and foreign trade, and create a national currency. Following Montesquieu's principle of a "separation of powers" to provide a system of "checks and balances," the central or federal government was divided into three branches, each with some power to check the functioning of the others. A president would serve as the chief executive with the power to execute laws, veto the legislature's acts, make judicial and executive appointments, supervise foreign affairs, and direct military forces. Legislative power was vested in the second branch of government, a bicameral legislature composed of a Senate elected by the state legislatures and a House of Representatives elected directly by the people. The federal judiciary, embodied in a Supreme Court and other courts "as deemed necessary" by Congress, provided the third branch of government. With judges nominated by the executive and approved by the legislative branch, the federal judiciary would enforce the Constitution as the "supreme law of the land."

The constitutional convention had stipulated that the new Constitution would have to be ratified by popularly chosen conventions in nine of the thirteen states before it would take effect. After fierce contests, the Federalists, who favored the new Constitution, won, although the margin of victory was quite slim. Important to their success had been a promise to add a Bill of Rights to the Constitution as the new government's first piece of business. Accordingly, in March of 1789, the new Congress enacted the first ten amendments to the Constitution, ever since known as the Bill of Rights. These guaranteed freedom of religion, speech, press, petition, and assembly, as well as the right to bear arms, the right to be protected against unreasonable searches and arrests, trial by jury, due process of law, and the protection of property rights. Although many of these rights had their origins in English law, others were derived from the natural rights philosophy of the eighteenth-century philosophes and the American experience. Is it any wonder that many European intellectuals saw the American Revolution as the embodiment of the Enlightenment's political dreams?

Toward a New Political Order

The year 1789 witnessed two far-reaching events, the beginning of a new United States of America and the eruption of the French Revolution. Compared to the American Revolution, the French Revolution was more complex, more violent, and far more radical with its attempt to reconstruct both a new political order and a new social order. But while the French were trying to create a new kind of state and a new kind of society, the rulers of other European states were attempting to come to terms with the ideas of the Enlightenment. Their failure helped ensure that the lessons of the French Revolution would find willing listeners elsewhere in Europe.

Background: Enlightened Absolutism in the Eighteenth Century

There is no doubt that Enlightenment thought had some impact on the political development of European states in the eighteenth century. Closely related to the Enlightenment idea of natural laws was the belief in natural rights, which were thought to be inalienable privileges that ought not to be withheld from any person. These natural rights included equality before the law, freedom of religious worship, freedom of speech and press, and the right to assemble, hold property, and pursue happiness. The American Declaration of Independence summarized the Enlightenment concept of natural rights in its opening paragraph: "We hold these truths to be self-evident, that all men are created equal; that they are endowed by their creator with certain unalienable rights; that among these are life, liberty and the pursuit of happiness."

But how were these natural rights to be established and preserved? In the opinion of many philosophes, most people needed the direction provided by an enlightened ruler. What, however, made rulers enlightened? They must allow religious toleration, freedom of speech and press, and the rights of private property. They must foster the arts, sciences, and education. Above all, they must not be arbitrary in their rule; they must obey the laws and enforce them fairly for all subjects. Only strong monarchs seemed capable of overcoming vested interests and effecting the reforms society needed. Reforms then should come from above—from the rulers—rather than from the people below. Distrustful of the masses, the philosophes believed that absolute rulers, swayed by enlightened principles, were the best hope of reforming their societies.

The extent to which rulers actually put these principles into practice has been much discussed. Many historians once assumed that a new type of monarchy emerged in the later eighteenth century, which they called "enlightened despotism" or "enlightened absolutism." Monarchs such as Frederick II of Prussia, Catherine the Great of Russia, and Joseph II of Austria supposedly followed the advice of the philosophes and ruled by enlightened principles, creating a path to modern nationhood. Recently, however, scholars have questioned the usefulness of the concept of "enlightened absolutism." We can best determine the extent to which it can be applied by examining the major "enlightened absolutists" of the later eighteenth century.

Two able Prussian kings in the eighteenth century, Frederick William I and Frederick II, further developed the two major institutions—the army and the bureaucracy—that were the backbone of Prussia. Frederick William I (1713–1740) promoted the evolution of Prussia's highly efficient civil bureaucracy by establishing the General Directory. Its supervision of military, police, economic, and financial affairs made it the chief administrative agent of the central government. Because Prussia's disjointed territories could hardly have been governed without a centralized administrative machine, Frederick William strove to maintain a highly efficient bureaucracy of civil service workers. It became a special kind of organization with its own code in which the supreme values were obedience, honor, and service to the king as the highest duty. As Frederick William asserted: "One must serve the king with life and limb, with goods and chattels, with honor and conscience, and surrender everything except salvation. The latter is reserved for God. But everything else must be mine."[3] Close, personal supervision of the bureaucracy became a hallmark of the eighteenth-century Prussian rulers.

The nobility or landed aristocracy known as Junkers, who owned large estates with many serfs, continued to play a dominating role in the Prussian state. The Junkers held a complete monopoly over the officer corps of the Prussian army, which Frederick William passionately continued to expand. By the end of his reign, the army had grown from 45,000 to 83,000 men. Though tenth in physical size and thirteenth in population in Europe, Prussia had the fourth largest army after France, Russia, and Austria.

As officers, the Junker nobility became imbued with a sense of service to the king or state. All the virtues of the Prussian nobility were, in effect, military virtues: duty, obedience, sacrifice. At the same time, because of its size and reputation as one of the best armies in Europe, the Prussian army was the most important institution in the state. "Prussian militarism" became synonymous with the extreme exaltation of military virtues. Indeed, one Prussian minister remarked around 1800 that "Prussia was not a country with an army, but an army with a country which served as headquarters and food magazine."[4]

Frederick the Great (1740–1786) was one of the best educated and most cultured monarchs in the eighteenth century. He was well versed in Enlightenment thought and even invited Voltaire to live at his court for several years. A believer in the king as the "first servant of the state," Frederick the Great became a conscientious ruler who made few innovations in administration. His diligence in overseeing its operation, however, made the Prussian bureaucracy famous for both efficiency and honesty.

For a time, Frederick seemed quite willing to follow the philosophes' recommendations for reform. He established a single code of laws for his territories that eliminated the use of torture except in treason and murder cases. He also granted a limited freedom of speech and press as well as complete religious toleration, no difficult task since he had no strong religious convictions anyway. Although Frederick was well aware of the philosophes' condemnation of serfdom, he was too dependent on the Prussian nobility to interfere with it or with the hierarchical structure of Prussian society. In fact, Frederick II was a social conservative who made Prussian society even more aristocratic than it had been before. Frederick reversed his father's policy of allowing commoners to have

CHRONOLOGY

The European States—Enlightened Absolutism in the Eighteenth Century

Prussia	
Frederick William I	1713–1740
Frederick II the Great	1740–1786
The Austrian Empire	
Maria Theresa	1740–1780
Joseph II	1780–1790
Russia	
Peter III	1762
Catherine II the Great	1762–1796
Pugachev's rebellion	1773–1775
Charter of the Nobility	1785
Poland	
First partition	1772
Second partition	1793
Third partition	1795

power in the civil service and reserved the higher positions in the bureaucracy for members of the nobility. The upper ranks of the bureaucracy came close to constituting a hereditary caste over time.

Like his predecessors, Frederick the Great took a great interest in military affairs and enlarged the Prussian army (to 200,000 men). Unlike his predecessors, he had no objection to using it. As we have seen, Frederick did not hesitate to take advantage of a succession crisis in the Habsburg monarchy to seize the Austrian province of Silesia for Prussia. This act led to Austria's bitter hostility to Prussia and Frederick's engagement in two major wars, the War of the Austrian Succession and the Seven Years' War. Although the latter war left his country exhausted, Frederick succeeded in keeping Silesia. After the wars, the first partition of Poland with Austria and Russia in 1772 gave him the Polish territory between Prussia and Brandenburg, which linked some of the scattered lands of Prussia. By the end of his reign, Prussia was recognized as a great European power.

The Austrian Empire had become one of the great European states by the beginning of the eighteenth century. The city of Vienna, center of the Habsburg monarchy, was filled with magnificent palaces and churches built in the Baroque style and became the music capital of

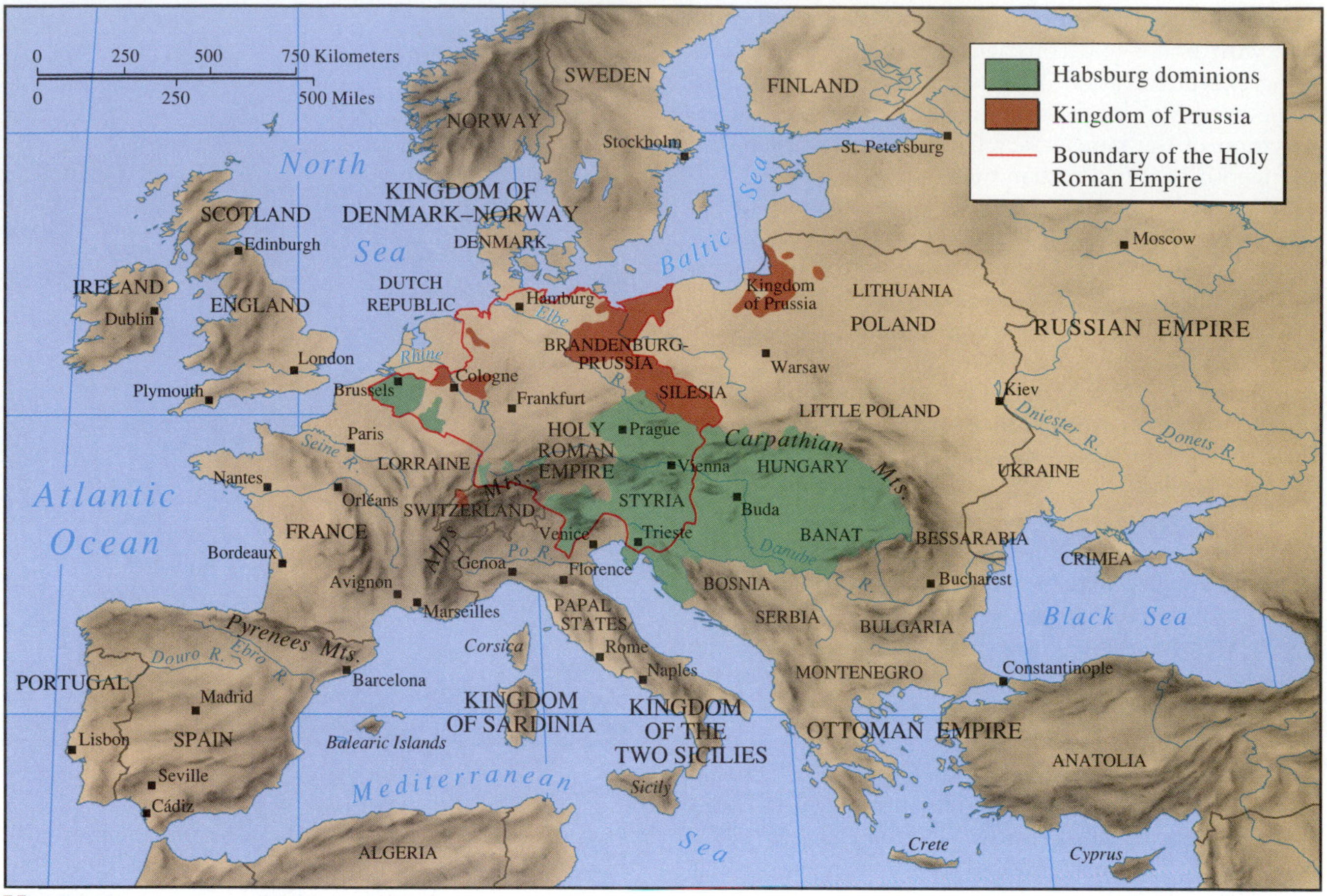

Map 19.5 Europe in 1763.

Europe. And yet Austria, by its very nature as a sprawling empire composed of many different nationalities, languages, religions, and cultures, found it difficult to provide common laws and administrative centralization for its people. Although Empress Maria Theresa (1740–1780) managed to make administrative reforms that helped centralize the Austrian Empire, these reforms were done for practical reasons—to strengthen the power of the Habsburg state—and were accompanied by an enlargement and modernization of the armed forces. Maria Theresa remained staunchly conservative and was not open to the philosophes' calls for wider reform. But her successor was.

Joseph II (1780–1790) was determined to make changes; at the same time, he carried on his mother's chief goal of enhancing Habsburg power within the monarchy and Europe. Joseph II was an earnest man who believed in the need to sweep away anything standing in the path of reason. As Joseph expressed it: "I have made Philosophy the lawmaker of my empire, her logical applications are going to transform Austria."

Joseph's reform program was far-reaching. He abolished serfdom and tried to give the peasants hereditary rights to their holdings. An exponent of Physiocratic ideas, he abandoned economic restraints by eliminating internal trade barriers, ending monopolies, and removing guild restrictions. A new penal code was instituted that abrogated the death penalty and established the principle of equality of all before the law. Joseph produced drastic religious reforms as well, including complete religious toleration and restrictions on the Catholic church. Altogether, Joseph II issued 6,000 decrees and 11,000 laws in his effort to transform Austria.

Joseph's reform program proved overwhelming for Austria, however. He alienated the nobility by freeing the serfs and alienated the church by his attacks on the monastic establishment. Even the serfs were unhappy, unable to comprehend the drastic changes inherent in

The Proposals of Catherine II for a New Law Code

Catherine II the Great of Russia appeared for a while to be an enlightened ruler. In 1767, she convened a legislative commission to prepare a new code of laws for Russia. In her famous Instruction, she gave the delegates a detailed guide to the principles they should follow. Although the guidelines were obviously culled from the liberal ideas of the philosophes, the commission itself accomplished nothing, and Catherine's Instruction was soon forgotten.

Catherine II, Proposals for a New Law Code

13. What is the true End of Monarchy? Not to deprive People of their natural Liberty; but to correct their Actions, in order to attain the supreme good.

33. The Laws ought to be so framed, as to secure the Safety of every Citizen as much as possible.

34. The Equality of the Citizens consists in this; that they should all be subject to the same Laws.

38. A Man ought to form in his own Mind an exact and clear Idea of what Liberty is. Liberty is the Right of doing whatsoever the Laws allow: And if any one Citizen could do what the Law forbid, there would be no more Liberty; because others would have an equal Power of doing the same.

123. The Usage of Torture is contrary to all the Dictates of Nature and Reason; even Mankind itself cries out against it, and demands loudly the total Abolition of it.

180. That Law, therefore, is highly beneficial to the Community where it is established, which ordains that every Man shall be judged by his Peers and Equals. For when the Fate of a Citizen is in Question, all Prejudices arising from the Difference of Rank or Fortune should be stifled; because they ought to have no Influence between the Judges and the Parties accused.

194. No Man ought to be looked upon as guilty, before he has received his judicial Sentence; nor can the Laws deprive him of their Protection, before it is proved that he has forfeited all Right to it. What Right therefore can Power give to any to inflict Punishment upon a Citizen at a Time, when it is yet dubious, whether he is Innocent or guilty?

270. It is highly necessary that the Law should prescribe a Rule to the Lords, for a more judicious Method of raising their Revenues; and oblige them to levy such a Tax, as tends least to separate the Peasant from His House and Family; this would be the Means by which Agriculture would become more extensive, and Population be more increased in the Empire.

Joseph's policies. His attempt to rationalize the administration of the empire by imposing German as the official bureaucratic language alienated the non-German nationalities. As Joseph complained, there were not enough people for the kind of bureaucracy he needed. He realized his failure when he wrote his own epitaph for his gravestone: "Here lies Joseph II who was unfortunate in everything that he undertook." His successors undid many of his reform efforts.

In Russia, Peter the Great was followed by a series of six weak successors who were made and unmade by the palace guard. After the last of these weak tsars, Peter III, was murdered by a faction of nobles, his German wife emerged as autocrat of all the Russias. Catherine II the Great (1762–1796) was an intelligent woman who was familiar with the works of the philosophes. It is possible that like Joseph II she wished to reform Russia along the lines of Enlightenment ideas, but she was always shrewd enough to realize that her success depended upon the support of the palace guard and the gentry class from which it stemmed. She could not afford to alienate the Russian nobility.

Initially, Catherine seemed eager to pursue reform. She called for the election of an assembly in 1767 to debate the details of a new law code. In her Instruction, written as a guide to the deliberations, Catherine questioned the institution of serfdom, torture, and capital punishment and even advocated the principle of the equality of all people in the eyes of the law (see the box above). But one and one-half years of negotiation produced little real change.

In fact, Catherine's subsequent policies had the effect of strengthening the hands of the landholding class at the expense of all others, especially the Russian serfs. In order to reorganize local government, Catherine divided Russia into fifty provinces, each of which in turn was subdivided into districts whose ruling officials were chosen by the nobles. In this way, the local nobility became responsible for the day-to-day governing of Russia. Moreover, the gentry were now formed into corporate groups with special legal privileges, including the right to trial by peers and exemption from personal taxation and corporal punishment. These rights were formalized in 1785 by a Charter of the Nobility.

Catherine's policy of favoring the landed nobility led to even worse conditions for the Russian peasantry. In 1767, serfs were forbidden to appeal to the state against their masters. The attempt of the Russian government to impose restrictions upon free peasants in the border districts of the Russian empire soon led to a full-scale revolt that spread to the Volga valley. It was intensified by the support of the Cossacks, independent tribes of fierce warriors who had at times fought for the Russians against the

◆ **Catherine the Great.**   Autocrat of Russia, Catherine was an intelligent ruler who favored reform. She found it expedient, however, to retain much of the old system in order to keep the support of the landed nobility. This portrait by Dmitry Levitsky shows her in legislative regalia in the Temple of Justice in 1783.

Turks but who now resisted the government's attempt to absorb them into the empire.

The elements of discontent were welded into a mass revolt by an illiterate Cossack, Emelyan Pugachev. Beginning in 1773, Pugachev's rebellion spread across southern Russia from the Urals to the Volga River. Initially successful, Pugachev won the support of many peasants when he issued a manifesto in July 1774, freeing all peasants from oppressive taxes and military service. The rebellion soon faltered, however, as government forces became more effective. Betrayed by his own subordinates, Pugachev was captured, tortured, and executed. The rebellion collapsed completely, and Catherine responded with even greater repression of the peasantry. All rural reform was halted, serfdom was expanded into newer parts of the empire, and peasants on crown lands were also reduced to serfdom.

Above all, Catherine proved a worthy successor to Peter the Great in her policies of territorial expansion westward (into Poland) and southward (to the Black Sea). Russia spread southward by defeating the Turks and gaining some land and the privilege of protecting Greek Orthodox Christians in the Ottoman Empire. Russian expansion westward occurred at the expense of neighboring Poland. In the three partitions of Poland, Russia gained about 50 percent of Polish territory.

Of the three major rulers most closely associated traditionally with enlightened absolutism—Joseph II, Frederick II, and Catherine the Great—only Joseph II sought truly radical changes based on Enlightenment ideas. Both Frederick and Catherine liked to be cast as disciples of the Enlightenment, expressed interest in enlightened reforms, and even attempted some. But the policies of neither seemed seriously affected by Enlightenment thought. Necessities of state and maintenance of the existing system took precedence over reform. Indeed, many historians maintain that Joseph, Frederick, and Catherine were all primarily guided by a concern for the power and well-being of their states and that their policies were not all that different from those of their predecessors. In the final analysis, heightened state power was used to create armies and wage wars to gain more power. Nevertheless, in their desire to build stronger state systems, these rulers did pursue such enlightened measures as legal reform, religious toleration, and the extension of education because these served to create more satisfied subjects and strengthened the state in significant ways.

It would be foolish, however, to overlook the fact that the ability of enlightened rulers to make reforms was also limited by political and social realities. Everywhere in Europe the hereditary aristocracy was still the most powerful class in society. Enlightened reforms were often limited to those administrative and judicial reforms that did not seriously undermine the powerful interests of the European nobility. As the chief beneficiaries of a system based on traditional rights and privileges for their class, they were certainly not willing to support a political ideology that trumpeted the principle of equal rights for all. The first serious challenge to their supremacy would come in the French Revolution, which opened the door to a more modern world of politics.

The French Revolution

Although we associate events like the French Revolution with sudden changes, the causes of such events involve long-range problems as well as immediate, precipitating forces. Hence the causes of the French Revolution must be found in a multifaceted examination of French society and its problems in the late eighteenth century.

FROM DISCONTENT TO THE DESTRUCTION OF THE OLD REGIME

The long-range or indirect causes of the French Revolution must first be sought in the condition of French society. Before the Revolution, France was a society grounded in the inequality of rights or the idea of privilege. Its population of 27 million was divided, as it had been since the Middle Ages, into three orders or estates.

The First Estate consisted of the clergy and numbered about 130,000 people who owned approximately 10 percent of the land. Clergy were exempt from the *taille*, France's chief tax, although the church had agreed to pay a "voluntary" contribution every five years to the state. The clergy were also radically divided: the higher clergy, stemming from aristocratic families, shared the interests of the nobility while the parish priests were often poor and from the class of commoners.

The Second Estate was the nobility, composed of 120,000 to 350,000 people who nevertheless owned about 25 to 30 percent of the land. The nobility had continued to play an important and even crucial role in French society in the eighteenth century, holding many of the leading positions in the government, the military, the law courts, and the higher church offices. The French nobility was also divided. The nobility of the robe derived their status from officeholding, which had often opened the doors for commoners to receive noble status. These nobles now dominated the royal law courts and important administrative offices. The nobility of the sword claimed to be descended from the original me-

dieval nobility. The nobles as a whole sought to expand their power at the expense of the monarchy—to defend liberty by resisting the arbitrary actions of the crown, as some nobles asserted—and to maintain their monopolistic control over positions in the military, church, and government. Moreover, the possession of privileges remained a hallmark of the nobility. Common to all nobles were tax exemptions, especially from the *taille*.

The Third Estate, or the commoners of society, constituted the overwhelming majority of the French population. They were divided by vast differences in occupation, level of education, and wealth. The peasants who alone constituted 75 to 80 percent of the total population were by far the largest segment of the Third Estate. They owned about 35 to 40 percent of the land, although their landholdings varied from area to area and over half had no or little land on which to survive. Serfdom no longer existed on any large scale in France, but French peasants still had obligations to their local landlords that they deeply resented. These "relics of feudalism," survivals from an earlier age, included the payment of fees for the use of village facilities, such as the flour mill, community oven, and winepress, as well as tithes to the clergy.

Another part of the Third Estate consisted of skilled artisans, shopkeepers, and other wage earners in the cities. Although the eighteenth century had been a period of rapid urban growth, 90 percent of French towns had fewer than 10,000 inhabitants while only nine cities had more than 50,000. In the eighteenth century, consumer prices rose faster than wages, causing these urban groups to experience a noticeable decline in purchasing power. In Paris, for example, income lagged behind food prices and especially behind a 140 percent rise in rents for working people in skilled and unskilled trades. The economic discontent of this segment of the Third Estate and often simply their struggle to survive led them to play an important role in the Revolution, especially in the city of Paris.

About 8 percent or 2.3 million people constituted the bourgeoisie or middle class who owned about 20 to 25 percent of the land. This group included merchants, industrialists, and bankers who controlled the resources of trade, manufacturing, and finance and benefited from the economic prosperity after 1730. The bourgeoisie also included professional people—lawyers, holders of public offices, doctors, and writers. Many members of the bourgeoisie sought security and status through the purchase of land. They had their own set of grievances because they were often excluded from the social and political privileges monopolized by the nobles. At the same time, remarkable similarities existed at the upper levels of society between the wealthier bourgeoisie and the nobility. It was still possible for wealthy middle-class individuals to enter the ranks of the nobility by obtaining public offices and entering the nobility of the robe. During the eighteenth century, 6,500 new noble families were created. Moreover, the new and critical ideas of the Enlightenment proved attractive to both aristocrats and bourgeoisie. Members of both groups shared a common world of liberal political thought. Both aristocratic and bourgeois elites, long accustomed to a new socioeconomic reality based on wealth and economic achievement, were increasingly frustrated by a monarchical system resting on privileges and an old and rigid social order based on the concept of estates. The opposition of these elites to the old order ultimately led them to take drastic action against the monarchical regime, although they soon split over the problem of how far to proceed in eliminating traditional privileges. In a real sense, the Revolution had its origins in political grievances.

The inability of the French monarchy to deal with new social realities and problems was exacerbated by specific problems in the 1780s. Although France had enjoyed fifty years of economic expansion, the French economy still experienced periodic crises. Bad harvests in 1787 and 1788 and the beginnings of a manufacturing depression resulted in food shortages, rising prices for food and other necessities, and unemployment in the cities. The number of poor, estimated by some at almost one-third of the population, reached crisis proportions on the eve of the Revolution.

The immediate cause of the French Revolution was the near collapse of government finances. French governmental expenditures continued to grow due to costly wars and royal extravagance. On the verge of a complete financial collapse, the government of Louis XVI (1774–1792) was finally forced to call a meeting of the Estates-General, the French parliamentary body that had not met since 1614. The Estates-General consisted of representatives from the three orders of French society. In the elections for the Estates-General, the government had ruled that the Third Estate should get double representation (it did, after all, constitute 97 percent of the population). Consequently, while both the First Estate (the clergy) and the Second (the nobility) had about 300 delegates each, the commoners had almost 600 representatives. Two-thirds of the latter were people with legal training while three-fourths were from towns of over 2,000 inhabitants, giving the Third Estate a particularly strong legal and urban representation. Most members of the Third Estate advocated a regular constitutional government that would abolish the fiscal privileges of the church and nobility as the major way to regenerate France.

The Estates-General opened at Versailles on May 5, 1789. It was troubled from the start with the problem of whether voting should be by order or by head (each delegate having one vote). Traditionally, each order would vote separately; each would have veto power over the other two, thus guaranteeing aristocratic control over reforms. But the Third Estate was opposed to this approach and pushed its demands for voting by head. Since it had double representation, with the assistance of liberal nobles and clerics, it could turn the three estates into a single-chamber legislature that would reform France in its own way. Most delegates still desired to make changes within a framework of respect for the authority of the king; revival or reform did not mean the overthrow of traditional institutions. But when the First Estate declared in favor of voting by order, the Third Estate felt compelled to respond in a significant fashion. On June 17, 1789, the Third Estate voted to constitute itself a "National Assembly" and decided to draw up a constitution. This declaration of June 17 represents the first step in the French Revolution because the Third Estate had no legal right to act as the National Assembly. This revolution, largely the work of the lawyers of the Third Estate, was soon in jeopardy, however, as the king sided with the First Estate and threatened to dissolve the Estates-General. Louis XVI now prepared to use force.

The intervention of the common people, however, in a series of urban and rural uprisings in July and August of 1789 saved the Third Estate from the king's attempted counterrevolution. The most famous of the urban risings was the fall of the Bastille. Parisians organized a popular force and on July 14 attacked the Bastille, a royal armory. But the Bastille had also been a state prison, and though it now contained only seven prisoners, its fall quickly became a popular symbol of triumph over despotism. Paris was abandoned to the insurgents, and Louis XVI was soon informed that the royal troops were unreliable. Louis's acceptance of that reality signaled the collapse of royal authority; the king could no longer enforce his will. The fall of the Bastille had saved the National Assembly.

At the same time, independently of what was going on in Paris, popular revolutions broke out in numerous cities. The collapse of royal authority in the cities was paralleled by peasant revolutions in the countryside. Behind the popular uprisings was a growing resentment of the entire landholding system with its fees and obligations. With the fall of the Bastille and the king's apparent capitulation to the demands of the Third Estate, the peasants decided to take matters into their own hands.

From July 19 to August 3, peasant rebellions occurred throughout France. The agrarian revolts served as a backdrop to the Great Fear, a vast panic that spread like wildfire through France between July 20 and August 6. The fear of invasion by foreign troops, aided by a supposed aristocratic plot, encouraged the formation of citizens' militias and permanent committees. The greatest impact of the agrarian revolts and the Great Fear was on the National Assembly meeting in Versailles.

One of the first acts of the National Assembly was to destroy the relics of feudalism or aristocratic privileges. On the "night of 4 August" 1789, the National Assembly in an astonishing session voted to abolish landlords' feudal rights as well as the fiscal privileges of nobles, clergy, towns, and provinces. On August 26, the assembly provided the ideological foundation for its actions and an educational device for the nation by adopting the Declaration of the Rights of Man and the Citizen (see the box on p. 708). This charter of basic liberties began with a ringing affirmation of "the natural and imprescriptible rights of man" to "liberty, property, security and resistance to oppression." It went on to affirm the destruction of aristocratic privileges by proclaiming an end to exemptions from taxation, freedom and equal rights for all men, and access to public office based on talent. The monarchy was restricted, and all citizens were to have the

◆ **Storming of the Bastille.** Louis XVI planned to use force to dissolve the Estates-General, but a number of rural and urban uprisings by the common people prevented this action. The fall of the Bastille, pictured here in an anonymous painting, is perhaps the most famous of the urban risings.

Declaration of the Rights of Man and the Citizen

One of the important documents of the French Revolution, the Declaration of the Rights of Man and the Citizen was adopted in August 1789 by the National Assembly. The declaration affirmed that "men are born and remain free and equal in rights," that governments must protect these natural rights, and that political power is derived from the people.

Declaration of the Rights of Man and the Citizen

The representatives of the French people, organized as a national assembly, considering that ignorance, neglect, and scorn of the rights of man are the sole causes of public misfortunes and of corruption of governments, have resolved to display in a solemn declaration the natural, inalienable, and sacred rights of man, so that this declaration, constantly in the presence of all members of society, will continually remind them of their rights and their duties. . . . Consequently, the National Assembly recognizes and declares, in the presence and under the auspices of the Supreme Being, the following rights of man and citizen:

1. Men are born and remain free and equal in rights; social distinctions can be established only for the common benefit.
2. The aim of every political association is the conservation of the natural and imprescriptible rights of man; these rights are liberty, property, security, and resistance to oppression.
3. The source of all sovereignty is located in essence in the nation; no body, no individual can exercise authority which does not emanate from it expressly.
4. Liberty consists in being able to do anything that does not harm another person. . . .
6. The law is the expression of the general will; all citizens have the right to concur personally or through their representatives in its formation; it must be the same for all, whether it protects or punishes. All citizens being equal in its eyes are equally admissible to all honors, positions, and public employments, according to their capabilities and without other distinctions than those of their virtues and talents.
7. No man can be accused, arrested, or detained except in cases determined by the law, and according to the forms which it has prescribed. . . .
10. No one may be disturbed because of his opinions, even religious, provided that their public demonstration does not disturb the public order established by law.
11. The free communication of thoughts and opinions is one of the most precious rights of man: every citizen can therefore freely speak, write, and print. . . .
12. The guaranteeing of the rights of man and citizen necessitates a public force; this force is therefore instituted for the advantage of all, and not for the private use of those to whom it is entrusted. . . .
14. Citizens have the right to determine for themselves or through their representatives the need for taxation of the public, to consent to it freely, to investigate its use, and to determine its rate, basis, collection, and duration.
15. Society has the right to demand an accounting of his administration from every public agent.
16. Any society in which guarantees of rights are not assured nor the separation of powers determined has no constitution.
17. Property being an inviolable and sacred right, no one may be deprived of it unless public necessity, legally determined, clearly requires such action, and then only on condition of a just and prior indemnity.

right to take part in the legislative process. Freedom of speech and press were guaranteed, and arbitrary arrests were outlawed.

The declaration also raised another important issue. Did the ideal of equal rights for all men extend to women? Many deputies insisted that it did, at least in terms of civil liberties, provided that, as one said, "women do not aspire to exercise political rights and functions." Olympe de Gouges, a playwright and pamphleteer, refused to accept this exclusion of women from political rights. Echoing the words of the official declaration, she penned a Declaration of the Rights of Woman and the Female Citizen, in which she insisted that women should have all the same rights as men (see the box on p. 709). The National Assembly ignored her demands.

Declaration of the Rights of Woman and the Female Citizen

Olympe de Gouges (a pen name for Marie Gouze) was a butcher's daughter who wrote plays and pamphlets. She argued that the Declaration of the Rights of Man and the Citizen did not apply to women and composed her own Declaration of the Rights of Woman.

Declaration of the Rights of Woman and the Female Citizen (1791)

Mothers, daughters, sisters and representatives of the nation demand to be constituted into a national assembly. Believing that ignorance, omission, or scorn for the rights of woman are the only causes of public misfortunes and of the corruption of governments, the women have resolved to set forth in a solemn declaration the natural, inalienable, and sacred rights of woman in order that this declaration, constantly exposed before all the members of the society, will ceaselessly remind them of their rights and duties. . . .

Consequently, the sex that is as superior in beauty as it is in courage during the sufferings of maternity recognizes and declares in the presence and under the auspices of the Supreme Being, the following Rights of Woman and of Female Citizens.

1. Woman is born free and lives equal to man in her rights. Social distinctions can be based only on the common utility.

2. The purpose of any political association is the conservation of the natural and imprescriptible rights of woman and man; these rights are liberty, property, security, and especially resistance to oppression.

3. The principle of all sovereignty rests essentially with the nation, which is nothing but the union of woman and man; no body and no individual can exercise any authority which does not come expressly from it [the nation].

4. Liberty and justice consist of restoring all that belongs to others; thus, the only limits on the exercise of the natural rights of woman are perpetual male tyranny; these limits are to be reformed by the laws of nature and reason.

6. The law must be the expression of the general will; all female and male citizens must contribute either personally or through their representatives to its formation; it must be the same for all: male and female citizens, being equal in the eyes of the law, must be equally admitted to all honors, positions, and public employment according to their capacity and without other distinctions besides those of their virtues and talents.

7. No woman is an exception; she is accused, arrested, and detained in cases determined by law. . . .

10. No one is to be disquieted for his very basic opinions; woman has the right to mount the scaffold; she must equally have the right to mount the rostrum, provided that her demonstrations do not disturb the legally established public order.

11. The free communication of thoughts and opinions is one of the most precious rights of woman, since that liberty assured the recognition of children by their fathers. . . .

12. The guarantee of the rights of woman and the female citizen implies a major benefit; this guarantee must be instituted for the advantage of all, and not for the particular benefit of those to whom it is entrusted.

14. Female and male citizens have the right to verify, either by themselves or through their representatives, the necessity of the public contribution. This can only apply to women if they are granted an equal share, not only of wealth, but also of public administration, and in the determination of the proportion, the base, the collection, and the duration of the tax.

15. The collectivity of women, joined for tax purposes to the aggregate of men, has the right to demand an accounting of his administration from any public agent.

16. No society has a constitution without the guarantee of rights and the separation of powers; the constitution is null if the majority of individuals comprising the nation have not cooperated in drafting it.

17. Property belongs to both sexes whether united or separate; for each it is an inviolable and sacred right; no one can be deprived of it, since it is the true patrimony of nature. . . .

In the meantime, Louis XVI had remained inactive at Versailles. He did refuse to promulgate the decrees on the abolition of feudalism and the Declaration of Rights, but an unexpected turn of events soon forced the king to change his mind. On October 5, crowds of Parisian women, numbering in the thousands and described by one eyewitness as "detachments of women coming up from every direction, armed with broomsticks, lances, pitchforks, swords, pistols and muskets," marched to Versailles and forced the king to accept the constitutional decrees. The crowd now insisted that the royal family return to Paris. On October 6, the king complied. As a goodwill gesture, he brought along wagonloads of flour from the palace stores, escorted by women armed with pikes singing, "We are bringing back the baker, the baker's wife, and the baker's boy" (the king, queen, and their son). The king was virtually a prisoner in Paris, and the National Assembly, now meeting in Paris, would also feel the influence of Parisian insurrectionary politics.

Because the Catholic church was viewed as an important pillar of the old order, reforms soon overtook it. Most of the lands of the church were confiscated to pay state debts, and the church was also secularized. In July 1790, a new Civil Constitution of the Clergy was put into effect. Both bishops and priests were to be elected by the people and paid by the state. All clergy were also required to swear an oath of allegiance to the Civil Constitution. Only 54 percent of the French parish clergy took the oath while the majority of bishops refused. The Catholic church, still an important institution in the life of the French people, now became an enemy of the Revolution.

By 1791, the National Assembly had finally completed a new constitution that established a limited, constitutional monarchy. There was still a monarch (now called king of the French), but he enjoyed few powers not subject to review by the new Legislative Assembly. The Legislative Assembly, in which sovereign power was vested, was to sit for two years and consist of 745 representatives chosen by an indirect system of election that preserved power in the hands of the more affluent members of society. Only active citizens (those men over the age of twenty-five paying in taxes the equivalent of three days' unskilled labor) could vote for electors (those men paying taxes equal in value to ten days' labor). This relatively small group of 50,000 electors then chose the deputies. To qualify as a deputy, one had to pay taxes equal in value to fifty-four days' labor.

Thus, by 1791 a revolutionary consensus, largely the work of the wealthier bourgeoisie, had moved France to a drastic reordering of the old regime. By mid-1791, however, this consensus faced growing opposition from clerics opposed to the Civil Constitution of the Clergy, lower classes hurt by a rise in the cost of living, peasants angry that some dues still had not been abandoned, and political clubs like the Jacobins that offered more radical solutions to France's problems. In addition, by mid-1791, the government was still facing several financial difficulties due to massive tax evasion. Despite all of their problems, however, the bourgeois politicians in charge remained relatively unified on the basis of their trust in the king. But Louis XVI disastrously undercut them. Quite upset with the whole turn of revolutionary events, he sought to flee France in June 1791 and almost succeeded before being recognized, captured, and brought back to Paris. In this unsettled situation, with a discredited and seemingly disloyal monarch, the new Legislative Assembly held its first session in October 1791. France's relations with the rest of Europe soon led to Louis's downfall.

Meanwhile, some other European rulers had become concerned about the French example and feared that revolution would spread to their countries. On August 27, 1791, the monarchs of Austria and Prussia invited other European monarchs to use force to reestablish monarchical authority in France. Insulted by this threat, the Legislative Assembly declared war on Austria on April 20, 1792. The French fared badly in the initial fighting, and loud recriminations were soon heard in Paris. A frantic search for scapegoats began; as one observer noted, "Everywhere you hear the cry that the king is betraying us, the generals are betraying us, that nobody is to be trusted; . . . that Paris will be taken in six weeks by the Austrians . . . we are on a volcano ready to spout flames."[5] Defeats in war coupled with economic shortages in the spring reinvigorated popular groups that had been dormant since the previous summer and led to renewed political demonstrations, especially against the king. Radical Parisian political groups, declaring themselves an insurrectionary commune, organized a mob attack on the royal palace and Legislative Assembly in August 1792, took the king captive, and forced the Legislative Assembly to suspend the monarchy and call for a National Convention, chosen on the basis of universal male suffrage, to decide on the future form of government. The French Revolution was about to enter a more radical stage.

FROM RADICAL REVOLUTION TO REACTION

In September 1792, the newly elected National Convention began its sessions. Although it was called to draft a new constitution, it also acted as the sovereign ruling body of France. Socially, the composition of the National Convention was similar to its predecessors. Dominated by lawyers, professionals, and property owners, two-thirds of its deputies were under the age of forty-five, and almost all had had political experience as a result of the Revolution. Almost all were also intensely distrustful of the king and his activities. It was therefore no surprise that the convention's first major step on September 21 was to abolish the monarchy and establish a republic. At the beginning of 1793, the convention passed a decree condemning Louis XVI to death. On January 21, 1793, the king was executed and the destruction of the old regime was complete. There could be no turning back. But the execution of the king produced new challenges by creating new enemies for the Revolution both at home and abroad while strengthening those who were already its enemies.

Within Paris the local government known as the Commune, which drew a number of its leaders from the working classes, favored radical change and put constant pressure on the convention, pushing it to ever more radical positions. Moreover, the National Convention itself still did not rule all France. Peasants in western France as well as inhabitants of France's major provincial cities refused to accept its authority. Domestic turmoil was paralleled by a foreign crisis. By the beginning of 1793, after the king had been executed, most of Europe—an informal coalition of Austria, Prussia, Spain, Portugal, Britain, the Dutch Republic, and even Russia—was pitted against France. Grossly overextended, the French armies began to experience reverses, and by late spring some members of the anti-French coalition were poised for an invasion of France. If it succeeded, both the Revolution and the revolutionaries would be destroyed and the old regime reestablished.

To meet these crises, the convention gave broad powers to an executive committee of twelve known as the Committee of Public Safety, which came to be dominated by Maximilien Robespierre, the leader of the Jacobins. For a twelve-month period, from 1793 to 1794, virtually the same twelve members were reelected and gave the country the leadership it needed to weather the domestic and foreign crises of 1793.

To meet the foreign crisis and save the republic from its foreign enemies, the Committee of Public Safety decreed a universal mobilization of the nation on August 23, 1793:

> Young men will fight, young men are called to conquer. Married men will forge arms, transport military baggage and guns and will prepare food supplies. Women, who at

◆ **Citizens Enlist in the New French Army.**   To save the Republic from its foreign enemies, the National Convention created a new revolutionary army of unprecedented size. In this painting, citizens joyfully hasten to sign up at the recruitment tables set up in the streets. On this occasion, officials are distributing coins to those who have enrolled.

long last are to take their rightful place in the revolution and follow their true destiny, will forget their futile tasks: their delicate hands will work at making clothes for soldiers; they will make tents and they will extend their tender care to shelters where the defenders of the Patrie will receive the help that their wounds require. Children will make lint of old cloth. It is for them that we are fighting: children, those beings destined to gather all the fruits of the revolution, will raise their pure hands toward the skies. And old men, performing their missions again, as of yore, will be guided to the public squares of the cities where they will kindle the courage of young warriors and preach the doctrines of hate for kings and the unity of the Republic.[6]

In less than a year, the French revolutionary government had raised an army of 650,000; by September 1794, it numbered 1,169,000. The Republic's army was the largest ever seen in European history. It now pushed the allies back across the Rhine and even conquered the Austrian Netherlands.

Historians have focused on the French revolutionary army as an important step in the creation of modern nationalism. Previously, wars had been fought between governments or ruling dynasties by relatively small armies of professional soldiers. Although innocent civilians had suffered in those struggles, all parties had considered them noncombatants with no direct involvement in the conflicts. The new French army, however, was the creation of a "people's" government; its wars were now "people's" wars. The entire nation was to be involved in the war. But when dynastic wars became people's wars, warfare increased in ferocity and restraints disappeared. The wars of the French revolutionary era opened the door to the total war of the modern world.

To meet the domestic crisis, the National Convention and the Committee of Public Safety initiated the "Reign of Terror." Revolutionary courts were instituted to protect the revolutionary Republic from its internal enemies. In the course of nine months, 16,000 people were officially killed under the blade of the guillotine, the latter a revolutionary device for the quick and efficient separation of heads from bodies. But the true number of the Terror's victims was probably closer to 30,000. The bulk of the Terror's executions took place in cities and districts that had been in open rebellion against the authority of the National Convention. The Terror demonstrated no class prejudice. Estimates are that the nobles constituted 8 percent of its victims, the middle classes, 25, the clergy, 6, and the peasant and laboring classes, 60. To the Committee of Public Safety, this bloodletting was only a temporary expedient. Once the war and domestic emergency were over, "the republic of virtue" would follow, and the

Declaration of the Rights of Man and the Citizen would be fully established.

Military force in the form of revolutionary armies was used to bring recalcitrant cities and districts back under the control of the National Convention. The Committee of Public Safety decided to make an example of Lyons, which was France's second city after Paris and had defied the National Convention during a time when the Republic was in peril. By April 1794, 1,880 citizens of Lyons had been executed. When guillotining proved too slow, cannon fire and grapeshot were used to blow condemned men into open graves. A German observed:

> . . . whole ranges of houses, always the most handsome, burnt. The churches, convents, and all the dwellings of the former patricians were in ruins. When I came to the guillotine, the blood of those who had been executed a few hours beforehand was still running in the street . . . I said to a group of sansculottes that it would be decent to clear away all this human blood. Why should it be cleared? one of them said to me. It's the blood of aristocrats and rebels. The dogs should lick it up.[7]

Along with the Terror, the Committee of Public Safety took other steps to control France. By spring 1793, they were sending "representatives on mission" as agents of the central government to all parts of the country to implement the laws dealing with the wartime emergency. The committee also attempted to provide some economic controls by establishing price limits on goods declared of first necessity ranging from food and drink to fuel and clothing. The controls failed to work very well, however, because the government lacked the machinery to enforce them.

The National Convention also pursued a policy of dechristianization. A new calendar was instituted in which years were no longer numbered from the birth of Christ but from September 22, 1792, the first day of the French Republic. The new calendar also eliminated Sundays and church holidays. In Paris, the cathedral of Notre Dame was designated a Temple of Reason; in November 1793, a public ceremony dedicated to the worship of reason was held in the former cathedral in which patriotic maidens clad in white dresses paraded before a temple of reason where the high altar once stood.

By the summer of 1794, the French had been successful on the battlefield against their foreign foes. The military successes meant that there was now less need for the Terror. But the Terror continued because Robespierre, who had become a figure of power and authority, had become obsessed with purifying the body politic of all the corrupt. Many deputies in the National Convention began to fear that they were not safe while he was free to act. Forming an anti-Robespierre coalition in the National Convention, they soon gathered enough votes to condemn him. Robespierre was guillotined on July 28, 1794.

After the death of Robespierre, a reaction set in called the Thermidorean Reaction, named after the month of Thermidor on the new French calendar. The Terror came to a halt. The National Convention reduced the power of the Committee of Public Safety, closed the Jacobin club, and tried to provide better protection for its deputies against the Parisian mobs. Churches were allowed to reopen for public worship. Economic regulation was dropped in favor of *laissez-faire* policies, another clear indication that moderate forces were again gaining control of the Revolution. In addition, a new constitution was framed in August 1795 that reflected this more conservative republicanism or a desire for a stability that did not sacrifice the ideals of 1789. The constitution provided for five directors to act as the executive authority or Directory.

The period of the Revolution under the government of the Directory was an era of stagnation, corruption, and graft, a materialistic reaction to the sufferings and sacrifices that had been demanded in the Reign of Terror. Speculators made fortunes in property by taking advantage of the Republic's severe monetary problems. At the same time, the government of the Directory was faced with political enemies from both the left and the right of the political spectrum. On the right, royalists who desired the restoration of the monarchy continued their agitation. On the left, Jacobin hopes of power were revived by continuing economic problems. Battered by the left and right, unable to find a definitive solution to the country's economic problems, and still carrying on the wars left from the Committee of Public Safety, the Directory increasingly relied on the military to maintain its power. This led to a coup d'etat in 1799 in which the successful and popular military general Napoleon Bonaparte was able to seize power.

The Age of Napoleon

Napoleon dominated both French and European history from 1799 to 1815. He was born in Corsica in 1769, only a few months after France had annexed the island. The son of a lawyer whose family stemmed from the Florentine nobility, the young Napoleon obtained a royal scholarship to study at a military school in France. When the revolution broke out in 1789, Napoleon was a lieutenant. The French Revolution and the European war that followed broadened his sights and presented him with new opportunities. Napoleon rose quickly through the ranks. In 1794, at the age of only twenty-five, he was promoted

◆ **Women Patriots.**   Women played a variety of roles in the events of the French Revolution. This picture shows a women's patriotic club discussing the decrees of the National Convention, an indication that some women became highly politicized by the upheavals of the revolution.

The French Revolution

	1789
Meeting of Estates-General	May 5
Formation of National Assembly	June 17
Fall of the Bastille	July 14
Great Fear	Summer
Abolition of feudalism	August 4
Declaration of the Rights of Man and the Citizen	August 26
March to Versailles; king's return to Paris	October 5–6
	1790
Civil Constitution of the Clergy	July 12
	1791
Flight of the king	June 20–21
	1792
France declares war on Austria	April 20
Attack on the royal palace	August 10
Abolition of monarchy	September 21
	1793
Execution of the king	January 21
Levy-in-mass	August 23
	1794
Execution of Robespierre	July 28
	1795
Constitution of 1795 is adopted—the Directory	August 22

to the rank of brigadier general by the Committee of Public Safety. Two years later, he was made commander of the French army in Italy (see the box on p. 715) where he won a series of victories and dictated peace to the Austrians in 1797. He returned to France as a conquering hero. After a disastrous expedition to Egypt, Napoleon returned to Paris where he participated in the coup d'etat that ultimately led to his virtual dictatorship of France. He was only thirty years old at the time.

With the coup d'etat of 1799, a new form of the Republic was proclaimed in which, as first consul, Napoleon directly controlled the entire executive authority of government. He had overwhelming influence over the legislature, appointed members of the administrative bureaucracy, controlled the army, and conducted foreign affairs. In 1802, Napoleon was made consul for life, and in 1804 he returned France to monarchy when he had himself crowned as Emperor Napoleon I. The revolutionary era that had begun with an attempt to limit arbitrary government had ended with a government far more autocratic than the monarchy of the old regime.

One of Napoleon's first domestic moves was to establish peace with the oldest and most implacable enemy of the Revolution, the Catholic church. In 1801, Napoleon arranged a Concordat with the pope that recognized Catholicism as the religion of a majority of the French people. Although the Catholic church was permitted to hold processions again and reopen the seminaries, the pope agreed not to raise the question of the church lands confiscated during the Revolution. As a result of the Concordat, the Catholic church was no longer an enemy of the French government. At the same time, the agreement reassured those who had acquired church lands during the Revolution that they would not be taken away, an assurance that obviously made the new owners supporters of the Napoleonic regime.

Napoleon's most famous domestic achievement was his codification of the laws. Before the Revolution, France did not have a single set of laws, but rather virtually three hundred different legal systems. During the Revolution, efforts were made to prepare a codification of the laws for the entire nation, but it remained for Napoleon to bring the work to completion in the famous Civil Code. This preserved most of the revolutionary gains by recognizing the principle of the equality of all citizens before the law, the right of the individual to choose his profession, religious toleration, and the abolition of serfdom and feudalism. Property rights continued to be carefully protected while the interests of employers were safeguarded by outlawing trade unions and strikes. The Civil Code clearly reflected the revolutionary aspirations for a uniform legal system, legal equality, and protection of property and individuals.

At the same time, the Civil Code strictly curtailed the rights of some people. During the radical phase of the French Revolution, new laws had made divorce an easy process for both husbands and wives, restricted the rights of fathers over their children (they could no longer have their children put in prison arbitrarily), and allowed all children (including daughters) to inherit property equally. The Civil Code undid most of this legislation. The control of fathers over their families was restored.

In 1796, at the age of twenty-seven, Napoleon Bonaparte was given command of the French army in Italy where he won a series of stunning victories. His use of speed, deception, and surprise to overwhelm his opponents is well known. In this selection from a proclamation to his troops in Italy, Napoleon also appears as a master of psychological warfare.

Napoleon Bonaparte, Proclamation to French Troops in Italy (April 26, 1796)

Soldiers:

In a fortnight you have won six victories, taken twenty-one standards, fifty-five pieces of artillery, several strong positions, and conquered the richest part of Piedmont [in northern Italy]; you have captured 15,000 prisoners and killed or wounded more than 10,000 men. . . . You have won battles without cannon, crossed rivers without bridges, made forced marches without shoes, camped without brandy and often without bread. Soldiers of liberty, only republican troops could have endured what you have endured. Soldiers,

you have our thanks! The grateful Patrie [nation] will owe its prosperity to you. . . .

The two armies which but recently attacked you with audacity are fleeing before you in terror; the wicked men who laughed at your misery and rejoiced at the thought of the triumphs of your enemies are confounded and trembling.

But, soldiers, as yet you have done nothing compared with what remains to be done. . . . Undoubtedly the greatest obstacles have been overcome; but you still have battles to fight, cities to capture, rivers to cross. Is there one among you whose courage is abating? No. . . . All of you are consumed with a desire to extend the glory of the French people; all of you long to humiliate those arrogant kings who dare to contemplate placing us in fetters; all of you desire to dictate a glorious peace, one which will indemnify the Patrie for the immense sacrifices it has made; all of you wish to be able to say with pride as you return to your villages, "I was with the victorious army of Italy!"

Divorce was still allowed, but made more difficult for women to obtain. A wife caught in adultery, for example, could be divorced by her husband and even imprisoned. A husband, however, could be accused of adultery only if he moved his mistress into his home. Women were now "less equal than men" in other ways as well. When they married, their property came under the control of their husbands. In lawsuits they were treated as minors, and their testimony was regarded as less reliable than that of men.

Napoleon also worked on rationalizing the bureaucratic structure of France by developing a powerful, centralized administrative machine. Administrative centralization required a bureaucracy of capable officials, and Napoleon worked hard to develop one. Early on, the regime showed its preference for experts and cared little whether that expertise had been acquired in royal or revolutionary bureaucracies. Promotion, whether in civil or military offices, was to be based not on rank or birth but only on demonstrated abilities. This was, of course, what many bourgeoisie had wanted before the Revolution. Napoleon, however, also created a new aristocracy based on merit in the state service. Napoleon created 3,263 no-

bles between 1808 and 1814; nearly 60 percent were military officers while the remainder came from the upper ranks of the civil service and other state and local officials. Socially, only 22 percent of Napoleon's aristocracy came from the nobility of the old regime; almost 60 percent were bourgeois in origin.

In his domestic policies, then, Napoleon both destroyed and preserved aspects of the Revolution. Liberty had been replaced by an initially benevolent despotism that grew increasingly arbitrary as the demands of war overwhelmed Napoleon and the French. While equality was preserved in the law code and the opening of government offices to talent, the creation of a new aristocracy and the strong protection accorded to property rights make it clear that a loss of equality accompanied the loss of liberty.

NAPOLEON'S EMPIRE AND THE EUROPEAN RESPONSE

When Napoleon became consul in 1799, France was at war with a second European coalition of Russia, Great Britain, and Austria. Napoleon realized the need for a pause and achieved a peace treaty in 1802 that left

◆ **The Coronation of Napoleon.**   In 1804, Napoleon restored monarchy to France when he had himself crowned as emperor. In the coronation scene painted by Jacques-Louis David, Napoleon is shown crowning the empress Josephine while the pope looks on. The painting shows Napoleon's mother seated in the box in the background, even though she was not at the ceremony.

France with new frontiers and a number of client territories from the North Sea to the Adriatic. But the peace did not last, and in 1803 war was renewed with Britain, which was soon joined by Austria, Russia, and Prussia in the Third Coalition. In a series of battles from 1805 to 1807, Napoleon's Grand Army defeated the continental members of the coalition, giving Napoleon the opportunity to create a new European order. The Grand Empire was composed of three major parts: the French empire, dependent states, and allied states. The French empire, the inner core of the Grand Empire, consisted of an enlarged France extending to the Rhine in the east and including the western half of Italy north of Rome. Dependent states were kingdoms under the rule of Napoleon's relatives; these came to include Spain, Holland, the kingdom of Italy, the Swiss Republic, the Grand Duchy of Warsaw, and the Confederation of the Rhine, the latter a union of all German states except Austria and Prussia. Allied states were those defeated by Napoleon and forced to join his struggle against Britain; they included Prussia, Austria, Russia, and Sweden.

Within his empire, Napoleon sought acceptance everywhere of certain revolutionary principles, including legal equality, religious toleration, and economic freedom. As he explained to his brother Jerome after he had made him king of the new German state of Westphalia:

> What the peoples of Germany desire most impatiently is that talented commoners should have the same right to your esteem and to public employments as the nobles, that any trace of serfdom and of an intermediate hierarchy between the sovereign and the lowest class of the people should be completely abolished. The benefits of the Code Napoléon, the publicity of judicial procedure, the creation of juries must be so many distinguishing marks of your

monarchy. . . . What nation would wish to return under the arbitrary Prussian government once it had tasted the benefits of a wise and liberal administration? The peoples of Germany, the peoples of France, of Italy, of Spain all desire equality and liberal ideas. I have guided the affairs of Europe for many years now, and I have had occasion to convince myself that the buzzing of the privileged classes is contrary to the general opinion. Be a constitutional king.[8]

In the inner core and dependent states of his Grand Empire, Napoleon tried to destroy the old order. Nobility and clergy everywhere in these states lost their special privileges. He decreed equality of opportunity with offices open to talent, equality before the law, and religious

✖ **Map 19.6**   Napoleon's Grand Empire.

toleration. This spread of French revolutionary principles was an important factor in the development of liberal traditions in these countries.

Like Hitler one hundred and thirty years later, Napoleon hoped that his Grand Empire would last for centuries; like Hitler's empire, it collapsed almost as rapidly as it had been formed. Two major reasons help to explain this: the survival of Great Britain and the force of nationalism. Britain's survival was primarily due to its seapower. As long as Britain ruled the waves, it was almost invulnerable to military attack. Although Napoleon contemplated an invasion of Britain and even collected ships for it, he could not overcome the British navy's decisive defeat of a combined French-Spanish fleet at Trafalgar in 1805. Napoleon then turned to his Continental System to defeat Britain. Put into effect between 1806 and 1808, it attempted to prevent British goods from reaching the European continent in order to weaken Britain economically and destroy its capacity to wage war. But the Continental System failed. Allied states resented the ever-tightening French economic hegemony; some began to cheat and others to resist, thereby opening the door to collaboration with the British. New markets in the Levant and in Latin America also provided compensation for the British. Indeed, by 1809–1810, British overseas exports were at near-record highs.

A second important factor in the defeat of Napoleon was nationalism. This political creed had arisen during the French Revolution in the French people's emphasis on brotherhood (*fraternité*) and solidarity against other peoples. Nationalism involved the unique cultural identity of a people based on common language, religion, and national symbols. The spirit of French nationalism had made possible the mass armies of the revolutionary and Napoleonic eras. But by extending the principles of the French Revolution beyond France, Napoleon had inadvertently spread nationalism as well. The French aroused nationalism in two ways: by making themselves hated oppressors and thus arousing the patriotism of others in opposition to French nationalism, and by showing the people of Europe what nationalism was and what a nation in arms could do. It was a lesson not lost on other peoples and rulers. A Spanish uprising against Napoleon's rule, aided by the British, kept a French force of 200,000 pinned down for years.

The beginning of Napoleon's downfall came in 1812 with the invasion of Russia. The latter's defection from the Continental System left Napoleon with little choice. Although aware of the risks in invading such a large country, he also knew that if the Russians were allowed to challenge the Continental System unopposed, others would soon follow suit. In June 1812, he led a Grand Army of over 600,000 men into Russia. Napoleon's hopes for victory depended on quickly meeting and defeating the Russian armies, but the Russian forces refused to give battle and retreated for hundreds of miles, torching their own villages and countryside to prevent Napoleon's army from finding food and forage. When the Russians did stop to fight at Borodino, Napoleon's forces won an indecisive and costly victory. When the remaining forces of the Grand Army arrived in Moscow, they found the city ablaze. Lacking food and supplies, Napoleon abandoned Moscow late in October and made the "Great Retreat" across Russia in terrible winter conditions. Only 40,000 out of the original army managed to arrive back in Poland in January 1813. This military disaster then led to a war of liberation all over Europe, culminating in Napoleon's defeat in April 1814.

The defeated emperor of the French was allowed to play ruler on the island of Elba, off the coast of Tuscany, while the Bourbon monarchy was restored to France in the person of Louis XVIII, brother of the executed king. But the new king had little support, and Napoleon, bored on the island of Elba, slipped back into France. The troops sent to capture him went over to his side, and Napoleon entered Paris in triumph on March 20, 1815. The powers who had defeated him pledged once more to fight this person they called the "Enemy and Disturber of the Tranquility of the World." Having decided to strike first at his enemies, Napoleon raised yet another army and moved to attack the nearest allied forces stationed in Belgium. At Waterloo on June 18, Napoleon met a combined British and Prussian army under the Duke of Wellington and suffered a bloody defeat. This time the victorious allies exiled him to St. Helena, a small, forsaken island in the south Atlantic. Only Napoleon's memory would continue to haunt French political life.

Conclusion

Everywhere in Europe at the beginning of the eighteenth century, the old order remained strong. Nobles, clerics, towns, provinces all had privileges. Everywhere in the eighteenth century, monarchs sought to enlarge their bureaucracies to raise taxes to support the new large standing armies that had originated in the seventeenth century. The existence of these armies guaranteed wars. The existence of five great powers, with two of them (France and Britain) in conflict in the Far East and the New World, initiated a new scale of conflict; the Seven Years' War could legitimately be viewed as the first world war. Although the wars changed little on the European continent, British victories enabled Great Britain to emerge as the world's greatest naval and colonial power. Everywhere in Europe, increased demands for taxes to support these conflicts led to attacks on the privileged orders and a desire for change not met by the ruling monarchs. At the same time, sustained population growth and dramatic changes in finance, trade, and industry created tensions that undermined the traditional foundations of the old order. The inability of that old order to deal meaningfully with these changes led to a revolutionary outburst at the end of the eighteenth century that marked the beginning of the end for the old order.

The revolutionary era of the late eighteenth century witnessed a dramatic political transformation. Revolutionary upheavals, beginning in North America and continuing in France, produced movements for political liberty and equality. The documents created by these revolutions, the Declaration of Independence and the Declaration of the Rights of Man and the Citizen, embodied the fundamental ideas of the Enlightenment and created a liberal political agenda based on a belief in popular sovereignty—the people are the source of political power—and the principles of liberty and equality. Liberty, frequently limited in practice, meant, in theory, freedom from arbitrary power as well as the freedom to think, write, and worship as one chose. Equality meant equality in rights and the equality of opportunity based on talent rather than birth. In practice, equality remained limited; those who owned property had greater opportunities for voting and officeholding while there was certainly no equality between men and women.

The French Revolution created a modern revolutionary concept. No one had foreseen or consciously planned the upheaval that began in 1789, but after 1789 "revolutionaries" knew that the proper use of mass uprisings could produce the overthrow of unwanted governments. The French Revolution became the classical political and social model for revolution. At the same time, the liberal and national political ideals created by the Revolution dominated the political landscape of the nineteenth and early twentieth centuries. A new era had begun and the world would never again be the same.

CHAPTER NOTES

1. Igor Vinogradoff, "Russian Missions to London, 1711–1789: Further Extracts from the Cottrell Papers," *Oxford Slavonic Papers*, New Series (1982), 15:76.

2. Quoted in E. Bradford Burns, *Latin America: A Concise Interpretative History*, 4th ed. (Englewood Cliffs, N.J., 1986), p. 62.

3. Quoted in Reinhold A. Dorwart, *The Administrative Reforms of Frederick William I of Prussia* (Cambridge, Mass., 1953), p. 36.

4. Quoted in Hans Rosenberg, *Bureaucracy, Aristocracy, and Autocracy: The Prussian Experience, 1660–1815* (Cambridge, Mass., 1958), p. 40.

5. Quoted in William Doyle, *The Oxford History of the French Revolution* (Oxford, 1989), p. 184.

6. Quoted in Leo Gershoy, *The Era of the French Revolution* (Princeton, N.J., 1957), p. 157.

7. Quoted in Doyle, *The Oxford History of the French Revolution*, p. 254.

8. Quoted in J. Christopher Herold, ed., *The Mind of Napoleon* (New York, 1955), pp. 74–75.

SUGGESTED READINGS

For a good introduction to the history of eighteenth-century Europe, see the relevant chapters in the general works by Woloch and Anderson listed in Chapter 18. See also G. Treasure, *The Making of Modern Europe, 1648–1780* (London, 1985) and O. Hufton, *Europe: Privilege and Protest, 1730–1789* (London, 1980). A good introduction to European population can be found in M. W. Flinn, *The European Demographic System, 1500–1820* (Brighton, 1981). A different perspective on economic history can be found in F. Braudel's *Capitalism and Material Life, 1400–1800* (New York, 1973). The subject of mercantile empires and worldwide trade is covered in J. H. Parry, *Trade and Dominion: European Overseas Empires in the Eighteenth Century* (London, 1971) and D. K. Fieldhouse, *The Colonial Empires* (New York, 1971). Eighteenth-century cottage industry and the beginnings of industrialization are examined in the early chapters of D. Landes, *The Unbound Prometheus: Technological Change and Industrial Development in Western Europe from 1750 to the Present* (New York, 1969).

For an introduction to the social order of the eighteenth century, see G. Rudé, *Europe in the Eighteenth Century: Aristocracy and the Bourgeois Challenge* (London, 1972) and P. Laslett, *The World We Have Lost*, 3d ed. (New York, 1984). The warfare of this period is examined in J. Childs, *Armies and Warfare in Europe, 1648–1789* (Manchester, 1982). There is no better work on the problem of poverty in the eighteenth century than O. Hufton, *The Poor of Eighteenth-Century France* (Oxford, 1974).

For a brief survey of Latin America, see E. B. Burns, *Latin America: A Concise Interpretative History*, 4th ed. (Englewood Cliffs, N.J., 1986). More detailed works on colonial Latin American history include S. J. Stein and B. H. Stein, *The Colonial Heritage of Latin America* (New York, 1970) and J. Lockhardt and S. B. Schwartz, *Early Latin America: A History of Colonial Spanish America and Brazil* (New York, 1983). A good, brief survey of the revolutionary era in America can be found in E. S. Morgan, *Birth of the Republic, 1763–1789*, rev. ed. (New York, 1977). The importance of ideology is treated in B. Bailyn, *The Ideological Origins of the American Revolution* (Cambridge, 1966). For an interesting comparative study, see the stimulating work by P. Higonnet, *Sister Republics: Origins of the French and American Revolutions* (Cambridge, Mass., 1988).

For a brief study of the practice of enlightened absolutism, see J. Gagliardo, *Enlightened Despotism* (New York, 1967). Good biographies of some of Europe's monarchs include R. Asprey, *Frederick the Great: The Magnificent Enigma* (New York, 1986); I. de Madariaga, *Russia in the Age of Catherine the Great* (New Haven, Conn., 1981); and the first volume of a major work on Joseph II by D. Deales, *Joseph II* (Cambridge, 1987).

A well written, up-to-date introduction to the French Revolution can be found in W. Doyle, *The Oxford History of the French Revolution* (Oxford, 1989). For the entire revolutionary and Napoleonic eras, see O. Connelly, *The French Revolution and Napoleonic Era*, 2d ed. (Fort Worth, 1991) and D. M. G. Sutherland, *France 1789–1815: Revolution and Counter-Revolution* (London, 1985). Although controversial, the massive and beautifully written work by S. Schama, *Citizens* (New York, 1989), makes exciting reading. A different approach to the French Revolution can be found in E. Kennedy, *A Cultural History of the French Revolution* (New Haven, Conn., 1989).

The origins of the French Revolution are examined in W. Doyle, *Origins of the French Revolution* (Oxford, 1988). On the early years of the Revolution, see J. Egret, *The French Pre-Revolution, 1787–88* (Chicago, 1977) and N. Hampson, *Prelude to Terror* (Oxford, 1988). Important works on the radical stage of the French Revolution include N. Hampson, *The Terror in the French Revolution* (London, 1981); R. R. Palmer, *Twelve Who Ruled* (Princeton, N.J., 1941); and R. Cobb, *The People's Armies* (London, 1987). The importance of the revolutionary wars in the radical stage of the Revolution is underscored in T. C. W. Blanning, *The Origins of the French Revolutionary Wars* (London, 1986). On the Directory, see M. Lyons, *France under the Directory* (Cambridge, 1975). On the Great Fear, there is the classic work by G. Lefebvre, *The Great Fear of 1789: Rural Panic in Revolutionary France* (London, 1973). Two recent works that take rather different approaches to the French Revolution are W. H. Sewell, *Work and Revolu-*

tion in France (Cambridge, 1980) and P. Higonnet, *Class, Ideology and the Rights of Nobles during the French Revolution* (Oxford, 1981). On the role of women in revolutionary Paris, there is much to be found in the collection of documents edited by D. G. Levy, H. B. Applewhite, and M. D. Johnson, *Women in Revolutionary Paris 1789–1795* (Urbana, Ill., 1979). The best brief biography of Napoleon is F. Markham, *Napoleon* (New York, 1963). A good recent treatment is L. Bergeron, *France under Napoleon* (Princeton, N.J., 1981). On Napoleon's military campaigns see D. Chandler, *The Campaigns of Napoleon* (London, 1966).

The Emergence of New World Patterns
(1500–1800)

Historians often refer to the period from the end of the fifteenth to the end of the eighteenth century as the early modern era. The phrase is not chosen lightly, for it was during these years that several factors were at work that created the conditions of our own time. It was during that era that maritime exploration opened the entire world to trade and colonization. It was then that centralized monarchies—and later nation-states—formed that led to the modern concept of statehood. It was then that an intellectual revolution laid the foundations for a modern worldview based on rationalism and secularism. And it was at the close of that era that technological advances began to lay the basis for the Industrial Revolution.

In a global perspective, perhaps the most noteworthy event of the period was the extension of the maritime trade network throughout the entire populated world. The primary instrument of that expansion, of course, was a resurgent Europe, which exploded onto the world scene with the initial explorations of the Portuguese and the Spanish at the end of the fifteenth century and then gradually came to dominate shipping on international trade routes during the next three centuries.

Some contemporary historians argue that it was this sudden burst of energy from Europe that created the first truly global economic system. According to the historian Immanuel Wallerstein, one of the leading proponents of this theory, the age of exploration led to the creation of a new "world system" characterized by the emergence of global trade networks dominated by the rising force of European capitalism.

Strictly speaking, this is true in that only in the sixteenth century did trade patterns first encircle the earth. In the view of other contemporary historians, however, this view must be qualified. Some point to the Mongol expansion beginning in the thirteenth century, or even to the rise of the Arab empire in the Middle East a few centuries earlier, as early signs of the creation of the first global communications network enabling goods and ideas to travel from one end of the Eurasian supercontinent to the other.

Others take issue with the assertion that modern capitalism was the exclusive product of Europe during the fif-

teenth and sixteenth centuries and argue that its roots can be found in earlier centuries and in other environments as well as Europe. Finally, as noted previously, some historians point to the continuing vitality of many traditional Asian civilizations and dispute the view of world system theorists that the year 1500 inaugurated an era of European dominance.

Whatever the truth of these assertions, there are still many reasons for considering the end of the fifteenth century as a crucial date in world history. In the most basic sense, it marked the end of the long isolation of the Western Hemisphere from the rest of the inhabited world. In so doing, it led to the creation of the first truly global network of ideas and commodities, which would introduce plants, ideas, and (unfortunately) many new diseases to all humanity. Secondly, the period gave birth to a stunning increase in trade and manufacturing that stimulated major economic changes not only in Europe but in other parts of the world as well. The world would never be the same again.

The period from 1500 to 1800, then, was an incubation period for the modern world and the launching pad for an era of Western domination that began in the nineteenth century. To understand why the West emerged as the leading force in the world at that time, it is necessary to understand what factors at work in Europe led to the scientific and industrial revolutions and why such factors were absent in other major civilizations around the globe.

Historians have identified the technological changes that took place in Europe in the early modern era as an essential element in that Age of Exploration. And it is certainly true that technology—in the form of improvements in navigation, shipbuilding, and weaponry—was a significant factor in the European ability to encircle the earth and establish dominance over the seas. But it is also true that many of these technological advances had taken place elsewhere—in China, India, and the Middle East—and had then been brought to Europe on Muslim ships or along the trade routes through Central Asia. No doubt, the firearms and artillery of European nations enabled them to dominate international sea-lanes and create vast colonial empires in the New World. But gunpowder was also crucial to other civilizations as well in the early modern era. The rise of a Russian empire in Europe and Asia depended in large part on Peter the Great's importation of Western military technology. The Muslim empires of the Ottomans, Safavids, and Mughals, as well as the Manchu dynasty in China, were all dependent on the new military hardware. In the late fifteenth century, then, Europe was only one of many centers of civilization, and certainly not the most advanced, in the world. It was the capacity and desire of the Europeans to enhance their wealth and power by making practical use of the discoveries of others that was the significant factor in the equation.

Technological innovations, then, cannot provide the final answer to the question of why at this time in history Europe suddenly became the engine for rapid global change. Another factor, certainly, was the change in the European worldview, the shift from a metaphysical to a materialist perspective and the growing inclination among European intellectuals to question first principles. Whereas in China, for example, the "investigation of things" had been put to the use of analyzing and confirming principles first established by Confucius during the Chinese "Golden Age," in early modern Europe, empirical scientists rejected received religious ideas, developed a new conception of the universe, and sought ways to improve material conditions around them.

But why were European thinkers more interested in practical applications for their discoveries than their counterparts elsewhere? One explanation, certainly, lies in the growing strength of the urban bourgeoisie in many areas of early modern Europe and the deliberate appeal that early scientists made to the literate mercantile elites of Europe when they showed how the new scientific ideas could be applied directly to specific technological needs. As we have seen, thriving commercial and manufacturing communities existed in the countries of East Asia, India, Central and East Africa, and the Middle East and were playing an increasingly important role in the life of their societies. But the European mercantile sector had begun to carve out an independent existence in the autonomous cities of southern and central Europe as early as the eleventh and twelfth centuries and by the eve of the early modern era suffered from few of the political and economic restrictions imposed on their counterparts elsewhere. By the sixteenth century, these affluent sectors of the community were enjoying increasing wealth and prosperity.

A final factor can be attributed to political changes that were beginning to take place in Europe during this period. The breakup of the world of Christendom, a consequence of the religious wars of the sixteenth and seventeenth centuries, helped to give birth to independent and relatively centralized monarchies in many areas of Europe. In the eighteenth century, the process of centralization that had characterized the growth of states since the Middle Ages continued as most European states enlarged their bureaucratic machinery and consolidated their governments in order to collect the revenues and amass the manpower they needed to compete militarily with the other European states. In this highly competitive environment—evident in the wars of the century—political leaders desperately sought ways to enhance their wealth and power at the expense of rivals and grasped eagerly at whatever tools were available to guarantee their survival and prosperity. Where necessary and appropriate, they were more than willing to form alliances with the urban bourgeoisie to enhance state power and the prosperity of the people.

At the end of the eighteenth century, profound political upheavals led to additional political change and the emergence of a new political order. In discussing the upheavals of the late eighteenth century, it is appropriate to speak of a liberal movement to extend political rights and power to the bourgeoisie "possessing capital," namely, those besides the aristocracy who were literate and had become wealthy through capitalist enterprises in trade, industry, and finance. The years preceding and accompanying the French Revolution included attempts at reform and revolt in the North American colonies, Britain, the Dutch Republic, some Swiss cities, and the Austrian Netherlands. The success of the revolutionary upheavals in North America and France created a liberal political agenda based on principles of liberty and equality and a new sense of nationhood. The identity of citizens with their nation rather than their monarch created a new and powerful force—nationalism—that would lead to revolutionary movements throughout the world in the nineteenth and twentieth centuries.

Conditions in many areas of Asia and Africa were less conducive to these economic and political developments. In China, a centralized monarchy continued to rely on a prosperous agricultural sector as the economic foundation of the empire. Though Emperor Yongle briefly toyed with the idea of expanding China's commercial contacts with the outside world, his successor, urged on by domestic interests, reversed the process and unilaterally brought China's own Age of Exploration to an end. In Japan, power was centralized under the powerful Tokugawa shogunate, and the era of peace and stability that ensued saw an increase in manufacturing and commercial activity. But Japanese elites, after initially expressing interest in the outside world, abruptly shut the door on European trade and ideas in an effort to protect "the land of the gods" from external contamination.

In India and the Middle East, commerce and manufacturing had played a vital role in the life of societies since the emergence of the Indian Ocean trade network in the first centuries C.E. And while India was still a predominantly agricultural society, commerce was almost literally the life blood of many states in the Middle East, including the powerful Abbasid caliphate that had dominated the entire area during its apogee in the eight and ninth centuries. But beginning in the eleventh century, the area had suffered through an extended period of political instability, marked by invasions by nomadic peoples from Central Asia. Although the Turks and the Mongols eventually formed their own states in the area and continued to promote trade with countries outside the region, the violence of the period and the local rulers' lack of experience in promoting maritime commerce had a severe depressing effect on urban manufacturing and commerce.

In the meantime, the countries of sub-Saharan Africa had their own problems. A number of trading states had begun to emerge in West Africa and along the eastern coast of the continent in the seventh and eighth centuries C.E., a process that was accelerated by Muslim penetration of the area in later centuries. But except for the eastern fringes, most parts of the continent still lacked the necessary infrastructure in terms of means of transportation, technology, and centralized states to compete aggressively for an active role in the regional trade passing through the area. For the most part, African states were suppliers rather than carriers of goods and remained too isolated from the main trade routes to benefit substantially from the technological and cultural diffusion that was taking place in many other areas of the world.

In the early modern era, then, Europe was best placed to take advantage of the technological innovations that had now become increasingly available throughout the Old World. It possessed the political stability, the capital, and what today might be called the "modernizing elite" that provided the spur to active efforts to take advantage of new conditions for their own benefit. Where other regions were still beset by internal obstacles or had deliberately "turned inward" to seek their destiny, Europe now turned outward to seek a new and dominant position in the world.

European expansion was not fueled solely by economic considerations, however. As had been the case with the rise of Islam in the seventh and eighth centuries, religion played a major role in motivating the European Age of Exploration in the early modern era. Although Christianity was by no means a new religion in the fifteenth century (as Islam had been at the moment of Arab expansion), the world of Christendom was in the midst of a major period of rivalry with the forces of Islam, a rivalry that was severely exacerbated by the conquest of the Byzantine Empire by the Ottoman Turks in the mid-fifteenth century.

Although the claims of Portuguese and Spanish adventurers that their activities were motivated primarily by a desire to bring the word of God to non-Christian peoples undoubtedly included a considerable measure of self-delusion and hypocrisy, there seems no reason to doubt that religious motives played a meaningful part in the European Age of Exploration. A perusal of the diaries of such famous explorers as Columbus, Vasco da Gama, and Francisco Pizarro attests to the sincerity and depth of their Christian beliefs. Religion undoubtedly provided a moral justification for some of the more heinous acts that were committed by Europeans in distant lands.

Religious motives were perhaps less evident in the activities of the non-Catholic powers that entered the competition beginning in the seventeenth century. English and Dutch merchants and officials were more inclined to be motivated purely by the pursuit of economic profit or by the prevailing "beggar thy neighbor" mercantile philosophy of the day. Eventually, however, the idea that trade benefits all participants provided a new moral justification, especially in the last quarter of the eighteenth century, when the free trade philosophy of Adam Smith became accepted wisdom in official and mercantile circles throughout much of Europe. The importance of free trade as a prerequisite for economic prosperity and political democracy became a common tenet of enlightened thinking in the colonial era in the nineteenth century and continues to be influential in our own day.

In the West, then, the Age of Exploration has traditionally been viewed essentially in a positive sense, as the first step in a process that would lead eventually to the emergence of economic well-being and political democracy in societies throughout the world. Recently, however, that assumption has come under sharp attack from those who claim that the primary legacy of the European Age of Exploration was not widespread global prosperity but harsh colonial exploitation. The brunt of that criticism has been directed at Christopher Columbus, one of the initiators of the European expansion and a leader in the discovery and conquest of the Americas. Taking issue with the prevailing image of Columbus as a heroic figure in world history, critics view him as a symbol of colonial repression and a prime mover in the virtual extinction of the peoples and cultures of the New World.

There is no doubt that the record of the Portuguese and the Spanish—as well as of other European states—leaves much to be desired, and certainly, the voyages of Columbus were not of universal benefit to his contemporaries or to the generations later to come. But to focus solely on the evils that were committed in the name of exploration and the propagation of Christianity distorts the realities of the era. In the first place, the consequences of European expansion into such regions were not universally pernicious. In some cases, the Europeans brought economic benefit to particular groups in society, while laying the basis for expanded production and trade in the future. As with the nomadic invasions and Islamic conquests of an earlier period, the legacy of the period of European expansion is too complex to be summed up in moral or ideological simplifications. Whether Christopher Columbus was a hero or a villain is a matter of debate. That he and his contemporaries suffered from the common state of the human condition is a matter on which there can be little doubt.

In the second place, as we have seen, the impact of European expansion on the rest of the world was still limited, at least in the period prior to the end of the eighteenth century. While European political authority was firmly established in a few key areas, such as the Spice Islands and Latin America, and existing trade patterns were severely disrupted in much of the world, in most regions of Africa and Asia traditional societies remained relatively intact. And processes at work in these societies were operating independently of events in Europe and later gave birth to forces that acted to limit or shape the Western impact.

One of these processes was the progressive emergence of centralized states, some of them built on the concept of ethnic or cultural unity. This process was at work in East Asia and in mainland Southeast Asia, as well as in India, where a centralized empire had been created for the first time since the fall of the Mauryas in the era of antiquity. It was somewhat less apparent in the Middle East, where the Ottoman Empire still laid claim to universal hegemony over the entire eastern Mediterranean and Mesopotamia, and in sub-Saharan Africa, where the forces of state building were still in an embryonic stage. But the concept of statehood was strengthening and laid the basis for the spread of nationalism in the twentieth century.

Another interesting point is that the growth of commerce and manufacturing was not exclusively a product of European expansion. A number of Asian societies made technological advances during this period and witnessed the emergence of a more visible and articulate urban bourgeoisie, developments that could provide the basis for a possible industrial revolution in the future. This process was especially evident in China and Japan, but also occurred in India, the Middle East, and parts of North Africa. The restraints on industrial growth were political, social, and intellectual, not economic or technological.

For the moment, however, such forces were mere portents for the future, not signs of an imminent industrial revolution. At the beginning of the nineteenth century, the primary fact of life for most Asian and African societies was the expansionist power of an industrializing and ever more aggressive Europe. The power and ambition of the West posed an immediate challenge to the independence and the destiny of societies throughout the rest of the world. The nature of that challenge will be the subject of our next section.

PART

IV

Modern Patterns of World History (1800–1945)

The period of world history from 1800 to 1945 was characterized, above all, by two major developments: the growth of industrialization and Western domination of the world. The two developments were, of course, directly interconnected. The Industrial Revolution became one of the major forces for change in the nineteenth century as it led Western civilization into the industrial era that has characterized the modern world. Beginning in Britain, it spread to the Continent and the Western Hemisphere in the course of the nineteenth century. At the same time, the Industrial Revolution created the technological means by which the Western world achieved domination of much of the rest of the world by the end of the nineteenth century.

Europeans had begun to explore the world in the fifteenth century, but even as late as 1870, they had not yet completely penetrated North America, South America, and Australia. In Asia and Africa, with a few notable exceptions, the Western presence was limited to trading posts. Between 1870 and 1914, Western civilization expanded into the rest of the Americas and Australia while most of Africa and Asia was divided into European colonies or spheres of influence. Two major events explain this remarkable expansion: the migration of many Europeans to other parts of the world due to population growth and the revival of imperialism, which was made possible by the West's technological advances.

The European population increased dramatically between 1850 and 1910, rising from 270 million to over 460 million by 1910. Although growing agricultural and industrial prosperity supported an increase in the European population, it could not do so indefinitely, especially in areas that had little industry and a severe problem of rural overpopulation. Some of the excess labor from underdeveloped areas migrated to the industrial regions of Europe. By 1913, for example, over 400,000

1800	1810	1820	1830	1840	1850	1860	1870

AFRICA

Slave trade declared illegal in Great Britain

Boers' Great Trek in South Africa

French seizure of Algeria

Completion of Suez Canal

INDIA AND THE MIDDLE EAST

Decline of Ottoman Empire in the Middle East

Sepoy Mutiny

EAST AND SOUTHEAST ASIA

Opium War

Commodore Perry arrives in Tokyo Bay

Fall of Tokugawa shogunate

EUROPE AND THE WESTERN HEMISPHERE

Latin American movements for independence

Unification of Italy and Germany

Poles were working in the heavily industrialized Ruhr region of western Germany. But the industrialized regions of Europe were not able to absorb the entire surplus population of the agricultural regions. A booming American economy after 1898 and cheap shipping fares after 1900 led to mass emigration from southern and eastern Europe to America at the beginning of the twentieth century. In 1880, on average around 500,000 people departed annually from Europe, but between 1906 and 1910, their numbers increased to 1,300,000, many of them from southern and eastern Europe. Altogether, between 1846 and 1932 probably 60 million Europeans left Europe, half of them bound for the United States and most of the rest for Canada or Latin America.

Beginning in the 1880s, European states began an intense scramble for overseas territory. This revival of imperialism, or the "new imperialism" as some have called it, led Europeans to carve up Asia and Africa. Imperialism was not a new phenomenon. Since the crusades of the Middle Ages and the overseas expansion between 1500 and 1800, when Europeans established colonies in North and South America and trading posts around Africa and the Indian Ocean, Europeans had shown a marked proclivity for the domination of less technologically oriented, non-European peoples. Nevertheless, the imperialism of the late nineteenth century was different from the earlier European imperialism. It occurred after a period in which Europeans had reacted against imperial expansion. Between 1775 and 1875, European states had lost

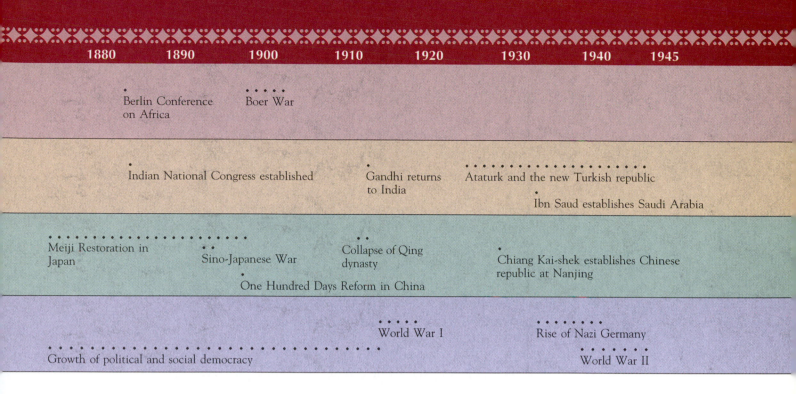

| 1880 | 1890 | 1900 | 1910 | 1920 | 1930 | 1940 | 1945 |

Berlin Conference on Africa • • • • • Boer War

Indian National Congress established • Gandhi returns to India • • • • • • • • • • • Ataturk and the new Turkish republic • Ibn Saud establishes Saudi Arabia

• • • • • • • • • • • • • • • Meiji Restoration in Japan • • • Sino-Japanese War • • Collapse of Qing dynasty • Chiang Kai-shek establishes Chinese republic at Nanjing • One Hundred Days Reform in China

• • • • • World War I • • • • • • • • Rise of Nazi Germany • Growth of political and social democracy • • • • • • • • World War II

more colonial territory than they acquired as many Europeans had actually come to regard colonies as expensive and useless. The new imperialism was also more rapid and resulted in greater and deeper penetrations into non-European societies. Finally, most of the new imperialism was directed toward the domination of Africa and Asia, two regions that had been largely ignored until then.

The new imperialism had a dramatic effect on Africa and Asia as European powers competed for control of these two continents. A major exception was Latin America, which was able to achieve political independence from its colonial rulers in the course of the nineteenth century and embark upon the building of new nations. Nevertheless, like the Ottoman Empire, Latin America still remained subject to commercial penetration by Western merchants.

Another part of the world that escaped total domination by the West was East Asia, where China and Japan were able to maintain at least the substance of national independence during the height of the Western onslaught at the end of the nineteenth century. For China, once the most advanced country in the world, survival was very much in doubt for many decades as the wave of Western political, military, and economic influence lapped at the edges of the Chinese empire and appeared to be on the verge of dividing up the Chinese heartland into separate spheres of influence. Only Japan responded with vigor and effectiveness, launching a comprehensive reform program that by the end of the century transformed the island nation into an emerging member of the imperialist club.

When Europeans imposed their culture upon peoples they considered inferior, how did the conquered peoples respond? Initial attempts to expel the foreigners only led to devastating defeats at the hands of Westerners, whose industrial technology gave them modern weapons of war that could be used to crush the natives. Accustomed to rule by small elites, many native peoples then simply accepted their new governors, making Western colonial rule relatively easy. Others tried to counter foreign rule, but in different ways. Traditionalists sought to maintain their cultural traditions while modernizers believed that adoption of Western ways would enable them to reform their societies and subsequently challenge Western rule.

For advocates of change, Western ideas were a two-edged sword, a symbol of both oppression and liberation. Many Asian and African leaders resented Western attitudes of superiority and demanded human dignity for the indigenous people, but they nevertheless adopted the West's own ideologies for change. Liberalism, with its parliamentary institutions and doctrine of civil rights and political self-determination, and nationalism, with its emphasis on the right of peoples to have their own nations, were used to foster independence movements wherever native people suffered under foreign oppression.

Modern nationalism, of course, had developed first in Europe during the French Revolution, and it proved to be an especially powerful force. But its political orientation varied according to time and place. In the first half of the nineteenth century, nationalism in Europe was closely identified with liberals who pursued both individual rights and national unification and independence. Liberal nationalists maintained that unified, independent nation-states could best preserve individual rights.

After the unification of Italy and Germany in 1871, however, nationalism entered a new stage of development. The new nationalism of the late nineteenth century, tied to conservatism, was loud and chauvinistic. As one exponent expressed it, "a true nationalist places his country above everything"; he believes in the "exclusive pursuit of national policies" and "the steady increase in national power—for a nation declines when it loses military might." But while the national aspirations of European powers led them to acquire colonies abroad, the colonists soon learned the power of nationalism, and in the twentieth century, nationalism would become a powerful force in the rest of the world as nationalist revolutions moved through Asia, Africa, and the Middle East.

By 1945, the era of European hegemony over world affairs was severely shaken. As World War I was followed by revolutions, the

Great Depression, the mass murder machines of totalitarian regimes, and the destructiveness of World War II, it appeared to many that European civilization had become a nightmare. Europeans, who had been accustomed to dominating the world at the beginning of the twentieth century, now watched helplessly at mid-century as the two new superpowers—the United States and the Soviet Union—created by their two world wars took control of their destinies. Moreover, the power of the European states had been destroyed by the exhaustive struggles of World War II, and the colonial powers no longer had the energy or wealth to maintain their colonial empires after the war. With the decline of Western power, a new era of global relationships was about to begin.

CHAPTER
20

The Beginnings of Modernization: Industrialization and Nationalism, 1800–1870

In September 1814, hundreds of foreigners began to converge on Vienna, the capital city of the Austrian Empire. Many were members of European royalty—kings, archdukes, princes, and their wives—accompanied by their diplomatic advisers and scores of servants. Their congenial host was the Austrian emperor Francis I, who never tired of providing Vienna's guests with concerts, glittering balls, sumptuous feasts, and an endless array of hunting parties. One participant remembered, "Eating, fireworks, public illuminations. For eight or ten days, I haven't been able to work at all. What a life!" Of course, not every waking hour was spent in pleasure during this gathering of notables, known to history as the Congress of Vienna. These people were also representatives of all the states that had fought Napoleon, and their real business was to arrange a final peace settlement after almost a decade of war. On June 8, 1815, they finally completed their task.

The forces of upheaval unleashed during the French revolutionary and Napoleonic eras were temporarily quieted in 1815 as monarchs sought to restore stability by reestablishing much of the old order to a Europe ravaged by war. Kings and landed and bureaucratic elites regained their control over domestic governments while internationally the forces of conservatism attempted to maintain the new status quo. But the Western world had been changed, and it would not readily go back to the old system. New ideologies of change, espe-

Bolívar and San Martín lead Latin American
independence movements

Revolutions of 1848

Congress of Vienna

American Civil War

Beginning of Industrial
Revolution in Britain

Stephenson's *Rocket*

Emancipation of Russian serfs

Chadwick's report on cities

Romantic poetry: Wordsworth

Charles Darwin, *On the Origin of Species*

Beethoven, Ninth Symphony   Realism: Dickens

cially liberalism and nationalism, products of the revolutionary upheaval initiated in France, had become too powerful to be contained forever. Not content with the status quo, the forces of change called forth revolts and revolutions that periodically shook the West in the 1820s and 1830s and culminated in the widespread revolutions of 1848. Some of the revolutions and revolutionaries were successful; most were not. And yet within twenty-five years, many of the goals sought by the liberals and nationalists during the first half of the nineteenth century seemed to have been achieved. National unity became a reality in Italy and Germany while many Western states developed constitutional-parliamentary features.

Reinforcing the forces unleashed by the French Revolution were the changes wrought by the Industrial Revolution. The Industrial Revolution transformed the economic and social structure of Europe and led Western civilization into the industrial era that has characterized the modern world.

The Industrial Revolution and Its Impact

The period of the Industrial Revolution witnessed a quantum leap in industrial production. New sources of energy and power, especially coal and steam, replaced wind and water to create machines that dramatically decreased the use of human and animal labor and, at the same time, increased the level of productivity. New ways of organizing human labor were required, in turn, to maximize the benefits and profits from the new machines; accordingly, factories replaced shop and home workrooms. Farming very gradually lost its place as the largest employer of labor. During the Industrial Revolution, Europe experienced a shift from a traditional, labor-intensive economy based on agriculture and handicrafts to a more capital-intensive economy based on manufacturing by machines, specialized labor, and industrial factories.

Although the Industrial Revolution took decades to spread, it was truly revolutionary in that it fundamentally changed Europeans, their society, their relationship to other peoples, and the world itself. The development of large factories encouraged mass movements of people from the countryside to urban areas where impersonal coexistence replaced the traditional intimacy of rural life. Higher levels of productivity led to a search for new sources of raw materials, new consumption patterns, and a revolution in transportation that allowed raw materials and finished products to be moved quickly around the world. The creation of a wealthy industrial middle class and a huge industrial working class (or proletariat) substantially transformed traditional social relationships.

Finally, the Industrial Revolution fundamentally altered how people related to nature, ultimately producing an environmental crisis that in the twentieth century has finally been recognized as a danger to human existence itself.

The Industrial Revolution in Great Britain

The Industrial Revolution had its beginnings in Britain in the 1780s. A number of factors or conditions coalesced there to produce the first Industrial Revolution. The agricultural revolution of the eighteenth century led to a significant increase in food production. British agriculture could now feed more people at lower prices with less labor; even ordinary British families did not have to use most of their income to buy food, giving them the potential to purchase manufactured goods. At the same time, the rapid growth of population in the second half of the eighteenth century provided a pool of surplus labor for the new factories of the emerging British industry.

Britain had a ready supply of capital for investment in the new industrial machines and the factories that were needed to house them. In addition to profits from trade and cottage industry, Britain possessed an effective central bank and well-developed, flexible credit facilities. Many early factory owners were merchants and entrepreneurs who had profited from eighteenth-century cottage industry. But capital alone is only part of the story. Britain also had a fair number of individuals who were interested in making profits if the opportunity presented itself. The British were a people, as one historian has said, "fascinated by wealth and commerce, collectively and individually."

Britain was richly supplied with important mineral resources, such as coal and iron ore, needed in the manufacturing process. Britain was also a small country, and the relatively short distances made transportation facilities readily accessible. In addition to nature's provision of abundant rivers, from the mid-seventeenth century onward, both private and public investment poured into the construction of new roads, bridges, and canals. By 1780, roads, rivers, and canals linked the major industrial centers of the North, the Midlands, London, and the Atlantic coast.

Finally, a supply of markets gave British industrialists a ready outlet for their manufactured goods. British exports quadrupled between 1660 and 1760. In the course of its eighteenth-century wars and conquests, Great Britain had developed a vast colonial empire at the expense of its leading continental rivals, the Dutch Republic and France. Britain also possessed a well-developed merchant marine that was able to transport goods to any place in the world. A crucial factor in Britain's successful industrialization was the ability to produce cheaply those articles most in demand abroad. And the best markets abroad were not in Europe, where countries protected their own incipient industries, but in the Americas, Africa, and the Far East, where people wanted sturdy, inexpensive clothes rather than costly, highly finished, luxury items. Britain's machine-produced textiles fulfilled that demand. Nor should we overlook the British domestic market. Britain had the highest standard of living in Europe and a rapidly growing population. It was the demand from both domestic and foreign markets and the inability of the old system to meet it that led entrepreneurs to seek and accept the new methods of manufacturing that a series of inventions provided. In so doing, these individuals produced the Industrial Revolution.

TECHNOLOGICAL CHANGES AND NEW FORMS OF INDUSTRIAL ORGANIZATION

Already in the eighteenth century, Great Britain had surged ahead in the production of cheap cotton goods using the traditional methods of cottage industry. The development of the flying shuttle had sped the process of weaving on a loom and enabled weavers to double their output. This, however, created shortages of yarn until James Hargreaves's spinning jenny, perfected by 1768, allowed spinners to produce yarn in greater quantities. Edmund Cartwright's power loom, invented in 1787, allowed the weaving of cloth to catch up with the spinning of yarn and presented new opportunities to entrepreneurs. It was much more efficient to bring workers to the machines and organize their labor collectively in factories located next to rivers and streams, the sources of power for many of these early machines. The concentration of labor in the new factories also brought the laborers and their families to live in the new towns that rapidly grew up around the factories.

The cotton industry was pushed to even greater heights of productivity by the invention of the steam engine, which played a major role in the Industrial Revolution. It revolutionized the production of cotton goods and caused the factory system to spread to other areas of production, thereby creating whole new industries. The steam engine secured the triumph of the Industrial Revolution.

In the 1760s, a Scottish engineer, James Watt (1736–1819), devised an engine powered by steam that could pump water from mines three times as quickly as previous engines. In 1782, Watt enlarged the possibilities

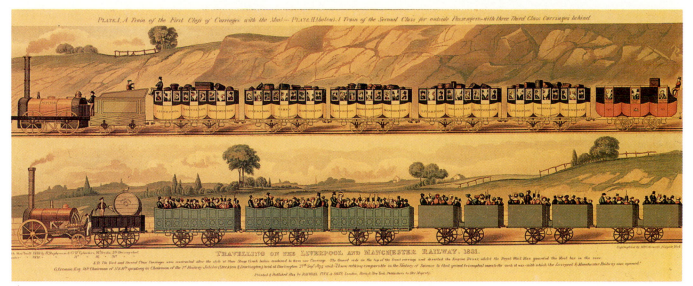

♦ **Railroad Line from Liverpool to Manchester.** The railroad line from Liverpool to Manchester, first opened in 1830, relied on steam locomotives. As is evident in this illustration, carrying passengers was the railroad's main business. First-class passengers rode in covered cars; second- and third-class passengers in open cars.

of the steam engine when he developed a rotary engine that could turn a shaft and thus drive machinery. Steam power could now be applied to spinning and weaving cotton, and before long cotton mills using steam engines were multiplying across Britain. Because steam engines were fired by coal, they did not have to be located near rivers, giving entrepreneurs greater flexibility in choosing sites for their factories.

The new boost given to cotton textile production by technological changes was readily apparent. In 1760, Britain had imported 2.5 million pounds of raw cotton, which was farmed out to cottage industries. In 1787, the British imported 22 million pounds of cotton; most of it was spun on machines, some powered by water in large mills. By 1840, 366 million pounds of cotton—now Britain's most important product in value—were imported annually, much of it from the American South where it was grown by slaves. By this time, most cotton industry employees worked in factories. The cheapest labor in India could not compete in quality or quantity with British workers. British cotton goods sold everywhere in the world.

The steam engine proved invaluable to Britain's Industrial Revolution. Unlike horses, the steam engine was a tireless source of power and depended for fuel on a substance—namely, coal—that seemed then to be available in unlimited quantities. The popular saying that "Steam is an Englishman" had real significance by 1850. The success of the steam engine increased the demand for coal and led to an expansion in coal production; between 1815 and 1850, the output of coal quadrupled. In turn, new processes using coal furthered the development of an iron industry.

The British iron industry was radically transformed during the Industrial Revolution. Britain had large resources of iron ore, but at the beginning of the eighteenth century, the basic process of producing iron had altered little since the Middle Ages and still depended heavily on charcoal. In the early eighteenth century, new methods of smelting iron ore to produce cast iron were devised based on the use of coke derived from coal. A better quality of iron was still not possible, however, until the 1780s when Henry Cort developed a system called puddling, in which coke was used to burn away impurities in pig iron and produce an iron of high quality. A boom then ensued in the British iron industry. In 1740, Britain produced 17,000 tons of iron; by the 1840s, over two million tons; and by 1852, almost three million tons, more than the rest of the world combined.

The high-quality wrought iron produced by the Cort process encouraged the growth of machinery in other industries, most noticeably in such new means of transportation as steamboats and railroads. In 1804, Richard Trevithick pioneered the first steam-powered locomotive on an industrial rail-line in south Wales. It pulled ten tons of ore and seventy people at five miles per hour. Better locomotives soon followed. The engines built by George Stephenson and his son proved superior, and it was in their workshops in Newcastle upon Tyne that the locomotives for the first modern railways in Britain were built. George Stephenson's *Rocket* was used on the first public railway line, which opened in 1830, extending thirty-two miles from Liverpool to Manchester. *Rocket* sped along at sixteen miles per hour. Within twenty years, locomotives had reached fifty miles per hour, an incredible speed to contemporary passengers. During the same period, new companies were formed to build additional railroads as the infant industry proved to be not only technically but financially successful. In 1840, Britain had almost 2,000 miles of railroads; by 1850, 6,000 miles of railroad track crisscrossed much of the country.

The railroad was an important element in the success and maturing of the Industrial Revolution. The demands of railroads for coal and iron furthered the growth of those industries. Railway construction created new job opportunities, especially for farm laborers and peasants who had long been accustomed to finding work outside their local villages. Perhaps most importantly, the cheaper and faster means of transportation provided by the railroads had a rippling effect on the industrial economy. Reductions in the price of goods created larger markets; increased sales meant more factories and more machinery, thereby reinforcing the self-sustaining aspect of the Industrial Revolution that marked a fundamental break with the traditional European economy. The great productivity of the Industrial Revolution enabled entrepreneurs to reinvest their profits in new capital equipment, further expanding the productive capacity of the economy. Continuous, even rapid, self-sustaining economic growth came to be seen as a fundamental characteristic of the new industrial economy.

The railroad was the perfect symbol of this aspect of the Industrial Revolution. The ability to transport goods and people at dramatic speeds also provided visible confirmation of a new sense of power. When railway engineers pierced mountains with tunnels and spanned chasms with breathtaking bridges, contemporaries experienced a sense of power over nature not felt before in civilization.

Another visible symbol of the Industrial Revolution was the factory, which became the chief means of organizing labor for the new machines. From its beginning, the factory system demanded a new type of discipline from its employees. Once factory owners purchased machinery, it had to be used constantly to enable them to profit from their investment. Workers were forced to work regular hours and in shifts to keep the machines producing at a steady pace for maximum output. This represented a massive adjustment for the first factory laborers.

Pre-industrial workers were not accustomed to a "timed" format. Agricultural laborers had always kept irregular hours; hectic work at harvest time might be followed by periods of inactivity. Even in the burgeoning cottage industry of the eighteenth century, wool weavers and spinners who worked at home might fulfill their weekly quotas by working around the clock for two or three days and then proceed at a leisurely pace until the next week's demands forced another work spurt.

Factory owners, therefore, faced a formidable task. They had to create a system of work discipline in which employees became accustomed to working regular, unvarying hours during which they performed a set number of tasks over and over again as efficiently as possible. One early industrialist said that his aim was "to make such machines of the men as cannot err." Such work, of course, tended to be repetitive and boring, and factory owners resorted to tough methods to accomplish their goals. Factory regulations were minute and detailed (see the box on p. 737). Adult workers were fined for a wide variety of minor infractions, such as being a few minutes late for work, and dismissed for more serious offenses, especially drunkenness. The latter was viewed as particularly offensive because it set a bad example for younger workers and also courted disaster in the midst of dangerous machinery. Employers found that dismissals and fines worked well for adult employees; in a time when great population growth had produced large masses of unskilled labor, dismissal meant disaster. Children were less likely to understand the implications of dismissal so they were sometimes disciplined more directly—by beating. In one crucial sense, the efforts of the early industrialists proved successful. As the nineteenth century progressed, the second and third generations of workers came to view a regular working week as a natural way of life. It was, of course, an attitude that made possible Britain's incredible economic growth in that century.

By the mid-nineteenth century, Great Britain had become the world's first and richest industrial nation. Britain was the "workshop, banker, and trader of the world." It produced half of the world's coal and manufactured goods; in 1850, its cotton industry alone was equal in size to the industries of all other European countries combined. No doubt, Britain's certainty about its mission in the world in the nineteenth century was grounded in its incredible material success story.

❧ *Discipline in the New Factories* ❧

Workers in the new factories of the Industrial Revolution had been accustomed to a lifestyle free of overseers. Unlike the cottages, where workers spun thread and wove cloth in their own rhythm and time, the factories demanded a new, rigorous discipline geared to the requirements of the machines. This selection is taken from a set of rules for a factory in Berlin in 1844. They were typical of company rules everywhere the factory system had been established.

The Foundry and Engineering Works of the Royal Overseas Trading Company, Factory Rules

In every large works, and in the co-ordination of any large number of workmen, good order and harmony must be looked upon as the fundamentals of success, and therefore the following rules shall be strictly observed.

1. The normal working day begins at all seasons at 6 A.M. precisely and ends, after the usual break of half an hour for breakfast, an hour for dinner and half an hour for tea, at 7 P.M., and it shall be strictly observed. . . .
2. Workers arriving 2 minutes late shall lose half an hour's wages; whoever is more than 2 minutes late may not start work until after the next break, or at least shall lose his wages until then. Any disputes about the correct time shall be settled by the clock mounted above the gatekeeper's lodge. . . .
3. No workman, whether employed by time or piece, may leave before the end of the working day, without having first received permission from the overseer and having given his name to the gatekeeper. Omission of these two actions shall lead to a fine of ten silver groschen [pennies] payable to the sick fund.
4. Repeated irregular arrival at work shall lead to dismissal. This shall also apply to those who are found idling by an official or overseer, and refused to obey their order to resume work. . . .
6. No worker may leave his place of work otherwise than for reasons connected with his work.
7. All conversation with fellow-workers is prohibited; if any worker requires information about his work, he must turn to the overseer, or to the particular fellow-worker designated for the purpose.
8. Smoking in the workshops or in the yard is prohibited during working hours; anyone caught smoking shall be fined five silver groschen for the sick fund for every such offense. . . .
10. Natural functions must be performed at the appropriate places, and whoever is found soiling walls, fences, squares, etc., and similarly, whoever is found washing his face and hands in the workshop and not in the places assigned for the purpose, shall be fined five silver groschen for the sick fund. . . .
12. It goes without saying that all overseers and officials of the firm shall be obeyed without question, and shall be treated with due deference. Disobedience will be punished by dismissal.
13. Immediate dismissal shall also be the fate of anyone found drunk in any of the workshops. . . .
14. Every workman is obliged to report to his superiors any acts of dishonesty or embezzlement on the part of his fellow workmen. If he omits to do so, and it is shown after subsequent discovery of a misdemeanor that he knew about it at the time, he shall be liable to be taken to court as an accessory after the fact and the wage due to him shall be retained as punishment.

The Spread of Industrialization

Beginning first in Great Britain, industrialization spread to the continental countries of Europe and the United States at different times and speeds during the nineteenth century. First to be industrialized on the Continent were Belgium, France, and the German states and in North America, the new nation of the United States.

Not until after 1850 did the Industrial Revolution spread to the rest of Europe and other parts of the world.

Industrialization on the Continent faced numerous hurdles, and as it proceeded in earnest after 1815, it did so along lines that were somewhat different from Britain's. Lack of technical knowledge was a first major obstacle to industrialization. But the continental countries possessed an advantage here; they could simply borrow British techniques and practices. Gradually, however, the Continent achieved technological independence as local people learned all the skills they could from their British teachers. By the 1840s, a new generation of skilled mechanics from Belgium and France was spreading technological knowledge east and south. More importantly, continental countries, especially France and the German states, began to establish a wide range of technical schools to train engineers and mechanics.

That government played an important role in this regard brings us to a second difference between British and continental industrialization. Governments on much of the Continent were accustomed to playing a significant role in economic affairs. Furthering the development of industrialization was a logical extension of that attitude. Hence governments provided for the costs of technical education; awarded grants to inventors and foreign entrepreneurs; exempted foreign industrial equipment from import duties; and, in some places, even financed factories. Of equal if not greater importance in the long run, governments actively bore much of the cost of building roads and canals, deepening and widening river channels, and constructing railroads. By 1850, a network of iron rails had spread across Europe, although only Germany and Belgium had completed major parts of their systems by that time.

Map 20.1 The Industrialization of Europe by 1850.

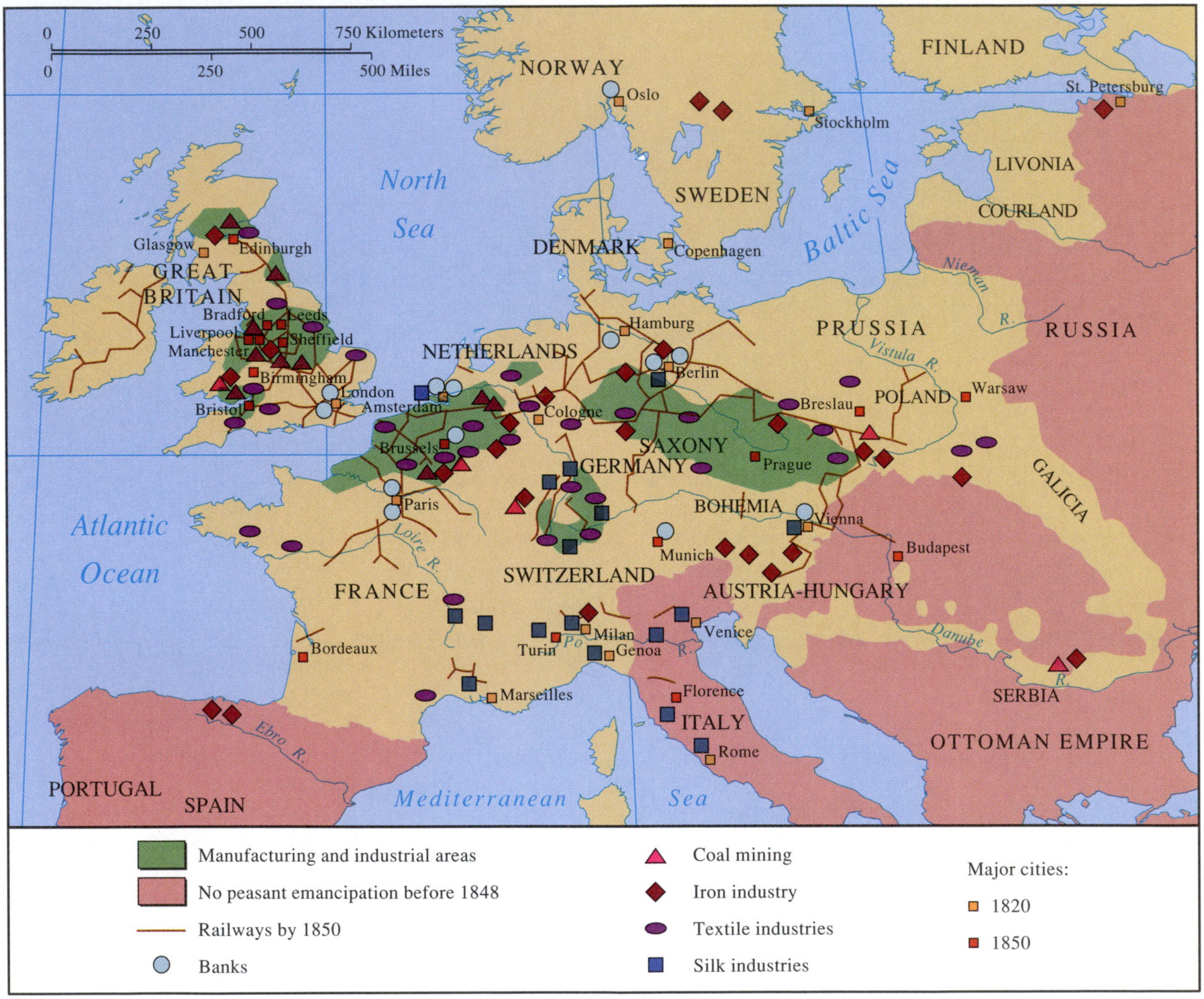

Like Belgium, France, and the German states, the United States experienced an industrial revolution and the urbanization that accompanied it during the first half of the nineteenth century. In 1800, society in the United States was agrarian. There were no cities over 100,000, and six out of every seven American workers were farmers. By 1860, the population had grown from 5 to 30 million people, larger than Great Britain. Almost half of them lived west of the Appalachian Mountains. There were now thirty-four instead of sixteen states, and nine American cities had populations over 100,000. Only 50 percent of American workers were farmers.

The initial application of machinery to production was accomplished—as it had been in continental Europe—by borrowing from Great Britain. Soon, however, Americans began to equal or surpass British technical inventions. The Harpers Ferry arsenal, for example, built muskets with interchangeable parts. Because all the individual parts of a musket were identical (e.g., all triggers were the same), the final product could be put together quickly and easily; this enabled Americans to avoid the more costly system in which skilled craftsmen fitted together individual parts made separately. The so-called American system reduced costs and revolutionized production by saving labor, an important consideration in a society that had few skilled artisans.

Unlike Britain, the United States was a large country. The lack of a good system of internal transportation seemed to limit American economic development by making the transport of goods prohibitively expensive. This was gradually remedied, however. Thousands of miles of roads and canals were built linking east and west. The steamboat facilitated transportation on the Great Lakes, Atlantic coastal waters, and rivers. It was especially important to the Mississippi valley; by 1860, a thousand steamboats plied that river (see the box on p. 740). Most important of all in the development of an American transportation system was the railroad. Beginning with 100 miles in 1830, by 1860 there were over 27,000 miles of railroad track covering the United States. This transportation revolution turned the United States into a single massive market for the manufactured goods of the Northeast, the early center of American industrialization.

Labor for the growing number of factories in this area came primarily from rural New England. The United States did not possess a large number of craftsmen, but it did have a rapidly expanding farm population; its size in the Northeast soon outstripped the available farmland. While some of this excess population, especially men, went west, others, mostly women, found work in the new textile and shoe factories of New England. Indeed, women made up more than 80 percent of the laboring force in the large textile factories. In Massachusetts mill towns, company boarding houses provided rooms for large numbers of young women who worked for several years before marriage. Outside Massachusetts, factory owners sought entire families including children to work in their mills; one mill owner ran this advertisement in a newspaper in Utica, New York: "Wanted: A few sober and industrious families of at least five children each, over the age of eight years, are wanted at the Cotton Factory in Whitestown. Widows with large families would do well to attend this notice." When a decline in rural births threatened to dry up this labor pool in the 1830s and 1840s, European immigrants, especially poor and unskilled Irish, English, Scottish, and Welsh, appeared in large numbers to replace American women and children in the factories.

By 1860, the United States was well on its way to being an industrial nation. In the Northeast, the most industrialized section of the country, per capita income was 40 percent higher than the national average. Diets, it has been argued, were better and more varied; machine-made clothing was more abundant. Nevertheless, despite a growing belief in a myth of social mobility based upon equality of economic opportunity, the reality was that the richest 10 percent of the population in the cities held 70 to 80 percent of the wealth compared to 50 percent in 1800. Nevertheless, American historians generally argue that while the rich got richer, increased purchasing power at least prevented the poor from getting poorer.

The Social Impact of the Industrial Revolution

Eventually, the Industrial Revolution revolutionized the social life of Europe and the world. Although much of Europe remained bound by its traditional ways, already in the first half of the nineteenth century, the social impact of the Industrial Revolution was being felt, and future avenues of growth were becoming apparent. Vast changes in the numbers of people and where they lived were already dramatically evident.

POPULATION GROWTH AND URBANIZATION

Population increases had already begun in the eighteenth century, but they became dramatic in the nineteenth century. In 1750, the total European population stood at an estimated 140 million; by 1800, it had increased to 187 million, and by 1850, the population had almost doubled since 1750 to 266 million. The key to the rise in

≋ S–t–e–a–m–Boat a–Comin'!" ≋

Steamboats and railroads were crucial elements in a transportation revolution that enabled industrialists to expand markets by shipping goods cheaply and efficiently. At the same time, these marvels of technology aroused a sense of power and excitement that was an important aspect of the triumph of industrialization. The American novelist Mark Twain captured this sense of excitement in this selection from Life on the Mississippi.

Mark Twain, *Life on the Mississippi*

After all these years I can picture that old time to myself now, just as it was then: the white town drowsing in the sunshine of a summer's morning; the streets empty, or pretty nearly so; one or two clerks sitting in front of the Water Street stores, with their splint-bottomed chairs tilted back against the wall, chins on breasts, hats slouched over their faces, asleep; . . . two or three lonely little freight piles scattered about the "levee"; a pile of "skids" on the slope of the stone-paved wharf, and the fragrant town drunkard asleep in the shadow of them; . . . the great Mississippi, the majestic, the magnificent Mississippi, rolling its mile-wide tide along, shining in the sun; the dense forest away on the other side; the "point" above the town, and the "point" below, bounding the river-glimpse and turning it into a sort of sea, and withal a very still and brilliant and lonely one. Presently a film of dark smoke appears above one of those remote "points"; instantly a Negro drayman, famous for his quick eye and prodigious voice, lifts up the cry, "S–t–e–a–m–boat a–comin'!" and the scene changes! The town drunkard stirs, the clerks wake up, a furious clatter of drays follows, every house and store pours out a human contribution, and all in a twinkling the dead town [Hannibal, Missouri] is alive and moving. Drays, carts, men, boys, all go hurrying from many quarters to a common center, the wharf. Assembled there, the people fasten their eyes upon the coming boat as upon a wonder they are seeing for the first time. And the boat *is* rather a handsome sight, too. She is long and sharp and trim and pretty; she has two tall, fancy-topped chimneys, with a gilded device of some kind swung between them; a fanciful pilot-house, all glass and "gingerbread," perched on top of the "texas" deck behind them; the paddle-boxes are gorgeous with a picture or with gilded rays above the boat's name; the boiler deck, the hurricane deck, and the texas deck are fenced and ornamented with clean white railings; there is a flag gallantly flying from the jack-staff; the furnace doors are open and the fires glaring bravely; the upper decks are black with passengers; the captain stands by the big bell, calm, imposing, the envy of all; great volumes of the blackest smoke are rolling and tumbling out of the chimneys—a husbanded grandeur created with a bit of pitch pine just before arriving at a town; the crew are grouped on the forecastle; the broad stage is run far out over the port bow, and an envied deck-hand stands picturesquely on the end of it with a coil of rope in his hand; the pent steam is screaming through the gauge-cocks; the captain lifts his hand, a bell rings, the wheels stop; then they turn back, churning the water to foam, and the steamer is at rest. Then such a scramble as there is to get aboard, and to get ashore, and to take in freight and to discharge freight, all at one and the same time; and such a yelling and cursing as the mates facilitate it all with! Ten minutes later the steamer is under way again, with no flag on the jack-staff and no black smoke issuing from the chimneys. After ten more minutes the town is dead again, and the town drunkard asleep by the skids once more.

---

population was the decline in death rates evident throughout Europe. There was a drop in the number of deaths from famines, epidemics, and war. Major epidemic diseases in particular, such as plague and smallpox, declined noticeably, although small-scale epidemics continued. There was also a decline in the ordinary death rate as a general increase in the food supply, already evident in the agricultural revolution of Britain in the late eighteenth century, spread to more areas. More food enabled a greater number of people to be better fed and therefore more resistant to disease. Famine largely disappeared from western Europe, although there were dramatic exceptions in isolated areas where overpopulation magnified the already existing problem of rural poverty. In Ireland, it produced the century's great catastrophe.

Irish peasants lived in mud hovels in desperate poverty. Cultivation of the potato, a nutritious and relatively easy food to grow that produced three times as much food per acre as grain, gave the peasants a basic staple that enabled them to survive and even expand in numbers. Between 1781 and 1845, the Irish population doubled from four to eight million. Probably half of this population depended on the potato for survival. In the summer of 1845, the potato crop in Ireland was struck by blight in the form of a fungus that turned the potatoes black. Between 1845 and 1851, the Great Famine decimated the Irish population. Over one million died of starvation and disease while almost two million emigrated to the United States and Britain. Of all the European nations, only Ireland had a declining population in the nineteenth century.

The flight of so many Irish to America reminds us that the traditional safety valve for overpopulation has always been emigration. Between 1821 and 1850, the number of emigrants from Europe averaged about 110,000 a year. More often than emigrating, however, the rural masses sought a solution to their poverty by moving to towns and cities within their own countries to find work. It should not astonish us then that the first half of the nineteenth century was a period of rapid urbanization.

Cities and towns grew dramatically in the first half of the nineteenth century, a phenomenon related to industrialization. Cities had traditionally been centers for princely courts, government and military offices, churches, and commerce. By 1850, especially in Great Britain and Belgium, they were rapidly becoming places for manufacturing and industry. With the steam engine, entrepreneurs could locate their manufacturing plants in urban centers where they had ready access to transportation facilities and unemployed people from the country looking for work.

In 1800, Great Britain had one major city, London, with a population of one million, and six cities between 50,000 and 100,000. Fifty years later, London's population had swelled to 2,363,000 while there were nine cities over 100,000 and eighteen cities with populations between 50,000 and 100,000. When the populations of cities under 50,000 are added to these, we realize that over 50 percent of the British population lived in towns and cities by 1850. Urban populations also grew on the Continent, but less dramatically.

The dramatic growth of cities in the first half of the nineteenth century produced miserable living conditions for many of the inhabitants. Of course, this had been true for centuries in European cities, but the rapid urbanization associated with the Industrial Revolution intensified the problems in the first half of the nineteenth century and made these appalling living conditions all the more apparent. Wealthy, middle-class inhabitants, as usual, insulated themselves as best they could, often living in suburbs or the outer ring of the city where they could have

♦ **A New Industrial Town.** Cities and towns grew dramatically in Britain in the first half of the nineteenth century, largely as a result of industrialization. Pictured here is Saltaire, a model textile factory and town founded near Bradford by Titus Salt in 1851. To facilitate the transportation of goods, the town was built on the Leeds and Liverpool canals.

individual houses and gardens. In the inner ring of the city stood the small row houses, some with gardens, of the artisans and lower middle class. Finally, located in the center of most industrial towns were the row houses of the industrial workers. This report on working-class housing in the British city of Birmingham in 1843 gives an idea of the general conditions they faced:

The courts [of working class row houses] are extremely numerous; . . . a very large portion of the poorer classes of the inhabitants reside in them. . . . The courts vary in the number of the houses which they contain, from four to twenty, and most of these houses are three stories high, and built, as it is termed, back to back. There is a washhouse, an ash-pit, and a privy at the end, or on one side of the court, and not unfrequently one or more pigsties and heaps of manure. Generally speaking, the privies in the old courts are in a most filthy condition. Many which we have inspected were in a state which renders it impossible for us to conceive how they could be used; they were without doors and overflowing with filth.

Rooms were not large and were frequently overcrowded, as this government report of 1838 revealed: "I entered several of the tenements. In one of them, on the ground floor, I found six persons occupying a very small room, two in bed, ill with fever. In the room above this were two more persons in one bed, ill with fever." Another report said: "There were 63 families where there were at least five persons to one bed; and there were some in which even six were packed in one bed, lying at the top and bottom—children and adults."[1]

Sanitary conditions in these towns were appalling. Due to the lack of municipal direction, sewers and open drains were common on city streets: "In the center of this street is a gutter, into which potato parings, the refuse of animal and vegetable matters of all kinds, the dirty water from the washing of clothes and of the houses, are all poured, and there they stagnate and putrefy."[2] Unable to deal with human excrement, cities in the new industrial era smelled horrible and were extraordinarily unhealthy. Towns and cities were fundamentally death traps. As deaths outnumbered births in most large cities in the first half of the nineteenth century, only a constant influx of people from the country kept them alive and growing.

To many of the well-to-do middle classes, this situation presented a clear danger to society. Were not these masses of workers, sunk in crime, disease, and immorality, a potential threat to their own well-being? Might not the masses be organized and used by unscrupulous demagogues to overthrow the established order? Some observers, however, wondered if the workers could be held responsible for their fate. One of the best of a new breed of urban reformers was Edwin Chadwick (1800–1890). Chadwick became obsessed with eliminating the poverty and squalor of the metropolitan areas. As secretary of the Poor Law Commission, he initiated a passionate search for detailed facts about the living conditions of the working classes. After three years of investigation, Chadwick summarized the results in his *Report on the Condition of the Labouring Population of Great Britain*, published in 1842. In it he concluded that "the various forms of epidemic, endemic, and other disease" were directly caused by the "atmospheric impurities produced by decomposing animal and vegetable substances, by damp and filth, and close overcrowded dwellings [prevailing] amongst the population in every part of the kingdom." Such conditions, he argued, could be eliminated. As to the means: "The primary and most important measures, and at the same time the most practicable, and within the recognized province of public administration, are drainage, the removal of all refuse of habitations, streets, and roads, and the improvement of the supplies of water."[3] In other words, Chadwick was advocating a system of modern sanitary reforms including efficient sewers and a supply of piped water. Six years after his report and largely due to his efforts, Britain's first Public Health Act created a National Board of Health empowered to form local boards that would establish modern sanitary systems.

Fear of cholera convinced many middle-class citizens to support the public health reforms advocated by men like Chadwick. Outbreaks of this deadly disease ravaged Europe in the early 1830s and late 1840s and were especially rampant in overcrowded cities. As city authorities and wealthier residents became convinced that filthy conditions helped to spread the disease, they began to support the call for new public health measures.

NEW SOCIAL CLASSES

The rise of industrial capitalism produced a new industrial middle-class group. The bourgeois or middle class was not new; it had existed since the emergence of cities in the Middle Ages. Originally, the bourgeois was a burgher or town dweller, whether active as a merchant, official, artisan, lawyer, or man of letters, who enjoyed a special set of rights from the charter of his town. As wealthy townspeople bought land, the original meaning of the word *bourgeois* became lost, and the term came to include people involved in commerce, industry, and banking as well as professionals, such as lawyers, teachers, and physicians, and government officials at varying levels. At the lower end of the economic scale were master craftsmen and shopkeepers.

Lest we make the industrial middle class too much of an abstraction, we need to look at who the new industrial entrepreneurs actually were. These were the people who constructed the factories, purchased the machines, and figured out where the markets were. Their qualities included resourcefulness, single-mindedness, resolution, initiative, vision, ambition, and often, of course, greed. As Jedediah Strutt, a cotton manufacturer said, "Getting of money . . . is the main business of the life of men." But this was not an easy task. The early industrial entrepreneurs were called upon to superintend an enormous array of functions that are handled today by teams of managers; they raised capital, determined markets, set company objectives, organized the factory and its labor, and trained supervisors who could act for them. The opportunities for making money were great, but the risks were also tremendous.

By 1850, in Britain at least, the kind of traditional entrepreneurship that had created the Industrial Revolution was declining and was being replaced by a new business aristocracy. This new generation of entrepreneurs stemmed from the professional and industrial middle classes, especially as sons inherited the successful businesses established by their fathers. Increasingly, the new industrial entrepreneurs—the bankers and owners of factories and mines—came to amass much wealth and play an important role alongside the traditional landed elites of their societies. The Industrial Revolution began at a time when the pre-industrial agrarian world was still largely dominated by these landed elites. As the new bourgeoisie bought great estates and acquired social respectability, they also sought political power, and in the course of the nineteenth century, their wealthiest members would merge with those old elites.

At the same time that the members of the industrial middle class sought to reduce the barriers between themselves and the landed elite, they were also trying to separate themselves from the laboring classes below them. The working class was actually a mixture of different groups in the first half of the nineteenth century. In the course of the nineteenth century, factory workers would form an industrial proletariat, but in the first half of that century, they by no means constituted a majority of the working class in any major city, even in Britain. According to the 1851 census in Britain, while there were 1.8 million agricultural laborers and 1 million domestic servants, there were only 811,000 workers in the cotton and woolen industries. Even one-third of these were still working in small workshops or in their own homes.

Industrial workers faced wretched working conditions. In the early decades of the Industrial Revolution "places of work," as early factories were called, were dreadful. Work hours ranged from twelve to sixteen hours a day, six days a week, with half an hour for lunch and dinner. There was no security of employment and no minimum wage. The worst conditions were in the cotton mills where temperatures were especially debilitating. One report noted that "in the cotton-spinning work, these creatures are kept, fourteen hours in each day, locked up, summer and winter, in a heat of from eighty to eighty-four degrees." Mills were also dirty, dusty, and unhealthy:

> Not only is there not a breath of sweet air in these truly infernal scenes, but . . . there is the abominable and pernicious stink of the gas to assist in the murderous effects of the heat. In addition to the noxious effluvia of the gas, mixed with the steam, there are the dust, and what is called cotton-flyings or fuz, which the unfortunate creatures have to inhale; and . . . the notorious fact is that well constituted men are rendered old and past labour at forty years of age, and that children are rendered decrepit and deformed, and thousands upon thousands of them slaughtered by consumptions, before they arrive at the age of sixteen.[4]

Thus ran a report on working conditions in the cotton industry in 1824.

Conditions in the coal mines were also harsh. The introduction of steam power meant only that steam-powered engines mechanically lifted coal to the top. Inside the mines, men still bore the burden of digging the coal out while horses, mules, women, and children hauled coal carts on rails to the lift. Dangerous conditions abounded in coal mines; cave-ins, explosions, and gas fumes (called "bad air") were a way of life. The cramped conditions in the mines—tunnels often did not exceed three or four feet in height—and their constant dampness resulted in deformed bodies and ruined lungs.

Both children and women were employed in large numbers in early factories and mines. Children had been an important part of the family economy in pre-industrial times, working in the fields or carding and spinning wool at home with the growth of cottage industry. In the Industrial Revolution, however, child labor was exploited more than ever and in a considerably more systematic fashion (see the box on p. 744). The owners of cotton factories appreciated certain features of child labor. Children had a particular delicate touch as spinners of cotton. Their smaller size made it easier for them to move under machines to gather loose cotton. Moreover, children were more easily broken to factory work. Above all, children represented a cheap supply of labor. In 1821, 49 percent of the British people were under twenty years of age. Hence children made up a particularly abundant supply of labor, and they were paid only about one-sixth or one-third of what a man was paid. In the cotton factories in 1838,

◆ **Women in the Mines.** Both women and children were often employed in the early factories and mines of the nineteenth century. As is evident in this illustration of a woman dragging a cart loaded with coal behind her, they often worked under very trying conditions.

⇒ Child Labor: Discipline in the Textile Mills ⇐

Child labor was certainly not new, but in the early Industrial Revolution it was exploited more systematically. These selections are taken from the Report of Sadler's Committee, which was commissioned in 1832 to inquire into the condition of child factory workers.

How They Kept the Children Awake

It is a very frequent thing at Mr. Marshall's [at Shrewsbury] where the least children were employed (for there were plenty working at six years of age), for Mr. Horseman to start the mill earlier in the morning than he formerly did; and provided a child should be drowsy, the overlooker walks round the room with a stick in his hand, and he touches that child on the shoulder, and says, "Come here." In a corner of the room there is an iron cistern; it is filled with water; he takes this boy, and takes him up by the legs, and dips him over head in the cistern, and sends him to work for the remainder of the day. . . .

What means were taken to keep the children to their work?—Sometimes they would tap them over the head, or nip them over the nose, or give them a pinch of snuff, or throw water in their faces, or pull them off where they were, and job them about to keep them waking.

The Sadistic Overlooker

Samuel Downe, age 29, factory worker living near Leeds; at the age of about ten began work at Mr. Marshall's mill at Shrewsbury, where the customary hours when work was brisk were generally 5 A.M. to 8 P.M., sometimes from 5:30 A.M. to 8 or 9:

What means were taken to keep the children awake and vigilant, especially at the termination of such a day's labour as you have described?—There was generally a blow or a box, or a tap with a strap, or sometimes the hand.

Have you yourself been strapped?—Yes, most severely, till I could not bear to sit upon a chair without having pillows, and through that I left. I was strapped both on my own legs, and then I was put upon a man's back, and then strapped and buckled with two straps to an iron pillar, and flogged, and all by one overlooker; after that he took a piece of tow, and twisted it in the shape of a cord, and put it in my mouth, and tied it behind my head.

He gagged you?—Yes; and then he ordered me to run round a part of the machinery where he was overlooker, and he stood at one end, and every time I came there he struck me with a stick, which I believe was an ash plant, and which he generally carried in his hand, and sometimes he hit me, and sometimes he did not; and one of the men in the room came and begged me off, and that he let me go, and not beat me any more, and consequently he did.

You have been beaten with extraordinary severity?—Yes, I was beaten so that I had not power to cry at all, or hardly speak at one time. What age were you at that time?—Between 10 and 11.

---

children under eighteen made up 29 percent of the total workforce; children as young as seven worked twelve to fifteen hours per day six days a week in cotton mills.

By 1830, women and children made up two-thirds of the cotton industry's labor. As the number of children employed declined under the Factory Act of 1833, which established nine as the minimum work age, their places were taken by women, who came to dominate the labor forces of the early factories. Women made up 50 percent of the labor force in textile (cotton and woolen) factories before 1870. They were mostly unskilled labor and were paid half or less of what men received. Excessive working hours for women were outlawed in 1844, but only in textile factories and mines; not until 1867 were they outlawed in craft workshops.

The employment of children and women in large part represents a continuation of a pre-industrial kinship pattern. Cottage industry had always involved the efforts of the entire family, and it seemed perfectly natural to continue this pattern. Men migrating from the countryside to industrial towns and cities took their wives and children with them into the factory or into the mines. Of 136 employees in Robert Peel's factory at Bury in 1801, 95 belonged to twenty-six families. The impetus for this family work often came from the family itself. The factory owner Jedediah Strutt was opposed to child labor under ten but was forced by parents to take children as young as seven.

The employment of large numbers of women in factories did not produce a significant transformation in female working patterns, as was once assumed. Studies of urban households in France and Britain, for example, have revealed that throughout the nineteenth century traditional types of female labor still predominated in the women's work world. In 1851, fully 40 percent of the female workforce in Britain consisted of domestic servants. In France, the largest group of female workers, 40 percent, worked in agriculture. In addition, only 20 percent of female workers labored in Britain's factories, only 10 percent in France. Regional and local studies have also indicated that most of these workers were single women. Few married women worked outside their homes.

The Factory Acts that limited the work hours of children and women also began to break up the traditional kinship pattern of work and led to a new pattern based on a separation of work and home. Men came to be expected to be responsible for the primary work obligations while women assumed daily control of the family and performed low-paying jobs such as laundry work that could be done in the home. Domestic industry made it possible for women to continue their contributions to family survival.

Reaction and Revolution: The Growth of Nationalism

During the first half of the nineteenth century, liberals and nationalists attempted—generally unsuccessfully—to overthrow many of the authoritarian governments that had been reestablished after the defeat of Napoleon. The failure of liberals and nationalists in the revolutions between 1820 and 1848 did not mean the demise of liberalism and nationalism, however. After 1850, a new generation of conservative leaders made use of both ideologies to cement their power and achieve nationalist goals. Because of their efforts between 1850 and 1871, the national state increasingly became the focus of people's loyalties.

The Conservative Order

The immediate response to the defeat of Napoleon was the desire to contain revolution and the revolutionary forces by restoring much of the old order. This was the goal of the great powers—Great Britain, Austria, Prussia, and Russia—when they met at a congress in Vienna in

✖ **Map 20.2**   Europe after the Congress of Vienna.

September 1814 to arrange a final peace settlement after the Napoleonic wars. The congress was dominated by the Austrian foreign minister, Prince Klemens von Metternich (1773–1859), who claimed that he was guided at Vienna by the principle of legitimacy. To reestablish peace and stability in Europe, he considered it necessary to restore the legitimate monarchs who would preserve traditional institutions. This had already been done in France with the restoration of the Bourbons, but elsewhere the principle of legitimacy was in fact largely ignored and completely overshadowed by more practical considerations of power. The great powers all grabbed lands to add to their states. In making these territorial rearrangements, the powers at Vienna believed they were following the familiar eighteenth-century practice of maintaining a balance of power or equilibrium among the great powers. Essentially, this meant a balance of political and military forces that guaranteed the independence of the great powers by ensuring that no one country could dominate Europe. For example, to balance Russian gains, Prussia and Austria had been strengthened. According to Metternich, this arrangement had clearly avoided a great danger: "Prussia and Austria are completing their systems of defense; united, the two monarchies form an unconquerable barrier against the enterprises of any conquering prince who might perhaps once again occupy the throne of France or that of Russia."[5]

The Vienna peace settlement of 1815 has sometimes been criticized for its failure to recognize the liberal and national forces unleashed by the French revolutionary and Napoleonic eras. But containing these revolutionary forces was precisely what the diplomats at Vienna hoped to achieve. Their transfers of territories and peoples to the victors to create a new balance of power, with little or no regard for the wishes of the people themselves, were in accord with long-standing European diplomatic traditions. One could hardly expect Metternich, foreign minister of the Austrian Empire, a dynastic state composed of many different peoples, to espouse a principle of self-determination for European nationalities. Whatever its weaknesses, the Congress of Vienna has received credit for establishing a European order that managed to avoid a general European conflict for almost a hundred years.

The peace arrangements of 1815 were but the beginning of a conservative reaction determined to contain the liberal and nationalist forces unleashed by the French Revolution. Metternich and his kind were representatives of the ideology known as conservatism. Most conservatives favored obedience to political authority, believed that organized religion was crucial to social order, hated revolutionary upheavals, and were unwilling to accept either the liberal demands for civil liberties and representative governments or the nationalistic aspirations generated by the French revolutionary era. The community took precedence over individual rights; society must be organized and ordered, and tradition remained the best guide for order. After 1815, the political philosophy of conservatism was supported by hereditary monarchs, government bureaucracies, landowning aristocracies, and revived churches, be they Protestant or Catholic. Although not unopposed, both internationally and domestically the conservative forces appeared dominant after 1815.

One method used by the great powers to maintain the new status quo they had constructed was the Concert of Europe, according to which Great Britain, Russia, Prussia, and Austria (and later France) agreed to meet periodically in conferences to discuss their common interests and examine measures that "will be judged most salutary for the repose and prosperity of peoples, and for the maintenance of peace in Europe." Eventually, the great powers adopted a principle of intervention, which meant that they claimed the right to use force to restore legitimate monarchs who had been toppled from their thrones by revolutions. Britain refused to agree to the principle, arguing that it had never been the intention of the great powers to interfere in the internal affairs of other states. Ignoring the British position, Austria, Prussia, Russia, and France used military intervention to defeat revolutionary movements in Spain and Italy and to restore legitimate (and conservative) monarchs to their thrones.

Revolutionary Outbursts

Between 1815 and 1830, the conservative domination of Europe evident in the Concert of Europe was also apparent in domestic affairs as conservative governments throughout Europe worked to maintain the old order. But powerful movements for change were also at work. These depended on ideas embodied in a series of political philosophies or ideologies—liberalism and nationalism—that came into their own in the first half of the nineteenth century. They continue to affect the entire world.

One of these was liberalism. Liberalism owed much to the Enlightenment of the eighteenth century and the American and French Revolutions at the end of that century. In addition, liberalism became increasingly important as the Industrial Revolution progressed because the developing industrial middle class largely adopted it as its own. There were divergencies of opinion among people classified as liberals, but all began with a common denominator, a conviction that people should be as free from restraint as possible. This belief is evident in both economic and political liberalism.

Also called classical economics, economic liberalism was based on the primary tenet of *laissez-faire*, or the belief that the state should not interrupt the free play of natural economic forces, especially supply and demand. Government should not interfere with the economic liberty of the individual and should restrict itself to only three primary functions: defense of the country, police protection of individuals, and the construction and maintenance of public works too expensive for individuals to undertake. If individuals were allowed economic liberty, ultimately they would bring about the maximum good for the maximum number and benefit the general welfare of society.

In political as in economic liberalism, liberals stressed that people should be free from restraint. Politically, liberals came to hold a common set of beliefs. Chief among them was the protection of civil liberties or the basic rights of all people, which included equality before the law, freedom of assembly, speech, and press, and freedom from arbitrary arrest. All of these freedoms should be guaranteed by a written document, such as the American Bill of Rights or the French Declaration of the Rights of Man and the Citizen. In addition to religious toleration for all, most liberals advocated separation of church and state. The right of peaceful opposition to the government in and out of parliament and the making of laws by a representative assembly (legislature) elected by qualified voters constituted two other liberal demands. Many liberals believed, then, in a constitutional monarchy or constitutional state with limits on the powers of government to prevent despotism, and in written constitutions that would also help to guarantee these rights.

Many liberals also advocated ministerial responsibility or a system in which ministers of the king were responsible to the legislature rather than to the king, giving the legislative branch a check upon the power of the executive. Liberals in the first half of the nineteenth century also believed in a limited suffrage. While all people were entitled to equal civil rights, they should not have equal political rights. The right to vote and hold office would be open only to men who met certain property qualifications. As a political philosophy, liberalism was tied to middle-class, and especially industrial middle-class, men who favored the extension of voting rights so that they could share power with the landowning classes. They had little desire to let the lower classes share that power. Liberals were not democrats.

Nationalism was an even more powerful ideology for change in the nineteenth century. Nationalism arose out of an awareness of being part of a community that has common institutions, traditions, language, and customs. This community is called a "nation," and the primary political loyalty of individuals would be to the nation rather than to a dynasty or a city-state or other political unit. Nationalism did not become a popular force for change until the French Revolution, and even then nationalism was not so much political as cultural with its emphasis upon the uniqueness of a particular nationality. Cultural nationalism, however, evolved into political nationalism. The latter advocated that governments should coincide with nationalities. Thus, a divided people such as the Germans wanted national unity in a German nation-state with one central government. Subject peoples, such as the Hungarians, wanted national self-determination or the right to establish their own autonomy rather than be subject to a German minority in a multinational empire.

Nationalism threatened to upset the existing political order, both internationally and nationally, making nationalism fundamentally radical. A united Germany or united Italy would upset the balance of power established in 1815. By the same token, an independent Hungarian state would mean the breakup of the Austrian Empire. The prospect of such dramatic change makes it evident why conservatives tried so hard to repress nationalism.

At the same time, in the first half of the nineteenth century, nationalism found a strong ally in liberalism. Most liberals believed that freedom could only be realized by peoples who ruled themselves. Each people should have its own country; no state should try to dominate others. The alliance with liberalism also gave nationalism a cosmopolitan dimension. Many nationalists believed that once each people obtained its own state, all nations could be linked together into a broader community of all humanity.

Beginning in 1830, the forces of change began to break through the conservative domination of Europe, more successfully in some places than in others. In France, the attempt of the ultraroyalists under the Bourbon monarch Charles X (1824–1830) to restore the old regime as far as possible led to a revolt by liberals in 1830. After the overthrow of Charles, a limited constitutional monarchy was established under Louis-Philippe (1830–1848), soon called the bourgeois monarch because political support for his rule came from the upper middle class.

Supporters of liberalism played a primary role in the revolution in France, but nationalism was the crucial force in three other revolutionary outbursts in 1830. The

Belgians, who had been annexed to the Dutch Republic in 1815 to create a larger state to act as a barrier to French aggression, rebelled against the Dutch and established an independent constitutional monarchy. The revolutionary scenarios in Poland and Italy were much less successful. Russian forces crushed the Poles' attempt to liberate themselves from foreign domination, while Austrian troops intervened in Italy to uphold reactionary governments in a number of Italian states.

THE REVOLUTIONS OF 1848

Despite the liberal and nationalist successes in France and Belgium, the conservative order continued to dominate much of Europe. But the forces of liberalism and nationalism, first generated by the French Revolution, continued to grow as a second great revolution—the Industrial Revolution—expanded and gave rise to new groups of people who wanted change. In 1848, these forces of change erupted once more. As usual, revolution in France provided the spark for other countries, and soon most of central and southern Europe was ablaze with revolutionary fires. Tsar Nicholas I of Russia lamented to Queen Victoria in April 1848, "What remains standing in Europe? Great Britain and Russia."

In France, a severe industrial and agricultural depression beginning in 1846 brought untold hardship to the lower middle class, workers, and peasants. Scandals, graft, and corruption were rife while the government's persistent refusal to extend the suffrage angered the disfranchised members of the middle class. As Louis-Philippe's government continued to refuse to make changes, opposition grew and finally overthrew the monarchy on February 24, 1848. A group of moderate and radical republicans established a provisional government and called for the election by universal manhood suffrage of a Constituent Assembly that would draw up a new constitution.

The provisional government also established national workshops, which were supposed to be cooperative factories run by the workers. In fact, the workshops became unemployment compensation units or public works, except that they provided little work beyond leaf raking and ditch digging. The cost of the program became increasingly burdensome to the government. The result was a growing split between the moderate republicans, who had the support of most of France, and the radical republicans, whose main support came from the Parisian working class. From March to June, the number of unemployed enrolled in the national workshops rose from 6,100 to almost 120,000, emptying the treasury and frightening the moderates who responded by closing the workshops on June 21. The workers refused to accept this decision and poured into the streets. Four days of bitter and bloody fighting by government forces crushed the working-class revolt. Thousands were killed, and 11,000

◆ **The 1830 Revolution of Paris.** In 1830, the forces of change began to undo the conservative domination of Europe. In France, the reactionary Charles X was overthrown. In this painting, students, former soldiers of the Empire, and middle-class citizens are seen joining the rebels who are marching on city hall to demand a republic. The forces of Charles X, seen firing from a building above, failed to halt the rebels.

prisoners were deported to the French colony of Algeria in northern Africa.

The new constitution, ratified on November 4, 1848, established a republic (Second Republic) with a single legislature elected by universal male suffrage for three years and a president, also elected by universal male suffrage, for four years. In the elections for the presidency held in December 1848, four republicans who had been associated with the early months of the Second Republic were resoundingly defeated by Charles Louis Napoleon Bonaparte, the nephew of the famous French ruler. Within four years President Napoleon had become Emperor Napoleon. The French had once again made their journey from republican chaos to authoritarian order, a pattern that was becoming all too common in French history.

News of the February revolution in Paris led to upheaval in central Europe as well (see the box on p. 750). The Vienna settlement in 1815 had recognized the existence of thirty-eight sovereign states (called the Germanic Confederation) in what had once been the Holy Roman Empire. Austria and Prussia were the two great powers while the other states varied considerably in size. In 1848, revolutionary cries for change caused many German rulers to promise constitutions, a free press, jury trials, and other liberal reforms. In Prussia concessions were also made to appease the revolutionaries. King Frederick William IV (1840–1861) agreed to abolish censorship, establish a new constitution, and work for a united Germany. The latter promise had its counterpart throughout all the German states as governments allowed elections by universal male suffrage for deputies to an all-German parliament. Its purpose was to fulfill a liberal and nationalist dream—the preparation of a constitution for a new united Germany.

But the Frankfurt Assembly (as the all-German parliament was called) soon disbanded. Although some members spoke of using force, they had no real means of compelling the German rulers to accept the constitution they had drawn up. The attempt of the German liberals at Frankfurt to create a German state had failed, and leadership for unification would now pass to the Prussian military monarchy.

The Austrian Empire also had its social, political, and nationalist grievances and needed only the news of the revolution in Paris to encourage it to erupt in flames in March 1848. The Austrian Empire was a multinational state, a collection of eleven different peoples including Germans, Czechs, Magyars (Hungarians), Slovaks, Romanians, Slovenes, Poles, Serbians, and Italians. Only the Habsburg emperor provided a common bond. The Germans, though only a quarter of the population, were the most advanced economically and played a leading role in governing Austria. The Hungarian liberal gentry agitated for "commonwealth" status; they were willing to keep the Habsburg monarch, but they wanted their own legislature. In March, demonstrations in Budapest, Prague, and Vienna led to Metternich's dismissal. The arch-symbol of the conservative order fled abroad. In Vienna, revolutionary forces, carefully guided by the educated and propertied classes, took control of the capital and insisted that a constituent assembly be summoned to draw up a liberal constitution. Hungary's demands for its own legislature, a separate national army, and control over its foreign policy and budget were granted. In Bohemia, the Czechs began to clamor for their own government as well.

Although Austrian officials had made concessions to appease the revolutionaries, they awaited an opportunity to reestablish their firm control. Like the rulers of the German states, they were increasingly encouraged by the divisions between radical and moderate revolutionaries and played upon the middle-class fear of a working-class social revolution. The counterrevolutionaries' first success came in June 1848 when Austrian military forces ruthlessly suppressed the Czech rebels in Prague. By the end of October, radical rebels had been crushed in Vienna, but it was only with the assistance of a Russian army of 140,000 men that the Hungarian revolution was finally crushed in 1849. The revolutions in the Austrian Empire had also failed. Autocratic government was restored; the emperor and propertied classes remained in control while the numerous nationalities remained subject to the Austrian government.

The revolutions in Italy also failed. The Congress of Vienna had established nine states in Italy, including the kingdom of Piedmont in the north ruled by the house of Savoy; the kingdom of the Two Sicilies (Naples and Sicily); the Papal States; a handful of small duchies ruled by relatives of the Austrian emperor; and the important northern provinces of Lombardy and Venetia, which were now part of the Austrian Empire. Italy was largely under Austrian domination while all the states had extremely reactionary governments eager to smother any liberal or nationalist sentiment. Attempts at change were ruthlessly crushed. But under the leadership of a new movement for Italian unity known as Young Italy, revolts against the foreigners were initially successful in 1848. By 1849, however, the Austrians had reestablished complete control over Lombardy and Venetia, and counterrevolutionary forces also prevailed elsewhere in Italy.

Revolutionary Excitement: Carl Schurz and the Revolution of 1848 in Germany

The excitement with which German liberals and nationalists received the news of the February revolution in France and their own expectations for Germany are well captured in this selection from the Reminiscences of Carl Schurz (1829–1906). Schurz made his way to the United States after the failure of the German revolution and eventually became a U.S. senator.

Carl Schurz, *Reminiscences*

One morning, toward the end of February, 1848, I sat quietly in my attic-chamber, working hard at my tragedy of "Ulrich von Hutten" [sixteenth-century German humanist and knight], when suddenly a friend rushed breathlessly into the room, exclaiming: "What, you sitting here! Do you not know what has happened?"

"No; what?"

"The French have driven away Louis Philippe and proclaimed the republic."

I threw down my pen—and that was the end of "Ulrich von Hutten." I never touched the manuscript again. We tore down the stairs, into the street, to the market-square, the accustomed meeting-place for all the student societies after their midday dinner. Although it was still forenoon, the market was already crowded with young men talking excitedly. There was no shouting, no noise, only agitated conversation. What did we want there? This probably no one knew. But since the French had driven away Louis Philippe and proclaimed the republic, something of course must happen here, too. . . . We were dominated by a vague feeling as if a great outbreak of elemental forces had begun, as if an earthquake was impending of which we had felt the first shock, and we instinctively crowded together. . . .

The next morning there were the usual lectures to be attended. But how profitless! The voice of the professor sounded like a monotonous drone coming from far away. What he had to say did not seem to concern us. The pen that should have taken notes remained idle. At last we closed with a sigh the notebook and went away, impelled by a feeling that now we had something more important to do—to devote ourselves to the affairs of the fatherland. And this we did by seeking as quickly as possible again the company of our friends, in order to discuss what had happened and what was to come. In these conversations, excited as they were, certain ideas and catchwords worked themselves to the surface, which expressed more or less the feelings of the people. Now had arrived in Germany the day for the establishment of "German Unity," and the founding of a great, powerful national German Empire. In the first line the convocation of a national parliament. Then the demands for civil rights and liberties, free speech, free press, the right of free assembly, equality before the law, a freely elected representation of the people with legislative power, responsibility of ministers, self-government of the communes, the right of the people to carry arms, the formation of a civic guard with elective officers, and so on—in short, that which was called a "constitutional form of government on a broad democratic basis." Republican ideas were at first only sparingly expressed. But the word democracy was soon on all tongues, and many, too, thought it a matter of course that if the princes should try to withhold from the people the rights and liberties demanded, force would take the place of mere petition. Of course the regeneration of the fatherland must, if possible, be accomplished by peaceable means. . . . Like many of my friends, I was dominated by the feeling that at last the great opportunity had arrived for giving to the German people the liberty which was their birthright and to the German fatherland its unity and greatness, and that it was now the first duty of every German to do and to sacrifice everything for this sacred object.

Throughout Europe in 1848, popular revolts had initiated revolutionary upheavals that had led to liberal constitutions and liberal governments. But the failure of the revolutionaries to stay united soon led to the reestablishment of authoritarian regimes. In other parts of the Western world, revolutions had taken somewhat different directions.

Independence and the Development of the National State in Latin America

The Spanish and Portuguese colonial empires in Latin America had been integrated into the traditional monarchical structure of Europe for centuries. When that structure was challenged, first by the ideas of the Enlightenment and then by the upheavals of the Napoleonic era, Latin America encountered the possibility of change. How it responded to that possibility, however, was determined in part by conditions unique to the region.

REVOLT IN LATIN AMERICA

By the end of the eighteenth century, the creole elites (descendants of Europeans who had become permanent inhabitants of Latin America) were being influenced by the ideas of the Enlightenment and the new political ideals stemming from the successful revolution in North America (see Chapters 18 and 19). They were particularly attracted to the idea of broadening education and the principles of the equality of all people in the eyes of the law, free trade, and a free press. Sons of creoles, such as Simón Bolívar and José de San Martín, who became leaders of the independence movement, even went to European universities where they imbibed the ideas of the Enlightenment. These Latin American elites, joined by a growing class of merchants, especially resented the domination of their trade by Spain and Portugal.

The creole elites soon began to use their new ideas to denounce the rule of the Iberian monarchs and the peninsulars (Spanish and Portuguese immigrants who resided temporarily in Latin America for political and economic gain). As Bolívar said in 1815, "the hatred that the peninsular has inspired in us is greater than the ocean that separates us." Bolívar reflected the growing nativism among the creole elites who resented the peninsulars who dominated Latin America and drained the Americas of their wealth. At the beginning of the nineteenth century, Napoleon's continental wars provided the creoles with an opportunity for change. When Bonaparte toppled the monarchies of Spain and Portugal, the authority of the Spaniards and Portuguese in their colonial empires was severely weakened. Between 1807 and 1825, a series of revolts enabled most of Latin America to become independent.

An unusual revolution preceded the main independence movements. Saint Domingue—the western third of Hispaniola—was a French sugar colony. Led by Toussaint L'Ouverture (c. 1743–1803), a son of African slaves, over 100,000 black slaves rose in revolt and seized control of all of Hispaniola. An army sent by Napoleon captured L'Ouverture, but the French soldiers, weakened by disease, soon succumbed to the slave forces. On January 1, 1804, the western part of Hispaniola, now called Haiti, announced its freedom and became the first independent state in Latin America.

Beginning in 1810, Mexico, too, experienced a revolt, fueled initially by the desire of the creole elites to overthrow the rule of the peninsulars. But when Indians and mestizos joined the revolt, both creoles and peninsulars, fearful of the masses, cooperated in defeating the popular revolutionary forces. Nevertheless, independence still came to Mexico, but now it was the conservative elites—both creoles and peninsulars—who decided to overthrow Spanish rule as a way of preserving their own power. They selected a creole military leader, Augustín de Iturbide (1783–1824), as their leader and the first emperor of Mexico in 1821. But the new government fostered neither political nor economic changes, and it soon became apparent that Mexican independence benefited primarily the creole elite.

Independence movements elsewhere in Latin America were also the work of elites—primarily creoles—who overthrew Spanish rule and created new governments that they could dominate. The masses of people—Indians, blacks, mestizos, and mulattoes—gained little from the revolts as the independence movements fell into the hands of a few elitist leaders. Two of the most prominent were both members of the creole elite—José de San Martín (1778–1850) of Argentina and Simón Bolívar (1783–1830) of Venezuela.

By 1810, the forces of San Martín had freed Argentina from Spanish authority while Bolívar, hailed as the Liberator, led the bitter struggle for independence in Venezuela. San Martín, who believed that the Spaniards must be removed from all South America if any nation was to be free, led his forces into Chile in 1817 and then, in 1821, moved on to Lima, Peru, the center of Spanish authority. He was soon joined by Bolívar who assumed the task of crushing the last significant Spanish army in 1824. By then, Peru, Uruguay, Paraguay, Colombia, Venezuela, Argentina, Bolivia, and Chile had all become free states. In 1822, the Central American states had

◆ **José de San Martín.** José de San Martín of Argentina was one of the famous leaders of the Latin American independence movement. His forces liberated Argentina, Chile, and Peru from Spanish authority. In this painting by Theodore Géricault, San Martín is shown leading his troops at the Battle of Chacabuco in Chile.

decided to ally themselves with Mexico, but one year later, they separated and became independent. In 1838–1839, the United Provinces of Central America divided into five republics (Guatemala, El Salvador, Honduras, Costa Rica, and Nicaragua). Earlier, in 1822, the prince regent of Brazil had declared Brazil's independence from Portugal.

In the early 1820s, only one major threat remained to the newly won independence of the Latin American states. Flushed by their success in crushing rebellions in Spain and Italy, the victorious continental powers favored the use of troops to restore Spanish control in Latin America. This time British opposition to intervention prevailed. Eager to gain access to an entire conti-

nent for investment and trade, the British proposed joint action with the United States against European interference in Latin America. Distrustful of British motives, President James Monroe acted alone in 1823, guaranteeing the independence of the new Latin American nations and warning against any further European intervention in the New World in the famous Monroe Doctrine. Actually more important to Latin American independence than American words was Britain's navy. All of the continental powers were reluctant to challenge British naval power, which stood between Latin America and any European invasion force.

THE DIFFICULTIES OF NATION BUILDING

The new Latin American nations, most of which began their existence as republics, faced a number of serious problems between 1830 and 1870. The wars for independence had themselves resulted in a staggering loss of population, property, and livestock. Despite the Monroe Doctrine, fear of European intervention persisted, and disputes often arose between the new nations over their precise boundaries. Poor transportation and communication systems fostered regionalism and made national unity difficult.

Severe struggles between church and state were common occurrences in the new nations. The Catholic church had enormous landholdings in Latin America and through its amassed wealth exercised great power. After independence, clerics often took positions in the new governments and wielded considerable influence. Throughout Latin America, a division arose between liberals who wished to curtail the temporal powers of the church and conservatives who hoped to maintain all of the church's privileges and prerogatives. In Mexico, this division even led to civil war, the bloody War of Reform fought between 1858 and 1861, in which Catholic clergy and the military lined up against a liberal government.

The insecurities prevalent after independence produced a new phenomenon—the rise of the caudillo or strong leader. Although caudillos could be found at both the regional and the national level, national caudillos generally fell into one of two types. One group, who supported the elites, were autocrats who controlled (and often abused) state revenues, centralized power, and kept the new national states together. Sometimes they were also modernizers who built roads and canals, ports, and schools. Others were destructive, such as Antonio López de Santa Anna who ruled Mexico from 1829 to 1855. He misused state funds, curtailed reforms, created chaos, and helped lose some of Mexico's territory to the United

✳ Map 20.3 Latin America in the First Half of the Nineteenth Century.

States. Caudillos were usually supported by the Catholic church, the rural aristocracy, and the army, which emerged from the wars of independence as a powerful political force that often made and deposed governments. Many caudillos, in fact, were former army leaders.

In contrast, other caudillos were supported by the masses, became extremely popular, and served as an instrument for radical change. Juan Manuel de Rosas, for example, who led Argentina from 1829 to 1852, became very popular by favoring Argentine interests against foreigners. Rafael Carrera, who ruled Guatemala from 1839 to 1865, supported native Indian cultures and pursued a

policy of land redistribution to aid the Indians. But he was disliked by the elites who wanted to Europeanize the economy and Guatemalan culture, and his efforts were undone by his successor, Justo Rufino Barrios (1873–1885). A caudillo who was supported by the elites, Barrios pushed the economy to coffee production and forced the Indians to give up their lands and become wage laborers to serve the interests of large plantation owners.

Although political independence brought economic independence, old patterns were quickly reestablished. Instead of Spain and Portugal, Great Britain now dominated the Latin American economy. British merchants moved in in large numbers, while British investors poured in funds, especially into the mining industry. Old trade patterns soon reemerged. Because Latin America served as a source of raw materials and foodstuffs for the industrializing nations of Europe and the United States, exports—especially wheat, tobacco, wools, sugar, coffee, and hides—to the North Atlantic countries increased noticeably. At the same time, finished consumer goods, especially textiles, were imported in increasing quantities, causing a decline in industrial production in Latin America. The emphasis on exporting raw materials and importing finished products ensured the ongoing domination of the Latin American economy by foreigners.

A fundamental, underlying problem for all of the new Latin American nations was the persistent domination of society by the landed elites. Large estates remained an important aspect of Latin America's economic and social life (see the box on p. 755). After independence, the size of these estates even expanded. By 1848, the Sánchez Navarro family in Mexico owned seventeen haciendas comprising 16 million acres. Governments facilitated this process by selling off church lands, public domains, and the lands of Indian communities. In Argentina, five hundred people bought 21 million acres of public land. Estates were often so large that they could not be farmed efficiently. As one Latin American newspaper put it: "The huge fortunes have the unfortunate tendency to grow even larger, and their owners possess vast tracts of land, which lie fallow and abandoned. Their greed for land does not equal their ability to use it intelligently and actively."[6]

Land remained the basis of wealth, social prestige, and political power throughout the nineteenth century. The Latin American elites tended to identify with European standards of progress, which worked to their benefit, while the masses gained little. Landed elites ran governments, controlled courts, and maintained the system of debt peonage that provided large landowners with a supply of cheap labor. These landowners made enormous profits by concentrating on specialized crops for export, such as coffee, while the masses, left without land to grow basic food crops, lived in dire poverty.

Upheaval in the Ottoman Empire: The Eastern Question

The Ottoman Empire had long been in control of much of southeastern Europe. By the beginning of the nineteenth century, however, when the Ottoman Empire was in decline and authority over its outlying territories in southeastern Europe waned, European governments began to take an active interest in its disintegration. The "Eastern Question," as it came to be called, troubled European diplomats throughout the nineteenth century. Russia's proximity to the Ottoman Empire and the religious bonds between the Russians and the Greek Orthodox Christians in Turkish-dominated southeastern Europe naturally gave it special opportunities to enlarge its sphere of influence. Other European powers feared Russian ambitions and had their own interest in the apparent demise of the Ottoman Empire. Austria craved more land in the Balkans, a desire that inevitably meant conflict with Russia, while France and Britain were interested in commercial opportunities and naval bases in the eastern Mediterranean.

In 1821, the Greeks revolted against their Turkish masters. Although subject to Muslim control for four hundred years, the Greeks had been allowed to maintain their language and their Greek Orthodox faith. A revival of Greek national sentiment at the beginning of the nineteenth century added to the growing desire for "the liberation of the fatherland from the terrible yoke of Turkish oppression." The Greek revolt was soon transformed into a noble cause by an outpouring of European sentiment for the Greeks' struggle. In 1827, a combined British and French fleet went to Greece and defeated a large Turkish fleet. A year later, Russia declared war on the Ottoman Empire and invaded its European provinces of Moldavia and Walachia. By the Treaty of Adrianople in 1829, which ended the Russian-Turkish War, the Russians received a protectorate over the two provinces. By the same treaty, the Turks agreed to allow Russia, France, and Britain to decide the fate of Greece. In 1830, the three powers declared Greece an independent kingdom, and two years later a new royal dynasty was established.

The Crimean War was yet another episode in the story of the Eastern Question. In 1853, war had erupted again between the Russians and Turks over Russian demands for the right to protect Christian shrines in Palestine, a privilege that had already been extended to the French. When the Turks refused, the Russians invaded Turkish Moldavia and Walachia. Failure to resolve the problem by negotiations led the Turks to declare war on Russia on October 4, 1853. In the following year, on March 28, Great Britain and France, fearful that the Russians would gain at the expense of the disintegrating Ottoman Empire, declared war on Russia.

The Crimean War was poorly planned and poorly fought. Britain and France decided on an attack on Russia's Crimean peninsula in the Black Sea. After a long siege and at a terrible cost in manpower for both sides,

A Radical Critique of the Land Problem in Mexico

The domination of Mexico by elites who owned large estates remained a serious problem throughout the nineteenth century. Conservatives, of course, favored the great estates as the foundation stones of their own political power, while even liberals shied away from any extremist attack on property rights. Nevertheless, there were some strong voices of protest, as this excerpt from a speech delivered in 1857 by Ponciano Arriaga demonstrates. Arriaga's appeal went unheeded; conservatives called him a "Communist."

Ponciano Arriaga, Speech to the Constitutional Convention of 1856–1857

One of the most deeply rooted evils of our country—an evil that merits the close attention of legislators when they frame our fundamental law—is the monstrous division of landed property.

While a few individuals possess immense areas of uncultivated land that could support millions of people, the great majority of Mexicans languish in a terrible poverty and are denied property, homes, and work. . . .

There are Mexican landowners who occupy (if one can give that name to a purely imaginary act) an extent of land greater than the areas of some of our sovereign states, greater even than that of one of several European states.

In this vast area, much of which lies idle, deserted, abandoned, awaiting the arms and labor of men, live four or five million Mexicans who know no other industry than agriculture, yet are without land or the means to work it, and who cannot emigrate in the hope of bettering their fortunes. They must either vegetate in idleness, turn to banditry, or accept the yoke of a landed monopolist who subjects them to intolerable conditions of life. . . .

How can a hungry, naked, miserable people practice popular government? How can we proclaim the equal rights of men and leave the majority of the nation in conditions worse than those of helots or pariahs? How can we condemn slavery in words, while the lot of most of our fellow citizens is more grievous than that of the black slaves of Cuba or the United States? . . .

With some honorable exceptions, the rich landowners of Mexico, or the administrators who represent them, resemble the feudal lords of the Middle Ages. On his seignorial land, . . . the landowner makes and executes laws, administers justice and exercises civil power, imposes taxes and fines, has his own jails and irons, metes out punishments and tortures, monopolizes commerce, and forbids the conduct without his permission of any business but that of the estate. The judges or officials who exercise on the hacienda the powers attached to public authority are usually the master's servants or tenants, his retainers, incapable of enforcing any law but the will of the master.

An astounding variety of devices are employed to exploit the peons or tenants, to turn a profit from their sweat and labor. They are compelled to work without pay even on days traditionally set aside for rest. They must accept rotten seeds or sick animals whose cost is charged to their miserable wages. They must pay enormous parish fees that bear no relation to the scale of fees that the owner or majordomo has arranged beforehand with the parish priest. They must make all their purchases on the hacienda, using tokens or paper money that do not circulate elsewhere. At certain seasons of the year they are assigned articles of poor quality, whose price is set by the owner or majordomo, constituting a debt which they can never repay. They are forbidden to use pastures and woods, firewood and water, or even the wild fruit of the fields, save with the express permission of the master. In fine, they are subject to a completely unlimited and irresponsible power.

the main Russian fortress of Sevastopol fell in September 1855, and the Russians soon sued for peace. By the Treaty of Paris, signed in March 1856, Russia was forced to give up Bessarabia at the mouth of the Danube and accept the neutrality of the Black Sea. In addition, the Danubian principalities of Moldavia and Walachia were placed under the protection of all the great powers.

The Crimean War broke up long-standing European power relationships and effectively destroyed the Concert of Europe. Austria and Russia, the two chief powers maintaining the status quo in the first half of the nineteenth century, were now enemies because of Austria's unwillingness to support Russia in the war. Russia, defeated, humiliated, and weakened by the obvious failure of its armies, withdrew from European affairs for the next two decades. Great Britain, disillusioned by its role in the war, also pulled back from continental affairs. Austria, paying the price for its neutrality, was now without friends among the great powers. Not until the 1870s were new combinations formed to replace those that had disappeared, but in the meantime the European international situation remained fluid. Those willing to pursue the "politics of reality" found themselves presented with a situation filled with opportunity. It was this new international situation that made possible the unification of Italy and Germany.

National Unification: Italy and Germany

The breakdown of the Concert of Europe opened the way for the Italians and the Germans to establish national states. Their successful unifications transformed the power structure of the Continent. Well into the twentieth century, Europe and the world would still be dealing with the consequences.

The Italians were the first people to benefit from the breakdown of the Concert of Europe. In 1850, Austria was still the dominant power on the Italian peninsula. After the failure of the revolution of 1848–1849, a growing number of advocates for Italian unification now focused on the northern Italian state of Piedmont as their best hope to achieve their goal. The royal house of Savoy ruled the kingdom of Piedmont, which also included the island of Sardinia. It appeared doubtful, however, that the little state could provide the leadership needed to unify Italy until King Victor Emmanuel II (1849–1878) named Count Camillo di Cavour (1810–1861) as his prime minister in 1852.

Cavour was a consummate politician with the ability to persuade others about the rightness of his own convictions. After becoming prime minister in 1852, he pursued a policy of economic expansion that increased government revenues and enabled him to pour money into equipping a large army. Cavour, however, had no illusions about Piedmont's military strength and was only too well aware that he could not challenge Austria directly. Consequently, he made an alliance with the French emperor Louis Napoleon and then provoked the Austrians into invading Piedmont in 1859. In the initial stages of fighting, the Austrians were defeated in two major battles by mostly French armies. A peace settlement gave the French Nice and Savoy, which they had been promised for making the alliance, and awarded Lombardy to Cavour and the Piedmontese. More importantly, however, Cavour's success caused nationalists in some north-

ern Italian states (Parma, Modena, and Tuscany) to overthrow their governments and join their states to Piedmont.

Italian unification might have stopped here since there is little indication that Cavour envisioned uniting all of Italy in the spring of 1860. But the forces of romantic republican nationalism forced him to act. Giuseppe Garibaldi (1807–1882), a dedicated Italian patriot who had supported the republican cause of Young Italy, raised an army of a thousand Red Shirts, as his volunteers were called because of their distinctive dress, and landed in Sicily where a revolt had broken out against the Bourbon king of the Two Sicilies. By the end of July 1860, most of Sicily had been pacified under Garibaldi's control (see the box on p. 757). In August, Garibaldi and his forces crossed over to the mainland and began a victorious march up the Italian peninsula. Naples, and with it the Kingdom of the Two Sicilies, fell in early September. Ever the patriot, Garibaldi chose to turn over his conquests to Cavour's Piedmontese forces. On March 17, 1861, a new kingdom of Italy was proclaimed under a centralized government subordinated to the control of Piedmont and King Victor Emmanuel II (1861–1878) of the house of Savoy. Worn out by his efforts, Cavour died three months later.

Despite the proclamation of a new kingdom, the task of unification was not yet complete as Venetia in the north was still held by Austria and Rome was under papal control, supported by French troops. To attack either one meant war with a major European state, which the Italian army was not prepared to handle. Instead, it was the Prussian army that indirectly completed the task of Italian unification. In the Austro-Prussian War of 1866, the new Italian state became an ally of Prussia. Although the Italian army was defeated by the Austrians, Prussia's victory left the Italians free to annex Venetia. In 1870, the Franco-Prussian War resulted in the withdrawal of French troops from Rome. The Italian army then annexed the city on September 20, 1870, and Rome became the new capital of the united Italian state.

THE UNIFICATION OF GERMANY

After the failure of the Frankfurt Assembly to achieve German unification in 1848–1849, German nationalists focused on Austria and Prussia as the only two states powerful enough to dominate German affairs. Austria had long controlled the existing Germanic Confederation, but Prussian power had grown, strongly reinforced by economic expansion in the 1850s. Industrial growth made rapid strides in Germany, especially within the *Zoll-*

❧ *Garibaldi and Romantic Nationalism* ❧

Giuseppe Garibaldi was one of the more colorful figures involved in the unification of Italy. Accompanied by only a thousand of his famous "Red Shirts," the Italian soldier of fortune left Genoa on the night of May 5, 1860, for an invasion of the kingdom of the Two Sicilies. The ragged band entered Palermo, the chief city on the island of Sicily, on May 31. This selection is taken from an account by a correspondent for The Times *of London, the Hungarian-born Nandor Eber.*

The Times, June 13, 1860

Palermo, May 31—Anyone in search of violent emotions cannot do better than set off at once for Palermo. However blasé he may be, or however milk-and-water his blood, I promise it will be stirred up. He will be carried away by the tide of popular feeling. . . .

In the afternoon Garibaldi made a tour of inspection round the town. I was there, but find it really impossible to give you a faint idea of the manner in which he was received everywhere. It was one of those triumphs which seem to be almost too much for a man. . . . The popular idol, Garibaldi, in his red flannel shirt, with a loose colored handkerchief round his neck, and his worn "wide-awake" [a soft-brimmed felt hat], was walking on foot among those cheering, laughing, crying, mad thousands; and all his few followers could do was to prevent him from being bodily carried off the ground. The people threw themselves forward to kiss his hands, or, at least, to touch the hem of his garment, as if it contained the panacea for all their past and perhaps coming suffering. Children were brought up, and mothers asked on their knees for his blessing; and all

this while the object of this idolatry was calm and smiling as when in the deadliest fire, taking up the children and kissing them, trying to quiet the crowd, stopping at every moment to hear a long complaint of houses burned and property sacked by the retreating soldiers, giving good advice, comforting, and promising that all damages should be paid for. . . .

One might write volumes of horrors on the vandalism already committed, for every one of the hundred ruins has its story of brutality and inhumanity. . . . In these small houses a dense population is crowded together even in ordinary times. A shell falling on one, and crushing and burying the inmates, was sufficient to make people abandon the neighboring one and take refuge a little further on, shutting themselves up in the cellars. When the Royalists retired they set fire to those of the houses which had escaped the shells, and numbers were thus burned alive in their hiding places. . . .

If you can stand the exhalation, try and go inside the ruins, for it is only there that you will see what the thing means and you will not have to search long before you stumble over the remains of a human body, a leg sticking out here, an arm there, a black face staring at you a little further on. You are startled by a rustle. You look round and see half a dozen gorged rats scampering off in all directions, or you see a dog trying to make his escape over the ruins. . . . I only wonder that the sign of these scenes does not convert every man in the town into a tiger and every woman into a fury. But these people have been so long ground down and demoralized that their nature seems to have lost the power of reaction.

verein, a German customs union that had been formed in 1834 under Prussian leadership. By eliminating tolls on rivers and roads among member states, the *Zollverein* had stimulated trade and added to the prosperity of its members. By 1853, all the German states except Austria had joined the Prussian-dominated customs union. Austria was rapidly being excluded from a new Germany based on common economic ties. Prussia benefited the most from this development, as even middle-class liberals began to find some good things in the Prussian state.

In the 1860s, King William I (1861–1888) attempted to enlarge and strengthen the Prussian army. When the

Prussian legislature refused to levy new taxes for the proposed military changes, William I appointed a new prime minister, Count Otto von Bismarck (1815–1898). Bismarck came to determine the course of modern German history and dominated both German and European politics until 1890.

Bismarck ignored the legislative opposition to the military reforms, arguing instead that, "Germany does not look to Prussia's liberalism but to her power. . . . Not by speeches and majorities will the great questions of the day be decided—that was the mistake of 1848–1849—but by iron and blood."[7] Bismarck went ahead, collected the taxes, and reorganized the army anyway, blaming the liberals for causing the breakdown of constitutional government. From 1862 to 1866, Bismarck governed Prussia by simply ignoring parliament. Unwilling to revolt and unable to force people not to pay their taxes, parliament did nothing. In the meantime, opposition to his domestic policy determined Bismarck to engage in an active foreign policy, which led to war and German unification.

Because Bismarck succeeded in guiding Prussia's unification of Germany, it is often assumed that he had determined upon a course of action that led precisely to that goal. That is hardly the case. Bismarck was a consummate politician and opportunist. He was not a political gambler, but a moderate who waged war only when all other diplomatic alternatives had been exhausted and when he was reasonably sure that all the military and diplomatic advantages were on his side. Bismarck has often been portrayed as the ultimate realist, the foremost nineteenth-century practitioner of *realpolitik*—the "politics of reality." His ability to manipulate people and power justifies that claim, but unlike Hitler in the twentieth cen-

tury, Bismarck also recognized the limitations of power. When he perceived that the advantages to be won from war "no longer justified the risks involved," he became an ardent defender of peace.

Bismarck's first war was against Denmark and was fought over the duchies of Schleswig and Holstein. Bismarck persuaded the Austrians to join Prussia in declaring war on Denmark on February 1, 1864. The Danes were quickly defeated and surrendered Schleswig and Holstein to the victors. Austria and Prussia then agreed to divide the administration of the two duchies; Prussia took Schleswig while Austria administered Holstein. But Bismarck used the joint administration of the two duchies to create friction with the Austrians and goad them into a war that began on June 14, 1866.

Many Europeans expected a quick Austrian victory, but they overlooked the effectiveness of the Prussian military reforms of the 1860s. The Prussian breech-loading needle gun had a much faster rate of fire than the Austrian muzzle-loader, and a superior network of railroads enabled the Prussians to mass troops quickly. At König-

✖ Map 20.4 The Unification of Italy.

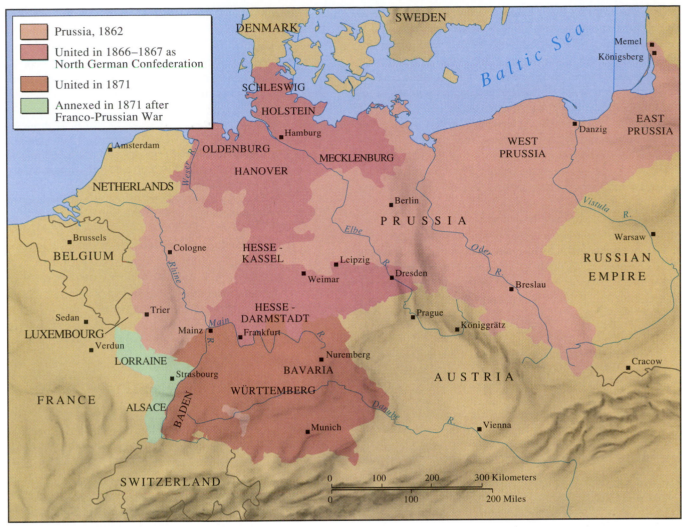

✳ **Map 20.5**   The Unification of Germany.

grätz (or Sadowa) on July 3, the Austrian army was decisively defeated. Austria was now excluded from German affairs, and the German states north of the Main River were organized into a North German Confederation controlled by Prussia. Each German state kept its own local government, but the king of Prussia was head of the confederation while the chancellor (Bismarck) was responsible directly to the king. Both the army and foreign policy remained in the hands of the king and his chancellor. The south German states, largely Catholic, remained independent but were coerced into signing military agreements with Prussia.

Bismarck and William I had achieved a major goal by 1866. Prussia now dominated all of northern Germany, and Austria had been excluded from any significant role

in German affairs. At the same time, unsettled business led to new international complications and further change. Bismarck realized that France would never be content with a strong German state to its east because of the potential threat to French security. At the same time, after a series of setbacks, Napoleon III, the French ruler, needed a diplomatic triumph to offset his serious domestic problems. The French were not happy with the turn of events in Germany and looked for opportunities to humiliate the Prussians.

In 1870, Prussia and France became embroiled in a dispute over the candidacy of a relative of the Prussian king for the throne of Spain. Bismarck manipulated the misunderstandings between the French and Prussians to goad the French into declaring war on Prussia on July 15,

1870. The French proved no match for the better led and organized Prussian forces. The south German states honored their military alliances with Prussia and joined the war effort against the French. The Prussian armies advanced into France, and at Sedan, on September 2, 1870, an entire French army and Napoleon III himself were captured. Paris finally capitulated on January 28, 1871, and an official peace treaty was signed in May. France had to pay an indemnity of five billion francs (about one billion dollars) and give up the provinces of Alsace and Lorraine to the new German state. The loss of Alsace-Lorraine rankled the French and left them burning for revenge.

Even before the war had ended, the south German states had agreed to enter the North German Confederation. On January 18, 1871, in the Hall of Mirrors in Louis XIV's palace at Versailles, William I was proclaimed kaiser or emperor of the Second German Empire (the first was the medieval Holy Roman Empire). German unity

◆ **The Unification of Germany.** Under Prussian leadership, a new German empire was proclaimed on January 18, 1871, in the Hall of Mirrors in the palace at Versailles. King William of Prussia became Emperor William I of the Second German Empire. Otto von Bismarck, the man who had been so instrumental in creating the new German state, is shown here, resplendently attired in his white uniform, standing at the foot of the throne.

had been achieved by the Prussian monarchy and the Prussian army. In a real sense, Germany had been merged into Prussia, not Prussia into Germany. German liberals also rejoiced. They had dreamed of unity and freedom, but the achievement of unity now seemed much more important. One old liberal proclaimed:

> I cannot shake off the impression of this hour. I am no devotee of Mars; I feel more attached to the goddess of beauty and the mother of graces than to the powerful god of war, but the trophies of war exercise a magic charm even upon the child of peace. One's view is involuntarily chained and one's spirit goes along with the boundless row of men who acclaim the god of the moment—success.[8]

The Prussian leadership of German unification meant that authoritarian, militaristic values would triumph over liberal, constitutional sentiments in the development of the new German state. With its industrial resources and military might, the new state had become the strongest power on the Continent. A new European balance of power was at hand.

Nationalism and Reform: The National State in Mid-Century

While European affairs were dominated by the unification of Italy and Germany, other states in the Western world were also undergoing transformations. War, civil war, and changing political alignments served as catalysts for domestic reforms.

Unlike the nations on the Continent, Great Britain managed to avoid the revolutionary upheavals of the first half of the nineteenth century. In 1815, Britain was still governed by the aristocratic landowning classes that dominated both houses of Parliament. But in 1832, to prevent revolutionary turmoil like that on the Continent, Parliament passed a Reform Bill that increased the numbers of male voters, primarily benefiting the upper middle class. A significant step had been taken. Now the "monied, manufacturing, and educated elite" would join with the landed interests in ruling Britain.

As a result of such reforms, Britain experienced no revolutionary disturbances during 1848. The Reform Act of 1832 had opened the door to political representation for the industrial middle class, and in the 1850s and 1860s, the British liberal parliamentary system demonstrated once more its ability to make both social and political reforms that enabled the country to remain stable and prosperous. One of the reasons for Britain's stability was its continuing economic growth. After 1850, middle-class prosperity was at last coupled with some improvements for the working classes as well. Real wages for laborers increased over 25 percent between 1850 and 1870. The British sense of national pride was well reflected in Queen Victoria (1837–1901), whose self-contentment and sense of moral respectability reflected the attitudes of her time, which has ever since been known as the Victorian Age.

Meanwhile France in the aftermath of the revolution of 1848 had moved toward the restoration of monarchy. Even after his election as the president of the French Republic, many of his contemporaries dismissed Napoleon "the Small" as a nonentity whose success was due only to his name. But Louis Napoleon was a clever politician who was especially astute at understanding the popular forces of his day. Four years after his election as president, Louis Napoleon returned to the people to ask for the restoration of the empire. Ninety-seven percent responded affirmatively, and on December 2, 1852, Louis Napoleon assumed the title of Napoleon III (the first Napoleon had abdicated in favor of his son, Napoleon II, on April 6, 1814). The Second Empire had begun.

The government of Napoleon III was clearly authoritarian in a Bonapartist sense. As chief of state, Napoleon III controlled the armed forces, police, and civil service. Only he could introduce legislation and declare war. The Legislative Corps gave an appearance of representative government since its members were elected by universal male suffrage for six-year terms. But they could neither initiate legislation nor affect the budget.

The first five years of Napoleon III's reign were a spectacular success as he reaped the benefits of worldwide economic prosperity, although the government's policies also contributed to French economic renewal. Napoleon believed in using the resources of government to encourage the national economy and took many steps to expand industrial growth. Government subsidies were used to foster the rapid construction of railroads, harbors, roads, and canals. The major French railway lines were completed during Napoleon's reign while industrial expansion was evident in the tripling of iron production. In the midst of this economic expansion, Napoleon III also undertook a vast reconstruction of the city of Paris. The medieval Paris of narrow streets and old city walls was destroyed and replaced by a modern Paris of broad boulevards, spacious buildings, circular plazas, public squares, an underground sewage system, a new public water supply, and gaslights.

In the 1860s, as opposition to some of Napoleon's policies began to mount, his sensitivity to the change in the public mood led him to undertake new measures liberal-

♦ **Emperor Napoleon III.** On December 2, 1852, Louis Napoleon took the title of Napoleon III and then proceeded to create an authoritarian monarchy. As opposition to his policies intensified in the 1860s, Napoleon III began to liberalize his government. However, a disastrous military defeat at the hands of Prussia in 1870–1871 brought the collapse of his regime.

izing his regime. Napoleon III reached out to the working class by legalizing trade unions and granting them the right to strike. He also began to liberalize the political process. The Legislative Corps was permitted more say in affairs of state, including debate over the budget. Initially, these liberalization policies did serve to strengthen the hands of the government. In May 1870, in a plebiscite on whether to accept a new constitution that might have inaugurated a parliamentary regime, the French people gave Napoleon another resounding victory. This triumph was short-lived, however. Foreign

Developments in Europe, 1800–1871

Great Britain

Reform Act	1832
Queen Victoria	1837–1901

France

Charles X	1824–1830
July Revolution	1830
Louis-Philippe	1830–1848
Abdication of Louis-Philippe; formation of provisional government	February 22–24, 1848
Formation of national workshops	February 26, 1848
"June Days": Workers' revolt in Paris	1848 (June)
Establishment of Second Republic	1848 (November)
Election of Louis Napoleon as French president	1848 (December)
Coup d'etat by Louis Napoleon	1851
Creation of the Second Empire	1852
Emperor Napoleon III	1852–1870

Germany

Germanic Confederation established	1815
Frederick William IV of Prussia	1840–1861
Revolution in Germany	1848
Frankfurt Assembly	1848–1849
Unification of Germany	
King William I of Prussia	1861–1888
The Danish War	1864
The Austro-Prussian War	1866
The Franco-Prussian War	1870–1871
German Empire is proclaimed	January 18, 1871

The Austrian Empire

Revolt in Austrian Empire; Metternich dismissed	1848 (March)
Austrian forces crush Czech rebels	1848 (June)
Viennese rebels crushed	1848 (October)
Defeat of Hungarians with help of Russian troops	1849
Ausgleich: The dual monarchy	1867

Italy

Revolutions in Italy	1848
Austria reestablishes control in Lombardy and Venetia	1849
Unification of Italy	
Victor Emmanuel II	1849–1878
Count Cavour becomes prime minister of Piedmont	1852
The Austrian War	1859
Plebiscites in the northern Italian states	1860
Garibaldi's invasion of the Two Sicilies	1860
Kingdom of Italy is proclaimed	March 17, 1861
Italy's annexation of Venetia	1866
Italy's annexation of Rome	1870

Russia

Tsar Alexander II	1855–1881
Emancipation edict	March 3, 1861

The Ottoman Empire: The Eastern Question

The Greek revolt	1821–1830
The Crimean War	1853–1856

policy failures led to growing criticism, and war with Prussia in 1870 turned out to be the death blow for Napoleon III's regime. Napoleon was ousted, and a republic proclaimed.

Although nationalism was a major force in nineteenth-century Europe, one of Europe's most powerful states—the Austrian Empire—was a multinational empire that managed to frustrate the desires of its ethnic groups for self-determination. After the Habsburgs had crushed the revolutions of 1848–1849, they restored centralized, autocratic government to the empire. But failure in war had severe internal consequences for Austria. The defeat at the hands of the Prussians in 1866 forced the Austrians to deal with the fiercely nationalistic Hungarians. The result was the negotiated *Ausgleich*, or Compromise, of 1867, which created the dual monarchy of Austria-Hungary. Each part of the empire now had its own constitution, its own bicameral legislature, its own governmental machinery for domestic affairs, and its own capital (Vienna for Austria and Budapest for Hungary). Holding the two states together were a single monarch—Francis Joseph (1848–1916) was emperor of Austria and king of Hungary—and a common army, foreign policy, and system of finances. In domestic affairs, the Hungarians had become an independent nation. The *Ausgleich* did not, however, satisfy the other nationalities that made up the multinational Austro-Hungarian Empire. The dual monarchy simply enabled the German-speaking Austrians and Hungarian Magyars to dominate the minorities, especially the Slavs, in their respective states.

At the beginning of the nineteenth century, Russia was overwhelmingly rural, agricultural, and autocratic. The Russian tsar was still regarded as a divine-right monarch with unlimited power although the extent of the Russian empire made the claim impractical. The Russian imperial autocracy, based on soldiers, secret police, repression, and censorship, had withstood the revolutionary fervor of the first half of the nineteenth century and even served as the "arsenal of autocracy" in crushing revolutions elsewhere in Europe. But the defeat at the hands of the British and French in the Crimean War in 1856 revealed the blatant deficiencies behind the facade of absolute power and made it clear even to staunch conservatives that Russia was falling hopelessly behind the western European powers. Tsar Alexander II (1855–1881) turned his energies to a serious overhaul of the Russian system. Following the autocratic procedures of his predecessors, he attempted to impose reforms upon the Russian people.

Serfdom was the most burdensome problem in tsarist Russia. The continuing subjugation of millions of peasants to the land and their landlords was an obviously corrupt and failing system. On March 3, 1861, Alexander issued his emancipation edict (see the box on p. 764). Peasants were now free to own property, marry as they chose, and bring suits in the law courts. But the system of land redistribution instituted after emancipation was not particularly favorable to them. The government provided land for the peasants by purchasing it from the landlords, but the landowners often chose to keep the best lands. The Russian peasants soon found that they had inadequate amounts of good arable land to support themselves, a situation worsened by the rapidly increasing peasant population in the second half of the nineteenth century.

Nor were the peasants completely free. The state compensated the landowners for the land given to the peasants, but the peasants, in turn, were expected to repay the state in long-term installments. To ensure that the payments were made, peasants were subjected to the authority of their *mir* or village commune, which was collectively responsible for the land payments to the government. In a very real sense, then, the village commune, not the individual peasants, owned the land the peasants were purchasing. And since the village communes were responsible for the payments, they were reluctant to allow peasants to leave their land. Emancipation, then, led not to free, landowning peasants as in western Europe, but to unhappy, land-starved peasants who largely followed the old ways of agricultural production.

Alexander II attempted other reforms as well, including the election of local assemblies that provided a moderate degree of self-government and legal reforms that created a regular system of local and provincial courts. But even the autocratic tsar was unable to control the forces he unleashed by his reform program. Reformers wanted more and rapid change; conservatives opposed what they perceived as the tsar's attempts to undermine the basic institutions of Russian society. By 1870, Russia was witnessing increasing levels of dissatisfaction. When one group of radicals assassinated Alexander II in 1881, his son and successor, Alexander III, turned against reform and returned to the traditional methods of repression.

THE GROWTH OF THE UNITED STATES

The U.S. Constitution, ratified in 1789, committed the United States to two of the major forces of the first half of the nineteenth century, liberalism and nationalism. Initially, this constitutional commitment to national unity was challenged by disagreements over the power of the

❧ *Emancipation: Serfs and Slaves* ❧

Although overall their histories have been quite different, Russia and the United States shared a common feature in the 1860s. They were the only states in the Western world that still had large enslaved populations (the Russian serfs were virtually slaves). The leaders of both countries issued emancipation proclamations within two years of each other. The first excerpt is taken from the Imperial Decree of March 3, 1861, which freed the Russian serfs. The second excerpt is from Abraham Lincoln's Emancipation Proclamation, issued on January 1, 1863.

The Imperial Decree, March 3, 1861

By the grace of God, we, Alexander II, Emperor and Autocrat of all the Russias, King of Poland, Grand Duke of Finland, etc., to all our faithful subjects, make known:

Called by Divine Providence and by the sacred right of inheritance to the throne of our ancestors, we took a vow in our innermost heart to respond to the mission which is intrusted to us as to surround with our affection and our Imperial solicitude all our faithful subjects of every rank and of every condition, from the warrior, who nobly bears arms for the defense of the country to the humble artisan devoted to the works of industry; from the official in the career of the high offices of the State to the laborer whose plough furrows the soil. . . .

We thus came to the conviction that the work of a serious improvement of the condition of the peasants was a sacred inheritance bequeathed to us by our ancestors, a mission which, in the course of events, Divine Providence called upon us to fulfill. . . .

In virtue of the new dispositions above mentioned, the peasants attached to the soil will be invested within a term fixed by the law with all the rights of free cultivators. . . .

At the same time, they are granted the right of purchasing their close, and, with the consent of the proprietors, they may acquire in full property the arable lands and other appurtenances which are allotted to them as a permanent holding. By the acquisition in full property of the quantity of land fixed, the peasants are free from their obligations toward the proprietors for land thus purchased, and they enter definitely into the condition of free peasants-landholders.

The Emancipation Proclamation, January 1, 1863

Now therefore, I, Abraham Lincoln, President of the United States, by virtue of the power in me vested as Commander-in-Chief of the Army and Navy of the United States in time of actual armed rebellion against the authority and government of the United States, and as a fit and necessary war measure for suppressing such rebellion, do, on this 1st day of January, A.D. 1863, and in accordance with my purpose to do so, . . . order and designate as the States and parts of States wherein the people thereof, respectively, are this day in rebellion against the United States the following, to wit:

Arkansas, Texas, Louisiana, . . . Mississippi, Alabama, Florida, Georgia, South Carolina, North Carolina, and Virginia . . .

And by virtue of the power for the purpose aforesaid, I do order and declare that all persons held as slaves within said designated States and parts of States are, and henceforward shall be free; and that the Executive Government of the United States, including the military and naval authorities thereof, will recognize and maintain the freedom of said persons.

federal government vis-à-vis the individual states. Bitter conflict erupted between the Federalists and the Republicans. Led by Alexander Hamilton (1757–1804), the Federalists favored a financial program that would establish a strong central government. The Republicans, guided by Thomas Jefferson (1743–1826) and James Madison (1751–1836), feared centralization and its consequences for popular liberties. These divisions were intensified by European rivalries as the Federalists were pro-British and the Republicans pro-French. The suc-

cessful conclusion of the War of 1812 brought an end to the Federalists, who had opposed the war, while the surge of national feeling generated by the war served to heal the nation's divisions.

Another strong force for national unity came from the Supreme Court under the leadership of John Marshall (1755–1835), who was chief justice from 1801 to 1835. Marshall made the Supreme Court into an important national institution by asserting its right to overrule an act of Congress if the Court found it to be in violation of the

Constitution. Under Marshall, the Supreme Court contributed further to establishing the supremacy of the national government by curbing the actions of state courts and legislatures.

The election of Andrew Jackson (1767–1845) as president in 1828 opened a new era in American politics. Jacksonian democracy introduced a mass democratic politics. The electorate was expanded by dropping traditional property qualifications; by the 1830s, suffrage had been extended to almost all adult white males. During the period from 1815 to 1850, the traditional liberal belief in the improvement of human beings was also given concrete expression. Americans developed detention schools for juvenile delinquents and new penal institutions, both motivated by the liberal belief that the right kind of environment would rehabilitate those in need of it.

By the mid-nineteenth century, however, American national unity was increasingly threatened by the issue of slavery. Like the North, the South had grown dramatically in population during the first half of the nineteenth century. But its development was quite different. Its cotton economy and social structure were based on the exploitation of enslaved black Africans and their descendants. The importance of cotton is evident from production figures. In 1810, the South produced a raw cotton crop of 178,000 bales worth $10 million. By 1860, it was generating 4.5 million bales of cotton with a value of $249 million. Ninety-three percent of southern cotton in 1850 was produced by a slave population that had grown dramatically in fifty years. Although new slave imports had been barred in 1808, there were four million Afro-American slaves in the South by 1860 compared to one million in 1800. The cotton economy and plantation-based slavery were intimately related, and the attempt to maintain them in the course of the first half of the nineteenth century led the South to become increasingly defensive, monolithic, and isolated. At the same time, the growth of an abolitionist movement in the North challenged the southern order and created an "emotional chain reaction" that led to civil war.

The push of Americans westward was a major factor in bringing the issue of slavery to the forefront of American politics. A debate arose over whether to admit new states to the Union as free or slave states. The issue had already arisen in the 1810s as new states were being created by the rush of settlers beyond the Mississippi. The free states of the North feared the creation of a slave-state majority in the national government. Attempts at compromise did not solve this divisive issue, but merely postponed it. By the 1850s, slavery had caused the Whig Party to be-

come defunct and the Democrats (the descendants of Jefferson's Republicans) to split along North-South lines while angry northerners created a new one-issue party. The Republicans were united by antislavery and were especially driven by the fear that the "slave power" of the South would attempt to spread the slave system throughout the country.

As polarization over the issue of slavery intensified, compromise became less feasible. When Abraham Lincoln, the man who had said in a speech in Illinois in 1858 that "this government cannot endure permanently half slave and half free," was elected president in November 1860, the die was cast. Lincoln carried only 2 of the 1,109 counties in the South; the Republicans were not even on the ballot in ten southern states. On December 20, 1860, a South Carolina convention voted to repeal ratification of the Constitution of the United States. In February 1861, six more southern states did the same, and a rival nation—the Confederate States of America—was formed. In March, fighting erupted between North and South.

The American Civil War (1861–1865) was an extraordinarily bloody struggle, a clear foretaste of the total war to come in the twentieth century. Over 600,000 soldiers died, either in battle or from deadly infectious diseases spawned by filthy camp conditions. This figure exceeds the combined American casualties of World War I and World War II. Over a period of four years, the Union states mobilized their superior assets and gradually wore down the South. As the war dragged on, it had the effect of radicalizing public opinion in the North. What began as a war to save the Union became a war against slavery. On January 1, 1863, Lincoln's Emancipation Proclamation made most of the nation's slaves "forever free" (see the box on p. 764). The increasingly effective Union blockade of the South combined with a shortage of fighting men made the Confederate cause desperate by the end of 1864. The final push of Union troops under General Ulysses S. Grant forced General Robert E. Lee's army to surrender on April 9, 1865. Although the problems of reconstruction lay ahead, the Union victory confirmed that the United States would be "one nation, indivisible." National unity, not particularism, had prevailed in the United States.

THE EMERGENCE OF A CANADIAN NATION

By the Treaty of Paris in 1763, Canada—or New France as it was called—passed into the hands of the British. By 1800, most Canadians favored more autonomy, although the colonists disagreed on the form this autonomy should take. Upper Canada (now Ontario) was predominantly English-speaking while Lower Canada (now Quebec) was dominated by French Canadians. Increased immigration to Canada after 1815 also fueled the desire for self-government. After two short rebellions against the government broke out in Upper and Lower Canada in 1837 and 1838, the British agreed to make some changes. In 1840, the British Parliament formally joined Upper and Lower Canada into the United Provinces of Canada. But

Parliament failed to grant self-government, and Canada remained but a group of provinces with little sense of unity.

The head of Upper Canada's Conservative Party, John Macdonald, became an avid apostle for union and self-government. Fearful of American designs on Canada, the British government finally capitulated to Macdonald's campaign, and in 1867, Parliament passed the British North American Act, which established a Canadian na-

Map 20.6 The United States and Canada in the Nineteenth Century.

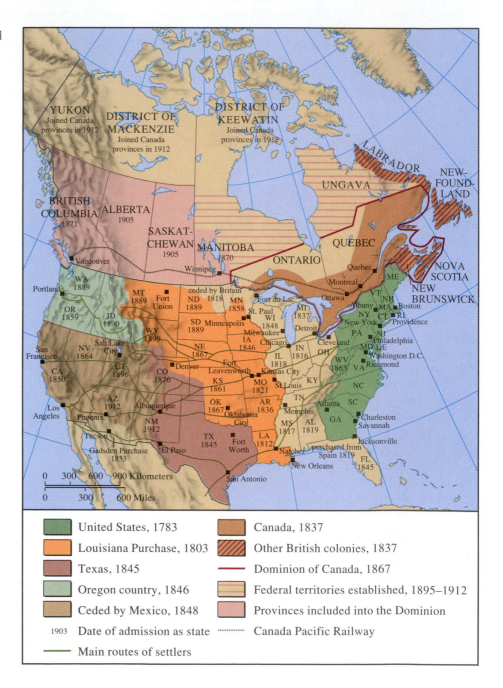

United States, 1783

Louisiana Purchase, 1803

Texas, 1845

Oregon country, 1846

Ceded by Mexico, 1848

1903 Date of admission as state

Main routes of settlers

Canada, 1837

Other British colonies, 1837

Dominion of Canada, 1867

Federal territories established, 1895–1912

Provinces included into the Dominion

Canada Pacific Railway

tion—the Dominion of Canada—with its own constitution. John Macdonald became the first prime minister of the Dominion. Although Canada now possessed a parliamentary system and ruled itself as a national federation, provincial legislatures were given considerable latitude in local affairs, and foreign affairs still remained the preserve of the British government.

Cultural Life: Romanticism and Realism in the Western World

At the end of the eighteenth century, a new intellectual movement known as Romanticism was developing as a reaction against the Enlightenment's preoccupation with reason in discovering truth. While the Romantics, especially the early Romantics, by no means disparaged reason, they tried to balance its use by stressing the importance of feeling, emotion, and imagination as sources of knowing.

The Characteristics of Romanticism

Romantic writers emphasized emotion and sentiment and believed that these inner feelings were only understandable to the person experiencing them. An important model for Romantics was the tragic figure in *The Sorrows of Young Werther*, a novel by the great German writer, Johann Wolfgang von Goethe (1749–1832), who later rejected Romanticism in favor of classicism. Werther was a Romantic figure who sought freedom in order to fulfill himself. Misunderstood and rejected by society, he continued to believe in his own worth through his inner feelings, but his deep love for a girl who did not love him finally led him to commit suicide. After Goethe's *The Sorrows of Young Werther*, numerous novels and plays appeared whose plots revolved around young maidens tragically carried off at an early age (twenty-three was most common) by disease (usually tuberculosis, at that time a protracted disease that was usually fatal) to the sorrows and sadness of their male lovers.

Another important characteristic of Romanticism was individualism or an interest in the unique traits of each person. The Romantics' desire to follow their inner drives led them to rebel against middle-class conventions. Long hair, beards, and outrageous clothes served to reinforce the individualism that young Romantics were trying to express.

Many Romantics also possessed a passionate interest in the past. This historical mindedness was furthered in many ways. In Germany, the Grimm brothers collected

and published their nation's fairy tales. The revival of medieval Gothic architecture left European countrysides adorned with pseudo-medieval castles and cities bedecked with grandiose neo-Gothic cathedrals, city halls, parliamentary buildings, and even railway stations. Literature, too, reflected this historical consciousness. The

Gothic Literature: Edgar Allan Poe

American writers and poets made significant contributions to the movement of Romanticism. Although Edgar Allan Poe (1809–1849) was influenced by the German Romantic school of mystery and horror, many literary historians give him the credit for pioneering the modern short story. This selection from the conclusion of "The Fall of the House of Usher" gives a feeling for the nature of so-called Gothic literature.

Edgar Allan Poe, "The Fall of the House of Usher"

No sooner had these syllables passed my lips, than—as if a shield of brass had indeed, at the moment, fallen heavily upon a floor of silver—I became aware of a distinct, hollow, metallic, and clangorous, yet apparently muffled, reverberation. Complete unnerved, I leaped to my feet; but the measured rocking movement of Usher was undisturbed. I rushed to the chair in which he sat. His eyes were bent fixedly before him, and throughout his whole countenance there reigned a stony rigidity. But, as I placed my hand upon his shoulder, there came a strong shudder over his whole person; a sickly smile quivered about his lips; and I saw that he spoke in a low, hurried, and gibbering murmur, as if unconscious of my presence. Bending closely over him, I at length drank in the hideous import of his words.

"Not hear it?—yes, I hear it, and *have* heard it. Long-long-long-many minutes, many hours, many days, have I heard it—yet I dared not—oh, pity me, miserable wretch that I am!—I dared not—I *dared* not speak! *We have put her living in the tomb!* Said I not that my senses were acute? I *now* tell you that I heard her first feeble movements in the hollow coffin. I heard them—many, many days ago—yet I dared not—*I dared not speak!* And now—to-night—. . . the rending of her coffin, and the grating of the iron hinges of her prison, and her struggles within the coppered archway of the vault! Oh whither shall I fly? Will she not be here anon? Is she not hurrying to upbraid me for my haste? Have I not heard her footstep on the stair? Do I not distinguish that heavy and horrible beating of her heart? MADMAN!"—here he sprang furiously to his feet, and shrieked out his syllables, as if in the effort he were giving up his soul—"MADMAN! I TELL YOU THAT SHE NOW STANDS WITHOUT THE DOOR!"

As if in the superhuman energy of his utterance there had been found the potency of a spell, the huge antique panels to which the speaker pointed threw slowly back, upon the instant, their ponderous and ebony jaws. It was the work of the rushing gust—but then without those doors there DID stand the lofty and enshrouded figure of the lady Madeline of Usher. There was blood upon her white robes, and the evidence of some bitter struggle upon every portion of her emaciated frame. For a moment she remained trembling and reeling to and fro upon the threshold, then, with a low moaning cry, fell heavily inward upon the person of her brother, and in her violent and now final death-agonies, bore him to the floor a corpse, and a victim to the terrors he had anticipated.

novels of Walter Scott (1771–1832) became European best-sellers in the first half of the nineteenth century. *Ivanhoe*, in which Scott tried to evoke the clash between Saxon and Norman knights in medieval England, was one of his most popular works.

To the historical mindedness of the Romantics could be added an attraction to the bizarre and unusual. In an exaggerated form, this preoccupation gave rise to so-called Gothic literature (see the box above), chillingly evident in short stories of horror by the American Edgar Allan Poe (1809–1849) and in *Frankenstein* by Mary Shelley (1797–1851). Her novel was the story of a mad scientist who brings into being a humanlike monster who goes berserk. Some Romantics even sought the unusual in their own lives by pursuing extraordinary states of experience in dreams, nightmares, frenzies, and suicidal depression or by experimenting with cocaine, opium, and hashish to produce drug-induced, altered states of consciousness.

To the Romantics, poetry ranked above all other literary forms because it was regarded as the direct expression of one's soul. The Romantic poets were viewed as seers who could reveal the invisible world to others. Their incredible sense of drama made some of them the most colorful figures of their era, living intense but short lives. Percy Bysshe Shelley (1792–1822), expelled from school for advocating atheism, set out to reform the world. His *Prometheus Unbound*, completed in 1820, is a portrait of the revolt of human beings against the laws and customs that oppress them. He drowned in a storm in the

Mediterranean. Lord Byron (1788–1824) dramatized himself as the melancholy Romantic hero that he had described in his own work, *Childe Harold's Pilgrimage*. He joined the movement for Greek independence and died in Greece fighting the Turks.

Romantic poetry gave full expression to one of the most important characteristics of Romanticism: love of nature, especially evident in William Wordsworth (1770–1850), the foremost Romantic prophet of nature. His experience of nature was almost mystical as he claimed to receive "authentic tidings of invisible things":

> *One impulse from a vernal wood*
> *May teach you more of man,*
> *Of moral evil and of good,*
> *Than all the sages can.*[9]

To Wordsworth, nature contained a mysterious force that the poet could perceive and learn from. Nature served as a mirror into which humans could look to learn about themselves. Nature was, in fact, alive and sacred:

> *To every natural form, rock, fruits, or flower,*
> *Even the loose stones that cover the highway,*
> *I gave a moral life: I saw them feel,*
> *Or link'd them to some feeling: the great mass*
> *Lay bedded in a quickening soul, and all*
> *That I beheld, respired with inward meaning.*[10]

Other Romantics carried this worship of nature further into pantheism by identifying the great force in nature with God.

Romanticism was not only prevalent in Europe and the United States but also remained a dominant force in Latin American literary circles for much of the nineteenth century. Perhaps the best-known Romantic novel in Latin America was *María*, the work of the Colombian Jorge Isaacs. *María* was a Romantic, idealized account of hacienda life. Isaacs's portrayal of the beauties of nature and his account of individual suffering easily touched the emotions of his readers.

Like the literary arts, the visual arts were also deeply affected by Romanticism. Although they varied widely in what they produced, Romantic artists shared at least two fundamental characteristics. All artistic expression to them was a reflection of the artist's inner feelings; a painting should mirror the artist's vision of the world and be the instrument of his own imagination. Moreover, Romantic artists deliberately rejected the principles of classicism. Beauty was not a timeless thing; its expression depended on one's own culture and one's age. The Romantics abandoned classical restraint for warmth, emotion, and movement.

The early life experiences of Caspar David Friedrich (1774–1840) left him with a lifelong preoccupation with God and nature. Friedrich painted many landscapes but with an interest that transcended the mere presentation of natural details. His portrayals of mountains shrouded in mist, gnarled trees bathed in moonlight, and the stark ruins of monasteries surrounded by withered trees all

◆ **Casper David Friedrich, *Man and Woman Gazing at the Moon.*** The German artist Caspar David Friedrich sought to express in painting his own mystical view of nature. "The divine is everywhere," he once wrote, "even in a grain of sand." In this painting, two solitary wanderers are shown from the back gazing at the moon. Overwhelmed by the all-pervasive presence of nature, the two figures express the human longing for infinity.

♦ **Eugène Delacroix, *Women of Algiers*.** Also characteristic of Romanticism was its love of the exotic and unfamiliar. In his *Women of Algiers*, Delacroix reflected this fascination with the exotic in his portrayal of harem concubines in North Africa. At the same time, Delacroix's painting reflects his preoccupation with light and color.

conveyed a feeling of mystery and mysticism. For Friedrich, nature was a manifestation of divine life. As in *Man and Woman Gazing at the Moon*, he liked to depict one or two solitary figures gazing upon the grandeur of a natural scene with their backs to the viewer. Not only were his human figures dwarfed by the overwhelming presence of nature, but they expressed the human yearning for infinity, the desire to lose oneself in the universe. To Friedrich, the artistic process depended upon the use of an unrestricted imagination that could only be achieved through inner vision.

Eugène Delacroix (1798–1863) was one of the most famous French exponents of the Romantic school of painting. Delacroix's paintings exhibited two primary characteristics, a fascination with the exotic and a passion for color. Both are visible in his *Women of Algiers*. Significant for its use of light and its patches of interrelated color, this portrayal of the world of harem concubines in exotic North Africa was actually somewhat scandalous to the early nineteenth century. In Delacroix, theatricality and movement combined with a daring use of color. Many of his works reflect his own belief that "a painting should be a feast to the eye."

To many Romantics, music was the most Romantic of the arts because it enabled the composer to probe deeply into human emotions. Music historians have called the eighteenth century an age of classicism and the nineteenth the era of Romanticism. One of the greatest com-

posers of all time, Ludwig van Beethoven, served as a bridge between classicism and Romanticism.

Beethoven (1770–1827) was born in Bonn (Germany) but soon made his way to Vienna, then the musical capital of Europe, where he studied briefly under Mozart. Beginning in 1792, Vienna became his permanent residence although he was barely tolerated by Viennese society because of his unruly manner. During his first major period of composing from 1792 to 1802, his work was still largely within the classical framework of the eighteenth century, and his style differed little from that of Mozart and Haydn. But with his Third Symphony, the *Eroica*, originally intended for Napoleon, Beethoven broke through to the elements of Romanticism in his use of uncontrolled rhythms to create dramatic struggle and uplifted resolutions. E. T. A. Hoffman, a contemporary composer and writer, said, "Beethoven's music opens the flood gates of fear, of terror, of horror, of pain, and arouses that longing for the eternal which is the essence of Romanticism. He is thus a pure Romantic composer."[11]

A New Age of Science

Between 1850 and 1870, two major intellectual developments stand out: the growth of scientific knowledge with its rapidly increasing impact on the Western worldview, and the shift from Romanticism with its emphasis on the inner world of reality to Realism with its focus on the outer, material world.

By the mid-nineteenth century, as theoretical discoveries in science led to an increased number of derived practical benefits, science came to have a greater and greater impact on European life. The Scientific Revolution of the sixteenth and seventeenth centuries had fundamentally transformed the Western worldview and initiated a modern, rational approach to the study of natural phenomena. Even in the eighteenth century, however, these intellectual developments had remained the preserve of an educated elite and resulted in few practical benefits. Moreover, the technical advances of the early Industrial Revolution had depended little on pure science and much more on the practical experiments of technologically oriented amateur inventors. Advances in industrial technology, however, fed an interest in basic scientific research, which, in turn, in the 1830s and afterward resulted in a rash of basic scientific discoveries that were soon transformed into technological improvements that affected everybody.

The development of the steam engine was important in encouraging scientists to work out its theoretical foundations, a preoccupation that led to thermodynamics, the science of the relationship between heat and mechanical energy. The laws of thermodynamics were at the core of nineteenth-century physics. In biology, the Frenchman Louis Pasteur discovered the germ theory of disease, which had enormous practical applications in the development of modern, scientific medical practices. In chemistry, the Russian Dmitri Mendeleyev in the 1860s classified all the material elements then known on the basis of their atomic weights and provided the systematic foundation for the periodic law. The Briton Michael Faraday discovered the phenomenon of electromagnetic induction and put together a primitive generator that laid the foundation for the use of electricity, although economically efficient generators were not built until the 1870s.

The steadily increasing and often dramatic material benefits generated by science and technology led Europeans to have a growing faith in the benefits of science. The popularity of scientific and technological achievement led to a widespread acceptance of the scientific method, based on observation, experiment, and logical analysis, as the only path to objective truth and objective reality. This, in turn, undermined the faith of many people in religious revelation and truth. It is no accident that the nineteenth century was an age of increasing secularization, particularly evident in the growth of materialism or the belief that everything mental, spiritual, or ideal was simply an outgrowth of physical forces. Truth was to be found in the concrete material existence of human beings, not as Romanticists imagined in revelations gained by feeling or intuitive flashes. The importance of materialism was strikingly evident in the most important scientific event of the nineteenth century, the development of the theory of organic evolution according to natural selection. On the theories of Charles Darwin could be built a picture of humans as material beings that were simply part of the natural world.

In 1859, Charles Darwin (1809–1882) published his celebrated book, *On the Origin of Species by Means of Natural Selection*. The basic idea of this book was that all plants and animals had evolved over a long period of time from earlier and simpler forms of life, a principle known as organic evolution. Darwin was important in explaining how this natural process worked. In every species, he argued, "many more individuals of each species are born than can possibly survive." This results in a "struggle for existence." "As more individuals are produced than can possibly survive, there must in every case be a struggle for existence, either one individual with another of the same species, or with the individuals of distinct species, or with the physical conditions of life." Those who succeeded in this struggle for existence had adapted better to their environment, a process made possible by the appearance of "variants." Chance variations occurred in the process of inheritance, he thought, that enabled some organisms to be more adaptable to the environment than others, a process that Darwin called natural selection:

> Owing to this struggle [for existence], variations, however slight. . . , if they be in any degree profitable to the individuals of a species, in their infinitely complex relations to other organic beings and to their physical conditions of life, will tend to the preservation of such individuals, and will generally be inherited by the offspring.[12]

Those that were naturally selected for survival ("survival of the fit") survived. The unfit did not and became extinct. The fit who survived, in turn, propagated and passed on the variations that enabled them to survive until, from Darwin's point of view, a new separate species emerged.

In *On the Origin of Species,* Darwin discussed plant and animal species only. He was not concerned with humans themselves and only later applied his theory of natural selection to humans. In *The Descent of Man,* published in 1871, he argued for the animal origins of human beings: "man is the co-descendant with other mammals of a common progenitor." Humans were not an exception to the rule governing other species.

Although Darwin's ideas were eventually accepted, initially they were highly controversial. Some people objected to what they considered Darwin's debasement of humans; his theory, they claimed, made human beings ordinary products of nature rather than unique beings. Others were disturbed by the implications of life as a struggle for survival, of "nature red in tooth and claw." Was there a place in the Darwinian world for moral values? For those who believed in a rational order in the world, Darwin's theory seemed to eliminate purpose and design from the universe. Gradually, however, Darwin's theory was accepted by scientists and other intellectuals although Darwin was somewhat overly optimistic when he wrote in 1872 that "almost every scientist admits the principle of evolution." In the process of accepting Darwin's ideas, some people even tried to apply them to society, yet another example of science's increasing prestige.

Realism in Literature and Art

Closely related to the materialistic outlook was the belief that the world should be viewed realistically, an idea that was frequently expressed after 1850. The word *Realism* was first employed in 1850 to describe a new style of painting and soon spread to literature. The literary Realists of the mid-nineteenth century were distinguished by their deliberate rejection of Romanticism. The literary Realists wanted to deal with ordinary characters from actual life rather than Romantic heroes in exotic settings. They also sought to avoid exaggerated and emotional language by using close observation and precise description, an approach that led them to eschew poetry in favor of prose and the novel. Realists often combined their interest in everyday life with a searching examination of social questions. Even then they tried not to preach but to allow their characters to speak for themselves. Although the French were preeminent in literary Realism, it also proved to be international in scope.

The leading novelist of the 1850s and 1860s, the Frenchman Gustave Flaubert (1821–1880), perfected the Realist novel. His *Madame Bovary* (1857) was a straightforward description of barren and sordid provincial life in France. Emma Bovary, a woman of some vitality, is trapped in a marriage to a drab provincial doctor. Impelled by the images of romantic love she has read about in novels, she seeks the same thing for herself in adulterous love affairs. Unfulfilled, she is ultimately driven to suicide, unrepentant to the end for her lifestyle. Flaubert's hatred of bourgeois society was evident in his portrayal of middle-class hypocrisy and smugness.

The British novelist Charles Dickens (1812–1870) achieved extraordinary success with his realistic novels focusing on the lower and middle classes in Britain's early industrial age. His descriptions of the urban poor and the brutalization of human life were vividly realistic. But Dickens also demonstrated an interesting facet of Realism—a streak of Romantic imagery that permeated his descriptions of the sordid and commonplace. Nowhere is this more evident than in *The Old Curiosity Shop* where his description of an industrial nightmare conjures up the imagery of Dante's Hell (see the box on p. 773).

Realism also made inroads into the Latin American literary scene by the second half of the nineteenth century. There, Realist novelists focused on the injustices of their society, evident in the work of Clorinda Matto de Turner (1852–1909). Her *Aves sin Nido (Birds without a Nest)* was a brutal revelation of the pitiful living conditions of the Indians in Peru. She especially blamed the Catholic church for much of their misery.

In art, too, Realism became dominant after 1850, although Romanticism was by no means dead. Realist art demonstrated three major characteristics: a desire to depict the everyday life of ordinary people, whether peasants, workers, or prostitutes; an attempt at photographic realism; and an interest in the natural environment. The French became leaders in Realist painting.

Gustave Courbet (1819–1877) was the most famous artist of the realist school. In fact, the word *Realism* was first coined in 1850 to describe one of his paintings. Courbet reveled in a realistic portrayal of everyday life. His subjects were factory workers, peasants, and the wives of saloon keepers. "I have never seen either angels or goddesses, so I am not interested in painting them," he exclaimed. One of his famous works, *The Stonebreakers*, painted in 1849, shows two road workers engaged in the deadening work of breaking stones to build a road. This representation of human misery was a scandal to those who objected to his "cult of ugliness." To Courbet, no subject was too ordinary, too harsh, or too ugly to interest him.

◆ **Gustave Courbet,** *The Stonebreakers.*   Realism, largely developed by French painters, aimed at a lifelike portrayal of the daily activities of ordinary people. Gustave Courbet was the most famous of the Realist artists. As is evident in *The Stonebreakers*, he sought to portray things as they really appear. He shows an old road builder and his young assistant in their tattered clothes, engrossed in their dreary work of breaking stones to construct a road.

Realism: Charles Dickens and an Image of Hell on Earth

Charles Dickens was a highly successful English novelist. While he realistically portrayed the material, social, and psychological milieu of his time, an element of Romanticism still pervaded his novels. This is evident in this selection from The Old Curiosity Shop *in which his description of the English mill town of Birmingham takes on the imagery of Dante's Hell.*

Charles Dickens, *The Old Curiosity Shop*

A long suburb of red brick houses,—some with patches of garden ground, where coal-dust and factory smoke darkened the shrinking leaves, and coarse rank flowers; and where the struggling vegetation sickened and sank under the hot breath of kiln and furnace, making them by its presence seem yet more blighting and unwholesome than in the town itself,—a long, flat, straggling suburb passed, they came by slow degrees upon a cheerless region, where not a blade of grass was seen to grow; where not a bud put forth its promise in the spring; where nothing green could live but on the surface of the stagnant pools, which here and there lay idly sweltering by the black roadside.

Advancing more and more into the shadow of this mournful place, its dark depressing influence stole upon their spirits, and filled them with a dismal gloom. On every side, and as far as the eye could see into the heavy distance, tall chimneys, crowding on each other, and presenting that endless repetition of the same dull, ugly form, which is the horror of oppressive dreams, poured out their plague of smoke, obscured the light, and made foul the melancholy air. On mounds of ashes by the wayside, sheltered only by a few rough boards, or rotten pent-house roofs, strange engines spun and writhed like tortured creatures; clanking their iron chains, shrieking in their rapid whirl from time to time as though in torment unendurable, and making the ground tremble with their agonies. Dismantled houses here and there appeared, tottering to the earth, propped up by fragments of others that had fallen down, unroofed, windowless, blackened, desolate, but yet inhabited. Men, women, children, wan in their looks and ragged in attire, tended the engines, fed their tributary fires, begged upon the road, or scowled half-naked from the doorless houses. Then came more of the wrathful monsters, whose like they almost seemed to be in their wildness and their untamed air, screeching and turning round and round again; and still, before, behind, and to the right and left, was the same interminable perspective of brick towers, never ceasing in their black vomit, blasting all things living or inanimate, shutting out the face of day, and closing in on all these horrors with a dense dark cloud.

But night-time in this dreadful spot!—night, when the smoke was changed to fire; when every chimney spurted up its flame; and places, that had been dark vaults all day, now shone red-hot, with figures moving to and from within their blazing jaws, and calling to one another with hoarse cries—night, when the noise of every strange machine was aggravated by the darkness; when the people near them looked wilder and more savage; when bands of unemployed labourers paraded the roads, or clustered by torch-light round their leaders, who told them in stern language of their wrongs, and urged them on to frightful cries and threats; when maddened men, armed with sword and firebrand, spurning the tears and prayers of women who would restrain them, rushed forth on errands of terror and destruction, to work no ruin half so surely as their own—night, when carts came rumbling by, filled with rude coffins (for contagious disease and death had been busy with the living crops); when orphans cried, and distracted women shrieked and followed in their wake—night, when some called for bread, and some for drink to drown their cares, and some with tears, and some with staggering feet, and some with bloodshot eyes, went brooding home—night, which, unlike the night that Heaven sends on earth, brought with it no peace, nor quiet, nor signs of blessed sleep—who shall tell the terrors of the night to the young wandering child!

Conclusion

Between 1800 and 1870, the forces unleashed by two revolutions—the French Revolution and the Industrial Revolution—transformed much of the world. The Industrial Revolution seemed to prove to Europeans the underlying assumption of the Scientific Revolution of the seventeenth century—that human beings were capable of dominating nature. By rationally manipulating the material environment for human benefit, people could create new levels of material prosperity and produce machines not dreamed of in their wildest imaginings. Lost in the excitement of the Industrial Revolution were the voices that pointed to the dehumanization of the workforce and the alienation from one's work, one another, one's self, and the natural world.

In 1815, a conservative order had been reestablished throughout Europe, and the great powers cooperated to try to ensure its durability. But the revolutionary waves in Latin America and Europe in the first half of the nineteenth century made it clear that the ideologies of liberalism and nationalism, unleashed by the French Revolution and now reinforced by the spread of the Industrial Revolution, were still alive and active in the Western world. Between 1850 and 1871, the national state became the focus of people's loyalty. Wars, both foreign and civil, were fought to create unified nation-states, while both wars and changing political alignments served as catalysts for domestic reforms that made the nation-state the center of attention. In 1870, however, the political transformations stimulated by the force of nationalism were by no means complete. Significantly large minorities, especially in the polyglot empires controlled by the Austrians, Ottoman Turks, and Russians, had not achieved the goal of their own national states. Moreover, the nationalism that had triumphed by 1870 was no longer the nationalism that had been closely identified with liberalism. Liberal nationalists had believed that unified nation-states would preserve individual rights and lead to a greater community of peoples. But the new nationalism of the late nineteenth century, loud and chauvinistic, did not unify peoples, but divided them as the new national states became embroiled in bitter competition after 1870.

Many people, however, were hardly aware of nationalism's dangers in 1870. The spread of industrialization and the growing popularity of scientific and technological achievements were sources of optimism, not pessimism. After the revolutionary and military upheavals of the mid-century decades, many Westerners undoubtedly believed that they stood on the verge of a new age of progress.

CHAPTER NOTES

1. Quotations can be found in E. Royston Pike, *Human Documents of the Industrial Revolution in Britain* (London, 1966), pp. (in order of quotations) 320, 314, 343.
2. Ibid., p. 315.
3. Ibid., pp. 343–44.
4. Ibid., pp. 60–61.
5. Quoted in M. S. Anderson, *The Ascendancy of Europe, 1815–1914,* 2d ed. (London, 1985), p. 1.
6. Quoted in E. Bradford Burns, *Latin America: A Concise Interpretative History,* 4th ed. (Englewood Cliffs, N.J., 1986), p. 116.
7. Louis L. Snyder, ed., *Documents of German History* (New Brunswick, N.J., 1958), p. 202.
8. Quoted in Otto Pflanze, *Bismarck and the Development of Germany: The Period of Unification, 1815–1871* (Princeton, N.J., 1963), p. 327.
9. William Wordsworth, "The Tables Turned," *Poems of Wordsworth,* ed. Matthew Arnold (London, 1963), p. 138.
10. William Wordsworth, *The Prelude* (Harmondsworth, 1971), p. 109.
11. Quoted in Siegbert Prawer, ed., *The Romantic Period in Germany* (London, 1970), p. 285.
12. Charles Darwin, *On the Origin of Species* (New York, 1872), 1:77, 79.

SUGGESTED READINGS

For a good, up-to-date survey of the entire nineteenth century, see R. Gildea, *Barricades and Borders, Europe 1800–1914* (Oxford, 1987) in the Short Oxford History of the Modern World series. Also valuable is M. S. Anderson, *The Ascendancy of Europe, 1815–1914,* 2d ed. (London, 1985). The well-written work by D. Landes, *The Unbound Prometheus: Technological Change and In-* *dustrial Development in Western Europe from 1750 to the Present* (Cambridge, 1969), is still a good introduction to the Industrial Revolution. Although more technical, also of value are S. Pollard, *Peaceful Conquest: The Industrialization of Europe, 1760–1970* (Oxford, 1981) and P. Mathias and J. A. Davis, eds., *The First Industrial Revolutions* (Oxford, 1989). For an introduction to the Industrial Revolution in Britain, see P. Mathias, *The First Industrial Nation: An Economic History of Britain, 1700–1914,* 2d ed. (New York, 1983). Given the importance of Great Britain in the Industrial Revolution, a good book for placing the Industrial Revolution in Britain into a broader context is E. J. Evans, *The Forging of the Modern State: Early Industrial Britain, 1783–1870* (London, 1983).

A general discussion of population growth in Europe can be found in T. McKeown, *The Modern Rise of Population* (London, 1976). For an examination of urban growth, see the work by A. R. Sutcliffe, *Towards the Planned City: Germany, Britain, the United States and France, 1780–1914* (Oxford, 1981). On the social impact of the Industrial Revolution, see C. Morazé, *The Triumph of the Middle Classes* (London, 1966); F. Crouzet, *The First Industrialists: The Problems of Origins* (Cambridge, 1985), on British entrepreneurs; and E. Gauldie, *Cruel Habitations, A History of Working-Class Housing, 1790–1918* (London, 1974). G. Himmelfarb, *The Idea of Poverty: England in the Early Industrial Age* (New York, 1984) traces the concepts of poverty and poor from the mid-eighteenth century to the mid-nineteenth century. A valuable work on female labor patterns is L. A. Tilly and J. W. Scott, *Women, Work, and Family* (New York, 1978).

A concise summary of the international events of the entire nineteenth century can be found in R. Bullen and F. R. Bridge, *The Great Powers and the European State System, 1815–1914* (London, 1980). There are some useful books on individual countries that cover more than the subject of this chapter. These include R. Magraw, *France, 1815–1914: The Bourgeois Century* (London, 1983); H. Seton-Watson, *The Russian Empire, 1801–1917* (Oxford, 1967); H. Holborn, *A History of Modern Germany,* vol. 2, *1648–1840* (New York, 1964); and C. A. Macartney, *The Habsburg Empire, 1790–1918* (London, 1971).

On the man whose conservative policies dominated this era, see the brief but good biography by A. Palmer, *Metternich* (New York, 1972). On the revolutions in Europe in 1830, see C. Church, *Europe in 1830: Revolution and Political Change* (Chapel Hill, N.C., 1983). The best introduction to the Revolutions of 1848 is P. Stearns, *1848: The Revolutionary Tide in Europe* (New York, 1974).

For a comprehensive survey of Latin American history, see E. Williamson, *The Penguin History of Latin America* (London, 1992). On the revolts in Latin America, see J. Lynch, *The Spanish American Revolutions, 1808–1826* (New York, 1973). A good survey of nineteenth-century developments can be found in D. Bushnell and N. Macaulay, *The Emergence of Latin America in the Nineteenth Century* (Oxford, 1988). For a detailed account of the Ottoman Empire in the nineteenth century, see S. Shaw, *History of the Ottoman Empire and Modern Turkey,* vol. 2 (Cambridge, 1977).

The unification of Italy can best be examined in the works of D. M. Smith, *Victor Emmanuel, Cavour and the Risorgimento* (London, 1971) and *Cavour* (London, 1985). The unification of Germany can be pursued first in two good biographies of Bismarck, E. Crankshaw, *Bismarck* (New York, 1981) and G. O. Kent, *Bismarck and His Times* (Carbondale, Ill., 1978). For a good introduction to the French Second Empire, see A. Plessis, *The Rise and Fall of the Second Empire, 1852–1871,* trans. J. Mandelbaum (New York, 1985). Louis Napoleon's role can be examined in W. H. C. Smith, *Napoleon III* (New York, 1972). On the emancipation of the Russian serfs, see D. Field, *The End of Serfdom: Nobility and Bureaucracy in Russia, 1855–1861* (Cambridge, 1976). The evolution of British political parties in mid-century is examined in H. J. Hanham, *Elections and Party Management: Politics in the Time of Disraeli and Gladstone,* 2d ed. (London, 1978). A good one-volume survey of the Civil War can be found in P. J. Parish, *The American Civil War* (New York, 1975). For a general history of Canada, see C. Brown, ed., *The Illustrated History of Canada* (Toronto, 1991).

G. L. Mosse, *The Culture of Western Europe: The Nineteenth and Twentieth Centuries* (Chicago, 1961) remains a good introduction to the cultural history of Europe. For an introduction to the intellectual changes of the nineteenth century, see O. Chadwick, *The Secularization of the European Mind in the Nineteenth Century* (Cambridge, 1975). A beautifully illustrated introduction to Romanticism can be found in H. Honour, *Romanticism* (New York, 1979). On the ideas of the Romantics, see H. G. Schenk, *The Mind of the European Romantics* (Garden City, N.Y., 1969) and M. Cranston, *The Romantic Movement* (Oxford, 1994). A detailed biography of Darwin can be found in R. W. Clark, *The Survival of Charles Darwin* (New York, 1984). On Realism, there is a good introduction in L. Nochlin, *Realism* (Harmondsworth, 1971).

CHAPTER
21

The Emergence of Mass Society in the Western World

During the fifty years before 1914, the Western world witnessed a dynamic age of material prosperity. With new industries, new sources of energy, and new goods, a Second Industrial Revolution transformed the human environment and led people to believe that material progress meant human progress. Scientific and technological achievements, many naively believed, would improve humanity's condition and solve all human problems. The doctrine of progress became an article of great faith.

The new urban and industrial world created by the rapid economic changes of the nineteenth century led to the emergence of a mass society by the late nineteenth century. A mass society meant improvements for the lower classes who benefited from the extension of voting rights, a better standard of living, and mass education. It also brought mass leisure. New work patterns established the "weekend" as a distinct time of recreation and fun while new forms of mass transportation—railroads and streetcars—enabled even workers to make brief excursions to amusement parks. Coney Island was only eight miles from central New York City; Blackpool in England was a short train ride from nearby industrial towns. With their Ferris wheels and other daring rides that threw young men and women together, amusement parks offered a whole new world of entertainment. Thanks to the railroad, seaside resorts, once the preserve of the wealthy, also became accessible to more people for weekend visits, much to the disgust of one upper-class regular who complained about the

Beginning of Third Republic in France

Mexican Revolution begins

Triple Alliance

Triple Entente

Bell invents the telephone

Women's Social and Political Union founded in Britain

Emergence of mass newspapers

Mass production of Ford's Model T

Impressionism

Freud, *The Interpretation of Dreams*

Beginning of abstract painting

Einstein's special theory of relativity

new "day-trippers": "They swarm upon the beach, wandering listlessly about with apparently no other aim than to get a mouthful of fresh air." Enterprising entrepreneurs in resorts like Blackpool welcomed the masses of new visitors, however, and built piers laden with food, drink, and entertainment to serve them.

The coming of mass society also created new roles for the governments of European nation-states, which now fostered national loyalty, created mass armies by conscription, and took more responsibility for public health and housing measures in their cities. By 1871, the national state had become the focus of Europeans' lives. Within many of these nation-states, the growth of the middle class had led to the triumph of liberal practices: constitutional governments, parliaments, and principles of equality. The period after 1871 also witnessed the growth of political democracy as the right to vote was extended to all adult males; women, though, would still have to fight for the same political rights. With political democracy came a new mass politics and a new mass press. Both would become regular features of the twentieth century.

The period between 1870 and 1914 was also a time of great tension as imperialist adventures, international rivalries, and cultural uncertainties disturbed the apparent calm. Europeans engaged in a great race for colonies that greatly intensified existing antagonisms among European states, while the creation of mass conscript armies and enormous military establishments served to further the tensions among the major powers. At the same time, despite the appearance of progress, Western philosophers, writers, and artists were creating modern cultural expressions that questioned traditional ideas and values and increasingly provoked a crisis of confidence. Before 1914, many intellectuals had a sense of unease about the direction society was headed, accompanied by a feeling of imminent catastrophe. They proved remarkably prophetic.

The Growth of Industrial Prosperity

At the heart of Europe's belief in progress between 1870 and 1914 was the stunning material growth produced by what historians have called the Second Industrial Revolution. The first Industrial Revolution had given rise to textiles, railroads, iron, and coal. In the second revolution, steel, chemicals, electricity, and petroleum led the way to new industrial frontiers.

New Products and New Patterns

The first major change in industrial development between 1870 and 1914 was the substitution of steel for iron. New methods for rolling and shaping steel made it useful in the construction of lighter, smaller, and faster machines and engines as well as for railways, shipbuilding, and armaments. In 1860, Great Britain, France, Germany, and Belgium produced 125,000 tons of steel; by 1913, the total was 32 million tons. By 1910, German

steel production was double that of Great Britain, and both had been surpassed by the United States.

Electricity was a major new form of energy that proved to be of great value because it could be easily converted into other forms of energy, such as heat, light, and motion, and moved relatively effortlessly through space by means of transmitting wires. The first commercially practical generators of electrical current were not developed until the 1870s. By 1910, hydroelectric power stations and coal-fired steam-generating plants enabled entire dis-

Map 21.1   The Industrial Regions of Europe by 1914.

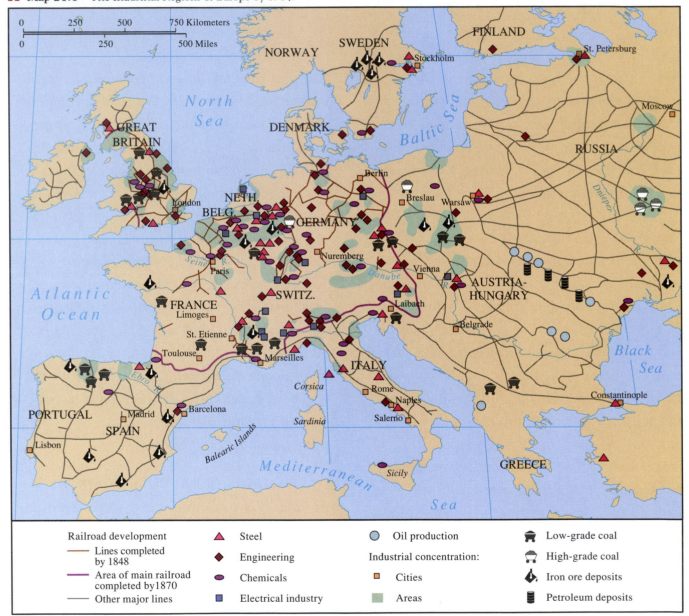

tricts to be tied into a single power distribution system that provided a common source of power for homes, shops, and industrial enterprises.

Electricity spawned a whole series of new products. The invention of the lightbulb by the American Thomas Edison and the Briton Joseph Swan opened homes and cities to illumination by electric lights. A revolution in communications was fostered when Alexander Graham Bell invented the telephone in 1876 and Guglielmo Marconi sent the first radio waves across the Atlantic in 1901. Although most electricity was initially used for lighting, it was eventually put to use in transportation. By the 1880s, streetcars and subways had appeared in major European cities. Electricity also transformed the factory. Conveyor belts, cranes, machines, and machine-tools could all be powered by electricity and located anywhere. Thanks to electricity, all countries could now enter the industrial age.

The development of the internal combustion engine had a similar effect. The processing of liquid fuels, namely, petroleum and its distilled derivatives, made possible the widespread use of the internal combustion engine as a source of power in transportation. An oil-fired engine was made in 1897, and by 1902, the Hamburg-Amerika Line had switched from coal to oil on its new ocean liners. By the beginning of the twentieth century, some naval fleets had been converted to oil burners as well.

The internal combustion engine gave rise to the automobile and airplane. In 1900, world production stood at 9,000 cars; by 1906, Americans had overtaken the initial lead of the French. It was an American, Henry Ford, who revolutionized the car industry with the mass production of the Model T. By 1916, Ford's factories were producing 735,000 cars a year. In the meantime, air transportation had emerged with the Zeppelin airship in 1900. In 1903, at Kitty Hawk, North Carolina, the Wright brothers made the first flight in a fixed-wing plane powered by a gasoline engine. It took World War I, however, to stimulate the aircraft industry, and it was not until 1919 that the first regular passenger air service was established.

The growth of industrial production depended upon the development of markets for the sale of manufactured goods. After 1870, the best foreign markets were already heavily saturated, forcing Europeans to take a renewed look at their domestic markets. Between 1850 and 1900, real wages had increased in Britain by two-thirds and in Germany by one-third. A decline in the cost of food combined with lower prices for manufactured goods because of reduced transportation costs made it easier for Europeans to buy consumer products. Businesses soon

perceived the value of using new techniques of mass marketing to sell the consumer goods made possible by the development of the steel and electrical industries. By bringing together a vast array of new products in one place, they created the department store (see the box on p. 780). The desire to own sewing machines, clocks, bicycles, electric lights, and typewriters rapidly created a new consumer ethic that became a crucial part of the modern economy.

Meanwhile, increased competition for foreign markets and the growing importance of domestic demand led to a reaction against the free trade that had characterized much of the European economy between 1820 and 1870. To many industrial and political leaders, protective tariffs guaranteed domestic markets for the products of their own industries. By the 1870s, Europeans were returning to the practice of tariff protection. At the same time, cartels were being formed to decrease competition internally. In a cartel, independent enterprises worked together to control prices and fix production quotas, thereby restraining the kind of competition that led to reduced prices. Cartels were especially strong in Germany, where banks moved to protect their investments by eliminating the "anarchy of competition." Founded in 1893, the Rhenish-Westphalian Coal Syndicate controlled 98 percent of Germany's coal production by 1904.

The formation of cartels was paralleled by a move toward ever-larger manufacturing plants, especially in the iron and steel, machinery, heavy electrical equipment, and chemical industries. This growth in the size of industrial plants led to pressure for greater efficiency in factory production at the same time that competition led to demands for greater economy. The result was a desire to streamline or rationalize production as much as possible. The development of precision tools enabled manufacturers to produce interchangeable parts, which in turn led to the creation of the assembly line for production. First used in the United States for small arms and clocks, the assembly line had moved to Europe by 1850. In the last half of the nineteenth century, it was primarily used in manufacturing nonmilitary goods, such as sewing machines, typewriters, bicycles, and finally the automobile.

The emergence of protective tariffs and cartels was clearly a response to the growth of the multinational industrial system. Economic competition intensified the political rivalries of the age. The growth of the national state, which had seemed in the mid-nineteenth century to be the answer to old problems, now seemed to be creating new ones.

Between 1870 and 1914, Germany replaced Great Britain as the industrial leader of Europe. Already in the

The Department Store and the Beginnings of Mass Consumerism

Domestic markets were especially important for the sale of the goods being turned out by Europe's increasing number of industrial plants. New techniques of mass marketing arose to encourage the sale of the new consumer goods. The Parisians pioneered in the development of the department store, and this selection is taken from a contemporary's account of the growth of these stores in the French capital city.

E. Lavasseur, On Parisian Department Stores, 1907

It was in the reign of Louis-Phillippe that department stores for fashion goods and dresses, extending to material and other clothing, began to be distinguished. The type was already one of the notable developments of the Second Empire; it became one of the most important ones of the Third Republic. These stores have increased in number and several of them have become extremely large. Combining in their different departments all articles of clothing, toilet articles, furniture and many other ranges of goods, it is their special object so to combine all commodities as to attract and satisfy customers who will find conveniently together an assortment of a mass of articles corresponding to all their various needs. They attract customers by permanent display, by free entry into the shops, by periodic exhibitions, by special sales, by fixed prices, and by their ability to deliver the goods purchased to customers' homes, in Paris and to the provinces. Turning themselves into direct intermediaries between the producer and the consumer, even producing sometimes some of their articles in their own workshops, buying at lowest prices because of their large orders and because they are in a position to profit from bargains, working with large sums, and selling to most of their customers for cash only, they can transmit these benefits in lowered selling prices. They can even decide to sell at a loss, as an advertisement or to get rid of out-of-date fashions. Taking 5–6 per cent on 100 million brings them in more than 20 per cent would bring to a firm doing a turnover of 50,000 francs.

The success of these department stores is only possible thanks to the volume of their business and this volume needs considerable capital and a very large turnover. Now capital, having become abundant, is freely combined nowadays in large enterprises, although French capital has the reputation of being more wary of the risks of industry than of State or railway securities. On the other hand, the large urban agglomerations, the ease with which goods can be transported by the railways, the diffusion of some comforts to strata below the middle classes, have all favored these developments.

As example we may cite some figures relating to these stores, since they were brought to the notice of the public in the *Revue des Deux-Mondes*. . . .

Le Louvre, dating to the time of the extension of the rue de Rivoli under the Second Empire, did in 1893 a business of 120 million at a profit of 6.4 per cent. *Le Bon-Marché*, which was a small shop when Mr. Boucicaut entered it in 1852, already did a business of 20 million at the end of the Empire. During the republic its new buildings were erected; Mme. Boucicaut turned it by her will into a kind of co-operative society, with shares and an ingenious organization; turnover reached 150 million in 1893, leaving a profit of 5 per cent. . . .

According to the tax records of 1891, these stores in Paris, numbering 12, employed 1,708 persons and were rated on their site values at 2,159,000 francs; the largest had then 542 employees. These same stores had, in 1901, 9,784 employees; one of them over 2,000 and another over 1,600; their site value has doubled (4,089,000 francs).

1890s, Germany's superiority was evident in new areas of manufacturing, such as organic chemicals and electrical equipment, and increasingly apparent in its ever-greater share of worldwide trade. But the struggle for economic (and political) supremacy between Great Britain and Germany should not cause us to overlook the other great polarization of the age. By 1900, Europe was divided into two economic zones. Great Britain, Belgium, France, the Netherlands, Germany, the western part of the Austro-Hungarian Empire, and northern Italy constituted an advanced industrialized core that had a high standard of living, decent systems of transportation, and relatively healthy and educated peoples. Another part of Europe, the backward and little industrialized area to the south and east, consisting of southern Italy, most of Austria-Hungary, Spain, Portugal, the Balkan kingdoms, and Russia, was still largely agricultural and relegated by the industrial countries to the function of providing food and raw materials. The presence of Romanian oil, Greek olive oil, and Serbian pigs and prunes in western Europe served as reminders of an economic division of Europe that continued well into the twentieth century.

Toward a World Economy

The economic developments of the late nineteenth century, combined with the transportation revolution that saw the growth of marine transport and railroads, fostered a true world economy. By 1900, Europeans were receiving beef and wool from Argentina and Australia, coffee from Brazil, nitrates from Chile, iron ore from Algeria, and sugar from Java. European capital was also invested abroad to develop railways, mines, electrical power plants, and banks. High rates of return, such as 11.3 percent on Latin American banking shares that were floated in London, provided plenty of incentive. Of course, foreign countries also provided markets for the surplus manufactured goods of Europe. With its capital, industries, and military might, Europe dominated the world economy by the beginning of the twentieth century.

Women and Work: New Job Opportunities

The Second Industrial Revolution had an enormous impact on the position of women in the labor market. During the course of the nineteenth century, considerable controversy erupted over a woman's "right to work." Working-class organizations tended to reinforce the underlying ideology of domesticity; women should remain at home to bear and nurture children and not be allowed in the industrial workforce. Working-class men argued that keeping women out of industrial work would ensure the moral and physical well-being of families. In reality, keeping women out of the industrial workforce simply made it easier to exploit them when they needed income to supplement their husbands' wages or to support their families when their husbands were unemployed. The desperate need to work at times forced women to do marginal work at home or labor as pieceworkers in sweatshops.

After 1870, however, new job opportunities for women became available. The development of larger industrial plants and the expansion of government services created a variety of service or white-collar jobs. The increased demand for white-collar workers at relatively low wages coupled with a shortage of male workers led employers to hire women. Big businesses and retail shops needed clerks, typists, secretaries, file clerks, and salesclerks. The expansion of government services created opportunities for women to be secretaries and telephone operators and to take jobs in health and social services. Compulsory education necessitated more teachers while the development of modern hospital services opened the way for an increase in nurses.

Many of the new white-collar jobs were by no means exciting. The work was routine and, except for teaching

◆ **An Age of Progress.**   Between 1871 and 1914, a Second Industrial Revolution led many Europeans to believe that they were living in an age of progress when most human problems would be solved by scientific achievements. This illustration is taken from a special issue of *The Illustrated London News* celebrating the Diamond Jubilee of Queen Victoria in 1897. On the left are scenes from 1837, when Victoria came to the British throne; on the right are scenes from 1897. The vivid contrast underscored the magazine's conclusion: "The most striking . . . evidence of progress during the reign is the ever increasing speed which the discoveries of physical science have forced into everyday life. Steam and electricity have conquered time and space to a greater extent during the last sixty years than all the preceding six hundred years witnessed."

and nursing, required few skills beyond basic literacy. Although there was little hope for advancement, these jobs had distinct advantages for the daughters of the middle classes and especially the upward-aspiring working classes. For some middle-class women, the new jobs offered freedom from the domestic patterns expected of them. Most of the jobs, however, were filled by working-class females who saw the job as an opportunity to escape from the "dirty" work of the lower-class world.

Organizing the Working Classes

The desire to improve their working and living conditions led many industrial workers to form socialist political parties and socialist labor unions. These emerged after 1870, but the theory that made them possible had already been developed by mid-century in the work of Karl Marx.

Marxism made its first appearance on the eve of the revolutions of 1848 with the publication of a short treatise entitled *The Communist Manifesto*, written by two Germans, Karl Marx (1818–1883) and Friedrich Engels (1820–1895). The work became one of the most influential political treatises in modern European history. At the same time, it contained the substance of the basic economic and political ideas that Marx elaborated upon during the rest of his life.

What, then, was the basic picture of historical development that Marx and Engels offered in *The Communist Manifesto*? They began their treatise with the statement that "the history of all hitherto existing society is the history of class struggles." Throughout history, then, oppressor and oppressed have "stood in constant opposition to one another." In an earlier struggle, the feudal classes of the Middle Ages were forced to accede to the emerging middle class or bourgeoisie. As the bourgeoisie took control in turn, their ideas became the dominant views of the era, and government became their instrument. Marx and Engels declared: "The executive of the modern State is but a committee for managing the common affairs of the whole bourgeoisie."[1] In other words, the government of the state reflected and defended the interests of the industrial middle class and its allies.

Although bourgeois society had emerged victorious out of the ruins of feudal society, Marx and Engels insisted that it had not triumphed completely. Now once again the bourgeoisie were antagonists in an emerging class struggle, but this time they faced the proletariat, or the industrial working class. The struggle would be fierce; in fact, Marx and Engels predicted that the workers would eventually overthrow their bourgeois masters. After their victory, the proletariat would form a dictatorship

to reorganize the means of production. Then, a classless society would emerge, and the state—itself an instrument of the bourgeoisie—would wither away because it no longer represented the interests of a particular class. Class struggles would then be over (see the box on p. 783). Marx believed that the emergence of a classless society would lead to progress in science, technology, and industry and to greater wealth for all.

After the failure of the revolutions of 1848, Marx returned to Britain, where he spent the rest of his life in exile. Marx continued his writing on political economy, especially his famous work, *Das Kapital (Capital)*, but his preoccupation with organizing the working-class movement kept him from ever finishing *Capital*. In *The Communist Manifesto*, Marx had defined the communists as "the most advanced and resolute section of the working-class parties of every country." Their advantage was their ability to understand "the line of march, the conditions, and the ultimate general results of the proletarian movement." Marx saw his role in this light and participated enthusiastically in the activities of the International Working Men's Association. Formed in 1864 by British and French trade unionists, this "First International" served as an umbrella organization for working-class interests. Marx was the dominant personality on the organization's General Council and devoted much time to its activities. Internal dissension, however, soon damaged the organization, and it failed in 1872. A Second International was not formed until 1889, six years after Marx's death, but by that time the working men's movement had undergone a significant growth and transformation with the rise of socialist parties and trade unions, most of which were Marxist in orientation.

The growth of socialist parties after the demise of the First International was rapid and widespread. Most important was the formation of a socialist party in Germany. The German Social Democratic Party (SPD) emerged in 1875. Under the direction of its two Marxist leaders, Wilhelm Liebknecht and August Bebel, the SPD espoused revolutionary Marxist rhetoric while organizing itself as a mass political party to compete in elections for the Reichstag. Once in the Reichstag, SPD delegates worked to achieve legislation to improve the condition of the working class. As August Bebel explained, "Pure negation would not be accepted by the voters. The masses demand that something should be done for today irrespective of what will happen on the morrow."[2] Despite government efforts to destroy it, the SPD continued to grow. In 1890, it received 1.5 million votes and thirty-five seats in the Reichstag. When it received 4 million votes in the 1912 elections, it became the largest single party in Germany.

≫ The Classless Society ≪

In The Communist Manifesto, *Karl Marx and Friedrich Engels projected as the final end product of the struggle between the bourgeoisie and the proletariat the creation of a classless society. In this selection, they discuss the steps by which that classless society would be reached.*

Karl Marx and Friedrich Engels,
The Communist Manifesto

We have seen above, that the first step in the revolution by the working class, is to raise the proletariat to the position of ruling class. . . . The proletariat will use its political supremacy to wrest, by degrees, all capital from the bourgeoisie, to centralize all instruments of production in the hands of the State, i.e., of the proletariat organized as the ruling class; and to increase the total of productive forces as rapidly as possible.

Of course, in the beginning, this cannot be effected except by means of despotic inroads on the rights of property, and on the conditions of bourgeois production; by means of measures, therefore, which appear economically insufficient and untenable, but which, in the course of the movement, outstrip themselves, necessitate further inroads upon the old social order, and are unavoidable as a means of entirely revolutionizing the mode of production.

These measures will of course be different in different countries.

Nevertheless, in the most advanced countries, the following will be pretty generally applicable:

1. Abolition of property in land and application of all rents of land to public purposes.
2. A heavy progressive or graduated income tax.
3. Abolition of all right of inheritance. . . .
5. Centralization of credit in the hands of the State, by means of a national bank with State capital and an exclusive monopoly.
6. Centralization of the means of communication and transport in the hands of the State.
7. Extension of factories and instruments of production owned by the State. . . .
8. Equal liability of all to labor. Establishment of industrial armies, especially for agriculture.
9. Combination of agriculture with manufacturing industries; gradual abolition of the distinction between town and country, by a more equable distribution of the population over the country.
10. Free education for all children in public schools. Abolition of children's factory labor in its present form. . . .

When, in the course of development, class distinctions have disappeared, and all production has been concentrated in the whole nation, the public power will lose its political character. Political power, properly so called, is merely the organized power of one class for oppressing another. If the proletariat during its contest with the bourgeoisie is compelled, by the force of circumstances, to organize itself as a class, if, by means of a revolution, it makes itself the ruling class, and, as such, sweeps away by force the old conditions of production, then it will, along with these conditions, have swept away the conditions for the existence of class antagonisms and of classes generally, and will thereby have abolished its own supremacy as a class.

In place of the old bourgeois society, with its classes and class antagonisms, we shall have an association, in which the free development of each is the condition for the free development of all.

Socialist parties emerged in other European states, although not with the kind of success achieved by the German Social Democrats. As the socialist parties grew, agitation for an international organization that would strengthen their position against international capitalism intensified. In 1889, leaders of the various socialist parties formed the Second International. Significantly, while the First International had been formed by individuals and had been highly centralized, the Second International was created by representatives of national working-class parties and was organized as a loose association of national groups. Although the Second International took some coordinated actions—May Day (May 1), for example, was made an international labor day to be marked by strikes and mass labor demonstrations—differences often wreaked havoc at the congresses of the organization.

One divisive issue for international socialism was nationalism. Despite the belief of Karl Marx and Friedrich Engels that "the working men have no country," in truth,

♦ **"Proletarians of the World, Unite."**   To improve their working and living conditions, many industrial workers, inspired by the ideas of Karl Marx, joined working-class or socialist parties. Pictured here is a socialist-sponsored poster that proclaims in German the closing words of *The Communist Manifesto:* "Proletarians of the World, Unite!"

socialist parties varied from country to country and remained tied to national interests and issues. Nationalism proved to be a much more powerful force than socialism. Marxist parties also divided over the issue of revisionism. Some Marxists believed in a pure Marxism that accepted the imminent collapse of capitalism and the need for socialist ownership of the means of production. But others rejected the revolutionary approach and argued in a revisionist direction that the workers must continue to organize in mass political parties and even work together with the other progressive elements in a nation to gain reform. With the extension of the right to vote, workers were in a better position than ever to achieve their aims through democratic channels. Evolution by democratic means, rather than revolution, would achieve the desired goal of socialism.

Another force working for evolutionary rather than revolutionary socialism and at the same time an expression of a nationalistically oriented socialism was the development of trade unions. Attempts to organize the masses of unskilled and semiskilled workers in factory industries did not come in Great Britain until the last two decades of the nineteenth century, after unions had won the right to strike in the 1870s. Strikes proved necessary to achieve the goals of these workers. A walkout by female workers in the match industry in 1888 and another by dock workers in London the following year led to the establishment of trade unions for both groups. By 1900, there were two million workers in British trade unions, and by the outbreak of World War I, between three and four million workers, less than one-fifth of the total workforce, were collectively organized. By 1914, the German trade union movement with its three million members was the second largest in Europe after Great Britain's.

The Structure of Mass Society

The new urban and industrial world created by the rapid economic and social changes of the nineteenth century has led historians to speak of the emergence of a mass society by the late nineteenth century. A mass society meant new forms of expression for the lower classes as they benefited from the extension of voting rights, an improved standard of living, and compulsory elementary education. However, mass society also made possible the development of organizations that manipulated and controlled the populations of the nation-states. Governments fostered national loyalty and created mass armies by conscription. A mass press swayed popular opinion by flamboyant journalistic practices. To understand this mass society, we need to examine some aspects of the structure that made it up.

The New Urban Environment

By far one of the most important consequences of industrialization and the population explosion of the nineteenth century was urbanization. In the course of the nineteenth century, urban inhabitants came to make up an ever-increasing percentage of the European population. In 1800, they constituted 40 percent of the population in Britain, 25 percent in France and Germany, and only 10 percent in eastern Europe. By 1914, urban inhabitants had increased to 80 percent of the population in Britain, 45 percent in France, 60 percent in Germany, and 30 percent in eastern Europe. The size of cities also expanded dramatically, especially in industrialized countries. Between 1800 and 1900, London's population grew from 960,000 to 6,500,000 and Berlin's from 172,000 to 2,700,000.

Urban populations grew faster than the general population primarily because of the vast migration from rural areas to cities. People were driven by sheer economic necessity—unemployment, land hunger, and physical want—from the countryside to the city. Urban centers offered something positive as well, usually mass employment in factories and later in service trades and professions. But cities also grew faster in the second half of the nineteenth century because health and the conditions of urban life were improving as reformers and city officials used new technology to improve the urban landscape.

In the 1840s, a number of urban reformers had pointed to filthy living conditions as the primary cause of epidemic diseases and urged sanitary reforms to correct the problem. Soon, legislative acts created boards of health that brought governmental action to bear on public health issues. Urban medical officers and building inspectors were authorized to inspect dwellings for public health hazards. New building regulations made it more difficult for private contractors to construct shoddy housing. The Public Health Act of 1875 in Britain, for example, prohibited the construction of new buildings without running water and an internal drainage system. For the first time in Western history, the role of municipal governments had been expanded to include detailed regulations for the improvement of the living conditions of urban dwellers.

Essential to the public health of the modern European city was the ability to bring clean water to it and to expel sewage from it. The accomplishment of those two tasks was a major engineering feat in the last half of the nineteenth century. The problem of fresh water was solved by a system of dams and reservoirs that stored the water and aqueducts and tunnels that carried it from the countryside to the city and into individual dwellings. By the second half of the nineteenth century, regular private baths became accessible to many people as gas heaters in the 1860s and later electric heaters made hot baths possible. The treatment of sewage was also improved by laying mammoth underground pipes that carried raw sewage far from the city for disposal. In the late 1860s, a number of German cities began to construct sewer systems. Frankfurt began its program after a lengthy public campaign enlivened by the slogan "from the toilet to the river in half an hour." London devised a system of five enormous sewers that discharged their loads twelve miles from the city where the waste was chemically treated. Unfortunately, in many places the new underground sewers simply continued to discharge their raw sewage into what soon became highly polluted lakes and rivers. Nevertheless, the development of pure water and sewerage systems dramatically improved the public health of European cities by 1914.

◆ **Working-Class Housing in London.** Although urban workers experienced some improvements in the material conditions of their lives after 1871, working-class housing remained drab and depressing. This 1912 photograph of working-class housing in the East End of London shows rows of similar-looking buildings on treeless streets. Most often, these buildings had no gardens or green areas.

Middle-class reformers who denounced the unsanitary living conditions of the working class also focused on their housing needs. Overcrowded, disease-ridden slums were viewed as dangerous not only to physical health, but to the political and moral health of the entire nation. V. A. Huber, the foremost early German housing reformer, wrote in 1861: "Certainly it would not be too much to say that the home is the communal embodiment of family life. Thus the purity of the dwelling is almost as important for the family as is the cleanliness of the body for the individual."[3] To Huber, good housing was a prerequisite for stable family life, and without stable family life one of the "stabilizing elements of society" would be dissolved, much to society's detriment.

Early efforts to attack the housing problem emphasized the middle-class, liberal belief in the efficacy of private enterprise. Reformers such as Huber believed that the construction of model dwellings renting at a reasonable price would force other private landlords to elevate their housing standards. A fine example of this approach was the work of Octavia Hill (see the box on p. 787). With the financial assistance of a friend, she rehabilitated some old dwellings and constructed new ones to create housing for 3,500 tenants.

As the number and size of cities continued to mushroom, governments by the 1880s came to the conclusion—although reluctantly—that private enterprise could not solve the housing crisis. In 1890, a British Housing Act empowered local town councils to construct cheap housing for the working classes. London and Liverpool were the first communities to take advantage of their new powers. Similar activity had been set in motion in Germany by 1900. Everywhere, however, these lukewarm measures failed to do much to meet the real housing needs of the working classes. Nevertheless, by the start of World War I, the need for planning had been recognized, and after the war municipal governments moved into housing construction on a large scale. In housing, as in so many other areas of life in the late nineteenth and early twentieth centuries, the liberal principle that the government that governs least governs best had simply proved untrue. More and more, governments were stepping into areas of activity that they would have never touched earlier.

The Social Structure of Mass Society

At the top of European society stood a wealthy elite, constituting but 5 percent of the population while controlling between 30 and 40 percent of its wealth. This nineteenth-century elite was an amalgamation of the traditional landed aristocracy that had dominated European society for centuries and the wealthy upper middle class. In the course of the nineteenth century, aristocrats coalesced with the most successful industrialists, bankers, and merchants to form a new elite. The growth of big business had created this group of wealthy plutocrats while aristocrats, whose income from landed estates declined, invested in railway shares, public utilities, government bonds, and even businesses, sometimes on their own estates. Gradually, the greatest fortunes shifted into the hands of the upper middle class. In Great Britain, for example, landed aristocrats constituted 73 percent of the country's millionaires in mid-century while the commercial and financial magnates made up 14 percent. By the period 1900–1914, landowners had declined to 27 percent.

Increasingly, aristocrats and plutocrats fused as the members of the wealthy upper middle class purchased landed estates to join the aristocrats in the pleasures of country living while the aristocrats bought lavish town houses for part-time urban life. Common bonds were also created when the sons of wealthy middle-class families were admitted to the elite schools dominated by the children of the aristocracy. This educated elite, whether aristocratic or middle class in background, assumed leadership roles in government bureaucracies and military hierarchies. Marriage also served to unite the two groups. Daughters of tycoons gained titles while aristocratic heirs gained new sources of cash. Wealthy American heiresses were in special demand. When Consuelo Vanderbilt married the duke of Marlborough, the new duchess brought £2 million (approximately $10 million) to her husband.

The middle classes consisted of a variety of groups. Below the upper middle class was a middle level that included such traditional groups as professionals in law, medicine, and the civil service as well as moderately well-to-do industrialists and merchants. The industrial expansion of the nineteenth century also added new groups to the middle middle class. These included business managers and new professionals, such as the engineers, architects, accountants, and chemists who formed professional associations as the symbols of their newfound importance. Beneath this solid and comfortable middle middle class was a lower middle class of small shopkeepers, traders, manufacturers, and prosperous peasants. Their chief preoccupation was the provision of goods and services for the classes above them.

Standing between the lower middle class and the lower classes were new groups of white-collar workers who were the product of the Second Industrial Revolution. They were the traveling salesmen, bookkeepers,

The Housing Venture of Octavia Hill

Octavia Hill was a practical-minded British housing reformer who believed that workers and their families were entitled to happy homes. At the same time, she was convinced that the poor needed guidance and encouragement, not charity. In this selection, she describes her housing venture.

Octavia Hill, *Homes of the London Poor*

About four years ago I was put in possession of three houses in one of the worst courts of Marylebone. Six other houses were bought subsequently. All were crowded with inmates.

The first thing to be done was to put them in decent tenantable order. The set last purchased was a row of cottages facing a bit of desolate ground, occupied with wretched, dilapidated cow-sheds, manure heaps, old timber, and rubbish of every description. The houses were in a most deplorable condition—the plaster was dropping from the walls; on one staircase a pail was placed to catch the rain that fell through the roof. All the staircases were perfectly dark; the banisters were gone, having been burnt as firewood by tenants. The grates, with large holes in them, were falling forward into the rooms. The washhouse, full of lumber belonging to the landlord, was locked up; thus the inhabitants had to wash clothes, as well as to cook, eat and sleep in their small rooms. The dust-bin, standing in the front part of the houses, was accessible to the whole neighbourhood, and boys often dragged from it quantities of unseemly objects and spread them over the court. The state of the drainage was in keeping with everything else. The pavement of the backyard was all broken up, and great puddles stood in it, so that the damp crept up the outer walls. . . .

As soon as I entered into possession, each family had an opportunity of doing better: those who would not pay, or who led clearly immoral lives, were ejected.

The rooms they vacated were cleansed; the tenants who showed signs of improvement moved into them, and thus, in turn, an opportunity was obtained for having each room distempered and papered. The drains were put in order, a large slate cistern was fixed, the wash-house was cleared of its lumber, and thrown open on stated days to each tenant in turn. The roof, the plaster, the woodwork was repaired; the staircase walls were distempered; new grates were fixed; the layers of paper and rag (black with age) were torn from the windows, and glass was put in; out of 192 panes only eight were found unbroken. The yard and footpath were paved.

The rooms, as a rule, were re-let at the same prices at which they had been let before; but tenants with large families were counselled to take two rooms, and for these much less was charged than if let singly: this plan I continue to pursue. In-coming tenants are not allowed to take a decidedly insufficient quantity of room, and no sub-letting is permitted. . . .

The pecuniary result has been very satisfactory. Five per cent has been paid on all the capital invested. A fund for the repayment of capital is accumulating. A liberal allowance has been made for repairs. . . .

My tenants are mostly of a class far below that of mechanics. They are, indeed, of the very poor. And yet, although the gifts they have received have been next to nothing, none of the families who have passed under my care during the whole four years have continued in what is called "distress," except such as have been unwilling to exert themselves. Those who will not exert the necessary self-control cannot avail themselves of the means of livelihood held out to them. But, for those who are willing, some small assistance in the form of work has, from time to time, been provided—not much, but sufficient to keep them from want or despair.

---

bank tellers, telephone operators, department store salespeople, and secretaries. Although largely propertyless and often paid little more than skilled laborers, these white-collar workers were often committed to middle-class ideals and optimistic about improving their status.

The moderately prosperous and successful middle classes shared a certain style of life, one whose values tended to dominate much of nineteenth-century society.

The members of the middle class were especially active in preaching their worldview to their children and to the upper and lower classes of their society. This was especially evident in Victorian Britain, often considered a model of middle-class society. It was the European middle classes who accepted and promulgated the importance of progress and science. They believed in hard work, which they viewed as the primary human good, open to everyone and guaranteed to have positive results. They were also regular churchgoers who believed in the good conduct associated with traditional Christian morality. The middle class was concerned with propriety, the right way of doing things, which gave rise to an incessant number of books aimed at the middle-class market with such titles as *The Habits of Good Society* or *Don't: A Manual of Mistakes and Improprieties More or Less Prevalent in Conduct and Speech.*

The working classes of European society constituted almost 80 percent of the population. Many of them were landholding peasants, agricultural laborers, and sharecroppers, especially in eastern Europe. This was less true, however, in western and central Europe. About 10 percent of the British population worked in agriculture, while in Germany the figure was 25 percent.

There was no such thing as a homogeneous urban working class. The elite of the working class included, first of all, skilled artisans in such traditional handicraft trades as cabinetmaking, printing, and jewelry making. As the production of more items was mechanized in the course of the nineteenth century, these highly skilled workers found their economic security threatened. The Second Industrial Revolution, however, also brought new entrants into the group of highly skilled workers, such as machine-tool specialists, shipbuilders, and metalworkers. Many of the skilled workers attempted to pattern themselves after the middle class by seeking good housing and educating their children.

Semiskilled laborers, who included such people as carpenters, bricklayers, and many factory workers, earned wages that were about two-thirds of those of highly skilled workers. At the bottom of the working-class hierarchy stood the largest group of workers, the unskilled laborers. They included day laborers, who worked irregularly for very low wages, and large numbers of domestic servants. One out of every seven employed persons in Great Britain in 1900 was a domestic servant. Most of them were women.

Urban workers did experience a real betterment in the material conditions of their lives after 1870. For one thing, urban improvements meant better living conditions. A rise in real wages, accompanied by a decline in many consumer costs, especially in the 1880s and 1890s, made it possible for workers to buy more than just food and housing. Workers' budgets now included money for more clothes and even leisure at the same time that strikes and labor agitation were winning ten-hour days and Saturday afternoons off. The combination of more income and more free time produced whole new patterns of mass leisure.

The "Woman Question": The Role of Women

The "woman question" was the term used to identify the debate over the role of women in society. In the nineteenth century, women remained legally inferior, economically dependent, and largely defined by family and household roles. Many women still aspired to the ideal of femininity popularized by writers and poets. Alfred Lord Tennyson's *The Princess* expressed it well:

> *Man for the field and woman for the hearth:*
> *Man for the sword and for the needle she:*
> *Man with the head and woman with the heart:*
> *Man to command and woman to obey;*
> *All else confusion.*

This traditional characterization of the sexes, based on gender-defined social roles, was virtually elevated to the status of universal male and female attributes in the nineteenth century, largely due to the impact of the Industrial Revolution on the family. As the chief family wage earners, men worked outside the home while women were left with the care of the family for which they were paid nothing. Of course, the ideal did not always match reality, especially for the lower classes, where the need for supplemental income drove women to do "sweated" work.

For most women, marriage was viewed as the only honorable and available career throughout most of the nineteenth century. While the middle class glorified the ideal of domesticity (see the box on p. 789), for most women marriage was a matter of economic necessity. The lack of meaningful work and the lower wages paid to women for their work made it difficult for single women to earn a living. Most women chose to marry, which was reflected in the increase in marriage rates and a decline in illegitimacy rates over the course of the nineteenth century.

Birthrates also dropped significantly in the nineteenth century. The most significant development in the modern family was the decline in the number of offspring born to the average woman. The change was not necessarily due to new technology. Although the invention of vulcanized rubber in the 1840s made possible the production of condoms and diaphragms, they were not widely used as effective contraceptive devices until the era of World War I. Some historians maintain that the change in attitude that led parents to limit the number of offspring deliberately was more important than the method used. While some historians attribute increased birth control to more widespread use of coitus interruptus, or

Advice to Women: Be Dependent

Industrialization had a strong impact on middle-class women as gender-based social roles became the norm. Men worked outside the home to support the family while women provided for the needs of their children and husband at home. In this piece, one woman gives advice to middle-class women on their proper role and behavior.

Elizabeth Poole Sanford, *Woman in Her Social and Domestic Character*

The changes wrought by Time are many. It influences the opinions of men as familiarity does their feelings; it has a tendency to do away with superstition, and to reduce every thing to its real worth.

It is thus that the sentiment for woman has undergone a change. The romantic passion which once almost deified her is on the decline; and it is by intrinsic qualities that she must now inspire respect. She is no longer the queen of song and the star of chivalry. But if there is less of enthusiasm entertained for her, the sentiment is more rational, and, perhaps, equally sincere; for it is in relation to happiness that she is chiefly appreciated.

And in this respect it is, we must confess, that she is most useful and most important. Domestic life is the chief source of her influence; and the greatest debt society can owe to her is domestic comfort: for happiness is almost an element of virtue; and nothing conduces more to improve the character of men than domestic peace. A woman may make a man's home delightful, and may thus increase his motives for virtuous exertion. She may refine and tranquillize his mind,—may turn away his anger or allay his grief. Her smile may be the happy influence to gladden his heart, and to disperse the cloud that gathers on his brow. And in proportion to her endeavors to make those around her happy, she will be esteemed and loved. She will secure by her excellence that interest and that regard which she might formerly claim as the privilege of her sex, and will really merit the deference which was then conceded to her as a matter of course. . . .

Perhaps one of the first secrets of her influence is adaptation to the tastes, and sympathy in the feelings, of those around her. This holds true in lesser as well as in graver points. It is in the former, indeed, that the absence of interest in a companion is frequently most disappointing. Where want of congeniality impairs domestic comfort, the fault is generally chargeable on the female side. It is for woman, not for man, to make the sacrifice, especially in indifferent matters. She must, in a certain degree, be plastic herself if she would mould others. . . .

Nothing is so likely to conciliate the affections of the other sex as a feeling that woman looks to them for support and guidance. In proportion as men are themselves superior, they are accessible to this appeal. On the contrary, they never feel interested in one who seems disposed rather to offer than to ask assistance. There is, indeed, something unfeminine in independence. It is contrary to nature, and therefore it offends. We do not like to see a woman affecting tremors, but still less do we like to see her acting the amazon. A really sensible woman feels her dependence. She does what she can; but she is conscious of inferiority, and therefore grateful for support. She knows that she is the weaker vessel, and that as such she should receive honor. In this view, her weakness is an attraction, not a blemish.

In every thing, therefore, that women attempt, they should show their consciousness of dependence. If they are learners, let them evince a teachable spirit; if they give an opinion, let them do it in an unassuming manner. There is something so unpleasant in female self-sufficiency that it not unfrequently deters instead of persuading, and prevents the adoption of advice which the judgment even approves.

male withdrawal before ejaculation, others have emphasized female control of family size through abortion and even infanticide or abandonment. That a change in attitude occurred was apparent in the development of a movement to increase awareness of birth control methods. Europe's first birth control clinic opened in Amsterdam in 1882.

The family was the central institution of middle-class life. Men provided the family income while women focused on household and child care. The use of domestic servants in many middle-class homes, made possible by an abundant supply of cheap labor, reduced the amount of time middle-class women had to spend on household work. At the same time, by reducing the number of

♦ **A Middle-Class Family.** Nineteenth-century middle-class moralists considered the family the fundamental pillar of a healthy society. The family was a crucial institution in middle-class life, and togetherness constituted one of the important ideals of the middle-class family. This painting by William P. Frith, entitled *Many Happy Returns of the Day*, shows a family birthday celebration for a little girl in which grandparents, parents, and children take part. The servant at the left holds the presents for the little girl.

children in the family, mothers could devote more time to child care and domestic leisure.

The middle-class family fostered an ideal of togetherness. The Victorians created the family Christmas with its yule log, Christmas tree, songs, and exchange of gifts. In the United States, Fourth of July celebrations changed from drunken revels to family picnics by the 1850s. The education of middle-class females in domestic crafts, singing, and piano playing prepared them for their function of providing a proper environment for home recreation.

Women in working-class families were more accustomed to hard work. Daughters in working-class families were expected to work until they married; even after marriage, they often did piecework at home to help support the family. For the children of the working classes, childhood was over by the age of nine or ten when they became apprentices or were employed in odd jobs.

Between 1890 and 1914, however, family patterns among the working class began to change. High-paying jobs in heavy industry and improvements in the standard of living made it possible for working-class families to depend on the income of husbands and the wages of grown children. By the early twentieth century, some working-class mothers could afford to stay at home, following the pattern of middle-class women. At the same time, new consumer products, such as sewing machines, clocks, bicycles, and cast-iron stoves, created a new mass consumer society whose focus was on higher levels of consumption.

These working-class families also followed the middle classes in limiting the size of their families. Children began to be viewed as dependents rather than wage earners as child labor laws and compulsory education took children out of the workforce and into schools. Improvements in public health as well as advances in medicine and a better diet resulted in a decline in infant mortality rates for the lower classes, especially noticeable in the cities after 1890, and made it easier for working-class families to choose to have fewer children. At the same time, strikes and labor agitation led to laws that reduced work hours to ten per day by 1900 and eliminated work on Saturday afternoons, which enabled working-class parents to devote more attention to their children and develop more emotional ties with them.

THE RISE OF THE FEMINIST MOVEMENT

In the 1830s, a number of women in the United States and Europe, who worked together in several reform movements, became frustrated by the apparent prejudices against females. They sought improvements for women by focusing on family and marriage law because it was difficult for women to secure divorces and property laws gave husbands almost complete control over the property of their wives. These early efforts were not overly successful, however. For example, women did not gain the right to their own property until 1870 in Britain, 1900 in Germany, and 1907 in France.

Custody and property rights were only a beginning for the women's movement, however. Some middle- and upper-middle-class women gained access to higher education while others sought entry into occupations dominated by men. The first to fall was teaching. As medical training was largely closed to women, they sought alternatives in the development of nursing. A nursing pioneer in Germany was the upper-class spinster Amalie Sieveking (1794–1859), who founded the Female Association for the Care of the Poor and Sick in Hamburg. As she explained: "To me, at least as important were the benefits which [work with the poor] seemed to promise for those of my sisters who would join me in such a work of charity. The higher interests of my sex were close to my heart."[4] Sieveking's work was followed by the more famous British nurse, Florence Nightingale, whose efforts during the Crimean War (1854–1856), combined with those of Clara Barton in the American Civil War (1861–1865), transformed nursing into a profession of trained, middle-class "women in white."

By the 1840s and 1850s, the movement for women's rights had entered the political arena with the call for equal political rights. Many feminists believed that the right to vote was the key to all other reforms to improve the position of women. Suffragists had one basic aim, the right of women to full citizenship in the nation-state (see the box on p. 792).

The British women's movement was the most vocal and active in Europe, but divided over tactics. Moderates believed that women must demonstrate that they would use political power responsibly if they wanted Parliament to grant them the right to vote. Another group, however, favored a more radical approach. Emmeline Pankhurst (1858–1928) and her daughters, Christabel and Sylvia, founded the Women's Social and Political Union in 1903, which enrolled mostly middle- and upper-class women. Pankhurst's organization realized the value of the media and used unusual publicity stunts to call attention to its demands. Derisively labeled suffragettes by male politicians, its members pelted government officials with eggs, chained themselves to lampposts, smashed the windows of department stores on fashionable shopping streets, burned railroad cars, and went on hunger strikes in jail.

Before World War I, the demands for women's rights were being heard throughout Europe and the United States, although only in Norway and some American states did women actually receive the right to vote before 1914. It would take the dramatic upheaval of World War I before male-dominated governments capitulated on this basic issue.

Education and Leisure in an Age of Mass Society

Between 1870 and 1914, Europe witnessed the emergence of a mass society. Trade unions and political parties gave an economic and political voice to many workers. Mass conscription created mass armies and possibilities for warfare on a scale never before imagined. The masses became a fresh force in Western society as mass education and mass leisure created new forms of popular culture.

MASS EDUCATION

Mass education was a product of the "mass society" of the late nineteenth and early twentieth centuries. Being "educated" in the early nineteenth century meant attending a secondary school or possibly even a university. Secondary schools mostly emphasized a classical education based on the study of Greek and Latin. Secondary and university education were primarily for the elite, the sons

of government officials, nobles, or the wealthier middle class. After 1850, secondary education was expanded as more middle-class families sought employment in public service and the professions or entry into elite scientific and technical schools. Existing secondary schools also placed more emphasis on practical and scientific education by adding foreign languages and natural sciences to their curriculum.

In the decades after 1870, the functions of the state were extended to include the development of mass education in state-run systems. Between 1870 and 1914, most Western governments began to offer at least primary education to both boys and girls between the ages of six and twelve. States also assumed responsibility for better training of teachers by establishing teacher-training schools.

By the beginning of the twentieth century, many European states, especially in northern and western Europe, had provided state-financed primary schools, salaried and trained teachers, and free, compulsory mass elementary education. Why did European states make this commitment to mass education? Liberals believed that education was important to personal and social improvement and in Catholic countries sought to supplant Catholic education with moral and civic training based on secular values. Even conservatives, however, were attracted to mass education as a means of improving the quality of military recruits and training people in social discipline. In 1875, a German military journal stated: "We in Germany consider education to be one of the principal ways of promoting the strength of the nation and above all military strength."[5]

Another incentive for mass education came from industrialization. In the early Industrial Revolution, unskilled labor was sufficient to meet factory needs, but the new firms of the Second Industrial Revolution demanded skilled labor. Diversification of the economic and social structure provided incentives to learn new skills. Both boys and girls with an elementary education had new possibilities of jobs beyond their villages or small towns, including white-collar jobs in railways, new metro stations, post offices, banking and shipping firms, teaching, and nursing. To industrialists, then, mass education furnished the trained workers they needed.

Nevertheless, the chief motive for mass education was political. For one thing, the increase in suffrage created the need for a more educated electorate. Even more important, however, mass compulsory education instilled patriotism and nationalized the masses, providing an opportunity for even greater national integration. As people lost their ties to local regions and even to religion,

Advice to Women: Be Independent

Although a majority of women probably followed the nineteenth-century middle-class ideal of women as keepers of the household and nurturers of husband and children, an increasing number of women fought for the rights of women. This selection is taken from Act III of Henrik Ibsen's A Doll's House (1879), in which the character Nora Helmer declares her independence from her husband's control over her life.

Henrik Ibsen: A Doll's House

NORA: *(Pause)* Does anything strike you as we sit here?

HELMER: What should strike me?

NORA: We've been married eight years; does it not strike you that this is the first time we two, you and I, man and wife, have talked together seriously?

HELMER: Seriously? What do you mean, *seriously?*

NORA: For eight whole years, and more—ever since the day we first met—we have never exchanged one serious word about serious things. . . .

HELMER: Why, my dearest Nora, what have you to do with serious things?

NORA: There we have it! You have never understood me. I've had great injustice done to me, Torvald; first by father, then by you.

HELMER: What! Your father *and* me? We, who have loved you more than all the world?

NORA *(Shaking her head):* You have never loved me. You just found it amusing to think you were in love with me.

HELMER: Nora! What a thing to say!

NORA: Yes, it's true, Torvald. When I was living at home with father, he told me his opinions and mine were the same. If I had different opinions, I said nothing about them, because he would not have liked it. He used to call me his doll-child and played with me as I played with my dolls. Then I came to live in your house.

HELMER: What a way to speak of our marriage!

NORA *(Undisturbed):* I mean that I passed from father's hands into yours. You arranged everything to your taste and I got the same tastes as you; or pretended to—I don't know which—both, perhaps; sometimes one, sometimes the other. When I look back on it now, I seem to have been living here like a beggar, on hand-outs. I lived by performing tricks for you, Torvald. But that was how you wanted it. You and father have done me a great wrong. It is your fault that my life has come to naught.

HELMER: Why, Nora, how unreasonable and ungrateful! Haven't you been happy here?

NORA: No, never. I thought I was, but I never was.

HELMER: Not—not happy! . . .

NORA: I must stand quite alone if I am ever to know myself and my surroundings; so I cannot stay with you.

HELMER: Nora! Nora!

NORA: I am going at once. I daresay [my friend] Christina will take me in for tonight.

HELMER: You are mad! I shall not allow it! I forbid it!

NORA: It's no use your forbidding me anything now. I shall take with me only what belongs to me; from you I will accept nothing, either now or later.

HELMER: This is madness!

NORA: Tomorrow I shall go home—I mean to what was my home. It will be easier for me to find a job there.

HELMER: Oh, in your blind inexperience—

NORA: I must try to gain experience, Torvald.

HELMER: Forsake your home, your husband, your children! And you don't consider what the world will say.

NORA: I can't pay attention to that. I only know that I must do it.

HELMER: This is monstrous! Can you forsake your holiest duties?

NORA: What do you consider my holiest duties?

HELMER: Need I tell you that? Your duties to your husband and children.

NORA: I have other duties equally sacred.

HELMER: Impossible! What do you mean?

NORA: My duties toward myself.

HELMER: Before all else you are a wife and a mother.

NORA: That I no longer believe. Before all else I believe I am a human being, just as much as you are—or at least that I should try to become one. I know that most people agree with you, Torvald, and that they say so in books. But I can no longer be satisfied with what most people say and what is in books. I must think things out for myself and try to get clear about them.

nationalism supplied a new faith. The use of a single national language created greater national unity than did loyalty to a ruler.

A nation's motives for universal elementary education largely determined what was taught in the elementary schools. Obviously, indoctrination in national values took on great importance. At the core of the academic curriculum were reading, writing, arithmetic, national history, especially geared to a patriotic view, geography, literature, and some singing and drawing. The education of boys and girls differed, however. Where possible, the sexes were separated. Girls did less math and no science but concentrated on such domestic skills as sewing, washing, ironing, and cooking, all prerequisites for providing a good home for husband and children. Boys were taught some practical skills, such as carpentry, and even some military drill. Most of the elementary schools also inculcated the middle-class virtues of hard work, thrift, sobriety, cleanliness, and respect for the family. For most students, elementary education led to apprenticeship and a job.

The development of compulsory elementary education created a demand for teachers, and most of them were female. In the United States, for example, females constituted two-thirds of all teachers by the 1880s. Many men viewed teaching children as an extension of women's "natural role" as nurturers of children. Moreover, females were paid lower salaries, in itself a considerable incentive for governments to encourage the establishment of teacher-training institutes for women. The first female colleges were really teacher-training schools. It was not until the beginning of the twentieth century that women were permitted to enter the male-dominated universities. In France, 3 percent of university students in 1902 were women; by 1914, their number had increased to 10 percent of the total.

The most immediate result of mass education was an increase in literacy. In Germany, Great Britain, France, and the Scandinavian countries, adult illiteracy was virtually eliminated by 1900. Where there was less schooling, the story is very different. Adult illiteracy rates were 79 percent in Serbia, 78 percent in Romania, and 79 percent in Russia. These were all countries where little had been invested in compulsory mass education.

With the dramatic increase in literacy after 1871 came the rise of mass newspapers, such as the *Evening News* (1881) and *Daily Mail* (1896) in London, which sold millions of copies a day. Known as the "yellow press" in the United States, these newspapers shared some common characteristics. They were written in an easily understood style and tended to be extremely sensational. Un-

◆ **A Women's College.** Women were largely excluded from male-dominated universities before 1900. Consequently, the demand of women for higher education led to the establishment of women's colleges, most of which were primarily teacher-training schools. This photograph shows a group of women in an astronomy class at Vassar College in the United States in 1878. Maria Mitchell, a famous female astronomer, was head of the department.

like eighteenth-century newspapers, which were full of serious editorials and lengthy political analysis, these tabloids provided lurid details of crimes, jingoistic diatribes, gossip, and sports news. There were other forms of cheap literature as well. Specialty magazines, such as the *Family Herald* for the entire family, and women's magazines began in the 1860s. Pulp fiction for adults included the extremely popular westerns with their innumerable variations on conflicts between cowboys and Indians. Literature for the masses was but one feature of a new mass culture; another was the emergence of new forms of mass leisure.

MASS LEISURE

In the preindustrial centuries, play or leisure activities had been closely connected to work patterns based on the seasonal or daily cycles typical of agricultural and even artisanal life. The process of industrialization in the nineteenth century had an enormous impact upon that traditional pattern. The factory imposed new work patterns that were determined by the rhythms of machines and clocks and removed work time completely from the family environment of farms and workshops. Work and leisure became opposites as leisure was viewed as what people do for fun after work. In fact, the new leisure hours created by the industrial system—evening hours after work, weekends, and later a week or two in the summer—largely determined the contours of the new mass leisure.

At the same time, the influx of rural people into industrial towns eventually caused the demise of traditional village culture, especially the fairs and festivals that had formed such an important part of that culture. Industrial progress, of course, demanded that such traditional celebrations as Whitsuntide, which had occasioned thirteen days of games and drinking, be eliminated or reduced. In fact, Whitsuntide had been reduced to a single one-day holiday by the 1870s.

New technology and business practices also determined the forms of the new mass leisure. The new technology created novel experiences for leisure, such as the Ferris wheel at amusement parks, while the mechanized urban transportation systems of the 1880s meant that even the working classes were no longer dependent on neighborhood bars, but could make their way to athletic games, amusement parks, and dance halls. Likewise, railroads could take people to the beaches on weekends.

Music and dance halls appeared in the last half of the nineteenth century. By the 1880s, there were five hundred music halls in London. Promoters gradually made them more respectable and broadened their fare to entice women and children as well as men to attend the programs. The new dance halls, which were all the rage by 1900, were more strictly oriented toward adults. Contemporaries were often shocked by the sight of young people engaged in sexually suggestive dancing.

The upper and middle classes had created the first market for tourism, but as wages increased and workers were given paid vacations, tourism, too, became another form of mass leisure. Thomas Cook (1808–1892) was a British pioneer of mass tourism. Secretary to a British temperance group, Cook had accepted responsibility for organizing a railroad trip to temperance gatherings in 1841. This experience led him to offer trips on a regular basis after he found that he could make substantial profits by renting special trains, lowering prices, and increasing the number of passengers.

By the late nineteenth century, team sports had also developed into yet another important form of mass leisure. Unlike the old rural games, they were no longer chaotic and spontaneous activities, but became strictly organized with sets of rules and officials to enforce them. These rules were the products of organized athletic groups, such as the English Football Association (1863) and the American Bowling Congress (1895).

The new team sports rapidly became professionalized. In Britain, soccer had its Football Association in 1863 and rugby its Rugby Football Union in 1871. In the United States, the first National Association to recognize professional baseball players was formed in 1863. By 1900, the National League and American League had a monopoly over professional baseball. The development of urban transportation systems made possible the construction of stadiums where thousands could attend, making mass spectator sports into a big business. Professional teams became objects of mass adulation by crowds of urbanites who compensated for their lost sense of identity in mass urban areas by developing these new loyalties.

The new forms of popular leisure were standardized amusements that drew mass audiences. Although some argued that they were important for improving people, in truth, they mostly served to provide entertainment and distract people from the realities of their work lives. Much of mass leisure was secular. Churches found that they had to compete with popular amusements for people's attention on Sundays. The new mass leisure also represented a significant change from earlier forms of popular culture. Festivals and fairs had been based on an ethos of active community participation, whereas the new forms of mass leisure were standardized for largely passive mass audiences. Amusement parks and professional sports teams were, after all, big businesses organized to make profits.

The National State

Throughout much of the Western world by 1870, the national state had become the focus of people's loyalties and the arena for political activity. Only in Russia, eastern Europe, Austria-Hungary, and Ireland did national groups still struggle for independence.

Change and Tradition in Latin America

In the three decades after 1870, Latin America began to experience an era of prosperity with results that were by no means beneficial for all of its people. As industrialization progressed in Europe and the United States, those countries experienced an ever-greater need for food and raw materials. Latin American nations provided these goods, and their increasing prosperity was based to a large extent on the export of one or two commodities from each region, such as wheat and beef from Argentina, coffee from Brazil, nitrates from Chile, coffee and bananas from Central America, and sugar and silver from Peru. Exports from Argentina doubled between 1873 and 1893; Mexican exports quadrupled between 1877 and 1900. These foodstuffs and raw materials were largely exchanged for finished goods—textiles, machines, and luxury products—from Europe and the United States. With economic growth came a boom in foreign investment. Between 1870 and 1913, British investments—mostly in railroads, mining, and public utilities—grew from £85 million to £757 million, which constituted two-thirds of all foreign investment in Latin America. As Latin Americans struggled to create more balanced economies after 1900, they concentrated on increasing industrialization, especially by building textile, food-processing, and construction material factories.

Nevertheless, the growth of the Latin American economy largely came from the export of raw materials, and economic modernization in Latin America simply added to the growing dependency of Latin America on the capitalist nations of the West. Modernization was basically a surface feature of Latin American society, where past patterns still largely prevailed. Rural elites dominated their estates and their rural workers. Although slavery was abolished by 1888, former slaves and their descendants were still at the bottom of society. The Indians remained poverty-stricken, debt servitude was still a way of life, and Latin America remained economically dependent on foreigners. Despite its economic growth, Latin America was still an underdeveloped region of the world.

The prosperity that resulted from the development of an export economy had both social and political repercussions. One result socially was the modernization of the elites, who grew determined to pursue their vision of modern progress. Large landowners increasingly sought ways to rationalize their production methods in order to make greater profits. As a result, cattle ranchers in Argentina and coffee barons in Brazil became more aggressive entrepreneurs.

Another result of the new prosperity was the growth in the middle sectors of Latin American society—lawyers, merchants, shopkeepers, businessmen, schoolteachers, professors, bureaucrats, and military officers. These middle sectors, which made up only 5 to 10 per-

cent of the population, depending on the country, were hardly large enough in numbers to constitute a true middle class. As one contemporary observer remarked, "In the cities there exists, between the wealthy and the workingmen, a considerable body of professional men, shopkeepers, and clerks, who are rather less of a defined middle class than they might be in European countries." Nevertheless, after 1900, the middle sectors continued to expand. Regardless of the country, they shared some common characteristics. They lived in the cities, sought education and decent incomes, and increasingly saw the United States as the model to emulate, especially in regard to industrialization and education.

The middle sectors in Latin America sought liberal reform, not revolution, and the elites found it relatively easy to co-opt them by extending them the right to vote. Although the middle sectors were not large and remained dependent on the agrarian sector of the economy, in some places they were able to enlarge their political power. In Costa Rica, the middle sectors played an important role in maintaining a constitutional government from 1882 to 1917. An alliance of the middle sectors with the working classes won control of Chile's government in 1918. In Argentina, the extension of suffrage to the middle sectors in 1912 enabled a middle party to win power in 1916.

As Latin American export economies boomed, the working class expanded, which in turn led to the growth of labor unions, especially after 1914. Radical unions often advocated the use of the general strike as an instrument for change. By and large, however, the governing elites succeeded in stifling the political influence of the working class by restricting their right to vote. The need for industrial labor also led Latin American countries to encourage European immigrants. Between 1880 and 1914, three million Europeans, primarily Italians and Spaniards, settled in Argentina. Over 100,000 Europeans, mostly Italian, Portuguese, and Spanish, arrived in Brazil each year between 1891 and 1900.

As in Europe and the United States, industrialization led to urbanization, evident in both the emergence of new cities and the rapid growth of old ones. Buenos Aires (the "Paris" of South America) had 750,000 inhabitants by 1900 and two million by 1914, which constituted a fourth of Argentina's population. By that time, urban dwellers made up 53 percent of Argentina's population overall. Brazil and Chile also witnessed a dramatic increase in the number of urban dwellers.

Latin America also experienced a political transformation after 1870. Large landowners began to take a more direct interest in national politics, sometimes expressed by a direct involvement in governing. In Argentina and Chile, for example, landholding elites controlled the governments, and although they produced constitutions similar to those of the United States and Europe, they were careful to ensure their power by regulating voting rights.

In some countries, large landowners made use of dictators to maintain the interests of the ruling elite. Porfirio Díaz, who ruled Mexico from 1876 to 1910, established a conservative, centralized government with the support of the army, foreign capitalists, large landowners, and the Catholic church. All of them benefited from their alliance. But there were forces for change in Mexico that precipitated a true social revolution. The Mexican Revo-

♦ **Emiliano Zapata.** The inability of Francisco Madero to carry out far-reaching reforms led to a more radical upheaval in the Mexican countryside. Emiliano Zapata led a band of Indians in a revolt against the large landowners of southern Mexico and issued his own demands for land reform.

lution has long been considered a model for nationalistic revolutionary change.

Under Díaz's dictatorial regime, the real wages of the working class had declined. Moreover, 95 percent of the rural population owned no land while about one thousand families owned almost all of Mexico. When a liberal landowner, Francisco Madero, forced Díaz from power, he opened the door to a wider revolution. Madero's ineffectiveness triggered a demand for agrarian reform led by Emiliano Zapata, who aroused the masses of landless peasants and began to seize the haciendas of the wealthy landholders (see the box on p. 797). Between 1910 and 1920, the revolution caused untold destruction to the Mexican economy. Finally, a new constitution in 1917 established a strong presidency, initiated land reform policies, established limits on foreign investors, and set an agenda for social welfare for workers. The revolution also led to an outpouring of nationalistic pride. Intellectuals and artists in particular sought to capture what was unique about Mexico with special emphasis on its Indian past. As the Mexican minister of education said, "Tired, disgusted of all this copied civilization, . . . we wish to cease being Europe's spiritual colonies."

By this time, a new power had begun to wield its influence over Latin America. At the beginning of the twentieth century, the United States, which had begun to emerge as a great world power, increasingly interfered in the affairs of its southern neighbors. As a result of the Spanish-American War (1898), Cuba became an American protectorate while Puerto Rico was annexed outright to the United States. American investments in Latin America soon followed; so too did American resolve to protect these investments. Between 1898 and 1934, U.S. military forces were sent to Cuba, Mexico, Guatemala, Honduras, Nicaragua, Panama, Colombia, Haiti, and the Dominican Republic to protect American interests. Some expeditions remained for many years; U.S. Marines were in Haiti from 1915 to 1934 while Nicaragua was occupied from 1909 to 1933. At the same time, the United States became the chief foreign investor in Latin America.

The United States and Canada

Four years of bloody civil war had preserved American national unity. The old South had been destroyed; one-fifth of its adult white male population had been killed, and four million black slaves had been freed. For a while at least, a program of radical change in the South was attempted. Slavery was abolished by the Thirteenth Amendment to the U.S. Constitution in 1865 while the

❧ Zapata and Land Reform ❧

Emiliano Zapata was a sharecropper on a sugar planta-
tion in Morelos, a mountainous state in southern Mex-
ico. Using the slogan "Land and Liberty," Zapata formed a
guerrilla band of Indians and led them in revolt against the
haciendas of southern Mexico, burning the houses and sugar
refineries. Convinced that the new president of Mexico,
Francisco Madero, would not go far enough with land re-
form, Zapata issued his own plan, the Plan of Ayala, from
which these excerpts are taken.

The Plan of Ayala

The Liberating Plan of the sons of the State of Morelos,
members of the insurgent army that demands the . . .
reforms that it judges convenient and necessary for the
welfare of the Mexican Nation.

We, the undersigned, constituted as a Revolutionary Junta, in order to maintain and obtain the fulfillment of the promises made by the revolution of November 20, 1910, solemnly proclaim in the face of the
civilized world. . . , so that it may judge us, the principles that we have formulated in order to destroy the
tyranny that oppresses us. . . .

1. Considering that the President of the Republic,
   Don Francisco I. Madero, has made a bloody mockery of Effective Suffrage by . . . entering into an
   infamous alliance with the . . . enemies of the Revolution that he proclaimed, in order to forge the
   chains of a new dictatorship more hateful and terrible than that of Porfirio Díaz. . . . For these reasons
   we declare the said Francisco I. Madero unfit to
   carry out the promises of the Revolution of which
   he was the author. . . .
4. The Revolutionary Junta of the State of Morelos
   formally proclaims to the Mexican people:

That it endorses the Plan of San Luis Potosí
[Madero's revolutionary plan] with the additions
stated below for the benefit of the oppressed peoples, and that it will defend its principles until
victory or death. . . .

6. As an additional part of the plan we proclaim, be it
   known: that the lands, woods, and waters usurped
   . . . through tyranny and venal justice henceforth
   belong to the towns or citizens who have corresponding titles to those properties, of which they
   were despoiled by the bad faith of our oppressors.
   They shall retain possession of the said properties at
   all costs, arms in hand. The usurpers who think
   they have a right to the said lands may state their
   claims before special tribunals to be established
   upon the triumph of the Revolution.
7. Since the immense majority of Mexican towns and
   citizens own nothing but the ground on which they
   stand and endure a miserable existence, denied the
   opportunity to improve their social condition or to
   devote themselves to industry or agriculture because a few individuals monopolize the lands,
   woods, and waters—for these reasons the great
   estates shall be expropriated, with indemnification
   to the owners of one third of such monopolies, in
   order that the towns and citizens of Mexico may
   obtain colonies, town sites, and arable lands. Thus
   the welfare of the Mexican people shall be promoted in all respects.
8. The properties of those [landowners] who directly
   or indirectly oppose the present Plan shall be seized
   by the nation, and two thirds of their value shall be
   used for war indemnities and pensions for the widows and orphans of the soldiers who may perish in
   the struggle for this Plan.

Fourteenth and Fifteenth Amendments extended citizenship to blacks and guaranteed them the right to vote.
Radical Reconstruction in the early 1870s tried to create
a new South based on the principle of the equality of
black and white people, but the changes were soon
largely undone. Militia organizations, such as the Ku
Klux Klan, used violence to discourage blacks from voting. A new system of sharecropping made blacks once
again economically dependent on white landowners.
New state laws stripped blacks of their right to vote. By

the end of the 1870s, supporters of white supremacy were
back in power everywhere in the South.

Between 1860 and World War I, the United States
made the shift from an agrarian to a mighty industrial nation. American heavy industry stood unchallenged in
1900. In that year, the Carnegie Steel Company alone
produced more steel than Great Britain's entire steel industry. Industrialization also led to urbanization. While
established cities, such as New York, Philadelphia, and
Boston, grew even larger, other moderate-size cities, such

as Pittsburgh, grew by leaps and bounds because of industrialization. Whereas 20 percent of Americans lived in cities in 1860, over 40 percent did in 1900.

By 1900, the United States had become the world's richest nation and greatest industrial power. Yet serious questions remained about the quality of American life. In 1890, the richest 9 percent of Americans owned an incredible 71 percent of all the wealth. Labor unrest over unsafe working conditions, strict work discipline, and periodic cycles of devastating unemployment led workers to organize. By the turn of the century, one national organization, the American Federation of Labor, emerged as labor's dominant voice. Its lack of real power, however, is reflected in its membership figures. In 1900, it constituted but 8.4 percent of the American industrial labor force.

During the so-called Progressive Era after 1900, the reform of many features of American life became a primary issue. At the state level, reforming governors sought to achieve clean government by introducing elements of direct democracy, such as direct primaries for selecting nominees for public office. State governments also enacted economic and social legislation, such as laws that governed hours, wages, and working conditions, especially for women and children. The realization that state laws were ineffective in dealing with nationwide problems, however, led to a progressive movement at the national level.

National progressivism was evident in the administrations of both Theodore Roosevelt and Woodrow Wilson. Under Roosevelt (1901–1909), the Meat Inspection Act and Pure Food and Drug Act provided for a limited degree of federal regulation of corrupt industrial practices. Roosevelt's expressed principle, "We draw the line against misconduct, not against wealth," guaranteed that public protection would have to be within limits tolerable to big corporations. Wilson (1913–1921) was responsible for the creation of a graduated federal income tax and a Federal Reserve System that permitted the federal government to have a role in important economic decisions formerly made by bankers. Like European states, the United States was moving slowly into policies that extended the functions of the state.

Canada, too, faced problems of national unity between 1870 and 1914. At the beginning of 1870, the Dominion of Canada had only four provinces: Quebec, Ontario, Nova Scotia, and New Brunswick. With the addition of two more provinces in 1871—Manitoba and British Columbia—the Dominion of Canada now extended from the Atlantic Ocean to the Pacific. But real unity was difficult to achieve because of the distrust between the English-speaking and French-speaking peoples of Canada. Fortunately for Canada, Wilfred Laurier, who became the first French-Canadian prime minister in 1896, was able to reconcile Canada's two major groups and resolve the issue of separate schools for French-Canadians. Lanier's administration also witnessed increased industrialization and successfully encouraged immigrants from central and eastern Europe to help populate Canada's vast territories.

THE UNITED STATES AS A WORLD POWER

By the end of the nineteenth century, many Americans, especially businessmen and political leaders, believed that the United States was ready to expand. The Pacific islands were the scene of great power competition and witnessed the entry of the United States on the imperialistic stage. The Samoan Islands became the first important American colony; the Hawaiian Islands were the next to fall. Soon after Americans had made Pearl Harbor into a naval station in 1887, American settlers gained control of the sugar industry on the islands. When Hawaiian natives tried to reassert their authority, the U.S. Marines were brought in to "protect" American lives. Hawaii was annexed by the United States in 1898 during the era of American nationalistic fervor generated by the Spanish-American War. The American defeat of Spain encouraged Americans to extend their empire by acquiring Puerto Rico, Guam, and the Philippine Islands. Although the Filipinos hoped for independence, the Americans refused to grant it. As President William McKinley said, the United States had the duty "to educate the Filipinos and uplift and Christianize them," a remarkable statement in view of the fact that most of them had been Roman Catholics for centuries. It took three years and 60,000 troops to pacify the Philippines and establish American control. By the first decade of the twentieth century, American possessions in the Caribbean and Asia had made the United States another Western imperialist power.

Europe

The domestic policies of the major European states focused on five major themes: the achievement of liberal practices (constitutions, parliaments, and individual liberties); the growth of political democracy through universal male suffrage; the organization of mass political parties as a result of a widened electorate; the rise of socialist, working-class parties; and the enactment of social welfare measures to meet the demands of the working classes. These developments varied in expression from place to place. In general, western European states (France and Britain) had the greatest success with the growth of parliamentary governments. Central European states (Germany, Austria-Hungary) had the trappings of parliamentary government, but authoritarian forces, especially powerful monarchies and conservative social groups, remained strong. In eastern Europe, especially Russia, the old system of autocracy was barely touched by the winds of change.

By 1871, Great Britain had a functioning two-party parliamentary system. For fifty years, the Liberals and Conservatives alternated in power at regular intervals, although they also shared some common features. Both were dominated by a ruling class comprised of a coalition of aristocratic landowners frequently involved in industrial and financial activities and upper-middle-class businessmen. And both competed with each other in supporting legislation that expanded the right to vote. Reform Acts in 1867 and 1884 greatly expanded the number of adult males who could vote, and by the end of World War I, all males over twenty-one and women over thirty could vote. In 1911, parliamentary legislation curtailed the power of the House of Lords and instituted the payment of salaries to members of the House of Commons, which further democratized that institution by at least opening the door to people other than the wealthy. By the beginning of World War I, political democracy had become well entrenched and was soon accompanied by social welfare measures for the working class.

The growth of trade unions, which began to advocate more radical change of the economic system, and the emergence in 1900 of the Labour Party, which dedicated itself to workers' interests, caused the Liberals to favor new social legislation. The Liberals, who held the government from 1906 to 1914, perceived that they would have to initiate a program of social welfare or lose the support of the workers. Therefore, they abandoned the classical principles of *laissez-faire* and voted for a series of social reforms. The National Insurance Act of 1911 provided benefits for workers in case of sickness and unemployment, to be paid for by compulsory contributions from workers, employers, and the state. Additional legislation provided a small pension for those over seventy and compensation for those injured in accidents while at work. While the benefits of the program and tax increases were both modest, they were the first hesitant steps toward the future British welfare state.

In France, the confusion that ensued after the collapse of the Second Empire finally ended in 1875 when an improvised constitution established a republican form of government. This constitution established a bicameral legislature with an upper house or Senate elected indirectly and a lower house or Chamber of Deputies chosen by universal male suffrage. The powers of the president, chosen by the legislature to be the executive of the government for seven years, were deliberately left vague. The premier (or prime minister) led the government, and he and his ministers were responsible not to the president, but to the Chamber of Deputies. The Constitution of 1875, intended only as a stopgap measure, solidified the republic—the Third Republic—which lasted sixty-five years. France failed, however, to develop a strong parliamentary system on the British two-party model because the existence of a dozen political parties forced the premier to depend upon a coalition of parties to stay in power. The Third Republic was notorious for its changes of government. Between 1875 and 1914, there were no fewer than fifty cabinet changes; during the same period, the British had eleven. Nevertheless, the government's moderation gradually encouraged more and more middle-class and peasant support, and by 1914, the Third Republic commanded the loyalty of most French people.

By 1870, Italy had emerged as a geographically united state with pretensions to great power status. Its internal weaknesses, however, gave that claim a particularly hollow ring. Sectional differences—a poverty-stricken south and an industrializing north—weakened any sense of community. Chronic turmoil between labor and industry undermined the social fabric. The Italian government was unable to deal effectively with these problems because of the extensive corruption among government officials and the lack of stability created by ever-changing government coalitions. Even Italy's pretensions to great power status proved hollow when Italy became the first European power to lose to an African state, Ethiopia, a disgrace that later led to the costly (but successful) attempt to compensate by conquering Libya in 1911 and 1912.

The constitution of the new imperial Germany begun by Bismarck in 1871 provided for a federal system with a bicameral legislature. The lower house of the German parliament, known as the Reichstag, was elected on the basis of universal male suffrage, but it did not have ministerial responsibility. Ministers of government, among whom the most important was the chancellor, were responsible not to the parliament, but to the emperor. The emperor also commanded the armed forces and controlled foreign policy and internal administration. Although the creation of a parliament elected by universal male suffrage presented opportunities for the growth of a real political democracy, it failed to develop in Germany before World War I. Bismarck's high-handed tactics and the army's independence were two major reasons why it did not.

During the reign of Emperor William II (1888–1918), the new imperial Germany begun by Bismarck continued as an "authoritarian, conservative, military-bureaucratic power state." By the end of William's reign, Germany had become the strongest military and industrial power on the Continent. Over 50 percent of German workers had jobs in industry while only 30 percent of the workforce was still in agriculture. Urban centers had mushroomed in number and size. These rapid changes in Wilhelmine Germany helped to produce a society torn between modernization and traditionalism. With the expansion of industry and cities came demands for more political participation and growing sentiment for reforms that would produce greater democratization. Conservative forces, especially the landowning nobility and representatives of heavy industry, two of the powerful ruling groups in Germany, tried to block it by supporting William II's activist foreign policy of finding Germany's "place in the sun." Expansionism, they believed, would divert people from demands for further democratization.

The tensions in German society created by the conflict between modernization and traditionalism were also manifested in a new, radicalized, right-wing politics. A

Map 21.2 Europe in 1871.

number of nationalist pressure groups arose to support nationalistic goals. Antisocialist and antiliberal, such groups as the Pan-German League stressed strong German nationalism and advocated imperialism as a tool to overcome social divisions and unite all classes. They were also anti-Semitic and denounced Jews as the destroyers of national community.

After the creation of the dual monarchy of Austria-Hungary in 1867, the Austrian part received a constitution that theoretically recognized the equality of the nationalities and established a parliamentary system with the principle of ministerial responsibility. However, Emperor Francis Joseph (1848–1916) largely ignored ministerial responsibility by personally appointing and dismissing his ministers and ruling by decree when parliament was not in session.

The problem of the various nationalities remained a difficult one. The German minority that governed Austria felt increasingly threatened by the Czechs, Poles, and other Slavic groups within the empire. The granting of universal male suffrage in 1907 served only to exacerbate the problem when nationalities that had played no role in the government now agitated in the parliament for autonomy. This led prime ministers after 1900 to ignore the parliament and rely increasingly on imperial emergency decrees to govern. On the eve of World War I, the Austro-Hungarian Empire was as far away as ever from solving its minorities problem.

In Russia, the assassination of Alexander II in 1881 convinced his son and successor, Alexander III (1881–1894), that reform had been a mistake, and he quickly returned to the repressive measures of earlier tsars. Advocates of constitutional monarchy and social reform, along with revolutionary groups, were persecuted. Entire districts of Russia were placed under martial law if the government suspected the inhabitants of treason. When Alexander III died, his weak son and successor, Nicholas II (1894–1917), began his rule with his father's conviction that the absolute power of the tsars should be preserved: "I shall maintain the principle of autocracy just as firmly and unflinchingly as did my unforgettable father."[6] But conditions were changing, especially with the growth of industrialization, and the tsar's approach was not realistic in view of the new circumstances he faced.

Although industrialization came late to Russia, it progressed rapidly after 1890, especially with the assistance of foreign investment capital. By 1900, Russia had become the fourth largest producer of steel behind the United States, Germany, and Great Britain. At the same time, Russia was turning out half of the world's produc-

CHRONOLOGY

The National State: 1870–1914

Great Britain	
Reform Act	1884
Formation of Labour Party	1900
Restriction of power of the House of Lords	1911
National Insurance Act	1911
France	
Surrender of French Provisional Government to Germany	1871 (Jan. 28)
Republican constitution (Third Republic)	1875
Germany	
Bismarck as chancellor	1871–1890
Emperor William II	1888–1918
Austria-Hungary	
Emperor Francis Joseph	1848–1916
Imperial Russia	
Tsar Alexander III	1881–1894
Tsar Nicholas II	1894–1917
First Congress of Social Democratic Party	1898
Russo-Japanese War	1904–1905
Revolution	1905
Latin America	
Rule of Porfirio Díaz in Mexico	1876–1910
Mexican Revolution begins	1910
United States	
Spanish-American War	1898
Theodore Roosevelt	1901–1909
Woodrow Wilson	1913–1921

tion of oil. With industrialization came factories, an industrial working class, and the development of socialist parties, although repression in Russia soon forced them to go underground and be revolutionary. The Marxist Social Democratic Party, for example, held its first congress in Minsk in 1898, but the arrest of its leaders caused the next one to be held in Brussels in 1903, attended by Russian émigrés. The Social Revolutionaries worked to overthrow the tsarist autocracy and establish peasant socialism. Having no other outlet for opposition to the regime, they advocated political terrorism and attempted to assassinate government officials and members of the ruling dynasty. The growing opposition to the tsarist regime finally exploded into revolution in 1905.

The defeat of the Russians by the Japanese in 1904–1905 encouraged antigovernment groups to rebel against the tsarist regime. Nicholas II granted civil liberties and agreed to create a Duma or legislative assembly elected directly by a broad franchise. But real constitutional monarchy proved short-lived. Already by 1907, the tsar had curtailed the power of the Duma, and fell back on the army and bureaucracy to rule Russia.

International Rivalry and the Coming of War

Between 1871 and 1914, Europeans experienced a long period of peace. There were wars (including wars of conquest in the non-Western world) but none involved the great powers. There were, however, a series of crises that might easily have led to general war. Until 1890, Bismarck, the chancellor of Germany, exercised a restraining influence on Europeans. He realized that the emergence in 1871 of a unified Germany as the most powerful state on the Continent had upset the balance of power established at Vienna in 1815. Bismarck knew that Germany's success frightened Europeans. Fearful of a possible anti-German alliance between France and Russia and possibly even Austria, Bismarck made a defensive alliance with Austria in 1879. Both powers agreed to sup-

port each other in the event of an attack by Russia. In 1882, this German-Austrian alliance was enlarged with the entrance of Italy, angry with the French over conflicting colonial ambitions in North Africa. The Triple Alliance of 1882 committed the three powers to support the existing political and social order while providing a defensive alliance against France. At the same time, Bismarck maintained a separate treaty with Russia and tried to remain on good terms with Great Britain.

When Emperor William II cashiered Bismarck in 1890 and took over direction of Germany's foreign policy, he embarked upon an activist foreign policy dedicated to enhancing German power by finding, as he put it, Germany's rightful "place in the sun." One of his changes in Bismarck's foreign policy was to drop the treaty with Russia, which he viewed as being at odds with Germany's alliance with Austria. The ending of the alliance achieved what Bismarck had feared: it brought France and Russia together. Republican France leapt at the chance to draw closer to tsarist Russia, and in 1894 the two powers concluded a military alliance. During the next ten years, German policies abroad caused the British to draw closer to France. By 1907, a loose confederation of Great Britain, France, and Russia—known as the Triple Entente—stood opposed to the Triple Alliance of Germany, Austria-Hungary, and Italy. Europe became divided into two opposing camps that became more and more inflexible and unwilling to compromise. When the members of the two alliances became involved in a new series of crises between 1908 and 1913 over the remnants of the Ottoman Empire in the Balkans, the stage was set for World War I.

The Ottoman Empire and Nationalism in the Balkans

Like the Austro-Hungarian Empire, the Ottoman Empire was severely troubled by the nationalist aspirations of its subject peoples, especially in the Balkans. Corruption and inefficiency had so weakened the Ottoman Empire that only the interference of the great European powers, who were fearful of each other's designs on the empire, kept it alive.

In the course of the nineteenth century, the Balkan provinces of the Ottoman Empire gradually gained their freedom, although the rivalry in the region between Austria and Russia complicated the process. Serbia had already received a large degree of autonomy in 1829, although it remained a province of the Ottoman Empire until 1878. Greece became an independent kingdom in

1830 after its successful revolt. By the Treaty of Adrianople in 1829, Russia received a protectorate over the principalities of Moldavia and Walachia, but was forced to give them up after the Crimean War. In 1861, Moldavia and Walachia were merged into the state of Romania. Not until Russia's defeat of the Ottoman Empire in 1878, however, was Romania recognized as completely independent, as was Serbia at the same time. Although freed from Turkish rule, Montenegro was placed under an Austrian protectorate while Bulgaria achieved autonomous status under Russian protection. The other Balkan territories of Bosnia and Herzegovina were placed under Austrian protection; Austria could occupy but not annex them. Despite these gains, by the end of the nineteenth century, the forces of Balkan nationalism were by no means stilled.

CRISES IN THE BALKANS, 1908–1913

The Bosnian Crisis of 1908–1909 began a chain of events that eventually spun out of control. Since 1878, Bosnia and Herzegovina had been under the protection of Austria, but in 1908 Austria took the the drastic step of annexing these two Slavic-speaking territories. Serbia was outraged at this action because it dashed the Serbs' hopes of creating a large Serbian kingdom that would include most of the south Slavs. But this possibility was precisely why the Austrians had annexed Bosnia and Herzegovina. The creation of a large Serbia would be a threat to the unity of their empire with its large Slavic population. The Russians, as protectors of their fellow Slavs and also desiring to increase their own authority in the Balkans, supported the Serbs and opposed the Austrian action. Backed by the Russians, the Serbs prepared for war against Austria. At this point, William II intervened and demanded that the Russians accept Austria's annexation of Bosnia and Herzegovina or face war with Germany. Weakened from their defeat in the Russo-Japanese War in 1904–1905, the Russians were afraid to risk war and backed down. Humiliated, the Russians vowed revenge.

European attention returned to the Balkans in 1912 when Serbia, Bulgaria, Montenegro, and Greece organized a Balkan League and defeated the Turks in the First Balkan War. When the victorious allies were unable to agree on how to divide the conquered Turkish provinces of Macedonia and Albania, a second Balkan War erupted in 1913. Greece, Serbia, Romania, and the Ottoman Empire attacked and defeated Bulgaria. As a result, Bulgaria obtained only a small part of Macedonia, and most of the

♦ **Ottoman Army in Retreat.** In 1912, a coalition of Serbia, Bulgaria, Montenegro, and Greece defeated the Turks and took possession of the Ottoman provinces of Macedonia and Albania. This picture shows the Ottoman army in retreat, pursued by Bulgarian forces.

rest was divided between Serbia and Greece. Yet Serbia's aspirations remained unfulfilled. The two Balkan wars left the inhabitants embittered and created more tensions among the great powers.

One of Serbia's major ambitions had been to acquire Albanian territory that would give it a port on the Adriatic. At the London Conference arranged by Austria at the end of the two Balkan wars, the Austrians had blocked Serbia's wishes by creating an independent Albania. The Germans, as Austrian allies, had supported this move. In their frustration, Serbian nationalists increasingly portrayed the Austrians as evil monsters who were keeping the Serbs from becoming a great nation. As Serbia's chief supporters, the Russians were also upset by the turn of events in the Balkans. A feeling had grown among Russian leaders that they could not back down again in the event of a confrontation with Austria or Germany in the Balkans. Moreover, as a result of the Balkan wars, both Russia and Austria expressed discontent that their supposed friends and allies, Great Britain and Germany, had not done enough to support them. This made the British and Germans more determined to support their allies in order to avoid endangering their alliances.

Austria-Hungary had achieved another of its aims, but it was left convinced that Serbia was a mortal threat to its empire and must at some point be crushed. Meanwhile, the French and Russian governments renewed their alliance and promised each other that they would not back down at the next crisis. Britain drew closer to France. By the beginning of 1914, two armed camps viewed each other with suspicion. The European "age of progress" was about to come to an inglorious and bloody end.

Toward the Modern Consciousness: Intellectual and Cultural Developments

Before 1914, most Westerners continued to believe in the values and ideals that had been generated by the impact of the Scientific Revolution and Enlightenment. *Reason*, *science*, and *progress* were still important words in the European vocabulary. The ability of human beings to improve themselves and achieve a better society seemed to be well demonstrated by a rising standard of living, urban improvements, and mass education. Such products of modern technology as electric lights, phonographs, and automobiles reinforced the popular prestige of science

Map 21.3   The Balkans in 1913.

and the belief in the ability of the human mind to understand the universe. Between 1870 and 1914, however, a dramatic transformation in the realm of ideas and culture challenged many of these assumptions. A new view of the physical universe, alternative views of human nature, and radically innovative forms of literary and artistic expression shattered old beliefs and opened the way to a modern consciousness. Although the real impact of many of these ideas was not felt until after World War I, they served to provoke a sense of confusion and anxiety before 1914 that would become even more pronounced after the war.

Developments in the Sciences: The Emergence of a New Physics

Science was one of the chief pillars underlying the optimistic and rationalistic view of the world that many Westerners shared in the nineteenth century. Supposedly based on hard facts and cold reason, science offered a certainty of belief in the orderliness of nature that was comforting to many people for whom traditional religious beliefs no longer had much meaning. Many naively believed that the application of already known scientific laws would give humanity a complete understanding of the physical world and an accurate picture of reality. The new physics dramatically altered that perspective.

Throughout much of the nineteenth century, Westerners adhered to the mechanical conception of the universe postulated by the classical physics of Isaac Newton. In this perspective, the universe was viewed as a giant machine in which time, space, and matter were objective realities that existed independently of those observing them. Matter was thought to be composed of indivisible and solid material bodies called atoms.

These views were first seriously questioned at the end of the nineteenth century. Some scientists had discovered that certain elements such as radium and polonium spontaneously gave off rays or radiation that apparently came from within the atom itself. Atoms were not simply hard, material bodies but small worlds containing such subatomic particles as electrons and protons that behaved in seemingly random and inexplicable fashion. Inquiry into the disintegrative process within atoms became a central theme of the new physics.

Building upon this work, in 1900 a Berlin physicist, Max Planck (1858–1947), rejected the belief that a heated body radiates energy in a steady stream but maintained instead that it did so discontinuously, in irregular packets of energy that he called "quanta." The quantum theory raised fundamental questions about the subatomic realm of the atom. By 1900, the old view of atoms as the basic building blocks of the material world was being seriously questioned, and the world of Newtonian physics was in trouble.

Albert Einstein (1879–1955), a German-born patent officer working in Switzerland, pushed these new theories of thermodynamics into new terrain. In 1905, Einstein published a paper entitled "The Electro-dynamics of Moving Bodies" that contained his special theory of relativity. According to relativity theory, space and time are not absolute, but relative to the observer, and both are interwoven into what Einstein called a four-dimensional space-time continuum. Neither space nor time had an existence independent of human experience. As Einstein later explained simply to a journalist: "It was formerly believed that if all material things disappeared out of the universe, time and space would be left. According to the relativity theory, however, time and space disappear together with the things."[7] Moreover, matter and energy reflected the relativity of time and space. Einstein concluded that matter was nothing but another form of energy. His epochal formula $E = mc^2$—that each particle of matter is equivalent to its mass times the square of the velocity of light—was the key theory explaining the vast energies contained within the atom. It led to the atomic age.

Sigmund Freud and the Emergence of Psychoanalysis

Although poets and mystics had revealed a world of unconscious and irrational behavior, many scientifically oriented intellectuals under the impact of Enlightenment thought continued to believe that human beings responded to conscious motives in a rational fashion. At the end of the nineteenth and beginning of the twentieth century, the Viennese doctor Sigmund Freud (1856–1939) put forth a series of theories that undermined optimism about the rational nature of the human mind. Freud's thought, like the new physics, added to the uncertainties of the age. His major ideas were published in 1900 in his *Interpretation of Dreams*, which laid the basic foundation for what came to be known as psychoanalysis.

According to Freud, human behavior was strongly determined by the unconscious, by former experiences and inner drives of which people were largely oblivious. To explore the contents of the unconscious, Freud relied on both hypnosis and dreams, but the latter were dressed in an elaborate code that needed to be deciphered if the contents were to be properly understood.

But why did some experiences whose influence persisted in controlling an individual's life remain unconscious? According to Freud, this was repression (see the box on p. 807), a process by which unsettling experiences were blotted from conscious awareness but still continued to influence behavior because they had become part of the unconscious. To explain how repression worked, Freud elaborated an intricate theory of the inner life of human beings.

According to Freud, a human being's inner life was a battleground of three contending forces, the id, ego, and superego. The id was the center of unconscious drives and was ruled by what Freud termed the pleasure principle. As creatures of desire, human beings directed their energy toward pleasure and away from pain. The id contained all kinds of lustful drives and desires, crude appetites and impulses, love and hates. The ego was the seat of reason and hence the coordinator of the inner life. It was governed by the reality principle. Although humans were dominated by the pleasure principle, a true pursuit of pleasure was not feasible. The reality principle meant that people rejected pleasure so that they might live together in society; reality thwarted the unlimited pursuit of pleasure. The superego was the locus of conscience and represented the inhibitions and moral values that society in general and parents in particular imposed upon people. The superego served to force the ego to curb the unacceptable pressures of the id.

Thus, the conflict among the id, ego, and superego dominated the human being's inner life. The ego and superego exerted restraining influences on the unconscious id and repressed or kept out of consciousness what they wanted to. Repression began in childhood, and psychoanalysis was accomplished through a dialogue between psychotherapist and patient in which the therapist probed deeply into memory in order to retrace the chain of repression all the way back to its childhood origins. By making the conscious mind aware of the unconscious and its repressed contents, the patient's psychic conflict was resolved.

◆ **Sigmund Freud.** Freud was one of the intellectual giants of the nineteenth century. His belief that unconscious forces strongly determine human behavior formed the foundation for twentieth-century psychoanalysis.

The Impact of Darwin: Social Darwinism and Racism

In the second half of the nineteenth century, scientific theories were sometimes wrongly applied to achieve other ends. The application of Darwin's principle of organic evolution to the social order came to be known as Social Darwinism. The most popular exponent of Social Darwinism was the British philosopher Herbert Spencer (1820–1903). Using Darwin's terminology, Spencer argued that societies were organisms that evolved through time from a struggle with their environment. Progress came from "the struggle for survival," as the "fit"—the strong—advanced while the weak declined. The state, then, should not intervene in this natural process. Some prominent businessmen used Social Darwinism to explain their success in the competitive business world. The strong and fit, the able and energetic had risen to the top; the stupid and lazy had fallen by the wayside.

Darwin's ideas were also applied to human society in an even more radical way by rabid nationalists and racists. In their pursuit of national greatness, extreme nationalists often insisted that nations, too, were engaged

Freud and the Concept of Repression

Freud's psychoanalytical theories resulted from his attempt to understand the world of the unconscious. This excerpt is taken from a lecture given in 1909 in which Freud describes how he arrived at his theory of the role of repression. Although Freud valued science and reason, his theories of the unconscious produced a new image of the human being as governed less by reason than by irrational forces.

Sigmund Freud, *Five Lectures on Psychoanalysis*

I did not abandon it [his technique of encouraging patients to reveal forgotten experiences], however, before the observations I made during my use of it afforded me decisive evidence. I found confirmation of the fact that the forgotten memories were not lost. They were in the patient's possession and were ready to emerge in association to what was still known by him; but there was some force that prevented them from becoming conscious and compelled them to remain unconscious. The existence of this force could be assumed with certainty, since one became aware of an effort corresponding to it if, in opposition to it, one tried to introduce the unconscious memories into the patient's consciousness. The force which was maintaining the pathological condition became apparent in the form of resistance on the part of the patient.

It was on this idea of resistance, then, that I based my view of the course of psychical events in hysteria. In order to effect a recovery, it had proved necessary to remove these resistances. Starting out from the mechanism of cure, it now became possible to construct quite definite ideas of the origin of the illness. The same forces which, in the form of resistance, were now offering opposition to the forgotten material's being made conscious, must formerly have brought about the forgetting and must have pushed the pathogenic experiences in question out of consciousness. I gave the name of "repression" to this hypothetical process, and I considered that it was proved by the undeniable existence of resistance.

The further question could then be raised as to what these forces were and what the determinants were of the repression in which we now recognized the pathogenic mechanism of hysteria. A comparative study of the pathogenic situations which we had come to know through the cathartic procedure made it possible to answer this question. All these experiences had involved the emergence of a wishful impulse which was in sharp contrast to the subject's other wishes and which proved incompatible with the ethical and aesthetic standards of his personality. There had been a short conflict, and the end of this internal struggle was that the idea which had appeared before consciousness as the vehicle of this irreconcilable wish fell a victim to repression, was pushed out of consciousness with all its attached memories, and was forgotten. Thus the incompatibility of the wish in question with the patient's ego was the motive for the repression; the subject's ethical and other standards were the repressing forces. An acceptance of the incompatible wishful impulse or a prolongation of the conflict would have produced a high degree of unpleasure; this unpleasure was avoided by means of repression, which was thus revealed as one of the devices serving to protect the mental personality.

---

in a "struggle for existence" in which only the fittest would survive. The German general Friedrich von Bernhardi gave war a Darwinist interpretation in his book, *Germany and the Next War,* published in 1907. He argued that:

> War is a biological necessity of the first importance, a regulative element in the life of mankind which cannot be dispensed with, since without it an unhealthy development will follow, which excludes every advancement of the race, and therefore all real civilization. "War is the father of all things." The sages of antiquity long before Darwin recognized this.[8]

Numerous nationalist organizations preached the same doctrine as Bernhardi.

Although certainly not new to Western society, racism, too, was dramatically revived and strengthened by new biological arguments. Perhaps nowhere was the combination of extreme nationalism and racism more evident and more dangerous than in Germany where racist nationalism was expressed in volkish thought. The concept of the *Volk* (nation, people, or race) had been an underlying idea in German history since the beginning of the nineteenth century. One of the chief propagandists for German volkish ideology at the turn of the century was Houston Stewart Chamberlain (1855–1927), an Englishman who became a German citizen. His book, *The Foundations of the Nineteenth Century*, published in 1899, made a special impact on Germany. Modern-day Germans, according to Chamberlain, were the only pure successors of the Aryans who were portrayed as the true and original creators of Western culture. The Aryan race, under German leadership, must be prepared to fight for Western civilization and save it from the destructive assaults of such lower races as Jews, Negroes, and Orientals. Increasingly, Jews were singled out by German volkish nationalists as the racial enemy in biological terms and as parasites who wanted to destroy the Aryan race.

ANTI-SEMITISM

Anti-Semitism was not new to European civilization. Since the Middle Ages, Jews had been portrayed as the murderers of Christ and subjected to mob violence; their rights had been restricted, and they had been physically separated from Christians in quarters known as ghettos.

In the nineteenth century, as a result of the ideals of the Enlightenment and the French Revolution, Jews were increasingly granted legal equality in many European countries. Nevertheless, Jews were not completely accepted, and this ambivalence was apparent throughout Europe. In Prussia, for example, Jews were emancipated in 1812 but still faced certain restrictions. They could not hold government offices or take advanced degrees in universities. After the revolutions of 1848, emancipation became a fact of life for Jews throughout western and central Europe. For many Jews, emancipation enabled them to leave the ghetto and become assimilated as hundreds of thousands of Jews entered what had been the closed worlds of parliaments and universities. Many Jews became eminently successful as bankers, lawyers, scientists, scholars, journalists, and stage performers. In 1880, for example, Jews made up 10 percent of the population of the city of Vienna, Austria, but accounted for 39 percent of its medical students and 23 percent of its law students.

These achievements represent only one side of the picture, however. In Germany and Austria during the 1880s and 1890s, conservatives founded right-wing anti-Semitic parties that used anti-Semitism to win the votes of traditional lower-middle-class groups who felt threatened by the new economic forces of the times. These German anti-Semitic parties were based on race. To modern racial anti-Semites, one could not be both German and Jew. The worst treatment of Jews in the last two decades of the nineteenth century and the first decade of the twentieth occurred in eastern Europe where 72 percent of the entire world Jewish population lived. Russian Jews were admitted to secondary schools and universities only under a quota system and were forced to live in certain regions of the country. Persecutions and pogroms were so widespread that hundreds of thousands of Jews decided to emigrate. Between 1881 and 1899, an average of 23,000 Jews left Russia each year. Many of them went to the United States, although some (probably about 25,000) moved to Palestine, which soon became the focus for a Jewish nationalist movement called Zionism.

The emancipation of the nineteenth century had presented vast opportunities to some Jews, but dilemmas to others. Did emancipation mean full assimilation, and did assimilation mean the disruption of traditional Jewish life? Many paid the price willingly, but others questioned its value and advocated a different answer, a return to Palestine. For many Jews, Palestine had long been the land of their dreams. During the nineteenth century, as nationalist ideas spread and Italians, Poles, Irish, Greeks, and others sought national emancipation, so too did the idea of national independence capture the imagination of some Jews. A key figure in the growth of political Zionism was Theodor Herzl (1860–1904). In 1896, he published a book called *The Jewish State* (see the box on p. 809) in which he straightforwardly advocated that "The Jews who wish it will have their state." Financial support for the development of *yishuvs* or settlements in Palestine came from wealthy Jewish banking families, who wanted a refuge in Palestine for persecuted Jews, not a political Jewish state. Even settlements were difficult because Palestine was then part of the Ottoman Empire and Turkish authorities were opposed to Jewish immigration. Despite the problems, however, the First Zionist Congress, which met in Switzerland in 1897, proclaimed as its aim the creation of a "home in Palestine secured by public law" for the Jewish people. In 1900, 1,000 Jews migrated to Palestine. And although 3,000 Jews went annually to Palestine between 1904 and 1914, the Zionist dream remained just that on the eve of World War I.

The Attack on Christianity and the Response of the Churches

The growth of scientific thinking as well as the forces of modernization presented new challenges to the Christian churches. Industrialization and urbanization had an

The Voice of Zionism: Theodor Herzl and the Jewish State

The Austrian Jewish journalist Theodor Herzl wrote The Jewish State in the summer of 1895 in Paris while he was covering the Dreyfus case for his Vienna newspaper. (Alfred Dreyfus, a French army officer who was also Jewish, was wrongly convicted of selling military secrets. Although he was later exonerated, the case revealed the depth of anti-Semitism in France.) In several weeks, during a period of feverish composition, he set about to analyze the fundamental causes of anti-Semitism and devise a solution to the "Jewish problem." In this selection, he discusses two of his major conclusions.

Theodor Herzl, *The Jewish State*

I do not intend to arouse sympathetic emotions on our behalf. That would be a foolish, futile, and undignified proceeding. I shall content myself with putting the following questions to the Jews: Is it true that, in countries where we live in perceptible numbers, the position of Jewish lawyers, doctors, technicians, teachers, and employees of all descriptions becomes daily more intolerable? True, that the Jewish middle classes are seriously threatened? True, that the passions of the mob are incited against our wealthy people? True, that our poor endure greater sufferings than any other proletariat?

I think that this external pressure makes itself felt everywhere. In our economically upper classes it causes discomfort, in our middle classes continual and grave anxieties, in our lower classes absolute despair.

Everything tends, in fact, to one and the same conclusion, which is clearly enunciated in that classic Berlin phrase: "Juden 'raus!" (Out with the Jews!)

I shall now put the Jewish Question in the curtest possible form: Are we to "get out" now? And if so, to what place?

Or, may we yet remain? And if so, how long?

Let us first settle the point of staying where we are. Can we hope for better days, can we possess our souls in patience, can we wait in pious resignation till the princes and peoples of this earth are more mercifully disposed toward us? I say that we cannot hope for a change in the current of feeling. And why not? Were we as near to the hearts of princes as are their other subjects, even so they could not protect us. They would only feed popular hatred of Jews by showing us too much favor. By "too much," I really mean less than is claimed as a right by every ordinary citizen, or by every race. The nations in whose midst Jews live are all, either covertly or openly, Anti-Semitic. . . .

The whole plan is in its essence perfectly simple, as it must necessarily be if it is to come within the comprehension of all.

Let the sovereignty be granted us over a portion of the globe large enough to satisfy the rightful requirements of a nation; the rest we shall manage for ourselves.

The creation of a new State is neither ridiculous nor impossible. We have in our day witnessed the process in connection with nations which were not in the bulk of the middle class, but poorer, less educated, and consequently weaker than ourselves. The Governments of all countries scourged by Anti-Semitism will be keenly interested in assisting us to obtain the sovereignty we want. . . .

Palestine is our ever-memorable historic home. The very name of Palestine would attract our people with a force of marvellous potency. Supposing his Majesty the Sultan were to give us Palestine, we could in return undertake to regulate the whole finances of Turkey. We should there form a portion of the rampart of Europe against Asia, an outpost of civilization as opposed to barbarism. We should as a neutral State remain in contact with all Europe, which would have to guarantee our existence. The sanctuaries of Christendom would be safeguarded by assigning to them an extra-territorial status such as is well known to the law of nations. We should form a guard of honor about these sanctuaries, answering for the fulfillment of this duty with our existence. This guard of honor would be the great symbol of the solution of the Jewish Question after eighteen centuries of Jewish suffering.

adverse effect on religious institutions. The mass migration of people from the countryside to the city meant a change from the close-knit, traditional ties of the village in which the church had been a key force to new urban patterns of social life from which the churches were often excluded. The established Christian churches had a weak hold on workers. For one thing, new churches were rarely built in working-class neighborhoods. Although workers were not atheists, as is sometimes claimed, they tended to develop their own culture in which organized religion played little role.

Science became one of the chief threats to all the Christian churches and even to religion itself in the nineteenth century. Darwin's theory of evolution, accepted by ever-larger numbers of educated Europeans, seemed to contradict the doctrine of divine creation. Some Christian churches responded by rejecting modern ideas outright. Protestant fundamentalist sects were especially active in maintaining a literal interpretation of the Bible. By suppressing Darwin's books and forbidding the teaching of the evolutionary hypothesis, however, the churches often caused even larger numbers of educated people to reject established religions.

Other churches sought compromise, an approach especially evident in the Catholic church during the pontificate of Leo XIII (1878–1903). Pope Leo permitted the teaching of evolution as a hypothesis in Catholic schools and also responded to the challenges of modernization in the economic and social spheres. In his encyclical *De Rerum Novarum,* issued in 1891, he upheld the individual's right to private property but at the same time criticized "naked" capitalism for the poverty and degradation in which it had left the working classes. Much in socialism, he declared, was Christian in principle, but he condemned Marxian socialism for its materialistic and antireligious foundations. The pope recommended that Catholics form socialist parties and labor unions of their own.

The Culture of Modernity

The revolution in physics and psychology was paralleled by a revolution in literature and the arts. Before 1914, writers and artists were rebelling against the traditional literary and artistic styles that had dominated European cultural life since the Renaissance. The changes that they produced have since been called Modernism.

Throughout much of the late nineteenth century, literature was dominated by Naturalism. Naturalists accepted the material world as real and felt that literature should be realistic. By addressing social problems, writers could contribute to an objective understanding of the world. Although Naturalism was a continuation of Realism, it lacked the underlying note of liberal optimism about people and society that had still been prevalent in the 1850s. The Naturalists were pessimistic about Europe's future. They doubted the existence of free will and portrayed characters caught in the grip of forces beyond their control.

The novels of the French writer Émile Zola (1840–1902) provide a good example of Naturalism. Against a backdrop of the urban slums and coal fields of northern France, Zola showed how alcoholism and different environments affected people's lives. The materialistic science of his age had an important influence on Zola. He had read Darwin's *Origin of Species* and had been impressed by its emphasis on the struggle for survival and the importance of environment and heredity. These themes were central to his *Rougon-Macquart,* a twenty-volume series of novels on the "natural and social history of a family." Zola maintained that the artist must analyze and dissect life as a biologist would a living organism. He said, "I have simply done on living bodies the work of analysis which surgeons perform on corpses."

At the turn of the century, a new group of writers, known as the Symbolists, reacted against Realism. Primarily interested in writing poetry, the Symbolists believed that an objective knowledge of the world was impossible. The external world was not real but only a collection of symbols that reflected the true reality of the individual human mind. Art, they believed, should function for its own sake instead of serving, criticizing, or seeking to understand society. In the works of the Symbolist poets W. B. Yeats and Rainer Maria Rilke, poetry ceased to be part of popular culture because only through a knowledge of the poet's personal language could one hope to understand what the poet was saying (see the box on p. 811). Symbolism began in France, and its founder, Stéphane Mallarmé (1842–1898), attempted to summarize its poetic theory in one sentence: "It is not description which can unveil the efficacy and beauty of monuments, seas, or the human face in all their maturity and native state, but rather evocation, allusion, suggestion."

Since the Renaissance, the task of artists had been to represent reality as accurately as possible. By the late nineteenth century, however, artists were seeking new forms of expression. The period from 1870 to 1914 was one of the most fertile in the history of art and witnessed three major movements: Impressionism, Post-Impressionism, and abstract painting.

The preamble to modern painting can be found in Impressionism, a movement that originated in France in the

Symbolist Poetry: Art for Art's Sake

The Symbolist movement was an important foundation for Modernism. The Symbolists believed that the working of the mind was the proper study of literature. Arthur Rimbaud was one of Symbolism's leading practitioners in France. Although his verses seem to have little real meaning, they were not meant to describe the external world precisely, but to enchant the mind. Art was not meant for the masses, but only for "art's sake." Rimbaud wrote, "By the alchemy of the words, I noted the inexpressible. I fixed giddiness."

Arthur Rimbaud, The Drunken Boat

As I floated down impassible rivers,
I felt the boatmen no longer guiding me:
After them came redskins who with war cries
Nailed them naked to the painted poles.

I was oblivious to the crew,
I who bore Flemish wheat and English cotton.
When the racket was finished with my boatmen,
The waters let me drift my own free way.

In the tide's furious pounding,
I, the other winter, emptier than children's minds,
I sailed! And the unmoored peninsulas
Have not suffered more triumphant turmoils.

The tempest blessed my maritime watches.
Lighter than a cork I danced on the waves,
Those eternal rollers of victims,
Ten nights, without regretting the lantern-foolish eye!

Sweeter than the bite of sour apples to a child,
The green water seeped through my wooden hull,
Rinsed me of blue wine stains and vomit,
Broke apart grappling iron and rudder.

And then I bathed myself in the poetry
Of the star-sprayed milk-white sea,
Devouring the azure greens; where, pale
And ravished, a pensive drowned one sometimes floats;

Where, suddenly staining the blueness, frenzies
And slows rhythms in the blazing of day,
Stronger than alcohol, vaster than our lyres,
The russet bitterness of love ferments. . . .

I have dreamed of the green night bedazzled with snow,
A kiss climbing slowly to the eyes of the sea,
The flow of unforgettable sap,
And the yellow-blue waking of singing phosphorous!

Long months I have followed, like maddened cattle,
The surge assaulting the rocks
Without dreaming that the Virgin's luminous feet
Could force a muzzle on the panting ocean!

I have struck against the shares of incredible Floridas
Mixing panther-eyed flowers like human skins!
Rainbows stretched like bridle reins
Under the ocean's horizon, toward sea-green troops!

I have seen the fermenting of monstrous marshes,
Nets where a whole Leviathan rots in the reeds!
The waters collapsing in the middle of the calm,
And horizons plunging toward the abyss!

Glaciers, silver suns, waves of pearl, charcoal skies,
Hideous beaches at the bottom of brown gulfs
Where giant serpents devoured by vermin
Tumble from twisted trees with black perfumes!

I would have liked to show the children those dolphins
On the blue waves, those golden singing fish.
—The froth of flowers lulled my voyagings,
Ineffable winds gave me wings by the moment. . . .

◆ **Claude Monet,** *Impression, Sunrise.* Impressionists rejected "rules and principles" and sought to paint what they observed and felt in order "not to lose the first impression." As is evident in *Impression, Sunrise,* Monet sought to capture his impression of the fleeting moments of sunrise through the simple interplay of light, water, and atmosphere.

1870s when a group of artists rejected the studios and museums and went out into the countryside to paint nature directly. Camille Pissarro (1830–1903), one of Impressionism's founders, expressed what they sought:

> Precise drawing is dry and hampers the impression of the whole, it destroys all sensations. Do not define too closely the outlines of things; it is the brush stroke of the right value and color which should produce the drawing. . . . The eye should not be fixed on one point, but should take in everything, while observing the reflections which the colors produce on their surroundings. Work at the same time upon sky, water, branches, ground, keeping everything going on an equal basis and unceasingly rework until you have got it. . . . Don't proceed according to rules and principles, but paint what you observe and feel. Paint generously and unhesitatingly, for it is best not to lose the first impression.[9]

Above all, said, Pissarro, "Don't be timid in front of nature: one must be bold, at the risk of being deceived, and making mistakes. One must have only one master—nature; she is the one always to be consulted."

Pissarro's suggestions are visibly portrayed in the work of Claude Monet (1840–1926). He was especially enchanted with water and painted many pictures in which he sought to capture the interplay of light, water, and at-

mosphere, especially evident in *Impression, Sunrise.* But the Impressionists did not just paint scenes from nature. Streets and cabarets, rivers, and busy boulevards—wherever people congregated for work and leisure—formed their subject matter.

By the 1880s, a new movement known as Post-Impressionism arose in France but soon spread to other European countries. Post-Impressionism retained the Impressionist emphasis upon light and color but revolutionized it even further by paying more attention to structure and form. Post-Impressionists sought to use both color and line to express inner feelings and produce a personal statement of reality rather than an imitation of objects. Impressionist paintings had retained a sense of realism, but the Post-Impressionists shifted from objective reality to subjective reality and, in so doing, began to withdraw from the artist's traditional task of depicting the external world. Post-Impressionists were the real forerunners of modern art.

A famous Post-Impressionist was the tortured and tragic figure Vincent van Gogh (1853–1890). For van Gogh, art was a spiritual experience. He was especially interested in color and believed that it could act as its own form of language. Van Gogh maintained that artists should paint what they feel. In his *Starry Night,* he painted a sky alive with whirling stars that overwhelm the huddled buildings in the village below.

By the beginning of the twentieth century, the belief that the task of art was to represent "reality" had lost much of its meaning. By that time, the new psychology and the new physics had made it evident that many people were not sure what constituted reality anyway. Then, too, the growth of photography gave artists another reason to reject visual realism. First invented in the 1830s, photography became popular and widespread after George Eastman created the first Kodak camera for the mass market in 1888. What was the point of an artist doing what the camera did better? Unlike the camera, which could only mirror reality, artists could create reality. As in literature, so also in modern art, individual consciousness became the source of meaning. Between 1905 and 1914, this search for individual expression produced a great variety of painting schools that had their greatest impact after World War I.

By 1905, one of the most important figures in modern art was just beginning his career. Pablo Picasso (1881–1973) was from Spain but settled in Paris in 1904. Picasso was extremely flexible and painted in a remarkable variety of styles. He was instrumental in the development of a new style called Cubism that used geometric

♦ **Vincent van Gogh, *The Starry Night.*** The Dutch painter Vincent van Gogh was a major figure among the Post-Impressionists. His originality and power of expression made a strong impact upon his artistic successors. In *The Starry Night*, van Gogh's subjective vision was given full play as the dynamic swirling forms of the heavens above overwhelmed the village below. The heavens seem alive with a mysterious spiritual force.

designs as visual stimuli to recreate reality in the viewer's mind. Picasso's 1907 work *Les Demoiselles d'Avignon* has been called the first Cubist painting.

The modern artist's flight from "visual reality" reached a high point in 1910 with the beginning of abstract painting. A Russian who worked in Germany, Vasily Kandinsky (1866–1944) was one of the founders of Abstract Expressionism. As is evident in his *Painting with White Border*, Kandinsky sought to avoid representation altogether. He believed that art should speak directly to the soul. To do so, it must avoid any reference to visual reality and concentrate on color.

Modernism in the arts revolutionized architecture and architectural practices. A new principle known as functionalism motivated this revolution. Functionalism meant that buildings, like the products of machines, should be "functional" or useful, fulfilling the purpose for which they were constructed. Art and engineering were

◆ **Pablo Picasso,** *Les Demoiselles d'Avignon.*   Pablo Picasso, a major pioneer and activist of modern art, experimented with a remarkable variety of modern styles. His *Les Demoiselles d'Avignon* was the first great example of Cubism, which one art historian has called "the first style of this century to break radically with the past." Geometric shapes replace traditional forms, forcing the viewer to recreate reality in his or her own mind.

to be unified, and all unnecessary ornamentation was to be stripped away.

The United States was a leader in these pioneering architectural designs. Unprecedented urban growth and the absence of restrictive architectural traditions allowed for new building methods, especially in the relatively "new city" of Chicago. The Chicago school of the 1890s, led by Louis H. Sullivan (1856–1924), used reinforced concrete, steel frames, and electric elevators to build skyscrapers virtually free of external ornamentation. One of Sullivan's most successful pupils was Frank Lloyd Wright (1869–1959), who became known for innovative designs in domestic architecture. Wright's private houses, built chiefly for wealthy patrons, featured geometric structures with long lines, overhanging roofs, and severe planes of brick and stone. The interiors were open spaced and included cathedral ceilings and built-in furniture and lighting features. Wright pioneered the modern American house.

At the beginning of the twentieth century, developments in music paralleled those in painting. Expressionism in music was a Russian creation, the product of the composer Igor Stravinsky (1882–1971) and the Ballet Russe, the dancing company of Sergei Diaghilev (1872–1929). Together they revolutionized the world of music with Stravinsky's ballet *The Rite of Spring.* When it was performed in Paris in 1913, the savage and

◆ **Vasily Kandinsky,** *Composition VIII, No. 2 (Painting with White Border).*   One of the founders of Abstract Expressionism was the Russian Vasily Kandinsky, who sought to eliminate representation altogether by focusing on color and avoiding any resemblance to visual reality. In *Painting with White Border,* Kandinsky used color "to send light into the darkness of men's hearts." He believed that color, like music, could fulfill a spiritual goal of appealing directly to the human being.

primitive sounds and beats of the music and dance caused a near riot from an audience outraged at its audacity.

Conclusion

Between 1870 and 1914, the national state began to expand its functions beyond all previous limits. Fearful of the growth of socialism and trade unions, governments attempted to appease the working masses by adopting such social insurance measures as protection against accident, illness, and old age. These social welfare measures were narrow in scope and limited in benefits before 1914. Moreover, they failed to halt the growth of socialism. Nevertheless, they signaled a new direction for state action to benefit the mass of its citizens.

This extension of state functions took place in an atmosphere of increased national loyalty. After 1870, nation-states increasingly sought to solidify the social order and win the active loyalty and support of their citizens by deliberately cultivating national feelings. Yet this policy contained potentially great dangers. Nations had discovered once again that imperialistic adventures and military successes could arouse nationalistic passions and smother domestic political unrest. But they also found—belatedly in 1914—that nationalistic feelings could also lead to intense international rivalries that made war almost inevitable.

What many Europeans liked to call their "age of progress" between 1870 and 1914 was also an era of anxiety. Frenzied imperialist expansion had created vast European empires and spheres of influence around the globe. This feverish competition for colonies, however, had markedly increased the existing antagonisms among the European states. At the same time, the Western treatment of native peoples as racial inferiors caused educated, non-Western elites in these colonies to initiate movements for national independence. Before these movements could be successful, however, the power that Europeans had achieved through their mass armies and technological superiority had to be weakened. The Europeans inadvertently accomplished this task for their colonial subjects by demolishing their own civilization on the battlegrounds of Europe in World War I and World War II.

CHAPTER NOTES

1. Karl Marx and Friedrich Engels, *The Communist Manifesto* (Harmondsworth, 1967), pp. (in order of quotations) 79, 81, 102, 82.
2. Quoted in W. L. Guttsman, *The German Social Democratic Party, 1875–1933* (London, 1981), p. 63.
3. Quoted in Nicholas Bullock and James Read, *The Movement for Housing Reform in Germany and France, 1840–1914* (Cambridge, 1985), p. 42.
4. Quoted in Catherine M. Prelinger, "Prelude to Consciousness: Amalie Sieveking and the Female Association for the Care of the Poor and the Sick," in John C. Fout, ed., *German Women in the Nineteenth Century: A Social History* (New York, 1984), p. 119.
5. Quoted in Robert Gildea, *Barricades and Borders: Europe, 1800–1914* (Oxford, 1987), p. 249.
6. Quoted in Shmuel Galai, *The Liberation Movement in Russia, 1900–1905* (Cambridge, 1973), p. 26.
7. Quoted in Arthur E. E. McKenzie, *The Major Achievements of Science* (New York, 1960), 1:310.
8. Friedrich von Bernhardi, *Germany and the Next War*, trans. Allen H. Powles (New York, 1914), pp. 18–19.
9. Quoted in John Rewald, *History of Impressionism* (New York, 1961), pp. 456–58.

SUGGESTED READINGS

The subject of the Second Industrial Revolution is well covered in D. Landes, *The Unbound Prometheus*, cited in Chapter 20. For a fundamental survey of European industrialization, see A. S. Milward and S. B. Saul, *The Development of the Economies of Continental Europe, 1850–1914* (Cambridge, Mass., 1977). The impact of the new technology on European thought is imaginatively discussed in S. Kern, *The Culture of Time and Space, 1880–1918* (Cambridge, Mass., 1983).

On Marx, there is the standard work by D. McLellan, *Karl Marx: His Life and Thought* (New York, 1974). For an introduction to international socialism, see J. Joll, *The Second International, 1889–1914*, 2d ed. (New York, 1975) and L. Derfler, *Socialism since Marx: A Century of the European Left* (New York, 1973). On the emergence of German social democracy, there is W. L. Guttsman, *The German Social Democratic Party, 1875–1933* (London, 1981).

For a good introduction to housing reform on the Continent, see N. Bullock and J. Read, *The Movement for Housing Reform in Germany and France, 1840–1914* (Cambridge, 1985). An interesting work on aristocratic life is G. D. Philips, *The Diehards: Aristocratic Society and Politics in Edwardian England* (Cambridge, 1979). On the working classes, see L. Berlanstein, *The Working People of Paris, 1871–1914* (Baltimore, 1984). The transformation of the French peasants into good French citizens is examined in E. Weber, *Peasants into Frenchmen: The Modernization of Rural France, 1870–1914* (Stanford, Calif., 1976). There are good overviews of women's experiences in the nineteenth century in B. S. Anderson and J. P. Zinsser, *A History of Their Own*, vol. 2 (New York, 1988) and M. J. Boxer and J. H. Quataert, eds., *Connecting Spheres: Women in the Western World, 1500 to the Present* (Oxford, 1987). The world of women's work is examined in L. A. Tilly and J. W. Scott, *Women, Work, and Family* (New York, 1978). The rise of feminism is examined in J. Rendall, *The Origins of Modern Feminism: Women in Britain, France and the United States* (London, 1985). On the family and children, see M. Mitterauer and R. Sieder, *The European Family* (Chicago, 1982). On various aspects of education, see M. J. Maynes, *Schooling in Western Europe: A Social History* (Albany, N.Y., 1985) and J. S. Hurt, *Elementary Schooling and the Working Classes, 1860–1918* (London, 1979). A concise and well-presented survey of leisure patterns is G. Cross, *A Social History of Leisure since 1600* (State College, Pa., 1989).

The domestic politics of the period can be examined in the general works listed in the bibliography for Chapter 20. There are also specialized works on aspects of each country's history. On the problem of British industrial decline, see M. J. Wiener, *English Culture and the Decline of the Industrial Spirit, 1850–1980* (Cambridge, 1981). For a detailed examination of French history from 1871 to 1914, see J.-M. Mayeur and M. Reberioux, *The Third Republic from its Origins to the Great War, 1871–1914* (Cambridge, 1984). There is a good introduction to the political world of William II's Germany in J. C. G. Röhl, *Germany without Bismarck* (Berkeley, Calif., 1965). An important study on right-wing German politics is G. Eley, *Reshaping the German Right: Radical Nationalism and Political Change after Bismarck* (New Haven, Conn., 1980). On the nationalities problem in the Austro-Hungarian Empire, see R. Kann, *The Multinational Empire: Nationalism and National Reform in the Habsburg Monarchy, 1848–1918*, 2 vols. (New York, 1950). On aspects of Russian history, see H. Rogger, *Russia in the Age of Modernization and Revolution, 1881–1917* (London, 1983) and A. Ascher, *The Revolution of 1905: Russia in Disarray* (New York, 1988). On the United States, see D. Cashman, *America in the Gilded Age: From the Death of Lincoln to the Rise of Theodore Roosevelt* (New York, 1984) and J. W. Chambers, *The Tyranny of Change: America in the Progressive Era, 1900–1917* (New York, 1980). On Latin American economic developments, see B. Albert, *South America and the World Economy from Independence to 1930* (London, 1983). For a comprehensive examination of the Mexican Revolution, see A. Knight, *The Mexican Revolution*, 2 vols. (Cambridge, 1986). Two fundamental works on the diplomatic history of the period are W. L. Langer, *European Alliances and Alignments*, 2d ed. (New York, 1966), and *The Diplomacy of Imperialism*, 2d ed. (New York, 1965).

A well-regarded study of Freud is P. Gay, *Freud: A Life for Our Time* (New York, 1988). Also see R. Clark, *Freud: The Man and the Cause* (New York, 1980).

The subject of modern anti-Semitism is covered in J. Katz, *From Prejudice to Destruction* (Cambridge, Mass., 1980). European racism is analyzed in G. L. Mosse, *Toward the Final Solution* (New York, 1980). For a recent biography of Theodor Herzl, see J. Kornberg, *Theodor Herzl: From Assimilation to Zionism* (London, 1993). A good introduction to the challenge of scientific movements to the established churches is J. W. Burrow, *Evolution and Society: A Study in Victorian Social Theory* (London, 1966). Very valuable on modern art are J. Rewald, *The History of Impressionism*, 4th ed. (New York, 1973) and *Post-Impressionism*, 3d ed. (New York, 1962). On literature, see R. Pascal, *From Naturalism to Expressionism: German Literature and Society, 1880–1918* (New York, 1973).

The High Tide of Imperialism

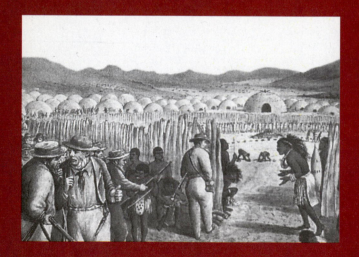

In 1877, the young British empire builder Cecil Rhodes drew up his last will and testament. He bequeathed his fortune, achieved as a diamond magnate in South Africa, to two of his close friends and acquaintances. He also instructed them to use the inheritance to form a secret society with the aim of bringing about "the extension of British rule throughout the world, the perfecting of a system of emigration from the United Kingdom . . . especially the occupation of the whole continent of Africa, the Holy Land, the valley of the Euphrates, the Islands of Cyprus and Candia [Crete], the whole of South America. . . . The ultimate recovery of the United States as an integral part of the British Empire . . . then finally the foundation of so great a power to hereafter render wars impossible and promote the best interests of humanity."[1]

Preposterous as such ideas appear to us today, they serve as a graphic reminder of the hubris that characterized the worldview of Rhodes and many of his contemporaries during the age of imperialism, as well as the complex union of moral concern and vaulting ambition that motivated their actions on the world stage.

Through their efforts, Western colonialism spread throughout much of the non-Western world during the nineteenth and early twentieth centuries. Spurred by the demands of the Industrial Revolution, a few powerful Western states, notably Great Britain, France, Germany, Russia, and the United States, competed avariciously for consumer markets and raw materials for their expanding economies. By the end of the

Slave trade declared
illegal in Great Britain

French seize Algeria

Berlin
Conference
on Africa

Boer War

Sepoy Mutiny

Indian National
Congress established

Gandhi
returns
to India

British rail network opened in northern India

Stamford Raffles
founds Singapore

French attack
Vietnam

Commodore Dewey defeats Spanish fleet in Manila Bay

French and British agree to neutralize Thailand

nineteenth century, virtually all of the traditional societies in Asia and Africa were under direct or indirect colonial rule. As the new century began, the Western imprint on Asian and African societies, for better or for worse, appeared to be a permanent feature of the political and cultural landscape.

The Spread of Colonial Rule

In the nineteenth century, a new phase of Western expansion into Asia and Africa began. Whereas European aims in the East before 1800 could be summed up in Vasco da Gama's famous phrase "Christians and spices," in the early nineteenth century a new relationship took shape, as European nations began to view Asian and African societies as sources of industrial raw materials and a market for Western manufactured goods. No longer were Western gold and silver exchanged for cloves, pepper, tea, silk, and porcelain. Now the prodigious output of European factories was sent to Africa and Asia in return for oil, tin, rubber, and the other resources needed to fuel the Western industrial machine.

The reason for this change, of course, was the Industrial Revolution, which began in England in the late eighteenth century and spread to the Continent a few decades later. Now industrializing countries in the West needed vital raw materials that were not available at home as well as a reliable market for the goods produced in their factories. The latter factor became increasingly crucial as capitalist societies began to discover that their home markets could not always absorb domestic output.

When consumer demand lagged, economic depression threatened.

As Western economic expansion into Asia and Africa gathered strength during the last quarter of the nineteenth century, it became fashionable to call the process imperialism. Although the term *imperialism* has many meanings, in this instance it referred to the efforts of capitalist states in the West to seize markets, cheap raw materials, and lucrative sources for the investment of capital in the countries beyond Western civilization. In this interpretation, the primary motives behind the Western expansion were economic. The best-known promoter of this view was the British political economist John A. Hobson, who published a major analysis entitled *Imperialism: A Study* in 1902. In this influential book, Hobson maintained that modern imperialism was a direct consequence of the modern industrial economy.

As in the earlier phase of Western expansion, however, the issue was not simply an economic one. As Hobson himself conceded, economic concerns were inevitably tinged with political ones and with questions of national grandeur and moral purpose as well. In nineteenth-century Europe, economic wealth, national status, and political power went hand in hand with the possession of a colonial empire, at least in the minds of observers at the time. To nineteenth-century global strategists, colonies brought tangible benefits in the world of balance of power politics as well as economic profits, and many nations became involved in the pursuit of colonies as much to gain advantage over their rivals as to acquire territory for its own sake.

The relationship between colonialism and national survival was expressed directly in a speech by French politician Jules Ferry in 1885. A policy of "containment or abstinence," he warned, would set France on "the broad road to decadence" and initiate its decline into a "third-or-fourth-rate power." British imperialists agreed. To Cecil Rhodes, the most famous empire builder of his day, the extraction of material wealth from the colonies was only a secondary matter. "My ruling purpose," he remarked, "is the extension of the British Empire."[2] That British Empire, on which (as the saying went) "the sun never set," was the envy of its rivals and was viewed as the primary source of British global dominance during the latter half of the nineteenth century.

With the change in European motives for colonization came a corresponding shift in tactics. Earlier, when their economic interests were more limited, European states had generally been satisfied to deal with existing independent states rather than attempting to establish direct control over vast territories. There had been exceptions where state power at the local level was at the point of collapse (as in India), where European economic interests were especially intense (as in Latin America and the East Indies), or where there was no centralized authority (as in North America and the Philippines). But for the most part, the Western presence in Asia and Africa had been limited to controlling the regional trade network and establishing a few footholds where the foreigners could carry on trade and missionary activity.

After 1800, the demands of industrialization in Europe created a new set of dynamics. Maintaining access to industrial raw materials such as oil and rubber and setting up reliable markets for European manufactured products required more extensive control over colonial territories. As competition for colonies increased, the colonial powers sought to solidify their hold over their territories to protect them from attack by their rivals. During the last two decades of the nineteenth century, the quest for colonies became a scramble, as all the major European states, now joined by the United States and Japan, engaged in a global land grab. In many cases, economic interests were secondary to security concerns or the requirements of national prestige. In Africa, for example, the British engaged in a struggle with their rivals to protect their interests in the Suez Canal and the Red Sea. In Southeast Asia, the United States seized the Philippines from Spain at least partly to keep them out of the hands of the Japanese, while the French took over Indochina for fear that it would otherwise be occupied by Germany, Japan, or the United States.

✖ Map 22.1 Colonial Southeast Asia.

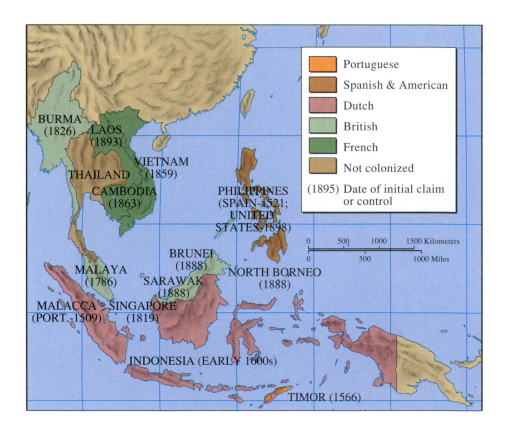

By 1900, almost all the societies of Africa and Asia were either under full colonial rule or, as in the case of China and the Ottoman Empire, at a point of virtual collapse. Only a handful of states, such as Japan in East Asia, Thailand in Southeast Asia, Afghanistan and Iran in the Middle East, and mountainous Ethiopia in East Africa, managed to escape internal disintegration or political subjection to colonial rule. For the most part, the exceptions were the result of good fortune rather than design. Thailand escaped subjugation primarily because officials in London and Paris found it more convenient to transform the country into a buffer state than to fight over it. Ethiopia and Afghanistan survived due to their remote location and mountainous terrain. Only Japan managed to avoid the common fate through a concerted strategy of political and economic reform.

"Opportunity in the Orient": The Colonial Takeover in Southeast Asia

In 1800, only two societies in Southeast Asia were under effective colonial rule: the Spanish Philippines and the Dutch East Indies. The British had been driven out of the Spice Island trade in the seventeenth century and possessed only a small enclave on the southern coast of the island of Sumatra in addition to territory on the Malay peninsula. The French had actively engaged in trade with states on the Asian mainland, but were eventually reduced to a small missionary effort run by the Society for Foreign Missions. The only legacy of Portuguese expansion in the region was their possession of half of the small island of Timor.

During the last half of the nineteenth century, however, European interest in Southeast Asia increased rapidly, and by 1900 virtually the entire area was under colonial rule. The process began after the end of the Napoleonic Wars, when the British, by agreement with the Dutch, abandoned their claims to territorial possessions in the East Indies in return for a free hand in the Malay peninsula. In 1819, the colonial administrator Sir Stamford Raffles founded a new British colony on a small island at the tip of the peninsula. Called Singapore (city of the lion), it had previously been used by Malay pirates as a base for raids on shipping passing through the Strait of Malacca. When the invention of steam power enabled merchant ships to save time and distance by passing through the strait rather than sailing with the westerlies across the southern Indian Ocean, Singapore became a major stopping point for traffic en route to and from China and other commercial centers in the region. Raffles, an official with the East India Company who had

urged his government to launch a vigorous effort to counter Dutch moves in the area, showed an understandable paternal pride in "this my almost only child." He wrote to a friend in England that "here all is life and activity; and it would be difficult to name a place on the face of the globe with brighter prospects or more present satisfaction."[3]

During the next few decades, the pace of European penetration into Southeast Asia accelerated. At the beginning of the nineteenth century, the British had sought and received the right to trade with the kingdom of Burma. A few decades later, the British began to consolidate a more direct presence in the area to protect the eastern flank of their possessions in India (see Chapter 16) and to explore the possibility of a land route into South China. The latter effort failed because of the tortuous terrain along the frontier between Burma and China and the inhospitable reception given to outsiders by hill peoples in the region (the members of the first British exploratory team, for example, were reportedly beheaded by natives). But British activities in the area did lead to the destruction of the Burmese monarchy and the establishment of British control over the entire country, which was eventually placed under the colonial administration in India.

The British advance into Burma was watched nervously in Paris, where French geopoliticians were ever anxious at British operations in Asia and Africa. The French still maintained a clandestine missionary organization in Vietnam despite harsh persecution by the local authorities, who viewed Christianity as a threat to Confucian doctrine. But Vietnamese efforts to prohibit Christian missionary activities were hindered by internal rivalries that had earlier divided the country into two separate and mutually hostile governments in the north and south.

French religious interests had intervened in the Vietnamese civil war in the late eighteenth century in the hope of regaining access to the country, but the Nguyen dynasty, which came to power with French assistance in 1802, continued to persecute French priests operating in Vietnam. In 1857, the French government decided to force the Vietnamese to accept French protection in order to prevent the British from obtaining a monopoly of trade in South China. A naval attack launched a year later was not a total success, but the French eventually forced the Vietnamese court to cede territories in the Mekong River delta. A generation later, French rule was extended over the remainder of the country. By the end of the century, French seizure of neighboring Cambodia and Laos had led to the creation of the French-ruled Indochinese Union.

With the French conquest of Indochina, Thailand was the only remaining independent state on the Southeast Asian mainland. During the last quarter of the century, British and French rivalry threatened to place the Thai, too, under colonial rule. But under the astute leadership of two remarkable rulers, King Mongkut (familiar to millions of theatergoers as the king in *The King and I*) and his son King Chulalongkorn, the Thai attempted to introduce Western learning and maintain relations with the major European powers without undermining internal stability or inviting an imperialist attack. In 1896, the British and the French agreed to preserve Thailand as an independent buffer zone between their possessions in Southeast Asia.

The final piece in the colonial edifice in Southeast Asia was put in place in 1898, when U.S. naval forces under Commodore George Dewey defeated the Spanish fleet in Manila Bay. President William McKinley agonized over the fate of the Philippines, but ultimately decided that the moral thing to do was to turn the islands into an American colony to prevent them from falling into the hands of the Japanese. In fact, the Americans (like the Spanish before them) found the islands convenient as a jumping-off point for the China trade (see Chapter 23). The mixture of moral idealism and the desire for profit was reflected in a speech that was given in the Senate in January 1900 by Senator Albert Beveridge of Indiana:

> Mr. President, the times call for candor. The Philippines are ours forever, "territory belonging to the United States," as the Constitution calls them. And just beyond the Philippines are China's illimitable markets. We will not retreat from either. We will not repudiate our duty in the archipelago. We will not abandon our opportunity in the Orient. We will not renounce our part in the mission of our race, trustee, under God, of the civilization of the world. And we will move forward to our work, not howling out regrets like slaves whipped to their burdens, but with gratitude for a task worthy of our strength, and thanksgiving to Almighty God that He has marked us as His chosen people, henceforth to lead in the regeneration of the world.[4]

Not all Filipinos agreed with Senator Beveridge's portrayal of the situation. Under the leadership of Emilio Aguinaldo, guerrilla forces fought bitterly against U.S. troops to establish their independence from both Spain and the United States. But America's first war against guerrilla forces in Asia was a success, and the bulk of the resistance collapsed in 1901. President McKinley had his stepping-stone to the rich markets of China.

Empire Building in Africa

Up to the beginning of the nineteenth century, the relatively limited nature of European economic interests in Africa had provided little temptation for the penetration of the interior or the political takeover of the coastal areas. The slave trade, the main source of European profit during the eighteenth century, could be carried on by using African rulers and merchants as intermediaries. Disease, political instability, the lack of transportation, and the generally unhealthy climate all served as obstacles to European efforts to extort a profit from dealings in Africa.

THE GROWING EUROPEAN PRESENCE IN WEST AFRICA

As the new century dawned, the slave trade itself was in a state of decline. One reason was the growing sense of outrage among humanitarians in several European countries over the purchase, sale, and exploitation of human beings (see the box on p. 823). Dutch merchants effectively ceased trafficking in slaves in 1795, and the Danes stopped in 1803. A few years later, the slave trade was declared illegal in both Great Britain and the United States. The British began to apply pressure on other nations to follow suit, and most did so after the end of the Napoleonic Wars in 1815, leaving only Portugal and Spain as practitioners of the trade south of the equator. In the meantime, the demand for slaves began to decline in the Western Hemisphere, and by the 1880s slavery had been abolished in all major countries of the world.

Economic as well as humanitarian interests contributed to the end of the slave trade. The cost of slaves had begun to rise after the middle of the eighteenth century, while the growth of the slave population reduced the need for additional labor on the plantations in the Americas. The British, with some reluctant assistance from France and the United States, added to the costs by actively using their navy to capture slave ships and free the occupants. When slavery was abolished in the United States in 1863 and in Cuba and Brazil seventeen years later, the slave trade across the Atlantic was effectively brought to an end.

Paradoxically, the decline of the slave trade in the Atlantic during the first half of the nineteenth century did not lead to an overall reduction in the European presence in West Africa. To the contrary, European interest in what was sometimes called "legitimate trade" in natural resources increased. Exports of peanuts, timber, hides, and palm oil increased substantially during the first decades of the century, while imports of textile goods and other manufactured products rose. The increasing pace of

❧ A Horror Almost Inconceivable ❧

By the early nineteenth century, human rights groups in Great Britain and on the Continent had begun to speak out vocally against the evils of the slave trade. By mid-century, the trade had been abolished by many colonial powers and was openly practiced only in East Africa, where it was a primary source of income for Muslim rulers along the Swahili coast. The following passages provide brief descriptions of the horrors of the experience. As the first excerpt shows, mistreatment began even before the ships set sail. The second passage, written by an Ibo captured by British slavers in the late eighteenth century, describes the unspeakable conditions on board the ships en route to America.

In Harbor in Africa

When our slaves are aboard we shackle the men two and two, while we lie in port, and in sight of their own country, for 'tis then they attempt to make their escape, and mutiny . . . they are fed twice a day . . . which is the time they are aptest to mutiny, being all upon deck; therefore all that time, what of our men are not em-ploy'd in distributing their victuals to them, and settling them, stand to their arms; and some with lighted matches at the great guns that yawn upon them, loaden with partridge, till they have done and gone down to their kennels between decks.

The Voyage to America

The closeness of the place, and the heat of the climate, added to the number in the ship, which was so crowded that each had scarcely room to turn himself, almost suffocated us. This produced copious perspirations, so that the air soon become unfit for respiration, from a variety of loathsome smells, and brought on a sickness amongst the slaves, of which many died. . . . This wretched situation was again aggravated by the galling of the chains, now become insupportable; and the filth of the necessary tubs, into which the children often fell, and were almost suffocated. The shrieks of the women, and the groans of the dying, rendered the whole a scene of horror almost inconceivable.

---

interregional commerce benefited rulers and merchants, of course, but in some cases it also worked to the advantage of farmers and artisans who were fortunate enough to be involved in that trade.

Stimulated by growing commercial interests in the area, European governments began to push for a more permanent presence along the coast. During the first decades of the nineteenth century, the British established settlements along the Gold Coast and in Sierra Leone, where they attempted to set up agricultural plantations for freed slaves who had returned from the Western Hemisphere or had been liberated by British ships while en route to the Americas. A similar haven for ex-slaves was developed with the assistance of the United States in Liberia. The French occupied the area around the Senegal River near Cape Verde, where they attempted to develop peanut plantations.

Europeans also began to press inward beyond the coastal jungles and swamps in search of new riches in the interior. An expedition led by the Scottish surgeon Mungo Park established that the Niger River ran eastward rather than westward, as had previously been believed. Park and his party were killed by natives, but a second mission was sent out in the 1820s, and after further tribulations the entire course of the Niger to the Gulf of Benin was charted.

The growing European presence in West Africa led to the emergence of a new class of Afro-Europeans educated in Western culture and often employed by Europeans. Many became Christians and some studied in European or American universities. At the same time, the European presence inevitably led to increasing tensions with African governments in the area. British efforts to increase trade with Ashanti led to conflict in the 1820s, but British influence in the area intensified in later decades. Most African states, especially those with a fairly high degree of political integration, were able to maintain their independence from this creeping European encroachment, called "informal empire" by some historians, but the prospects for the future were ominous. When Afro-European groups attempted to organize to protect their own interests, the British stepped in and annexed the coastal states as the British colony of Gold Coast in 1874. At about the same time, the British extended an informal protectorate over warring tribal groups in the Niger delta.

IMPERIALIST SHADOW OVER THE NILE

A similar process was underway in the Nile valley. Ever since the voyages of the Portuguese explorers at the close of the fifteenth century, European trade with the east had been carried on almost exclusively by the route around the Cape of Good Hope. But from the outset there was some interest in shortening the route by digging a canal east of Cairo, where only a low, swampy isthmus separated the Mediterranean from the Red Sea. The Turks had considered constructing a canal from Cairo to Suez in the sixteenth century, as had the French king Louis

XIV a century later, but the French did nothing about it until the end of the eighteenth century. At that time, Napoleon planned a military takeover of Egypt to cement French power in the eastern Mediterranean and open a faster route to India.

Napoleon's plan proved abortive. French troops landed in Egypt in 1798 and destroyed the ramshackle Mamluk regime in Cairo, but the British counterattacked, destroying the French fleet in Aboukir Bay, off the Egyptian coast, and eventually forcing the French to evacuate in disorder. The British restored the Mamluks to power, but in 1805 elements in the Ottoman army

✴ Map 22.2   Africa in 1914.

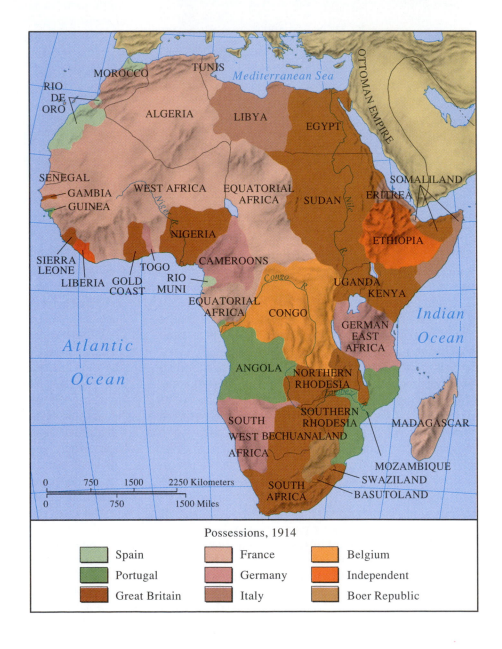

seized power under Muhammad Ali, an officer of either Turkish or Albanian extraction. Muhammad Ali then turned against the Ottomans for reneging on a promise to give him the island of Crete and sought to establish Egyptian autonomy from Turkish rule.

During the next three decades, Muhammad Ali introduced a series of reforms to bring Egypt into the modern world. He modernized the army, set up a public educational system (supplementing the traditional religious education provided in Muslim schools), and sponsored the creation of a small industrial sector. Refined sugar, textiles, munitions, and even ships were among the products. Muhammad Ali also extended Egyptian authority southward into the Sudan and across the Sinai peninsula into Arabia, Syria, and northern Iraq and even briefly threatened to seize Istanbul itself. To prevent the possible collapse of the Ottoman Empire, the British and the French recognized Muhammad Ali as the hereditary pasha (later to be known as the *khedive*) of Egypt under the loose authority of the Ottoman government.

The growing economic importance of the Nile valley, along with the development of steam navigation, made the heretofore visionary plans for a Suez Canal more urgent. In 1854, the French entrepreneur Ferdinand de Lesseps signed a contract to begin construction of the canal, and it was completed in 1869. The project brought little immediate benefit to Egypt, however. The construction not only cost thousands of lives but left the Egyptian government deep in debt, forcing it to depend increasingly on foreign financial support. When an army revolt

against growing foreign influence broke out in 1881, the British stepped in to protect their investment (they had bought Egypt's canal company shares in 1875) and establish an informal protectorate that would last until World War I.

Rising discontent in the Sudan added to Egypt's growing internal problems. In 1881, the Muslim cleric Muhammad Ahmad, known as the Mahdi (in Arabic, the "rightly guided one"), led a religious revolt that brought much of the upper Nile under his control. The famous British general Charles Gordon, who had earlier commanded Manchu armies fighting against the Taiping Rebellion in China (see Chapter 23), led a military force to Khartoum to restore Egyptian authority, but his besieged army was captured in 1885 by the Mahdi's troops, thirty-six hours before a British rescue mission reached Khartoum. Gordon himself died in the battle, which became one of the most dramatic news stories of the last quarter of the century.

The weakening of Turkish rule in the Nile valley had a parallel further to the west, where local viceroys in Tripoli, Tunis, and Algiers had begun to establish their autonomy. In 1830, the French, on the pretext of protecting European shipping in the Mediterranean from pirates, seized the area surrounding Algiers and integrated it into the French Empire. By the mid-1850s, more than 150,000 Europeans had settled in the fertile region adjacent to the coast, although Berber elements in the desert to the south continued to resist. In 1881, the French imposed a protectorate on neighboring Tunisia. Only

◆ **The Opening of the Suez Canal.** The Suez Canal, which connected the Mediterranean and the Red Seas for the first time, was constructed under the direction of the French promoter, Ferdinand de Lesseps. Still in use today, the canal is Egypt's greatest revenue producer. This sketch shows the ceremonial passage of the first ships through the canal in 1869.

◆━━━━━◆━━━━━◆━━━━━◆

Imperialism in Africa

Dutch abolish slave trade in Africa	1795
Napoleonic invasion of Egypt	1798
Slave trade declared illegal in Great Britain	1808
British-Ashanti War	1820s
Boers' Great Trek in South Africa	1830s
French seize Algeria	1830
Sultan of Oman establishes capital at Zanzibar	1840
David Livingstone arrives in Africa	1841
Slavery abolished in the United States	1863
Completion of Suez Canal	1869
Zanzibar slave market closed	1873
British establish Gold Coast colony	1874
British establish informal protectorate over Egypt	1881
Berlin Conference on Africa	1884
Charles Gordon killed at Khartoum	1885
Confrontation at Fashoda	1898
Boer War	1899–1902
Union of South Africa established	1910

Tripoli and Cyrenaica (the Ottoman provinces that comprise modern-day Libya) remained under Turkish rule until the Italians took them in 1911–1912.

ARAB MERCHANTS AND EUROPEAN MISSIONARIES IN EAST AFRICA

As always, events in East Africa followed their own distinctive pattern of development. In another of the paradoxes of the time, the decline in the Atlantic slave trade led to an increase in slavery on the other side of the continent. One reason may simply have been the tendency for the commerce in slaves to drift to a new source of supply. But a second reason was the sudden growth of plantation agriculture in the region and in the islands off the coast. The French introduced sugar to the island of Réunion early in the century, while clove plantations (the clove was first introduced from the Moluccas in the

eighteenth century) were established under Omani Arab ownership on the island of Zanzibar. Zanzibar itself became the major shipping port along the entire east coast during the early part of the century, and the sultan of Oman, who had reasserted Arab suzerainty over the region in the aftermath of the collapse of Portuguese authority, established his capital at Zanzibar in 1840.

From Zanzibar, Arab merchants fanned out into the interior plateaus in search of slaves, ivory, and other local products. The government in Zanzibar made no attempt to establish political hegemony on the continent, but Arab traders, relying on the superiority of firearms over the spear and the bow, became a dominant force in the region, which was now characterized by growing violence and tribal warfare. The competition for slaves spread as far as the Lake District and the lower Sudan, as traders from the north launched their own raids to obtain conscripts for the Egyptian army. The khedive sent General Charles Gordon to Uganda to stop the practice, but in the absence of alternative sources of income, such as mechanized agriculture or ivory, local merchants could not easily be persuaded to give up a lucrative occupation.

The tenacity of the slave trade in East Africa—Zanzibar had now become the largest slave market in Africa—was undoubtedly a major reason for the rise of Western interest and Christian missionary activity in the region during the middle of the century. The most renowned symbol of European humanitarianism in nineteenth-century Africa was the Scottish missionary David Livingstone. Livingstone had first arrived in Africa as a medical missionary in 1841. For years he trekked through unchartered regions in the central part of the continent, preaching Christianity to the local African population and becoming a celebrity in Europe as well as Africa. Because Livingstone spent much of his time exploring the interior of the continent, discovering Victoria Falls in the process, he was occasionally criticized for being more explorer than missionary. But Livingstone was convinced that it was his divinely appointed task to bring Christianity to the far reaches of the continent, and his passionate opposition to the institution of slavery did far more to win public support for the abolitionist cause than did the efforts of any other figure of his generation. Public outcries provoked the British to redouble their efforts to bring the slave trade in East Africa to an end, and in 1873 the slave market at Zanzibar was finally closed as the result of pressure from London. Shortly before, Livingstone had died of illness in central Africa, but some of his followers brought his body to the coast for burial. His legacy is still visible today in the form of an Anglican cathedral that was erected on the site of the slave market at Zanzibar.

BANTUS, BOERS, AND BRITISH IN THE SOUTH

Nowhere in Africa did the European presence grow more rapidly than in the south. During the eighteenth century, European settlers began to migrate eastward from the Cape Colony into territory inhabited by local Khoisan and Bantu-speaking peoples entering the area from the north. Internecine warfare among the Bantus had largely depopulated the region, facilitating occupation of the land by the Boers, the Afrikaans-speaking farmers who were descended from the original Dutch settlers in the seventeenth century. But in the early nineteenth century, a local people called the Zulus, under a talented ruler named Shaka, counterattacked, setting off a series of wars between the Europeans and the Zulus. Eventually, Shaka was overthrown, and the Boers continued their relentless advance northeastward during the so-called Great Trek in the mid-1830s. By 1865, the total white population of the area had risen to nearly 200,000 people.

The Boers' eastward migration was provoked in part by the British seizure of the cape from the Dutch during the Napoleonic Wars and by the different attitude of the British to the native population. Slavery was abolished in the British Empire in 1834, and the British government was generally more sympathetic to the rights of the local African population than were the Afrikaners, many of whom saw white superiority as ordained by God and fled from British rule to control their own destiny. Eventually, the Boers formed their own independent republics—called the Orange Free State and the South African Republic (usually known as Transvaal). When arriving

♦ **A Slave Raid on the Lualaba River.** By the mid-nineteenth century, most European nations had prohibited the trade in African slaves, but slavery continued in East Africa under the sponsorship of the sultan of Zanzibar. In this sketch, slave traders massacre Africans in an 1871 slave raid on the Lualaba River, just west of Lake Tanganyika. Wrote David Livingstone of the occasion, "It gave me the impression of being in Hell."

Boers drove many of the remaining Khoisan off their grazing lands, the Khoisan sometimes reacted with violence. One Dutch official complained that the Khoisan were driving settlers from their farms "for no other reason than because they saw that we were breaking up the best land and grass, where their cattle were accustomed to graze."[5] Ultimately, most of the blacks in the Boer republics were confined to reservations.

♦ **A Zulu Encampment in South Africa.** When white settlers moved beyond the original Cape Colony in search of good farmland, they encountered the Zulus, a Bantu-speaking people living in the lands northeast of the cape. Often the encounter was quite brutal on both sides. In this illustration from 1838, Boer leaders are entering a Zulu settlement to take part in a ceremony in their honor. Instead, they were executed by Zulu warriors.

THE SCRAMBLE FOR AFRICA

At the beginning of the 1880s, most of Africa was still independent. European rule was still limited to the fringes of the continent, such as Algeria, the Gold Coast, and South Africa. Other areas like Egypt, lower Nigeria, Senegal, and Mozambique were under various forms of loose protectorate. But the trends were ominous, as the pace of European penetration was accelerating, and the constraints that had limited European rapaciousness were fast disappearing.

The scramble began in the mid-1880s, when several European states, including Belgium, France, Germany, Great Britain, and Portugal, engaged in what today would be called a feeding frenzy to seize a piece of African territory before the carcass had been picked clean. By 1900, virtually all of the continent had been placed under one form or another of European rule. The British had consolidated their authority over the Nile valley and seized additional territories in East Africa. When the British received the German colony of Tanganyika as a trust territory after World War I, they had created an unbroken band from "Cape to Cairo" under the rule of the British crown. The French retaliated by advancing eastward from Senegal into the central Sahara, where they eventually came eyeball to eyeball with the British at Fashoda on the Nile. They also occupied the island of Madagascar and other coastal territories in West and Central Africa. In between, the Germans claimed the hinterland opposite Zanzibar, as well as coastal strips in West and Southwest Africa north of the Cape, while King Leopold II of Belgium claimed the Congo. Eventually, Italy entered the contest and seized modern-day Libya and some of the Somali coast.

◆ **Serving the White Ruler.**   Although European governments claimed to be carrying out the civilizing mission in Africa, all too often the local population was forced to labor in degrading conditions to serve the economic interests of occupying power. Here African workers are depicted as they transport goods for a European merchant. Note the whimsical touch with the dog on the top of the cart.

What had happened to spark the sudden imperialist hysteria that brought an end to African independence? Clearly, economic interests in the narrow sense were not at stake as they had been in South and Southeast Asia. The level of trade between Europe and Africa was simply not sufficient to justify the risks and the expense of conquest.

There were, in fact, a number of other reasons. And perhaps the most important was to be found not in Africa, but in Europe itself. Until the 1870s, competition among the European states had not been particularly intense. But during the last quarter of the century, mutual rivalries had sharpened, leading to growing competition among Great Britain, France, Germany, and Russia over the extension of European control into the non-Western world. We have already seen the consequences of this heightened rivalry in Southeast Asia. It had an impact on Africa as well.

The intensified rivalries among the European states meant that they might be provoked into an imperialist takeover, not by strictly economic considerations, but by the fear that another state might do so, leaving them at a disadvantage. As one British diplomatic official remarked, a protectorate at the mouth of the Niger River would be an "unwelcome burden," but a French protectorate there would be "fatal." In such circumstances, statesmen felt compelled to protect possible future interests and security concerns even where they had no current rationale for action. In the most famous example, the British solidified their control over the entire Nile valley to protect the Suez Canal. The French, fearful of being left out, moved into Tunisia and the Sahara to protect their own interests. King Leopold of Belgium had coveted the Congo primarily for reasons of prestige (Belgium, he commented, is "a small country, with a small people," and needed a colony to enhance its image), while the Germans joined the scramble to become a legitimate member of the imperialist club.[6]

Another consideration might be called the "missionary factor," as European missionary interests lobbied with their governments for colonial takeovers to facilitate their efforts to convert the African population to Christianity. In fact, considerable moral complacency was inherent in the process. The concept of social Darwinism and the "White Man's Burden" persuaded many that it was in the interests of the African people, as well as their conquerors, to be introduced more rapidly to the benefits of Western civilization. Even David Livingstone had become convinced that missionary work and economic development had to go hand in hand, pleading to his fellow Europeans to introduce the "three Cs" (Christianity, commerce, and civilization) to the continent. How much easier such a task would be if African peoples were under benevolent European rule!

There were more prosaic reasons as well. Advances in Western technology and European superiority in firearms made it easier than ever for a small European force to defeat superior numbers. Furthermore, life expectancy for Europeans living in Africa had improved. With the discovery that quinine (extracted from the bark of the cinchona tree) could provide partial immunity from the ravages of malaria, the mortality rate for Europeans living in Africa dropped dramatically in the 1840s. By the end of the century, European residents in tropical Africa faced only slightly higher risks of death by disease than individuals living in Europe.

It has been said that the European conquest of Africa was not inevitable and was primarily the result of the entry of new European contestants (Belgium and Germany) into a previously stable environment, which had been marked by mutual restraint. This argument is not convincing. What took place in Africa was part of a larger process that was occurring throughout the world. As tensions among European states intensified, concerns for present and future markets and sources of raw materials increased, and there was a growing psychological predisposition to obtain colonies as a hedge against future actions by rivals.

In the case of Africa, the immediate justification was Belgium's claim to the Congo. When Leopold used missionary activities as an excuse to claim the vast territories in the Congo River basin, he aroused widespread concern that other European nations would act quickly to protect their own interests. Belgium and France sent their representatives on a desperate race to plant the national flag in the heart of Africa. Leopold ended up with the territories south of the Congo River, while France occupied areas to the north (Leopold later bequeathed the Congo to Belgium on his death). Meanwhile, on the eastern side of the continent, Germany (through the activities of an ambitious missionary and with the agreement of the British, who needed German support against the French) annexed the colony of Tanganyika. To avert the possibility of violent clashes among the great powers, the German chancellor Otto von Bismarck convened a conference in Berlin in 1884 to set ground rules for future annexations of African territory by European nations. Like the famous Open Door Notes fifteen years later (see Chapter 23), the conference combined high-minded resolutions with a hardheaded recognition of practical interests. The delegates called for liberty of commerce in the Congo and along the Niger River as well as for further efforts to end the slave trade. At the same time, they recognized the inevitability of the imperialist dynamic, agreeing only that future annexations of African territory should not be given international recognition until effective occupation had been demonstrated. No African delegates were present.

The Berlin Conference had been convened to avert war and reduce tensions among European nations competing for the spoils of Africa. It proved reasonably successful at achieving the first objective but less so at the second. During the next few years, African territories were annexed without provoking a major confrontation between the Western powers, but in the late 1890s, Britain and France reached the brink of conflict at Fashoda, a small town on the Nile River in the Sudan. The French had been advancing eastward across the Sahara with the transparent objective of controlling the re-

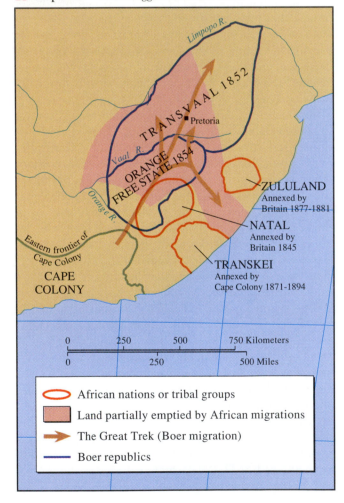

⚜ Map 22.3 The Struggle for South Africa.

Limpopo R.

TRANSVAAL 1852

Pretoria

Vaal R.

ORANGE
FREE STATE 1854

Orange R.

Eastern frontier of
Cape Colony

CAPE
COLONY

ZULULAND
Annexed by
Britain 1877-1881

NATAL
Annexed by
Britain 1845

TRANSKEI
Annexed by
Cape Colony 1871-1894

| 0 | 250 | 500 | 750 Kilometers |
| 0 | | 250 | 500 Miles |

⬭ African nations or tribal groups

▦ Land partially emptied by African migrations

➡ The Great Trek (Boer migration)

— Boer republics

gions around the upper Nile. In 1898, British and Egyptian troops seized the Sudan from successors of the Mahdi and then marched southward to head off the French. After a tense face-off between units of the two European countries at Fashoda, the French government backed down, and British authority over the area was secured. Except for the Mediterranean littoral and their small possessions of Djibouti and a portion of the Somali coast, the French were restricted to equatorial Africa.

Ironically, the only major clash between Europeans over Africa took place in South Africa, where competition among the powers was almost nonexistent. The discovery of gold and diamonds in the Boer republic of the Transvaal was the source of the problem. Clashes between the Afrikaner population and foreign (mainly British) miners and developers led to an attempt by Cecil Rhodes, prime minister of the Cape Colony and a prominent entrepreneur in the area, to subvert the Transvaal and bring it under British rule. In 1899, the so-called Boer War broke out between Britain and the Transvaal, which was backed by its fellow republic, the Orange Free State. Guerrilla resistance by the Boers was fierce, but the vastly superior forces of the British were able to prevail by 1902. To compensate the defeated Afrikaner population for the loss of independence, the British government agreed that only whites would vote in the now essentially self-governing colony. The Boers were placated, but the brutalities committed during the war (the British introduced an institution later to be known as the concentration camp) created bitterness on both sides that continued to fester through future decades.

The Colonial System

Now that they were in control of most of the world, what did the colonial powers do with it? As we have seen, their primary objective was to exploit the natural resources of the subject areas and to open up markets for manufactured goods and capital investment from the mother country. In some cases, that goal could be realized in cooperation with local political elites, whose loyalty could be earned, or purchased, by economic rewards or by confirming them in their positions of authority and status in a new colonial setting. Sometimes, however, this policy, known as "indirect rule," was not feasible because local leaders refused to cooperate with their colonial masters or even actively resisted the foreign conquest. In such cases, the local elites were removed from power and replaced with a new set of officials recruited from the mother country.

Several factors determined whether colonial rule would be direct or indirect. In general, active resistance to colonial conquest came primarily from societies with a long tradition of national cohesion and independence, such as China, Burma, and Vietnam in Asia and the African Muslim states in northern Nigeria and Morocco. In those areas, the colonial power was likely to dispense with local collaborators and govern directly. Indirect rule, on the other hand, was often applied in societies where the local authorities, for whatever reason, were willing to collaborate with the imperialist powers. Such was the case in parts of Africa and the Indian subcontinent and in the Malay peninsula.

The distinctions between direct and indirect rule were not merely academic and often had fateful consequences for the peoples involved. Where colonial powers encountered resistance and were forced to overthrow local political elites, they often adopted policies designed to eradicate the source of resistance and destroy the traditional culture. Such policies often had quite corrosive effects on the indigenous societies and provoked resentment and resistance that not only marked the colonial relationship but even affected relations after the restoration of national independence. The bitter struggles after World War II in Algeria, the Dutch East Indies, and Vietnam can be ascribed in part to that phenomenon.

The Philosophy of Colonialism

To justify their conquests, the colonial powers appealed, in part, to the time-honored maxim of "might makes right." In a manner reminiscent of the Western attitude toward the oil reserves in the Persian Gulf today, the European powers viewed industrial resources as vital to national survival and security and felt that no moral justification was needed for any action to protect access to them. By the end of the nineteenth century, that attitude received pseudoscientific validity from the concept of social Darwinism, which maintained that only societies that moved aggressively to adapt to changing circumstances would survive and prosper in a world governed by the Darwinist law of "survival of the fittest."

Some people, however, were uncomfortable with such a brutal view of the law of nature and sought a moral justification that appeared to benefit the victim. Here again the concept of social Darwinism pointed the way. According to social Darwinists, human societies, like living organisms, must adapt to survive. Thus, the advanced nations of the West were obliged to assist the backward nations of Asia and Africa so that they, too, could adjust to the challenges of the modern world. Few expressed this

view as graphically as the English poet Rudyard Kipling, who called on the Anglo-Saxon peoples (in particular, the United States) to take up the "White Man's Burden" in Asia (see the box on p. 832).

Buttressed by such comforting theories, humane and sympathetic souls in Western countries could ignore the brutal aspects of the colonial process and persuade themselves that in the long run the results would be beneficial to both sides. Some, like their antecedents in the sixteenth and seventeenth centuries, saw the issue primarily in religious terms. During the nineteenth century, Christian missionaries by the thousands went to Asia and Africa to bring the Gospel to the "heathen masses." To others, the objective was the more secular one of bringing the benefits of Western democracy and capitalism to the feudalistic and tradition-ridden societies of the Orient. Either way, sensitive Western minds could console themselves with the belief that their governments were bringing civilization to the primitive peoples of the world. If commercial profit and national prestige happened to be by-products of that effort, so much the better.

Few were as good at expressing such a "civilizing mission" as the French administrator and twice governor-general of French Indochina Albert Sarraut. Admitting that colonialism was originally an "act of force" undertaken for commercial profit, he declared that it resulted in a "work of human solidarity":

> More important than any other rights is the right of all human beings to live a better life on this planet through the more effective utilization of material goods and moral wealth susceptible to be distributed to all living persons. This process can only take place through the solid collaboration of all races, liberally exchanging their natural resources and the creative faculties of their own genius. Nature has divided these faculties and these resources unequally across the surface of the globe through the unequal influence of climate, of fertility and hereditary values. Its arbitrary devolution has localized, here and there, one from another, in the diversity, the dispersion and the contrast. Is it just, is it legitimate that such a state of things should be indefinitely prolonged? In the name of humanity, one can respond forcefully: No! A right which results in undermining the right of universal well-being is not a right. Humanity is universal throughout the globe. No race, no people has the right or the power to isolate itself egotistically from the movements and necessities of the universal life.[7]

Here, claimed Sarraut, was the "broad and generous idea" on which colonialism, "the agent of civilization," must be founded as it took charge of the wealth of the earth so that it could be distributed to the profit of all.

≽ The White Man's Burden ≼

One of the justifications for European imperialism was the notion that the allegedly "more advanced" white peoples had the moral responsibility to raise ignorant native peoples to a higher level of civilization. Few captured this notion better than the British poet Rudyard Kipling (1865–1936) in his famous poem, The White Man's Burden. His appeal was addressed to the United States.

Rudyard Kipling, *The White Man's Burden*

Take up the White Man's burden—
Send forth the best ye breed—
Go bind your sons to exile
To serve your captives' need;
To wait in heavy harness,
On fluttered folk and wild—
Your new-caught sullen peoples,
Half-devil and half-child.

Take up the White Man's burden—
In patience to abide,
To veil the threat of terror
And check the show of pride;
By open speech and simple,
An hundred times made plain
To seek another's profit,
And work another's gain.

Take up the White Man's burden—
The savage wars of peace—
Fill full the mouth of Famine
And bid the sickness cease;
And when your goal is nearest
The end for others sought,
Watch Sloth and heathen Folly
Bring all your hopes to nought.

Take up the White Man's burden—
No tawdry rule of kings,
But toil of serf and sweeper—
The tale of common things.
The ports ye shall not enter,
The roads ye shall not tread,
Go mark them with your living,
And mark them with your dead!

Take up the White Man's burden—
And reap his old reward:
The blame of those ye better,
The hate of those ye guard—
The cry of hosts ye humour
(Ah, slowly!) toward the light:—
'Why brought ye us from bondage,
'Our loved Egyptian night?'

Take up the White Man's burden—
Ye dare not stoop to less—
Nor call too loud on Freedom
To cloak your weariness;
By all ye cry or whisper,
By all you leave or do,
The silent, sullen peoples
Shall weigh your Gods and you.

Take up the White Man's burden—
Have done with childish days—
The lightly proffered laurel,
The easy, ungrudged praise.
Comes now, to search your manhood
Through all the thankless years,
Cold-edged with dear-bought wisdom,
The judgment of your peers!

But what about the possibility that historically and culturally the societies of Asia and Africa were fundamentally different from those of the West and could not, or would not, be persuaded to transform themselves along Western lines? After all, even Kipling had remarked that "East is East and West is West, and ne'er the twain shall meet." Was the human condition universal, in which case the Asian and African peoples could be transformed, in the quaint American phrase for their subject Filipinos, into "little brown Americans"? Or were human beings so shaped by their history and geographical environment that their civilizations would inevitably remain distinct from those of the West? In that case, a policy of cultural transformation could not be expected to succeed and could even lead to disaster.

In fact, colonial theory never decided this issue one way or another. The French, who were most inclined to philosophize about the problem, adopted the terms *assimilation* (which implied an effort to transform colonial societies in the Western image) and *association* (by which they meant collaboration with local elites, while leaving local traditions alone) to describe the two alternatives and then proceeded to vacillate from one approach to the other. French policy in Indochina, for example, began as one of association, but switched to assimilation under pressure from liberal elements who felt that colonial powers owed a debt to their subject peoples. But assimilation (which in any case was never accepted as feasible or desirable by many colonial officials) aroused resentment among the local population, many of whom opposed the destruction of their native traditions. In the end, the French abandoned the attempt to justify their presence and fell back on a policy of ruling by force of arms.

Not all colonial powers were as inclined to debate the theory of colonialism as were the French. The British,

whether out of a sense of pragmatism or of racial superiority, refused to entertain the possibility of assimilation and treated their subject peoples as culturally and racially distinct. In formulating a colonial policy for the Philippines, the United States adopted a policy of assimilation in theory, but was not always so quick to put it into practice.

To many of the colonial peoples, such questions must have appeared academic, since the primary objectives of all the colonial states were economic exploitation and the retention of power (see the box on p. 834). Like the British soldier in Kipling's poem "On the Road to Mandalay," all too many Westerners living in the colonies believed that the Great Lord Buddha was nothing but a "bloomin' idol made of mud, what they call the great god Bud."

The Dilemmas of Colonial Responsibility

Whatever their ultimate intentions, most colonial governments sought to justify their presence by promising to

◆ **"Old and New Generations,** each in its own time." In the French colonial period the difference between young and old

Vietnamese was evident in virtually everything from clothing and hair styles to furniture, as shown here.

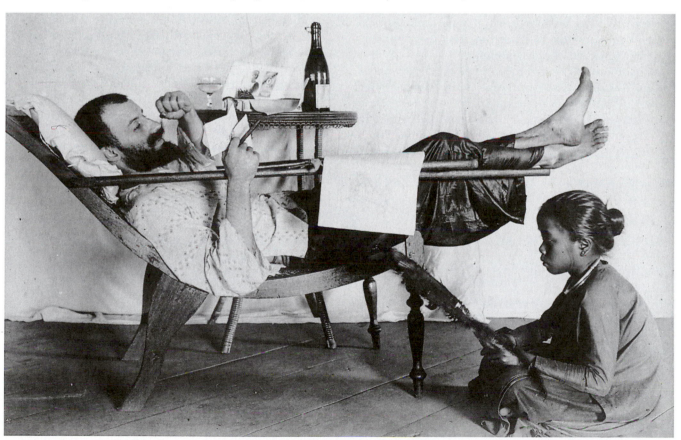

The Black Man's Burden

The Western justification of imperialism that was based on a sense of moral responsibility, evident in Rudyard Kipling's poem, was often hypocritical. Edmund Morel, a British journalist who spent time in the Congo, pointed out the destructive effects of Western imperialism on native Africans in his book, The Black Man's Burden.

Edmund Morel, *The Black Man's Burden*

It is [the Africans] who carry the "Black man's burden." They have not withered away before the white man's occupation. Indeed . . . Africa has ultimately absorbed within itself every Caucasian and, for that matter, every Semitic invader, too. In hewing out for himself a fixed abode in Africa, the white man has massacred the African in heaps. The African has survived, and it is well for the white settlers that he has. . . .

What the partial occupation of his soil by the white man has failed to do; what the mapping out of European political "spheres of influence" has failed to do; what the Maxim [machine gun] and the rifle, the slave gang, labour in the bowels of the earth and the lash, have failed to do; what imported measles, smallpox and syphilis have failed to do; whatever the overseas slave trade failed to do; the power of modern capitalistic exploitation, assisted by modern engines of destruction, may yet succeed in accomplishing.

For from the evils of the latter, scientifically applied and enforced, there is no escape for the African. Its destructive effects are not spasmodic; they are permanent. In its permanence resides its fatal consequences. It kills not the body merely, but the soul. It breaks the spirit. It attacks the African at every turn, from every point of vantage. It wrecks his polity, uproots him from the land, invades his family life, destroys his natural pursuits and occupations, claims his whole time, enslaves him in his own home.

In Africa, especially in tropical Africa, which a capitalistic imperialism threatens and has, in part, already devastated, man is incapable of reacting against unnatural conditions. In those regions man is engaged in a perpetual struggle against disease and an exhausting climate, which tells heavily upon childbearing; and there is no scientific machinery for saving the weaker members of the community. The African of the tropics is capable of tremendous physical labours. But he cannot accommodate himself to the European system of monotonous, uninterrupted labour, with its long and regular hours, involving, moreover, as it frequently does, severance from natural surroundings and nostalgia, the condition of melancholy resulting from separation from home, a malady to which the African is specially prone. Climatic conditions forbid it. When the system is forced upon him, the tropical African droops and dies.

Nor is violent physical opposition to abuse and injustice henceforth possible for the African in any part of Africa. His chances of effective resistance have been steadily dwindling with the increasing perfectibility in the killing power of modern armament.

Thus the African is really helpless against the material gods of the white man, as embodied in the trinity of imperialism, capitalistic exploitation, and militarism. . . .

To reduce all the varied and picturesque and stimulating episodes in savage life to a dull routine of endless toil for uncomprehended ends; to dislocate social ties and disrupt social institutions; to stifle nascent desires and crush mental development; to graft upon primitive passions the annihilating evils of scientific slavery, and the bestial imaginings of civilized man, unrestrained by convention or law; in fine, to kill the soul in a people—this is a crime which transcends physical murder.

introduce the blessings of advanced Western civilization. In the United States and Britain, the task was commonly known as the "White Man's Burden." In France and the Netherlands, it was called the "Civilizing Mission."

EXPORTING DEMOCRACY?

The problem with such a lofty goal was that all too often it conflicted with practical considerations. That was certainly the case in the area of political reform. The civilizing mission postulated that the colonial powers would introduce representative institutions and educate the native peoples in the democratic process. In fact, however, colonial officials understandably feared that native elements with full powers of political representation (especially educated ones) would be only too likely to demand full participation in the government or even the restoration of national independence.

Faced with a contradiction between moral purpose and practical needs, colonial governments routinely opted for the latter. In directly ruled societies, power was placed entirely in the hands of high European officials appointed by the colonial government and assisted by an advisory council composed mainly of Europeans. In societies under indirect rule, the colonial power ruled through the native rulers, who retained at least a semblance of their formerly supreme authority. Key decisions, however, were usually made by the ruler's colonial advisers.

In time, pressure from educated elements within the indigenous population compelled colonial governments to introduce political reforms. In the early years of the twentieth century, legislative councils with limited representation for native elements were established in Egypt, India, the Dutch East Indies, French Indochina, and the Gold Coast. The powers of these fledgling parliamentary bodies were limited, however, and the franchise was restricted to a wealthy elite. As time passed, such advisory councils gradually evolved into full legislative assemblies. Native participation in the colonial bureaucracies also tended to increase, although senior positions were usually held by Europeans, and salaries for native officials were lower than for their European counterparts.

A key aspect of the colonial enterprise, of course, was education, and all colonial governments set up new school systems to introduce the subject peoples to the rudiments of Western culture and institutions. In general, only native elites attended such schools, where the primary goal was to train native officials for the colonial bureaucracy. Some went abroad to receive higher education at Oxford, Cambridge, the Sorbonne, or similar institutions in Belgium, the Netherlands, or the United States. A few were sent by their governments, but more commonly they went at their families' expense.

Educational opportunities for the common people were harder to come by. In French-controlled Vietnam, for example, in 1917 only 3,000 out of a total of 23,000 villages in the country had a public school. The French had opened a university in Hanoi, but it was immediately closed as a result of student demonstrations. In some cases, missionary schools filled the gap, providing sound instruction at the elementary and secondary level for the fortunate few in many colonial societies.

By the second quarter of the twentieth century, then, a framework of representative government had been put into place in most if not all the colonial territories, and a native elite trained in the democratic process was beginning to play a role in decision making. Yet most decisions continued to be made by the colonial power in its own

interests. In that sense, colonial rule had not essentially transformed the traditional political culture. It was still fundamentally paternalistic and elitist. The main difference now was that the new ruling class was not only foreign but also lacked the mystique and semidivine quality that had been a characteristic of traditional leadership. Where authority in traditional societies in Asia and Africa had been legitimized by religion or hallowed tradition, authority in colonial societies was based on military force alone.

CAUGHT BETWEEN OLD AND NEW: COLONIAL ECONOMIC POLICY

In the field of economics, the objective of the civilizing mission was to integrate native societies into the global economic market. Those believing in Adam Smith's philosophy of laissez-faire economics maintained that the division of labor on the basis of free trade principles would eventually redound to the benefit of all. "Open new channels," advised one British writer in the 1830s, "for the most productive employment of English capital. Let the English buy bread from every people that has bread to sell cheap. Make England, for all that is produced by steam, the workshop of the world. If, after this, there be capital and people to spare, . . . find room for both by means of colonization."[8] In this view, the increasing wealth accumulated in colonial territories would nurture a native middle class, which in turn would spur the growth and maturation of democratic institutions. Many Western observers believed that a strong middle class was a prerequisite for the emergence of liberal democracy.

It was therefore in the interests of the general good that the economic relationship between the mother country and the colonial society should be governed by the laws of the marketplace. In practice, that normally meant that manufactured goods from the former would be exchanged for raw materials exported by the latter. The problem with this relationship was that due to high labor costs, prices for manufactured goods were much higher than for the raw materials exported from the colonies, and it was obviously in the interest of the colonial government to keep them that way. Simply put, the system exploited the colonial peoples.

To native producers, the obvious answer was to develop their own technology for refining raw materials and producing their own manufactured goods, which could then be exported on a competitive basis to other countries. But such a policy would threaten the economic interests of the colonial power, which benefited from keeping the price of raw materials low and maintaining a lucrative colonial market for the manufactures of the home country. Not surprisingly, in this clash of economic interests, those of the colonial power triumphed. Colonial governments generally located refining facilities in the home country and discouraged the development of a native manufacturing sector.

This is not to say that no economic changes took place in the colonies. To facilitate the production and flow of goods, colonial governments built railroads and highways, telegraph lines, radio transmitters, modern power plants, and airports. Although these facilities were designed primarily for the benefit of European interests, they did provide an economic infrastructure that future independent governments would inherit and could use for the benefit of the native peoples.

Moreover, in major urban conglomerations from Dakar to Batavia, Saigon to Bombay, and Calcutta to Cairo, a lively commercial and manufacturing sector began to develop almost despite the restrictive efforts of the colonial bureaucracy. Some of the wealth resulting from increased economic activity enriched an affluent and well-educated middle class. All too often, however, the most enterprising and successful entrepreneurs were not members of the majority population. In some cases, they were Europeans. In others, they were Indians in East Africa and Burma; Persian Parsis in Bombay; Jews, Syrians and Armenians as well as Greeks and Italians in Egypt; and Chinese in Kuala Lumpur, Batavia, and Saigon. In most colonial cities, foreign interests controlled banking, major manufacturing activities, and the import-export trade. The natives were more apt to work in a family business, at handicrafts, in factory or assembly plants, or as peddlers, day laborers, or rickshaw pullers (i.e., at less profitable and less capital-intensive businesses). Many of them lived in dismal conditions in urban slums or in squatter settlements along the edge of the cities.

Despite the growth of an urban economy, the vast majority of colonial peoples continued to farm the land. Many continued to live by subsistence agriculture, growing dry crops or wet rice as they had for centuries. But the colonial era brought changes here as well. In some areas, the livelihood of the rural population was affected by the colonial power's interest in producing cash crops for the export market. Peasants in the Dutch East Indies, for example, were forced to devote some of their ricelands to growing sugarcane in order to pay their taxes. Other areas previously occupied by private farms were turned into plantations for growing cotton, rubber trees, palm trees for oil, tropical fruits, or spices. In some cases, farmers benefited from the new situation. But others who had previously possessed tenure rights to their land risked eviction by landlords who turned the land to commercial use.

The situation was made even more difficult by the steady growth of the population. Peasants in Asia and Africa had always had large families on the assumption that a high proportion of their children would die in infancy. Large families, and especially sons, provided labor for the present and security for old age. But improved sanitation and medical treatment resulted in lower rates of infant mortality and a staggering increase in population. The population of the island of Java, for example, increased from about a million in the precolonial era to about 40 million at the end of the nineteenth century.

Under these conditions, the rural areas could no longer support the growing populations, and many young people fled to the cities to seek jobs in factories or shops. This migratory pattern gave rise to the squatter settlements in the suburbs of the major cities. A similar process had occurred in Europe during the early stages of the Industrial Revolution, when changes in agricultural practices forced many peasants off the land. At first, the transition had been painful, but eventually it led to more efficient farming and an available labor force for the growing industrial base.

The problem in colonial societies was that there was no such light at the end of the tunnel. Because colonial policies limited the growth of the domestic industrial economy, no jobs were available for the migrants to the cities. And the lack of capital and a local manufacturing base meant that few farmers could afford to mechanize. The end result was that the colonial peoples, unlike their Western counterparts, suffered for nothing. As the sociologist Clifford Geertz has said, the colonial peoples were caught between the old and new. The old system was collapsing, but a new system did not emerge to take its place.

SOCIAL AND CULTURAL CHANGES

The Western presence also had an impact on the social mores and religious beliefs of the colonial peoples. It was difficult for many Westerners who visited or lived in Asia or Africa to avoid an attitude of condescension toward the customs and institutions of non-Western societies. Even well-meaning European or American observers viewed strange customs as the remnants of a primitive or feudal legacy destined to be wiped out by the inexorable march of modern civilization. In some cases, the results were beneficial, as in the efforts to end child marriage and *sati* in India and the practice of cannibalism among upland peoples on the island of Sumatra. All too often, however, the Western attitude was expressed in blatant cultural arrogance personified by the colonial habit of addressing natives by their first names or calling an adult male "boy."

Nowhere were such attitudes more pronounced than in South Africa. The Afrikaners' ideas of racial superiority were deeply rooted, and they kept virtually the entire black population of the Cape Colony in the condition of slavery. Most slaves were laborers, few had families, and because of the increasingly strict racial segregation between master and slave, few achieved manumission. After the British government abolished slavery in 1838, many blacks sought employment in cities and towns, but racial prejudice and lack of job skills condemned them to menial employment and ghetto conditions.

Although such attitudes were often bitterly resented, at the same time many Asian and African elites found European civilization irresistible and began to hold their own traditional cultures in contempt. In the colonial cities, many native elites aped the behavior and dress of their rulers, speaking European languages, drinking European wines, and dancing to Western tunes in modern nightclubs built for the pleasure of the affluent. Outside the urban areas, though, traditional mores continued to survive.

How is one to evaluate the colonial experience? Defenders of colonialism point to the undeniable technological benefits that it brought to many a preindustrial

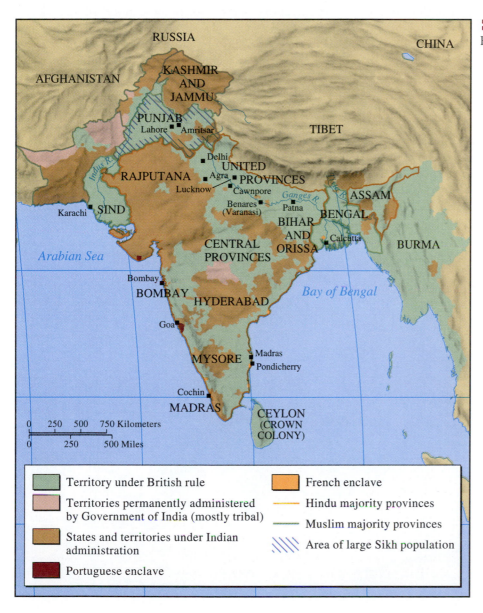

✖ **Map 22.4**   India Under British Rule, 1805–1931.

society. They note that, however painful, the experience represented the first stage in the nation-building process. Critics deny that colonialism was the handmaiden of modernization and argue that in many ways it actively delayed the process of change. No final answer to this controversy is likely to appear, since, unlike a scientific experiment, history can never be repeated. What can be said is that because economic self-interest usually had more power than high moral purpose, the colonial experience for most of the peoples of Asia and Africa was unnecessarily painful and protracted. It is a keen historical irony that most of the major colonial powers were practicing democracies. But their constituencies were in London and Paris, Birmingham and Brussels, Amsterdam, Pittsburgh, and Dubuque, not in Jakarta, Dakar, Cairo, or Manila.

Colonialism in Action

In practice, colonialism in India, Southeast Asia, and Africa exhibited many similarities but also some differences. Some of these variations can be traced to political or social differences among the colonial powers themselves. The French, for example, often tried to impose a centralized administrative system on their colonies that mirrored the system in use in France while the British sometimes attempted to transform local aristo-crats into the equivalent of the landed gentry at home in Britain. Other differences stemmed from conditions in the colonies themselves and the colonizers' aspirations for them. For instance, the Western powers believed that their economic interests were far more limited in Africa than elsewhere and therefore treated their African colonies somewhat differently than those in India or Southeast Asia. The result was to introduce a degree of variation within the general pattern of colonialism that we have described.

INDIA UNDER THE BRITISH RAJ

At the beginning of the nineteenth century, Indian society was at one of the lowest points in its historical development. The once glorious empire of the Mughals had been debased and humiliated and was now reduced by British military power to a shadow of its former greatness. During the next few decades, the British sought to consolidate their control over the subcontinent, expanding from their base areas along the coast into the interior. Some territories were taken over directly first by the East India Company and later by the British crown, while others were ruled indirectly through their local maharajas and rajas. In the 1820s, the British began to move into lower Burma in an attempt to find a land route to China, and twenty years later British troops fought in

◆ **Gateway to India?** Built by the British to commemorate the visit to India of King George V and Queen Mary in 1911, the Gateway of India was erected at the water's edge in the harbor of Bombay, India's greatest port city. For thousands of British citizens arriving in India, the Gateway of India was the first view of their new home and a symbol of the power and majesty of the British raj.

Afghanistan to solidify India's northwestern frontier against Russian penetration.

Not all of the effects of British rule were bad. British governance over the subcontinent brought order and stability to a society that had been rent by civil war even before the effects of Western intrusion had been strongly felt. By the early nineteenth century, British control had been consolidated and led to a relatively honest and efficient government that in many respects operated to the benefit of the average Indian. One of the benefits of the period was the heightened attention given to education. Through the efforts of the British administrator and historian Thomas Babington Macaulay, a new school system was established to train the children of Indian elites, and the British civil service examination was introduced. Macaulay's attitude, however, was unashamedly Anglocentric (see the box on p. 840).

British rule also brought an end to some of the more inhumane aspects of Indian tradition. The practice of *sati* was outlawed, and widows were legally permitted to remarry. The British also attempted to put an end to the endemic brigandage (known as thuggee, which gave rise to the English word "thug") that had plagued travelers in India since time immemorial. Railroads, the telegraph, and the postal service were introduced to India shortly after they appeared in Great Britain itself. Work began on the main highway from Calcutta to Delhi in 1839, and the first rail network was opened in 1853. A new penal code based on the British model was adopted, and health and sanitation conditions were improved.

But the Indian people paid a high price for the peace and stability brought by the British raj (from the Indian *raja*, or prince). Perhaps the most flagrant cost was economic. While British entrepreneurs and a small percent-

◆ **An English Nabob in Colonial India.** When the British took over India in the late eighteenth and nineteenth centuries, many Indians began to imitate European customs for prestige or social advancement. Sometimes, however, the cultural influence went the other way. Here an English nabob, as European residents in the colonies were often called, apes the manner of an Indian aristocrat, complete with harem and hookah, the Indian water pipe.

⋟ Indian in Blood, English in Taste and Intellect ⋞

Thomas Babington Macaulay (1800–1859) was named a member of the Supreme Council of India in the early 1830s. In that capacity he was responsible for drawing up a new educational policy for British subjects in the area. In his Minute on Education, *he considered the claims of English and various local languages to become the vehicle for educational training and decided in favor of the former. It is better, he argued, to teach Indian elites about Western civilization so as "to form a class who may be interpreters between us and the millions whom we govern; a class of persons, Indian in blood and color, but English in taste, in opinions, in morals, and in intellect." Later Macaulay became a prominent historian.*

Thomas Babington Macaulay, *Minute on Education*

We have a fund to be employed as government shall direct for the intellectual improvement of the people of this country. The simple question is, what is the most useful way of employing it?

All parties seem to be agreed on one point, that the dialects commonly spoken among the natives of this part of India contain neither literary or scientific information, and are, moreover so poor and rude that, until they are enriched from some other quarter, it will not be easy to translate any valuable work into them. It seems to be admitted on all sides that the intellectual improvement of those classes of the people who have the means of pursuing higher studies can at present be affected only by means of some language not vernacular amongst them.

What, then, shall that language be? One half of the Committee maintain that it should be the English. The other half strongly recommend the Arabic and Sanskrit. The whole question seems to me to be, which language is the best worth knowing?

I have no knowledge of either Sanskrit or Arabic—but I have done what I could to form a correct esti-

mate of their value. I have read translations of the most celebrated Arabic and Sanskrit works. I have conversed both here and at home with men distinguished by their proficiency in the Eastern tongues. I am quite ready to take the Oriental learning at the valuation of the Orientalists themselves. I have never found one among them who could deny that a single shelf of a good European library was worth the whole native literature of India and Arabia. . . .

It will hardly be disputed, I suppose, that the department of literature in which the Eastern writers stand highest is poetry. And I certainly never met with any Orientalist who ventured to maintain that the Arabic and Sanskrit poetry could be compared to that of the great European nations. But, when we pass from works of imagination to works in which facts are recorded and general principles investigated, the superiority of the Europeans becomes absolutely immeasurable. It is, I believe, no exaggeration to say, that all the historical information which has been collected from all the books written in the Sanskrit language is less valuable than what may be found in the most paltry abridgments used at preparatory schools in England. In every branch of physical or moral philosophy the relative position of the two nations is nearly the same. . . .

To sum up what I have said: I think it clear that we are free to employ our funds as we choose; that we ought to employ them in teaching what is best worth knowing; that English is better worth knowing than Sanskrit or Arabic; that the natives are desirous to be taught English, and are not desirous to be taught Sanskrit or Arabic; that neither as the languages of law, nor as the languages of religion, have the Sanskrit and Arabic any peculiar claim to our encouragement; that it is possible to make natives of this country thoroughly good English scholars, and that to this end our efforts ought to be directed.

age of the Indian population attached to the imperial system reaped financial benefits from British rule, it brought hardship to millions of others in both the cities and the rural areas. The introduction of British textiles put thousands of Bengali women out of work and severely damaged the local textile industry.

In rural areas, the British introduced the *zamindar* system (see Chapter 16) in the misguided expectation that

it would not only facilitate the collection of agricultural taxes but would also create a new landed gentry who could, as in Britain itself, become the conservative foundation of imperial rule. But the local gentry took advantage of their new authority to increase taxes and force the less fortunate peasants to become tenants or lose their land entirely. When rural unrest threatened, the government passed legislation protecting farmers against evic-

❧ The Effects of Dutch Colonialism in Java ❧

E. Douwes Dekker was a Dutch colonial official who served in the East Indies for nearly twenty years. In 1860, he published a critique of the Dutch colonial system that had an impact in the Netherlands similar to that of Harriet Beecher Stowe's Uncle Tom's Cabin in the United States. In the following excerpt from his book Max Havelaar, or Coffee Auctions of the Dutch Trading Company, Dekker described the system as it was applied on the island of Java, in the Indonesian archipelago.

E. Douwes Dekker, *Max Havelaar*

The Javanese is by nature a husbandman; the ground whereon he is born, which gives much for little labor, allures him to it, and, above all things, he devotes his whole heart and soul to the cultivating of his rice-fields, in which he is very clever. He grows up in the midst of his sawahs [rice fields] . . . ; when still very young, he accompanies his father to the field, where he helps him in his labor with plough and spade, in constructing dams and drains to irrigate his fields; he counts his years by harvests; he estimates time by the color of the blades in his field; he is at home amongst the companions who cut paddy with him; he chooses his wife amongst the girls of the dessah [village], who every evening tread the rice with joyous songs. The possession of a few buffaloes for ploughing is the ideal of his dreams. The cultivation of rice is in Java what the vintage is in the Rhine provinces and in the south of France. But there came foreigners from the West, who made themselves masters of the country. They wished to profit by the fertility of the soil, and ordered the native to devote a part of his time and labor to the cultivation of other things which should produce higher profits in the markets of Europe. To persuade the lower orders to do so, they had only to follow a very simple policy. The Javanese obeys his chiefs; to win the chiefs, it was only necessary to give them a part of the gain,—and success was complete.

To be convinced of the success of that policy we need only consider the immense quantity of Javanese products sold in Holland; and we shall also be convinced of its injustice, for, if anybody should ask if the husbandman himself gets a reward in proportion to that quantity, then I must give a negative answer. The Government compels him to cultivate certain products on his ground; it punishes him if he sells what he has produced to any purchaser but itself; and it fixes the price actually paid. The expenses of transport to Europe through a privileged trading company are high; the money paid to the chiefs for encouragement increases the prime cost; and because the entire trade *must* produce profit, that profit cannot be got in any other way than by paying the Javanese just enough to keep him from starving, which would lessen the producing power of the nation.

---

tion and unreasonable rent increases, but this measure had little effect outside the southern provinces, where it had originally been enacted.

British colonialism was also remiss in bringing the benefits of modern science and technology to India. Some limited forms of industrialization took place, notably in the manufacturing of textiles and jute (used in making rope). The first textile mill opened in 1856. Seventy years later, there were eighty mills in the city of Bombay alone. Nevertheless, the lack of local capital and the advantages given to British imports prevented the emergence of other vital new commercial and manufacturing operations.

Foreign rule also had a psychological effect on the psyche of the Indian people. While many British colonial officials sincerely tried to improve the lot of the people under their charge, British arrogance and contempt for native tradition cut deeply into the pride of many Indians, especially those of high caste who were accustomed to a position of superior status in India. Educated Indians trained in the Anglo-Indian school system for a career in the civil service, as well as Eurasians born to mixed marriages, rightfully wondered where their true cultural loyalties lay. This cultural collision was poignantly described in the novel *A Passage to India* by the British writer E. M. Forster.

COLONIAL REGIMES IN SOUTHEAST ASIA

In Southeast Asia, economic profit was the immediate and primary aim of colonial enterprise. For that purpose, colonial powers tried wherever possible to work with local elites to facilitate the exploitation of natural resources. Indirect rule reduced the cost of training European administrators and had a less corrosive impact on the local culture. In the Dutch East Indies, for example, officials of the Dutch East India Company (VOC) entrusted local administration to the indigenous landed aristocracy, known as the *priyayi*. The *priyayi* maintained law and order and collected taxes in return for a payment from the VOC (see the box on p. 843). The British followed a similar practice in Malaya. While establishing direct rule over areas of crucial importance, such as the commercial centers of Singapore and Malacca and the island of Penang, the British signed agreements with local Muslim rulers to maintain princely power in the interior of the peninsula.

Indirect rule, however convenient and inexpensive, was not always feasible. In some instances, local resistance to the colonial conquest made such a policy impossible. In Burma, the staunch opposition of the monarchy and other traditionalist forces caused the British to abolish the monarchy and administer the country directly through their colonial government in India. In Indochina, the French used both direct and indirect means. They imposed direct rule on the southern provinces in the Mekong delta, which had been ceded to France as a colony after the first war in 1858–1860. The northern parts of the country, seized in the 1880s, were governed as a protectorate, with the emperor retaining titular authority from his palace in Huê. The French adopted a similar policy in Cambodia and Laos, where local rulers were left in charge with French advisers to counsel them. Even the Dutch were eventually forced into a more direct approach. When the development of plantation agriculture and the extraction of oil in Sumatra made effective exploitation of local resources more complicated, they dispensed with indirect rule and tightened their administrative control over the archipelago.

Whatever method was used, colonial regimes in Southeast Asia, as elsewhere, were slow to create democratic institutions. The first legislative councils and assemblies were composed almost exclusively of European residents in the colony. The first representatives from the indigenous population were wealthy and conservative in their political views. When Southeast Asians began to complain, colonial officials gradually and reluctantly began to broaden the franchise, but even such liberal thinkers as Albert Sarraut advised patience in awaiting the full benefits of colonial policy. "I will treat you like my younger brothers," he promised, "but do not forget that I am the older brother. I will slowly give you the dignity of humanity."[9]

There was some logic to the view that education in democratic institutions must precede the granting of greater political rights. But here, too, concerns that more knowledge of Western freedoms might spark greater resistance to foreign rule led colonial officials to adopt a cautious attitude toward educational reform. While the in-

◆ **Royal Palace at Bangkok.** Few societies in Asia have been as adept at absorbing Western influence without destroying their own institutions and customs as the Thai. In some cases this talent has extended to the field of architecture. The illustration shown here depicts a late nineteenth century building on the grounds of the royal palace in Bangkok. Note the way in which the architect has attempted to synthesize Western classical techniques with the rooftop design and Buddhist stupas characteristic of traditional religious buildings in Thailand.

troduction of Western educational systems was one of the dominant themes of the concept of civilizing missions, colonial officials soon discovered that educating native elites could backfire. Often there were few jobs for highly trained lawyers, engineers, and architects in colonial societies, leading to the threat of an indigestible mass of unemployed intellectuals who would take out their frustrations on the colonial regime. By the mid-1920s, many colonial governments in Southeast Asia began to limit education to a small and, they hoped, docile elite. As one French official noted in voicing his opposition to increasing the number of schools in Vietnam, educating the natives did not mean "one coolie less, but one rebel more."

Colonial powers were equally reluctant to take up the White Man's Burden in the area of economic development. As we have seen, their primary goals were to secure a source of cheap raw materials and to maintain markets for manufactured goods. Such objectives would be undermined by the emergence of advanced industrial economies. So colonial policy concentrated on the export of raw materials—teakwood from Burma, rubber and tin from Malaya, spices, tea and coffee, and palm oil from the East Indies, and sugar and copra from the Philippines. In many instances, this policy resulted in the creation of a form of plantation agriculture in which peasants were recruited to work as wage laborers on rubber and tea plantations owned by foreign interests.

In some Southeast Asian colonial societies, a measure of industrial development did take place to meet the needs of the European population and local elites. Major manufacturing cities like Rangoon in lower Burma, Batavia on the island of Java, and Saigon in French Indochina grew rapidly. Such forms of light industry as textile-processing plants, cement and brick works, and factories for bicycle and auto assembly were established, and some were run by local entrepreneurs. New lands were opened for cultivation in the Mekong and Irrawaddy deltas, and modern banking and transportation networks began to appear.

Despite such fragile signs of economic development, in practice colonial policy tended to lock the local population into the status of permanent economic inferiority relative to their colonial masters. To slake their desire for profits and maintain a competitive edge, plantation owners kept the wages of their workers at poverty levels. Many plantation workers were "shanghaied" (the English term originated from the practice of recruiting laborers, often from the docks and streets of Shanghai, by unscrupulous means such as the use of force, alcohol, or drugs) to work on plantations where conditions were often so inhumane that thousands died. High taxes, en-

CHRONOLOGY

Imperialism in Asia

Stamford Raffles arrives in Singapore	1819
British attack lower Burma	1826
British rail network opened in northern India	1853
Sepoy Mutiny	1857
French attack Vietnam	1858
Indian National Congress established	1885
British and French agree to neutralize Thailand	1896
Commodore Dewey defeats Spanish fleet in Manila Bay	1898
Gandhi returns to India	1913

acted by colonial governments to pay for administrative costs or improvements in the local infrastructure, were a heavy burden for poor peasants.

Colonial policy was often equally harmful in urban areas. There was usually a local middle class that benefited in various ways from the Western presence, but most industrial and commercial establishments were owned and managed by Europeans or, in some cases, by Indian or Chinese merchants. In Saigon, for example, even the manufacture of *nuoc mam*, the traditional Vietnamese fish sauce, was under Chinese ownership. Most urban residents were coolies (the term itself, used contemptuously by Westerners, means "bitter labor" in Chinese), factory workers, or rickshaw pullers or eked out a living in family shops as they had during the traditional era.

As in India, colonial rule did bring some benefits to Southeast Asia. It led to the beginnings of a modern economic infrastructure and to what is sometimes called a "modernizing elite" dedicated to the creation of an advanced industrialized society. The development of an export market helped to create an entrepreneurial class in rural areas. This happened, for example, on the outer islands of the Dutch East Indies (such as Borneo and Sumatra), where small growers of rubber trees, palm trees for oil, coffee, tea, and spices began to share in the profits of the colonial enterprise. A Dutch sociologist, reporting on conditions in western Sumatra in the 1920s, noted that the development of small coffee plantations in the area had brought considerable benefits to local planters.

♦ **A Rubber Tree.** Natural rubber was one of the most important cash crops in European colonies in Asia. Rubber trees, native to the Amazon River basin in Brazil, were eventually transplanted to Southeast Asia, where they became a major source of profit. Workers on the plantations received few benefits, however, for once the sap of the tree (known as latex and shown here) was extracted, the bulk of the refining process took place in Europe.

Children and even teachers stayed away from school, he remarked, because "they see that a coffee farmer earns more than a miserable petty official, who is, moreover, obliged to work away from his native village."[10] Local residents who had previously migrated to Malaya to find employment were now returning to work in their native villages.

A balanced assessment of the colonial legacy in Southeast Asia must take into account that the early stages of industrialization are difficult in any society. Even in Western Europe, industrialization led to the creation of an impoverished and powerless proletariat, urban slums, and displaced peasants driven from the land. In much of Europe and Japan, however, the bulk of the population eventually enjoyed better material conditions as the profits from manufacturing and plantation agriculture were reinvested in the national economy and gave rise to increased consumer demand. In contrast, in Southeast Asia, most of the profits were repatriated to the colonial mother country, while displaced peasants fleeing to cities like Rangoon, Batavia, and Saigon found little opportunity for employment. Many were left with

seasonal employment, with one foot on the farm and one in the factory. The old world was being destroyed, while the new had yet to be born.

COLONIALISM IN AFRICA

Colonialism had similar consequences in Africa, although with some changes in emphasis. As we have seen, European economic interests were more limited in Africa than elsewhere. Having seized the continent in what could almost be described as a fit of hysteria, the European powers had to decide what to do with it. With economic concerns relatively limited except for isolated areas like the gold mines in the Transvaal and copper deposits in the Belgian Congo, interest in Africa declined, and most European governments settled down to govern their new territories with the least effort and expense possible. In many cases, this meant a form of indirect rule similar to what the British used in the princely states in India. The British with their tradition of decentralized government at home were especially prone to adopt this approach.

In the minds of British administrators, the stated goal of indirect rule was to preserve African political traditions. The desire to limit cost and inconvenience was one reason for this approach, but it may also have been due to the conviction that Africans were inherently inferior to the white race and thus incapable of adopting European customs and institutions. In any event, indirect rule entailed relying to the greatest extent possible on existing political elites and institutions. Initially, in some areas the British simply asked a local ruler to formally accept British authority and to fly the Union Jack over official buildings. Sometimes it was the Africans who did the bidding, as in the case of the African leaders in the Cameroon who wrote to Queen Victoria:

> We *wish* to have your laws in our towns. We want to have every *fashion* altered, also we will do according to your Consul's *word*. Plenty wars here in our country. Plenty murder and plenty idol worshippers. Perhaps these *lines* of our writing will *look* to you as an *idle* tale.
> We have *spoken* to the English consul plenty times about having an English *government* here. We never have answer from you, so we wish to write you *ourselves*.
> We are, etc.
> King Acqua
> Prince Dido Acqua
> Prince Blakc
> Prince Go Garner
> etc.[11]

The concept of indirect rule was introduced in the Islamic state of Sokoto in northern Nigeria in 1900. British administration under European officials operated at the central level, but local authority was assigned to native chiefs, with British district officers serving as intermediaries with the central administration. Where a local aristocracy did not exist, the British assigned administrative responsibility to clan heads from communities in the vicinity. The local authorities were expected to maintain law and order and to collect taxes from the native population. As a general rule, indigenous customs were left undisturbed; a dual legal system was instituted that applied African laws to Africans and European laws to foreigners (see the box on p. 846).

One advantage of such an administrative system was that it did not severely disrupt local customs and institutions. In fact, however, it had several undesirable consequences. In the first place, it was essentially a fraud, since all major decisions were made by the British administrators while the native authorities served primarily as the means of enforcing decisions. Moreover, indirect rule served to perpetuate the autocratic system often in use prior to colonial takeover. It was official policy to inculcate respect for authority in areas under British rule, and there was a natural tendency to view the local aristocracy as the African equivalent of the traditional British ruling class. Such a policy provided few opportunities for ambitious and talented young Africans from outside the traditional elite and thus sowed the seeds for class tensions after the restoration of independence in the twentieth century.

The situation was somewhat different in East Africa, especially in Kenya, which had a relatively large European population attracted by the temperate climate in the central highlands. The local government had encouraged white settlers to migrate to the area as a means of promoting economic development and encouraging financial self-sufficiency. To attract Europeans, fertile farmlands in the central highlands were reserved for European settlement while, as in South Africa, specified reserve lands were set aside for Africans. The presence of a substantial European minority (although, in fact, they represented only about one percent of the entire population) had an impact on Kenya's political development. The white settlers actively sought self-government and dominion status similar to that granted to such former British possessions as Canada and Australia. The British government, however, was not willing to run the risk of provoking racial tensions with the African majority and agreed only to establish separate government organs for the European and African populations.

The situation in South Africa, of course, was unique, not only because of the high percentage of European settlers but also because of the division between English-speaking and Afrikaner elements within the European population. In 1910, the British agreed to the creation of an independent Union of South Africa that combined the old Cape Colony and Natal with the Boer republics. The new union adopted a representative government, but only for the European population, while the African reserves of Basutoland (now Lesotho), Bechuanaland (now Botswana), and Swaziland were subordinated directly to the crown. The union was now free to manage its own domestic affairs and possessed considerable autonomy in foreign relations. Formal British rule was also extended to the remaining lands south of the Zambezi River, which were eventually divided into the territories of Northern and Southern Rhodesia. Southern Rhodesia attracted many British immigrants, and in 1922, after a popular referendum, it became a crown colony.

Most other European nations governed their African possessions through a form of direct rule. The prototype was the French system, which reflected the centralized administrative system introduced in France itself by Napoleon. As in the British colonies, at the top of the pyramid was a French official, usually known as a governor-general, who was appointed from Paris and governed with the aid of a bureaucracy in the capital city. At the provincial level, French commissioners were assigned to deal with local administrators, but the latter were required to be conversant in French and could be transferred to a new position at the needs of the central government.

Moreover, the French ideal was to assimilate their African subjects into French culture rather than preserving their native traditions. Africans were eligible to run for office and to serve in the French National Assembly, and a few were appointed to high positions in the colonial administration. Such policies reflected the relative absence of racist attitudes in French society, as well as the French conviction of the superiority of Gallic culture and their revolutionary belief in the universality of human nature.

After World War I, European colonial policy in Africa entered a new and more formal phase. The colonial administrative network was extended to a greater degree into outlying areas, where it was represented by a district official and defended by a small native army under European command. Greater attention was given to improving social services, including education, medicine and sanitation, and communications. The colonial system was now viewed more formally as a moral and social responsibility, a "sacred trust" to be maintained by the

A Guide for Peace in Africa: A British Point of View

John Frederick Lugard (1858–1945) was the governor of British Nigeria prior to World War II. Earlier he had set forth the principles of indirect rule that became the foundation of British policy in Africa during the colonial era. In this short excerpt from his book The Dual Mandate in Tropical Africa, *Lord Lugard explained that effective policies could only be achieved if the British government and the native rulers established a cooperative arrangement, where each authority would govern within its own domain. The result, he argued, would be a careful balance between tradition and modernity that would maintain law and order and bring about evolutionary change in African society.*

John Frederick Lugard, *The Dual Mandate in Tropical Africa*

1. Native rulers are not permitted to raise and control armed forces, or to grant permission to carry arms. . . . The evils which result in Africa from an armed population were evident in Uganda before it fell under British control, and are very evident in Abyssinia today. No one with experience will deny the necessity of maintaining the strictest military discipline over armed forces or police in Africa if misuse of power is to be avoided, and they are not to become a menace and a terror to the native population and a danger in case of religious excitement—a discipline which an African ruler is incapable of appreciating or applying. For this reason native levies should never be employed in substitution for or in aid of troops. On the other hand, the government armed police are never quartered in native towns, where their presence would interfere with the authority of the chiefs.

2. The sole right to impose taxation in any form is reserved to the suzerain power. This fulfills the bilateral understanding that the peasantry . . . should be free of all other exactions whatsoever (including—unpaid labor), while a sufficient proportion of the tax is assigned to the native treasuries to meet the expenditure of the native administration. . . .

3. The right to legislate, is reserved. That this should remain in the hands of the central government . . . cannot be questioned. The native authority, how-

ever, exercises very considerable power in this regard. A native ruler, and the native courts, are empowered to enforce native law and custom, provided it is not repugnant to humanity, or in opposition to any ordinance.

4. The right to appropriate land on equitable terms for public purposes and for commercial requirements is vested in the governor. . . . In practice this does not interfere with the power of the native ruler (as the delegate of the governor) to assign lands to the natives under his rule, in accordance with native law and custom, or restrict him or the native courts from adjudicating between natives regarding occupancy rights in land. No rents are levied on lands in occupation by indigenous natives. Leases to aliens are granted by the central government.

   If the pressure of population in one community makes it necessary to assign to it a portion of the land belonging to a neighbor with a small and decreasing population the governor (to whom appeal may be made) would decide the matter. These reservations were set out in the formal letter of appointment given to each chief in Northern Nigeria.

5. In order to maintain intact the control of the central government over all aliens, and to avoid friction and difficulties, it has been the recognized rule that the employees of the native administration should consist entirely of natives subject to the native authority. If aliens are required for any skilled work by the native administration, government servants may be employed and their salaries reimbursed by the native treasury. For a like reason, whenever possible, all non-natives and natives not subject to the local native jurisdiction live in the "township," from which natives subject to the native administration are as far as possible excluded.

6. Finally, in the interests of good government, the right of confirming or otherwise the choice of the people of the successor to a chiefship, and of deposing any ruler for misrule or other adequate cause, is reserved to the governor.

civilized countries until the Africans became capable of self-government. More emphasis was placed on economic development and on the exploitation of natural resources to provide the colonies with the means of achieving self-sufficiency. More Africans were now serving in colonial administrations, although relatively few were placed in positions of responsibility. On the other hand, race consciousness probably increased during this period. Segregated clubs, schools, and churches were established as more European officials brought their wives and began to raise families in the colonies.

The Rise of Nationalism

Thus far we have looked at the colonial experience primarily from the point of view of the colonial powers, examining why the Western states wanted colonies and how they administered their colonial possessions. Equally important is the way the subject peoples reacted to the experience. From the perspective of nearly half a century, it seems clear that their primary response was to turn to nationalism, which might well be called the most powerful idea of the twentieth century.

Nationalism, of course, is not a uniquely twentieth-century phenomenon, nor is it the exclusive preserve of the non-Western world. Some historians believe that the concept of nationalism first emerged with the rise of linguistic and ethnic consciousness in eighteenth-century Europe. It eventually resulted in the breakup of the multiracial empires of the Ottomans and the Habsburgs and the creation of such modern "nations" as Italy, Germany, Hungary, and Poland. Others see the origins of nationalism in the decline in religious belief and the need for a new sense of community to replace the concept of heavenly salvation.

As we have seen, nationalism refers to a state of mind rising out of an awareness of being part of a community that possesses common institutions, traditions, language, and customs. Few nations in the world today meet such criteria. Most modern states contain a variety of ethnic, religious, and linguistic communities, each with its own sense of cultural and national identity. Should Canada, for example, which includes peoples of French, English and Native American heritage, be considered a nation? Another question is how nationalism differs from other forms of tribal, religious, or linguistic affiliation. Should every group that resists assimilation into a larger cultural unity be called nationalist?

Such questions complicate the study of nationalism even in Europe and North America and make agreement on a definition elusive. They create even greater dilemmas in discussing Asia and Africa, where most societies are deeply divided by ethnic, linguistic, and religious differences and the very term *nationalism* is a foreign phenomenon imported from the West (see the box on p. 848). Prior to the colonial era, most traditional societies in Africa and Asia were formed on the basis of religious beliefs, tribal loyalties, or devotion to hereditary monarchies. Although individuals in some countries may have identified themselves as members of a particular national group, others viewed themselves as subjects of a king, members of a tribe, or adherents to a particular religion.

The advent of European colonialism brought the consciousness of modern nationhood to many of the societies of Asia and Africa. The creation of European colonies with defined borders and a powerful central government led to the weakening of tribal and village ties and a significant reorientation in the individual's sense of political identity. The introduction of Western ideas of citizenship and representative government produced a new sense of participation in the affairs of government. At the same time, the appearance of a new elite class based not on hereditary privilege or religious sanction but on alleged racial or cultural superiority aroused a shared sense of resentment among the subject peoples who felt a common commitment to the creation of an independent society. By the first quarter of the twentieth century, political movements dedicated to the overthrow of colonial rule had arisen throughout much of the non-Western world.

Modern nationalism, then, was a product of colonialism and, in a sense, a reaction to it. But a sense of nationhood does not emerge full-blown in a given society. The rise of modern nationalism is a process that begins among a few members of the educated elite (most commonly among articulate professionals such as lawyers, teachers, journalists, and doctors) and then spreads only gradually to the mass of the population. Even after national independence has been realized, as we shall see, it is often questionable whether a mature sense of nationhood has been created.

Traditional Resistance: A Precursor to Nationalism

If we view the concept of nationalism as a process by which people in a given society gradually become aware of themselves as members of a particular nation with its own culture and aspirations, then it is reasonable to seek the beginnings of modern nationalism in the initial resistance by the indigenous peoples to the colonial conquest

⇒ A Critique of Indian Nationalism ⇐

Rabindranath Tagore, one of India's greatest writers, was a prominent spokesman for the Indian people under colonial rule. While indisputably a patriot, like many intellectuals he was torn between his commitment to his native land and his awareness of the benefits of Western civilization. In this passage from a book written at the height of World War I, he seeks to persuade his readers that the common destiny of all humanity is more important than that of an individual nation or people. The message still has considerable relevance today.

Rabindranath Tagore, *Nationalism in India*

India has never had a real sense of nationalism. Even though from childhood I had been taught that idolatry of the nation is almost better than reverence for God and humanity, I believe I have outgrown that teaching, and it is my conviction that my countrymen will truly gain their India by fighting against the education which teaches them that a country is greater than the ideals of humanity. . . .

We must recognize that it is providential that the West has come to India. And yet someone must show the East to the West, and convince the West that the East has her contribution to make to the history of civilization. India is no beggar of the West. And yet even though the West may think she is, I am not for thrusting off Western civilization and becoming segregated in our independence. Let us have a deep association. If providence wants England to be the channel of that communication, of that deeper association, I am willing to accept it with all humility. I have great faith in human nature, and I think the West will find its true mission. I speak bitterly of Western civilization when I am conscious that it is betraying its trust and thwarting its own purpose. The West must not make herself a curse to the world by using her power for her own selfish needs, but by teaching the ignorant and helping the weak, she should save herself from the worst danger that the strong is liable to incur, by making the feeble acquire power enough to resist her intrusion. And also she must not make her materialism to be the final thing, but must realize that she is doing a service in freeing the spiritual being from the tyranny of matter. . . .

Once again I draw your attention to the difficulties India has had to encounter and her struggle to overcome them. Her problem was the problem of the world in miniature. India is too vast in its area and too diverse in its races. It is many countries packed in one geographical receptacle. It is just the opposite of what Europe truly is, namely, one country made into many. Thus, Europe in its culture and growth has had the advantage of the strength of the many as well as the strength of the one. India, on the contrary, being naturally many, yet adventitiously one, has all along suffered from the looseness of its diversity and the feebleness of its unity. A true unity is like a round globe, it rolls on, carrying its burden easily; but diversity is a many cornered thing which has to be dragged and pushed with all force. Be it said to the credit of India that this diversity was not her own creation; she has had to accept it as a fact from the beginning of her history. . . .

---

itself. Strictly speaking, such resistance cannot be described as "nationalist," since it was essentially motivated by the desire to defend traditional institutions. Still, at a minimum it reflected a primitive concept of nationhood in that it aimed at protecting the homeland from the invader; later spokespersons for patriotic groups have often hailed such resistance movements as the precursors of more modern nationalist movements that have arisen in the twentieth century. Thus, traditional resistance to colonial conquest may logically be viewed as the first stage in the development of modern nationalism.

Such resistance took various forms. For the most part, it was led by the existing ruling class. In the Ashanti kingdom in Africa and in Burma and Vietnam in Southeast Asia, the resistance to Western domination was initially directed by the imperial courts themselves. In some cases, however, traditionalist elements continued to oppose foreign conquest even after resistance had collapsed at the center. In Japan, conservative elements led by nobles under Saigo Takamori opposed the decision of the Tokugawa shogunate in Tokyo to accommodate the Western presence and launched an abortive movement to defeat the foreigners and restore Japan to its previous policy of isolation (see Chapter 23). In India, Tipu Sultan resisted the British in the Deccan after the collapse of the Mughal dynasty. Similarly, after the decrepit monarchy in Vietnam had bowed to French pressure and agreed to the concession of territory in the south and the establishment of a protectorate over the remainder of the country, a number of civilian and military officials set up an organization called Can Vuong (literally "save the king") and continued their resistance without imperial sanction (see the box on p. 850).

The first stirrings of nationalism in India took place in the early nineteenth century with the search for a renewed sense of cultural identity. In 1828, Ram Mohan Roy, a brahmin from Bengal, founded the Brahmo Samaj (Society of Brahma). Roy probably had no intention of promoting Indian national independence, but had established the new organization as a means of helping his fellow-religionists defend the Hindu religion against verbal attacks by their British acquaintances. Roy was by no means a hidebound traditionalist. He opposed such cruel practices as *sati* and recognized the benefit of introducing the best aspects of European culture into Indian society.

Sometimes traditional resistance to Western penetration went beyond elite circles. Most commonly, it appeared in the form of peasant revolts. Rural rebellions were not uncommon in traditional Asian societies as a means of expressing peasant discontent with high taxes, official corruption, rising rural debt, and famine in the countryside. Under colonialism, rural conditions often deteriorated, as land hunger increased and peasants were driven off the land to make way for plantation agriculture. Angry peasants then vented their frustration at the foreign invaders. For example, in Burma, the Buddhist monk Saya San led a peasant uprising against the British many years after they had completed their takeover. Similar forms of unrest occurred in various parts of India, where *zamindars* and rural villagers alike resisted government attempts to increase tax revenues. Yet another peasant uprising took place in Algeria in 1840 under the leadership of Abdel Qadir.

Sometimes the resentment had a religious basis, as in the Sudan where the revolt led by the Mahdi had strong

◆ **Vietnamese Prisoners in Stocks.** Whereas some Vietnamese took up Western ways, others resisted the foreign incursion but were vigorously suppressed by the French. In this photograph, Vietnamese prisoners, who had plotted against the French, are held in stocks in preparation for trial in 1907.

≽ A Call to Arms ≼

In 1862, the Vietnamese imperial court at Huê ceded three provinces in southern Vietnam to the French. In outrage, many patriotic Vietnamese military officers and government officials appealed to their compatriots to rise up spontaneously and resist the foreigners. The following passage is from an anonymous document written in 1864.

An Appeal to Resist the French

This is a general proclamation addressed to the scholars and the people.

Our country is about to undergo dangerous upheavals.

Certain persons are plotting treason.

Our people are now suffering through a period of anarchy and disorder.

That is but Heaven's will.

Nonetheless, even in times of confusion, there remain books that teach us how to overcome disorder.

Past generations can still be for us examples of right and wrong.

Intelligent persons should meditate on them with care.

Let us now consider our situation with the French today.

We are separated from them by thousands of mountains and seas.

By hundreds of differences in our daily customs.

Although they were very confident in their copper battleships surmounted by chimneys,

Although they had a large quantity of steel rifles and lead bullets,

These things did not prevent the loss of some of their best generals in these last years, when they attacked our frontier in hundreds of battles.

The sun and the moon have always shown us the right way; shall we now suffer that a flock of birds come to sing and dictate our behavior?

Heaven will not leave our people enchained very long.

Heaven will not allow them [the French] the free enjoyment of their lives.

From antiquity to the present day, who could lay claim to the strength of Heaven.

At the end, everything shall encounter its master.

You, officials of the country,

Do not let your resistance to the enemy be blunted by the peaceful stand of the court.

Do not take the lead from the three subjected provinces and leave hatred unavenged.

Alas!

Such a hostility, such a hatred, such an enmity; our heart will be quieted before we are avenged.

So many years of labor, of energy, of suffering—shall we now abandon all?

Rather, we should go to the far ends of jungles or to the high peaks of mountains in search of heroes.

Rather, we should go to the shores of the sea in search of talented men.

Do not envy the scholars who now become provincial or district magistrates [in the French administration]. They are decay, garbage, filth, swine.

Do not imitate some who hire themselves out to the enemy. They are idiots, fools, lackeys, scoundrels.

At the beginning, you followed the way of righteousness. From beginning to end you ought to behave according to the moral obligations which bind you to your king.

Life has fame, death too has fame. Act in such a way that your life and your death will be a fragrant ointment to your families and to your country.

Islamic overtones, although it was initially provoked by Turkish misrule in Egypt. More significant than Roy's Brahmo Samaj in its impact on British policy was the famous Sepoy Mutiny of 1857 in India. The sepoys (derived from *sipahi*, a Turkish word meaning horseman or soldier) were native troops hired by the East India Company to protect British interests in the region. Unrest within Indian units of the colonial army had been common since early in the century, when it had been sparked by economic issues, religious sensitivities, or nascent anticolonial sentiment. Such attitudes intensified in the mid-1850s when the British instituted a new policy of shipping Indian troops abroad—a practice that exposed Hindus to pollution by foreigners. In 1857, tension erupted when the British adopted the new Enfield rifle for use by sepoy infantrymen. The new weapon was a muzzle-loader that used paper cartridges covered with animal fat and lard; because the cartridge had to be bitten off, it broke strictures against high-class Hindus eating animal products and Muslim prohibitions against eating pork. Protests among sepoy units in northern India turned into a full-scale mutiny, supported by risings in rural districts in various parts of the country. But the revolt lacked a clear sense of goals, while rivalries between Hindus and Muslims and discord among the leaders within each community prevented coordination of operations. Although Indian troops often fought bravely and outnumbered the British by 240,000 to 40,000, they were poorly organized, and the British forces (supplemented in many cases by sepoy troops) suppressed the rebellion.

Still, the revolt frightened the British and led to a number of major reforms. The proportion of native troops relative to those from Great Britain was reduced, and precedence was given to ethnic groups likely to be loyal to the British, such as the Sikhs of Punjab and the Gurkhas, an upland people from Nepal in the Himalaya Mountains. To avoid religious conflicts, ethnic groups were spread throughout the service rather than assigned to special units. The British also decided to suppress the final remnants of the hapless Mughal dynasty, which had supported the mutiny.

As we have noted, such forms of resistance cannot properly be called nationalist, since they were essentially attempts to protect or restore traditional society and its institutions and were not motivated by the desire to create a "nation" in the modern sense of the word. In any event, such movements usually met with little success. Peasants armed with pikes and spears were no match for Western armies possessing the most terrifying weapons then known to human society. In a few cases, such as the revolt of the Mahdi at Khartoum, the natives were able to defeat the invaders temporarily. But such successes were rare, and the late nineteenth century witnessed the seemingly inexorable march of the Western powers, armed with the Gatling gun (the first rapid-fire weapon and the precursor of the modern machine gun), to mastery of the globe.

Conclusion

By the first quarter of the twentieth century, virtually all of Africa and a good part of South and Southeast Asia were under some form of colonial rule. With the advent of the age of imperialism, a global economy was finally established, and the domination of Western civilization over those of Africa and Asia appeared to be complete.

Defenders of colonialism argue that the system was a necessary if sometimes painful stage in the evolution of human societies. Although its immediate consequences were admittedly sometimes unfortunate, Western imperialism was ultimately beneficial to colonial powers and subjects alike, since it created the conditions for global economic development and the universal application of democratic institutions. Critics, however, charge that the Western colonial powers were driven by an insatiable lust for profits. They dismiss the Western civilizing mission as a fig leaf to cover naked greed and reject the notion that imperialism played a salutary role in hastening the adjustment of traditional societies to the demands of industrial civilization. In the blunt words of two recent Western critics of imperialism: "Why is Africa (or for that matter Latin America and much of Asia) so poor? . . . The answer is very brief: we have made it poor."[12]

Between these two irreconcilable views, where does the truth lie? This chapter has contended that neither extreme position is justified. The sources of imperialism lie not simply in the demands of industrial capitalism, but in the search for security, national greatness, and even such psychological factors as the spirit of discovery and the drive to excel. While some regard the concept of the White Man's Burden as a hypocritical gesture to moral sensitivities, others see it as a meaningful reality justifying a lifelong commitment to the colonialist enterprise. Although the "civilizing urge" of missionaries and officials may have been tinged with self-interest, it was nevertheless often sincerely motivated.

Similarly, the consequences of colonialism have been more complex than either its defenders or its critics would have us believe. While the colonial peoples received little immediate benefit from the imposition of foreign rule, overall the imperialist era brought about a vast expansion of the international trade network and created at least the potential for societies throughout Africa and Asia to play an active and rewarding role in the new global economic arena. If, as the world historian William McNeill believes, the introduction of new technology through cross-cultural encounters is the driving force of change in world history, then Western imperialism, whatever its faults, served a useful purpose in opening the door to such change, much as the rise of the Arab empire and the Mongol invasions hastened the process of global economic development in an earlier time.

Still, the critics have a point. Although colonialism did introduce the peoples of Asia and Africa to new technology and the expanding economic marketplace, it was unnecessarily brutal in its application and all too often failed to realize the exalted claims and objectives of its promoters. Existing economic networks—often potentially valuable as a foundation for later economic development—were ruthlessly swept aside in the interests of providing markets for Western manufactured goods. Potential sources of native industrialization were nipped in the bud to avoid competition for factories in Amsterdam, London, Pittsburgh, or Manchester. Training in Western democratic ideals and practices was ignored out of fear that the recipients might use them as weapons against the ruling authorities.

The fundamental weakness of colonialism, then, was that it was ultimately based on the self-interests of the citizens of the colonial powers. Where those interests collided with the needs of the colonial peoples, those of the former always triumphed. Much the same might have been said about earlier periods in history, when Assyrians, Arabs, Mongols, and Chinese turned their conquests to their own profit. Where modern imperialism differed was in its tendency to cloak naked self-interest in the cloak of a moral obligation. However sincerely the David Livingstones, Albert Sarrauts, and William McKinleys of the world were convinced of the rightness of their civilizing mission, the ultimate result was to deprive the colonial peoples of the right to make their own choices about their own destiny.

Did the system serve the interests of the colonial powers? On the face of it, the answer seems obvious, since it provided cheap raw materials and markets for Western manufactured goods, both essential to the effective operation of the capitalist system. But some recent observers of the phenomenon have concluded that the possession of colonies was not always beneficial to those who possessed them. According to the French economic historian Jacques Marseille, for example, the cost of maintaining the French colonial empire, on balance, exceeded the economic benefits it provided, especially since the maintenance of a protected market in the colonies hindered the French effort to create an industrial sector capable of competing in the global marketplace. Such costs did not become fully apparent until after World War II, however, as we shall see in future chapters.

In one area of Asia, the spreading tide of imperialism did not result in the establishment of formal Western colonial control. In East Asia, the traditional societies of China and Japan were buffeted by the winds of Western expansionism during the nineteenth century but successfully resisted foreign conquest. In the next chapter, we will see how they managed to retain their independence while attempting to cope with the demands of a changing world.

CHAPTER NOTES

1. J. G. Lockhart and C. M. Wodehouse, *Rhodes* (1963), pp. 69–70, cited in Thomas Pakenham, *The Scramble for Africa* (New York, 1991), pp. 376–77.
2. Quoted in Henry Braunschwig, *French Colonialism, 1871–1914* (London, 1961), p. 80.
3. Quoted in C. M. Turnbull, *A History of Singapore, 1819–1975* (Kuala Lumpur, 1977), p. 19.
4. Quoted in Ruhl Bartlett, ed., *The Record of American Diplomacy: Documents and Readings in the History of American Foreign Relations* (New York, 1952), p. 385.
5. Quoted in John Iliffe, *Africans: The History of a Continent* (Cambridge, 1995), p. 124.
6. Pakenham, *The Scramble for Africa*, p. 13.
7. Quoted in Georges Garros, *Forceries Humaines* (Paris, 1926).

8. Quoted in Winfred Baumgart, *Imperialism: The Idea and Reality of British and French Colonial Expansion, 1880–1914* (Oxford, 1982), p. 137.

9. Sarraut's comment is quoted in Louis Roubaud, *Vietnam: La Tragédie Indochinoise* (Paris, 1926), p. 80.

10. Quoted in Clifford Geertz, *Agricultural Involution: The Process of Ecological Change in Indonesia* (Berkeley, Calif., 1963), p. 119.

11. Quoted in Pakenham, *The Scramble for Africa*, p. 182, citing a letter to Queen Victoria, 7 Aug 1879.

12. Peter C. W. Gutkind and Immanuel Wallerstein, eds., *The Political Economy of Contemporary Africa* (Beverly Hills, 1976), p. 14, cited in Tony Smith, *The Pattern of Imperialism: The United States, Great Britain, and the Late-industrial World since 1815* (Cambridge, 1981), p. 81.

SUGGESTED READINGS

There are a number of good recent works on the subject of imperialism and colonialism. For example, see W. Baumgart, *Imperialism: The Idea and Reality of British and French Colonial Expansion, 1880–1914* (Oxford, 1982); M. Edwardes, *The West in Asia, 1850–1914* (New York, 1967); and H. M. Wright, ed., *The "New Imperialism": Analysis of Late Nineteenth Century Expansion* (New York, 1976). On technology, see D. R. Headrick, *The Tentacles of Progress: Technology Transfer in the Age of Imperialism, 1850–1940* (Oxford, 1988). For readings, see L. J. Snyder, *The Imperialism Reader* (New York, 1962).

On the imperialist age in Africa, above all see R. Robinson and J. Gallagher, *Africa and the Victorians: The Official Mind of Imperialism* (London, 1961). Also see B. Davidson, *Modern Africa: A Social and Political History* (London, 1989); T. Pakenham, *The Scramble for Africa* (New York, 1991); and his *The Boer War* (London, 1979). On South Africa, see J. Guy, *The Destruction of the Zulu Kingdom* (London, 1979) and D. Nenoon and B. Nyeko, *Southern Africa since 1800* (London, 1984). Also useful is R. O. Collins, ed., *Historical Problems of Imperial Africa,* (Princeton, N.J., 1994).

For an overview of the British takeover and administration of India, see S. Wolpert, *A New History of India* (New York, 1989). C. A. Bayly, *Indian Society and the Making of the British Empire* (Cambridge, 1988) is a scholarly analysis of the impact of British conquest on the Indian economy. For a comparative approach, see R. Murphey, *The Outsiders: The Western Experience in China and India* (Ann Arbor, Mich., 1977).

General studies of the colonial period in Southeast Asia are rare because most authors focus on specific areas. For some stimulating essays on a variety of aspects of the topic, see *Continuity and Change in Southeast Asia: Collected Journal Articles of Harry J. Benda* (New Haven, Conn., 1972). The role of religion is examined in F. von der Mehden, *Religion and Nationalism in Southeast Asia* (Madison, Wis., 1963). On nationalist movements, see also R. Emerson's classic *From Empire to Nation* (Boston, 1960). For a view of the region from the inside, see D. J. Steinberg, et al., eds., *In Search of Southeast Asia* (New York, 1986). On the French conquest of Indochina, see M. O. Osborne, *The French Presence in Cochin China and Cambodia* (Ithaca, 1969).

CHAPTER
23

Shadows over the Pacific: East Asia under Challenge

In August 1793, a British diplomatic mission led by Lord Macartney arrived at the North Chinese port of Taku and embarked on the road to Beijing. His caravan, which included six hundred cases of gifts for the emperor, bore flags and banners provided by the Chinese that proclaimed in Chinese characters "Ambassador bearing tribute from the country of England." Macartney chose to ignore the slight, but on arriving in the capital, he refused his hosts' demand that he perform the kowtow symbolizing his country's submission to the emperor. Eventually, a compromise was reached—Macartney agreed to bend on one knee, a courtesy that he displayed to his own sovereign—and the dispute over protocol was resolved.

In other respects, however, the mission was a failure. Macartney carried a British request for an increase in trade between the two countries, but the appeal was flatly rejected, and he left Beijing in October with nothing to show for his efforts. Not until half a century later would the Qing dynasty—at the point of a gun—agree to the British demand for an expansion of commercial ties.

Historians have often viewed the failure of the Macartney mission as a reflection of the disdain of Chinese rulers toward their counterparts in other countries and their serene confidence in the superiority of Chinese civilization in a world inhabited by barbarians, and of course it was. But in retrospect, it is clear that the Chinese concern was justified. At the beginning of the nineteenth century, China faced a growing challenge from

Manchus suppress
Taiping rebellion

Sun Yat-sen's forces overthrow Manchu dynasty

One Hundred Days Reform

Commodore Perry
arrives in Tokyo Bay

Collapse of Tokugawa shogunate

Meiji Constitution
adopted

Abolition of Civil Service
Examination

Abolition of feudalism in Japan

Opium War

Sino-Japanese
War

Russo-Japanese War

the escalating power and ambitions of the West. Backed by European guns, European merchants and missionaries pressed insistently for the right to carry out their activities in China and the islands of Japan. Despite their initial reluctance, the Chinese and Japanese governments were eventually forced to open their doors to the foreigners, whose presence escalated rapidly during the final years of the century.

Unlike other Asian societies, both Japan and China were able to maintain their national independence against the Western onslaught. In other respects, however, the results in Japan and China were strikingly different. Japan responded quickly to the challenge by adopting Western institutions and customs and eventually becoming a significant competitor for the spoils of empire. In contrast, China grappled unsuccessfully with the problem, which eventually undermined the foundations of the Qing dynasty and brought it to an unceremonious conclusion. For the next two decades, Chinese society followed the familiar pattern of an interdynastic interregnum, as Chinese political forces competed desperately to fill the vacuum left by the collapse of the old order.

The Decline of the Manchus

In 1800, the Qing (Ch'ing) or Manchu dynasty appeared to be at the height of its power. China had experienced a long period of peace and prosperity under the rule of two great emperors, Kangxi and Qianlong. Its borders were secure, and its culture and intellectual achievements were the envy of the world. Its rulers, hidden behind the walls of the Forbidden City in Beijing, had every reason to describe their patrimony as the "Central Kingdom." But a little over a century later, humiliated and harassed by the black ships and big guns of the Western powers, the Qing dynasty, the last in a series that had endured for more than two thousand years, collapsed in the dust.

Historians once assumed that the primary reason for the rapid decline and fall of the Manchu dynasty was the intense pressure applied to a proud but somewhat complacent traditional society by the modern West. Now, however, most historians believe that internal changes played a role in the dynasty's collapse and point out that at least some of the problems suffered by the Manchus during the nineteenth century were self-inflicted.

Both explanations have some validity. Like so many of its predecessors, after an extended period of growth, the Qing dynasty began to suffer from the familiar dynastic ills of official corruption, peasant unrest, and incompetence at court. Such weaknesses were probably exacerbated by the rapid growth in population. The long era of peace and stability, the introduction of new crops from the Americas, and the cultivation of new, fast-ripening strains of rice enabled the Chinese population to double between 1550 and 1800. The population continued to grow, reaching the unprecedented level of 400 million by the end of the nineteenth century. Even without the irritating presence of the Western powers, the Manchus were probably destined to repeat the fate of their imperial predecessors. The ships, guns, and ideas of the foreigners simply highlighted the growing weakness of the Manchu dynasty and likely hastened its demise. In doing so, Western imperialism still exerted an indelible impact on the history of modern China, but as a contributing, not a causal, factor.

Opium and Rebellion

By 1800, Westerners had been in contact with China for more than two hundred years, but after an initial period of flourishing relations, Western traders had been limited to a small commercial outlet at Canton. This arrangement was not acceptable to the British, however. They chafed at being restricted to a tiny enclave on the muddy banks of the Pearl River, while the growing British appetite for Chinese tea created a severe balance of payments problem. At first, officials of the East India Company attempted to reduce the deficit by shipping raw cotton from India in exchange for Chinese tea, but eventually increased cotton production in North China cut into this market and forced the company to pay with silver bullion imported from Mexico.

♦ **Haggling over the Price of Tea.**   An important item in the China trade of the eighteenth and early nineteenth centuries was tea, which had become extremely popular in Great Britain. This painting depicts the various stages of growing, processing, and marketing tea leaves. In the background, workers are removing tender young leaves from the bushes. After being dried, the leaves are packed into chests and loaded on vessels for shipment abroad.

As the balance of trade in China worsened, the British tried negotiations, dispatching Lord Macartney to Beijing in 1793 and another mission led by Lord Amherst in 1816. But both missions foundered on the rock of protocol and managed only to worsen the already strained relations between the two countries. The British solution was opium. A product more addictive than tea, opium was grown under company sponsorship in northeastern India and then shipped directly to the Chinese market. Opium had been grown in southwestern China for several hundred years, but had been used primarily for medicinal purposes. Now, as imports increased, popular demand for the product in South China became insatiable despite an official prohibition on its use. Soon bullion was flowing out of the Chinese imperial treasury into the pockets of company officials.

The Chinese became concerned and tried to negotiate. In 1839, Lin Zexu (Lin Tse-hsu; 1785–1850), a Chinese official appointed by the court to curtail the opium trade, appealed to Queen Victoria on both moral and practical grounds and threatened to prohibit the sale of rhubarb (widely used as a laxative in nineteenth-century Europe) to Great Britain if she did not respond (see the box on p. 857). But moral principles, then as now, paled before the lure of commercial profits, and company merchants continued to promote the opium trade, arguing that if the Chinese did not want the opium, they did not have to buy it. Lin Zexu attacked on three fronts, imposing penalties on smokers, arresting dealers, and seizing supplies from importers as they attempted to smuggle the drug into China. The last tactic caused his downfall. When he blockaded the foreign factory area in Canton to force traders to hand over their remaining chests of opium, the British government, claiming that it could not permit British subjects "to be exposed to insult and injustice," launched a naval expedition to punish the Manchus and force the court to open China to foreign trade.[1]

The Opium War (1839–1842) lasted for three years and demonstrated the superiority of British firepower and military tactics (including the use of a shallow-draft steamboat that effectively harassed Chinese coastal defenses). British warships destroyed Chinese coastal and river forts and seized the offshore island of Chusan. When a British fleet sailed virtually unopposed up the Yangtze River to Nanjing and cut off the supply of "tribute grain" from South to North China, the Qing finally agreed to British terms. In the Treaty of Nanjing in 1842, the Chinese agreed to open five coastal ports to British trade, limit tariffs on imported British goods, grant extraterritorial rights to British citizens in China, and pay a

A Letter of Advice to the Queen

Lin Zexu was the Chinese imperial commissioner in Canton at the time of the Opium War. Prior to the conflict, he attempted to use reason and the threat of retaliation to persuade the British to cease importing opium illegally into South China. The following excerpt is from a letter that he wrote to Queen Victoria. In it, he appeals to her conscience while showing the condescension that the Chinese traditionally displayed to the rulers of other countries.

Lin Zexu, Letter to Queen Victoria

The kings of your honorable country by a tradition handed down from generation to generation have always been noted for their politeness and submissiveness. We have read your successive tributary memorials saying, "In general our countrymen who go to trade in China have always received His Majesty the Emperor's gracious treatment and equal justice," and so on. Privately we are delighted with the way in which the honorable rulers of your country deeply understand the grand principles and are grateful for the Celestial grace. For this reason the Celestial Court in soothing those from afar has redoubled its polite and kind treatment. The profit from trade has been enjoyed by them continuously for two hundred years. This is the source from which your country has become known for its wealth.

But after a long period of commercial intercourse, there appear among the crowd of barbarians both good persons and bad, unevenly. Consequently there are those who smuggle opium to seduce the Chinese people and so cause the spread of the poison to all provinces. Such persons who only care to profit themselves, and disregard their harm to others, are not tolerated by the laws of heaven and are unanimously hated by human beings. His Majesty the Emperor, upon hearing of this, is in a towering rage. He has especially sent me, his commissioner, to come to Kwangtung, and together with the governor-general and governor jointly to investigate and settle this matter.

We find that your country is sixty or seventy thousand li [three li make one mile, ordinarily] from China. Yet there are barbarian ships that strive to come here for trade for the purpose of making a great profit. The wealth of China is used to profit the barbarians. That is to say, the great profit made by barbarians is all taken from the rightful share of China. By what right do they then in return use the poisonous drug to injure the Chi-

nese people? Even though the barbarians may not necessarily intend to do us harm, yet in coveting profit to an extreme, they have no regard for injuring others. Let us ask, where is your conscience? I have heard that the smoking of opium is very strictly forbidden by your country; that is because the harm caused by opium is clearly understood. Since it is not permitted to do harm to your own country, then even less should you let it be passed on to the harm of other countries—how much less to China! Of all that China exports to foreign countries, there is not a single thing which is not beneficial to people: they are of benefit when eaten, or of benefit when used, or of benefit when resold: all are beneficial. Is there a single article from China which has done any harm to foreign countries? Take tea and rhubarb, for example; the foreign countries cannot get along for a single day without them. . . . On the other hand, articles coming from the outside to China can only be used as toys. We can take them or get along without them. Since they are not needed by China, what difficulty would there be if we closed the frontier and stopped the trade? Nevertheless our Celestial Court lets tea, silk, and other goods be shipped without limit and circulated everywhere without begrudging it in the slightest. This is for no other reason but to share the benefit with the people of the whole world.

Our Celestial Dynasty rules over and supervises the myriad states, and surely possesses unfathomable spiritual dignity. Yet the Emperor cannot bear to execute people without having first tried to reform them by instruction. Therefore he especially promulgates these fixed regulations. The barbarian merchants of your country, if they wish to do business for a prolonged period, are required to obey our statutes respectfully and to cut off permanently the source of opium. . . . May you, O King, check your wicked and sift your vicious people before they come to China, in order to guarantee the peace of your nation, to show further the sincerity of your politeness and submissiveness, and to let the two countries enjoy together the blessings of peace. . . . After receiving this dispatch will you immediately give us a prompt reply regarding the details and circumstances of your cutting off the opium traffic. Be sure not to put this off. The above is what has to be communicated.

substantial indemnity to cover the costs of the war. China also agreed to cede the island of Hong Kong (dismissed by a senior British official as a "barren rock") to Great Britain. Nothing was said in the treaty about the opium trade, which continued unabated until it was brought under control through Chinese government efforts in the early twentieth century.

The Opium War has traditionally been considered the beginning of modern Chinese history. This view seems plausible, since the war marked the first major stage in the Western penetration of China, a process that eventually led to the collapse of the Qing dynasty in 1911. At the time, however, it is unlikely that many Chinese would have seen it that way. This was not the first time that a ruling dynasty had been forced to make concessions to foreigners, and the opening of five coastal ports to the British hardly constituted a serious threat to the security of the empire. Although a few concerned Chinese argued that the court should learn more about European civilization to find the secret of British success, others contended that China had nothing to learn from the barbarians and that borrowing foreign ways would undercut the purity of Confucian civilization (see the box on p. 859).

For the time being, the Manchus attempted to deal with the problem in the traditional way of playing the foreigners off against each other. Concessions granted to the British were offered to other Western nations, including the United States, and soon thriving foreign concession areas were operating in treaty ports along the southern Chinese coast from Canton in the south to Shanghai, a bustling new port on a tributary of the Yangtze, in the center. Like Britain, other Western countries received the right of extraterritoriality, which meant that if any of their citizens were charged with a crime in China, they could be tried by a consular court under the laws of their own country.

In the meantime, the Qing court's failure to deal with pressing internal economic problems led to a major peasant revolt that shook the foundations of the empire. On the surface, the so-called Taiping (T'ai p'ing) Rebellion owed something to the Western incursion; the leader of the uprising, Hong Xiuquan (Hung Hsiu-ch'uan), a failed examination candidate, was a Christian convert who viewed himself as a younger brother of Jesus Christ and hoped to establish what he referred to as a "Heavenly Kingdom of Supreme Peace" in China. But there were many local causes as well. The rapid increase in population forced millions of peasants to eke out a living as sharecroppers or landless laborers. Official corruption and incompetence led to the whipsaw of increased taxes and a decline in government services, such as the dredging of the Grand Canal. The silting up of the canal not only hindered the shipment of grain from south to north, but also drove countless barge people out of work.

Throughout the southern provinces, impoverished peasants and other discontented elements flocked to join the rebels. Then, as Hong Xiuquan proclaimed his intention of destroying the corrupt Qing and founding a new

◆ **The Opium War.** The Opium War, waged between China and Great Britain between 1839 and 1842, was China's first conflict with a European power. Lacking modern military technology, the Chinese suffered a humiliating defeat. In this painting, heavily armed British steamships destroy unwieldy Chinese junks along the Chinese coast.

❧ Europe in Chinese Eyes ❧

Until the mid-nineteenth century, the Chinese expressed little interest in Europe and its people. In the aftermath of the Opium War, however, Chinese intellectuals gradually began to explore Western society and its underpinnings. In 1891, a Chinese named Wang Hsi-ch'i published a compilation of descriptions of foreign countries for the edification of his compatriots. The following excerpt from this volume provides a general description of Europe through the eyes of an anonymous Chinese writer. Note the author's assumption that civilization came to Europe from the Orient. The final paragraph pays tribute to European persistence in seeking scientific truth.

A Chinese Description of Europe

Europe (Ou-lo-pa) is one of the five great continents. . . . Though it is smaller than the other four continents, its soil is fertile, its products are plentiful, it has many talented people and many famous places. For this reason, Europe's power in the present world is pre-eminent, and it has become a leading force in the five continents. Yet in ancient times its people hunted for a living, ate meat, and wore skins. Their customs were barbaric, and their spirit was wild and free. But during our own Shang period (2000 B.C.) Greece and other countries gradually came under the influence of the Orient. For the first time they began to till fields and manufacture products, build cities and dig lakes. They began to do all kinds of things. Before long, writing and civilization began to flourish. Thus they became beautiful like the countries of the East. . . .

Europe's people are all tall and white. Only those who live in the northeast where it is very cold are short, and dwarfish. They have big noses and deep eyes. But their eyes are not of the same color, with brown, green, and black being most frequent. They have heavy beards that go up to their temples, or are wound around their jaws. Some of their beards are straight like those of Chinese. Some are crooked and twisted like curly hairs. Some shave them all off. . . .

For their eating and drinking utensils they use gold, silver, and ceramics. When they eat they use knife and fork, and they do not use chopsticks. They eat mainly bread. Potatoes are staple. They mostly roast or broil fowl and game. They usually season it with preserves or olive oil. They drink spirits and soda water, as well as coffee in which they mix sugar. Its fragrance enlivens teeth and jaws, and makes the spirit fresh and clear.

Now as to the way they build houses. On the outside they have no surrounding walls, and inside they have no courts. They do not pay much attention to the exact direction and position (geomancy), they do not have fixed standards; square or round, concave or convex—all depends on the discretion of the owner. Sometimes they have many-storied buildings that go up for five or six, or seven or eight floors. They usually also dig out another underground floor; they use it for storage or go there to escape the heat. Their foundations are deep and solid. Their walls are substantial and thick. In hot or in cold weather nothing comes through them. In the winter they are warm inside and in the summer cool. They are very convenient. The upper classes use stone. The middle classes use brick. The lower classes use earth. For covering tiles, they use lead or sometimes ceramic pieces or light stones and boards. They make them depending on how wealthy they are. . . .

Now for their machines. When they first invented them, they just relied on common sense. They tried this and rejected that, without ever finding out from anyone else how it ought to be done. However, they did some research and found people who investigated the fine points and propagated their usage. In this way they gradually developed all their machines such as steamships, steam trains, spinning machines, mining and canal-digging machines, and all machines for making weapons and gunpowder. Things improved day by day and helped enrich the nation and benefit the people. Day by day they became more prosperous and will keep on becoming so.

dynasty, the rebellion swept northward. The rebels seized the old Ming capital of Nanjing in March 1853. The revolt continued for ten more years, but the seizure of the central Yangtze valley was its high-water mark. Plagued by factionalism that led to an internal civil war and the death of thousands, the rebellion gradually lost momentum. In 1864 the Qing, although weakened, retook Nanjing and destroyed the remnants of the rebel force.

One reason for the dynasty's failure to deal effectively with the internal unrest was its continuing difficulties with the Western imperialists. In 1856, the British and the French, still smarting from trade restrictions and limitations on their missionary activities, launched a new series of attacks against China and seized the capital of Beijing in 1860. As punishment, British troops destroyed the imperial summer palace just outside the city. In the ensuing Treaty of Tianjin (Tientsin), the Qing agreed to humiliating new concessions: the legalization of the opium trade, the opening of additional ports to foreign trade, and the cession of the peninsula of Kowloon (opposite the island of Hong Kong) to the British. Additional territories in the north were ceded to Russia.

The Climax of Imperialism in China

The continuing failure of traditional methods to deal with the Western threat gradually persuaded some thoughtful officials and intellectuals that China must learn from the West in order to survive. At first that point of view had little impact at court, where the initial reaction to the occupation of the capital was to seek a return to Confucian purity. But Confucian precepts by themselves were of little use against European guns, and the glories of the past could not be conjured up at will to restore China to the Golden Age of the early Zhou.

By the late 1870s, the old dynasty was well on the road to internal disintegration. In fending off the Taiping Rebellion, the Manchus had been compelled to rely for support on armed forces under regional command, since the banner and Green Standard troops were insufficient by themselves to restore order. After quelling the revolt, many of these regional commanders refused to disband

Map 23.1 Canton and Hong Kong.

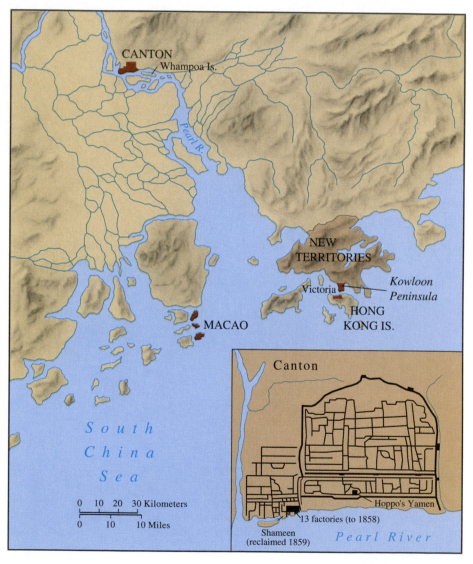

their units and, with the support of the local gentry, continued to collect local taxes for their own use. The dreaded pattern of imperial breakdown, so familiar in Chinese history, was beginning to appear once again.

In its weakened state, the court finally began to listen to the appeals of reform-minded officials, who called for a new policy of "self-strengthening," in which Western technology would be adopted while Confucian principles and institutions were maintained intact. This policy, popularly known by its slogan "East for Essence, West for Practical Use," remained the guiding standard for Chinese foreign and domestic policy for nearly a quarter of a century. Some even called for reforms in education and in China's hallowed political institutions. Pointing to the power and prosperity of Great Britain, the journalist Wang Tao (Wang T'ao; 1828–1897) remarked: "The real strength of England . . . lies in the fact that there is a sympathetic understanding between the governing and the

governed, a close relationship between the ruler and the people. . . . My observation is that the daily domestic political life of England actually embodies the traditional ideals of our ancient Golden Age."[2] Wang Tao was especially impressed with the principle of majority rule, although he apparently did not understand how it worked and confused unanimity with majority; according to him, when an important issue was at stake in Great Britain, it would be taken before Parliament, where all had to agree before any action could be taken. Such ideas were too radical for most reformers, however. One of the leading court officials of the day, Zhang Zhidong (Chang Chihtung), countered:

The doctrine of people's rights will bring us not a single benefit but a hundred evils. Are we going to establish a parliament? Among the Chinese scholars and people there are still many today who are content to be vulgar and

Map 23.2 The Qing Empire in the Early Twentieth Century.

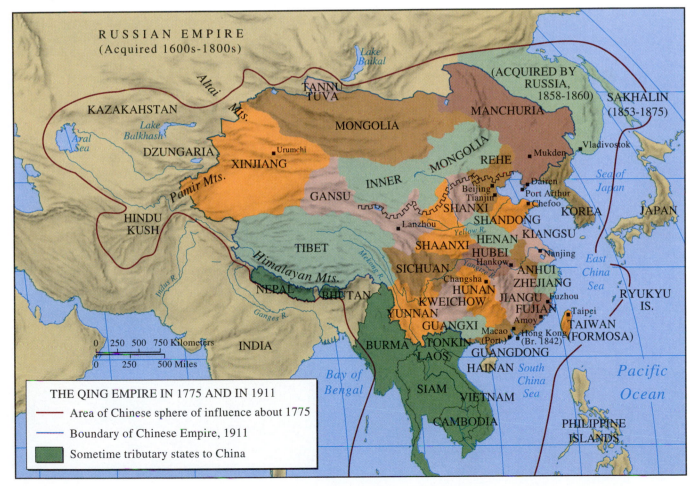

rustic. They are ignorant of the general situation in the world, they do not understand the basic system of the state. They have not the most rudimentary idea about foreign countries—about the schools, the political systems, military training, and manufacture of armaments. Even supposing the confused and clamorous people are assembled in one house, for every one of them who is clear-sighted, there will be a hundred others whose vision is beclouded; they will converse at random and talk as if in a dream—what use will it be?[3]

For the time being, Zhang Zhidong's arguments won the day. During the last quarter of the century, the Manchus attempted to modernize their military establishment and build up an industrial base without touching the essential elements of traditional Chinese civilization. Railroads,

weapons arsenals, and shipyards were built, but the value system remained essentially unchanged.

In the end, the results spoke for themselves. During the last two decades of the nineteenth century, the European penetration of China, both political and military, intensified. Rapacious imperialists began to bite off the outer edges of the Qing Empire. The Gobi Desert north of the Great Wall, Chinese Central Asia, and Tibet, all inhabited by non-Chinese peoples and never fully assimilated into the Chinese Empire, were now gradually removed totally from Beijing's control. In the north and northwest, the main beneficiary was Russia, which took advantage of the dynasty's weakness to force the cession of territories north of the Amur River in Siberia. In Tibet, competition between Russia and Great Britain

◆ **The Empress Dowager's Navy.**   Historians have often interpreted the stone pavilion shown above as a symbol of the Qing dynasty's inability to comprehend the nature of the threat to its survival. Funds meant to strengthen the Chinese navy

against imperious Westerns were used instead to construct this stone pleasure boat on the shore of a lake at the Summer Palace west of Beijing. Today the lake is a popular place for Chinese tourists.

prevented either power from seizing the territory outright, but at the same time enabled Tibetan authorities to revive local autonomy never recognized by the Chinese. On the southern borders of the empire, British and French advances in mainland Southeast Asia removed Burma and Vietnam from their traditional vassal relationship to the Manchu court.

Even more ominous developments were taking place in the Chinese heartland, where European economic penetration led to the creation of so-called spheres of influence dominated by diverse foreign powers. These spheres, normally composed of one or more Chinese administrative provinces, had originated with the rise of autonomous regional forces after the Taiping Rebellion. Local commanders began to negotiate directly with foreign political and economic interests, providing them with exclusive commercial, railroad-building, or mining privileges in return for financial compensation. Although the imperial court retained theoretical sovereignty throughout the country, in practice its political, economic, and

administrative influence beyond the region of the capital was increasingly circumscribed.

The breakup of the Manchu dynasty accelerated during the last five years of the nineteenth century. In 1894, the Qing went to war with Japan over Japanese incursions into the Korean peninsula, which threatened China's long-held suzerainty over the area (see Joining the Imperialist Club later in this chapter). To the surprise of many observers, the Chinese were roundly defeated, confirming to some critics the devastating failure of the policy of self-strengthening by halfway measures. As a reward, Japan demanded and received the island of Taiwan (known to Europeans at the time as Formosa) and the Liaodong (Liaotung) peninsula, which is strategically located at the entrance to the Gulf of Bohai in southern Manchuria. The emergence of Japan as an imperialist power aroused concern in European capitals, and a consortium composed of Germany, France, and Russia forced the Japanese to renounce their seizure of the Liaodong peninsula. But European statesmen were not concerned

✖ **Map 23.3**   Foreign Possessions and Spheres of Influence About 1900.

with preventing the collapse of the Chinese Empire. Before the end of the century, the peninsula once again fell under foreign control.

The process began in 1897, when Germany, a new entry in the race for spoils in East Asia, used the pretext of the murder of two German missionaries by Chinese rioters to demand the cession of territories in the Shandong (Shantung) peninsula. The approval of the demand by the imperial court set off a scramble for territory by other interested powers. Russia now demanded the Liaodong peninsula with its ice-free port at Port Arthur, and Great Britain weighed in with a request for a coaling station in North China at Weihaiwei, near the eastern tip of the Shandong peninsula.

The latest scramble for territory had taken place at a time of internal crisis in China. In the spring of 1898, an outspoken advocate of reform, the progressive Confucian scholar Kang Youwei (K'ang Yu-wei), won the support of the young Emperor Guangxu (Kuang Hsu) for a comprehensive reform program patterned after recent changes initiated in Japan. During the next several weeks, the emperor issued edicts calling for major political, administrative, and educational reforms. Kang's appeal to the emperor was simple and direct:

> A survey of all states in the world will show that those states which undertook reforms became strong while those states which clung to the past perished. The consequences of clinging to the past and the effects of opening up new ways are thus obvious. If Your Majesty, with your discerning brilliance, observes the trends in other countries, you will see that if we can change, we can preserve ourselves. But if we cannot change, we shall perish. Indeed, if we can make a complete change, we shall become strong, but if we only make limited changes, we shall still perish. If Your Majesty and his ministers investigate the source of the disease, you will know that this is the right prescription.[4]

Not surprisingly, Kang's ideas for reform were opposed by many conservatives, who saw little advantage to copying the West. "An examination of the causes of success and failure in government," said one, "reveals that in general the upholding of Confucianism leads to good government while the adoption of foreignism leads to disorder."[5] What was necessary, he concluded, was to reform existing ways (i.e., to follow the "Kingly Way") rather than abandoning the tried and true rules of the past.

Most important, the new program was opposed by the emperor's aunt, the Empress Dowager Cixi (Tz'u Hsi), the real source of power at court. Cixi had begun her political career as a concubine to an earlier emperor. After his death, she became a dominant force at court and in 1878 placed her infant nephew Guangxu on the throne. For two decades, she ruled in his name as regent. Cixi interpreted Guangxu's action as a British-supported effort to reduce her influence at court. With the aid of conservatives in the army, she arrested and executed several of the reformers and had the emperor incarcerated in the palace. Kang Youwei succeeded in fleeing abroad. With Cixi's palace coup, the so-called One Hundred Days of reform came to an end.

OPENING THE DOOR TO CHINA

During the next two years, foreign pressure on the dynasty intensified. With encouragement from the British, who hoped to avert a total collapse of the Manchu Empire, U.S. Secretary of State John Hay presented the

♦ **Empress Dowager Cixi.**   Cixi was the most powerful figure in late nineteenth-century China. Originally a concubine at the imperial court, she later placed a nephew on the throne and dominated the political scene for a quarter of a century until her death in 1908. Conservative in her views, she staunchly resisted her advisers' suggestions for changes to help China face the challenge posed by the West. Note the long fingernails, a symbol of the privileged class, in this photograph taken in her final years.

other imperialist powers with a proposal to ensure equal economic access to the China market for all states. Hay also suggested that all powers join together to guarantee the territorial and administrative integrity of the Chinese Empire. He requested that each power observe the following restrictions within its own sphere of influence:

1. Will in no way interfere with any treaty port or any vested interest within any so-called sphere of interest or leased territory it may have in China.
2. That only the Chinese government should collect duty and according to the Chinese treaty tariff.
3. That no preferential harbor dues or railway charges should benefit its own subjects.[6]

When none of the other governments flatly opposed the idea, Hay issued a second note declaring that all major states with economic interests in China had agreed to an "Open Door" policy in China.

In later years, the Open Door policy would be praised in American history books as an indication of U.S. benevolence and support for the survival of China. While many Americans did sympathize with China's struggle against rapacious colonial powers, it is undeniable that the United States was also motivated by self-interest. Trading interests in the United States preferred to operate in open markets and disliked the existing division of China into separate spheres of influence dominated by individual powers. The Open Door policy did not formally end the system of spheres of influence, but it did reduce the number of tariffs or quotas on foreign imports imposed by the dominating power within each sphere.

Whatever the underlying motivations for their promulgation, the Open Door Notes did have the practical effect of reducing the imperialist hysteria over access to the China market. That hysteria, a product of decades of mythologizing among Western commercial interests about the "four hundred million" Chinese customers, had accelerated at the end of the century as fear of China's imminent collapse increased. The "gentlemen's agreement" about the Open Door (it was not a treaty, but merely a pious and nonbinding expression of intent) served to deflate fears in Britain, France, Germany, and Russia that other powers would take advantage of China's weakness to dominate the China market for themselves.

In the long run, then, the Open Door was a positive step that brought a measure of sanity to imperialist behavior in East Asia. Unfortunately, it came too late to stop the domestic explosion known as the Boxer Rebel-

China in the Era of Imperialism

Lord Macartney's mission to China	1793
Opium War	1839–1842
Taiping rebels seize Nanjing	1853
Taiping Rebellion suppressed	1864
Cixi becomes regent for nephew Guangxu	1878
Sino-Japanese War	1894–1895
One Hundred Days Reform	1898
Open Door Notes	1899
Boxer Rebellion	1900
Commission to study constitution formed	1905
Deaths of Cixi and Guangxu	1908
Revolution in China	1911

lion. The Boxers, so-called because of the physical exercises they performed, were members of a secret society operating primarily in rural areas in North China. Provoked by a damaging drought and high levels of unemployment caused in part by foreign economic activity (the introduction of railroads and steamships, for example, undercut the livelihood of boatworkers who traditionally carried merchandise on the rivers and canals), the Boxers attacked foreign residents and besieged the foreign legation quarter in Beijing until the foreigners were rescued by an international expeditionary force in the late summer of 1900. As punishment, the foreign troops destroyed a number of temples in the capital suburbs, while the Chinese government was compelled to pay a heavy indemnity to the foreign governments involved in suppressing the uprising.

The Collapse of the Old Order

During the next few years, the old dynasty tried desperately to reform itself. The empress dowager, who had long resisted change, now embraced a number of reforms in education, administration, and the legal system. The venerable civil service examination system was replaced by a new educational system based on the Western model. In 1905, a commission was formed to study constitutional changes, and over the next few years, legislative assemblies were established at the provincial

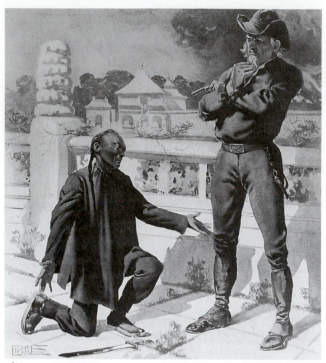

◆ **Justice or Mercy: Uncle Sam Decides.**   In the summer of 1900, Chinese rebels called Boxers besieged Western embassies in the imperial capital of Beijing. Western nations, including the United States, dispatched troops to North China to rescue their compatriots. In this cartoon, which appeared in a contemporary American news magazine, China figuratively seeks pardon from a stern Uncle Sam.

level, while elections for a national assembly were held in 1910.

Such moves won at least temporary support for the dynasty among progressive elements in the country. But history shows that the most dangerous period for an authoritarian system is when it begins to reform itself, because change breeds instability and performance rarely matches rising expectations. Such was the case in China. The emerging new provincial elite, composed of merchants, professionals, and reform-minded gentry, soon became impatient with the slow pace of political change and were disillusioned to find that the new assemblies, severely limited in their franchise in any case, were intended to be primarily advisory rather than legislative. The government also alienated influential elements by financing railway development projects through lucrative contracts with foreign firms rather than by turning to local investors.

These reforms also had little meaning for peasants, artisans, miners, and transportation workers whose living conditions were being eroded by rising taxes and official venality. Rising rural unrest, as yet poorly organized and

often centered on secret societies such as the Boxers, was an ominous sign of deep-seated resentment to which the dynasty would not, or could not, respond.

To China's reformist elite, such signs of social unrest were a threat to be avoided. To its tiny revolutionary movement, they were a harbinger of promise. The first physical manifestations of future revolution appeared during the last decade of the nineteenth century with the formation of the Revive China Society by the young radical Sun Yat-sen (1866–1925). Born to a peasant family in a village south of Canton, Sun was educated in Hawaii and returned to China to practice medicine. Soon he turned his full attention to the ills of Chinese society.

Sun Yat-sen disagreed with Kang Youwei's plan to use the young Manchu emperor as the engine of change. When you decide to build a railroad, he pointed out, you should find the most modern locomotive. He was convinced that the Qing dynasty was in a state of irreparable decay and lacked the capacity to become the vehicle for an effective program of national revival. The Chinese people, he lamented, are like "a sheet of loose sand."[7] Until they were united under a strong government, they would be at the mercy of other countries. Accordingly, Sun believed that China should follow the pattern of the Western democracies.

Gathering support from radical students, merchants, and secret society members in South China, as well as Chinese living in Europe, the United States, or elsewhere in Asia, Sun launched a series of local insurrections to topple the Qing and establish a republic on the Western model. He was not blind to Kang's point that the Chinese people were not yet sophisticated enough to put Western democracy into practice, so he called for a three-stage process beginning with a military takeover and ending with a constitutional democracy. Thus, for Sun his own revolutionary party, rather than the monarchy, would be the vehicle for change during a transitional stage that he labeled the period of political tutelage. During that stage, the revolutionary party would try to repair the defects in Chinese society and prepare the people for the next stage of constitutionalism.

At first, Sun's efforts yielded few positive results except to create a symbol of resistance and a pantheon of revolutionary martyrs. But in a convention in Tokyo in 1905, Sun managed to unite radical groups from across China in a Revolutionary Alliance (Tongmenghui, or T'ung Meng Hui). The new organization's program was based on Sun's so-called Three People's Principles of Nationalism (meaning primarily the destruction of Manchu rule over China), Democracy, and People's Livelihood (see the box on p. 867). Although the new organization

A Program for a New China

In 1905, Sun Yat-sen united a number of anti-Manchu groups into a single patriotic organization called the Revolutionary Alliance (Tongmenghui). The new organization eventually formed the basis of his Guomindang, or Nationalist Party. This excerpt is from the organization's manifesto, published in 1905 in Tokyo.

Sun Yat-sen, Manifesto for the Tongmenghui

By order of the Military Government, . . . the Commander-in-Chief of the Chinese National Army proclaims the purposes and platform of the Military Government to the people of the nation:

Therefore we proclaim to the world in utmost sincerity the outline of the present revolution and the fundamental plan for the future administration of the nation.

1. *Drive out the Tartars:* The Manchus of today were originally the eastern barbarians beyond the Great Wall. They frequently caused border troubles during the Ming dynasty; then when China was in a disturbed state they came inside Shanhaikuan, conquered China, and enslaved our Chinese people. . . . The extreme cruelties and tyrannies of the Manchu government have now reached their limit. With the righteous army poised against them, we will overthrow that government, and restore our sovereign rights.
2. *Restore China:* China is the China of the Chinese. The government of China should be in the hands of the Chinese. After driving out the Tartars we must restore our national state. . . .
3. *Establish the Republic:* Now our revolution is based on equality, in order to establish a republican government. All our people are equal and all enjoy political rights. The president will be publicly chosen by the people of the country. The parliament will be made up of members publicly chosen by the people of the country. A constitution of the Chinese Republic will be enacted, and every person must abide by it. . . .
4. *Equalize land ownership:* The good fortune of civilization is to be shared equally by all the people of the nation. We should improve our social and economic organization, and assess the value of all the land in the country. Its present price shall be received by the owner, but all increases in value resulting from reform and social improvements after the revolution shall belong to the state, to be shared by all the people, in order to create a socialist state, where each family within the empire can be well supported, each person satisfied, and no one fail to secure employment. . . .

The above four points will be carried out in three steps in due order. The first period is government by military law. When the righteous army has arisen, various places will join the cause. The local administration, in areas where the enemy has been either already defeated or not yet defeated, will be controlled in general by the Military Government, so that step by step the accumulated evils can be swept away. Evils like the oppression of the government, the greed and graft of officials, . . . the cruelty of tortures and penalties, the tyranny of tax collections, the humiliation of the queue—shall all be exterminated together with the Manchu rule. Evils in social customs, such as the keeping of slaves, the cruelty of foot-binding, the spread of the poison of opium, should also all be prohibited. . . .

The second period is that of government by a provisional constitution. When military law is lifted in each *hsien*, the Military Government shall return the right of self-government to the local people. . . . Six years after the securing of peace in the nation the provisional constitution shall be annulled and the constitution shall be promulgated.

The third period will be government under the constitution. Six years after the provisional constitution has been enforced a constitution shall be made. The military and administrative powers of the Military Government shall be annulled; the people shall elect the president, and elect the members of parliament to organize the parliament. The administrative matters of the nation shall proceed according to the provisions of the constitution.

was small and relatively inexperienced, it benefited from rising popular discontent with the failure of Manchu reforms to improve conditions in China. The dynasty, in fact, was about to commit suicide. In 1908, the dowager empress died. Mysteriously, her nephew Guangxu, imprisoned in the imperial palace since the failure of the One Hundred Day Reforms, had died the day before. The throne was now occupied by China's "last emperor," the infant Henry Puyi (P'u Yi).

In October 1911, followers of Sun Yat-sen launched yet another uprising in the industrial center of Wuhan, on the Yangtze River in central China. With Sun traveling in the United States, the insurrection lacked leadership, but the decrepit government's inability to react quickly encouraged political forces at the provincial level to take measures into their own hands. The dynasty was

◆ **Sun Yat-sen, Father of Modern China.**   The son of a peasant in South China, Sun Yat-sen rose to become a prominent revolutionary and the founder of the first Chinese republic. This photograph shows Sun as he assumed office as provisional president in January 1912. Shortly after, he was forced to resign in favor of General Yuan Shikai who moved the capital from Nanjing to Beijing.

now in a state of virtual collapse, opening the way for new political forces to fill the vacuum, but Sun's party had neither the military strength nor the political base necessary to seize the initiative and was forced to turn to a representative of the old order, General Yuan Shikai (Yuan Shih-k'ai). A prominent figure in military circles since the beginning of the century, Yuan had been placed in charge of the imperial forces sent to suppress the rebellion, but now he abandoned the Manchus and acted on his own behalf. In negotiations with representatives of Sun Yat-sen's party (Sun himself had arrived in China in January 1912), he agreed to serve as president of a new Chinese republic. The old dynasty and the age-old system that it had attempted to preserve were no more.

Propagandists for Sun Yat-sen's party have often portrayed the events of 1911 as a glorious revolution that brought two thousand years of imperial tradition to an end, and indeed they did finish off the old dynastic system. But a true revolution does not just destroy an old order, it also brings new political and social forces into power and creates new institutions and values that provide a new framework for a changing society. If these are the prerequisites for revolution, then the 1911 revolution did not live up to its name. Sun Yat-sen and his followers were unable to consolidate their gains. The Revolutionary Alliance found the bulk of its support in an emerging urban middle class and set forth a program based generally on Western liberal democratic principles. That class and that program had provided the foundation for the capitalist democratic revolutions in Western Europe and North America in the late eighteenth and nineteenth centuries, but the bourgeois class in China was still too small to form the basis for a new post-Confucian political order. The vast majority of the Chinese people still lived on the land. Sun Yat-sen had hoped to win their support with a land reform program that relied on fiscal incentives to persuade landlords to sell excess lands to their tenants, but few peasants had participated in the 1911 revolution, although rural unrest was on the rise. In effect, then, the events of 1911 were less a revolution than a collapse of the old order. Weakened by imperialism and its own internal weaknesses, the old dynasty had come to an abrupt end before new political and social forces were ready to fill the vacuum.

What China had experienced was part of a historical process that was bringing down traditional empires across the globe both in those regions threatened by Western imperialism and in Europe itself, where tsarist Russia, the Austro-Hungarian Empire, and the Ottoman Empire all came to an end within a few years of the collapse of the Qing. The circumstances of their demise were not all the same. The Austro-Hungarian Empire, for example, was dismembered by the victorious allies after World War I, while the fate of tsarist Russia was directly linked to that conflict. Still, all four regimes shared the responsibility for their common fate, in that they had failed to meet the challenges posed by the times. All had responded to the forces of industrialization and popular participation in the political process with hesitation and reluctance, and their attempts at reform were too little and too late. All paid the supreme price for their folly.

Chinese Society in Transition

The growing Western presence in China during the late nineteenth and early twentieth centuries obviously had a major impact on Chinese society; hence many historians have asserted that the arrival of the Europeans shook China out of centuries of slumber and launched it on the road to revolutionary change. In fact, when the European economic penetration into China began to accelerate in the mid-nineteenth century, Chinese society was already in a state of transition. The growth of industry and trade was particularly noticeable in the cities, where a national market for such commodities as oil, copper, salt, tea, and porcelain had developed. The foundation of an infrastructure more conducive to the rise of a money economy appeared to be in place. In the countryside, new crops introduced from abroad significantly increased food production and aided population growth. The Chinese economy had never been more productive or complex.

Whether these changes by themselves would eventually have led to an industrial revolution and the rise of a capitalist society on the Western model in the absence of Western intervention is a question that historians cannot answer with assurance. Certainly, a number of obstacles would have made it difficult for China to embark on the Western path if it had wished to do so.

Although industrial production was on the rise, it was still based almost entirely on traditional methods of production. There was no uniform system of weights and measures, and the banking system was still primitive by European standards. The use of paper money, invented by the Chinese centuries earlier, had essentially been abandoned. The transportation system, which had been neglected since the end of the Yuan dynasty, was increasingly chaotic. There were few paved roads, and the Grand Canal, long the most efficient means of carrying goods from north to south, was silting up. As a result, merchants had to rely more and more on the coastal route, where they faced increasing competition from foreign shipping.

Although foreign concession areas in the coastal cities provided a conduit for the importation of Western technology and modern manufacturing methods, the Chinese borrowed less than they might have. Foreign manufacturing enterprises could not legally operate in China until the last decade of the nineteenth century, and their methods had little influence beyond the concession areas. Chinese efforts to imitate Western methods, notably in shipbuilding and weapons manufacture, were dominated by the government and often suffered from mismanagement.

Equally serious problems persisted in the countryside. The rapid increase in population had led to smaller plots and growing numbers of tenant farmers. Whether per capita consumption of food was on the decline is not clear from the available evidence, but apparently rice as a staple of the diet was increasingly being replaced by less nutritious foods. Some farmers benefited from switching to commercial agriculture to supply the markets of the growing coastal cities, but the shift entailed a sizable investment. Many farmers went so deeply into debt that they eventually lost their land. In the meantime, the traditional patron-client relationship was frayed, as landlords moved to the cities to take advantage of the glittering urban lifestyle.

Most important, perhaps, was that the Qing dynasty was still locked into a traditional mindset that discouraged commercial activities and prized the time-honored virtues of preindustrial agrarian society. China also lacked the European tradition of a vigorous and self-confident merchant class based in cities that were autonomous or even independent of the feudal political leader in the surrounding areas.

In any event, the advent of the imperialist era in the last half of the nineteenth century made such questions academic; imperialism created serious distortions in the local economy that resulted in massive changes in Chinese society during the twentieth century. Whether the Western intrusion was beneficial or harmful is debated to this day. The Western presence undoubtedly accelerated the development of the Chinese economy in some ways: the introduction of modern means of production, transport, and communications; the appearance of an export market; and the steady integration of the Chinese market into the nineteenth-century global economy. To many Westerners at the time, it was self-evident that such changes would ultimately benefit the Chinese people. Western civilization represented the most advanced stage of human development. By supplying (in the catch phrase of the day) "oil for the lamps of China," it was providing a backward society with an opportunity to move up a notch or two on the ladder of human evolution.

Not everyone agreed. The Marxist Vladimir Lenin contended that Western imperialism actually hindered the process of structural change in preindustrial societies because it thwarted the rise of a local industrial and commercial sector in order to maintain colonies and semicolonies as a market for Western manufactured goods and a source of cheap labor and materials. Fellow Marxists in China such as Mao Zedong later took up Lenin's charge and asserted that if the West had not intervened, China would have found its own road to capitalism and thence to socialism and communism.

Many historians today would say that the answer was a little of both. By shaking China out of its traditional mindset, imperialism accelerated the process of change that had begun in the late Ming and early Qing periods and forced the Chinese to adopt new ways of thinking and acting. At the same time, China paid a heavy price in the destruction of its local industry, while many of the profits flowed abroad. Although the industrial revolution is a painful process whenever and wherever it occurs, the Chinese found the experience doubly painful because it was foisted on China from the outside.

Daily Life

At the beginning of the nineteenth century, daily life for most Chinese was not substantially different from what it had been for centuries. Most were farmers, living in millions of villages in rice fields and on hillsides throughout the countryside. Their lives were governed by the harvest cycle, village custom, and family ritual. Their roles in society were firmly fixed by the time-honored principles of Confucian social ethics. Male children, at least the more fortunate ones, were educated in the Confucian classics, while females remained in the home or in the fields. All children were expected to obey their parents, and wives to submit to their husbands.

A visitor to China a hundred years later would have seen a very different society, although it would have still been recognizably Chinese. The changes were most striking in the coastal cities, where the educated and affluent had been visibly affected by the growing Western cultural presence. Confucian social institutions and behavioral norms were declining rapidly in influence while those of Europe and North America were on the ascendant. Changes were much less noticeable in the countryside, but even there the customary bonds had been dangerously frayed by the rapidly changing times.

Some of the change can be traced to the educational system. During the nineteenth century, the importance of a Confucian education steadily declined, as up to half of the degree holders had purchased their degrees. After 1906, when the government abolished the civil service examinations, a Confucian education ceased to be the key to a successful career, and Western-style education became more desirable. The old dynasty attempted to modernize by establishing an educational system on the Western model with universal education at the elementary level. Such plans had some effect in the cities, where public schools, missionary schools and other private institutions educated a new generation of Chinese with little knowledge or respect for the past.

The status of women was also in transition. During the mid-Qing era, women were still expected to remain in the home. Their status as useless sex objects was painfully symbolized by the practice of foot-binding, a custom that had probably originated among court entertainers in the Tang dynasty and later spread to the common people. By the mid-nineteenth century, more than half of all adult women probably had bound feet.

During the late nineteenth century, the first signs of change began to appear. Christian missionaries began to open girls' schools, mainly in the foreign concession areas. Although only a relatively small number of women were educated in these schools, they had a significant impact on Chinese society. By the end of the century, progressive intellectuals had begun to argue that ignorant women produced ignorant children. In 1905, the court announced its intention to open public schools for girls, but few such schools ever materalized. Private schools for girls were established in some urban areas. The government also began to take steps to discourage the practice of foot-binding, although initially with only minimal success.

A Rich Country and a Strong State: The Rise of Modern Japan

By the beginning of the nineteenth century, the Tokugawa shogunate had ruled the Japanese islands for two hundred years. It had revitalized the old governmental system, which had virtually disintegrated under its predecessors. It had driven out the foreign traders and missionaries and isolated the country from virtually all contacts with the outside world. The Tokugawa maintained formal relations only with Korea, although informal trading links with Dutch and Chinese merchants continued at

Nagasaki. Isolation, however, did not mean stagnation. Under the Tokugawa, Japanese society had begun to undergo deep-seated changes that eventually ended Tokugawa rule and destroyed the traditional feudal system itself.

Those changes were social and economic as well as political. Under the centralized system of the Tokugawa, political power was largely concentrated in the hands of the *bakufu* in Edo, and the daimyo, at least in theory, were directly subordinated to the shogunate. In the meantime, the long period of peace and prosperity saw the emergence of a vigorous manufacturing and commercial sector that promised to change the face of Japanese society. The vast majority of Japanese still engaged in agriculture for their livelihood, and a theoretically rigid class hierarchy of samurai, artisans, farmers, and merchants continued to shape the legal climate and cultural habits of the population. Nevertheless, Japanese society was rapidly changing, and traditional class distinctions were becoming blurred.

Some historians speculate that the Tokugawa system was beginning to come apart, just as the medieval order in Europe had begun to disintegrate at the beginning of the Renaissance. Certainly, there were signs that the shogunate was becoming less effective. Factionalism and corruption plagued the central bureaucracy, while rural unrest, provoked by a series of poor harvests brought about by bad weather, swept the countryside. Farmers fled to the towns, where anger was already rising as a result of declining agricultural incomes and shrinking stipends for the samurai. Many of the samurai lashed out at the perceived incompetence and corruption of the government. In response, the *bakufu* retreated into ideological rigidity, persecuting its critics and attempting to force fleeing peasants to return to their lands. In the meantime, the government intensified its efforts to maintain the nation's isolation from the outside world, driving away foreign ships that were beginning to prowl along the Japanese coast in increasing numbers.

An End to Isolation

Japan, then, was ripe for change. Some historians maintain that Japan was poised to experience an industrial revolution under the stimulus of internal conditions. As in China, the resumption of contacts with the West in the middle of the nineteenth century rendered such questions somewhat academic. To the Western powers, the continued isolation of Japanese society was an affront and a challenge. Driven by growing rivalry among themselves and convinced by their own propaganda and the ideology of world capitalism that the expansion of trade on a global basis would benefit all nations, Western nations began to approach Japan in the hope of opening up the hermit kingdom to foreign economic interests.

◆ **Commodore Perry Arrives in Japan.** In July 1853, U.S. Commodore Matthew Perry arrived in Tokyo Bay in command of a fleet of black ships. His goal was to open Japan to Western trade. In this painting by a Japanese artist, Perry is greeted by his Japanese host, both in full regalia. The U.S. fleet sits at anchor in the background.

The first to succeed was the United States. American whalers and clipper ships following the northern route across the Pacific needed a fueling station before completing their long journey to China and other ports in the area. The first efforts to pry the Japanese out of their cloistered existence in the 1830s and 1840s failed, but the Americans persisted. In the summer of 1853, an American fleet of four warships under Commodore Matthew C. Perry arrived in Edo Bay (now Tokyo Bay) with a letter from President Millard Fillmore addressed to the shogun. The letter requested better treatment for sailors shipwrecked on the Japanese islands and the opening of foreign relations between the two countries (see the box on p. 872).

A few months later, Perry returned with an even larger fleet for an answer. In his absence, shogunate officials had discussed the issue, but without reaching a decision. The question had then been referred to the leading daimyo for

A Letter to the Shogun

When U.S. Commodore Matthew Perry arrived in Tokyo Bay on his first visit to Japan in July 1853, he carried a letter from the president of the United States, Millard Fillmore. The letter requested that trade relations between the two countries be established. Little did the president know how momentous the occasion was.

A Letter from the President of the United States

Millard Fillmore
President of the United States of America,
To His Imperial Majesty,
The Emperor of Japan.
Great and Good Friend!
I send you this public letter by Commodore Matthew C. Perry, an officer of the highest rank in the Navy of the United States, and commander of the squadron now visiting your Imperial Majesty's dominions.

I have directed Commodore Perry to assure your Imperial Majesty that I entertain the kindest feelings towards your Majesty's person and government; and that I have no other object in sending him to Japan, but to propose to your Imperial Majesty that the United States and Japan should live in friendship, and have commercial intercourse with each other.

The constitution and laws of the United States forbid all interference with the religious or political concerns of other nations. I have particularly charged Commodore Perry to abstain from every act which could possibly disturb the tranquillity of your Imperial Majesty's dominions.

The United States of America reach from ocean to ocean, and our territory of Oregon and state of California lie directly opposite to the dominions of your Imperial Majesty. Our steam-ships can go from California to Japan in eighteen days.

Our great state of California produces about sixty millions of dollars in gold, every year, besides silver, quicksilver, precious stones, and many other valuable articles. Japan is also a rich and fertile country, and produces many very valuable articles. . . . I am desirous that our two countries should trade with each other, for the benefit both of Japan and the United States.

We know that the ancient laws of your Imperial Majesty's government do not allow of foreign trade except with the Dutch. But as the state of the world changes, and new governments are formed, it seems to be wise from time to time to make new laws. . . . If your Imperial Majesty were so far to change the ancient laws as to allow a free trade between the two countries, it would be extremely beneficial to both.

If your Imperial Majesty is not satisfied that it would be safe, altogether, to abrogate the ancient laws which forbid foreign trade, they might be suspended for five or ten years, so as to try the experiment. If it does not prove as beneficial as was hoped, the ancient laws can be restored. . . .

I have directed Commodore Perry to mention another thing to your Imperial Majesty. Many of our ships pass every year from California to China; and great numbers of our people pursue the whale fishery near the shores of Japan. It sometimes happens in stormy weather that one of our ships is wrecked on your Imperial Majesty's shores. In all such cases we ask and expect, that our unfortunate people should be treated with kindness, and that their property should be protected, till we can send a vessel and bring them away. . . .

Commodore Perry is also directed by me to represent to your Imperial Majesty that we understand there is a great abundance of coal and provisions in the empire of Japan. Our steam-ships, in crossing the great ocean, burn a great deal of coal, and it is not convenient to bring it all the way from America. We wish that our steam-ships and other vessels should be allowed to stop in Japan and supply themselves with coal, provisions and water. They will pay for them, in money, or anything else your Imperial Majesty's subjects may prefer; and we request your Imperial Majesty to appoint a convenient port in the southern part of the empire, where our vessels may stop for this purpose. . . .

May the Almighty have your Imperial Majesty in his great and holy keeping! . . .

Your Good Friend,
Millard Fillmore

debate, but they were ambivalent. Some argued that contacts with the West would be both politically and morally disadvantageous to Japan, while others pointed to U.S. military superiority and recommended concessions. For the shogunate in Edo, the big black guns of Commodore Perry's ships proved decisive, and Japan agreed to the Treaty of Kanagawa, which provided for the return of American sailors, the opening of two ports, and the establishment of a U.S. consulate on Japanese soil. In 1858, U.S. Consul Townsend Harris negotiated a more elaborate commercial treaty calling for the opening of several ports to U.S. trade and residence, the exchange of ministers, and the granting of extraterritorial privileges for U.S. residents in Japan. Similar treaties were soon signed with several European nations.

In his remarks to the Japanese officials, Townsend Harris artfully combined implied threats with persuasion. The advent of the steamship, he said, had made the world "like one family." No country could expect to remain isolated from others in the future. Noting that Great Britain was prepared to use force to open Japan as it had recently done against China, he concluded:

> If Japan should make a treaty with the ambassador of the United States, who has come unattended by military force, her honor will not be impaired. There will be a great difference between a treaty made with a single individual, unattended, and one made with a person who should bring fifty men-of-war to these shores.

The U.S. consul's Japanese hosts were impressed by his arguments. As one senior official noted to his colleagues:

> I am therefore convinced that our policy should be to stake everything on the present opportunity, to conclude friendly alliances, to send ships to foreign countries everywhere and conduct trade, to copy the foreigners where they are at their best and so repair our own shortcomings, to foster our national strength and complete our armaments, and so gradually subject the foreigners to our influence until in the end . . . our hegemony is acknowledged throughout the globe.[8]

The decision to open relations with the Western barbarians was highly unpopular in some quarters, particularly in regions distant from the shogunate headquarters in Edo. Resistance was especially strong in two of the key outside daimyo territories in the south, Satsuma and Choshu. Both had strong military traditions (the former, on Kyushu, was a center of pirate activity, while the latter dominated the strategically located Strait of Shi-

monoseki, leading into the Sea of Japan), and neither was at first exposed to heavy Western military pressure. In 1863, the "Sat-Cho" alliance forced the hapless shogun to promise to bring relations with the West to an end. The shogun eventually reneged on the agreement, but the rebellious groups soon disclosed their own weakness. When Choshu troops fired on Western ships in the Strait of Shimonoseki, the Westerners fired back and destroyed the Choshu fortifications. The incident convinced the rebellious samurai of the need to strengthen their own military and intensified their unwillingness to give in to the West. Accordingly, Sat-Cho elements continued to insist that the shogunate should take a stronger line with the foreigners. Having strengthened their influence at the imperial court in Kyoto, they demanded the shogun's resignation and the restoration of the emperor's power. The reigning shogun agreed to resign in favor of a council composed of daimyo that would function under the chairmanship of the emperor with the shogun serving as prime minister. But this arrangement was unsatisfactory to leading members of the Sat-Cho faction, and in January 1868 rebel armies attacked the shogunate's palace in Kyoto and proclaimed the restored authority of the emperor. After a few weeks resistance collapsed, and the venerable shogunate system was brought to an end.

The Meiji Restoration

Although the victory of the Sat-Cho faction over the shogunate had appeared on the surface to be a struggle between advocates of tradition and proponents of conciliation of the West, in fact, the new leadership soon embarked on a policy of comprehensive reform that would lay the foundations of a modern industrial nation within a generation. Although the Sat-Cho leaders had genuinely mistrusted the West, they soon realized that Japan must change to survive.

The symbol of the new era was the young emperor himself, who had taken the reign name Meiji (enlightened rule) on ascending the throne after the death of his father in 1867. Although the post-Tokugawa period was termed a "restoration," the Meiji ruler, who shared the modernist outlook of the Sat-Cho group, was controlled by the new leadership just as the shogunate had controlled his predecessors. In tacit recognition of the real source of political power, the new capital was located at Edo (now renamed Tokyo, or "Eastern Capital"), and the imperial court was moved to the shogun's palace in the center of the city.

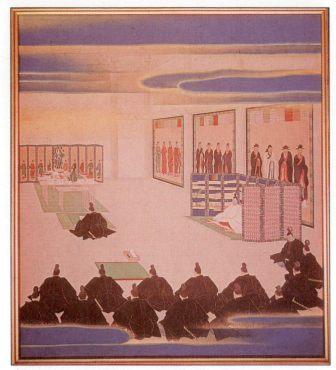

◆ **Empire Meiji and the Charter Oath.** In 1868, reformist elements overthrew the Tokugawa shogunate in an era of rapid modernization in Japanese Society. Their intentions were announced in a Charter Oath of five articles promulgated in April 1868. In this contemporary print, the young emperor Meiji listens to the reading of the Charter Oath in his palace in Kyoto.

THE TRANSFORMATION OF JAPANESE POLITICS

Once in power, the new leaders launched a comprehensive reform of Japanese political, social, economic, and cultural institutions and values. They moved first to abolish the remnants of the old order and strengthen executive power in their hands. To undercut the power of the daimyo, hereditary privileges were abolished in 1871, and the great lords lost title to their lands. As compensation, they were given government bonds and were named governors of the territories formerly under their control, but now reorganized as prefectures. Noble titles were retained, but the *eta*, the traditional slave class, were granted legal equality. The samurai, comprising about 8 percent of the total population, received a lump sum payment to replace their traditional stipends, but they were forbidden to wear the sword, the symbol of their hereditary status.

The abolition of the legal underpinnings of the Tokugawa system permitted the Meiji modernizers to embark on the creation of a modern political system based on the Western model. In 1868, the new leaders enacted a Charter Oath, in which they promised to create a new delib-

erative assembly within the framework of continued imperial rule (see the box on p. 875). An advisory council of state was established the same year. Although senior positions in the new government were given to the daimyo, the key posts were dominated by modernizing samurai from the Sat-Cho clique. The leading faction in the new highly centralized government was known as the *genro*, or elder statemen. The country was divided into seventy-five prefectures (the number was reduced to forty-five in 1889 and remains at that number today).

During the next two decades, the Meiji government undertook a systematic study of Western political systems. A constitutional commission under Prince Ito Hirobumi traveled to several Western countries to study their political systems and expressed particular interest in those of Great Britain, Germany, Russia, and the United States. As the process evolved, a number of factions appeared, each representing different political ideas within the ruling clique. The most prominent were the Liberal Party and the Progressive Party. The Liberal Party was led by Itagaki Taisuke, who favored political reform on the Western liberal democratic model with supreme authority vested in the parliament as the representative of the people. The Progressive Party was led by Okuma Shigenobu, who called for the distribution of power between the legislative and executive branches, with a slight nod to the latter. There was also an imperial party that advocated the retention of supreme authority exclusively in the hands of the emperor.

During the 1870s and 1880s, these factions competed for preeminence. In the end, the Progressives emerged victorious. The Meiji Constitution, which was adopted in 1890, was based on the Bismarckian model with authority vested in the executive branch; the imperialist faction was pacified by the statement that the constitution was the gift of the emperor. Members of the cabinet were to be handpicked by the Meiji oligarchs. The upper house of parliament was to be appointed and have equal legislative powers with the lower house, called the Diet, whose members would be elected. An interesting feature of the new constitution was that the Diet had the power to appropriate funds, but if no agreement was reached, the budget would remain the same as in the previous year, thus permitting the executive branch to continue in operation. The core ideology of the state was called the *kokutai* (national polity), which embodied (although in very imprecise form) the concept of the uniqueness of the Japanese system based on the supreme authority of the emperor.

The result was a system that was democratic in form but despotic in practice, modern in external appearance

A Program for Reform in Japan

In the spring of 1868, the reformers drew up a program for transforming Japanese society along Western lines in the post-Tokugawa era. Though vague in its essentials, the Charter Oath is a good indication of the plans that were carried out during the Meiji Restoration.

The Charter Oath of Emperor Meiji

By this oath we set up as our aim the establishment of the national weal on a broad basis and the framing of a constitution and laws.

1. Deliberative assemblies shall be widely established and all matters decided by public discussion.
2. All classes, high and low, shall unite in vigorously carrying out the administration of affairs of state.
3. The common people, no less than the civil and military officials, shall each be allowed to pursue his own calling so that there may be no discontent.
4. Evil customs of the past shall be broken off and everything based upon the just laws of Nature.
5. Knowledge shall be sought throughout the world so as to strengthen the foundations of imperial rule.

but still recognizably traditional in that power remained in the hands of a ruling oligarchy. The system permitted the traditional ruling class to retain its influence and economic power while acquiescing in the emergence of a new set of institutions and values. In fact, some historians have contended that the Meiji ruling clique deliberately exaggerated the hierarchical character of Japanese society during the Tokugawa era in order to further its goal of strengthening the state and increasing its wealth and power.

MEIJI ECONOMICS

With the end of the daimyo domains, the government needed to establish a new system of land ownership that would transform the mass of the rural population from indentured serfs into citizens. To do so, it enacted a land reform program that redefined the domain lands as the private property of the tillers, while compensating the previous owner with government bonds. One reason for the new policy was that the government needed operating revenues. At the time, public funds came mainly from the customs, which were limited by agreement with the foreign powers to 5 percent of the value of the product. To remedy the problem, the Meiji leaders added a new agriculture tax, which was set at an annual rate of 3 percent of the estimated value of the land. The new tax proved to be a lucrative and dependable source of income for the government, but it was quite onerous for the farmers, who previously had paid a fixed percentage of their harvest to the landowner. As a result, in bad years, many taxpaying peasants were unable to pay their taxes and were forced to sell their lands to wealthy neighbors. Eventually, the government reduced the tax to 2.5 per-

cent of the land value. Still, by the end of the century, about 40 percent of all farmers were tenants.

With its budget needs secured, the government turned to the promotion of industry. The basic objective of the Meiji reformers was to create a "rich country and strong state" (*fukoku kyohei*) in order to guarantee Japan's survival against the challenge of Western imperialism. In a broad sense, they very single-mindedly copied the process of development followed by the nations of Western Europe. An advantage, of course, was that a small but growing industrial economy already existed under the Tokugawa. In its early stages, manufacturing in Japan had been the exclusive responsibility of an artisan caste, who often worked for the local daimyo. Eventually, these artisans began to expand their activities, hiring workers and borrowing capital from merchants. By the end of the seventeenth century, substantial manufacturing centers had developed in Japan's growing cities, such as Edo, Kyoto, and Osaka. According to one historian, by 1700 Japan had four cities with a population over 100,000 and was one of the most urbanized societies in the world.

Japan's industrial revolution received a massive stimulus from the Meiji Restoration. The government provided financial subsidies to needy industries, training, foreign advisers, improved transport and communications, and a universal educational system emphasizing applied science. In contrast to China, Japan was able to achieve results with minimum reliance on foreign capital. Although the first railroad—built in 1872—was financed by a loan from Great Britain, future projects were all financed by local funds. The foreign currency holdings came largely from tea and silk, which were exported in significant quantities during the latter half of the nineteenth century.

During the late Meiji era, Japan's industrial sector began to grow. Besides tea and silk, other key industries were weaponry, shipbuilding, and *sake* (Japanese rice wine). From the start, the distinctive feature of the Meiji model was the intimate relationship between government and private business in terms of operations and regulations. Once an individual enterprise or industry was on its feet (or, sometimes, when it had ceased to make a profit), it was turned over entirely to private ownership, although the government often continued to play some role even after its direct involvement in management was terminated. One historian has explained the process:

> It [the Meiji government] pioneered many industrial fields and sponsored the development of others, attempting to cajole businessmen into new and risky kinds of endeavor, helping assemble the necessary capital, forcing weak companies to merge into stronger units, and providing private entrepreneurs with aid and privileges of a sort that would be corrupt favoritism today. All this was in keeping with Tokugawa traditions that business operated under the tolerance and patronage of government. Some of the political leaders even played a dual role in politics and business.[9]

Also noteworthy is the effect that the Meiji reforms had on rural areas. As we have seen, the new land tax provided the government with funds to subsidize the industrial sector, but it imposed severe hardship on the rural population, many of whom abandoned their farms and fled to the cities in search of jobs. This influx of people, in turn, benefited Japanese industry, because it provided an abundant source of cheap labor. As in early modern Europe, the industrial revolution was built on the strong backs of the long-suffering peasantry.

♦ **The Ginza in Downtown Tokyo.** This 1877 woodblock print shows the Ginza in downtown Tokyo, with modern brick buildings, rickshaws, and a horse-drawn streetcar.

The Rules of Good Citizenship in Meiji Japan

After seizing power from the Tokugawa shogunate in 1868, the new Japanese leaders turned their attention to the creation of a new political system that would bring the country into the modern world. After exploring various systems in use in the West, a constitutional commission decided to adopt the system used in imperial Germany because of its paternalistic character. To promote civic virtue and obedience among the citizenry, the government then drafted an imperial rescript that was to be taught to every school-child in the country. The rescript instructed all children to obey their sovereign and place the interests of the community and the state above their own personal desires.

Imperial Rescript on Education of 1890

Know ye, Our subjects:
Our Imperial Ancestors have founded Our Empire on a basis broad and everlasting, and have deeply and firmly implanted virtue. Our subjects ever united in loyalty and filial piety have from generation to generation illustrated the beauty thereof. This is the glory of the fundamental character of Our Empire, and herein also lies the source of Our education. Ye, Our subjects, be filial to your parents, affectionate to your brothers and sisters, as husbands and wives be harmonious, as friends true; bear yourselves in modesty and moderation; extend your benevolence to all; pursue learning and cultivate arts, and thereby develop intellectual faculties and perfect moral powers; furthermore, advance public good and promote common interests; always respect the Constitution and observe the laws; should emergency arise, offer yourselves to the State; and thus guard and maintain the prosperity of Our Imperial Throne coeval with heaven and earth. So shall ye not only be Our good and faithful subjects, but render illustrious the best traditions of your forefathers.

BUILDING A MODERN SOCIAL STRUCTURE

The Meiji reformers also transformed several other feudal institutions. A key focus of their attention was the army. The Sat-Cho reformers had been struck by the weakness of the Japanese armed forces in clashes with the Western powers and embarked on a major program to create a modern military force that could compete in a Darwinist world governed by survival of the fittest. The old feudal army based on the traditional warrior class was abolished, and an imperial army based on universal conscription was formed in 1871. The army also played an important role in Japanese society, becoming a route of upward mobility for many rural males.

Education also underwent major changes. The Meiji leaders recognized the need for universal education including instruction in modern technology, and after a few years of experiment, they adopted the American model of a three-tiered system culminating in a series of universities and specialized institutes. In the meantime, they sent bright students to study abroad and brought foreign specialists to Japan to teach in their new schools. Much of the content of the new system was Western in inspiration. Yet, in a Japanese equivalent to the Chinese "essence versus practical use" concept, its ethical foundations had a distinctly Confucian orientation. The traditional flavor of the new system was demonstrated in the Imperial Rescript on Education, which was displayed in every school in Japan and recited by the students (see the box above).

SPROUTS OF MODERNITY

By the early nineteenth century, the old social order was already showing signs of impending disintegration. Despite the efforts of the Tokugawa, the rigidly hierarchical system was becoming frayed at the edges. Rich merchants were buying their way into the ranks of the samurai, while Japanese of all classes were beginning to abandon their rice fields and move into the growing cities.

Nevertheless, Japanese society in the late Tokugawa era could still be accurately described by two terms, community and hierarchy. The lives of all Japanese were determined by their membership in various social organizations—the family (*ie*), the village, and their social class. At the same time, Japanese society continued to be highly hierarchical. Membership in a particular social class determined a person's occupation and social relationships with others. Women in particular were constrained by the "three obediences" imposed on their sex:

child to father, wife to husband, and widow to son. Husbands could easily obtain a divorce, but wives could not (one regulation issued by the shogunate allegedly decreed that a husband could divorce his spouse if she drank too much tea or talked too much). Marriages were arranged, and the average age at marriage for females was sixteen years. Females did not share inheritance rights with males, and few received any education outside the family.

The Meiji Restoration had a corrosive effect on the traditional social system in Japan. With the abolition of hereditary rights in 1871, the legal restrictions of the past were brought to an end with a single stroke. Special privileges for the aristocracy were abolished, as were the legal restrictions on the *eta* (numbering about 400,000 in the 1870s). Women for the first time were given an opportunity to obtain an education. As the economy shifted from an agricultural to an industrial base, thousands of Japanese began to enter new occupations and establish new social relationships. Western fashions became the rage in elite circles, and the ministers of the first Meiji government were known as the "dancing cabinet" because of their addiction to Western-style ballroom dancing. Young people were increasingly exposed to Western culture and values. A new generation of modern boys and girls (*modan boyu* and *modan garu*) began to imitate the clothing styles, eating habits, and social practices of their European and American counterparts. One colorful example was the introduction of baseball.

But the social changes brought about by the Meiji Restoration also had a less attractive side. Many commoners were ruthlessly exploited in the coal mines and textile mills in the interests of building a "rich country and strong state." Farmers, remarked one Japanese official of the time, "are the fertilizer of the nation." Workers labored up to twenty hours a day, often in conditions of incredible hardship. According to the film series *The Pacific Century*, coal miners employed on a small island in the harbor of Nagasaki worked naked in temperatures up to 130 degrees Fahrenheit. When they tried to escape, they were shot.

Popular resistance to such conditions was not unknown. The makers of *The Pacific Century* pointed out that in many areas villagers became actively involved in the search for a new political culture, in some cases drafting "people's constitutions" to demand increased attention to human rights. Women took part in this process, forming a "Freedom and People's Rights Movement" that demanded female suffrage as early as 1876.

The self-proclaimed transformation of Japan into a "modern society," however, by no means detached the country entirely from its traditional moorings. Although an educational order of 1872 substantially increased the percentage of Japanese women exposed to education (see the box on p. 879), a decade later conservatives began to impose restrictions and bring about a return to more traditional social relationships. The importance of traditional values was underlined by the Imperial Rescript on Education in 1890, which stressed the virtues of filial piety, patriotism, and loyalty to the family and community. Traditional values were given a firm legal basis in the Constitution of 1890, which restricted the franchise to males and defined individual liberties as "subject to the limitations imposed by law," and by the Civil Code of 1898, which de-emphasized individual rights and essentially placed women within the context of their role in the family.

Joining the Imperialist Club

Japan's rapid advance was an impressive achievement and was viewed with proprietary pride and admiration by sympathetic observers in the United States. Unfortunately, the Japanese did not just imitate the domestic policies of their Western mentors, they also emulated the Western approach to foreign affairs. This is perhaps not surprising. In their own minds, the Japanese were particularly vulnerable in the world economic arena. Their territory was small, lacking in resources, and densely populated, and they had no natural outlet for expansion. To observant Japanese, the lessons of history were clear. Western nations had amassed wealth and power not only because of their democratic systems and high level of education, but also because of their colonies, which provided them with sources of raw materials, cheap labor, and markets for their manufactured products.

Traditionally, Japan had not been an expansionist country. As we have seen, the Japanese had generally been satisfied to remain on their home islands and had even deliberately isolated themselves from their neighbors during the Tokugawa era. On the other hand, Japanese pirates were active throughout the region, and at times, notably during the period of Toyotomi Hideyoshi, Japanese militarist elements had attempted to extend Japanese control over the Korean peninsula.

The Japanese began their program of territorial expansion close to home. In 1874, the Japanese claimed compensation from China for fifty-four sailors from the Ryukyu Islands who had been killed by aborigines on the island of Taiwan and sent a Japanese fleet to Taiwan to punish the perpetrators. When the Qing dynasty evaded responsibility for the incident while agreeing to pay an indemnity to Japan to cover the cost of the expedition, it weakened its claim to ownership of the island of Taiwan. Japan was then able to claim suzerainty over the Ryukyu Islands, long tributary to the Chinese Empire. Two years later, Japanese naval pressure forced Korea to open three ports to Japanese commerce.

In the Beginning, We Were the Sun

One aspect of Western thought that the genro leadership in Meiji Japan did not seek to imitate was the idea of sexual equality. Although Japanese women sometimes tried to be "modern" like their male counterparts, Japanese society as a whole continued to treat women differently, as had been the case during the Tokugawa era. In 1911, a young woman named Hiratsuka Raicho founded a journal named Seito (Blue Stockings) to promote the liberation of women in Japan. The goal of the new movement was to encourage women to develop their own latent talents, rather than to demand legal changes in Japanese society. The following document is the proclamation that was issued at the creation of the Seito Society.

Hiratsuka Raicho, Proclamation at the Founding of the Seito Society

In the beginning, woman was truly the sun, and a true being. Now woman is the moon. She lives by others, and shines through the light of others. Her countenance is pale, like a patient.

We must now restore the sun, which has been hidden from us.

"Let the hidden talent, our hidden sun, re-emerge!" This has been our continuous outcry directed inwardly to ourselves. It represents our insatiable longing, our final instinctive feeling encompassing our total beings, unifying all our different sentiments. . . .

Freedom and Liberation! Oftentimes we have heard the term "liberation of women." But what is it then? Are we not seriously misunderstanding the term freedom or liberation? Even if we call the problem the liberation of women, are there not many other issues involved. Assuming that women are freed from external oppression, liberated from constraint, given the so-called higher education, employed in various occupations, given franchise, and provided an opportunity to be independent from the protection of their parents and husbands, and to be freed from the little confinement of their homes, can all of these be called liberation of women? They may provide proper surroundings and opportunities to let us fulfill the true goal of liberation. Yet they remain merely the means, and do not represent our goal or ideals.

However, I am unlike many intellectuals in Japan who suggest that higher education is not necessary for women. Men and women are endowed by nature to have equal faculties. Therefore, it is odd to assume that one of the sexes requires education while the other does not. This may be tolerated in a given country and in a given age, but it is fundamentally a very unsound proposition.

I bemoan the facts that there is only one private college for women in Japan, and that there is no tolerance on man's part to permit entrance of women into many universities maintained for men. However, what benefit is there when the intellectual level of women becomes similar to that of men? Men seek knowledge in order to escape from their lack of wisdom and lack of enlightenment. They want to free themselves. . . . Yet multifarious thought can darken true wisdom, and lead men away from nature. Men who live by playing with knowledge may be called scholars, but they can never be men of wisdom. Nay, on the contrary, they are almost like blind men, who lack the perception to see the things in front of their eyes as what they are. . . .

Now, what is the true liberation which I am seeking? It is none other than to provide an opportunity for women to develop fully their hidden talents and hidden abilities. We must remove all the hindrances that stand in the way of women's development, whether they be external oppression or lack of knowledge. And above and beyond these factors, we must realize that we are the masters in possession of great talents, for we are the bodies which enshrine the great talents. . . .

During the early decades of the nineteenth century, Korea had followed Japan's example and attempted to isolate itself from outside contact except for periodic tribute missions to China. Christian missionaries, mostly Chinese or French, were vigorously persecuted. But Korea's problems were basically internal. In the early 1860s, a peasant revolt, inspired in part by the Taiping Rebellion in China, caused considerable devastation before being crushed in 1864. In succeeding years, the Yi dynasty sought to strengthen the country by returning to traditional values and fending off outside intrusion, but rural poverty and official corruption remained rampant. A U.S. fleet, following the example of Commodore Perry in Japan, sought to open the country in 1871, but was driven off with considerable loss of life.

Korea's most persistent suitor, however, was Japan, which was determined to bring an end to Korea's dependency status with China and modernize it along Japanese lines. In 1876, the two countries signed an agreement opening three treaty ports to Japanese commerce in return for Japanese recognition of Korean independence. During the 1880s, Sino-Japanese rivalry over Korea intensified. China supported conservatives at the Korean court, while Japan promoted a more radical faction that was determined to break loose from lingering Chinese influence. When a new peasant rebellion broke out in Korea in 1894, China and Japan intervened on opposite sides. During the war, the Japanese navy destroyed the Chinese fleet and seized the Manchurian city of Port Arthur (see the box on p. 880). In the Treaty of Shimonoseki, the Manchus were forced to recognize the independence of Korea and cede Taiwan and the Liaodong peninsula with its strategic naval base at Port Arthur to Japan.

Shortly thereafter, under pressure from the European powers, the Japanese returned the Liaodong peninsula to China, but in the early twentieth century, they returned to the offensive. Rivalry with Russia over influence in Korea led to increasingly strained relations between the

Map 23.4 Japanese Overseas Expansion During the Meiji Era.

two countries. In 1904, Japan launched a surprise attack on the Russian naval base at Port Arthur, which Russia had taken from China in 1898. The Japanese armed forces were weaker, but Russia faced difficult logistical problems along its new Trans-Siberian Railway and severe political instability at home. In 1905, after Japanese warships sunk almost the entire Russian fleet off the coast of Korea, the Russians agreed to a humiliating peace, ceding the strategically located Liaodong peninsula back to Japan, as well as southern Sakhalin and the Kurile Islands. Russia also agreed to abandon its political and economic influence in Korea and southern Manchuria, which now came increasingly under Japanese control. The Japanese victory stunned the world, including the colonial peoples of Southeast Asia, who now began to realize that the white race was not necessarily invincible.

During the next few years, the Japanese consolidated their position in northeastern Asia, annexing Korea in 1908 as an integral part of Japan. When the Koreans protested the seizure, Japanese reprisals resulted in thousands of deaths. The United States was the first nation to recognize the annexation in return for Tokyo's declaration of respect for U.S. authority in the Philippines. In 1908, the two countries reached an agreement in which the United States recognized Japanese interests in the region in return for Japanese acceptance of the principles of the Open Door. But mutual suspicion between the two countries was growing, sparked in part by U.S. efforts to restrict immigration from all Asian countries. President Theodore Roosevelt, who mediated the Russo-Japanese War, had aroused the anger of many Japanese by turning down a Japanese demand for reparations from Russia. In turn, some Americans began to fear the rise of a "Yellow Peril" manifested by Japanese expansion in East Asia.

Japanese Culture in an Era of Transition

The wave of Western technology and ideas that entered Japan in the last half of the nineteenth century greatly altered the shape of traditional Japanese culture. Literature in particular was affected as European models eclipsed the repetitive and frivolous tales of the Tokugawa era. Dazzled by this "new" literature, Japanese authors began translating and imitating the imported models. Experimenting with Western verse, Japanese poets were at first influenced primarily by the British, but eventually adopted such French styles as Symbolism, Dadaism, and Surrealism, although some traditional poetry was still composed.

The novel and the short story exhibited the greatest degree of transformation. In the last decades of the

❧ Two Views of the World ❧

During the nineteenth century, China's hierarchical way of looking at the outside world came under severe challenge, not only from European countries avid for new territories in Asia, but also from the rising power of Japan, which accepted the Western view that a colonial empire was the key to national greatness. Japan's first objective was Korea, long a dependency of China, and in 1894 the competition between China and Japan in the peninsula led to war. The following declarations of war by the rulers of the two countries are revealing. Note the Chinese use of the derogatory term wojen (dwarf people) in referring to Japan.

Declaration of War against China

We, by the grace of Heaven, Emperor of Japan, seated on a Throne occupied by the same dynasty from time immemorial, do hereby make proclamation to all our loyal and brave subjects, as follows:— . . .

Korea is an independent state. She was first introduced into the family of nations by the advice and guidance of Japan. It has, however, been China's habit to designate Korea as her dependency, and both openly and secretly to interfere with her domestic affairs. At the time of the recent insurrection in Korea, China despatched troops thither, alleging that her purpose was to afford a succor to her dependent state. We, in virtue of the treaty concluded with Korea in 1882, and looking to possible emergencies, caused a military force to be sent to that country.

Wishing to procure for Korea freedom from the calamity of perpetual disturbance, and thereby to maintain the peace of the East in general, Japan invited China's co-operation for the accomplishment of the object. But China, advancing various pretexts, declined Japan's proposal. China's plain object is to make it uncertain where the responsibility resides of preserving peace and order in Korea, and not only to weaken the position of that state in the family of nations—a position obtained for Korea through Japan's efforts—but also to obscure the significance of the treaties recognizing and confirming that position. Such conduct on the part of China is not only a direct injury to the rights and interests of this Empire, but also a menace to the permanent peace and tranquility of the Orient. Judging from her actions, it must be concluded that China from the beginning has been bent upon sacrificing peace to the attainment of her sinister object.

In this situation, . . . we find it impossible to avoid a formal declaration of war against China. It is our earnest wish that, by the loyalty and valor of our faithful subjects, peace may soon be permanently restored and the glory of the Empire be augmented and completed.

Declaration of War against Japan

Korea has been our tributary for the past two hundred odd years. She has given us tribute all this time, which is a matter known to the world. For the past dozen years or so Korea has been troubled by repeated insurrections and we, in sympathy with our small tributary, have as repeatedly sent succor to her aid, eventually placing a Resident in her capital to protect Korea's interests. In the fourth moon (May) of this year another rebellion was begun in Korea, and the King repeatedly asked again for aid from us to put down the rebellion. We then ordered Li Hung-chang to send troops to Korea; and they having barely reached Yashan the rebels immediately scattered. But the *Wojen*, without any cause whatever, suddenly sent their troops to Korea, and entered Seoul, the capital of Korea, reinforcing them constantly until they have exceeded ten thousand men. In the meantime the Japanese forced the Korean king to change his system of government, showing a disposition every way of bullying the Koreans.

It was found a difficult matter to reason with the *Wojen*. . . . Japan's treaty with Korea was as one country with another; there is no law for sending large armies to bully a country in this way, and compel it to change its system of government. . . .

As Japan has violated the treaties and not observed international laws, and is now running rampant with her false and treacherous actions commencing hostilities herself, and laying herself open to condemnation by the various powers at large, we therefore desire to make it known to the world that we have always followed the paths of philanthropy and perfect justice throughout the whole complications, while the *Wojen*, on the other hand, have broken all the laws of nations and treaties which it passes our patience to bear with. Hence we commanded Li Hung-chang to give strict orders to our various armies to hasten with all speed to root the *Wojen* out of their lairs.

nineteenth century, the "I novel," or fictionalized autobiography, which allowed authors to express their traditional poetic sensitivity in prose, became popular. Relating the author's personal tribulations, these "diaries" greatly appealed to the sensibilities and concerns facing the traditional Japanese of the Meiji era. Another significant genre was the naturalistic novel, patterned on the French tradition of Émile Zola. Naturalist Japanese authors attempted to present society, the human condition, and the realities of war as objectively as possible.

Other aspects of Japanese culture were also affected by the vast social upheaval that struck post-Tokugawa Japan. The Japanese invited technicians, engineers, architects, and artists from Europe and the United States to teach their "modern" skills to a generation of eager students. The Meiji era was a time of massive consumption of Western artistic techniques and styles. Japanese architects and artists created huge buildings of steel and reinforced concrete adorned with Greek columns and cupolas, oil paintings reflecting the European concern with depth perception and shading, and bronze sculptures of secular subjects. All expressed the individual creator's emotional and aesthetic preferences.

Cultural exchange also went the other way, as Japanese arts and crafts, porcelains, textiles, fans, folding screens, and woodblock prints became the vogue in Europe and North America. Japanese art influenced Western painters such as Vincent van Gogh, Edgar Degas, and the American James Whistler who experimented with flatter compositional perspectives and unusual poses. Japanese gardens, with their exquisite attention to the positioning of rocks and falling water, became especially popular in the United States.

After the initial period of mass absorption of Western art, a national reaction occurred at the end of the nineteenth century as many artists returned to pre-Meiji techniques. In 1889, the Tokyo School of Fine Arts (today the Tokyo National University of Fine Arts and Music) was founded to promote traditional Japanese art. Over the next several decades, Japanese art underwent a dynamic resurgence reflecting the nation's emergence as a prosperous and powerful state. Japanese artists fervently searched for a new but authentically Japanese means of expression. While some attempted to synthesize native and foreign techniques, others returned to past artistic traditions for inspiration.

In architecture, Japan's split personality revealed itself most effectively in the Diet building. As the home of the new Japanese parliament, it was supposed to reflect both progress and the nation and culture of Japan. For half a century, conflicting views over the priority of these concepts delayed its construction. After a number of proposals were rejected, the government held a competition in

♦ **A View of Mount Fuji.** During the nineteenth century, the woodblock print continued to be one of the favored forms of illustration in Japan. A very successful example is the series Thirty-six Views of Mount Fuji by Hokusai. Each view of the mountain differs in perspective, season, time of day, and general composition. Several portray Fujiyama in the background, while the foreground depicts everyday Japanese in various trades, as in this print of a fisherman fighting the waves as he seeks to obtain his catch.

1919, but none of the designs won general approval. Finally, in 1936 the government decided on the final design, which followed neither traditional styles nor European architecture of the period.

Woodblock prints continued to be popular with both indigenous and foreign audiences. But the subjects became more diverse, including political cartoons and commissioned depictions of battle scenes for the newspapers.

The Meiji Restoration: A Revolution from Above

Japan's transformation from a feudal, agrarian society to an industrializing, technologically advanced society in little more than half a century has frequently been described by outside observers (if not by the Japanese themselves) in almost miraculous terms. Some historians have questioned this characterization, pointing out that the achievements of the Meiji leaders were spotty. In his book, *Japan's Emergence as a Modern State,* the Canadian historian E. H. Norman lamented that the Meiji Restoration was an "incomplete revolution" because it had not ended the economic and social inequities of feudal society or enabled the common people to participate fully in the governing process. Although the *genro* were enlightened in many respects, they were also despotic and elitist, and the distribution of wealth remained as unequal as it had been under the old system.[10]

These criticisms are persuasive, although they could also be applied to most other societies going through the early stage of industrialization. In any event, from an economic perspective, the Meiji Restoration was certainly one of the great success stories of modern times. Not only did the Meiji leaders put Japan firmly on the path to economic and political development, they also managed to remove the unequal treaty provisions that had been imposed at mid-century. Japanese achievements are especially impressive when compared with the difficulties experienced by China, which was not only unable to realize significant changes in its traditional society, but had not even reached a consensus on the need for doing so. Japan's achievements more closely resemble those of Europe, but whereas the West needed a century and a half to achieve a significant level of industrial development, the Japanese realized it in forty years.

One of the distinctive features of Japan's transition from a traditional to a modern society during the Meiji era was that it took place for the most part without violence or the kind of major social or political revolution that occurred in so many other countries. The Meiji Restoration, which began the process, has been called a "revolution from above," a comprehensive restructuring of Japanese society by its own ruling group.

Technically, of course, the Meiji Restoration was not a revolution, since it was not violent and did not result in the displacement of one ruling class by another. The existing elites undertook to carry out a series of major reforms that transformed society but left their own power intact. In the words of one historian, it was "a kind of amalgamation, in which the enterprising, adaptable or lucky individuals of the old privileged classes [were] for most practical purposes tied up with those individuals of the old submerged classes, who, probably through the same gifts, were able to rise." In that respect, the Meiji Restoration resembles the American Revolution more than the French Revolution; it was a "conservative revolution" that resulted in gradual change rather than rapid and violent change.[11]

The differences between the Japanese response to the West and that of China and many other nations in the region have sparked considerable debate among students of comparative history, and a number of explanations have been offered. Some have argued that Japan's success was partly due to good fortune. Lacking abundant natural resources, it was exposed to less pressure from the West than many of its neighbors. That argument is problematical, however, and would probably not have been accepted by Japanese observers at the time. Nor does it explain why nations under considerably less pressure such as Laos and Nepal did not advance even more quickly. All in all, the "good luck" hypothesis is not very persuasive.

Some explanations have already been suggested in this book. Japan's unique geographical position in Asia was certainly a factor. China, a continental nation with a heterogeneous ethnic composition, was distinguished from its neighbors by its Confucian culture. By contrast, Japan was an island nation, ethnically and linguistically homogeneous, and had never been conquered. Unlike the Chinese or many other peoples in the region, the Japanese had little to fear from cultural change in terms of its effect on their national identity. If Confucian culture, with all its accoutrements, was what defined the Chinese gentleman, his Japanese counterpart, in the familiar image, could discard his sword and kimono and don a modern military uniform or a Western business suit and still feel comfortable in both worlds.

Whatever the case, as the historian W. G. Beasley has noted, the Meiji Restoration was possible because aristocratic and capitalist elements managed to work together in a common effort to bring about national wealth and power. The nature of the Japanese value system, with its emphasis on practicality and military achievement, may also have contributed. Finally, the Meiji also benefited from the fact that the pace of urbanization and commercial and industrial development had already begun to quicken under the Tokugawa. Japan, it was said, was ripe for change, and nothing could have been more suitable as an antidote for the collapsing old system than the Western emphasis on wealth and power. It was a classic example of challenge and response.

The final product was an amalgam of old and new, native and foreign, forming a new civilization that was still uniquely Japanese. There were some undesirable consequences, however. Because Meiji politics was essentially despotic, Japanese leaders were able to fuse key traditional elements such as the warrior ethic and the concept of feudal loyalty with the dynamics of modern industrial capitalism to create a state totally dedicated to the possession of material wealth and national power. This combination of *kokutai* and capitalism, which one scholar has described as a form of "Asian fascism," was highly effective, but explosive in its international manifestation. Like modern Germany, which also entered the industrial age directly from feudalism, Japan eventually engaged in a policy of repression at home and expansion abroad in order to achieve its national objectives. In Japan, as in Germany, it took defeat in war to disconnect the drive for national development from the feudal ethic and bring about the transformation to a pluralistic society dedicated to living in peace and cooperation with its neighbors. Whether that transformation has been completed in Japan only the future will tell.

Conclusion

Few areas of the world resisted the Western incursion as stubbornly and effectively as East Asia. Although military, political, and economic pressure by the European powers was relatively intense during this era, two of the main states in the area were able to retain their independence, while the third—Korea—was temporarily absorbed by one of its larger neighbors. Why the Chinese and the Japanese were able to prevent a total political and military takeover by foreign powers is an interesting question. Certainly, a key reason was that both had a long history as well-defined states with a strong sense of national community and territorial cohesion. Although China had frequently been conquered, it had retained its sense of unique culture and identity. Geography, too, was in its favor. As a continental nation, China was able to survive partly because of its sheer size, while Japan possessed the advantage of an island location.

Even more striking, however, is the different way in which the two states attempted to deal with the challenge. While the Japanese chose to face the problem in a pragmatic manner, borrowing foreign ideas and institutions that appeared to be of value and at the same time not in conflict with traditional attitudes and customs, China agonized over the issue for half a century, while conservative elements fought a desperate battle to retain a maximum of the traditional heritage intact.

This chapter has discussed some of the possible reasons for those differences. In retrospect, it is difficult to avoid the conclusion that the Japanese approach was the more effective one. While the Meiji leaders were able to set in motion an orderly transition from a traditional to an advanced society, in China the old system collapsed in disorder, leaving chaotic conditions that were still not rectified a generation later. China would pay a heavy price for its failure to respond coherently to the challenge.

But the Japanese "revolution from above" was by no means an unalloyed success. Ambitious efforts by Japanese leaders to carve out a share in the spoils of empire led to escalating conflict with China as well as with rival Western powers, and in the early 1940s to global war. We will deal with that issue in Chapter 26. Meanwhile, in Europe, a combination of old rivalries and the effects of the Industrial Revolution were leading to a bitter regional conflict that eventually engulfed the entire world.

CHAPTER NOTES

1. From Hosea Ballou Morse, *The International Relations of the Chinese Empire* (Shanghai and London, 1910–1918), 2:622, quoted in Jonathan D. Spence, *The Search for Modern China* (New York, 1990), p. 154.
2. Quoted in Ssu-yu Teng and John K. Fairbank, eds., *China's Response to the West: A Documentary Survey, 1839–1923* (New York, 1970), p. 140
3. Ibid., p. 167.
4. Quoted in William Theodore de Bary et al., eds., *Sources of Chinese Tradition* (New York, 1963), p. 733.
5. Ibid., p. 472.
6. Morse, *International Relations of the Chinese Empire*, 3:126.
7. Quoted in Teng and Fairbank, *China's Response to the West*, p. 263.

8. Quoted in John W. Hall, et al., eds., *The Cambridge History of Japan* (Cambridge, 1989), 6:278.
9. John K. Fairbank, Albert M. Craig, and Edwin O. Reischauer, *East Asia: Tradition and Transformation* (Boston, 1973), p. 514.
10. Quoted in John W. Dower, ed., *The Origins of the Modern Japanese State: Selected Writings of E. H. Norman* (New York, 1975), p. 13.
11. Crane Brinton, *The Anatomy of Revolution* (New York, 1965), quoted in W. G. Beasley, *The Meiji Restoration* (Stanford, Calif., 1972), p. 423.

SUGGESTED READINGS

For a general overview of this period of East Asian history, see C. Schirokauer, *Modern China and Japan: A Brief History* (New York, 1982) and J. K. Fairbank, A. M. Craig, and E. O. Reischauer, *East Asia: Tradition and Transformation* (Boston, 1973). See also J. Spence's highly stimulating *The Search for Modern China* (New York, 1990); *The Cambridge History of China*, vols. 10–11 (Cambridge, 1978–80), dealing with the Qing period; and *The Cambridge History of Japan*, vols. 5–6 (Cambridge, 1988).

On the Western intrusion into China during the nineteenth century, see the classic work by J. K. Fairbank, *Trade and Diplomacy on the China Coast* (Cambridge, 1953), and F. Wakeman, *Strangers at the Gate: Social Disorder in South China, 1839–1861* (Berkeley, Calif., 1966). On the Opium War, see A. Waley, *The Opium War through Chinese Eyes* (London, 1958), and P. W. Fay, *The Opium War, 1840–1842* (Chapel Hill, N.C., 1975). On the Taiping Rebellion, see F. Michael and C. Chung-li, *The Taiping Rebellion: History and Documents*, 3 vols. (Seattle, 1966–1971).

There are a number of important works on the final decades of the Chinese Empire. For a general overview, see F. Wakeman, Jr., *The Fall of Imperial China* (New York, 1975). For economic developments, see A. Feuerwerker's classic *China's Early Industrialization: Sheng Hsuan-huai and Mandarin Enterprise* (Cambridge, 1958). China's response to the Western challenge is chronicled in S. Teng and J. K. Fairbank, eds., *China's Response to the West: A Documentary Survey, 1839–1923* (New York, 1970).

On the 1911 Revolution, see M. C. Wright, ed., *China in Revolution: The First Phase, 1900–1913* (New Haven, Conn., 1968). Sun Yat-sen's early career is explored in H. Z. Schiffren, *Sun Yat-sen and the Origins of the Chinese Revolution* (Berkeley, Calif., 1970). On the

Boxer Rebellion, the definitive study is J. Esherick, *The Origins of the Boxer Uprising* (Berkeley, Calif., 1987).

For a recent survey of modern Japanese history, see J. Hunter, *The Emergence of Modern Japan: An Introductory History since 1853* (London, 1989). For a provocative treatment in a comparative context, see A. M. Craig, ed., *Japan: A Comparative View* (Princeton, N.J., 1979). See also J. W. Dower, ed., *The Origins of the Modern Japanese State: Selected Writings of E. H. Norman* (New York, 1975).

The Meiji period is discussed in W. G. Beasley, *The Meiji Restoration* (Stanford, Calif., 1972). An earlier and more controversial view is E. H. Norman, *Japan's Emergence as a Modern State: Political and Economic Problems of the Meiji Period* (New York, 1940). See also C. Gluck, *Japan's Modern Myths: Ideology in the Late Meiji Period* (Princeton, N.J., 1985), and C. Totman, *The Collapse of the Tokugawa Bakufu, 1862–1868* (Honolulu, 1980).

On the economy, see R. Smethurst, *Agricultural Development and Tenancy Disputes in Japan, 1870–1940* (Princeton, N.J., 1986), and G. C. Allen, *A Short Economic History of Japan, 1867–1937* (London, 1972). Social developments are examined in R. Dore, ed., *Aspects of Social Change in Modern Japan* (Princeton, N.J., 1967). The rise of the modern Japanese army is chronicled in R. F. Hackett, *Yamagata Aritomo and the Rise of Meiji Japan* (Cambridge, 1971). For the best introduction to Japanese art, consult P. Mason, *History of Japanese Art* (New York, 1993). See also J. S. Baker's concise *Japanese Art* (London, 1984).

On Japan's emergence as an imperialist power, see A. Iriye, *Pacific Estrangement: Japanese and American Expansion, 1897–1911* (Cambridge, 1972); M. R. Peattie and R. Myers, *The Japanese Colonial Empire, 1895–1945* (Princeton, N.J., 1984); and M. B. Jansen, *Japan and Its World: Two Centuries of Change* (Princeton, N.J., 1980).

CHAPTER
24

The Beginning of the Twentieth-Century Crisis: War and Revolution

On July 1, 1916, British and French infantry forces attacked German defensive lines along a twenty-five-mile front near the Somme River in France. Each soldier carried almost seventy pounds of equipment, making it "impossible to move much quicker than a slow walk." German machine guns soon opened fire: "We were able to see our comrades move forward in an attempt to cross No-Man's Land, only to be mown down like meadow grass," recalled one British soldier. "I felt sick at the sight of this carnage and remember weeping." In one day more than 21,000 British soldiers died. After six months of fighting, the British had advanced five miles; one million British, French, and German soldiers had been killed or wounded.

World War I (1914–1918) was the defining event of the twentieth century. It devastated the prewar economic, social, and political order of Europe while its uncertain outcome served to prepare the way for an even more destructive war. Overwhelmed by the scale of its battles, the extent of its casualties, and the effects of its impact on all facets of life, contemporaries referred to it simply as the "Great War."

The Great War was all the more disturbing to Europeans because it came after a period that many believed to have been an age of progress. There had been international crises before 1914, but somehow Europeans had managed to avoid serious and prolonged military confrontations. Material prosperity and a fervid belief in scientific and technological progress had convinced many people that the world stood on the verge of creat-

Assassination of Archduke Francis Ferdinand · Battle of Verdun · Paris Peace Conference · Treaty of Locarno

Bolshevik Revolution ·· Lenin adopts New Economic Policy · Stalin establishes dictatorship in Russia

··········· Civil war in Russia

United States enters the war · Dawes Plan · Germany enters League of Nations · Great Depression begins

ing the utopia that humans had dreamed of for centuries. The historian Arnold Toynbee expressed what the pre–World War I era had meant to his generation:

> [it was expected] that life throughout the World would become more rational, more humane, and more democratic and that, slowly, but surely, political democracy would produce greater social justice. We had also expected that the progress of science and technology would make mankind richer, and that this increasing wealth would gradually spread from a minority to a majority. We had expected that all this would happen peacefully. In fact we thought that mankind's course was set for an earthly paradise.[1]

After 1918, it was no longer possible to maintain naive illusions about the progress of Western civilization. As World War I was followed by revolutionary upheavals, the mass murder machines of totalitarian regimes, and the destructiveness of World War II, it became all too apparent that instead of a utopia, Western civilization had become a nightmare. World War I and the revolutions it spawned can properly be seen as the first stage in the crisis of the twentieth century.

The Road to World War I

On June 28, 1914, the heir to the Austrian throne, the Archduke Francis Ferdinand, was assassinated in the Bosnian city of Sarajevo. Although this event precipitated the confrontation between Austria and Serbia that led to World War I, there were also long-range, underlying forces that were propelling Europeans toward armed conflict.

Nationalism and Internal Dissent

In the first half of the nineteenth century, liberals had maintained that the organization of European states along national lines would lead to a peaceful Europe based on a sense of international fraternity. They had been very wrong. The system of nation-states that had emerged in Europe in the last half of the nineteenth century led not to cooperation but to competition. Rivalries over colonial and commercial interests intensified during an era of frenzied imperialist expansion while the division of Europe's great powers into two loose alliances (Germany, Austria, and Italy and France, Great Britain, and Russia) only added to the tensions. The series of crises that tested these alliances in the 1900s and early 1910s had left European states with a dangerous lesson. Those governments that had exercised restraint in order to avoid war wound up being publicly humiliated, while those that went to the brink of war to maintain their national interests had often been praised for having preserved national honor. In either case, by 1914, the major European states had come to believe that their allies were important and that their security depended on supporting those allies, even when they took foolish risks.

Diplomacy based on brinkmanship was especially frightening in view of the nature of the European state system. Each nation-state regarded itself as sovereign, subject to no higher interest or authority. Each state was motivated by its own self-interest and success. Such attitudes made war an ever-present possibility, particularly since most statesmen considered war an acceptable way to preserve the power of their national states.

The growth of nationalism in the nineteenth century had yet another serious consequence. Not all ethnic groups had achieved the goal of nationhood. Slavic minorities in the Balkans and the polyglot Habsburg empire, for example, still dreamed of creating their own national states. So did the Irish in the British Empire and the Poles in the Russian Empire.

National aspirations, however, were not the only source of internal strife at the beginning of the twentieth century. Socialist labor movements had grown more powerful and were increasingly inclined to use strikes, even violent ones, to achieve their goals. Some conservative leaders, alarmed at the increase in labor strife and class division, even feared that European nations were on the verge of revolution. Did these statesmen opt for war in 1914 because they believed that "prosecuting an active foreign policy," as some Austrian leaders expressed it, would smother "internal troubles"? Some historians have argued that the desire to suppress internal disorder may have encouraged some leaders to take the plunge into war in 1914.

Militarism

The growth of large mass armies after 1900 not only heightened the existing tensions in Europe, but made it inevitable that if war did come it would be highly destructive. Conscription had been established as a regular practice in most Western countries before 1914 (the United States and Britain were major exceptions). European military machines had doubled in size between 1890 and 1914. With its 1.3 million men, the Russian

Map 24.1 Europe in 1914.

army had grown to be the largest, but the French and Germans were not far behind with 900,000 each. The British, Italian, and Austrian armies numbered between 250,000 and 500,000 soldiers.

Militarism, however, involved more than just large armies. As armies grew, so too did the influence of military leaders who drew up vast and complex plans for quickly mobilizing millions of men and enormous quantities of supplies in the event of war. Fearful that changing these plans would cause chaos in the armed forces, military leaders insisted that the plans could not be altered. In the crises during the summer of 1914, the generals' lack of flexibility forced European political leaders to make decisions for military instead of political reasons.

The Outbreak of War: The Summer of 1914

Militarism, nationalism, and the desire to stifle internal dissent may all have played a role in the coming of World War I, but the decisions made by European leaders in the summer of 1914 directly precipitated the conflict. It was another crisis in the Balkans that forced this predicament upon European statesmen.

As we have seen, states in southeastern Europe had struggled to free themselves from Ottoman rule in the course of the nineteenth and early twentieth centuries. But the rivalry between Austria-Hungary and Russia for domination of these new states created serious tensions in the region. By 1914, Serbia, supported by Russia, was determined to create a large, independent Slavic state in the Balkans, while Austria, which had its own Slavic minorities to contend with, was equally set on preventing that possibility. Many Europeans perceived the inherent dangers in this combination of Serbian ambition bolstered by Russian hatred of Austria and Austrian conviction that Serbia's success would mean the end of its empire. The British ambassador to Vienna wrote in 1913:

> Serbia will some day set Europe by the ears, and bring about a universal war on the Continent. . . . I cannot tell you how exasperated people are getting here at the continual worry which that little country causes to Austria under encouragement from Russia. . . . It will be lucky if Europe succeeds in avoiding war as a result of the present crisis. The next time a Serbian crisis arises . . . , I feel sure that Austria-Hungary will refuse to admit of any Russian interference in the dispute and that she will proceed to settle her differences with her little neighbor by herself.[2]

It was against this backdrop of mutual distrust and hatred between Austria-Hungary and Russia, on the one hand, and Austria-Hungary and Serbia, on the other, that the events of the summer of 1914 were played out.

The assassination of the Austrian Archduke Francis Ferdinand and his wife Sophia on June 28, 1914, was carried out by a Bosnian activist who worked for the Black Hand, a Serbian terrorist organization dedicated to the creation of a pan-Slavic kingdom. Although the Austrian government did not know whether the Serbian government had been directly involved in the archduke's assassination, it saw an opportunity to "render Serbia innocuous once and for all by a display of force," as the Austrian foreign minister put it. Fearful of Russian intervention on Serbia's behalf, Austrian leaders sought the backing of their German allies. Emperor William II and his chancellor gave their assurance that Austria-Hungary could rely on Germany's "full support," even if "matters went to the length of a war between Austria-Hungary and Russia."

Strengthened by German support, Austrian leaders issued an ultimatum to Serbia on July 23 in which they made such extreme demands that Serbia had little choice but to reject some of them in order to preserve its sovereignty. Austria then declared war on Serbia on July 28. Still smarting from its humiliation in the Bosnian crisis of 1908, Russia was determined to support Serbia's cause. On July 28, Tsar Nicholas II ordered partial mobilization of the Russian army against Austria. At this point, the rigidity of the military war plans played havoc with diplomatic and political decisions. The Russian General Staff informed the tsar that their mobilization plans were based on a war against both Germany and Austria simultaneously. They could not execute partial mobilization without creating chaos in the army. Consequently, the Russian government ordered full mobilization of the Russian army on July 29, knowing that the Germans would consider this an act of war against them (see the box on p. 890). Germany responded to Russian mobilization with its own ultimatum that the Russians must halt their mobilization within twelve hours. When the Russians ignored it, Germany declared war on Russia on August 1.

At this stage of the conflict, German war plans determined whether or not France would become involved in the war. Under the guidance of General Alfred von Schlieffen, chief of staff from 1891 to 1905, the German General Staff had devised a military plan based on the assumption of a two-front war with France and Russia, because the two powers had formed a military alliance in 1894. The Schlieffen Plan called for a minimal troop deployment against Russia while most of the German army would make a rapid invasion of France before Russia could become effective in the east or before the British could cross the English Channel to help France. This meant invading France by advancing through neutral

❧ "You Have to Bear the Responsibility for War or Peace" ❧

After Austria declared war on Serbia on July 28, 1914, Russian support of Serbia and German support of Austria threatened to escalate the conflict in the Balkans into a wider war. As we can see in these last-minute telegrams between the Russians and Germans, neither side was able to accept the other's line of reasoning.

Communications between Berlin and St. Petersburg on the Eve of World War I

Emperor William II to Tsar Nicholas II, July 28, 10:45 P.M.

I have heard with the greatest anxiety of the impression which is caused by the action of Austria-Hungary against Servia [Serbia]. The inscrupulous agitation which has been going on for years in Servia, has led to the revolting crime of which Archduke Franz Ferdinand has become a victim. The spirit which made the Servians murder their own King and his consort still dominates that country. Doubtless You will agree with me that both of us, You as well as I, and all other sovereigns, have a common interest to insist that all those who are responsible for this horrible murder shall suffer their deserved punishment. . . .

Your most sincere and devoted friend and cousin

(Signed) WILHELM

Tsar Nicholas II to Emperor William II, July 29, 1 P.M.

I am glad that you are back in Germany. In this serious moment I ask You earnestly to help me. An ignominious war has been declared against a weak country and in Russia the indignation which I full share is tremendous. I fear that very soon I shall be unable to resist the pressure exercised upon me and that I shall be forced to take measures which will lead to war. To prevent a calamity as a European war would be, I urge You in the name of our old friendship to do all in Your power to restrain Your ally from going too far.

(Signed) NICOLAS

Emperor William II to Tsar Nicholas II, July 29, 6:30 P.M.

I have received Your telegram and I share Your desire for the conservation of peace. However: I cannot—as I told You in my first telegram—consider the action of Austria-Hungary as an "ignominious war." Austria-Hungary knows from experience that the promises of Servia as long as they are merely on paper are entirely unreliable. . . . I believe that a direct understanding is possible and desirable between Your Government and Vienna, an understanding which—as I have already telegraphed You—my Government endeavors to aid with all possible effort. Naturally military measures by Russia, which might be construed as a menace by Austria-Hungary, would accelerate a calamity which both of us desire to avoid and would undermine my position as mediator which—upon Your appeal to my friendship and aid—I willingly accepted.

(Signed) WILHELM

Emperor William II to Tsar Nicholas II, July 30, 1 A.M.

My Ambassador has instructions to direct the attention of Your Government to the dangers and serious consequences of a mobilization. I have told You the same in my last telegram. Austria-Hungary has mobilized only against Servia, and only a part of her army. If Russia, as seems to be the case, according to Your advice and that of Your Government, mobilizes against Austria-Hungary, the part of the mediator with which You have entrusted me in such friendly manner and which I have accepted upon Your express desire, is threatened if not made impossible. The entire weight of decision now rests upon Your shoulders, You have to bear the responsibility for war or peace.

(Signed) WILHELM

German Chancellor to German Ambassador at St. Petersburg, July 31, URGENT

In spite of negotiations still pending and although we have up to this hour made no preparations for mobilization, Russia has mobilized her entire army and navy, hence also against us. On account of these Russian measures, we have been forced, for the safety of the country, to proclaim the threatening state of war, which does not yet imply mobilization. Mobilization, however, is bound to follow if Russia does not stop every measure of war against us and against Austria-Hungary within 12 hours, and notifies us definitely to this effect. Please to communicate this at once to M. Sazonoff and wire hour of communication.

Belgium with its level coastal plain where the army could move faster than on the rougher terrain to the southeast. After the planned quick defeat of the French, the German army expected to redeploy to the east against Russia. Under the Schlieffen Plan, Germany could not mobilize its troops solely against Russia and therefore declared war on France on August 3 after it had issued an ultimatum to Belgium on August 2 demanding the right of German troops to pass through Belgian territory. On August 4, Great Britain declared war on Germany, officially over this violation of Belgian neutrality, but in fact over the British desire to maintain their world power. As one British diplomat argued, if Germany and Austria were to win the war, "what would be the position of a friendless England?" By August 4, all the great powers of Europe were at war.

The War

Before 1914, many political leaders had become convinced that war involved so many political and economic risks that it was not worth fighting. Others had believed that "rational" diplomats could control any situation and prevent the outbreak of war. At the beginning of August 1914, both of these prewar illusions were shattered, but the new illusions that replaced them soon proved to be equally foolish.

1914–1915: Illusions and Stalemate

Europeans went to war in 1914 with remarkable enthusiasm (see the box on p. 892). Government propaganda had been successful in stirring up national antagonisms before the war. Now in August of 1914, the urgent pleas of governments for defense against aggressors fell on receptive ears in every belligerent nation. Most people seemed genuinely convinced that their nation's cause was just. A new set of illusions also fed the enthusiasm for war. In August 1914, almost everyone believed that the war would be over in a few weeks. People were reminded that all European wars since 1815 had, in fact, ended in a matter of weeks, conveniently overlooking the American Civil War (1861–1865), which was the "real prototype" for World War I. Both the soldiers who exuberantly boarded the trains for the war front in August 1914 and the jubilant citizens who bombarded them with flowers as they departed believed that the warriors would be home by Christmas.

German hopes for a quick end to the war rested upon a military gamble. The Schlieffen Plan had called for the

◆ **The Excitement of War.** World War I was greeted with incredible enthusiasm. Each of the major belligerents was convinced of the rightness of its cause. Everywhere in Europe, jubilant civilians sent their troops off to war with joyous fervor. Their belief that the soldiers would be home by Christmas proved to be a pathetic illusion.

German army to make a vast encircling movement through Belgium into northern France that would sweep around Paris and encircle most of the French army. But the German advance was halted only twenty miles from Paris at the First Battle of the Marne (September 6–10). The war quickly turned into a stalemate as neither the Germans nor the French could dislodge the other from the trenches they had begun to dig for shelter. Two lines of trenches soon extended from the English Channel to the frontiers of Switzerland. The Western Front had become bogged down in a trench warfare that kept both sides immobilized in virtually the same positions for four years.

In contrast to the west, the war in the east was marked by much more mobility, although the cost in lives was equally enormous. At the beginning of the war, the Russian army moved into eastern Germany but was decisively defeated at the Battles of Tannenberg on August 30 and the Masurian Lakes on September 15. The Russians were no longer a threat to German territory.

The Austrians, Germany's allies, fared less well initially. They had been defeated by the Russians in Galicia and thrown out of Serbia as well. To make matters worse, the Italians betrayed the Germans and Austrians and entered the war on the Allied side by attacking Austria in

The incredible outpouring of patriotic enthusiasm that greeted the declaration of war at the beginning of August 1914 demonstrated the power that nationalistic feeling had attained at the beginning of the twentieth century. Many Europeans seemingly believed that the war had given them a higher purpose, a renewed dedication to the greatness of their nation. This selection is taken from the autobiography of Stefan Zweig, an Austrian writer who captured well the orgiastic celebration of war in Vienna in 1914.

Stefan Zweig, The World of Yesterday

The next morning I was in Austria. In every station placards had been put up announcing general mobilization. The trains were filled with fresh recruits, banners were flying, music sounded, and in Vienna I found the entire city in a tumult. . . . There were parades in the street, flags, ribbons, and music burst forth everywhere, young recruits were marching triumphantly, their faces lighting up at the cheering. . . .

And to be truthful, I must acknowledge that there was a majestic, rapturous, and even seductive something in this first outbreak of the people from which one could escape only with difficulty. And in spite of all my hatred and aversion for war, I should not like to have missed the memory of those days. As never before, thousands and hundreds of thousands felt what they should have felt in peace time, that they belonged together. A city of two million, a country of nearly fifty million, in that hour felt that they were participating in world history, in a moment which would never recur, and that each one was called upon to cast his infini-tesimal self into the glowing mass, there to be purified of all selfishness. All differences of class, rank, and language were flooded over at that moment by the rushing feeling of fraternity. Strangers spoke to one another in the streets, people who had avoided each other for years shook hands, everywhere one saw excited faces. Each individual experienced an exaltation of his ego, he was no longer the isolated person of former times, he had been incorporated into the mass, he was part of the people, and his person, his hitherto unnoticed person, had been given meaning. . . .

What did the great mass know of war in 1914, after nearly half a century of peace? They did not know war, they had hardly given it a thought. It had become legendary, and distance had made it seem romantic and heroic. They still saw it in the perspective of their school readers and of paintings in museums; brilliant cavalry attacks in glittering uniforms, the fatal shot always straight through the heart, the entire campaign a resounding march of victory—"We'll be home at Christmas," the recruits shouted laughingly to their mothers in August of 1914. . . . A rapid excursion into the romantic, a wild, manly adventure—that is how the war of 1914 was painted in the imagination of the simple man, and the young people were honestly afraid that they might miss this most wonderful and exciting experience of their lives; that is why they hurried and thronged to the colors, and that is why they shouted and sang in the trains that carried them to the slaughter; wildly and feverishly the red wave of blood coursed through the veins of the entire nation.

May 1915. By this time, the Germans had come to the aid of the Austrians. A German-Austrian army defeated and routed the Russian army in Galicia and pushed the Russians back three hundred miles into their own territory. Russian casualties stood at 2.5 million killed, captured, or wounded; the Russians had almost been knocked out of the war. Buoyed by their success, the Germans and Austrians, joined by the Bulgarians in September 1915, attacked and eliminated Serbia from the war.

1916–1917: The Great Slaughter

The successes in the east enabled the Germans to move back to the offensive in the west. The early trenches dug in 1914 had by now become elaborate systems of defense. Both lines of trenches were protected by barbed wire entanglements three to five feet high and thirty yards wide, concrete machine-gun nests, and mortar batteries, supported further back by heavy artillery. Troops lived in holes in the ground, separated from each other by a "no man's land."

The unexpected development of trench warfare baffled military leaders who had been trained to fight wars of movement and maneuver. The only plan generals could devise was to attempt a breakthrough by throwing masses of men against enemy lines that had first been battered by artillery barrages. Once the decisive breakthrough had been achieved, they thought, they could then return to the war of movement that they knew best. Periodically, the high command on either side would order an offensive that would begin with an artillery barrage to flatten the enemy's barbed wire and leave the enemy in a state of shock. After "softening up" the enemy in this fashion, a mass of soldiers would climb out of their trenches with fixed bayonets and hope to work their way toward the enemy trenches. The attacks rarely worked, as the machine gun put hordes of men advancing unprotected across open fields at a severe disadvantage. In 1916 and 1917, millions of young men were sacrificed in the search for the elusive breakthrough. In ten months at Verdun, 700,000 men lost their lives over a few miles of terrain.

Warfare in the trenches of the Western Front produced unimaginable horrors (see the box on p. 894). Battlefields were hellish landscapes of barbed wire, shell holes, mud, and injured and dying men. The introduction of poison gas in 1915 produced new forms of injuries, as one British writer described them:

> I wish those people who write so glibly about this being a holy war could see a case of mustard gas . . . could see the poor things burnt and blistered all over with great mustard-coloured suppurating blisters with blind eyes all sticky . . . and stuck together, and always fighting for breath, with voices a mere whisper, saying that their throats are closing and they know they will choke.[3]

Soldiers in the trenches also lived with the persistent presence of death. Since combat went on for months, soldiers had to carry on in the midst of countless bodies of dead men or the remains of men dismembered by artillery barrages. Many soldiers remembered the stench of decomposing bodies and the swarms of rats that grew fat in the trenches.

The Widening of the War

As another response to the stalemate on the Western Front, both sides looked for new allies who might provide a winning advantage. The Ottoman Empire had already come into the war on Germany's side in August 1914. Russia, Great Britain, and France declared war on the Ottoman Empire in November. Although the Allies attempted to open a Balkan front by landing forces at Gallipoli, southwest of Constantinople, in April 1915, the entry of Bulgaria into the war on the side of the Central Powers (as Germany, Austria-Hungary, and the Ottoman Empire were called) and a disastrous campaign at Gallipoli caused them to withdraw. The Italians, as we have seen, also entered the war on the Allied side after France and Britain promised to further their acquisition of Austrian territory. In the long run, however, Italian military incompetence forced the Allies to come to the assistance of Italy.

By 1917, the war that had originated in Europe had truly become a world conflict. In the Middle East, a British officer who came to be known as Lawrence of Arabia (1888–1935) incited Arab princes to revolt against their Ottoman overlords in 1917. In 1918, British forces from Egypt destroyed the rest of the Ottoman Empire in the Middle East. For their Middle East campaigns, the British mobilized forces from India, Australia, and New Zealand. The Allies also took advantage of Germany's preoccupations in Europe and lack of naval strength to seize German colonies in the rest of the world. Japan seized a number of German-held islands in the Pacific while Australia took over German New Guinea.

Most important to the Allied cause was the entry of the United States into the war. At first, the United States tried to remain neutral in the Great War, but that became more difficult as the war dragged on. The immediate cause of American involvement grew out of the naval conflict between Germany and Great Britain. Britain used its superior naval power to maximum effect by imposing a naval blockade on Germany. Germany retaliated with a counterblockade enforced by the use of unrestricted submarine warfare. Strong American protests over the German sinking of passenger liners, especially

◆ **The Horrors of War.** The slaughter of millions of men in the trenches of World War I created unimaginable horrors for the participants. For the sake of survival, many soldiers learned to harden themselves against the stench of decomposing bodies and the sight of bodies horribly dismembered by artillery barrages.

The Reality of War: Trench Warfare

The romantic illusion about the excitement and adventure of war that filled the minds of so many young men who marched off to battle quickly disintegrated after a short time in the trenches on the Western Front. This description of trench warfare is taken from the most famous novel that emerged from World War I, Erich Maria Remarque's All Quiet on the Western Front, *written in 1929. Remarque had fought in the trenches in France.*

Erich Maria Remarque,
All Quiet on the Western Front

We wake up in the middle of the night. The earth booms. Heavy fire is falling on us. We crouch into corners. We distinguish shells of every calibre.

Each man lays hold of his things and looks again every minute to reassure himself that they are still there. The dug-out heaves, the night roars and flashes. We look at each other in the momentary flashes of light, and with pale faces and pressed lips shake our heads.

Every man is aware of the heavy shells tearing down the parapet, rooting up the embankment and demolishing the upper layers of concrete. . . . Already by morning a few of the recruits are green and vomiting. They are too inexperienced. . . .

The bombardment does not diminish. It is falling in the rear too. As far as one can see it spouts fountains of mud and iron. A wide belt is being raked.

The attack does not come, but the bombardment continues. Slowly we become mute. Hardly a man speaks. We cannot make ourselves understood.

Our trench is almost gone. At many places it is only eighteen inches high, it is broken by holes, and craters, and mountains of earth. A shell lands square in front of our post. At once it is dark. We are buried and must dig ourselves out. . . .

Towards morning, while it is still dark, there is some excitement. Through the entrance rushes in a swarm of fleeing rats that try to storm the walls. Torches light up the confusion. Everyone yells and curses and slaughters. The madness and despair of many hours unloads itself in this outburst. Faces are distorted, arms strike out, the beasts scream; we just stop in time to avoid attacking one another. . . .

Suddenly it howls and flashes terrifically, the dug-out cracks in all its joints under a direct hit, fortunately only a light one that the concrete blocks are able to withstand. It rings metallically, the walls reel, rifles, helmets, earth, mud, and dust fly everywhere. Sulphur fumes pour in. . . . The recruit starts to rave again and two others follow suit. One jumps up and rushes out, we have trouble with the other two. I start after the one who escapes and wonder whether to shoot him in the leg—then it shrieks again, I fling myself down and when I stand up the wall of the trench is plastered with smoking splinters, lumps of flesh, and bits of uniform. I scramble back.

The first recruit seems actually to have gone insane. He butts his head against the wall like a goat. We must try tonight to take him to the rear. Meanwhile we bind him, but so that in case of attack he can be released.

Suddenly the nearer explosions cease. The shelling continues but it has lifted and falls behind us, our trench is free. We seize the hand-grenades, pitch them out in front of the dug-out and jump after them. The bombardment has stopped and a heavy barrage now falls behind us. The attack has come.

No one would believe that in this howling waste there could still be men; but steel helmets now appear on all sides out of the trench, and fifty yards from us a machine-gun is already in position and barking.

The wire-entanglements are torn to pieces. Yet they offer some obstacle. We see the storm-troops coming. Our artillery opens fire. Machine-guns rattle, rifles crack. The charge works its way across. Haie and Kropp begin with the hand-grenades. They throw as fast as they can, others pass them, the handles with the strings already pulled. Haie throws seventy-five yards, Kropp sixty, it has been measured, the distance is important. The enemy as they run cannot do much before they are within forty yards.

We recognize the distorted faces, the smooth helmets: they are French. They have already suffered heavily when they reach the remnants of the barbed-wire entanglements. A whole line has gone down before our machine-guns; then we have a lot of stoppages and they come nearer.

I see one of them, his face upturned, fall into a wire cradle. His body collapses, his hands remain suspended as though he were praying. Then his body drops clean away and only his hands with the stumps of his arms, shot off, now hang in the wire.

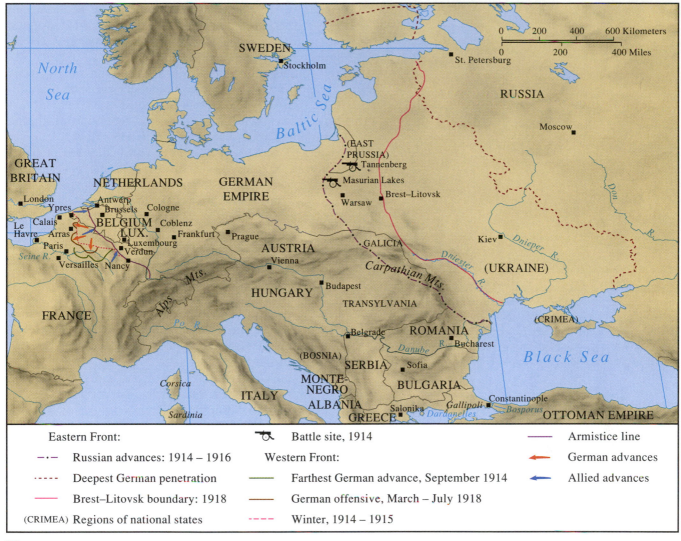

✦ Map 24.2   World War I, 1914–1918.

the British ship *Lusitania* on May 7, 1915, where over a hundred Americans lost their lives, forced the German government to suspend unrestricted submarine warfare in September 1915 to avoid further antagonizing the Americans.

In January 1917, however, eager to break the deadlock in the war, the Germans decided on another military gamble by returning to unrestricted submarine warfare. German naval officers convinced Emperor William II that the use of unrestricted submarine warfare could starve the British into submission within five months, certainly before the Americans could act. The return to unrestricted submarine warfare brought the United States into the war on April 6, 1917. Although American troops did not arrive in Europe in large num-

bers until 1918, the entry of the United States into the war in 1917 gave the Allied powers a psychological boost when they needed it. The year 1917 was not a good year for them. Allied offensives on the Western Front were disastrously defeated. The Italian armies were smashed in October, and in November 1917 the Bolshevik Revolution in Russia (see The Russian Revolution later in this chapter) led to Russia's withdrawal from the war and left Germany free to concentrate entirely on the Western Front. The cause of the Central Powers looked favorable, although war weariness in the Ottoman Empire, Bulgaria, Austria-Hungary, and Germany was beginning to take its toll. The home front was rapidly becoming a cause for as much concern as the war front.

◆ **Impact of the Machine Gun.** The development of trench warfare on the Western Front stymied military leaders who had expected to fight a war based on movement and maneuver. Their efforts to effect a breakthrough by sending masses of men against enemy lines was the height of folly in view of the machine gun. Masses of men advancing across open land made magnificent targets.

The Home Front: The Impact of Total War

The prolongation of World War I made it a total war that affected the lives of all citizens, however remote they might be from the battlefields. The need to organize masses of men and matériel for years of combat (Germany alone had 5.5 million men in active units in 1916) led to increased centralization of government powers, economic regimentation, and manipulation of public opinion to keep the war effort going.

Because the war was expected to be short, little thought had been given to economic problems and long-term wartime needs. Governments had to respond quickly, however, when the war machines failed to achieve their knockout blows and made ever-greater demands for men and matériel. The extension of government power was a logical outgrowth of these needs. Most European countries had already devised some system of mass conscription or military draft. It was now carried to unprecedented heights as countries mobilized tens of millions of young men for that elusive breakthrough to victory. Even countries that continued to rely on volunteers (Great Britain had the largest volunteer army in modern history—one million men—in 1914 and 1915) were forced to resort to conscription, especially to ensure that skilled laborers did not enlist but remained in factories that were important to the production of munitions. In 1916, despite widespread resistance to this extension of government power, compulsory military service was introduced in Great Britain.

Throughout Europe, wartime governments expanded their powers over their economies. Free-market capitalistic systems were temporarily shelved as governments experimented with price, wage, and rent controls, the rationing of food supplies and materials, the regulation of imports and exports, and the nationalization of transportation systems and industries. Some governments even moved toward compulsory labor employment. In effect, in order to mobilize the entire resources of their nations for the war effort, European nations had moved toward planned economies directed by government agencies. Under total war mobilization, the distinction between soldiers at war and civilians at home was narrowed. In the view of political leaders, all citizens constituted a national army dedicated to victory. As the American president Woodrow Wilson expressed it, the men and women "who remain to till the soil and man the factories are no less a part of the army than the men beneath the battle flags."

As the Great War dragged on and both casualties and privations worsened, internal dissatisfaction replaced the patriotic enthusiasm that had marked the early stages of the conflict. By 1916, there were numerous signs that civilian morale was beginning to crack under the pressure of total war. War governments, however, fought back against the growing opposition to the war. Authoritarian regimes, such as those of Germany, Russia, and Austria-Hungary, had always relied on force to subdue their populations. Under the pressures of the war, however, even parliamentary regimes resorted to an expansion of police powers to stifle internal dissent. The British Parliament passed a Defence of the Realm Act (DORA) at the very beginning of the war that allowed the public authorities to arrest dissenters as traitors. The act was later extended to authorize public officials to censor newspapers by deleting objectionable material and even to suspend newspaper publication. In France, government authorities had initially been lenient about public opposition to the war. But by 1917, they began to fear that open opposition to the war might weaken the French will to fight. When Georges Clemenceau (1841–1929) became premier near the end of 1917, the lenient French policies came to an end, and basic civil liberties were suppressed for the duration of the war. When a former premier publicly advocated a negotiated peace, Clemenceau's government had him sentenced to prison for two years for treason.

Wartime governments made active use of propaganda to arouse enthusiasm for the war. At the beginning, public officials needed to do little to achieve this goal. The British and French, for example, exaggerated German atrocities in Belgium and found that their citizens were only too willing to believe these accounts. But as the war dragged on and morale sagged, governments were forced to devise new techniques for stimulating declining enthusiasm. In one British recruiting poster, for example, a small daughter asked her father, "Daddy, what did YOU do in the Great War?" while her younger brother played with toy soldiers and cannon.

Total war made a significant impact on European society, most visibly by bringing an end to unemployment. The withdrawal of millions of men from the labor market to fight, combined with the heightened demand for wartime products, led to jobs for everyone able to work.

World War I also created new roles for women. Because so many men went off to fight at the front, women were called upon to take over jobs and responsibilities that had not been available to them before. Overall, the number of women employed in Britain who held new jobs or replaced men rose by 1,345,000. Women were also now employed in jobs that had been considered beyond the "capacity of women." These included such occupations as chimney sweeps, truck drivers, farm laborers, and, above all, factory workers in heavy industry (see the box on p. 898). Thirty-eight percent of the workers in the Krupp Armaments works in Germany in 1918 were women.

While male workers expressed concern that the employment of females at lower wages would depress their own wages, women began to demand equal pay legislation. A law passed by the French government in July 1915 established a minimum wage for women homeworkers in textiles, an industry that had grown dramatically because of the need for military uniforms. Later in 1917 the government decreed that men and women should receive equal rates for piecework. Despite the noticeable increase in women's wages that resulted from government regulations, women's industrial wages still were not equal to men's wages by the end of the war.

Even worse, women's place in the workforce was far from secure. Both men and women seemed to assume that many of the new jobs for women were only temporary, an expectation quite evident in the British poem "War Girls," written in 1916:

> There's the girl who clips your ticket for the train,
> And the girl who speeds the lift from floor to floor,
> There's the girl who does a milk-round in the rain,
> And the girl who calls for orders at your door.
> Strong, sensible, and fit,
> They're out to show their grit,
> And tackle jobs with energy and knack.
> No longer caged and penned up,
> They're going to keep their end up
> Till the khaki soldier boys come marching back.[4]

At the end of the war, governments moved quickly to remove women from the jobs they had encouraged them to take earlier. By 1919, there were 650,000 unemployed women in Britain while wages for women who were still employed were also lowered. The work benefits for women from World War I seemed to be short-lived as demobilized men returned to the job market.

◆ **British Recruiting Poster.** As the conflict persisted month after month, governments resorted to active propaganda campaigns to generate enthusiasm for the war. In this British recruiting poster, the government tried to pressure men into volunteering for military service. By 1916, the British were forced to adopt compulsory military service.

✦ Women in the Factories ✦

During World War I, women were called upon to assume new job responsibilities, including factory work. In this selection, Naomi Loughnan, a young, upper-middle-class woman, describes the experiences in a munitions plant that considerably broadened her perspective on life.

Naomi Loughnan, "Munition Work"

We little thought when we first put on our overalls and caps and enlisted in the Munition Army how much more inspiring our life was to be than we had dared to hope. Though we munition workers sacrifice our ease we gain a life worth living. Our long days are filled with interest, and with the zest of doing work for our country in the grand cause of Freedom. As we handle the weapons of war we are learning great lessons of life. In the busy, noisy workshops we come face to face with every kind of class, and each one of these classes has something to learn from the others. . . .

Engineering mankind is possessed of the unshakable opinion that no woman can have the mechanical sense. If one of us asks humbly why such and such an alteration is not made to prevent this or that drawback to a machine, she is told, with a superior smile, that a man has worked her machine before her for years, and that therefore if there were any improvement possible it would have been made. As long as we do exactly what we are told and do not attempt to use our brains, we give entire satisfaction, and are treated as nice, good children. Any swerving from the easy path prepared for us by our males arouses the most scathing contempt in their manly bosoms. . . . Women have, however, proved that their entry into the munition world has increased the output. Employers who forget things personal in their patriotic desire for large results are enthusiastic over the success of women in the shops. But their workmen have to be handled with the utmost tenderness and caution lest they should actually imagine it was being suggested that women could do their work equally well, given equal conditions of training—at least where muscle is not the driving force. . . .

The coming of the mixed classes of women into the factory is slowly but surely having an educative effect upon the men. "Language" is almost unconsciously becoming subdued. There are fiery exceptions who make our hair stand up on end under our close-fitting caps, but a sharp rebuke or a look of horror will often straighten out the most savage. . . . It is grievous to hear the girls also swearing and using disgusting language. Shoulder to shoulder with the children of the slums, the upper classes are having their eyes opened at last to the awful conditions among which their sisters have dwelt. Foul language, immorality, and many other evils are but the natural outcome of overcrowding and bitter poverty. . . . Sometimes disgust will overcome us, but we are learning with painful clarity that the fault is not theirs whose actions disgust us, but must be placed to the discredit of those other classes who have allowed the continued existence of conditions which generate the things from which we shrink appalled.

Nevertheless, in some countries the role played by women in the wartime economies did have a positive impact on the women's movement for social and political emancipation. The most obvious gain was the right to vote that was given to women in Germany and Austria immediately after the war (in Britain already in January 1918). Contemporary media, however, tended to focus on the more noticeable, yet in some ways more superficial, social emancipation of upper- and middle-class women. In ever-larger numbers, these young women took jobs, had their own apartments, and showed their new independence by smoking in public and wearing shorter dresses, cosmetics, and new hair styles.

The Last Year of the War

For Germany, the withdrawal of the Russians from the war in March 1918 (see The Russian Revolution later in this chapter) offered renewed hope for a favorable end to the war. The victory over Russia persuaded Erich von Ludendorff (1865–1937), who guided German military operations, and most German leaders to make one final military gamble—a grand offensive in the west to break the military stalemate. The German attack was launched in March and lasted into July, but an Allied counterattack, supported by the arrival of 140,000 fresh American troops, defeated the Germans at the Second Battle of the

CHRONOLOGY

World War I

The path to war	**1914**	Italy declares war on Austria-Hungary	May 23
Assassination of Archduke Francis Ferdinand	June 28	Entry of Bulgaria into the war	September
Austria's ultimatum to Serbia	July 23		
Austria declares war on Serbia	July 28		**1916**
Russia mobilizes	July 29	Battle of Verdun	February 21– December 18
Germany's ultimatum to Russia	July 31	Battle of Jutland	May 31
Germany declares war on Russia	August 1		**1917**
Germany declares war on France	August 3	Germany returns to unrestricted submarine warfare	January
German troops invade Belgium	August 4	United States enters the war	April 6
Great Britain declares war on Germany	August 4		**1918**
The war	**1914**	Last German offensive	March 21–July 18
Battle of Tannenberg	August 26–30	Second Battle of the Marne	July 18
First Battle of the Marne	September 6–10	Allied counteroffensive	July 18–November 10
Battle of Masurian Lakes	September 15	Armistice between Allies and Germany	November 11
Russia, Great Britain, and France declare war on Ottoman Empire	November		**1919**
		Paris Peace Conference begins	January 18
	1915	Peace of Versailles	June 28
Battle of Gallipoli begins	April 25		

Marne on July 18. Ludendorff's gamble had failed. With the arrival of two million more American troops on the Continent, Allied forces began to advance steadily toward Germany.

On September 29, 1918, General Ludendorff informed German leaders that the war was lost and demanded that the government sue for peace at once. When German officials discovered, however, that the Allies were unwilling to make peace with the autocratic imperial government, reforms were instituted to create a liberal government. But these constitutional reforms came too late for the exhausted and angry German people. On November 3, naval units in Kiel mutinied, and within days councils of workers and soldiers were forming throughout northern Germany and taking over the supervision of civilian and military administrations. William II capitulated to public pressure and abdicated on November 9, while the Socialists under Friedrich Ebert (1871–1925) announced the establishment of a republic. Two days later, on November 11, 1918, the new German government agreed to an armistice. The war was over.

The Peace Settlement

In January 1919, the delegations of twenty-seven victorious Allied nations gathered in Paris to conclude a final

⇒ *The Voice of Peacemaking: Woodrow Wilson* ⇐

"We are fighting for the liberty, the self-government, and the undictated development of all peoples. . . ."

When the Allied powers met in Paris in January 1919, it soon became apparent that the victors had different opinions on the kind of peace they expected. These excerpts are from the speeches of Woodrow Wilson in which the American president presented his idealistic goals for a peace based on justice and reconciliation.

Woodrow Wilson: May 26, 1917

We are fighting for the liberty, the self-government, and the undictated development of all peoples, and every feature of the settlement that concludes this war must be conceived and executed for that purpose. Wrongs must first be righted and then adequate safeguards must be created to prevent their being committed again. . . .

No people must be forced under sovereignty under which it does not wish to live. No territory must change hands except for the purpose of securing those who inhabit it a fair chance of life and liberty. No indemnities must be insisted on except those that constitute payment for manifest wrongs done. No readjustments of power must be made except such as will tend to secure the future peace of the world and the future welfare and happiness of its peoples.

And then the free peoples of the world must draw together in some common covenant, some genuine and practical cooperation that will in effect combine their force to secure peace and justice in the dealings of nations with one another.

April 6, 1918

We are ready, whenever the final reckoning is made, to be just to the German people, deal fairly with the German power, as with all others. There can be no difference between peoples in the final judgment, if it is indeed to be a righteous judgment. To propose anything but justice, even-handed and dispassionate justice, to Germany at any time, whatever the outcome of the war, would be to renounce and dishonor our own cause. For we ask nothing that we are not willing to accord.

January 3, 1919

Our task at Paris is to organize the friendship of the world, to see to it that all the moral forces that make for right and justice and liberty are united and are given a vital organization to which the peoples of the world will readily and gladly respond. In other words, our task is no less colossal than this, to set up a new international psychology, to have a new atmosphere.

settlement of the Great War. Some delegates believed that this conference would avoid the mistakes made at Vienna in 1815 by aristocrats who rearranged the map of Europe to meet the selfish desires of the great powers. Harold Nicolson, one of the British delegates, expressed what he believed this conference would achieve instead: "We were journeying to Paris not merely to liquidate the war, but to found a New Order in Europe. We were preparing not Peace only, but Eternal Peace. There was about us the halo of some divine mission. . . . For we were bent on doing great, permanent and noble things."[5]

National expectations, however, made Nicolson's quest for "eternal peace" a difficult one. Over the years, the reasons for fighting World War I had been transformed from selfish national interests to idealistic principles. No one expressed the latter better than Woodrow Wilson. The American president outlined "Fourteen Points" to the U.S. Congress that he believed justified the

enormous military struggle then being waged. Later, Wilson spelled out additional steps for a truly just and lasting peace. Wilson's proposals included "open covenants of peace, openly arrived at" instead of secret diplomacy; the reduction of national armaments to a "point consistent with domestic safety"; and the self-determination of people so that "all well-defined national aspirations shall be accorded the utmost satisfaction." Wilson characterized World War I as a people's war waged against "absolutism and militarism," two scourges of liberty that could only be eliminated by creating democratic governments and a "general association of nations" that would guarantee the "political independence and territorial integrity to great and small states alike" (see the box above). As the spokesman for a new world order based on democracy and international cooperation, Wilson was enthusiastically cheered by many Europeans when he arrived in Europe for the peace conference.

Wilson soon found, however, that other states at the Paris Peace Conference were guided by considerably more pragmatic motives. The secret treaties and agreements that had been made before the war could not be totally ignored, even if they did conflict with the principle of self-determination enunciated by Wilson. National interests also complicated the deliberations of the Paris Peace Conference. David Lloyd George (1863–1945), prime minister of Great Britain, had won a decisive electoral victory in December of 1918 on a platform of making the Germans pay for this dreadful war.

France's approach to peace was primarily determined by considerations of national security. To Georges Clemenceau, the feisty French premier who had led his country to victory, the French people had borne the brunt of German aggression. They deserved revenge and security against future German aggression. Clemenceau wanted a demilitarized Germany, vast German reparations to pay for the costs of the war, and a separate Rhineland as a buffer state between France and Germany, demands that Wilson viewed as vindictive and contrary to the principle of national self-determination.

Although twenty-seven nations were represented at the Paris Peace Conference, the most important decisions were made by Wilson, Clemenceau, and Lloyd George. Italy was considered one of the so-called Big Four powers, but played a much less important role than the other three countries. Germany, of course, was not invited to attend and Russia could not because of its civil war.

In view of the many conflicting demands at Versailles, it was inevitable that the Big Three would quarrel. Wilson was determined to create a League of Nations to prevent future wars. Clemenceau and Lloyd George were equally determined to punish Germany. In the end, only compromise made it possible to achieve a peace settlement. Wilson's wish that the creation of an international peacekeeping organization be the first order of business was granted, and already on January 25, 1919, the conference adopted the principle of a League of Nations. The details of its structure were left for later sessions, and Wilson willingly agreed to make compromises on territorial arrangements to guarantee the establishment of the league, believing that a functioning league could later rectify bad arrangements. Clemenceau also compromised to obtain some guarantees for French security. He renounced France's desire for a separate Rhineland and instead accepted a defensive alliance with Great Britain and the United States. Both states pledged to help France if it were attacked by Germany.

The final peace settlement of Paris consisted of five separate treaties with the defeated nations—Germany, Austria, Hungary, Bulgaria, and Turkey. The Treaty of Versailles with Germany, signed on June 28, 1919, was by far the most important one. The Germans considered it a harsh peace and were particularly unhappy with Article 231, the so-called War Guilt Clause, which declared Germany (and Austria) responsible for starting the war and ordered Germany to pay reparations for all the damage to which the Allied governments and their people were subjected as a result of the war "imposed upon them by the aggression of Germany and her allies."

The military and territorial provisions of the treaty also rankled the Germans, although they were by no means as harsh as the Germans claimed. Germany had to lower its army to 100,000 men, reduce its navy, and eliminate its air force. German territorial losses included the return of Alsace and Lorraine to France and sections of Prussia to the new Polish state. German land west and as far as thirty miles east of the Rhine was established as a demilitarized zone and stripped of all armaments or fortifications to serve as a barrier to any future German military moves westward against France. Outraged by the "dictated peace," the new German government complained but accepted the treaty.

The separate peace treaties made with the other Central Powers (Austria, Hungary, Bulgaria, and Turkey) extensively redrew the map of eastern Europe. Many of these changes merely ratified what the war had already

◆ **The Big Four at Paris.** Shown here are the Big Four at the Paris Peace Conference: David Lloyd George of Britain, Vittorio Orlando of Italy, Georges Clemenceau of France, and Woodrow Wilson of the United States. Although Italy was considered one of the Big Four powers, Britain, France, and the United States (the Big Three) made the major decisions at the peace conference.

Map 24.3 Territorial Changes in Europe and the Middle East after World War I.

accomplished. Both the German and Russian Empires lost considerable territory in eastern Europe while the Austro-Hungarian Empire disappeared altogether. New nation-states emerged from the lands of these three empires: Finland, Latvia, Estonia, Lithuania, Poland, Czechoslovakia, Austria, and Hungary. Territorial rearrangements were also made in the Balkans. Romania acquired additional lands from Russia, Hungary, and Bulgaria. Serbia formed the nucleus of a new South Slav state, called Yugoslavia, which combined Serbs, Croats, and Slovenes. Although the Paris Peace Conference was supposedly guided by the principle of self-determination, the mixtures of peoples in eastern Europe made it impossible to draw boundaries along neat ethnic lines. Compromises had to be made, sometimes to satisfy the national interest of the victors. France, for example, had lost Russia as its major ally on Germany's eastern border and wanted to strengthen and expand Poland, Czechoslovakia, Yugoslavia, and Romania as much as possible so that those states could serve as barriers against Germany and Communist Russia. As a result of compromises, virtually every eastern Europe state was left with a minorities problem that could lead to future conflicts. Germans in Poland, Hungarians, Poles, and Germans in Czechoslovakia, and the combination of Serbs, Croats, Slovenes, Macedonians, and Albanians in Yugoslavia all became sources of later conflict. Moreover, the new map of eastern Europe was based upon the temporary collapse of power in both Germany and Russia. As neither country accepted the new eastern frontiers, it seemed only a matter of time before a resurgent Germany or Russia would make changes.

Yet another centuries-old empire—the Ottoman Empire—was dismembered by the peace settlement after the war. To gain Arab support against the Turks during the war, the Western allies had promised to recognize the independence of Arab states in the Middle Eastern lands of the Ottoman Empire. But the imperialist habits of Western nations died hard. After the war, France took control of Lebanon and Syria while Britain received Iraq and Palestine. Officially, both acquisitions were called mandates. Because Woodrow Wilson had opposed the outright annexation of colonial territories by the Allies, the peace settlement had created a system of mandates whereby a nation officially administered a territory on behalf of the League of Nations. The system of mandates could not hide the fact that the principle of national self-determination at the Paris Peace Conference was largely for Europeans.

The peace settlement negotiated at Paris soon came under attack, not only by the defeated Central Powers, but by others who felt that the peacemakers had been shortsighted. The famous British economist John Maynard Keynes, for example, condemned the preoccupation with frontiers at the expense of economic issues that left Europe "inefficient, unemployed, disorganized." Despite the criticisms, the peace settlement was a sensible one. Self-determination had served reasonably well as a central organizing principle while the establishment of the League of Nations gave some hope that future conflicts could be resolved peacefully. And yet, within twenty years after the signing of the peace treaties, Europe was again engaged in deadly conflict. As some historians have suggested, perhaps the cause of the failure of the peace of 1919 was less in its structure than in its lack of enforcement.

Succcessful enforcement of the peace necessitated the active involvement of its principal architects, especially in assisting the new German state in developing a peaceful and democratic republic. The failure of the U.S. Senate to ratify the Treaty of Versailles, however, meant that the United States never joined the League of Nations. In addition, the U.S. Senate also rejected Wilson's defensive alliance with Great Britain and France. Already by the end of 1919, the United States was retreating into isolationism.

This retreat had dire consequences. American withdrawal from the defensive alliance with Britain and France led Britain to withdraw as well. By removing itself from European affairs, the United States forced France to face its old enemy alone, leading the embittered nation to take strong actions against Germany that only intensified German resentment. By the end of 1919, it appeared that the peace of 1919 was already beginning to unravel.

ℛevolution and the Futile Search for a New Stability

Only twenty years after the Treaty of Versailles, the world was again at war. Yet, in the 1920s, many people continued to assume that Europe and the world were about to enter a new era of international peace, economic growth, and political democracy. In all of these areas, the optimistic hopes of the 1920s failed to be realized.

An Uncertain Peace: The Search for Security

The peace settlement at the end of World War I had tried to fulfill the nineteenth-century dream of nationalism by creating new boundaries and new states. From its inception, however, this peace settlement had left nations unhappy. Conflicts over disputed border regions between Germany and Poland, Poland and Lithuania, Poland and Czechoslovakia, Austria and Hungary, and Italy and Yugoslavia poisoned mutual relations in eastern Europe for years. Many Germans viewed the Peace of Versailles as a dictated peace and vowed to seek its revision.

The American president Woodrow Wilson had recognized that the peace treaties contained unwise provisions that could serve as new causes for conflicts and had placed many of his hopes for the future in the League of Nations. The league, however, was not particularly effective in maintaining the peace. The failure of the United States to join the league and the subsequent American retreat into isolationism undermined the effectiveness of the league from its beginning. Moreover, the league could use only economic sanctions to halt aggression. The French attempt to strengthen the league's effectiveness as an instrument of collective security by creating some kind of international army was rejected by nations that feared giving up any of their sovereignty to a larger international body.

The weakness of the League of Nations and the failure of both the United States and Great Britain to honor their defensive military alliances with France left France embittered and alone. France's search for security between 1919 and 1924 was founded primarily upon a strict enforcement of the Treaty of Versailles. This tough policy toward Germany began with the issue of reparations, or the payments that the Germans were supposed to make to compensate for the "damage done to the civilian population of the Allied and Associated Powers and to their property," as the treaty asserted. In April 1921, the Allied Reparations Commission settled on a sum of 132 billion marks ($33 billion) for German reparations, payable in annual installments of 2.5 billion (gold) marks. Allied threats to occupy the Ruhr valley, Germany's chief indus-trial and mining center, led the new German republic to accept the reparations settlement and make its first pay-ment in 1921. By the following year, however, faced with rising inflation, domestic turmoil, and lack of revenues due to low tax rates, the German government announced that it was unable to pay more. Outraged by what they considered to be Germany's violation of one aspect of the peace settlement, the French government sent troops to occupy the Ruhr valley. Since the Germans would not pay reparations, the French would collect reparations in kind by operating and using the Ruhr mines and facto-ries.

Both Germany and France suffered from the French occupation of the Ruhr. The German government adopted a policy of passive resistance to French occupa-tion that was largely financed by printing more paper money. This only intensified the inflationary pressures that had already begun in Germany by the end of the war. The German mark became worthless. Economic disaster fueled political upheavals as Communists staged upris-ings in October and Adolf Hitler's band of Nazis at-tempted to seize power in Munich in 1923. All the na-tions, including France, were happy to cooperate with the American suggestion for a new conference of experts to reassess the reparations problem. By the time the con-ference did its work in 1924, both France and Germany were opting to pursue a more conciliatory approach to-ward each other.

The formation of liberal-socialist governments in both Great Britain and France opened the door to conciliatory approaches to Germany and the reparations problem. At the same time, a new German government led by Gustav Stresemann (1878–1929) ended the policy of passive re-sistance and committed Germany to carry out the provi-sions of the Versailles Treaty while seeking a new settle-ment of the reparations question.

In August 1924, an international commission pro-duced a new plan for reparations. Named the Dawes Plan after the American banker who chaired the commission, it reduced reparations and stabilized Germany's payments on the basis of its ability to pay. The Dawes Plan also granted an initial $200 million loan for German recov-ery, which opened the door to heavy American invest-ments in Europe that helped create a new era of Euro-pean prosperity between 1924 and 1929.

A new age of European diplomacy accompanied the new economic stability. A spirit of international cooper-ation was fostered by the foreign ministers of Germany and France, Gustav Stresemann and Aristide Briand

(1862–1932), who concluded the Treaty of Locarno in 1925. This guaranteed Germany's new western borders with France and Belgium. Although Germany's new east-ern borders with Poland were conspicuously absent from the agreement, the Locarno pact was viewed by many as the beginning of a new era of European peace. On the day after the pact was concluded, the headline in the *New York Times* ran "France and Germany Ban War For-ever," while the London *Times* declared, "Peace at Last."[6]

Germany's entry into the League of Nations in March 1926 soon reinforced the new spirit of conciliation en-gendered at Locarno. Two years later, similar optimistic attitudes prevailed in the Kellogg-Briand pact, drafted by the American secretary of state Frank B. Kellogg and the French foreign minister Aristide Briand. Sixty-three na-tions signed this accord, in which they pledged "to re-nounce war as an instrument of national policy." Noth-ing was said, however, about what would be done if anyone violated the treaty.

The spirit of Locarno was based on little real sub-stance. Germany lacked the military power to alter its western borders even if it wanted to. Pious promises to re-nounce war without mechanisms to enforce them were virtually worthless. And the issue of disarmament soon proved that even the spirit of Locarno could not bring nations to cut back on their weapons. The League of Na-tions Covenant had suggested the "reduction of national armaments to the lowest point consistent with national safety." Germany, of course, had been disarmed with the expectation that other states would do likewise. Numer-ous disarmament conferences, however, failed to achieve anything substantial as states proved unwilling to trust their security to anyone but their own military forces. When a World Disarmament Conference finally met in Geneva in 1932, the issue was already dead.

The Great Depression

After World War I, most European states hoped to return to the liberal ideal of a private-enterprise, market econ-omy largely free of state intervention. But the war had vastly strengthened business cartels and labor unions, making some government regulation of these powerful organizations necessary. At the same time, reparations and war debts had severely damaged the postwar interna-tional economy, making the prosperity that did occur be-tween 1924 and 1929 at best a fragile one and the dream of returning to the liberal ideal of a self-regulating market economy merely an illusion. What destroyed the concept altogether was the Great Depression.

Two factors played a major role in the coming of the Great Depression: a downturn in domestic economies and an international financial crisis created by the collapse of the American stock market in 1929. Already in the mid-1920s, prices for agricultural goods were beginning to decline rapidly due to overproduction of basic commodities, such as wheat. In 1925, states in central and eastern Europe began to impose tariffs to close their markets to other countries' goods. An increase in the use of oil and hydroelectricity led to a slump in the coal industry even before 1929.

In addition to these domestic economic troubles, much of the European prosperity between 1924 and 1929 had been built upon American bank loans to Germany. Twenty-three billion marks had been invested in German municipal bonds and German industries since 1924. Already in 1928 and 1929, American investors had begun to pull money out of Germany in order to invest in the booming New York stock market. The crash of the American stock market in October 1929 led panicky American investors to withdraw even more of their funds from Germany and other European markets. The withdrawal of funds seriously weakened the banks of Germany and other central European states. The Credit-Anstalt, Vienna's most prestigious bank, collapsed on May 31, 1931. By that time, trade was slowing down, industrialists were cutting back production, and unemployment was increasing as the ripple effects of international bank failures had a devastating impact on domestic economies.

Economic depression was by no means a new phenomenon in European history. But the depth of the economic downturn after 1929 fully justifies the label Great Depression. During 1932, the worst year of the depression, one British worker in four was unemployed, while six million or 40 percent of the German labor force were out of work. Between 1929 and 1932, industrial production plummeted almost 50 percent in the United States and over 40 percent in Germany. The unemployed and homeless filled the streets of the cities throughout the advanced industrial countries (see the box on p. 906).

Governments seemed powerless to deal with the crisis. The classical liberal remedy for depression, a deflationary policy of balanced budgets, which involved cutting costs by lowering wages and raising tariffs to exclude other countries' goods from home markets, only served to worsen the economic crisis and create even greater mass discontent. This, in turn, led to serious political repercussions. Increased government activity in the economy was one reaction, even in countries like the United States that had a strong *laissez-faire* tradition. Another effect was a renewed interest in Marxist doctrines because Marx had predicted that capitalism would destroy itself through overproduction. Communism took on new popularity, especially with workers and intellectuals. Finally, the Great Depression increased the attractiveness of simplistic dictatorial solutions, especially from a new movement known as fascism. Everywhere, democracy seemed on the defensive in the 1930s.

◆ **The Great Depression: Bread Lines in Paris.** The Great Depression devastated the European economy and had serious political repercussions. Because of its more balanced economy, France did not feel the effects of the depression as quickly as other European countries. By 1931, however, even France was experiencing lines of unemployed people at free-food centers.

➤ The Great Depression: Unemployed and Homeless in Germany ⇐

In 1932, Germany had six million unemployed workers, many of them wandering aimlessly about the country, begging for food and seeking shelter in city lodging houses for the homeless. The Great Depression was an important factor in the rise to power of Adolf Hitler and the Nazis. This selection presents a description of the unemployed homeless in 1932.

Heinrich Hauser, "With Germany's Unemployed"

An almost unbroken chain of homeless men extends the whole length of the great Hamburg-Berlin highway. . . . All the highways in Germany over which I have traveled this year presented the same aspect. . . .

Most of the hikers paid no attention to me. They walked separately or in small groups, with their eyes on the ground. And they had the queer, stumbling gait of barefooted people, for their shoes were slung over their shoulders. Some of them were guild members—carpenters . . . milkmen . . . and bricklayers . . . —but they were in a minority. Far more numerous were those whom one could assign to no special profession or craft—unskilled young people, for the most part, who had been unable to find a place for themselves in any city or town in Germany, and who had never had a job and never expected to have one. There was something else that had never been seen before—whole families that had piled all their goods into baby carriages and wheelbarrows that they were pushing along as they plodded forward in dumb despair. It was a whole nation on the march.

I saw them—and this was the strongest impression that the year 1932 left with me—I saw them, gathered into groups of fifty or a hundred men, attacking fields of potatoes. I saw them digging up the potatoes and throwing them into sacks while the farmer who owned the field watched them in despair and the local policeman looked on gloomily from the distance. I saw them staggering toward the lights of the city as night fell, with their sacks on their backs. What did it remind me of? Of the War, of the worst periods of starvation in 1917 and 1918, but even then people paid for the potatoes. . . .

I saw that the individual can know what is happening only by personal experience. I know what it is to be a tramp. I know what cold and hunger are. . . . But there are two things that I have only recently experienced—begging and spending the night in a municipal lodging house.

I entered the huge Berlin municipal lodging house in a northern quarter of the city. . . .

Distribution of spoons, distribution of enameled-ware bowls with the words "Property of the City of Berlin" written on their sides. Then the meal itself. A big kettle is carried in. Men with yellow smocks have brought it in and men with yellow smocks ladle out the food. These men, too, are homeless and they have been expressly picked by the establishment and given free food and lodging and a little pocket money in exchange for their work about the house.

Where have I seen this kind of food distribution before? In a prison that I once helped to guard in the winter of 1919 during the German civil war. There was the same hunger then, the same trembling, anxious expectation of rations. Now the men are standing in a long row, dressed in their plain nightshirts that reach to the ground, and the noise of their shuffling feet is like the noise of big wild animals walking up and down the stone floor of their cages before feeding time. The men lean far over the kettle so that the warm steam from the food envelops them and they hold out their bowls as if begging and whisper to the attendant, "Give me a real helping. Give me a little more." A piece of bread is handed out with every bowl.

My next recollection is sitting at table in another room on a crowded bench that is like a seat in a fourth-class railway carriage. Hundreds of hungry mouths make an enormous noise eating their food. The men sit bent over their food like animals who feel that someone is going to take it away from them. They hold their bowl with their left arm part way around it, so that nobody can take it away, and they also protect it with their other elbow and with their head and mouth, while they move the spoon as fast as they can between their mouth and the bowl.

The Democratic States

According to Woodrow Wilson, World War I had been fought to make the world safe for democracy. In 1919, there seemed to be some justification for his claim. Four major European states and a host of minor ones had functioning political democracies. In a number of states, universal male suffrage had even been replaced by universal suffrage as male politicians rewarded women for their contributions to World War I by granting them the right to vote (except in Italy, Switzerland, France, and Spain where women had to wait until the end of World War II). In the 1920s, Europe seemed to be returning to the political trends of the prewar era—the broadening of parliamentary regimes and the fostering of individual liberties. But it was not an easy process; four years of total war and four years of postwar turmoil made the desire for a "return to normalcy" a difficult and troublesome affair.

After World War I, Great Britain went through a period of painful readjustment and serious economic difficulties. During the war, Britain had lost many of the markets for its industrial products, especially to the United States and Japan. The postwar decline of such staple industries as coal, steel, and textiles led to a rise in unemployment, which reached the two million mark in 1921. But Britain soon rebounded and experienced an era of renewed prosperity between 1925 and 1929. This prosperity, however, was relatively superficial. British exports in the 1920s never compensated for the overseas investments lost during the war, and even in these so-called prosperous years, unemployment remained at a startling 10 percent level. Coal miners were especially affected by the decline of the antiquated and inefficient British coal mines, which also suffered from a world glut of coal.

By 1929, Britain was faced with the growing effects of the Great Depression. The Labour Party, which had now become the largest party in Britain, failed to solve the nation's economic problems and fell from power in 1931. A National Government, dominated by the Conservatives, claimed credit for bringing Britain out of the worst stages of the depression, primarily by using the traditional policies of balanced budgets and protective tariffs. British politicians largely ignored the new ideas of a Cambridge economist, John Maynard Keynes (1883–1946). In 1936, Keynes published his *General Theory of Employment, Interest, and Money*. Contrary to the traditional view that depressions should be left to work themselves out through the self-regulatory mechanisms of a free economy, Keynes argued that unemployment stemmed not from overproduction but from a decline in demand, and that demand could be increased by public works, financed, if necessary, through deficit spending to stimulate production. These policies, however, could only be accomplished by government intervention in the economy, and Britain's political leaders were unwilling to go that far in the 1930s.

After the defeat of Germany and the demobilization of the German army, France had become the strongest power on the European continent. Its biggest problem involved the reconstruction of the devastated areas of northern and eastern France. But neither the conservative National Bloc government nor a government coalition of leftist parties (the Cartel of the Left) seemed capable of solving France's financial problems between 1921 and 1926. The failure of the Cartel of the Left led to the return of the conservative Raymond Poincaré (1860–1934), whose government from 1926 to 1929 stabilized the French economy by a substantial increase in taxes during a period of relative prosperity.

France did not feel the effects of the depression as soon as other countries because of its more balanced economy. The French population was almost evenly divided between urban and agricultural pursuits while a slight majority of French industrial plants were small enterprises. Consequently, France did not begin to feel the full effects of the Great Depression until 1932, but then economic instability soon had political repercussions. During a nineteenth-month period in 1932 and 1933, six different cabinets were formed as France faced political chaos. Finally, in June 1936, fearful that rightists intended to seize power, a coalition of leftist parties—Communists, Socialists, and Radicals—formed a Popular Front government.

The Popular Front succeeded in initiating a program for workers that some have called the French New Deal. It included the right of collective bargaining, a forty-hour work week, two-week paid vacations, and minimum wages. The Popular Front's policies failed to solve the problems of the depression, however. Although the Popular Front survived in name until 1938, it was for all intents and purposes dead before then. By 1938, the French were experiencing a serious decline of confidence in their political system that left them unprepared to deal with their aggressive Nazi enemy to the east.

After the Imperial Germany of William II had come to an end with Germany's defeat in World War I, a German democratic state known as the Weimar Republic had been established. From its beginnings, the Weimar Republic was plagued by a series of problems. The republic had no truly outstanding political leaders. Even its more able leaders, such as Friedrich Ebert, who served as president, and Gustav Stresemann, the foreign minister and chancellor, died in the 1920s. When Ebert died in 1925, Paul von Hindenburg (1847–1934), the World War I military hero, was elected president. Hindenburg was a traditional military man, monarchist in sentiment, who at heart was not in favor of the republic. The young republic also suffered politically from attempted uprisings and attacks from both the left and right.

The Weimar Republic also faced serious economic difficulties. Germany experienced runaway inflation in 1922 and 1923 with grave social effects. Widows, orphans, the retired elderly, army officers, teachers, civil servants, and others who lived on fixed incomes all watched their monthly stipends become worthless or their lifetime savings disappear. Their economic losses increasingly pushed the middle class to the rightist parties that were hostile to the republic. To make matters worse, after a period of prosperity from 1924 to 1929, Germany faced the Great Depression. Unemployment increased to 3 million in March 1930 and 4.38 million by December of the same year. The depression paved the way for social discontent, fear, and extremist parties. The political, economic, and social problems of the Weimar Republic help us to understand the environment in which Adolf Hitler and the Nazis were able to rise to power.

After Germany, no Western nation was more affected by the Great Depression than the United States. The full force of the depression had struck the United States by 1932. In that year industrial production fell to 50 percent of what it had been in 1929. By 1933, there were 15 million unemployed. Under these circumstances, the Democrat Franklin Delano Roosevelt (1882–1945) was able to win a landslide electoral victory in 1932. Following the example of the American experience during World War I, he and his advisers pursued a policy of active government intervention in the economy that came to be known as the New Deal.

Initially, the New Deal attempted to restore prosperity by creating the National Recovery Administration (NRA), which required government, labor, and industrial leaders to work out regulations for each industry. Declared unconstitutional by the Supreme Court in 1935, the NRA was soon superseded by other efforts collectively known as the Second New Deal. These included a stepped-up program of public works, such as the Works Progress Administration (WPA) established in 1935. This government organization employed between two and three million people who worked at building bridges, roads, post offices, and airports. The Roosevelt administration was also responsible for new social legislation that launched the American welfare state. In 1935, the Social Security Act created a system of old age pensions and unemployment insurance. Moreover, the National Labor Relations Act of 1935 encouraged the rapid growth of labor unions.

No doubt, the New Deal provided some social reform measures that perhaps averted the possibility of social revolution in the United States. It did not, however, solve the unemployment problems of the Great Depression. In May 1937, during what was considered a period of full recovery, American unemployment still stood at 7 million. A recession the following year increased that number to 11 million. Only World War II and the subsequent growth of armaments industries brought American workers back to full employment.

The Russian Revolution

By 1917, total war was creating serious domestic turmoil in all of the European belligerent states. Only one, however, experienced the kind of complete collapse that others were predicting might happen throughout Europe. Out of Russia's collapse came the Russian Revolution, whose impact would be widely felt in Europe for decades to come.

After the Revolution of 1905 had failed to bring any substantial changes to Russia, Tsar Nicholas II fell back on the army and bureaucracy as the basic props for his autocratic regime. But World War I magnified Russia's problems and put the tsarist government to a test that it could not meet. Russia was unprepared both militarily and technologically for the total war of World War I. Competent military leadership was lacking. Even worse, the tsar, alone of all European monarchs, insisted upon taking personal charge of the armed forces despite his obvious lack of ability and training for such an awesome burden. Russian industry was unable to produce the weapons needed for the army. Ill-led and ill-armed, Russian armies suffered incredible losses. Between 1914 and 1916, two million soldiers were killed while another four to six million were wounded or captured. By 1917, the Russian will to fight had vanished.

The tsarist government was totally inadequate for the tasks that it faced in 1914. Even conservative aristocrats were appalled by the incompetent and inefficient bureaucracy that controlled the political and military system. In the meantime, Tsar Nicholas II was increasingly insulated from events by his German-born wife Alexandra, a willful woman who had fallen under the influence of Rasputin, a Siberian peasant who belonged to a religious sect that indulged in sexual orgies. Rasputin's influence made him an important power behind the throne, and he did not hesitate to interfere in government affairs. As the leadership at the top stumbled its way through a series of military and economic disasters, the middle class, aristocrats, peasants, soldiers, and workers grew more and more disenchanted with the tsarist regime. Even conservative aristocrats who supported the monarchy felt the need to do something to reverse the deteriorating situation. For a start, they assassinated Rasputin in December 1916. By then it was too late to save the monarchy, and its fall came quickly.

At the beginning of March 1917, a series of strikes broke out in the capital city of Petrograd (formerly St. Petersburg). Here the actions of working-class women helped to change the course of Russian history. In February of 1917, the government had introduced bread rationing in the capital city after the price of bread had skyrocketed. Many of the women who stood in the lines waiting for bread were also factory workers who had put in twelve-hour days. The Russian government had become aware of the volatile situation in the capital from a police report:

> Mothers of families, exhausted by endless standing in line at stores, distraught over their half-starving and sick children, are today perhaps closer to revolution than [the liberal opposition leaders] and of course they are a great deal more dangerous because they are the combustible material for which only a single spark is needed to burst into flame.[7]

On March 8, about ten thousand Petrograd women marched through the city demanding "Peace and Bread" and "Down with Autocracy." Soon the women were joined by other workers, and together they called for a general strike that succeeded in shutting down all the factories in the city on March 10. Nicholas ordered the troops to disperse the crowds by shooting them if necessary, but soon significant numbers of the soldiers joined the demonstrators. The Duma or legislative body, which the tsar had tried to dissolve, met anyway and on March 12 established a Provisional Government that urged the tsar to abdicate. He did so on March 15.

The Provisional Government headed by Alexander Kerensky (1881–1970) decided to carry on the war to preserve Russia's honor—a major blunder because it satisfied neither the workers nor the peasants who above all wanted an end to the war. The Provisional Government was also faced with another authority, the soviets, or councils of workers' and soldiers' deputies. The Petrograd soviet had been formed in March 1917; at the same time, soviets sprang up spontaneously in army units, factory towns, and rural areas. The soviets represented the more radical interests of the lower classes and were largely composed of socialists of various kinds. One group—the Bolsheviks—came to play a crucial role.

The Bolsheviks were a small faction of Marxist Social Democrats who had come under the leadership of Vladimir Ulianov, known to the world as V. I. Lenin (1870–1924). Arrested for his revolutionary activity, Lenin was shipped to Siberia. After his release, he chose to go into exile in Switzerland and eventually assumed the leadership of the Bolshevik wing of the Russian Social Democratic Party. Under Lenin's direction, the Bolsheviks became a party dedicated to violent revolution. He believed that only a violent revolution could destroy the capitalist system and that a "vanguard" of activists must form a small party of well-disciplined professional revolutionaries to accomplish the task. Between 1900 and 1917, Lenin spent most of his time in Switzerland. When the Provisional Government was formed in March 1917, he believed that an opportunity for the Bolsheviks to seize power had come. In April 1917, with the connivance of the German High Command, who hoped to create disorder in Russia, Lenin was shipped to Russia in a "sealed train" by way of Finland.

Lenin's arrival in Russia opened a new stage of the Russian Revolution. Lenin maintained that the soviets of soldiers, workers, and peasants were ready-made instruments of power. The Bolsheviks must work toward gaining control of these groups and then use them to overthrow the Provisional Government. At the same time, Bolshevik propaganda must seek mass support through

◆ **Lenin Addresses a Crowd.** V. I. Lenin was the driving force behind the success of the Bolsheviks in seizing power in Russia and creating the Union of Soviet Socialist Republics. Here Lenin is seen addressing a rally in Moscow in 1917.

Ten Days That Shook the World: Lenin and the Bolshevik Seizure of Power

John Reed was an American journalist who helped to found the American Communist Labor Party. Accused of sedition, he fled the United States and went to Russia. In Ten Days That Shook the World, Reed left an impassioned eyewitness account of the Russian Revolution. It is apparent from his comments that Reed considered Lenin the indispensable hero of the Bolshevik success.

John Reed, *Ten Days That Shook the World*

It was just 8:40 when a thundering wave of cheers announced the entrance of the presidium, with Lenin—great Lenin—among them. A short, stocky figure, with a big head set down in his shoulders, bald and bulging. Little eyes, a snubbish nose, wide, generous mouth, and heavy chin; clean-shaven now, but already beginning to bristle with the well-known beard of his past and future. Dressed in shabby clothes, his trousers much too long for him. Unimpressive, to be the idol of a mob, loved and revered as perhaps few leaders in history have been. A strange popular leader—a leader purely by virtue of intellect; colorless, humorless, uncompromising and detached; without picturesque idiosyncrasies—but with the power of explaining profound ideas in simple terms, of analyzing a concrete situation. And combined with shrewdness, the greatest intellectual audacity. . . .

Now Lenin, gripping the edge of the reading stand, letting his little winking eyes travel over the crowd as he stood there waiting, apparently oblivious to the long-rolling ovation, which lasted several minutes. When it finished, he said simply, "We shall now proceed to construct the Socialist order!" Again that overwhelming human roar.

"The first thing is the adoption of practical measures to realize peace. . . . We shall offer peace to the peoples of all the belligerent countries upon the basis of the Soviet terms—no annexations, no indemnities, and the right of self-determination of peoples. At the same time, according to our promise, we shall publish and repudiate the secret treaties. . . . The question of War and Peace is so clear that I think that I may, without preamble, read the project of a Proclamation to the Peoples of All the Belligerent Countries. . . ."

His great mouth, seeming to smile, opened wide as he spoke; his voice was hoarse—not unpleasantly so, but as if it had hardened that way after years and years of speaking—and went on monotonously, with the effect of being able to go forever. . . . For emphasis he bent forward slightly. No gestures. And before him, a thousand simple faces looking up in intent adoration.

[Reed then reproduces the full text of the Proclamation.]

When the grave thunder of applause had died away, Lenin spoke again: "We propose to the Congress to ratify this declaration. . . . This proposal of peace will meet with resistance on the part of the imperialist governments—we don't fool ourselves on that score. But we hope that revolution will soon break out in all the belligerent countries; that is why we address ourselves especially to the workers of France, England and Germany. . . .

"The revolution of November 6th and 7th," he ended, "has opened the era of the Social Revolution. . . . The labor movement, in the name of peace and Socialism, shall win, and fulfill its destiny. . . ."

There was something quiet and powerful in all this, which stirred the souls of men. It was understandable why people believed when Lenin spoke.

promises geared to the needs of the people: an end to the war; redistribution of all land to the peasants; the transfer of factories and industries from capitalists to committees of workers; and the relegation of government power from the Provisional Government to the soviets. Three simple slogans summed up the Bolshevik program: "Peace, Land, Bread," "Worker Control of Production," and "All Power to the Soviets."

By the end of October, the Bolsheviks had achieved a slight majority in the Petrograd and Moscow soviets. The number of party members had also grown from 50,000 to 240,000. With the close cooperation of Leon Trotsky (1877–1940), a fervid revolutionary, Lenin organized a Military Revolutionary Committee within the Petrograd soviet to plot the overthrow of the government. On the night of November 6–7, Bolshevik forces seized the Winter Palace, seat of the Provisional Government. The Provisional Government quickly collapsed with little bloodshed. This coup d'etat had been timed to coincide with a meeting in Petrograd of the all-Russian Congress of Soviets representing local soviets from all over the country. Lenin nominally turned over the sovereignty of the Provisional Government to this Congress of Soviets. Real power, however, passed to a Council of People's Commissars, headed by Lenin (see the box on p. 910).

But the Bolsheviks, soon renamed the Communists, still had a long way to go. For one thing, Lenin had promised peace, and that, he realized, was not an easy task because of the humiliating losses of Russian territory that it would entail. There was no real choice, however. On March 3, 1918, Lenin signed the Treaty of Brest-Litovsk with Germany and gave up eastern Poland, Ukraine, Finland, and the Baltic provinces. To his critics, Lenin argued that it made no difference because the spread of socialist revolution throughout Europe would make the treaty largely irrelevant. In any case, he had promised peace to the Russian people, but real peace did not come, for the country soon sank into civil war.

There was great opposition to the new Bolshevik or Communist regime, not only from groups loyal to the tsar but also from bourgeois and aristocratic liberals and anti-Leninist socialists. In addition, thousands of Allied troops were eventually sent to different parts of Russia in the hope of bringing Russia back into the war.

Between 1918 and 1921, the Bolshevik (or Red) Army was forced to fight on many fronts. The first serious threat to the Bolsheviks came from Siberia where a White (anti-Bolshevik) force attacked westward and advanced almost to the Volga River before being stopped. Attacks also came from the Ukrainians in the southeast and from the Baltic regions. In mid-1919, White forces swept through Ukraine and advanced almost to Moscow. At one point by late 1919, three separate White armies seemed to be closing in on the Bolsheviks, but were eventually pushed back. By 1920, the major White forces had been defeated, and Ukraine retaken. The next year, the Communist regime regained control over the independent nationalist governments in the Caucasus: Georgia, Russian Armenia, and Azerbaijan.

How had Lenin and the Bolsheviks triumphed over what seemed at one time to be overwhelming forces? For one thing, the Red Army became a well-disciplined and formidable fighting force, largely due to the organizational genius of Leon Trotsky. As commissar of war, Trotsky reinstated the draft and insisted on rigid discipline; soldiers who deserted or refused to obey orders were summarily executed.

The disunity of the anti-Communist forces seriously weakened the efforts of the Whites. Political differences created distrust among the Whites and prevented them from cooperating effectively with each other. Some

Whites insisted on restoring the tsarist regime, while others understood that only a more liberal democratic program had any chance of success. It was difficult enough to achieve military cooperation; political differences made it virtually impossible.

The Whites' inability to agree on a common goal was in sharp contrast to the Communists' single-minded sense of purpose. Inspired by their vision of a new socialist order, the Communists had the advantage of possessing the determination that comes from revolutionary fervor and revolutionary convictions.

The Communists also succeeded in translating their revolutionary faith into practical instruments of power. A policy of "war communism," for example, was used to ensure regular supplies for the Red Army. War communism included the nationalization of banks and most industries, the forcible requisition of grain from peasants,

♦ **"Agit-Prop" in the Civil War.** During the civil war in Russia, the Communists made effective use of agitational propaganda, or "agit-prop." Vibrant posters with brief slogans were used to educate the masses in the ideas of the Communists. The "agit-prop" poster shown here used the Red Army star to remind the people that Russia had become an armed camp.

The Russian Revolution

	1916
Murder of Rasputin	December
	1917
March of women in Petrograd	March 8
General strike in Petrograd	March 10
Establishment of Provisional Government	March 12
Tsar Nicholas II abdicates	March 15
Formation of Petrograd soviet	March
Lenin arrives in Russia	April 3
Bolsheviks gain majority in Petrograd soviet	October
Bolsheviks overthrow Provisional Government	November 6–7
	1918
Lenin disbands the Constituent Assembly	January
Treaty of Brest-Litovsk	March 3
Civil war	1918–1921
Lenin adopts New Economic Policy	1921
Lenin dies	1924
Trotsky is expelled from the Communist Party	1927

and the centralization of state administration under Bolshevik control. Another Bolshevik instrument was "revolutionary terror." Although the old tsarist secret police had been abolished, a new Red secret police—known as the Cheka—replaced it. The Red Terror instituted by the Cheka aimed at nothing less than the destruction of all those who opposed the new regime. The Red Terror added an element of fear to the Bolshevik regime.

Finally, the intervention of foreign armies enabled the Communists to appeal to the powerful force of Russian patriotism. Although the Allied powers had intervened initially in Russia to encourage the Russians to remain in the war, the end of the war on November 11, 1918, had made that purpose inconsequential. Nevertheless, Allied troops remained, and more were even sent as Allied countries did not hide their anti-Bolshevik feelings. At one point, over 100,000 foreign troops, mostly Japanese,

British, American, and French, were stationed on Russian soil. These forces rarely engaged in pitched battles, however, nor did they pursue a common strategy, although they gave material assistance to anti-Bolshevik forces. This intervention by the Allies enabled the Communist government to appeal to patriotic Russians to fight the foreign invaders. Allied interference was never substantial enough to make a military difference in the civil war, but it did serve indirectly to help the Bolshevik cause.

By 1921, the Communists had succeeded in retaining control of Russia. In the course of the civil war, the Bolshevik regime had also transformed Russia into a bureaucratically centralized state dominated by a single party. It was also a state that was largely hostile to the Allied powers that had sought to assist the Bolsheviks' enemies in the civil war.

But the civil war in Russia had taken an enormous toll of life. During the civil war, Lenin had pursued a policy of war communism, but once the war was over, peasants began to sabotage the program by hoarding food. Added to this problem was drought, which caused a great famine between 1920 and 1922 that claimed as many as five million lives. Industrial collapse paralleled the agricultural disaster. By 1921, industrial output was only 20 percent of its 1913 levels. Russia was exhausted. As Leon Trotsky said, "the collapse of the productive forces surpassed anything of the kind that history had ever seen. The country, and the government with it, were at the very edge of the abyss."[8]

In March 1921, Lenin pulled Russia back from the abyss by aborting war communism in favor of his New Economic Policy (NEP). Lenin's NEP was a modified version of the old capitalist system. Forced requisitioning of food from the peasants was halted, and peasants were now allowed to sell their produce openly. Retail stores as well as small industries that employed fewer than twenty employees could now operate under private ownership, although heavy industry, banking, and mines remained in the hands of the government. Already by 1922, a revived market and good harvest had brought an end to famine; Soviet agriculture climbed to 75 percent of its prewar level. Industry, especially state-owned heavy industry, fared less well and continued to stagnate. Only coal production had reached prewar levels by 1926. Overall, the NEP had saved Communist Russia from complete economic disaster even though Lenin and other leading Communists intended it to be only a temporary, tactical retreat from the goals of communism.

Lenin's death in 1924 inaugurated a struggle for power among the seven members of the Politburo, the institution that had become the leading organ of the party. The Politburo was severely divided over the future direction of Soviet Russia. The Left, led by Leon Trotsky, wanted to end the NEP and launch Russia on the path of rapid industrialization, primarily at the expense of the peasantry. This same group wanted to carry the revolution on, believing that the survival of the Russian Revolution ultimately depended on the spread of communism abroad. Another group in the Politburo, called the Right, rejected the cause of world revolution and wanted to concentrate instead on constructing a socialist state in Russia. This group also favored a continuation of Lenin's NEP because they believed that too rapid industrialization would harm the living standards of the Soviet peasantry.

These ideological divisions were underscored by an intense personal rivalry between Leon Trotsky and Joseph Stalin. In 1924, Trotsky held the post of commissar of war and was the leading spokesman for the Left in the Politburo. Joseph Stalin (1879–1953) was content to hold the dull bureaucratic job of party general secretary while other Politburo members held party positions that enabled them to display their brilliant oratorical abilities. But Stalin was a good organizer (his fellow Bolsheviks called him "Comrade Card-Index"), and the other members of the Politburo soon found that the position of party secretary was really the most important in the party hierarchy. Stalin used his post as party general secretary to gain complete control of the Communist Party. Trotsky was expelled from the party in 1927. By 1929, Stalin had succeeded in eliminating the Old Bolsheviks of the revolutionary era from the Politburo and establishing a dictatorship so powerful that the Russian tsars of old would have been envious.

Conclusion

World War I shattered the liberal, rational society of late nineteenth- and early twentieth-century Europe. The incredible destruction and the death of almost 10 million people undermined the whole idea of progress. New propaganda techniques had manipulated entire populations into sustaining their involvement in a meaningless slaughter.

World War I was a total war and involved an unprecedented mobilization of resources and populations and increased government centralization of power over the lives of its citizens. Civil liberties, such as freedom of the press, speech, assembly, and movement, were circumscribed in the name of national security. World War I made the practice of strong central authority a way of life.

The turmoil wrought by World War I seemed to open the door to even greater insecurity. Revolutions in Russia and the Middle East dismembered old empires and created new states that gave rise to unexpected problems. Expectations that Europe and the world would return to normalcy were soon dashed by the failure to achieve a lasting peace, economic collapse, and the rise of authoritarian governments that not only restricted individual freedoms, but sought even greater control over the lives of their subjects in order to manipulate and guide them to achieve the goals of their totalitarian regimes.

Finally, World War I ended the age of European hegemony over world affairs. By demolishing their own civilization on the battlegrounds of Europe in World War I, Europeans inadvertently encouraged the subject peoples of their vast colonial empires to initiate movements for national independence. In the next chapter, we examine some of those movements.

CHAPTER NOTES

1. Arnold Toynbee, *Surviving the Future* (New York, 1971), pp. 106–7.
2. Quoted in Joachim Remak, "1914—The Third Balkan War: Origins Reconsidered," *Journal of Modern History* 43 (1971): 364–65.
3. Quoted in J. M. Winter, *The Experience of World War I* (New York, 1989), p. 142.
4. Quoted in Catherine W. Reilly, ed., *Scars upon My Heart: Women's Poetry and Verse of the First World War* (London, 1981), p. 90.
5. Harold Nicolson, *Peacemaking, 1919* (Boston and New York, 1933), pp. 31–32.
6. Quoted in Robert Paxton, *Europe in the Twentieth Century,* 2d ed. (San Diego, 1985), p. 237.
7. Quoted in William M. Mandel, *Soviet Women* (Garden City, N.Y., 1975), p. 43.
8. Irving Howe, ed., *The Basic Writings of Trotsky* (London, 1963), p. 162.

SUGGESTED READINGS

The historical literature on the causes of World War I is enormous. A good starting point is the work by J. Joll, *The Origins of the First World War* (London, 1984). The belief that Germany was primarily responsible for the war was argued vigorously by the German scholar F. Fischer, *Germany's Aims in the First World War* (New York, 1967); *World Power or Decline: The Controversy over Germany's Aims in World War I* (New York, 1974); and *War of Illusions: German Policies from 1911 to 1914* (New York, 1975). The role of each great power has been reassessed in a series of books on the causes of World War I. They include V. R. Berghahn, *Germany and the Approach of War in 1914* (London, 1973); Z. S. Steiner, *Britain and the Origins of the First World War* (New York, 1977); J. F. Keiger, *France and the Origins of the First World War* (New York, 1984); and D. C. B. Lieven, *Russia and the Origins of the First World War* (New York, 1984). The theory of the domestic origins of the war is probed in A. Mayer, *The Persistence of the Old Regime* (New York, 1981).

There are two good recent accounts of World War I in M. Gilbert, *The First World War* (New York, 1994) and the lavishly illustrated book by J. M. Winter, *The Experience of World War I* (New York, 1989). For an account of the military operations of the war, see the classic work by B. H. Liddell-Hart, *History of the First World War* (Boston, 1970). The nature of trench warfare is examined in T. Ashworth, *Trench Warfare, 1914–1918: The Live and Let-Live System* (London, 1980). On the morale of World War I soldiers, see J. Keegan, *The Face of Battle* (London, 1975). The war at sea is studied in R. Hough, *The Great War at Sea, 1914–18* (Oxford, 1983). In *The Great War and Modern Memory* (London, 1975), P. Fussell attempted to show how British writers described their war experiences. Although scholars do not always agree with her conclusions, B. Tuchman's *The Guns of August* (New York, 1962) is a magnificently written account of the opening days of the war. For an interesting perspective on World War I and the beginnings of the modern world, see M. Eksteins, *Rites of Spring: The Great War and the Birth of the Modern Age* (Boston, 1989).

For a good account of the economic consequences of the war for the European states, see G. Hardach, *The First World War, 1914–1918* (London, 1976). On the role of women in World War I, see G. Braybon, *Women Workers in the First World War: The British Experience* (London, 1981) and J. M. Winter and R. M. Wall, eds., *The Upheaval of War: Family, Work and Welfare in Europe, 1914–1918* (Cambridge, 1988).

The role of war aims in shaping the peace settlement is examined in V. H. Rothwell, *British War Aims and Peace Diplomacy, 1914–1918* (Oxford, 1971) and D. R. Stevenson, *French War Aims against Germany, 1914–1919* (New York, 1982). That fear of Bolshevism was a factor at the Paris Peace Conference is argued in A. Mayer, *The Politics and Diplomacy of Peacemaking: Containment and Counter-Revolution at Versailles, 1918–1919* (New York, 1967).

For a general introduction to the interwar period, see R. J. Sontag, *A Broken World, 1919–39* (New York, 1971). On European security issues after the Peace of Paris, see S. Marks, *The Illusion of Peace: Europe's International Relations, 1918–1933* (New York, 1976). The Locarno agreements have been well examined in J. Jacobson, *Locarno Diplomacy* (Princeton, N. J., 1972). The important role of French diplomacy in the 1920s is examined in J. M. Hughes, *To the Maginot Line: The Politics of French Military Preparations in the 1920s* (Cambridge, Mass., 1971). On German foreign policy, see the older but valuable work of H. W. Gatzke, *Stresemann and the Rearmament of Germany* (Baltimore, Md., 1965). The best study on the problem of reparations is now M. Trachtenberg, *Reparations in World Politics* (New York, 1980), which paints a more positive view of French policies. The "return to normalcy" after the war is analyzed in C. S. Maier, *Recasting Bourgeois Europe: Stabilization in France, Germany, and Italy in the Decade after World War I* (Princeton, N.J., 1975). Also valuable is D. P. Silverman, *Reconstructing Europe after the Great War* (Cambridge, Mass., 1982). On the Great Depression, see C. P. Kindleberger, *The World in Depression, 1929–39*, rev. ed. (Berkeley, Calif., 1986).

A good introduction to the Russian Revolution can be found in S. Fitzpatrick, *The Russian Revolution, 1917–1932* (New York, 1982) and R. V. Daniels, *Red October* (New York, 1967). On Lenin, see R. W. Clark, *Lenin* (New York, 1988) and the valuable work by A. B.

Ulam, *The Bolsheviks* (New York, 1965). The role of workers in the events of Russian Revolution is examined in D. Koenker, *Moscow Workers and the 1917 Revolution* (Princeton, N.J., 1981). On Allied intervention in the civil war, see M. Kettle, *Russia and the Allies, 1917–1920* (Minneapolis, 1981). There is now a comprehensive study of the Russian civil war in W. B. Lincoln, *Red Victory: A History of the Russian Civil War* (New York, 1989).

World War I and the Russian Revolution are also well covered in two good general surveys, R. Paxton, *Europe in the Twentieth Century*, 2d ed. (San Diego, 1985) and A. Rudhart, *Twentieth Century Europe* (Englewood Cliffs, N.J., 1986).

CHAPTER
25

Nationalism, Revolution, and Dictatorship: Africa, Asia, and Latin America from 1919 to 1939

In 1930, Mohandas Gandhi, the sixty-one-year-old leader of the nonviolent movement for Indian independence from British rule, began a march to the sea with seventy-eight followers. Their destination was Dandi, a little coastal town some 240 miles away. The group covered about twelve miles a day. As they went, Gandhi preached his doctrine of nonviolent resistance to British rule in every village he passed through: "Civil disobedience is the inherent right of a citizen. He dare not give it up without ceasing to be a man." By the time he reached Dandi, twenty-four days later, his small group had become a nonviolent army of thousands. When they arrived at Dandi Gandhi picked up a pinch of salt from the sand. All along the coast, thousands did likewise, openly breaking British laws that prohibited Indians from making their own salt. The British had long profited from their monopoly on the making and sale of salt, an item much in demand in a tropical country. By their simple acts of disobedience, Gandhi and the Indian people had taken yet another step on their long march to independence.

The salt march was but one of many nonviolent activities that Mohandas Gandhi undertook between World War I and World War II to win India's goal of national independence from British rule. World War I had not only deeply affected the lives of Europeans, but it had also ended the age of European domination over world affairs. When Europeans devastated their own civilization on the battlefields of Europe, the subject peoples of their vast colonial empires were quick to understand what it meant. In Africa and

Reza Khan seizes power in Iran

Creation of Turkey
under Ataturk

Jewish settlers arrive in Palestine

Ibn Saud establishes Saudi Arabia

Formation of Chinese Communist Party

Northern Expedition in China

Creation of Nanjing Republic

The Long March

Formation of the Comintern

Gandhi's march
to the sea

American Good Neighbor Policy
begins

Vargas establishes
New State in Brazil

Asia, movements for national independence began to take shape. Some were inspired by the nationalist and liberal movements of the West, while others began to look toward the new Marxist model provided by the victory of the Communists in the Soviet Union, who soon worked to spread their revolutionary vision to African and Asian societies. In the Middle East, World War I ended the rule of the Ottoman Empire and created new states, some of which adopted Western features in order to modernize their countries. For some Latin American countries, the fascist dictatorships of Italy and Germany provided models for change.

The Rise of Nationalism

Although the West had emerged from its recent bloodletting relatively intact, its political and social foundations and its self-confidence had been severely undermined by the experience. Doubts about the future viability of Western civilization were widespread among Europeans, especially the intellectual elite. Perceptive observers in Asia and Africa quickly sensed the Europeans' declining confidence, and this in turn contributed to a rising tide of unrest against Western political domination throughout the colonial and semicolonial world. That unrest took a variety of forms, but was most evident in increasing worker activism, rural protest, and a rising national fervor among anticolonialist intellectuals. Even in those areas in Asia, Africa, and Latin America where independent states had successfully resisted the Western onslaught, the discontent fostered by the Great Depression led to a loss of confidence in democratic institutions and the rise of political dictatorships.

Modern Nationalism

The first stage of resistance to the West in Asia and Africa had met with humiliation and failure and must have confirmed many Westerners' conviction that colonial peoples lacked both the strength and the know-how to create modern states and govern their own destinies. In fact, the process was just beginning. The next phase, which can be described as the rise of modern nationalism, began to take shape at the beginning of the twentieth century and was the product of the convergence of several factors. The primary sources of anticolonialist sentiment were found in a new class of Westernized intellectuals in the urban centers created by colonial rule. In many cases, this new urban middle class, composed of merchants, petty functionaries, clerks, students, and professionals, had been educated in Western-style schools. A few had spent time in the West. In either case, they were the first generation of Asians and Africans to possess more than a rudimentary understanding of the institutions and values of the modern West. Many spoke Western languages, wore Western clothes, and worked in occupations connected with the colonial regime. Some, like Mahatma Gandhi in India, José Rizal in the Philippines, and Kwame Nkrumah in the Gold Coast, even wrote in the languages of their colonial masters.

The results were paradoxical. On the one hand, this "new class" admired Western culture and sometimes harbored a deep sense of contempt for traditional ways. On the other hand, many strongly resented the foreigners and their arrogant contempt for colonial peoples. While eager to introduce Western ideas and institutions into their own society, these intellectuals often resented the gap between ideal and reality, theory and practice, in colonial policy. Although Western political thought exalted democracy, equality, and individual freedom, these values were generally not applied in the colonies. Democratic institutions were primitive or nonexistent, and colonial subjects usually had access to only the most menial positions in the colonial bureaucracy. Equally important, the economic prosperity of the West was only imperfectly reflected in the colonies. To many Asians and Africans, colonialism meant the loss of their farmlands or demeaning and brutal employment on plantations or in sweatshops and factories run by foreigners.

Normally, middle-class Asians did not suffer in the same manner as impoverished peasants or menial workers on sugar or rubber plantations, but they, too, had complaints. They usually qualified only for menial jobs in the government or business. Even when employed, their salaries were normally lower than those of Europeans in similar occupations. The superiority of the Europeans over the natives was expressed in a variety of ways, including "whites only" clubs and the forms of language used to address colonial subjects. For example, Europeans would characteristically use the familiar form (normally used by adults to children) when talking to members of the local population.

Such conditions led many of the new urban educated class to be very ambivalent toward their colonial masters and the civilization that they represented. While willing to concede the superiority of many aspects of Western culture, these new intellectuals fiercely resented colonial rule and were determined to assert their own nationality and cultural destiny. Out of this mixture of hopes and resentments emerged the first stirrings of modern nationalism in Asia and Africa. During the first quarter of the century, in colonial and semicolonial societies across the entire arc of Asia from the Suez Canal to the shores of the Pacific Ocean, educated native peoples began to organize political parties and movements seeking reforms or the end of foreign rule and the restoration of independence.

RELIGION AND NATIONALISM

At first, many of the leaders of these movements did not focus clearly on the idea of nationhood, but tried to defend the economic interests or religious beliefs of the native population. In Burma, for example, the first expression of modern nationalism came from students at the University of Rangoon who formed an organization to protest against official persecution of the Buddhist religion and British lack of respect for local religious traditions. Calling themselves "Thakin" (a polite term in the Burman language meaning "lord" or "master," thus emphasizing their demand for the right to rule themselves), they protested against British arrogance and failure to observe local customs in Buddhist temples (visitors are expected to remove their footwear in a temple, a custom that was widely ignored by Europeans in colonial Burma). Only in the 1930s did they begin to focus specifically on the issue of national independence.

A similar example occurred in the Dutch East Indies, where the first quasi-political organization dedicated to the creation of a modern Indonesia, the Sarekat Islam (Islamic Association), began as a self-help society among Muslim merchants to fight against domination of the local economy by Chinese interests. Eventually, activist elements began to realize that the source of the problem was not the Chinese merchants, but the colonial presence, and in the 1920s Sarekat Islam was transformed into a new organization that focused on the issue of national independence—the Nationalist Party of Indonesia (PNI). Like the Thakins in Burma, this party would eventually lead the country to independence after World War II.

INDEPENDENCE OR MODERNIZATION?
THE NATIONALIST QUANDARY

Building a new nation, however, requires more than a shared sense of grievances against the foreign invader. By what means was independence to be achieved? Was independence or modernization the more important objective? What kind of political and economic system should be adopted once colonial rule had been overthrown? What national or cultural concept should be adopted as the symbol of the new nation, and which institutions and values should be preserved from the past?

Questions such as these created lively and sometimes acrimonious debate among patriotic elements throughout the colonial world. If national independence was the desired end, how could it be achieved? Could the Westerners be persuaded to leave by nonviolent measures, or would force be required? If the Western presence could be beneficial in terms of introducing much-needed reforms in traditional societies, then a gradualist approach made sense, but if the colonial regime was primarily an impediment to social and political change, then the first priority was to bring it to an end.

Another problem was how to adopt modern Western ideas and institutions while at the same time preserving the essential values that defined the indigenous culture. The vast majority of patriotic intellectuals were convinced that to survive, their societies must move with the times and adopt much of the Western way of life. The programs adopted by most nationalist parties displayed a devotion to such Western concepts as political democracy, economic industrialization, and national unity. Yet many were equally determined that the local culture could not, and should not, become simply a carbon copy of the West. What was the national identity, after all, if it did not incorporate some elements from the traditional way of life?

One of the reasons for using traditional values was to provide ideological symbols that the common people could understand. If the desired end was national independence, then, almost by definition, the new political parties needed to enlist the mass of the population in the common struggle. But how could ignorant peasants, plantation workers, fishermen, and sheepherders be made to understand complicated and unfamiliar concepts like democracy, industrialization, and nationhood? The problem was often one of communication, for most urban intellectuals had little in common with the teeming population in the countryside. As the Indonesian intellectual Sutan Sjahrir lamented, many Westernized intellectuals had more in common with their colonial rulers than with the native population in the rural villages (see the box on p. 919). As one French colonial official remarked in some surprise to a Vietnamese reformist, "Why, monsieur, you are more French than I am!"

Gandhi and the Indian National Congress

Nowhere in the colonial world were these issues debated more vigorously than in India. Before the Sepoy Mutiny, as we have seen, Indian consciousness had focused primarily on the question of religious identity (see Chapter 17). But in the latter half of the nineteenth century, a stronger sense of national consciousness began to arise, provoked by the conservative policies and racial arrogance of the British colonial authorities.

The first Indian nationalists were almost invariably upper class and educated. Many of them were from urban areas such as Bombay, Madras, and Calcutta. Some were trained in law and were members of the civil service. At first, many tended to prefer reform to revolution and accepted the idea that India needed modernization before it could handle the problems of independence. Otherwise, it would slip back into traditionalism. An exponent of this view was Gopal Gokhale (1866–1915), a moderate nationalist who hoped that he could convince the British to bring about needed reforms in Indian society. Gokhale and other like-minded reformists did have some effect. In the 1880s, the government launched a series of reforms introducing a measure of self-government for the first time. All too often, however, such efforts were sabotaged by local British officials.

The slow pace of reform convinced many Indian nationalists that relying on British benevolence was futile. In 1885, a small group of Indians, with some British participation, met in Bombay to form the Indian National Congress (INC). They hoped to speak for all India, but most were high-caste English-trained Hindus. Like their reformist predecessors, members of the INC did not demand immediate independence and accepted the need for reforms to end traditional abuses like child marriage and *sati*. At the same time, they called for an Indian share in the governing process and more spending on economic development and less on military campaigns along the frontier.

The British responded with a few concessions, such as accepting the principle of elective Indian participation on government councils, but in general change was glacially slow. As impatient members of the INC became disillusioned, radical leaders like Balwantrao Tilak (1856–1920) openly criticized the British while defending traditional customs like child marriage to solicit support from conservative elements within the local population. Tilak's activities split the INC between moderates and radicals, and he and his followers formed the New Party, which called for the use of terrorism and violence to achieve national independence. Tilak was eventually convicted of sedition.

The INC also had difficulty reconciling religious differences within its ranks. The stated goal of the INC was to seek self-determination for all Indians regardless of class or religious affiliation, but many of its leaders were Hindu and inevitably reflected Hindu concerns. By the first decade of the twentieth century, Muslims began to

≈ The Dilemma of the Intellectual ≈

Sutan Sjahrir (1909–1966) was a prominent leader of the Indonesian nationalist movement who briefly served as prime minister of the Republic of Indonesia in the 1950s. Like many Western-educated Asian intellectuals, he was tortured by the realization that by education and outlook he was closer to his colonial masters than to his own people. He wrote the following passage in a letter to his wife in 1935 and later included it in his book Out of Exile.

Sutan Sjahrir, *Out of Exile*

Am I perhaps estranged from my people? Why am I vexed by the things that fill their lives, and to which they are so attached? Why are the things that contain beauty for them and arouse their gentler emotions only senseless and displeasing for me? In reality, the spiritual gap between my people and me is certainly no greater than that between an intellectual in Holland and, for example, a Drents farmer, or even between the intellectual and the undeveloped people of Holland in general. The difference is rather, I think, that the intellectual in Holland does not feel this gap because there is a portion—even a fairly large portion—of his own people on approximately the same intellectual level as himself. And that portion is, moreover, precisely what constitutes the cultural life of Holland; namely, the intellectuals, the scientists, the artists, the writers.

This is what we lack here. Not only is the number of intellectuals in this country smaller in proportion to the total population—in fact, very much smaller—but in addition, the few who are here do not constitute any single entity in spiritual outlook, or in any spiritual life or single culture whatsoever. From the point of view of culture, they are still unconscious, and are only beginning to seek a form and a unity. It is for them so much more difficult than for the intellectuals in Holland. In Holland they build—both consciously and uncon-

sciously—on what is already there. They stand on and push forward from their past and their tradition; and even if they oppose it, they do so as a method of application or as a starting point.

In our country this is not the case. Here there has been no spiritual or cultural life, and no intellectual progress for centuries. There are the much-praised Eastern art forms but what are these except bare rudiments from a feudal culture that cannot possibly provide a dynamic fulcrum for people of the twentieth century? What can the puppet and other simple and mystical symbols offer us in a broad and intellectual sense? Our spiritual needs are needs of the twentieth century; our problems and our views are of the twentieth century. Our inclination is no longer toward the mystical, but toward reality, clarity, and objectivity.

In substance, we can never accept the essential difference between the East and the West, because for our spiritual needs we are in general dependent on the West, not only scientifically but culturally.

We intellectuals here are much closer to Europe or America than we are to the Borobudur or Mahabharata or to the primitive Islamic culture of Java and Sumatra. Which is our basis: the West, or the rudiments of feudal culture that are still to be found in our Eastern society?

So, it seems, the problem stands in principle. It is seldom put forth by us in this light, and instead most of us search unconsciously for a synthesis that will leave us internally tranquil. We want to have both Western science and Eastern philosophy, the Eastern "spirit," in the culture. But what is this Eastern spirit? It is, they say, the sense of the higher, of spirituality, of the eternal and religious, as opposed to the materialism of the East. I have heard this countless times, but it has never convinced me.

call for the creation of a separate Muslim League to represent the interests of the millions of Muslims in Indian society.

In 1913, a young Hindu lawyer returned from South Africa to become active in the INC; his work would transform the movement and galvanize India's struggle for independence and identity. Mohandas Gandhi (1869–1948) was born in Gujarat, in western India, the

son of a government minister. In the late nineteenth century, he studied in London and became a lawyer. In 1893, he went to South Africa to work in a law firm serving Indian emigrés working as laborers there. He soon became aware of the racial prejudice and exploitation experienced by Indians living in the territory and tried to organize them to improve their living conditions.

On his return to India, Gandhi immediately became

active in the independence movement. Using his experience in South Africa, he set up a movement based on nonviolent resistance (the Indian term was *satyagraha*, "hold fast to the truth") to try to force the British to improve the lot of the poor and grant independence to India. His goal was twofold: to convert the British to his views while simultaneously strengthening the unity and sense of self-respect of his compatriots. Gandhi was particularly concerned about the plight of the millions of untouchables, whom he called *harijans*, or "children of God." When the British attempted to suppress dissent, he called on his followers to refuse to obey British regulations. He began to manufacture his own clothes (Gandhi now dressed in a simple *dhoti* made of coarse homespun cotton) and adopted the spinning wheel as a symbol of Indian resistance to imports of British textiles.

Gandhi, now increasingly known as India's "Great Soul" (*Mahatma*), organized mass protests to achieve his aims, but in 1919 they got out of hand and led to violence and British reprisals. British troops killed hundreds of unarmed protesters in the enclosed square in the city of Amritsar in northwestern India. When the protests spread, Gandhi was horrified at the violence and briefly retreated from active politics. Nevertheless, he was arrested for his role in the protests and spent several years in prison.

Gandhi combined his anticolonial activities with an appeal to the spiritual instincts of all Indians. Though born and raised a Hindu, he possessed a universalist approach to the idea of God that transcended individual religion, although it was shaped by the historical themes of Hindu religious belief. At a speech given in London in September 1931, he expressed his view of the nature of God as "an indefinable mysterious power that pervades everything. . . , an unseen power which makes itself felt and yet defies all proof. . . ."[1]

While Gandhi was in prison, the political situation continued to evolve. In 1921, the British passed the Government of India Act to expand the role of Indians in the governing process and transform the heretofore advisory Legislative Council into a bicameral parliament, two-thirds of whose members would be elected. Similar bodies were created at the provincial level. In a stroke, five million Indians were enfranchised. But such reforms were no longer enough for many members of the INC, which under its new leader Motilal Nehru wanted to push aggressively for full independence. The British exacerbated the situation by increasing the salt tax and prohibiting the Indian people from manufacturing or harvesting their own salt. Gandhi, now released from prison, returned to

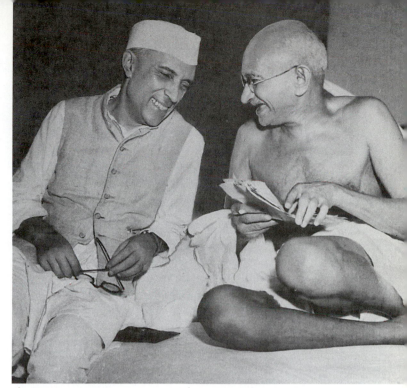

◆ **Gandhi and Nehru.** Mahatma Gandhi, India's "Great Soul," became the emotional leader of India's struggle for independence from British colonial rule. Unlike many other nationalist leaders, Gandhi rejected the materialistic culture of the West and urged his followers to return to the native traditions of the Indian village. To illustrate his point, Gandhi dressed in the simple Indian *dhoti* rather than in the Western fashion favored by many of his colleagues. Along with Gandhi, Jawaharlal Nehru was a leading figure in the Indian struggle for independence. Unlike Gandhi, however, his goal was to transform India into a modern industrial society. After independence, he became the nation's prime minister until his death in 1964.

his earlier policy of civil disobedience by openly joining several dozen supporters in a 240-mile walk to the sea, where he picked up a lump of salt and urged Indians to ignore the law. Gandhi and many other members of the INC were arrested (see the box on p. 922).

In the 1930s, a new figure entered the movement in the person of Jawaharlal Nehru (1889–1964), son of the INC leader Motilal Nehru. Educated in the law in Great Britain and a brahmin by birth, Nehru personified the new Anglo-Indian politician: secular, rational, upper class, and intellectual. In fact, he appeared to be everything that Gandhi was not. With his emergence, the independence movement embarked on two paths, religious and secular, native and Western, traditional and modern. The dual character of the INC leadership may well have strengthened the movement by bringing together the two primary impulses behind the desire for

❧ Gandhi and Civil Disobedience ❧

After his return to India in 1913, Mahatma Gandhi gradually became convinced that only a policy of civil disobedience could effectively bring an end to British rule in the subcontinent. In this letter to Lord Irwin, the viceroy of India, he sought to persuade the British to take the necessary actions to avoid future conflict.

Mahatma Gandhi: Letter to Lord Irwin

Dear Friend,

Before embarking on civil disobedience and taking the risk I have dreaded to take all these years, I would fain approach you and find a way out.

My personal faith is absolutely clear. I cannot intentionally hurt anything that lives, much less fellow human beings, even though they may do the greatest wrong to me and mine. Whilst, therefore, I hold the British rule to be a curse, I do not intend harm to a single Englishman or to any legitimate interest he may have in India.

I must not be misunderstood. Though I hold the British rule in India to be a curse, I do not, therefore, consider Englishmen in general to be worse than any other people on earth. I have the privilege of claiming many Englishmen as dearest friends. Indeed much that I have learnt of the evil of British rule is due to the writings of frank and courageous Englishmen who have not hesitated to tell the unpalatable truth about that rule.

And why do I regard the British rule as a curse?

It has impoverished the dumb millions by a system of progressive exploitation and by a ruinously expensive military and civil administration which the country can never afford.

It has reduced us politically to serfdom. It has sapped the foundations of our culture. And, by the policy of cruel disarmament, it has degraded us spiritually. Lacking the inward strength, we have been reduced, by all but universal disarmament, to a state bordering on cowardly helplessness.

. . . .

Let me put before you some of the salient points.

The terrific pressure of land revenue, which furnishes a large part of the total, must undergo considerable modification in an independent India. Even the much vaunted permanent settlement benefits the few rich samindars, not the ryots. The ryot [farmer] has remained as helpless as ever. He is a mere tenant at will.

Not only, then, has the land revenue to be considerably reduced, but the whole revenue system has to be so revised as to make the ryot's good its primary concern. But the British system seems to be designed to crush the very life out of him. Even the salt he must use to live is so taxed as to make the burden fall heaviest on him, if only because of the heartless impartiality of its incidence. The tax shows itself still more burdensome on the poor man when it is remembered that salt is the one thing he must eat more than the rich man both individually and collectively. The drink and drug revenue is derived from the poor. It saps the foundations too, both of their health and morals. It is defended under the false plea of individual freedom, but, in reality, is maintained for its own sake. . . .

It is common cause that, however disorganized and, for the time being, insignificant it may be, the party of violence is gaining ground and making itself felt. Its end is the same as mine. But I am convinced that it cannot bring the desired relief to the dumb millions. And the conviction is growing deeper and deeper in me that nothing but unadulterated non-violence can check the organized violence of the British Government. Many think that non-violence is not an active force. My experience, limited though it undoubtedly is, shows that non-violence can be an intensely active force. It is my purpose to set in motion that force as well against the organized violent force of the British rule as [against] the unorganized violent force of the growing party of violence. To sit still would be to give rein to both the forces above mentioned. Having an unquestioning and immovable faith in the efficacy of non-violence as I know it, it would be sinful on my part to wait any longer.

This non-violence will be expressed through civil disobedience, for the moment confined to the inmates of the Satyagraha Ashram, but ultimately designed to cover all those who choose to join the movement with its obvious limitations.

I know that in embarking on non-violence I shall be running what might fairly be termed a mad risk. But the victories of truth have never been won without risks, often of the gravest character. Conversion of a nation that has consciously or unconsciously preyed upon another, far more numerous, far more ancient and no less cultured than itself, is worth any amount of risk.

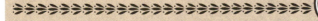

A Call for a Muslim State

Mohammed Iqbal, a well-known Muslim poet in colonial India, was also a prominent advocate of the creation of a separate state for Muslims in South Asia. In this passage from an address he presented to the All-India Muslim League in December 1930, he explained the rationale for his proposal.

Mohammed Iqbal, Speech to the All-India Muslim League

It cannot be denied that Islam, regarded as an ethical ideal plus a certain kind of polity—by which expression I mean a social structure regulated by a legal system and animated by a specific ethical ideal—has been the chief formative factor in the life-history of the Muslims of India. It has furnished those basic emotions and loyalties which gradually unify scattered individuals and groups and finally transform them into a well-defined people. Indeed it is no exaggeration to say that India is perhaps the only country in the world where Islam, as a people-building force, has worked at its best. In India, as elsewhere, the structure of Islam as a society is almost entirely due to the working of Islam as a culture inspired by a specific ethical ideal. What I mean to say is that Muslim society, with its remarkable homogeneity and inner unity, has grown to be what it is under the pressure of the laws and institutions associated with the culture of Islam.

Communalism in its higher aspect, then, is indispensable to the formation of a harmonious whole in a country like India. The units of Indian society are not territorial as in European countries. India is a continent of human groups belonging to different religions.

Their behavior is not at all determined by a common race-consciousness. Even the Hindus do not form a homogeneous group. The principle of European democracy cannot be applied to India without recognizing the fact of communal groups. The Muslim demand for the creation of a Muslim India within India is, therefore, perfectly justified.

The idea need not alarm the Hindus or the British. India is the greatest Muslim country in the world. The life of Islam, as a cultural force, in this country very largely depends on its centralization in a specified territory. This centralization of the most living portion of the Muslims of India, whose military and police service has, notwithstanding unfair treatment from the British, made the British rule possible in this country, will eventually solve the problem of India as well as of Asia. It will intensify their sense of responsibility and deepen their patriotic feeling. Thus possessing full opportunity of development within the body politic of India, the North-West India Muslims will prove the best defenders of India against a foreign invasion, be the invasion one of ideas or of bayonets. . . .

I therefore demand the formation of a consolidated Muslim State in the best interests of India and Islam. For India it means security and peace resulting from an internal balance of power; for Islam an opportunity to rid itself of the stamp that Arabian imperialism was forced to give it, to mobilize its law, its education, its culture, and to bring them into closer contact with its own original spirit and with the spirit of modern times.

independence: elite nationalism and the primal force of Indian traditionalism. But it portended trouble for the nation's new leadership in defining India's future path in the contemporary world. In the meantime, Muslim discontent with Hindu dominance over the INC was increasing. In 1930, the Muslim League called for the creation of a separate Muslim state of Pakistan (meaning "the land of the pure") in the northwest. As communal strife between Hindus and Muslims increased, many Indians came to realize with sorrow (and some British colonialists with satisfaction) that British rule was all that stood between peace and civil war (see the box above).

The Nationalist Revolt in the Middle East

In the Middle East, as in Europe, World War I hastened the collapse of old empires. The Ottoman Empire had been growing steadily weaker since the end of the eighteenth century, troubled by rising governmental corruption, a decline in the effectiveness of the sultans, and the loss of considerable territory in the Balkans and southwestern Russia. In North Africa, Ottoman authority, tenuous at best, had disintegrated in the nineteenth century, enabling the French to seize Algeria and Tunisia and the British to establish a protectorate over the Nile River valley.

MUSTAPHA KEMAL AND THE MODERNIZATION OF TURKEY

Reformist elements in Istanbul, to be sure, had tried to resist the trend. The first phase had taken place in the eighteenth century, when Westernizing forces, concerned at the shrinkage of the empire, had tried to modernize the army. But, as other traditional forces would later discover, a modern army cannot compensate for decrepit political and social institutions. One energetic sultan, Selim III (1789–1807), tried to establish a "new order" that would streamline both the civilian and military bureaucracies, but janissary forces (the sultan's private guard recruited from among Christian subjects in the Balkans), alarmed at the potential loss of their power, revolted and brought the experiment to an end. Further efforts during the first half of the nineteenth century were somewhat more successful and resulted in the removal of the janissaries from power and the institution of a series of bureaucratic, military, and educational reforms. New roads were built, the power of local landlords was reduced, and an Imperial Rescript issued in 1856 granted equal rights to all subjects of the empire, whatever their religious preference.

◆ **Mustapha Kemal Ataturk.** The war hero Mustapha Kemal took the initiative in creating a new Republic of Turkey. As president of the new republic, Ataturk (or "father Turk" as he came to be called) worked hard to transform Turkey into a modern secular state by modernizing the economy, adopting Western styles of dress, and breaking the powerful hold of Islamic traditions.

But military defeats continued, as Greece declared its independence and Ottoman power declined steadily in the Middle East. A rising sense of nationality among Serbs, Armenians, and other minority peoples threatened the internal stability and cohesion of the empire. In the 1870s, a new generation of Ottoman reformers seized power in Istanbul and pushed through a constitution aimed at forming a legislative assembly that would represent all the peoples in the state. But the sultan they placed on the throne, Abdulhamid (1876–1909), suspended the new charter and attempted to rule by traditional authoritarian means.

By the end of the nineteenth century, the defunct 1876 constitution had become a symbol of change for reformist elements, now grouped together under the common name "Young Turks" (undoubtedly borrowed from the "Young Italy" nationalist movement earlier in the century). Leading members of the group established a so-called Committee of Union and Progress (CUP), which found support within the Ottoman army and administration and among Turks living in exile. In 1908, Young Turk elements forced the sultan to restore the constitution. He was removed from power the following year.

But the Young Turks had appeared at a moment of extreme fragility for the empire. Internal rebellions, combined with Austrian annexations of Ottoman territories in the Balkans, undermined the support for the new government and provoked the army to step in. With most minorities from the old empire now removed from Istanbul's authority, many ethnic Turks began to embrace a new concept of a Turkish state based on all those of Turkish nationality.

The final blow to the old empire came in World War I, when the Ottoman government decided to ally with Germany in the hope of driving the British from Egypt and restoring Ottoman rule over the Nile valley. The new sultan called for a holy war by Muslim subjects in Russian and in British- and French-ruled territories in the Middle East. In response, the British declared an official protectorate over Egypt and, aided by the efforts of the dashing if eccentric British adventurer T. E. Lawrence (popularly known as "Lawrence of Arabia"), sought to undermine Ottoman rule in the Arabian peninsula by encouraging Arab nationalist activities there. In 1916, the local governor of Mecca, encouraged by the British, declared Arabia independent from Ottoman rule, while British troops, advancing from Egypt, seized Palestine. In October 1918, having suffered over 300,000 casualties during the war, the Ottoman Empire negotiated an armistice with the Allied powers.

During the next few years, the tottering empire began

to fall apart, as the British and the French made plans to divide up Ottoman territories in the Middle East and the Greeks won Allied approval to seize the western parts of the Anatolian peninsula for their dream of re-creating the substance of the old Byzantine Empire. The impending collapse energized key elements in Turkey under the leadership of war hero Colonel Mustapha Kemal (1881–1938), who had commanded Turkish forces in their heroic defense of the Dardanelles against a British invasion during World War I. Now he resigned from the army and convoked a National Congress that called for the creation of an elected government and the preservation of the remaining territories of the old empire in a new Republic of Turkey. Establishing his new capital at Ankara, Kemal's forces drove the Greeks from the Anatolian peninsula and persuaded the British to agree to a new treaty. In 1923, the last of the Ottoman sultans fled the country, which was now declared a Turkish republic. The Ottoman Empire had finally come to an end.

During the next few years, President Mustapha Kemal (now popularly known as Ataturk or "father Turk") attempted to transform Turkey into a modern secular republic. The trappings of a democratic system were put in place, centered on an elected Grand National Assembly, but the president was relatively intolerant of opposition and harshly suppressed critics of his rule. Turkish nationalism was emphasized, and the Turkish language, now written in the roman alphabet, was shorn of many of its Arabic elements. Popular education was emphasized, old aristocratic titles like pasha and bey were abolished, and all Turkish citizens were given family names in the European style.

Ataturk also took steps to modernize the economy. A light industrial sector, consisting of factories producing textiles, glass, paper, and cement, was established, and a five-year plan on the Soviet model was drawn up to provide for state direction over the economy. Ataturk was no admirer of Soviet communism, however, and the Turkish economy can be better described as a form of state capitalism. He also encouraged the modernization of the agricultural sector through the establishment of training institutions and model farms, but such reforms had relatively little effect among the nation's predominantly conservative peasantry.

Perhaps the most significant aspect of Ataturk's reform program was his attempt to break the power of the Islamic religion and transform Turkey into a secular state. The caliphate was formally abolished in 1924 (see the box on p. 926), and the *Shari'ya* was replaced by a revised version of the Swiss law code. The fez (the brimless cap worn by Turkish Muslims) was abolished as a form of

headdress, and women were forbidden to wear the veil in the traditional Islamic custom. Women received the right to vote in 1934 and were legally guaranteed equal rights with men in all aspects of marriage and inheritance. Education and the professions were now open to citizens of both sexes, and some women even began to take part in politics. All citizens were given the right to convert to another religion at will.

Finally, Ataturk attempted to break the waning power of the various religious orders of Islam, abolishing all monasteries and brotherhoods and declaring that "the straightest, truest way is the way of civilization. To be a man," he said, "it is enough to do as civilization requires. The heads of the brotherhoods will understand this truth I have uttered in all its clarity, and will of their own accord at once close their convents, and accept the fact that their disciples have at last come of age."[2] The legacy of Mustapha Kemal Ataturk was enormous. Although not all of his reforms were widely accepted in practice, especially by devout Muslims, the bulk of the changes that he introduced were retained after his death in 1938. In virtually every respect, the Turkish republic was the product of his determined efforts to create a modern Turkish nation.

MODERNIZATION IN IRAN

In the meantime, a similar process was underway in Persia. Under the Qajar dynasty (1794–1925), the country had not been very successful in resisting Russian advances in the Caucasus or resolving its domestic problems. To secure themselves against foreign influence, the shahs moved the capital from Tabriz to Tehran, in a mountainous area just south of the Caspian Sea. During the mid-nineteenth century, one modernizing shah attempted to introduce political and economic reforms, but was impeded by resistance from tribal and religious—predominantly Shi'ite—forces. To buttress its rule, the dynasty turned increasingly to Russia and Great Britain to protect itself from its own people.

Eventually, the growing foreign presence led to the rise of a native Persian nationalist movement. Its efforts were largely directed against Russian advances in the northwest and the growing European influence within the small modern industrial sector, the profits from which left the country or disappeared into the hands of the dynasty's ruling elite. Supported actively by Shi'ite religious leaders, opposition to the regime rose steadily among both peasants and merchants in the cities, and in 1906 popular pressures forced the reigning shah to grant a constitution on the Western model. It was an eerie foretaste of the revolution of 1979.

≽ Mustapha Kemal's Case against the Caliphate ≼

As part of his plan to transform Turkey into a modern society, Mustapha Kemal Ataturk proposed to bring an end to the caliphate, which had been in the hands of Ottoman sultans since the formation of the empire. In the following passage from a speech to the National Assembly, he gives his reasons.

Ataturk's Speech to the Assembly, October 1924

I must call attention to the fact that Hodja Shukri Effendi [a pious Muslim who opposed Mustapha Kemal's religious policy] as well as the politicians who pushed forward his person and signature, had intended to substitute the sovereign bearing the title of Sultan or Padishah by a monarch with the title of Caliph. The only difference was that, instead of speaking of a monarch of this or that country or nation, they now spoke of a monarch whose authority extended over a population of three hundred million souls belonging to manifold nations and dwelling in different continents of the world. Into the hands of this great monarch, whose authority was to extend over the whole of Islam, they placed as the only power that of the Turkish people, that is to say, only from 10 to 15 millions of these three hundred million subjects. The monarch designated under the title of Caliph was to guide the affairs of these Muslim peoples and to secure the execution of the religious prescriptions which would best correspond to their worldly interests. He was to defend the rights of all Muslims and concentrate all the affairs of the Muslim world in his hands with effective authority.

The sovereign entitled Caliph was to maintain justice among the three hundred million Muslims on the terrestrial globe, to safeguard the rights of these peoples, to prevent any event that could encroach upon order and security, and confront every attack which the Muslims would be called upon to encounter from the side of other nations. It was to be part of his attributes to preserve by all means the welfare and spiritual development of Islam. . . .

If the Caliph and Caliphate, as they maintained, were to be invested with a dignity embracing the whole of Islam, ought they not to have realized in all justice that a crushing burden would be imposed on Turkey, on her existence; her entire resources and all her forces would be placed at the disposal of the Caliph? . . .

For centuries our nation was guided under the influence of these erroneous ideas. But what has been the result of it? Everywhere they have lost millions of men. "Do you know," I asked, "how many sons of Anatolia have perished in the scorching deserts of the Yemen? Do you know the losses we have suffered in holding Syria and Egypt and in maintaining our position in Africa? And do you see what has come out of it? Do you know?

"Those who favor the idea of placing the means at the disposal of the Caliph to brave the whole world and the power to administer the affairs of the whole of Islam must not appeal to the population of Anatolia alone but to the great Muslim agglomerations which are eight or ten times as rich in men.

"New Turkey, the people of New Turkey, have no reason to think of anything else but their own existence and their own welfare. She has nothing more to give away to others."

As in the Ottoman Empire and Manchu China, however, the modernizers had moved too soon, before the power base was secure. With the support of the Russians and the British, the shah was able to retain control, while the two foreign powers began to divide the country into separate spheres of influence. One reason for the growing foreign presence in Persia was the discovery of oil reserves in the southern part of the country in 1908. Within a few years, oil exports increased rapidly, with the bulk of the profits going into the pockets of British investors.

In 1921, an officer in the Persian army by the name of Reza Khan (1878–1944) led a mutiny that seized power in Tehran. The new ruler's original intention had been to establish a republic, but resistance from traditional forces impeded his efforts, and in 1925 a new Pahlavi dynasty, with Reza Khan as shah, replaced the now defunct Qajar dynasty. During the next few years, Reza Khan attempted to follow the example of Mustapha Kemal Ataturk in Turkey by introducing a number of reforms to strengthen the central government, modernize the civilian and military bureaucracy, and establish a modern economic infrastructure.

Unlike Mustapha Kemal Ataturk, Reza Khan did not attempt to destroy the power of Islamic beliefs, but he did encourage the establishment of a Western-style educational system and forbade women to wear the veil in public. To strengthen the sense of Persian nationalism and reduce the power of Islam, he attempted to popularize the symbols and beliefs of pre-Islamic times. Like his Qajar predecessors, however, Reza Khan was hindered by the continuation of strong foreign influence, and when the Soviet Union and Great Britain decided to send troops to the country during World War II, he resigned in protest and died three years later.

THE RISE OF ARAB NATIONALISM AND THE PROBLEM OF PALESTINE

As we have seen, the Arab uprising during World War I helped bring about the demise of the Ottoman Empire. Actually, unrest against Ottoman rule had existed in the Arabian peninsula since the eighteenth century, when the Wahhabi revolt attempted to drive out the outside influences and cleanse Islam of corrupt practices that had developed in past centuries. The revolt was eventually suppressed, but the influence of the Wahhabi movement persisted, revitalized in part by resistance to the centralizing and modernizing efforts of reformist elements in the nineteenth century.

World War I offered an opportunity for the Arabs to throw off the shackles of Ottoman rule—but what would replace them? The Arabs were not a nation, but an idea,

a loose collection of peoples who often do not see eye to eye on what constitutes their common sense of community. Disagreement over what constitutes an Arab has plagued generations of political leaders who have sought unsuccessfully to knit together the disparate peoples of the region into a single Arab nation.

When the Arab leaders in Mecca declared their independence from Ottoman rule in 1916, they had hoped for British support, but they were to be sorely disappointed.

◆ **The Impact of Oil.** Oil discoveries early in the twentieth century began to bring wealth to Persia. Shown here are workers developing the oil fields at Petroleum Springs, Dalaki, in Persia.

♦ **European Jewish Refugees.** European Jewish refugees emigrated to Palestine both before and after World War II. They had one goal: to build a new life in a Jewish homeland. Like the refugees aboard this ship, they all celebrated as they reached the safety of Palestine. The sign reads "Keep the gates open."

At the close of the war, the British and French agreed to create a number of mandates in the area to be placed under the general supervision of the League of Nations. Iraq and Jordan were assigned to the British, and Syria and Lebanon (the two areas were separated so that Christian peoples in Lebanon could be placed under Christian administration) were given to the French.

The land of Palestine—once the home of the Jews but now inhabited primarily by Muslim Palestinians—was made into a separate mandate. According to the Balfour Declaration, issued by the British foreign secretary Lord Balfour in November 1917, Palestine was to be a national home for the Jews. The declaration was ambiguous on the legal status of the territory and promised that the decision would not undermine the rights of the non-Jewish peoples currently living in the area. But Arab nationalists were incensed. How could a national home for the Jewish people be established in a territory where 90 percent of the population were Muslims?

In the early 1920s, a leader of the Wahhabi movement, Ibn Saud (1880–1953), united Arab tribes in the northern part of the Arabian peninsula and drove out the remnants of Ottoman rule. Ibn Saud was a descendant of the family that had led the Wahhabi revolt in the eighteenth century. Devout and gifted, he won broad support among Arab tribal peoples and established the kingdom

of Saudi Arabia throughout much of the peninsula in 1932.

At first his new kingdom, consisting essentially of the vast wastes of central Arabia, was desperately poor. Its financial resources were limited to the income from Muslim pilgrims visiting the holy sites in Mecca and Medina. But during the 1930s, American oil prospectors began to explore for oil, and Standard Oil made a successful strike at Dahran, on the Persian Gulf, in 1938. Soon an Arabian-American oil conglomerate, popularly called Aramco, was established, and the isolated kingdom was suddenly inundated by Western oilmen and untold wealth.

In the meantime, Jewish settlers began to arrive in Palestine in response to the promises made in the Balfour Declaration. As tensions between the new arrivals and existing Muslim residents began to escalate during the 1930s, the British tried to restrict Jewish immigration into the territory and rejected the concept of a separate state. The stage was set for the conflicts that would take place in the region after World War II.

Nationalism and Revolution in Asia and Africa

Before the Russian Revolution, to most intellectuals in Asia and Africa, Westernization meant the capitalist democratic civilization of Western Europe and the United States, not the doctrine of social revolution developed by Karl Marx. Until 1917, Marxism was regarded as a utopian idea rather than a concrete system of government. Moreover, to many intellectuals Marxism appeared to have little relevance to conditions in Asia and Africa. Marxist doctrine, after all, declared that a communist society would only arise in the ashes of an advanced capitalism that had already passed through the stage of industrial revolution. From the perspective of Marxist historical analysis, most societies in Asia and Africa were still at the feudal stage of development and lacked the economic conditions and political awareness to achieve a socialist revolution that would bring the working class to power. Finally, the Marxist view of nationalism and religion had little appeal to many patriotic intellectuals in the non-Western world. Marx believed that nationhood and religion were essentially false ideas that diverted the attention of the oppressed masses from the critical issues of class struggle and, in his phrase, the exploitation of one person by another. Instead Marx stressed the importance of an "internationalist" outlook based on class consciousness and the eventual creation of a classless society with no artificial divisions based on culture, nation, and religion.

For these reasons, many patriotic non-Western intellectuals initially found Marxism to be both irrelevant and unappealing. That situation began to change after the Russian Revolution in 1917. The rise to power of Lenin's Bolsheviks demonstrated that a revolutionary party espousing Marxist principles could overturn a corrupt, outdated system and launch a new experiment dedicated to ending human inequality and achieving a paradise on earth. In 1920, Lenin proposed a new revolutionary strategy designed to relate Marxist doctrine and practice to non-Western societies. His reasons were not entirely altruistic. Soviet Russia, surrounded by capitalist powers, desperately needed allies in its struggle to survive in a hostile world. To Lenin, the anticolonial movements emerging in North Africa, Asia, and the Middle East after World War I were natural allies of the beleaguered new regime in Moscow. Lenin was convinced that only the ability of the imperialist powers to find markets, raw materials, and sources of capital investment in the non-Western world kept capitalism alive. If the tentacles of capitalist influence in Asia and Africa could be severed, then imperialism itself would ultimately weaken and collapse.

Establishing such an alliance was not easy, however. Most nationalist leaders in colonial countries belonged to the urban middle class, and many abhorred the idea of a comprehensive revolution to create a totally egalitarian society. In addition, many still adhered to traditional religious beliefs and were opposed to the atheistic principles of classic Marxism.

Because it was unrealistic to expect bourgeois nationalist support for social revolution, Lenin sought a compromise by which Communist Parties could be organized among the working classes in the preindustrial societies of Asia and Africa. These parties would then forge informal alliances with existing middle-class parties to struggle against the common enemies of feudal reaction (the remnants of the traditional ruling class) and Western imperialism. Such an alliance could not be permanent, of course, as many bourgeois nationalists in Asia and Africa would reject an egalitarian classless society. Once the imperialists had been overthrown, therefore, the Communist Parties should turn against their erstwhile nationalist partners to seize power on their own and carry out the socialist revolution. Lenin thus proposed a two-stage revolution: an initial "national democratic" stage followed by a "proletarian socialist" stage.

Lenin's strategy became a major element in Soviet foreign policy in the 1920s. Soviet agents fanned out across the world to carry Marxism beyond the boundaries of industrial Europe. The primary instrument of this effort was the Communist International, or Comintern for short.

♦ **Jomo Kenyatta.**   By the 1930s, calls for the independence of African states came from a new generation of young African leaders who had been educated abroad, in Europe and the United States. Jomo Kenyatta, pictured here, had been educated in Great Britain. He became an eloquent spokesperson for independence of Kenya from British rule.

Formed in 1919 at Lenin's prodding, the Comintern was a worldwide organization of Communist Parties dedicated to advancing world revolution. At Comintern headquarters in Moscow, agents from around the world were trained in the precepts of world communism and then sent back to their own countries to form Marxist parties and promote the cause of social revolution. By the end of the 1920s, almost every colonial or semicolonial society in Asia had a party based on Marxist principles. The Soviets had less success in the Middle East, where Marxist ideology appealed mainly to minorities such as Jews and Armenians in the cities, or in black Africa, where Soviet strategists in any case did not feel conditions were sufficiently advanced for the creation of communist organizations. Later on, they had some success in the labor unions of countries like the Sudan and the Ivory Coast.

⇒ *The Path of Liberation* ⇐

In 1919, the Vietnamese revolutionary Ho Chi Minh (1890–1969) was living in exile in France where he first became acquainted with the new revolutionary experiment in Bolshevik Russia. He became a leader of the Vietnamese Communist movement. In the following passage, written in 1960, he reminisces about his reasons for becoming a Communist.

Ho Chi Minh, "The Path Which Led Me to Leninism"

After World War I, I made my living in Paris, now as a retoucher at a photographer's, now as a painter of "Chinese antiquities" (made in France!). I would distribute leaflets denouncing the crimes committed by the French colonialists in Vietnam.

At that time, I supported the October Revolution only instinctively, not yet grasping all its historic importance. I loved and admired Lenin because he was a great patriot who liberated his compatriots; until then, I had read none of his books.

The reason for my joining the French Socialist Party was that these "ladies and gentlemen"—as I called my comrades at that moment—had shown their sympathy toward me, toward the struggle of the oppressed peoples. But I understood neither what was a party, a trade-union, nor what was Socialism nor Communism.

Heated discussions were then taking place in the branches of the Socialist Party, about the question whether the Socialist Party should remain in the Sec-

ond International, should a Second-and-a-half International be founded or should the Socialist Party join Lenin's Third International? I attended the meetings regularly, twice or three times a week, and attentively listened to the discussion. First, I could not understand thoroughly. Why were the discussions so heated? Either with the Second, Second-and-a-half or Third International, the revolution could be waged. What was the use of arguing then? As for the First International, what had become of it?

What I wanted most to know—and this precisely was not debated in the meetings—was: which International sides with the peoples of colonial countries?

I raised this question—the most important in my opinion—in a meeting. Some comrades answered: It is the Third, not the Second International. And a comrade gave me Lenin's "Thesis on the national and colonial questions," published by *l'Humanité*, to read.

There were political terms difficult to understand in this thesis. But by dint of reading it again and again, finally I could grasp the main part of it. What emotion, enthusiasm, clear-sightedness, and confidence it instilled in me! I was overjoyed to tears. Though sitting alone in my room, I shouted aloud as if addressing large crowds: "Dear martyrs, compatriots! This is what we need, this is the path to our liberation!"

After that, I had entire confidence in Lenin, in the Third International.

According to Marxist doctrine, the rank and file of Communist Parties should be urban factory workers alienated from capitalist society by inhuman working conditions. In practice, many of the leading elements even in European Communist Parties tended to be urban intellectuals or members of the lower middle class (in Marxist parlance, the "petty bourgeoisie"). That phenomenon was even more true in the non-Western world, where most early Marxists were rootless intellectuals. Some were probably drawn into the movement for patriotic reasons and saw Marxist doctrine as a new, more effective means of modernizing their societies and removing the power of exploitative colonialism (see the box above). Others were attracted by the basic message of egalitarian communism and the utopian dream of a class-

less society. All who joined found it a stirring message of release from oppression and a practical strategy for the liberation of their society from colonial rule. For those who had lost their faith in traditional religion, it often served as a new secular ideology, dealing not with the hereafter but with the here and now or, indeed, with a remote future when the state would wither away and the "classless society" would replace the lost truth of traditional faiths.

Of course, the new doctrine's appeal was not the same in all non-Western societies. In Confucian societies such as China and Vietnam, where traditional belief systems had been badly discredited by their failure to counter the Western challenge, communism had an immediate impact and rapidly became a major factor in the anticolonial movement. In Buddhist and Muslim societies, where traditional religion remained strong and actually became a cohesive factor within the resistance movement, communism had less success and was forced to adapt to local conditions in order to survive.

Sometimes, as in Malaya (where the sense of nationhood was weak) or Thailand (which, alone in Southeast Asia, had not fallen under colonial rule), support for the local Communist Party came from minority groups such as the overseas Chinese community in the cities. In Egypt and Syria, the Marxists often found adherents among the sons of wealthy merchants and landowners. To maximize their appeal and minimize potential conflict with traditional ideas, Communist Parties frequently attempted to adjust Marxist doctrine to indigenous values and institutions. In the Middle East, for example, the Ba'ath Party in Syria adopted a hybrid socialism combining Marxism with Arab nationalism. In Africa, radical intellectuals talked vaguely of a uniquely "African road to socialism."

The degree to which these parties were successful in establishing alliances with existing nationalist parties and building a solid base of support among the mass of the population also varied from place to place. In some instances, the local Communists were briefly able to establish a cooperative relationship with bourgeois parties in the struggle against Western imperialism. The most famous example was the alliance between the Chinese Communist Party (CCP) and Sun Yat-sen's Nationalist (*Kuomintang,* or *Guomindang*) Party.

In the Dutch East Indies, the Indonesian Communist Party (known as the PKI) allied with the middle-class nationalist group Sarekat Islam, but later broke loose in an effort to organize its own mass movement among the poor peasants. Similar problems were encountered in French Indochina where Vietnamese Communists organized by the Moscow-trained revolutionary Ho Chi Minh sought to cooperate with bourgeois nationalist parties against the colonial regime. In 1928, these efforts were abandoned, as the Comintern, reacting to Chiang Kai-shek's betrayal of the alliance with the CCP (see Revolution in China later in the chapter), declared that Communist Parties should restrict their recruiting efforts to the most revolutionary elements in society, notably, the urban intellectuals and the working class. Harassed by colonial authorities and saddled with strategic directions from Moscow that often had little relevance to local conditions, Communist Parties in most colonial societies had little success in the 1930s and failed to build a secure base of support among the mass of the population.

Revolution in China

Overall, revolutionary Marxism had its greatest impact in China. There, in 1921, a group of young radicals, including several faculty and staff members from prestigious Peking University, had founded the Chinese Communist Party.

The rise of the CCP was a consequence of the failed revolution of 1911. When political forces are too weak or divided to consolidate their power during a period of instability, the military usually steps in to fill the vacuum. As we have seen, Sun Yat-sen (1866–1925) and his colleagues had accepted General Yuan Shikai (1859–1916) as president of the new Chinese republic in 1911 because they lacked the military force to compete with his control over the army (see Chapter 17). Moreover, many feared, perhaps rightly, that if the revolt lapsed into chaos, the Western powers would intervene and the last shreds of Chinese sovereignty would be lost. But some had misgivings about Yuan's intentions. As one remarked in a letter to a friend, "we don't know whether he will be a George Washington or a Napoleon."

As it turned out, he was neither. Understanding little of the new ideas sweeping into China from the West, Yuan ruled in a traditional manner, reviving Confucian rituals and institutions and eventually trying to found a new imperial dynasty. Yuan's dictatorial inclinations rapidly led to clashes with Sun's party, now renamed the *Guomindang* (*Kuomintang*) or Nationalist Party. When Yuan dissolved the new parliament, the Nationalists launched a rebellion. When it failed, Sun Yat-sen fled to Japan.

Yuan was strong enough to brush off the challenge from the revolutionary forces, but not to turn back the clock of history. He died in 1916 (apparently of natural causes, although legend holds that his heart was broken by growing popular resistance to his imperial pretensions) and was succeeded by one of his military subordinates. For the next several years, China slipped into semi-anarchy, as the power of the central government disintegrated and military warlords seized power in the provinces.

Mr. Science and Mr. Democracy: The New Culture Movement

Although the failure of the 1911 Revolution was a clear sign that China was not yet ready for radical change, discontent with existing conditions continued to rise in various sectors of Chinese society. The most vocal protests came from radical intellectuals who opposed Yuan Shikai's conservative rule but were now convinced that political change could not take place until the Chinese people were more familiar with the trends in the outside world. Braving the displeasure of Yuan Shikai and his successors, progressive intellectuals at Peking University launched a New Culture Movement aimed at abolishing the remnants of the old system and introducing Western values and institutions into China. Using the classrooms of China's most prestigious university as well as the pages of newly established progressive magazines and newspapers, Chinese intellectuals presented the Chinese people with a bewildering mix of new ideas, from the philosophy of Friedrich Nietszche and Bertrand Russell to the educational views of the American John Dewey and the feminist plays of Henrik Ibsen. As such ideas flooded into China, they stirred up a new generation of educated Chinese youth, who chanted "down with Confucius and Sons" and talked of a new era dominated by "Mr. Sai" (Mr. Science) and "Mr. De" (Mr. Democracy). No one was a greater defender of free thought and speech than the chancellor of Peking University, Cai Yuanpei (Ts'ai Yuan-p'ei):

> So far as theoretical ideas are concerned, I follow the principles of "freedom of thought" and an attitude of broad tolerance in accordance with the practice of universities the world over.... Regardless of what school of thought a person may adhere to, so long as that person's ideas are justified and conform to reason and have not been passed by through the process of natural selection, although there may be controversy, such ideas have a right to be presented.[3]

The problem was that appeals for American-style democracy and women's liberation had little relevance to Chinese peasants, most of whom were still illiterate and concerned above all with survival. Consequently, the New Culture Movement did not win widespread support outside the urban areas. It certainly earned the distrust of conservative military officers, one of whom threatened to lob artillery shells into Peking University to destroy the poisonous new ideas and their advocates.

Discontent among intellectuals, however, was soon joined by the rising chorus of public protest against Japan's efforts to expand its influence on the mainland. During the first decade of the twentieth century, Japan had taken advantage of the Qing's decline to extend its domination over Manchuria and Korea (see Joining the Imperialist Club in Chapter 23). In 1915, the Japanese government insisted that Yuan Shikai accept a series of "twenty-one demands" that would have given Japan a

virtual protectorate over the Chinese government and economy. Yuan was able to fend off the most far-reaching Japanese demands by arousing popular outrage in China, but at the Paris Peace Conference four years later, Japan demanded and received Germany's sphere of influence in Shandong province as a reward for its support of the Allied cause in World War I. On hearing the news that the Chinese government had accepted the decision, on May 4, 1919, patriotic students, supported by other sectors of the urban population, demonstrated in Beijing and other major cities of the country. Although this May Fourth Movement did not result in a reversal of the decision to award Shandong to Japan, it did alert a substantial part of the politically literate population to the threat to national survival and the incompetence of the warlord government.

By 1920, central authority had almost ceased to exist in China. Two political forces now began to emerge as competitors for the right to bring order to the chaos of the early republican era. One was Sun Yat-sen's Nationalist Party. Driven from the political arena seven years earlier by Yuan Shikai, the party now reestablished itself on the mainland by making an alliance with the warlord ruler of Guangdong (Kuangtung) province in South China. From Canton, Sun sought international assistance to carry out his national revolution. The other political force was the Chinese Communist Party, formed by radical intellectuals in Shanghai in the summer of 1921. Following Lenin's strategy, Comintern agents soon advised the new party to link up with the more experienced Nationalists. Sun Yat-sen himself needed the expertise and the diplomatic support that the Soviet Union could provide, as his anti-imperialist rhetoric had alienated many Western powers; one English-language newspaper in the international concession in Shanghai remarked: "All his life, all his influence, are devoted to ideas which keep China in turmoil, and it is utterly undesirable that he should be allowed to prosecute those aims here."[4] In 1923, the two parties formed an alliance to oppose the warlords and drive the imperialist powers out of China.

For three years, with the assistance of a Comintern mission in Canton, the two parties submerged their mutual suspicions and mobilized and trained a revolutionary army to march north and seize control of China. The so-called Northern Expedition began in the summer of 1926. By the following spring, revolutionary forces were in control of all Chinese territory south of the Yangtze River, including the major river ports of Wuhan and Shanghai. But tensions between the two parties now surfaced. Sun Yat-sen had died of cancer in 1925 and was succeeded as head of the Nationalist Party by his military subordinate Chiang Kai-shek (1887–1975). Chiang feigned support for the alliance with the Communists but actually planned to destroy them. In April 1927, he struck against the Communists and their supporters in Shanghai, killing thousands. The CCP responded by encouraging revolts in central China and Canton, but the uprisings were defeated and their leaders killed or forced into hiding.

The Nanjing Republic

In 1928, Chiang Kai-shek founded a new Chinese republic at Nanjing, and over the next three years, he managed to reunify China by a combination of military operations and inducements (known as "silver bullets") to various northern warlords to join his movement. One of his key targets was the warlord Zhang Zuolin (Chang Tso-lin), who controlled Manchuria under the tutelage of Japan. When Zhang allegedly agreed to throw in his lot with the Nationalists, the Japanese had him assassinated by placing a bomb under his train as he was returning to Manchuria. The Japanese hoped that Zhang Zuolin's son and successor Zhang Xueliang (Chang Hsueh-liang) would be more cooperative, but they had miscalculated. Promised a major role in Chiang Kai-shek's government, Zhang began instead to integrate Manchuria politically and economically into the Nanjing Republic.

Chiang Kai-shek saw the Japanese as a serious threat to Chinese national aspirations, but considered them less dangerous than the Communists (he once remarked to an American reporter that "the Japanese are a disease of the skin, but the Communists are a disease of the heart"). After the Shanghai massacre of April 1927, most of the Communist leaders had gone into hiding in the city, where they attempted to revive the movement in its traditional base among the urban working class. Shanghai was a rich recruiting ground for the party. A city of millionaires, paupers, prostitutes, gamblers, and adventurers, it had led one pious Christian missionary to comment that "if God lets Shanghai endure, He owes an apology to Sodom and Gomorrah."[5] Some party members, however, led by the young Communist organizer Mao Zedong (Mao Tse-Tung), fled to the hilly areas south of the Yangtze River.

Unlike most other CCP leaders, Mao (1893–1976) was convinced that the Chinese revolution must be based on the impoverished peasants in the countryside.

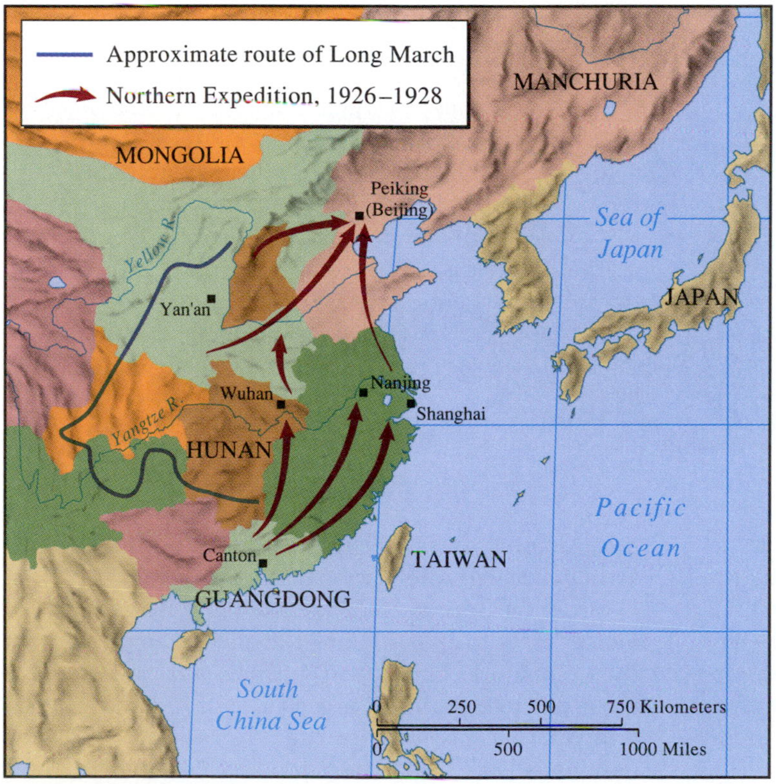

Map 25.1 The Northern Expedition.

≽ A Call for Revolt ≼

In the fall of 1926, Nationalist and Communist forces moved north from Canton on their Northern Expedition in an effort to defeat the warlords. The young Communist Mao Zedong accompanied revolutionary troops into his home province of Hunan, where he submitted a report to the CCP Central Committee calling for a massive peasant revolt against the ruling order. The report shows his confidence that peasants could play an active role in the Chinese revolution despite the skepticism of many of his colleagues.

Mao Zedong, "The Peasant Movement in Hunan"

During my recent visit to Hunan I made a first-hand investigation of conditions in the five counties of Hsiangtan, Hsianghsiang, Hengshan, Liling, and Changsha. In a very short time, in China's Central, Southern, and Northern provinces, several hundred million peasants will rise like a mighty storm, like a hurricane, a force so swift and violent that no power, however great, will be able to hold it back. They will smash all the trammels that bind them and rush forward along the road to liberation. They will sweep all the imperialists, warlords, corrupt officials, local tyrants, and evil gentry into their graves. Every revolutionary party and every revolutionary comrade will be put to the test, to be accepted or rejected as they decide. There are three alternatives. To march at their head and lead them? To trail behind them, gesticulating and criticizing? Or to stand in their way and oppose them? Every Chinese is free to choose, but events will force you to make the choice quickly.

The main targets of attack by the peasants are the local tyrants, the evil gentry and the lawless landlords, but in passing they also hit out against patriarchal ideas and institutions, against the corrupt officials in the cities and against bad practices and customs in the rural areas. In force and momentum the attack is tempestuous; those who bow before it survive and those who resist perish. As a result, the privileges which the feudal landlords enjoyed for thousands of years are being shattered to pieces. Every bit of the dignity and prestige built up by the landlords is being swept into the dust. With the collapse of the power of the landlords, the peasant associations have now become the sole organs of authority and the popular slogan "All power to the peasant associations" has become a reality.

The peasants' revolt disturbed the gentry's sweet dreams. When the news from the countryside reached the cities, it caused immediate uproar among the gentry. Soon after my arrival in Changsha, I met all sorts of people and picked up a good deal of gossip. From the middle social strata upwards to the Kuomintang right-wingers, there was not a single person who did not sum up the whole business in the phrase, "It's terrible!" Under the impact of the views of the "It's terrible!" school then flooding the city, even quite revolutionary-minded people became downhearted as they pictured the events in the countryside in their mind's eye; and they were unable to deny the word "terrible." Even quite progressive people said, "Though terrible, it is inevitable in a revolution." In short, nobody could altogether deny the word "terrible." But as already mentioned, the fact is that the great peasant masses have risen to fulfill their historic mission and that the forces of rural democracy have risen to overthrow the forces of rural feudalism. What the peasants are doing is absolutely right; what they are doing is fine! "It's fine!" is the theory of the peasants and of all other revolutionaries. Every revolutionary comrade should know that the national revolution requires a great change in the countryside. The Revolution of 1911 did not bring about this change, hence its failure. This change is now taking place, and it is an important factor for the completion of the revolution. Every revolutionary comrade must support it, or he will be taking the stand of counter-revolution.

The son of a prosperous peasant, Mao had helped to organize a peasant movement in South China during the early 1920s, and then served as an agitator in rural villages in his native province of Hunan during the Northern Expedition in the fall of 1926. At that time he wrote a famous report to the party leadership suggesting that the CCP support peasant demands for a land revolution (see the box above). But his superiors refused, fearing that adopting excessively radical policies would destroy the alliance with the Nationalists.

After the spring of 1927, the CCP-Nationalist alliance ceased to exist. Chiang Kai-shek attempted to root the Communists out of their urban base in Shanghai and their rural redoubt in the rugged hills of Jiangxi (Kiangsi) province. He succeeded in the first task in 1931, when most party leaders were forced to flee Shanghai for Mao's base in South China. Three years later, using their superior military strength, Chiang's troops surrounded the Communist base in Jiangxi, inducing Mao's young People's Liberation Army (PLA) to abandon its guerrilla lair and embark on the famous "Long March," an arduous journey of thousands of miles on foot through mountains, marshes, and deserts to the small provincial town of Yan'an (Yenan) two hundred miles north of the modern-day city of Xian in the dusty hills of North China. Of the 90,000 who embarked on the journey in October 1934, only 10,000 arrived in Yan'an a year later. Contemporary observers must have thought that the Communist threat to the Nanjing regime had been averted forever.

In the meantime, Chiang Kai-shek had also been trying to build a new nation. When the Nanjing Republic was established in 1928, Chiang had publicly declared his commitment to Sun Yat-sen's Three People's Principles. In a program announced in 1918, Sun had written about the all-important second stage of "political tutelage":

> China . . . needs a republic government just as a boy needs school. As a schoolboy must have good teachers and helpful friends, so the Chinese people, being for the first time under republican rule, must have a farsighted revolutionary government for their training. This calls for the period of political tutelage, which is a necessary transitional stage from monarchy to republicanism. Without this, disorder will be unavoidable.[6]

In keeping with Sun's program, Chiang announced a period of political indoctrination to prepare the Chinese people for a final stage of constitutional government. In the meantime, the Nationalists would use their dictatorial power to carry out a land reform program and modernize the urban industrial sector.

But it would take more than paper plans to create a new China. Years of neglect and civil war had severely frayed the political, economic, and social fabric of the nation. There were faint signs of an impending industrial revolution in the major urban centers, but most of the people in the countryside, drained by warlord exactions and civil strife, were still grindingly poor and overwhelmingly illiterate. A Westernized middle class had begun to emerge in the cities and formed much of the natural constituency of the Nanjing government. But this new Westernized elite, preoccupied with bourgeois values of individual advancement and material accumulation, had few links with the peasants in the countryside or the rickshaw drivers "running in this world of suffering," in the poignant words of a Chinese poet. In an expressive

◆ **Mao Zedong at Yan'an.**   In 1934, Mao Zedong led his bedraggled forces on a famous "Long March" from South China to a new location at Yan'an, in the hills just south of the Gobi Desert. Here Chairman Mao, next to one of his generals, poses for a photograph at his new headquarters. Note the thick padded jackets to keep out the cold.

phrase, some critics dismissed Chiang Kai-shek and his chief followers as "banana Chinese," yellow on the outside, white on the inside.

Chiang Kai-shek was aware of the difficulty of introducing exotic foreign ideas into a society still culturally conservative. While building a modern industrial sector, he attempted to synthesize modern Western ideas with traditional Confucian values of hard work, obedience, and moral integrity. In the officially promoted "New Life Movement," sponsored by his Wellesley-educated wife Mei-ling Soong, Chiang sought to propagate traditional Confucian social ethics such as integrity, propriety, and righteousness, while rejecting what he considered the excessive individualism and material greed of Western capitalism.

Unfortunately for Chiang Kai-shek, Confucian ideas—at least in their institutional form—had been

◆◆◆◆◆◆◆◆◆◆◆◆◆◆◆◆◆◆◆

Revolution in China

Formation of Chinese Communist Party	1921
Northern Expedition	1926
Chiang Kai-shek establishes the Nanjing Republic	1928
Long March	1934–1935

widely discredited by the failure of the traditional system to solve China's growing problems. With only a tenuous hold over the Chinese provinces (the Nanjing government had total control over only a handful of provinces in the Yangtze valley), a growing Japanese threat in the north (see Chapter 26), and a world suffering from the Great Depression, Chiang made little progress with his program. Lacking the political sensitivity of Sun Yat-sen and fearing Communist influence, Chiang repressed all opposition and censored free expression, thereby alienating many intellectuals and political moderates. Since the urban middle class and landed gentry were his natural political constituency, he shunned programs that would lead to a redistribution of wealth. A land reform program was enacted in 1930 but had little effect.

Chiang Kai-shek's government had little more success in promoting industrial development. During the decade of precarious peace following the Northern Expedition, industrial growth averaged only about 1 percent annually. Much of the national wealth was in the hands of the so-called four families, composed of senior officials and close subordinates of the ruling elite. Military expenses consumed half the budget, and distressingly little was devoted to social and economic development.

The new government, then, had little success in dealing with the deep-seated economic and social problems that affected China during the interwar years. The deadly combination of internal disintegration and foreign pressure now began to coincide with the virtual collapse of the global economic order during the Great Depression and the rise of militant political forces in Japan determined to extend Japanese influence and power in an unstable Asia. These forces and the turmoil they unleashed will be examined in the next chapter.

Down with Confucius and Sons: Economic and Social Change in Republican China

The transformation of the old order that had begun at the end of the Qing era continued into the period of the early Chinese republic. The industrial sector continued to grow, albeit slowly; its growth was aided by the decline in competition from European firms during World War I. Although many Chinese firms faced severe competition from Western rivals after the war, they enjoyed the advantages of experience and local connections and in general were able to hold their own. Nevertheless, in the early 1930s, about 75 percent of all industrial production was still carried out by hand in small workshops.

Mechanization, however, was gradually beginning to replace manual labor in a number of traditional industries, notably the manufacture of textile goods. Sometimes technological advances undoubtedly led to a loss of jobs, but as in many other industrializing societies, the overall impact was probably beneficial in terms of cheaper products and increased output. Traditional Chinese exports, such as silk and tea, were hard hit by the Great Depression, however, and manufacturing suffered a decline during the 1930s.

It is difficult to gauge conditions in the countryside during the early republican era. Scholars disagree over whether overall per capita consumption declined during this period, and if so, what the primary causes were. Whatever the statistical evidence for agricultural production, there is no doubt that farmers were often victimized by high taxes imposed by local warlords and the endemic political and social conflict that marked the period.

Social changes followed shifts in the economy and the political culture. By 1915, the assault on the old system and values by educated youth was intense. The main focus of the attack was the Confucian concept of the family, in particular, filial piety and the subordination of women. Young people demanded the right to choose their own mates and their own careers. Women demanded rights and opportunities equal to those enjoyed by men.

More broadly, progressives called for an end to the concept of duty to the community and praised the Western individualist ethos. The prime spokesman for such views was the popular writer Lu Xun (Lu Hsun), whose short stories criticized the Confucian concept of family as a "man-eating" system that degraded humanity. In a famous short story entitled "Diary of a Madman," the protagonist remarks:

I remember when I was four or five years old, sitting in the cool of the hall, my brother told me that if a man's parents were ill, he should cut off a piece of his flesh and boil it for them if he wanted to be considered a good son. I have only just realized that I have been living all these years in a place where for four thousand years they have been eating human flesh.[7]

Such criticisms did have some beneficial results. During the early republic, the tyranny of the old family system began to decline, at least in urban areas, under the impact of economic changes and the urgings of the New Culture intellectuals. Women, long consigned to an inferior place in the Confucian world order, began to escape their cloistered existence and seek education and employment alongside their male contemporaries. Free choice in marriage and a more relaxed attitude toward sex became commonplace among affluent families in the cities, where the teenage children of Westernized elites aped the clothing, social habits, and even the musical tastes of their contemporaries in Europe and the United States.

But as a rule, the new consciousness of individualism and women's rights that marked the early republican era in the major cities did not penetrate to the villages. Here traditional attitudes and customs held sway. Arranged marriages continued to be the rule rather than the exception, and concubinage remained common. According to a survey taken in the 1930s, well over two-thirds of the marriages even among urban couples had been arranged by their parents (see the box on p. 938), while in one rural area, only 3 villagers out of 170 who were interviewed had even heard of the idea of "modern marriage." Even the tradition of binding the feet of female children continued despite efforts by the Nationalist government to eradicate the practice.

China's Changing Culture

Nowhere was the struggle between traditional and modern more visible than in the field of culture. Beginning with the New Culture era during the early years of the first Chinese republic, radical reformists criticized traditional culture as the symbol and instrument of feudal oppression that must be entirely eradicated in order to create a new China that could stand on its feet with dignity in the modern world.

The first cracks in the edifice of traditional culture had actually come in the late nineteenth century when progressive elements began to introduce Western books, paintings, music, and ideas into China. By the first quarter of the new century, the trickle became a flood, as progressive intellectuals called for a new culture based on that of the modern West. During the 1920s and 1930s,

◆ **Student Demonstrations in Beijing.** The massive popular demonstrations in Tiananmen Square in downtown Beijing in 1989 were not the first of their kind in China. On May 4, 1919, students gathered at the same spot to protest against the Japanese takeover of Shandong peninsula after World War I. The event triggered the famous May Fourth Movement, which highlighted the demand of progressive forces in China for political and social reforms.

⟩ An Arranged Marriage ⟨

Under Western influence, Chinese social customs changed dramatically for many urban elites in the early twentieth century. But life was generally unaffected in the villages where traditional patterns held sway. This often created severe tensions between the older and younger generations, as this passage from the pen of the popular twentieth-century novelist Ba Jin shows.

Ba Jin, *Family*

Brought up with loving care, after studying with a private tutor for a number of years, Chueh-hsin entered middle school. One of the school's best students, he graduated four years later at the top of his class. He was very interested in physics and chemistry and hoped to study abroad, in Germany. His mind was full of beautiful dreams. At that time he was the envy of his classmates.

In his fourth year at middle school, he lost his mother. His father later married again, this time to a younger woman who had been his mother's cousin. Chueh-hsin was aware of his loss, for he knew full well that nothing could replace the love of a mother. But her death left no irreparable wound in his heart; he was able to console himself with rosy dreams of his future. Moreover, he had someone who understood him and could comfort him—his pretty cousin Mei, "mei" for "plum blossom."

But then, one day, his dreams were shattered, cruelly and bitterly shattered. The evening he returned home carrying his diploma, the plaudits of his teachers and friends still ringing in his ears, his father called him into his room and said:

"Now that you've graduated, I want to arrange your marriage. Your grandfather is looking forward to having a great-grandson, and I, too, would like to be able to hold a grandson in my arms. You're old enough to be married; I won't feel easy until I fulfill my obligation to find you a wife. Although I didn't accumulate much money in my years away from home as an official, still I've put by enough for us to get along on. My health isn't what it used to be; I'm thinking of spending my time at home and having you help me run the household affairs. All the more reason you'll be needing a wife. I've already arranged a match with the Li family. The thirteenth of next month is a good day. We'll announce the engagement then. You can be married within the year. . . ."

Chueh-hsin did not utter a word of protest, nor did such a thought ever occur to him. He merely nodded to indicate his compliance with his father's wishes. But after he returned to his own room, and shut the door, he threw himself down on his bed, covered his head with the quilt and wept. He wept for his broken dreams.

He was deeply in love with Mei, but now his father had chosen another, a girl he had never seen, and said that he must marry within the year. What's more, his hopes of continuing his studies had burst like a bubble. It was a terrible shock to Chueh-hsin. His future was finished, his beautiful dreams shattered.

He cried his disappointment and bitterness. But the door was closed and Chueh-hsin's head was beneath the bedding. No one knew. He did not fight back, he never thought of resisting. He only bemoaned his fate. But he accepted it. He complied with his father's will without a trace of resentment. But in his heart he wept for himself, wept for the girl he adored—Mei, his "plum blossom."

Western literature and art became highly popular in China, especially among the urban middle class. Traditional culture continued to prevail among more conservative elements of the population, while some intellectuals argued for the creation of a new art that would synthesize the best of Chinese and foreign culture. But the most creative artists were interested in imitating foreign trends, while traditionalists were more concerned with preservation.

Literature in particular was influenced by foreign ideas as Western genres like the novel and the short story attracted a larger audience. Although most Chinese novels written after World War I dealt with Chinese subjects, they reflected the Western tendency toward social realism and often dealt with the new Westernized middle class (Mao Dun's *Midnight,* for example, described the changing mores of Shanghai's urban elites) or the disintegration of the traditional Confucian family (Ba Jin's famous novel *Family* is an example). Most of China's modern authors displayed a clear contempt for the past.

Japan between the Wars

During the first two decades of the twentieth century, Japan made remarkable progress toward the creation of an advanced society on the Western model. The political system based on the Meiji Constitution of 1890 began to evolve along Western pluralistic lines, and a multiparty system took shape, while the economic and social reforms launched during the Meiji era led to increasing prosperity and the development of a modern industrial and commercial sector. Optimists had reason to hope that Japan was on the road to becoming a full-fledged democracy.

Experiment in Democracy

During the first quarter of the twentieth century, the Japanese political system appeared to evolve significantly toward the Western democratic model; political parties expanded their popular following and became increasingly competitive while universal male suffrage was instituted in the 1920s. Individual pressure groups began to appear in Japanese society along with an independent press and a bill of rights. The influence of the old ruling oligarchy, the *genro*, had not yet been significantly challenged, however, nor had that of its ideological foundation, the *kokutai* (the national polity, embodying the concept of the uniqueness of the Japanese system based on the supreme authority of the emperor).

The fragile flower of democratic institutions was able to survive throughout the 1920s (often called the era of "Taisho democracy" from the reign title of the ruling emperor). During that period, the military budget was reduced, and a suffrage bill enacted in 1925 continued the process of democratization that had begun earlier in the century.

But the era was also marked by growing social turmoil, and two opposing forces within the system were gearing up to challenge the prevailing wisdom. On the left, a Marxist labor movement, which reflected the tensions within the working class and the increasing radicalism among the rural poor, began to take shape in the early 1920s in response to growing economic difficulties. Attempts to suppress labor disturbances led to further radicalization. On the right, ultranationalist groups called for a rejection of Western models of development and a more militant approach to realizing national objectives. In 1919, the radical nationalist Kita Ikki called for a military takeover and the establishment of a new system bearing strong resemblance to what would later be called National Socialism in Germany (see Chapter 26).

This cultural conflict between old and new, native and foreign, was reflected in the world of literature. The victories over China and Russia in 1895 and 1905 had somewhat restored Japanese self-confidence and sparked a great age of creativity in the early twentieth century. Now more adept at handling European literary forms, Japanese writers blended Western psychology with Japanese sensibility in exquisite novels reeking with nostalgia for the old Japan. A well-known example is Junichiro Tanizaki's *Some Prefer Nettles*, published in 1928, which delicately juxtaposed the positive aspects of both traditional and modern Japan (see the box on p. 940). By the 1930s, however, military censorship increasingly inhibited free literary expression. Many authors continued to write privately, producing works that reflected the gloom of the era. This attitude was perhaps best exemplified by Shiga Naoya's *A Dark Night's Journey*, written during the early 1930s and capturing a sense of the approaching global catastrophe. It is regarded as the masterpiece of modern Japanese literature.

A ZAIBATSU ECONOMY

Japan also continued to make impressive progress in economic development. Spurred by rising domestic demand as well as a continued high rate of government investment in the economy, the production of raw materials tripled between 1900 and 1930, while industrial production increased over twelvefold. Much of the increase went into the export market, and Western manufacturers began to complain about the rising competition for markets from the Japanese.

As often happens, rapid industrialization was accompanied by some hardship and rising social tensions. A characteristic of the Meiji model was the concentration of various manufacturing processes within a single enterprise, the so-called *zaibatsu*, or financial clique. Some of these firms were existing merchant companies such as Mitsui and Sumitomo that had the capital and the foresight to move into new areas of opportunity. Others were formed by enterprising samurai, who used their status and experience in management to good stead in a new environment. Whatever their origins, these firms gradually developed, often with official encouragement, into large conglomerates that controlled a major segment of the Japanese industrial sector. According to one source, by 1937 the four largest *zaibatsu* (Mitsui, Mitsubishi, Sumitomo, and Yasuda) controlled 21 percent of the banking industry, 26 percent of mining, 35 percent of shipbuilding, 38 percent of commercial shipping, and over 60 percent of paper manufacturing and insurance.

◈ In Search of Old Japan ◈

Their confidence restored after victories over China and Russia, Japanese authors produced a host of superb works in the early twentieth century. Many authors blended Western psychology with Japanese sensibility in novels of yearning for old Japan. Here novelist Junichiro Tanizaki recalls the charm of an island as yet untouched and unpolluted by modernization.

Junichiro Tanizaki, *Some Prefer Nettles*

The island of Awaji showed not very large on the map, and its harbor very possibly consisted of but this one road. You go straight down, the inn manager had said, till you come out at the river, and the theater is in the flats beyond. The rows of houses therefore most probably ended at the river. This may have been the seat of some minor baron a century ago—even then it could hardly have been imposing enough to be called a castle town—and it had probably changed little since. A modern coating goes no farther than the large cities that are a country's arteries, and there are not many such cities anywhere. In an old country with a long tradition, China and Europe as well as Japan—any country, in fact, except a very new one like the United States—the smaller cities, left aside by the flow of civilization, retain the flavor of an earlier day until they are overtaken by catastrophe.

This little harbor, for instance: it had its electric wires and poles, its painted billboards, and here and there a display window, but one could ignore them and find on every side townsmen's houses that might have come from an illustration to a seventeenth-century novel. The earthen walls covered to the eaves with white plaster, the projecting lattice fronts with their solid, generous slats of wood, the heavy tiled roofs held down by round ridge-tiles, the shop signs—"Lacquer," "Soy," "Oil"—in fading letters on fine hardwood grounds, and inside, beyond earth-floored entrances, the shop names printed on dark-blue half-curtains—it was not the old man's remark this time but every detail brought back—how vividly!—the mood and air of old Japan. Kaname felt as if he were being drunk up into the scene, as if he were losing himself in the clean white walls and the brilliant blue sky. Those walls were a little like the sash around O-hisa's waist: their first luster had disappeared in long years under the fresh sea winds and rains, and bright though they were, their brightness was tempered by a certain reserve, a soft austerity.

Kaname felt a deep repose come over him. "These old houses are so dark you have no idea what's inside."

"Partly it's because the road is so bright." The old man had come up beside them. "The ground here seems almost white."

Kaname thought of the faces of the ancients in the dusk behind their shop curtains. Here on this street people with faces like theater dolls must have passed lives like stage lives. The world of the plays—of O-yumi, Jurobei of Awa, the pilgrim O-tsuru, and the rest—must have been just such a town as this. And wasn't O-hisa a part of it? Fifty years ago, a hundred years ago, a woman like her, dressed in the same kimono, was perhaps going down this same street in the spring sun, lunch in hand, on her way to the theater beyond the river. Or perhaps, behind one of these latticed fronts, she was playing "Snow" on her koto. O-hisa was a shade left behind by another age.

This concentration of power and wealth in the hands of a few major industrial combines created problems in Japanese society. In the first place, it resulted in the emergence of a form of dual economy: on the one hand, a modern industry characterized by up-to-date methods and massive government subsidies, and on the other, a traditional manufacturing sector characterized by conservative methods and small-scale production techniques.

Concentration of wealth also led to growing economic inequalities. As we have seen, economic growth had been achieved at the expense of the peasants, many of whom fled to the cities to escape rural poverty. That labor surplus benefited the industrial sector, but the urban proletariat was still poorly paid and ill-housed. Rampant inflation in the price of rice led to food riots shortly after World War I. A rapid increase in population (the total population of the Japanese islands increased from an estimated 43 million in 1900 to 73 million in 1940) led to food shortages and the threat of rising unemployment. Intense competition and the global recession in the early 1920s led to an increased concentration of industry and a perceptible rise in urban radicalism, marked by the appearance of a Marxist labor movement. In the meantime, those left on the farm continued to suffer. As late as the beginning of World War II, an estimated one-half of all Japanese farmers were tenants.

SHIDEHARA DIPLOMACY

A final problem for Japanese leaders in the post-Meiji era was the familiar colonial dilemma of finding sources of raw materials and foreign markets for the nation's manufactured goods. Until World War I, Japan had dealt with the problem by seizing territories like Formosa, Korea, and southern Manchuria and transforming them into colonies or protectorates of the growing Japanese Empire. That policy had succeeded brilliantly, but it had also begun to arouse concern and, in some cases, hostility among the Western nations. China also was becoming apprehensive, and as we have seen, Japanese demands for Shandong province at the Paris Peace Conference in 1919 had aroused massive protests in major Chinese cities.

The United States was especially concerned about Japanese aggressiveness. Although the United States had been less active than some European states in pursuing colonies in the Pacific, it had a strong interest in keeping the area open for U.S. commercial activities. American anxiety about Tokyo's "twenty-one demands" on China in 1915 led to a new agreement in 1917, which essentially repeated the compromise provisions of the agreement reached nine years earlier.

In 1922, in Washington, D.C., the United States convened a major conference of nations with interests in the Pacific to discuss problems of regional security. The Washington Conference led to agreements on several issues, but the major accomplishment was the conclusion of a nine-power treaty recognizing the territorial integrity of China and the maintenance of the Open Door. The other participants induced Japan to accept the provisions by accepting its special position in Manchuria.

During the remainder of the 1920s, Japanese governments attempted to play by the rules laid down by the Washington Conference. Known as "Shidehara diplomacy" from the name of the foreign minister (and later prime minister) who attempted to carry it out, this policy sought to use diplomatic and economic means to realize Japanese interests in Asia. But this approach came under severe pressure as Japanese industrialists began to move into new areas of opportunity, such as heavy industry, chemicals, mining, and the manufacturing of appliances and automobiles. Because such industries desperately needed resources not found in abundance locally, the Japanese government came under increasing pressure to find new sources abroad.

The fragile flower of democratic institutions was able to survive growing social turmoil throughout the 1920s, while Japan sought to operate within a cooperative framework with other nations. In the early 1930s, however, with the onset of the Great Depression and growing tensions in the international arena, nationalist forces rose to dominance in the government. As one historian has recently noted, the changes taking place in the 1930s were not in the constitution or the institutional structure, which remained essentially intact, but in the composition and attitudes of the ruling group. Party leaders during the 1920s had attempted to realize Japanese aspirations within the existing global political and economic framework. The dominant elements in the government in the 1930s, a mixture of military officers and ultranationalist politicians, were convinced that the diplomacy of the 1920s had failed and advocated a more aggressive approach to protecting national interests in a brutal and competitive world.

Historians argue over whether Taisho democracy was merely a fragile period of comparative liberalization within a framework dominated by the Meiji vision of empire and *kokutai* or whether the militant nationalism of the 1930s was an aberration brought on by the depression, which caused the emerging Japanese democracy to wilt. Perhaps both contentions contain a little truth. A process of democratization was taking place in Japan during the first decades of the twentieth century, but without shaking the essential core of the Meiji concept of the state. When the "liberal" approach of the 1920s failed to solve the problems of the day, the shift toward a more aggressive approach was inevitable.

Nationalism and Dictatorship in Latin America

Although the nations of Latin America played little role in World War I, that conflict nevertheless had an impact on the region, especially on its economy. The Great Depression also had a profound effect on both the economic and the political life of the nations of Latin America.

The Economy and the United States

By the beginning of the twentieth century, the Latin American economy was based largely on the export of foodstuffs and raw materials. Many countries had only one or two products that they relied on for sale abroad. Argentina sent beef and wheat; Chile, nitrates and copper; Brazil, sugar; Central America, bananas; and Cuba and the Caribbean, sugar. At the end of the nineteenth and beginning of the twentieth centuries, these exports brought a certain level of prosperity to Latin America, although it varied from country to country. Large landowners in Argentina, for example, grew rich from selling beef and wheat abroad.

During World War I, the demand of the European states for Latin America's raw materials increased substantially. For example, exports of Chilean nitrates, a mineral used to make explosives, tripled during the war. But the war years also saw the beginning of a decline in European investment in Latin America and a corresponding rise in U.S. investment.

In the 1920s, the United States began to replace Britain as the foremost investor in Latin America. Unlike the British, however, American investors put funds directly into production enterprises, causing large segments of Latin America's export industries to fall into American hands. A number of Central American states, for example, became "banana republics," where land, packing plants, and railroads were all owned by the American-owned United Fruit Company. U.S. companies also gained control of the copper mining industry in Chile and Peru and the oil industry in Mexico, Peru, and Bolivia.

The United States had always cast a large shadow over Latin America and for years had intervened militarily in Latin American affairs, especially in Central America and the Caribbean, regions that many Americans considered their backyard and thus vital to U.S. security. The control of many industries by American investors added to Latin American hostility toward the Americans. A growing nationalist consciousness led many Latin Americans to view the United States as an imperialist power. It was not difficult for Latin American nationalists to show that profits from American businesses were often used to keep ruthless dictators in power. In Venezuela, for example, the American oil companies enjoyed a close relationship with the dictator Juan Vicente Gómez. But the United States also tried to pursue a new relationship with Latin America. In 1935, President Franklin Roosevelt announced the "Good Neighbor" policy, which rejected the use of U.S. military forces in Latin America. Adhering to his word, the president withdrew the last marines from Haiti in 1936. For the first time in thirty years, there were no U.S. troops in Latin America.

The Great Depression of the 1930s underscored a basic weakness of the Latin American economy. At the beginning of the decade, Latin America was still dependent on an export-import economy in which Latin Americans exported raw materials while importing the manufactured goods of Europe and the United States. The depression proved disastrous for this kind of economy. The decline of the American and European economies led to a decreased demand for Latin American foodstuffs and raw materials, especially coffee, sugar, metals, and meat.

◆ **Getúlio Vargas.** Shown here is Getúlio Vargas, a rancher and lawyer who turned to politics and became president of Brazil after a military coup in 1930. Vargas's New State imitated some of the features of Fascist Italy and Nazi Germany.

The total value of Latin American exports in 1930 was almost 50 percent below the figures for the years between 1925 and 1929. The situation was especially dire for countries dependent on only one export.

But the Great Depression also had one positive effect on the Latin American economy. With the decline in exports, Latin Americans no longer had the revenues to buy manufactured goods, which led many Latin American countries to encourage the development of new industries to produce the goods that were formerly imported. This industrial development was supposed to achieve greater economic independence for Latin America, but due to a shortage of capital in the private sector, governments often invested in the new industries. This led to government-run steel industries in Chile and Brazil and oil industries in Argentina and Mexico.

The Move to Authoritarianism

Most Latin American countries had begun their existence in the nineteenth century with republican forms of government. In reality, a relatively small group of church officials, military leaders, and large landowners dominated their countries. They controlled the masses of people, who were mostly poverty-stricken peasants. Military forces were often crucial in keeping these special interests in power. Indeed, military leaders often ruled as strongmen while foreign investors, either British or American, supported these oligarchies for the sake of order.

The trend toward authoritarianism increased in the 1930s, largely because of the impact of the Great Depression. Domestic instability from economic crises led to military coups and the creation of military dictatorships at the beginning of the 1930s in Argentina, Brazil, Chile, Peru, Guatemala, El Salvador, and Honduras. These were not totalitarian states, but traditional authoritarian regimes. This trend toward authoritarianism was especially evident in Argentina, Brazil, and Mexico, three countries that together possessed over half of the land and wealth of Latin America.

Argentina had grown wealthy from the export of beef and wheat while a conservative oligarchy of large landowners basically controlled the country. Their chief concern was to continue Argentina's export economy, which, of course, was the source of their wealth. But the members of the oligarchy failed to realize the growing importance of industry and the cities. They ignored the growing middle class, which reacted by forming the Radical Party in 1890. In 1916, its leader, Hipólito Irigoyen (1852–1933), was chosen president of Argentina. But

the Radical Party achieved little. Fearful of industrial workers, who were using strikes to improve their conditions, the Radical Party drew ever closer to the large landowners. It also grew more corrupt and by the end of the 1920s was no longer able to lead.

In 1930, the Argentinian military stepped in. It overthrew President Irigoyen and reestablished the power of the large landowners. By this policy, the military hoped to continue the old export economy and thus avoid the growth of working-class power that would come with more industrialization. During World War II, restless military officers formed a new organization, known as the Group of United Officers (GOU). Unhappy with the civilian oligarchy, they overthrew it in June 1943. Three years later, one of its own members, Juan Perón, established sole power (see Chapter 29).

Brazil also followed an authoritarian path. In 1889, the army overthrew the Brazilian monarchy and established a republic, which was controlled chiefly by the landed elites, especially the coffee barons. By 1900, three-quarters of the world's coffee was grown in Brazil. As long as coffee prices remained high, the republican oligarchy was able to maintain its power. The oligarchy largely ignored the growth of urban industry and the working class that came with it.

But the Great Depression devastated the coffee industry. Already by the end of 1929, coffee prices had hit a record low. In 1930, a military coup made Getúlio Vargas (1883–1954), a wealthy rancher, president of Brazil. Vargas ruled Brazil from 1930 to 1945. Early in his rule, Vargas appeased the workers with an eight-hour day and a minimum wage. Faced with strong opposition in 1937, Vargas established himself as a dictator.

Between 1938 and 1945, Vargas established his New State, basically an authoritarian, fascist-like state that outlawed political parties and restricted civil rights. A secret police force used torture to silence his opponents. Vargas also pursued a policy of stimulating new industries. The government established the Brazilian steel industry and set up a company to explore for oil. By the end of World War II, Brazil was becoming Latin America's chief industrial power. In 1945, the army, fearing that Vargas might prolong his power illegally after calling for new elections, forced him to resign.

Mexico was not an authoritarian state, but neither was it democratic. The Mexican Revolution at the beginning of the twentieth century had been the first significant effort in Latin American history to overturn the system of large landed estates and improve the living standards of the masses (see Chapter 22). Out of the political revolution emerged a relatively stable political order. Although democratic in form, the official political party of the Mexican Revolution, known as the Institutional Revolutionary Party or PRI, controlled the major groups within Mexican society. Every six years, party bosses of the PRI chose the party's presidential candidate who was then dutifully elected by the people.

A new wave of change began with Lázaro Cárdenas (1895–1970), who was president of Mexico from 1934 to 1940. He moved to fulfill some of the original goals of the revolution by distributing 44 million acres of land to landless peasants, an action that made him enormously popular with the peasants. Cárdenas also took a stronger

◆ **Rivera's Mural Art.**   Diego Rivera was an important figure in the development of Mexico's mural art in the 1920s and 1930s. One of Rivera's goals—to portray Mexico's past and native traditions—is evident in this mural that conveys the complexity and variety of Aztec civilization. When the Spanish arrived, they were amazed at the variety of foods and merchandise for sale in the marketplace in Tenochtitlan (present-day Mexico City).

stand with the United States, especially over oil. By 1900, it had become known that Mexico had enormous oil reserves, and over the next thirty years, foreign oil companies, some British, but mostly American, made large investments in Mexico. After a dispute with the foreign-owned oil companies over workers' wages, the Cárdenas government seized control of the oilfields and the property of the oil companies. The American oil companies were furious and asked President Roosevelt to intervene. He refused, reminding them of his promise in the "Good Neighbor" policy not to send U.S. troops into Latin America. Mexicans were delighted with Cárdenas, who was cheered as the president who had stood up to the Americans. Eventually, the Mexican government did pay the oil companies for the property it had taken and then set up PEMEX, a national oil company, to run the oil industry.

Culture in Latin America

Two major factors influenced cultural development in Latin America in the early twentieth century. One was the influence of the modern artistic and literary movements that had developed in Europe. Symbolism and Surrealism were especially important in setting new directions in both art and literature. Especially in the cities, such as Buenos Aires and São Paulo, wealthy elites expressed a great interest in the work of avant-garde artists. Others, however, became concerned about following European models. Latin American artists who went abroad brought back modern techniques, but often then adapted them to their own native roots.

Nationalism was the other factor that influenced culture in Latin America. In the 1900s, people in the various countries of Latin America began to seek their national essence, a search that by the 1920s had led intellectuals to rediscover popular traditions and ethnic lore. For the rest of the twentieth century, the quest for national identity dominated cultural life in Latin America. Writers and artists became especially important as the people who helped to define the new national culture in the making.

This attempt to create a national art that would combine new techniques and old traditions was especially evident in the mural art of Mexico, where the government provided funds for painting murals on the walls of public buildings, including schools and government offices. One artist was especially prominent in the development of Mexico's mural art: Diego Rivera (1886–1957).

Rivera had studied in Europe, where he was especially influenced by fresco painting in Italy. Upon his return to Mexico, he worked his way toward a monumental style that filled wall after wall with murals. Rivera sought to create a national art that served two purposes. One was to illustrate Mexico's past by portraying Aztec legends as well as Mexican festivals and folk customs. But Rivera's national art also had a political and social message. He wanted the masses to be aware of the new Mexican political order and not to forget the Mexican Revolution that had overthrown the large landowners and the foreign interests that supported them. Indeed, his works were not for a cultivated audience, but for the masses of people, many of whom could not even read. His wall paintings can be found in such diverse places as the Ministry of Education, the Chapel of the Agriculture School at Chapingo, and the Social Security Hospital.

Conclusion

The turmoil brought by World War I seemed to open the door to upheaval throughout the world. In the Middle East, the decline and fall of the Ottoman Empire led, first of all, to the creation of a new secular Republic of Turkey. Arab states, too, emerged with the collapse of Ottoman power, but were only given mandate status under the British and the French. A new state of Saudi Arabia emerged in the Arabian peninsula while Palestine became a source of tension between newly arrived Jewish settlers and longtime Muslim Palestinians.

Africa and Asia also witnessed movements for national independence. In Africa, these movements were led by native Africans who were educated in Europe and the United States. In India, Gandhi and his campaign of civil disobedience played a crucial role in that country's bid to be free of British rule. Communist movements also began to emerge in Asian societies as instruments for the overthrow of Western imperialism while Japan followed its own path to an authoritarian and militaristic system.

Between 1919 and 1939, China experienced a dramatic struggle to establish a modern nation. Two forces—the Nationalists and the Communists—first cooperated and then fought for control of China. The Nationalists emerged supreme, but found it difficult to control all of China and bring about the kind of modernization they wanted. Japanese interference in Chinese affairs complicated these events.

During the interwar years, the nations of Latin America faced economic problems due to their dependence on the export of foodstuffs and raw materials. Increasing U.S. investments in Latin America contributed to growing hostility against the powerful neighbor to the north.

The Great Depression had two important effects on Latin Americans. It forced them to begin the development of new industries, but it also led to military dictatorships and authoritarian governments, some of them modeled after the fascist regimes of Italy and Germany.

By demolishing their own civilization on the battlefields of Europe in World War I, Europeans had indirectly helped the subject peoples of the vast colonial empires to begin their movements for national independence. And once Europeans had again weakened themselves in the even more destructive conflict of World War II, the hopes for national freedom could at last be realized. It is to that devastating world conflict that we must now turn.

CHAPTER NOTES

1. Speech by Mahatma Gandhi, delivered in London in September 1931 during his visit for the first Roundtable Conference.
2. Quoted in Bernard Lewis, *The Emergence of Modern Turkey*, 2d ed. (London, 1968), pp. 410–11.
3. Ts'ai Yuan-p'ei, "Ta Lin Ch'in-nan Han," in *Ts'ai Yuan-p'ei Hsien-sheng Ch'uan-chi* (Collected Works of Mr. Ts'ai Yuan-p'ei) (Taipei, 1968), pp. 1057–58.

4. Quoted in Nicholas Rowland Clifford, *Spoilt Children of Empire: Westerners in Shanghai and the Chinese Revolution of the 1920s* (Hanover, N.H., 1991), p. 93.
5. Ibid., p. 16.
6. Quoted in William Theodore de Bary et al., ed., *Sources of Chinese Tradition* (New York, 1963), p. 783.
7. Lu Xun, "Diary of a Madman," in *Selected Works of Lu Hsun* (Peking, 1957), 1:20.

SUGGESTED READINGS

The classic study of nationalism in the non-Western world is R. Emerson, *From Empire to Nation* (Boston, 1960). Also see F. von der Mehden, *Religion and Nationalism in Southeast Asia* (Madison, Wis., 1963). For a recent approach, see B. Anderson, *Imagined Communities: Reflections on the Origin and Spread of Nationalism* (London, 1983). On nationalism in India, see S. Wolpert, *Congress and Indian Nationalism: The Pre-independence Phase* (New York, 1988). Also see P. Chatterjee's interesting *The Nation and Its Fragments: Colonial and Postcolonial Histories* (Princeton, N.J., 1993).

There have been a number of studies of Mahatma Gandhi and his ideas. See, for example, J. M. Brown, *Gandhi: Prisoner of Hope* (New Haven, Conn., 1989) and the psychohistorical study by E. Erikson, *Gandhi's Truth: On the Origins of Militant Nonviolence* (New York, 1969). Also see *All Men Are Brothers: The Life and Thought of Mahatma Gandhi as Told in His Own Words* (New York, 1960). For a recent study of Nehru, see S. Gopal, *Jawaharlal Nehru: A Biography*, vol. 1, 1889–1947 (Cambridge, 1976).

For a general survey of events in the Middle East, see H. M. Sachar, *The Emergence of the Middle East, 1914–1924* (New York, 1969). On modernization in Iran, see J. M. Upton, *The History of Modern Iran* (Cambridge, Mass., 1960). The role of Ataturk is examined in J. P. Balfour, *Ataturk: The Rebirth of a Nation* (London, 1964).

On the early republic in China, see L. Yu-sheng, *The Crisis of Chinese Consciousness: Radical Antitraditionalism in the May Fourth Era* (Madison, Wis., 1979). The rise of the Chinese Communist Party is discussed in B. Schwartz, *Chinese Communism and the Rise of Mao* (Cambridge, 1958) and A. Dirlik, *The Origins of Chinese Communism* (Oxford, 1989). There are a number of biographies of Mao Zedong. For a readable and informative version, see S. Schram, *Mao Tse-tung: A Political Biography* (Baltimore, 1966). Also see the same author's *The Political Thought of Mao Tse-tung* (New York, 1966). For an inside account of the movement by a sympathetic Western journalist, see E. Snow's *Red Star over China* (New York, 1938). The early Chiang

Kai-shek period is dealt with persuasively in L. Eastman's *The Abortive Revolution: China under Nationalist Rule, 1927–1937* (Cambridge, 1974).

For an overview of Latin American history in the 1920s and 1930s, see E. Williamson, *The Penguin History of Latin America* (Harmondsworth, 1992). On U.S.–Latin American relations, see the classic study by B. Wood, *The Making of the Good Neighbor Policy* (New York, 1960). On Argentina, Brazil, and Mexico, see D. Rock, *Argentina, 1516–1982* (London, 1986); E. B. Burns, *A History of Brazil*, 2d ed. (New York, 1980); and M. C. Meyer and W. L. Sherman, *The Course of Mexican History*, 3d ed. (New York, 1987). On Getúlio Vargas, see R. Bourne, *Getúlio Vargas of Brazil, 1883–1954: Sphinx of the Pampas* (London, 1974). On culture, see J. Franco, *The Modern Culture of Latin America: Society and the Artist* (Harmondsworth, 1970).

CHAPTER
26

The Crisis Deepens: World War II

On February 3, 1933, only four days after he had been appointed chancellor of Germany, Adolf Hitler met secretly with Germany's leading generals. He revealed to them his desire to remove the "cancer of democracy," create a new authoritarian leadership, and forge a new domestic unity. All Germans would need to realize that "only a struggle can save us and that everything else must be subordinated to this idea." Youth especially must be trained and their wills strengthened "to fight with all means." Since Germany's living space was too small for its people, Hitler said, above all, Germany must rearm and prepare for "the conquest of new living space in the east and its ruthless Germanization." Even before he had consolidated his power, Adolf Hitler had a clear vision of his goals, and their implementation meant another war. World War II in Europe was clearly Hitler's war. Although other countries may have helped to make the war possible by not resisting Hitler's Germany earlier, it was Nazi Germany's actions that made World War II inevitable.

World War II was more than just Hitler's war, however. World War II consisted of two conflicts: one provoked by the ambitions of Germany in Europe, the other by the ambitions of Japan in Asia. By 1941, with the involvement of the United States in both wars, the two had merged into a single global conflict.

Although World War I had been described as a total war, World War II was even more so and was fought on a scale unheard of in history. Almost everyone in the warring countries was in-

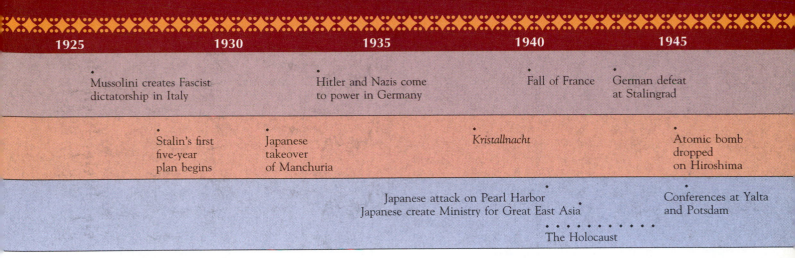

Mussolini creates Fascist dictatorship in Italy

Hitler and Nazis come to power in Germany

Fall of France

German defeat at Stalingrad

Stalin's first five-year plan begins

Japanese takeover of Manchuria

Kristallnacht

Atomic bomb dropped on Hiroshima

Japanese attack on Pearl Harbor
Japanese create Ministry for Great East Asia

Conferences at Yalta and Potsdam

The Holocaust

volved in one way or another: as soldiers; as workers in wartime industries; as ordinary citizens subject to invading armies, military occupation, or bombing raids; as refugees; or as victims of mass extermination. The world had never witnessed such widespread human-made death and destruction.

The Retreat from Democracy: Dictatorial Regimes

There was a close relationship between the rise of dictatorial regimes in the 1930s and the coming of World War II. The apparent triumph of liberal democracy in 1919 proved extremely short-lived. By 1939, only two major states in Europe, France and Great Britain, and a host of minor ones remained democratic. Italy and Germany had succumbed to the political movement called fascism while Soviet Russia under Joseph Stalin moved toward a repressive totalitarian state. A host of other European states and Latin American countries as well adopted authoritarian structures of various kinds while a militarist regime in Japan moved that country down the path of war.

The dictatorial regimes between the wars assumed both old and new forms. Dictatorship was by no means a new phenomenon, but the modern totalitarian state was. The totalitarian regimes, whose best examples can be found in Stalinist Russia and Nazi Germany, extended the functions and power of the central state far beyond

what they had been in the past. The immediate origins of totalitarianism can be found in the total warfare of World War I when governments exercised controls over economic, political, and personal freedom in order to achieve victory.

The modern totalitarian state soon moved beyond the ideal of passive obedience expected in a traditional dictatorship or authoritarian monarchy. The new "total states" expected the active loyalty and commitment of their citizens to the regime's goals. They used modern mass propaganda techniques and high-speed communications to conquer the minds and hearts of their subjects. The total state aimed to control not only the economic, political, and social aspects of life, but the intellectual and cultural aspects as well. But that control also had a purpose: the active involvement of the masses in the achievement of the regime's goals, whether they be war, a socialist state, or a thousand-year Reich.

The modern totalitarian state was to be led by a single leader and single party. It ruthlessly rejected the liberal ideal of limited government power and constitutional guarantees of individual freedoms. Indeed, individual freedom was to be subordinated to the collective will of the masses, organized and determined for them by a leader or leaders. Modern technology also gave total states the ability to use unprecedented police powers to impose their wishes on their subjects.

Totalitarianism is an abstract term, and no state followed all its theoretical implications. The fascist states—Italy and Nazi Germany—as well as Stalin's Communist Russia have all been labeled totalitarian, although their regimes exhibited significant differences and met with varying degrees of success. Totalitarianism transcended traditional political labels. Fascism in Italy and Nazism in

Germany grew out of extreme rightist preoccupations with nationalism and, in the case of Germany, with racism. Communism in Soviet Russia emerged out of Marxian socialism, a radical leftist program. Thus, totalitarianism could and did exist in what were perceived as extreme right-wing and extreme left-wing regimes. This fact helped bring about a new concept of the political spectrum in which the extremes were no longer seen as opposites on a linear scale, but came to be viewed as being similar to each other in at least some respects.

The Birth of Fascism

In the early 1920s, in the wake of economic turmoil, political disorder, and the general insecurity and fear stemming from World War I, Benito Mussolini burst upon the Italian scene with the first Fascist movement in Europe. Mussolini (1883–1945) began his political career as a socialist, but was expelled from the socialist party after supporting Italy's entry into World War I, a position contrary to the socialist position of ardent neutrality. In 1919, Mussolini established a new political group, the *Fascio di Combattimento*, or League of Combat. It received little attention in the elections of 1919, but political stalemate in Italy's parliamentary system and strong nationalist sentiment saved Mussolini and the Fascists.

The new parliament elected in November 1919 quickly proved to be incapable of governing Italy, as the three major parties were unable to form an effective governmental coalition. Meanwhile the socialists, who had become the largest party, spoke theoretically of the need for revolution and alarmed conservatives who quickly associated them with Bolsheviks or Communists. Thousands of industrial and agricultural strikes in 1919 and 1920 created a climate of class warfare and continual violence. In 1920 and 1921, bands of armed Fascists called *squadristi* were formed and turned loose to attack socialist offices and newspapers. Strikes by trade unionists and socialist workers and peasant leagues were broken up by force. Mussolini's Fascist movement began to gain support from middle-class industrialists fearful of working-class agitation and large landowners who objected to the agricultural strikes. Mussolini also perceived that Italians were angry over Italy's failure to receive more fruits of victory in the form of territorial acquisitions after World War I. By 1922, Mussolini's nationalist rhetoric and ability to play to middle-class fears of socialism, Communist revolution, and disorder were attracting even more adherents. On October 29, 1922, after Mussolini and the Fascists threatened to march on Rome if they were not given power, King Victor Emmanuel III

(1900–1946) capitulated and made Mussolini prime minister of Italy.

By 1926, Mussolini had established the institutional framework for his Fascist dictatorship. Press laws gave the government the right to suspend any publications that fostered disrespect for the Catholic church, the monarchy, or the state. The prime minister was made "Head of Government" with the power to legislate by decree. A police law empowered the police to arrest and confine anybody for both nonpolitical and political crimes without due process of law. The government was given the power to dissolve political and cultural associations. In 1926, all anti-Fascist parties were outlawed. A secret police, known as the OVRA, was also established. By the end of 1926, Mussolini ruled Italy as *Il Duce*, the leader.

Mussolini conceived of the Fascist state as totalitarian: "Fascism is totalitarian, and the Fascist State, the synthesis and unity of all values, interprets, develops and gives strength to the whole life of the people."[1] He did try to create a totalitarian apparatus for police surveillance and for controlling mass communications, but this machinery was not all that effective. Police activities in Italy were never as repressive, efficient, or savage as those of Nazi Germany. Likewise, the Italian Fascists' attempt to exercise control over all forms of mass media, including newspapers, radio, and cinema, in order to use propaganda as an instrument to integrate the masses into the state failed to achieve its major goals. Most commonly, Fascist propaganda was disseminated by plastering simple slogans, such as "Mussolini is always right," on walls all over Italy.

Mussolini and the Fascists also attempted to mold Italians into a single-minded community by developing Fascist organizations. Because the secondary schools maintained considerable freedom from Fascist control, the regime relied more and more on the activities of Fascist youth organizations known as the Young Fascists to indoctrinate the young people of the nation in Fascist ideals. By 1939, about 6,800,000 children, teenagers, and young adults of both sexes, or 66 percent of the population between eight and eighteen, were enrolled in some kind of Fascist youth group. Activities for these groups included Saturday afternoon marching drills and calisthenics, seaside and mountain summer camps, and youth contests. An underlying motif for all of these activities was the Fascist insistence on militarization. Beginning in the 1930s, all male groups were given some kind of premilitary exercises to develop discipline and provide training for war. Results were mixed. Italian teenagers, who liked neither military training nor routine discipline of any kind, simply refused to attend Fascist youth group meetings on a regular basis.

The Fascist organizations hoped to create a new Italian, who would be hard-working, physically fit, disciplined, intellectually sharp, and martially inclined. In practice, the Fascists largely reinforced traditional social attitudes in Italy, as is evident in their policies toward women. The Fascists portrayed the family as the pillar of the state and women as the basic foundation of the family. "Woman into the home" became the Fascist slogan. Women were to be homemakers and baby producers, "their natural and fundamental mission in life," according to Mussolini, who viewed population growth as an indicator of national strength. Employment outside the home was an impediment distracting from conception. "It forms an independence and consequent physical and moral habits contrary to child bearing."[2] A practical consideration also underlay the Fascist attitude toward women. Working women would compete with males for jobs in the depression economy of the 1930s. Eliminating women from the market reduced male unemployment figures.

Despite the instruments of repression, the use of propaganda, and the creation of numerous Fascist organizations, Mussolini never really achieved the degree of totalitarian control accomplished in Hitler's Germany or Stalin's Soviet Union. Mussolini and the Fascist Party never really destroyed the old power structure. Some institutions, including the armed forces and monarchy, were never absorbed into the Fascist state and mostly managed to maintain their independence. Mussolini had boasted that he would help workers and peasants, but instead he generally allied himself with the interests of industrialists and large landowners at the expense of the lower classes.

Even more indicative of Mussolini's compromise with the traditional institutions of Italy was his attempt to gain the support of the Catholic church. In the Lateran Accords of February 1929, Mussolini's regime recognized the sovereign independence of a small enclave of 109 acres within Rome, known as Vatican City, which had remained in the church's possession since the unification of Italy in 1870; in return, the papacy recognized the Italian state. The Lateran Accords also guaranteed the church a large grant of money and recognized Catholicism as the "sole religion of the state." In return, the Catholic church urged Italians to support the Fascist regime.

In all areas of Italian life under Mussolini and the Fascists, there was a noticeable dichotomy between Fascist ideals and practice. The Italian Fascists promised much but actually delivered considerably less, and they were soon overshadowed by a much more powerful Fascist movement to the north. Adolf Hitler was a great admirer of Benito Mussolini, but the German pupil soon proved to be far more adept in the use of power than his Italian teacher.

◆ **Mussolini—The Dynamic Duce.** Mussolini worked hard to portray himself as a dynamic and virile leader. He created numerous poses for photographers that were supposed to reinforce this image of himself. Here Mussolini is shown leading his officers on a jog in full uniform.

Hitler and Nazi Germany

In 1923, a small, south German rightist party, known as the Nazis, led by an obscure Austrian rabble-rouser named Adolf Hitler, created a stir when it tried to seize power in southern Germany in conscious imitation of Mussolini's march on Rome in 1922. Although the attempt failed, Adolf Hitler and the Nazis achieved sudden national prominence. Within ten years, Hitler and the Nazis had taken over complete power.

Born on April 20, 1889, Adolf Hitler was the son of an Austrian customs official. He was a total failure in secondary school and eventually made his way to Vienna to become an artist. In Vienna, Hitler established the basic ideas of an ideology from which he never deviated for the rest of his life. At the core of Hitler's ideas was racism, especially his anti-Semitism. His hatred of the Jews lasted to the very end of his life. Hitler also became an extreme German nationalist who learned from the mass politics of Vienna how political parties could use propaganda and terror effectively. Finally, in his Viennese years, Hitler also came to a firm belief in the need for struggle, which he saw as the "granite foundation of the world."

At the end of World War I, after four years of service on the Western Front, Hitler went to Munich and decided to enter politics. Between 1919 and 1923, Hitler accomplished a great deal as a Munich politician. He joined the obscure German Workers' Party, one of a number of right-wing extreme nationalist parties in Munich. By the summer of 1921, he had assumed total control over the party, which he renamed the National Socialist German Workers' Party (NSDAP), or Nazi for short. His idea was that the party's name would distinguish the Nazis from the socialist parties while gaining support from both working-class and nationalist circles. Hitler worked assiduously to develop the party into a mass political movement with flags, party badges, uniforms, its own newspaper, and its own police force or party militia known as the SA, the *Sturmabteilung*, or Storm Troops. The SA was used to defend the party in meeting halls and break up the meetings of other parties. It added an element of force and terror to the growing Nazi movement. Hitler's own oratorical skills were largely responsible for attracting an increasing number of followers. By 1923, the party had grown from its early hundreds into a membership of 55,000 with 15,000 SA members.

Overconfident, Hitler staged an armed uprising against the government in Munich in November 1923. The Beer Hall Putsch was quickly crushed, and Hitler was sentenced to prison. During his brief stay in jail, he wrote *Mein Kampf*, an autobiographical account of his movement and its underlying ideology. Extreme German nationalism, virulent anti-Semitism, and vicious anti-communism are linked together by a Social Darwinian theory of struggle that stresses the right of superior nations to *Lebensraum* (living space) through expansion and the right of superior individuals to secure authoritarian leadership over the masses. What is perhaps most remarkable about *Mein Kampf* is its elaboration of a series of ideas that directed Hitler's actions once he took power. That others refused to take Hitler and his ideas seriously was one of his greatest advantages.

During his imprisonment, Hitler also came to the realization that the Nazis would have to come to power by constitutional means, not by overthrowing the Weimar Republic. This implied the formation of a mass political party that would actively compete for votes with the other political parties. After his release from prison, Hitler worked assiduously to build such a party. He reorganized the Nazi Party on a regional basis and expanded it to all parts of Germany. By 1929, the Nazi Party had a national party organization. It also grew from 27,000 members in 1925 to 178,000 by the end of 1929. Especially noticeable was the youthfulness of the regional, district, and branch leaders of the Nazi organization. Many were between the ages of twenty-five and thirty and were fiercely committed to Hitler because he gave them the kind of active politics they sought. Rather than democratic debate, they wanted brawls in beer halls, enthusiastic speeches, and comradeship in building a new Germany. One new, young Nazi member expressed his excitement about the party:

> For me this was the start of a completely new life. There was only one thing in the world for me and that was service in the movement. All my thoughts were centered on the movement. I could talk only politics. I was no longer aware of anything else. At the time I was a promising athlete; I was very keen on sport, and it was going to be my career. But I had to give this up too. My only interest was agitation and propaganda.[3]

Such youthful enthusiasm gave the Nazi movement the aura of a "young man's movement" and a sense of dynamism that the other parties could not match.

By 1932, the Nazi Party had 800,000 members and had become the largest party in the Reichstag. No doubt, Germany's economic difficulties were a crucial factor in the Nazi rise to power. Unemployment rose dramatically, from 4.35 million in 1931 to 6 million by the winter of 1932. The economic and psychological impact of the Great Depression made extremist parties more attractive. The Nazis were especially effective in developing modern electioneering techniques. In their election campaigns, party members pitched their themes to the needs and fears of different social groups. In working-class districts, for example, the Nazis attacked international high finance, while in middle-class neighborhoods, they exploited fears of a Communist revolution and its threat to private property. At the same time that the Nazis made blatant appeals to class interests, they were denouncing conflicts of interest and maintaining that they stood above classes and parties. Hitler, in particular, claimed to stand above all differences and promised to create a new Germany free of class differences and party infighting. His appeal to national pride, national honor, and traditional militarism struck chords of emotion in his listeners.

Increasingly, the right-wing elites of Germany, the industrial magnates, landed aristocrats, military establishment, and higher bureaucrats, came to see Hitler as the man who had the mass support to establish a right-wing, authoritarian regime that would save Germany and their privileged positions from a Communist takeover. Under pressure, since the Nazi Party had the largest share of seats in the Reichstag, President Paul von Hindenburg agreed to allow Hitler to become chancellor (on January 30, 1933) and create a new government.

Within two months, Hitler had laid the foundations for the Nazis' complete control over Germany. On the day after a fire broke out in the Reichstag building (February 27), supposedly caused by the Communists, Hitler convinced President Hindenburg to issue a decree that gave the government emergency powers. It suspended all basic rights for the full duration of the emergency and thus enabled the Nazis to arrest and imprison anyone without redress. The crowning step in Hitler's "legal seizure" of power came on March 23 when the Reichstag passed the Enabling Act by a two-thirds vote. This legislation, which empowered the government to dispense with constitutional forms for four years while it issued laws that dealt with the country's problems, provided the legal basis for Hitler's subsequent acts. He no longer needed either the Reichstag or President Hindenburg. In effect, Hitler became a dictator appointed by the parliamentary body itself.

With their new source of power, the Nazis acted quickly to enforce *Gleichschaltung*, or the coordination of all institutions under Nazi control. The civil service was purged of Jews and democratic elements, concentration camps were established for opponents of the new regime, the autonomy of the federal states was eliminated, trade unions were dissolved, and all political parties except the Nazis were abolished. By the end of the summer of 1933, within seven months of being appointed chancellor,

Hitler and the Nazis had established the foundations for a totalitarian state. When Hindenburg died on August 2, 1934, the office of Reich president was abolished, and Hitler became sole ruler of Germany. Public officials and soldiers were all required to take a personal oath of loyalty to Hitler as the "Führer of the German Reich and people."

THE NAZI STATE, 1933–1939

Having smashed the parliamentary state, Hitler now felt the real task was at hand: to develop the "total state." Hitler's aims had not been simply power for power's sake or a tyranny based on personal power. He had larger ideological goals. The development of an Aryan racial state that would dominate Europe and possibly the world for generations to come required a movement in which the German people would be actively involved, not passively cowed by force. Hitler stated:

> We must develop organizations in which an individual's entire life can take place. Then every activity and every need of every individual will be regulated by the collectivity represented by the party. There is no longer any arbitrary will, there are no longer any free realms in which the individual belongs to himself.... The time of personal happiness is over.[4]

The Nazis pursued the creation of this totalitarian state in a variety of ways.

Mass demonstrations and spectacles were employed to integrate the German nation into a collective fellowship and to mobilize it as an instrument for Hitler's policies (see the box on p. 955). These mass demonstrations, especially the Nuremberg party rallies that were held every September, combined the symbolism of a religious service with the merriment of a popular amusement. They had great appeal and usually evoked mass enthusiasm and excitement.

Some features of the state apparatus of Hitler's "total state" seem contradictory. One usually thinks of Nazi Germany as having an all-powerful government that maintained absolute control and order. In truth, Nazi Germany was the scene of almost constant personal and institutional conflict, which resulted in administrative chaos. In matters such as foreign policy, education, and economics, parallel government and party bureaucracies competed with each other over spheres of influence. Incessant struggle characterized relationships within the party, within the state, and between party and state. Some historians assume that Hitler's aversion to making decisions resulted in the chaos that subverted his own authority and made him a "weak dictator," while others maintain that Hitler deliberately created this institutional confusion. By fostering rivalry within the party and between party and state, he would be the ultimate decision maker and absolute ruler.

In the economic sphere, Hitler and the Nazis also established control. Although the regime pursued the use of public works projects and "pump-priming" grants to private construction firms to foster employment and end the depression, there is little doubt that rearmament contributed far more to solving the unemployment problem. Unemployment, which had stood at 6 million in 1932, dropped to 2.6 million in 1934 and less than 500,000 in 1937. The regime claimed full credit for solving Germany's economic woes, and this was an important factor in convincing many Germans to accept the new regime, despite its excesses.

For those who needed coercion, the Nazi total state had its instruments of terror and repression. Especially important was the SS. Originally created as Hitler's personal bodyguard, the SS, under the direction of Heinrich Himmler (1900–1945), came to control all of the regular and secret police forces. Himmler and the SS functioned on the basis of two principles: terror and ideology. Terror included the instruments of repression and murder: the secret police, criminal police, concentration camps, and later the execution squads and death camps for the extermination of the Jews. For Himmler, the SS was a crusading order whose primary goal was to further the Aryan master race. SS members, who constituted a carefully chosen elite, were thoroughly indoctrinated in racial ideology.

Other institutions, such as the Catholic and Protestant churches, primary and secondary schools, and universities, were also brought under the control of the Nazi totalitarian state. Nazi professional organizations and leagues were formed for civil servants, teachers, women, farmers, doctors, and lawyers. Since the early indoctrination of youth would create the foundation for a strong totalitarian state for the future, youth organizations, the *Hitler Jugend* (Hitler Youth) and its female counterpart, the *Bund deutscher Mädel* (League of German Maidens), were given special attention. The oath required of Hitler Youth members demonstrates the degree of dedication expected of youth in the Nazi state: "In the presence of this blood banner, which represents our Führer, I swear to devote all my energies and my strength to the savior of our country, Adolf Hitler. I am willing and ready to give up my life for him, so help me God."

The creation of the Nazi total state also had an impact on women. The Nazi attitude toward women was largely determined by ideological considerations. Women played a crucial role in the Aryan racial state as bearers of the children who would bring about the triumph of the Aryan race. To the Nazis, the differences between men and women were quite natural. Men were warriors and political leaders while women were destined to be wives and mothers. By maintaining this clear distinction, each could best serve to "maintain the whole community."

Nazi ideas determined employment opportunities for women. The Nazis hoped to drive women out of certain areas of the labor market, including heavy industry or other jobs that might hinder women from bearing healthy children. Certain professions, including univer-

♦ **The Nazi Mass Spectacle.** Hitler and the Nazis made clever use of mass spectacles to rally the German people behind the Nazi regime. These mass demonstrations evoked intense enthusiasm, as is evident in this photograph of Hitler arriving at the Bückeberg near Hamelin for the Harvest Festival in 1937. Almost one million people were present for the celebration.

≫ Propaganda and Mass Meetings in Nazi Germany ≪

Propaganda and mass rallies were two of the chief instruments that Hitler used to prepare the German people for the tasks he set before them. In the first selection, taken from Mein Kampf, Hitler explains the psychological importance of mass meetings in creating support for a political movement. In the second excerpt, taken from his speech to a crowd at Nuremberg, he describes the kind of mystical bond he hoped to create through his mass rallies.

Adolf Hitler, *Mein Kampf*

The mass meeting is also necessary for the reason that in it the individual, who at first, while becoming a supporter of a young movement, feels lonely and easily succumbs to the fear of being alone, for the first time gets the picture of a larger community, which in most people has a strengthening, encouraging effect.... When from his little workshop or big factory, in which he feels very small, he steps for the first time into a mass meeting and has thousands and thousands of people of the same opinions around him, when, as a seeker, he is swept away by three or four thousand others into the mighty effect of suggestive intoxication and enthusiasm, when the visible success and agreement of thousands confirm to him the rightness of the new doctrine and for the first time arouse doubt in the truth of his previous conviction—then he himself has suc-

cumbed to the magic influence of what we designate as "mass suggestion." The will, the longing, and also the power of thousands are accumulated in every individual. The man who enters such a meeting doubting and wavering leaves it inwardly reinforced: he has become a link in the community.

Adolf Hitler, Speech at the Nuremberg Party Rally, 1936

Do we not feel once again in this hour the miracle that brought us together? Once you heard the voice of a man, and it struck deep into your hearts; it awakened you, and you followed this voice. Year after year you went after it, though him who had spoken you never even saw. You heard only a voice, and you followed it. When we meet each other here, the wonder of our coming together fills us all. Not everyone of you sees me, and I do not see everyone of you. But I feel you, and you feel me. It is the belief in our people that has made us small men great, that has made us poor men rich, that has made brave and courageous men out of us wavering, spiritless, timid folk; this belief made us see our road when we were astray; it joined us together into one whole! ... You come, that ... you may, once in a while, gain the feeling that now we are together; we are with him and he with us, and we are now Germany!

---

sity teaching, medicine, and law, were also considered inappropriate for women, especially married women. Instead the Nazis encouraged women to pursue professional occupations that had direct practical application, such as social work and nursing. In addition to restrictive legislation against females, the Nazi regime pushed its campaign against working women with such poster slogans as "Get ahold of pots and pans and broom and you'll sooner find a groom!"

The Nazi total state was intended to be an Aryan racial state. From its beginning, the Nazi Party reflected the strong anti-Semitic beliefs of Adolf Hitler. Once in power, the Nazis translated anti-Semitic ideas into anti-Semitic policies. In September 1935, the Nazis announced new racial laws at the annual party rally in Nuremberg. These "Nuremberg laws" excluded German Jews from German citizenship and forbade marriages and extramarital relations between Jews and German citizens. The "Nuremberg laws" essentially separated Jews

from the Germans politically, socially, and legally and were the natural extension of Hitler's stress upon the creation of a pure Aryan race.

Another, considerably more violent phase of anti-Jewish activity took place in 1938 and 1939. It was initiated on November 9–10, 1938, the infamous *Kristallnacht*, or night of shattered glass. The assassination of a third secretary in the German embassy in Paris became the occasion for a Nazi-led destructive rampage against the Jews in which synagogues were burned, 7,000 Jewish businesses were destroyed, and at least one hundred Jews were killed. Moreover, 20,000 Jewish males were rounded up and sent to concentration camps. *Kristallnacht* also led to further drastic steps. Jews were barred from all public buildings and prohibited from owning, managing, or working in any retail store. Finally, under the direction of the SS, Jews were encouraged to "emigrate from Germany." After the outbreak of World War II, the policy of emigration was replaced by a more gruesome one.

The Stalinist Era in the Soviet Union

The Stalinist era marked the beginning of an economic, social, and political revolution in Russia that was more sweeping in its results than the revolutions of 1917. Joseph Stalin made a significant shift in economic policy in 1928 when he launched his first five-year plan. Its real goal was nothing less than the transformation of Russia from an agricultural into an industrial country virtually overnight. Instead of consumer goods, the first five-year plan emphasized maximum production of capital goods and armaments and succeeded in quadrupling the production of heavy machinery and doubling oil production. Between 1928 and 1937, during the first two five-year plans, steel production increased from 4 to 18 million tons per year while hard coal output went from 36 to 128 million tons. At the same time, new industrial cities, located near iron ore and coal deposits, sprang up overnight in the Urals and Siberia.

The social and political costs of industrialization were enormous. Little provision was made for absorbing the expanded labor force into the cities. While the industrial labor force increased by millions between 1932 and 1940, total investment in housing actually declined after 1929, with the result that millions of workers and their families lived in pitiful conditions. Real wages in industry also declined by 43 percent between 1928 and 1940 while strict laws limited workers' freedom of movement. To inspire and pacify the workers, government propaganda stressed the need for sacrifice to create the new socialist state.

Rapid industrialization was accompanied by an equally rapid collectivization of agriculture. Its goal was to eliminate private farms and push people into collective farms (see the box on p. 957). Strong resistance from peasants who hoarded crops and killed livestock only led Stalin to step up the program. By 1930, 10 million peasant households had been collectivized; by 1934, Russia's 26 million family farms had been collectivized into 250,000 units. This was done at tremendous cost, as the hoarding of food and the slaughter of livestock produced widespread famine. Stalin himself is supposed to have told Winston Churchill during World War II that 10 million peasants died in the artificially created famines of 1932 and 1933. The only concession Stalin made to the peasants was that each collective farm worker was allowed to have one tiny, privately owned garden plot.

Stalin's program of rapid industrialization entailed other costs as well. To achieve his goals, Stalin strengthened the Communist Party bureaucracy under his control. Those who resisted were sent into forced labor camps in Siberia. Stalin's desire for sole control of decision making also led to purges of the Old Bolsheviks. Between 1936 and 1938, the most prominent Old Bolsheviks were put on trial and condemned to death. During this same time, Stalin undertook a purge of army officers, diplomats, union officials, party members, intellectuals, and numerous ordinary citizens. Estimates are that eight million Russians were arrested; millions were sent to Siberian forced labor camps, from which they never returned.

The Stalinist era also reversed much of the permissive social legislation of the early 1920s. Advocating complete equality of rights for women, the Communists had made divorce and abortion easy to obtain while also encouraging women to work outside the home and liberate themselves sexually. After Stalin came to power, the family was praised as a miniature collective in which parents

⇒ The Formation of Collective Farms ⇐

Accompanying the rapid industrialization of the Soviet Union was the collectivization of agriculture, a feat that involved nothing less than transforming Russia's 26 million family farms into 250,000 collective farms (kolkhozes). This selection provides a firsthand account of how the process worked.

Max Belov, *The History of a Collective Farm*

General collectivization in our village was brought about in the following manner: Two representatives of the [Communist] Party arrived in the village. All the inhabitants were summoned by the ringing of the church bell to a meeting at which the policy of general collectivization was announced.... The upshot was that although the meeting lasted two days, from the viewpoint of the Party representatives nothing was accomplished.

After this setback the Party representatives divided the village into two sections and worked each one separately. Two more officials were sent to reinforce the first two. A meeting of our section of the village was held in a stable which had previously belonged to a kulak. The meeting dragged on until dark. Suddenly someone threw a brick at the lamp, and in the dark the peasants began to beat the Party representatives who jumped out the window and escaped from the village barely alive. The following day seven people were arrested. The militia was called in and stayed in the village until the peasants, realizing their helplessness, calmed down....

By the end of 1930 there were two kolkhozes in our village. Though at first these collectives embraced at most only 70 percent of the peasant households, in the months that followed they gradually absorbed more and more of them.

In these kolkhozes the great bulk of the land was held and worked communally, but each peasant household owned a house of some sort, a small plot of ground and perhaps some livestock. All the members of the kolkhoz were required to work on the kolkhoz a certain number of days each month; the rest of the time they were allowed to work on their own holdings. They derived their income partly from what they grew on their garden strips and partly from their work in the kolkhoz.

When the harvest was over, and after the farm had met its obligations to the state and to various special funds (for insurance, seed, etc.) and had sold on the market whatever undesignated produce was left, the remaining produce and the farm's monetary income were divided among the kolkhoz members according to the number of "labor days" each one had contributed to the farm's work.... It was in 1930 that the kolkhoz members first received their portions out of the "communal kettle." After they had received their earnings, at the rate of 1 kilogram of grain and 55 kopecks per labor day, one of them remarked, "You will live, but you will be very, very thin."

In the spring of 1931 a tractor worked the fields of the kolkhoz for the first time. The tractor was "capable of plowing every kind of hard soil and virgin sod," as Party representatives told us at the meeting in celebration of its arrival. The peasants did not then know that these "steel horses" would carry away a good part of the harvest in return for their work....

By late 1932 more than 80 percent of the peasant households . . . had been collectivized.... That year the peasants harvested a good crop and had hopes that the calculations would work out to their advantage and would help strengthen them economically. These hopes were in vain. The kolkhoz workers received only 200 grams of flour per labor day for the first half of the year; the remaining grain, including the seed fund, was taken by the government. The peasants were told that industrialization of the country, then in full swing, demanded grain and sacrifices from them.

---

were responsible for inculcating values of duty, discipline, and hard work. Abortion was outlawed while divorced fathers who did not support their children were fined heavily. The new divorce law of June 1936 imposed fines for repeated divorces. This return of social conservatism was paralleled by official encouragement of Soviet patriotism. Even the tsars were rehabilitated as Russian heroes.

Authoritarian States in Europe

A number of other European states were not totalitarian but did possess conservative authoritarian governments. These states adopted some of the trappings of totalitarian states, especially their wide police powers, but their greatest concern was not the creation of a mass movement aimed at the establishment of a new kind of society, but rather the defense of the existing social order. Consequently, the authoritarian states tended to limit the participation of the masses and were content with passive obedience rather than demanding active involvement in the goals of the regime.

Nowhere had the map of Europe been more drastically altered by World War I than in eastern Europe. The new states of Austria, Poland, Czechoslovakia, and Yugoslavia (known as the kingdom of the Serbs, Croats, and Slovenes until 1929) adopted parliamentary systems while the preexisting kingdoms of Romania and Bulgaria gained new parliamentary constitutions in 1920. Greece became a republic in 1924. Hungary's government was parliamentary in form, but controlled by its landed aristocrats. Thus, at the beginning of the 1920s, political democracy seemed well established, but almost everywhere in eastern Europe, parliamentary governments soon gave way to authoritarian regimes.

Several problems helped to create this situation. Eastern European states had little tradition of liberalism or parliamentary politics and no substantial middle class to support them. Then, too, these states were largely rural and agrarian in character. While many of the peasants were largely illiterate, much of the land was still dominated by large landowners who feared the growth of agrarian peasant parties with their schemes for land redistribution. Ethnic conflicts also threatened to tear these countries apart. Fearful of land reform, Communist agrarian upheaval, and ethnic conflict, powerful landowners, the churches, and even some members of the small middle class looked to authoritarian governments to maintain the old system. Only Czechoslovakia, with its substantial middle class, liberal tradition, and strong industrial base, maintained its political democracy.

In Spain, political democracy also failed to survive. Led by General Francisco Franco (1892–1975), Spanish military forces revolted against the democratic government in 1936 and inaugurated a brutal and bloody civil war that lasted three years. Foreign intervention complicated the Spanish Civil War. Franco's forces were aided by arms, money, and men from the Fascist regimes of Italy and Germany while the government was assisted by 40,000 foreign volunteers and trucks, planes, tanks, and military advisers from the Soviet Union. After Franco's forces captured Madrid on March 28, 1939, the Spanish Civil War finally came to an end. General Franco soon established a dictatorship that favored large landowners, businessmen, and the Catholic clergy. It was yet another example of a traditional, conservative, authoritarian regime.

◆ **Stalin Signs a Death Warrant.** Terror played an important role in the totalitarian system established by Joseph Stalin. In this photograph, Stalin is shown signing what is supposedly a death warrant in 1933. As the terror increased in the late 1930s, Stalin signed such lists every day.

The Rise of a Militarist Japan

The rise of militant forces in Japan was not the result of a takeover of power by a new political party, but of the increasing influence of militant elements at the top of the political hierarchy. Some, like the publicist Kita Ikki, were civilians convinced that the parliamentary system had been corrupted by materialism and Western values and should be replaced by a system that would return to traditional Japanese values and imperial authority. Others were military men who were angered at budget cuts in military expenditures and the pacifist policies followed by the government during the 1920s.

During the early 1930s, extremist patriotic organizations were formed within the civilian population as well as within the army and the navy. One such organization composed of middle-level army officers secured the takeover of Manchuria in the fall of 1931. Others terrorized Japanese society by assassinating businessmen and public figures identified with the Shidehara policy of conciliation toward the outside world. Moderates were intimidated into silence, and individuals tried for their part in assassination attempts portrayed themselves as selfless patriots and received light sentences. National elections continued to be held, but the cabinets were dominated by the military or advocates of Japanese expansionism.

As war approached in the late 1930s, Japanese society was placed on a wartime footing. A conscription law was passed in 1938, and economic resources were placed under strict government control. Two years later, all political parties were merged into an Imperial Rule Assistance Association that served as a mouthpiece for expansionist elements within the government and the military establishment. Labor unions were dissolved, and education and culture were purged of all corrupt Western ideas in favor of traditional values emphasizing the divinity of the emperor and the higher spirituality of Japanese civilization.

The Path to War

Only twenty years after the war to end war, the world plunged back into the nightmare of total war. The efforts at collective security in the 1920s—the League of Nations, the attempts at disarmament, the pacts and treaties—all proved meaningless in view of the growth of Nazi Germany and the rise of Japan.

The German Path to War

World War II in Europe had its beginnings in the ideas of Adolf Hitler, who believed that only the Aryans were capable of building a great civilization. But to Hitler, the Germans (the leading group of Aryans) were threatened from the east by a large mass of inferior peoples, the Slavs, who had learned to use German weapons and technology. Germany needed more land to support a larger population and be a great power. Already in the 1920s, in the second volume of *Mein Kampf*, Hitler had indicated where a National Socialist regime would find this land: "And so we National Socialists . . . take up where we broke off six hundred years ago. We stop the endless German movement to the south and west, and turn our gaze toward the land in the east. . . . If we speak of soil in Europe today, we can primarily have in mind only Russia and her vassal border states."[5] Once Russia had been conquered, its land could be resettled by German peasants while the Slavic population could be used as slave labor to build the Aryan racial state that would dominate Europe for a thousand years. Hitler's conclusion was apparent: Germany must prepare for its inevitable war with the Soviet Union. Hitler's ideas were by no means secret. He had spelled them out in *Mein Kampf*, a book readily available to anyone who wished to read it.

When Hitler became chancellor on January 30, 1933, Germany's situation in Europe seemed weak. The Versailles treaty had created a demilitarized zone on Germany's western border that would allow the French to move into the heavily industrialized parts of Germany in the event of war. To Germany's east, the smaller states, such as Poland and Czechoslovakia, had defensive treaties with France. The Versailles treaty had also limited Germany's army to 100,000 troops with no air force and only a small navy.

Posing as the man of peace in his public speeches, Hitler emphasized that Germany wished only to revise the unfair provisions of Versailles by peaceful means and achieve Germany's rightful place among the European states. On March 9, 1935, he announced the creation of a new air force and, one week later, the introduction of a military draft that would expand Germany's army from 100,000 to 550,000 troops. Hitler's unilateral repudiation of the Versailles treaty brought a swift reaction as France, Great Britain, and Italy condemned Germany's action and warned against future aggressive steps. But nothing concrete was done.

On March 7, 1936, buoyed by his conviction that the Western democracies had no intention of using force to maintain the Treaty of Versailles, Hitler sent German troops into the demilitarized Rhineland. According to the Versailles treaty, the French had the right to use force against any violation of the demilitarized Rhineland. But France would not act without British support, and the British viewed the occupation of German territory by German troops as reasonable action by a dissatisfied power. The London *Times* noted that the Germans were only "going into their own back garden."

Meanwhile, Hitler gained new allies. In October 1935, Benito Mussolini had committed Fascist Italy to imperial expansion by invading Ethiopia. Angered by French and British opposition to his invasion, Mussolini welcomed Hitler's support and began to draw closer to the German dictator he had once called a buffoon. The joint intervention of Germany and Italy on behalf of General Francisco Franco in the Spanish Civil War in 1936 also drew the two nations closer together. In October 1936, Mussolini and Hitler concluded an agreement that recognized their common political and economic interests, and one month later, Mussolini referred publicly to the new Rome-Berlin Axis. Also in November, Germany and Japan (the rising military power in the Far East) concluded the Anti-Comintern Pact and agreed to maintain a common front against communism.

By the end of 1936, Hitler and Nazi Germany had achieved a "diplomatic revolution" in Europe. The Treaty of Versailles had been virtually scrapped and Germany was once more a "World Power," as Hitler proclaimed. Hitler was convinced that neither the French nor the British would provide much opposition to his plans and decided in 1938 to move on Austria. By threatening Austria with invasion, Hitler coerced the Austrian chancellor into putting Austrian Nazis in charge of the government. The new government promptly invited German troops to enter Austria and assist in maintaining law and order. One day later, on March 13, 1938, after his triumphal return to his native land, Hitler formally annexed Austria to Germany. Great Britain's ready acknowledgment of Hitler's action only increased the German dictator's contempt for Western weakness.

The annexation of Austria improved Germany's strategic position in central Europe and put Germany in position for Hitler's next objective—the destruction of Czechoslovakia. This goal might have seemed unrealistic since democratic Czechoslovakia was quite prepared to defend itself and was well supported by pacts with France and the Soviet Union. Hitler believed, however, that France and Britain would not use force to defend Czechoslovakia.

He was right again. On September 15, 1938, Hitler demanded the cession of the Sudetenland (an area in northwestern Czechoslovakia that was inhabited largely by ethnic Germans) to Germany and expressed his willingness to risk "world war" to achieve his objective. Instead of objecting, the British, French, Germans, and Italians—at a hastily arranged conference at Munich—reached an agreement that essentially met all of Hitler's demands. German troops were allowed to occupy the Sudetenland as the Czechs, abandoned by their Western allies, stood by helplessly. The Munich Conference was the high point of Western appeasement of Hitler. When Neville Chamberlain, the British prime minister, returned to England from Munich, he boasted that the

◆ **Hitler Enters the Sudetenland.** The Sudetenland was an area of Czechoslovakia inhabited by 3.5 million ethnic Germans. The Munich Conference allowed Germany to occupy the Sudetenland. This picture shows Hitler and his entourage arriving at Eger (now Cheb) in October 1938 to the cheers of an enthusiastic crowd.

≈ The Munich Conference ≈

At the Munich Conference, the leaders of France and Great Britain capitulated to Hitler's demands on Czechoslovakia. While the British prime minister, Neville Chamberlain, defended his actions at Munich as necessary for peace, another British statesman, Winston Churchill, characterized the settlement at Munich as "a disaster of the first magnitude."

Winston Churchill, Speech to the House of Commons (October 5, 1938)

I will begin by saying what everybody would like to ignore or forget but which must nevertheless be stated, namely, that we have sustained a total and unmitigated defeat, and that France has suffered even more than we have. . . . The utmost my right honorable Friend the Prime Minister . . . has been able to gain for Czechoslovakia and in the matters which were in dispute has been that the German dictator, instead of snatching his victuals from the table, has been content to have them served to him course by course. . . . And I will say this, that I believe the Czechs, left to themselves and told they were going to get no help from the Western Powers, would have been able to make better terms than they have got. . . .

We are in the presence of a disaster of the first magnitude which has befallen Great Britain and France. Do not let us blind ourselves to that. . . .

And do not suppose that this is the end. This is only the beginning of the reckoning. This is only the first sip, the first foretaste of a bitter cup which will be proffered to us year by year unless by a supreme recovery of moral health and martial vigor, we arise again and take our stand for freedom as in the olden time.

Neville Chamberlain, Speech to the House of Commons (October 6, 1938)

That is my answer to those who say that we should have told Germany weeks ago that, if her army crossed the border of Czechoslovakia, we should be at war with her. We had no treaty obligations and no legal obligations to Czechoslovakia. . . . When we were convinced, as we became convinced, that nothing any longer would keep the Sudetenland within the Czechoslovakian State, we urged the Czech Government as strongly as we could to agree to the cession of territory, and to agree promptly. . . . It was a hard decision for anyone who loved his country to take, but to accuse us of having by that advice betrayed the Czechoslovakian State is simply preposterous. What we did was to save her from annihilation and give her a chance of new life as a new State, which involves the loss of territory and fortifications, but may perhaps enable her to enjoy in the future and develop a national existence under a neutrality and security comparable to that which we see in Switzerland today. Therefore, I think the Government deserve the approval of this House for their conduct of affairs in this recent crisis which has saved Czechoslovakia from destruction and Europe from Armageddon.

Munich agreement meant "peace for our time." Hitler had promised Chamberlain that he had made his last demand. Like scores of German politicians before him, Chamberlain had believed Hitler's promises (see the box above).

In fact, Munich confirmed Hitler's perception that the Western democracies were weak and would not fight. Increasingly, Hitler was convinced of his own infallibility, and he had by no means been satisfied at Munich. In March 1939, Hitler occupied the Czech lands (Bohemia and Moravia) while the Slovaks, with his encouragement, declared their independence of the Czechs and became a puppet state (Slovakia) of Nazi Germany. On the evening of March 15, 1939, Hitler triumphantly declared in Prague that he would be known as the greatest German of them all.

At last, the Western states reacted vigorously to the Nazi threat. Hitler's naked aggression had made clear that his promises were utterly worthless. When he began to demand the return of Danzig (which had been made a free city by the Treaty of Versailles to serve as a seaport for Poland) to Germany, Britain recognized the danger and offered to protect Poland in the event of war. At the same time, both France and Britain realized that only the Soviet Union was powerful enough to help contain Nazi aggression and began political and military negotiations with Joseph Stalin and the Soviets. Their distrust of Soviet communism, however, made an alliance unlikely.

Meanwhile, Hitler pressed on in the belief that Britain and France would not really fight over Poland. To preclude an alliance between the western European states and the Soviet Union, which would create the danger of a two-front war, Hitler, ever the opportunist, negotiated his own nonaggression pact with Stalin and shocked the world with its announcement on August 23, 1939. The treaty with the Soviet Union gave Hitler the freedom to attack Poland. He told his generals: "Now Poland is in the position in which I wanted her . . . I am only afraid that at the last moment some swine or other will yet submit to me a plan for mediation."[6] He need not have worried. On September 1, German forces invaded Poland; two days later, Britain and France declared war on Germany. Europe was again at war.

The Japanese Path to War

In September 1931, on the pretext that the Chinese had attacked a Japanese railway near Mukden (the "Mukden incident" had actually been carried out by Japanese saboteurs), Japanese military units seized Manchuria. Japanese officials in Tokyo were divided over the wisdom of the takeover, but the moderates were unable to control the army. Eventually, worldwide protests against the Japanese action led the League of Nations to send an investigative commission to Manchuria. When the commission issued a report condemning the seizure, Japan withdrew from the league. Over the next several years, the Japanese consolidated their hold on Manchuria, renaming it Manchukuo and placing it under the titular authority of the former Chinese emperor and now Japanese puppet Henry Pu Yi. Japan now began to expand into North China.

Not all politicians in Tokyo agreed with this aggressive policy, but right-wing terrorists assassinated some of the key critics and intimidated others into silence. By the mid-1930s, militants connected with the government and the armed forces were effectively in control of Japanese politics. The United States refused to recognize the Japanese takeover of Manchuria, but was unwilling to threaten the use of force. Instead the Americans attempted to appease Japan in the hope of encouraging moderate forces in Japanese society. As a senior U.S. diplomat with long experience in Asia warned in a memorandum to the president: "Utter defeat of Japan would be no blessing to the Far East or to the world. It would merely create a new set of stresses, and substitute for Japan the USSR as the successor to Imperial Russia—as a contestant (and at least an equally unscrupulous and

◆ **A Japanese Victory in China.** After consolidating its authority over Manchuria, Japan began to expand into North China. Direct hostilities between Japanese and Chinese forces began in 1937. By 1939, Japan had conquered most of eastern China. This photograph shows victorious Japanese soldiers amid the ruins of the railway station in Hankou, which became China's temporary capital after the fall of Nanjing.

dangerous one) for the mastery of the East. Nobody except perhaps Russia would gain from our victory in such a war."[7]

For the moment, the prime victim of Japanese aggression was China. Chiang Kai-shek attempted to avoid a confrontation with Japan so that he could deal with what he considered the greater threat from the Communists. When clashes between Chinese and Japanese troops broke out, he sought to appease the Japanese by granting them the authority to administer areas in North China. But as Japan moved steadily southward, popular protests in Chinese cities against Japanese aggression intensified. In December 1936, Chiang was briefly kidnapped by military forces commanded by General Zhang Xueliang, who compelled him to end his military efforts against the Communists in Yan'an and form a new united front against the Japanese. After Chinese and Japanese forces clashed at Marco Polo Bridge, south of Beijing, in July 1937, China refused to apologize and hostilities spread.

A MONROE DOCTRINE FOR ASIA

Japan had not planned to declare war on China, but neither side would compromise, and the 1937 incident eventually turned into a major conflict. The Japanese advanced up the Yangtze valley and seized the Chinese capital of Nanjing in December, but Chiang Kai-shek refused to capitulate and moved his government upriver to Hankou. When the Japanese seized that city, he moved on to Chongqing, in remote Sichuan province. Japanese strategists had hoped to force Chiang to join a new Japanese-dominated New Order in East Asia, comprising Japan, Manchuria, and China. This was part of a larger plan to seize Soviet Siberia with its rich resources and create a new "Monroe Doctrine for Asia," in which Japan would guide its Asian neighbors on the path to development and prosperity (the box on p. 964). After all, who better to instruct Asian societies on modernization than the one Asian country that had already achieved it?

During the late 1930s, Japan began to cooperate with Nazi Germany on the assumption that the two countries would ultimately launch a joint attack on the Soviet Union and divide up its resources between them. But when Germany surprised the world by signing a nonaggression pact with the Soviets in August 1939, Japanese strategists were compelled to reevaluate their long-term objectives. Japan was not strong enough to defeat the Soviet Union alone, as a small but bitter border war along the Siberian frontier near Manchukuo had amply demonstrated. So the Japanese began to shift their eyes

south to the vast resources of Southeast Asia—the oil of the Dutch East Indies, the rubber and tin of Malaya, and the rice of Burma and Indochina.

A move southward, of course, would risk war with the European colonial powers and the United States. Japan's attack on China in the summer of 1937 had already aroused strong criticism abroad, particularly from the United States, where President Franklin D. Roosevelt threatened to "quarantine" the aggressors after Japanese military units bombed an American naval ship operating in China. Public fear of involvement forced the president to draw back, but when Japan suddenly demanded the right to occupy airfields and exploit economic resources in French Indochina in the summer of 1940, the United States warned the Japanese that it would impose

CHRONOLOGY

The Path to War, 1931–1939

Japan seizes Manchuria	September 1931
Hitler becomes chancellor	January 30, 1933
Hitler announces a German air force	March 9, 1935
Hitler announces military conscription	March 16, 1935
Mussolini invades Ethiopia	October 1935
Hitler occupies demilitarized Rhineland	March 7, 1936
Mussolini and Hitler intervene in Spanish Civil War	1936
Rome-Berlin Axis	October 1936
Anti-Comintern Pact (Japan and Germany)	November 1936
Japan invades China	1937
Germany annexes Austria	March 13, 1938
Munich Conference: Sudetenland goes to Germany	September 29, 1938
Germany occupies the rest of Czechoslovakia	March 1939
German-Soviet Nonaggression Pact	August 23, 1939
Germany invades Poland	September 1, 1939
Britain and France declare war on Germany	September 3, 1939

Japan's Justification for Expansion

Advocates of Japanese expansion justified their proposals by claiming both economic necessity and moral imperatives. Note the familiar combination of motives in this passage written by an extremist military leader in the late 1930s.

Hashimoto Kingoro, The Need for Emigration and Expansion

We have already said that there are only three ways left to Japan to escape from the pressure of surplus population. We are like a great crowd of people packed into a small and narrow room, and there are only three doors through which we might escape, namely emigration, advance into world markets, and expansion of territory. The first door, emigration, has been barred to us by the anti-Japanese immigration policies of other countries. The second door, advance into world markets, is being pushed shut by tariff barriers and the abrogation of commercial treaties. What should Japan do when two of the three doors have been closed against her?

It is quite natural that Japan should rush upon the last remaining door.

It may sound dangerous when we speak of territorial expansion, but the territorial expansion of which we speak does not in any sense of the word involve the occupation of the possessions of other countries, the planting of the Japanese flag thereon, and the declaration of their annexation to Japan. It is just that since the Powers have suppressed the circulation of Japanese materials and merchandise abroad, we are looking for some place overseas where Japanese capital, Japanese skills and Japanese labor can have free play, free from the oppression of the white race.

We would be satisfied with just this much. What

moral right do the world powers who have themselves closed to us the two doors of emigration and advance into world markets have to criticize Japan's attempt to rush out of the third and last door?

If they do not approve of this, they should open the door which they have closed against us and permit the free movement overseas of Japanese emigrants and merchandise. . . .

At the time of the Manchurian incident, the entire world joined in criticism of Japan. They said that Japan was an untrustworthy nation. They said that she had recklessly brought cannon and machine guns into Manchuria, which was the territory of another country, flown airplanes over it, and finally occupied it. But the military action taken by Japan was not in the least a selfish one. Moreover, we do not recall ever having taken so much as an inch of territory belonging to another nation. The result of this incident was the establishment of the splendid new nation of Manchuria. The Powers are still discussing whether or not to recognize this new nation, but regardless of whether or not other nations recognize her, the Manchurian empire has already been established, and now, seven years after its creation, the empire is further consolidating its foundations with the aid of its friend, Japan.

And if it is still protested that our actions in Manchuria were excessively violent, we may wish to ask the white race just which country it was that sent warships and troops to India, South Africa, and Australia and slaughtered innocent natives, bound their hands and feet with iron chains, lashed their backs with iron whips, proclaimed these territories as their own, and still continues to hold them to this very day.

economic sanctions unless Japan withdrew from the area and returned to its borders of 1931.

The Japanese viewed the American threat of retaliation as a threat to their long-term objectives. Japan badly needed liquid fuel and scrap iron from the United States. Should they be cut off, Japan would have to find them elsewhere. The Japanese were thus caught in a vise. To obtain guaranteed access to natural resources that were necessary to fuel the Japanese military machine, Japan must risk being cut off from its current source of raw materials that would be needed in case of a conflict. After much debate, the Japanese decided to launch a surprise

attack on American and European colonies in Southeast Asia in the hope of a quick victory that would evict the United States from the region.

The Course of World War II

Using *Blitzkrieg,* or "lightning war," Hitler stunned Europe with the speed and efficiency of the German attack. Armored columns or panzer divisions (a panzer division was a strike force of about three hundred tanks and accompanying forces and supplies) supported by airplanes broke quickly through Polish lines and encircled the bewildered Polish troops. Conventional infantry units then moved in to hold the newly conquered territory. Within four weeks, Poland had surrendered. On September 28, 1939, Germany and the Soviet Union officially divided Poland between them.

Europe at War

Although Hitler's hopes to avoid a war with the western European states were dashed when France and Britain declared war on September 3, he was confident that he could control the situation. After a winter of waiting (called the "phony war"), Hitler resumed the war on April 9, 1940, with another *Blitzkrieg* against Denmark and Norway. One month later, on May 10, the Germans launched their attack on the Netherlands, Belgium, and France. The main assault through Luxembourg and the Ardennes forest was completely unexpected by the French and British forces. German panzer divisions broke through the weak French defensive positions there and raced across northern France, splitting the Allied armies and trapping French troops and the entire British army on the beaches of Dunkirk. Only by heroic efforts did the British succeed in a gigantic evacuation of 330,000 Allied (mostly British) troops. The French capitulated on June 22. German armies occupied about three-fifths of France while the French hero of World War I, Marshal Henri Pétain (1856–1951), established an authoritarian regime (known as Vichy France) over the remainder. Germany was now in control of western and central Europe, but Britain had still not been defeated.

As Hitler realized, an amphibious invasion of Britain would only be possible if Germany gained control of the air. At the beginning of August 1940, the *Luftwaffe* (the German air force) launched a major offensive against British air and naval bases, harbors, communication centers, and war industries. The British fought back doggedly, supported by an effective radar system that gave them early warning of German attacks. Nevertheless, the British air force suffered critical losses by the end of August and was probably saved by Hitler's change in strategy. In September, in retaliation for a British attack on Berlin, Hitler ordered a shift from military targets to massive bombing of British cities to break British morale. The British rebuilt their air strength quickly and were soon inflicting major losses on *Luftwaffe* bombers. By the end of September, Germany had lost the Battle of Britain, and the invasion of Britain had to be postponed.

At this point, Hitler pursued the possibility of a Mediterranean strategy, which would involve capturing Egypt and the Suez Canal and closing the Mediterranean to British ships, thereby shutting off Britain's supply of oil. Hitler's commitment to the Mediterranean was never wholehearted, however. His initial plan was to let the Italians defeat the British in North Africa, but this strategy failed when the British routed the Italian army. Although Hitler then sent German troops to the North African theater of war, his primary concern lay elsewhere; he had already reached the decision to fulfill his lifetime obsession with the acquisition of territory in the east.

Although he had no desire for a two-front war, Hitler became convinced that Britain was remaining in the war only because it expected Soviet support. If the Soviet Union were smashed, Britain's last hope would be eliminated. Moreover, Hitler had convinced himself that the Soviet Union, with what he regarded as its Jewish-Bolshevik leadership and a pitiful army, could be defeated quickly and decisively. Although the invasion of the Soviet Union was scheduled for spring 1941, the attack was delayed because of problems in the Balkans. Hitler had already obtained the political cooperation of Hungary, Bulgaria, and Romania, but Mussolini's disastrous invasion of Greece in October 1940 exposed Hitler's southern flank to British air bases in Greece. To secure his Balkan flank, German troops seized both Yugoslavia and Greece in April 1941. Now reassured, Hitler turned to the east and invaded the Soviet Union on June 22, 1941, in the belief that the Soviets could still be decisively defeated before winter set in.

The massive attack stretched out along an 1,800-mile front. German troops advanced rapidly, capturing two million Russian soldiers. By November, one German army group had swept through Ukraine, while a second was besieging Leningrad; a third approached within twenty-five miles of Moscow, the Russian capital. An early winter and unexpected Soviet resistance, however, brought a halt to the German advance. For the first time in the war, German armies had been stopped. A Soviet counterattack in December 1941 by a Soviet army supposedly exhausted by Nazi victories came as an ominous ending to the year for the Germans. By that time, another of Hitler's decisions—the declaration of war on the United States—probably made his defeat inevitable and turned another European conflict into a global war.

Japan at War

On December 7, 1941, Japanese carrier-based aircraft attacked the U.S. naval base at Pearl Harbor in the Hawaiian Islands. The same day, other units launched assaults on the Philippines and began advancing toward the British colony of Malaya. Shortly thereafter, Japanese forces invaded the Dutch East Indies and occupied a number of islands in the Pacific Ocean. In some cases, as on the Bataan peninsula and the island of Corregidor in the Philippines, resistance was fierce, but by the spring of 1942, almost all of Southeast Asia and much of the western Pacific had fallen into Japanese hands. Japan declared the creation of a Great East-Asia Co-prosperity Sphere of the entire region under Japanese tutelage and announced its intention to liberate the colonies of Southeast Asia from Western rule. For the moment, however, Japan needed the resources of the region for its war machine and placed its conquests under its rule on a wartime basis.

Japanese leaders had hoped that their lightning strike at American bases would destroy the U.S. Pacific Fleet and persuade the Roosevelt administration to accept Japanese domination of the Pacific. The American people, in the eyes of Japanese leaders, had been made soft by material indulgence. But the Japanese had miscalculated. The attack on Pearl Harbor galvanized American opinion and won broad support for Roosevelt's war policy. The United States now joined with European nations and Nationalist China in a combined effort to defeat Japan and bring an end to its hegemony in the Pacific. Believing the American involvement in the Pacific would render the United States ineffective in the European theater of war, Hitler declared war on the United States four days after Pearl Harbor.

The Turning Point of the War, 1942–1943

The entry of the United States into the war created a coalition (the Grand Alliance) that ultimately defeated the Axis powers (Germany, Italy, Japan). Nevertheless,

the three major Allies, Britain, the United States, and the Soviet Union, had to overcome mutual suspicions before they could operate as an effective alliance. Two factors aided that process. First, Hitler's declaration of war on the United States made it easier for the Americans to accept the British and Russian contention that the defeat of Germany should be the first priority of the United States. For that reason, the United States, under its Lend-Lease program, sent large amounts of military aid, including $50 billion worth of trucks, planes, and other arms, to the British and Soviets. Also important to the alliance was the tacit agreement of the three chief Allies to stress military operations while ignoring political differences and larger strategic issues concerning any postwar settlement. At the beginning of 1943, the Allies agreed to fight until the Axis powers surrendered unconditionally. Although this principle of unconditional surrender prevented a repeat of the mistake of World War I, which was ended in 1918 with an armistice rather than a total victory, it likely discouraged dissident Germans and Japanese from overthrowing their governments in order to arrange a negotiated peace. At the same time, it did have the effect of cementing the Grand Alliance by making it nearly impossible for Hitler to divide his foes.

Defeat, however, was far from Hitler's mind at the beginning of 1942. As Japanese forces advanced into Southeast Asia and the Pacific after crippling the American naval fleet at Pearl Harbor, Hitler and his European allies continued the war in Europe against Britain and the Soviet Union. Until the fall of 1942, it appeared that the Germans might still prevail on the battlefield. Reinforcements in North Africa enabled the Afrika Korps under General Erwin Rommel to break through the British

◆ **German Panzer Troops in Russia.** At first, the German attack on Russia was enormously successful, leading one German general to remark in his diary, "It is probably no overstatement to say that the Russian campaign has been won in the space of two weeks." This picture shows German panzer troops jumping from their armored troop carriers to attack Red Army snipers who had taken refuge in a farmhouse.

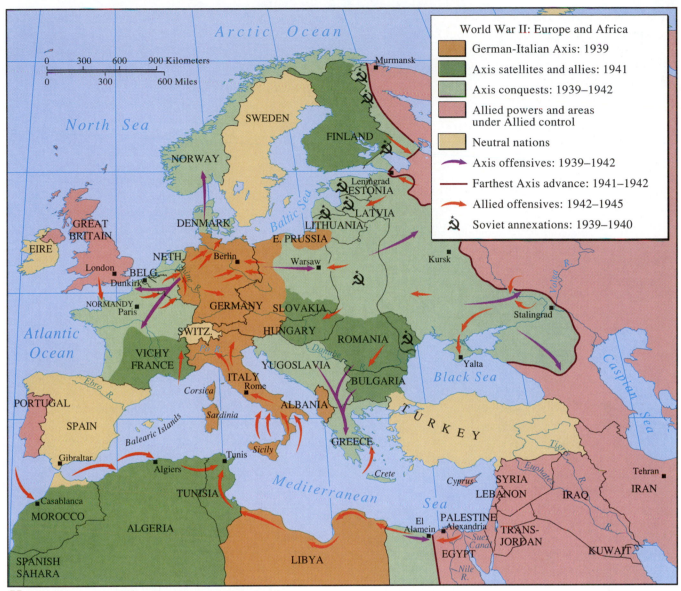

Map 26.1   World War II in Europe and North Africa.

defenses in Egypt and advance toward Alexandria. In the spring of 1942, a renewed German offensive in the Soviet Union led to the capture of the entire Crimea, causing Hitler to boast in August 1942:

> As the next step, we are going to advance south of the Caucasus and then help the rebels in Iran and Iraq against the English. Another thrust will be directed along the Caspian Sea toward Afghanistan and India. Then the English will run out of oil. In two years we'll be on the borders of India. Twenty to thirty elite German divisions will do. Then the British Empire will collapse.[8]

But this would be Hitler's last optimistic outburst. By the fall of 1942, the war had turned against the Germans.

In North Africa, British forces had stopped Rommel's troops at El Alamein in the summer of 1942 and then forced them back across the desert. In November 1942, British and American forces invaded French North Africa and forced the German and Italian troops to surrender in May 1943. On the Eastern Front, the turning point of the war occurred at Stalingrad. After the capture of the Crimea, Hitler's generals wanted him to concentrate on the Caucasus and its oil fields, but Hitler decided that Stalingrad, a major industrial center on the Volga,

❧ A German Soldier at Stalingrad ❧

The Soviet victory at Stalingrad was a major turning point in World War II. This excerpt comes from the diary of a German soldier who fought and died in the Battle of Stalingrad. His dreams of victory and a return home with medals are soon dashed by the realities of Soviet resistance.

Diary of a German Soldier

Today, after we'd had a bath, the company commander told us that if our future operations are as successful, we'll soon reach the Volga, take Stalingrad and then the war will inevitably soon be over. Perhaps we'll be home by Christmas.

July 29. The company commander says the Russian troops are completely broken, and cannot hold out any longer. To reach the Volga and take Stalingrad is not so difficult for us. The Führer knows where the Russians' weak point is. Victory is not far away. . . .

August 10. The Führer's orders were read out to us. He expects victory of us. We are all convinced that they can't stop us.

August 12. This morning outstanding soldiers were presented with decorations. . . . Will I really go back to Elsa without a decoration? I believe that for Stalingrad the Führer will decorate even me. . . .

September 4. We are being sent northward along the front toward Stalingrad. We marched all night and by dawn had reached Voroponovo Station. We can already see the smoking town. It's a happy thought that the end of the war is getting nearer. That's what everyone is saying. . . .

September 8. Two days of non-stop fighting. The Russians are defending themselves with insane stubbornness. Our regiment has lost many men. . . .

September 16. Our battalion, plus tanks, is attacking the [grain storage] elevator, from which smoke is pouring—the grain in it is burning, the Russians seem to

have set light to it themselves. Barbarism. The battalion is suffering heavy losses. . . .

October 10. The Russians are so close to us that our planes cannot bomb them. We are preparing for a decisive attack. The Führer has ordered the whole of Stalingrad to be taken as rapidly as possible. . . .

October 22. Our regiment has failed to break into the factory. We have lost many men; every time you move you have to jump over bodies. . . .

November 10. A letter from Elsa today. Everyone expects us home for Christmas. In Germany everyone believes we already hold Stalingrad. How wrong they are. If they could only see what Stalingrad has done to our army. . . .

November 21. The Russians have gone over to the offensive along the whole front. Fierce fighting is going on. So, there it is—the Volga, victory and soon home to our families! We shall obviously be seeing them next in the other world.

November 29. We are encircled. It was announced this morning that the Führer has said: "The army can trust me to do everything necessary to ensure supplies and rapidly break the encirclement."

December 3. We are on hunger rations and waiting for the rescue that the Führer promised. . . .

December 14. Everybody is racked with hunger. Frozen potatoes are the best meal, but to get them out of the ice-covered ground under fire from Russian bullets is not so easy. . . .

December 26. The horses have already been eaten. I would eat a cat; they say its meat is also tasty. The soldiers look like corpses or lunatics, looking for something to put in their mouths. They no longer take cover from Russian shells; they haven't the strength to walk, run away and hide. A curse on this war!

should be taken first. Between November 1942 and February 1943, German troops were stopped, then encircled, and finally forced to surrender on February 2, 1943 (see the box above). The entire German Sixth Army of 300,000 men was lost. By February 1943, German forces in Russia were back to their positions of June 1942. By the spring of 1943, long before Allied troops returned to the European continent, even Hitler knew that the Germans would not defeat the Soviet Union.

The tide of battle in the Far East also turned dramatically in 1942. In the Battle of the Coral Sea on May 7–8, 1942, American naval forces stopped the Japanese advance and temporarily relieved Australia of the threat of invasion. On June 4, at the Battle of Midway Island, American carrier planes destroyed all four of the attacking Japanese aircraft carriers and established American naval superiority in the Pacific. The victory was especially remarkable in that almost all the American planes

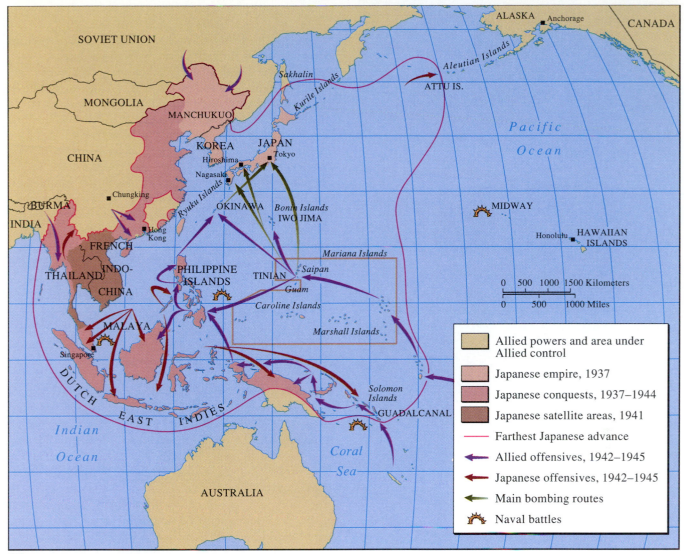

Map 26.2 World War II in Asia and the Pacific.

were shot down in the encounter. By the fall of 1942, Allied forces were beginning to gather for offensive operations into South China from Burma, through the Indonesian islands by a process of "island hopping" by troops commanded by the American general Douglas MacArthur, and across the Pacific with a combination of U.S. Army, Marine, and Navy attacks on Japanese-held islands. After a series of bitter engagements in the waters of the Solomon Islands from August to November 1942, Japanese fortunes began to fade.

The Last Years of the War

By the beginning of 1943, the tide of battle had turned against Germany, Italy, and Japan. After the Axis forces had surrendered in Tunisia on May 13, 1943, the Allies crossed the Mediterranean and carried the war to Italy. After taking Sicily, Allied troops began the invasion of mainland Italy in September. In the meantime, after the ouster and arrest of Benito Mussolini, a new Italian government offered to surrender to Allied forces. But Mussolini was liberated by the Germans in a daring raid and then set up as the head of a puppet German state in northern Italy while German troops moved in and occupied much of Italy. The new defensive lines established by the Germans in the hills south of Rome were so effective that the Allied advance up the Italian peninsula was a painstaking affair accompanied by heavy casualties. Rome did not fall to the Allies until June 4, 1944. By that time, the Italian war had assumed a secondary role

CHRONOLOGY

The Course of World War II

Germany and the Soviet Union divide Poland	September 28, 1939
Blitzkrieg against Denmark and Norway	April 1940
Blitzkrieg against Belgium, Netherlands, France	May 1940
France surrenders	June 22, 1940
Battle of Britain	Fall 1940
Nazi seizure of Yugoslavia and Greece	April 1941
Germany invades the Soviet Union	June 22, 1941
Japanese attack on Pearl Harbor	December 7, 1941
Battle of the Coral Sea	May 7–8, 1942
Battle of Midway Island	June 4, 1942
Allied invasion of North Africa	November 1942
German surrender at Stalingrad	February 2, 1943
Axis forces surrender in North Africa	May 1943
Battle of Kursk	July 5–12, 1943
Invasion of mainland Italy	September 1943
Allied invasion of France	June 6, 1944
Hitler commits suicide	April 30, 1945
Surrender of Germany	May 7, 1945
Atomic bomb dropped on Hiroshima	August 6, 1945
Japan surrenders	August 14, 1945

anyway as the Allies opened their long-awaited "second front" in western Europe.

Since the autumn of 1943, the Allies had been planning a cross-channel invasion of France from Britain. Under the direction of the American general Dwight D. Eisenhower (1890–1969), the Allies landed five assault divisions on the Normandy beaches on June 6, 1944, in history's greatest naval invasion. An initially indecisive German response enabled the Allied forces to establish a beachhead. Within three months, they had landed two million men and a half-million vehicles that pushed inland and broke through German defensive lines.

After the breakout, Allied troops moved south and east and liberated Paris by the end of August. By March 1945, they had crossed the Rhine River and advanced further into Germany. At the end of April 1945, Allied armies in northern Germany moved toward the Elbe River where they finally linked up with the Soviets. The Soviets had come a long way since the Battle of Stalingrad in 1943. In the summer of 1943, Hitler gambled on taking the offensive by making use of newly developed heavy tanks. German forces were soundly defeated by the Soviets at the Battle of Kursk (July 5–12), the greatest tank battle of World War II. Soviet forces now began a relentless advance westward. The Soviets had reoccupied Ukraine by the end of 1943 and lifted the siege of Leningrad and moved into the Baltic states by the beginning of 1944. Advancing along a northern front, Soviet troops occupied Warsaw in January 1945 and entered Berlin in April. Meanwhile, Soviet troops along a southern front swept through Hungary, Romania, and Bulgaria.

In January 1945, Adolf Hitler had moved into a bunker fifty-five feet under Berlin to direct the final stages of the war. In his final political testament, Hitler, consistent to the end in his rabid anti-Semitism, blamed the Jews for the war: "Above all I charge the leaders of the nation and those under them to scrupulous observance of the laws of race and to merciless opposition to the universal poisoner of all peoples, international Jewry."[9] Hitler committed suicide on April 30, two days after Mussolini had been shot by partisan Italian forces. On May 7, German commanders surrendered. The war in Europe was over.

The war in Asia continued. Beginning in 1943, American forces had gone on the offensive and advanced their way, slowly at times, across the Pacific. American forces took an increasing toll of enemy resources, especially at sea and in the air. As Allied military power drew inexorably closer to the main Japanese islands in the first months of 1945, President Harry Truman, who had succeeded to the presidency on the death of Franklin Roosevelt in April, had an excruciatingly difficult decision to make. Should he use atomic weapons (at the time, only two bombs were available, and their effectiveness had not been demonstrated) to bring the war to an end without the necessity of an Allied invasion of the Japanese homeland? As the world knows, Truman answered that question in the affirmative. The first bomb was dropped on the city of Hiroshima on August 6. Truman then called on Japan to surrender or expect a "rain of ruin from

♦ **Refugees Flee Yokohama.** American bombing attacks on Japanese cities began in earnest in November 1944. Built of flimsy materials, Japan's crowded cities were soon devastated by these air raids. This photograph shows a homeless family fleeing Yokohama, a shelter for refugees until American bombers devastated the city on May 29, 1945.

the air." When the Japanese did not respond, a second bomb was dropped on Nagasaki. Japan surrendered unconditionally on August 14. World War II, in which 17 million men died in battle and perhaps 18 million civilians perished as well (some estimate total losses at 50 million), was finally over.

*T*he New Order

The initial victories of the Germans and Japanese gave them the opportunity to create new orders in Europe and Asia. Although both countries presented positive images of these new orders for publicity purposes, in practice both followed policies of ruthless domination of their subject peoples.

The New Order in Europe

After the German victories in Europe, Nazi propagandists created glowing images of a new European order based on "equal chances" for all nations and an integrated economic community. This was not Hitler's conception of a European New Order. He saw the Europe he had conquered simply as subject to German domination. Only the Germans, he once said, "can really organize Europe."

The Nazi empire stretched across continental Europe from the English Channel in the west to the outskirts of Moscow in the east. In no way was this empire organized systematically or governed efficiently. Nazi-occupied Europe was largely organized in one of two ways. Some areas, such as western Poland, were directly annexed by

Nazi Germany and made into German provinces. Most of occupied Europe was administered by German military or civilian officials in combination with varying degrees of indirect control from collaborationist regimes.

Racial considerations played an important role in how conquered peoples were treated. German civil administrations were established in Norway, Denmark, and the Netherlands because the Nazis considered their peoples to be Aryan or racially akin to the Germans and hence worthy of more lenient treatment. "Inferior" Latin peoples, such as the occupied French, were given military administrations. By 1943, however, as Nazi losses continued to multiply, all the occupied territories of northern and western Europe were ruthlessly exploited for material goods and manpower for Germany's labor needs.

Because the conquered lands in the east contained the living space for German expansion and were populated in Nazi eyes by racially inferior Slavic peoples, Nazi administration there was considerably more ruthless. Hitler's racial ideology and his plans for an Aryan racial empire were so important to him that he and the Nazis began to implement their racial program soon after the conquest of Poland. Heinrich Himmler, a strong believer in Nazi racial ideology and the leader of the SS, was put in charge of German resettlement plans in the east. Himmler's task was to evacuate the inferior Slavic peoples and replace them with Germans, a policy first applied to the new German provinces created from the lands of western Poland. One million Poles were uprooted and dumped in southern Poland. Hundreds of thousands of ethnic Germans (descendants of Germans who had migrated years ago from Germany to different parts of southern and eastern Europe) were encouraged to colonize designated areas in Poland. By 1942, two million ethnic Germans had been settled in Poland.

The invasion of the Soviet Union inflated Nazi visions of German colonization in the east. Hitler spoke to his intimate circle of a colossal project of social engineering after the war, in which Poles, Ukrainians, and Russians would become slave labor while German peasants settled on the abandoned lands and Germanized them (see the box on p. 973). Nazis involved in this kind of planning were well aware of the human costs. Himmler told a gathering of SS officers that although the destruction of 30 million Slavs was a prerequisite for German plans in the east, "Whether nations live in prosperity or starve to death interests me only insofar as we need them as slaves for our culture. Otherwise it is of no interest."[10]

Labor shortages in Germany led to a policy of ruthless mobilization of foreign labor for Germany. After the invasion of the Soviet Union, the four million Russian prisoners of war captured by the Germans along with more than two million workers conscripted in France became a major source of heavy labor, but it was wasted by allowing more than three million of them to die from neglect. In 1942, a special office was created to recruit labor for German farms and industries. By the summer of 1944, seven million foreign workers were laboring in Germany and constituted 20 percent of Germany's labor force. At the same time, another seven million workers were supplying forced labor in their own countries on farms, in industries, and even in military camps. Forced labor, however, often proved counterproductive because it created economic chaos in occupied countries and disrupted industrial production that could have helped Germany. The brutal character of Germany's recruitment policies often led more and more people to resist the Nazi occupation forces.

The Holocaust

No aspect of the Nazi New Order was more terrifying than the deliberate attempt to exterminate the Jewish people of Europe. Racial struggle was a key element in Hitler's ideology and meant to him a clearly defined conflict of opposites: the Aryans, creators of human cultural development, against the Jews, parasites who were trying to destroy the Aryans. By the beginning of 1939, Nazi policy focused on promoting the "emigration" of German Jews from Germany. Once the war began in September 1939, the so-called Jewish problem took on new dimensions. For a while there was discussion of the Madagascar Plan, which aspired to the mass shipment of Jews to the African island of Madagascar. When war contingencies made this plan impractical, an even more drastic policy was conceived.

Heinrich Himmler and the SS organization closely shared Hitler's racial ideology. The SS was given responsibility for what the Nazis called their Final Solution to the Jewish problem, that is, the annihilation of the Jewish people. Reinhard Heydrich (1904–1942), head of the SS's Security Service, was given administrative responsibility for the Final Solution. After defeating Poland, Heydrich ordered the special strike forces (*Einsatzgruppen*) that he had created to round up all Polish Jews and concentrate them in ghettos established in a number of Polish cities.

In June 1941, the *Einsatzgruppen* were given new responsibilities as mobile killing units. These SS death squads followed the regular army's advance into the Soviet Union. Their job was to round up Jews in the villages and execute and bury them in mass graves, often giant pits dug by the victims themselves before they were shot.

Hitler's Plans for a New Order in the East

Hitler's nightly monologues to his postdinner guests, which were recorded by the Führer's private secretary, Martin Bormann, reveal much about the New Order he wished to create. On the evening of October 17, 1941, Hitler expressed his views on what the Germans would do with their newly conquered territories in the east.

Hitler's Secret Conversations, October 17, 1941

In comparison with the beauties accumulated in Central Germany, the new territories in the East seem to us like a desert. . . . This Russian desert, we shall populate it. . . . We'll take away its character of an Asiatic steppe, we'll Europeanize it. With this object, we have undertaken the construction of roads that will lead to the southernmost point of the Crimea and to the Caucasus. These roads will be studded along their whole length with German towns, and around these towns our colonists will settle.

As for the two or three million men whom we need to accomplish this task, we'll find them quicker than we think. They'll come from Germany, Scandinavia, the Western countries and America. I shall no longer be here to see all that, but in twenty years the Ukraine will already be a home for twenty million inhabitants besides the natives. In three hundred years, the country will be one of the loveliest gardens in the world.

As for the natives, we'll have to screen them carefully. The Jew, that destroyer, we shall drive out. . . .

We shan't settle in the Russian towns, and we'll let them fall to pieces without intervening. And, above all, no remorse on this subject! We're not going to play at children's nurses; we're absolutely without obligations as far as these people are concerned. To struggle against the hovels, chase away the fleas, provide German teachers, bring out newspapers—very little of that for us! We'll confine ourselves, perhaps, to setting up a radio transmitter, under our control. For the rest, let them know just enough to understand our highway signs, so that they won't get themselves run over by our vehicles. . . . There's only one duty: to Germanize this country by the immigration of Germans, and to look upon the natives as Redskins. If these people had defeated us, Heaven have mercy! But we don't hate them. That sentiment is unknown to us. We are guided only by reason. . . .

All those who have the feeling for Europe can join in our work.

In this business I shall go straight ahead, cold-bloodedly. What they may think about me, at this juncture, is to me a matter of complete indifference. I don't see why a German who eats a piece of bread should torment himself with the idea that the soil that produces this bread has been won by the sword.

Such constant killing produced morale problems among the SS executioners. During a visit to Minsk in the Soviet Union, Himmler tried to build morale by pointing out that "he would not like it if Germans did such a thing gladly. But their conscience was in no way impaired, for they were soldiers who had to carry out every order unconditionally. He alone had responsibility before God and Hitler for everything that was happening, . . . and he was acting from a deep understanding of the necessity for this operation."[11]

Although it has been estimated that as many as one million Jews were killed by the *Einsatzgruppen*, this approach to solving the Jewish problem was soon perceived as inadequate. Instead, the Nazis opted for the systematic annihilation of the European Jewish population in specially built death camps. The plan was basically simple.

Jews from countries occupied by Germany (or sympathetic to Germany) would be rounded up, packed like cattle into freight trains, and shipped to Poland, where six extermination centers were built for this purpose. The largest and most famous was Auschwitz-Birkenau. Medical technicians chose Zyklon B (the commercial name for hydrogen cyanide) as the most effective gas for quickly killing large numbers of people in gas chambers designed to look like "shower rooms" to facilitate the cooperation of the victims. After gassing, the corpses would be burned in specially built crematoria.

By the spring of 1942, the death camps were in operation. Although initial priority was given to the elimination of the ghettos in Poland, by the summer of 1942, Jews were also being shipped from France, Belgium, and Holland. Even as the Allies were making significant

◆ **The Holocaust: Activities of the *Einsatzgruppen*.** The activities of the mobile killing units known as the *Einsatzgruppen* were the first stage in the mass killings of the Holocaust. This picture shows the execution of a Jew by a member of one of these SS killing squads. Onlookers include members of the German Army, the German Labor Service, and even Hitler Youth. When it became apparent that this method of killing was inefficient, it was replaced by the death camps.

advances in 1944, Jews were being shipped from Greece and Hungary. These shipments depended on the cooperation of Germany's Transport Ministry, but despite desperate military needs, the Final Solution had priority in using railroad cars for the transportation of Jews to death camps.

A harrowing experience awaited the Jews when they arrived at one of the six death camps. Rudolf Höss, commandant at Auschwitz-Birkenau, described it:

> We had two SS doctors on duty at Auschwitz to examine the incoming transports of prisoners. The prisoners would be marched by one of the doctors who would make spot decisions as they walked by. Those who were fit for work were sent into the camp. Others were sent immediately to the extermination plants. Children of tender years were invariably exterminated since by reason of their youth they were unable to work. . . . at Auschwitz we endeavored to fool the victims into thinking that they were to go through a delousing process. Of course, frequently they realized our true intentions and we sometimes had riots and difficulties due to that fact.[12]

About 30 percent of the arrivals at Auschwitz were sent to a labor camp, while the remainder went to the gas chambers (see the box on p. 975). After they had been gassed, the bodies were burned in the crematoria. The victims' goods and even their bodies were used for economic gain. Female hair was cut off, collected, and turned into mattresses or cloth. Some inmates were also subjected to cruel and painful "medical" experiments. The Germans killed between five and six million Jews, over three million of them in the death camps. Virtually 90 percent of the Jewish populations of Poland, the Baltic countries, and Germany were exterminated. Overall, the Holocaust was responsible for the death of nearly two out of every three European Jews.

The Nazis were also responsible for another Holocaust, the death by shooting, starvation, or overwork of at least another 9 to 10 million people. Because the Nazis also considered the Gypsies of Europe (like the Jews) a race containing alien blood, they were systematically rounded up for extermination. About 40 percent of Europe's one million Gypsies were killed in the death camps. The leading elements of the "subhuman" Slavic peoples—the clergy, intelligentsia, civil leaders, judges, and lawyers—were arrested and deliberately killed. Probably an additional four million Poles, Ukrainians, and Belorussians lost their lives as slave laborers for Nazi Germany while at least three to four million Soviet prisoners of war were killed in captivity. The Nazis also singled out homosexuals for persecution, and thousands lost their lives in concentration camps.

The New Order in Asia

Once the takeover was completed, Japanese war policy in the occupied areas in Asia became essentially defensive, as Japan hoped to use its new possessions to meet its burgeoning needs for raw materials, such as tin, oil, and rubber, as well as an outlet for Japanese manufactured goods. To provide an organizational structure for the arrangement, Japanese leaders set up the Great East-Asia Co-prosperity Sphere, a self-sufficient economic community

The Holocaust: The Camp Commandant and the Camp Victims

The systematic annihilation of millions of men, women, and children in extermination camps makes the Holocaust one of the most horrifying events in history. The first document is taken from an account by Rudolf Höss, commandant of the extermination camp at Auschwitz-Birkenau. In the second document, a French doctor explains what happened at one of the crematoria described by Höss.

Commandant Höss Describes the Equipment

The two large crematoria, Nos. I and II, were built during the winter of 1942–43. . . . They each . . . could cremate c. 2,000 corpses within twenty-four hours. . . . Crematoria I and II both had underground undressing and gassing rooms which could be completely ventilated. The corpses were brought up to the ovens on the floor above by lift. The gas chambers could hold c. 3,000 people.

The firm of Topf had calculated that the two smaller crematoria, III and IV, would each be able to cremate 1,500 corpses within twenty-four hours. However, owing to the wartime shortage of materials, the builders were obliged to economize and so the undressing rooms and gassing rooms were built above ground and the ovens were of a less solid construction. But it soon became apparent that the flimsy construction of these two four-retort ovens was not up to the demands made on it. No. III ceased operating altogether after a short time and later was no longer used. No. IV had to be repeatedly shut down since after a short period in operation of 4–6 weeks, the ovens and chimneys had burnt out. The victims of the gassing were mainly burnt in pits behind crematorium IV.

The largest number of people gassed and cremated within twenty-four hours was somewhat over 9,000.

A French Doctor Describes the Victims

It is mid-day, when a long line of women, children, and old people enter the yard. The senior official in charge . . . climbs on a bench to tell them that they are going to have a bath and that afterward they will get a drink of hot coffee. They all undress in the yard. . . . The doors are opened and an indescribable jostling begins. The first people to enter the gas chamber begin to draw back. They sense the death which awaits them. The SS men put an end to this pushing and shoving with blows from their rifle butts beating the heads of the horrified women who are desperately hugging their children. The massive oak double doors are shut. For two endless minutes one can hear banging on the walls and screams which are no longer human. And then—not a sound. Five minutes later the doors are opened. The corpses, squashed together and distorted, fall out like a waterfall. . . . The bodies which are still warm pass through the hands of the hairdresser who cuts their hair and the dentist who pulls out their gold teeth. . . . One more transport has just been processed through No. IV crematorium.

---

designed to provide mutual benefits to the occupied areas and the home country (see the box on p. 976). A Ministry for Great East Asia, staffed by civilians, was established in Tokyo in October 1942 to handle arrangements between Japan and the conquered territories.

The Japanese conquest of Southeast Asia had been accomplished under the slogan "Asia for the Asiatics," and many Japanese probably sincerely believed that their government was bringing about the liberation of the Southeast Asian peoples from European colonial rule. Japanese officials in the occupied territories quickly made contact with anticolonialist elements and promised that independent governments would be established under Japanese tutelage. Such governments were eventually established in Burma, the Dutch East Indies, Vietnam, and the Philippines.

In fact, however, real power rested with the Japanese military authorities in each territory, and the local Japanese military command was directly subordinated to the Army General Staff in Tokyo. The economic resources of the colonies were exploited for the benefit of the Japanese war machine, while natives were recruited to serve in local military units or conscripted to work on public works projects. In some cases, the people living in the occupied areas were subjected to severe hardships. In Indochina, for example, forced requisitions of rice by the local Japanese authorities for shipment abroad created a food shortage that caused the starvation of over a million Vietnamese in 1944 and 1945.

The Japanese planned to implant a new moral and social order as well as a new political and economic order in the occupied areas. Occupation policy stressed

The Japanese objective in World War II was to create a vast Great East-Asia Co-prosperity Sphere to provide Japan with needed raw materials and a market for its exports. The following passage is from a secret document produced by a high-level government committee in January 1942.

Draft Plan for the Establishment of a Great East-Asia Co-prosperity Sphere

The Plan. The Japanese empire is a manifestation of morality and its special characteristic is the propagation of the Imperial Way. It is necessary to foster the increased power of the empire, to cause East Asia to return to its original form of independence and co-prosperity by shaking off the yoke of Europe and America, and to let its countries and peoples develop their respective abilities in peaceful cooperation and secure livelihood.

The Form of East Asiatic Independence and Co-prosperity. The states, their citizens, and resources, comprised in those areas pertaining to the Pacific, Central Asia, and the Indian Oceans formed into one general union are to be established as an autonomous zone of peaceful living and common prosperity on behalf of the peoples of the nations of East Asia. The area in-

cluding Japan, Manchuria, North China, lower Yangtze River, and the Russian Maritime Province, forms the nucleus of the East Asiatic Union. The Japanese empire possesses a duty as the leader of the East Asiatic Union.

The above purpose presupposes the inevitable emancipation or independence of Eastern Siberia, China, Indo-China, the South Seas, Australia, and India.

Regional Division in the East Asiatic Union. In the Union of East Asia, the Japanese empire is at once the stabilizing power and the leading influence. To enable the empire actually to become the central influence in East Asia, the first necessity is the consolidation of the inner belt of East Asia; and the East Asiatic Sphere shall be divided as follows for this purpose:

The Inner Sphere—the vital sphere for the empire—includes Japan, Manchuria, North China, the lower Yangtze Area and the Russian Maritime area.

The Smaller Co-prosperity Sphere—the smaller self-supplying sphere of East Asia—includes the inner sphere plus Eastern Siberia, China, Indo-China and the South Seas.

The Greater Co-prosperity Sphere—the larger self-supplying sphere of East Asia—includes the smaller co-prosperity sphere, plus Australia, India, and island groups in the Pacific.

traditional values such as obedience, community spirit, filial piety, and discipline that reflected the prevailing political and cultural bias in Japan, while supposedly Western values such as materialism, liberalism, and individualism were strongly discouraged. In order to promote the creation of this New Order, as it was called, occupation authorities gave particular support to local religious organizations, but discouraged the formation of formal political parties.

At first, many Southeast Asian nationalists took Japanese promises at face value and agreed to cooperate with their new masters. In Burma, an independent government was established in 1943 and subsequently declared war on the Allies. But as the exploitative nature of Japanese occupation policies became increasingly clear, sentiment turned against the New Order. Japanese officials sometimes unwittingly provoked resentment by their arrogance and contempt for local customs. In the

Dutch East Indies, for example, Indonesians were required to bow in the direction of Tokyo and recognize the divinity of the Japanese emperor, practices that were repugnant to Muslims. In Burma, Buddhist pagodas were sometimes used as military latrines.

Such Japanese behavior created a dilemma for many nationalists, who had no desire to see the return of the colonial powers. Some turned against the Japanese while others lapsed into inactivity. Indonesian patriots tried to have it both ways, feigning support for Japan while attempting to sabotage the Japanese administration. In French Indochina, Ho Chi Minh's Indochinese Communist Party established contacts with American military units in South China and agreed to provide information on Japanese troop movements and rescue downed American fliers in the area. In Malaya, where Japanese treatment of ethnic Chinese residents was especially harsh, many joined a guerrilla movement against the occupying

Outline of East Asiatic Administration. It is intended that the unification of Japan, Manchoukuo, and China in neighborly friendship be realized by the settlement of the Sino-Japanese problems through the crushing of hostile influences in the Chinese interior, and through the construction of a new China. . . . Aggressive American and British influences in East Asia shall be driven out of the area of Indo-China and the South Seas, and this area should be brought into our defense sphere. The war with Britain and America shall be prosecuted for that purpose. . . .

Chapter 3: Political Construction

Basic Plan. The realization of the great ideal of constructing Greater East Asia Co-prosperity requires not only the complete prosecution of the current Greater East Asia War but also presupposes another great war in the future. Therefore, the following two points must be made during the course of the next twenty years: (1) Preparation for war with the other spheres of the world; and (2) Unification and construction of the East Asia Smaller Co-prosperity Sphere.

The following are the basic principles for the political construction of East Asia, when the above two points are taken into consideration. . . .

The desires of the peoples in the sphere for their independence shall be respected and endeavors shall be made for their fulfillment, but proper and suitable forms of government shall be decided for them in consideration of military and economic requirements and of the historical, political and cultural elements peculiar to each area.

It must also be noted that the independence of various peoples of East Asia should be based upon the idea of constructing East Asia as "independent countries existing within the New Order of East Asia" and that this conception differs from an independence based on the idea of liberalism and national self-determination. . . .

Occidental individualism and materialism shall be rejected and a moral world view, the basic principle of whose morality shall be the Imperial Way, shall be established. The ultimate object to be achieved is not exploitation but co-prosperity and mutual help, not competitive conflict but mutual assistance and mild peace, not a formal view of equality but a view of order based on righteous classification, not an idea of rights but an idea of service, and not several world views but one unified world view.

forces. By the end of the war, little support remained in the region for the erstwhile "liberators."

The Home Front

World War II was even more of a total war than World War I. Fighting was much more widespread and covered most of the world. Economic mobilization was more extensive; so too was the mobilization of women. The number of civilians killed was far higher; almost 20 million were killed from bombing raids, mass extermination policies, and attacks by invading armies.

The Mobilization of Peoples: Four Examples

The home fronts of the major belligerents varied considerably, based on local circumstances. World War II had an enormous impact on the Soviet Union. Known to the Soviets as the Great Patriotic War, the German-Soviet war witnessed the greatest land battles in history as well as incredible ruthlessness. To Nazi Germany, it was a war of oppression and annihilation that called for merciless measures. Two out of every five persons killed in World War II were Soviet citizens.

The initial defeats of the Soviet Union led to drastic emergency mobilization measures that affected the civilian population. Leningrad, for example, experienced 900 days of siege, during which its inhabitants became so desperate for food that they ate dogs, cats, and mice. As the German army made its rapid advance into Soviet territory, the factories in the western part of the Soviet Union were dismantled and shipped to the interior—to the Urals, western Siberia, and the Volga region. Machines were placed on the bare ground, and walls went up around them as workers began their work.

This widespread military, industrial, and economic mobilization created yet another industrial revolution for the Soviet Union. Stalin labeled it a "battle of machines," and the Soviets won, producing 78,000 tanks and 98,000 artillery pieces. Fifty-five percent of Soviet national income went for war materials compared to 15 percent in 1940. As a result of the emphasis on military goods, Soviet citizens experienced incredible shortages of both food and housing.

Soviet women played a major role in the war effort. Women and girls worked in industries, mines, and railroads. Overall, the number of women working in industry increased almost 60 percent. Soviet women were also expected to dig antitank ditches and work as air-raid wardens. In addition, the Soviet Union was the only country in World War II to use women as combatants. Soviet women functioned as snipers and also as aircrews in bomber squadrons. The female pilots who helped to defeat the Germans at Stalingrad were known as the "Night Witches."

The home front in the United States was quite different from those of its chief wartime allies, largely because the United States faced no threat of war in its own territory. Although the economy and labor force were slow to mobilize, eventually the United States became the arsenal of the Allied powers, producing the military equipment they needed. At the height of war production in 1943, the nation was constructing six ships a day and $6 billion worth of war-related goods a month.

The mobilization of the American economy produced social problems. The construction of new factories created boom towns where thousands came to work but then faced a shortage of houses, health facilities, and schools. The dramatic expansion of small towns into large cities often brought a breakdown in traditional social mores, especially evident in the increase in teenage prostitution. Economic mobilization also led to extensive movements of people, which in turn created new social tensions. Sixteen million men and women were enrolled in the military, while another 16 million, mostly wives and sweethearts of the servicemen or workers looking for jobs, also relocated. Over one million blacks migrated from the rural South to the industrial cities of the North and West, looking for jobs in industry. The presence of blacks in areas where they had not been present before led to racial tensions and sometimes even racial riots. In Detroit in June 1943, white mobs roamed the streets attacking blacks. Many of the one million blacks who enrolled in the military, only to be segregated in their own battle units, were angered by the way they were treated. Some became militant and prepared to fight for their civil rights.

Japanese Americans were treated even more shabbily. On the West Coast, 110,000 Japanese Americans, 65 percent of whom had been born in the United States, were removed to camps encircled by barbed wire and made to take loyalty oaths. Although public officials claimed this policy was necessary for security reasons, no similar treatment of German Americans or Italian Americans ever took place. The racism inherent in this treatment of Japanese Americans was evident when the California governor, Culbert Olson, said: "You know, when I look out at a group of Americans of German or Italian descent, I can tell whether they're loyal or not. I can tell how they think and even perhaps what they are thinking. But it is impossible for me to do this with inscrutable orientals, and particularly the Japanese."[13]

In August 1914, Germans had enthusiastically cheered their soldiers marching off to war. In September 1939, the streets were quiet. Many Germans were apathetic or, even worse for the Nazi regime, had a foreboding of disaster. Hitler was very aware of the importance of the home front. He believed that the collapse of the home front in World War I had caused Germany's defeat, and in his determination to avoid a repetition of that experience, he adopted economic policies that may indeed have cost Germany the war.

To maintain the morale of the home front during the first two years of the war, Hitler refused to cut the production of consumer goods or increase the production of armaments. *Blitzkrieg* allowed the Germans to win quick victories, after which they believed they could plunder the food and raw materials of the conquered countries to avoid diverting resources away from the civilian economy. After German defeats on the Russian front and the American entry into the war, the economic situation changed. Early in 1942, Hitler finally ordered a massive increase in armaments production and in the size of the army. Hitler's architect, Albert Speer, was made minister for armaments and munitions in 1942. By eliminating waste and rationalizing procedures, Speer was able to triple the production of armaments between 1942 and 1943 despite the intense Allied air raids. Speer's urgent plea for a total mobilization of resources for the war effort went unheeded, however. Hitler, fearful of civilian morale problems that would undermine the home front, refused any dramatic cuts in the production of consumer goods. A total mobilization of the economy was not implemented until 1944, when schools, theaters, and cafes were closed and Speer was finally permitted to use all remaining resources for the production of a few basic military items. By that time, it was in vain. Total war mobilization in July 1944 was too little too late to save Germany from defeat.

The war produced a reversal in Nazi attitudes toward women. Nazi resistance to female employment declined as the war progressed and more and more men were called up for military service. Nazi magazines now proclaimed: "We see the woman as the eternal mother of our people, but also as the working and fighting comrade of the man."[14] But the number of women working in industry, agriculture, commerce, and domestic service increased only slightly. The total number of employed women in September 1944 was 14.9 million compared to 14.6 in May 1939. Many women, especially those of the middle class, resisted regular employment, particularly in factories. Even the introduction of labor conscription for women in January 1943 failed to achieve much as women found ingenious ways to avoid the regulations.

Wartime Japan was a highly mobilized society. To guarantee its control over all national resources, the government established a planning board to control prices, wages, the utilization of labor, and the allocation of resources. Traditional habits of obedience and hierarchy, buttressed by the concept of imperial divinity, were emphasized to encourage citizens to sacrifice their resources, and sometimes their lives, for the national cause. The calls for sacrifice culminated in the final years of the war, when young Japanese were encouraged to volunteer en masse to serve as pilots in the suicide missions (known as kamikaze, or "divine wind") against American fighting ships.

Japan was extremely reluctant to mobilize women on behalf of the war effort. General Hideki Tojo, prime minister from 1941 to 1944, opposed female employment, arguing that "the weakening of the family system would be the weakening of the nation . . . we are able to do our duties only because we have wives and mothers at home."[15] Women should remain at home and fulfill their responsibilities by bearing more children. Female employment increased during the war, but only in areas, such as the textile industry and farming, where women traditionally had worked. Instead of using women to meet labor shortages, the Japanese government brought in Korean and Chinese laborers.

The Frontline Civilians: The Bombing of Cities

Bombing was used in World War II in a variety of ways: against nonhuman military targets, against enemy troops, and against civilian populations. The latter made World War II as devastating for civilians as for frontline soldiers (see the box on p. 980). A small number of bombing raids in the last year of World War I had given rise to the argument, crystallized in 1930 by the Italian general

Giulio Douhet, that the public outcry created by the bombing of civilian populations would be an effective way to coerce governments into making peace. Consequently, European air forces began to develop long-range bombers in the 1930s.

The first sustained use of civilian bombing contradicted Douhet's theory. Beginning in early September, the German *Luftwaffe* subjected London and many other British cities and towns to nightly air raids, making the Blitz (as the British called the German air raids) a national experience. Londoners took the first heavy blows and set the standard for the rest of the British population by keeping up their spirits. But London morale was helped by the fact that German raids were widely dispersed over a very large city. Smaller communities were more directly affected by the devastation. On November 14, 1940, for example, the *Luftwaffe* destroyed hundreds of shops and a hundred acres of the city center of Coventry. The destruction of smaller cities did produce morale problems as wild rumors of social collapse spread quickly in these communities. Nevertheless, morale was soon restored. War production in these areas, in any case, seems to have been little affected by the raids.

The British failed to learn from their own experience, however, and soon proceeded with the bombing of Germany. Prime Minister Winston Churchill (1874–1965) and his advisers believed that destroying German communities would break civilian morale and bring victory. Major bombing raids began in 1942 under the direction of Arthur Harris, the wartime leader of the British air force's Bomber Command, which was rearmed with four-engine heavy bombers capable of taking the war into the center of occupied Europe. On May 31, 1942, Cologne became the first German city to be subjected to an attack by a thousand bombers.

The entry of the Americans into the war produced a new bombing strategy. American planes flew daytime missions aimed at the precision bombing of transportation facilities and wartime industries, while the British Bomber Command continued nighttime saturation bombing of all German cities with populations over 100,000. Bombing raids added an element of terror to circumstances already made difficult by growing shortages of food, clothing, and fuel. Germans especially feared the incendiary bombs that created firestorms that swept destructive paths through the cities. Four raids on Hamburg in August 1943 produced temperatures of 1,800 degrees Fahrenheit, obliterated half the city's buildings, and killed 50,000 civilians. The ferocious bombing of Dresden for three days in 1945 (February 13–15) created a firestorm that may have killed as many

❧ The Bombing of Civilians ❧

The home front became a battlefront when civilian populations became the targets of mass bombing raids. Many people believed that mass bombing could effectively weaken the morale of the people and shorten the war. Rarely did it achieve its goal. In these selections, British, German, and Japanese civilians relate their experiences during bombing raids.

London (1940)

Early last evening, the noise was terrible. My husband and Mr. P. were trying to play chess in the kitchen. I was playing draughts with Kenneth in the cupboard. . . . Presently I heard a stifled voice "Mummy! I don't know what's become of my glasses." "I should think they are tied up in my wool." My knitting had disappeared and wool seemed to be everywhere! We heard a whistle, a bang which shook the house, and an explosion. . . . Well, we straightened out, decided draughts and chess were no use under the circumstances, and waited for a lull so we could have a pot of tea.

Hamburg (1943)

As the many fires broke through the roofs of the burning buildings, a column of heated air rose more than two and a half miles high and one and a half miles in diameter. . . . This column was turbulent, and it was fed from its base by in-rushing cooler ground-surface air. One and one-half miles from the fires this draught increased the wind velocity from eleven to thirty-three miles per hour. At the edge of the area the velocities must have been appreciably greater, as trees three feet in diameter were uprooted. In a short time the temperature reached ignition point for all combustibles, and the entire area was ablaze. In such fires complete burnout occurred; that is, no trace of combustible material remained, and only after two days were the areas cool enough to approach.

Hiroshima (August 6, 1945)

I heard the airplane; I looked up at the sky, it was a sunny day, the sky was blue. . . . Then I saw something drop—and pow!—a big explosion knocked me down. Then I was unconscious—I don't know for how long. Then I was conscious but I couldn't see anything. . . . Then I see people moving away and I just follow them. It is not light like it was before, it is more like evening. I look around; houses are all flat! . . . I follow the people to the river. I couldn't hear anything, my ears are blocked up. I am thinking—a bomb has dropped! . . . I didn't know my hands were burned, nor my face. . . . My eyes were swollen and felt closed up.

as 100,000 inhabitants and refugees. Even some Allied leaders began to criticize what they saw as the unnecessary terror bombing of German cities.

Germany suffered enormously from the Allied bombing raids. Millions of buildings were destroyed, and possibly half a million civilians died from the raids. Nevertheless, it is highly unlikely that Allied bombing sapped the morale of the German people. Instead, Germans, whether pro-Nazi or anti-Nazi, fought on stubbornly, often driven simply by a desire to live. Nor did the bombing destroy Germany's industrial capacity. The Allied Strategic Bombing survey revealed that the production of war materials actually increased between 1942 and 1944. Even in 1944 and 1945, Allied raids cut German armaments production by only 7 percent. Nevertheless, the widespread destruction of transportation systems and fuel supplies made it extremely difficult for the new materials to reach the German military.

In Japan, the bombing of civilians reached a new level with the use of the first atomic bomb. Japan was especially vulnerable to air raids because its air force had been virtually destroyed in the course of the war, and its crowded cities were built of flimsy materials. Attacks on Japanese cities by the new American B-29 Superfortresses, the biggest bombers of the war, began on November 24, 1944. By the summer of 1945, many of Japan's industries had been destroyed along with one-fourth of its dwellings. After the Japanese government decreed the mobilization of all people between the ages of thirteen and sixty into a People's Volunteer Corps, President Truman and his advisers feared that Japanese fanaticism might mean a million American casualties. This concern led them to drop the atomic bomb on Hiroshima (August 6) and Nagasaki (August 9). The destruction was incredible. Of 76,000 buildings near the hypocenter of the explosion in Hiroshima, 70,000 were flattened, while

140,000 of the city's 400,000 inhabitants died by the end of 1945. By the end of 1950, another 50,000 had perished from the effects of radiation. The dropping of the first atomic bomb introduced the world to the nuclear age.

The Aftermath of the War: The Emergence of the Cold War

The total victory of the Allies in World War II was not followed by a real peace, but by the beginnings of a new conflict known as the Cold War that dominated world politics until the end of the 1980s. The origins of the Cold War stemmed from the military, political, and ideological differences, especially between the Soviet Union and the United States, that became apparent at the Allied war conferences held in the last years of the war. Although Allied leaders were mostly preoccupied with how to end the war, they also were strongly motivated by differing, and often conflicting, visions of the postwar world.

The Conferences at Tehran, Yalta, and Potsdam

Stalin, Roosevelt, and Churchill, the leaders of the Big Three of the Grand Alliance, met at Tehran (the capital of Iran) in November 1943 to decide the future course of the war. Their major tactical decision concerned the final assault on Germany. Stalin and Roosevelt argued successfully for an American-British invasion of the Continent through France, which they scheduled for the spring of 1944. The acceptance of this plan had important consequences. It meant that Soviet and British-American forces would meet in defeated Germany along a north-south dividing line and that, most likely, Eastern Europe would be liberated by Soviet forces. The Allies also agreed to a partition of postwar Germany until denazification could take place.

By the time of the conference at Yalta in southern Russia in February 1945, the defeat of Germany was a foregone conclusion. The Western powers, which had earlier believed that the Soviets were in a weak position, were now faced with the reality of 11 million Red Army soldiers taking possession of Eastern and much of central Europe. Stalin was still operating under the notion of spheres of influence. He was deeply suspicious of the Western powers and desired a buffer to protect the Soviet Union from possible future Western aggression. At the same time, however, Stalin was eager to obtain economically important resources and strategic military positions. Roosevelt by this time was moving away from the notion of spheres of influence to the more Wilsonian ideal of self-determination. He called for "the end of the system of unilateral action, exclusive alliances, and spheres of influence." The Grand Alliance approved a "Declaration on Liberated Europe." This was a pledge to assist liberated Europe in the creation of "democratic institutions of their own choice." Liberated countries were to hold free elections to determine their political systems.

At Yalta, Roosevelt sought Soviet military help against Japan. The atomic bomb was not yet assured, and American military planners feared the possible loss of as many as one million men in amphibious assaults on the Japanese home islands. Roosevelt therefore agreed to Stalin's price for military assistance against Japan: possession of Sakhalin and the Kurile Islands, as well as two warm water ports and railroad rights in Manchuria.

The creation of the United Nations was a major American concern at Yalta. Roosevelt hoped to ensure the participation of the Big Three powers in a postwar international organization before difficult issues divided them into hostile camps. After a number of compromises, both Churchill and Stalin accepted Roosevelt's plans for a United Nations organization and set the first meeting for San Francisco in April of 1945.

✦ **Hiroshima.** The most devastating destruction of civilians came near the end of World War II when the United States dropped atomic bombs on the Japanese cities of Hiroshima and Nagasaki. This panoramic view of Hiroshima after the bombing shows the incredible devastation produced by the atomic bomb.

◆ **The Victorious Allied Leaders at Yalta.** Even before World War II ended, the leaders of the Big Three of the Grand Alliance, Churchill, Roosevelt, and Stalin (shown from left to right), met in wartime conferences to plan the final assault on Germany and negotiate the outlines of the postwar settlement. At the Yalta meeting (February 5–11, 1945), the three leaders concentrated on postwar issues. The American president, who died two months later, was already a worn-out man at Yalta.

The issues of Germany and Eastern Europe were treated less decisively. The Big Three reaffirmed that Germany must surrender unconditionally and created four occupation zones. German reparations were set at $20 billion. A compromise was also worked out in regard to Poland. Stalin agreed to free elections in the future to determine a new government. But the issue of free elections in Eastern Europe caused a serious rift between the Soviets and the Americans. The principle was that Eastern European governments would be freely elected, but they were also supposed to be pro-Soviet. As Churchill expressed it: "The Poles will have their future in their own hands, with the single limitation that they must honestly follow in harmony with their allies, a policy friendly to Russia."[16] This attempt to reconcile two irreconcilable goals was doomed to failure, as soon

became evident at the next conference of the Big Three powers.

Even before the conference at Potsdam took place in July 1945, Western relations with the Soviets were deteriorating rapidly. The Grand Alliance had been one of necessity in which ideological incompatibility had been subordinated to the pragmatic concerns of the war. The Allied powers' only common aim was the defeat of Nazism. Once this aim had all but been accomplished, the many differences that antagonized East-West relations came to the surface.

The Potsdam conference of July 1945 consequently began under a cloud of mistrust. Roosevelt had died on April 12 and had been succeeded as president by the somewhat less flexible Harry Truman. During the conference, Truman received word that the atomic bomb had been successfully tested. Some historians have argued that this knowledge resulted in Truman's stiffened resolve against the Soviets. Whatever the reasons, there was a new coldness in the relations between the Soviets and Americans. At Potsdam, Truman demanded free elections throughout Eastern Europe. Stalin responded: "A freely elected government in any of these East European countries would be anti-Soviet, and that we cannot allow."[17] After a bitterly fought and devastating war, Stalin sought absolute military security. To him, it could only be gained by the presence of Communist states in Eastern Europe. Free elections might result in governments hostile to the Soviets. By the middle of 1945, only an invasion by Western forces could undo developments in Eastern Europe, and after the world's most destructive conflict had ended, few people favored such a policy.

As the war slowly receded into the past, the reality of conflicting ideologies had reappeared. Many in the West interpreted Soviet policy as part of a worldwide Communist conspiracy. The Soviets, on the other hand, viewed Western, especially American, policy as nothing less than global capitalist expansionism or, in Leninist terms, nothing less than economic imperialism. Vyacheslav Molotov, the Russian foreign minister, referred to the Americans as "insatiable imperialists" and "war-mongering groups of adventurers."[18] In March 1946, in a speech to an American audience, the former British prime minister Winston Churchill declared that "an iron curtain" had "descended across the continent," dividing Germany and Europe into two hostile camps. Stalin branded Churchill's speech a "call to war with the Soviet Union." Only months after the world's most devastating conflict had ended, the world seemed once again to be bitterly divided.

Map 26.3 Territorial Changes in Europe after World War II.

Conclusion

World War II was the most devastating total war in human history. Germany, Italy, and Japan had been utterly defeated. Perhaps as many as 40 million people—both soldiers and civilians—had been killed in only six years. In Asia and Europe, cities had been reduced to rubble, and millions of people faced starvation as once fertile lands stood neglected or wasted. Untold millions of people had become refugees.

The Germans, Italians, and Japanese had lost, but only after tremendous sacrifices and costs. Europeans, who had been accustomed to dominating the world at the begin-

ning of the twentieth century, now watched helplessly at mid-century as the two new superpowers created by their two world wars took control of their destinies. Even before the last battles had been fought, the United States and the Soviet Union had arrived at different visions of the postwar world. No sooner had the war ended than their differences created a new and potentially even more devastating conflict known as the Cold War. And even though Europeans seemed merely pawns in the struggle between the two superpowers, they managed to stage a remarkable recovery of their own civilization. In Asia, defeated Japan made a miraculous economic recovery while an era of European domination finally came to an end.

CHAPTER NOTES

1. Benito Mussolini, "The Doctrine of Fascism," in Adrian Lyttleton, ed., *Italian Fascisms from Pareto to Gentile* (London, 1973), p. 42.
2. Quoted in Alexander De Grand, "Women under Italian Fascism," *Historical Journal* 19 (1976): 958–59.
3. Quoted in Jeremy Noakes and Geoffrey Pridham, eds., *Nazism, 1919–1945* (Exeter, 1983), 1:50–51.
4. Quoted in Joachim Fest, *Hitler,* trans. Richard and Clara Winston (New York, 1974), p. 418.
5. Adolf Hitler, *Mein Kampf,* trans. Ralph Manheim (Boston, 1971), p. 654.
6. *Documents on German Foreign Policy* (London, 1956), Series D, 7:204.
7. Memorandum by John Van Antwerp MacMurray, quoted in Arthur Waldron, *How the Peace Was Lost: The 1935 Memorandum* (Stanford, Calif., 1992), p. 5.
8. Albert Speer, *Spandau,* trans. Richard and Clara Winston (New York, 1976), p. 50.
9. *Nazi Conspiracy and Aggression* (Washington, D.C., 1946), 6:262.
10. International Military Tribunal, *Trial of the Major War Criminals* (Nuremberg, 1947–1949), 22:480.
11. Quoted in Raul Hilberg, *The Destruction of the European Jews,* rev. ed. (New York, 1985), 1:332–33.
12. *Nazi Conspiracy and Aggression,* 6:789.
13. Quoted in John Campbell, *The Experience of World War II* (New York, 1989), p. 170.
14. Quoted in Claudia Koonz, "Mothers in the Fatherland: Women in Nazi Germany," in Renate Bridenthal and Claudia Koonz, eds., *Becoming Visible: Women in European History* (Boston, 1977), p. 466.
15. Quoted in Campbell, *The Experience of World War II,* p. 143.
16. Quoted in Norman Graebner, *Cold War Diplomacy, 1945–1960* (Princeton, N.J., 1962), p. 117.
17. Quoted in ibid.
18. Quoted in Wilfried Loth, *The Division of the World, 1941–1955* (New York, 1988), p. 81.

SUGGESTED READINGS

For a general study of fascism, see S. G. Payne, *A History of Fascism* (Madison, Wis., 1996). The best biography of Mussolini is now D. Mack Smith, *Mussolini* (New York, 1982). Two brief but excellent surveys of Fascist Italy are A. Cassels, *Fascist Italy,* 2d ed. (Arlington Heights, Ill., 1985) and A. De Grand, *Italian Fascism* (Lincoln, Neb., 1982). On propaganda and other aspects of cultural life in Fascist Italy, see E. R. Tannenbaum, *Italian Society and Culture, 1922–1945* (New York, 1972).

Two brief but sound surveys of Nazi Germany are J. Spielvogel, *Hitler and Nazi Germany: A History,* 3d ed. (Englewood Cliffs, N.J., 1996); and J. Bendersky, *A History of Nazi Germany* (Chicago, 1985). The best biographies of Hitler are A. Bullock, *Hitler: A Study in Tyranny* (New York, 1964) and J. Fest, *Hitler,* trans. R. and C. Winston (New York, 1974). On the Nazi administration of the state, see M. Broszat, *The Hitler State: The Foundations and Development of the Internal Structure of the Third Reich* (New York, 1981). Basic studies of the SS include R. Koehl, *The Black Corps: The Structure and Power Struggles of the Nazi SS* (Madison, Wis., 1983) and H. Krausnick and M. Broszat, *Anatomy of the SS State* (London, 1970). On women, see C. Koonz, *Mothers in the Fatherland: Women, the Family, and Nazi Politics* (New York, 1987). The Hitler Youth is examined in H. W. Koch, *The Hitler Youth* (New York, 1976). On Nazi anti-Jewish policies between 1933 and 1939, see S. Friedländer, *Nazi Germany and the Jews,* vol. 1, *The Years of Persecution 1933–1939* (New York, 1997).

The collectivization of agriculture in the Soviet Union is examined in R. W. Davies, *The Socialist Offensive: The Collectivization of Soviet Agriculture, 1929–30* (Cambridge, Mass., 1980). Industrialization is covered in H. Kuromiya, *Stalin's Industrial Revolution, Politics and Workers, 1928–1932* (New York, 1988). Stalin's purges are examined in R. Conquest, *The Great Terror: Stalin's*

Purge of the Thirties, rev. ed. (New York, 1973). For a biography of Stalin, see R. H. McNeal, *Stalin, Man and Ruler* (New York, 1988).

The basic study of Germany's foreign policy from 1933 to 1939 can be found in G. Weinberg, *The Foreign Policy of Hitler's Germany: Diplomatic Revolution in Europe, 1933–36* (Chicago, 1970) and *The Foreign Policy of Hitler's Germany: Starting World War II, 1937–1939* (Chicago, 1980). Japan's march to war is examined in J. B. Crawley, *Japan's Quest for Autonomy: National Security and Foreign Policy, 1930–1938* (Princeton, N.J., 1966).

General works on World War II include M. K. Dziewanowski, *War at Any Price: World War II in Europe, 1939–1945*, 2d ed. (Englewood Cliffs, N.J., 1991); the comprehensive study by G. Weinberg, *A World at Arms: A Global History of World War II* (Cambridge, 1994); and J. Campbell, *The Experience of World War II* (New York, 1989). On Hitler as a military leader, see R. Lewin, *Hitler's Mistakes* (New York, 1986). On battles, see J. Keegan, *The Second World War* (New York, 1990).

A standard work on the German New Order in Russia is A. Dallin, *German Rule in Russia, 1941–1945*, rev. ed. (London, 1981). The best studies of the Holocaust include R. Hilberg, *The Destruction of the European Jews*, rev. ed., 3 vols. (New York, 1985) and L. Yahil, *The Holocaust* (New York, 1990). There is a good overview of the scholarship on the Holocaust in M. Marrus, *The Holocaust in History* (New York, 1987). On the problem of what the Allied countries knew about the Holocaust, see D. Wyman, *The Abandonment of the Jews: America*

and the Holocaust (New York, 1984) and M. Gilbert, *Auschwitz and the Allies* (New York, 1981). The other holocaust is examined in B. Wytwycky, *The Other Holocaust* (Washington, D.C., 1980).

General studies on the impact of total war include J. Costello, *Love, Sex and War: Changing Values, 1939–1945* (London, 1985) and M. R. Marrus, *The Unwanted: European Refugees in the Twentieth Century* (New York, 1985). On the home front in Germany, see E. R. Beck, *Under the Bombs: The German Home Front, 1942–1945* (Lexington, Ky., 1986). The Soviet Union during the war is examined in M. Harrison, *Soviet Planning in Peace and War, 1938–1945* (Cambridge, 1985). On the American home front, see G. Perrett, *Days of Sadness, Years of Triumph: The American People, 1939–1945* (New York, 1973). The Japanese home front is examined in T. R. H. Havens, *The Valley of Darkness: The Japanese People and World War Two* (New York, 1978).

On the destruction of Germany by bombing raids, see H. Rumpf, *The Bombing of Germany* (London, 1963). The German bombing of Britain is covered in T. Harrisson, *Living through the Blitz* (London, 1985). On Hiroshima, see A. Chisholm, *Faces of Hiroshima* (London, 1985).

On the emergence of the Cold War, see W. Loth, *The Division of the World, 1941–1955* (New York, 1988). On the wartime summit conferences, see H. Feis, *Churchill, Roosevelt, Stalin: The War They Waged and the Peace They Sought*, 2d ed. (Princeton, N.J., 1967) and D. Clemens, *Yalta* (New York, 1970).

Modern Patterns of World History
(1800–1945)

At the outset of Part IV, we remarked that two of the most significant developments during the nineteenth and early twentieth centuries were the Industrial Revolution and the European domination of the world. Of these two factors, the first was clearly the more important, for it created the conditions for the latter. It was, of course, the major industrial powers—Great Britain, France, and later Germany, Japan, and the United States—that took the lead in building large colonialist empires. Those European nations that did not achieve a high level of industrial advancement, such as Spain and Portugal, clearly declined in importance as colonial powers.

Why some societies were able to master the challenge of industrialization and others were not has been a matter of considerable scholarly debate. Some observers have found the answer in the cultural characteristics of individual societies, such as the Protestant work ethic in parts of Europe or the tradition of social discipline and class hierarchy in Japan. Others have placed more emphasis on practical considerations, such as the lack of an urban market for agricultural goods in China (which reduced the landowners' incentives to introduce mechanized farming) or the absence of a foreign threat in Japan (which provided increased opportunities for local investment). Whatever the truth of such speculations, it is clear that there was more than one road to industrialization. In his highly respected work on the subject entitled *Social Origins of Dictatorship and Democracy*, sociologist Barrington Moore found at least three paths of economic modernization: the bourgeois capitalist route followed in Great Britain, France, and the United States, the "revolution from above" approach adopted by traditional elites in Germany and Japan, and the Marxist-Leninist strategy used in the Soviet Union. While all three approaches led to a significant level of industrial development, the overall consequences for these societies have been strikingly different.

The advent of the industrial age had a number of lasting consequences for the world at large. On the one hand, the material wealth of those nations that successfully passed through the process increased significantly. In many cases, the creation of advanced industrial societies strengthened democratic institutions and led to a higher standard of living for the majority of the population. The spread of technology and trade outside of Europe created the basis for a new international economic order based on the global exchange of goods.

On the other hand, as we have seen, not all the consequences of the Industrial Revolution were beneficial. In the industrializing societies themselves, rapid economic change often led to widening disparities in the distribution of wealth and a sense of rootlessness and alienation among much of the population. While some societies were able to manage these problems with some degree of success, others experienced a breakdown of social values and the rise of widespread political instability. In Imperial Russia, internal tensions became too much for the traditional landholding elites to handle, leading to social revolution and the rise of the Soviet state. In other cases, such as Germany, deep-seated ethnic and class antagonisms remained under the surface until conditions of economic depression led to the rise of militant fascist regimes.

Industrialization also had destabilizing consequences on the global scene. Rising economic competition among the industrial powers was a major contributor to heightened international competition and ultimately to global war. For many at the time, the dream of universal affluence that had been aroused by the age of industrialization had turned into a nightmare.

Of course, other forces were also at work in Western society during this period. A second development that had a major impact on the era was the rise of nationalism. Like the Industrial Revolution, the idea of nationalism originated in eighteenth-century Europe, where it was a product of the secularization of the age and the experiences of the French revolutionary and Napoleonic eras. Although the concept provided the basis for a new sense of community and the rise of the modern nation-state, it also gave birth to ethnic tensions and hatred that resulted in bitter disputes and civil strife in a number of countries and contributed to the competition among nations that eventually erupted into world war.

Finally, industrialization and the rise of national consciousness transformed the nature of war itself. New weapons of mass destruction created the potential for a new kind of warfare that reached beyond the battlefield into the very heartland of the enemy's territory, while the concept of nationalism transformed war from the sport of kings to a matter of national honor and commitment. Since the French Revolution, when the revolutionary government in Paris had mobilized the entire country by a levy-in-mass (mass conscription) to fight against the forces that opposed the Revolution, governments had relied on mass conscription to defend the national cause while their engines of destruction reached far into enemy territory to destroy the industrial base and undermine the will to fight. This trend was amply demonstrated in the two world wars of the twentieth century. Each was a product of antagonisms that had been unleashed by economic competition and growing national consciousness. Each resulted in a level of destruction that severely damaged the material foundations and eroded the popular spirit of the participants, the victors as well as the vanquished.

In the end, then, industrial power and the driving force of nationalism, the very factors that had created the conditions for European global dominance, contained the seeds for the decline of that dominance. These seeds germinated during the 1930s, when the Great Depression sharpened international competition and mutual antagonisms, and then sprouted in the ensuing conflict, which for the first time embraced the entire globe. By the time World War II came to an end, the once-powerful countries of Europe were exhausted, leaving the door ajar for the emergence of two new global superpowers, the United States and the Soviet Union, which dominated the postwar political scene. Although the new superpowers were both products of modern European civilization, they were physically and politically separate from it, and their intense competition, which marked the postwar period, threatened to transform the old map of Europe into a battleground for a new and even more destructive ideological conflict.

If in Europe the dominant fact of the era was the Industrial Revolution, in the rest of the world it was undoubtedly the sheer fact of Western imperialism. Between the end of the Napoleonic wars and the end of the nineteenth century, European powers, or their rivals in Japan and the United States, achieved political mastery over virtually the entire remainder of the world.

What was the overall effect of imperialism on the subject peoples? It seems clear from this narrative that for most of the population in colonial areas Western domination was rarely beneficial and was often destructive.

Although a limited number of merchants, large landowners, and traditional hereditary elites undoubtedly prospered under the umbrella of the expanding imperialist economic order, the majority of people, urban and rural alike, probably suffered considerable hardship as a result of the policies adopted by their foreign rulers. The effects of the Industrial Revolution on the poor had been felt in Europe, too, but there the pain was eased somewhat by the fact that the industrial era had laid the foundations for future technological advances and material abundance. In the colonial territories, the importation of modern technology was limited, while most of the profits from manufacturing and commerce fled abroad. For too many, the White Man's Burden was shifted to the shoulders of the colonial peoples.

Some historians point out, however, that for all the inequities of the colonial system, the colonial experience had another side as well. It provided some marginal benefits such as expanded markets and the beginnings of a modern transportation and communications network. The Western intruders also introduced a number of new ideas to the peoples of Asia and Africa and provided new ways of looking at human society and its relationship with the individual.

Perhaps the most influential concept introduced from the West was nationalism. The concept of nationalism often served a useful role in many countries in Asia and Africa, where it provided colonial peoples with a sense of common purpose that later proved vital in knitting together the coherent elements in their societies to oppose colonial regimes and create the conditions for future independent states. At first such movements achieved relatively little success, but they began to gather momentum in the second quarter of the twentieth century, when full-fledged nationalist movements began to appear throughout the colonial world to lead their people in the struggle for independence.

Another idea that gained currency in colonial areas was that of democracy. As a rule, colonial regimes did not make a serious attempt to introduce democratic institutions to their subject populations; understandably, they feared that such institutions would inevitably undermine colonial authority. Nevertheless, Western notions of representative government and individual freedom had their advocates in India, Vietnam, China, and Japan well before the end of the nineteenth century. Later, countless Asians and Africans were exposed to such ideas in schools set up by the colonial regime or in the course of travel to Europe or the United States. Most of the nationalist parties founded in colonial territories espoused democratic principles and attempted to apply them when they took power after the restoration of independence.

As we shall see later, in most instances such programs were premature. For the most part, the experiment with democracy in postwar African and Asian societies was a brief one. But the popularity of democratic ideals among educated elites in colonial societies was a clear indication of democracy's universal appeal and a sign that it would become a meaningful part of the political culture after the dismantling of the colonial regimes. The idea of the nation, composed of free, educated, and politically active citizens, was now widely accepted throughout much of the non-Western world.

How are we to draw up a final balance sheet on the era of Western imperialism? To its defenders, it was a necessary stage in the evolution of the human race, a flawed but essentially humanitarian effort to provide the backward peoples of Africa and Asia with a boost up the ladder of evolution. To its critics, it was a tragedy of major proportions. The insatiable drive of the advanced economic powers for access to raw materials and markets resulted in the widespread destruction of traditional cultures and created an exploitative environment that transformed the vast majority of colonial peoples into a permanent underclass, while restricting the benefits of modern technology to a privileged few. Sophisticated, age-old societies that should have been left to respond to the technological revolution in their own way were subjected to foreign rule and squeezed dry of precious national resources under the guise of the "civilizing mission."

In this debate, the critics surely have the best of the argument. All in all, the colonial experience was a brutal one, and its benefits accrued almost entirely to citizens of the ruling power. The argument that the Western societies had a "White Man's Burden" to civilize the world was all too often a hypocritical gesture to salve the guilty feelings of those who recognized imperialism for what it was—a savage act of rape.

But as with earlier periods of conquest and empire, not all the consequences were unfortunate ones. Because the ruling colonial powers did make a halfhearted gesture to introduce the technology and ideas that had accompanied the rise of modern Europe, they left behind a legacy that their subject peoples might hope to exploit once they had a chance to determine their own destinies. However slightly, the concept of the civilizing mission did have a mitigating effect on the enormity of the tragedy.

The final judgment on the age of European dominance, then, must be a mixed one. It was a time of unfulfilled expectations, of altruism and greed, of bright promise and tragic failure. The fact is, human beings had learned how to master some of the forces of nature before they had learned how to order relations among themselves or temper their own natures for the common good. The consequences were painful, for European and non-European peoples alike.

But although the experience was a painful one, human societies were able to survive it and to earn a second chance to make better use of the stunning promise of the industrial era. How they have fared in that effort will be the subject of the final section of this book.

Toward a Global Civilization?
The World since 1945

From a broad historical perspective, World War II can be seen to represent the logical culmination of the imperialist era. Competition among the European powers for markets and sources of raw materials had begun to accelerate during the early years of the nineteenth century and intensified as the effects of the Industrial Revolution made their way through western and central Europe. By the end of the century, virtually all of Asia and Africa had come under some degree of formal or informal colonial control. World War I weakened the European powers but did not bring the era to an end, and the seeds of a second world confrontation started to sprout in the 1930s when Hitler's Germany sought to recoup its losses and Japan became an active participant in the race for spoils in the Pacific region.

When the American president Franklin D. Roosevelt and the British prime minister Winston Churchill met off the coast of Newfoundland in August 1941 to discuss their common objectives in a postwar world, they appeared to recognize that imperialist rivalry was at the root of the problem. The Atlantic Charter stated that the two countries hoped to realize equality of economic opportunity, abandonment of force, and friendly collaboration among the peoples of the world, as well as the right of nations to choose their own form of government.

In many respects, the wartime allies achieved their peace aims. The rapacious efforts of Germany and Japan to dominate the world were brought to an end, and both states were eventually restored to the family of nations. The intense rivalry that had characterized relations among the Western powers dissipated, and a lengthy period of mutual cooperation and peaceful development began. Outside Europe, the colonial system was gradually dismantled, and the peoples of Asia and Africa were granted self-determination in the form of independent states.

	1945	1950	1955	1960	1965

AFRICA

Brazzaville Declaration • Ghana obtains independence • Formation of Organization for African Unity •

INDIA AND SOUTHEAST ASIA

India and Pakistan become independent • Geneva Conference divides Vietnam • Indo-Pakistani War •

Military seizes power in Indonesia •

EAST ASIA

Communists come to power in China • Sino-Soviet dispute breaks into the open •

End of U.S. occupation of Japan •

Korean War begins •

THE MIDDLE EAST

Formation of state of Israel • Egypt nationalizes the Suez Canal •

EUROPE AND THE WESTERN HEMISPHERE

Cold War in Europe: Formation of NATO • Cuban Missile Crisis •

Cold War in Europe: Formation of Warsaw Pact •

But there were some disappointments. In wartime conferences, Roosevelt had tried to win the confidence of Joseph Stalin in order to link the Soviet Union with the Western Allies in an effort to build a peaceful and democratic world after the end of the war. For a variety of reasons, that effort failed, and even before the final defeat of Japan, tension had begun to build in Europe between the Soviet Union and the Western powers. By the end of the decade, that tension had spread throughout the world, and the Cold War had begun.

In the meantime, the end of colonial empires did not mean that the peoples of Asia and Africa enjoyed political stability, peaceful cooperation, and material prosperity. Economic difficulties, a product of both their own inexperience and continued Western domination of the global economy, led to internal factionalism, military rule, and sometimes regional conflict. Competition between capitalist and socialist power blocs led by the United States and the Soviet Union compounded the problem.

In the late 1980s, the Soviet empire began to come apart. In December 1991, the Soviet Union itself became a memory, as onetime Soviet republics established independent states. The development was greeted with relief throughout much of the world, because it brought an end to

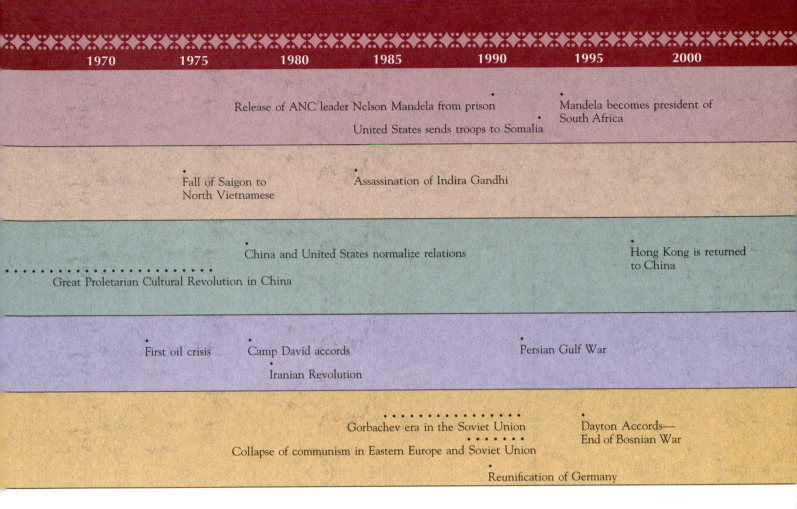

| 1970 | 1975 | 1980 | 1985 | 1990 | 1995 | 2000 |

Release of ANC leader Nelson Mandela from prison

Mandela becomes president of South Africa

United States sends troops to Somalia

Fall of Saigon to North Vietnamese

Assassination of Indira Gandhi

China and United States normalize relations

Hong Kong is returned to China

Great Proletarian Cultural Revolution in China

First oil crisis

Camp David accords

Persian Gulf War

Iranian Revolution

Gorbachev era in the Soviet Union

Dayton Accords— End of Bosnian War

Collapse of communism in Eastern Europe and Soviet Union

Reunification of Germany

the ideological Cold War and initiated a new stage of cooperation between the successor states of the old Soviet Union and the nations of the West. In the meantime, many Asian nations have apparently become advanced industrial countries and embarked on the road to political democracy. Half a century after the end of World War II, some of the dreams embodied in the Atlantic Charter appear to be reaching fruition.

But challenges remain, and many of them appear intimidating. The breakup of the Soviet empire has led to the emergence of squabbling nationalities throughout Eastern Europe, while in other parts of the world, including the Middle East, Africa, and Northern Ireland, age-old rivalries and ethnic and religious suspicions continue to create sources of potential bitter conflict. A global economic slowdown brought recession to the advanced nations and severe political and economic difficulties to many societies in the rest of the world. In the meantime, the effects of untrammeled industrial development are coming home to roost in the form of growing environmental pollution. Ethnic and religious differences, as well as intense competition for markets, put a severe strain on efforts to achieve global cooperation in solving the common problems of humanity.

In the Grip of the Cold War: The Breakdown of the Yalta System

Our meeting here in the Crimea has reaffirmed our common determination to maintain and strengthen in the peace to come that unity of purpose and of action which has made victory possible and certain for the United Nations in this war. We believe that this is a sacred obligation which our Governments owe to our peoples and to all the peoples of the world.[1]

With these ringing words, drafted at the Yalta Conference in February 1945, President Franklin D. Roosevelt, Soviet leader Joseph Stalin, and British prime minister Winston Churchill affirmed their common hope that the Grand Alliance that had achieved victory in World War II could be sustained into the postwar era. Only through continuing and growing cooperation and understanding among the three victorious allies, the statement asserted, could a secure and lasting peace be realized that, in the words of the Atlantic Charter, would "afford assurance that all the men in all the lands may live out their lives in freedom from fear and want."

Roosevelt had hoped that the decisions reached at the Yalta Conference would provide the basis for a stable peace in the postwar era. Allied occupation forces—American, British, and French in the west and Soviet in the east—were to bring an end to Axis administration, and free elections were to be held throughout Europe to create democratic governments. To foster mutual trust and put an end to the suspicions that had marked relations between the capitalist world and the Soviet Union prior to World War II, Roosevelt tried to reassure Stalin that the peace settlement

1945	1955	1965	1975	1985	1995

NATO formed

Warsaw Pact created

Cuban Missile Crisis

SALT pact signed

Soviet invasion of Afghanistan

Gorbachev announces "New Thinking"

Yalta Conferences

Marhall Plan

Spirit of Camp David

Tito expelled from Soviet bloc

Hungarian revolution fails

"Prague Spring" Europe

Solidarity movement in Poland

Collapse of Soviet power in Eastern Europe

Civil War in China

Korean War

Geneva Conference ends conflict in Indochina

Sino-Soviet dispute breaks into open

U.S. sends combat troops to Viernam

Nixon visit to China

Communists seize power in South Vietnam

Sino-Vietnamese border conflict

would make adequate provision for the Soviets' legitimate territorial aspirations and genuine security needs.

But the stable peace never materialized. Within months after the German surrender, the mutual trust among the victorious allies—if it had ever existed—rapidly disintegrated, and the dream of a durable peace was replaced by the specter of a nuclear holocaust. As the Cold War conflict between the Soviet Union and the United States intensified, Europe was divided into two armed camps, while the two superpowers, glaring at each other across a deep ideological divide, held the survival of the entire world in their hands.

The Collapse of the Yalta System

The problem started in Europe. At the end of the war, Soviet military forces occupied all of Eastern Europe and the Balkans (except for Greece, Albania, and Yugoslavia), while U.S. and other Allied forces occupied the west. Roosevelt had assumed that free elections administered by "democratic and peace-loving forces" would lead to democratic governments responsive to the aspirations of the local populations. But it soon became clear that the Soviet Union and the United States interpreted the Yalta agreement differently. When Soviet occupation authorities set about forming a new Polish government in Warsaw, Stalin refused to accept the legitimacy of the Polish government-in-exile—which had spent the war years in London—and instead installed a new government composed of Communists who had spent the war in Moscow. Roosevelt complained, but he was preoccupied with other problems and eventually agreed to a compromise whereby two members of the London government were included in a new regime dominated by the Communists. A week later, Roosevelt was dead.

Similar developments took place elsewhere in Eastern Europe, as all of the states occupied by Soviet troops were brought within Moscow's sphere of influence. Coalitions of all political parties (except fascist or right-wing parties) were formed to run the government, but within a year or two, the Communist parties in these coalitions had assumed the lion's share of power. The next step was the creation of one-party Communist governments. The timetable in these takeovers varied from country to country, but between 1945 and 1947, Communist governments became firmly entrenched in East Germany, Bulgaria, Romania, Poland, and Hungary. In Czechoslovakia, where there was a stronger tradition of democratic institutions, the Communists did not achieve their goals until 1948. In the elections of 1946, the Communist Party of Czechoslovakia had become the largest party.

But it was not all-powerful and shared control of the government with the non-Communist parties. When it appeared that the latter might win new elections early in 1948, the Communists seized control of the government on February 25. All other parties were dissolved, and Klement Gottwald, the leader of the Communists, became the new president of Czechoslovakia.

Albania and Yugoslavia were notable exceptions to the growing Soviet dominance in Eastern Europe. In both countries, the Communist Party had led the resistance to the Nazis during the war, and it simply took over power when the war ended. In Albania, local Communists established a rigidly Stalinist regime, but one that grew increasingly independent of the Soviet Union.

In Yugoslavia, Josip Broz, known as Tito (1892–1980), the leader of the Communist resistance movement, seemed to be a loyal Stalinist. After the war, however, he moved toward the establishment of an independent Communist state in Yugoslavia. Stalin hoped to take control of Yugoslavia, just as he had done in other Eastern European countries, but Tito refused to capitulate to Soviet demands and gained the support of the people by portraying the struggle as one of Yugoslav national freedom. In 1958, the Yugoslav party congress asserted that Yugoslav Communists did not see themselves as deviating from communism, only from Stalinism. They considered their way closer to the Marxist-Leninist ideal. Yugoslav communism included a more decentralized economic and political system in which workers could manage themselves and local communes could exercise some political power.

In establishing pliant pro-Soviet regimes throughout Eastern Europe, Stalin may simply have been following his interpretation of the Yalta peace agreement; thus, to him these client states may have represented compensation for Soviet sacrifices during the war, as well as a means of providing a buffer zone against the capitalist West. If the Soviet leader had any intention of promoting future Communist revolutions in Western Europe— and there is some indication that he did—they would have to await the appearance of a new capitalist crisis a decade or more into the future. Lenin had always maintained that revolutions come in waves.

The Truman Doctrine and the Marshall Plan

To the United States, however, the Soviet takeover of Eastern Europe represented an ominous development that threatened Roosevelt's vision of a durable peace. President Harry S Truman (1884–1972), whose views on foreign policy were less nuanced than those of his predecessor, was quick to express his discontent at recent Soviet policies. At the Potsdam Conference in late July 1945, Truman demanded free elections throughout Eastern Europe. Stalin responded: "A freely elected government in any of these European countries would be anti-Soviet, and that we cannot allow." After the bitterly fought and devastating war, Stalin sought absolute military security. To him, it could only be gained by the presence of Communist states in Eastern Europe.

In the United States, public suspicion of Soviet intentions escalated rapidly, especially among the millions of Americans who had relatives in Eastern Europe. Winston Churchill was quick to put such fears into words. In a highly publicized speech to an American audience at Westminster College in Fulton, Missouri, in March 1946, the former British prime minister declared that "an iron curtain" had "descended across the continent," dividing Germany and Europe into two hostile camps. Stalin responded by branding Churchill's speech a "call to war with the Soviet Union." But he need not have worried. Although public opinion in the United States placed increasing pressure on Truman to devise an effective strategy to counter Soviet advances abroad, the American people were in no mood for another war. By the middle of 1945, only an invasion by Western forces could have reversed the Soviet takeover in Eastern Europe, and after the world's most destructive conflict had ended, few people favored such a policy.

A civil war in Greece created another arena for confrontation between the superpowers and an opportunity for the Truman administration to take a stand. Communist guerrilla forces supported by Tito's Yugoslavia had taken up arms against the pro-Western government in Athens. Great Britain had initially assumed primary responsibility for promoting postwar reconstruction in the eastern Mediterranean, but in 1947 continued postwar economic problems caused the British to withdraw from the active role they had been playing in both Greece and Turkey. Alarmed by British weakness and the possibility of Soviet expansion into the eastern Mediterranean, Truman responded with the Truman Doctrine (see the box on p. 975). According to the president, "It must be the policy of the United States to support free peoples who are resisting attempted subjugation by armed minorities or by outside pressures." This statement was made to the U.S. Congress in March 1947 when Truman requested $400 million in economic and military aid for Greece and Turkey. The Truman Doctrine said in essence that the United States would provide money to countries that claimed they were threatened by Communist expansion. If the Soviets were not stopped in Greece, the Truman ar-

❧ *The Truman Doctrine* ❧

B y 1947, *the battle lines had been clearly drawn in the Cold War. This excerpt is taken from a speech by President Harry Truman to the U.S. Congress in which he justified his request for aid to Greece and Turkey. Truman expressed the urgent need to contain the expansion of communism.*

Truman's Speech to Congress, March 12, 1947

The peoples of a number of countries of the world have recently had totalitarian regimes forced upon them against their will. The Government of the United States has made frequent protests against coercion and intimidation, in violation of the Yalta agreement, in Poland, Rumania, and Bulgaria. I must also state that in a number of other countries there have been similar developments.

At the present moment in world history nearly every nation must choose between alternative ways of life. The choice is too often not a free one.

One way of life is based upon the will of the majority, and is distinguished by free institutions, representative government, free elections, guaranties of individual liberty, freedom of speech and religion, and freedom from political oppression.

The second way of life is based upon the will of a minority forcibly imposed upon the majority. It relies upon terror and oppression, a controlled press and radio, fixed elections, and the suppression of personal freedoms.

I believe that it must be the policy of the United States to support free peoples who are resisting attempted subjugation by armed minorities or by outside pressures.

I believe that we must assist free people to work out their own destinies in their own way.

I believe that our help should be primarily through economic and financial aid which is essential to economic stability and orderly political processes. . . . I therefore ask the Congress for assistance to Greece and Turkey in the amount of $400,000,000.

---

gument ran, the United States would have to face the spread of communism throughout the free world. As Dean Acheson, the U.S. secretary of state, explained, "Like apples in a barrel infected by disease, the corruption of Greece would infect Iran and all the East . . . likewise Africa . . . Italy . . . France. . . . Not since Rome and Carthage had there been such a polarization of power on this earth."[2]

The proclamation of the Truman Doctrine was soon followed in June 1947 by the European Recovery Program, better known as the Marshall Plan, which provided $13 billion for the economic recovery of war-torn Europe. Underlying the program was the belief that Communist aggression fed off economic turmoil. In a commencement speech at Harvard, General George C. Marshall described the purpose of the program: "Our policy is not directed against any country or doctrine but against hunger, poverty, desperation and chaos."[3] From the Soviet perspective, though, the Marshall Plan was nothing less than capitalist imperialism, a thinly veiled attempt to buy the support of the smaller European countries, which in return would be expected to submit to economic exploitation by the United States. A Soviet spokesman described the United States as the "main force in the imperialist camp," whose ultimate goal was "the strengthening of imperialism, preparation for a new imperialist war, a struggle against socialism and democracy, and the support of reactionary and antidemocratic, pro-fascist regimes and movements." The Marshall Plan did not intend to shut out either the Soviet Union or its Eastern European satellite states, but they refused to participate. According to the Soviet view, the Marshall Plan aimed at "the construction of a bloc of states bound by obligations to the USA" and guaranteed "the American loans in return for the relinquishing by the European states of their economic and later also their political independence."[4] The Soviets, however, were in no position to compete financially with the United States and could do little to counter the Marshall Plan.

Crisis in Berlin

By 1947, the split in Europe between East and West had become a fact of life. At the end of World War II, the United States had favored a quick end to its commitments in Europe. But U.S. fears of Soviet aims caused the United States to play an increasingly important role in European affairs. In an important article in *Foreign Affairs* in July 1947, George Kennan, a well-known U.S.

◆ A Call to Arms.   In March, 1946 former British Prime Minister Winston Churchill gave a speech before a college audience in Fulton, Missouri, which electrified the world. Soviet occupation of the countries of Eastern Europe, he declared, had divided the continent into two conflicting halves, separated by an "Iron Curtain." Churchill's speech has often been described as the opening salvo in the Cold War. In the photo above, Churchill, with President Harry S. Truman behind him, prepares to give his address.

diplomat with much knowledge of Soviet affairs, advocated a policy of containment against further aggressive Soviet moves. Kennan favored the "adroit and vigilant application of counter-force at a series of constantly shifting geographical and political points, corresponding to the shifts and manoeuvres of Soviet policy." After the Soviet blockade of Berlin in 1948, containment of the Soviet Union became formal American policy.

The fate of Germany had become a source of heated contention between East and West. Besides denazification and the partitioning of Germany (and Berlin) into four occupied zones, the Allied powers had agreed on little with regard to the conquered nation. Even denazification proceeded differently in the various zones of occupation. The Americans and British proceeded methodically—the British had tried two million cases by 1948—while

the Soviets (and French) went after major criminals and allowed lesser officials to go free. The Soviet Union, hardest hit by the war, took reparations from Germany in the form of booty. The technology-starved Soviets dismantled and removed to Russia 380 factories from the western zones of Berlin before transferring their control to the Western powers. By the summer of 1946, two hundred chemical, paper, and textile factories in the East German zone had likewise been shipped to the Soviet Union. At the same time, the German Communist Party was reestablished under the control of Walter Ulbricht (1893–1973) and was soon in charge of the political reconstruction of the Soviet zone in eastern Germany.

Although the foreign ministers of the four occupying powers (the United States, the Soviet Union, Great Britain, and France) kept meeting in an attempt to arrive at a final peace treaty with Germany, they moved further and further apart. At the same time, the British, French, and Americans gradually began to merge their zones economically and, by February 1948, were making plans for the unification of these three western sections of Germany and the formal creation of a West German federal government. The Soviet Union responded with a blockade of West Berlin that allowed neither trucks nor trains to enter the city's three western zones. The Soviets hoped to secure economic control of all Berlin and force the Western powers to stop the creation of a separate West German state.

The Western powers were faced with a dilemma. Direct military confrontation seemed dangerous, and no one wished to risk World War III. Therefore, an attempt to break through the blockade with tanks and trucks was ruled out. The solution was the Berlin Air Lift. At its peak, 13,000 tons of supplies were flown daily to Berlin. The Soviets, also not wanting war, did not interfere and finally lifted the blockade in May 1949. Nevertheless, the blockade had severely increased tensions between the United States and the Soviet Union and brought the separation of Germany into two states. In September 1949, the German Federal Republic was formally created from the three sections occupied by the Western powers, and a month later, a separate German Democratic Republic was established in East Germany. Berlin remained a divided city and the source of much contention between East and West.

Military Alliances and Superpower Rivalry

The search for security in the new world of the Cold War also led to the formation of military alliances. The North Atlantic Treaty Organization (NATO) was formed in April 1949 when Belgium, Luxembourg, the Netherlands, France, Britain, Italy, Denmark, Norway, Portugal, and Iceland signed a treaty with the United States and Canada. All the powers agreed to provide mutual assistance if any one of them was attacked. A few years later, West Germany and Turkey joined NATO.

The Eastern European states soon followed suit. In 1949, they had already formed the Council for Mutual Economic Assistance (COMECON) for economic cooperation. Then in 1955, Albania, Bulgaria, Czechoslovakia, East Germany, Hungary, Poland, Romania, and the Soviet Union organized a formal military alliance in the Warsaw Pact. Once again, Europe was tragically divided into hostile alliance systems.

By the end of the 1940s, then, the dream of a stable peace in Europe had been obliterated. There has been considerable historical debate over who bears the most

CHRONOLOGY

The Cold War in the West

Truman Doctrine	1947
Formation of NATO	1949
Soviet Union explodes first nuclear device	1949
Warsaw Pact created	1955
Khrushchev calls for peaceful coexistence	1956
Cuban Missile Crisis	1962
SALT Treaty signed	1972
Soviet invasion of Afghanistan	1979
Gorbachev announces "New Thinking" in Moscow	1985

responsibility for starting the Cold War. In the 1950s, most scholars in the West assumed that the bulk of the blame must fall on the shoulders of Stalin, whose determination to impose Soviet rule on the countries of Eastern Europe snuffed out hopes for freedom and self-determination there and aroused justifiable fears of Communist expansion in the Western democracies. During the next decade, however, a new school of revisionist historians—provoked by aggressive U.S. policies to prevent a Communist victory in Southeast Asia—began to argue that the fault lay primarily with Truman and his anti-Communist advisers, who abandoned the precepts of Yalta and sought to encircle the Soviet Union with a tier of pliant U.S. client states.

No doubt, both the United States and the Soviet Union took steps at the end of World War II that were unwise or might have been avoided. Both nations, however, were working within a framework conditioned by the past. Ultimately, the rivalry between the two superpowers stemmed from their different historical perspectives and their irreconcilable political ambitions. Intense competition for political and military supremacy had long been a regular feature of Western civilization. The United States and the Soviet Union were the heirs of that European tradition of power politics, and it should not surprise us that two such different systems would seek to extend their way of life to the rest of the world. Because of its need to feel secure on its western border, the Soviet Union was not prepared to give up the advantages it had gained in Eastern Europe from Germany's defeat. But neither were U.S. leaders willing to give up the power and prestige the United States had gained throughout the world. Suspicious of each other's motives, the United States and the Soviet Union soon raised their mutual fears to a level of intense competition.

The East is Red: Cold War In Asia

The Cold War was somewhat slower to make its appearance in Asia. The Yalta agreement had provided a structure for postwar cooperation among the victorious Allied powers. Stalin had formally agreed to enter the Pacific war against Japan three months after the end of the conflict with Germany. As a reward for Soviet participation in the struggle against Japan, Roosevelt promised that the Soviet Union would be granted "preeminent interests" in Manchuria (interests reminiscent of those possessed by imperial Russia prior to its defeat by Japan in 1904–1905) and allowed to establish a naval base at Port Arthur. In return, Stalin agreed to sign a treaty of alliance with Chiang Kai-shek's Republic of China, thus implicitly promising not to support the Chinese Communists in a possible future civil war.

Although many observers would later question Stalin's sincerity in making such a commitment to the vocally anti-Communist Chiang Kai-shek, the decision probably had a logic of its own. The Soviet Union had provided diplomatic support and military assistance to Chiang's Nanjing Republic during the 1930s, when Stalin viewed Chiang as a potentially useful bulwark against Japanese expansion in East Asia. Although that policy was abandoned in 1941 when the Soviet Union signed a treaty of nonaggression with Japan to protect its eastern flank, Stalin had good reason to seek to resurrect the relationship after the close of the Pacific conflict. He had no particular liking for the independent-minded Mao Zedong and indeed did not anticipate a Communist victory in the eventuality of a civil war in China. Only an agreement with Chiang Kai-shek could provide the Soviet Union with a strategically vital economic and political presence in North China.

In spite of such commitments, Allied agreements aimed at creating a stable peace in East Asia soon broke down, and by 1950 the region had been sucked into the vortex of the Cold War. The root of the problem could be found in the underlying weakness of Chiang Kai-shek's regime.

The Chinese Civil War

As World War II came to an end in the Pacific, Chiang Kai-shek's government had a powerful ally. During the two years after the Japanese attack on Pearl Harbor, the United States had attempted to strengthen Chiang to provide a base in southern and central China from which to attack Japan. President Roosevelt had also hoped Republican China would be the keystone of his plan for peace and stability in Asia after the war. Eventually, however, U.S. officials became disillusioned with the corruption of Chiang's government and his unwillingness to risk his forces against the Japanese (he hoped to save them for use against the Communists after the war in the Pacific ended), and China became a backwater as the war came to a close. Nevertheless, U.S. military and economic aid to China had been substantial, and at war's end the new Truman administration still hoped that it could rely on Chiang to support U.S. postwar goals in the region.

While Chiang Kai-shek wrestled with Japanese aggression and problems of national development, the Communists had been building up their liberated base in North China. An alliance with Chiang in December 1936 had relieved them from the threat of immediate attack from the south, although Chiang was chronically suspicious of the Communists and stationed troops near Xian to prevent them from infiltrating into areas under his control.

He had good reason to fear for the future. During the war, the Communists had patiently penetrated Japanese lines and built up their strength in North China. To enlarge their political base, they carried out a "mass line" policy (from the masses, to the masses), reducing land rents and confiscating the lands of wealthy landlords. According to Communist estimates, 20 to 30 million Chinese were living under their administration by the end of World War II, and their People's Liberation Army included nearly one million troops.

As the war came to an end, world attention began to focus on the prospects for renewed civil strife in China. Members of a U.S. liaison team stationed in Yan'an during the last months of the war were impressed by the performance of the Communists, and some recommended that the United States should support them or at least remain neutral in a possible conflict between Communists and Nationalists for control of China. The Truman administration, though skeptical of Chiang's ability to forge a strong and prosperous country, was increasingly concerned about the spread of communism in Europe and tried to find a peaceful solution through the formation of a coalition government of all parties in China.

The effort failed. By 1946, full-scale war between the Nationalist government, now reinstalled in Nanjing, and the Communists resumed. The Communists, having taken advantage of the Soviet occupation of

Manchuria in the last days of the war, occupied rural areas in the region and laid siege to Nationalist garrisons hastily established there. Now Chiang Kai-shek's errors came home to roost. In the countryside, millions of peasants, attracted to the Communists by promises of land and social justice, flocked to serve in Mao Zedong's People's Liberation Army (PLA). In the cities, middle-class Chinese, who were normally hostile to communism, were alienated by Chiang's brutal suppression of all dissent and his government's inability to slow the ruinous rate of inflation or solve the economic problems it caused. With morale dropping in the cities, Chiang's troops began to defect to the Communists. Sometimes whole divisions, officers as well as ordinary soldiers, changed sides. By 1948, the PLA was advancing south out of Manchuria and had encircled Beijing. Communist troops took the old imperial capital, crossed the Yangtze the following spring, and occupied the commercial hub of Shanghai. During the next few months, Chiang's government and two million of his followers fled to Taiwan, which the Japanese had returned to Chinese control after World War II.

The Truman administration had reacted to the spread of Communist power in China with acute discomfort. It had no desire to see a Communist government on the mainland, but had little confidence in Chiang Kai-shek's ability to realize Roosevelt's dream of a strong, united, and prosperous China. In December 1945, Truman sent General George C. Marshall to China in a last-ditch effort to avoid civil war and bring about a peaceful settlement. But anti-Communist elements within the Republic of China resisted U.S. efforts to create a coalition government with the Chinese Communist Party (CCP), and in December 1946 Marshall, arguing that neither side was cooperating in the effort, sought and received Truman's permission to abandon the mission. During the next two years, the United States gave limited military support to Chiang Kai-shek's regime, but refused to commit U.S. power to guarantee its survival. This hands-off policy deeply angered many in Congress, who charged that the Truman administration was "soft on communism" and that Roosevelt had betrayed Chiang Kai-shek at Yalta by granting privileges in Manchuria to the Soviet Union. In their view, Soviet troops had hindered the dispatch of Chiang's forces to the area and supplied the soldiers of the People's Liberation Army with weapons to use against their rivals.

In later years, sources in both Moscow and Beijing suggested that the Soviet Union gave little assistance to the CCP in its struggle against Chiang Kai-shek's regime. In fact, Stalin periodically advised Mao against undertaking the effort. Although Communist forces undoubtedly received some assistance from Soviet occupation troops in Manchuria, the underlying causes of their victory stemmed from conditions inside China, and not from the intervention of outside powers. So indeed argued the Truman administration in 1949, when it issued a White Paper that placed most of the blame for the debacle at the foot of Chiang Kai-shek's regime. Essentially, the paper claimed, nothing that the United States could have done would have changed the outcome (see the box on p. 1000–1001).

Many Americans, however, did not agree. The Communist victory on the mainland of China injected Asia directly into American politics as an integral element of the Cold War. During the spring of 1950, under pressure from Congress and public opinion to define U.S. interests in Asia, the Truman administration adopted a new national security policy that implied that the United States would take whatever steps were necessary to stem the further expansion of communism in the region.

◆ **Chiang Kai-shek and Mao Zedong Exchange a Toast.** After World War II, the United States sent General George C. Marshall to China in an effort to prevent civil war between Chiang Kai-shek's government and the Communists. Marshall's initial success was symbolized by this toast between Chiang and Mao. But suspicion ran too deep, and soon conflict ensued, leading to a Communist victory in 1949. Chiang Kai-shek's government retreated to the island of Taiwan.

➣ It's Not Our Fault ➣

In 1949, with China about to fall under the control of the Communists, President Harry S Truman instructed the State Department to prepare a White Paper explaining why the U.S. policy of seeking to avoid a Communist victory in China had failed. The authors of the White Paper concluded that responsibility lay at the door of Nationalist Chinese leader Chiang Kai-shek, and that there was nothing the United States could have reasonably done to alter the result. Most China observers today would accept that assessment, but it did little at the time to deflect criticism of the administration for selling out the interests of our ally in China.

U.S. State Department White Paper on China, 1949

When peace came the United States was confronted with three possible alternatives in China: (1) it could have pulled out lock, stock and barrel; (2) it could have intervened militarily on a major scale to assist the Nationalists to destroy the Communists; (3) it could, while assisting the Nationalists to assert their authority over as much of China as possible, endeavor to avoid a civil war by working for a compromise between the two sides.

The first alternative would, and I believe American public opinion at the time so felt, have represented an abandonment of our international responsibilities and of our traditional policy of friendship for China before we had made a determined effort to be of assistance. The second alternative policy, while it may look attractive theoretically, in retrospect, was wholly impracticable. The Nationalists had been unable to destroy the Communists during the 10 years before the war. Now after the war the Nationalists were, as indicated above, weakened, demoralized, and unpopular. They had quickly dissipated their popular support and prestige in the areas liberated from the Japanese by the conduct of their civil and military officials. The Communists on the other hand were much stronger than they had ever been and were in control of most of North China. Because of the ineffectiveness of the Nationalist forces which was later to be tragically demonstrated, the Communists probably could have been dislodged only by American arms. It is obvious that the American people would not have sanctioned such a colossal commitment of our armies in 1945 or later. We therefore came to the third alternative policy whereunder we faced the facts of the situation and attempted to assist in working out a *modus vivendi* which would avert civil war but nevertheless preserve and even increase the influence of the National Government. . . .

The Korean War

Communist leaders in China in their new capital of Beijing hoped that their accession to power in 1949 would bring about an era of peace in the region that would permit their new government to concentrate on domestic goals. But the desire for peace was tempered by their determination to erase a century of humiliation at the hands of imperialist powers and to restore the traditional outer frontiers of the empire. In addition to recovering territories that had been part of the Manchu empire such as Manchuria, Taiwan, and Tibet, the Chinese leaders also hoped to restore Chinese influence in former tributary areas such as Korea and Vietnam.

It soon became clear that these two goals were not always compatible. Negotiations with the Soviet Union led to Soviet recognition of Chinese sovereignty over Manchuria and Xinjiang (the desolate lands north of Tibet that were known as Chinese Turkestan because many of the peoples in the area were of Turkish origin), although the Soviets retained a measure of economic influence in both areas. Chinese troops occupied Tibet in 1950 and brought it under Chinese administration for the first time in over a century. But in Korea and Taiwan, China's efforts to re-create the imperial buffer zone provoked new conflicts with foreign powers.

The problem of Taiwan was a consequence of the Cold War. As the civil war in China came to an end, the Truman administration appeared determined to avoid entanglement in China's internal affairs and indicated that it would not prevent a Communist takeover of the island, now occupied by Chiang Kai-shek's Republic of China. But as tensions between the United States and the new Chinese government escalated during the winter of 1949–1950, influential figures in the United States be-

Fully recognizing that the heads of the Chinese Communist Party were ideologically affiliated with Moscow, our Government nevertheless took the view, in the light of the existing balance of forces in China, that peace could be established only if certain conditions were met. The Kuomintang would have to set its own house in order and both sides would have to make concessions so that the Government of China might become, in fact as well as in name, the Government of all China and so that all parties might function within the constitutional system of the government. Both internal peace and constitutional development required that the progress should be rapid from one-party government with a large opposition party in armed rebellion, to the participation of all parties, including the moderate non-communist elements, in a truly national system of government.

None of these conditions has been realized. The distrust of the leaders of both the Nationalist and Communist Parties for each other proved too deep-seated to permit final agreement, notwithstanding temporary truces and apparently promising negotiations. The Nationalists, furthermore, embarked in 1946 on an over-ambitious military campaign in the face of warnings by General Marshall that it not only would fail but would plunge China into economic chaos and eventually destroy the National Government. General Marshall pointed out that though Nationalist armies could, for a period, capture Communist-held cities, they could not destroy the Communist armies. Thus every Nationalist advance would expose their communications to attack by Communist guerrillas and compel them to retreat or to surrender their armies together with the munitions which the United States has furnished them. No estimate of a military situation has ever been more completely confirmed by the resulting facts. . . .

The unfortunate but inescapable fact is that the ominous result of the civil war in China was beyond the control of the government of the United States. Nothing that this country did or could have done within the reasonable limits of its capabilities could have changed that result; nothing that was left undone by this country has contributed to it. It was the product of internal Chinese forces, forces which this country tried to influence but could not. A decision was arrived at within China, if only a decision by default.

---

gan to argue that Taiwan was crucial to U.S. defense strategy in the Pacific.

The outbreak of war in Korea also helped bring the Cold War to East Asia. After the Sino-Japanese War in 1894–1895, Korea, long a Chinese tributary, had fallen increasingly under the rival influence of Japan and Russia. After the Japanese defeated the Russians in 1905, Korea was incorporated into the Japanese Empire where it remained until 1945. The removal of Korea from Japanese control had been one of the stated objectives of the Allies in World War II, and on the eve of Japanese surrender in August 1945, the Soviet Union and the United States agreed to divide the country into two separate occupation zones at the 38th parallel. They originally planned to hold national elections after the restoration of peace to reunify Korea under an independent government. But as U.S.-Soviet relations deteriorated, two separate governments emerged in Korea, a Communist one in the north and an anti-Communist one in the south.

Tensions between the two governments ran high along the dividing line, and on June 25, 1950, with Stalin's apparent approval, North Korean troops invaded the south. The Truman administration immediately ordered U.S. naval and air forces to support South Korea, and the United Nations Security Council passed a resolution calling on member nations to jointly resist the invasion. By September, United Nations (UN) forces under the command of U.S. General Douglas MacArthur marched northward across the 38th parallel with the aim of unifying Korea under a single non-Communist government.

President Truman worried that, by approaching the Chinese border at the Yalu River, the UN troops could trigger Chinese intervention, but was assured by MacArthur that China would not respond. In November,

Conflict in Indochina

During the mid-1950s, China sought to build contacts with the nonsocialist world. A cease-fire agreement brought the Korean War to an end in July 1953, and China signaled its desire for peaceful coexistence with other independent countries in the region. But a relatively minor conflict in French Indochina on Beijing's southern flank now began to intensify. The struggle had begun after World War II, when a multiparty nationalist alliance called the Vietminh Front, which was led by Ho Chi Minh's Indochinese Community Party, seized power in northern and central Vietnam after the surrender of imperial Japan. After abortive negotiations with the returning French, war broke out in December 1946. French forces occupied the cities and the densely populated lowlands, while the Vietminh took refuge in the mountains.

Over the next three years, the Vietminh gradually increased in size and effectiveness. Then, in the early 1950s, what had begun as an anticolonial struggle against the French became entangled in the Cold War as both the United States and the new Communist government

✖ **Map 27.1** The Korean Peninsula.

however, Chinese "volunteer" forces intervened in force on the side of North Korea and drove the UN troops southward in disarray. A static defense line was eventually established near the original dividing line at the 38th parallel, although the war continued.

To many Americans, the Chinese intervention in Korea was clear evidence that China intended to promote communism throughout Asia. In fact, China's decision to enter the war was probably motivated in large part by the fear that hostile U.S. forces might be stationed on the Chinese frontier and perhaps even launch an attack across the border. MacArthur had intensified such fears by calling publicly for air attacks on Manchurian cities in preparation for an attack on Communist China. In any case, the outbreak of the Korean War was particularly unfortunate for China. Immediately after the invasion, President Truman dispatched the U.S. Seventh Fleet to the Taiwan Strait to prevent a possible Chinese invasion of Taiwan. Even more unfortunate, the invasion hardened Western attitudes against the new Chinese government and led to China's isolation from the major capitalist powers for two decades. As a result, China was cut off from all forms of economic and technological assistance and was forced to rely almost entirely on the Soviet Union with which it had signed a pact of friendship and cooperation in early 1950.

in China began to intervene in the conflict to promote their own national security objectives. China began to provide military assistance to the Vietminh to protect its own borders from hostile forces. The Americans supported the French, but pressured the French government to prepare for an eventual transition to non-Communist governments in Vietnam, Laos, and Cambodia.

At the Geneva Conference in 1954, with the French public tired of fighting the "dirty war" in Indochina, the French agreed to a peace settlement with Ho Chi Minh's Vietminh. Vietnam was temporarily divided into a northern Communist half (known as the Democratic Republic of Vietnam, or DRV) and a non-Communist southern half based in Saigon (eventually to be known as

the Republic of Vietnam, or RVN). Elections were to be held in two years to create a unified government. Cambodia and Laos were both declared independent under neutral governments.

China had played an active role in bringing about the settlement, but subsequent efforts to improve relations between China and the United States foundered on the issue of Taiwan. In the fall of 1954, the United States and the Republic of China on Taiwan signed a mutual security treaty that guaranteed U.S. military support in case of an invasion of Taiwan. When Beijing demanded a U.S. withdrawal from Taiwan as the price for improved relations, diplomatic talks between the two countries failed.

◆ **Ho Chi Minh Plans an Attack on the French.** Unlike many peoples in Southeast Asia, the Vietnamese had to fight for their independence after World War II. That fight was led by the talented Communist leader Ho Chi Minh. In this photograph, Ho, assisted by his chief strategist Vo Nguyen Giap, plans an attack on French positions in Vietnam.

From Confrontation to Coexistence

The decade of the 1950s opened with the world teetering on the edge of a nuclear holocaust. The Soviet Union had detonated its first nuclear device in 1949, and relations between the capitalist and socialist blocs grew increasingly bitter with each passing year. Yet as the decade drew to a close, a measure of sanity had crept into the Cold War, and the leaders of the major world powers had begun to seek ways to coexist in a peaceful and stable world.

Ferment in Eastern Europe

The keystone of the Soviet Union's security belt along its western frontier was the string of satellite states that had been created in Eastern Europe in the aftermath of World War II. Once Communist power had been assured in Poland, Czechoslovakia, Bulgaria, Hungary, Romania, and East Germany, a series of "little Stalins" installed by Moscow instituted Soviet-type five-year plans that emphasized heavy industry rather than consumer goods and called for the collectivization of agriculture and the na-

Map 27.2 The New European Alliance Systems in the 1950s and 1960s.

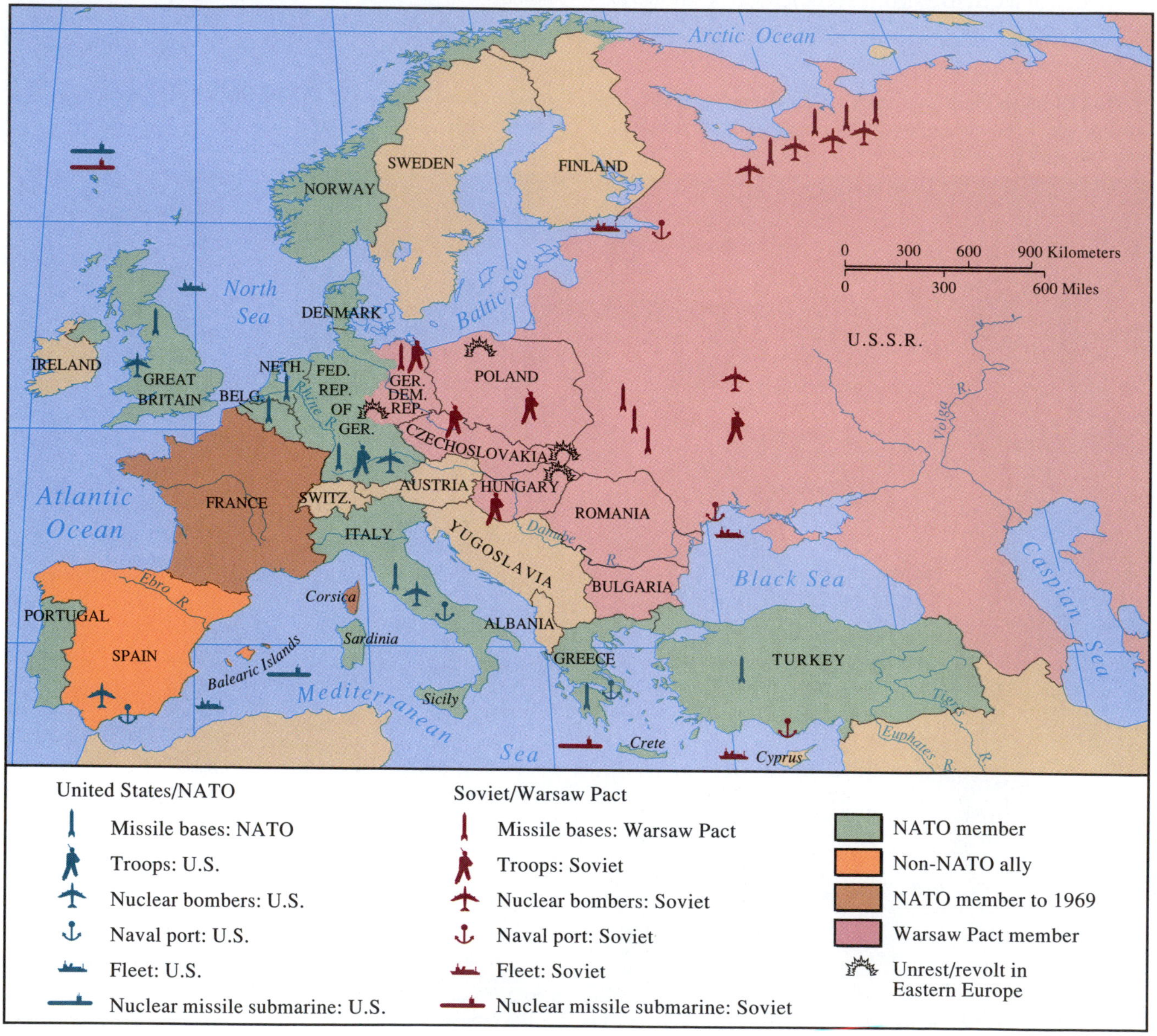
Arctic Ocean
SWEDEN
FINLAND
NORWAY
North Sea
Baltic Sea
DENMARK
0 300 600 900 Kilometers
0 300 600 Miles
U.S.S.R.
IRELAND
GREAT BRITAIN
BELG.
NETH.
FED. REP. OF GER.
GER. DEM. REP.
POLAND
Rhine R.
CZECHOSLOVAKIA
Volga R.
Atlantic Ocean
FRANCE
SWITZ.
AUSTRIA
HUNGARY
ROMANIA
ITALY
YUGOSLAVIA
Danube R.
Caspian Sea
Ebro R.
Corsica
BULGARIA
Black Sea
PORTUGAL
Sardinia
ALBANIA
SPAIN
Balearic Islands
GREECE
TURKEY
Mediterranean Sea
Sicily
Crete
Cyprus
Tigris R.
Euphrates R.
United States/NATO
Missile bases: NATO
Troops: U.S.
Nuclear bombers: U.S.
Naval port: U.S.
Fleet: U.S.
Nuclear missile submarine: U.S.
Soviet/Warsaw Pact
Missile bases: Warsaw Pact
Troops: Soviet
Nuclear bombers: Soviet
Naval port: Soviet
Fleet: Soviet
Nuclear missile submarine: Soviet
NATO member
Non-NATO ally
NATO member to 1969
Warsaw Pact member
Unrest/revolt in Eastern Europe

tionalization of industry. They also appropriated the political tactics that Stalin had perfected in the Soviet Union, eliminating all non-Communist parties and establishing the classical institutions of repression—the secret police and military forces. Dissidents were tracked down and thrown into prison, while "national Communists" who resisted total subservience to the Soviet Union were charged with treason in mass show trials and executed.

Despite these efforts at repression, however, Soviet-style policies aroused growing discontent in several Eastern European societies. Countries such as Hungary, Poland, and Romania harbored bitter memories of past Russian domination and suspected that Stalin, under the pose of proletarian internationalism, was seeking to revive the empire of the Romanovs. For the vast majority of peoples in Eastern Europe, the imposition of the so-called people's democracies (a term invented by Moscow to refer to a society in the early stage of socialist transition) had resulted in economic hardship and severe threats to the most basic political liberties.

The first signs of unrest appeared in 1953, when popular riots broke out against Communist rule in East Berlin. Georgy Malenkov (1902–1988), who had seized power in Moscow after Stalin's death in March (see Chapter 28), tried to deflect the discontent by announcing a "new course" in the Soviet Union's relations with its Eastern European allies. Malenkov's objective was to bring about political and economic reforms in the region before full-scale rebellion broke out.

The riots in East Berlin eventually subsided, but the virus had begun to spread to neighboring countries. Several of the "little Stalins" had ignored the ominous warnings of public discontent, and in 1956 popular dissatisfaction erupted in Poland and Hungary. In Poland, public demonstrations against an increase in food prices escalated into widespread protests against the regime's economic policies, restrictions on the freedom of Catholics to practice their religion, and the continued presence of Soviet troops (as called for by the Warsaw Pact) on Polish soil.

In a desperate effort to defuse the unrest, in October the first secretary of the Polish Workers' Party (the official name of the ruling party in Poland) stepped down and was replaced by Wladyslaw Gomulka (1905–1982), a popular figure who had previously been demoted for his "nationalist" tendencies. When Gomulka took steps to ease the crisis, the new Soviet party chief Nikita Khrushchev (1894–1971) flew to Warsaw to warn his Polish colleague against adopting policies that could undermine the dictatorship of the proletariat (a classic

Marxist phrase to express the political dominance of the party) and even weaken security links with the Soviet Union. After a brief confrontation during which both sides threatened to use military force to punctuate their demands, Gomulka and Khrushchev reached a compromise, according to which Poland would adopt a policy labeled "internal reform, external loyalty." Poland agreed to remain in the Warsaw Pact and to maintain the sanctity of party rule. In return, Gomulka was authorized to adopt domestic reforms, such as easing restrictions on religious practice and ending the policy of forced collectivization in rural areas, as a gesture to ease popular discontent.

The developments in Poland sent shock waves throughout the region. The impact was the strongest in neighboring Hungary, where the methods of the local "little Stalin," Matyas Rakosi, had been so brutal that he had been summoned to Moscow for a lecture. In late October, student-led popular riots broke out in the capital of Budapest and soon spread to other towns and villages throughout the country. Rakosi was forced to resign and was replaced by Imre Nagy (1896–1958), a "national Communist" who attempted to satisfy popular demands without arousing Soviet anger. Unlike Gomulka, however, Nagy was unable to contain the zeal of leading members of the protest movement, who sought major political reforms and Hungary's resignation from the Warsaw Pact. On November 1, Nagy promised free elections, which, given the mood of the country, would probably have led to an end to Communist rule. After a brief moment of uncertainty, Khrushchev decided on firm action. Soviet troops, recently withdrawn at Nagy's request, returned to Budapest and installed a new government under the more pliant party leader János Kádár (1912–1989). While Kádár rescinded many of the measures that Nagy had adopted, the latter sought refuge in the Yugoslavian Embassy. A few weeks later he left the embassy under the promise of safety, but was quickly arrested, convicted of treason, and executed (see the box on p. 1007).

The dramatic events in Poland and Hungary had graphically demonstrated the underlying vulnerability of the Soviet satellite system in Eastern Europe, and many observers throughout the world anticipated that the United States would attempt to intervene on behalf of the freedom fighters in Hungary. After all, the Eisenhower administration had promised that it would "roll back" communism, and radio broadcasts by the U.S.-sponsored Radio Liberty and Radio Free Europe had encouraged the peoples of Eastern Europe to rise up against Soviet domination. In reality, the United States was well

◆ **How the Mighty Have Fallen.**　In the fall of 1956, Hungarian freedom fighters rose up against Communist domination of their country in the short-lived Hungarian revolution. Their actions threatened Soviet hegemony in Eastern Europe, however, and in late October Soviet leader Nikita Khrushchev dispatched troops to quell the uprising. In the meantime, the Hungarian people had voiced their discontent by toppling a gigantic statue of Joseph Stalin in the capital of Budapest.

aware that intervention could lead to nuclear war and limited itself to protests against Soviet brutality in crushing the uprising.

The year of discontent was not without consequences, however. Soviet leaders now recognized that Moscow could maintain control over its satellites in Eastern Europe only by granting them the leeway to adopt domestic policies appropriate to local conditions. Khrushchev had already embarked on this path in 1955 when, during a visit to Belgrade, he assured Josip Tito that there were "different roads to socialism." That willingness to compromise had been confirmed to Gomulka in Warsaw the following year. Eastern European Communist leaders now took Khrushchev at his word and adopted reform programs to make socialism more palatable to their sub-

ject populations. Even János Kádár, popularly labeled the "butcher of Budapest," managed to preserve many of Imre Nagy's reforms and allowed a measure of capitalist incentive and freedom of expression in Hungary.

Khrushchev and the Era of Peaceful Coexistence

The brutality employed by Moscow in reinforcing its domination over the Eastern European satellites disguised a historic shift that was taking place in Soviet foreign policy. Soviet leaders were beginning to reassess their postwar objectives and to conclude that their purposes would best be served by improving relations with the capitalist world. The first clear sign had taken place after Stalin's death in early 1953. His successor, Georgy

Soviet Repression in Eastern Europe: Hungary, 1956

Developments in Poland in 1956 inspired the Communist leaders of Hungary to begin to remove their country from Soviet control. But there were limits to Khrushchev's tolerance, and he sent Soviet troops to crush Hungary's movement for independence. The first selection is a statement by the Soviet government justifying its use of troops, while the second is the brief and tragic final statement from Imre Nagy, the Hungarian leader.

Statement of the Soviet Government, October 30, 1956

The Soviet Government regards it as indispensable to make a statement in connection with the events in Hungary.

The course of the events has shown that the working people of Hungary, who have achieved great progress on the basis of their people's democratic order, correctly raise the question of the necessity of eliminating serious shortcomings in the field of economic building, the further raising of the material well-being of the population, and the struggle against bureaucratic excesses in the state apparatus.

However, this just and progressive movement of the working people was soon joined by forces of black reaction and counterrevolution, which are trying to take advantage of the discontent of part of the working people to undermine the foundations of the people's democratic order in Hungary and to restore the old landlord and capitalist order.

The Soviet Government and all the Soviet people deeply regret that the development of events in Hungary has led to bloodshed. On the request of the Hungarian People's Government the Soviet Government consented to the entry into Budapest of the Soviet Army units to assist the Hungarian People's Army and the Hungarian authorities to establish order in the town.

The Last Message of Imre Nagy, November 4, 1956

This fight is the fight for freedom by the Hungarian people against the Russian intervention, and it is possible that I shall only be able to stay at my post for one or two hours. The whole world will see how the Russian armed forces, contrary to all treaties and conventions, are crushing the resistance of the Hungarian people. They will also see how they are kidnapping the Prime Minister of a country which is a Member of the United Nations, taking him from the capital, and therefore it cannot be doubted at all that this is the most brutal form of intervention. I should like in these last moments to ask the leaders of the revolution, if they can, to leave the country. I ask that all that I have said in my broadcast, and what we have agreed on with the revolutionary leaders during meetings in Parliament, should be put in a memorandum, and the leaders should turn to all the peoples of the world for help and explain that today it is Hungary and tomorrow, or the day after tomorrow, it will be the turn of other countries because the imperialism of Moscow does not know borders, and is only trying to play for time.

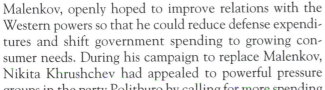

Malenkov, openly hoped to improve relations with the Western powers so that he could reduce defense expenditures and shift government spending to growing consumer needs. During his campaign to replace Malenkov, Nikita Khrushchev had appealed to powerful pressure groups in the party Politburo by calling for more spending on defense, but once in power, he resumed the efforts of his predecessor to reduce tensions with the West and improve the living standards of the Soviet people.

In an adroit public relations touch, Khrushchev publicized Moscow's appeal for a new policy of "peaceful coexistence" with the West. In 1955, he surprisingly agreed to negotiate an end to the postwar occupation of Austria by the victorious Allies and allow the creation of a neutral country with strong cultural and economic ties with the West. He also called for a cut in defense expenditures and reduced the size of the Soviet armed forces.

At first, the United States was suspicious of Khrushchev's motives, especially after the Soviet crackdown in Hungary in the fall of 1956. A new crisis over Berlin added to the tension. The Soviet Union had launched its first intercontinental ballistic missile (ICBM) in August 1957. This success aroused U.S. fears, fueled by a partisan political debate, of a missile gap between the United States and the Soviet Union. Khrushchev attempted to take advantage of the American frenzy over missiles to solve the problem of West Berlin. West Berlin had remained a "Western island" of prosperity inside the relatively poverty-stricken East Germany. Many East Germans sought to escape to West Germany by fleeing through West Berlin.

In November 1958, Khrushchev announced that unless the Western powers removed their forces from West Berlin within six months, he would turn over control of the access routes to Berlin to the East Germans. Unwilling to accept an ultimatum that would have abandoned West Berlin to the Communists, President Dwight D. Eisenhower (1890–1969) and the West stood firm, and Khrushchev eventually backed down.

Despite such periodic crises in East-West relations, there was rising optimism that an era of true peaceful coexistence between the two power blocs could be achieved. In the late 1950s, the United States and the Soviet Union initiated a cultural exchange program that helped to acquaint the peoples of one bloc with the nature of life in the other. While the Leningrad Ballet appeared at theaters in the United States, Benny Goodman and the film *West Side Story* with Leonard Bernstein's music played in Moscow. In 1958, Khrushchev visited the United States and had a brief friendly encounter with President Eisenhower at the presidential retreat in northern Maryland. Predictions of improved future relations led reporters to laud "the spirit of Camp David."

Yet Khrushchev could rarely avoid the temptation to gain an advantage over the United States in the competition for influence throughout the world, and the result was an unstable relationship that prevented a lasting accommodation between the two superpowers. West Berlin was an area of persistent tension (a boil on the foot of the United States, Khrushchev derisively termed it), and in January

1961, just as President John F. Kennedy (1917–1963) came into office, Moscow threatened once again to turn over responsibility for access to the East German government.

The Soviet Union also took every opportunity to promote its interests in the Third World, as the countries of Asia, Africa, and Latin America were now popularly called. Unlike Stalin, Khrushchev viewed the dismantling of colonial regimes in the area as a potential advantage for the Soviet Union and sought especially to exploit the deep suspicions of the United States in Latin America. To improve Soviet influence in such areas, Khrushchev established alliances with key Third World leaders such as Sukarno in Indonesia, Gamal Abdul Nasser in Egypt, Jawaharlal Nehru in India, and Fidel Castro in Cuba. In January 1961, Khrushchev unnerved the recently inaugurated President Kennedy at an informal summit meeting in Vienna by declaring that the Soviet Union would provide active support to national liberation movements throughout the world. Such statements increased U.S. fears of Soviet meddling in such sensitive trouble spots as Southeast Asia, Central Africa, and the Caribbean.

The Cuban Missile Crisis and the Move toward Détente

The Cold War confrontation between the United States and the Soviet Union reached frightening levels during the Cuban Missile Crisis. In 1959, a left-wing revolutionary named Fidel Castro (b. 1927) had overthrown the Cuban dictator Fulgencio Batista and established a Soviet-supported totalitarian regime (see Chapter 29). After the utter failure of a U.S.-supported attempt (the "Bay

◆ **The Kitchen Debate.** During the late 1950s, the United States and the Soviet Union sought to defuse Cold War tensions by encouraging cultural exchanges between the two countries. On one occasion, U.S. Vice President Richard M. Nixon visited Moscow in conjunction with the arrival of an exhibit to introduce U.S. culture and society to the Soviet people. Here Nixon lectures Soviet party chief Nikita Khrushchev on the technology of the U.S. kitchen. To Nixon's left is future Soviet president Leonid Brezhnev.

of Pigs" incident) to overthrow Castro's regime in 1961, the Soviet Union decided to place nuclear missiles in Cuba in 1962. The United States was not prepared to allow nuclear weapons to be within such close striking distance of the American mainland, although it had placed nuclear weapons in Turkey within easy range of the Soviet Union. Khrushchev was quick to point out that "your rockets are in Turkey. You are worried by Cuba . . . because it is 90 miles from the American coast. But Turkey is next to us."[5] When U.S. intelligence discovered that a Soviet fleet carrying missiles was heading to Cuba, President Kennedy decided to blockade Cuba and prevent the fleet from reaching its destination. This approach to the problem had the benefit of delaying confrontation and giving the two sides time to find a peaceful solution. Khrushchev agreed to turn back the fleet if Kennedy pledged not to invade Cuba. In a conciliatory letter to Kennedy, Khrushchev wrote, "We and you ought not to pull on the ends of the rope in which you have tied the knot of war, because the more the two of us pull, the tighter that knot will be tied. And a moment may come when that knot will be tied too tight that even he who tied it will not have the strength to untie it. . . . Let us not only relax the forces pulling on the ends of the rope, let us take measures to untie that knot. We are ready for this."[6]

The intense feeling that the world might have been annihilated in a few days had a profound influence on both sides. A hotline communications system between Moscow and Washington was installed in 1963 to expedite rapid communications between the two superpowers in a time of crisis. In the same year, the two powers agreed to ban nuclear tests in the atmosphere, a step that at least served to lessen the tensions between the two nations.

The Sino-Soviet Dispute

Khrushchev had called for peaceful coexistence as a means of improving relations with the capitalist powers. Ironically, one result of the campaign was to undermine Moscow's ties with its close ally China. During Stalin's

Map 27.3 The Global Cold War in the 1950s and 1960s.

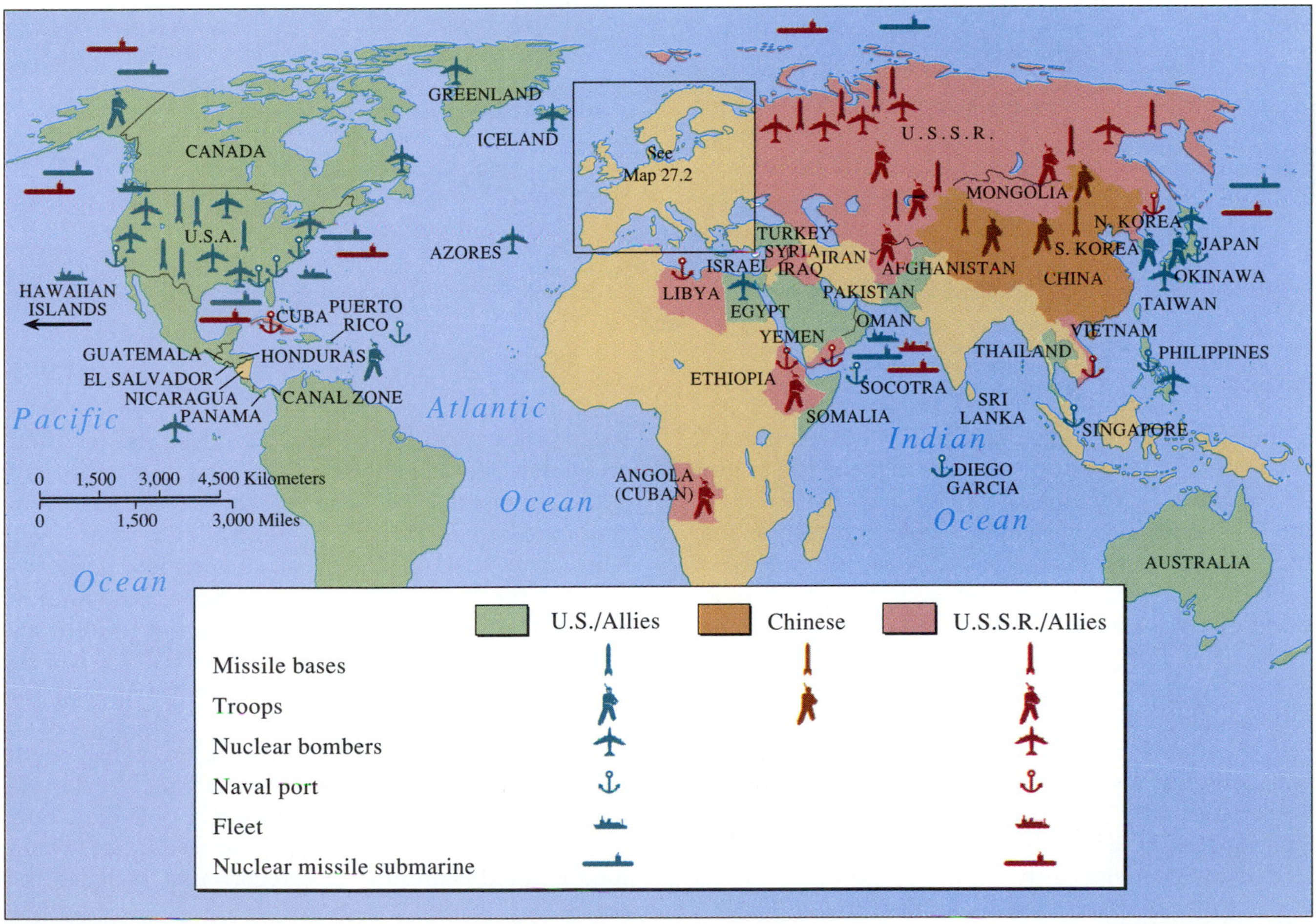

❧ A Plea for Peaceful Coexistence ❧

The Soviet leader Vladimir Lenin had contended that war between the socialist and imperialist camps was inevitable, because the imperialists would never give up without a fight. That assumption had probably guided the thoughts of Joseph Stalin, who told colleagues shortly after World War II that a new war would break out in fifteen to twenty years. But Stalin's successor Nikita Khrushchev feared that a new world conflict could result in a nuclear holocaust and contended that the two sides must learn to coexist, although peaceful competition would continue. In this speech given in Beijing in 1959, Khrushchev attempted to persuade the Chinese to accept his views. But Chinese leaders argued that the "imperialist nature" of the United States would never change and warned that they would not accept any peace agreement in which they had no part. China was undoubtedly angered that the United States continued to occupy Taiwan, which Beijing considered part of its own sacred territory.

Khrushchev's Speech to the Chinese, 1959

Comrades! Socialism brings to the people peace—that greatest blessing. The greater the strength of the camp of socialism grows, the greater will be its possibilities for successfully defending the cause of peace on this earth. The forces of socialism are already so great that real possibilities are being created for excluding war as a means of solving international disputes.

In our time the leaders of governments in some capitalist countries have begun to show a certain tendency towards a realistic understanding of the situation that has emerged in the world.

When I spoke with President Eisenhower—and I have just returned from the United States of America—I got the impression that the President of the U.S.A.—and not a few people support him—understands the need to relax international tension.

Perhaps not every bourgeois leader can pronounce the words "peaceful co-existence" well, but they cannot deny that two systems exist in the world—the socialist and the capitalist. The recognition of this fact ran like a red thread through all the talks; this was repeatedly spoken about by the President and other leaders. Therefore we on our part must do all we can to exclude war as a means of settling disputed questions, and settle these questions by negotiations.

The leaders of the capitalist countries cannot but take account of such a decisive factor of modern times as the existence of the powerful world camp of socialism. There is only one way of preserving peace—that is the road of peaceful co-existence of states with different social systems. The question stands thus: either peaceful co-existence or war with its catastrophic consequences. Now, with the present relation of forces between socialism and capitalism being in favor of socialism, he who would continue the "cold war" is moving towards his own destruction. The "cold war" warriors are pushing the world towards a new world war in the fires of which those who light it will be the first to get burned.

Already in the first years of the Soviet power the

---

lifetime, Beijing had accepted the Soviet Union as the acknowledged leader of the socialist camp. After Stalin's death, however, relations began to deteriorate. Part of the reason may have been Mao Zedong's contention that he, as the most experienced leading Marxist, should now be acknowledged as Stalin's successor and the most authoritative voice within the socialist community. But another determining factor was that just as Soviet policies were moving toward moderation, those of China were becoming more radical.

Several other issues were involved as well, including territorial disputes and China's unhappiness with limited Soviet economic assistance. But the key sources of disagreement involved ideology and the Cold War. Chinese leaders were convinced that the successes of the Soviet space program confirmed that the socialists were now technologically superior to the capitalists (the East Wind, trumpeted the Chinese official press, had now triumphed over the West Wind), and they urged Khrushchev to go on the offensive to promote world revolution. Specifically, China wanted Soviet assistance in retaking Taiwan from Chiang Kai-shek. But Khrushchev was trying to improve relations with the West and rejected Chinese demands for support against Taiwan (see the box above and on p. 1011).

By the end of the 1950s, the Soviet Union had begun to remove its advisers from China, and in 1961 the dispute broke into the open. Increasingly isolated, China voiced its hostility to what Mao described as the "urban industrialized countries" (a category that included the

great Lenin defined the general line of our foreign policy as being directed towards the peaceful co-existence of states with different social systems. For a long time, the ruling circles of the Western Powers rejected these truly humane principles. Nevertheless the principles of peaceful co-existence made their way into the hearts of the vast majority of mankind.

The leaders of many capitalist states are being forced more and more to take account of realities, and to recast their international relations because in our century it is impossible to resolve questions of relations between two systems successfully other than on the basis of the principles of peaceful co-existence. There is no other way.

We are convinced that the peaceful foreign policy of the socialist states, defending peace on earth, will continue to gain new victories. No small efforts will have to be exerted to achieve this. But it is well worth fighting for such a high aim with unsparing efforts.

Comrades! The socialist countries have achieved great successes in developing their economies and as a consequence have created mighty potential forces on the basis of which they can successfully continue their advance. They have the means to defend themselves from the attacks of the imperialist aggressors if these should attempt by interference in our countries' affairs to force them to leave the socialist path and return to capitalism. That old time has gone never to return.

But we must think realistically and understand the contemporary situation correctly. This, of course, does not by any means signify that if we are so strong, then we must test by force the stability of the capitalist system. This would be wrong: the peoples would not understand and would never support those who would think of acting in this way. We have always been against wars of conquest. Marxists have recognized, and recognize, only liberating, just wars; they have always condemned, and condemn, wars of conquest, imperialist wars. This is one of the characteristic features of Marxist-Leninist theory.

It is not at all because capitalism is still strong that the socialist countries speak out against war, and for peaceful co-existence. No, we have no need of war at all. If the people do not want it, even such a noble and progressive system as socialism cannot be imposed by force of arms. The socialist countries therefore, while carrying through a consistently peace-loving policy, concentrate their efforts on peaceful construction, they fire the hearts of men by the force of their example in building socialism, and thus lead them to follow in their footsteps. The question of when this or that country will take the path to socialism is decided by its own people. This, for us, is the holy of holies. . . .

Soviet Union) and portrayed itself as the leader of the "rural underdeveloped countries" of Asia, Africa, and Latin America in a global struggle against imperialist oppression. In effect, China had now applied Mao Zedong's famous concept of people's war in an international framework (see the box on p. 1012).

Events elsewhere in the socialist camp added to Beijing's concern. In the late summer of 1968, Soviet and other Warsaw Pact troops invaded Czechoslovakia to topple a new government led by the reform Communist Alexander Dubcek (1921–1992). Czechoslovakia had not shared in the thaw of the mid-1950s and remained under the rule of Antonin Novotny (1904–1975), who had been placed in power by Stalin himself. By the late 1960s, however, Novotny's policies had led to widespread popular alienation, and in 1968, with the support of intellectuals and reformist party members, Dubcek was elected first secretary of the Communist Party. He immediately attempted to create what was popularly called "socialism with a human face," relaxing restrictions on freedom of speech and the press and the right to travel abroad. Economic reforms were announced, and party control over all aspects of society was reduced. A period of euphoria erupted that came to be known as the "Prague Spring."

It proved to be short-lived. Encouraged by Dubcek's actions, some called for more far-reaching reforms, including neutrality and withdrawal from the Soviet bloc. To forestall the spread of this "spring fever," the Soviet Red Army, supported by troops from other Warsaw Pact

A Manual for Revolutionaries

In the 1920s, Mao Zedong formulated his theory of people's war, which held that in preindustrial societies revolution could be more readily fomented in the countryside than in the cities. Forty years later, Lin Biao, Mao's colleague and the minister of defense, placed the concept in an international framework, arguing that the rural nations of the world (led, of course, by China) would defeat the industrialized "urban" nations (represented by the United States and the Soviet Union). This is an excerpt from the article in which Lin Biao presented his thesis.

Lin Biao, "Long Live the Victory of People's War"

Many countries and peoples in Asia, Africa and Latin America are now being subjected to aggression and enslavement on a serious scale by the imperialists headed by the United States and their lackeys. The basic political and economic conditions in many of these countries have many similarities to those that prevailed in old China. As in China, the peasant question is extremely important in these regions. The peasants constitute the main force of the national-democratic revolution against the imperialists and their lackeys. In committing aggression against these countries, the imperialists usually begin by seizing the big cities and the main lines of communication. But they are unable to bring the vast countryside completely under their control. The countryside, and the countryside alone, can provide the broad areas in which the revolutionaries can maneuver freely. The countryside, and the countryside alone, can provide the revolutionary basis from which the revolutionaries can go forward to final victory. Precisely for this reason, Mao Tse-tung's theory of establishing revolutionary base areas in the rural districts and encircling the cities from the countryside is attracting more and more attention among the people in these regions.

Taking the entire globe, if North America and Western Europe can be called "the cities of the world," then Asia, Africa and Latin America constitute "the rural areas of the world." Since World War II, the proletarian revolutionary movement has for various reasons been temporarily held back in the North American and West European capitalist countries, while the people's revolutionary movement in Asia, Africa and Latin America has been growing vigorously. In a sense, the contemporary world revolution also presents a picture of the encirclement of cities by the rural areas. In the final analysis, the whole cause of world revolution hinges on the revolutionary struggles of the Asian, African and Latin American peoples, who make up the overwhelming majority of the world's population. The socialist countries should regard it as their internationalist duty to support the people's revolutionary struggles in Asia, Africa and Latin America. . . .

Ours is the epoch in which world capitalism and imperialism are heading for their doom and communism is marching to victory. Comrade Mao Tse-tung's theory of people's war is not only a product of the Chinese revolution, but has also the characteristic of our epoch. The new experience gained in the people's revolutionary struggles in various countries since World War II has provided continuous evidence that Mao Tse-tung's thought is a common asset of the revolutionary people of the whole world. This is the great international significance of the thought of Mao Tse-tung. . . .

---

states, invaded Czechoslovakia in August of 1968 and crushed the reform movement. Gustav Husák (1913–1991), a committed Stalinist, replaced Dubcek and restored the old order. To justify their action, the Soviets announced the "Brezhnev Doctrine," according to which socialist nations were obliged to cooperate in the spirit of "proletarian internationalism" to restore socialism in any country where its survival was threatened (see the box on p. 1013). The message was undoubtedly not lost on Beijing.

The Second Indochina War

China's radicalism was intensified in the early 1960s by the outbreak of renewed war in Indochina. The Eisenhower administration had opposed the peace settlement at Geneva in 1954, which had divided Vietnam temporarily into two separate regroupment zones, specifically because the provision for future national elections opened up the possibility that the entire country might come under Communist rule. But President Eisenhower

The Brezhnev Doctrine

In the summer of 1968, when the new Communist Party leaders in Czechoslovakia were giving serious considera- tion to proposals for reforming the totalitarian system there, the Warsaw Pact nations met under the leadership of Soviet party chief Leonid Brezhnev to assess the threat to the so- cialist camp. Shortly after, military forces of several Soviet bloc nations entered Czechoslovakia and imposed a new government subservient to Moscow. The move was justified by the spirit of "proletarian internationalism" and was widely viewed as a warning to China and other socialist states not to stray too far from Marxist-Leninist orthodoxy, as interpreted by the Soviet Union.

A Letter to Czechoslovakia

To the Central Committee of the Communist Party of Czechoslovakia
Dear comrades!

On behalf of the Central Committees of the Com- munist and Workers' Parties of Bulgaria, Hungary, the German Democratic Republic, Poland and the Soviet Union, we address ourselves to you with this letter, prompted by a feeling of sincere friendship based on the principles of Marxism-Leninism and proletarian inter- nationalism and by the concern of our common affairs for strengthening the positions of socialism and the se- curity of the socialist community of nations.

The development of events in your country evokes in us deep anxiety. It is our firm conviction that the offensive of the reactionary forces, backed by imperial- ists, against your Party and the foundations of the social system in the Czechoslovak Socialist Republic, threat- ens to push your country off the road of socialism and that consequently it jeopardizes the interests of the en- tire socialist system. . . .

We neither had nor have any intention of inter- fering in such affairs as are strictly the internal business of your Party and your state, nor of violating the princi- ples of respect, independence and equality in the re- lations among the Communist Parties and socialist countries. . . .

At the same time we cannot agree to have hostile forces push your country from the road of socialism and create a threat of severing Czechoslovakia from the so- cialist community. . . . This is the common cause of our countries, which have joined in the Warsaw Treaty to ensure independence, peace and security in Europe, and to set up an insurmountable barrier against the in- trigues of the imperialist forces, against aggression and revenge. . . . We shall never agree to have imperialism, using peaceful or non-peaceful methods, making a gap from the inside or from the outside in the socialist sys- tem, and changing in imperialism's favor the correla- tion of forces in Europe. . . .

That is why we believe that a decisive rebuff of the anti-communist forces, and decisive efforts for the preservation of the socialist system in Czechoslovakia are not only your task but ours as well. . . .

We express the conviction that the Communist Party of Czechoslovakia, conscious of its responsibility, will take the necessary steps to block the path of reac- tion. In this struggle you can count on the solidarity and all-round assistance of the fraternal socialist coun- tries.

Warsaw, July 15, 1968

had been unwilling to introduce U.S. military forces to continue the conflict without the full support of the British and the French, who preferred to seek a negoti- ated settlement. In the end, the United States promised not to break the provisions of the Geneva agreement but refused to commit itself to the results.

In the months after the agreement was concluded, the United States began to provide aid to a new government in South Vietnam. Under the leadership of the anti- Communist politician Ngo Dinh Diem, the South Viet- namese government began to root out dissidents. With the tacit approval of the United States, Diem refused to hold the national elections called for by the Geneva Ac- cords. It was widely anticipated, even in Washington, that the Communists would win such elections. In 1959, Ho Chi Minh, despairing of the peaceful unification of the country under Communist rule, returned to a policy of revolutionary war in the south.

By 1963, South Vietnam was on the verge of collapse. Diem's autocratic methods and inattention to severe eco- nomic inequality had alienated much of the population, and revolutionary forces, popularly known as the Viet

❧ The Sampan Girl ❧

Women played an active role in the insurgent movement in South Vietnam. Some were guerrilla fighters, others were spies, and still others served as transport workers carrying provisions to Viet Cong units in the field. In this poem by the young poet Giang Nam, a young woman transports guerrilla fighters across a river in her sampan. The poem promoted the cause of patriotism, but also reminded readers of their loved ones back home.

Giang Nam, Night Crossing

In the midst of the night, a sampan glides toward us.
Dark bamboos on the bank, swift current . . .
An oar shatters the star-studded firmament.
A bird wanders in the dark and disappears.
Silently the sampan glides between the palms
Whose crests are swept by a searchlight from the outpost.

Loaded rifles, all hands on alert,
We await the moment to dart across the river.

Tucking her black trousers up to her thigh
The boat-girl, smelling of grass and flowers, helps us
Unload our motley bundles.
In the dark, we imagine her red cheeks;
Holding her hand
We breathe her breath, sense her brisk gestures.

Loudly, the water clatters against the sampan.
Heavily loaded, it rolls and leaves the bank so slowly.
"Comrade" asks a voice, "can I help you?"
Shaking her head, she swings the bow.
In the midst of enemy outposts she lives
Keeping for herself the sorrow and joys of her heart.
The sampan emerges from the dark
Challenging the current, the onrushing wave,

Again the oar shatters the sky and the stars.
The other bank is silent, a palm greets us.
Standing still, our boat-girl is watching the guardpost
at the hamlet's entrance.
Her arms still swinging the oar.
Her slender silhouette looms over the river.
One more effort, and we will reach the bank;
A feeling of tender joy flushes our bodies.

A long burst has been fired from the outpost,
Red and white tracers thunder everywhere.
"Be quiet," she says, "don't be afraid,"
And the sampan swiftly
Darts toward the enemy, defying its bullets.
Silhouetted in the sky, what a dashing figure;
"Lie down," she whispers, "let me maneuver,
Don't be worried!" The boat moves ahead;
Emotion packs the night.
Our hearts are pinching; anger fills our eyes.
Bullets rain in the river.
In our hands, our rifles burn with anger.

In safe haven, the sampan is tied to a tree.
Slowly, we shake the girl's hand.
"Thank you," we say. . . . A smile lights
her face; "I belong to the youth corps,
And I only do my duty," she answers.
We press our march across the village.

Still thinking, still hearing
The light tread of her walk.

Valiant image, valiant girl
In future battles come with us.

Cong (Vietnamese Communists), expanded their influence throughout much of the country (see the box above). In the fall of 1963, with the approval of the Kennedy administration, senior military officers overthrew the Diem regime. But factionalism kept the new military leadership from reinvigorating the struggle against the insurgent forces, and the situation in South Vietnam grew worse. By early 1965, the Viet Cong, whose ranks were now swelled by military units infiltrated from North Vietnam, were on the verge of seizing control of the entire country. In March, President Lyndon Johnson decided to send U.S. combat troops to South Vietnam to prevent a total defeat for the anti-Communist government in Saigon.

Chinese leaders must have observed the gradual escalation of the conflict in South Vietnam with mixed feelings. They were undoubtedly pleased to have a firm Communist ally—and indeed one that had in so many ways followed the path of Mao Zedong—just beyond their southern frontier. Yet they could hardly have relished the possibility that renewed bloodshed in South Vietnam could enmesh China in a new conflict with the United States. Nor could they have welcomed the specter of a powerful and ambitious united Vietnam that might wish to extend its influence throughout mainland Southeast Asia, an area that Beijing regarded as its own backyard.

Chinese leaders therefore tiptoed delicately through the minefield of the Indochina conflict, trying to maintain good relations with their ally in Hanoi while avoiding a confrontation with the United States. As the war escalated in 1964 and 1965, they publicly announced that the Chinese people would give their full support to their fraternal comrades seeking national liberation in South Vietnam, but privately they assured Washington that China would not directly enter the conflict unless U.S. forces threatened its southern border. China also refused to cooperate fully with the Soviet Union in shipping Soviet goods to North Vietnam through Chinese territory.

Despite their dismay at the lack of full support from their powerful Chinese ally, the Communist leaders in North Vietnam responded to U.S. escalation by infiltrating more of their own regular force troops into the south, and by 1968 the war had reached a stalemate. The Communists were not strong enough to overthrow the

◆ **War in the Rice Paddies.** In the spring of 1965, Lyndon Johnson ordered U.S. combat troops to South Vietnam in a desperate bid to prevent a Communist victory in that beleaguered country. For the next seven years, American GIs fought against Viet Cong guerrillas and North Vietnamese regular forces until they were finally withdrawn as a result of the Paris Agreement reached in January 1973. Two years later, South Vietnam fell to a Communist offensive.

◆ **A Bridge Across the Cold War Divide.** In January 1972, U.S. President Richard Nixon startled the world by visiting mainland China and beginning the long process of restoring normal relations between the two countries. Despite Nixon's reputation as a devout anti-Communist, the visit was a success, as the two sides agreed to put aside their most bitter differences in an effort to reduce tensions in Asia. Here Nixon and Chinese leader Mao Zedong exchange an historic handshake in Beijing.

government in Saigon, but President Johnson was reluctant to engage in all-out war on North Vietnam for fear of provoking a global nuclear conflict. In the fall, after the Communist-led Tet offensive aroused heightened antiwar protests in the United States, peace negotiations began in Paris.

Richard Nixon (1913–1994) came into the White House in 1969 on a pledge to bring an honorable end to the Vietnam War. With U.S. public opinion sharply divided on the issue, he began to withdraw U.S. troops while continuing to hold peace talks in Paris. But the centerpiece of his strategy was to improve relations with China and thus undercut Chinese support for the North Vietnamese war effort. During the 1960s, relations between Moscow and Beijing had reached a point of extreme tension, and thousands of troops were stationed on both sides of their long common frontier. To intimidate their Communist rivals, Soviet sources hinted that they

might decide to launch a preemptive strike to destroy Chinese nuclear facilities in Xinjiang. Sensing an opportunity to split the onetime allies, Nixon sent his emissary Henry Kissinger on a secret trip to China. Responding to assurances from Washington that the United States was determined to withdraw from Indochina and hoped to improve relations with the mainland regime, Chinese leaders invited President Nixon to visit China in early 1972 (see the box on p. 1017).

Incensed at the apparent betrayal by their close allies, North Vietnamese leaders decided to seek a peaceful settlement of the war in the south. In January 1973, a peace treaty was signed in Paris calling for the removal of all U.S. forces from South Vietnam. In return, the Communists agreed to seek a political settlement of their differences with the Saigon regime. But negotiations between north and south over the political settlement soon broke down, and in early 1975 the Communists resumed the of-

Nixon Plays His China Card

*I*n *February 1972, President Richard Nixon visited mainland China, ending twenty years of U.S. unwillingness to recognize the existence of the Communist regime. In a joint communiqué issued in Shanghai at the close of the visit, the two nations agreed to set aside the question of Taiwan, which could not be resolved, and to seek common ground on other issues. In the communiqué, Nixon agreed that the Taiwan issue had to be resolved by the Chinese people themselves.*

The Shanghai Communiqué

The sides reviewed the long-standing serious disputes between China and the United States.

The Chinese side reaffirmed its position: The Taiwan question is the crucial question obstructing the normalization of relations between China and the United States; the Government of the People's Republic of China is the sole legal government of China; Taiwan is a province of China which has long been returned to the motherland; the liberation of Taiwan is China's internal affair in which no other country had the right to interfere; and all U.S. forces and military installations must be withdrawn from Taiwan. The Chinese government firmly opposes any activities which aim at the creation of "one China, one Taiwan," "one China, two governments," "two Chinas" and "independent Taiwan" or advocate that "the status of Taiwan remains to be determined."

The U.S. side declared: The United States acknowledges that all Chinese on either side of the Taiwan Strait maintain there is but one China and that Taiwan is a part of China. The United States Government does not challenge that position. It reaffirms its interest in a peaceful settlement of the Taiwan question by the Chinese themselves. With this prospect in mind, it affirms the ultimate objective of the withdrawal of all U.S. forces and military installations from Taiwan. In the meantime, it will progressively reduce its forces and military installations on Taiwan as the tension in the area diminishes.

The two sides agreed that it is desirable to broaden the understanding between the two peoples. To this end, they discussed specific areas in such fields as science, technology, culture, sports and journalism, in which people-to-people contacts and exchanges would be mutually beneficial. Each side undertakes to facilitate the further development of such contacts and exchanges.

Both sides view bilateral trade as another area from which mutual benefits can be derived and agree that economic relations based on equality and mutual benefit are in the interest of the peoples of the two countries. They agree to facilitate the progressive development of trade between their two countries.

The two sides agree that they will stay in contact through various channels, including the sending of a senior U.S. representative to Peking from time to time for concrete consultations to further the normalization of relations between the two countries and continue to exchange views on issues of common interest.

---

fensive. At the end of April, under a massive assault by North Vietnamese military forces, the South Vietnamese government surrendered. A year later, the country was unified under Communist rule.

During the next decade, Sino-American relations continued to improve. In 1979, the two countries established diplomatic ties after the United States renounced its mutual security treaty with the Republic of China in return for a pledge from China to seek reunification by peaceful means. By the end of the 1970s, China and the United States had forged a "strategic relationship" by which each would cooperate with the other against the common threat of Soviet "hegemonism" (as China described Soviet policy) in Asia.

An Era of Equivalence

The Johnson administration had sent U.S. combat troops to South Vietnam in 1965 in an effort to prevent the expansion of communism in Southeast Asia. The administration's primary concern, however, was China, not the Soviet Union. By the mid-1960s, U.S. officials viewed the Soviet Union as an essentially conservative power, more concerned with protecting its vast empire than with expanding its borders. In fact, U.S. policymakers periodically sought Soviet assistance in bringing about a peaceful settlement of the Vietnam War. So long as Khrushchev was in power, they found a receptive ear in Moscow. Khrushchev was firmly dedicated to promoting peaceful coexistence (at least on his terms) and sternly advised the North Vietnamese against a resumption of revolutionary war in South Vietnam.

After October 1964, when Khrushchev was replaced by a new leadership headed by party chief Leonid Brezhnev (1906–1982) and Prime Minister Alexei Kosygin (1904–1980), Soviet attitudes about Vietnam became more ambivalent. The new Soviet leaders had no desire to see the Vietnam conflict poison relations between the great powers. On the other hand, Moscow was anxious to demonstrate its support for the North Vietnamese and their struggle for reunification with the south in order to deflect Chinese charges that the Soviet Union had betrayed the interests of the oppressed peoples of the world. As a result, Soviet officials publicly voiced sympathy for the U.S. predicament in Vietnam, but put no pressure on their allies to bring an end to the war. Indeed, the Soviet Union became Hanoi's main supplier of advanced military equipment in the final years of the war.

Still, under Brezhnev and Kosygin the Soviet Union continued to pursue the Khrushchev line of peaceful coexistence with the West and adopted a generally cautious posture in foreign affairs. By the early 1970s, a new age in Soviet-American relations had emerged. Called détente, it was characterized by a reduction of tensions between the Soviet Union and the United States. One appropriate symbol of the new relationship was the Antiballistic Missile (ABM) Treaty, often called SALT I (for the Strategic Arms Limitation Talks), signed in 1972. Despite some lessening of tensions after the Cuban Missile Crisis, both superpowers had continued to expand their nuclear arsenals, while seeking to enhance the destructive power of their missiles by arming them with multiple warheads. By 1970, the United States had developed the capacity to arm its intercontinental ballistic missiles (ICBMs) with "multiple independently targeted re-entry vehicles" (MIRVs) that enabled one missile to hit ten different targets. The Soviet Union soon followed suit. Between 1968 and 1972, both sides had also developed antiballistic missiles whose purpose was to hit and destroy incoming missiles. In the 1972 SALT I treaty, the two nations agreed to limit their antiballistic missile systems.

Washington's objective in pursuing such a treaty was to make a nuclear exchange so unprofitable that neither superpower could believe that it could win by launching a preemptive strike against the other. U.S. officials believed that a policy of "equivalence," according to which there was a roughly equal power balance on each side of the Cold War, was the best way to avoid a nuclear confrontation. Détente was pursued in other ways as well.

When President Nixon took office in 1969, he sought to increase trade and cultural contacts with the Soviet Union. His purpose was to set up a series of "linkages" in U.S.-Soviet relations that would persuade Moscow of the economic and social benefits of maintaining good relations with the West.

A symbol of that new relationship was the Helsinki Agreement of 1975. Signed by the United States, Canada, and all European nations on both sides of the Iron Curtain, these accords recognized all borders in central and eastern Europe that had been established since the end of World War II, thereby formally acknowledging for the first time the Soviet sphere of influence in Eastern Europe. The Helsinki Agreement also committed the signatory powers to recognize and protect the human rights of their citizens, a clear effort by the Western states to improve the performance of the Soviet Union and its allies in that arena.

An End to Détente?

Protection of human rights became one of the major foreign policy goals of the next U.S. president, Jimmy Carter (b. 1924). Ironically, just at the point when U.S. involvement in Vietnam came to an end and relations with China had begun to improve, U.S.-Soviet relations began to sour. During the 1976 presidential campaign, the Republican nominee Gerald Ford (b. 1913), who had become president after Nixon resigned under pressure in August 1974, refused to categorize the relationship with the Soviet Union under the label of détente.

A variety of factors were involved. For one thing, some Americans had become increasingly concerned about aggressive new tendencies in Soviet foreign policy. The first indication came in Africa. Soviet influence was on the rise in Somalia, in South Yemen across the Red Sea, and later in Ethiopia. Soviet involvement was also on the increase in southern Africa, where an insurgent movement supported by Cuban troops came to power in Angola, once a colony of Portugal. Then, in 1979 Soviet troops were sent to neighboring Afghanistan to protect a newly installed Marxist regime that faced rising internal resistance from fundamentalist Muslims. The latter had been provoked by the Marxist government's effort to abolish traditional Islamic customs.

Some observers suspected that the Soviet advance into hitherto neutral Afghanistan was timed to take advantage of the revolution led by traditionalist Muslim forces loyal to the Ayatollah Khomeini in Iran (see Chapter 30) and that its ultimate objective was to extend Soviet power into the oil fields of the Persian Gulf. To deter such a possibility, the White House promulgated the Carter Doctrine, which stated that, if necessary, the United States would use its military power to safeguard Western access to the oil reserves in the Middle East. In fact, sources in Moscow later disclosed that the Soviet advance into Afghanistan had little to do with a strategic drive toward the Persian Gulf; rather, it represented an effort to take advantage of the recent disarray in U.S. foreign policy in the aftermath of the defeat in Vietnam to expand Soviet influence in a sensitive region increasingly beset with Islamic fervor. Soviet officials feared that the wave of Islamic activism could spread to the Muslim populations in the Soviet republics in Central Asia and were confident that the United States was too distracted by the "Vietnam syndrome" (meaning the public fear of U.S. involvement in another Vietnam-type conflict) to respond.

Other factors also contributed to the growing suspicion of the Soviet Union in the United States. During the era of détente, Washington officials, believing that each side possessed sufficient strength to destroy the other in the event of a surprise attack, had assumed that Moscow accepted the U.S. doctrine of equivalence. By the end of the decade, however, some U.S. defense analysts began to charge that the Soviet Union was seeking strategic superiority in nuclear weapons and therefore argued for a substantial increase in U.S. defense spending. Such charges, combined with evidence of Soviet efforts in Africa and the Middle East and reports of the persecution of Jews and dissidents in the Soviet Union, helped to sour public support for détente in the United States. Such attitudes were reflected in the failure of the Carter administration to obtain congressional approval of the SALT II agreement, signed with the Soviet Union in 1979.

Countering the "Evil Empire"

The early years of the administration of President Ronald Reagan (b. 1911) witnessed a return to the harsh rhetoric, if not all of the harsh practices, of the Cold War. Reagan's anti-Communist credentials were well known. In a speech given shortly after his election, he referred to the Soviet Union as an "evil empire" and frequently voiced his suspicion of its motives in foreign affairs. In an effort to eliminate perceived Soviet advantages in strategic weaponry, the White House began a military buildup that stimulated a renewed arms race. In 1982, the Reagan administration introduced the nuclear-tipped cruise missile, whose ability to fly at low altitudes made it difficult to detect by enemy radar. Reagan also became an ardent

◆ **Reagan and Gorbachev.** The willingness of Mikhail Gorbachev and Ronald Reagan to dampen the arms race was a significant factor in ending the Cold War confrontation between the United States and the Soviet Union. Reagan and Gorbachev are shown here standing before St. Basil's Cathedral during Reagan's visit to Moscow in 1988.

exponent of the Strategic Defense Initiative (SDI), nicknamed "Star Wars," whose purpose was to create a space shield that could destroy incoming missiles. By pushing for SDI, the administration also hoped to force Moscow into an arms race that it could not hope to win.

The Reagan administration also adopted a more activist, if not confrontational, stance in the Third World. The fruit of that attitude was most directly demonstrated in Central America, where the consolidation of power in Nicaragua by the revolutionary Sandinista regime (the Sandinistas had come to power with the overthrow of the Somoza dictatorship in 1979) aroused concern in

⋟ From Cold War to Peace: The Challenge of the New Order ⋞

In May 1992, Mikhail Gorbachev gave an address at Westminster College in Fulton, Missouri, the same location where Winston Churchill had announced the opening of the Cold War nearly half a century before. With the Cold War at an end, Gorbachev spoke of the possibilities of a new era, but he warned of the multiple dangers that threatened the peace, including the rising force of nationalism and the growing gap between rich and poor countries. As the century nears an end, his words appear prophetic.

Gorbachev's Speech in Fulton, Missouri, 1992

More than 46 years ago, Winston Churchill spoke in Fulton, and in my country this speech was singled out as the formal declaration of the cold war. This was, indeed, the first time the words Iron Curtain were pronounced, and the whole Western world was challenged to close ranks against the threat of tyranny in the form of the Soviet Union and Communist expansion. . . .

Since that time, the world in which we live has undergone tremendous changes. Even so . . . , however paradoxical it may sound, there is a certain similarity between the situation then and today. Then, the prewar structure of international relations had virtually collapsed, and new pattern [sic] of forces had emerged, along with a new set of interests and claims. Different trends in world development could be discerned, but their prospects were not clearly outlined. New possibilities for progress had appeared. Answers had to be found to the challenges posed by new subjects of international law. . . .

The U.S.S.R. and the U.S. missed that chance, the chance to establish their relationship on a basis of principle, and thereby to initiate a world order different from that which existed before the war. . . . It would be a supreme tragedy if the world, having overcome the 1946 model, were to find itself once again in a 1914 model. A major international effort will be needed to render irreversible the shift in favor of a democratic world, one which is democratic for the whole of humanity, not just for half of it. . . .

The very fact that the two world blocs are no longer in confrontation and that the collapse of totalitarian regimes has released centrifugal forces which had been temporarily frozen—territorial and intergovernmental contradictions and claims—has encouraged an exaggerated nationalism, and that has already led to much bloodshed.

The ending of the global confrontation of the nuclear superpowers . . . has rendered even more visible today's major contradictions between the rich and the poor countries, between the North and the South. . . . Thus we live today in a watershed era. One epoch has ended and a second is commencing. No one yet knows how concrete it will be—no one. Having long been orthodox Marxists, we were sure that we knew. But life once again has refuted those who claim to be know-it-alls and messiahs.

the White House about the further spread of international communism in the Western Hemisphere. Charging that the Sandinista regime was supporting a guerrilla insurgency movement in nearby El Salvador, the Reagan administration began to provide material aid to the government in El Salvador, while simultaneously applying pressure on the Sandinistas by giving support to an anti-Communist guerrilla movement (called the Contras) in Nicaragua. The administration's Central American policy aroused considerable controversy in Congress, as some charged that growing U.S. involvement there could lead to a repeat of the nation's bitter experience in Vietnam.

The Reagan administration also took the offensive in other areas. By providing military support to the anti-Soviet insurgents in Afghanistan, the White House helped to maintain a Vietnam-like war in Afghanistan that entangled the Soviet Union in its own quagmire. Like the Vietnam War, the conflict in Afghanistan resulted in heavy casualties and demonstrated that the might of a superpower was actually limited in the face of strong nationalist, guerrilla-type opposition.

The End of the Cold War

The accession of Mikhail Gorbachev (b. 1931) to power in the Soviet Union in 1985 eventually brought a dramatic end to the Cold War. Gorbachev was willing to rethink many of the fundamental assumptions underlying Soviet foreign policy, and his "New Thinking," as it was called, opened the door to a series of stunning changes. For one, Gorbachev initiated a plan for arms limitation that led in 1987 to an agreement with the United States to eliminate intermediate-range nuclear weapons (the INF Treaty). Both sides had incentives to dampen the expensive arms race. Gorbachev hoped to make extensive economic and internal reforms while the United States had serious deficit problems. During the Reagan years, the United States had moved from being a creditor nation to the world's biggest debtor nation. By 1990, both countries were becoming aware that their large military budgets were making it difficult for them to solve their serious social problems.

During 1989 and 1990, much of the Cold War's reason for being disappeared as a mostly peaceful revolutionary upheaval swept through Eastern Europe (see the box on p. 1020). Gorbachev's policy of allowing greater autonomy for the Communist regimes of Eastern Europe meant that the Soviet Union would no longer militarily support Communist governments that were faced with internal revolt. The unwillingness of the Soviet regime to use force to maintain the status quo, as it had in Hungary in 1956 and in Czechoslovakia in 1968, opened the door to the overthrow of the Communist regimes. The reunification of Germany on October 3, 1990, also destroyed one of the most prominent symbols of the Cold War era. The disintegration of the Soviet Union at the end of 1991 made impossible any renewal of the global rivalry between two competing superpowers. Although the United States emerged as the world's leading military power by

1992, its role in the creation of the "New World Order" that President George Bush (b. 1924) advocated at the time of the Persian Gulf War (see Chapter 30) is not yet clear.

During the first administration of President Bill Clinton (b. 1946), the United States sought to involve Russia as well as its NATO allies in resolving the numerous brushfire conflicts that have arisen in various parts of the world since the end of the Cold War (see Chapters 30 and 31). As yet, however, the framework for achieving a stable world in the aftermath of the long postwar ideological conflict remains fragile.

The Shifting Power Balance in Asia

The end of the Cold War had less impact in Asia, where relations among the major countries in the area had been essentially delinked from ideological concerns as a result of the improvement in U.S.-Chinese relations after Nixon's visit to Beijing. Still, the situation in the Pacific region was in flux. During the 1980s, China began to emerge as an independent power less closely tied to the United States. Chinese relations with the Soviet Union gradually improved, while relations with the United States were impeded by a variety of issues, including continuing U.S. military aid to Taiwan, Chinese arms sales to Middle Eastern countries, and the Chinese government's suppression of human rights after the Tiananmen Square demonstrations in 1989. Today, China conducts an independent foreign policy and is playing an increas-

◆ **And the Wall Came Tumbling Down.** The Berlin Wall, long a symbol of Europe's Cold War divisions, became the site of massive celebrations after the East German government opened its border with the West. The activities included spontaneous acts of demolition as Germans used sledgehammers and crowbars to tear down parts of the wall.

ingly active role in the region. To some of its neighbors, including Japan, India, and post-Soviet Russia, China's new posture is cause for disquiet and gives rise to suspicions that it is once again preparing to assert its muscle as in the imperial era. A striking example of this new attitude took place as early as 1979, when Chinese forces briefly invaded Vietnam as punishment for the Vietnamese occupation of neighboring Cambodia (see Chapter 31). In the 1990s, China has aroused concern in the region by claiming sole ownership over the Spratly Islands in the South China Sea and over Diaoyu Island (also claimed by Japan) near Taiwan.

To Chinese leaders, however, such actions simply represent legitimate efforts to resume China's rightful role in the affairs of the region. After a century of humiliation at the hands of the Western powers and neighboring Japan, the nation, in Mao's famous words in 1949, "has stood up" and no one will be permitted to humiliate it again. For the moment, at least, China appears to be experiencing a rise in fervent patriotism, a phenomenon that is actively promoted by the party as a means of holding the country together in uncertain times. Pride in the achievement of national sports teams is intense, and two young authors recently won wide acclaim for a book entitled *The China That Can Say No*, an obvious response to recent criticism of the country in the United States and Europe.

Conclusion

At the end of World War II, a new conflict erupted in the Western world as the new superpowers, the United States and the Soviet Union, competed for political domina-

tion. Soon, this ideological division spread to the rest of the world as the United States fought in Korea and Vietnam to prevent the spread of communism, promoted by the new Maoist government in China, while the Soviet Union used its armies to prop up pro-Soviet regimes in Eastern Europe.

By the end of the 1980s and the beginning of the 1990s, profound changes in the Soviet Union and China brought an end to the Cold War. Although the power of the Soviet Union seemed secure and its control of its Eastern European satellites appeared certain, forces of disintegration had clearly been at work for some time in the Soviet bloc. Peoples in Eastern Europe had always viewed communism as an alien system imposed on them by wartime circumstances. Within the Soviet Union itself, failure to deal with a growing number of economic and structural problems only led to further decay of the system. The rapid collapse of Communist governments in Eastern Europe was clearly due to Gorbachev's reversal of Soviet postwar policy as he decided not to interfere in the internal turmoil of the Soviet satellites. Quite unexpectedly, the forces of change that enabled Communist regimes in Eastern Europe to give way to popular demands for political reforms and restructuring also spread to the Soviet Union and brought its demise as well. Although China remained in Communist hands, its leaders adopted policies in foreign affairs that reflected their national interests, rather than their ideological orientation. The stage was now set for cooperative efforts within the United Nations or other multinational organizations to attack the common problems that afflicted all the peoples of the world, including environmental pollution, overpopulation, climatic changes, and widespread hunger.

CHAPTER NOTES

1. *Department of State Bulletin* 12 (February 11, 1945), pp. 213–16.
2. Quoted in Joseph M. Jones, *The Fifteen Weeks (February 21–June 5, 1947)*, 2d ed. (New York, 1964), pp. 140–41.
3. Quoted in Walter Laqueur, *Europe in Our Time* (New York, 1992), p. 111.
4. Quoted in Wilfried Loth, *The Division of the World, 1941–1955* (New York, 1988), pp. 160–61.
5. Quoted in Peter Lane, *Europe since 1945: An Introduction* (Totowa, N.J.; 1985), p. 248.
6. Quoted in Robert F. Kennedy, *Thirteen Days: A Memoir of the Cuban Missile Crisis* (New York, 1969), pp. 89–90.

SUGGESTED READINGS

There is a detailed literature on the Cold War. Two general accounts are R. B. Levering, *The Cold War, 1945–1972* (Arlington Heights, Ill., 1982) and B. A. Weisberger, *Cold War, Cold Peace: The United States and Russia since 1945* (New York, 1984). There is a brief survey of the early Cold War in M. Dockrill, *The Cold War, 1945–1963* (Atlantic Highlands, N.J., 1988). The following works maintain that the Soviet Union was chiefly responsible for the Cold War: H. Feis, *From Trust to Terror: The Onset of the Cold War, 1945–1950* (New York, 1970) and A. Ulam, *The Rivals: America and Russia since World War II* (New York, 1971). Revisionist studies on the Cold War have emphasized the responsibility of the United States for the Cold War, especially its global aspects. These works include J. and G. Kolko, *The Limits of Power: The World and United States Foreign Policy, 1945–1954* (New York, 1972); W. LaFeber, *America, Russia and the Cold War, 1945–1966*, 2d ed. (New York, 1972); and M. Sherwin, *A World Destroyed: The Atomic Bomb and the Grand Alliance* (New York, 1975). For a critique of the revisionist studies, see R. L. Maddox, *The New Left and the Origins of the Cold War* (Princeton, N.J., 1973). R. Garthoff, *Détente and Confrontation: American-Soviet Relations from Nixon to Reagan* (Washington, D.C., 1985) provides a detailed analysis of U.S.-Soviet relations in the 1970s and 1980s. See also F. Halliday, *The Making of the Second Cold War*, 2d ed. (New York, 1986).

There have been a number of recent studies of the early stages of the Cold War based on newly released documents. See, for example, O. A. Westad, *Cold War and Revolution: Soviet-American Rivalry and the Origins of the Chinese Civil War* (New York, 1993); D. A. Mayers, *Cracking the Monolith: U.S. Policy against the Sino-Soviet Alliance, 1949–1955* (Baton Rouge, 1986); and S. Gon-

charov, J. W. Lewis, and Xue Litai, *Uncertain Partners: Stalin, Mao, and the Korean War* (Stanford, Calif., 1993). The latter provides a fascinating view of the war from several perspectives.

On the end of the Cold War, see B. Denitch, *The End of the Cold War* (Minneapolis, Minn., 1990); W. G. Hyland, *The Cold War Is Over* (New York, 1990); and W. Laqueur, *Soviet Union 2000: Reform or Revolution?* (New York, 1990). For important studies of Soviet foreign policy, see A. B. Ulam, *Expansion and Coexistence: Soviet Foreign Policy, 1917–1973*, 2d ed (New York, 1974) and *Dangerous Relations: The Soviet Union in World Politics, 1970–1982* (New York, 1983). The effects of the Cold War on Germany are examined in J. H. Backer, *The Decision to Divide Germany: American Foreign Policy in Transition* (Durham, N.C., 1978). On atomic diplomacy in the Cold War, see G. F. Herken, *The Winning Weapon: The Atomic Bomb in the Cold War, 1945–1950* (New York, 1981). For a good introduction to the arms race, see E. M. Bottome, *The Balance of Terror: A Guide to the Arms Race*, rev. ed. (Boston, 1986).

There are several surveys of Chinese foreign policy since the Communist rise to power. For the revolutionary period, see P. Van Ness, *Revolution and Chinese Foreign Policy* (Berkeley, Calif., 1971) and J. Gittings, *The World and China* (New York, 1974). For more recent developments, see R. G. Sutter, *Chinese Foreign Policy: Developments after Mao* (New York, 1986) and H. Harding, *Chinese Foreign Policy during the 1980s* (New Haven, Conn., 1984). On Sino-U.S. relations, see H. Harding, *A Fragile Relationship: The United States and China since 1972* (Washington, D.C., 1992). On Chinese policy in Korea, see the classic by A. S. Whiting, *China Crosses the Yalu* (Stanford, Calif., 1960).

CHAPTER

28

Brave New World: Communism

According to Karl Marx, capitalism is a system that involves the exploitation of man by man. Under socialism, it is the other way around. That wry joke, an ironic twist on the familiar Marxist remark a century earlier, was typical of popular humor in post-World War II Moscow, where the dreams of a future Communist utopia had faded in the grim reality of life in the Soviet Union.

Grim though life in the Soviet Union might be, the Communist monopoly on power seemed secure, as did the Soviet Union's hold over its client states in Eastern Europe. And yet, within the brief period between 1989 and 1991, the Communist regimes in Eastern Europe were toppled, and the long-standing division of postwar Europe came to an end. Even the Soviet Union ceased to exist as a single nation, as Russia and other former Soviet republics declared their separate independence. Although the Communist Party survived the demise of the Soviet Union and even showed signs of new vigor in the Russian elections of 1996, its monopoly is gone, and it is only one of many parties competing for power.

The fate of communism in China has been quite different. Despite some turbulence, communism has survived in China, even as that nation takes giant strides toward becoming an economic superpower. Yet as China's aging leaders struggle to prepare for the twenty-first century, many of the essential principles of Marxist-Leninist dogma have been tacitly abandoned, and cynicism among the nation's youth is widespread. It remains an open question whether

Death of Stalin and emergence of Khrushchev

Era of Brezhnev

Dissolution of the Soviet Union

The Gorbachev years

Communist governments established in Eastern Europe

"Prague Spring"

Revolutions in Eastern Europe

Dissolution and civil war in Yugoslavia

Creation of People's Republic of China

Death of Mao Zedong

Period of New Democracy

Rise to power of Deng Xiaoping

Tiananmen Square incident

Great Leap Forward

Great Proletarian Cultural Revolution

Era of "Four Modernizations"

communism will continue to provide a usable framework for the challenges that lie ahead.

The Soviet Union and Its Eastern European Satellites, 1945–1970

World War II had left the Soviet Union as one of the world's two superpowers and its leader, Joseph Stalin, at the height of his power. As a result of the war, Stalin and his Soviet colleagues were now in control of a vast empire that included Eastern Europe, much of the Balkans, and new territory gained from Japan in the Far East.

From Stalin to Khrushchev

World War II devastated the Soviet Union. Twenty million citizens had lost their lives while cities like Kiev, Kharkov, and Leningrad had suffered enormous physical destruction. As the lands that had been occupied by the German forces were liberated, the Soviet government turned its attention to the restoration of their economic structures. Nevertheless, in 1945, agricultural production was only 60 percent and steel output only 50 percent of prewar levels. The Soviet people faced incredibly difficult conditions: they worked longer hours than before the war, they ate less, and they were ill-housed and poorly clothed.

In the immediate postwar years, the Soviet Union removed goods and materials from occupied Germany and extorted valuable raw materials from its satellite states in Eastern Europe. More importantly, however, to create a new industrial base, Stalin returned to the method that he had used in the 1930s—the acquisition of development capital from Soviet labor. Working hard for little pay and for precious few consumer goods, Soviet laborers were expected to produce goods for export with little in return for themselves. The incoming capital from abroad could then be used to purchase machinery and Western technology. The loss of millions of men in the war meant that much of this tremendous workload fell upon Soviet women, who performed almost 40 percent of the heavy manual labor.

Economic recovery in the Soviet Union was nothing less than spectacular. By 1947, Russian industrial production had attained 1939 levels; three years later, it had surpassed those levels by 40 percent. New power plants, canals, and giant factories were built while new industrial enterprises and oil fields were established in Siberia and Soviet Central Asia. Stalin's new five-year plan, announced in 1946, reached its goals in less than five years.

Although Stalin's economic recovery policy was successful in promoting growth in heavy industry, primarily for the benefit of the military, consumer goods remained scarce. While the development of thermonuclear weapons, MiG fighters, and the first space satellite (*Sputnik*) in the 1950s elevated the Soviet state's reputation as a world power abroad, domestically the Soviet people were shortchanged. Heavy industry grew at a rate three times that of personal consumption. Moreover, the housing shortage was acute. A British military attaché in Moscow reported that "all houses, practically without exception, show lights from every window after dark. This seems to indicate that every room is both a living room by day and a bedroom by night. There is no place in overcrowded Moscow for the luxury of eating and sleeping in separate rooms."[1]

When World War II ended in 1945, Stalin had been in power for more than fifteen years. During that time, he had removed all opposition to his rule and remained the undisputed master of the Soviet Union. Other leading members of the Communist Party were completely obedient to his will. Increasingly distrustful of competitors, Stalin exercised sole authority and pitted his subordinates against one another. One of these subordinates, Lavrenti Beria, head of the secret police, controlled a force of several hundred thousand agents.

Stalin's morbid suspicions added to the constantly increasing repression of the regime. In 1946, government decrees subordinated all forms of literary and scientific expression to the political needs of the state. Along with the anti-intellectual campaign came political terror. By the late 1940s, there were an estimated nine million people in Siberian concentration camps. Stalin's distrust of potential threats to his power even extended to some of his closest colleagues. In 1948, Andrey Zhdanov (1896–1948), his presumed successor and head of the Leningrad party organization, died under mysterious circumstances, but presumably at Stalin's order. Within weeks, the Leningrad party organization was purged of several top leaders, many of whom were charged with traitorous connections with Western intelligence agencies. In succeeding years, Stalin directed his suspicion at other members of the inner circle, including Foreign Minister Vyacheslav Molotov (1890–1986). Known as "old stone butt" in the West for his stubborn defense of Soviet security interests, Molotov had been a loyal lieutenant since the early years of Stalin's rise to power. Now Stalin distrusted Molotov and had his Jewish wife sent to a Siberian concentration camp.

Stalin died in 1953, and after some bitter infighting within the party leadership, he was succeeded by Georgy Malenkov, a veteran administrator and ambitious member of the Politburo. Malenkov came to power with a clear agenda. In foreign affairs, he hoped to promote a decline in Cold War tensions and improve relations with the Western powers (see Chapter 27). To Moscow's Eastern European allies, he advocated a "new course" in mutual relations and a decline in Stalinist methods of rule. Inside the Soviet Union, he hoped to reduce defense expenditures and make improving the standard of living a higher priority for government spending. Such goals were laudable and probably had the support of the majority of the Russian people, but they were not necessarily appealing to key pressure groups within the Soviet Union—the army, the party, the managerial elite, and the security services (known as the Committee of Government Security, or KGB). In 1953, Malenkov was removed from his position of prime minister, and power shifted to his rival—the new party general secretary, Nikita Khrushchev (1894–1971).

During his struggle for power with Malenkov, Khrushchev had outmaneuvered the latter by calling for heightened defense expenditures and a continuing emphasis on heavy industry. Once in power, however, Khrushchev showed the political dexterity displayed by many a U.S. politician and reversed his priorities. He now resumed the efforts of his predecessor to reduce tensions with the West and improve the standard of living of the Russian people. He moved vigorously to improve the performance of the Soviet economy and revitalize Soviet society. By nature, Khrushchev was a man of enormous energy as well as an innovator. In an attempt to release the stranglehold of the central bureaucracy over the national economy, he abolished dozens of government ministries and split up the party and government apparatus. Khrushchev also attempted to rejuvenate the stagnant agricultural sector, long the Achilles heel of the Soviet economy. He attempted to spur production by increasing profit incentives and opened "virgin lands" in Soviet Kazakhstan to bring thousands of acres of new land under cultivation.

Like any innovator, Khrushchev had to overcome the inherently conservative instincts of not only the Soviet bureaucracy but also the mass of the Soviet population. His plan to remove the "dead hand" of the state, however laudable in intent, alienated much of the Soviet official class, while his effort to split the party angered those who saw it as the central force in the Soviet system. Khrushchev's agricultural schemes aroused equal opposition. Although the Kazakhstan wheat lands would eventually demonstrate their importance in the overall agricultural picture, progress was slow, while his effort to persuade the Russian people to eat more corn (an idea he had apparently picked up during a visit to the United States) led to the mocking nickname of "Cornman." Disappointing agricultural production, combined with high military spending, hurt the Soviet economy. The industrial growth rate, which had soared in the early 1950s, now declined dramatically from 13 percent in 1953 to 7.5 percent in 1964.

Khrushchev was probably best known for his policy of de-Stalinization. Khrushchev had risen in the party hierarchy as a Stalin protégé, but he had been deeply disturbed by his mentor's excesses and, once in a position of authority, moved to excise the Stalinist legacy from Soviet society. The campaign began at the Twentieth

Khrushchev Denounces Stalin

Three years after Stalin's death, the new Soviet premier, Nikita Khrushchev, addressed the Twentieth Congress of the Communist Party and denounced the former Soviet dictator for his crimes. This denunciation was the beginning of a policy of de-Stalinization.

Khrushchev Addresses the Twentieth Party Congress, February 1956

Comrades, . . . quite a lot has been said about the cult of the individual and about its harmful consequences. . . . The cult of the person of Stalin . . . became at a certain specific stage the source of a whole series of exceedingly serious and grave perversions of Party principles, of Party democracy, of revolutionary legality.

Stalin absolutely did not tolerate collegiality in leadership and in work and . . . practiced brutal violence, not only toward everything which opposed him, but also toward that which seemed to his capricious and despotic character, contrary to his concepts.

Stalin abandoned the method of ideological struggle for that of administrative violence, mass repressions and terror. . . . Arbitrary behavior by one person encouraged and permitted arbitrariness in others. Mass arrests and deportations of many thousands of people, execution without trial and without normal investigation created conditions of insecurity, fear and even desperation.

Stalin showed in a whole series of cases his intolerance, his brutality and his abuse of power. . . . He often chose the path of repression and annihilation, not only against actual enemies, but also against individuals who had not committed any crimes against the Party and the Soviet government. . . .

Many Party, Soviet and economic activists who were branded in 1937–8 as "enemies" were actually never enemies, spies, wreckers and so on, but were always honest communists; they were only so stigmatized, and often, no longer able to bear barbaric tortures, they charged themselves (at the order of the investigative judges-falsifiers) with all kinds of grave and unlikely crimes.

This was the result of the abuse of power by Stalin, who began to use mass terror against the Party cadres. . . . Stalin put the Party and the NKVD up to the use of mass terror when the exploiting classes had been liquidated in our country and when there were no serious reasons for the use of extraordinary mass terror. The terror was directed . . . against the honest workers of the Party and the Soviet state. . . .

Stalin was a very distrustful man, sickly suspicious. . . . Everywhere and in everything he saw "enemies," "two-facers" and "spies." Possessing unlimited power, he indulged in great willfulness and choked a person morally and physically. A situation was created where one could not express one's own will. When Stalin said that one or another would be arrested, it was necessary to accept on faith that he was an "enemy of the people." What proofs were offered? The confession of the arrested. . . . How is it possible that a person confesses to crimes that he had not committed? Only in one way—because of application of physical methods of pressuring him, tortures, bringing him to a state of unconsciousness, deprivation of his judgment, taking away of his human dignity.

National Congress of the Communist Party in February 1956, when Khrushchev gave a long secret speech criticizing some of Stalin's major shortcomings (see the box above). The speech had apparently not been intended for public distribution, but it was quickly leaked to the Western press and created a sensation throughout the world. During the next few years, Khrushchev encouraged more freedom of expression for writers, artists, and composers, arguing that "readers should be given the chance to make their own judgments" regarding the acceptability of controversial literature, and that "police measures shouldn't be used."[2]

At Khrushchev's instructions, thousands of prisoners were released from concentration camps. In 1962, he allowed the publication of Alexander Solzhenitsyn's *One Day in the Life of Ivan Denisovich*, a grim portrayal of the horrors of Russia's forced-labor camps (see the box on p. 1028).

Khrushchev's personality, however, did not endear him to the higher Soviet officials who frowned at his tendency to crack jokes and play the clown. Nor were the higher members of the party bureaucracy pleased when Khrushchev tried to curb their privileges. Foreign policy failures caused additional damage to Khrushchev's

≽ One Day in the Life of Ivan Denisovich ≼

On November 20, 1962, a Soviet magazine published a work by Alexander Solzhenitsyn that created a literary and political furor. The short novel related one day in the life of its chief character, Ivan Denisovich, at a Siberian concentration camp, to which he had been sentenced at the end of World War II for supposedly spying for the Germans while a Soviet soldier. This excerpt narrates the daily journey from the prison camp to a work project through the 17 degrees-below-zero cold of Siberia. Many Soviets identified with Ivan as a symbol of the suffering they had endured under Stalin.

Alexander Solzhenitsyn, One Day in the Life of Ivan Denisovich

There were escort guards all over the place. They flung a semicircle around the column on its way to the power station, their machine guns sticking out and pointing right at your face. And there were guards with gray dogs. One dog bared its fangs as if laughing at the prisoners. The escorts all wore short sheepskins, except for half a dozen whose coats trailed the ground. The long sheepskins were interchangeable: they were worn by anyone whose turn had come to man the watchtowers.

And once again as they brought the squads together the escort recounted the entire power-station column by fives. . . .

Out beyond the camp boundary the intense cold, accompanied by a headwind, stung even Shukhov's face, which was used to every kind of unpleasantness. Realizing that he would have the wind in his face all the way to the power station, he decided to make use of his bit of rag. To meet the contingency of a headwind he, like many other prisoners, had got himself a cloth with a long tape on each end. The prisoners admitted that these helped a bit. Shukhov covered his face up to the eyes, brought the tapes around below his ears, and fastened the ends together at the back of his neck. Then he covered his nape with the flap of his hat and raised his coat collar. The next thing was to pull the front flap of the hat down into his brow. Thus in front only his eyes remained unprotected. He fixed his coat tightly at the waist with the rope. Now everything was in order except for his hands, which were already stiff with cold (his mittens were worthless). He rubbed them, he clapped them together, for he knew that in a moment he'd have to put them behind his back and keep them there for the entire march.

The chief of the escort guard recited the "morning prayer," which every prisoner was heartily sick of:

"Attention, prisoners. Marching orders must be strictly obeyed. Keep to your ranks. No hurrying, keep a steady pace. No talking. Keep your eyes fixed ahead and your hands behind your backs. A step to right or left is considered an attempt to escape and the escort has orders to shoot without warning. Leading guards, on the double."

The two guards in the lead of the escort must have set out along the road. The column heaved forward, shoulders swaying, and the escorts, some twenty paces to the right and left of the column, each man at a distance of ten paces from the next, machine guns held at the ready, set off too.

reputation among his colleagues. His plan to place missiles in Cuba was the final straw (see Chapter 27). While he was away on vacation in 1964, a special meeting of the Soviet Politburo voted him out of office (because of "deteriorating health") and forced him into retirement. Although a group of leaders succeeded him, real power came into the hands of Leonid Brezhnev (1906–1982), the "trusted" supporter of Khrushchev who had engineered his downfall.

The Brezhnev Years (1964–1982)

The overthrow of Nikita Khrushchev in October 1964 vividly demonstrated the challenges that would be encountered by any Soviet leader sufficiently bold to try to reform the Soviet system. In democratic countries, pressure on the executive and the legislative branches comes from various sources within society at large—from the business community and the labor unions, from innumerable pressure groups created to represent the particular needs of interest groups in society, and of course from the general public as well. In the Soviet Union, pressure on government and party leaders originated from sources essentially operating inside the system—from the government bureaucracy, the party apparatus, the KGB, and the armed forces.

Leonid Brezhnev, the new party chief, was undoubtedly aware of these realities of Soviet politics, and his long tenure in power was marked, above all, by the desire to avoid changes that might provoke instability, either at home or abroad. Brezhnev was himself a product of the Soviet system. He had entered the ranks of the party leadership under Joseph Stalin, and although he was not a particularly avid believer in party ideology (indeed, while he was in power, there were innumerable stories about his addiction to "bourgeois pleasures" like expensive country houses in the elite Moscow suburb of Zhukovka and fast cars, many of them gifts from foreign leaders), he was no partisan of reform.

Instead, Brezhnev's domestic goal was stability. He and his prime minister, Alexei Kosygin, undertook what might be described as a program of "de-Khrushcheviza-tion," returning the responsibility for long-term planning to the central ministries and reuniting the Communist Party apparatus. The leaders did make some cautious attempts to stimulate the stagnant farm sector by increasing capital investment in agriculture and raising food prices to increase rural income and provide additional incentives to collective farmers. But no attempt was made to revise the basic structure of the collective system. In the industrial sector, the regime launched a series of reforms designed to give factory managers (themselves employees of the state) more responsibility for setting prices, wages, and production quotas. These "Kosygin reforms" had little effect, however, because they were stubbornly resisted by the bureaucracy and ultimately were adopted by relatively few enterprises within the vast state-owned industrial sector.

A CONTROLLED SOCIETY

Brezhnev also initiated a significant retreat from Khrushchev's policy of de-Stalinization. Criticism of the memory and record of the country's "Great Leader" had angered conservatives both within the party hierarchy and among the public at large, many of whom still revered Stalin as a hero of the Soviet system and a defender of the Russian people against Nazi Germany. Many influential figures in the Kremlin feared that de-Stalinization could lead to internal instability and a decline in public trust in the legitimacy of party leadership—the hallowed "dictatorship of the proletariat." Early in Brezhnev's tenure, Stalin's reputation began to be revived. Although his alleged "shortcomings" were not totally ignored, he was now described in the official press as "an outstanding party leader" who had been primarily responsible for the successes achieved by the Soviet Union.

The regime also adopted a more restrictive policy toward free expression and dissidence in Soviet society. Critics of the Soviet system, such as the physicist Andrey Sakharov, were harassed and arrested or, like the famous

♦ **The Portals of Doom.**   Perhaps the most feared location in the Soviet Union was Lyubyanka Prison, an ornate pre-revolutionary building in the heart of Moscow. Taken over by the Bolsheviks after the 1917 revolution, it became the headquarters of the Soviet secret police, the Cheka, later to be known as the KGB. It was here that many Soviet citizens accused of "counter-revolutionary acts" were imprisoned and executed.

writer Alexander Solzhenitsyn, forced to leave the Soviet Union. There was also a qualified return to the anti-
Semitic policies and attitudes that had marked the Stalin
era. Such indications of renewed repression aroused concern in the West and were instrumental in the inclusion
of a statement on human rights (the so-called "basket
three") in the 1975 Helsinki Agreement, which guaranteed the sanctity of international frontiers throughout
the European continent (see Chapter 27). Soviet performance in human rights continued to be spotty, however,
and the repressive character of Soviet society was not significantly alleviated.

The political stamp of the Brezhnev era was formally
enshrined in a new state constitution promulgated in
1977. Although the preamble declared that the Soviet
Union was no longer a proletarian dictatorship, but a
"state of all the people," comprising workers, farmers, and
"socialist intellectuals," it confirmed the leading role of
the party as "the predominant force" in Soviet society.
Article 49 stated that "persecution for criticism shall be
prohibited," but Article 39 qualified the rights of the individual by declaring that "the exercise by citizens of
their rights and freedoms *should not harm the interests of
society and the state* or the rights of other citizens [italics
added]." Article 62 was even more explicit about the priority of national interests over those of the individual:
"The citizens of the USSR shall be obligated to safeguard
the interests of the Soviet state and to contribute to the
strength of its might and prestige."

There were, of course, no interest groups to compete
with the party and the government in defining national
interests. The media were controlled by the state and
presented only what it wanted the people to hear. The
two major newspapers, *Pravda* (Truth) and *Izvestiya*
(News), were the agents of the party and the government, respectively. Cynics joked that there was no news
in *Pravda*, and no truth in *Izvestiya*. According to Western journalists, airplane accidents in the Soviet Union
were rarely publicized on the grounds that such stories
would raise questions about the quality of the Soviet airline industry. The government made strenuous efforts to
prevent the Soviet people from exposure to harmful foreign ideas, especially modern art, literature, and contemporary Western rock music. When the Summer Olympic
Games were held in Moscow in 1980, Soviet newspapers
advised citizens to keep their children indoors to protect
them from being polluted with "bourgeois" ideas passed
on by foreign visitors.

For citizens in Western democracies, such a political
atmosphere would seem highly oppressive, but for the
Russian people, the emphasis on law and order was an accepted aspect of everyday life inherited from the tsarist
period. Conformism was the rule in virtually every corner
of Soviet society, from the educational system (dedicated
at all levels to rote memorization and political indoctrination), to child rearing (it was forbidden, for example,
to be left-handed), and even to yearly vacations (most
workers took their vacations at resorts run by their employer, where the daily schedule of activities was highly
regimented). Young Americans studying in the Soviet
Union reported that their Soviet friends were often
shocked to hear U.S. citizens criticizing their own president and to learn that they did not routinely carry identity cards.

A STAGNANT ECONOMY

Soviet leaders also failed to achieve their objective of re-
vitalizing the national economy. Although growth rates
during the early Khrushchev era had been impressive
(prompting Khrushchev during one visit to the United
States in the late 1950s to chortle that "we will bury
you"), during the Brezhnev years industrial growth continued to decline to an annual rate of under 4 percent in
the early 1970s and to less than 3 percent in the period
1975–1980. Successes in the agricultural sector were
equally meager. Grain production, which had risen from
less than 90 million tons in the early 1950s to nearly 200
million tons in the 1970s, then stagnated at that level.

What were the major causes of the overall slowdown
in the Soviet economy? One of the primary problems was
certainly the absence of incentives. Under the Soviet system, the people lacked the motivation to produce and to
create, activities that Karl Marx had described as the
most fundamental aspirations of human nature. In most
sectors of the Soviet economy, salary levels for most
workers offered little reward for hard labor and extraordinary achievement. The range of pay differentials in the
Soviet Union was much narrower than in most Western
societies, and there was little danger of being dismissed.
After all, the Soviet constitution guaranteed every Soviet citizen an opportunity to work.

There were, of course, some exceptions to this general
rule. Athletic achievement was highly prized, and a gym-
nast of Olympic stature would reap great rewards in the
form of prestige and lifestyle. Senior officials did not receive high salaries, but were provided with countless
perquisites, such as access to foreign goods, an official
automobile with a chauffeur, and entry into prestigious
institutions of higher learning for their children. For the
elite, it was *blat* (influence) that most often differenti-
ated them from the rest of the population. The average

citizen, however, whether clerk, factory laborer, collective farmer, or waitress, had little material incentive to produce beyond the minimum acceptable level. It is hardly surprising that overall per capita productivity was only about half that realized in most capitalist countries. At the same time, the rudeness of Soviet clerks and waiters toward their customers became legendary.

Incentives were lacking at the managerial level as well, where centralized planning discouraged initiative and innovative techniques. Factory managers, for example, were assigned monthly and annual quotas by the Gosplan (the "state plan," drawn up by the central planning commission). Because state-owned factories were not subjected to the competition characteristic of a free market system, it was of relatively little concern to factory managers whether their products were competitive in terms of price and quality, so long as the quota was attained. One of the key complaints of Soviet citizens was the low quality of most locally made consumer goods. Knowledgeable consumers were aware that products manufactured at the end of the month were often of lower quality (because of the practice of "storming," in which factory workers rushed to meet their quotas at the end of their production cycle and thus produced shoddy goods) and attempted to avoid purchasing them.

Often, consumer goods were simply not available on the shelves. Soviet citizens automatically got in line when they observed a queue forming in front of a store, because they never knew when something might be available again. When they reached the head of the line, most would purchase several of the same item so they could swap with their friends and neighbors. A popular

◆ **How to Shop in Moscow.** Because of the policy of state control over the Soviet economy, the availability of goods was a consequence not of market factors but of decisions made by government bureaucrats. As a result, needed goods were often in short supply. When Soviet citizens heard that a shipment of a particular product had arrived at a state store, they queued up to buy it. Here shoppers line up in front of a store selling dinnerware in Moscow.

joke at the time was that a Soviet inventor had managed to produce an airplane that was cheap enough to be purchased by every citizen. Everyone was delighted because now when they heard that a particular item was available for sale anywhere in the country, they would be able to fly to the proper location to buy it. This "queue psychology," of course, was time-consuming and inevitably served to reduce the per capita rate of productivity.

Soviet citizens often tried to overcome the shortcomings of the system by operating "on the left" (i.e., engaging in black market activities). Private economic activities, of course, were illegal in the socialized Soviet system, but many workers took to "moonlighting" to augment their meager salaries. An employee in a state-run appliance store, for example, would promise to repair a customer's television set on his own time in return for a payment "under the table." Otherwise servicing the set might require several weeks. Knowledgeable observers estimated that as much as one-third of the entire Soviet economy operated outside the legal system.

Another major obstacle to economic growth was inadequate technology. Except for national defense, the overall level of Soviet technology was not comparable to that in the West or in the advanced industrial societies of East Asia. Part of the problem, of course, stemmed from the issues already mentioned. Factory managers had little incentive to improve the quality of their products, because they had no competition. But another reason was the high priority assigned to defense in the Soviet Union. The military sector of the economy regularly received the most resources from the government and attracted the cream of the scientific talent in the country.

There were yet other underlying reasons for the gradual slowdown in the Soviet economy. Coal mining was highly inefficient, and it was estimated that only one-third of the coal extracted ever reached its final destination. Although the Soviet Union's liquid energy reserves were estimated to be the largest in the world, for the most part they were located in inaccessible areas of Siberia where extraction facilities and transportation were inadequate. U.S. intelligence reports estimated that a leveling off of oil and gas production could cause a severe problem for the future growth of the Soviet economy. Government planners hoped that nuclear energy could eventually take up the slack, but the highly publicized meltdown of a nuclear reactor at Chernobyl in 1986 vividly demonstrated that Soviet technology was encountering difficulties there as well. There were also serious underlying structural problems in agriculture. Climatic difficulties (frequent floods, droughts, and a short growing season) and a lack of fertile soil, except in the renowned "black earth" regions of Ukraine, combined with a chronic shortage of mechanized farm equipment and a lack of incentives to prevent the growth of an advanced agricultural economy.

PROBLEMS OF GERONTOCRACY

Such problems would be intimidating for any government and were particularly so for the generation of elderly party leaders surrounding Leonid Brezhnev, many of whom were cautious to a fault. While some undoubtedly recognized the need for reform and innovation, they were paralyzed by fear of instability and change. The problem worsened during the late 1970s, when Brezhnev's health began to deteriorate. According to one authoritative source in Moscow, during the last years of his life he was mentally as well as physically incapacitated, as the use of sedatives gradually destroyed his grip on reality. Brezhnev's mental and physical ailments inspired a new round of popular humor, but for the average citizen, conditions in Soviet society were no laughing matter.

Brezhnev died in November 1982 and was succeeded by Yuri Andropov (1914–1984), a party veteran and head of the Soviet secret services. During his brief tenure as party chief, Andropov was a vocal advocate of reform, but most of his initiatives were limited to the familiar nostrums of punishment for wrongdoers and moral exhortations to Soviet citizens to work harder. At the same time, material incentives were still officially discouraged and generally ineffective. Andropov had been ailing when he was selected to succeed Brezhnev as party chief, and when he died after only a few months in office, little had been done to change the system. He in turn was succeeded by a mediocre party stalwart, the elderly Konstantin Chernenko (1911–1985). With the Soviet system in crisis, Moscow seemed stuck in a time warp. As one concerned observer told an American journalist, "I had a sense of foreboding, like before a storm. That there was something brewing in people and there would be a time when they would say, 'That's it. We can't go on living like this. We can't. We need to redo everything.' "[3]

Culture in the Soviet Bloc

In his occasional musings about the future Communist utopia, Karl Marx had predicted the emergence of a new classless society to replace the exploitative and hierarchical system of the past. Workers would engage in productive activities and share equally in the fruits of their labor. In their free time, they would help to produce a new advanced culture, proletarian in character and egalitarian in content.

The reality in the post–World War II Soviet Union and in Eastern Europe was somewhat different. Under

Stalin, the Soviet cultural scene was a wasteland. Beginning in 1946, a series of government decrees made all forms of literary and scientific expression dependent on the state. All Soviet culture was expected to follow the party line. Historians, philosophers, and social scientists all grew accustomed to quoting Marx, Lenin, and above all, Stalin as their chief authorities. Novels and plays, too, were supposed to portray Communist heroes and their efforts to create a better society. No criticism of existing social conditions was permitted. Even distinguished composers such as Dimitry Shostakovich were compelled to heed Stalin's criticisms, such as his view that contemporary Western music was nothing but a "mishmash." Some areas of intellectual activity were virtually abolished; the science of genetics disappeared, and few movies were made during Stalin's final years.

Stalin's death brought a modest respite to cultural repression. Writers and artists who had been banned from expression during Stalin's years were again allowed to publish. Still, Soviet authorities, including Khrushchev, were reluctant to allow cultural freedom to move far beyond official Soviet ideology.

These restrictions did not prevent the emergence of some significant Soviet literature, although authors paid a heavy price if they alienated the Soviet authorities. The writer Ilya Ehrenburg (1891–1967) set the tone with his novel, significantly titled *The Thaw*. Boris Pasternak (1890–1960), who began his literary career as a poet, won the Nobel Prize in 1958 for his celebrated novel, *Doctor Zhivago*, which had been written between 1945 and 1956 and published in Italy in 1957. But the Soviet government condemned Pasternak's anti-Soviet tendencies, banned the novel from Russia, and would not allow him to accept the prize. The author had alienated the authorities by describing a society scarred by the excesses of Bolshevik revolutionary zeal.

Map 28.1 The States of Eastern Europe and the Former Soviet Union.

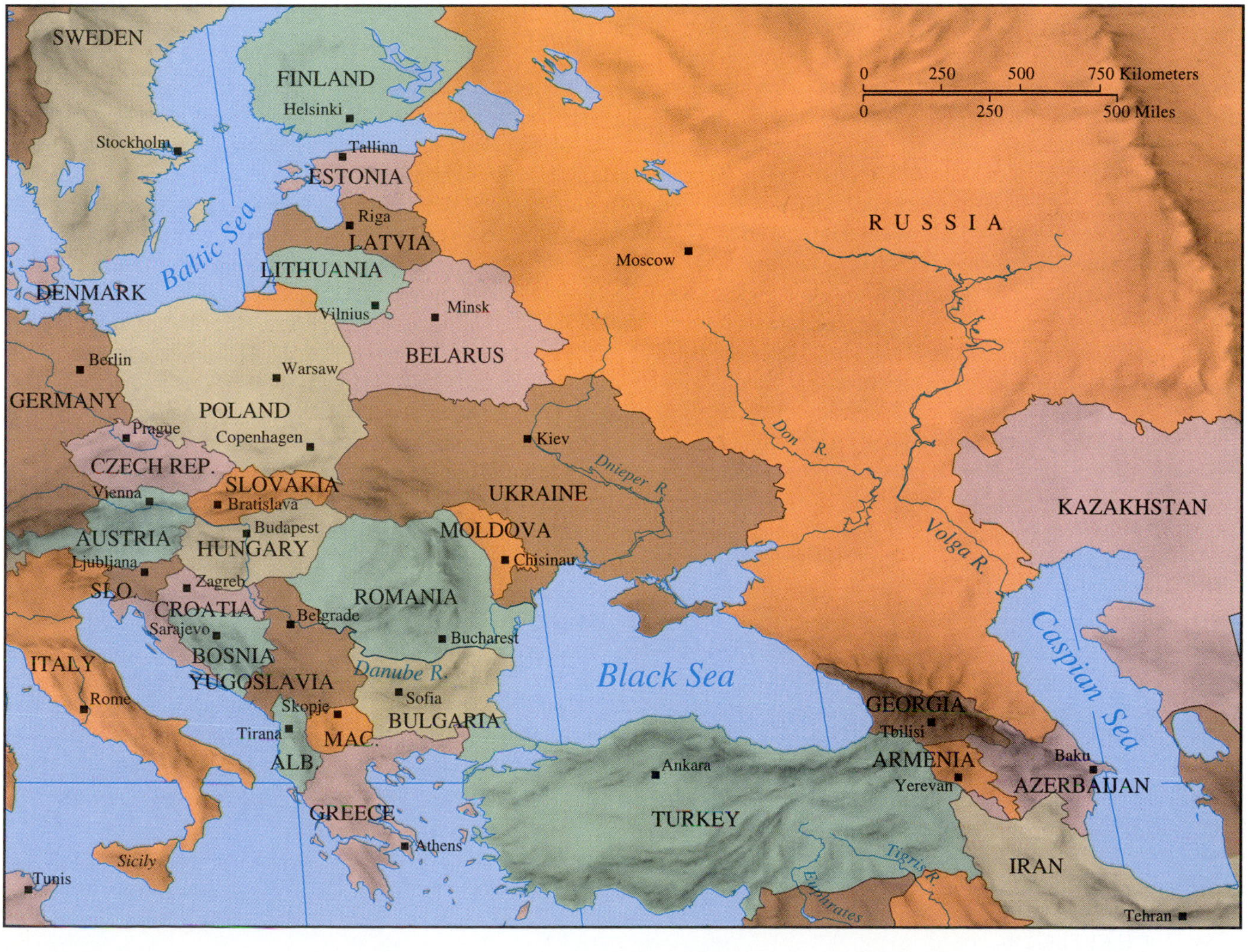

Alexander Solzhenitsyn (b. 1918) created an even greater furor than Pasternak. Solzhenitsyn had spent eight years in forced-labor camps for criticizing Stalin, and his *One Day in the Life of Ivan Denisovich,* which won him the Nobel Prize in 1970, was an account of life in those camps (see the box on p. 1028). Khrushchev allowed the book's publication as part of his de-Stalinization campaign. Later, Solzhenitsyn wrote *The Gulag Archipelago,* a detailed indictment of the whole system of Soviet oppression. Soviet authorities viciously denounced Solzhenitsyn's efforts to inform the world of Soviet crimes against humanity and arrested and expelled him from the Soviet Union after he published *The Gulag Archipelago* abroad in 1973.

Exile abroad rather than imprisonment in forced-labor camps was, of course, some kind of cultural progress. But even the limited freedom that had arisen during Khrushchev's years was rejected after his fall from power. Cultural controls were reimposed, de-Stalinization was broken off, and authors were again sent to labor camps for expressing outlawed ideas. These restrictive policies continued until the late 1980s when Gorbachev's policy of *glasnost* (see The Gorbachev Era later in this chapter) opened the doors to a new cultural freedom and new opportunities for expression.

In the Eastern European satellites, cultural freedom varied considerably from country to country. In Poland, intellectuals had access to Western publications as well as greater freedom to travel to the West. Hungarian and Yugoslavian Communists, too, tolerated a certain level of intellectual activity that was not liked, but at least not prohibited. Elsewhere, intellectuals were forced to conform to the regime's demands. After the Soviet invasion of Czechoslovakia in 1968 (see Chapter 27), Czech Communists pursued a policy of strict cultural control. This did not stop a number of intellectuals from opposing the regime, however. Dissident writers and professionals, including the dramatist Vaclav Havel, the current president of the Czech Republic, formed Charter 77 in January 1977 to protest human rights violations by the Communist regime. Although the regime struck back by prohibiting them from working in their professions, members of Charter 77 persisted and eventually founded Civic Forum, the political organization that guided the ouster of the Communist regime in the revolution of 1989.

The socialist camp also experienced the many facets of modern popular culture. By the early 1970s, there were 28 million television sets in the Soviet Union, although state authorities controlled the content of the programs that the Soviet people watched. Modern tourism, too, made inroads into the Communist world as state-run industries provided vacation time and governments facilitated the establishment of resorts for workers on the Black Sea and Adriatic coasts. In Poland, the number of vacationers who used holiday retreats increased from 700,000 in 1960 to 2.8 million in 1972.

Spectator sports became a large industry and were also highly politicized as the result of Cold War divisions. In 1948, the Soviet Communist Party called upon the nation "to spread physical culture and sport to every corner of the land, and to raise the level of skill, so that Soviet sportsmen might win world supremacy in the major sports in the immediate future." "Each new victory," one party leader stated, "is a victory for the Soviet form of society and the socialist sport system; it provides irrefutable proof of the superiority of socialist culture over the decaying culture of the capitalist states."[4] Accordingly, the state supported athletics by providing money for the construction of gymnasia and training camps and portrayed athletes as superheroes.

A Classless Society? Social Changes in the Soviet Union and Eastern Europe

The imposition of socialist systems in Eastern Europe had far-reaching social consequences. Most Eastern European countries made the change from peasant societies to modern, industrialized economies. In Bulgaria, for example, while 80 percent of the labor force was in agriculture in 1950, only 20 percent was still there by 1980. Although the Soviet Union and its Eastern European satellites never achieved the high standards of living of the West, they did experience some improvement. In 1960, the average real income of Polish peasants was four times higher than before World War II. Consumer goods also became more widespread. In East Germany, only 17 percent of families had television sets in 1960, but 75 percent had acquired them by 1972.

According to Communist ideology, government control of industry and the elimination of private property were supposed to lead to a classless society. Although the classless society was never achieved, that ideal did have important social consequences in the Soviet Union and Eastern Europe. For one thing, traditional ruling classes in the Soviet Union and Eastern European countries were stripped of their special status after 1945. The Potocki family in Poland, for example, which had owned nine million acres of land before the war, lost all of its possessions while the family members were reduced to the ranks of common laborers.

The desire to create a classless society led to noticeable changes in education. In some countries, the desire to provide equal educational opportunities led to laws that mandated quota systems based on class. In East Germany, for example, 50 percent of the students in secondary schools had to be children of workers and peasants. The sons of manual workers constituted 53 percent of university students in Yugoslavia in 1964 and 40 percent in East Germany, compared to only 15 percent in Italy and 5.3 percent in West Germany. Social mobility also increased. In 1961, 50 percent of white-collar workers in Poland came from blue-collar families. A significant number of judges, professors, and industrial managers stemmed from working-class backgrounds.

Education became crucial in preparing for new jobs in the Communist system and led to higher enrollments in both secondary schools and universities. In Czechoslovakia, for example, the number of students in secondary schools tripled between 1945 and 1970, while the number of university students quadrupled between the 1930s and the 1960s. The type of education that students received also changed. In Hungary before World War II, 40 percent of students studied law, 9 percent engineering and technology, and 5 percent agriculture. In 1970, the figures were 35 percent in engineering and technology, 9 percent in agriculture, and only 4 percent in law.

By the 1970s, the new managers of society, regardless of their class background, realized the importance of higher education and used their power to gain special privileges for their children. By 1971, 60 percent of the children of white-collar workers attended university, and even though blue-collar families constituted 60 percent of the population, only 36 percent of their children attended institutions of higher learning. Even East Germany dropped its requirement that 50 percent of secondary students had to be the offspring of workers and peasants.

Ideals of equality certainly did not include women. Men dominated the leadership positions of the Communist Parties in the Soviet Union and Eastern Europe. Women did have greater opportunities in the workforce and even in the professions, however. In the Soviet Union, women comprised 51 percent of the labor force in 1980; by the mid-1980s, they constituted 50 percent of the engineers, 80 percent of the doctors, and 75 percent of the teachers and teachers' aides. But many of these were low-paying jobs; most female doctors, for example, worked in primary care and were paid less than skilled machinists. The chief administrators in hospitals and schools were still men.

Moreover, although women were part of the workforce, they were never freed of their traditional roles in the home (see the box on page 1036). Most women con-

fronted what came to be known as the "double shift." After working eight hours in their jobs, they came home to do the housework and care for the children. They might spend two hours a day in long lines at a number of stores waiting to buy food and clothes. Because of the housing situation, they were forced to use kitchens that were shared by a number of families.

Nearly three-quarters of a century after the Bolshevik Revolution, then, the Marxist dream of an advanced egalitarian society was as far away as ever. Although in some respects conditions in the socialist camp were a distinct improvement over those before World War II, many problems and inequities were as intransigent as ever.

The Disintegration of the Soviet Empire

On the death of Konstantin Chernenko in 1985, party leaders selected Mikhail Gorbachev to succeed him. His appointment initiated a period of revolutionary upheaval that ended the Cold War and dramatically altered the European scene.

The Gorbachev Era

Born into a peasant family in 1931, Mikhail Gorbachev combined farm work with school and received the Order of the Red Banner for his agricultural efforts. This award and his good school record enabled him to study law at the University of Moscow. After receiving his law degree in 1955, he returned to his native southern Russia, where

Soviet Women: "It's So Difficult to Be a Woman Here"

One of the major problems for Soviet women was the balancing of work and family roles, a problem noticeably ignored by authorities. This excerpt is taken from a series of interviews of thirteen women in Moscow conducted in the late 1970s by Swedish investigators. As is evident in this interview with Anna, a young wife and mother, these Soviet women took pride in their achievements but were also frustrated with their lives. At the same time, they maintained traditional views of women's roles.

Moscow Women: Interview with Anna

[Anna is twenty-one and married, has a three-month-old daughter, and lives with her husband and daughter in a one-room apartment with a balcony and a large bathroom. Anna works as a hairdresser; her husband is an unemployed writer.]

Are there other kinds of jobs dominated by women?
Of course! Preschool teachers are exclusively women. Also beauticians. But I guess that's about all. Here women work in every profession, from tractor drivers to engineers. But I think there ought to be more jobs specifically for women so that there are *some* differences. In this century women have to be equal to men. Now women wear pants, have short hair, and hold important jobs, just like men. There are almost no differences left. Except in the home.

Do women and men have the same goal in life?
Of course. Women want to get out of the house and have careers, just the same as men do. It gives women a lot of advantages, higher wages, and so on. In that sense we have the same goal, but socially I don't think so. The family is, after all, more important for a woman. A man can live without a family; all he needs is for a woman to come from time to time to clean for him and do his laundry. He sleeps with her if he feels like it. Of course, a woman can adopt this lifestyle, but I still think that most women want their own home, family, children. From time immemorial, women's instincts have been rooted in taking care of their families, tending to their husbands, sewing, washing—all the household chores. Men are supposed to provide for the family; women should keep the home fires burning. This is so deeply ingrained in women that there's no way of changing it.

Whose career do you think is the most important?
The man's, naturally. The family is often broken up because women don't follow their men when they move where they can get a job. That was the case of my in-laws. They don't live together any longer because my father-in-law worked for a long time as far away as Smolensk. He lived alone, without his family, and then, of course, it was only natural that things turned out the way they did. It's hard for a man to live without his family when he's used to being taken care of all the time. Of course there are men who can endure, who continue to be faithful, etc., but for most men it isn't easy. For that reason I think a woman ought to go where her husband does. . . .

That's the way it is. Women have certain obligations, men others. One has to understand that at an early age. Girls have to learn to take care of a household and help at home. Boys too, but not as much as girls. Boys ought to be with their fathers and learn how to do masculine chores. . . .

It's so difficult to be a woman here. With emancipation, we lead such abnormal, twisted lives, because women have to work the same as men do. As a result, women have very little time for themselves to work on their femininity.

---

he eventually became first secretary of the Communist Party in the city of Stavropol (he had joined the Communist Party in 1952) and then first secretary of the regional party committee. In 1978, Gorbachev was made a member of the party's Central Committee in Moscow. Two years later, he became a full member of the ruling Politburo and secretary of the Central Committee. In March 1985, party leaders elected him general secretary of the party, and he became the new leader of the Soviet Union.

Educated during the reform years under Khrushchev, Gorbachev seemed intent on taking earlier reforms to their logical conclusions. By the 1980s, Soviet economic problems were obvious. Rigid, centralized planning led to mismanagement and stifled innovation. Although the Soviets still excelled in space exploration, they had fallen behind the West in high technology, especially in the development and production of computers for private and public use. Most noticeable to the Soviet people was the actual decline in the standard of living.

The cornerstone of Gorbachev's radical reforms was *perestroika* or "restructuring." At first this meant only a reordering of economic policy as Gorbachev called for the beginning of a market economy with limited free enterprise and some private property. Initial economic reforms were difficult to implement, however. Radicals demanded decisive measures; conservatives feared that rapid changes would be too painful. In his attempt to achieve compromise, Gorbachev often pursued partial liberalization, which satisfied neither faction and also failed to work, producing only more discontent

Gorbachev soon perceived that in the Soviet system, the economic sphere was intimately tied to the social and political spheres. Any efforts to reform the economy without political or social reform would be doomed to failure. One of the most important instruments of *perestroika* was *glasnost* or "openness." Soviet citizens and officials were encouraged to discuss openly the strengths and weaknesses of the Soviet Union. This policy could be seen in *Pravda*, the official newspaper of the Communist Party, where disasters such as the nuclear accident at Chernobyl in 1986 and collisions of ships in the Black Sea received increased coverage. Soon this type of reporting was extended to include reports of official corruption, sloppy factory work, and protests against government policy. The arts also benefited from the new policy as previously banned works were now published, and motion pictures began to depict negative aspects of Soviet life. Music based on Western styles, such as jazz and rock, began to be performed openly.

◆ **Behind the Mask.** After the Bolshevik Revolution, Soviet writers and artists were compelled to follow the dictates of socialist realism. All creative work was expected to glorify the state and the superiority of the socialist system. As official restrictions began to loosen under Gorbachev's policy of glasnost, however, books and paintings began to demonstrate a more critical view of the Soviet system. In the paintings shown here, displayed at an exhibit in Moscow in 1989, an artist seeks to expose the harsh inner nature of hallowed Soviet leaders.

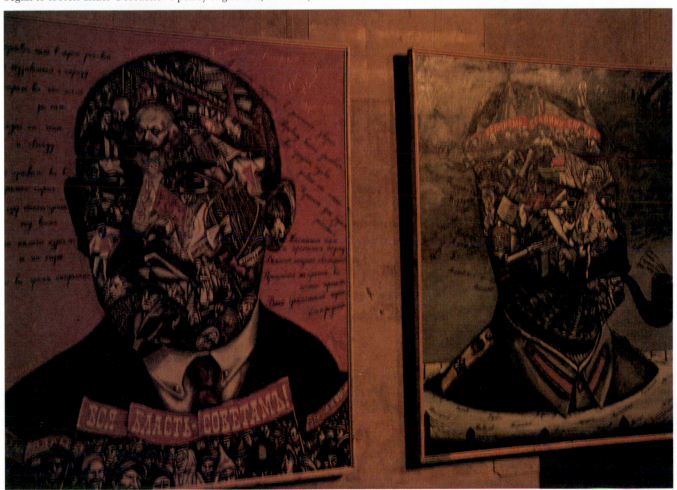

♦ **Tovarishchi, Get Out and Vote!**   In 1989, the Soviet Union held its first free national elections since the election for the Constituent Assembly in January 1918. Under Gorbachev's polling of glasnost, Soviet citizens elected a Congress of People's Deputies to help create a more open system of government in the USSR. In this poster, voters are encouraged to elect deputies who will support the policy of perestroika.

Political reforms were equally revolutionary. In June 1987, the principle of two-candidate elections was introduced, whereas previously voters were presented with only one candidate. Most dissidents, including Andrey Sakharov, who had spent years in internal exile, were released. At the Communist Party conference in 1988, Gorbachev called for the creation of a new Soviet parliament, the Congress of People's Deputies, whose members were to be chosen in competitive elections. It convened in 1989, the first such meeting in Russia since 1918. Because of its size, the Congress chose a Supreme Soviet of 450 members to deal with day-to-day activities. The revolutionary nature of Gorbachev's political reforms was evident in Sakharov's rise from dissident to an elected member of the Congress of People's Deputies. As a leader of the dissident deputies, Sakharov called for

an end to the Communist monopoly of power and, on December 11, 1989, the day he died, urged the creation of a new non-Communist party. Early in 1990, Gorbachev legalized the formation of other political parties and struck out Article 6, which had guaranteed the "leading role" of the Communist Party, from the Soviet constitution. At the same time, Gorbachev attempted to consolidate his power by the creation of a new state presidency. This was a consequence of the dissociation of the state and the Communist Party. Hitherto, the position of first secretary of the party was the most important post in the Soviet Union, but as the Communist Party became less closely associated with the state, the powers of this office diminished correspondingly. In March 1990, Gorbachev became the Soviet Union's first president.

One of Gorbachev's most serious problems stemmed from the character of the Soviet Union. The Union of Soviet Socialist Republics was a truly multiethnic country, containing 92 nationalities and 112 recognized languages. Previously, the iron hand of the Communist Party, centered in Moscow, had kept a lid on the centuries-old ethnic tensions that had periodically erupted throughout the history of this region. As Gorbachev released this iron grip, tensions resurfaced, a by-product of *glasnost* that Gorbachev had not anticipated. Ethnic groups took advantage of the new openness to protest what they perceived to be ethnically motivated slights. As violence erupted, the Soviet army, in disrepair since the Soviet intervention in Afghanistan in 1979, had difficulty controlling the situation. In some cases, independence movements and ethnic causes became linked, as in Azerbaijan where the National Front became the spokesgroup for the Muslim Azerbaijanis in their conflict with Christian Armenians.

The period 1988 to 1990 also witnessed the appearance of nationalist movements throughout the republics of the Soviet Union. Many were motivated by ethnic concerns and called for sovereignty of the republics and independence from the Russian-based rule centered in Moscow. These movements sprang up first in Georgia in late 1988 and then in Latvia, Estonia, Moldavia, Uzbekistan, Azerbaijan, and most dramatically in Lithuania.

In December of 1989, the Communist Party of Lithuania declared itself independent of the Communist Party of the Soviet Union. Then, on March 11, 1990, the Lithuanian Supreme Council unilaterally declared Lithuania independent. Its formal name was now the Lithuanian Republic; the adjectives Soviet and Socialist had been dropped. On March 15, the Soviet Congress of People's Deputies, though recognizing a general right to secede from the Union of Soviet Socialist Republics, declared the Lithuanian declaration null and void; the congress stated that proper procedures must be established and followed before secession would be acceptable.

During 1990 and 1991, Gorbachev struggled to deal with Lithuania and the other problems unleashed by his reforms. On the one hand, he tried to appease the conservative forces who complained about the growing disorder within the Soviet Union. On the other hand, he tried to accommodate the liberal forces, especially those in the Soviet republics, who increasingly favored a new kind of decentralized Soviet federation. Gorbachev especially labored to cooperate more closely with Boris Yeltsin, who had been elected president of the Russian Republic in June 1991.

By 1991, the conservative leaders of the traditional Soviet institutions—the army, government, KGB, and military industries—had grown increasingly worried about the impending dissolution of the Soviet Union and its impact on their own fortunes. On August 19, 1991, a group of these discontented rightists arrested Gorbachev and attempted to seize power. Gorbachev's unwillingness to work with the conspirators and the brave resistance in Moscow of Yeltsin and thousands of Russians who had grown accustomed to their new liberties caused the coup to disintegrate rapidly. The actions of these right-wing plotters, however, served to accelerate the very process they had hoped to stop—namely, the disintegration of the Soviet Union.

Despite desperate pleas from Gorbachev, the Soviet republics soon moved for complete independence. Ukraine voted for independence on December 1, 1991, and, a week later, the leaders of Russia, Ukraine, and Belarus announced that the Soviet Union had "ceased to exist" and would be replaced by a Commonwealth of Independent States. Gorbachev resigned on December 25, 1991, and turned over his responsibilities as commander-in-chief to Boris Yeltsin, the president of Russia. By the end of 1991, one of the largest empires in world history had come to an end, and a new era had begun in its lands.

Within Russia, a new power struggle soon ensued. Yeltsin was committed to introducing a free market economy as quickly as possible. In December 1991, Yeltsin had been granted temporary power to rule by decree by the Congress of People's Deputies, the Soviet-era parliament that had been elected in 1989. Dominated by former Communist Party members and their allies, who were opposed to many of Yeltsin's economic reforms, the Congress tried to place new limits on his powers. Yeltsin fought back. After winning a vote of confidence, both in himself and in his economic reforms on April 25, 1993, Yeltsin pushed ahead on plans for a new constitution for Russia that would abolish the Congress of People's Deputies, create a two-chamber parliament, and establish a strong presidency.

Nevertheless, the conflict between Yeltsin and the Congress continued and turned violent. On September 21, Yeltsin issued a decree dissolving the Congress of People's Deputies and scheduling new parliamentary elections for December. A hard-line parliamentary minority resisted and even took the initiative by urging supporters to take over government offices and the central television station. On October 4, Yeltsin responded by ordering military forces to storm the parliament building and arrest hard-line opponents. Yeltsin used his victory to consolidate his power; at the same time, he remained

◆ **Something Old, Something New.**   Under Soviet rule, church weddings were declared illegal and marriage became a simple civil ceremony, lacking the ritual solemnity that religious sanctions had previously provided. With the disintegration of the USSR in 1991, many people began to return to pre-revolutionary practice. Here two newlyweds in the Ukrainian port city of Odessa celebrate their marriage ties in the traditional manner.

committed to holding new parliamentary elections on December 12.

During the mid-1990s, Yeltsin was able to maintain a precarious grip on power while seeking to implement reforms that would place Russia on a firm course toward a pluralistic political system and a market economy. But the new post-Communist Russia remains as fragile as ever. Burgeoning economic inequality and rampant corruption have aroused widespread criticism and shaken the confidence of the Russian people in the superiority of the capitalist system over what they had under Communist rule. A nagging war in the Caucasus—where the people of Chechnya have resolutely sought to obtain their national independence from Russia—has drained the government budget and exposed the decrepit state of the once vaunted Red Army. In presidential elections held in 1996, Yeltsin was reelected, but the rising popularity of a revived Communist Party and the growing strength of nationalist elements led by General Alexander Lebed, combined with Yeltsin's precarious health, have raised serious questions about the future of the country.

The demise of the Soviet Union came with a rapidity that few had expected. Gorbachev had hoped that he could institute economic and political reforms while retaining the Communist framework and preserving the Soviet Empire, but those goals proved incompatible. The new Russia that emerged from the ruins of the Soviet

Union has yet to show, however, that it can solve the economic and social problems that led to its predecessor's collapse. The new market economy has enabled some entrepreneurs to make fortunes but has also removed much of the safety net that protected many workers and pensioners. The result has been a growing disparity in wealth, combined with a rising crime rate, that has led some to yearn for the "good old days" of communism.

Eastern Europe: From Soviet Satellites to Sovereign Nations

Stalin's postwar order had imposed Communist regimes throughout Eastern Europe. The process of sovietization seemed so complete that few people believed that the new order could be undone. But discontent with their Soviet-style regimes always simmered beneath the surface of these satellite states, and after Mikhail Gorbachev made it clear that his government would not intervene militarily, their Communist regimes fell quickly in the revolutions of 1989. As had happened previously, the initial steps took place in Poland.

Under Wladyslaw Gomulka, Poland had achieved a certain stability in the 1960s, but economic problems brought his ouster in 1971. His replacement, Edward Gierek, attempted to solve Poland's economic problems by borrowing heavily from the West. But in 1980, when he announced huge increases in food prices in an effort to pay off part of the Western debt, workers' protests erupted once again. This time, however, the revolutionary demands of the workers led directly to the rise of an independent labor movement called Solidarity. Led by Lech Walesa (b. 1943), Solidarity represented 10 million of Poland's 35 million people. Almost instantly, Solidarity became a tremendous force for change and a threat to the government's monopoly of power. With the support of the workers, many intellectuals, and the Catholic church, Solidarity was able to win a series of concessions. The Polish government seemed powerless to stop the flow of concessions until December 1981, when it arrested Walesa and other Solidarity leaders, outlawed the union, and imposed military rule under General Wojciech Jaruzelski (b. 1923).

But martial rule did not solve Poland's serious economic problems. In 1988, new demonstrations broke out. After much maneuvering and negotiating with Solidarity, the Polish regime finally consented to free parliamentary elections—the first free elections in Eastern Europe for forty years—that led to even greater strength for Solidarity. Bowing to the inevitable, Jaruzelski's regime allowed the Solidarity-led coalition in the lower house of

the new legislature to elect Tadeusz Mazowiecki, a leading member of Solidarity, as prime minister. The Communist monopoly of power in Poland had come to an end after forty-five years. In April 1990, it was decided that a new president would be freely elected by the populace by the end of the year, and in December Lech Walesa was chosen the new Polish president.

Poland's new path has not been an easy one. The existence of over one hundred political parties has fragmented the political process and created the danger of parliamentary stalemate, while rapid free market reforms have created severe unemployment and popular discontent. At the same time, the effort of the powerful Catholic church to secure abortion law reform and religious education in the schools has raised new issues to divide the Polish people.

Similar developments took place in other countries in the region. In Hungary, János Kádár tried to keep up with the changing mood by enacting the most far-reaching economic reforms in Eastern Europe. In the early 1980s, he legalized small private enterprises to give communism "a capitalist facelift." Multicandidate elections with at least two candidates per seat were held for the first time on June 8, 1985.

As the 1980s progressed, however, the economy sagged, and Kádár fell from power in 1988. By 1989, the Hungarian Communist Party was aware of the growing dissatisfaction and changed its name to the Hungarian Socialist Party in order to have a greater chance of success in new elections scheduled for March 25, 1990. The party came in fourth, however, winning only 8.5 percent of the vote, a clear repudiation of communism. The Democratic Forum, a right-of-center, highly patriotic party, won the election and formed a new coalition government that committed Hungary to democratic government and the institution of a free market economy.

Communist regimes in Poland and Hungary had attempted to make some political and economic reforms in the 1970s and 1980s, but this was not the case in Czechoslovakia. After Soviet troops had crushed the reform movement in 1968, hard-line Czech Communists under Gustav Husák purged the party and followed a policy of massive repression to maintain their power. In January 1977, dissident intellectuals formed Charter 77 as a vehicle for protest against human rights violations. By the 1980s, Charter 77 members were also presenting their views on the country's economic and political problems, despite the government's harsh response to their movement.

Regardless of the atmosphere of repression, dissident movements continued to grow in the late 1980s. In

❧ Vaclav Havel: The Call for a New Politics ❧

In their attempt to deal with the world's problems, some European leaders have pointed to the need for a new perspective, especially a moral one, if people are to live in a sane world. These two excerpts are taken from two speeches by Vaclav Havel, who was elected the new president of Czechoslovakia at the end of 1989. The first is from his inaugural address as president of Czechoslovakia on January 1, 1990; the second is from a speech to the U.S. Congress.

Address to the People of Czechoslovakia, January 1, 1990

But all this is still not the main problem [the environmental devastation of the country by its Communist leaders]. The worst thing is that we live in a contaminated moral environment. We fell morally ill because we became used to saying something different from what we thought. We learned not to believe anything, to ignore each other, to care only about ourselves. Concepts such as love, friendship, compassion, humility, or forgiveness lost their depth and dimensions, and for many of us they represented only psychological peculiarities, or they resembled gone-astray greetings from ancients, a little ridiculous in the era of computers and spaceships. Only a few of us were able to cry out loud that the powers that be should not be all-powerful, and that special farms, which produce ecologically pure and top-quality food just for them, should send their produce to schools, children's homes, and hospitals if our agriculture was unable to offer them to all. The previous regime—armed with its arrogant and intolerant ideology—reduced man to a force of production and nature to a tool of production. In this it attacked both their very substance and their mutual relationship. It reduced gifted and autonomous people, skillfully working in their own country, to nuts and bolts of some monstrously huge, noisy, and stinking machine, whose real meaning is not clear to anyone.

Speech to Congress, February 21, 1990

For this reason, the salvation of this human world lies nowhere else than in the human heart, in the human power to reflect, in human meekness and in human responsibility.

Without a global revolution in the sphere of human consciousness, nothing will change for the better in the sphere of our being as humans, and the catastrophe toward which this world is headed—be it ecological, social, demographic or a general breakdown of civilization—will be unavoidable. . . .

We are still a long way from that "family of man." In fact, we seem to be receding from the ideal rather than growing closer to it. Interests of all kinds—personal, selfish, state, nation, group, and if you like, company interests—still considerably outweigh genuinely common and global interests. We are still under the sway of the destructive and vain belief that man is the pinnacle of creation and not just a part of it and that therefore everything is permitted. . . .

In other words, we still don't know how to put morality ahead of politics, science and economics. We are still incapable of understanding that the only genuine backbone of all our actions, if they are to be moral, is responsibility.

Responsibility to something higher than my family, my country, my company, my success—responsibility to the order of being where all our actions are indelibly recorded and where and only where they will be properly judged.

The interpreter or mediator between us and this higher authority is what is traditionally referred to as human conscience.

December 1989, the Communist government, lacking any real support, collapsed. President Husák resigned and at the end of December was replaced by Vaclav Havel, a dissident playwright who had been a leading figure in Charter 77 and had played an important role in bringing down the Communist government (see the box above).

The shift to non-Communist rule, however, was complicated by old problems, especially ethnic issues. Czechs and Slovaks disagreed over the makeup of the new state but were able to agree to a peaceful division of the country. On January 1, 1993, Czechoslovakia split into the Czech Republic and Slovakia.

THE REUNIFICATION OF GERMANY

The ruling Communist government in East Germany, led by Walter Ulbricht, consolidated its position in the early

1950s and became a faithful Soviet satellite. Industry was nationalized and agriculture collectivized. After a workers' revolt in 1953 was crushed by Soviet tanks, a steady flight of East Germans to West Germany ensued, primarily through the city of Berlin. This exodus of mostly skilled laborers created economic problems and, in 1961, led the East German government to build the infamous Berlin Wall separating West from East Berlin, as well as equally fearsome barriers along the entire border with West Germany.

After building the wall, East Germany succeeded in developing the strongest economy among the Soviet Union's Eastern European satellites. In 1971, Walter Ulbricht was succeeded by Erich Honecker (b. 1912), a party hard-liner who was deeply committed to the ideological battle against détente. Propaganda increased, and the use of the *Stasi*, the secret police, became a hallmark of Honecker's virtual dictatorship. Honecker ruled unchallenged for the next eighteen years.

In 1988, however, popular unrest, fueled by the persistent economic slump of the 1980s (which affected most of Eastern Europe) as well as the ongoing oppressiveness of Honecker's regime, caused another mass exodus of East German refugees. Violent repression as well as Honecker's refusal to institute reforms only led to a larger exodus and mass demonstrations against the regime in the summer and fall of 1989. By the beginning of November 1989, the Communist government had fallen into complete disarray. Capitulating to popular pressure on November 9, it opened the entire border with the West. Hundreds of thousands of Germans swarmed across the borders, mostly to visit and return. The Berlin Wall, long the symbol of the Cold War, became the site of a massive celebration. By December, new political parties had emerged, and on March 18, 1990, in East Germany's first free elections ever, the Christian Democrats won almost 50 percent of the vote. The Christian Democrats supported rapid monetary unification followed shortly by political unification with West Germany. On July 1, 1990, the economies of West and East Germany were united with the West German deutsche mark becoming the official currency of the two countries. Political reunification was achieved on October 3, 1990. What had seemed almost impossible at the beginning of 1989 had become a reality by the end of 1990. The country of East Germany had ceased to exist.

YUGOSLAVIA: A TRAGEDY IN THE MAKING

From its beginning in 1919, Yugoslavia had been an artificial creation. After World War II, Josip Tito had served as a cohesive force for the six republics and two autonomous provinces that constituted Yugoslavia. In the 1970s, Tito had become concerned that decentralization had gone too far in creating too much power at the local level and encouraging regionalism. As a result, he purged thousands of local Communist leaders who seemed more involved with local affairs than national concerns.

After Tito's death in 1980, no strong leader emerged, and his responsibilities passed to a collective state presidency and the presidium of the League of Communists of Yugoslavia (LCY). At the end of the 1980s, Yugoslavia was caught up in the reform movements sweeping through Eastern Europe. On January 20, 1990, the League of Communists called for an end to authoritarian socialism and proposed the creation of a pluralistic political system with freedom of speech and other civil liberties, free elections, an independent judiciary, and a mixed economy with equal status for private property. But divisions between Slovenes who wanted a loose federation and Serbians who wanted to retain the centralized system caused the collapse of the party congress, and hence the Communist Party. New parties quickly emerged. In multiparty elections held in the republics of Slovenia and Croatia in April and May of 1990 (the first multiparty elections in Yugoslavia in fifty-one years), the Communists fared poorly.

The Yugoslav political scene was complicated by the development of separatist movements that brought the disintegration of Yugoslavia in the 1990s. When new non-Communist parties won elections in the republics of Slovenia, Croatia, Bosnia-Herzegovina, and Macedonia in 1990, they began to lobby for a new federal structure of Yugoslavia that would fulfill their separatist desires. Slobodan Milosevic, who had become the leader of the Serbian Communist Party in 1987 and had managed to stay in power by emphasizing his Serbian nationalism, rejected these efforts. He maintained that these republics could only be independent if new border arrangements were made to accommodate the Serb minorities in those republics who did not want to live outside the boundaries of a Greater Serbian state. Serbs constituted 11.6 percent of Croatia's population and 32 percent of Bosnia-Herzegovina's population in 1981.

After negotiations among the six republics failed, Slovenia and Croatia declared their independence in June 1991. Milosevic's government sent the Yugoslavian army, which it controlled, into Slovenia, but without much success. In September 1991, it began a full assault against Croatia. Increasingly, the Yugoslavian army was the Serbian army, and the Serbian irregular forces played an important role in military operations. Before a cease-fire was arranged, the Serbian forces had captured one-third of Croatia's territory in brutal and destructive fighting.

The recognition of Slovenia, Croatia, and Bosnia-Herzegovina by many European states and the United States early in 1992 did not stop the Serbs from turning their guns on Bosnia-Herzegovina. By mid-1993, Serbian forces had acquired 70 percent of Bosnian territory. The Serbian policy of "ethnic cleansing"—killing or forcibly removing Bosnian Muslims from their lands—revived memories of Nazi atrocities in World War II. Nevertheless, despite worldwide outrage, European governments failed to take a decisive and forceful stand against these Serbian activities, and by the spring of 1993, the Muslim population of Bosnia-Herzegovina was in desperate straits. As the fighting spread, European nations and the United States began to intervene to stop the bloodshed, and in the fall of 1995, a fragile cease-fire was reached at a conference held in Dayton, Ohio. An international peacekeeping force was stationed in the area to maintain tranquillity and monitor the accords. Implementation has been difficult, however, as ethnic antagonisms continue to flare, and a lasting peace seems as far away as ever.

After the Fall

In Eastern Europe, the fall of Communist governments during the revolutions of 1989 brought a wave of euphoria. The new structures meant an end to a postwar European order that had been imposed on unwilling peoples by the victorious forces of the Soviet Union. In 1989 and 1990, new governments throughout Eastern Europe worked diligently to scrap the remnants of the old system and introduce the democratic procedures and market systems that they believed would revitalize their scarred lands. But the process proved to be neither simple nor easy, and the mood of euphoria had largely faded by 1992.

Most Eastern European countries had little or virtually no experience with democratic systems. Moreover, under Communist rule most people had had no chance to participate in public life in general and in democratic debate in particular. Then, too, ethnic divisions that had troubled these areas before World War II and had been forcibly submerged under Communist rule reemerged with a vengeance, making political unity almost impossible. While Czechoslovakia resolved its differences peacefully, Yugoslavia descended into the kind of brutal warfare that had not been experienced in Europe since World War II.

The rapid conversion to market economies has also proved painful. The adoption of "shock-therapy" austerity measures produced much suffering and uncertainty. Un-

employment climbed to over 15 percent in the former East Germany and 13 percent in Poland in 1992. Wages remained low while prices skyrocketed. At the same time, in many countries former Communists were able to retain important positions of power or become the new owners of private property. Resentment against former Communists has provided yet another source of social instability. For both political and economic reasons, the new non-Communist states of Eastern Europe, like the former Soviet Union, face dangerous and uncertain futures.

The East is Red: China Under Communism

In the fall of 1949, China was at peace for the first time in twelve years. The newly victorious Communist Party, under the leadership of its chairman Mao Zedong, turned its attention to consolidating its power base and healing the wounds of war. Its long-term goal was to construct a socialist society, but its leaders realized that popular support for the revolution had been based on the party's platform of honest government, land reform, social justice, and peace, rather than on the utopian goal of a classless society. Accordingly, the new regime followed Soviet precedent in adopting a moderate program of political and economic recovery known as New Democracy.

◆ **Speaking Bitterness.**   One of the primary methods used by the Communists to win the support of Chinese peasants was to confiscate the land of the wealthy and distribute it to the poor. The program had its violent side. In this photograph, a peasant accuses a landlord of crimes against the people at a tribunal held in a Chinese village. Up to one million landlords were reportedly executed after such trials.

⨠ Consolidating Power in China ⨠

After the Communists came to power in China in 1949, Mao Zedong and his colleagues adopted a relatively moderate program designed to win the support of the Chinese people. Although major industries were to be placed under state ownership, the bulk of the manufacturing and commercial sector was to remain in private hands, while land would be confiscated from wealthy landlords and redistributed to the poor. In this excerpt from an article written in 1940, Mao predicted this policy.

Mao Zedong, "On New Democracy"

We must establish in China a republic that is politically new-democratic as well as economically new-democratic.

Big banks and big industrial and commercial enterprises shall be owned by this republic.

"Enterprises, whether Chinese-owned or foreign-owned, which are monopolistic in character or which are on too large a scale for private management, such as banks, railways and air lines, shall be operated by the state so that private capital cannot dominate the livelihood of the people: This is the main principle of the control of capital."

. . . The state-operated enterprises of the new-democratic republic under the leadership of the proletariat are socialist in character and constitute the leading force in the national economy as a whole; but this republic does not take over other forms of capitalist private property, or forbid the development of capitalist production that "cannot dominate the livelihood of the people," for China's economy is still very backward.

This republic will adopt certain necessary measures to confiscate the land of landlords and distribute it to those peasants having no land or only a little land, carry out Dr. Sun Yat-sen's slogan of "land to the tillers," abolish the feudal relations in the rural areas, and turn the land into the private property of the peasants. In the rural areas, rich peasant economic activities will be tolerated. This is the line of "equalization of land ownership." The correct slogan for this line is "land to the tillers." In this stage, socialist agriculture is in general not yet to be established, though the various types of co-operative enterprises developed on the basis of "land to the tillers" will contain elements of socialism.

China's economy must develop along the path of "control of capital" and "equalization of land ownership," and must never be "monopolist by a few"; we must never let the few capitalists and landlords "dominate the livelihood of the people"; we must never establish a capitalist society of the European-American type, nor allow the old semi-feudal society to remain. Whoever dares to run counter to this line will certainly fail to attain his aim, and will be knocked on the head.

New Democracy

Under New Democracy, which was patterned essentially after Lenin's New Economic Policy in Soviet Russia in the 1920s (see Chapter 24), the capitalist system of ownership was retained in the industrial and commercial sectors, and a program of land redistribution to the poor was adopted, but the collectivization of agriculture was postponed. Only after the party had consolidated its rule and brought a reasonable degree of prosperity to the national economy would the difficult transformation to a socialist society begin (see the box above).

In following Soviet precedent, the new Chinese leader tacitly recognized that time and extensive indoctrination would be needed to convince the Chinese people of the superiority of socialism. In the meantime, the party would rely on capitalist profit incentives to spur productivity. Manufacturing and commercial firms were permitted to remain under private ownership, although they were placed under stringent government regulations, and some were encouraged to form "joint enterprises" with the government. To win the support of the poorer peasants, who made up the majority of the population, the land reform program that had long been in operation in "liberated areas" was now expanded throughout the entire country. This strategy was designed not only to win the gratitude of the rural masses, but also to undermine and destroy the political and economic influence of counterrevolutionary elements still loyal to Chiang Kai-shek.

In a number of key respects, New Democracy was a success. About two-thirds of the peasant households in the country received land under the land reform program and thus had reason to be grateful to the new regime. Spurred by the benign official tolerance for capitalist activities and the end of internal conflict, the national economy began to rebound, although agricultural production still lagged behind both official targets and the growing population, which was increasing at an annual rate of more than 2 percent. But there was a darker side to the picture. In the course of carrying out land redistribution, thousands if not millions of landlords and rich farmers lost their lands, their personal property, their freedom, and sometimes their lives. Many of those who died had been tried and convicted of "crimes against the people" in people's tribunals set up under official sponsorship in towns and villages around the country. As Mao himself conceded, many were innocent of any crime, but in the eyes of the party, their deaths were necessary to destroy the power of the landed gentry in the countryside (see the box on p. 1047).

The Transition to Socialism

Originally, party leaders intended to follow the Leninist formula of delaying the building of a fully socialist society until China had a sufficient industrial base to permit the mechanization of agriculture. In 1953, the nation's first five-year plan (patterned after similar Soviet plans) was inaugurated. It called for substantial increases in industrial output. Lenin had believed that the lure of mechanization would provide Russian peasants with an incentive to join collective farms, which, because of their greater size and efficiency, could better afford to purchase expensive farm machinery. But the enormity of the challenge of providing tractors and reapers for millions of rural villages eventually convinced Mao Zedong and some of his colleagues that collectivization should be undertaken immediately in the hope that collective farms would increase food production and release land, labor, and capital for the industrial sector.

Accordingly, in 1955, when it felt secure from foreign threats, the Chinese government launched a new program to build a socialist society. Beginning in that year, virtually all private farmland was collectivized, although peasant families were allowed to retain small plots for their private use (a Chinese version of the private plots in the Soviet Union). In addition, most industry and commerce were nationalized.

Collectivization was achieved without provoking the massive peasant unrest that had taken place in the Soviet Union during the 1930s, perhaps because the Chinese government followed a policy of persuasion rather than compulsion (Mao Zedong said that Stalin had "drained the pond to catch the fish") and because the Communist land redistribution program had already earned the support of millions of rural Chinese. But the hoped-for production increases did not materialize, and in 1958 party leaders, at Mao's insistent urging, approved a more radical program known as the Great Leap Forward. Existing rural collectives, normally the size of the traditional village, were combined into vast "people's communes," each

Map 28.2 The People's Republic of China

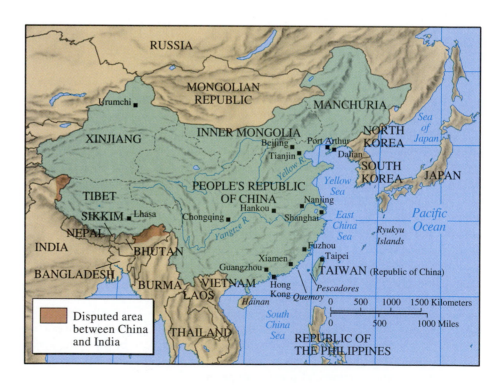

Disputed area between China and India

Land Reform in Action

One of the great achievements of the new Communist regime was the land reform program, which resulted in the distribution of farmland to almost two-thirds of the rural population in China. The program consequently won the gratitude of millions of Chinese. But it also had a dark side, as local land reform tribunals routinely convicted "wicked landlords" of crimes against the people and then put them to death. The following passage, written by a foreign observer, describes the process in one village.

Revolution in a Chinese Village

T'ien-ming [a Party cadre] called all the active young cadres and the militiamen of Long Bow [village] together and announced to them the policy of the county government, which was to confront all enemy collaborators and their backers at public meetings, expose their crimes, and turn them over to the county authorities for punishment. He proposed that they start with Kuo Te-yu, the puppet village head. Having moved the group to anger with a description of Te-yu's crimes, T'ien-ming reviewed the painful life led by the poor peasants during the occupation and recalled how hard they had all worked and how as soon as they harvested all the grain the puppet officials, backed by army bayonets, took what they wanted, turned over huge quantities to the Japanese devils, forced the peasants to haul it away, and flogged those who refused.

As the silent crowd contracted toward the spot where the accused man stood, T'ien-ming stepped forward . . . "This is our chance. Remember how we were oppressed. The traitors seized our property. They beat us and kicked us. . . .

Let us speak out the bitter memories. Let us see that the blood debt is repaid. . . ."

He paused for a moment. The peasants were listening to every word but gave no sign as to how they felt. . . .

"Come now, who has evidence against this man?"

Again there was silence.

Kuei-ts'ai, the new vice-chairman of the village, found it intolerable. He jumped up, struck Kuo Te-yu on the jaw with the back of his hand, "Tell the meeting how much you stole," he demanded.

The blow jarred the ragged crowd. It was as if an electric spark had tensed every muscle. Not in living memory had any peasant ever struck an official. . . .

The people in the square waited fascinated as if watching a play. They did not realize that in order for the plot to unfold they themselves had to mount the stage and speak out what was on their minds. No one moved to carry forward what Kuei-ts'ai had begun.

That evening T'ien-ming and Kuei-ts'ai called together the small groups of poor peasants from various parts of the village and sought to learn what it was that was really holding them back. *They soon found the root of the trouble was fear* of the old established political forces, and their military backers. The old reluctance to move against the power of the gentry, the fear of ultimate defeat and terrible reprisal that had been seared into the consciousness of so many generations lay like a cloud over the peasants' minds and hearts.

. . . The mobilization of the population could spread only slowly and in concentric circles like the waves on the surface of a pond when a stone is thrown in. The stone in this case was a small group of *chi-chi-fen-tzu* or "activists," as the cadres of the new administration and the core of its militia were called.

Emboldened by T'ien-ming's words other peasants began to speak out. They recalled what Te-yu had done to them personally. Several vowed to speak up and accuse him the next morning. After the meeting broke up, the passage of time worked its own leaven. In many a hovel and tumbledown house talk continued well past midnight. Some people were so excited they did not sleep at all. . . .

On the following day the meeting was livelier by far. It began with a sharp argument as to who would make the first accusation and T'ien-ming found it difficult to keep order. Before Te-yu had a chance to reply to any questions, a crowd of young men, among whom were several militiamen, surged forward ready to beat him.

containing more than 30,000 people. These communes were to be responsible for all administrative and economic tasks at the local level. The party's official slogan promised "Hard work for a few years, happiness for a thousand."[5]

Mao Zedong hoped this program would mobilize the population for a massive effort to accelerate economic growth and ascend to the final stage of communism before the end of the twentieth century. It is better, he said, to "strike while the iron is hot" and advance the revolution without interruption. Some party members were concerned that this ambitious program would threaten the government's rural base of support, but Mao argued that Chinese peasants were naturally revolutionary in spirit. The Chinese rural masses, he said, are "first of all, poor, and secondly, blank. That may seem like a bad

thing, but it is really a good thing. Poor people want change, want to do things, want revolution. A clean sheet of paper has no blotches, and so the newest and most beautiful words can be written on it, the newest and most beautiful pictures can be painted on it."[6] Those words, of course, were socialism and communism.

The Great Leap Forward was a disaster. Administrative bottlenecks, bad weather, and peasant resistance to the new system (which, among other things, attempted to eliminate work incentives and destroy the traditional family as the basic unit in Chinese society) combined to drive food production downward, and over the next few years, as many as 15 million people may have died of starvation. Many peasants were reportedly reduced to eating the bark off trees and in some cases to allowing infants to starve. In 1960, the commune experiment was essentially abandoned, and although the commune structure was retained, ownership and management were returned to the collective level. Mao Zedong was severely criticized by some of his more pragmatic colleagues (one remarked bitingly that "one cannot reach Heaven in a single step"), provoking him to complain that he had been relegated to the sidelines "like a Buddha on a shelf."

The Great Proletarian Cultural Revolution

But Mao was not yet ready to abandon either his power or his dream of a totally egalitarian society. In 1966, he returned to the attack, mobilizing discontented youth and disgruntled party members into revolutionary units known as Red Guards who were urged to take to the streets to cleanse Chinese society—from local schools and factories to government ministries in Beijing—of impure elements who (in Mao's mind, at least) were guilty of "taking the capitalist road." Supported by his wife Jiang Qing and other radical party figures, Mao launched China on a new forced march toward communism.

The so-called Great Proletarian Cultural Revolution (literally, great revolution to create a proletarian culture) lasted for ten years, from 1966 to 1976. Some Western observers interpreted it as a simple power struggle between Mao Zedong and some of his key rivals such as Liu Shaoqi (Liu Shao-ch'i), Mao's designated successor, and Deng Xiaoping (Teng Hsiao-p'ing), the party's general secretary. Both were removed from their positions, and Liu later died, allegedly of torture, in a Chinese prison. But real policy disagreements were involved. One reason Mao Zedong had advocated the Great Leap Forward was to bypass the party and government bureaucracy, which, in his view, had lost their revolutionary zeal and were pri-

♦ **Punishing Chinese Enemies during the Cultural Revolution.** The Cultural Revolution, which began in 1966, was a massive effort by Mao Zedong and his radical supporters to eliminate rival elements within the Chinese Communist party and the government. Accused of being "capitalist roaders," such individuals were subjected to public criticism and removed from their positions. Some were imprisoned or executed. Here Red Guards parade a victim wearing a dunce cap through the streets of Beijing.

marily concerned with protecting their power. Now he and his supporters feared that capitalist values and the remnants of "feudalist" Confucian ideas and practices would undermine ideological fervor and betray the revolutionary cause. Mao himself was convinced that only an atmosphere of constant revolutionary fervor could enable the Chinese to overcome the lethargy of the past and achieve the final stage of utopian communism. "I care not," he once wrote, "that the winds blow and the waves beat. It is better than standing idly in a courtyard."

His opponents, on the other hand, worried that Mao's "heaven-storming" approach could delay economic growth and antagonize the people, and they argued for a more pragmatic strategy that gave priority to nation building over the ultimate Communist goal of spiritual transformation. But with Mao's supporters now in power, the party carried out vast economic and educational reforms that virtually eliminated any remaining profit incentives and established a new school system that emphasized "Maozedong Thought" and stressed practical education at the elementary level at the expense of specialized training in science and the humanities in the universities. School learning was discouraged as a legacy of capitalism, and Mao's famous *Little Red Book* (a slim volume of Maoist aphorisms to encourage good behavior and revolutionary zeal) was hailed as the most important source of knowledge in all areas.

The radicals' efforts to destroy all vestiges of traditional society are reminiscent of the Reign of Terror in revolutionary France (see Chapter 19). Red Guards rampaged through the country attempting to eradicate the "four olds" (old thought, old culture, old customs, and old habits). They destroyed temples and religious sculptures and tore down street signs and replaced them with new ones carrying revolutionary names. At one point the city of Shanghai even ordered that the significance of colors in stoplights be changed, so that red (the revolutionary color) would indicate that traffic could move.

But a mood of revolutionary ferment and enthusiasm is difficult to sustain. Key groups, such as party bureaucrats, urban professionals, and many military officers, did not share Mao's belief in the benefits of "permanent revolution" and constant turmoil. Many were alienated by the arbitrary actions of the Red Guards, who indiscriminately accused and brutalized their victims in a society where legal safeguards had almost entirely vanished (see the box on p. 1050). Whether the Cultural Revolution led to declining productivity is a matter for debate. Inevitably, however, the sense of anarchy and uncertainty caused popular support for the movement to erode, and when the end came with Mao's death in 1976, the vast

majority of the population may well have welcomed its demise. Personal accounts by young Chinese who took part in the Cultural Revolution clearly show that their initial enthusiasm often turned to disillusionment. According to Liang Heng, author of a book entitled *Son of the Revolution,* at first he helped friends organize Red Guard groups:

> I thought it was a great idea. We would be following Chairman Mao just like the grownups, and Father would be proud of me. I suppose I too resented the teachers who had controlled and criticized me for so long, and I looked forward to a little revenge.[7]

Later, he had reason to repent. His sister ran off to join the local Red Guard group. Prior to her departure, she denounced her mother and the rest of her family as "rightists" and enemies of the revolution. Their home was regularly raided by Red Guards, and the father was severely beaten and tortured for having three neckties and "Western shirts." Books, paintings, and writings were piled in the center of the floor and burned before his eyes. On leaving, a few of the Red Guards helped themselves to his monthly salary and his transistor radio.

China after Mao

In September 1976, Mao Zedong died at the age of eighty-three. After a short but bitter succession struggle, the pragmatists led by Deng Xiaoping (1904–1997) seized power from the radicals and formally brought the Cultural Revolution to an end. Mao's widow, Jiang Qing, and three other radicals (derisively called the "gang of four") were placed on trial and sentenced to death or to long terms in prison. The egalitarian policies of the previous decade were reversed, and a new program emphasizing economic modernization was introduced.

Under the leadership of Deng Xiaoping, who placed his supporters in key positions throughout the party and the government, attention focused on what were called the "four modernizations" in industry, agriculture, technology, and national defense. Deng Xiaoping had been a leader of the faction that opposed Mao's program of rapid socialist transformation, and during the Cultural Revolution he had been forced to undergo menial labor to "sincerely correct his errors." But Deng continued to espouse the pragmatic approach and reportedly once remarked, "Black cat, white cat, what does it matter so long as it catches the mice?" Under the program of four modernizations, many of the restrictions against private activities and profit incentives were eliminated, and people were

☙ Make Revolution! ❧

In 1966, Mao Zedong unleashed the power of revolution on China. Rebellious youth in the form of Red Guards rampaged through all levels of society, exposing anti-Maoist elements, suspected "capitalist roaders," and those identified with the previous ruling class. In this poignant excerpt, Nien Cheng, the widow of an official of Chiang Kai-shek's regime, describes a visit by Red Guards to her home during the height of the Cultural Revolution.

Nien Cheng, *Life and Death in Shanghai*

From the direction of the street, faint at first but growing louder, came the sound of a heavy motor vehicle slowly approaching. I listened and waited for it to speed up and pass the house. But it slowed down, and the motor was cut off. I knew my neighbor on the left was also expecting the Red Guards. Dropping the book on my lap and sitting up tensely, I listened, wondering which house was to be the target.

Suddenly the doorbell began to ring incessantly. At the same time, there was furious pounding of many fists on my front gate, accompanied by the confused sound of hysterical voices shouting slogans. The cacophony told me that the time of waiting was over and that I must face the threat of the Red Guards and the destruction of my home. Lao-zhao came up the stairs

breathlessly. Although he had known the Red Guards were sure to come eventually and had been waiting night after night just as I had, his face was ashen.

"They have come!" His unsteady voice was a mixture of awe and fright.

"Please keep calm, Lao-zhao! Open the gate but don't say anything. Take Chen-ma with you to your room and stay there," I told him.

Outside, the sound of voices became louder. "Open the gate! Open the gate! Are you all dead? Whey don't you open the gate?" Someone was swearing and kicking the wooden gate. The horn of the truck was blasting too.

Lao-zhao ran downstairs. I stood up to put the book on the shelf. A copy of the Constitution of the People's Republic caught my eye. Taking it in my hand and picking up the bunch of keys I had ready on my desk, I went downstairs.

At the same moment, the Red Guards pushed open the front door and entered the house. There were thirty or forty senior high school students, aged between fifteen and twenty, led by two men and one woman much older.

The leading Red Guard, a gangling youth with angry eyes, stepped forward and said to me, "We are the

---

encouraged to work hard to benefit themselves and Chinese society.

Crucial to the program's success was the government's ability to attract foreign technology and capital. For over two decades, China had been isolated from technological advances taking place elsewhere in the world (see The Korean War in Chapter 27). Although China's leaders understandably prided themselves on their nation's capacity for "self-reliance," their isolationist policy had been exceedingly costly for the national economy. While China's post-Mao leaders blamed the country's backwardness on the "ten lost years" of the Cultural Revolution, the "lost years," at least in technological terms, extended back to the end of the Civil War in 1949 and in some respects even before. Now, to make up for lost time, the government encouraged foreign investment and sent thousands of students and specialists abroad to study capitalist techniques.

By adopting this pragmatic approach, in the years after 1976 China made great strides in ending its chronic problems of poverty and underdevelopment. Per capita

income roughly doubled during the 1980s; housing, education, and sanitation improved; and both agricultural and industrial output skyrocketed. Clearly, China had begun to enter the industrial age.

But critics, both Chinese and foreign, complained that Deng Xiaoping's program had failed to achieve a "fifth modernization"—that of democracy. Official sources denied such charges and spoke proudly of restoring "socialist legality" by doing away with the arbitrary punishments applied during the Great Proletarian Cultural Revolution. Deng Xiaoping himself encouraged the Chinese people to speak out against earlier excesses, particularly in the late 1970s when ordinary citizens pasted "big character posters" criticizing the abuses of the past on the so-called Democracy Wall near Tiananmen Square in downtown Beijing.

Yet it soon became clear that the new leaders would not tolerate any direct criticism of the Communist Party or of Marxist-Leninist ideology. Dissidents who called for the institution of the fifth modernization of democracy

Red Guards. We have come to take revolutionary action against you!"

Though I knew it was futile, I held up the copy of the Constitution and said calmly, "It's against the Constitution of the People's Republic of China to enter a private house without a search warrant."

The young man snatched the document out of my hand and threw it on the floor. With his eyes blazing, he said, "The Constitution is abolished. It was a document written by the Revisionists within the Communist Party. We recognize only the teachings of our Great Leader Chairman Mao."

"Only the People's Congress has the power to change the Constitution," I said.

"We have abolished it. What can you do about it?" he said aggressively while assuming a militant stance with feet apart and shoulders braced.

Another young man used a stick to smash the mirror hanging over the blackwood chest facing the front door.

Mounting the stairs, I was astonished to see several Red Guards taking pieces of my porcelain collection out of their padded boxes. One young man had arranged a set of four Kangxi winecups in a row on the floor and was stepping on them. I was just in time to

hear the crunch of delicate porcelain under the sole of his shoe. The sound pierced my heart. Impulsively I leapt forward and caught his leg just as he raised his foot to crush the next cup. He toppled. We fell in a heap together. My eyes searched for the other winecups to make sure we had not broken them in our fall, and momentarily distracted, I was not able to move aside when the boy regained his feet and kicked me right in my chest. I cried out in pain. The other Red Guards dropped what they were doing and gathered around us, shouting at me angrily for interfering in their revolutionary activities.

The young man whose revolutionary work of destruction I had interrupted said angrily, "You shut up! These things belong to the old culture. They are the useless toys of the feudal emperors and the modern capitalist class and have no significance to us, the proletarian class. They cannot be compared to cameras and binoculars, which are useful for our struggle in time of war. Our Great Leader Chairman Mao taught us, 'If we do not destroy, we cannot establish.' The old culture must be destroyed to make way for the new socialist culture."

---

were suppressed, and some were sentenced to long terms in prison. Among them was the well-known astrophysicist Fang Lizhi (Fang Li-chih), a longtime critic of Stalinism and Maoist "leftism." Fang spoke out publicly against official corruption and the continuing influence of Marxist-Leninist concepts in post-Mao China, telling an audience in Hong Kong that "China will not be able to modernize, if it does not break the shackles of Maoist and Stalinist-style socialism." Fang immediately felt the weight of official displeasure. He was refused permission to travel abroad, and articles that he submitted to official periodicals were rejected. Deng Xiaoping himself reportedly remarked: "We will not suppress people who hold differing political views from our own. But as for Fang Lizhi, he has been indulging in mudslinging and spreading slander without any basis, and we should take legal action against him." Replied Fang: "I have never criticized any Chinese leader by name, nor accused any of them of illegal acts or immoral activities. But some perhaps feel guilty. If the cap fits, wear it."[8]

The problem began to intensify in the late 1980s, as more Chinese began to study abroad, and more information about Western society reached educated individuals inside the country. Rising expectations aroused by the economic improvements of the early 1980s led in turn to increasing pressure from students and other urban residents for better living conditions, relaxed restrictions on study abroad, and increased freedom to select employment after graduation.

As long as economic conditions for the majority of Chinese were improving, other classes did not share the students' discontent, and the government was able to isolate them from other elements in society. But in the late 1980s, an overheated economy led to rising inflation and growing discontent among salaried workers, especially in the cities. At the same time, corruption, nepotism, and favored treatment for senior officials and party members were provoking increasing criticism. In May 1989, student protesters carried placards demanding Science and Democracy (reminiscent of the slogan of the May Fourth

◆ Give Me Liberty—or Give Me Death! The demonstrations that erupted in Tiananmen Square in the spring of 1989 spread rapidly to other parts of the country, where students and other local citizens gave their vocal support to the popular movement in Beijing. Here students from a high school march to the nearby city of Guilin to display their own determination to take part in the reform of Chinese society. Their call to "give me liberty or give me death" (in Patrick Henry's famous phrase) echoes the determination expressed by many of their counterparts in Beijing.

Movement, whose seventieth anniversary was celebrated in the spring of 1989) and an end to official corruption and the resignation of China's aging party leadership. These demands received widespread support from the urban population (although notably less in rural areas) and led to massive demonstrations in Tiananmen Square.

The demonstrations divided the Chinese leaders. Reformist elements around party general secretary Zhao Ziyang (b. 1919) were sympathetic to the protesters, but veteran leaders like Deng Xiaoping saw the student demands for more democracy as a disguised call for an end to Communist Party rule. After some hesitation, the government sent tanks and troops into Tiananmen Square to crush the demonstrators. Dissidents were arrested, and the regime once again began to stress ideological purity and socialist values. Although the crackdown provoked widespread criticism abroad, Chinese leaders insisted that economic reforms could only take place in conditions of party leadership and political stability.

During the next few years, the party cracked down vigorously on all signs of incipient opposition, while making strenuous efforts to alleviate urban discontent by stabilizing prices and increasing the availability of consumer goods. The fifth modernization demanded by the demonstrators in Tiananmen Square remained a chimera.

Serve the People: Chinese Society under Communism

Enormous changes have taken place in Chinese society since the Communist rise to power in 1949. Under the Nanjing regime, Sun Yat-sen's ideology of the Three People's Principles had replaced the Confucian values that had endured since the ancient Zhou dynasty. When that failed, China turned to the ideology of Marxism-Leninism, patterned after the socialist experiment in the Soviet Union. No longer a fundamentally agrarian and self-sufficient society, China today is launching its own version of the Industrial Revolution with all of the political, social, and cultural implications that process entails.

Yet, beneath the surface of rapid change, there are tantalizing hints of the survival of elements of the old China. Despite all the efforts of Sun Yat-sen, Mao Zedong, and their followers, the ideas of "Confucius and Sons" have still not irrevocably been thrown into the trashcan. China today remains a society that in many respects is in thrall to its past.

THE POLITICS OF THE MASS LINE

Nowhere is this uneasy balance between the old and the new more clearly demonstrated than in politics and government. The Chinese Communist Party (CCP) came to power in 1949 dedicated to eradicating what it described as the remnants of the feudalistic Confucian system and to building a set of political institutions based on Marxist principles. As Mao Zedong had declared in a speech to the CCP Central Committee in March:

> The Chinese revolution is great, but the road after the revolution will be longer, the work greater and more arduous. This must be made clear now in the Party. The comrades must be helped to remain modest, prudent, and free from arrogance and rashness in their style of work. The comrades must be helped to preserve the style of plain living and hard struggle.[9]

In its broad outlines, the new political system followed the Soviet pattern. Yet from the start, the Communist leaders made it clear that the Chinese model would differ from the Soviet in important respects. Whereas the Bolsheviks had severely distrusted nonrevolutionary elements in Russia and established a minority government based on the radical left, Mao Zedong and his colleagues were more confident that they possessed the basic support of the majority of the Chinese people. In New Democracy, the party attempted to reach out to all progressive classes in the population to maintain the alliance that had brought it to power in the first place.

As a symbolic confirmation of this broad-based policy, the CCP permitted minor political parties (the Democratic Party, the Socialist Party, and the so-called Revolutionary Branch of the Guomindang under Sun Yat-sen's widow, Soong Qingling) to represent the interests of progressive intellectuals and the bourgeoisie. But the primary link between the regime and the population was the system of "mass organizations," representing peasants, workers, women, religious groups, writers, and artists. The party had established these associations during the

CHRONOLOGY

China under Communist Rule

New Democracy	1949–1955
The Era of Collectivization	1955–1958
The 100 Flowers Campaign	1956–1957
The Great Leap Forward	1958–1960
The Great Proletarian Cultural Revolution	1966–1976
Death of Mao Zedong	1976
The Era of Deng Xiaoping	1978–1997
The Tiananmen Incident	1989

1920s to mobilize support for the revolution. Now they served as a conduit between party and people, enabling the leaders to assess the attitude of the masses while at the same time seeking their support for the party's programs. Behind this facade of representative institutions stood the awesome power of the CCP.

Initially, this "mass line" system worked fairly well. True, there was a human cost since opposition to the regime was ruthlessly suppressed, but on the positive side, China finally had a government that appeared to be for the people. Although there was no pretense at Western-style democracy, and official corruption and bureaucratic mismanagement and arrogance had by no means been entirely eliminated, the new ruling class came preponderantly from workers and peasants and, at least by comparison with its predecessors, was willing to listen to the complaints and aspirations of its constituents.

But the failure of the Great Leap Forward betrayed a fundamental weakness in the policy of the mass line. While party leaders declared their willingness to listen to the concerns of the population, they were also determined to build a utopian society based on Marxist-Leninist principles. The popular acceptance of nationalization and collectivization during the mid-1950s indicates that the Chinese people were not entirely hostile to socialism, but when those programs were carried to an extreme during the Great Leap Forward, many, even within the party, resisted and forced the government to abandon the program.

The failure of the Great Leap Forward split the CCP and led to the revolutionary disturbances of the following decade. The Cultural Revolution, which Mao launched in 1966, can be seen above all as his attempt to cleanse the system of its impurities and put Chinese society back on the straight road to egalitarian communism. Many of his compatriots evidently shared his beliefs. Young people in particular, alienated by the lack of job opportunities, flocked to his cause and served with enthusiasm in the Red Guard organizations that became the shock troops of the revolution. As we have seen, the enthusiasms aroused by the Cultural Revolution did not last. As in the French Revolution, the efforts to achieve revolutionary purity eventually alienated all except the most radical elements in the country, and a period of reaction inevitably set in. In China, revolutionary fervor has given way to a new era in which belief in socialist ideals has been replaced by a more practical desire for material benefits.

After Mao's death, the new Chinese leadership under Deng Xiaoping recognized the need to restore a sense of "socialist legality" and credibility to a system that was on the verge of breakdown. Deng's encouragement of Democracy Wall in 1979 was an attempt to rebuild the links between the party and the masses. But like other Communist leaders, Deng soon discovered that once the people have been encouraged to criticize current conditions, it is difficult to prevent them from focusing on the linchpin of the entire Marxist-Leninist system, the dictatorship of the proletariat and the party's domination of power.

The regime attempted to suppress the criticism by closing down Democracy Wall and providing new guidelines—called the "Four Cardinal Principles"—that prohibited criticism of the socialist system, the dictatorship of the proletariat, Marxist-Leninist-Maoist thought, and the final goal of communism. But the credibility of Marxist thought, and of the CCP itself, had been severely shaken by recent events. Although the demonstrations at Tiananmen Square in 1989 were not aimed directly at the party's authority, many of the demonstrators viewed its dominant role in political affairs as the heart of the problem.

Deng Xiaoping and other aging party leaders turned to the army to protect their base of power and suppress what they described as "counterrevolutionary elements." Deng was undoubtedly counting on the fact that many Chinese, particularly in rural areas, feared a recurrence of the disorder of the Cultural Revolution and craved economic prosperity more than political reform. In the months following the confrontation, the government issued new regulations requiring courses on Marxist-Leninist ideology in the schools, sought out dissidents within the intellectual community, and made it clear that while economic reforms would continue, the CCP's monopoly of power would not be allowed to decay. During the 1990s, the government has imposed harsh punishment on those accused of undermining the Communist system and supporting its enemies abroad.

Whether the current leaders will be able to prevent the further erosion of the party's power and prestige is unclear. Dissatisfaction with the CCP and alienation from the socialist system are running high in China, notably among the educated youth, the professionals, and the middle ranks of the bureaucracy. Although a disintegration of the authority of the Communist regime in China as in the Soviet Union cannot be predicted, the trend toward a greater popular role in the governing process will be difficult to reverse.

ECONOMICS IN COMMAND

During the late 1950s, Mao Zedong began to maintain that political considerations were more important than economic ones in building a socialist society. This attitude had been symbolized by the well-known catch phrase "politics in command" and had been a major factor in the abandonment of the mass line policy in the late 1950s. After 1976 Deng Xiaoping and other party leaders were obviously hoping that rapid economic growth would satisfy the Chinese people and prevent them from demanding political reforms. Here the post-Mao leadership has shown a clear willingness to place economic performance over ideological purity. Deng Xiaoping and his colleagues rapidly dismantled many of the official restrictions on private economic activities that had hindered productivity since the mid-1950s. To stimulate the stagnant industrial sector, which had been under state control since the end of the era of New Democracy, they reduced bureaucratic controls over state industries and allowed local managers to have more say over prices, salaries, and quality control. Productivity was encouraged by permitting bonuses to be paid for extra effort, a policy that had been discouraged during the Cultural Revolution. State firms were no longer guaranteed access to precious resources and were told to compete with each other for public favor and even to export goods on their own initiative.

The regime also tolerated the emergence of a small private sector. Unemployed youth were encouraged to set up restaurants, bicycle or radio repair shops, and handicraft shops on their own initiative. At first, the government insisted that all participants should be considered joint owners, making the ventures a form of collective, but eventually the new businesses were permitted to hire workers. Attempts to restrict the number of salaried workers were generally ignored.

Finally, the regime opened up the country to foreign investment and technology. The Maoist policy of self-reliance was abandoned, and China openly sought the advice of foreign experts and the money of foreign capitalists. Special economic zones were established in urban centers near the coast (ironically, many were located in the old nineteenth-century treaty ports), where lucrative concessions were offered to encourage foreign firms to build factories. The tourist industry was encouraged, and students were sent abroad to study.

The new leaders especially stressed educational reform. The system adopted during the Cultural Revolution, which emphasized practical education and ideology at the expense of higher education and modern science, was rapidly abandoned (the *Little Red Book* itself was withdrawn from circulation and could no longer be found on bookshelves), and a new system based generally on the Western model was instituted. Admission to higher education was based on success in merit examinations, and courses on science and mathematics received high priority.

No economic reform program could succeed unless it included the countryside. Three decades of socialism had done little to increase food production or to lay the basis for a modern agricultural sector. The initial effort to follow the Leninist-Stalinist model had been abandoned, and the Maoist attempt to utilize the labor power of the rural masses had fared no better. China, with a population now numbering one billion, could still barely feed itself. Peasants had little incentive to work and few opportunities to increase production through mechanization, the use of fertilizer, or better irrigation.

Under Deng Xiaoping, agricultural policy made a rapid about-face. Under the new "rural responsibility system," adopted shortly after Deng Xiaoping had consolidated his authority, collectives leased land on contract to peasant families, who paid a quota in the form of rent to the collective. Anything produced on the land above that payment could be sold on the private market or consumed. To soak up excess labor in the villages, the government encouraged the formation of so-called sideline industries, a modern equivalent of the traditional cottage industries in premodern China. Peasants raised fish or shrimp, made consumer goods, and even assembled living room furniture and appliances for sale to their newly affluent compatriots.

The reform program had a striking effect on rural production. Grain production increased rapidly and farm income doubled during the 1980s. Yet it also created problems. In the first place, income at the village level became more unequal as some enterprising farmers

(known locally as "ten thousand dollar" households) earned profits several times those realized by their less fortunate or less industrious neighbors. When some farmers discovered they could earn more by growing cash crops or other specialized commodities, they devoted less land to rice and other grain crops, thus threatening to reduce the supply of China's most crucial staple. Finally, the agricultural policy threatened to undermine the government's population control program, which party leaders viewed as crucial to the success of the four modernizations.

Since a misguided period in the mid-1950s when Mao Zedong had argued that more labor would result in higher productivity, China had been attempting to limit its population growth. By 1970, the government had launched a stringent family planning program, including education, incentives, and penalties for noncompliance, to persuade the Chinese people to limit themselves to one child per family. The program did have some success, and population growth was reduced drastically in the early 1980s. The rural responsibility system, however, undermined the program, because it encouraged farm families to pay the penalties for having additional children in the belief that their labor would increase family income and provide the parents with a form of social security for their old age.

Still, the overall effects of the modernization program were impressive. The standard of living had improved for the majority of the population. Whereas a decade earlier the average Chinese had struggled to earn enough to buy a bicycle, radio, watch, or washing machine, by the late 1980s many were beginning to purchase videocassette recorders, refrigerators, and color television sets. The government popularized the idea that all Chinese would prosper, although not necessarily at the same speed. Earlier slogans such as "serve the people" and "uphold the banner of Marxist-Leninist-Maoist thought" were replaced by others that announced that "time is money" and instructed citizens to "create wealth for the people." The party announced that China was still at the "primary stage of socialism" and might not reach the state of utopian communism for generations.

Yet the rapid growth of the economy created its own problems of inflationary pressures, greed and envy, increased corruption, and—most dangerous of all for the regime—rising expectations. Young people in particular resented restrictions on employment (most young people in China are still required to accept the jobs that are offered to them by the government or school officials) and opportunities to study abroad. Disillusionment ran high, especially in the cities where high living by officials and

♦ **Student Fashions: Before and after Deng.**   The increasing affluence of Chinese society is evident in the changes in clothing styles since the end of the Cultural Revolution. The picture on the left shows student dress in the late 1970s. Ten years of modernization under Deng Xiaoping have led to more sophisticated styles, as the photo on the right attests. (One of the authors—William Duiker—is pictured on the left.)

rising prices for goods aroused widespread alienation and cynicism. Such attitudes undoubtedly contributed to the anger and frustration that burst out during the spring of 1989, when many workers, peasants, and functionaries joined the demonstrations against official corruption and one-party rule in Tiananmen Square.

In the 1990s, the government began to nurture urban support by controlling the rate of inflation and guaranteeing the availability of the consumer goods that were in great demand among the growing middle class. That policy has paid dividends in bringing about a perceptible decline in alienation among the population in the cities. Industrial production has been increasing rapidly, leading to predictions that China may become one of the economic superpowers in the twenty-first century. But problems in rural areas are on the rise. Farm income has lagged behind in recent years, and high taxes and official corruption have sparked increasing resentment among the rural populace (see the box on p. 1057). In the meantime, food production has leveled off for a variety of reasons, prompting some observers to question whether China will be able to feed its growing population in the early years of the new century.

EAST FOR ESSENCE, WEST FOR PRACTICAL USE: ARE MARXISM AND AFFLUENCE COMPATIBLE?

These recent events have highlighted a serious dilemma facing China's aging leaders: How can they introduce Western technology and work habits without at the same time infecting the Chinese people with the virus of bourgeois individualism and the desire for personal profit and advancement? When the program of modernization was first launched in the late 1970s, conservative party officials warned that when the windows were opened, dust, flies, and all sorts of bad things would come in. Deng Xiaoping attempted to reassure them. In that case, he said, we will simply use our flyswatters. But will the flyswatters be enough? Or will the regime's current effort to introduce Western technology while preserving the essence of Chinese socialism go the way of the nineteenth-century slogan of East for Essence, West for Practical Use (see Chapter 23)?

From the start, the CCP intended to bring an end to the Confucian legacy in modern China. At the root of Marxist-Leninist ideology is the idea of building a new citizen free from the prejudices, ignorance, and superstition of the "feudal" era and the capitalist desire for self-gratification. This new citizen would be characterized not only by a sense of racial and sexual equality, but also by the selfless desire to contribute his or her utmost for the good of all. In the words of Mao Zedong's famous work "The Foolish Old Man Who Removed the Mountains," the people should "be resolute, fear no sacrifice, and surmount every difficulty to win victory."[10]

The new government wasted no time in keeping its promise. During the early 1950s, it took a number of steps to bring a definitive end to the old system in China. Women were permitted to vote and encouraged to become active in the political process. At the local level, an

Trouble in the Garlic Fields

Considered one of the masterpieces of recent Chinese literature, Mo Yan's The Garlic Ballads (1988) describes with passion and intimacy the suffering of contemporary Chinese peasants in North China. Based on real-life riots in North China in the summer of 1987, the novel is a plea for social reform, as it exposes the greed, corruption, and inhumanity of the local government and the legacy of the feudal mentality. Oppressed and betrayed by their cadres, a group of garlic farmers are swept up into a riot against the local administrator. Mo Yan depicts the resilience and courage of Chinese peasants in the face of incredible hardship and violent oppression. In the closing pages of the novel, at the trial of the peasant rioters, a young military officer, speaking for the author and human decency, accuses the local judge of turning the court into a travesty of justice.

Mo Yan, *The Garlic Ballads*

He turned to face the spectators, speaking with a passion that touched everyone who heard him. "Your Honors, ladies and gentlemen, the situation in our farming villages has changed drastically in the wake of the Party's Third Plenary Session of the Eleventh Central Committee, including those here in Paradise County. The peasants are much better off than they were during the Cultural Revolution. This is obvious to everyone. But the benefits they enjoyed as a result of rural economic reforms are gradually disappearing."

"Please don't stray too far from the subject," the presiding judge broke in.

"Thank you for reminding me, Your Honor: I'll get right to the point. In recent years the peasants have been called upon to shoulder ever heavier burdens: fees, taxes, fines, and inflated prices for just about everything they need. No wonder you hear them talk about plucking the wild goose's tail feathers as it flies by. Over the past couple of years these trends have gotten out of control, which is why, I believe, the Paradise County garlic incident should have come as no surprise."

The presiding judge glanced down at his wristwatch.

"Not being able to sell their crops was the spark that ignited this explosive incident, but the root cause was the unenlightened policies of the Paradise County government!" the officer continued. "Before Liberation only about a dozen people were employed by the district government, and things worked fine. Now even a township government in charge of the affairs of a mere thirty thousand people employs more than sixty people! And when you add those in the communes it's nearly a hundred, seventy percent of whose salaries are paid by peasants through township fees and taxes. Put in the bluntest possible terms, they are feudal parasites on the body of society! So in my view, the slogans 'Down with corrupt officials!' and 'Down with bureaucrats!' comprise a progressive call for the awakening of the peasants. . . .

"What I want to say is this," the young officer continued. "The people have the right to overthrow any party or government that disregards their well-being. If an official assumes the role of public master rather than public servant, the people have the right to throw him out! . . . In point of fact, things have improved in the wake of the party rectification, and most of Paradise County's responsible party members are doing a fine job. But one rat turd can spoil a whole pot of porridge, and the unprincipled behavior of a single party member adversely affects the party's reputation and the government's prestige. The people aren't always fair and discerning, and can be forgiven if their dissatisfaction with a particular official carries over into their attitudes toward officials in general. But shouldn't that be a reminder to officials to act in such a way as to best represent the party and the government?

". . . If we endorse the proposition that all people are equal under the law, then we must demand that the Paradise County People's Procuratorate indict Paradise County administrator Zhong Weimin on charges of official misconduct! I have nothing more to say."

The young officer remained standing for a moment before wearily taking a seat behind the defense table. Thunderous applause erupted from the spectator section behind him.

increasing number of women became active in the CCP and in collective organizations. In 1950, a new Marriage Law was passed, which guaranteed women equal rights with men. Most importantly, perhaps, it permitted women for the first time to initiate divorce proceedings against their husbands. Within a year, nearly one million divorces had been granted.

The regime also undertook to destroy the influence of the traditional family system. To the Communists, loyalty to the family, a crucial element in the Confucian social order, undercut loyalty to the state and to the dictatorship of the proletariat. Such concerns had been raised by reform-minded Chinese long before the Communists' rise to power. As we have seen, at the beginning of the century Sun Yat-sen had complained that China's family-oriented society lacked a concept of statehood, noting that the Chinese people were like "a sheet of loose sand." He believed loyalty to family undermined loyalty to the nation. Mao Zedong agreed. For Communist leaders, family loyalty contradicted the basic principle of Marxism—dedication to society at large.

At first, the new government moved carefully to avoid alienating its supporters in the countryside unnecessarily. When collective farms were established in the mid-1950s, each member of a collective accumulated "work points" based on the number of hours worked during a specified time period. Payment for work points was made not to the individual, but to the family head. The payments, usually in the form of ration coupons, could then be spent at the collective community store. Because the payments went to the head of the family, the traditionally dominant position of the patriarch was maintained. When people's communes were established in the late 1950s, payments went to the individual.

During the growing internal struggle and political radicalism of the Great Leap Forward, children were encouraged to report to the authorities any comments by their parents that criticized the system. Such practices continued during the Cultural Revolution, when young Red Guards were directed to root out all forms of reactionary thought from any source. Children were expected to report on their parents, students on their teachers, and employees on their superiors. Some have suggested that Mao deliberately encouraged such practices to bring an end to the traditional "politics of dependency." According to this theory, historically the famous "five relationships" forced individuals to swallow their anger and frustration and accept the hierarchical norms established by Confucian ethics (known in Chinese as "eat bitterness"). By encouraging the oppressed elements in society, such as the young, the female, and the poor, to voice their bitter-

ness, Mao was helping to break the tradition of dependency. Such denunciations had been issued against landlords and other "local tyrants" in the land reform tribunals of the late 1940s and early 1950s. Later, during the Cultural Revolution, they were applied to other authority figures in Chinese society.

At the time, many outside observers feared that the Cultural Revolution would transform the Chinese people into a race of automatons mindlessly spouting the slogans and the class hatred fed to them by their leaders. After the decline of the movement in the early 1970s, it became clear that such fears were exaggerated. In the end, the chaotic character of the Cultural Revolution doomed it to failure. Mao's gamble that the Chinese people would respond to his call for permanent revolution did not take into account their craving for order and their ultimately practical approach to the problems of human existence. After a decade of fear, turmoil, growing economic hardship, and arbitrary arrests, most Chinese probably greeted the end of the era with a great sense of exhaustion and relief.

The post-Mao era brought a decisive shift away from revolutionary utopianism and a return to the pragmatic approach to nation building. For most people, it meant improved living conditions and a qualified return to family traditions. Spurred by Deng Xiaoping's slogan "create wealth for the people," for the first time in more than a decade, enterprising Chinese began to concentrate on improving their standard of living. For the first time, millions of Chinese saw the prospect of a house or an urban flat with a washing machine, television set, and indoor plumbing. Married couples who had been given patriotic names such as "build the country," "protect Mao Zedong," and "assist Korea" by their parents began to choose more elegant and cosmopolitan names for their own children. Some names, such as "surplus grain" or "bring a younger brother," expressed hope for the future. One Western observer reported that he had encountered a young Chinese named Dian Shi, or "color television." When asked for an explanation, the father replied that if he had not had to pay a fine for having an extra child, he would have bought a color television set with the money.

The new attitudes are also reflected in physical appearance. For a generation after the civil war, clothing had been restricted to the traditional baggy "Mao suit" in olive drab or dark blue, but today young people crave such fashionable Western items as designer jeans, trendy sneakers, and sweat suits (or reasonable facsimiles). Cosmetic surgery to create a more buxom figure or a more Western facial look is increasingly common among affluent young women in the cities. Many have had the epicanthic fold over their eyelids removed or even added to their noses—a curious decision in view of the tradition of referring derogatorily to foreigners as "big noses."

Religious practices and beliefs have also changed. As the government has become more tolerant, some Chinese have been returning to the traditional Buddhist faith, and Buddhist and Taoist temples are once again crowded with worshipers. Christianity has become increasingly popular; like the "rice Christians" (persons who supposedly converted for economic reasons) of the past, many view it as a symbol of success and cosmopolitanism. Others have taken part in underground church activities as a form of protest against widespread corruption and the one-child policy. To control such practices, the government is attempting to register all churches and monitor the movements of foreign missionaries.

Such changes are much more prevalent among urban dwellers and China's still small middle class than among rural folk, who make up more than half the population. Although prosperity has come to some parts of the countryside—notably in areas located near the major metropolitan centers—the vast majority of peasants have been only superficially affected by the events since Mao's death. In that sense, the yawning gap that has always separated town and country in China still remains. Because of the growing problem of youthful unemployment, for example, young people in rural areas have been told that if they were born and raised on a farm, they are likely to remain there for the rest of their lives.

As with all social changes, China's reintegration into the outside world has had a price. Arranged marriages, nepotism, and mistreatment of females (for example, many parents in rural areas reportedly have killed female infants in the hope of having a son) have come back, although such behavior likely had survived under the cloak of revolutionary purity for a generation. Materialistic attitudes, including a desire for expensive weddings, are highly prevalent among young people along with a corresponding cynicism about politics and the CCP, and bribery and favoritism are all too frequent. Crime of all types, including prostitution and sex crimes against women, appears to be on the rise. To discourage violence against women, the government now tries to provide free legal services for women living in rural areas.

Partly out of fear that such changes could undermine the socialist system and the rule of the CCP, conservative leaders have attempted to curb Western influence and restore faith in Marxism-Leninism. Recently, in what may be a tacit recognition that Marxist exhortations are no longer an effective means of enforcing social discipline, the party has turned to Confucianism. Ceremonies celebrating the birth of Confucius now receive official sanction, and the virtues promoted by the Master, such as righteousness, propriety, and filial piety, are widely cited as antidotes to the tide of antisocial behavior. A recent article in *People's Daily* asserted that the current spiritual crisis in contemporary Western culture stems from the incompatibility of science and the Christian religion. The solution, the author maintained, was Confucianism, which is "a non-religious humanism that can provide the basis for morals and the value of life." Because a culture combining science and Confucianism is taking shape in

◆ **Downtown Beijing Today.** Deng Xiaoping's policy of four modernizations has had a dramatic visual effect on the capital city of Beijing, as evidenced by this photo of skyscrapers thrusting up beyond the walls of the fifteenth-century Imperial City. One of the heavy prices that the Chinese people pay for industrialization is environmental pollution, which, as here, frequently hovers as a dense haze over the entire city.

East Asia today, "it will thrive particularly well in the next century and will replace modern and contemporary Western culture."[11]

In the short term, such efforts may have some success in slowing down the rush toward Westernization because many Chinese are understandably fearful of punishment and concerned for their careers. But one is inevitably reminded of Chiang Kai-shek's failed attempt in the 1930s to revive Confucian ethics as a standard of behavior for modern China—dead ideologies cannot be revived by decree.

CHINA'S CHANGING CULTURE

The rise to power of the CCP in 1949 added a new dimension to the ongoing debate over the future of culture in China. Party leaders rejected the Western slogan of "art for art's sake" and, like their Soviet counterparts, viewed culture as an important instrument for indoctrination. The standard would no longer be aesthetic quality or the personal preference of the artist, but "art for life's safe," whereby culture would serve the interests of socialism. Through socialist realism, a concept borrowed from the Soviet Union, literature, art, and music would introduce the Chinese people to the superior virtues of socialist society.

At first, the new emphasis on socialist realism, which shared the Confucian conviction that culture must cultivate the mind, did not entirely extinguish the influence of traditional culture. Mao and his colleagues saw the importance of traditional values and culture in building a strong new China and tolerated—and in some cases even encouraged—efforts by artists to synthesize traditional ideas with socialist concepts and Western techniques. In the 1950s, for example, Chinese painting and classical music were highly syncretic. Under the surface, however, the debate over the role of tradition continued. During the 1960s, the issue became entwined in the political struggle between radicals and moderates over the future course of the Chinese revolution. The radicals around Mao Zedong who seized power during the Cultural Revolution viewed all forms of traditional culture as reactionary and wanted to create a new proletarian culture that would lead society toward communism. Socialist realism became the only standard for acceptability in literature, art, and music. All forms of traditional expression were forbidden.

Nowhere were the dilemmas of the new order more challenging than in literature. In the heady afterglow of the Communist victory in the civil war, many progressive writers supported the new regime and enthusiastically embraced Mao's exhortation to create a new Chinese literature for the edification of the masses. But in the harsher climate of the late 1950s and 1960s, many were criticized by the party for their excessive individualism and admiration for Western culture. Such writers either toed the new line and suppressed their doubts or were jailed and silenced.

A characteristic example of the changing cultural climate in China was the author Ding Ling. Born in 1904 and educated in a school for women set up by leftist intellectuals during the hectic years after the May Fourth Movement, she began writing in her early twenties. At first she was strongly influenced by prevailing Western styles, but after her husband, a struggling young poet and a member of the CCP, was executed by Chiang Kai-shek's government in 1931, she became active in party activities and sublimated her talent to the revolutionary cause.

In the late 1930s, Ding Ling settled in Yan'an, where she became a leader in the party's women's and literary associations. She remained dedicated to revolution, but years of service to the party had not stifled her individuality, and in 1942 she wrote critically of the incompetence, arrogance, and hypocrisy of many party officials, as well as the treatment of women in areas under Communist authority. Such conduct raised eyebrows, but she was able to survive criticism and in 1948 wrote her most famous novel, *The Sun Shines over the Sangan River,* which described the CCP's land reform program in favorable terms. It was awarded the Stalin Prize three years later.

During the early 1950s, Ding Ling was one of the most prominent literary lights of the new China, but in the more ideological climate at the end of the decade, she was attacked for her individualism and her previous criticism of the party. Although temporarily rehabilitated, during the Cultural Revolution she was sentenced to hard labor on a commune in the far north and was only released in the late 1970s after the death of Mao Zedong. Crippled and in poor health, she died in 1981.

Ding Ling's story was not unique and mirrors the fate of thousands of progressive Chinese intellectuals who, despite their efforts, were not able to satisfy the constantly changing demands of a repressive regime. Lionized during the conciliatory period of the early 1950s and encouraged to criticize society's shortcomings during a brief period of political relaxation called the One Hundred Flowers Movement in 1956, their voices were silenced during the Cultural Revolution, when only hymns of praise for revolutionary China and its "Great Helmsman" Mao Zedong were permitted.

After Mao's death, Chinese culture was once again released from the shackles of socialist realism. In painting, the new policies led to the revival of interest in both traditional and Western forms. The revival of interest in traditional art was in part a matter of practicality, as talented young Chinese had been trained to produce traditional paintings for export to earn precious foreign currency for the state. But the regime also showed a new tolerance for the imitation of Western styles as a necessary by-product of development. A new generation of Chinese painters began to emerge in the 1980s. Although some continued the attempt to blend Eastern and Western styles, others have imitated trends from abroad, experimenting with a wide range of previously prohibited art styles including Cubism and Abstract Expressionism. In recent years, Chinese folk art, often painted anonymously by older women in rural areas, has earned rising popularity.

In music, too, the post-Mao era brought significant changes. Music academies that had been closed during the Cultural Revolution for sowing the seeds of the bourgeois mentality were reopened. Students were permitted to study both Chinese and Western styles, but the vast majority selected the latter. To provide examples, leading musicians and composers like the violinist Isaac Stern were invited to China to lecture and perform before eager Chinese students. Western visitors could not but be aware of the trend, as Chinese orchestras greeted foreign tourist groups with earnest renditions of such old favorites as the "Red River Valley" and "Auld Lang Syne." By the late 1980s, popular music began to take on a more political orientation, as many rock musicians were active in the student protest movement. After Tiananmen, lyrics were often infused with social alienation, as in one hit song that closed by repeating the phrase, "What difference does it make?" As in the West, popular music has become part of the counterculture.

Today, as in earlier periods, the limits on freedom of expression are most apparent in literature. During the early 1980s, the party leaders encouraged Chinese writers to express their views on the shortcomings of the past, and a new "literature of the wounded" began to describe the violence, brutality, and arbitrary character of the Cultural Revolution. One of the most prominent writers was Bai Hua, whose script for the film *Bitter Love* described the life of a young Chinese painter who joined the revolutionary movement during the 1940s but was destroyed during the Cultural Revolution when his work was condemned as counterrevolutionary. The film depicts the condemnation through a view of a street in Beijing "full of people waving the *Quotations of Chairman Mao,* all those devout and artless faces fired by a feverish fanaticism." Driven from his home for posting a portrait of a third-century B.C.E. defender of human freedom on a

◆ **A Street Calligrapher.** During the Great Proletarian Cultural Revolution, all aspects of traditional culture were forbidden. Only items with revolutionary themes were permitted to be created or displayed. This elderly Chinese gentleman, a calligrapher by profession, had been prohibited from practicing his craft for two decades until the post-Mao era in the 1980s. He has now resumed his career at a roadside stand on a residential street in Beijing.

⇒ Marriage Chinese Style ⇐

"What men can do, women can also do." So said Chairman Mao as he "liberated" and masculinized Chinese women to work alongside men. Women's individuality and sexuality were sacrificed for the collective good of his new socialist society. Marriage, which had traditionally been arranged by families for financial gain, was now dictated by duty to the state. The Western concept of romantic love did not enter into a Chinese marriage, as this interview of a schoolteacher by the reporter Zhang Xinxin in the mid-1980s illustrates. According to recent surveys, the same is true today.

Zhang Xinxin, *Chinese Lives*

My husband and I never did any courting—honestly! We registered our marriage a week after we'd met. He was just out of the forces and a worker in a building outfit. They'd been given a foreign-aid assignment in Zambia, and he was selected. He wanted to get his private life fixed up before he went, and someone introduced us. Seeing how he looked really honest, I accepted him.

No, you can't say I didn't know anything about him. The person who introduced us told me he was a Party member who'd been an organization commissar. Any comrade who's good enough to be an organization cadre is politically reliable. Nothing special about our standing of living—it's what we've earned. He's still a worker, but we live all right, don't we?

He went off with the army as soon as we'd registered our marriage and been given the wedding certificates. He was away three years. We didn't have the wedding itself before he went because we hadn't got a room yet.

Those three years were a test for us. The main problem was that my family was against it. They thought I was still only a kid and I'd picked the wrong man. What did they have against him? His family was too poor. Of course I won in the end—we'd registered and got our wedding certificates. We were legally married whether we had the family ceremony or not.

We had our wedding after he came back in the winter of 1973. His leaders and mine all came to congratulate us and give us presents. The usual presents those days were busts of Chairman Mao. I was twenty-six and he was twenty-nine. We've never had a row.

Beijing wall, the artist flees the city. At the end of the film, he dies in a snowy field, where his corpse and a semicircle made by his footprints form a giant question mark.

In criticizing the excesses of the Cultural Revolution, Bai Hua was only responding to Deng Xiaoping's appeal for intellectuals to speak out, but like his counterparts during the Hundred Flowers era, he was soon criticized for failing to point out the essentially beneficial role of the CCP in recent Chinese history, and his film was withdrawn from circulation in 1981. Bai Hua was compelled to recant his errors and to state that the great ideas of Mao Zedong on art and literature were "still of universal guiding significance today."[12] Nevertheless, he was arrested during a 1996 campaign against "spiritual pollution" and criticized for being an "avant garde intellectual."

As the attack on Bai Hua illustrates, many party leaders remained suspicious of the impact that "decadent" bourgeois culture could have on the socialist foundations of Chinese society, and the official press periodically warned that China should adopt only the "positive" aspects of Western culture (notably, its technology and its work ethic) and not the "negative" elements such as drug use, pornography, and hedonism. Conservatives were es-

pecially incensed by the tendency of many writers to dwell on the shortcomings of the socialist system and to come uncomfortably close to direct criticism of the role of the CCP.

One author whose writings fell under the harsh glare of official disapproval was Zhang Xinxin (b. 1953). Her controversial novellas and short stories, which explored Chinese women's alienation and spiritual malaise, were viewed by many as a negative portrayal of contemporary society, and in 1984 the government prohibited her from publishing for a year. Determined and resourceful, Zhang turned to journalism. With a colleague she interviewed one hundred "ordinary" people to record their views on all aspects of everyday life (see the box above and on p. 1063).

The effort to restrict the freedom of China's writers, artists, and intellectuals has intensified since the Tiananmen Square demonstrations in 1989. Critics have been arrested or expelled from the party, and others (like Bai Hua) have been bullied into silence. But whether China's conservative leaders will be more successful at separating "essence" from "practical use" than their predecessors, the Self Strengtheners, a century ago (see Chapter 23) is not clear.

I never really wanted to take the college entrance exams. Then in 1978 the school leadership got us all to put our names forward. They said they weren't going to hold us back: the more of us who passed, the better it would be for the school. So I put my name forward, crammed for six weeks, and passed. I already had two kids then. . . .

I reckoned the chance for study was too good to miss. And my husband was looking after the kids all by himself. I usually only came back once a fortnight. So I couldn't let him down.

My instructors urged me to take the exams for graduate school, but I didn't. I was already thirty-four, so what was the point of more study? There was another reason too. I didn't want an even wider gap between us: he hadn't even finished junior middle school when he joined the army.

It's bad if the gap's too wide. For example, there's a definite difference in our tastes in music and art, I have to admit that. But what really matters? Now we've set up this family we have to preserve it. Besides, look at all the sacrifices he had to make to see me through col-

lege. Men comrades all like a game of cards and that, but he was stuck with looking after the kids. He still doesn't get any time for himself—it's all work for him.

We've got a duty to each other. Our differences? The less said about them the better. We've always treated each other with the greatest respect.

Of course some people have made suggestions, but my advice to him is to respect himself and respect me. I'm not going to be like those men who ditch their wives when they go up in the world.

I'm the head of our school now. With this change in my status I've got to show even more responsibility for the family. Besides, I know how much he's done to get me where I am today. I've also got some duties in the municipal Women's Federation and Political Consultative Conference. No, I'm not being modest. I haven't done anything worth talking about, only my duty.

We've got to do a lot more educating people. There have been two cases of divorce in our school this year.

Conclusion

Why has communism survived in China, albeit in a substantially altered form, when it collapsed in Eastern Europe and the Soviet Union? Although there may be many reasons, one of the primary causes is probably cultural. Although the doctrine of Marxism-Leninism originated in Europe, many of its main precepts, such as the primacy of the community over the individual and the denial of the concept of private property, run counter to the central trends in Western civilization. This is especially the case in the societies of Central Europe, which have been strongly influenced by Enlightenment philosophy and the Industrial Revolution. These forces are weaker in the countries further to the east, but both had begun to penetrate Tsarist Russia by the end of the nineteenth century.

By contrast, Marxism-Leninism found a more receptive climate in China. In political culture, the Communist system contains many of the same characteristics as State Confucianism (a single truth, an elite governing class, and an emphasis on obedience to the community and its governing representatives), while feudal attitudes

regarding female inferiority, loyalty to the family, and bureaucratic arrogance are hard to break. China today bears a number of uncanny similarities to the China of the past.

Yet these similarities should not blind us to the real changes that are taking place in Chinese society today. Although the youthful protesters in Tiananmen Square are comparable in some respects to the reformist elements of the 1890s or the New Culture intellectuals of the early republic—two generations of reformers whose passionate strivings to create a modern China on the Western model helped to destroy the old system but failed to lay firm foundations for a new one—the China of today is fundamentally different from that of the late Qing or even the early republic. Literacy rates and the standard of living, on balance, are far higher, the pressures of outside powers are less threatening, and China has entered the opening stages of its own industrial and technological revolution. Where Sun Yat-sen, Chiang Kai-shek, and even Mao Zedong broke their lances on the rocks of centuries of tradition, poverty, and ignorance, China's present leaders rule a country much more aware of the world and its place in it.

Such conditions will not guarantee a future of peace, political stability, and prosperity. We should not expect China to become, or necessarily even to seek to become, democratic and capitalist in form and content, at least not in the immediate future. The Chinese must find their own way to reconcile the challenge of modernity with the realities of the Chinese environment and history. Traditional ideas embodied in the age-old philosophy of Confucianism may well have a role to play in the future China. Building the new China is an intimidating task and may well lead to more turmoil and conflict. But it is clear that the journey has begun.

CHAPTER NOTES

1. R. Hilton, *Military Attaché in Moscow* (London, 1949), p. 41.
2. Nikita Khrushchev, *Khrushchev Remembers*, trans. Strobe Talbott (Boston, 1970), p. 77.
3. Cited in Hedrick Smith, *The New Russians* (New York, 1990) p. 30.
4. Quoted in Frank B. Tipton and Robert Aldrich, *An Economic and Social History of Europe from 1939 to the Present* (Baltimore, 1987), p. 193.
5. Quoted in Stanley Karnow, *Mao and China: Inside China's Cultural Revolution* (New York, 1972), p. 95.
6. Quoted from an article by Mao Zedong in the journal *Red Flag* (June 1, 1958). See Stuart R. Schram, *The Political Thought of Mao Tse-tung* (New York, 1963), p. 253. The quotation "strike while the iron is hot" is from Karnow, *Mao and China*, p. 93.
7. Liang Heng and Judith Shapiro, *Son of the Revolution* (New York, 1983).
8. Quoted in *Time*, March 13, 1989, pp. 10–11.
9. *Quotations from Chairman Mao Tse-tung* (Peking, 1976), p. 195, citing Mao's report to the CCP Central Committee, March 5, 1949.
10. "The Foolish Old Man Who Removed the Mountains," from ibid., p. 182.
11. Quoted in Frank Ching, "Confucius, the New Saviour," *Far Eastern Economic Review*, November 10, 1994, p. 37.
12. Quoted in Jonathan Spence, *Chinese Roundabout: Essays in History and Culture* (New York, 1992), p. 285.

SUGGESTED READINGS

For a general view of Soviet society, see D. K. Shipler, *Russia: Broken Idols, Solemn Dreams* (New York, 1983). On the Khrushchev years, see E. Crankshaw, *Khrushchev: A Career* (New York, 1966). Recent problems in the Soviet Union are analyzed in A. Brown and M. Kaser, *Soviet Policy for the 1980s* (London, 1983); S. F. Cohen, *Rethinking the Soviet Experience* (Oxford and New York, 1985); R. J. Hill, *The Soviet Union: Politics, Economics, and Society*, 2d ed. (London, 1989); M. Lewin, *The Gorbachev Phenomenon* (Berkeley, Calif., 1988); G. Hosking, *The Awakening of the Soviet Union* (London, 1990); and S. White, *Gorbachev and After* (Cambridge, 1991).

For a general study of the Soviet satellites in Eastern Europe, see A. Brown and J. Gary, *Culture and Political Changes in Communist States* (London, 1977) and S. Fischer-Galati, *Eastern Europe in the 1980s* (London, 1981). The unique path of Yugoslavia is examined in L. J. Cohen and P. Warwick, *Political Cohesion in a Fragile Mosaic: The Yugoslav Experience* (Boulder, Colo., 1983). On Romania, see L. S. Graham, *Rumania: A Developing Socialist State* (Boulder, Colo., 1978). On Hungary, see B. Kovrig, *The Hungarian People's Republic* (Baltimore, 1970). On East Germany, see C. B. Scharf, *Politics and Change in East Germany* (Boulder, Colo., 1984). Additional studies on the recent history of these countries include T. G. Ash, *The Polish Revolution: Solidarity* (New York, 1984); B. Kovrig, *Communism in Hungary from Kun to Kádár* (Stanford, Calif., 1979); T. G. Ash, *The Magic Lantern: The Revolution of '89 Witnessed in Warsaw, Budapest, Berlin and Prague* (New York, 1990); M. Shafir, *Romania: Politics, Economics and Society* (London, 1985); R. J. Crampton, *A Short History of Modern Bulgaria* (Cambridge, 1989); E. Biberaj, *Albania, A Socialist Maverick* (Boulder, Colo., 1990); and S. Ramet, *Nationalism and Federalism in Yugoslavia* (Bloomington, Ind., 1992).

A number of useful surveys deal with China after World War II. The most comprehensive treatment of the Communist period is M. Meisner, *Mao's China, and After: A History of the People's Republic* (New York, 1986). For shorter accounts of the period, see J. Grasso et al., *Modernization and Revolution in China* (Armonk, N.Y., 1991) and C. Dietrich, *People's China: A Brief History* (New York, 1986). For documents, see M. Selden, ed., *The People's Republic of China: A Documentary History of Revolutionary Change* (New York, 1978).

There are countless specialized studies on various aspects of the Communist period in China. For a detailed treatment of economic and political issues, see F. Schurmann, *Ideology and Organization in Communist China* (Berkeley, Calif., 1968). The Cultural Revolution is treated dramatically in S. Karnow, *Mao and China: Inside China's Cultural Revolution* (New York, 1972). For individual accounts of the impact of the revolution on people's lives, see the celebrated book by Nien Cheng, *Life and Death in Shanghai* (New York, 1986), and Liang Heng and J. Shapiro, *After the Revolution* (New York, 1986).

For the post-Mao period, see O. Schell, *To Get Rich Is Glorious* (New York, 1986) and the sequel, *Discoes and Democracy: China in the Throes of Reform* (New York, 1988). The 1989 demonstrations and their aftermath are chronicled in L. Feigon's eyewitness account, *China Rising: The Meaning of Tiananmen* (Chicago, 1990), and D. Morrison, *Massacre in Beijing* (New York, 1989). For commentary by Chinese dissidents, see Liu Binyan, *China's Crisis, China's Hope* (Cambridge, 1990) and Fang Lizhi, *Bringing Down the Great Wall: Writings on Science, Culture, and Democracy in China* (New York, 1991).

Several biographies of the Chinese party leaders are available. On Mao Zedong, see S. Schram, *Mao Tse-tung* (New York, 1966) and S. Uhalley, Jr., *Mao Tse-tung: A Critical Biography* (1977). For an interesting treatment of Mao's famous wife, a member of the gang of four, see R. Witke, *Comrade Chiang Ching* (Boston, 1972). On Deng Xiaoping, see R. Evans, *Deng Xiaoping and the Making of Modern China* (London, 1993).

On cultural issues, A. Chang's *Painting in the People's Republic of China* (Boulder, Colo., 1980) is a good survey of the modern period. On literature, see the interesting chapters on Ding Ling and her contemporaries in J. Spence, *The Gate of Heavenly Peace* (New York, 1981). See also Kai-yu Hsu and Ting Wang, eds., *Literature of the People's Republic of China* (Bloomington, Ind., 1980). For a comprehensive introduction to twentieth-century Chinese literature, consult E. Widmer and D. Der-Wei Wang, eds., *From May Fourth to June Fourth: Fiction and Film in Twentieth-Century China* (Cambridge, Mass., 1993). An excellent appraisal of Chinese women writers is found in M. S. Duke, ed., *Modern Chinese Women Writers: Critical Appraisals* (Armonk, N.Y., 1989).

Europe and the Western Hemisphere since 1945

The end of World War II in Europe had been met with great joy. One visitor in Moscow reported: "I looked out of the window [at 2 A.M.], almost everywhere there were lights in the windows—people were staying awake. Everyone embraced everyone else, someone sobbed aloud." But after the victory parades and celebrations, Europeans awoke to a devastating realization: their civilization was in ruins. Almost 40 million people (both soldiers and civilians) had been killed over the last six years. Massive air raids and artillery bombardments had reduced many of the great cities of Europe to heaps of rubble. An American general described Berlin: "Wherever we looked we saw desolation. It was like a city of the dead. Suffering and shock were visible in every face. Dead bodies still remained in canals and lakes and were being dug out from under bomb debris." Millions of Europeans faced starvation as grain harvests were only half of what they had been in 1939. Millions were also homeless. The destruction of bridges, roads, and railroads left transportation systems paralyzed. Untold millions of people had been uprooted by the war; now they became "displaced persons," trying to find food and then their way home.

Between 1945 and 1970, Europe not only recovered from the devastating effects of World War II, but also experienced an economic resurgence that seemed nothing less than miraculous to many people. Some historians have even labeled the years from 1950 to 1973 "the golden age of the European economy." Economic growth and virtually full employment continued so long that the first postwar recession in 1973

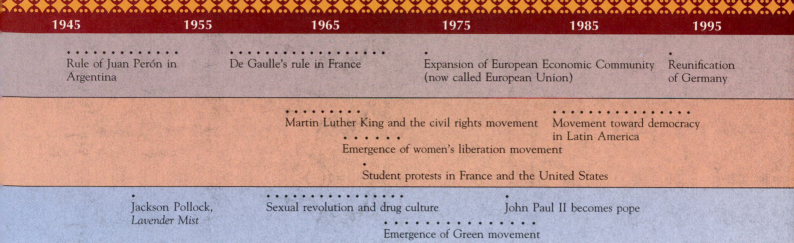

1945	1955	1965	1975	1985	1995

Rule of Juan Perón in Argentina

De Gaulle's rule in France

Expansion of European Economic Community (now called European Union)

Reunification of Germany

Martin Luther King and the civil rights movement

Movement toward democracy in Latin America

Emergence of women's liberation movement

Student protests in France and the United States

Jackson Pollock, *Lavender Mist*

Sexual revolution and drug culture

John Paul II becomes pope

Emergence of Green movement

came as a shock to Western Europe. Although economic growth resumed, Europeans faced a growing number of economic, social, and political problems in the 1980s and 1990s.

The most significant factor in the history of the Western world after 1945 was the emergence of the United States as the world's richest and most powerful nation. American prosperity reached new proportions in the two decades after World War II, but a series of economic and social problems—including racial division and staggering budget deficits—in the 1970s, 1980s, and early 1990s left the nation with an imposing array of difficulties that weakened its ability to function as the world's only superpower.

To the south of the United States lay the vast world of Latin America with its own unique heritage. Although some Latin Americans in the nineteenth century had looked to the United States as a model for their own development, in the twentieth century, many attacked the United States for its military and economic domination of Central and South America. Some states, such as Cuba, even adopted a Marxian path to building a new society and broke completely with

the United States. At the same time, many Latin American countries struggled with economic and political instability and all too often succumbed to the dictates of military regimes.

In the midst of the transformation from Cold War to post–Cold War realities, other changes also shaped a new Western world. New artistic and intellectual currents, the growth of science and technology, a religious revival, new threats from terrorists, the realization of environmental problems, the surge of a women's liberation movement—all of these spoke of a vibrant, ever-changing, and yet challenging new world.

Western Europe: Recovery and Renewal

All the nations of Western Europe faced similar kinds of problems at the end of World War II. Above all, they needed to rebuild their economies and recreate their democratic institutions. Within a few years after the defeat of Germany and Italy, an incredible economic revival brought a renewed growth to European society.

Western Europe: Domestic Politics

With the economic aid of the Marshall Plan, the countries of Western Europe recovered relatively rapidly from the devastation of World War II. Between 1947 and 1950, European countries received $9.4 billion to be used

De Gaulle Calls for French Autonomy

In the 1960s, the French president Charles de Gaulle sought to maintain France's independence from both the Soviet Union and the United States. In this 1966 speech, de Gaulle denounced those who were trying to subordinate France to international organizations.

A Speech of Charles de Gaulle (1966)

It is true that, among our contemporaries, there are many minds . . . who have envisaged that our country renounce its independence under the cover of one or another international group. Having thus handed over to foreign bodies the responsibility for our destiny, our leaders would . . . have nothing more to do than "plead France's case."

Thus some—exulting in the dream of the International—wanted to see our country itself, as they placed themselves, under the obedience of Moscow. Thus others—invoking either the supranational myth, or the danger from the East, or the advantage that the Atlantic West could derive from unifying its economy, or even the imposing utility of world arbitration—maintained that France should allow her policy to be dissolved in a tailor-made Europe, her defense in NATO, her monetary concepts in the Washington Fund, her personality in the United Nations.

Certainly, it is a good thing that such institutions exist, and it is only in our interest to belong to them; but if we had listened to their extreme apostles, these organs in which, as everyone knows, the political protection, military protection, economic power and multiform aid of the United States predominate—these organs would have been for us only a cover for our submission to American hegemony. Thus, France would disappear swept away by illusion.

---

for new equipment and raw materials. Between the early 1950s and late 1970s, industrial production surpassed all previous records, and Western Europe experienced virtually full employment. Social welfare programs—in the form of affordable health care, housing, family allowances to provide a minimum level of material care for children, increases in sickness, accident, unemployment, and old age benefits, and educational opportunities—helped create the modern welfare state. Despite economic recessions in the mid-1970s and early 1980s, especially after the dramatic increase in the price of oil in 1973, the economies of the Western European states recovered in the course of the 1980s, although problems remained. France had a 10.6 unemployment rate in 1993; it reached 11.7 percent in 1995. Despite their economic woes, Western Europeans were full participants in the technological advances of the age and seemed quite capable of standing up to American and Japanese economic competition.

Politically, Western Europe became accustomed to democracy. Even Spain and Portugal, which had retained their prewar dictatorial regimes until the mid-1970s, established democratic systems in the late 1970s. Moderate political parties, especially the Christian Democrats in Italy and Germany, played a particularly important role in achieving Europe's economic restoration. Overall, moderate yet ideologically oriented socialist parties declined, though reformist mass parties only slightly left of center, such as the Labour Party in Britain and the Social Democrats in West Germany, largely continued to share power. Western European Communist Parties declined drastically. During the mid-1970s, a new variety of communism called Eurocommunism briefly emerged when Communist Parties tried to work within the democratic system as mass movements committed to better government. But by the 1980s, internal political developments in Western Europe and events within the Communist world itself had combined to undermine the Eurocommunist experiment.

FRANCE: FROM DE GAULLE TO NEW UNCERTAINTIES

The history of France for nearly a quarter century after the war was dominated by one man—Charles de Gaulle (1890–1970)—who possessed an unshakable faith that he had a historical mission to reestablish the greatness of the French nation. During the war, de Gaulle had assumed leadership of some resistance groups and played an important role in ensuring the establishment of a French provisional government after the war. The creation of the Fourth Republic, with a return to a parliamentary system based on parties that de Gaulle considered weak, led him to withdraw from politics. Eventually, he formed the

French Popular Movement, a decidedly rightist organization. It blamed the parties for France's political mess and called for an even stronger presidency, a goal that de Gaulle finally achieved in 1958.

The fragile political stability of the Fourth Republic had been badly shaken by the Algerian crisis. The French army had suffered defeat in Indochina in 1954 and was determined to resist Algerian demands for independence. But a strong antiwar movement among French intellectuals and church leaders led to bitter divisions within France that opened the door to the possibility of civil war. The panic-stricken leaders of the Fourth Republic offered to let de Gaulle take over the government and revise the constitution.

In 1958, de Gaulle immediately drafted a new constitution for the Fifth Republic that greatly enhanced the power of the office of president, who now had the right to choose the prime minister, dissolve parliament, and supervise both defense and foreign policy. De Gaulle had always believed in strong leadership. The new Fifth Republic, while preserving the forms of democracy, lacked much of the substance of a democratic system. As the new president, de Gaulle sought to return France to a position of great power (see the box on p. 1068). He believed that playing a pivotal role in the Cold War might enhance France's stature. For that reason, he pulled France out of the NATO high command. He increased French prestige among the less-developed countries by consenting to Algerian independence despite strenuous opposition from the army. With an eye toward achieving the status of a world power, de Gaulle invested heavily in the nuclear arms race. France exploded its first nuclear bomb in 1960. Despite his successes, de Gaulle did not really achieve his ambitious goals of world power. Although his successors maintained that France was the "third nuclear power" after the United States and the Soviet Union, in truth France was too small for such global ambitions.

Although the cost of the nuclear program increased the defense budget, de Gaulle did not neglect the French economy. Economic decision making was centralized, a reflection of the overall centralization undertaken by the Gaullist government. Between 1958 and 1968, the French gross national product grew at an annual rate of 5.5 percent, faster than that of the United States. By the end of de Gaulle's era, France was a major industrial producer and exporter, particularly in such areas as automobiles and armaments. Nevertheless, problems remained. The expansion of traditional industries, such as coal, steel, and railroads, which had all been nationalized, led to large government deficits. The cost of living increased faster than in the rest of Europe.

♦ **Charles de Gaulle.** As president, Charles de Gaulle sought to revive the greatness of the French nation. He is shown here dressed in his military uniform participating in a formal state ceremony.

Increased dissatisfaction with the inability of de Gaulle's government to deal with these problems soon led to more violent action. In May 1968, a series of student protests, followed by a general strike by the labor unions, shook de Gaulle's government. Although he managed to restore order, the events of May 1968 had seriously undermined the French people's respect for their aloof and imperious president. Tired and discouraged, de Gaulle resigned from office in April 1969 and died within a year.

The worsening of France's economic situation in the 1970s brought a shift to the left politically. By 1981, the Socialists had become the dominant party in the National Assembly, and the Socialist leader, François Mitterrand (1916–1995), was elected president. His first concern was with France's economic difficulties. In 1982, Mitterrand froze prices and wages in the hope of reducing the huge budget deficit and high inflation. Mitterrand also passed a number of liberal measures to aid workers: an increased minimum wage, expanded social benefits, a mandatory fifth week of paid vacation for salaried workers, a thirty-nine-hour work week, and higher taxes for the rich. Mitterrand's administrative reforms included both centralization (nationalization of banks and industry) and decentralization (granting local governments greater powers). Their victory had also convinced the Socialists that they could enact some of their more radical reforms. Consequently, the government nationalized the steel industry, major banks, the space and electronics industries, and important insurance firms.

The Socialist policies largely failed to work, however, and within three years, faced with declining support, the Mitterrand government returned some of the economy to private enterprise. Some economic improvements in the late 1980s enabled Mitterrand to win a second seven-year term in the 1988 presidential election. But France's economic decline continued. In 1993, French unemployment stood at 10.6 percent, and in the elections in March of that year, the Socialists won only 28 percent of the vote while a coalition of conservative parties gained 80 percent of the seats in the National Assembly. The move to the right in France was strengthened when the conservative mayor of Paris, Jacques Chirac, was elected president in May 1995. After conservative policies failed to solve France's economic problems, the Socialists made a remarkable comeback in the elections of 1997.

FROM WEST GERMANY TO GERMANY

As a result of the pressures of the Cold War, the unification of the three Western zones into the West German Federal Republic became a reality in 1949. Konrad Adenauer (1876–1967), the leader of the Christian Democratic Union (CDU) who served as chancellor from 1949 to 1963, became the "founding hero" of the Federal Republic. Adenauer sought respect for Germany by cooperating with the United States and the other Western European nations. He was especially desirous of reconciliation with France—Germany's longtime enemy. The beginning of the Korean War in June of 1950 had unexpected repercussions for West Germany. The fear that South Korea might fall to the Communist forces of the north led many Germans and westerners to worry about the security of West Germany and led to calls for the rearmament of West Germany. Although many people, concerned about a revival of German militarism, condemned this proposal, Cold War tensions were decisive. West Germany rearmed in 1955 and became a member of NATO.

Adenauer's chancellorship is largely associated with the resurrection of the West German economy, often referred to as the "economic miracle." It was largely guided by the minister of finance, Ludwig Erhard. Although

West Germany had only 75 percent of the population and 52 percent of the territory of prewar Germany, by 1955 the West German gross national product exceeded that of prewar Germany. Real wages doubled between 1950 and 1965 even though work hours were cut by 20 percent. Unemployment fell from 8 percent in 1950 to 0.4 percent in 1965. In order to maintain its economic expansion, West Germany even imported hundreds of thousands of guest workers, primarily from Italy, Spain, Greece, Turkey, and Yugoslavia.

Throughout its postwar existence, West Germany was troubled by its Nazi past. The surviving major Nazi leaders had been tried and condemned as war criminals at the Nuremberg war crimes trials in 1945 and 1946. As part of the denazification of Germany, the victorious Allies continued to try lesser officials for war crimes, but these trials diminished as the Cold War produced a shift in attitudes. By 1950, German courts had begun to take over the war crimes trials, and the German legal machine persisted in prosecuting cases. Beginning in 1953, the West German government also began to make payments to Israel and to Holocaust survivors and their relatives in order to make some restitution for the crimes of the Nazi era. The German president Richard von Weizsäcker was especially eloquent in reminding Germans of their responsibility "for the unspeakable sorrow that occurred in the name of Germany."

After the Adenauer era, German voters moved politically from the center-right politics of the Christian Democrats to center-left politics, and in 1969 the Social Democrats became the leading party. By forming a ruling coalition with the small Free Democratic Party (FPD), the Social Democrats remained in power until 1982. The first Social Democratic chancellor was Willy Brandt (1913–1992). Brandt was especially successful with his "opening toward the east" (known as *Ostpolitik*), for which he received the Nobel Peace Prize in 1972. On March 19, 1971, Brandt met with Walter Ulbricht, the East German leader, and worked out the details of a Basic Treaty that was signed in 1972. This agreement did not establish full diplomatic relations with East Germany, but did call for "good neighborly" relations. As a result, it led to greater cultural, personal, and economic contacts between West and East Germany. Despite this success, the discovery of an East German spy among Brandt's advisers caused his resignation in 1974.

His successor, Helmut Schmidt (b. 1918), was more of a technocrat than a reform-minded socialist and concentrated primarily on the economic problems largely brought about by high oil prices between 1973 and 1975. Schmidt was successful in eliminating a deficit of 10 billion marks in three years. In 1982, when the coalition of Schmidt's Social Democrats with the Free Democrats fell apart over the reduction of social welfare expenditures, the Free Democrats joined with the Christian Democratic Union of Helmut Kohl (b. 1930) to form a new government.

Helmut Kohl was a clever politician who benefited greatly from an economic boom in the mid-1980s. Gradually, however, discontent with the Christian Democrats increased, and by 1988, their political prospects seemed diminished. But unexpectedly, the 1989 revolution in East Germany led to the reunification of the two Germanies, leaving the new Germany with its 79 million people the leading power in Europe. Reunification, accom-

plished during Kohl's administration, brought rich political dividends to the Christian Democrats. In the first all-German federal election, Kohl's Christian Democrats won 44 percent of the vote, while their coalition partners—the Free Democrats—received 11 percent.

But the excitement over reunification soon dissipated as new problems arose. All too soon, the realization set in that the revitalization of eastern Germany would take far more money than was originally thought, and Kohl's government was soon forced to face the politically undesirable task of raising taxes substantially. Moreover, the virtual collapse of the economy in eastern Germany led to extremely high levels of unemployment and severe discontent. One of the responses was an attack on

Map 29.1   The New Europe.

➤ *Violence against Foreigners in Germany* ◀

As the number of foreign guest workers and immigrants increased in Europe, violent attacks against them also escalated. Especially in the former East Germany, where unemployment rose dramatically after reunification, gangs of neo-Nazi youth have perpetrated violent attacks on foreigners. This document is taken from a German press account of an attack on guest workers from Vietnam and Mozambique who had originally been recruited by the East German government.

Knud Pries, "East Germans Have to Learn Tolerance"

The police headquarters in Dresden, the capital of Saxony, announced that "a political situation" had developed in the town of Hoyerswerda. Political leaders and the police needed to examine the problem and corresponding measures should be taken: "In the near future the residents of the asylum hostel will be moved."

The people of Hoyerswerda prefer to be more direct, referring to the problem of *Neger* (niggers) and *Fidschis* (a term for Asian foreigners). The loudmouths of the neo-fascist gangs make the message clear: "Niggers Go Home!"

It looks as if some Germans have had enough of bureaucratic officialese. What is more, they will soon make sure that no more foreign voices are heard in Hoyerswerda.

The municipality in northern Saxony has a population of just under 70,000, including 70 people from Mozambique and Vietnam who live in a hostel for foreigners and about 240 asylum-seekers in a hostel at the other end of town.

The "political situation" was triggered by an attack by a neo-Nazi gang on Vietnamese traders selling their goods on the market square on 17 September. After being dispersed by the police the Faschos carried out their first attack on the hostel for foreigners.

The attacks then turned into a regular evening "hunt" by a growing group of right-wing radicals, some of them minors, who presented their idea of a clean Germany by roaming the streets armed with truncheons, stones, steel balls, bottles and Molotov cocktails. Seventeen people were injured, some seriously.

After the police stepped in on a larger scale the extremists moved across the town to the asylum hostel.

To begin with, only the gang itself and onlookers were outside the building, but on the evening of 22 September members of the "Human Rights League" and about 100 members of "autonomous" groups turned up to help the foreigners who had sought refuge in the already heavily damaged block of flats.

A large police contingent, reinforced by men from Dresden and the Border Guard, prevented the situation from becoming even more critical. Two people were seriously injured. The mob was disbanded with the help of dogs, tear gas and water-cannons.

Thirty-two people were arrested, and blank cartridge guns, knives, slings and clubs were seized. On 23 September, a police spokesman announced that the situation was under control. It seems doubtful whether things will stay this way, since the pogroms have become an evening ritual. Politicians and officials are racking their brains about how to grapple with the current crisis and the basic problem. One thing is clear: without a massive intervention by the police the problem cannot even be contained. But what then?

Saxony's Interior Minister, Rudolf Krause, initially recommended that the hostels concerned should be "fenced in," but then admitted that this was "not the final solution." Providing the Defense Ministry approves, the "provisional solution" will be to move the foreigners to a barracks in Kamenz.

Even if this operation is completed without violence it would represent a shameful success for the right-wing radicals. Although the Africans and Asians still living in Hoyerswerda will have to leave at the end of November anyway once the employment contracts drawn up in the former [East Germany] expire, they are unwilling to endure the terror that long. "Even if we're going anyway—they want all foreigners to go now," says the 29-year-old Martinho from Mozambique.

His impression is that the gangs of thugs are doing something for which others are grateful: "The neighbors are glad when the skinheads arrive."

Interior Minister Krause feels that the abuse of asylum laws, the social problems in East Germany and an historically rooted deficit explain this situation: "The problem is that we were unable in the past to practice the tolerance needed to accept alien cultures."

foreigners (see the box on p. 1072). For years, foreigners seeking asylum and illegal immigrants had found haven in Germany because of its extremely liberal immigration laws. In 1992, more than 440,000 immigrants came to Germany seeking asylum; 123,000 came from former Yugoslavia alone. Attacks against foreigners by right-wing extremists—especially young neo-Nazis—became an all-too-frequent part of German life.

THE DECLINE OF GREAT BRITAIN

The end of World War II left Britain with massive economic problems. In elections held immediately after the war, the Labour Party overwhelmingly defeated Winston Churchill's Conservative Party. The Labour Party had promised far-reaching reforms, particularly in the area of social welfare, and in a country with a tremendous shortage of consumer goods and housing, its platform was quite appealing. The new Labour government proceeded to enact the reforms that created a modern welfare state. Clement Atlee (1883–1967), the new prime minister, was a pragmatic reformer and certainly not the leftist revolutionary that Churchill had warned against during the election campaign.

The establishment of the British welfare state began with the nationalization of the Bank of England, the coal and steel industries, public transportation, and public utilities, such as electricity and gas. In the area of social welfare, the new government enacted the National Insurance Act and the National Health Service Act, both in 1946. The insurance act established a comprehensive social security program and nationalized medical insurance, thereby enabling the state to subsidize the unemployed, the sick, and the aged. The health act created a system of socialized medicine that forced doctors and dentists to work with state hospitals, although private practices could be maintained. This measure was especially costly for the state, but within a few years 90 percent of the medical profession was participating. The British welfare state became the norm for most European states after the war.

The cost of building a welfare state at home forced the British to reduce expenses abroad. This meant dismantling the British Empire and reducing military aid to such countries as Greece and Turkey. Not a belief in the morality of self-determination, but economic necessity brought an end to the British Empire.

Continuing economic problems, however, brought the Conservatives back into power from 1951 to 1964. Although they favored private enterprise, the Conservatives accepted the welfare state and even extended it

✦ **Margaret Thatcher.** Great Britain's first female prime minister, Margaret Thatcher was a strong leader who dominated British politics in the 1980s. This picture of Thatcher was taken at the Chelsea Flower Show in May 1990. Six months later, a revolt within her own party caused her to resign as prime minister.

when they undertook an ambitious construction program to improve British housing. Although the British economy had recovered from the war, it had done so at a slower rate than other European countries. Moreover, the slow rate of recovery masked a long-term economic decline caused by a variety of factors. The demands of British trade unions for wages that rose faster than productivity were certainly a problem in the 1950s and 1960s. The unwillingness of the British to invest in modern industrial machinery and to adopt new methods also did not help. Underlying the immediate problems, however, was a deeper issue. As a result of World War II, Britain had lost much of its prewar revenues from abroad but was left with a burden of debt from its many international commitments. At the same time, with the rise of the United States and the Soviet Union, Britain's ability to play the role of a world power declined substantially.

Between 1964 and 1979, Conservatives and Labour alternated in power. Both parties had to face seemingly intractable problems. Although separatist movements in Scotland and Wales were overcome, fighting between Catholics and Protestants in Northern Ireland was not so easily settled. Violence increased as the Irish Republican

Army (IRA) staged a series of dramatic terrorist acts in response to the suspension of Northern Ireland's parliament in 1972 and the establishment of direct rule by London. The problems in Northern Ireland have not yet been solved. Nor was either party able to deal with Britain's ailing economy. Failure to modernize made British industry less and less competitive. Moreover,

Britain was hampered by frequent labor strikes, many of them caused by conflicts between rival labor unions.

In 1979, after Britain's economic problems had seemed to worsen during five years under a Labour government, the Conservatives returned to power under Margaret Thatcher (b. 1925). She became the first female prime minister in British history. Thatcher pledged to lower taxes, reduce government bureaucracy, limit social welfare, restrict union power, and end inflation. The "Iron Lady," as she was called, did break the power of the labor unions. While she did not eliminate the basic components of the social welfare system, she did use austerity measures to control inflation. "Thatcherism," as her economic policy was termed, improved the British economic situation but at a price. The south of England, for example, prospered, but the old industrial areas of the Midlands and north declined and were beset by high unemployment, poverty, and even violence. Cutbacks in funding for education seriously undermined the quality of British schools, long regarded as among the world's finest.

In foreign policy, Thatcher, like Ronald Reagan in the United States, took a hard-line approach against communism. She oversaw a large military buildup aimed at replacing older technology and reestablishing Britain as a world policeman. In 1982, when Argentina attempted to take control of the Falkland Islands (one of Britain's few remaining colonial outposts) three hundred miles off its coast, the British successfully rebuked the Argentines, although at great economic cost and the loss of 255 lives. The Falklands War, however, did generate much popular patriotic support for Thatcher.

Margaret Thatcher dominated British politics in the 1980s. The Labour Party, beset by divisions between moderate and radical wings, offered little effective opposition. Only in 1990 did Labour's fortunes seem to revive when Thatcher's government attempted to replace local property taxes with a flat-rate tax payable by every adult to his or her local authority. Although Thatcher argued that this would make local government more responsive to its electors, many argued that this was nothing more than a poll tax that would enable the rich to pay the same rate as the poor. In 1990, after antitax riots broke out, Thatcher's once remarkable popularity fell to all-time lows. At the end of November, a revolt within her own party caused Thatcher to resign as prime minister. She was replaced by John Major, whose Conservative Party won a narrow victory in the general elections held in April 1992. His government, however, failed to capture the imagination of most Britons. In new elections on May 1, 1997, the Labour Party won a landslide victory.

Western Europe: The Move Toward Unity

As we have seen, the divisions created by the Cold War led the nations of Western Europe to form the North Atlantic Treaty Organization (NATO) in 1949. But military unity was not the only kind of unity fostered in Europe after 1945. The destructiveness of two world wars caused many thoughtful Europeans to consider the need for some form of European unity. National feeling was still too powerful, however, for European nations to give up their political sovereignty. Consequently, the desire for unity was forced to focus primarily on the economic arena, not the political one.

In 1951, France, West Germany, the Benelux countries (Belgium, the Netherlands, and Luxembourg), and Italy formed the European Coal and Steel Community (ECSC). Its purpose was to create a common market for coal and steel products among the six nations by eliminating tariffs and other trade barriers. The success of the ECSC encouraged its members to proceed further, and in 1957 they created the European Atomic Energy Community (EURATOM) to further European research on the peaceful uses of nuclear energy.

In the same year, the same six nations signed the Rome Treaty, which created the European Economic Community (EEC), also known as the Common Market. The EEC eliminated customs barriers for the six member nations and created a large free-trade area protected from the rest of the world by a common external tariff. By promoting free trade, the EEC also encouraged cooperation and standardization in many aspects of the six nations' economies. All the member nations benefited economically.

Europeans also moved toward further integration of their economies after 1970. The EEC expanded in 1973 when Great Britain, Ireland, and Denmark gained membership in what its members now began to call the European Community (EC). By 1986, three additional members—Spain, Portugal, and Greece—had been added. The economic integration of the members of the EC led to cooperative efforts in international and political affairs as well. The foreign ministers of the twelve members consulted frequently and provided a common front for negotiations on important issues.

Nevertheless, the EC was still primarily an economic union, not a political one. By 1992, the EC comprised 344 million people and constituted the world's largest single trading entity, transacting almost one-fourth of the world's commerce. In the 1980s and 1990s, the EC moved toward even greater economic integration. A Treaty on European Union (also called the Maastricht Treaty after the city in the Netherlands where the agreement was reached) represented an attempt to create a true economic and monetary union of all EC members. The treaty did not go into effect until all members agreed. Finally, on January 1, 1994, the European Community became the European Union. One of its first goals was to introduce a common currency, called the "euro," by 2002.

The Emergence of the World's Superpower: The United States

At the end of World War II, the United States emerged as one of the world's two superpowers. Reluctantly, the United States remained involved in European affairs and, as its Cold War confrontation with the Soviet Union intensified, directed much of its energy toward combating the spread of communism throughout the world. With the collapse of the Soviet Union at the beginning of the 1990s, the United States emerged as the world's foremost military power. And yet, its own domestic problems led some to question whether the designation of sole remaining superpower would have any lasting significance. American domestic political life after 1945 was played out against a background of American military power abroad.

American Politics and Society through the Vietnam Era

Between 1945 and 1970, Franklin Roosevelt's New Deal largely determined the parameters of American domestic politics. The New Deal gave rise to a distinct pattern that signified a basic transformation in American society. This pattern included a dramatic increase in the role and power of the federal government; the rise of organized labor as a significant force in the economy and politics; a commitment to the welfare state, albeit a restricted one (Americans did not have access to universal health care as most other industrialized peoples did); a grudging acceptance of minority problems; and a willingness to experiment with deficit spending as a means of spurring the economy. The New Deal in American politics was bolstered by the election of Democratic presidents—Harry Truman in 1948, John F. Kennedy in 1960, and Lyndon B. Johnson in 1964. Even the election of a Republican president, Dwight D. Eisenhower, in 1952 and 1956 did not significantly alter the fundamental direction of the New Deal. As Eisenhower stated in 1954, "Should any political party attempt to abolish Social Security and eliminate labor laws and farm programs, you would not hear of that party again in our political history."

No doubt, the economic boom after World War II fueled confidence in the American way of life. A shortage of consumer goods during the war left Americans with both surplus income and the desire to purchase these goods after the war. Then, too, the development of organized labor enabled more and more workers to get the wage increases that fueled the growth of the domestic market. Government expenditures also indirectly subsidized the American private economy. Especially after the Korean War began in 1950, outlays on defense provided money for scientific research in the universities and mar-

kets for weapons industries. After 1955, tax dollars built a massive system of interstate highways while tax deductions for mortgages subsidized homeowners. Between 1945 and 1973, real wages grew at an average of 3 percent a year, the most prolonged advance in American history.

The prosperity of the 1950s and 1960s also translated into significant social changes. Work patterns changed as more and more people in the labor force left the factories and fields and moved into white-collar occupations, finding jobs as professional and technical workers, managers, proprietors, officials, and clerical and sales workers. In 1940, blue-collar workers made up 52 percent of the labor force; farmers and farm workers, 17 percent; and white-collar workers, 31 percent. By 1970, blue-collar workers

Map 29.2   The Economic Division of Europe during the Cold War.

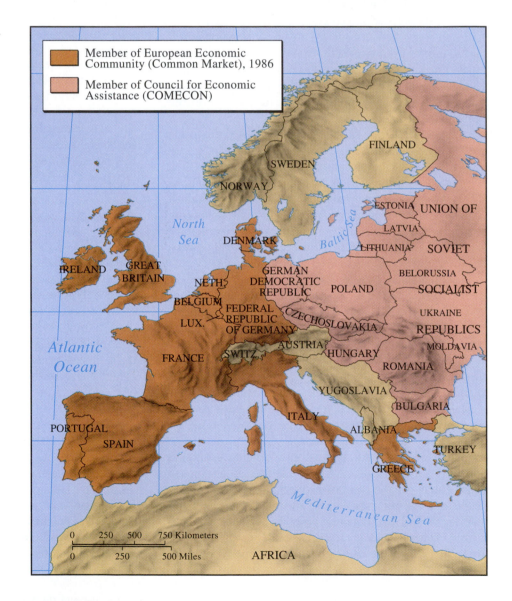

♦ **The Civil Rights Movement.**   In the early 1960s, Martin Luther King, Jr. and his Southern Christian Leadership Conference organized a variety of activities to pursue the goal of racial equality. He is shown here with his wife Coretta (right) and Rosa Parks and Ralph Abernathy (far left) leading a march in 1965 against racial discrimination.

constituted 50 percent; farmers and farm workers, 3 percent; and white-collar workers, 47 percent. Many of these white-collar workers now considered themselves middle class, and the growth of this middle class had other repercussions. From rural areas, small towns, and central cities, people moved to the suburbs. In 1940, 19 percent of the American population lived in suburbs, 49 percent in rural areas, and 32 percent in central cities. By 1970, those figures had changed to 38, 31, and 31 percent, respectively. The move to the suburbs also produced an imposing number of shopping malls and reinforced the American passion for the automobile, which provided the means of transport from suburban home to suburban mall and workplace. Finally, the search for prosperity led to new migration patterns. As the West and South experienced rapid economic growth through the development of new industries, especially in the defense field, massive numbers of people made the exodus from the cities of the Northeast and Midwest to the Sunbelt of the South and West. Between 1940 and 1980, cities like Chicago, Philadelphia, Detroit, and Cleveland lost between 13 and 36 percent of their populations, while Los Angeles, Dallas, and San Diego grew between 100 and 300 percent.

A new prosperity was not the only characteristic of the early 1950s. Cold War confrontations abroad had repercussions at home. The takeover of China by Mao Zedong's Communist forces in 1949 and Communist North Korea's invasion of South Korea in 1950 led to a fear that Communists had infiltrated the United States. President Truman's attorney general warned that Communists "are everywhere—in factories, offices, butcher stores, on street corners, in private businesses. And each carries in himself the germ of death for society." The demagogic senator from Wisconsin, Joseph McCarthy, helped to intensify a massive "Red Scare" with his exposés of hundreds of supposed Communists in high government positions. McCarthy went too far when he attacked alleged "Communist conspirators" in the U.S. army and was censured by Congress in 1954. Very quickly, his anti-Communist crusade came to an end.

While the 1950s has been characterized as a tranquil age, the period between 1960 and 1973 was a time of upheaval that brought to the fore problems that had been glossed over in the 1950s. The 1960s began on a youthful and optimistic note. At age forty-three, John F. Kennedy (1917–1963) became the youngest elected president in the history of the United States, and the first born in the twentieth century. His own administration, cut short by an assassin's bullet on November 22, 1963, focused primarily on foreign affairs. Kennedy's successor, Lyndon B. Johnson (1908–1973), who won a new term as president in a landslide in 1964, used his stunning mandate to pursue the growth of the welfare state, first begun in the New Deal. Johnson's programs included health care for the elderly; a War on Poverty to be fought with food stamps and a Job Corps; a new Department of Housing and Urban Development to deal with the problems of the cities; and federal assistance for education.

Lyndon Johnson's other domestic passion was the acquisition of equal rights for blacks. The civil rights movement had had its beginnings in 1954 when the U.S. Supreme Court took the dramatic step of striking down the practice of racially segregated public schools. According to Chief Justice Earl Warren, "separate educational facilities are inherently unequal." A year later, during a black boycott of segregated buses in Montgomery, Alabama, the eloquent Martin Luther King, Jr. (1929–1968) surfaced as the leader of a growing movement for racial equality.

By the early 1960s, a number of groups, including King's Southern Christian Leadership Conference (SCLC), were organizing demonstrations and sit-ins across the South to end racial segregation. In August 1963, King led a March on Washington for Jobs and Freedom that dramatized the blacks' desire for freedom. This march and King's impassioned plea for racial equality (see the box on p. 1079) had an electrifying effect on the American people. By the end of 1963, 52 percent of the American people called civil rights the most significant national issue; only 4 percent had done so eight months earlier.

President Johnson took up the cause of civil rights. As a result of his initiative, Congress enacted a Civil Rights Act in 1964, which created the machinery to end segregation and discrimination in the workplace and all public accommodations. A Voting Rights Act the following year eliminated obstacles to black participation in voting in southern states. But laws alone could not guarantee a Great Society, and Johnson soon faced bitter social unrest, both from blacks and from a burgeoning antiwar movement.

In the North and West, blacks had had voting rights for many years, but local patterns of segregation resulted in considerably higher unemployment rates for blacks (and Hispanics) than for whites and left blacks segregated in huge urban ghettos. In these ghettos, the calls for militant action of radical black nationalist leaders, such as Malcolm X of the Black Muslims, attracted more attention than the nonviolent appeals of Martin Luther King, Jr. Malcolm X's advice was straightforward: "If someone puts a hand on you, send him to the cemetery."

In the summer of 1965, race riots erupted in the Watts district of Los Angeles and resulted in thirty-four deaths and the destruction of over one thousand buildings.

Cleveland, San Francisco, Chicago, Newark, and Detroit likewise exploded in the summers of 1966 and 1967. After the assassination of Martin Luther King in 1968, over one hundred cities experienced rioting, including Washington, D.C., the nation's capital. The combination of riots and extremist comments by radical black leaders led to a "white backlash" and a severe division of American society. In 1964, 34 percent of American whites agreed with the statement that blacks were asking for "too much"; by late 1966, that number had risen to 85 percent, a figure not lost on politicians eager to achieve political office.

Antiwar protests also divided the American people after President Johnson committed American troops to a costly war in Vietnam (see Chapter 28). The antiwar movement arose out of the Free Speech Movement that began in 1964 at the University of California at Berkeley as a protest against the impersonality and authoritarianism of the large university (the "multiversity"). As the war progressed and a military draft ensued, protests escalated. Teach-ins, sit-ins, and occupations of university buildings alternated with more radical demonstrations that increasingly led to violence. The killing of four students at Kent State University in 1970 by the Ohio National Guard caused a reaction, and the antiwar movement began to decline. By that time, however, antiwar demonstrations had helped to weaken the willingness of many Americans to continue the war. But the combination of antiwar demonstrations and ghetto riots in the cities also prepared many people for "law and order," an appeal used by Richard Nixon (1913–1994), the Republican presidential candidate in 1968. With Nixon's election in 1968, a shift to the right in American politics had begun.

The Shift Rightward: The American Domestic Scene (1973 to the Present)

That shift was only a partial one during the Nixon years. Nixon eventually ended American involvement in Vietnam by gradually withdrawing American troops. Politically, he pursued a "southern strategy," carefully calculating that "law and order" issues and a slowdown in racial desegregation would appeal to southern whites. The South, which had once been a stronghold for the Democrats, began to form a new allegiance to the Republican Party. The Republican strategy, however, also gained support among white Democrats in northern cities, where court-mandated busing to achieve racial integration had produced a white backlash. But Nixon was less conservative on other social issues and, breaking with his own strong anti-Communist past, visited Communist China

"I Have a Dream"

In the spring of 1963, a bomb attack on a church that killed four children and the brutal fashion in which police handled black demonstrators brought the nation's attention to the policies of racial segregation in Birmingham, Alabama. A few months later, on August 28, 1963, Martin Luther King, Jr., led a march on Washington and gave an inspired speech that catalyzed the civil rights movement.

Martin Luther King, Jr., "I Have a Dream"

I am happy to join with you today in what will go down in history as the greatest demonstration for freedom in the history of our nation.

Five score years ago, a great American, in whose symbolic shadow we stand today, signed the Emancipation Proclamation. This momentous decree came as a great beacon light of hope to millions of Negro slaves who had been seared in the flames of withering injustice. It came as a joyous daybreak to end the long night of their captivity.

But one hundred years later, the Negro still is not free; one hundred years later, the life of the Negro is still sadly crippled by the manacles of segregation and the chains of discrimination; one hundred years later, the Negro lives on a lonely island of poverty in the midst of a vast ocean of material prosperity; one hundred years later, the Negro is still languished in the corners of American society and finds himself in exile in his own land. . . .

So we've come here today to dramatize a shameful condition. In a sense we've come to our nation's capital to cash a check. When the architects of our republic wrote the magnificent words of the Constitution and the Declaration of Independence, they were signing a promissory note to which every American was to fall heir. This note was the promise that all men, yes, black men as well as white men, would be guaranteed the unalienable rights of life, liberty, and the pursuit of happiness.

It is obvious today that America has defaulted on this promissory note in so far as her citizens of color are concerned. Instead of honoring this sacred obligation, America has given the Negro people a bad check, a check which has come back marked "insufficient funds." But we refuse to believe that the bank of justice is bankrupt. . . .

We have also come to this hallowed spot to remind America of the fierce urgency of now. This is no time to engage in the luxury of cooling off or to take the tranquilizing drug of gradualism. Now is the time to make real the promises of democracy; now is the time to rise from the dark and desolate valley of segregation to the sunlit path of racial justice; now is the time to lift our nation from the quicksands of racial injustice to the solid rock of brotherhood; now is the time to make justice a reality for all of God's children. It would be fatal for the nation to overlook the urgency of the moment. . . .

I say to you today, my friends, so even though we face the difficulties of today and tomorrow, I still have a dream. It is a dream deeply rooted in the American dream. I have a dream that one day this nation will rise up and live out the true meaning of its creed, "We hold these truths to be self-evident, that all men are created equal." I have a dream that one day on the red hills of Georgia, sons of former slaves and the sons of former slave owners will be able to sit down together at the table of brotherhood. . . . I have a dream that my four little children will one day live in a nation where they will not be judged by the color of their skin, but by the content of their character. . . .

This is our hope. This is the faith that I go back to the South with. With this faith we will be able to hew out of the mountain of despair a stone of hope. With this faith we will be able to transform the jangling discords of our nation into a beautiful symphony of brotherhood. With this faith we will be able to work together, to pray together, to struggle together, to go to jail together, to stand up for freedom together, knowing that we will be free one day. And this will be the day. This will be the day when all of God's children will be able to sing with new meaning, "My country 'tis of thee, sweet land of liberty, of thee I sing. Land where my father died, land of the pilgrims' pride, from every mountainside, let freedom ring." And if America is to be a great nation, this must become true. . . .

And when this happens, and when we allow freedom to ring, when we let it ring from every village and every hamlet, from every state and every city, we will be able to speed up that day when all of God's children, black men and white men, Jews and Gentiles, Protestants and Catholics, will be able to join hands and sing in the words of the old Negro spiritual: "Free at last. Free at last. Thank God Almighty, we are free at last."

CHRONOLOGY

American Society and Politics

Presidency of Harry S Truman	1945–1953
Presidency of Dwight D. Eisenhower	1953–1961
Presidency of John F. Kennedy	1961–1963
Assassination of Kennedy	1963
Presidency of Lyndon B. Johnson	1963–1969
Martin Luther King's March on Washington	1963
Civil Rights Act	1964
Watts riot	1965
Assassination of Martin Luther King	1968
Presidency of Richard M. Nixon	1969–1974
Killing of students at Kent State	1970
Resignation of Nixon in Watergate scandal	1974
Presidency of Gerald Ford	1974–1977
Presidency of Jimmy Carter	1977–1981
Presidency of Ronald Reagan	1981–1989
Presidency of George Bush	1989–1993
Election of Bill Clinton	1992
Reelection of Bill Clinton	1996

in 1972 and opened the door toward the eventual diplomatic recognition of that state.

As president, Nixon was also paranoid about conspiracies and began to use illegal methods of gaining political intelligence on his political opponents. One of the president's advisers explained that their intention was to "use the available Federal machinery to screw our political enemies." "Anyone who opposes us, we'll destroy," said another aide. Nixon's zeal led to the infamous Watergate scandal—the attempted bugging of Democratic National Headquarters. Although Nixon repeatedly lied to the American public about his involvement in the affair, secret tapes of his own conversations in the White House revealed the truth. On August 9, 1974, Nixon resigned in disgrace, an act that saved him from almost certain impeachment and conviction.

After Watergate, American domestic politics focused on economic issues. Gerald Ford (b. 1913) became president when Nixon resigned, only to lose in the 1976 election to the former governor of Georgia, Jimmy Carter (b. 1924), who campaigned as an outsider against the Washington establishment. Both Ford and Carter faced severe economic problems. The period from 1973 to the mid-1980s was one of economic stagnation, which came to be known as stagflation—a combination of high inflation and high unemployment. In 1984, median family income was 6 percent below that of 1973. In part, the economic downturn stemmed from a dramatic change in oil prices. Oil was considered a cheap and abundant source of energy in the 1950s, and Americans had grown dependent on its importation from the Middle East. By the late 1970s, 50 percent of the oil used in the United States came from the Middle East. But an oil embargo imposed by the Organization of Petroleum Exporting Countries (OPEC) as a result of the Arab-Israeli War in 1973 and OPEC's subsequent raising of prices led to a quadrupling of oil prices. As a result of additional price hikes, oil prices had increased twentyfold by the end of the 1970s, no doubt encouraging inflationary tendencies throughout the entire economy. Although the Carter administration produced a plan for reducing oil consumption at home while spurring domestic production, neither Congress nor the American people could be persuaded to follow what they regarded as drastic measures.

By 1980, the Carter administration was facing two devastating problems. High inflation and a noticeable decline in average weekly earnings were causing a perceptible drop in American living standards. At the same time, a crisis abroad had erupted when fifty-three Americans were held hostage by the Iranian government of Ayatollah Khomeini. Although Carter had little control over the situation, his inability to gain the release of the American hostages led to perceptions at home that he was a weak president. His overwhelming loss to Ronald Reagan (b. 1911) in the election of 1980 brought forward the chief exponent of right-wing Republican policies and a new political order.

The Reagan Revolution, as it has been called, changed the direction of American policy on many fronts. Reversing decades of the expanding welfare state, Reagan cut spending on food stamps, school lunch programs, and job programs. At the same time, his administration fostered the largest peacetime military buildup in American history. Total federal spending rose from $631 billion in 1981 to over a trillion dollars by 1986. But instead of raising taxes to pay for the new expenditures, which far outweighed the budget cuts in social areas, Reagan convinced Congress to support supply-side economics. Massive tax cuts would supposedly stimulate rapid economic growth and produce new revenues. Much of the tax cut went to the wealthy. Between 1980 and 1986, the income of the lower 40 percent of the workforce fell 9 percent, while the income of the highest 20 percent rose by 5 percent. Reagan's policies seemed to work in the short run as the United States experienced an economic upturn that lasted until the end of the 1980s. But the spending policies of the Reagan administration also produced record government deficits, which loomed as an obstacle to long-term growth. In the 1970s, the total deficit was $420 billion; between 1981 and 1987, Reagan budget deficits were three times that amount.

The inability of George Bush (b. 1924), Reagan's successor, to deal with the deficit problem or with the continuing economic downslide enabled a Democrat, William Clinton, to become president in November 1992. The new president was a southern Democrat who claimed to be a New Democrat—one who favored a number of the Republican policies of the 1980s. This was a clear indication that this Democratic victory had by no means ended the rightward drift in American politics. In fact, Clinton's reelection in 1996 was partially due to his adoption of Republican ideas and policies.

The Development of Canada

Canada experienced many of the same developments as the United States in the postwar years. For twenty-five years after World War II, Canada realized extraordinary economic prosperity as it set out on a new path of industrial development. Canada had always had a strong export economy based on its abundant natural resources. Now it also developed electronic, aircraft, nuclear, and chemical engineering industries on a large scale. Much of the Canadian growth, however, was financed by capital from the United States, which resulted in American ownership of Canadian businesses. While many Canadians welcomed the economic growth, others feared American economic domination of Canada and its resources.

These Canadian fears are a reminder that a notable feature of Canada's postwar history was its close relationship with the United States. In addition to fears of economic domination, Canadians have also worried about playing a subordinate role politically and militarily to the neighboring superpower. Canada agreed to join the North Atlantic Treaty Organization in 1949 and even sent military contingents to fight in Korea the following year. But to avoid subordination to the United States or any other great power, Canada has consistently and ac-

tively supported the United Nations. Nevertheless, concerns about the United States have not kept Canada from maintaining a special relationship with its southern neighbor. The North American Air Defense Command (NORAD), formed in 1957, was based on close cooperation between the air forces of the two countries for the defense of North America against missile attack. As another example of their close cooperation, in 1972, Canada and the United States signed the Great Lakes Water Quality Agreement to regulate pollution of the lakes that border both countries.

After 1945, the Liberal Party continued to dominate Canadian politics until 1957, when John Diefenbaker (1895–1979) achieved a Conservative victory. But a major recession returned the Liberals to power, and under Lester Pearson (1897–1972), they created Canada's welfare state by enacting a national social security system (the Canada Pension Plan) and a national health insurance program.

The most prominent Liberal government, however, was that of Pierre Trudeau (b. 1919), who came to power in 1968. Although French in background, Trudeau was dedicated to Canada's federal union, and in 1968 his government passed the Official Languages Act that created a bilingual federal civil service and encouraged the growth of French culture and language in Canada. Although Trudeau's government vigorously pushed an industrialization program, high inflation and Trudeau's efforts to impose the will of the federal government on the powerful provincial governments alienated voters and weakened his government. Economic recession in the early 1980s brought Brian Mulroney (b. 1939), leader of the Progressive Conservative Party, to power in 1984. Mulroney's government sought greater privatization of Canada's state-run corporations and negotiated a free trade agreement with the United States. Bitterly resented by many Canadians, the agreement cost Mulroney's government much of its popularity. In 1993, the ruling conservatives were drastically defeated. They won only two seats in the House of Commons, and the Liberal leader, Jean Chrétien, became prime minister.

Mulroney's government was also unable to settle the ongoing crisis over the French-speaking province of Quebec. In the late 1960s, the Parti Québécois, headed by René Lévesque, campaigned on a platform of Quebec's secession from the Canadian confederation. In 1970, the party won 24 percent of the popular vote in Quebec's provincial elections. To pursue their dream of separation, some underground separatist groups even used terrorist bombings and kidnapped two prominent government officials. In 1976, the Parti Québécois won Quebec's provincial elections and in 1980 called for a referendum that would enable the provincial government to negotiate Quebec's independence from the rest of Canada. Voters in Quebec narrowly rejected the plan in 1995, however, and debate over Quebec's status continues to divide Canada in the late 1990s.

Democracy, Dictatorship, and Development in Latin America since 1945

As a result of the Great Depression of the 1930s, many Latin American countries experienced political instability that led to military coups and militaristic regimes (see Chapter 25). But the Great Depression was also influential in transforming Latin America from a traditional to a modern economy. Since the nineteenth century, Latin Americans had exported raw materials, especially minerals and foodstuffs, while buying the manufactured goods of the industrialized countries, particularly Europe and the United States. Despite some industrialization, Latin America was still dependent on an export-import economy. As a result of the Great Depression, however, exports were cut in half, and the revenues available to buy manufactured goods declined. This led many Latin American countries to encourage the development of new industries that would produce goods that were formerly imported. This process of industrial development, known as "import-substituting industrialization" (ISI), was supposed to achieve greater economic independence for Latin America. Due to a shortage of capital in the private sector, governments often invested in the new industries, thereby leading, for example, to government-run steel industries in Chile and Brazil and petroleum industries in Argentina and Mexico.

By the 1960s, however, import-substituting industrialization had begun to fail. Despite their gains, Latin American countries were still dependent on the United States, Europe, and now Japan, especially for the advanced technology needed for modern industries. To make matters worse, the great poverty of Latin America limited the size of domestic markets, and many Latin American countries often failed to find markets abroad for their products. The failure of import-substituting industrialization led to instability and a new reliance on military regimes, especially to curb the new industrial middle class and working classes that had increased in size and power as a result of industrialization. Beginning in the 1960s, almost all economically advanced Latin American countries experienced domestic wars and military despotism. In the 1960s, repressive military regimes in Chile, Brazil, and Argentina even portrayed themselves as "antipolitical" as they abolished political parties and left few avenues for political opposition. These military regimes often returned to export-import economies financed by foreigners. They also encouraged multinational companies to come into their countries. Because these companies were primarily interested in taking advantage of Latin America's raw materials and abundant supply of cheap labor, their presence only contributed to the ongoing dependency of Latin America on the industrially developed nations.

In the decade of the 1970s, Latin American regimes, struggling to maintain their failing economies, grew even more dependent on borrowing from abroad, especially from banks in Europe and the United States. Between 1970 and 1982, debt to foreigners increased from $27 billion to $315.3 billion. By 1982, a number of governments announced that they could no longer pay interest on their debts to foreign banks, and their economies began to crumble. Wages fell and unemployment skyrocketed. Governments were forced to make fundamental reforms to qualify for additional loans and at the same time were encouraged to reevaluate the strategies they had used in their economic modernization. Many came to believe that the state sector had become too large and had overprotected domestic industries too long. The overly fast pace of industrialization had led to the decline of the rural economy as well, and many hoped that by improving agricultural production for home consumption, they could stem the flow of people from the countryside to the cities and at the same time strengthen the domestic market for Latin American industrial products.

In the 1980s, the debt crisis was paralleled by a movement toward democracy. In part, some military leaders were simply unwilling to deal with the monstrous debt problems. At the same time, many people realized that military power without popular consent was incapable of providing a strong state. Then, too, there was a swelling of popular support for basic rights and free and fair elections. The movement toward democracy was the most noticeable trend of the 1980s and early 1990s in Latin America. In the mid-1970s, only Colombia, Venezuela, and Costa Rica maintained democratic governments. In the mid-1980s, democratic regimes were everywhere except Cuba, some of the Central American states, Chile, and Paraguay. This revival of democracy is proving fragile, however. In 1992, for example, President Alberto Fujimori (b. 1938) undermined democracy and returned Peru to an authoritarian system.

Latin America's economic problems were made worse by a dramatic growth in population. In 1950, Latin America and North America (the United States and

Canada) had the same population—about 165 million people. By the mid-1980s, Latin America's population had exploded to 400 million while that of North America was about 270 million. Both a decline in death rates and an increase in birth rates led to this population explosion. With the increase in population came a rapid rise in the number and size of cities. In 1930, only one Latin American city had more than one million people. By 1990, there were twenty-nine, including Mexico City with 16 million inhabitants and Buenos Aires with 8 million. Cities grew in large part because poverty-stricken peasants fled there to seek a better life. Rarely did they find it. Population growth far outstripped economic growth, leaving millions without jobs. The inability of the cities to cope with the needs of these people led to the growth of slums that became part of virtually every Latin American city.

The gap between the poor and the rich had always been enormous in Latin American history, and it remained so after 1945. Landholding and urban elites, largely descendants of the Europeans who had colonized Latin America centuries before, still owned huge estates and businesses. A small but growing middle class consisted of businesspeople and office and government workers. Peasants and the urban poor struggled just to survive. Nevertheless, the lower classes became more and more vocal. Peasants called for land reforms that would give them more land while urban workers joined trade unions and demanded better wages and better working conditions.

The enormous gulf between rich and poor often undermined the stability of Latin American countries. So, too, did the international drug trade. Latin America's northern neighbor, the United States, was one of the world's largest consumers of drugs. Eighty percent of the cocaine and 90 percent of the marijuana used in the United States came from Latin America. Bolivia, Peru, and Colombia were especially big producers. For peasants in these countries, growing coca leaves and marijuana plants became an important part of their economic survival. In Columbia, drug traffickers became especially wealthy; they formed drug cartels that bribed and intimidated government officials and police officers into protecting their activities.

Other factors have also played important roles in the history of Latin America since 1945. The Catholic church had been a powerful force in Latin America for centuries, but its hold over people diminished as cities and industrial societies developed. By the beginning of the twentieth century, most Latin American governments had separated church and state, although the church remained a potent social and cultural force.

Eventually, the Catholic church pursued a middle way in Latin American society by advocating a moderate capitalist system that would respect workers' rights, institute land reform, and provide for the poor. This policy led to the formation of Christian Democratic Parties that had some success in the 1960s and 1970s. In the 1960s, however, some Catholics in Latin America took a more radical path to change by advocating a theology of liberation. Influenced by Marxist ideas, advocates of liberation theology believed that Christians must fight to free the oppressed, even using violence if necessary. Some Catholic clergy recommended armed rebellions and even teamed up with Marxist guerrillas in rural areas. Other radical priests worked in factories alongside workers or carried on social work among the poor in the slums. Although liberation theology attracted much attention, it was by no means the ideology of the majority of Latin American Catholics and was rejected by the church hierarchy. In the 1970s and 1980s, the Catholic church continued to play an important role in Latin America by becoming the advocate of human rights against authoritarian regimes.

In 1948, the states of the Western Hemisphere formed the Organization of American States (OAS), which was intended to eliminate unilateral action by one state within the internal or external affairs of any other state. Instead the OAS encouraged regional cooperation and allowed for group action to maintain peace. It certainly did not end the interference of the United States in Latin American affairs, however. Especially after World War II, as the Cold War between the United States and the Soviet Union intensified, American policymakers grew anxious about the possibility of Communist regimes in Central America and the Caribbean and returned to a policy of unilateral action when they believed that Soviet agents were attempting to utilize local Communists or radical reformers to establish governments hostile to American interests.

Especially after the success of Castro in Cuba (see The Cuban Revolution later in this chapter), the desire of the United States to prevent "another Cuba" largely determined American policy toward Latin America until the end of the Cold War in the 1990s. In the 1960s, President Kennedy's Alliance for Progress encouraged social reform and economic development by providing private and public funds to elected governments whose reform programs were acceptable to the United States. But the Alliance failed to work, and after the Cubans began to export the Cuban Revolution by starting guerrilla wars in other Latin American countries, Americans responded by providing massive military aid to anti-Communist regimes, regardless of their nature. By 1979, 83,000 military personnel from twenty-one Latin American countries had

◆ **Fidel Castro.** On January 1, 1959, a band of revolutionaries led by Fidel Castro overthrew the authoritarian government of Fulgencio Batista. Castro is shown here in 1957 with some of his followers at a secret base near the Cuban coast.

received American-assisted military training with special emphasis on antiguerrilla activity so that they could fight social revolutionaries.

The Threat of Marxist Revolutions

Until the 1960s, Marxism played little role in the politics of Latin America. The success of Fidel Castro in Cuba and his espousal of Marxism, however, opened the door for other Marxist movements that aimed to gain the support of peasants and industrial workers and bring radical change to Latin America. The United States portrayed these movements as Communist threats and provided substantial military assistance to fight them.

THE CUBAN REVOLUTION

An authoritarian regime, headed by Fulgencio Batista (1901–1973) and closely tied economically to American investors, had ruled Cuba since 1934. A strong opposition movement to Batista's government developed, led by Fidel Castro (b. 1926) and assisted by Ernesto "Ché" Guevara (1928–1967), an Argentinian who believed that revolutionary upheaval was necessary to change Latin America. Castro maintained that only armed force

could overthrow Batista, but when their initial assaults on Batista's regime brought little success, Castro's forces, based in the Sierra Maestra Mountains, turned to guerrilla warfare (see the box on p. 1085). As the rebels gained more support, Batista's regime responded with such brutality that he alienated his own supporters. The dictator fled in December 1958, and Castro's revolutionaries seized Havana on January 1, 1959.

The new government proceeded cautiously, but relations between Cuba and the United States quickly deteriorated. An agrarian reform law in May 1959 nationalized all landholdings over a thousand acres. A new source of antagonism between the United States and Cuba emerged early in 1960 when the Soviet Union agreed to buy Cuban sugar and provide $100 million in credits. On March 17, 1960, President Eisenhower directed the Central Intelligence Agency (CIA) to "organize the training of Cuban exiles, mainly in Guatemala, against a possible future day when they might return to their homeland."[1] Arms from Eastern Europe began to arrive in Cuba, the United States cut its purchases of Cuban sugar, and the Cuban government nationalized American companies and banks. In October 1960, the United States declared a trade embargo of Cuba, which drove Castro closer to the Soviet Union. In December 1960, Castro declared himself a Marxist.

On January 3, 1961, the United States broke diplomatic relations with Cuba. The new American president, John F. Kennedy, supported a coup attempt against Castro's government, but the landing of 1,400 CIA-assisted Cubans in Cuba on April 17, 1961, turned into a total military disaster (the infamous Bay of Pigs). This American fiasco encouraged the Soviets to make an even greater commitment to Cuban independence by placing nuclear missiles in the country, an act that led to a showdown with the United States (see Chapter 27). As its part of the bargain to defuse the Missile Crisis, the United States agreed not to invade Cuba.

But the Missile Crisis affected Cuba in another way as well. Castro realized that the Soviet Union had been unreliable. If revolutionary Cuba was to be secure and no longer encircled by hostile states tied to American interests, the Cubans would have to instigate social revolution in the rest of Latin America. Castro judged Bolivia, Haiti, Venezuela, Colombia, Paraguay, and a number of Central American states to be especially open to radical revolution. He believed that once guerrilla wars were launched, peasants would flock to the movement and overthrow the old regimes. Guevara began a guerrilla war in Bolivia but was caught and killed by the Bolivian army in the fall of 1967. The Cuban strategy had failed.

⇒ Castro's Revolutionary Ideals ⇐

On July 26, 1953, Castro and a small group of supporters launched an ill-fated attack on the Moncada Barracks in Santiago de Cuba. Castro was arrested and put on trial. This excerpt is taken from his defense speech in which he discussed the goals of the revolutionaries.

Fidel Castro, "History Will Absolve Me"

I stated that the second consideration on which we based our chances for success was one of social order because we were assured of the people's support. When we speak of the people we do not mean the comfortable ones, the conservative elements of the nation, who welcome any regime of oppression, any dictatorship, and despotism, prostrating themselves before the master of the moment until they grind their foreheads into the ground. When we speak of struggle, the people means the vast unredeemed masses, to whom all make promises and whom all deceive; we mean the people who yearn for a better, more dignified and more just nation; who are moved by ancestral aspirations of justice, for they have suffered injustice and mockery, generation after generation; who long for great and wise changes in all aspects of their life; people, who, to attain these changes, are ready to give even the very last breath of their lives—when they believe in something or in someone, especially when they believe in themselves.

In the brief of this cause there must be recorded the five revolutionary laws that would have been proclaimed immediately after the capture of the Moncada barracks and would have been broadcast to the nation by radio. . . .

The First Revolutionary Law would have returned power to the people and proclaimed the Constitution of 1940 the supreme Law of the land, until such time as the people should decide to modify or change it. . . .

The Second Revolutionary Law would have granted property, not mortgageable and not transferable, to all planters, sub-planters, lessees, partners and squatters who hold parcels of five or less "caballerias" [tract of land, about 33 acres] of land, and the state would indemnify the former owners on the basis of the rental which they would have received for these parcels over a period of ten years.

The Third Revolutionary Law would have granted workers and employees the right to share 30 percent of the profits of all the large industrial, mercantile and mining enterprises, including the sugar mills. . . .

The Fourth Revolutionary Law would have granted all planters the right to share 55 percent of the sugar production and a minimum quota of forty thousand "arrobas" [25 pounds] for all small planters who have been established for three or more years.

The Fifth Revolutionay Law would have ordered the confiscation of all holdings and ill-gotten gains of those who had committed frauds during previous regimes, as well as the holdings and ill-gotten gains of all their legatees and heirs. . . .

Furthermore, it was to be declared that the Cuban policy in the Americas would be one of close solidarity with the democratic people of this continent, and that those politically persecuted by bloody tyrants oppressing our sister nations would find generous asylum, brotherhood, and bread in [Cuba]. Not the persecution, hunger and treason that they find today. Cuba should be the bulwark of liberty and not a shameful link in the chain of despotism.

Nevertheless, within Cuba, Castro's socialist revolution proceeded, although with mixed results. The Cuban Revolution did secure some social gains for its people, especially in health care and education. The regime provided free medical services for all citizens, and the population's health improved noticeably. Illiteracy was wiped out by developing new schools and establishing teacher-training institutes that tripled the number of teachers within ten years. The theoretical equality of women in Marxist thought was put into practice in Cuba by new laws. One such law was the family code, which stated that husband and wife were equally responsible for the economic support of the family and household, as well as for child care. Such laws led to improvements but fell far short of creating full equality for women.

Eschewing the path of rapid industrialization, Castro encouraged agricultural diversification. Nevertheless, the Cuban economy continued to rely on the production and sale of sugar. Economic problems forced the Castro regime to depend on Soviet subsidies and the purchase of Cuban sugar by Soviet bloc countries. After the collapse of these Communist regimes in 1989, Cuba lost their support. Although economic conditions in Cuba have steadily declined without the Soviet subsidies, Castro manages to remain in power.

CHILE'S MARXIST ADVENTURE

Another challenge to American influence in Latin America came in 1970 when a Marxist, Salvador Allende (1908–1973), was elected president of Chile and attempted to create a Marxian socialist society by constitutional means. Chile had suffered from a series of economic problems. Much wealth was concentrated in the hands of large landowners and a select number of large corporations. Inflation, foreign debts, and a decline in the mining industry (copper exports accounted for 80 percent of Chile's export income) caused untold difficulties. Right-wing control of the government failed to achieve any solutions, especially since foreign investments were allowed to expand. There was already growing resentment of American corporations, especially Anaconda and Kennecott, which controlled the copper industry.

In the 1970 elections, a split in the moderate forces enabled Allende to become president of Chile as head of a coalition of Socialists, Communists, and Catholic radicals. A number of labor leaders, who represented the interests of the working classes, were given the ministries of labor, finance, public works, and interior in the new government. Allende increased the wages of industrial workers and began to move toward socialism by nationalizing the largest domestic and foreign-owned corporations.

♦ **Sandinista Victory in Nicaragua.** After a series of military victories that overthrew the Somoza dictatorship, the Sandinista National Liberation Front established a new government in Nicaragua. Triumphant Sandinistas are seen here celebrating their victory.

Nationalization of the copper industry—essentially without compensation for the owners—caused the Nixon administration to cut off all aid to Chile, creating serious problems for the Chilean economy. At the same time, the government offered only halfhearted resistance to radical workers who were beginning to take control of the landed estates.

These activities brought growing opposition from the upper and middle classes who began to organize strikes against the government (with support from the American CIA). Allende attempted to stop the disorder by bringing three military officers into his cabinet. They succeeded in ending the strikes, but when Allende's coalition increased its vote in the congressional elections of March 1973, the Chilean army, under the direction of General Augusto Pinochet (b. 1915), decided on a coup d'état. On September 11, 1973, military forces seized the presidential palace. Allende was shot to death. His wife publicly denounced the takeover and maintained that it had been financed by the United States. Contrary to the expectations of many right-wing politicians, the military remained in power and set up a dictatorship.

The Pinochet regime was one of the most brutal in Chile's history. Thousands of opponents were imprisoned, and thousands more were cruelly tortured and murdered. The regime also moved quickly to outlaw all political parties, remove the congress, and restore many nationalized industries and landowners' estates to their original owners. The copper industry, however, remained in government hands. The regime's horrible abuse of human rights led to growing unrest against the government in the mid-1980s. In 1989, free presidential elections led to the defeat of Pinochet. A Christian Democrat, Patricio Azócur, became president and restored a somewhat democratic system.

NICARAGUA: FROM THE SOMOZAS TO THE SANDINISTAS

The United States had intervened in Nicaraguan domestic affairs in the early twentieth century, and U.S. marines even remained there for long periods of time. After the leader of the American-supported National Guard, Anastasio Somoza, seized control of the government in 1937, his family remained in power for forty-three years. American support for the Somoza military regime enabled the family to overcome any opponents while enriching themselves at the expense of the state.

Opposition to the regime finally arose from Marxist guerrilla forces known as the Sandinista National Liberation Front. By mid-1979, military victories by the Sandinistas left them in virtual control of the country, and they organized a provisional government. The Sandinistas inherited a poverty-stricken nation. Their alignment with the Soviet Union caused the Reagan and Bush administrations to believe that Central America faced the danger of another Communist state and to finance contra rebels in a guerrilla war against the Sandinista government. The contra war and an American economic embargo damaged the Nicaraguan economy and undermined support for the Sandinistas. In 1990, they agreed to free elections and lost to a coalition headed by Violeta Barrios de Chamorro (b. 1929). Nevertheless, the Sandinistas remained the strongest single party in Nicaragua.

Nationalism and the Military: The Examples of Argentina and Brazil

The military became the power brokers of twentieth-century Latin America. Especially in the 1960s and 1970s, Latin American armies portrayed themselves as the guardians of national honor and orderly progress.

ARGENTINA

Fearful of the forces unleashed by the development of industry, the military intervened in Argentinian politics in 1930 and propped up the cattle and wheat oligarchy that had controlled politics since the beginning of the twentieth century. By this policy, the military hoped to continue the old import-export economy and thus avoid the growth of working-class power that would come with more industrialization. During World War II, restless military officers formed a new organization known as the Group of United Officers (GOU). Unhappy with the civilian oligarchy, they overthrew it in June 1943. But the new military regime was not sure how to deal with the working classes. One of its members, Juan Perón (1895–1974), thought that he could manage the workers and used his position as labor secretary in the military government to curry favor with the workers. He encouraged them to join labor unions and increased job benefits as well as the number of paid holidays and vacations. In 1944, Perón became vice-president of the military government and made sure that people knew he was responsible for the social welfare measures. But as Perón grew more popular, other army officers began to fear his power and arrested him. An uprising by workers forced the officers to back down, and in 1946, Perón was elected president.

Perón pursued a policy of increased industrialization in order to please his chief supporters—labor and the urban middle class. At the same time, he sought to free

◆ **The Peróns.** Elected president of Argentina in 1946, Juan Perón soon established an authoritarian regime that nationalized some of Argentina's basic industries and organized fascist gangs to overwhelm its opponents. He is shown here with his wife Eva during the inauguration ceremonies initiating his second term as president in 1952.

Argentina from foreign investors. The government bought the railways, took over the banking, insurance, shipping, and communications industries, and assumed regulation of imports and exports. But Perón's regime was also authoritarian. His wife, Eva Perón, organized women's groups to support the government while Perón created fascist gangs, modeled after Hitler's Brown Shirts, that used violence to overawe his opponents. But growing corruption in the Perón government and the alienation of more and more people by the regime's excesses encouraged the military to overthrow him in September 1955. Perón went into exile in Spain.

It had been easy for the military to seize power, but it was harder to rule, especially now that Argentina had a party of *Peronistas* clamoring for the return of the exiled leader. In the 1960s and 1970s, military and civilian governments (the latter closely watched by the military) alternated in power. Since neither was able to do much to provide economic stability, military leaders decided to allow Perón to come back from exile in Spain. Reelected president in September 1973, Perón died one year later. In 1976, the military installed a new regime. Tolerating no opposition, the military leaders encouraged the "disappearance" of their opponents. Perhaps 30,000 people, including 6,000 leftists, were killed as a result.

But economic problems remained. To divert people's attention, the military regime invaded the Falkland Islands off the coast of Argentina in April 1982. Great Britain, which had controlled the islands since the nineteenth century, sent ships and troops to defend the islands. When the Argentinian forces surrendered to the British in July, angry Argentinians denounced the military regime. The loss discredited the military and opened the door to civilian rule. In 1983, Raúl Alfonsín of the Radical Party was elected president and tried to restore democratic practices. In elections in 1989, the Peronist Carlos Saúl Menem (b. 1930) won. This peaceful transfer

Map 29.3 Political Trends in Latin America in the 1960s and 1970s.

( ) Date of independence

Urban terrorism 1960–1979

Rightist military coups 1960–1979

Leftist guerrilla warfare

European colonial possession

of power gave hope that Argentina was moving on a democratic path. Reelected in 1995, President Menem has pushed to control inflation and government spending.

BRAZIL

In 1889, a bloodless coup overthrew the Brazilian monarchy and established a republic controlled primarily by the landed elites, especially the coffee barons. The republic lasted until Getúlio Vargas (1883–1954) established his authoritarian New State between 1938 and 1945 (see Chapter 25). During this time Brazil made the shift from an export-import economy to one of state-supported import-substituting industrialization. In 1945, the army, fearing that Vargas might prolong his power illegally after calling for new elections, forced him to resign.

A second Brazilian republic came into being in 1946, and three years later, Vargas himself was elected to the presidency. But he was unable to solve Brazil's economic problems, especially its soaring inflation, and in 1954, after the armed forces called upon him to resign, he killed himself. Subsequent democratically elected presidents had no better success in controlling inflation while trying to push rapid industrialization. In the spring of 1964, the military decided to intervene and took over the government.

Unlike previous interventions by military leaders in politics, this time the armed forces remained in direct control of the country for twenty years. The military set course on a new economic direction, cutting back somewhat on state control of the economy and emphasizing market forces. Beginning in 1968, the new policies seemed to work, and Brazil experienced an "economic miracle" as it moved into self-sustaining economic growth, generally the hallmark of a modern economy. Economic growth also included the economic exploitation of the Amazon basin, which the regime opened to farming; some believe the corresponding destruction of the extensive Amazon rain forests, which is still going on, poses a threat to the ecological balance not only of Brazil but of the earth itself. Rapid economic growth had additional drawbacks. Ordinary Brazilians hardly benefited as the gulf between rich and poor, always wide, grew even wider. In 1960, the wealthiest 10 percent of Brazil's population received 40 percent of the nation's income; in 1980, they received 51 percent. Then, too, rapid development led to an inflation rate of 100 percent a year, while an enormous foreign debt added to the problems. By the early 1980s, the economic miracle was turning into an economic nightmare. Overwhelmed, the generals retreated and opened the door for a return to democracy in 1985.

CHRONOLOGY

Latin America

Presidency of Lázaro Cárdenas in Mexico	1934–1940
Vargas's New State in Brazil	1938–1945
Juan Perón becomes president of Argentina	1946
Creation of Organization of American States	1948
Perón goes into exile	1955
Castro's forces seize Cuba	1959
Bay of Pigs	1961
Cuban Missile Crisis	1962
Death of Ché Guevara in Bolivia	1967
Presidency of Luis Echeverría in Mexico	1970–1976
Overthrow of Salvador Allende in Chile	1973
Perón returns to power	1973
Presidency of José López Portillo in Mexico	1976–1982
Sandinistas establish provisional government	1979
Falklands War	1982
Election of Raúl Alfonsín in Argentina	1983
Election of Carlos Salinas in Mexico	1988
Resignation of Fernando Collor de Mello in Brazil	1992
Election of Fernando Cardoso in Brazil	1994
Reelection of Carlos Menem in Argentina	1995

The new democratic government faced herculean obstacles—a massive foreign debt, virtually runaway inflation, and the lack of any real social consensus. Presidential elections in 1990 brought a newcomer into office—Fernando Collor de Mello (b. 1949). He promised to end the inflation problem with a drastic reform program, based on squeezing money out of the economy by stringent controls on wages and prices, drastic reductions in public spendings, and cuts in the number of government employees. Collor de Mello's efforts were undermined by the corruption in his own administration, however, and he resigned from office at the end of 1992 after having been impeached. In new elections in 1994, Fernando Cardoso was elected president by an overwhelming majority of the popular vote.

The Mexican Way

The Mexican Revolution at the beginning of the twentieth century had been the first significant effort in Latin American history to overturn the system of large landed estates, limit foreign control over the country's resources, and increase the living standards of the masses (see Chapter 23). Out of the political revolution emerged a political order that has remained the most stable in Latin America. Lázaro Cárdenas (1895–1970), who was president from 1934 to 1940 (see Chapter 25), reorganized the official political party of the Mexican Revolution (known as the Institutional Revolutionary Party or PRI) to include separate divisions for the peasants, labor, the military, and the middle class. The revolutionary party thus became an umbrella organization that contained and controlled the major groups within Mexican society. Every six years, party bosses of the PRI chose the party's presidential candidate, who was then dutifully elected by the people.

During the 1950s and 1960s, Mexico's ruling party focused on a balanced industrial program. Fifteen years of steady economic growth combined with low inflation and real gains in wages for more and more people made those years appear to be a "golden age" in Mexico's economic development. But at the end of the 1960s, the true nature of Mexico's domination by one party became apparent with the student protest movement. On October 2, 1968, a demonstration of university students in Tlaltelolco Square in Mexico City was met by police forces who opened fire and killed hundreds of students (see the box on p. 1091). Leaders of the PRI became concerned about the need to change the system.

The next two presidents, Luis Echeverría (b. 1922) and José López Portillo (b. 1920), introduced political reforms. Rules for the registration of political parties were eased, making their growth more likely, and greater freedom of debate in the press and universities was allowed. But economic problems continued to trouble Mexico. In the late 1970s, vast new reserves of oil were discovered in Mexico. As the sale of oil abroad increased dramatically, the government became even more dependent on oil

revenues. When world oil prices dropped in the mid-1980s, Mexico was no longer able to make payments on its foreign debt, which had reached $80 billion in 1982. The government was forced to adopt new economic policies, including the increased sale of public-owned companies to private hands.

The debt crisis and rising unemployment left many people unhappy with the government, which was especially evident in the 1988 election. The PRI's choice for president was Carlos Salinas (b. 1948). Normally, he would have been expected to win in a landslide, but he received only 50.3 percent, a bare majority. The new president continued the economic liberalization of his predecessors and went even further by negotiating a free trade agreement with the United States and Canada, known as NAFTA (North American Free Trade Agreement). The success or failure of these economic policies will no doubt determine whether the PRI will continue to dominate Mexico politically. In 1995, a new challenge appeared when a group of rebels in the extreme south of Mexico led an armed revolt against the government.

Society and Culture in the Western World

Socially, culturally, and intellectually, the Western world during the last half of the twentieth century has been marked by much diversity. Although many trends represent a continuation of prewar modern developments, new directions in the last two decades have also led some to speak of a postmodern world.

New Directions and New Problems in Western Society

Dramatic social developments have accompanied political and economic changes since the end of World War II. A new society and new opportunities for women emerged, and a women's liberation movement sought to bring new meaning to the principle of equality with men. New problems for Western society also arose with the advent of terrorism and a growing awareness of environmental dangers.

THE EMERGENCE OF A NEW SOCIETY

During the postwar era, Western society witnessed remarkably rapid change. Such products of new technologies as computers, television, jet planes, contraceptive

Student Revolt in Mexico

A growing conflict between government authorities and university students in Mexico came to a violent and bloody climax on October 2, 1968, when army troops killed and wounded large numbers of students in Mexico City. This excerpt is taken from an account of the events by the student National Strike Council.

National Strike Council, Events of October 2–3

After an hour and a half of a peaceful meeting attended by ten thousand people and witnessed by scores of domestic and foreign reporters, a helicopter gave the army the signal to attack by dropping flares into the crowd. Simultaneously, the plaza was surrounded and attacked by members of the army and all police forces, using weapons of every caliber, up to 9 mm.

The local papers have given the following information about the attack, confirmed by firsthand witnesses:

1. Numerous secret policemen had infiltrated the meeting in order to attack it from within, with orders to kill. They were known to each other by the use of a white handkerchief tied around their right hands. . . .
3. High caliber weaponry and expansion bullets were used. Seven hours after the massacre began, tanks cleaned up the residential buildings of Nonoalco-Tlaltelolco with short cannon blasts and machine-gun fire.
4. On the morning of October 3, the apartments of supposedly guilty individuals were still being searched, without a search warrant.
5. Doctors in the emergency wards of the city hospitals were under extreme pressure, being forced to forgo attention to the victims until they had been interrogated and placed under guard. Various interns who attended the demonstration for the purpose of giving medical aid had since disappeared.
6. The results of this brutal military operation include hundreds of dead (including women and children), thousands of wounded, an unwarranted search of all the apartments in the area, and thousands of violent arrests. Those arrested were taken to various illegal locations, such as Military Camp No. 1. It should be added that members of the National Strike Council who were captured were stripped and herded into a small archaeological excavation at Tlaltelolco, converted for the moment into a dungeon. Some of them were put up against a wall and shot.
7. Onesimo Mason, the general who directed the operation, praised the preparedness of his men, in contrast to the obvious lack of preparedness on the part of the students.

All this has occurred only ten days before the start of the Olympics. The repression is expected to become even greater after the Games, in view of the fact that national public opinion and the protest from the provinces are unified against a regime whose only interest lies in demonstrating its power to control.

Already individual liberties have been suspended, and restricted zones have been created where all vehicles are searched at gun point and personal identification is demanded. The Secretary of Defense declared that the friendly disposition of the regime will solve the conflict.

WE ARE NOT AGAINST THE OLYMPIC GAMES. WELCOME TO MEXICO.

---

devices, and new surgical techniques all dramatically and quickly altered the pace and nature of human life. The rapid changes in postwar society, fueled by scientific advances and rapid economic growth, led many to view it as a new society. Called a technocratic society by some and the consumer society by others, postwar Western society was characterized by a changing social structure and new movements for change.

The structure of European society was altered after 1945. Especially noticeable were the changes in the middle class. Such traditional middle-class groups as businesspeople and professionals in law, medicine, and the universities were greatly augmented by a new group of managers and technicians, as large companies and government agencies employed increasing numbers of white-collar supervisory and administrative personnel. Whether in Eastern or Western Europe, the new managers and experts were very much alike. Everywhere their positions depended upon specialized knowledge acquired from some form of higher education. Everywhere they focused on the effective administration of their corporations. Since their positions usually depended upon their skills, they took steps to ensure that their children would be similarly educated.

Changes also occurred among the traditional lower classes. Especially noticeable was the dramatic shift of people from rural to urban areas. The number of people in agriculture declined drastically; by the 1950s, the number of peasants throughout most of Europe had dropped by 50 percent. Nor did the size of the industrial working class expand. In West Germany, industrial workers made up 48 percent of the labor force throughout the 1950s and 1960s. Thereafter, the number of industrial workers began to dwindle as the number of white-collar service employees increased. At the same time, a substantial increase in their real wages enabled the working classes to aspire to the consumption patterns of the middle class, leading to what some observers have called the "consumer society." Buying on the installment plan, which was introduced in the 1930s, became widespread beginning in the 1950s and gave workers a chance to imitate the middle class by buying such products as televisions, washing machines, refrigerators, vacuum cleaners, and stereos. But the most visible symbol of mass consumerism was the automobile. Before World War II, cars were reserved mostly for the European upper classes. In 1948, there were 5 million cars in all of Europe, but by 1957, the number had tripled. By the 1960s, there were almost 45 million cars.

Rising incomes, combined with shorter working hours, created an even greater market for mass leisure activities. Between 1900 and 1980, the work week was reduced from sixty hours to a little more than forty hours, and the number of paid holidays increased. All aspects of popular culture—music, sports, media—became commercialized and offered opportunities for leisure activities including concerts, sporting events, and television viewing.

Another very visible symbol of mass leisure was the growth of mass tourism. Before World War II, most persons who traveled for pleasure were from the upper and middle classes. After the war, the combination of more vacation time, increased prosperity, and the flexibility provided by package tours with their lower rates and low-budget rooms enabled millions to expand their travel possibilities. By the mid-1960s, one hundred million tourists were crossing European boundaries each year.

Social change was also evident in new educational patterns and student revolts. Before World War II, higher education had largely remained the preserve of Europe's wealthier classes. Even in 1950, for example, only 3 or 4 percent of West European young people were enrolled in a university. In addition, European higher education remained largely centered on the liberal arts, pure science, and preparation for the professions of law and medicine.

Much of this changed after World War II. European states began to foster greater equality of opportunity in higher education by eliminating fees, and universities experienced an influx of students from the middle and lower classes. Enrollments grew dramatically; in France, 4.5 percent of young people went to a university in 1950. By 1965, the figure had increased to 14.5 percent. Enrollments in European universities more than tripled between 1940 and 1960.

But there were problems. Overcrowded classrooms, professors who paid little attention to students, and administrators who acted in an authoritarian fashion aroused student resentment. In addition, despite changes in the curriculum, students often felt that the universities were not providing an education relevant to the modern age. This discontent led to an outburst of student revolts in the late 1960s. In part, these protests were an extension of the disruptions in American universities in the mid-1960s, which were often sparked by student opposition to the Vietnam War. Perhaps the most famous student revolt occurred in France in 1968. It erupted at the University of Nanterre outside Paris but soon spread to the Sorbonne, the main campus of the University of Paris. French students demanded a greater voice in the administration of the university, took over buildings, and then expanded the scale of their protests by inviting workers to support them. Half of France's workforce went on strike in May 1968. After the Gaullist government instituted a hefty wage hike, the workers returned to work, and the police repressed the remaining student protesters.

The student protest movement reached its high point in 1968, although scattered incidents lasted into the early 1970s. There were several reasons for the student radicalism. Some students were genuinely motivated by the desire to reform the university. Others were protesting the Vietnam War, which they viewed as a product of Western imperialism. They also attacked other aspects of Western society, such as its materialism, and expressed concern about becoming cogs in the large and impersonal bureaucratic jungles of the modern world. For many students, the calls for democratic decision making within the universities were a reflection of their deeper concerns about the direction of Western society. Although the student revolts fizzled out in the 1970s, the larger issues they raised have been increasingly revived in the 1990s.

THE PERMISSIVE SOCIETY

The "permissive society" was yet another term used by critics to describe the new society of postwar Europe. World War I had seen the first significant crack in the

◆ **Student Revolt in Paris, 1968.** The discontent of university students exploded in the late 1960s in a series of student revolts. Perhaps best known was the movement in Paris in 1968.

This photograph shows the barricades erected on a Parisian street on the morning of May 11 during the height of the revolt.

rigid code of manners and morals of the nineteenth century. Subsequently, the 1920s had witnessed experimentation with drugs, the appearance of hard-core pornography, and a new sexual freedom (police in Berlin, for example, issued cards that permitted female and male homosexual prostitutes to practice their trade). But these indications of a new attitude appeared mostly in major cities and touched only small numbers of people. After World War II, changes in manners and morals were far more extensive and far more noticeable.

Sweden took the lead in the propagation of the so-called sexual revolution of the 1960s, but the rest of Europe and the United States soon followed. Sex education in the schools and the decriminalization of homosexuality were but two aspects of Sweden's liberal legislation. The introduction of the birth control pill, which became widely available by the mid-1960s, gave people more freedom in sexual behavior. Meanwhile, sexually explicit movies, plays, and books broke new ground in the treatment of once-hidden subjects. Cities like Amsterdam, which allowed open prostitution and the public sale of hard-core pornography, attracted thousands of curious tourists.

The new standards were evident in the breakdown of the traditional family. Divorce rates increased dramatically, especially in the 1960s, while premarital and extramarital sexual experiences also rose substantially. A survey in the Netherlands in 1968 revealed that 78 percent of men and 86 percent of women had participated in extramarital sex.

The decade of the 1960s also saw the emergence of a drug culture. Marijuana was widely used among college and university students as the recreational drug of choice. For young people more interested in mind expansion into higher levels of consciousness, Timothy Leary, who had

◆ **The "Love-in."** In the 1960s, a number of outdoor public festivals for young people combined music, drugs, and sex. Flamboyant dress, facial painting, free-form dancing, and drugs were vital ingredients in creating an atmosphere dedicated to "love and peace." Shown here is a "love-in" that was held on the grounds of an English country estate in the Summer of Love, 1967.

done psychedelic research at Harvard on the effects of LSD (lysergic acid diethylamide), became the high priest of hallucinogenic experiences.

New attitudes toward sex and the use of drugs were only two manifestations of a growing youth movement in the 1960s that questioned authority and fostered rebellion against the older generation. Spurred on by the Vietnam War and a growing political consciousness, the youth rebellion became a youth protest movement by the second half of the 1960s (see the box on p. 1095).

NEW (AND OLD) PATTERNS: WOMEN IN
THE POSTWAR WORLD

After World War II, the trend toward earlier marriage continued. In Sweden, the average age of first marriage dropped from twenty-six in the 1940s to twenty-three in 1970. Although birthrates rose immediately after World War II, they have mostly declined since the war as contraceptive devices and abortion have become widely available. It is estimated that mothers need to average 2.1 children in order to ensure a natural replacement of a country's population. In many European countries, the population stopped growing in the 1960s, and the trend has continued since then. By 1992, fertility rates were down drastically; among the twelve nations of the European Community, the average number of children per mother was 1.58. No doubt, the trend toward early marriage and smaller families contributed to the changes in the character of women's employment in both Europe and the United States as women experienced considerably more years when they were not involved in rearing children.

The most important development was the increased number of married women in the workforce. At the beginning of the twentieth century, even working-class wives tended to stay at home if they could afford to do so. In the postwar period, this was no longer the case. In the United States, for example, married women made up about 15 percent of the female labor force in 1900; by 1970, their number had increased to 62 percent. The percentage of married women in the female labor force in Sweden increased from 47 to 66 percent between 1963 and 1975.

But the increased number of women in the workforce has not changed some old patterns. Working-class women in particular still earn salaries lower than those paid to men for equal work. Women still tend to enter traditionally female jobs. As one Swedish woman guidance counselor remarked in 1975: "Every girl now thinks in terms of a job. This is progress. They want children, but they don't pin their hopes on marriage. They don't intend to be housewives for some future husband. But there has been no change in their vocational choices."[2] A 1980 study of twenty-five European nations revealed

"The Times They Are a-Changin'": The Music of Youthful Protest

In the 1960s, the lyrics of rock music reflected the rebellious mood of many young people. Bob Dylan (b. 1941), a well-known recording artist, expressed the feelings of the younger generation. His song "The Times They Are a-Changin'," released in 1964, has been called an "anthem for the protest movement."

Bob Dylan, "The Times They Are a-Changin'"

Come gather 'round people
Wherever you roam
And admit that the waters
Around you have grown
And accept it that soon
You'll be drenched to the bone
If your time to you
Is worth savin'
Then you better start swimmin'
Or you'll sink like a stone
For the times they are a-changin'

Come writers and critics
Who prophesize with your pen
And keep your eyes wide
The chance won't come again
And don't speak too soon
For the wheel's still in spin
And there's no tellin' who
That it's namin'
For the loser now
Will be later to win
For the times they are a-changin'

Come senators, congressmen
Please heed the call

Don't stand in the doorway
Don't block up the hall
For he that gets hurt
Will be he who has stalled
There's a battle outside
And it is ragin'
It'll soon shake your windows
And rattle your walls
For the times they are a-changin'

Come mothers and fathers
Throughout the land
And don't criticize
What you can't understand
Your sons and your daughters
Are beyond your command
Your old road
Is rapidly agin'
Please get out of the new one
If you can't lend your hand
For the times they are a-changin'

The line it is drawn
The curse it is cast
The slow one now
Will later be fast
As the present now
Will later be past
The order is
Rapidly fadin'
And the first one now
Will later be last
For the times they are a-changin'

that women still made up over 80 percent of the typists, nurses, tailors, and dressmakers in those countries. Many European women also still faced the double burden of earning income on the one hand and raising a family and maintaining the household on the other. Such inequalities led increasing numbers of women to rebel.

The participation of women in World War I and II helped them achieve one of the major aims of the nineteenth-century feminist movement—the right to vote. Already after World War I, many governments acknowledged the contributions of women to the war effort by granting them the right to vote. Sweden, Great Britain, Germany, Poland, Hungary, Austria, and Czechoslovakia did so in 1918, followed by the United States in 1920. Women in France and Italy did not obtain the right to vote until 1945. After World War II, European women tended to fall back into the traditional roles expected of them, and little was heard of feminist concerns. But by the late 1960s,

The Voice of the Women's Liberation Movement

Simone de Beauvoir was an important figure in the emergence of the postwar women's liberation movement. This excerpt is taken from her influential book The Second Sex, *in which she argued that women have been forced into a position subordinate to men.*

Simone de Beauvoir, *The Second Sex*

Now, woman has always been man's dependent, if not his slave; the two sexes have never shared the world in equality. And even today woman is heavily handicapped, though her situation is beginning to change. Almost nowhere is her legal status the same as man's, and frequently it is much to her disadvantage. Even when her rights are legally recognized in the abstract, long-standing custom prevents their full expression in the mores. In the economic sphere men and women can almost be said to make up two castes; other things being equal, the former hold the better jobs, get higher wages, and have more opportunity for success than their new competitors. In industry and politics men have a great many more positions and they monopolize the most important posts. In addition to all this, they enjoy a traditional prestige that the education of children tends in every way to support, for the present enshrines the past—and in the past all history has been made by men. At the present time, when women are beginning to take part in the affairs of the world, it is still a world that belongs to men—they have no doubt of it at all and women have scarcely any. To decline to be the Other, to refuse to be a party to a deal—this would be for women to renounce all the advantages conferred upon them by their alliance with the superior caste. Man-the-sovereign will provide woman-the-liege with material protection and will undertake the moral justification of her existence; thus she can evade at once both economic risk and the metaphysical risk of a liberty in which ends and aims must be contrived without assistance. Indeed, along with the ethical urge of each individual to affirm his subjective existence, there is also the temptation to forgo liberty and become a thing. This is an inauspicious road, for he who takes it—passive, lost, ruined—becomes henceforth the creature of another's will, frustrated in his transcendence and deprived of every value. But it is an easy road; on it one avoids the strain involved in undertaking an authentic existence. When man makes of woman the *Other*, he may, then, expect her to manifest deep-seated tendencies toward complicity. Thus, woman may fail to lay claim to the status of subject because she lacks definite resources, because she feels the necessary bond that ties her to man regardless of reciprocity, and because she is often very well pleased with her role as the *Other*.

Now, what peculiarly signalizes the situation of woman is that she—a free and autonomous being like all human creatures—nevertheless finds herself living in a world where men compel her to assume the status of the Other.

---

women began to assert their rights again and speak as feminists. Along with the student upheavals of the late 1960s came renewed interest in feminism, or the women's liberation movement as it was now called. Increasingly, women protested that the acquisition of political and legal equality had not brought true equality with men:

> We are economically oppressed: in jobs we do full work for half pay, in the home we do unpaid work full time. We are commercially exploited by advertisement, television and the press; legally we often have only the status of children. We are brought up to feel inadequate, educated to narrower horizons than men. This is our specific oppression as women. It is as women that we are, therefore, organizing.[3]

These were the words of a British Women's Liberation Workshop in 1969.

Of great importance to the emergence of the postwar women's liberation movement was the work of Simone de Beauvoir (1908–1986). Born into a Catholic middle-class family and educated at the Sorbonne in Paris, she supported herself as a teacher and later as a novelist and writer. She maintained a lifelong relationship (but not marriage) with the philosopher Jean-Paul Sartre. Her involvement in the existentialist movement—the leading intellectual movement of its time—led her to become active in political causes. De Beauvoir believed that she lived a "liberated" life for a twentieth-century European woman, but for all her freedom, she still came to perceive that as a woman she faced limits that men did not. In 1949, she published her highly influential work, *The Second Sex*, in which she argued that as a result of male-dominated societies, women had been defined by their differences from men and consequently received second-class status: "What particularly signalizes the situation of woman is that she—a free autonomous being like all human creatures—nevertheless finds herself in a world where men compel her to assume the status of the Other."[4] De Beauvoir played an active role in the French women's movement of the 1970s, and her book was a major influence on both the American and the European women's movements (see the box on p. 1096).

Feminists in the women's liberation movement came to believe that women themselves must transform the fundamental conditions of their lives. They did so in a variety of ways. First, in the 1960s and 1970s, they formed numerous "consciousness-raising" groups to further awareness of women's issues. Women also sought and gained a measure of control over their own bodies by working for the legalization of both contraception and abortion. In the 1960s and 1970s, hundreds of thousands of European women worked to repeal the laws that outlawed contraception and abortion and began to meet with success. A French law in 1968 permitted the sale of contraceptive devices. In 1979, another French law legalized abortion. Even in Catholic countries, where the church remained strongly opposed to legalizing abortion, legislation allowing contraception and abortion was passed in the 1970s and 1980s.

As more women became activists, they also became involved in new issues. In the 1980s and 1990s, women faculty in universities concentrated on developing new cultural attitudes through the new academic field of "women's studies." Other women began to try to affect the political and natural environment by allying with the antinuclear and ecological movements. As one German writer who was concerned with environmental issues stated, it is women "who must give birth to children, willingly or unwillingly, in this polluted world of ours."

THE GROWTH OF TERRORISM

Acts of terror by those opposed to governments became a frightening aspect of modern Western society. During the late 1970s and early 1980s in particular, concern about terrorism was often at the top of foreign policy agendas in the United States and many European countries. Small bands of terrorists used assassination, indiscriminate killing of civilians, especially by bombing, the taking of hostages, and the hijacking of airplanes to draw attention to their demands or destabilize governments in the hope of achieving their political goals. Terrorist acts garnered considerable media attention. When Palestinian terrorists kidnapped and killed eleven Israeli athletes at the Munich Olympic games in 1972, hundreds of millions of people watched the drama unfold on

◆ **Women's Liberation Movement.**   In the late 1960s, as women began once again to assert their rights, a revived women's liberation movement emerged. Feminists in the movement maintained that women themselves must alter the conditions of their lives. During this women's liberation rally, some women climbed the statue of Admiral Farragut in Washington, D.C., to exhibit their signs.

television. Indeed, some observers believe that media exposure has been an important catalyst for some terrorist groups.

Motivations for terrorist acts varied considerably. Left- and right-wing terrorist groups flourished in the late 1970s and early 1980s. Left-wing groups, such as the Baader-Meinhof gang (also known as the Red Army Faction) in Germany and the Red Brigades in Italy, consisted chiefly of affluent middle-class young people who denounced the injustices of capitalism and supported acts of revolutionary terrorism in order to bring down the system. Right-wing terrorist groups, such as the New Order in Italy and the Charles Martel Club in France, used bombings to foment disorder and bring about authoritarian regimes. These groups received little or no public support, and authorities were able to crush them fairly quickly.

But terrorist acts also stemmed from militant nationalists who wished to create separatist states. Because they received considerable support from local populations sympathetic to their cause, these terrorist groups could maintain their activities over a long period of time. Most prominent was the Irish Republican Army (IRA), which resorted to vicious attacks against the ruling government and innocent civilians in Northern Ireland. Over a period of twenty years, IRA terrorists were responsible for the death of two thousand people in Northern Ireland; three-fourths of the victims were civilians.

Although left- and right-wing terrorist activities declined in Europe in the 1980s, international terrorism remained rather commonplace. Angered by the loss of their territory to Israel in 1967, some militant Palestinians responded with a policy of terrorist attacks against Israel's supporters. Palestinian terrorists operated throughout European countries, attacking both Europeans and American tourists; it was Palestinian terrorists who massacred vacationers at airports in Rome and Vienna in 1985. State-sponsored terrorism was often an integral part of international terrorism. Militant governments, especially in Iran, Libya, and Syria, assisted terrorist organizations that made attacks on Europeans and Americans. On December 21, 1988, Pan American flight 103 from Frankfurt to New York exploded over Lockerbie, Scotland, killing all 259 passengers and crew members. A massive investigation finally revealed that the bomb responsible for the explosion had been planted by two Libyan terrorists who were connected to terrorist groups based in Iran and Syria.

Governments fought back by creating special antiterrorist units that became extremely effective in responding to terrorist acts. In 1977, for example, the German special antiterrorist unit, known as GSG, rescued 91 hostages from a Lufthansa airplane that had been hijacked to Mogadishu in Somalia. Counterterrorism, or a calculated policy of direct retaliation against terrorists, also made states that sponsored terrorism more cautious. In 1986, the Reagan administration responded to the terrorist bombing of a West German disco club popular with American soldiers by launching an air attack on Libya, long suspected to be a major sponsor of terrorist organizations. Some observers attribute the overall decline in terrorist attacks in the late 1980s to the American action. In the 1990s, however, acts of terrorism have continued to be a disturbing element in Western life.

GUEST WORKERS AND IMMIGRANTS

As the economies of the Western European countries revived in the 1950s and 1960s, a severe labor shortage forced them to rely on foreign workers. Scores of Turks and eastern and southern Europeans came to Germany, North Africans to France, and people from the Caribbean, India, and Pakistan to Great Britain. Overall, there were probably 15 million guest workers in Europe in the 1980s. They constituted 17 percent of the labor force in Switzerland and 10 percent in Germany.

Although these workers were necessary for economic reasons, socially and politically their presence created problems for their host countries. Many foreign workers complained that they received lower wages and inferior social benefits. Moreover, their concentration in certain cities and even certain sections of those cities often created tensions with the local native populations. Foreign workers, many of them nonwhites, constituted almost one-fifth of the population in the German cities of Frankfurt, Munich, and Stuttgart. Having become settled in their new countries, many were unwilling to leave, even after the end of the postwar boom in the early 1970s led to mass unemployment. Moreover, as guest workers settled permanently in their host countries, additional family members migrated to join them. Although they had little success in getting guest workers already there to leave, some European countries passed legislation or took other measures to restrict new immigration.

In the 1980s, the problem of foreign workers was intensified by an influx of other refugees, especially to West Germany, which had liberal immigration laws that permitted people seeking asylum for political persecution to enter the country. During the 1970s and 1980s, West Germany absorbed over a million refugees from Eastern Europe and East Germany. In 1986 alone, two hundred thousand political refugees from Pakistan, Bangladesh, and Sri Lanka entered the country.

This great influx of foreigners, many of them nonwhite, strained not only the social services of European countries, but the patience of many native residents who opposed making their countries ethnically diverse. Antiforeign sentiment, especially in a time of growing unemployment, increased and was encouraged by new right-wing political parties that catered to people's complaints. Thus, the National Front in France, organized by Jean-Marie Le Pen, and the Republican Party in Germany, led by Franz Schönhuber, a former SS officer, advocated restricting all new immigration and limiting the assimilation of settled immigrants. Although these parties have had only limited success in elections so far, even that modest accomplishment has encouraged traditional conservative and even moderately conservative parties to adopt more nationalistic policies. Even more frightening, however, have been the organized campaigns of violence, especially against African and Asian immigrants, by radical, right-wing groups.

THE ENVIRONMENT AND THE GREEN MOVEMENTS

Beginning in the 1970s, environmentalism became a serious item on the European political agenda. By that time, serious ecological problems had become all too apparent. Air pollution, produced by nitrogen oxide and sulfur dioxide emissions from road vehicles, power plants, and industrial factories, was causing respiratory illnesses and having corrosive effects on buildings and monuments. Many rivers, lakes, and seas had become so polluted that they posed serious health risks. Dying forests and disappearing wildlife alarmed more and more people. The opening of Eastern Europe after the revolutions of 1989 brought to the world's attention the incredible environmental destruction of that region caused by unfettered industrial pollution. Communist governments had obviously operated under the assumption that production quotas were much more important than protection of the environment.

Environmental concerns forced the major political parties in Europe to advocate new regulations for the protection of the environment. The Soviet nuclear power disaster at Chernobyl in 1986 made Europeans even more aware of potential environmental hazards, and 1987 was touted as the "year of the environment." Many European states also established government ministries to oversee environmental issues.

Growing ecological awareness also gave rise to Green movements and Green Parties that emerged throughout Europe in the 1970s. The origins of these movements were by no means uniform. Some came from the antinuclear movement; others arose out of such causes as women's liberation and concerns for foreign workers. Most started at the local level and then gradually expanded to include activities at the national level, where they became formally organized as political parties. Most visible was the Green Party in Germany, which was officially organized in 1979 and, by 1987, had elected forty-two delegates to the West German parliament. Green Parties also competed successfully in Sweden, Austria, and Switzerland.

Despite their repressive policies, Communist countries in Eastern Europe also witnessed the formation of ecologically conscious groups. In the 1980s, environmental groups emerged in East Germany and Czechoslovakia, two especially environmentally devastated countries, as well as Poland and Hungary. The Czech dissident group, Charter 77, emphasized environmental damage as one of the chief crimes of its Communist government.

Although the Green movements and parties have played an important role in making people aware of ecological problems, they have by no means replaced the traditional political parties, as some political analysts in the mid-1980s forecast. For one thing, the coalitions that made up the Greens found it difficult to agree on all issues and tended to splinter into different cliques. Then, too, many of the founders of these movements, who often expressed a willingness to work with the traditional political parties, were ousted from their leadership positions by fundamentalists unwilling to compromise their principles in any way. Finally, traditional political parties have co-opted the environmental issues of the Greens. By the 1990s, more and more European governments were beginning to sponsor projects to safeguard the environment and clean up the worst sources of pollution.

Recent Trends in Art and Literature

Modern art continued to prevail at exhibitions and museums. For the most part, the United States dominated the art world, much as it did the world of popular culture. American art, often vibrantly colored and filled with activity, reflected the energy and exuberance of the postwar United States. After 1945, New York City became the artistic center of the Western world. The Guggenheim Museum, the Museum of Modern Art, and the Whitney Museum of American art, together with New York's numerous art galleries, promoted modern art and helped determine artistic tastes not only in New York and the United States, but throughout much of the world.

Abstractionism, especially Abstract Expressionism, emerged as the artistic mainstream. American exuberance in Abstract Expressionism is evident in the enormous canvases of Jackson Pollock (1912–1956). In such works as *Lavender Mist* (1950), paint seems to explode, assaulting the viewer with emotion and movement. Pollock's swirling forms and seemingly chaotic patterns broke all conventions of form and structure. His drip paintings, with their total abstraction, were extremely influential with other artists, although the public was initially quite hostile to his work.

The early 1960s saw the emergence of Pop Art, which took images of popular culture and transformed them into works of fine art. Andy Warhol (1930–1987), who began

◆ **Jackson Pollock Does a Painting.**   One of the best-known practitioners of Abstract Expressionism, which remained at the center of the artistic mainstream after World War II, was the American Jackson Pollock, who achieved his ideal of total abstraction in his drip paintings. He is shown here at work in his Long Island studio. Pollock found it easier to cover his large canvases with exploding patterns of color when he put them on the floor.

The most significant new trend in postwar literature has been called the "Theater of the Absurd." This new convention in drama began in France in the 1950s, although its most famous proponent was the Irishman Samuel Beckett (1906–1990), who lived in France. In Beckett's *Waiting for Godot* (1952), it is readily apparent that the action on the stage is not realistic. Two men wait incessantly for the appearance of someone, with whom they may or may not have an appointment. No background information on the two men is provided. During the course of the play, nothing seems to be happening. The audience is never told if the action in front of them is real or unreal. Unlike traditional theater, suspense is maintained not by having the audience wonder, "what is going to happen next?" but by having them wonder simply, "what is happening now?"

The Theater of the Absurd reflected its time. The postwar period was a time of disillusionment with fixed ideological beliefs in politics or religion. The same disillusionment that inspired the existentialism of Albert Camus (1913–1960) and Jean-Paul Sartre (1905–1980), with its sense of the world's meaninglessness, underscored the bleak worldview of absurdist drama and literature. The beginning point of the existentialism of Sartre and Camus was the absence of God in the universe. While the death of God was tragic, it meant that humans had no preordained destiny and were utterly alone in the universe with no future and no hope. As Camus expressed it:

> A world that can be explained even with bad reasons is a familiar world. But, on the other hand, in a universe suddenly divested of illusions and lights, man feels an alien, a stranger. His exile is without remedy since he is deprived of the memory of a lost home or the hope of a promised land. This divorce between man and his life, the actor and his setting, is properly the feeling of absurdity.[5]

According to Camus, then, the world was absurd and without meaning; humans, too, are without meaning and purpose. Reduced to despair and depression, humans have but one ground of hope—themselves.

The New World of Science and Technology

Since the Scientific Revolution of the seventeenth century and the Industrial Revolution of the nineteenth century, science and technology have played increasingly important roles in world civilization. Many of the scientific and technological achievements since World War II have revolutionized people's lives. When American astronauts walked on the moon, millions watched the event on their televisions in the privacy of their living rooms.

as an advertising illustrator, was the most famous of the pop artists. Warhol adapted images from commercial art, such as the Campbell soup cans, and photographs of such celebrities as Marilyn Monroe. Derived from mass culture, these works were mass produced and deliberately "of the moment," expressing the fleeting whims of popular culture.

In the 1980s, styles emerged that some have referred to as Postmodern. Although as yet ill-defined, Postmodernism tends to move away from the futurism or "cutting edge" qualities of Modernism. Instead it favors "utilizing tradition," whether that includes more styles of painting or elevating traditional craftsmanship to the level of fine art. Weavers, potters, glassmakers, metalsmiths, and furniture makers gained respect as artists.

Before World War II, theoretical science and technology were largely separated. Pure science was the domain of university professors who were quite far removed from the practical technological matters of technicians and engineers. But during World War II, university scientists were recruited to work for their governments and develop new weapons and practical instruments of war. British physicists played a crucial role in the development of an improved radar system that helped to defeat the German air force in the Battle of Britain in 1940. German scientists converted coal to gasoline to keep the German war machine moving and created self-propelled rockets as well as jet airplanes to keep Hitler's hopes alive for a miraculous turnaround in the war. The computer, too, was a wartime creation. The British mathematician Alan Turing designed a primitive computer to assist British intelligence in breaking the secret codes of German ciphering machines. The most famous product of wartime scientific research was the atomic bomb, created by a team of American and European scientists under the guidance of the physicist J. Robert Oppenheimer. Obviously, most wartime devices were created for destructive purposes, but merely to mention computers and jet airplanes demonstrates that they could easily be adapted for peacetime uses.

The sponsorship of research by governments and the military during World War II led to a new scientific model. Science had become very complex, and only large organizations with teams of scientists, huge laboratories, and complicated equipment could undertake such large-scale projects. Such facilities were so expensive, however, that they could only be provided by governments and large corporations. Because of its postwar prosperity, the United States was able to lead in the development of the new science. In 1965, almost 75 percent of all scientific research funds in the United States came from the government. Unwilling to lag behind, especially in military development, the Soviet Union was also forced to provide large outlays for scientific and technological research and development. In fact, the defense establishments of the United States and the Soviet Union generated much of postwar scientific research. One-fourth of the trained scientists and engineers after 1945 were utilized in the creation of new weapons systems. Universities found their research agendas increasingly determined by government funding for military-related projects.

There was no more stunning example of how the new scientific establishment operated than the space race of the 1960s. The announcement by the Soviets in 1957 that they had sent the first space satellite—*Sputnik I*—into orbit around the earth caused the United States to launch a gigantic project to land a manned spacecraft on the moon within a decade. Massive government funds financed the scientific research and technological advances that attained this goal in 1969.

The postwar alliance of science and technology led to an accelerated rate of change that became a fact of life in Western society. One product of this alliance—the computer—may yet prove to be the most revolutionary of all the technological inventions of the twentieth century. Early computers, which used thousands of vacuum tubes to function, were large and took up considerable room space. The development of the transistor and then the silicon chip produced a revolutionary new approach to computers. With the invention in 1971 of the microprocessor, a machine that combines the equivalent of thousands of transistors on a single, tiny silicon chip, the road was open for the development of the personal computer.

The computer is a new kind of machine whose chief function is to store and produce information, now considered a fundamental asset of our fast-paced civilization. By the 1990s, the personal computer had become a regular fixture in businesses, schools, and homes. It not only makes a whole host of tasks much easier, but it has also become an important tool in virtually every area of modern life. Indeed, other tools and machines now depend for their functioning on computers. Many of the minute-by-minute decisions required when flying an airplane, for example, are made by a computer.

Despite the marvels produced by the alliance of science and technology, some people came to question that underlying assumption of this alliance—that scientific knowledge gave human beings the ability to manipulate the environment for their benefit. They maintained that some technological advances had far-reaching side effects damaging to the environment. The chemical fertilizers, for example, that were touted for producing larger crops wreaked havoc with the ecological balance of streams, rivers, and woodlands. *Small Is Beautiful*, written by the British economist E. F. Schumacher (1911–1977), was a fundamental critique of the dangers of the new science and technology (see the box on p. 1102). The widespread proliferation of fouled beaches and dying forests and lakes made environmentalism one of the important issues of the 1990s.

The Revival of Religion

Existentialism was one response to the despair generated by the apparent collapse of civilized values in the twentieth century. The revival of religion has been another. Ever since the Enlightenment of the eighteenth century, Christianity and religion had been on the defensive. But in the twenti-

Small Is Beautiful: The Limits of Modern Technology

Although science and technology have produced an amazing array of achievements in the postwar world, some voices have been raised in criticism of their sometimes destructive aspects. In 1975, in his book Small Is Beautiful, *the British economist E. F. Schumacher examined the effects modern industrial technology has had on the earth's resources.*

E. F. Schumacher, *Small Is Beautiful*

Is it not evident that our current methods of production are already eating into the very substance of industrial man? To many people this is not at all evident. Now that we have solved the problem of production, they say, have we ever had it so good? Are we not better fed, better clothed, and better housed than ever before—and better educated? Of course we are: most, but by no means all, of us: in the rich countries. But this is not what I mean by "substance." The substance of man cannot be measured by Gross National Product. Perhaps it cannot be measured at all, except for certain symptoms of loss. However, this is not the place to go into the statistics of these symptoms, such as crime, drug addiction, vandalism, mental breakdown, rebellion, and so forth. Statistics never prove anything.

I started by saying that one of the most fateful errors of our age is the belief that the problem of production has been solved. This illusion, I suggested, is mainly due to our inability to recognise that the modern industrial system, with all its intellectual sophistication, consumes the very basis on which it has been erected.

To use the language of the economist, it lives on irreplaceable capital which it cheerfully treats as income. I specified three categories of such capital: fossil fuels, the tolerance margins of nature, and the human substance. Even if some readers should refuse to accept all three parts of my argument, I suggest that any one of them suffices to make my case.

And what is my case? Simply that our most important task is to get off our present collision course. And who is there to tackle such a task? I think every one of us. . . . To talk about the future is useful only if it leads to action *now*. And what can we do *now*, while we are still in the position of "never having had it so good"? To say the least . . . we must thoroughly understand the problem and begin to see the possibility of evolving a new life-style, with new methods of production and new patterns of consumption: a life-style designed for permanence. To give only three preliminary examples: in agriculture and horticulture, we can interest ourselves in the perfection of production methods which are biologically sound, build up soil fertility, and produce health, beauty and permanence. Productivity will then look after itself. In industry, we can interest ourselves in the evolution of small-scale technology, relatively nonviolent technology, "technology with a human face," so that people have a chance to enjoy themselves while they are working, instead of working solely for their pay packet and hoping, usually forlornly, for enjoyment solely during their leisure time.

---

eth century, a number of religious thinkers and leaders attempted to bring new life to Christianity. Despite the attempts of the Communist world to build an atheistic society and the West to build a secular society, religion continued to play an important role in the lives of many people.

One expression of this religious revival was the attempt by such theologians as the Protestant Karl Barth (1886–1968) and the Catholic Karl Rahner (1904–1984) to infuse traditional Christian teachings with new life. In his numerous writings, Barth attempted to reinterpret the religious insights of the Reformation era for the modern world. To Barth, the sinful and hence imperfect nature of human beings meant that humans could know religious truth not through reason, but only through the grace of God. Karl Rahner attempted to re-

vitalize traditional Catholic theology by incorporating aspects of modern thought. He was careful, however, to emphasize the continuity between ancient and modern interpretations of Catholic doctrine.

In the Catholic church, attempts at religious renewal also came from two charismatic popes—John XXIII and John Paul II. Pope John XXIII (1881–1963) reigned as pope for only a short time (1958–1963), but sparked a dramatic revival of Catholicism when he summoned the twenty-first ecumenical council of the Catholic church. Known as Vatican Council II, it liberalized a number of Catholic practices. The mass was henceforth to be celebrated in the vernacular languages rather than Latin. New avenues of communication with other Christian faiths were also opened for the first time since the Reformation.

John Paul II (b. 1920), who had been the archbishop of Cracow in Poland before his elevation to the papacy in 1978, was the first non-Italian to be elected pope since the sixteenth century. Although he alienated a number of people by reasserting traditional Catholic teaching on such issues as birth control, women in the priesthood, and clerical celibacy, John Paul's numerous travels around the world helped strengthen the Catholic church throughout the non-Western world. A strong believer in social justice, the charismatic John Paul II has been a powerful figure reminding Europeans of their spiritual heritage and the need to temper the pursuit of materialism with spiritual concerns.

The Explosion of Popular Culture

Popular culture in the twentieth century, especially since World War II, has played an important role in helping Western people define themselves. If on one level popular culture is but the history of the superficial and transient whims of mass taste, on another level "it is a history of how modern society has created images of itself and expressed its fantasies, its fears, its ambitions."[6]

The history of popular culture is also the history of the economic system that supports it, for this system manufactures, distributes, and sells the images that people consume as popular culture. As popular culture and its economic support system become increasingly intertwined, industries of leisure emerge. As one historian of popular culture has argued, "industrial societies turn the provision of leisure into a commercial activity, in which their citizens are sold entertainment, recreation, pleasure, and appearance as commodities that differ from the goods at the drugstore only in the way they are used."[7] Modern popular culture therefore is an integral part of the mass consumer society in which it has emerged, making it quite different from the folk culture of preceding centuries. Folk culture is something people make while popular culture is something people buy.

POPULAR CULTURE AND THE AMERICANIZATION OF THE WORLD

The United States has been the most influential force in shaping popular culture in the West and, to a lesser degree, the entire world. Through movies, music, advertising, and television, the United States has spread its particular form of consumerism and the American Dream to millions around the world. Already in 1923 the New York *Morning Post* noted that "the film is to America what the flag was once to Britain. By its means Uncle Sam may hope some day . . . to Americanize the world."[8] In movies, television, and popular music, the impact of American popular culture on the Western world is apparent.

Motion pictures were the primary vehicle for the diffusion of American popular culture in the years immediately following the war and continued to dominate both European and American markets in the next decades. Although developed in the 1930s, television did not become readily available until the late 1940s. By 1954, there were 32 million sets in the United States as television became the centerpiece of middle-class life. In the 1960s, as television spread around the world, American networks unloaded their products on Europe and developing countries at extraordinarily low prices. Only the establishment of quota systems prevented American television from completely inundating these countries. The United States has also dominated popular music since the end of World War II. Jazz, blues, rhythm and blues, rap, and rock and roll have been by far the most popular music forms in the Western world—and much of the non-Western world—during this time. All of them originated in the United States, and all are rooted in African-American musical innovations. These forms later spread to the rest of the world, inspiring local artists who then transformed the music in their own way.

In the postwar years, sports have become a major product of both popular culture and the leisure industry. The development of satellite television and various electronic breakthroughs helped make sports a global phenomenon. The Olympic Games could now be broadcast around the world from anyplace on earth. Sports became a cheap form of entertainment for consumers as fans did not have to leave their homes to enjoy athletic competitions. In fact, some sports organizations initially resisted television fearing that it would hurt ticket sales. The tremendous revenues possible from television contracts overcame this hesitation, however. As sports television revenue escalated, many sports came to receive the bulk of their yearly revenue from television contracts.

Sports have become big politics as well as big business. The politicization of sports has been one of the most significant trends in sports during the second half of the twentieth century. Football (soccer) remains the dominant world sport and more than ever has become a vehicle for nationalist sentiment and expression. The World Cup is the most watched event on television. Although the sport can be a positive outlet for national and local pride, all too often it has been marred by violence as nationalistic energies have overcome rational behavior.

Conclusion

Western Europe became a new community in the 1950s and 1960s as a remarkable economic recovery fostered a new optimism. Western European states became accustomed to political democracy, and with the development of the European Community, many of them began to move toward economic unity. But nagging economic problems, new ethnic divisions, resentment and violence toward immigrants, environmental degradation, and the inability to work together to stop a civil war in their own backyard have all indicated that what had been seen as a glorious new path for Europe in the 1950s and 1960s had become laden with pitfalls in the 1990s.

In the Western Hemisphere, the two North American countries—the United States and Canada—built prosperous economies and relatively stable communities in the 1950s, but there too new problems, including ethnic, racial, and linguistic differences as well as economic diffi-

culties, have dampened the optimism of the earlier decade. While some Latin American nations shared in the economic growth of the 1950s and 1960s, it was not matched by any real political stability. Only in the 1980s did democratic governments begin to replace oppressive military regimes with any consistency.

Western societies after 1945 were also participants in an era of rapidly changing international relationships. While Latin American countries struggled to find a new relationship with the colossus to the north, European states reluctantly let go of their colonial empires. Between 1947 and 1962, virtually every colony achieved independence and attained statehood. Although some colonial powers willingly relinquished their control, others, especially the French, had to be driven out by national wars of liberation. Decolonization was a difficult and even bitter process, but as we shall see in the next three chapters, it created a new world as the non-Western states ended the long-held ascendancy of the Western nations.

CHAPTER NOTES

1. Dwight Eisenhower, *The White House Years: Waging Peace, 1956–1961* (Garden City, N.Y., 1965), p. 533.
2. Quoted in Hilda Scott, *Sweden's 'Right to Be Human'—Sex-Role Equality: The Goal and the Reality* (London, 1982), p. 125.
3. Quoted in Marsha Rowe et al., *Spare Rib Reader* (Harmondsworth, 1982), p. 574.
4. Simone de Beauvoir, *The Second Sex*, trans. H. M. Parshley (New York, 1961), p. xxviii.
5. Quoted in Henry Grosshans, *The Search for Modern Europe* (Boston, 1970), p. 421.
6. Richard Maltby, ed., *Passing Parade: A History of Popular Culture in the Twentieth Century* (New York, 1989), p. 8.
7. Ibid.
8. Quoted in ibid., p. 11.

SUGGESTED READINGS

For a general perspective on the events covered in this chapter, see T. E. Vadney, *The World since 1945* (London, 1987). For a survey of postwar European history, see W. Laqueur, *Europe in Our Time* (New York, 1992). The rebuilding of postwar Europe is examined in A. S. Milward, *The Reconstruction of Western Europe, 1945–51* (Berkeley, Calif., 1984). On the building of common institutions in Western Europe, see J. Lodge, *Institutions and Policies of the European Community* (New York, 1983). For a survey of West Germany, see M. Balfour, *West Germany: A Contemporary History* (London, 1983). France under de Gaulle is examined in P. Williams and M. Harrison, *Politics and Society in de Gaulle's Republic* (New York, 1971). On Britain, see A. Sampson, *The Changing Anatomy of Britain* (New York, 1982). On the recent history of these countries, see P. Riddell, *The*

Thatcher Decade (Oxford, 1989); P. A. Hall, *Governing the Economy: The Politics of State Intervention in Britain and France* (New York, 1986); G. Ross, S. Hoffmann, and S. Malzacher, *The Mitterrand Experiment* (New York, 1987); R. J. Dalton, *Politics in West Germany* (Glenview, Ill., 1989); and K. Jarausch, *The Rush to German Unity* (New York, 1994).

For a general survey of American history, see Stephan Thernstrom, *A History of the American People*, 2d ed. (San Diego, 1989). The Truman administration is covered in R. J. Donovan, *Tumultuous Years: The Presidency of Harry S Truman* (New York, 1977). On the Eisenhower years, see S. Ambrose, *Eisenhower: The President* (New York, 1984). D. J. Garrow, *Martin Luther King, Jr., and the Southern Christian Leadership Conference* (New York, 1986) discusses the emergence of the civil rights movement. On the postwar social transformations in America, see W. Nugent, *Structures of American Social History* (Bloomington, Ind., 1981). On the turbulent decade of the 1960s, see W. O'Neill, *Coming Apart: An Informal History of America in the 1960s* (Chicago, 1971). On Nixon and Watergate, see J. Anthony Lukas, *Nightmare: The Underside of the Nixon Years* (New York, 1976). Works on recent events include B. Glad, *Jimmy Carter: From Plains to the White House* (New York, 1980) and G. Wills, *Reagan's America: Innocents at Home* (New York, 1987). On recent Canadian history, see R. Bothwell, I. Drummond, and J. English, *Canada since 1945* (Toronto, 1981).

For general surveys of Latin American history, see E. B. Burns, *Latin America: A Concise Interpretive Survey*, 4th ed. (Englewood Cliffs, N.J., 1986) and E. Williamson, *The Penguin History of Latin America* (London, 1992). The twentieth century is the focus of T. E. Skidmore and P. H. Smith, *Modern Latin America*, 3d ed. (New York, 1992). On the role of the military, see A. Rouquié, *The Military and the State in Latin America* (Berkeley, Calif., 1987). Recent United States–Latin American relations are examined in B. Wood, *The Dismantling of the Good Neighbor Policy* (Austin, Tex., 1985). Works on the countries examined in this chapter include L. A. Pérez, *Cuba: Between Reform and Revolution* (New York, 1988); B. Loveman, *Chile: The Legacy of Hispanic Capitalism*, 2d ed. (New York, 1988); J. A. Booth, *The End and the Beginning: The Nicaraguan Revolution* (Boulder, Colo., 1985); J. A. Page, *Perón: A Biog-*

raphy (New York, 1983); D. Rock, *Argentina, 1516–1987: From Spanish Colonization to Alfonsin*, 2d ed. (Berkeley, Calif., 1987); E. B. Burns, *A History of Brazil*, 2d ed. (New York, 1980); R. DaMatta, *Carnivals, Rogues, and Heroes: An Interpretation of the Brazilian Dilemma* (Notre Dame, Ind., 1991); and M. C. Meyer and W. L. Sherman, *The Course of Mexican History*, 4th ed. (New York, 1991).

For a survey of contemporary Western society, see A. Sampson, *The New Europeans* (New York, 1968). The student revolts of the late 1960s are put into a broader context in L. S. Feuer, *The Conflict of Generations* (New York, 1969). The changing role of women is examined in A. Cherlin, *Marriage, Divorce, Remarriage* (Cambridge, Mass., 1981). On the women's liberation movement, see D. Bouchier, *The Feminist Challenge: The Movement for Women's Liberation in Britain and the United States* (New York, 1983). More general works that include much information on the contemporary period are B. S. Anderson and J. P. Zinsser, *A History of Their Own*, vol. 2 (New York, 1988) and B. G. Smith, *Changing Lives: Women in European History since 1700* (Lexington, Mass., 1989). On terrorism, see W. Laqueur, *Terrorism*, 2d ed. (New York and London, 1988). The problems of guest workers and immigrants are examined in J. Miller, *Foreign Workers in Western Europe* (London, 1981). On the development of the Green parties, see F. Müller-Rommel, ed., *New Politics in Western Europe: The Rise and Success of Green Parties and Alternative Lists* (Boulder, Colo., 1989).

For a general view of postwar thought, see R. N. Stromberg, *European Intellectual History since 1789*, 5th ed. (Englewood Cliffs, N.J., 1990). On contemporary art, see R. Lambert, *Cambridge Introduction to the History of Art: The Twentieth Century* (Cambridge, 1981) and the general work by B. Cole and A. Gealt, *Art of the Western World* (New York, 1989). A physicist's view of science is contained in J. Ziman, *The Force of Knowledge: The Scientific Dimension of Society* (Cambridge, 1976). The space race is examined in W. A. McDougall, *The Heavens and the Earth: A Political History of the Space Age* (New York, 1984). There is an excellent survey of twentieth-century popular culture in R. Maltby, ed., *Passing Parade: A History of Popular Culture in the Twentieth Century* (New York, 1989).

Challenges of Nation Building in Africa and the Middle East

"If you educate a man, you educate an individual. If you educate a woman, you educate a nation." Ghanaian novelist Ama Ata Aidoo first heard that remark by the African educator Kwegyir Aggrey from her father when she was a child. In her own life, she has sought to live out the truth of that statement. After receiving her education at a girls' school in the Gold Coast and attending classes at Stanford University, she embarked on a writing career in which, as she notes, she has committed herself to the betterment of the African people. Every African woman and every man, she insists, *"should be a feminist, especially if they believe that Africans should take charge of our land, its wealth, our lives, and the burden of our development. Because it is not possible to advocate independence for our continent without also believing that African women must have the best that the environment can offer."*[1]

Since the end of World War II, the peoples of Africa and the Middle East have been liberated from the formal trappings of European colonialism. The creation of independent states in Africa began in the late 1950s and proceeded gradually over the next thirty years until the last colonial regime was finally dismantled. In the Middle East, the European mandates and protectorates of the prewar period gave way to independent states throughout the region.

But in both regions the transition to independence has not been an unalloyed success. In Africa, the legacy of colonialism in the form of arbitrary boundaries, political inexperience, and continued European economic domination has

• Statehood for Ghana   • Algeria receives independence from France   • Release of ANC chairman Nelson Mandela from prison

• Formation of the Organization for African Unity

• Egypt nationalizes the Suez Canal   • First oil crisis   • Iranian Revolution   • Iraqi invasion of Kuwait

• Formation of the state of Israel   • War between Israel and Egypt and other Arab states   • Camp David accords   • Agreement on Palestinian autonomy

• Founding of the Palestine Liberation Organization

combined with overpopulation and climatic disasters to frustrate the new states' ability to achieve political stability and economic prosperity. In the Middle East, deep-seated ethnic and religious disputes, superpower meddling, and the gross inequality in the distribution of oil resources throughout the region have led to a high degree of regional tension and conflict as well as a strong undercurrent of anti-Western sentiment. Today, the peoples of both Africa and the Middle East continue to search for a common identity beyond the framework of the nation-state—Africa in the concept of negritude (blackness) and the Middle East in a common devotion to the principles of a resurgent Islam. So far, however, neither color nor faith has proved to be a unifying factor, and the two regions remain among the most volatile and conflict-ridden in the world.

Emerging Africa

Under European colonial rule, which had been imposed on almost the entire continent by 1900, Africa was integrated into the global imperialist system. During the 1960s and 1970s, the Europeans finally retreated, and independent states emerged across the continent. But the process of building new nations has not been easy. The

peoples of Africa were ill-prepared for statehood, and even with political independence, they remained economically dependent upon their former masters. The Ivory Coast, for example, had more French residents in the early 1980s than it had before 1960. Even the geographical shape of the new states reflected colonial interests rather than African realities. Most of the colonial boundaries had been drawn for the convenience of European exploitation. Only rarely did they reflect the ethnic, cultural, or linguistic divisions of precolonial Africa.

African societies and their leaders have struggled for a generation to overcome these difficulties, but with only modest success. Many of the poorest nations in the world are in Africa. Several are threatened by mass starvation. AIDS is especially widespread in some African countries and, if unchecked, will wreak havoc on their populations early in the next century. Political stability is the exception rather than the rule, and civil wars are currently raging throughout the continent. Yet, for all its problems, Africa's natural and human resources give it enormous potential, and it is likely to play a major part in the history of the twenty-first century.

Uhuru: *The Struggle for Independence*

After World War II, Europeans reluctantly recognized that the end result of colonial rule in Africa would be African self-government, if not full independence. Accordingly, the African population would have to be trained to handle the responsibilities of representative government. In many cases, however, relatively little had been done to prepare the local population for self-rule. Early in the colonial era, during the mid-nineteenth century, African administrators had held influential positions in several British colonies, and one even served as governor of the Gold Coast. Legislative councils with limited African participation had been established in several colonies, although their functions were solely advisory. But with the formal institution of colonial rule, senior positions were reserved for the British, although local authority remained in the hands of native rulers.

After World War II, most British colonies introduced reforms that increased the representation of the local population. Members of legislative and executive councils were increasingly chosen through elections, and Africans came to constitute a majority. Elected councils at the local level were introduced in the 1950s to reduce the power of the tribal chiefs and clan heads, who had controlled local government under indirect rule. An exception was South Africa, where white domination continued. In the Union of South Africa, the franchise was restricted to whites except for the former territory of the Cape Colony, where persons of mixed ancestry had enjoyed the right to vote since the mid-nineteenth century. Black Africans did win some limited electoral rights in Northern and Southern Rhodesia (now Zambia and Zimbabwe), although whites generally dominated the political scene.

A similar process of political liberalization was taking place in the French colonies. At first, as we have seen, the French tried to assimilate the African peoples into French culture. By the 1920s, however, racist beliefs in Western cultural superiority and the tenacity of traditional beliefs and practices among Africans had somewhat discredited this ideal. The French therefore substituted a more limited program of assimilating African elites into Western culture and using them as administrators at the local level as a link to the remainder of the population. This policy resembled the British policy of indirect rule although it placed more emphasis on French culture in training local administrators. It had only limited success, however, because many Western-educated Africans refused to leave the urban centers to live in the countryside. Others, who were exposed to radical ideas while studying abroad, rejected the prevailing forms of Western civilization and called for the restoration of national independence.

The Nazi occupation of northern France had an effect on black Africans somewhat like that of the Japanese occupation of Southeast Asia on Asians (see Chapter 31). In 1944, the Free French movement under General Charles de Gaulle issued the Brazzaville Declaration, which promised equal rights, though not self-government, in a projected French Union composed of France and its overseas possessions. After the war, a legislative assembly for the new organization was created, although its political powers were limited. At the same time, African representatives were elected to the French National Assembly in Paris. But even this new community of nations had separate categories of citizenship based on education and ethnic background, and decisions on major issues were still made in France or by French officials in French Africa.

ROOTS OF REVIVAL

Colonial rule had a mixed impact on the societies and peoples of Africa. The Western presence brought a number of short-term and long-term benefits to Africa, such as improved transportation and communication facilities, and in a few areas laid the foundation for a modern industrial and commercial sector. Improved sanitation and medical care in all probability increased life expectancy. The introduction of selective elements of Western political systems laid the basis for the gradual creation of democratic societies.

Yet the benefits of Westernization were distributed highly unequally, and the vast majority of Africans found their lives little improved, if at all. Only South Africa and French-held Algeria, for example, developed modern industrial sectors, extensive railroad networks, and modern communications systems. In both countries, European settlers were numerous, most investment capital for industrial ventures was European, and whites comprised almost the entire professional and managerial class. Members of the native population were generally restricted to unskilled or semiskilled jobs at wages averaging less than one-fifth of those enjoyed by Europeans. Those who worked in industry or on infrastructure projects often suffered from inhuman working conditions. Several thousand African conscripts reportedly died on press gangs building the new railroad system.

Many colonies concentrated on export crops—peanuts from Senegal and Gambia, cotton from Egypt and Uganda, coffee from Kenya, and palm oil and cocoa products from the Gold Coast. Here the benefits of development were somewhat more widespread. In some cases, the crops were grown on plantations, which were usually owned by Europeans. But plantation agriculture was not always suitable in Africa, and much farming was done by free or tenant farmers. In some areas, where land ownership was traditionally vested in the community, the land was owned and leased by the corporate village.

Even here, however, the vast majority of the profits from the export of tropical products accrued to Europeans or to merchants from other foreign countries, such as India and the Arab emirates. While a fortunate few benefited from the increase in exports, the vast majority of Africans continued to be subsistence farmers growing food for their own consumption. The gap was particularly wide in places like Kenya, where the best lands had been reserved for European settlers to make the colony self-sufficient. As in other parts of the world, the early stages of the industrial revolution were especially painful for the rural population, and ordinary subsistence farmers reaped few benefits from colonial rule.

The African response to the loss of independence can be traced through several stages, beginning with resistance. In some cases, the opposition came from an organized state, such as Ashanti, which fought against the British takeover of the Gold Coast in the 1860s. Where formal states did not exist, the colonial takeover was often easier and more gradual; in a few instances, however, such as the Zulu tribesmen in South Africa in the 1880s and Abdel Qadir's rebellion against the French in Algeria, resistance to white rule was quite fierce.

But formal nationalist movements and parties generally arose later in Africa than in Asia (see Chapter 25). The first nationalist groups were formed in urban areas, primarily among peoples who had been exposed to Western civilization. The first Afro-Europeans, as such people are sometimes called, had often benefited from the European presence, and some, as we have seen, had held responsible positions in the colonial bureaucracy. But as the system became more formalized in the early twentieth century, more emphasis was placed on racial distinctions, and opportunities in government and other professional positions diminished, especially in the British colonies, where indirect rule had been based on collaboration with the local tribal aristocracy. The result was a dissatisfied urban educated elite, who were all the more angry when they realized they would not benefit from the improved conditions.

Political organizations for African rights did not arise until after World War I, and then only in a few areas, such as British-ruled Kenya and the Gold Coast. At first, organizations such as the National Congress of British West Africa (formed in 1919 in the Gold Coast) and Jomo Kenyatta's Kikuyu Central Association focused on improving African living conditions in the colonies rather than on national independence. After World War II, however, following the example of independence movements elsewhere, these groups became organized political parties with independence as their objective. In the Gold Coast, Kwame Nkrumah (1909–1972) led the Convention People's Party, the first formal African political party in black Africa. In the late 1940s, Jomo Kenyatta (1894–1978) founded the Kenya African National Union (KANU), which focused on economic issues but had an implied political agenda as well.

For the most part, these political activities were basically nonviolent and were led by Western-educated African intellectuals. Their constituents were primarily urban professionals, merchants, and members of labor unions. But the demand for independence was not entirely restricted to the cities. In Kenya, for example, the widely publicized Mau Mau movement among the Kikuyu peoples used terrorism as an essential element of its program to achieve *uhuru* (freedom) from the British. Although most of the violence was directed against other Africans (while only about 100 Europeans were killed in the violence, an estimated 1,700 Africans lost their lives at the hands of the rebels), the specter of Mau Mau terrorism alarmed the European population and in 1959 convinced the British government to promise eventual independence.

A similar process was occurring in Egypt, which had been a protectorate of Great Britain (and under loose Turkish suzerainty until the breakup of the Ottoman Empire) since the 1880s. National consciousness had existed in Egypt since well before the colonial takeover, and members of the legislative council were calling for independence even before World War I. In 1918, a formal political party called the Wafd was formed to promote Egyptian independence. The intellectuals were opposed as much to the local palace government as to the British, however, and in 1952 an army coup overthrew King Farouk, the grandson of Khedive Ismail, and established an independent republic.

In areas such as South Africa and Algeria, where the political system was dominated by European settlers, the transition to independence was more complicated. In South Africa, political activity by local blacks began with the formation of the African National Congress (ANC) in 1912. Initially, the ANC was dominated by Western-oriented intellectuals and had little mass support. Its goal was to achieve economic and political reforms, including full equality for educated Africans, within the framework of the existing system. But the ANC's efforts met with little success, while conservative white parties managed to stiffen the segregation laws. In response, the ANC became increasingly radicalized, and by the 1950s the prospects for a violent confrontation were growing.

In Algeria, resistance to French rule by Berbers and Arabs in rural areas had never ceased. After World War II, urban agitation intensified, leading to a widespread rebellion against colonial rule in the mid-1950s. At first, the French government tried to maintain its authority in Algeria, which was considered an integral part of metropolitan France. But when Charles de Gaulle became president in 1958, he reversed French policy, and Algeria became independent under President Ahmad Ben Bella (b. 1918) in 1962. The armed struggle in Algeria hastened the transition to statehood in its neighbors as well. Tunisia won its independence in 1956 after some urban agitation and rural unrest, but retained close ties with Paris. The French attempted to suppress the nationalist movement in Morocco by sending Sultan Muhammad V into exile, but the effort failed, and in 1956 he returned as the ruler of the independent state of Morocco.

Most black African nations achieved their independence in the late 1950s and 1960s, beginning with the Gold Coast, now renamed Ghana, in 1957. Nigeria, the Belgian Congo (renamed Zaire), Kenya, Tanganyika (later, when joined with Zanzibar, renamed Tanzania), and several other countries soon followed. Most of the French colonies agreed to accept independence within the framework of de Gaulle's French Community. By the late 1960s, only parts of southern Africa and the Portuguese possessions of Mozambique and Angola remained under European rule.

Yet independence had come later to Africa than to Asia, where most states had achieved independence by the early 1950s. Several factors help explain the delay. For one thing, colonialism had been established in Africa somewhat later than in most areas of Asia, and the inevitable reaction from the local population was consequently delayed. Furthermore, with the exception of a few areas in West Africa and along the Mediterranean, coherent states with a strong sense of cultural, ethnic, and linguistic unity did not exist in most of Africa. Most traditional states, such as Ashanti in West Africa, Songhai in the southern Sahara, and Bakongo in the Congo Basin, were collections of heterogeneous peoples with little sense of national or cultural identity. Even after colonies were established, the European powers often practiced a policy of "divide and rule," while the British encouraged political decentralization by retaining the authority of the traditional native chieftains. It is hardly surprising that when opposition to colonial rule emerged, unity was difficult to achieve.

The Era of Independence

The newly independent African states faced intimidating challenges. All of them had been profoundly affected by colonial rule, yet the experience had been highly unsatisfactory in most respects. Although Western political institutions, values, and technology had been introduced, at least into the cities, the exposure to European civilization had been superficial at best for most Africans and tragic for many. At the outset of independence, most African societies were still primarily agrarian and traditional, and their modern sectors depended heavily on imports from the West.

PAN-AFRICANISM AND NATIONALISM: THE DESTINY OF AFRICA

Most African leaders came from the urban middle class. They had studied in either Europe or the United States and spoke and read European languages. Although most were profoundly critical of colonial policies, they appeared to accept the relevance of the Western model to Africa and gave at least lip service to Western democratic values.

Their views on economics were somewhat more diverse. Some, like Jomo Kenyatta of Kenya and General Mobutu Sese Seko (b. 1930) of Zaire (previously the Belgian Congo), were advocates of Western-style capitalism. Others, like Julius Nyerere (b. 1922) of Tanzania, Kwame Nkrumah of Ghana, and Sékou Touré (1922–1984) of Guinea, preferred an "African form of socialism," which resembled the socialist trade union movement in Western Europe far more than the Marxist-Leninist socialism practiced in the Soviet Union. According to its advocates, it was descended from traditional communal practices in precolonial Africa.

Like the leaders of other developing countries, the new political leaders in Africa were highly nationalistic and generally accepted the colonial boundaries. But, as we have seen, these boundaries were artificial creations of the colonial powers. Virtually all of the new states included widely diverse ethnic, linguistic, and territorial groups. Zaire, for example, is composed of over two hundred different territorial groups speaking seventy-five different languages.

Some African leaders themselves harbored attitudes that undermined the fragile sense of common identity that was needed to knit together these diverse groups. A number of them, including Nkrumah of Ghana, Touré of Guinea, and Kenyatta of Kenya, were enticed by the dream of pan-Africanism, a concept of continental unity that transcended national boundaries and was to find its concrete manifestation in the Organization of African Unity (OAU), which was founded in Addis Ababa in 1963 (see the box on p. 1112).

Pan-Africanism originated among African intellectuals during the first half of the twentieth century. A basic element was the belief in negritude (blackness), the conviction that there was a distinctive "African personality" that owed nothing to Western materialism and provided a common sense of destiny for all black African peoples. According to Aimé Césaire, a West Indian of African descent and a leading ideologist of the movement, whereas Western civilization prized rational thought and material achievement, African culture emphasized emotional expression and a common sense of humanity. In a world where the Western drive for profit and political hegemony threatened to destroy civilization, Africans had an obligation to use their humanistic and spiritual qualities to help save the human race. The Ghanaian official Michael Francis Dei-Anang agreed.

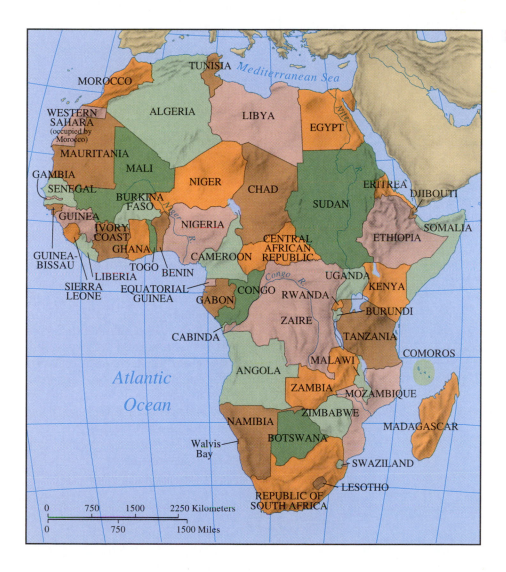

✖ **Map 30.1**   Modern Africa.

≈ Toward African Unity ≈

In May 1963, the leaders of thirty-two African states met in Addis Ababa, the capital of Ethiopia, to discuss the creation of an organization that would represent the interests of all the newly independent countries of Africa. The result was the Organization of African Unity. An excerpt from its charter is presented here. Although the organization has by no means realized all of the aspirations of its founders, it provides a useful forum for the discussion and resolution of its members' common problems.

The Charter of the Organization of African Unity

We, the Heads of African States and Governments assembled in the City of Addis Ababa, Ethiopia;
CONVINCED that it is the inalienable right of all people to control their own destiny;
CONSCIOUS of the fact that freedom, equality, justice and dignity are essential objectives for the achievement of the legitimate aspirations of the African peoples;
CONSCIOUS of our responsibility to harness the natural and human resources of our continent for the total advancement of our peoples in spheres of human endeavor;

INSPIRED by a common determination to promote understanding among our peoples and co-operation among our States in response to the aspirations of our peoples for brotherhood and solidarity, in a larger unity transcending ethnic and national differences;
CONVINCED that, in order to translate this determination into a dynamic force in the cause of human progress, conditions for peace and security must be established and maintained;
DETERMINED to safeguard and consolidate the hard-won independence as well as the sovereignty and territorial integrity of our States, and to fight against neo-colonialism in all its forms;
DEDICATED to the general progress of Africa; . . .
DESIROUS that all African States should henceforth unite so that the welfare and well-being of their peoples can be assured;
RESOLVED to reinforce the links between our states by establishing and strengthening common institutions;
HAVE agreed to the present Charter.

In *Whither Bound Africa*, written in 1946, he declared scathingly:

Forward! To What?
The Slums, where man is dumped upon man,
Where penury
And misery
Have made their hapless homes,
And all is dark and drear?
Forward! To what?
The factory
To grind hard hours
In an inhuman mill,
In one long ceaseless spell?

Forward! To what?
To the reeking round
Of medieval crimes,
Where the greedy hawks
Of Aryan stock
Prey with bombs and guns

On men of lesser breed?
Forward to CIVILIZATION [2]

The concept of negritude, as observers have pointed out, was in part a natural defensive response to the Social Darwinist concepts of Western racial superiority and African inferiority that were popular in Europe and the United States during the early years of the twentieth century. At the same time, it was stimulated by growing self-doubt among many European intellectuals after World War I who feared that Western civilization was on a path of self-destruction. African intellectuals such as Michael Dei-Anang and the West Indian Aimé Césaire shared such feelings and compared the white world:

Appallingly weary from its immense effort
The crack of its joints rebelling under the hardness
*   of the stars*

with the Africans:

Those who invented neither gunpowder nor compass
those who tamed neither steam nor electricity
those who explored neither sea nor sky
but those who know the humblest corners of the country
    suffering
those whose only journeys were uprooting
those who went to sleep on their knees
those who were domesticated and christianized
those who were inoculated with degeneration.[3]

Negritude had more appeal to Africans from French colonies than to those from British possessions. Yet it also found adherents in the British colonies as well as among blacks in the United States and elsewhere in the Americas. African-American intellectuals such as W.E.B. Dubois and George Padmore and the West Indian politician Marcus Garvey attempted to promote a "black renaissance" by popularizing the idea of a distinct African personality. Their views were shared by several of the new African leaders, including Leopold Senghor (b. 1906) of Senegal, Kwame Nkrumah of Ghana, and Jomo Kenyatta of Kenya. Nkrumah in particular appeared to hope that a pan-African union could be established that would unite all of the new countries of the continent in a broader community.

Dream and Reality: Political and Economic Conditions in Contemporary Africa

The program of the OAU had forecast a future Africa based on freedom, equality, justice, and dignity and on the unity, solidarity, and territorial integrity of African states. It did not take long for reality to set in. Vast disparities in education and income made it hard to establish democratic institutions in much of Africa. Expectations that independence would lead to stable political structures based on "one person, one vote" were soon disappointed, as the initial phase of pluralistic governments gave way to a series of military regimes and one-party states. Between 1957 and 1982, more than seventy leaders of African countries were overthrown by violence. In 1984, *Time* magazine reported that only seven of the forty-one major African states permitted opposition parties to operate legally. The remainder were under single-party regimes or were ruled by the military.[4]

Hopes that independence would inaugurate an era of economic prosperity and equality were similarly dashed. Part of the problem could be (and was) ascribed to the lingering effects of colonialism. Most newly independent countries in Africa were dependent upon the export of a single crop or natural resource. When prices fluctuated or dropped, they were at the mercy of the vagaries of the international market. In several cases, the resources were still controlled by foreigners, leading to the charge that colonialism had been succeeded by "neocolonialism," in which Western domination was maintained by economic rather than by political or military means. To make matters worse, most African states had to import technology and manufactured goods from the West, and the prices of those goods rose more rapidly than those of the export products.

The new states also contributed to their own problems. Scarce national resources were squandered on military equipment or expensive consumer goods rather than on building up their infrastructure to provide the foundation for an industrial economy. Corruption, a painful reality throughout the modern world, became almost a way of life in Africa, as bribery (known variously as *dash, chai,* or *bonsella*) became necessary to obtain even the most basic services (see the box on p. 1114). The Nigerian author Cyprian Ekwensi expressed his disillusionment with African politics in his novel *Jagua Nana.* When the heroine's boyfriend Freddie states, "I wan' money quick-quick; an' politics is de only hope," she replies, "No Freddie. I no wan' you to win. . . . Politics not for you, Freddie. You got education. You got culture. You're a gentleman an' proud. Politics be game for dog. And in dis Lagos, is a rough game. De roughest game in de whole worl'. Is smell an' dirty an' you too clean an' sweet."[5]

Finally, population growth, which more than anything else has hindered economic growth in the new nations of Asia and Africa, became a serious problem and crippled efforts to create modern economies. By the mid-1980s, population growth averaged nearly 3 percent throughout Africa, the highest rate of any continent. Drought conditions and the inexorable spread of the Sahara (usually known as desertification, a condition caused partly by overpopulation) have led to widespread hunger and starvation first in West African countries like Niger and Mali and then in Ethiopia, Somalia, and the Sudan. Despite global efforts to provide food, millions are in danger of starvation and malnutrition, and countless others have fled to neighboring countries in search of sustenance. In recent years, the spread of AIDS in Africa has reached epidemic proportions. According to one estimate, one-third of the entire population of sub-Saharan Africa is infected with the virus, including a high percentage of the urban middle class. Some observers believe that without measures to curtail the effect of the disease, it will have a significant influence on Africa's population, which is predicted to increase by at least 300 million in the next fifteen years.

Stealing the Nation's Riches

After 1965, African novelists transferred their anger from the foreign oppressor to their own national leaders, deploring their greed, corruption, and inhumanity. One of the most pessimistic expressions of this betrayal of newly independent Africa is found in The Beautiful Ones Are Not Yet Born, *a novel published by the Ghanaian author Ayi Kwei Armah in 1968. The author decries the government of Kwame Nkrumah and is unimpressed with the rumors of a military coup, which, he predicts, will simply replace the present regime with a new despot and his entourage of "fat men."*

Ayi Kwei Armah, *The Beautiful Ones Are Not Yet Born*

The net had been made in the special Ghanaian way that allowed the really big corrupt people to pass through it. A net to catch only the small, dispensable fellows, trying in their anguished blindness to leap and to attain the gleam and the comfort the only way these things could be done. And the big ones floated free, like all the slogans. End bribery and corruption. Build Socialism. Equality. Shit. A man would just have to make up his mind that there was never going to be anything but despair, and there would be no way of escaping it. . . .

. . . In the life of the nation itself, maybe nothing really new would happen. New men would take into their hands the power to steal the nation's riches and to use it for their own satisfaction. That, of course, was to be expected. New people would use the country's power to get rid of men and women who talked a language that did not flatter them. There would be nothing different in that. That would only be a continuation of the Ghanaian way of life. But here was the real change. The individual man of power now shivering, his head filled with the fear of the vengeance of those he had wronged. For him everything was going to change. And for those like him who had grown greasy and fat singing the praises of their chief, for those who had been getting themselves ready for the enjoyment of hoped-for favors, there would be long days of pain ahead. The flatterers with their new white Mercedes cars would have to find ways of burying old words. For those who had come directly against the old power, there would be much happiness. But for the nation itself there would only be a change of embezzlers and a change of the hunters and the hunted. A pitiful shrinking of the world from those days Teacher still looked back to, when the single mind was filled with the hopes of a whole people. A pitiful shrinking, to days when all the powerful could think of was to use the power of a whole people to fill their own paunches. Endless days, same days, stretching into the future with no end anywhere in sight.

The consequences of rapid population growth are depressing and familiar. Poverty is endemic in Africa, particularly among the three-quarters of the population still living off the land. Urban areas have grown tremendously, but as in much of Asia, most are surrounded by massive squatter settlements of rural peoples who had fled to the cities in search of a better life. The expansion of the cities has overwhelmed fragile transportation and sanitation systems and led to rising pollution and perpetual traffic jams, while millions are forced to live without water and electricity. In the meantime, the fortunate few (all too often government officials on the take) live the high life and emulate the consumerism of the West (in a particularly expressive phrase, the rich in many East African countries are known as the *wabenzi*, or Mercedes Benz people).

In "Pedestrian, to Passing Benz-man," the Kenyan poet Albert Ojuka voices the popular discontent with economic inequality:

You man, lifted gently
out of the poverty and suffering
we so recently shared; I say—
why splash the muddy puddle on to
my bare legs, as if, still unsatisfied
with your seated opulence
you must sully the unwashed
with your diesel-smoke and mud-water
and force him buy, beyond his means
a bar of soap from your shop?
a few years back we shared a master
today you have none, while I have
exchanged a parasite for something worse.
But maybe a few years is too long a time.[6]

THE SEARCH FOR SOLUTIONS

Concern over the dangers of economic inequality inspired a number of African leaders, such as Nkrumah in Ghana, Nyerere in Tanzania, and Samora Michel of Mozambique, to restrict foreign investment and nationalize the major industries and utilities while promoting social ideals and values. Nyerere was the most consistent, promoting the ideals of socialism and self-reliance through his Arusha Declaration of 1967 (see the box on p. 1116). Using the benefits of a single-party system, Nyerere placed limitations on income and established village collectives to avoid the corrosive effects of economic inequality and government corruption. Sympathetic foreign countries provided considerable economic aid to assist the experiment, and many observers noted that levels of corruption, political instability, and ethnic strife were lower in Tanzania than in many other African countries. Unfortunately, corruption has increased in recent years, while political elements in Zanzibar, citing the stagnation brought about by two decades of socialism, are agitating for autonomy or even total separation from the mainland. Tanzania also has poor soil, inadequate rainfall, and limited resources, all of which have contributed to its slow growth and continuing rural and urban poverty.

In 1985, Nyerere voluntarily retired from the presidency. In his farewell speech, he confessed that he had failed to achieve many of his ambitious goals to create a socialist society in Africa. In particular, he admitted that

◆ **The Arab Dhow.** Long the preferred mode of travel in the Indian Ocean, the Arab dhow, with its rakish lateen sail, remains in widespread use along the east coast of Africa. As this small sailing vessel in the Tanzanian port of Dar es Salaam demonstrates, such traditional craft still ply the waters off the continent from the Red Sea to the Strait of Madagascar.

❧ Socialism Is Not Racialism ❧

At Arusha, Tanzania, in 1967, Julius Nyerere, the president of Tanzania, set forth the principles for building a socialist society. Nyerere made it clear that he was talking about an African style of socialism that would put ownership of his country's wealth into the hands of the people rather than into the hands of foreign capitalists. Since then, Tanzania has taken a socialist approach to economic development. The results have been mixed: the country is not wealthy, but there are few extremes of rich and poor.

Julius Nyerere, The Arusha Declaration

The Arusha Declaration and the actions relating to public ownership were all concerned with ensuring that we can build socialism in our country. The nationalization and the taking of a controlling interest in many firms were a necessary part of our determination to organize our society in such a way that our efforts benefit all our people and that there is no exploitation of one man by another.

Yet these actions do not in themselves create socialism. They are necessary to it, but as the Arusha Declaration states, they could also be the basis for fascism—in other words, for the oppressive extreme of capitalism. For the words with which I began my pamphlet "Ujamaa" in 1962 remain valid; socialism is an attitude of mind. The basis of socialism is a belief in the oneness of man and the common historical destiny of mankind. Its basis, in other words, is human equality.

Acceptance of this principle is absolutely fundamental to socialism. The justification of socialism is Man—not the State, not the flag. Socialism is not for the benefit of black men, nor brown men, nor white men, nor yellow men. The purpose of socialism is the service of man, regardless of color, size, shape, skill, ability, or anything else. And the economic institutions of socialism, such as those we are now creating in accordance with the Arusha Declaration, are intended to serve man in our society. Where the majority of the people in a particular society are black, then most of those who benefit from socialism there will be black. But it has nothing to do with their blackness, only with their humanity. . . .

We in Tanzania have to hold fast to this lesson, especially now as we advance on the socialist road. For it is true that because of our colonial history the vast majority of the capitalist organizations in this country are owned and run by Asians or by Western Euro-

---

his plan to collectivize the traditional private farms (*shamba*) had encountered strong resistance from conservative peasants. "You can socialize what is not traditional," he remarked. "The *shamba* can't be socialized." But Nyerere insisted that many of his policies had succeeded in improving social and economic conditions, and he argued that the only real solution was to consolidate the multitude of small countries in the region into a larger East African Federation.[7]

The countries that opted for capitalism faced their own dilemmas. Tanzania's neighbor, Kenya, which was blessed with better soil in the highlands, a local tradition of aggressive commerce, and a residue of European settlers, welcomed foreign investment and profit incentives. The results have been mixed. Kenya has a strong current of indigenous African capitalism and a substantial middle class, mostly based in the capital of Nairobi. But landlessness, unemployment, and income inequities are high, even by African standards, and the rate of population growth—more than 4 percent annually—is one of the highest in the world. Eighty percent of the population re-

mains rural, and 40 percent live below the poverty line. The result has been widespread unrest in a country formerly admired for its successful development.

Beginning in the mid-1970s, a few African nations decided to adopt Soviet-style Marxism-Leninism. In Angola and Ethiopia, Marxist parties followed the Soviet model and attempted to create fully socialist societies with the assistance of Soviet experts and Cuban troops and advisers. Economically, the results were disappointing, and both countries faced severe internal opposition. In Ethiopia, the revolt by Muslim tribal peoples in the province of Eritrea led to the fall of the Marxist leader Mengistu and his regime in 1990. A similar revolt erupted against the government in Angola where the rebel group UNITA controlled much of the rural population and even threatened the capital city of Luanda.

Neither capitalism nor socialism could reverse Africa's downward spiral, however. According to recent statistics, eighteen of the world's twenty poorest countries are in Africa. Excluding South Africa, the gross national product in 1991 for all countries south of the Sahara, repre-

peans. Twenty years ago we could have said all the capitalists in this country were from those areas; we cannot say this now. For the truth is that capitalism and capitalist attitudes have nothing whatsoever to do with the race or national origin of those who believe in them or practice them. Indeed, nobody who was at Arusha needs any more proof that the temptations of capitalism ignore color boundaries. Even leaders of TANU [Tanzanian party of peasants and workers] were getting deeply involved in the practices of capitalism and landlordism. A few had started talking of "my company." And very many others would have done so if they could; they were capitalists by desire even when they could not be so in practice. Hence the resolution on leadership. Hence the difficulties we must expect in enforcing this resolution.

Socialism has nothing to do with race, nor with country of origin. In fact any intelligent man, whether he is a socialist or not, realizes that there are socialists in capitalist countries—and from capitalist countries. Very often such socialists come to work in newly independent and avowedly socialist countries like Tanzania because they are frustrated in their capitalist homeland. Neither is any intelligent man blind to the fact that there are frustrated capitalists in the communist countries—just as there will in time be frustrated capitalists in Tanzania. It may even be that some of those frustrated capitalists from Eastern countries come to work with us.

Neither is it sensible for a socialist to talk as if all capitalists are devils. It is one thing to dislike the capitalist system and to try and frustrate people's capitalist desires. But it would be as stupid for us to assume that capitalists have horns as it is for people in Western Europe to assume that we in Tanzania have become devils.

In fact the leaders in the capitalist countries have now begun to realize that communists are human beings like themselves—that they are not devils. . . . It would be very absurd if we react to the stupidity they are growing out of and become equally stupid ourselves in the opposite direction! We have to recognize in our words and our actions that capitalists are human beings as much as socialists. They may be wrong; indeed by dedicating ourselves to socialism we are saying that they are. But our task is to make it impossible for capitalism to dominate us. Our task is not to persecute capitalists or make dignified life impossible for those who would be capitalists if they could. . . .

senting almost 600 million people, was roughly equivalent to that of Belgium, with a population of about 10 million.

THE SEARCH FOR COMMUNITY

Finally, Africans have been disappointed that the dream of a united Africa has not been realized. No one skewered the pretensions of the apostles of negritude better than the Ugandan poet Taban Lo Liyong. In his poem "Negritude Is Crying Over Spilt Milk," he observed:

Strange mules called Negritude
and African Personality
Overran the terrain
And kicked wisdom down
Or above our heads.

Politicians quite unaware
How low we are
On the ladder universal

Decided to halt the race
And embrace the niches sure
Where we were stuck for the moment.[8]

But while some criticize the tendency to pursue what Taban called the "vanishing exotica" of the past, most Africans feel a shared sense of continuing victimization at the hands of the West and are convinced that independence has not ended Western interference in and domination of African affairs. Many African leaders were angered when Western powers led by the United States conspired to overthrow the radical Congolese politician Patrice Lumumba in Zaire in the early 1960s. The episode reinforced their desire to form the Organization of African Unity as a means of reducing Western influence. But aside from agreeing to adopt a neutral stance during the Cold War, African states have had difficulty achieving a united position on many issues, and their disagreements have left the region vulnerable to external influence and even led to conflict. During the late 1980s and early 1990s, border disputes festered in many areas of the continent and in some cases, as with Morocco and a rebel movement in the western Sahara, and between Kenya and Uganda, flared into outright war.

Even within many African nations, the concept of nationhood was undermined by the renascent force of regionalism or tribalism. Nigeria, with the largest population on the continent, was rent by civil strife during the late 1960s, when dissident Ibo groups in the southeast attempted unsuccessfully to form an independent state of Biafra. Ethnic conflicts broke out among hostile territorial groups in Zimbabwe (the new name for Southern Rhodesia) and in several nations in Central Africa. In Kenya, the Luo tribal leader Tom Mboya was assassinated, presumably because rival groups feared that he would be selected to succeed the charismatic president Jomo Kenyatta.

Another force that undermined nationalism in Africa was pan-Islamism. Its prime exponent in Africa was the Egyptian president Gamal Abdul Nasser (see Nasser and Pan-Arabism later in this chapter). After Nasser's death in 1970, the torch of Arab unity in Africa was carried by the Libyan president Muammar Qadhafi, whose ambitions to create a greater Muslim nation in the Sahara under his authority led to conflict with neighboring Chad. The Islamic resurgence also surfaced in Ethiopia, where Muslim tribesmen in Eritrea (the former Italian colony of Eritrea had been joined with Ethiopia in 1952) rebelled against the Marxist regime of Colonel Mengistu in Addis Ababa.

RECENT TRENDS

Not all the news in Africa has been bad. In recent years, popular demonstrations, fueled by stagnant economies, have led to the collapse of one-party regimes and the emergence of fragile democracies in several countries. Dictatorships were brought to an end in Ethiopia, Liberia, and Somalia, although in each case the fall of the regime was later followed by political instability or, in the latter two instances, by a bloody civil war. Perhaps the most notorious case was that of Idi Amin of Uganda. Colonel Amin had led a coup against Prime Minister Milton Obote in 1971. After ruling by terror and brutal repression of dissident elements, he was finally deposed in 1979. In recent years, stability has returned to Uganda, which held its first presidential elections in more than fifteen years in May 1996. In Eritrea, a popular Islamic government is gradually rebuilding the country and planning for the creation of a parliamentary system in 1997.

Africa has also benefited from the end of the Cold War, as the superpowers have virtually ceased to compete for power and influence there. When the Soviet Union withdrew its support from the Marxist government in Ethiopia, the United States allowed its right to maintain military bases in neighboring Somalia to lapse, resulting in the overthrow of the authoritarian government there. Unfortunately, clan rivalries led to such turbulence that many inhabitants were in imminent danger of starvation, and in the winter of 1992, U.S. military forces occupied the country in an effort to provide food to the starving population. Since the departure of foreign troops in 1993, the country has been divided into clan fiefdoms, while Islamist groups attempt to bring a return to law and order.

Yet foreign intervention in the internal affairs of African countries has by no means come to an end, especially in the ex-French colonies in central and western Africa. French troops have been stationed in a number of these countries for several years at the request of local governments. Opposition groups now contend that the French forces are being used to uphold dictatorial regimes and should be withdrawn.

Perhaps Africa's greatest success story is South Africa, where the white government, which long maintained its policy of apartheid and restricted black sovereignty to a series of small "Bantustans" in relatively infertile areas of the country, finally accepted the inevitability of African involvement in the political process and the national economy. In 1993, the government of President F. W. de Klerk (b. 1936) agreed with ANC leader Nelson Mandela (b. 1918) to hold democratic national elections the following spring. In the meantime, ANC representatives agreed to take part in a transitional coalition government with de Klerk's National Party. Those elections resulted in a substantial majority for the ANC, and Mandela became president. In May 1996, a new constitution that called for a multiracial state was approved. The National Party immediately went into opposition, claiming that the new charter did not adequately provide for joint decision making by members of the coalition.

The third group in the coalition government, the Zulu-based Inkatha Freedom Party, agreed to remain within the government, but rivalry between the ANC and Zulu elites intensified. Zulu chief Mangosuthu Buthelezi, drawing on the growing force of Zulu nationalism, has begun to invoke the memory of the great Zulu ruler Shaka in a possible bid for future independence. Although many Zulus currently support the ANC, the future of a multiracial society in the Republic of South Africa remains in doubt. Even with all its problems, however, it remains the wealthiest and most industrialized state on the continent.

If the situation in South Africa provides grounds for modest optimism, that in Nigeria, Africa's economic giant, provides reason for serious concern. With its substantial oil reserves, Nigeria is one of the wealthiest countries in Africa and has the largest population on the continent. In recent years, Nigeria has been in the grip of military rulers, most recently General Sani Abacha. General Abacha has ruthlessly suppressed opposition to his rule and in late 1995 ordered the execution of author Ken Saro-Wiwa despite widespread protests from human rights groups abroad. Saro-Wiwa had vocally criticized environmental damage caused by foreign oil interests in southern Nigeria, but the regime's major concern was his support for separatist activities in the area that had previously launched the Biafran insurrection. Wole Soyinka, a Nobel Prize–winning author now in exile, has published a stern protest against the brutality of the Abacha regime. Entitled *The Open Sore of a Continent: A Personal Narrative of the Nigerian Crisis*, the short book places the primary responsibility for the current crisis not on Nigeria's long list of dictators, but on the very concept of the modern nation-state, which was introduced arbitrarily by Europeans during the later stages of the colonial era. A nation, Soyinka contends, can only emerge from below,

◆ **From Rebel to Statesman.**
After spending many years in a South African prison after conviction for terrorist activities, African National Congress leader Nelson Mandela was finally released in the early 1990s. Shortly after, he signed an agreement with President F. W. de Klerk to create a multiracial state and bring an end to an era of apartheid. The historic moment is shown here.

as the expression of the moral and political will of the local inhabitants, and cannot be imposed artificially from above as was done throughout Africa.

Currently, the most tragic situation is in the central African states of Rwanda and Burundi, where a chronic conflict between the dominant minority Tutsis and the Hutu majority has led to a bitter civil war that sent thousands of refugees fleeing to neighboring Zaire. By the end of 1996, many of the refugees were beginning to return to their homes, but no political solution to the situation is in sight. In the meantime, the presence of large numbers of foreign troops and refugees has intensified centrifugal forces inside Zaire, where political elements led by Lauren Kabila have recently managed to topple the corrupt government of General Mobutu in the capital of Kinshasa.

It is clear that African societies have not yet begun to surmount the challenges that they have faced since independence. Most African states are still poor and their populations are mostly illiterate. But as Julius Nyerere and the Nigerian author Wole Soyinka have pointed out, a significant part of the problem is related to the inapplicability of the nation-state system to the African continent. Africans must find better ways to cooperate with each other and to protect and promote their own interests. A first step in that direction was taken in 1991, when the OAU agreed to establish a new African Economic Community (AEC). More recently, West African states have set up a peacekeeping force to monitor the fragile cease-fire in Liberia.

As Africa evolves, it is useful to remember that economic and political change is often an agonizingly slow and painful process. Introduced to industrialization and concepts of Western democracy only a century ago, African societies are still groping for ways to graft Western political institutions and economic practices onto a native structure still significantly influenced by traditional values and attitudes. As one African writer recently observed, it is easy to be cynical in Africa, because changes in political regimes have had little effect on people's livelihood. Still, he said, "let us welcome the wind of change. This, after all, is a continent of winds. The trick is to keep hope burning, like a candle protected from the wind."[9]

Continuity and Change in Modern African Societies

In general, the impact of the West has been greater on urban and educated Africans and more limited on their rural and illiterate compatriots. After all, the colonial presence was first and most firmly established in the cities. Many cities, including Dakar, Lagos, Johannesburg, Capetown, Brazzaville, and Nairobi, are direct products of the colonial experience. Most African cities today look like their counterparts elsewhere in the world. They have high-rise buildings, blocks of residential apartments, wide boulevards, neon lights, movie theaters, and traffic jams.

The cities are also where the African elites live and work. Affluent Africans, like their contemporaries in other developing countries, have been strongly attracted to the glittering material aspects of Western culture. They live in Western-style homes or flats and eat Western foods stored in Western refrigerators, and those who can afford it drive Western cars. It has been said, not wholly in praise, that there are more Mercedes Benzes in Nigeria than in Germany, where they are manufactured.

The furniture of the minds of the African elites has become increasingly Western as well, due in part to the educational system. In the precolonial era, education as we know it did not really exist in Africa except for parochial schools in Christian Ethiopia and academies to train young males in Islamic doctrine and law in Muslim societies in North and West Africa. For the average African, education took place at the home or in the village courtyard and stressed socialization and vocational training.

Traditional education in Africa was not necessarily inferior to that in Europe. Social values and customs were

◆ **Urban Affluence in Nigeria.**   In Africa, as in many countries of Asia and Latin America, affluent cities have emerged as a result of economic modernization and contact with the West. In this photograph two wealthy aristocrats from Nigeria, protected from the sun by a parasol, are emerging from their new Mercedes.

transmitted to the young by storytellers, often village elders who could gain considerable prestige through their performances. Among the Luo people in Kenya, for example, children were taught in a *siwindhe*, or the house of a widowed grandmother. Here they were instructed in the ways and thinking of their people. A favorite saying for those who behaved stupidly was "You are uneducated, like one who never slept in a *siwindhe*."[10]

Modern Western education was introduced into Africa in the nineteenth century by the Europeans, although some Africans had already become literate in one or more Western languages through taking part in commerce. The French set up the first state-run schools in Senegal in 1818. In British colonies and protectorates, the earliest schools were established by missionaries. At first, these schools concentrated on vocational training with some instruction in European languages and Western civilization. Most courses were taught in the vernacular, although later many schools switched to English or French. Eventually, pressure from Africans led to the introduction of professional training, and the first institutes of higher learning were established in the early twentieth century. Most college-educated Africans, called "been-to's," received their higher training abroad, however.

With independence, African countries established their own state-run schools. The emphasis was on the primary level, but high schools and universities were established in major cities. The basic objectives have been to introduce vocational training and improve literacy rates. Unfortunately, both funding and trained teachers are scarce in most countries, and few rural areas have schools. As a result, illiteracy remains high, estimated at about 70 percent of the population across the continent. There has been a perceptible shift toward education in the vernacular languages. In West Africa, only about one in four adults is conversant in a Western language.

One interesting vehicle for popular education that emerged during the transition to independence in Nigeria was the Onitsha market pamphlet. Produced primarily by the Igbo peoples in the south, who traditionally valued egalitarianism and individual achievement, the pamphlets were "how-to" books advising readers on how to succeed in a rapidly changing Africa. They tended to be short, inexpensive in price, and humorous in content, with flashy covers to attract the potential buyer's attention. One, entitled "The Nigerian Bachelor's Guide," sold 40,000 copies. Unfortunately, the Onitsha market and the pamphlet tradition were destroyed during the Nigerian civil war of the late 1960s, but the pamphlets undoubtedly played an important role during a crucial period in the country's history.

Christianity has also been a conduit for the introduction of Western ideas. Assisted by the strenuous efforts of missionaries, Christianity spread rapidly during the nineteenth century among the urban elites and in rural areas as well. By 1950, an estimated 50 million Africans, or about half the population outside the Muslim areas, were Christians. Although many accepted Western religious beliefs to advance their careers, sincere conversions were by no means uncommon.

Outside the major cities, in the rural areas where about three-quarters of the inhabitants of the continent live, Western influence has had less of an impact. Millions of people throughout Africa live much as their ancestors did in thatch huts without modern plumbing and electricity; they farm or hunt by traditional methods, practice time-honored family rituals, and believe in the traditional deities. Even here, however, change is taking place. Slavery, for the most part, has been eliminated, although there have been persistent reports of raids by slave traders on defenseless villages in the southern Sudan. Economic need, though, has brought about massive migrations; some leave to work on plantations, others move to the cities, and others flee to refugee camps to escape starvation. Migration itself is a wrenching experience, since it disrupts familiar family and village ties and enforces new social relationships.

Nowhere, in fact, is the dichotomy between the old and the new, the native and the foreign, the rural and the urban, so clear and painful as in Africa. Urban dwellers regard the village as the repository of all that is backward in the African past, while rural peoples view the growing urban areas as a source of corruption, prostitution, hedonism, and the destruction of time-honored communal customs and values. The tension between traditional ways and Western culture is particularly strong among many African intellectuals, who are torn between their admiration for things Western and their desire to retain an African identity. "Here we stand," said one:

infants overblown
poised between two civilizations
finding the balancing irksome,
itching for something to happen,
to tip us one way or the other,
groping in the dark for a helping hand
and finding none. . . .[11]

One of the consequences of colonialism and independence has been a change in the relationship between men and women. In precolonial Africa, as in traditional societies in Asia, men and women had distinctly different

◆ **Home Sweet Home.**   Although many of the large cities of Africa have taken on a modern character, with skyscrapers, environmental pollution, fashionable shops, and traffic jams, the African village has been relatively little affected by the winds of change sweeping parts of the continent. Shown here is a traditional thatched-roof hut in a village south of Dar es Salaam in Tanzania.

roles. Women in sub-Saharan Africa, however, generally did not live under the severe legal and social disabilities that we have seen in such societies as China and India. Their role, it has been said, was "complementary rather than subordinate to that of men."[12]

This complementary relationship existed at various levels. Within the family, wives normally showed a degree of deference to their husbands, and polygamy was not uncommon. But because society was usually arranged on communal lines, property was often held in common, and production tasks were divided on a cooperative rather than a hierarchical basis. The status of women tended to rise with the life cycle; women became more important as they reared children and reached an apex in old age, when they often became eligible to serve in senior roles within the family, lineage, or village. In some societies, such as the Ashanti kingdom in West Africa, women such as the queen mother were even eligible to hold senior political positions. Some observers argue that polygamy was beneficial for women because it promoted communal and cooperative attitudes within the community and divided up the task of motherhood among several wives.

Sexual relationships changed profoundly during the colonial era, sometimes in ways that could justly be described as beneficial. Colonial governments attempted to bring an end to forced marriage, bodily mutilation such as clitoridectomy, and polygamy. Missionaries introduced women to Western education and encouraged them to organize themselves to defend their interests.

But the new system had some unfavorable consequences as well. Like men, women now became a labor resource. As African males were taken from the villages to serve as forced labor on construction projects, the traditional division of labor was disrupted, and women were forced to play a more prominent role in the economy. At the same time, their role in the broader society was constricted. In British colonies, Victorian attitudes of sexual repression and female subordination led to constrictions on women's freedom, and the positions in government they had formerly held were closed to them.

Independence also had a significant impact on sexual relationships and roles in African society. Almost without exception, the new governments established the principle of sexual equality and permitted women to vote and run for political office. Yet, as elsewhere, women continue to operate at a disability in a world dominated by males. Politics remains a male preserve, and although a few professions such as teaching, child care, and clerical work are dominated by women, most African women are employed in menial positions such as agricultural labor, factory work, and retail trade or as domestics. Education is open to all at the elementary level, but women comprise less than 20 percent of students at the upper levels in most African societies today.

Not surprisingly, women have made the greatest strides in the cities. Most urban women, like men, now marry on the basis of personal choice, although a significant minority are still willing to accept the choice of their parents. After marriage, African women appear to occupy a more equal position than their counterparts in most Asian countries. Each marriage partner tends to maintain a separate income, and women often have the right to possess property separate from their husbands. While many wives still defer to their husbands in the traditional manner, others are like the woman in Abioseh Nicol's story "A Truly Married Woman" who, after years of living as a common law wife with her husband, is finally able to provide the price and finalize the marriage. After the wedding, she declares, "for twelve years I have got up every morning at five to make tea for you and breakfast. Now I am a truly married woman [and] you must treat me with a little more respect. You are now my husband and not a lover. Get up and make yourself a cup of tea."[13]

Sexual relationships between men and women in contemporary Africa are relatively relaxed, as they were in traditional society. Sexual activity among adolescents is customary in most societies, and only a minority of women are still virgins at the time of marriage. Most marriages are monogamous. Males seem to be more likely to have extramarital relationships, often with bar girls or prostitutes (sometimes known as "walk-about women"), but adultery on the part of women is not rare.

There is a growing feminist movement in Africa, but it is firmly based on conditions in the local environment. Many African women writers, for example, refuse to be defined by Western dogma and opt instead for a brand of African feminism much like that of Ama Ata Aidoo (see the opening of this chapter), whose ultimate objective is to free African society as a whole, not just its female inhabitants. "Women's liberation," said one, "is but an aspect of the need to liberate the total society from dehumanization."[14]

In a few cases, women are even going into politics. One example is Margaret Dongo of Zimbabwe, where black African government under Robert Mugabe (b. 1924) succeeded white rule in onetime Southern Rhodesia in 1980. Now an independent member of Zimbabwe's parliament, Dongo is called "the ant in the elephant's trunk" for her determined effort to root out corruption and bring about social and economic reforms to improve the lot of the general population. "We didn't fight to remove white skins," she remarks. "We fought discrimination against blacks in land distribution, education, employment. If we are being exploited again by our black leaders, then what did we fight for?"[15]

In general, then, women in urban areas in contemporary Africa have been able to hold their own. Although they are still sometimes held to different standards than men (African men often expect their wives to be both modern and traditional, fashionable and demure, wage earners and housekeepers) and do not possess the full range of career opportunities that men do, they are manifestly better off than women in many Asian societies.

The same cannot necessarily be said about women in rural areas, where traditional attitudes continue to exert a strong influence, and individuals may still be subordinated to communalism. In some societies, clitoridectomy is still widely practiced. Polygamy is also not uncommon, and arranged marriages are still the rule rather than the exception. As a father tells his son in Cyprian Ekwensi's *Iska*:

> We have our pride and must do as our fathers did. You see your mother? I did not pick her in the streets. When I wanted a woman I went to my father and told him about my need of her and he went to her father. . . . Marriage is a family affair. You young people of today may think you are clever. But marriage is still a family affair.[16]

Villagers in Africa as elsewhere often see cities as the fount of evil, decadence, and corruption. Women in particular have suffered from the tension between the pull of the city and the village. As men are drawn to the cities in

An African Lament

Like many other areas, Africa faces the challenge of adopting the technological civilization of the West while remaining true to its own cultural heritage. Often this challenge poses terrible personal dilemmas in terms of individual career choices and lifestyles. Few have expressed this dilemma more poignantly than the Ugandan writer p'Bitek Okot. In the following excerpts from two of his prose poems, Lawino laments that her husband is abandoning his African roots in a vain search for modernity. Ocol replies bitterly that African tradition is nothing but rotting buffalo and native villages in ruins.

p'Bitek Okot, I Do Not Know the Dances of White People

It is true
I am ignorant of the dances of foreigners
And how they dress
I do not know.
Their games
I cannot play,
I only know the dances of our people.

Song of Lawino

All I ask
Is that my husband should stop the insults,
My husband should refrain
From heaping abuses on my head.
Listen Ocol, my old friend,
The ways of your ancestors
Are good,
Their customs are solid
And not hollow
They are not thin, not easily breakable
They cannot be blown away
By the winds
Because their roots reach deep into the soil.

I do not understand
The ways of foreigners
But I do not despise their customs.
Why should you despise yours?
Listen, my husband,
You are the son of a Chief.
The pumpkin in the old homestead
Must not be uprooted!

Song of Ocol

Your song
Is rotting buffalo
Left behind by
Fleeing poachers,
Its nose blocked
With house-flies
Sucking bloody mucus, . . .
Of salty tears,
Maggots wallowing
In the pus
In the spear wounds;

Skinny-necked
Bald headed vultures
Hover above,
While aged stiff-jointed lions
And limping-hipped hyenas
Snarl over bones;
All the valley,
Make compost of the Pumpkins
And the other native vegetables,
The fence dividing
Family holdings
Will be torn down,
We will uproot
The trees demarcating
The land of clan from clan.

We will obliterate
Tribal boundaries
And throttle native tongues
To dumb death.

. . . .

Houseboy, Listen . . .
Help the woman
Pack her things,
Then sweep the house clean
And wash the floor,
I am off to Town
To fetch the painter.

search of employment and excitement, their wives and girlfriends are left behind, both literally and figuratively, in the native village. Nowhere has this been more vividly described than in the anguished cry of Lawino, the abandoned wife in Ugandan author p'Bitek Okot's *Song of Lawino*. Lawino laments not just her husband's decision to take a modern urban wife, who dusts powder over her face to look like a white woman and has red-hot lips like glowing charcoal, but his rejection of his roots. He in turn lashes out in frustration at what he considers the poverty, backwardness, and ignorance of the rural environment (see the box on p. 1124).

African Culture

Inevitably, the tension between traditional and modern, native and foreign, and individual and communal that has permeated contemporary African society has spilled over into culture. In general, in the visual arts and music, utility and ritual have given way to pleasure and decoration. In doing so, Africans have been affected to a certain extent by foreign influence, but have retained their distinctive characteristics. Wood carving, metalwork, painting, and sculpture, for example, have preserved their traditional forms, but are now increasingly adapted to serve the tourist industry and the export market. Some African art retains its traditional purpose, however. Reportedly, a foreign tourist displayed a wood carving he had purchased to a customs agent in an African country, only to find that an African woman standing nearby had knelt down to pay homage and address praise songs to the carving. The carving turned out to be a sacred headpiece that had been stolen from the woman's hometown a few days earlier.

Similar developments have taken place in music and dance. They retain their traditional popularity, although the earlier emphasis on religious ritual and the experience of the performer has been replaced to some degree by a new interest in the spectator. In the process, some of the social functions of traditional music and dance—to express grief or other emotions, to exorcise evil spirits, or to express community solidarity—have eroded, sometimes to the detriment of the society. To restore these activities to their traditional vigor or take advantage of the growing popularity of African dancing, several governments have sponsored traveling folk dance companies. African music has been exported to Europe and to North and Latin America and then has returned to Africa in a new synthesis with foreign styles like the cha cha and the samba.

No area of African culture has been so strongly affected by political and social events as literature. Except for Muslim areas in North and East Africa, precolonial Africans did not have a written literature, although their tradition of oral storytelling served as a rich repository of history, custom, and folk culture. The reason for the lack of a traditional African literature, of course, was the absence of written languages, although the first indications of writing were beginning to appear in pictographic or ideographic signs used for occult purposes in various areas of the continent. The first written literature in the vernacular or in European languages emerged during the nineteenth century in the form of novels, poetry, and drama.

Angry at the negative portrayal of Africa in Western literature, African authors initially wrote primarily for a European audience as a means of establishing black dignity and purpose. Embracing the ideals of negritude, many glorified the emotional and communal aspects of the traditional African experience.

◆ **The Art of West African Women.**   Whereas men have traditionally created art using stone, bronze, and wood, women have often expressed themselves through textiles, clay, woven fiber, paint, or other materials more accessible to the home. Their art is used to celebrate and appease the gods, beautify their surroundings, and introduce their children to color and design. Here two young women engage in the annual repainting of the carved door to their family meeting place in a compound in Nigeria. On the right, their mother imprints the "obo-aka," or print of the hand, which signifies a righteous person.

One of the first was the Guinean author Camara Lay (1928–1980), who in 1953 published *The Dark Child,* a touching and intimate initiation into village life in pre-colonial Africa. In the novel, which admitted the reader to the secret rituals and practices of daily life behind the protective hedges of an African village compound, the author openly regretted the passing of the ways of the African past, while conceding that they were not appropriate to the Guinea of tomorrow.

Another Francophone writer was Ousmane Sembène of Senegal. Not a member of the educated African elite, Sembène enlisted in the French army at the age of fifteen and fought in Europe during World War II. Afterward he participated in a rail workers' strike and later worked on the docks of Marseilles where he became the leader of a longshoremen's union. His novels, such as the renowned *God's Bits of Wood,* have often been compared to André Malraux's *Man's Fate* in their use of Marxist themes to promote the struggle of African workers against capitalist exploitation. Eventually, Sembène became one of Africa's first native film producers.

The Nigerian Chinua Achebe is considered the first major African novelist to write in the English language. In his writings he attempted to interpret African history from a native perspective and to forge a new sense of African identity. In his most famous novel, *Things Fall Apart* (1958), he recounted the story of a Nigerian who refused to submit to the new British order and eventually committed suicide. Criticizing those of his contemporaries who had accepted foreign rule, the protagonist lamented that the white man "has put a knife on the things that held us together and we have fallen apart."

After 1965, the African novel took a dramatic turn, shifting its focus from the brutality of the foreign oppressor to the shortcomings of the new native leadership that came into power after independence. African politicians were now portrayed as mimicking and even outdoing the injustices committed by their colonial predecessors. A prominent example of this genre is the Kenyan Ngugi Wa Thiong'o (b. 1938). His first novel, *A Grain of Wheat,* is set on the eve of *uhuru,* or independence. Although the novel mocks the racism, snobbishness, and superficiality of local British society, its chief interest lies in its unsentimental and even unflattering portrayal of ordinary Kenyans in their daily struggle for survival.

Like most of his predecessors, Ngugi initially wrote in English, but he eventually decided to write in his native Gikuyu as a means of broadening his readership. For that reason, perhaps, in the late 1970s, he was placed under house arrest for writing subversive literature. From prison he secretly wrote *Devil on the Cross,* which urged his compatriots to overthrow the government of Daniel Arap Moi. Published in 1980, the book sold widely and was eventually read aloud by storytellers throughout Kenya. Fearing an attempt on his life, in recent years Ngugi has lived abroad.

Many of Ngugi's contemporaries have followed his lead and focused their attention on the failure of the continent's new leaders to carry out the goals of independence. One of the most outstanding is the Nigerian Wole Soyinka (b. 1932). His novel *The Interpreters* (1965) lambasted the corruption and hypocrisy of Nigerian politics, a theme that continued in his later novels and plays. In 1986, Soyinka was awarded the Nobel Prize for literature. Like other recent writers, he also deals with problems of daily life in Africa and the alienation and estrangement that often characterize the shift from the traditional rural village to the impersonal modern city. In 1994, however, he barely managed to escape arrest and now lives abroad, whence he directs his satire at the inhumanity of the Abacha regime (see Recent Trends earlier in this chapter).

A number of Africa's most prominent writers today are women. Traditionally, African women were valued for their talents as storytellers, but writing was strongly discouraged by both traditional and colonial authorities on the grounds that women should occupy themselves with their domestic obligations. In recent years, however, several women have emerged as prominent writers of African fiction. Two examples are the Nigerian Buchi Emecheta (b. 1940) and Ama Ata Aidoo (b. 1942). Beginning with *Second Class Citizen* (1975), which chronicled the breakdown of her own marriage, Emecheta has published numerous works exploring the role of women in contemporary African society and decrying the practice of polygamy. In her own writings, the Ghanaian Ama Ata Aidoo (see the opening of this chapter) has focused on the identity of today's African women and the changing relations between men and women in society. In her recent novel *Changes: A Love Story* (1991), she chronicled the lives of three women. None was presented as a victim, but all three were caught in the struggle for survival and happiness. Sadly, the one who strays the furthest from traditional African values finds herself free but isolated and lonely.

One of the overriding concerns confronting African intellectuals since independence has been the problem of language. Unlike Asian societies, Africans have not inherited a long written tradition from the precolonial era. As a result, many intellectuals have written in the colonial language, a practice that sometimes results in guilt and anxiety (see the box on p. 1127). As we have seen, some have reacted by writing in their local languages to reach a native audience. The market for such works is

The Language of Colonialism

For African authors like the Kenyan Ngugi Wa Thiong'o, the adoption of the colonial usurper's written language has resulted in frustration and a feeling of guilt. In Decolonising the Mind: The Politics of Language in African Literature, Ngugi recalls with humiliation how Kenyan public school students caught speaking their native Gikuyu instead of the required English on the school premises would be caned and made to wear a sign saying "I am a Donkey." Equating language with culture, Ngugi goes on to explain the African's sense of cultural loss and alienation that resulted from the total immersion in Western instruction.

Ngugi Wa Thiong'o, *Decolonising the Mind*

So what was the colonialist imposition of a foreign language doing to us children?

The real aim of colonialism was to control the people's wealth: what they produced, how they produced it, and how it was distributed; to control, in other words, the entire realm of the language of real life. Colonialism imposed its control of the social production of wealth through military conquest and subsequent political dictatorship. But its most important area of domination was the mental universe of the colonised, the control, through culture, of how people perceived themselves and their relationship to the world. Economic and political control can never be complete or effective without mental control. To control a people's culture is to control their tools of self-definition in relationship to others.

For colonialism this involved two aspects of the same process: the destruction or the deliberate undervaluing of a people's culture, their art, dances, religions, history, geography, education, orature and literature, and the conscious elevation of the language of the coloniser. The domination of a people's language by the languages of the colonising nations was crucial to the domination of the mental universe of the colonised. . . .

But since the new, imposed languages could never completely break the native languages as spoken, their most effective area of domination was the third aspect of language as communication, the written. The language of an African child's formal education was foreign. The language of the books he read was foreign. The language of his conceptualisation was foreign. Thought, in him, took the visible form of a foreign language. So the written language of a child's upbringing in the school (even his spoken language within the school compound) became divorced from his spoken language at home. There was often not the slightest relationship between the child's written world, which was also the language of his schooling, and the world of his immediate environment in the family and the community. For a colonial child, the harmony existing between the three aspects of language as communication was irrevocably broken. This resulted in the disassociation of the sensibility of that child from his natural and social environment, what we might call colonial alienation. The alienation became reinforced in the teaching of history, geography, music, where bourgeois Europe was always the centre of the universe.

limited, however, because of the high illiteracy rate and also because novels written in African languages have no market abroad. Moreover, because of the deep financial crisis throughout the continent, there is little money for the publication of serious books. Many of Africa's libraries and universities are literally almost without books. It is little wonder that many African authors, to their discomfort, continue to write and publish in foreign languages.

Gathered at the Beach

Nowhere in the developing world is the dilemma of continuity and change more agonizing than in contemporary Africa. Mesmerized by the spectacle of Western afflu-ence, yet repulsed by the bloody trail from slavery to World War II and the atomic bombs over Hiroshima and Nagasaki, African intellectuals have been torn between the dual images of Western materialism and African negritude.

What is the destiny of Africa? Some still yearn for the dreams embodied in the program of the OAU. Novelist Ngugi Wa Thiong'o argues that for his country that starting point is a democratic Kenya. More broadly, he calls for "an internationalization of all the democratic and social struggles for human equality, justice, peace, and progress."[17] Some African political leaders, however, have apparently discarded the democratic ideal and turned their attention to what is sometimes called the "East Asian model," based on the Confucian tenet of subordination of the individual to the community as the guiding principle of national development (see Chapter 32). Whether African political culture today is well placed to imitate the strategy adopted by the fast-growing nations of East Asia is questionable, however. Like all peoples, Africans must ultimately find their solutions within the context of their own traditions, and not by seeking to imitate the example of others.

For the average African, of course, such intellectual dilemmas pale before the daily challenge of survival. But the fundamental gap between the traditional village and the modern metropolis is perhaps wider in Africa than anywhere else in the world and may well be harder to bridge. The solution is not yet visible. In the meantime, writes Ghanaian author George Awoonor-Williams, all Africans are exiles:

> The return is tedious
> And the exiled souls gathered at the beach
> Arguing and deciding their future
> Should they return home
> And face the fences the termites had eaten
> And see the dunghill that has mounted their birthplace?
> . . . The final strokes will land them on forgotten shores
> They committed the impiety of self-deceit
> Slashed, cut and wounded their souls
> And left the mangled remainder in manacles.
>
> The moon, the moon is our father's spirit
> At the stars entrance the night revellers gather
> To sell their chatter and inhuman sweat to the gateman
> And shuffle their feet in agonies of birth.
> Lost souls, lost souls, lost souls, that are
> still at the gate.[18]

Ferment in the Middle East

If the concept of negritude represented an alternative to the spread of a system of nation-states in the continent of Africa, in the Middle East a similar role was played by the forces of militant Islam. In both regions, a yearning for a sense of community beyond national borders tugged at the emotions and intellect of their inhabitants and counteracted the dynamic pull of nationalism that provoked political turmoil and conflict in much of the rest of the world.

For the Middle East, the period between the two world wars was an era of transition. With the fall of the Ottoman and Persian empires, new modernizing regimes emerged in Turkey and Iran, and a more traditionalist but fiercely independent government was established in Saudi Arabia. Elsewhere, European influence continued to be strong; the British and French had mandates in Syria, Lebanon, Jordan, and Palestine, and British influence persisted in Iraq, southern Arabia, and throughout the Nile valley. Pan-Arabism was on the rise, but it lacked focus and coherence.

During World War II, the region became the cockpit of European rivalries, as it had been during World War I. Germany no longer had a physical presence in the area since Turkey remained neutral, but it had a strong potential presence along the southern coast of the Mediterranean due to the Italian occupation of Libya and Vichy control over French colonies in North Africa. Moreover, the region was more significant to the warring powers than previously because of the growing importance of oil and the Suez Canal's position as a vital sea route.

During the war, the primary theater of Axis activity was along the Mediterranean coast rather than in the Middle East itself. For a brief period, the Afrika Korps under the command of the brilliant German general Erwin Rommel threatened to seize Egypt and the Suez Canal. Rommel's campaign was assisted by widespread sympathy for the Axis cause in Egypt, where nationalist forces in the Wafd Party agitated for complete independence and an end to the informal British protectorate. But the German forces were defeated by British troops at El Alamein, west of Alexandria, and were then gradually driven westward until their final defeat after the arrival of U.S. troops in Morocco under the field command of General George S. Patton. From that time, the entire region from the Mediterranean Sea eastward was under secure Allied occupation until the end of the war.

The Question of Palestine

As in other areas of Asia, the end of World War II led to the emergence of a number of independent states. Jordan, Lebanon, and Syria, all European mandates before the war, became independent. Egypt, Iran, and Iraq, though still under a degree of Western influence, became increasingly autonomous. Sympathy for the idea of Arab unity led to the formation of an Arab League in 1945, but different points of view among its members prevented it from achieving anything of substance.

The one issue on which all Arab states in the area could agree was the question of Palestine. As tensions between Jews and Arabs in that mandate intensified during the 1930s, the British reduced Jewish immigration into the area and firmly rejected proposals for independence. After World War II, the Zionists turned for support to the

United States, and in March 1948 the Truman administration approved the concept of an independent Jewish state, even though only about one-third of the local population were Jews. In May, the new state of Israel was formally established.

To its Arab neighbors, the new state represented a betrayal of the interests of the Palestinian people, 90 percent of whom were Muslim, and a flagrant disregard for the conditions set out in the Balfour Declaration of 1917. Outraged at the lack of Western support for Muslim interests in the area, several Arab countries invaded the new Jewish state. The invasion did not succeed because of internal divisions among the Arabs, but both sides remained bitter, and the Arab states refused to recognize Israel.

The war had other lasting consequences as well, because it led to the exodus of thousands of Palestinian refugees into neighboring Muslim states. Jordan, which had become independent under its Hashemite ruler, was now flooded by the arrival of one million urban Palestinians in a country occupied by half a million bedouins. To the north, the state of Lebanon had been created to provide the local Christian community with a country of their own, but the arrival of the Palestinian refugees upset the delicate balance between Christians and Muslims. In any event, the creation of Lebanon had angered the Syrians, who had lost it as well as other territories to Turkey as a result of European decisions before and after the war.

Nasser and Pan-Arabism

The dispute over Palestine placed Egypt in an uncomfortable position. Technically, Egypt was not an Arab state. King Farouk, who had acceded to power in 1936, had frequently declared support for the Arab cause, but the Egyptian peoples were not bedouins and shared little of the culture of the peoples across the Red Sea. Nevertheless, Farouk committed Egyptian armies to the disastrous war against Israel.

In 1952, King Farouk, whose corrupt habits had severely eroded his early popularity, was overthrown by a military coup engineered by young military officers ostensibly under the leadership of Colonel Muhammad Nagib. The real force behind the scenes was Colonel Gamal Abdul Nasser (1918–1970), the son of a minor government functionary who, like many of his fellow officers, had been angered by the army's inadequate preparation for the war against Israel four years earlier. In 1953, the monarchy was replaced by a republic.

In 1954, Nasser seized power in his own right and im-

mediately instituted a land reform program. He also adopted a policy of neutrality in foreign affairs and expressed sympathy for the Arab cause. The British presence had rankled many Egyptians for years, for even after granting Egypt independence, Britain had retained control over the Suez Canal to protect its route to the Indian Ocean. In 1956, Nasser suddenly nationalized the Suez Canal Company, which had been under British and French administration (see the box on p. 1130). Concerned at the threat to their route to the Indian Ocean, the British and the French launched a joint attack on Egypt to protect their investment. They were joined by Israel, whose leaders had grown exasperated at sporadic

♦ **Gamal Abdul Nasser.**   Gamal Abdul Nasser was a leading figure in the overthrow of King Farouk in 1953. Nasser's integrity, charisma, and program for government reform endeared him to the Egyptian people. In 1956, Nasser seized the Suez Canal from the British and the French who in turn mounted a joint attack on Egypt. They withdrew, however, when the United States supported Nasser. During his sixteen years as president, Nasser was an articulate spokesman for the Arab cause in the Middle East.

The Suez Canal Belongs to Egypt!

The Suez Canal was built between 1854 and 1869, using mainly French capital and Egyptian labor, under the direction of the French promoter Ferdinand de Lesseps. It was managed by a Paris-based limited liability corporation, called the Suez Canal Company, under a ninety-nine-year lease. Over time, the canal came to symbolize colonial exploitation in the minds of many Egyptians. In this excerpt from a speech given in July 1956, President Nasser declared that it was time for the canal to be owned and managed by Egyptians. The decision led to a brief invasion by Great Britain and France, but under pressure the European powers backed down, and Nasser got his way.

Nasser's Speech Nationalizing the Suez Canal Company

. . . The Suez Canal is an Egyptian canal built as a result of great sacrifices. The Suez Canal Company is an Egyptian company that was expropriated from Egypt by the British who, since the canal was dug, have been obtaining the profits of the Company. . . . And yet the Suez Canal Company is an Egyptian limited liability company. The annual Canal revenue is 35 million Egyptian pounds. From this sum Egypt—which lost 120,000 workers in digging the Canal—takes one million pounds from the Company. . . .

It is a shame when the blood of peoples is sucked, and it is no shame that we should borrow for construction. We will not allow the past to be repeated again, but we will cancel the past by restoring our rights in the Suez Canal. . . . We will build the High Dam, and we will obtain our rights. We will build it as we wish, and we are determined to do so. The 35 million pounds which the Company collects each year will be collected by us. . . . When we build the High Dam, we will be building the dam of prestige, freedom, and dignity, and we will be putting an end to the dams of humiliation. We announce that the whole of Egypt is one united national bloc. We will fight to the last drop of our blood . . . for the sake of our motherland.

. . . Now that the rights have been restored to their people after one hundred years, we are achieving true liberation. The Suez Canal Company was a state within a state, depending on the conspiracies of imperialism and its supporters. The Canal was built for the sake of Egypt, but it was a source of exploitation. There is no shame in being poor, but it is a shame to suck blood. Today we restore these rights, and I declare in the name of the Egyptian people that we will protect these rights with our blood and soul. The Suez Canal was one of the edifices of oppression. Now our funds are coming back to us. . . . With our sweat and tears and with the lives of our martyrs and their skulls in our memory, we can protect this country. . . .

. . . The people will stand united as one man to resist imperialist acts of treachery. We shall do whatever we like. When we restore all our rights, we shall become stronger and our production will increase. At this moment, some of your brethren, the sons of Egypt, are now taking over the Egyptian Suez Canal Company and directing it. We have taken this decision to restore part of the glories of the past and to safeguard our national dignity and pride. May God bless you and guide you in the path of righteousness.

Arab commando raids on Israeli territory and now decided to strike back. But the Eisenhower administration in the United States, concerned that the attack smacked of a revival of colonialism, supported Nasser and brought about the withdrawal of foreign forces from Egypt and of Israeli troops from the Sinai peninsula (see the box on p. 1131).

Nasser now turned to pan-Arabism. Egypt had won the approval of other Arab states in the area by its successful eviction of the British and the French from the Suez Canal and by its sponsorship of efforts to replace Israel by an independent Palestinian state. In 1958, Egypt united with Syria in a new United Arab Republic (UAR). The union had been proposed by the Ba'ath Party, which advocated the unity of all Arab states in a new socialist society. According to the constitution of the party: "The Arab nation has an immortal mission which has manifested itself in renewed and complete forms in the different stages of history and which aims at reviving human values, encouraging human development, and promoting harmony and cooperation among the nations of the world."[19] In 1957, the Ba'ath Party assumed power in Syria and opened talks with Egypt on a union between the two countries. It took place in March of 1958 after a plebiscite. Despite his reported ambiva-

❧ A Plea for Peace in the Middle East ❧

In an effort to end the Egyptian blockade of the Gulf of Aqaba against Israeli shipping, Israel joined Great Britain and France in attacking Egypt during the Suez Canal crisis in October 1956. Israel quickly captured the Sinai peninsula, but the United Nations condemned the attack and pressured Great Britain, France, and Israel to withdraw their troops. For four months Israel refused, demanding that the Arab states respect its right to use the Gulf of Aqaba. In March 1957, however, Golda Meir, Israel's foreign minister, announced that her government had agreed to withdraw from the Sinai and the Gaza Strip.

Golda Meir Announces an Israeli Withdrawal from Sinai

. . . Interference, by armed force, with ships of Israeli flag exercising free and innocent passage in the Gulf of Aqaba and through the Straits of Tiran, will be viewed by Israel as an attack entitling it to exercise its inherent right of self-defense under article 51 of the United Nations Charter and to take all such measures as are necessary to ensure the free and innocent passage of its ships in the Gulf and in the Straits. We make this announcement in accordance with the accepted principles of international law under which all states have an inherent right to use their forces to protect their ships and their rights against interference by armed force. My government naturally hopes that this contingency will not occur. In a public address on 20 February 1957, President Eisenhower states: "We should not assume that, if Israel withdraws, Egypt will prevent Israel shipping from using the Suez Canal or the Gulf of Aqaba." This declaration has weighed heavily with my government in determining its action today. Israel is now prepared to withdraw its forces from the regions of the Gulf of Aqaba and the Straits of Tiran in the confidence that there will be continued freedom of navigation for international and Israeli shipping in the Gulf of Aqaba and through the Straits of Tiran. . . .

May I now add these few words to the states in the Middle East area and, more specifically, to the neighbors of Israel. We all come from an area which is a very ancient one. The hills and the valleys have been witnesses to many wars and many conflicts. But that is not the only thing which characterizes the part of the world from which we come. It is also a part of the world which is of an ancient culture. It is that part of the world which has given to humanity three great religions. It is also that part of the world which has given a code of ethics to all humanity. In our countries, in the entire region, all our peoples are anxious for and in need of a higher standard of living, of great programs of development and progress. Can we, from now on—all of us— turn a new leaf and, instead of fighting with each other, can we all, united, fight poverty and disease and illiteracy? Is it possible for us to put all our efforts and all our energy into one single purpose, the betterment and progress and development of all our lands and all our peoples? I can here pledge the government and the people of Israel to do their part in this united effort. There is no limit to what we are prepared to contribute so that all of us, together, can live to see a day of happiness for our peoples and can see again from that region a great contribution to peace and happiness for all humanity.

lence about the union, Nasser was named president of the new state.

Egypt and Syria hoped that the union would eventually include all Arab states, but other Arab leaders, including young King Hussein of Jordan and the kings of Iraq and Saudi Arabia, were suspicious. The latter two in particular feared pan-Arabism on the reasonable assumption that they would be asked to share their vast oil revenues with the poorer states of the Middle East.

Nasser's concept of Arab socialism and his hopes for the union are more easily explained in terms of what he did not want than what he did. Nasser opposed existing relationships in which the world was dominated by two competing power blocs, while much of the wealth of the Middle East flowed into the treasuries of a handful of wealthy feudal states or, even worse, the pockets of foreign oil interests. In Nasser's view, through Arab unity, this wealth could be put to better use to improve the standard of living in the area. To achieve a more equitable division of the wealth of the region, natural resources and major industries would be nationalized; central planning would guarantee that resources were exploited efficiently, but private enterprise would continue at the local level.

In the end, however, Nasser's determination to extend state control over the economy brought an end to the UAR. When the government announced the nationalization of a large number of industries and utilities in 1961, a military coup overthrew the Ba'ath leaders in Damascus, and the new authorities declared that Syria would end its relationship with Egypt.

The breakup of the UAR did not necessarily end Nasser's dream of pan-Arabism. In 1962, Algeria finally received its independence from France and under its new president Ahmad Ben Bella established close relations with Egypt, as did a new republic in Yemen. During the mid-1960s, Egypt took the lead in promoting Arab unity against Israel. At a meeting of Arab leaders held in Jerusalem in 1964, the Palestine Liberation Organization (PLO) was set up under Egyptian sponsorship to represent the interests of the Palestinians. According to the charter of the PLO, only the Palestinian people (and thus not Jewish immigrants from abroad) had the right to form a state in the old British mandate. A guerrilla movement called al-Fatah led by the dissident PLO political leader Yasir Arafat (b. 1929) began to launch terrorist attacks on Israeli territory, prompting the Israeli government to raid PLO bases in Jordan in 1966.

The Arab-Israeli Dispute

The growing Arab hostility was a constant threat to the security of Israel. In the years after independence, Israeli leaders dedicated themselves to creating a Jewish homeland. Aided by reparations paid by the postwar German government of Chancellor Konrad Adenauer and private funds provided by Jews living abroad, notably in the United States, the government attempted to build a democratic and modern state that would be a magnet for Jews throughout the world and a symbol of Jewish achievement.

Ensuring the survival of the tiny state surrounded by antagonistic Arab neighbors was a considerable challenge, but it was made more difficult by divisions within the Israeli population. Some were immigrants from Europe, while others came from the countries of the Middle East. Some were secular and even socialist in their views, while others were politically conservative and stressed religious orthodoxy. There were also Christians as well as many Muslim Palestinians who had not fled to other countries. To balance these diverse interests, Israel established a parliament, called the Knesset, on the European model with proportional representation based on the number of votes each party received in the general election. The parties were so numerous that none ever re-

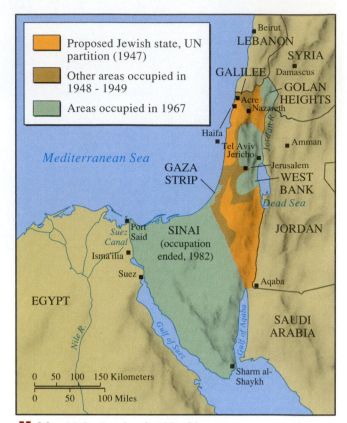

※ Map 30.2   Israel and its Neighbors.

ceived a majority of the votes, and all governments had to be formed from a coalition of several parties. As a result, moderate secular leaders like long-time prime minister David Ben Gurion (1886–1973) had to cater to more marginal parties composed of conservative religious groups.

During the late 1950s and 1960s, the dispute between Israel and other states in the Middle East escalated in intensity. Essentially alone except for the sympathy of the United States and several Western European countries, Israel adopted a policy of determined resistance to and immediate retaliation against alleged PLO and Arab provocations. By the spring of 1967, relations between Israel and its Arab neighbors had deteriorated, as Nasser attempted to improve his standing in the Arab world by intensifying military activities and imposing a blockade against Israeli commerce through the Gulf of Aqaba. In a speech before the Egyptian Popular Assembly he declared:

Israel used to boast a great deal, and the Western powers, headed by the United States and Britain, used to ignore and even despise us and consider us of no value. But now that the time has come—and I have already said in the past that we will decide the time and place and not allow them to decide—we must be ready for triumph and not for a recurrence of the 1948 comedies. We shall triumph, God willing.

Preparations have already been made. We are now ready to confront Israel. . . . Now we are ready for the confrontation. We are now ready to deal with the entire Palestine question.[20]

Concerned that it might be isolated and lacking firm support from Western powers (who had originally guaranteed Israel the freedom to use the Gulf of Aqaba), in June 1967 Israel suddenly launched air strikes against Egypt and several of its Arab neighbors. Israeli armies then broke the blockade at the head of the Gulf of Aqaba and occupied the Sinai peninsula. Other Israeli forces attacked Jordanian territory on the West Bank of the Jordan River (Jordan's King Hussein had recently signed an alliance with Egypt and placed his army under Egyptian command), occupied the whole of Jerusalem, and seized Syrian military positions on the Golan Heights along the Israeli-Syrian border.

Despite limited Soviet support for Egypt and Syria, in a brief six-day war, Israel had mocked Nasser's pretensions of Arab unity and tripled the size of its territory, thus enhancing its precarious security. Yet the new Israel also aroused even more bitter hostility among the Arabs and included an additional million Palestinians inside its borders, most of them living on the West Bank.

During the next few years, the focus of the Arab-Israeli dispute shifted, as Arab states demanded the return of the occupied territories. Meanwhile many Israelis argued that the new lands improved the security of the beleaguered state and should be retained. Concerned that the dispute might lead to a confrontation between the superpowers, the Nixon administration tried to achieve a peace settlement. The peace effort received a mild stimulus when Nasser died of a heart attack in September 1970 and was succeeded by his vice-president, ex-general Anwar al-Sadat (1918–1981). Sadat soon showed himself to be more pragmatic than his predecessor by dropping the now irrelevant name United Arab Republic in favor of the Arab Republic of Egypt and replacing Nasser's socialist policies with a new strategy based on free enterprise and encouragement of Western investment. He also agreed to sign a peace treaty with Israel on condition that the latter retire to its pre-1967 frontiers. Concerned that other Arab countries would refuse to make peace and take advantage of its weakness, Israel refused.

Rebuffed in his offer of peace to Israel, smarting from criticism of his moderate stand from other Arab leaders,

and increasingly concerned at Israeli plans to build permanent Jewish settlements in the occupied territories, Sadat attempted once again to renew Arab unity through a new confrontation with Israel. On Yom Kippur (the Jewish day of atonement), an Israeli national holiday, Egyptian forces suddenly launched an air and artillery attack on Israeli positions in the Sinai just east of the Suez Canal. Syrian armies attacked Israeli positions on the Golan Heights. After early Arab successes, the Israelis managed to recoup some of their losses on both fronts. As a superpower confrontation between the United States and the Soviet Union loomed, a cease-fire was finally reached.

In the next years, a fragile peace was maintained, marked by U.S. "shuttle diplomacy" (carried out by U.S. Secretary of State Henry Kissinger) and the rise to power in Israel of the militant Likud Party under Prime Minister Menachem Begin (1913–1992). The conflict now spread to Lebanon, where many Palestinians had found refuge and the PLO now set up its headquarters. Rising tension along the border was compounded by increasingly hostile disputes between Christians and Muslims over control of the capital of Beirut.

After his election as president in 1976, Jimmy Carter began to press for a compromise peace based on the return of occupied Arab territories and Arab recognition of the state of Israel, an idea originally proposed by Henry Kissinger. By now Sadat was anxious to reduce his military expenses and announced his willingness to visit Jerusalem to seek peace. The meeting took place in November 1977 and had no concrete results, but Sadat persisted. In September 1978, he and Begin met with Carter at Camp David in the United States. Israel agreed to withdraw from the Sinai, but not from other occupied territories unless it was recognized by other Arab countries.

The promise of the Camp David agreement was not fulfilled. One reason was the assassination of Sadat by Islamic militants in October 1981. But there were deeper causes, including the continued unwillingness of many Arab governments to recognize Israel and the Israeli government's encouragement of Jewish settlements on the occupied West Bank.

During the early 1980s, the militance of the Palestinians increased, leading to growing unrest, popularly called the *intifada* (uprising), among PLO supporters living inside Israel. To control the situation, a new Israeli government under Prime Minister Itzhak Shamir (b. 1914) invaded southern Lebanon to destroy PLO commando bases near the Israeli border. The invasion provoked international condemnation and further destabilized the

♦ **Bone of Contention.** The Golan Heights, a range of mountains to the east of the Sea of Galilee in northern Israel, has become a major bone of contention between the state of Israel and its neighbor Syria. In 1967, Israeli forces seized the area during the brief Arab-Israeli conflict and continue to occupy it today. As the photo above demonstrates, whoever controls the heights is in a position to dominate the Israeli lowlands below.

perilous balance between Muslims and Christians in Lebanon. As the 1990s began, U.S.-sponsored peace talks opened between Israel and a number of its neighbors. The first major breakthrough came in 1993, when Israel and the PLO reached an agreement calling for Palestinian autonomy in selected areas of Israel in return for PLO recognition of the legitimacy of the Israeli state.

Progress in implementing the agreement has been slow, however. Terrorist attacks by Palestinian militants have resulted in heavy casualties and shaken the confidence of many Jewish citizens that their security needs can be protected under the agreement. At the same time, Jewish residents on the West Bank have resisted the extension of Palestinian authority in the area. In November 1995, Prime Minister Yitzhak Rabin (1922–1995) was assassinated by an Israeli opponent of the accords. National elections held a few months later led to the formation of a new government under Benjamin Netanyahu that has adopted a tougher stance in negotiations with the Palestinian Authority under Yasir Arafat. For the moment, future progress in implementing the agreement is in doubt.

Oil Politics and Revolution in Iran

The Arab-Israeli dispute also provoked an international oil crisis. A number of oil-producing states had formed the Organization of Petroleum Exporting Countries (OPEC) in 1960 to gain control over oil prices, but the foreign oil companies did not recognize the organization.

In the 1970s, states established the Organization of Arab Petroleum Exporting Countries (OAPEC) in order to use oil as a weapon to force Western governments to abandon pro-Israeli policies. During the 1973 war, some OPEC nations announced significant increases in the price of oil to foreign countries. The price hikes led to an oil shortage and created serious economic problems in the United States and Europe as well as in the Third World. They also proved to be a boon to oil-exporting countries, such as Libya, now under Colonel Muammar Qadhafi (b. 1942).

One of the key oil-exporting countries was Iran. Under the leadership of Shah Mohammad Reza Pahlavi (1919–1980), who had taken over from his father in 1941, Iran had become one of the richest countries in the Middle East. Although relations with the West had occasionally been fragile (especially after Prime Minister Mossadeq had briefly attempted to nationalize the oil industry in 1951), during the next twenty years Iran had become a prime ally of the United States in the Middle East. With the encouragement of the United States, which hoped that Iran could become a force for stability in the Persian Gulf, the shah had attempted to carry through a series of social and economic reforms to transform the country into the most advanced in the region.

Statistical evidence indicated that his efforts were succeeding. Per capita income increased dramatically, literacy rates improved, a modern communications infrastructure took shape, and an affluent middle class emerged in the capital of Tehran. Under the surface, however, trouble was brewing. Despite an ambitious land reform program, many peasants were still landless, unemployment among intellectuals was dangerously high, and the urban middle class was squeezed by high inflation. Housing costs had skyrocketed, provoked in part by the massive influx of foreigners attracted by the oil money.

Some of the unrest took the form of religious discontent, as millions of devout Muslims looked with distaste at a new Iranian civilization based on greed, sexual license, and material accumulation. Conservative *ulama* opposed rampant governmental corruption, the ostentation of the shah's court, and the extension of voting rights to women. Some opposition elements took to terrorism against wealthy Iranians or foreign residents in an attempt to provoke social and political disorder. In response, the shah's U.S.-trained security police, the *Savak*, imprisoned and sometimes tortured thousands of dissidents.

Leading the opposition was the Ayatollah Ruholla Khomeini (1900–1989), an austere Shi'ite cleric who had been exiled to Iraq and then to France because of his

outspoken opposition to the shah's regime. From Paris, Khomeini continued his attacks in print and on television and radio broadcasts. By the late 1970s, large numbers of Iranians—students, peasants, and townspeople—began to respond to Khomeini's diatribes against the "satanic regime," and demonstrations by his supporters were repressed with ferocity by the police. But workers' strikes (some of them in the oil fields, thus reducing government revenue) grew in intensity, and in January 1979 the shah appointed a moderate, Shapur Bakhtiar, as prime minister and then left the country for medical treatment.

Bakhtiar attempted to conciliate the rising opposition and permitted Khomeini to return to Iran, where he presided over a new Islamic Revolutionary Council and demanded the resignation of the government. With rising public unrest and incipient revolt within the army, the government collapsed and was replaced by a hastily formed Islamic Republic. The new government, which was dominated by Shi'ite *ulama* under the guidance of

Ayatollah Khomeini, immediately began to introduce legislation to rid the country of Western influence and restore traditional Islamic law. At the same time, a new reign of terror ensued, as supporters of the shah were rounded up and executed. Along the borders, various ethnic groups like the Kurds and the Azerbaijanis rose in rebellion.

Though much of the outside world focused on the U.S. Embassy in Tehran, where militants held a number of foreign hostages, the Iranian Revolution involved much more. In the eyes of the ayatollah and his followers, the United States was "the great Satan," the powerful protector of Israel, and the enemy of Muslim peoples everywhere. Furthermore, it was responsible for the corruption of Iranian society under the shah. Now Khomeini demanded that the shah be returned to Iran for trial and that the United States apologize for its acts against the Iranian people. In response, the Carter administration stopped buying Iranian oil and froze Iranian assets in the United States.

The effects of the disturbances in Iran quickly spread beyond its borders. Sunni militants briefly seized the holy places in Mecca and began to appeal to their brothers to launch similar revolutions in Islamic countries around the world, including far-off Malaysia and Indonesia. At the same time, the ethnic unrest among the Kurdish minorities along the border continued. In July 1980, the shah died of cancer in Cairo. Two months later, Iraq and Iran went to war (see the next section). With economic conditions in Iran rapidly deteriorating, the Islamic revolutionary government finally agreed to free the hostages in return for the release of Iranian assets in the United States.

During the next few years, the intensity of the Iranian Revolution moderated slightly, and the government of President Hashemi Rafsanjani (b. 1934) displayed a modest tolerance for loosening clerical control over freedom of expression and social activities. But rising criticism of rampant official corruption and the high rate of inflation sparked a new wave of government repression in the mid-1990s; newspapers were censored, universities purged of disloyal or "un-Islamic" elements, and self-appointed religious militants raided private homes in search of blasphemous activities. "There is a deep fear and absolutely no freedom of expression," remarked an Iranian journalist.

Crisis in the Gulf

Although much of the Iranians' anger was directed against the United States during the early phases of the revolution, Iran had equally hated enemies closer to home. To the north, the immense power of the Soviet Union, driven by atheistic communism, was viewed as a modern-day version of the Russian threat of previous centuries. To the west was a militant and hostile Iraq, now under the leadership of the ambitious Saddam Hussein (b. 1937). Problems from both directions appeared shortly after Khomeini's rise to power. Soviet military forces occupied Afghanistan to prop up a weak Marxist regime there. The following year, Iraqi forces suddenly attacked along the Iranian border.

Iraq and Iran had long had an uneasy relationship, fueled by religious differences (Iranian Islam is predominantly Shi'ite, while the ruling caste in Iraq is Sunni) and a perennial dispute over borderlands adjacent to the Persian Gulf, the vital waterway for the export of oil from both countries. Like several of its neighbors, Iraq had long dreamed of unifying the Arabs, but had been hindered by internal factions and suspicion among its neighbors.

During the mid-1970s, Iran had given some support to a Kurdish rebellion in the mountains of Iraq. In 1975, the government of the shah agreed to stop aiding the rebels in return for territorial concessions at the head of the Gulf. Five years later, however, the Kurdish revolt had been suppressed, and President Saddam Hussein, who had assumed power in Baghdad in 1979, accused Iran of violating the territorial agreement and launched an attack on his neighbor. The war was a bloody one, involving the use of poison gas against civilians and the employment of children to clear minefields, and lasted for nearly ten years, while other countries including the two superpowers watched nervously in case the conflict spread throughout the region. With both sides virtually exhausted, a cease-fire was finally arranged in the fall of 1988.

The bitter conflict with Iran had not slaked Saddam Hussein's appetite for territorial expansion. In early August 1990, Iraqi military forces suddenly moved across the border and occupied the small neighboring country of Kuwait at the head of the Gulf. The immediate pretext was the claim that Kuwait was pumping oil from fields inside Iraqi territory. The Kuwaiti government's demands that Iraq repay loans it had received from Kuwait during the war with Iran had also angered the Iraqis. But the deeper reason was the Iraqi contention that Kuwait was legally a part of Iraq. Kuwait had been part of the Ottoman Empire until the opening of the twentieth century, when the local prince had agreed to place his patrimony under British protection. When Iraq became independent in 1932, it claimed the area on the grounds that the state of Kuwait had been created by British imperialism, but opposition from major Western powers and other countries in the region, which feared the consequences of a "Greater Iraq," prevented an Iraqi takeover.

The Iraqi invasion of Kuwait in 1990 sparked an international outcry, and the United States amassed an international force that liberated the country and destroyed a substantial part of Iraq's armed forces. President George Bush had promised the American people that U.S. troops would not fight with one hand tied behind their backs (a clear reference to the Vietnam War), but the allied forces did not occupy Baghdad at the end of the war, because the allies feared that doing so would cause the total breakup of the country, an eventuality that would operate to the benefit of Iran. The allies hoped instead that the Hussein regime would be ousted by an internal revolt. In the meantime, harsh economic sanctions were imposed on the Iraqi government as the condition for peace. The anticipated overthrow of Saddam Hussein did not materialize, however, and his tireless efforts to evade the conditions of the cease-fire continued to bedevil President Bill Clinton, who came into office in January 1993.

The dilemma for the leaders of the anti-Iraqi coalition is clear. They view Saddam Hussein as a dangerous and power-crazed dictator who oppresses his own people and threatens to seek dominance over the entire region, the world's chief source of oil. But a total collapse of Iraq would open the door for Iranian militants to move into the vacuum. The Shi'ite majority in Iraq might also seek to set up an "Islamic Republic" similar to that in neighboring Iran. The only practical solution is to maintain a balance among competing states to prevent a single power from dominating the region. Whether such a precarious balance can be maintained seems problematical, however, in light of the deep cultural and historical differences that divide the region today. The struggle for political and economic dominance in the Middle East has been going on for centuries.

Politics in the Contemporary Middle East

The Middle Eastern states that became independent after World War II exhibit a variety of forms of government. In some cases, the traditional leaders survived into the postwar period, notably on the Arabian peninsula, where the feudal rulers remained in power. The kings of Saudi Arabia, for example, continue to rule by traditional precepts and, citing the distinctive character of Muslim political institutions, have been reluctant to establish representative

 **Map 30.3** The Modern Middle East.

political institutions. As a general rule, these rulers maintain and even enforce the strict observance of traditional customs. Religious police in Saudi Arabia are responsible for enforcing the Muslim dress code, maintaining the prohibition against alcohol, and making sure offices close during the time for prayer. Reportedly, the government even forbade the airing of the U.S. program "The Muppets" on local television because its characters included a pig, which was considered offensive to Islamic strictures against eating pork.

In other societies, traditional authority has been replaced by charismatic one-party rule or military dictatorships. Nasser's regime in Egypt is a good example of a single-party state. Nasser clearly had immense appeal to the Egyptian people as a French observer explained:

> What first impresses you is his massive, thick-set build, the dazzlingly white smile in his dark face. He is tall, tough, African. As he comes toward you on the steps of his small villa on the outskirts of the city, or strides across his huge office at the presidency, he has the emphatic gait of some Covent Garden porter or some heavy feline creature, while he stretches his brawny hand out with the wide gesture of a reaper, completely sure of himself.[21]

Nasser was only the first of several Middle Eastern leaders who won political power by the force of their presence or personality. The Ayatollah Khomeini in Iran, Muammar Qadhafi in Libya, and Saddam Hussein in Iraq are other examples. Although their personal characteristics and images differ, they all have ruled by the force of their personalities.

In other instances, charismatic rule has given way to modernizing bureaucratic regimes. Examples include the governments of Syria, Yemen, Turkey, and Egypt since Nasser, where Anwar al-Sadat and his successor Hosni Mubarak (b. 1929) have avoided dramatic personal appeal in favor of a regime focused on performance. Sometimes the authoritarian character of the regimes has been modified by some democratic tendencies, especially in Turkey, where free elections and the sharing of power have become more prevalent in recent years.

Only in Israel, however, are democratic institutions firmly established. The Israeli system suffers from the proliferation of minor parties, some of which are able to dictate policy because their support is essential to keeping a government in power. In recent years, divisions between religious conservatives and secular elements within the Jewish community have become increasingly sharp, resulting in bitter disagreements over social policy and the negotiations with the Palestinians. Nevertheless, the Israeli government generally reflects the popular will, and power is transferred by peaceful and constitutional means.

The Economics of Oil

Few areas exhibit a greater disparity of individual and national wealth than the Middle East. While millions live in abject poverty, a fortunate few rank among the most wealthy people in the world. While the annual per capita income in Egypt is about $600 (in U.S. dollars), in the tiny states of Kuwait and the United Arab Emirates, it is nearly $20,000. Some of that disparity can be explained by the uneven distribution of fertile and barren land, but the primary answer, of course, is oil. Unfortunately for most of the peoples of the region, oil reserves are distributed unevenly and all too often are located in areas where the population density is low. Egypt and Turkey, with more than 50 million inhabitants apiece, have almost no oil reserves. The combined population of Kuwait, the United Arab Emirates, and Saudi Arabia is well under 10 million people. This disparity in wealth inspired Nasser's quest for Arab unity (and perhaps Saddam Hussein as well), but it has also posed a major obstacle to that unity.

The growing importance of petroleum was obviously a boon to several of the states in the region, but it has been an unreliable one. Because of the sharp fluctuations in the price of oil during the last twenty years, the income of oil-producing states has varied considerably. The spectacular increase in oil prices during the 1970s, when members of OPEC were able to raise the price of a barrel of oil from about $3 to $30, has not recurred, forcing a number of oil-producing countries to scale back their economic development plans.

Not surprisingly, considering their different resources and political systems, the states of the Middle East have adopted diverse approaches to the problem of developing strong and stable economies. Some, like Nasser in Egypt and the leaders of the Ba'ath Party in Syria, attempted to create a form of Arab socialism, involving a high level of government interference in the economy to relieve the inequities of the free enterprise system. Others turned to the Western capitalist model to maximize growth, while using taxes or massive development projects to build a modern infrastructure, redistribute wealth, and maintain political stability and economic opportunity for all.

Whatever their approach, all the states have attempted to develop their economies in accordance with Islamic beliefs. Although the Koran has little to say about economics and can be variously interpreted as capitalist or socialist, it is clear in its opposition to charging interest and in its concern for the material welfare of the Muslim community, the *umma*. How these goals are to be achieved, however, is a matter of interpretation.

Socialist theories of economic development such as Nasser's were often suggested as a way to promote economic growth while meeting the requirements of Islamic doctrine. State intervention in the economic sector would bring about rapid development, while land redistribution and the nationalization or regulation of industry would prevent or minimize the harsh inequities of the marketplace. In general, however, the socialist approach has had little success, and most governments, including those of Egypt and Syria, have recently shifted to a more free enterprise approach while encouraging foreign investment to compensate for a lack of capital or technology.

Although the amount of arable land is relatively small, most countries in the Middle East rely to a certain degree on farming to supply food for their growing populations. In some cases, as in Egypt, Iran, Iraq, and Turkey, farmers have until recently been a majority of the population. Often, much of the fertile land was owned by wealthy absentee landlords, but land reform programs in several countries have attempted to alleviate this problem.

The most comprehensive, and probably the most successful, land reform program was instituted in Egypt, where Nasser and his successors managed to reassign nearly a quarter of all cultivable lands by limiting the amount a single individual could hold. Similar programs in Iran, Iraq, Libya, and Syria generally had less effect. In Iran, large landlords at the local and national level managed to limit the effects of the shah's reform program. After the 1979 revolution, many farmers seized lands forcibly from the landlords, creating questions of ownership that the revolutionary government has tried with minimal success to resolve.

Agricultural productivity throughout the region has been plagued by the lack of water resources. With populations growing at more than 2 percent on average in the Middle East (more than 3 percent in some countries), several governments have tried to increase the amount of water available for irrigation. Many attempts have been sabotaged by government ineptitude, political disagreements, and territorial conflicts, however. The best-known example is the Aswan Dam, which was built by Soviet engineers in the 1950s. The project was designed to control the flow of water throughout the Nile valley, but has had a number of undesirable environmental consequences. Today, the dearth of water in the region is reaching crisis proportions.

Another way governments have attempted to deal with rapid population growth is to encourage emigration. Oil-producing states with small populations such as Saudi Arabia and the United Arab Emirates have imported labor from other countries in the region, mostly to work in the oil fields. By the mid-1980s, more than 40 percent of the population in those states was composed of foreign nationals, who often sent the bulk of their salaries back to their families in their home country. The decline in oil revenues since the mid-1980s, however, has forced several governments to take measures to stabilize or reduce the migrant population. Since the Iraqi invasion, Kuwait, for example, has expelled all Palestinians and restricted migrant workers from other countries to three-year stays.

The economies of the Middle Eastern countries, then, are in a state of rapid flux. Economic problems have been exacerbated by political and military conflicts, and in turn economic problems like the use of water have compounded political issues. For example, disputes between Israel and its neighbors over water rights and between Iraq and its neighbors over the exploitation of the Tigris and the Euphrates have caused serious tensions in recent years. In Saudi Arabia, declining oil revenues and corruption among Saudi elites have aroused a deep sense of anger among some segments of the populace and encouraged them to turn to radical politics.

The Islamic Revival

In recent years, many developments in the Middle East have been described in terms of a resurgence of traditional values and customs in response to the pressure of Western influence. Indeed, some conservative religious forces in the area have consciously attempted to replace foreign culture and values with allegedly "pure" Islamic forms of belief and behavior.

But the Islamic revival that has taken place in the contemporary Middle East is not a simple dichotomy between traditional and modern, native and foreign, or irrational and rational. In the first place, many Muslims in the Middle East believe that Islamic values and modern ways are not incompatible and may even be mutually reinforcing in some ways. Secondly, in the Middle Eastern context the resurgence of what are sometimes called "fundamentalist" Islamic groups may be a rational and practical response to destabilizing forces, such as corruption and hedonism, and self-destructive practices, such as drunkenness, prostitution, and the use of drugs. Finally, the reassertion of Islamic values can be a means of establishing cultural identity and fighting off the overwhelming impact of Western ideas.

Initially, many Muslim intellectuals responded to Western influence by trying to reconcile the perceived differences between tradition and modernity and by creating a "modernized" set of Islamic beliefs and practices that would not clash with the demands of the twentieth century. This process took place to some degree in most Islamic societies, but it was especially prevalent in Turkey, Egypt, and Persia. Mustapha Kemal Ataturk had embraced the strategy when he attempted to secularize the Islamic religion in the new Turkish republic. The Turkish model was followed by Shah Reza Khan and his son Mohammad Reza Pahlavi in Iran and then by Nasser in postwar Egypt, all of whom attempted to make use of

◆ **Following the Dress Code in Sana'a.** Throughout the Middle East, pressure has been increasing for Muslim women to adopt more traditional forms of dress and behavior. In some countries, such as Iran and Saudi Arabia, women are expected to wear a veil and avoid casual male companionship. In other Muslim countries, social conventions are less strict. In Sana'a, capital of North Yemen, these young women cover their heads in public, but are not required to wear the veil.

Islamic values while asserting the primacy of other issues such as political and economic development. Religion, in effect, had become the handmaiden of political power, national identity, and economic prosperity.

For obvious reasons, these secularizing trends were particularly noticeable among the political, intellectual, and economic elites in urban areas. They had less influence in the countryside, among the poor, and among devout elements within the *ulama*. Many of the latter believed that Western secular trends in the major cities had given birth to many regrettable and even repugnant social attitudes and behavioral patterns, such as political and economic corruption, sexual promiscuity, hedonism and individualism, and the use of alcohol, pornography, and drugs. Although such practices had long existed in the Middle East, they were now far more visible and socially acceptable.

This reaction began early in the century and intensified after World War I, when the Western presence increased. In 1928, devout Muslims in Egypt formed the Muslim Brotherhood as a means of promoting personal piety. Later the movement began to take a more activist approach, including eventually the use of terrorism by a radical minority. Despite Nasser's surface commitment to Islamic ideals and Arab unity, some Egyptians were fiercely opposed to his policies and regarded his vision of Arab socialism as a betrayal of Islamic principles. Nasser reacted harshly and executed a number of his leading opponents.

Of course, the movement to return to Islamic purity reached its zenith in Iran. It is not surprising that Iran took the lead in light of its long tradition of ideological purity within the Shi'ite sect as well as the uncompromisingly secular character of the shah's reforms in the postwar era. In revolutionary Iran, traditional Islamic beliefs have been all-pervasive and extend into education, clothing styles, social practices, and the legal system. In recent years, for example, Iranian women have been heavily fined or even flogged for violating the Islamic dress code.

While the political aspects of the Iranian Revolution inspired distrust and suspicion among political elites elsewhere in the region, its cultural and social effects have been profound. Although no other state in the Middle East has adopted the violent approach to cultural reform applied in Iran, Iranian ideas have spread throughout the area and affected social and cultural behavior in many ways. In Algeria, the political influence of fundamentalist Islamic groups has grown substantially and enabled them to win a stunning victory in the national elections in 1992. When the military stepped in to cancel the second round of elections and crack down on the militants, the latter responded with a campaign of terrorism against moderates that has claimed several thousand lives.

A similar trend has emerged in Egypt, where militant groups such as the Muslim Brotherhood have engaged in terrorism, including the assassination of Sadat and more recent attacks on foreign tourists, who are considered carriers of corrupt Western influence. In 1994, the prominent novelist Naguib Mahfouz (b. 1911) was stabbed outside his home, apparently because the militants considered his early writings to be blasphemous.

Even in Turkey, generally considered the most secular of Islamic societies, a militant political group, known as the Islamic Welfare Party, has taken power in a coalition government formed in 1996. The new prime minister, Necmettin Erbakan, has adopted a pro-Arab stance in foreign affairs and threatens to reduce the country's economic and political ties to Europe. Worried moderates express concern that the secular legacy of Mustapha Kemal Ataturk is being eroded.

Throughout the Middle East, even governments and individuals who do not support these efforts to return to pure Islamic principles have adjusted their behavior and beliefs in subtle ways. In Egypt, for example, the government now encourages television programs devoted to religion in preference to comedies and adventure shows imported from the West. Middle-class women in Cairo tend to dress more modestly than in the past, and alcohol is discouraged or at least consumed more discreetly.

Middle Eastern Societies and Women's Rights

Nowhere, in fact, have the fault lines between tradition and modernity within Muslim societies in the Middle East been so apparent as in the ongoing debate over the role of women. At the beginning of the twentieth century, women's place in Middle Eastern society had changed little since the death of the Prophet Muhammad. Women were secluded in their homes and had few legal, political, or social rights. Early in the twentieth century, inspired in part by the Western presence, a "modernist" movement arose in several countries in the Middle East with the aim of bringing Islamic social values and legal doctrine into line with Western values and attitudes. Advocates of modernist views contended that Islamic doctrine was not inherently opposed to women's rights and that the teachings of Muhammad and his suc-

cessors had actually broadened them in significant ways. To modernists, Islamic traditions such as female seclusion, wearing the veil, and even polygamy were pre-Islamic folk traditions that had been tolerated in the early Islamic era and continued to be practiced in later centuries.

During the first decades of the twentieth century, such views had considerable impact on a number of Middle Eastern societies, including Turkey and Persia. As we have seen, greater rights for women had been a crucial element in the social revolution promoted by Mustapha Kemal Ataturk in Turkey. In Iran, Shah Reza Khan and his son granted female suffrage and encouraged the education of women. In Egypt, a vocal feminist movement arose in educated women's circles in Cairo as early as the 1920s.

Modernist views had somewhat less effect in other Islamic states, such as Iraq, Jordan, Morocco, and Algeria, where traditional views of women continued to prevail in varying degrees. Particularly in rural areas, notions of women's liberation made little headway. Most conservative by far was Saudi Arabia, where women were not only segregated and expected to wear the veil in public, but were also restricted in education and forbidden to drive automobiles.

◆ **Gossip among the Pyramids.** In modern Cairo, the suburbs of the city creep up to the very feet of the ancient pyramids of Giza. Just beyond the pyramid in the background lies the Sahara, a vast wasteland that stretches unbroken for three thousand miles to the Atlantic Ocean. In the foreground, seemingly oblivious to the majesty of the ancient empire of the pharaohs, local residents discuss the events of the day on their return from the markets.

◆ **Golda Meir.** Golda Meir was one of the most beloved leaders of the new state of Israel. Born in Russia and raised in the United States, she became an ardent Zionist and immigrated to Palestine in the 1920s. An energetic pioneer with a dream and determination, Meir became Israel's fourth prime minister in 1969 and led her nation through a period of tension in Arab-Israeli relations.

Until recently, the general trend in urban areas of the Middle East was toward a greater role for women. With the exception of conservative religious communities, women in Israel have achieved substantial equality with men and are active in politics, the professions, and even the armed forces. Golda Meir (1898–1978), prime minister of Israel from 1969 to 1974, became an international symbol of the ability of women to be world leaders. But beginning in the 1970s, there was a noticeable shift toward a more traditional approach to sexual relationships in many Middle Eastern societies. It was accompanied by attacks on growing Western influence within the media and on the social habits of young people. The reactions were especially strong in Iran, where attacks by religious conservatives on the growing role of women contributed to the emotions underlying the Iranian Revolution of 1979.

The revolution caused Iranian women to return to more traditional forms of behavior. They were in-

structed to wear the veil and to dress modestly in public. Films produced in postrevolutionary Iran expressed the new morality. They rarely featured women, and when they did, physical contact between men and women was prohibited. Still, Iranian women have many freedoms that women had lacked before the twentieth century: for example, they can attend a university, receive military training, vote, practice birth control, and write fiction.

The Iranian Revolution helped to promote a revival of traditional attitudes toward women in other Islamic societies. Women in secular countries such as Egypt, Turkey, and far-off Malaysia have begun to dress more modestly in public, while public attacks on open sexuality in the media have become increasingly frequent (see the box on p. 1143).

Contemporary Literature and Art in the Middle East

As in other areas of Asia and Africa, the encounter with the West in the nineteenth and twentieth centuries stimulated a cultural renaissance in the Middle East. Muslim authors translated Western works into Arabic and Persian and began to experiment with new literary forms. The advent of modern newspapers and magazines eliminated the traditional differences between the oral and written languages. The resulting fused language included colloquial speech, borrowed Western words, and ancient words resurrected from indigenous languages. Turkish, however, was cleansed of its foreign borrowings by lexicographers who attempted to return it to its original pure form. Whereas in 1920 nearly three-quarters of all Turkish words had their roots in foreign languages, by 1970 the proportion had dropped to one-fifth.

The new literature dealt with a number of new themes. The rise in national consciousness stimulated interest in historical traditions. Writers also switched from religious to secular themes and addressed the problems of this world and the means of rectifying them. Furthermore, literature was no longer the exclusive domain of the elite, but was increasingly written for the broader mass of the population.

Iran has produced one of the most prominent national literatures in the contemporary Middle East. Since World War II, Iranian literature has been hampered somewhat by political considerations, since it has been expected to serve first the Pahlavi monarchy and more recently the Islamic Republic. Nevertheless, Iranian writers are among the most prolific in the region and

⇒ Keeping the Camel Out of the Tent ⇐

"Almighty God created sexual desire in ten parts; then he gave nine parts to women and one to men." So pronounced Ali, Muhammad's son-in-law, as he explained why women are held morally responsible as the instigators of sexual intercourse. Consequently, over the centuries Islamic women have been secluded, veiled, and in many cases genitally mutilated in order to safeguard male virtue. Women are forbidden to look directly at, speak to, or touch a man prior to marriage. Even today, they are often sequestered at home or limited to strictly segregated areas away from all male contact. Women normally pray at home or in an enclosed antechamber of the mosque so their physical presence will not disturb men's spiritual concentration.

Especially limiting today are the laws governing women's behavior in Saudi Arabia. Schooling for girls has never been compulsory, because fathers believe that "educating women is like allowing the nose of the camel into the tent; eventually the beast will edge in and take up all the room inside." The country did not establish its first girls' school until 1956. The following description of Saudi women is from Nine Parts Desire: The Hidden World of Islamic Women by the journalist Geraldine Brooks.

Geraldine Brooks, Nine Parts Desire

Women were first admitted to university in Saudi Arabia in 1962, and all women's colleges remain strictly segregated. Lecture rooms come equipped with closed-circuit TVs and telephones, so women students can listen to a male professor and question him by phone, without having to contaminate themselves by being seen by him. When the first dozen women graduated from university in 1973, they were devastated to find that their names hadn't been printed on the commencement program. The old tradition, that it dishonors women to mention them, was depriving them of recognition they believed they'd earned. The women and their families protested, so a separate program was printed and a segregated graduation ceremony was held for the students' female relatives. Two thousand women attended. Their celebratory ululations raised the roof.

But while the opening of women's universities widened access to higher learning for women, it also made the educational experience much shallower. Before 1962, many progressive Saudi families had sent their daughters abroad for education. They had returned to the kingdom not only with a degree but with experience of the outside world, whether in the West or in more progressive Arab countries such as Egypt, Lebanon or Syria, where they'd breathed the air of desegregation and even caught a breath of secular culture. Now a whole generation of Saudi women have completed their education entirely within the country. While thousands of Saudi men benefit from higher education abroad at government expense, women haven't been granted such scholarships since 1980. The government's position is that women's educational opportunities have improved within the kingdom to the point where a woman's needs can all be met within its borders. The definition of her educational needs, as set out in a Ministry of Higher Education policy paper, are "to bring her up in a sound Islamic way so that she can fulfill her role in life as a successful housewife, ideal wife and good mother, and to prepare her for other activities that suit her nature such as teaching, nursing and medicine." . . .

Lack of opportunity for education abroad means that Saudi women are trapped in the confines of an education system that still lags men's. Subjects such as geology and petroleum engineering—tickets to influential jobs in Saudi Arabia's oil economy—remain closed to women. Three of Saudi Arabia's seven universities—Imam Mohamed bin Saud Islamic University in Riyadh, the University of Petroleum and Minerals and the Islamic University in Medina—don't accept women. Few women's colleges have their own libraries, and libraries shared with men's schools are either entirely off limits to women or open to them only one day per week. Most of the time women can't browse for books but have to specify the titles they want and have them brought out to them.

But women and men sit the same degree examinations. Professors quietly acknowledge the women's scores routinely outstrip the men's. "It's no surprise," said one woman professor. "Look at their lives. The boys have their cars, they can spend the evenings cruising the streets with their friends, sitting in cafés, buying black-market alcohol and drinking all night. What do the girls have? Four walls and their books. For them, education is everything."

often write in prose, which has finally been accepted as the equal of poetry. Perhaps the most outstanding Iranian author of the twentieth century was the short story writer Sadeq Hedayat. Hedayat was obsessed with the frailty and absurdity of life and wrote with compassion about the problems of ordinary human beings. Frustrated and disillusioned at the government's suppression of individual liberties, he committed suicide in 1951. Like Japan's Yukio Mishima (see Chapter 32), Hedayat later became a cult figure among Iranian youth.

Sadeq Hedayat had a number of imitators, many of whom continued to write stories of everyday Iranian life. Some were preoccupied with the destructive effects of change on Iranian society and produced nostalgic works about the corrosive effects of contemporary ways on the family and other traditional institutions. Despite the male-oriented character of Iranian society, many of the new writers were women. One book by a woman writer was the best-selling Iranian novel in the 1970s. Many women understandably focused on the condition of women in Iran, with some favoring an extension of women's rights and others expressing more traditional views.

Since the revolution, the veil has become the central metaphor in Iranian women's writing. Those who favor the veil praise it as the last bastion of defense against Western cultural imperialism. Behind the veil, the Islamic woman can breathe freely, unpolluted by foreign exploitation and moral corruption. They see the veil as the courageous woman's weapon against Western efforts to dominate the Iranian soul. Other Iranian women, however, consider the veil a "mobile prison" or an oppressive anachronism from the Dark Ages. A few use the pen as a weapon in a crusade to liberate their sisters and enable them to make their own choices. As one recent writer expressed it:

> As I pulled the chador [the veil] over me, I felt a heaviness descending over me. I was hidden and in hiding. There was nothing visible left of Sousan Azadi. I felt like an animal of the light suddenly trapped in a cave. I was just another faceless Moslem woman carrying a whole inner world hidden inside the chador.[22]

Whether or not they accept the veil, women writers are a vital part of contemporary Iranian literature.

Like Iran, Egypt has experienced a flowering of literature in the twentieth century, which was accelerated by the establishment of the Egyptian republic in the early 1950s. As in Iran, the trend has been toward prose. Poetry is still composed, but classical meter and rhyme have been discarded for free verse and prose poetry.

The most illustrious contemporary Egyptian writer is Naguib Mahfouz, who won the Nobel Prize for literature in 1988. His *Cairo Trilogy*, published in 1952, is considered the finest writing in Arabic since World War II. With great compassion and energy, the novel chronicles three generations of a merchant family in Cairo during the tumultuous years between the two world wars. Mahfouz is particularly adept at blending panoramic historical events with the intimate lives of ordinary human beings. Unlike many other modern writers, his message is essentially optimistic and reflects his hope that religion and science can work together for the overall betterment of humankind.

The emergence of a modern Turkish literature can be traced to the establishment of the republic in 1923. As a national state replaced the multinational empire, writers began to return to Turkish folklore for inspiration. Turkish authors, both male and female, began to create a new "village literature" dealing with the lives of ordinary people in rural areas. One of the most popular and prolific was Aziz Nesin, who was born in 1915. Determined to free the common people from oppression, Nesin used humor and satire to ridicule bureaucratic inefficiency and corruption. His short stories have been translated into twenty-four languages and will bring a smile to anyone familiar with the frustrations of red tape and bureaucratic stupidity.

Although Israeli literature arises from a totally different tradition from that of its neighbors, it shares with them certain contemporary characteristics and a concern for ordinary human beings. Israeli writers have inherited not only a long tradition of Hebrew literature but also the various traditions of the country's multinational population. As they identify with the aspirations of the new nation, many Israeli writers try to find a sense of order in the new reality, voicing terrors from the past and hopes for the future.

Some contemporary Israeli authors have refused to serve as spokespersons for Zionism and are speaking out on sensitive national issues. In his writings, the internationally renowned novelist Amos Oz has examined the problems inherent in the kibbutz, one of Israel's most hallowed institutions. Other novels explore the psychological and sexual complexities of his characters; *My Michael* examines the emotional disintegration of a housewife, while *To Know a Woman* dissects a marriage. A vocal supporter of peace with the Palestinians, Oz is a member of Peace Now and the author of a political tract entitled *Israel, Palestine, and Peace*. Another of Israel's best-known novelists and poets is A. B. Yehoshua. With psychological insight, Yehoshua explores the way Israelis go about their daily lives surrounded by the threat of war, terrorism, and political turmoil.

The novels of David Grossman, another Israeli author strongly committed to peace in the region, have been made into films that have brought him international attention. In his nonfiction work *The Yellow Wind,* he attempted to understand the feelings of the Palestinian people living in the occupied territories; the book presents them empathetically as the reverse image of the Israelis, dreaming of their own homeland. Although he was criticized for such views by ultraconservative Jewish religious groups, Grossman wrote a sequel focusing on the many issues of identity, land, and language that Palestinians share with Israelis. Praising the 1993 peace agreement over Palestine, Grossman remarked that it would eventually bring the Palestinians "back into history, into time with all the clumsiness of reality." As for the Israelis, "peace will cure us from this profound disease of not trusting our own existence. . . . So finally this unbearable lightness of death will be over—not soon, but in fifty years it will be over."[23]

Like the literature, the art of the modern Middle East has been profoundly influenced by exposure to Western culture. At first artists tended to imitate Western models, but later they began to experiment with national styles, returning to earlier forms for inspiration. Some emulated the writers in returning to the village to depict peasants and shepherds, but others followed international trends and attempted to express the alienation and disillusionment that characterizes so much of modern life.

Reflecting their hopes for the new nation, Israeli painters sought to bring to life the sentiments of pioneers arriving in a promised land. Many attempted to capture the longing for community expressed in the Israeli commune, or kibbutz. Others searched for the roots of Israeli culture in the history of the Jewish people or in the horrors of the Holocaust. The experience of the Holocaust has attracted particular attention from sculptors, who work in wood and metal as well as stone.

Conclusion

Few regions in the world have had as much difficulty in adapting to the challenges of the twentieth century as the Middle East and the continent of Africa. In Africa, political turmoil, endemic poverty, and troubled relations among states have led many observers to adopt an attitude—sometimes called Afro-pessimism—that African societies, because of their distinct culture and history, lack the capacity to cope with the rapidly changing world of our day. In that view, Africans must seek the source of their salvation from within their own traditions, rather than by following the example of successful nations abroad.

The Middle East, like the continent of Africa, is one of the most unstable regions in the world today. In part, this turbulence is due to the continued interference of outsiders attracted by the massive oil reserves under the parched wastes of the Arabian peninsula and in the vicinity of the Persian Gulf. Oil indeed is both a blessing and a curse to the peoples of the region.

Another factor contributing to the volatility of the Middle East is the tug-of-war between the sense of ethnic identity in the form of nationalism and the intense longing to be part of a broader Islamic community, a dream that dates back to the time of the Prophet Muhammad. The desire to create that community inspired Gamal Abdul Nasser in the 1950s and the Ayatollah Khomeini in the 1970s and 1980s and—with all his faults—probably motivates many of the actions of Saddam Hussein today. Until the peoples of the Middle East are able to reconcile their desire for nationhood with their sense of a common religious experience, it seems unlikely that they will find true peace and political stability.

A final reason for the turmoil currently affecting the Middle East is the intense debate that is taking place there over the role of religion within civil society. In recent years, Western commentators have commonly labeled efforts by Muslims to return to a more pure form of Islam as fanatical and extremist and as a misguided attempt to reverse the course of history. Certainly, many of the legal and social restrictions now being enforced in various Muslim countries in the Middle East appear excessively harsh and often repugnant to outside observers. Nevertheless, it is important to remember that Muslim societies are not alone in deploring the sense of moral decline that is now allegedly taking place in societies throughout the world. Nor are they alone in advocating a restoration of traditional religious values as a means of reversing the trend. Movements dedicated to such purposes are appearing in many other societies (including, among others, Israel and the United States) and can be viewed as an understandable reaction to the rapid and often bewildering changes that are taking place in the contemporary world. Not infrequently, members of such groups turn to violence as a means of making their point. While the tensions between tradition and modernity appear to be strongest in the contemporary Middle East, they are hardly unique to that region. The consequences as yet cannot be foreseen.

CHAPTER NOTES

1. Ama Ata Aidoo, *Changes: A Love Story* (New York, 1991), p. 174; Aidoo, *No Sweetness Here* (New York, 1995), p. 136.
2. G.-C. M. Mutiso, *Socio-Political Thought in African Literature: Weusi?*, (New York, 1974), p. 117.
3. Aimé Césaire, *Cahier d'un retour du pays natal*, trans. John Berger and Anna Bostock (Harmondsworth, 1969), p. 10, cited in Emmanuel N. Obiechina, *Language and Theme: Essays on African Literature* (Washington, D.C., 1990), pp. 78–79.
4. *Time* Magazine, January 16, 1984.
5. Cyprian Ekwensi, *Jagua Nana* (Greenwich, 1961), pp.146–47.
6. Albert Ojuka, "Pedestrian, to Passing Benz-man," quoted in Adrian Roscoe, *Uhuru's Fire: African Literature East to South* (Cambridge, 1977), p. 103.
7. *New York Times*, September 1, 1996.
8. Taban Lo Liyong, "Student's Lament," quoted in Roscoe, *Uhuru's Fire*, pp. 120–21.
9. Dan Agbee, in *Newswatch* of Lagos, quoted in *World Press Review*, August 1991, p. 16.
10. Roscoe, *Uhuru's Fire*, p. 23.
11. Francis Ademola, *Reflections: Nigerian Prose and Verse* (Lagos, 1962), p. 65, quoted in Mutiso, *Socio-Political Thought in African Literature: Weusi?*, (New York, 1974), p. 117.
12. Kenneth Little, *African Women in Towns: An Aspect of Africa's Social Revolution* (Cambridge, 1973), p. 6.
13. Abioseh Nicol, *A Truly Married Woman and Other Stories* (London, 1965), p. 12.
14. Oyekan Owomoyela, ed., *A History of Twentieth-Century African Literature* (Lincoln, Neb., 1993), p. 339.
15. Quoted in *New York Times*, May 13, 1996.
16. Cyprian Ekwensi, *Iska* (London, 1966), p. 21.
17. Ngugi Wa-Thiong'o, *Decolonizing the Mind: The Politics of Language in African Literature* (Portsmouth, N.H., 1986), p. 103.
18. George Awoonor-Williams, *Rediscovery and Other Poems* (Ibadan, 1964), p. 11, quoted in Mutiso, *Socio-Political Thought in African Literature: Weusi?*, pp. 81–82.
19. Quoted in Arthur Goldschmidt, Jr., *A Concise History of the Middle East*, 4th ed. (Boulder, Colo., 1991), p. 280.
20. Walter Laqueur and Barry Rubin, eds., *The Israel-Arab Reader* (New York, 1984), pp. 186–89.
21. Roy R. Andersen, Robert F. Seibert, and Jon G. Wagner, *Politics and Change in the Middle East: Sources of Conflict and Accommodation*, 4th ed. (Englewood Cliffs, N.J., 1993), p. 200.
22. From Sousan Azadi, with Angela Ferrante, *Out of Iran* (London, 1987), p. 223, quoted in S. Sullivan, ed., *Stories by Iranian Women since the Revolution* (Austin, Tex., 1991), p. 13.
23. *New York Times*, February 7, 1996.

SUGGESTED READINGS

For general surveys of contemporary African history, see R. Oliver and J. D. Fage, *A Short History of Africa* (Harmondsworth, 1986); R. Oliver, *The African Experience* (New York, 1992), which contains interesting essays on a variety of themes; and K. Shillington, *History of Africa* (New York, 1989), which takes a chronological and geographical approach and includes excellent maps and illustrations.

Two recent treatments are B. Davidson, *Africa in History: Themes and Outlines*, rev. ed. (New York, 1991) and P. Curtin et al., *African History* (London, 1995).

On nationalist movements, see P. Gifford and W. R. Louis, eds., *The Transfer of Power in Africa* (New Haven, Conn., 1982) and J. D. Hargreaves, *Decolonisation in Africa* (London, 1988). For an African perspective, see K. Nkrumah, *Ghana* (London, 1959). For a poignant analysis of the hidden costs of nation building, see N. F. Mostert, *The Epic of South Africa's Creation and the Tragedy of the Xhosa People* (London, 1992).

For a survey of economic conditions in Africa, see *Sub-Saharan Africa: From Crisis to Sustainable Growth* (Washington, D.C., 1989), issued by the World Bank.

Also see A. O'Connor, *The African City* (London, 1983) and J. Illiffe, *The African Poor* (Cambridge, 1983).

Political events in Africa are often examined on a regional basis. For an overview, see A. Mazrui and M. Tidy, *Nationalism and New States in Africa* (Portsmouth, N.H., 1984). See also S. A. Akintoye, *The Emergent African States* (London, 1976) and S. Decalo, *Coups and Army Rule in Africa* (New Haven, Conn., 1990).

For a country-by-country survey of African literature, see L. S. Klein, ed., *African Literatures in the Twentieth Century: A Guide* (New York, 1986). On art, see F. Willett, *African Art: An Introduction* (New York, 1985). Of the many short story collections showcasing different African authors, we recommend C. Achebe and C. L. Innes, eds., *The Heinemann Book of Contemporary Short Stories* (Portsmouth, N.H., 1992); C. H. Bruner, ed., *Unwinding Threads: Writing by Women in Africa* (Oxford, 1983); and C. H. Bruner, ed., *The Heinemann Book of African Women's Writing* (Oxford, 1993). For a brief, intimate introduction to African culture, see *Sankofa: Stories, Proverbs and Poems of an African Childhood* by the Ghanaian D. Abdulai (Accra and Denver, 1995).

Good general surveys of the modern Middle East include A. Goldschmidt, Jr., *A Concise History of the Middle East* (Boulder, Colo., 1991) and G. E. Perry, *The Middle East: Fourteen Islamic Centuries* (Elizabeth City, N.J., 1992).

On Israel and the Palestinian question, see B. Reich, *Israel: Land of Tradition and Conflict* (Boulder, Colo., 1985) and C. C. O'Brien, *The Siege: The Saga of Israel and Zionism* (New York, 1986). On U.S.-Israeli relations, see S. Green, *Living by the Sword: America and Israel in the Middle East, 1968–1987* (London, 1988). Israeli politics are analyzed in D. Peretz, *The Government and Politics of Israel* (Boulder, Colo., 1983).

The issue of oil is examined in G. Luciani, *The Oil Companies and the Arab World* (New York, 1984) and P. Odell, *Oil and World Power* (New York, 1986). Also see M. H. Kerr and El Sayed Yassin, eds., *Rich and Poor States in the Middle East: Egypt and the New Arab Order* (Boulder, Colo., 1985). On Egypt, see A. Goldschmidt, Jr., *Modern Egypt: The Formation of a Nation-State* (Boulder, Colo., 1988).

On the Iranian Revolution, see S. Bakash, *The Reign of the Ayatollahs* (New York, 1984) and B. Rubin, *Iran since the Revolution* (Boulder, Colo., 1985). On Ayatollah Khomeini's role and ideas, see H. Algar, *Islam and Revolution: The Writings and Declarations of Imam Khomeini* (Berkeley, Calif., 1981). The Iran-Iraq War is discussed in C. Davies, ed., *After the War: Iran, Iraq and the Arab Gulf* (Chichester, 1990) and S. C. Pelletiere, *The Iran-Iraq War: Chaos in a Vacuum* (New York, 1992).

On the politics of the Middle East, see J. A. Bill and R. Springborg, *Politics in the Middle East* (London, 1990) and R. R. Anderson, R. F. Seibert, and J. G. Wagner, *Politics and Change in the Middle East: Sources of Conflict and Accommodation* (Englewood Cliffs, N.J., 1993). See also T. Ismael, *International Relations of the Contemporary Middle East* (Syracuse, 1986) and B. Reich, ed., *The Powers in the Middle East: The Ultimate Strategic Arena* (New York, 1987).

For a general anthology of Middle Eastern literature, see J. Kritzeck, *Modern Islamic Literature from 1800 to the Present* (New York, 1970). Also of interest is L. Hamalian and J. D. Yohannan, eds., *New Writing from the Middle East* (New York, 1978). For a scholarly but accessible overview of Arabic literature, see M. M. Badawi, *A Short History of Modern Arab Literature* (Oxford, 1993). For Iranian literature, see M. Southgate, *Modern Persian Short Stories* (Washington, D.C., 1980) and S. Sullivan and F. Milani, *Stories by Iranian Women since the Revolution* (Austin, Tex., 1991). For an accessible introduction to the life and work of Hedayat, see I. Bashiri, *The Fiction of Sadeq Hedayat* (Lexington, Ky., 1984). On Mahfouz, see M. N. Mikhail, *Studies in the Short Fiction of Mahfouz and Idris* (New York, 1992). See also T. S. Halman, *Contemporary Turkish Literature* (East Brunswick, N. J., 1982).

On women's issues, see G. Brooks, *Nine Parts Desire* (New York, 1995), a contemporary study by a journalist, and the Lebanese author H. al-Shaykh's *Women of Sand and Myrrh* (New York, 1989).

CHAPTER

31

Nationalism Triumphant: The Emergence of Independent States in South and Southeast Asia

In a letter to his friend and colleague Jawaharlal Nehru in October 1945, the Indian spiritual leader Mahatma Gandhi argued passionately against Nehru's dream of building a modern industrialized society in India. "I believe," he said, "that if India, and through India the world, is to achieve real freedom, then sooner or later we shall have to go and live in the villages—in huts, not in palaces."[1] Truth and nonviolence, he insisted, could be found only in the simplicity of village life, not in modern industrialized cities patterned after those in the West. Nehru did not agree, and after independence in 1947, he set his country on the path of industrial revolution. As we shall see, Nehru's decision did not end the debate, which continues today, as Indians seek to reconcile their traditional values with the demands of modern life.

The debate had its roots in the colonial era when the resources of South and Southeast Asia were systematically plundered by the Western colonial powers for more than a century. In the process, both regions were linked ever more closely to the global capitalist economy. Yet as in other areas of Africa and Asia, the experience brought only limited benefits to the local peoples, as little industrial development took place and the bulk of the profits went into the pockets of Western entrepreneurs.

Early in the twentieth century, nationalist forces had begun to seek reforms in colonial policy and the eventual overthrow of colonial power, but the peoples of South and Southeast Asia did not regain their national independence until after

1945	1955	1965	1975	1985	1995

India and Pakistan declare independence

Death of Jawaharlal Nehru

Era of Indira Gandhi

Destruction of mosque at Ayodhya

Southeast Asian states restore independence

Formation of ASEAN

Corazon Aquino elected president in the Philippines

Era of Guided Democracy in Indonesia

World War II. Finally, between 1945 and 1955, independent states emerged throughout the southern tier of Asia.

The leaders of these new nations were generally dedicated to building modern societies on the Western model. But escaping the legacy of the past was not easy. Most of the new states were weak and inexperienced and struggled with only limited success to develop advanced economies, establish stable political systems, and foster a sense of common identity among their diverse populations. Old animosities among the various ethnic groups reemerged and led to mutual suspicion and strife within the region. Half a century after independence, peace and prosperity are still more a dream than a reality for many peoples of the area.

The End of the British Raj

During the 1930s, the nationalist movement in India was severely shaken by factional disagreements between Hindus and Muslims within its own ranks. The outbreak of World War II interrupted these sectarian clashes and brought new problems. To the dismay of the leaders of the Indian National Congress, the British government committed India to the war without consulting its people or its elected leaders (the same thing had occurred during World War I). At the news, a number of Congress legislators resigned, and Muhammed Ali Jinnah

(1876–1948), leader of the Muslim League, demanded the creation of a separate state. Mahatma Gandhi started a new disobedience movement and demanded that the British "quit India." Jawaharlal Nehru (1889–1964) himself was arrested. To dampen the protests, the British offered India dominion status after the war and the right of secession for individual states, but the offer was rejected by the Congress.

When the war ended in 1945, the British sent a three-man commission to India to study the situation and make recommendations. The British government offered a complicated union arrangement with divided powers and a continued British presence, but Congress leaders were dubious. When clashes between Hindus and Muslims broke out in several cities, Jinnah called for "direct action," while British prime minister Clement Attlee announced that power would be transferred to "responsible Indian hands" by June 1948. To bring about the transferral of power, Lord Louis Mountbatten (1900–1979), a member of the British royal family, was appointed viceroy.

But the imminence of independence did not dampen communal strife. As riots escalated, Mountbatten reluctantly accepted the inevitability of partition, while the Congress and the Muslim League were reconciled to the division of Bengal and the Punjab, two provinces with Hindu and Muslim populations. Pakistan itself would be divided between the main area of Muslim habitation in the Indus River valley in the west and a separate territory two thousand miles away in east Bengal to the east. Among Congress leaders, Gandhi alone objected to the division of India. A Muslim woman criticized him for his opposition to partition, asking him "if two brothers were living together in the same house and wanted to separate and live in two different houses, would you object?" "Ah," Gandhi replied, "if only we could separate as two brothers. But we will not. It will be an orgy of blood. We shall tear ourselves asunder in the womb of the mother who bears us."[2]

But Gandhi was increasingly regarded as a figure of the past by many Indian leaders, and his views were ignored. On July 15, 1947, the British declared that one month later two independent nations—India and Pakistan—would be established. A boundary commission was formed, and Mountbatten instructed the rulers in the princely states to choose which state they would join by August 15. But problems arose in predominantly Hindu Hyderabad, where the maharaja was a Muslim, and in mountainous Kashmir, where a Hindu prince ruled over a Muslim population. Independence was declared on August 15, but the auguries were ominous. The flight of millions of Hindus and Muslims across the borders in Bengal and the Punjab led to violence and the death of over a million people. One of the casualties evoked widespread mourning. On January 30, 1948, a Hindu militant assassinated Gandhi as he was going to morning prayer. The assassin was apparently motivated by Gandhi's opposition to a Hindu India.

Independent India

With independence, the Indian National Congress, now renamed the Congress Party, moved from opposition to the responsibility of power. The prospect must have been intimidating. The vast majority of India's nearly 400 million people were poor and illiterate. There were a bewil-

✳ **Map 31.1**   Modern South Asia.

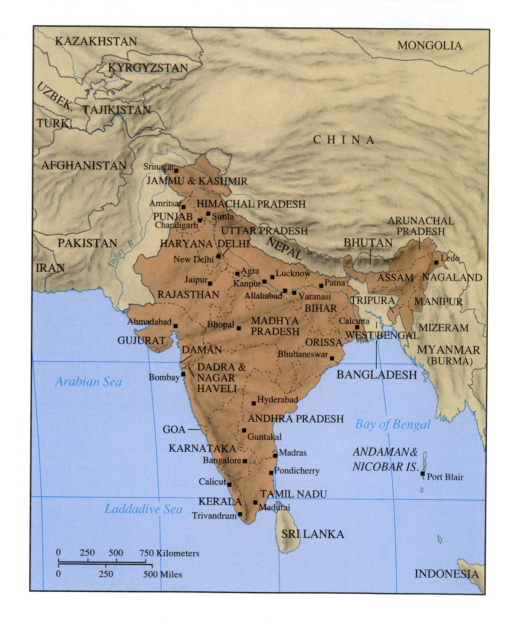

dering number of language and ethnic groups and fourteen major languages. Although Congress leaders spoke bravely of building a new nation, Indian society still bore many of the scars of past wars and divisions.

The new nation possessed one advantage in that it had an intelligent, self-confident, and reasonably united leadership. In the crucible years of colonialism, the Congress Party had gained experience in government, while the Indian civil service provided solid expertise in the arcane art of bureaucracy. Jawaharlal Nehru, the new prime minister, was a charismatic figure respected and often revered by millions of Indians.

The government's first problem was to resolve the border disputes left over from the transition period. The rulers of Hyderabad and Kashmir had both followed their own preferences rather than the wishes of their subject populations. Nehru was determined to include both states within India. In 1948, Indian troops invaded Hyderabad and annexed the area. India was also able to seize most of Kashmir, but at the cost of incurring the hostility of Pakistan's new leaders. An intractable problem had been created that poisoned relations between the two countries for the next generation.

An Experiment in Democratic Socialism

India's new leaders had strong ideas on the future of Indian society. Nehru himself was an admirer of British political institutions, but had also been influenced by the Socialist movement led by the Labour Party in England. With his dominating personality, he imposed his vision of an India with democratic political institutions but a moderately socialist economic structure and, in doing so, put a personal stamp on the country that would last long after his death (see the box on p. 1152).

Under Nehru's leadership, the new Republic of India adopted a political system on the British model with a figurehead president and a parliamentary form of government. A number of political parties operated legally, from the Indian Communist Party on the left to capitalist and religious parties on the right. But the Congress Party, with its enormous prestige and charismatic leadership, was dominant at both the central and the local levels. The Congress Party aspired to represent all Indians, from rich to poor, *brahmins* to *harijans* (untouchability was legally abolished by the new government), and Hindus to Muslims and other minority religious groups.

Economic policy was patterned roughly after the program of the British Labour Party with adjustments for local circumstances. The state took over ownership of the "commanding heights" of the economy, such as major industries and resources, transportation, and utilities, while private enterprise was permitted at the local and retail levels. Farmland remained in private hands, but rural cooperatives were officially encouraged.

In other respects, Nehru was a devotee of Western materialism. He was fully convinced that to succeed, India must industrialize. In advocating industrialization, Nehru departed sharply from Gandhi. Gandhi believed firmly that materialism was morally corrupting and that only simplicity and nonviolence (as represented by the traditional Indian village and his symbolic spinning wheel) could save India, and the world itself, from self-destruction (see the box on p. 1153). Nehru, however, had little fear of the corrupting consequences of material wealth and complained that Gandhi "just wants to spin and weave." Accordingly, Nehru actively pursued industrialization, although he recognized that a more efficient agricultural sector was a prerequisite for success. He attempted to bring about agricultural reforms through voluntary cooperatives and government assistance. Reflecting the strong anticolonialist views of the Congress leadership, the Indian government also sought to avoid excessive dependence upon foreign investment and technological assistance. All business enterprises were required by law to have majority Indian ownership.

LEADER OF THE THIRD WORLD

Nehru's staunch sense of morality was also apparent in his foreign policy. Under his guidance, India adopted a neutral posture in the Cold War and sought to provide leadership to all newly independent nations in Asia, Africa, and Latin America. The primary themes of Indian foreign policy were anticolonialism and antiracism. This neutral and independent stance quickly placed India in opposition to the United States, which during the 1950s was trying to mobilize all nations against what it viewed as the menace of international communism. India stood equidistant between the two superpowers and tried to establish good relations with the new People's Republic of China.

Although India sought to represent the needs and aspirations of all developing nations, this does not mean that Indian leaders did not look out for their country's own self-interest. In fact, like many other modern governments, India often used morality for its own purposes. Thus, India's opposition to the remnants of colonialism became a justification for resorting to force to evict the Portuguese from their tiny enclave in Goa in 1960. India also refused to consider Pakistan's claim to Kashmir even though the majority of the population there were

❧ Nehru's Program for India ❧

Before World War II, Jawaharlal Nehru was a leading member of the Indian National Congress and an outspoken advocate of independence from British colonial rule. He rejected not only Western imperialism, but also the capitalist system that underlay the drive for empire. Nehru saw socialism as the answer for India, but rejected the Soviet form in favor of a more moderate version that respected Western democratic principles and the concept of private property. The following excerpt is from a speech Nehru delivered to leading members of the Congress as its newly elected president in 1936.

Nehru's Socialist Creed

I am convinced that the only key to the solution of the world's problems and of India's problems lies in socialism, and when I use this word I do so not in a vague humanitarian way but in the scientific economic sense. Socialism is, however, something even more than an economic doctrine; it is a philosophy of life and as such also it appeals to me. I see no way of ending the poverty, the vast unemployment, the degradation and the subjection of the Indian people except through socialism. That involves vast and revolutionary changes in our political and social structure, the ending of vested interests in land and industry, as well as the feudal and autocratic Indian states system. That means the ending of private property, except in a restricted sense, and the replacement of the present profit system by a higher ideal of cooperative service. It means ultimately a change in our instincts and habits and desires. In short, it means a new civilization, radically different from the present capitalist order. Some glimpse we can have of this new civilization in the territories of the U.S.S.R. Much has happened there which has pained me greatly and with which I disagree, but I look upon that great and fascinating unfolding of a new order and a new civilization as the most promising feature of our dismal age. If the future is full of hope it is largely because of Soviet Russia and what it has done, and I am convinced that, if some world catastrophe does not intervene, this new civilization will spread to other lands and put an end to the wars and conflicts which capitalism feeds.

I do not know how or when this new order will come to India. I imagine that every country will fashion it after its own way and fit it in with its national genius. But the essential basis of that order must remain and be a link in the world order that will emerge out of the present chaos. Socialism is thus for me not merely an economic doctrine which I favor; it is a vital creed which I hold with all my head and heart. I work for Indian independence because the nationalist in me cannot tolerate an alien domination; I work for it even more because for me it is the inevitable step to social and economic change. I should like the Congress to become a socialist organization and to join hands with the other forces that in the world are working for the new civilization. But I realize that the majority in the Congress, as it is constituted today, may not be prepared to go thus far. We are a nationalist organization and we think and work on the nationalist plane. It is evident enough now that this is too narrow even for the limited objective of political independence, and so we talk of the masses and their economic needs. But still most of us hesitate, because of our nationalist backgrounds, to take a step which might frighten away some vested interests. Most of those interests are already ranged against us and we can expect little from them except opposition even in the political struggle.

Much as I wish for the advancement of socialism in this country, I have no desire to force the issue on the Congress and thereby create difficulties in the way of our struggle for independence. I shall cooperate gladly and with all the strength in me with all those who work for independence even though they do not agree with the socialist solution. But I shall do so stating my position frankly and hoping in course of time to convert the Congress and the country to it, for only thus can I see it achieving independence.

❧ Gandhi's Vision for India ❧

Where Nehru saw socialism as the answer for India's ills, Gandhi found it in the traditional village. Where Nehru favored industrialization to achieve material affluence, Gandhi praised the simple virtues of manual labor. Gandhi wrote this letter to Nehru in October 1945. A little over two years later, Gandhi was dead of an assassin's bullet, and Nehru was about to become prime minister of an independent Republic of India.

A Letter to Jawaharlal Nehru

Chi. Jawaharlal,

I have long been intending to write to you but can do so only today. I have also been wondering whether I should write in English or Hindustani. In the end I have decided to write in Hindustani.

I take first the sharp difference of opinion that has arisen between us. . . . I believe that if India, and through India the world, is to achieve real freedom, then sooner or later we shall have to go and live in the villages—in huts, not in palaces. Millions of people can never live in cities and palaces in comfort and peace. Nor can they do so by killing one another, that is, by resorting to violence and untruth. I have not the slightest doubt that, but for the pair, truth and non-violence, mankind will be doomed. We can have the vision of that truth and non-violence only in the simplicity of the villages. That simplicity resides in the spinning-wheel and what is implied by the spinning-wheel. It does not frighten me at all that the world seems to be going in the opposite direction. For the matter of that, when the moth approaches its doom it whirls round faster and faster till it is burnt up. It is possible that India will not be able to escape this moth-like circling. It is my duty to try, till my last breath, to save India and through it the world from such a fate. The sum and substance of what I want to say is that the individual person should have control over the things that are necessary for the sustenance of life. If he cannot have such control the individual can-

not survive. Ultimately, the world is made up only of individuals. If there were no drops there would be no ocean. . . .

You will not be able to understand me if you think that I am talking about the villages of today. My ideal village still exists only in my imagination. After all every human being lives in the world of his own imagination. In this village of my dreams the villager will not be dull—he will be all awareness. He will not live like an animal in filth and darkness. Men and women will live in freedom, prepared to face the whole world. There will be no plague, no cholera and no smallpox. Nobody will be allowed to be idle or to wallow in luxury. Everyone will have to do body labour. Granting all this, I can still envisage a number of things that will have to be organized on a large scale. Perhaps there will even be railways and also post and telegraph offices. I do not know what things there will be or will not be. Nor am I bothered about it. If I can make sure of the essential thing, other things will follow in due course. But if I give up the essential thing, I give up everything.

I want that we two should understand each other fully. And this for two reasons. Our bond is not merely political. It is much deeper. I have no measure to fathom that depth. This bond can never be broken. I therefore want that we should understand each other thoroughly in politics as well. The second reason is that neither of us considers himself as worthless. We both live only for India's freedom, and will be happy to die too for that freedom. We do not care for praise from any quarter. Praise or abuse are the same to us. They have no place in the mission of service. Though I aspire to live up to 125 years rendering service, I am nevertheless an old man, while you are comparatively young. That is why I have said that you are my heir. It is only proper that I should at least understand my heir and my heir in turn should understand me. I shall then be at peace.

Muslims. Tension between the two countries increased during the early 1960s, leading to war in 1965. India won a quick victory, and a cease-fire was signed in the Soviet city of Tashkent. Nevertheless, the sources of mutual hostility were not resolved, and when riots against the Pakistani government broke out in East Pakistan in 1971, India intervened on the side of East Pakistan, which declared its independence as the new nation of Bangladesh.

India also encountered difficulties with China. Nehru had attempted to conciliate the Chinese government by supporting its demand for admission into the United Nations and recognizing Chinese sovereignty over the province of Tibet. But when China cracked down on Tibetan autonomy in the late 1950s, India was severely critical. Shortly after, Nehru became aware that China was constructing a road in an area of Tibet claimed by India.

◆ **Portrait of Indira Gandhi.** After Nehru's death in 1964, India's next great leader was his daughter Indira Gandhi, who became prime minister in 1966. Gandhi sought to realize her father's ideal of building an industrialized society until her assassination by her own Sikh bodyguards in 1984.

When India sent troops to the area in the late summer of 1962, Chinese forces crossed the border and drove them back. A cease-fire was reached, but the border dispute, a consequence of boundaries drawn by a British surveying team at the beginning of the century, was not resolved.

The Post-Nehru Era

Nehru's death in 1964 aroused widespread anxiety, since many observers speculated that Indian democracy was dependent upon the Nehru mystique. When his successor, the soft-spoken Congress Party veteran Lal Bahadur Shastri, died in 1966, Congress leaders selected Nehru's daughter, Indira Gandhi (no relation to Mahatma Gandhi), as the new prime minister. Gandhi (1917–1984) was inexperienced in politics, and many thought the party bosses had chosen her because she would be easy to dominate, but she quickly showed the steely determination of her father.

In a number of respects, Gandhi followed her father's footsteps, embracing democratic socialism and a policy of neutrality in foreign affairs. If anything, she was more activist than her father. Concerned that rural poverty had become chronic, she launched a major program to reduce it, nationalizing banks, providing loans to peasants on easy terms, building low-cost housing, and distributing land to the landless. As part of the land redistribution program, she attempted to lower existing ceilings on landholdings to one hundred acres per family. She also introduced electoral reforms to enfranchise the poor.

Gandhi was especially worried by India's growing population, which was increasing at an annual rate of over 2 percent. To curb the rate of growth, she adopted a policy of enforced sterilization. This policy proved unpopular, however, and along with growing official corruption and Gandhi's authoritarian tactics and intolerance of opposition, led to her defeat in the general elections in 1975, the first time the Congress Party had failed to win a majority at the national level since independence. Congress also lost control of a number of state governments, where regional and ethnic parties were gaining strength.

A minority government of procapitalist parties was formed under Prime Minister Morarji Desai (b. 1896), who attempted to reverse India's steady drift toward socialism. But India's first non-Congress government lacked the competence and experience to handle the country's enormous problems, and within two years Gandhi was back in power with an increased electoral mandate. She now faced a new challenge, however, in the rise of ethnic and religious strife. The most dangerous situation was in the Punjab, where militant Sikhs were demanding autonomy or even independence for their province from India. Gandhi did not shrink from a confrontation and attacked Sikh rebels hiding in their Golden Temple in the city of Amritsar. The incident aroused widespread anger among the Sikh community, and in 1984 Sikh members of Gandhi's personal bodyguard assassinated her.

By now, Congress politicians were convinced that the party could not remain in power without a member of the Nehru family at the helm. Gandhi's son Sanjay, the original heir apparent, had been killed in a plane crash. Now her elder son Rajiv (1944–1991), a commercial airline pilot with little apparent interest in politics, was persuaded to replace his mother as prime minister. As a politician, Rajiv lacked the strong ideological and political convictions of his mother and grandfather and proceeded to allow a greater role for private enterprise. But his government was harshly criticized for cronyism, inefficiency, and corruption, as well as insensitivity to the poor. It steadily lost its political dominance over India, particularly at the local level.

In the late 1980s, India faced a new problem, as the neighboring island of Sri Lanka (previously known as Ceylon) was torn with violence between the majority Sinhalese, who are Buddhist, and the Tamils, a racial and religious minority (most Tamils are Hindus) living primarily in the northern part of the island. The leading Tamil rebel organization, which called itself the Elam Tigers of Tamil Elam, sought support and sanctuary in the southern Indian province of Tamil Nadu, where the population is ethnically related. In an effort to reduce the violence, India sent troops to Sri Lanka to suppress the rebels. While campaigning for reelection in the spring of 1991, Rajiv Gandhi was assassinated, reportedly by a member of the Tiger organization. For almost the first time since independence, India faced the future without a member of the Nehru family as prime minister. Desperate, Congress leaders even considered conferring the premiership on Rajiv's Italian widow.

In the years immediately following the assassination of Rajiv Gandhi, Congress remained the leading party, but the powerful hold it once enjoyed over the Indian electorate was gone. Rising new parties, such as the militantly Hindu Bharata Janata Party (BJP), actively vied with Congress for control of the central and state governments.

In national elections held in May 1996, the Congress Party was badly defeated and Prime Minister Narasimha Rao (b. 1921) resigned from office. But the BJP, which had failed to win a majority in the new legislature, was

CHRONOLOGY

South Asia

India and Pakistan become independent	1947
Assassination of Mahatma Gandhi	January 1948
Indian seizure of Goa	1960
Sino-Indian border war	1962
Death of Jawaharlal Nehru	1964
Indo-Pakistani War	1965
Indira Gandhi elected prime minister	1966
Bangladesh declares its independence	1971
Assassination of Indira Gandhi	1984
Rajiv Gandhi assassinated	1991
Destruction of mosque at Ayodhya	1992
Benazir Bhutto removed from power in Pakistan	1997

unable to form a government, and in the end a coalition government of left and center political groups was formed. Bickering within the coalition has been intense, however, while the Congress Party, with its president Narasimha Rao under investigation for corruption, tries to get its own house in order. Growing political instability at the center has been accompanied by rising ethnic tensions between Hindus and Muslims (see The Politics of Communalism later in this chapter). In the city of Bombay, the militantly Hindu Shiv Sena (Army of Siva) Party, which bluntly rejects the Gandhian vision of ethnic and racial harmony, has attacked Muslim and foreign interests. Although economic growth has continued at a gratifying pace, the growing signs of political and religious strife are disturbing.

The Land of the Pure: Pakistan since Independence

In August 1947, the new nation of Pakistan declared its independence. Unlike its neighbor India, Pakistan was in all respects a new nation, based on religious conviction rather than historical or ethnic tradition. Comprising

❧ The Soul of Islam ❧

The poet Muhammad Iqbal was the prophet of Islam in the Indian subcontinent and a major voice in the struggle for a Muslim state of Pakistan. In the following passage from his poem Mysteries of Selflessness, Iqbal called on his fellow Muslims to transcend the narrow bonds of regionalism and nationalism and find a sense of unity in the community of Islam.

Muhammad Iqbal, *The Mysteries of Selflessness*

A common aim shared by the multitude
Is unity which, when it is mature,
Forms the Community; the many live
Only by virtue of the single bond.
The Muslim's unity from natural faith
Derives, and this the Prophet taught us,
So that we lit a lantern on truth's way. . . .

Muslims Profess No Fatherland

Our Essence is not bound to any place;
The vigor of our wine is not contained
In any bowl; Chinese and Indian
Alike the shard that constitutes our jar,
Turkish and Syrian alike the clay
Forming our body; neither is our heart
Of India, or Syria, or Rum,
Nor any fatherland do we profess
Except Islam.

The Concept of Country Divides Humanity

Now brotherhood has been so cut to shreds
That in the stead of community

The country has been given pride of place
In men's allegiance and constructive work;
The country is the darling of their hearts,
And wide humanity is whittled down
Into dismembered tribes. . . .
Vanished is humankind; there but abide
The disunited nations. Politics
Dethroned religion. . . .

The Muslim Community Is Unbounded in Time

. . . When the burning brands
Of time's great revolution ring our mead,
Then Spring returns. The mighty power of Rome,
Conqueror and ruler of the world entire,
Sank into small account; the golden glass
Of the Sassanians was drowned in blood;
Broken the brilliant genius of Greece;
Egypt too failed in the great test of time,
Her bones lie buried neath the pyramids.
Yet still the voice of the muezzin rings
Throughout the earth, still the Community
Of World-Islam maintains its ancient forms.
Love is the universal law of life,
Mingling the fragmentary elements
Of a disordered world. Through our hearts' glow
Love lives, irradiated by the spark
There is no god but God.

two separate territories two thousand miles apart, Pakistan by its very nature was unique and distinctive. West Pakistan, including the basin of the Indus River and the West Punjab, was perennially short of water and was populated by dry crop farmers and peoples of the steppe. East Pakistan, comprising the eastern parts of the old Indian province of Bengal, was made up of the marshy deltas of the Ganges and Brahmaputra Rivers. Densely populated with rice farmers, it was the home of the artistic and intellectual Bengalis.

From its very origins, the new state was a product of the Muslims' wish to have their own state. Among the first to express this desire was Muhammad Iqbal

(1873–1938), who founded the Muslim League in 1907 and became one of South Asia's greatest poets. He helped keep the dream alive during the final years of colonial rule (see the box above).

Yet from the start, Pakistan's leaders made it clear that they did not intend to carry the logic of the Muslim League's demand for an Islamic state to extremes. Muhammed Ali Jinnah set the tone in a speech that he gave in August 1947 before a constitutional assembly convened to prepare for the transition to independence. Conceding that many had opposed the division of British India into two separate states, he argued that no other solution was possible. A united India, he maintained, would have been a "terrific disaster." Yet Jinnah insisted that now that the independence of Pakistan had been secured, it must "bury the hatchet" with the new Indian republic and concentrate on the well-being of the people. India had been conquered, he warned, because the Indian people had allowed themselves to be divided. Now Pakistan must assure freedom of religion and equal treatment for all.[3]

Muhammed Ali Jinnah's vision of a democratic society based on equal treatment for all citizens was only partly realized. The bitter division between advocates of a state based on Islamic principles and supporters of a Western-style democracy resulted in a compromise. The Constitution of 1956 described Pakistan as an "Islamic Republic, under the sovereignty of Allah," where Muslims could live their lives in accordance with "the Holy Qur'an and the Sunnah." Even though Pakistan was an essentially Muslim society, its first years were marked by intense internal conflicts over linguistic, religious, and regional issues. Most dangerous was the growing division between east and west. Many in East Pakistan felt that the government, based in the west, ignored the needs of the eastern section of the country. In 1952, riots erupted in East Pakistan over the government's decision to adopt Urdu (a Muslim version of Hindi) as the national language of the entire country. Most East Pakistanis spoke Bengali, an unrelated language. In 1958, the civilian government was overthrown by a military coup led by General Ayub Khan. Khan expressed his views as follows:

> My task, as I saw it, was to set up institutions which should enable the people of Pakistan to develop their material, moral and intellectual resources and capacities to the maximum extent. . . . I could not convince myself that we had become a nation in the real sense of the word; the whole spectacle was one of disunity and disintegration. We were divided in two halves, each half dominated by a distinct linguistic and cultural pattern. . . .[4]

Khan believed the answer to the disunity lay in a greater emphasis on law and order and less on Western-style democratic procedures. His regime dissolved the constitution and set up a new system called "Basic Democracy" with a strong central government and a limited franchise of under 100,000 voters. But the new military government was unable to curb the religious and ethnic tensions, and in 1969 Khan stepped down in favor of one of his key supporters, General Muhammad Yahya Khan.

In elections for the National Assembly in 1970, supporters of autonomy led by Sheikh Mujibur Rahman of the Awami League won a majority in East Pakistan. The Pakistani People's Party led by the populist Zulfikar Ali Bhutto (1928–1979) won a similar majority in the west, but the military government refused to step down and declared martial law. In March 1971, negotiations between representatives of east and west broke down, and East Pakistan declared its independence as the new nation of Bangladesh. Pakistani troops arrested Mujibur Rahman and attempted to restore central government authority in the capital of Dacca, but rebel forces supported by India went on the offensive, and General Yahya Khan, who had earlier declared that "no power on earth" could separate East and West Pakistan, bowed to the inevitable. Sheikh Mujibur Rahman was released and soon became the first prime minister of the new nation of Bangladesh.

The breakup of the union between East and West Pakistan undermined the fragile authority of the military regime and led to its replacement by a civilian government under Zulfikar Ali Bhutto. But the religious tensions persisted despite a new constitution that made a number of key concessions to conservative Muslims. In 1977, a new military government under General Zia Ul Ha'q came to power with a commitment to make Pakistan a truly Islamic state. Islamic law became the basis for social behavior as well as for the legal system. Laws governing the consumption of alcohol and the position of women were tightened in accordance with strict Muslim beliefs, and Zia promised a government that would conform to Islamic principles. But after Zia was killed in a plane crash, Pakistanis elected Benazir Bhutto (b. 1953), the daughter of Zulfikar Ali Bhutto and a supporter of secularism who had been educated in the United States. She too was removed from power by a military regime in 1990 on charges of incompetence and corruption. Reelected in 1993, she attempted to crack down on opposition forces, but was removed once again by President Farooq Leghari amid widespread jubilation and renewed charges of official corruption.

Problems of Poverty and Pluralism in South Asia

The leaders of the new states that emerged in South Asia after World War II all hoped that with independence their peoples would enjoy prosperity, popular participation, and national unity. Although their approaches varied, all declared their intention to build modern states based on some adaptation of the Western model. They faced a number of problems distinctive to their part of the world, however. A century of British rule had changed the subcontinent in many ways, but some basic historical realities remained. The peoples of South Asia were still overwhelmingly poor and illiterate, while the sectarian, ethnic, and cultural divisions that had plagued Indian society for centuries had not dissipated. It was a daunting challenge for even the most self-confident of political leaders.

The Politics of Communalism

Like most leaders throughout Asia and Africa, South Asian leaders tried to broaden popular participation in government and establish democratic institutions and values. Perhaps the most sincere effort was in India, where Nehru's government enacted a new constitution in 1950 that called for social justice, liberty, equality of status and opportunity, and fraternity.

The new Indian government followed the British parliamentary model. At the pinnacle was a president whose power, like that of the British monarch, was ceremonial. Executive authority was lodged in a prime minister operating through a cabinet called the Council of Ministers. Sovereignty was located in the lower house of parliament, called the Lok Sabha, or House of the Peoples. India became a federation with power divided between the central government and fifteen separate states; in addition, a number of "union territories" were administered by the central government. Residual powers were assigned to the central government. The one-time princely states remained under the authority of their maharajahs, while the president appointed governors for the other states for five-year terms. Regardless of population, all states had the same number of representatives in the Council of States, the upper chamber of parliament.

The constitution also reflected Western models in its protection of human rights. All citizens were guaranteed protection from discrimination on the grounds of religious belief, race, caste, sex, or place of birth. The curse of untouchability was expressly forbidden (the constitution had been drafted under the direction of an untouchable, Bhimrao Ambedkar). Another clause embodied an early form of affirmative action: if any group was inadequately represented in public service positions, the government was empowered to enact legislation that would allow citizens of that group to be favored in future appointments.

In theory, then, India became a full-fledged democracy on the Western model. In actuality, a number of distinctive characteristics may have made the system less than fully democratic (at least in the Western sense) but may also have enabled it to survive. Though pluralist in design, India became in essence a one-party state for several years. By leading the independence movement, the Congress Party had amassed massive public support, and in the first general elections in 1951, it won a smashing victory, securing three-quarters of the seats in the new Lok Sabha as well as control of the legislative assemblies in all the states.

The party retained its preeminent position in Indian politics over the next three decades, although the percentage of Congress representation in the Lok Sabha gradually began to decline. The party benefited from Nehru's personal popularity and from his ability to position the party in the middle of the political spectrum, while rivals like the Communist Party of India (CPI) on the left and the Swatantra Freedom Party on the right moved to the extremes. Congress also avoided being identified as a party exclusively for the Hindu majority by including prominent non-Hindus among its leaders and favoring measures to protect minority groups like the Sikhs and the Muslims from discrimination.

Through such adept maneuvering, Nehru kept his party in power through three general elections until his death in 1964; he also lost only one state election—to the Communists in the southern state of Kerala. But Nehru's success disguised the weakening of his party and the entire democratic political system that took place under his rule. Part of the problem was the familiar one of a party too long in power. Entering office with enthusiasm and high ideals, party officials became complacent in their secure positions and all too easily fell prey to the temptations of corruption and pork barrel politics. Although the Congress Party sincerely sought to speak for all people, especially the poor and disadvantaged, many party deputies came from privileged backgrounds and had little in common with their constituents.

Another problem was that of communalism. Beneath the surface unity of the new republic lay age-old ethnic, linguistic, and religious divisions. Although the government was reasonably successful in avoiding internecine religious conflict, regional and linguistic tensions were more difficult to surmount. Because of India's vast size and complex history, no national language had ever emerged from the plethora of tongues and dialects scattered throughout the subcontinent. Hindi, spoken mainly in the upper Ganges valley, was the most prevalent, but it was the native language of less than one-third of the population. During the colonial period, English had served as the official language of government, and many non-Hindi speakers in Bengal and the southern states preferred making it the official language of independent India to avoid favoring some Indians over others. But English had its own difficulties. It was spoken only by the educated elite, and it represented an affront to national pride. Eventually, India recognized fourteen official tongues, making the Lok Sabha sometimes sound like the proverbial Tower of Babel.

These problems increased after Nehru's death in 1964. Under his successors, official corruption grew, and Congress began to look like a tired party that had forgotten its ideals. Only the limited appeal of its rivals and the magic of the Nehru name carried on by his daughter Indira Gandhi kept the party in power. But Gandhi was unable to prevent the progressive disintegration of the party's power base at the state level, where regional parties (such as in Tamil Nadu in the south) or ideological ones (such as the Communists in Bengal) won the allegiance of the local population by exploiting ethnic or social revolutionary themes.

During the 1980s, religious tensions began to intensify, not only among Sikhs in the northwest but also between Hindus and Muslims. As we have seen, Gandhi's uncompromising approach to Sikh separatism led to her assassination in 1984. Under her son and successor Rajiv Gandhi, Hindu militants at Ayodhya in northern India demanded the destruction of a mosque built on the alleged site of King Rama's birthplace, where a Hindu temple had previously existed. The mosque had reportedly been built at the order of Emperor Babur, but was now little used. Eventually, the dispute became involved in national politics, as both the Congress Party and its rivals, hoping to cultivate support among the Muslim minority, leaned to the Muslim side. In 1992, Hindu demonstrators destroyed the mosque and erected a temporary temple at the site, provoking widespread clashes between Hindus and Muslims throughout the country and shaking the Congress government of Narasimha Rao. In protest, rioters in neighboring Pakistan destroyed a number of Hindu shrines in that country. As we have seen, India's involvement in similar ethnic strife in Sri Lanka may have led to the assassination of Rajiv Gandhi in 1991.

During the mid-1990s, communal divisions have continued to intensify. As we have seen, ethnic and religious tensions are one element in the debate. Militant Hindu groups centered around the figure of Shiv Sena leader Balasaheb Thackeray, the self-styled "Hitler of Bombay," have been agitating for a state that caters to the interests and aspirations of the Hindu majority, now numbering over 700 million people. During the recent parliamentary debate over the formation of a new government in May 1996 (see The Post-Nehru Era earlier in the chapter), opposition figures criticizes the BJP for its role in fomenting anti-Muslim riots during the Ayodhya incident, as well as for its demand that all education throughout the country take place in Hindi, even though that language is spoken widely only in areas with Hindu majorities in the north.

In recent years, the issue of caste has emerged as an equally serious source of tension in Indian politics. Inspired by political figures like the "bandit queen" Phoolan Devi, low-caste Indians are beginning to use the political process to struggle against the legacy of restrictions on their activities. Phoolan Devi spent several years in jail on the charge of taking part in the murder of twenty men from a landowning caste in the early 1980s. Members of the caste had allegedly gang-raped her when she was an adolescent. Her successful campaign for office during the 1996 elections was the occasion of violent arguments between her supporters and opponents.

One of Phoolan Devi's sponsors is Laloo Prasad Yadav, onetime chief minister of the state of Bihar in the Ganges River valley. Yadav openly invokes the memory of Mahatma Gandhi to promote the interests of the poor in his province. "I am fighting against evil," he remarked in a recent interview, "the evil of upper-caste domination of the backward and the downtrodden. And of course, the upper-caste people hate me. Now, they are thinking, he will be Prime Minister, and we will be slaves."[5]

Indian politics is thus assuming an increasingly class-based character, as members of the lower castes, who represent over 80 percent of the voting public, begin to demand affirmative action to relieve their disabilities and a more equal share of the national wealth. Officials at U.S. consulates in India have reportedly noticed an increase in applications for visas from members of the brahmin class, who claim that they have "no future" in the new India.

The Economy

India's new leaders after independence also realized the necessity of eliminating the social and economic inequality that had afflicted the subcontinent for centuries. Nehru's answer was socialism. Like many leaders of the Indian National Congress, he had been repelled by the excesses of European capitalism and impressed with the egalitarian principles of Marxism. Mahatma Gandhi had tapped similar sources of human idealism when he appealed for an end to the materialism, greed, and social inequality that plagued modern society. Gandhi, however, did not find the answer in Marx. In a letter to a friend in 1944, he remarked that during a recent stay in jail he had read about Marx and the Soviet experiment in Russia: "What a difference between our spinning-wheel and their machines driven by steam or electricity." Nevertheless, he added, "I prefer the snail-like speed of the spinning-wheel. The spinning-wheel is a symbol of *ahimsa* [nonviolence], and ultimately it is ahimsa that will triumph."[6]

As we have seen, Nehru did not share Gandhi's glorification of poverty. He wanted equality at a higher level of material affluence and was attracted by Lenin's effort to combine socialist ownership with industrialization (see the box on p. 1152). Nehru therefore instituted a series of five-year plans, which achieved some success. During the first decades of independence, India developed a relatively large and reasonably efficient industrial sector, centered on steel, vehicles, and textiles. Industrial production almost tripled between 1950 and 1965, while per capita income rose by 50 percent between 1950 and 1980, although it was still below U.S. $300.

By the 1970s, however, industrial growth had slowed down. The lack of a modern, efficient infrastructure (for transportation and communications, for example) was a problem, as was the rising price of oil, most of which had to be imported. Another problem was the relative weakness of the state-owned sector, which grew at an annual rate of only about 2 percent in the 1950s and 1960s while the private sector averaged rates of over 5 percent. By the 1980s, many Indian officials and economists began to recommend returning some state-owned enterprises to the private sector.

India's major economic weakness, however, was its agriculture. At independence, rural production techniques were still overwhelmingly primitive. Mechanization was almost unknown, fertilizer was rarely used, and most farms were small and uneconomical due to the Hindu tradition of dividing the land equally among all male children. As a result, the vast majority of the Indian people lived in conditions of abject poverty. Landless laborers outnumbered landowners by almost two to one.

The government attempted to relieve the problem by limiting the size of landholdings, thereby forcing a redistribution of land to the poor, while encouraging farmers to form voluntary cooperatives. But both programs ran into widespread opposition and apathy. The government encouraged the states to enact legislation restricting the maximum amount of land that an individual could possess, but many landlords evaded the law by distributing their lands among members of their family. As a result, in many instances tenants were evicted from lands they had farmed for years. In one village, the sociologist Kusum Nair found two hundred families who had been deprived of their tenancy rights and reduced to working as coolies. Nor was legal action a remedy. In *Blossoms in the Dust*, Nair quoted one man as saying: "Not a single man in this village has or will benefit by the land reforms. The tenants were so convinced that even if they went to court or to the tribunal the case would be decided in favour of the

◆ **An Indian Village.** Nearly 80 percent of the Indian people still live in traditional rural villages such as the one shown here. Housing styles, village customs, and methods of farming have changed little since they were first described by Portuguese travelers in the sixteenth century. Note the thatched roofs and the mud and straw walls plastered with dung that have been used in constructing these houses.

landowner that they thought it wiser to negotiate and come to terms with the landowner. So they got as much cash as they could out of him and surrendered their tenancy."[7]

Farmers were equally skeptical of the cooperatives. As one farmer said, many feared that "everyone will leave it to the other to do the work and shirk his own responsibility." Some complained that the government had attempted to consolidate landholdings by compulsory measures, and that the cooperatives were always tied up in red tape and litigation. Better, they said, to return to the old system of *zamindars*, which were at least considerate of the needs of the individual farmer. To a considerable extent, these views simply reflect the conservatism and suspicion of any change that are sometimes characteristic of farmers, but they also reveal the difficulty that the government encountered in changing attitudes in rural India.

Another crucial problem India faced was overpopulation. Even before independence, drought, soil erosion, and primitive mechanization made it difficult for the country to support its population of nearly 400 million. In the 1950s and 1960s, the population increased at a rate of over 2 percent annually. The annual rate of population growth increased from nine per thousand in the nineteenth century to over twenty per thousand in the 1960s. The fundamental problem, said economist Jan Myrdal, was not governmental indifference. Conditions in South Asian villages were not conducive to birth control:

Up to a point, bearing and rearing children can even be looked on as an investment; they offer a measure of security in illness and old age, and frequently begin to lighten their parents' work load while still in early childhood. Comparatively speaking, the setting of South Asian life is such that children are expected to fulfill obligations to parents more than parents to children.[8]

Beginning in the 1960s, the Indian government began to adopt stiff measures to curb population growth. Indira Gandhi instituted a program combining monetary rewards and compulsory sterilization. Males who had fathered too many children were sometimes forced to undergo a vasectomy. Popular resistance undermined the program, however, and the goals were scaled back in the 1970s. Despite such efforts, India has made little progress in holding down its burgeoning population, now estimated at over 700 million. One factor is the decline in the death rate and in the rate of infant mortality. Whereas life expectancy for the average Indian was less than thirty years in 1947, by the 1990s it had risen to nearly fifty.

The "Green Revolution" of the 1970s at least reduced the severity of the population problem. The introduction of new strains of rice and wheat that were more productive and more disease-resistant significantly increased grain production from about 50 million tons per year in 1950 to 100 million in 1970. But the Green Revolution

◆ **India's Hope, India's Sorrow.** In India, as in many other societies in southern Asia, overpopulation is a serious obstacle to economic development. The problem is particularly serious in large cities, where thousands of poor children are forced into begging or prostitution. Shown here are a few of the thousands of street children in Bombay.

exacted its own cost in the form of increased rural inequality. Only the wealthy and more enterprising peasants were able to master the new techniques and purchase the necessary fertilizer, while poor peasants were often driven off the land. Millions fled to the cities, where they live in vast slums, working at menial jobs or even begging for a living. After the death of Indira Gandhi in 1984, her son Rajiv proved more receptive to foreign investment and a greater role for the private sector in the economy. Limitations on imports of consumer goods from abroad were loosened, and beggars were driven away from the downtown streets of major cities. The results were quickly apparent. In urban areas, the pace of manufacturing and commercial activity quickened, and a newly affluent middle class began to take on the characteristics of a consumer society. India began to export more manufactured goods such as computer software and produced more motor scooters than any other country in the world.

The pace of change has accelerated under Rajiv Gandhi's successors, who have continued to transfer state-run industries into private hands and rely on the free market for the allocation of resources. This has stimulated the growth of India's new prosperous middle class, now estimated at over 100 million, or 12 percent of the entire population. Consumerism, reflected by the sight of Rajiv Gandhi abandoning the traditional *dhoti* and sport-ing designer loafers and sunglasses, has soared, and sales of television sets, automobiles, videocassette recorders, and telephones have increased dramatically in recent years. Equally important, Western imports are being replaced by new products manufactured in India with Indian brand names.

The trend toward privatization and the increase in foreign investment have probably helped to stimulate the growth of the industrial sector, estimated at over 8 percent in 1994 and 1995. But the pull of Nehru's dream of a socialist society remains strong. State-owned enterprises still account for about one-half of all goods produced in the country, while high tariffs continue to stifle imports. There is widespread concern about foreign influence over the economy, a fear eagerly exploited by nationalist parties, which have brought about the cancellation of some contracts with foreign companies and forced other foreign firms to relocate. In one celebrated case, a combination of religious and environmental groups attempted unsuccessfully to prevent Kentucky Fried Chicken from establishing outlets in major Indian cities (see the box on p. 1163).

As in the industrialized countries in the West, economic growth has been accompanied by environmental damage. Water and air pollution, as well as the leakage of chemicals in industrial zones, have led to illness and death for many people living in the vicinity, and a new

◆ **Bombay, Hollywood of the East.** India produces more movies than any other country in the world, including the United States. The capital of the Indian film industry is Bombay, which is sometimes dubbed India's "Bollywood." Shown here is a billboard in downtown Bombay.

❦ Say No to McDonald's! ❧

One of the consequences of Rajiv Gandhi's decision to deregulate the Indian economy has been an increase in the presence of foreign corporations, including the U.S. fast-food restaurants Pizza Hut and Kentucky Fried Chicken. Their arrival set off a storm of protest in India: from environmentalists concerned that raising grain for chickens is an inefficient use of land, from religious activists angry at the killing of animals for food, and from nationalists anxious to protect the domestic market from foreign competition. The author of this piece, which appeared in a June 1995 issue of the Hindustan Times, *was Maneka Gandhi, a daughter-in-law of Indira Gandhi and a onetime minister of the environment.*

Why India Doesn't Need Fast Food

India's decision to allow Pepsi Foods Ltd. to open 60 restaurants in India—30 each of Pizza Hut and Kentucky Fried Chicken—marks the first entry of multinational, meat-based junk-food chains into India. If this is allowed to happen, at least a dozen other similar chains will very quickly arrive, including the infamous McDonald's.

The implications of allowing junk-food chains into India are quite stark. As the name denotes, the foods served at Kentucky Fried Chicken (KFC) are chicken-based and fried. This is the worst combination possible for the body and can create a host of health problems, including obesity, high cholesterol, heart ailments, and many kinds of cancer. Pizza Hut products are a combination of white flour, cheese, and meat—again, a combination likely to cause disease.

A recent survey by the British Broadcasting Corp. (BBC) reported that, in America, 80 million people are obese and prone to cardiovascular and other diseases. These people spend almost one fifth of their incomes on medicines—often to cure ailments related to junk foods from chains such as KFC, Pizza Hut, and McDonald's. The BBC stated that a large number of diseases simply did not exist until these meat-based junk-food chains came in. Is this what we want for our new generation? . . .

Can our health systems take care of the fallout from these chicken restaurants? If you were to argue that everyone in America is eating such foods, I would point you toward a 1992 U.S. Senate investigation revealing that one American contracts cancer every seven seconds. The culprits identified: processed meats and chicken from the junk-food industry.

Then there is the issue of the environmental impact of junk-food chains. Modern meat production involves misuse of crops, water, energy, and grazing areas. In addition, animal agriculture produces surprisingly large amounts of air and water pollution.

KFC and Pizza Hut insist that their chickens be fed corn and soybeans. Consider the diversion of grain for this purpose. As the outlets of KFC and Pizza Hut increase in number, the poultry industry will buy up more and more corn to feed the chickens, which means that the corn will quickly disappear from the villages, and its increased price will place it out of reach for the common man. Turning corn into junk chicken is like turning gold into mud.

Animal farms use mountains of grain. Nearly 40 percent of the world's grain is fed to livestock, according to U.S. Department of Agriculture data. Can India afford to feed so much grain to animals? It is already shameful that, in a country plagued by famine and flood, we divert 37 percent of our arable land to growing animal fodder. Were all of that grain to be consumed directly by humans, it would nourish five times as many people as it does after being converted into meat, milk, and eggs. . . .

Of course, it is not just the KFC and Pizza Hut chains of Pepsi Foods Ltd. that will cause all of this damage. Once we open India up by allowing these chains, dozens more will be eagerly waiting to come in. Each city in America has an average of 5,000 junk-food restaurants. Is that what we want for India?

environmental movement has emerged taking its cue and its tactics from similar movements in Europe and the United States. Some critics, reflecting the traditional anti-imperialist attitude of Indian intellectuals, blame Western capitalist corporations for the problem, as in the highly publicized case of leakage from the foreign-owned chemical plant at Bhopal. Much of the problem, however, comes from state-owned factories erected with Soviet aid. A recent "Citizen's Report" from the southeastern state of Andhra Pradesh charged that local developers were part of "an international network of capitalists, capitalist governments, military power, and bureaucratic steel frame [an apparent reference to the entrenched power of Indian officialdom]." But not all the environmental damage can be ascribed to industrialization. The Ganges River is so polluted by human overuse that it is risky for Hindu believers to bathe in it.[9]

Moreover, many Indians have not benefited from the new prosperity. The average annual income remains under $300 per person (in U.S. dollars), and nearly one-third of the population lives below the national poverty line. Millions continue to live in rural slums, such as the famous "City of Joy" in Calcutta, where thousands of families live in primitive shacks and lean-tos, sharing water and toilet facilities. And while a leisured class has begun to appear in the countryside, most farm families remain desperately poor. Despite the socialist rhetoric of Indira Gandhi and other national leaders, the inequality of wealth in India is as pronounced as it is in capitalist nations like the United States. Indeed, India has been described as two nations: an educated urban India of 100 million people surrounded by 600 million impoverished peasants in the countryside.

Caste, Class, and Gender

Drawing generalizations about the effect of these changes on the life of the average Indian is difficult due to the ethnic, religious, and caste differences among Indians. Furthermore, these differences are compounded by the vast gulf between town and country.

The major lines of division in traditional Indian society, of course, were those of class and caste. Caste membership determined all the crucial issues in life, including marriage, occupation, moral and social obligations, social status, and even eating habits. During the colonial period, the British government sporadically attempted to reduce the tyrannical hold of class restrictions on Indian society, but for the most part, it took an attitude of benign indifference. Efforts by high-class Hindus to bring about social reforms or help untouchables sometimes led to excommunication from their own caste.

The Constitution of 1950 accepted the reality of caste distinctions, but tried to eliminate their worst consequences. It guaranteed equal treatment and opportunity for all, regardless of caste, and prohibited discrimination based on untouchability, such as barring *harijans* from the village well or local restaurants. It set quotas for government service and membership in legislative assemblies as well as admission to institutions of higher learning.

But prejudice is hard to eliminate. Untouchability still persists, particularly in the villages, where *harijans* still perform menial tasks and are often denied fundamental human rights. Mistreatment and exploitation by landlords or government officials have led to protests and even violence in the countryside and have become a major issue in national politics. In 1990, Prime Minister V. P. Singh (b. 1931) attempted to woo untouchables from their traditional support for the Congress Party by acceding to their demands for higher quotas for entrance into the bureaucracy and the universities. The measure led to widespread protests by members of higher castes, who claimed to be victims of reverse discrimination. As we have seen, caste again became an issue in the 1996 elections.

In the cities, there appears to be more reason for cautious optimism. In general, urban Indians appear less conscious of caste distinctions. Material wealth rather than caste identity is increasingly beginning to define status. The days when high-class Indians refused to eat in a restaurant unless assured that the cook was a *brahmin* are gone. Marriage and choice of occupation are more subject to individual preference than in the past. Still, the legacy of tradition is difficult to shake. Color consciousness based on the age-old distinctions between upper-class Aryans and lower-class Dravidians remains strong. Class-conscious Hindus still express a distinct preference for light-skinned marital partners. Young Indians looking for a wife or husband sometimes place detailed advertisements in the newspapers. Among the attributes most often mentioned is a light skin.

For most Indians, then, caste is simply the reality of the world they live in. Many do not question it and assume that it is the consequence of behavior in a past incarnation. As one farmer said, "How can we get other people's lands? If we are destined to be landless we must remain so."

In economic terms, life has changed for the urban middle class, though not necessarily for the better. More income, combined with the presence of more foreign goods on the shelves, means refrigerators, color television sets, and videocassette recorders. In turn that leads to a consumer-oriented society and greater homogenization of culture. Young Indians like their counterparts elsewhere are increasingly interested in rock music and contemporary clothing styles. In that sense, the traditional ways are being steadily eroded.

Such changes have had less impact in the villages. While the newly affluent have become active consumers and often send their children to the cities to study and to live, the rural poor appear to live in conditions little changed from past generations. Although some progress has been made in education since independence, rural education has been neglected and thousands of villages remain without schools, and the graduation rate from primary school is only 37 percent compared to over 60 percent for all Asia. According to recent statistics, nearly 40 percent of the rural population lives below the poverty level; the vast majority live in mud-and-thatch dwellings without running water and electricity, without education, and frequently without hope. Their lives have been affected only minimally by the changes taking place in the cities or in the world beyond.

Even the villages, however, have seen changes in the role of women and sexual relationships, although in this area as well the changes are more pronounced in the cities. In few societies had the life of women been more restricted than in traditional India. Hindu favoritism toward men was compounded by the Muslim custom of *purdah* to create a society where males were dominant in virtually all aspects of life. Females received no education and had no inheritance rights. They were restricted to the home and tied to their husbands for life. Widows were expected to shave their heads and engage in a life of religious meditation or even to immolate themselves on their husband's funeral pyre.

Stimulated in part by Mahatma Gandhi's efforts to improve the lot of Indian women and involve them in national affairs, many women took part in the anticolonialist activities that led to the British departure in 1947. After independence, India's leaders sought to equalize treatment of the sexes. The constitution expressly forbade discrimination based on sex and called for equal pay for equal work. Laws prohibited child marriage, *sati*, and the payment of a dowry by the bride's family. Women were encouraged to attend school and enter the labor market.

Such laws along with the dynamics of economic and social change have had a major impact on the life of many Indian women. Middle-class women in urban areas are much more likely to accept employment outside the home, and many hold managerial and professional positions. Before independence, a male's pride might have been offended if his wife were employed, but now the increasing demands of the consumer society lead many families to put their creature comforts first.

The sexual attitudes and practices of urban women have changed as well. While premarital sex is probably much less common than in most Western societies, it is becoming more frequent, and the mingling of the sexes in social situations is much more acceptable than in the past, even in high-class families. On the other hand, surveys suggest that many if not most young Indians still accept the idea of arranged marriages and will ultimately accede to the wish of their parents in the choice of a spouse.

In fact, Indian women like some Western women tend to play a modern role in their work and in the marketplace and a more submissive traditional one at home. The dichotomy is especially apparent in a country like India, where the choice is not simply between the traditional and the modern, but the native and the foreign (see the box on p. 1166). An Indian woman is often expected to be a professional executive at work and a loving dutiful wife and mother at home.

Such attitudes are also reflected in the Indian movie industry, where aspiring actresses must often brave family disapproval to enter the entertainment world. Before World War II, female actors were routinely viewed as prostitutes or "loose women," and even now, such views are prevalent among conservative Indian families. Even Karisma Kapoor, one of India's current film stars and a member of the Kapoor clan, which has produced several generations of actors, had to defy her family's ban on the family women entering show business.

Nothing more strikingly indicates the changing role of women in South Asia than the fact that in recent years three of the major countries in the area—India, Pakistan, and Sri Lanka—have had women as prime ministers. It is worthy of mention, however, that all three—Indira Gandhi, Benazir Bhutto, and Srimivao Bandaranaike—came from prominent political families and probably owed their initial success to a husband or a father who had served as prime minister before them.

Like other aspects of life, sexual relationships have changed much less in rural areas. In the early 1960s, many villagers still practiced and believed in the institution of *purdah*. A woman who went about freely in society would get a bad reputation. Female children are still much less likely to receive an education. The overall literacy rate in India today is less than 40 percent, but it is undoubtedly much lower among women. Laws relating to dowry, child marriage, and inheritance are routinely ignored in the countryside. Dowry costs have escalated rapidly in recent years and often take the form of crude bargaining between the families of the bride and the groom. All too often, families allow female children to die in the hope of later having a son. There have been a few highly publicized cases of *sati* still being practiced, although undoubtedly more women die of mistreatment or in kitchen fires. In a few instances, widows have been forcibly thrown on the funeral pyre by their in-laws.

Perhaps the most tragic aspect of continued sexual discrimination in India is the high mortality rate of young women. According to a recent UNICEF study,

≋ A Critique of Western Feminism ≋

Organized efforts to protect the rights of women have been underway in India since the 1970s, when the Progressive Organization for Women (POW) instituted a campaign against sexual harassment and other forms of discrimination against women in Indian society. Since then, women have become a vital force in the political process and have been active in attacking many social problems, including alcoholism, family violence, the dowry system, and poor education and sanitation. Like many of their counterparts in other parts of Asia and Africa, however, many activists for women's rights in India are critical of Western feminism, charging that it is irrelevant to their own realities. Although Indian feminists feel a bond with their sisters all over the world, they insist upon resolving Indian problems with Indian solutions. The author of this editorial is Madhu Kishwar, founder and editor of a women's journal in New Delhi.

Finding Indian Solutions to Women's Problems

Western feminism, exported to India and many other Third World countries in recent decades, has brought with it serious problems.

As products of a more homogenized culture, most Western feminists assume women's aspirations the world over must be quite similar. Yet a person's idea of a good life and her aspirations are closely related to what is valued in her particular society. This applies to feminism itself. An offshoot of individualism and liberalism, it posits that each individual is responsible primarily to herself.

At the same time, most feminists view the state as a vital agency for the protection of their individual rights. This view has served to atomize Western societies, often leaving people with only the authority and support of the state (and not even their family) for protection of their rights when they are violated by others.

In societies like India, most of us find it difficult to tune in to this extreme individualism. For instance, most Indian women are unwilling to assert rights in a way that estranges them not just from their family but also from their larger community. They want to ensure their rights are respected and acknowledged by their family and prefer to avoid asserting their rights in a way that isolates them.

This isn't slavery to social opinion. Rather, many of us believe life is a poor thing if our own dear ones don't honour and celebrate our rights, if our freedom cuts us off from others. In our culture, both men and women are taught to value the interests of our families more than our self-interest. (Most feminists consider this world view a product of low self-esteem).

Cultural issues aside, my most fundamental reservation regarding feminism is that it has strengthened the tendency among India's Western-educated elites to adopt the statist authoritarian route to social reform. The characteristic feminist response to most social issues affecting women—in the workplace, in the media, in the home—is to demand more and more stringent laws. The results in most cases do not better women's lives but rather facilitate a whole spate of vicious and harmful legislation which has put even more arbitrary powers in the hands of the police and government—powers that are routinely abused.

Most of the feminists' energies are spent appealing to governments to enforce the social reforms they've proposed. But dearly held and deeply cherished cultural norms cannot be changed simply by applying the instruments of state repression through legal punishment. Social reform is too complex and important a matter to be left to the police and courts. The best of laws will tend to fail if social opinion is contrary to them. Therefore, the statist route of using laws as a substitute for creating a new social consensus about women's rights tends to be counterproductive.

one-quarter of the female children born in India die before the age of fifteen due to neglect or even infanticide by their parents. Others are aborted before birth as the result of gender-detection examinations. Statistically, the results are striking. Whereas in most societies the number of women equals or exceeds that of men, in India, according to a 1981 estimate, the ratio was only 933 females to 1,000 males.

Indian Art and Literature since Independence

Recent decades have witnessed a prodigious outpouring of literature in India. Most works have been written in one of the Indian languages and have not been translated into a foreign tongue, although many authors choose to write in English. Known as Indo-Anglian literature, such works are written primarily for the Indian elite or for foreign audiences. For that reason, some charge that Indo-Anglian literature lacks authenticity and is polluted by market concerns and secular attitudes. Defenders respond that the English language is sufficiently flexible to express Indian idioms, style, and temperament. As the Indo-Anglian author Salman Rushdie wrote in 1982, the English language "now grows from many roots; and those whom it once colonized are carving out large territories within the language for themselves."

Because of the vast number of works published (India is currently the third largest publisher of English-language books in the world), only a few of the most prominent fictional writers can be mentioned here. One of the most popular is R. K. Narayan (b. 1907). Born of a *brahmin* family in Madras, Narayan was a prolific writer who appealed to readers by his use of traditional themes and the vivid descriptions of his characters.

Another popular writer today is Anita Desai. Born in New Delhi in 1937, Desai was one of the first prominent woman writers in contemporary India. Her writings focus on the struggle of Indian women of all classes and ages to achieve a degree of independence from the suffocating bondage imposed on them by traditional society. In Desai's first novel, *Cry, the Peacock,* the heroine finally sought liberation from the surrounding male-dominated society by murdering her husband, preferring freedom at any cost to remaining a captive of traditional society.

In recent years, many other women have taken up the cause. In "The Stars Are Trembling," for example, the Urdu writer Siddiqa Begum Sevharvi (b. 1925) relates the story of a man who forbids his sister to teach his young wife to read. The next thing you know, he grumbles, she will want to take up tennis. But the most famous woman writer in South Asia today is Taslima Nasrin from Bangladesh. She first became famous when she was sentenced to death for criticizing the Koran in one of her novels. Islam, she declared, obstructs human progress and women's equality. She now lives in exile in Europe.

Unquestionably, India's most controversial modern writer is Salman Rushdie (b. 1947). In *Midnight's Children,* published in 1980, Rushdie linked his protagonist, born on the night of independence, to the history of modern India, its achievements and its frustrations. Like his contemporary, the Colombian Gabriel García Márquez, Rushdie used the technique of magical realism to jolt his audience into recognizing the inhumanity of modern society and the need to develop a sense of moral concern for the fate of the Indian people and for the world as a whole. Rushdie's later novels have continued to attack such problems as religious intolerance, political tyranny, social injustice, and greed and corruption. His attack on Islamic fundamentalism in *The Satanic Verses* (1988) won plaudits from literary critics, but provoked widespread criticism among Muslims, including a death sentence by the Ayatollah Khomeini in Iran. Rushdie's latest novel, entitled *The Moor's Last Sigh,* turns its attention to the alleged excesses of Hindu nationalism and has been banned in India.

Like many other aspects of modern India, Indian art has been affected by the colonial experience. Like Chinese and Japanese artists, Indian artists have agonized for more than a century over how best to paint with a modern and yet indigenous mode of expression. Indeed, India's cultural schizophrenia was perhaps more poignant, since its artists had to search for identity and artistic expression while living under colonial domination.

During the colonial period, Indian art went in several directions at once. One school of painters favored sentimental renderings of traditional themes, while another experimented with a colorful primitivism founded in folk art. Many Indian artists painted representational social art extolling the suffering and silent dignity of India's impoverished millions. After 1960, however, most Indian artists adopted abstract art as their medium. Surrealism in particular, with its emphasis on spontaneity and the unconscious, appeared closer to the Hindu tradition of favoring intuition over reason. Yet Indian artists are still struggling to find the ideal way to be both modern and Indian.

Because of its representational character, sculpture was in eclipse during the centuries of Muslim rule. Since independence, however, sculpture and other forms of handicrafts have revived. The government has vigorously supported the revival, sponsoring local handicrafts and encouraging each village to produce its own unique artifacts in textiles, wood, clay, or metal. It is hardly surprising that India boasts an exceptional variety of folk art of high quality today.

The Vision of Mahatma Gandhi

Clearly, India like other non-Western countries is changing. Traditional ways are giving way to modern ones, and often the result is a society that looks increasingly Western in form, if not in content. In India, as in a number of other Asian and African societies, the distinction between traditional and modern or native and Westernized sometimes appears to be a simple dichotomy between

♦ **No Room in Paradise?**   The color and diversity of popular Hinduism are nowhere more fully displayed than on the gopuram, or gate tower, of the modern Hindu temple. The celestial figures shown here in rich profusion are located on the tower surmounting the entrance gate of a temple devoted to Siva in the south Indian city of Madras.

rural and urban areas. Downtown areas in the major cities are modern and Westernized in appearance, but the villages have changed little since precolonial days.

Yet it would be a mistake to draw simple comparisons between what is taking place in India and what is happening in other countries undergoing a similar transition into the industrial and technological age. In India, the past appears to be more resilient, and the result is often a synthesis rather than a frontal clash between conflicting institutions and values. Unlike China, India has not rejected its past, but merely adjusted it to meet the needs of the present. Clothing styles in the streets, where the *sari* and *dhoti* continue to be popular, religious practices in the temples, and social relationships in the home all testify to the greater role of tradition in India than in China or many other societies in the region.

One disadvantage of the eclectic approach that seeks to blend the old and the new rather than choosing one over the other is that sometimes contrasting traditions and customs cannot be reconciled. Such was the lesson of the failed experiment of self-strengthening in late nineteenth-century China (see Chapter 23). In his recent book *India: A Wounded Civilization*, author V. S. Naipaul, a West Indian of Indian descent, charged that Mahatma Gandhi's legacy of glorifying poverty and the simple Indian village was a severe obstacle to Indian efforts to overcome the poverty, ignorance, and degradation of its past and build a prosperous modern society. Gandhi's vision of a spiritual India, Naipaul complained, was a balm for defeatism and an excuse for failure.

Certainly, India faces a difficult and sometimes painful dilemma. Some of India's problems are undoubtedly a consequence of the colonial era, but the British cannot be blamed for all of the country's economic and social ills. To build a democratic, prosperous society, the Indian people must discard many of their traditional convictions and customs. Belief in *karma* and inherent class distinctions is incompatible with the democratic belief in equality before the law. These traditional beliefs also undercut the work ethic and the assumption, basic to modern Western society, that hard work earns concrete rewards. Identification with class or caste undermines the modern sentiment of nationalism.

So long as Indians accept their fate as predetermined, they will find it difficult to change their environment and create a new society. Yet their traditional beliefs provide a measure of identity and solace often lacking in other societies where such traditional spiritual underpinnings have eroded. Despite the difficulties the Indian people must surmount daily, they appear at least on the surface to be reasonably happy and content with their lot. Destroying India's traditional means of coping with a disagreeable reality without changing that reality would be cruel indeed. That, in a nutshell, is the cruel dilemma that India faces.

There is, of course, a final question that cannot be answered here. The vision of Mahatma Gandhi, maligned by some and treated with condescending amusement by others, was that materialism is ultimately a dead end. In light of contemporary concerns about the emptiness of life in the West and the self-destructiveness of material culture, can the Mahatma's message be ignored?

The Dismantling of Colonialism in Southeast Asia

First-time visitors to the Malaysian capital of Kuala Lumpur will be astonished to observe on the skyline a pair of twin towers rising above the surrounding buildings into the scudding monsoon clouds over the city. The Petronas towers, as they are called, rise 1,483 feet from ground level and are officially recognized as the world's tallest building—33 feet higher than the Sears Tower in Chicago.

The new building is more than an architectural achievement; it is a deliberate announcement of the emergence of Asia as a major player on the international scene and of the state of Malaysia as an aspiring member of the world's advanced nations. It is probably no accident that the foundations were laid on the site of the Selangor Cricket Club, symbol of colonial hegemony in

CHRONOLOGY

Southeast Asia

August Revolution in Vietnam	1945
Philippines become independent	1946
Beginning of Franco-Vietminh War	December 1946
Burma becomes independent	1948
Recognition of the Republic of Indonesia	1950
Malaya becomes independent	1957
Beginning of Sukarno's Guided Democracy in Indonesia	1959
Military comes to power in Burma	1962
Singapore declares its independence	1965
Military seizes power in Indonesia	1965
Foundation of ASEAN	1967
Fall of Saigon to North Vietnamese forces	1975
Vietnamese invade Cambodia	1978
Corazon Aquino elected president in the Philippines	1986
United Nations forces arrive in Cambodia	1991
Vietnam becomes a member of ASEAN	1996
Islamic and student protests in Indonesia	1996–1997

Southeast Asia. "These towers," commented one local official, "will do wonders for Asia's self-esteem and confidence, which I think is very important, and which I think at this moment are at the point of takeoff."[10]

As we have seen, Japanese wartime occupation had a great impact on attitudes among the peoples of Southeast Asia. It demonstrated the vulnerability of colonial rule in the region and showed that an Asian power could defeat Europeans. The Allied governments themselves also contributed—sometimes unwittingly—to rising aspirations for independence by promising self-determination for all peoples at the end of the war. Although British Prime Minister Winston Churchill later said that the Atlantic Charter he and President Franklin D. Roosevelt had signed in August 1941 did not apply to the colonial peoples, it would be difficult to put the genie back in the bottle again.

Some did not try. In July 1946, the United States lived up to the promise that it had made nearly ten years earlier and granted total independence to the Philippines. The Americans insisted on maintaining a military presence on the islands, and U.S. citizens were able to retain economic and commercial interests in the new country, a decision that would later spur charges of neocolonialism.

The British were equally willing to bring an end to a century of imperialism in the region. As prime minister, Churchill had made it clear that he did not intend to preside over the dissolution of the British Empire. But his successor from the Labour Party, Clement Attlee, had different views. The Labour Party had long been critical of the British colonial legacy on both moral and economic grounds and, once in power, moved rapidly to grant independence to those colonies prepared to accept it. In 1948, the Union of Burma received its independence. Malaya's turn came in 1957 after a Communist guerrilla movement had been suppressed.

Other European nations were less willing to abandon their colonial possessions in Southeast Asia. The French and the Dutch both regarded their colonies in the region as economic necessities as well as symbols of national grandeur and refused to turn them over to nationalist movements at the end of the war. The Dutch returned to the East Indies and attempted to suppress a new Indonesian republic established by Sukarno (1901–1970), leader of the Indonesian Nationalist Party (PNI). The PNI faced internal dissension within its own ranks as the Indonesian Communist Party (PKI) broke off its wartime alliance with the nationalist movement and launched its own abortive rebellion in central Java in 1948. But the United States, which feared a Communist victory in Indonesia, pressured the Dutch to grant independence to Sukarno and his non-Communist forces, and in 1950 the Dutch finally agreed to withdraw and recognize the new Republic of Indonesia.

The situation was somewhat different in Vietnam, where the leading force in the anticolonial movement was the local Indochinese Communist Party (ICP) led by the veteran Moscow-trained revolutionary Ho Chi Minh. In August 1945, virtually at the moment of the Japanese surrender, the Vietminh Front, an alliance of patriotic forces under secret ICP leadership that had been founded to fight the Japanese in 1941, launched a general uprising and seized power throughout most of Vietnam. In early September, Ho Chi Minh was elected president of a new provisional republic in Hanoi. The new government appealed to the victorious Allies for recognition but received no response, and by late fall the southern part of the country was back under French rule.

Ho signed a preliminary agreement with the French recognizing Vietnam as a "free state" within the French Union, but negotiations in France broke down in July 1946 and war broke out in December. At the time it was only an anticolonial war, but it would soon become much more (see Chapter 27).

The Era of Independent States

The leaders of the newly independent states in Southeast Asia had been members of nationalist movements before the war. Although many of them had dedicated their lives to ending colonial rule, in general they admired Western political principles and institutions and hoped to apply them, subject to historical and cultural differences, in their own countries. New constitutions were patterned on Western democratic models, and multiparty political systems quickly sprang into operation. Only in North Vietnam, where the Communist Party came to power after the Geneva Conference in 1954, did the local leadership firmly reject the Western historical experience and opt for the Soviet Leninist model.

By the end of the 1950s, most of these budding experiments in pluralist democracy had been abandoned or were under serious threat. Some had been replaced by military or one-party autocratic regimes. In Burma, a moderate government based on the British parliamentary system and dedicated to Buddhism and nonviolent Marxism had given way to a military government under General Ne Win. In Thailand, too, where traditional kingship had been replaced by a constitutional monarchy, the military now ruled. In the Philippines, a U.S.-style two-party presidential system survived, but democratic practices were undermined by the dominating presence of an influential landed elite.

But perhaps the most serious threat to democracy in the region arose in Indonesia. President Sukarno, exasperated at the incessant maneuvering among conservative Muslims, Communists, and the army, which had led to the overthrow of several cabinets and made long-term planning difficult if not impossible, dissolved the constitution and the pluralist political system that had functioned since independence and attempted to rule on his own through what he called "Guided Democracy." Highly suspicious of the West, Sukarno nationalized foreign-owned enterprises and sought economic aid from China and the Soviet Union.

In turning away from the Western concept of democracy, Sukarno explained to his people that his Guided Democracy was closer to Indonesian traditions and superior to the Western variety. Indonesian democracy, in his eyes, was neither Western liberal democracy nor Soviet socialist democracy. The weakness of Western democracy was that it provided for the domination of the majority over the minority, while Sukarno's Guided Democracy would attempt to reconcile different opinions and points of view in a government operated by consensus (see the box on p. 1172).

The collapse of democratic governments was accompanied by rising tensions among disparate interest groups inside the new countries. Ethnic disputes, notably in states with substantial minority populations such as Burma and Malaya, unleashed centrifugal forces that undermined the thrust for national unity and sometimes led to civil war. Communist Parties, many of which had cooperated with their non-Communist rivals in the struggle against the Japanese and the colonial power, now set out to seize power on their own. Ambitious hopes for rapid economic growth were sorely disappointed, and the economic disparity between the mass of the population and the affluent minority in the cities intensified.

In addition to these internal problems, Southeast Asian states were hampered by serious tensions among themselves. Some of these tensions were a consequence of historical rivalries and territorial disputes that had been submerged during the long era of colonial rule. Cambodia, for example, bickered with both of its neighbors, Thailand and Vietnam, over mutual frontiers drawn up originally by the French for their own convenience. A similar dispute erupted further to the south, when Sukarno of Indonesia unleashed a policy of *konfrontasi* (confrontation) against the Federation of Malaya.

⊠ Map 31.2   Modern Southeast Asia.

❧ The Golden Throat of President Sukarno ❧

President Sukarno of Indonesia was a spellbinding speaker and a charismatic leader of his nation's struggle for independence. These two excerpts are from speeches in which Sukarno promoted two of his favorite projects: Indonesian nationalism and Guided Democracy. The force that would guide Indonesia, of course, was to be Sukarno himself.

Sukarno on Nationalism and Democracy

Sukarno on Indonesian Greatness

What was Indonesia in 1945? What was our nation then? It was only two things, only two things. A flag and a song. That is all. (Pause, finger held up as afterthought) But no, I have omitted the main ingredient. I have missed the most important thing of all. I have left out the burning fire of freedom and independence in the breast and heart of every Indonesian. That is the most important thing—this is the vital chord—the spirit of our people, the spirit and determination to be free. This was our nation in 1945—the spirit of our people!

And what are we today? We are a great nation. We are bigger than Poland. We are bigger than Turkey.

We have more people than Australia, than Canada, we are bigger in area and have more people than Japan. In population now we are the fifth largest country in the world. In area, we are even bigger than the United States of America. The American Ambassador, who is here with us, admits this. Of course, he points out that we have a lot of water in between our thousands of islands. But I say to him—America has a lot of mountains and deserts, too!

Sukarno on Guided Democracy

Indonesia's democracy is not liberal democracy. Indonesian democracy is not the democracy of the world of Montaigne or Voltaire. Indonesia's democracy is not a la America, Indonesia's democracy is not the Soviet—NO! Indonesia's democracy is the democracy which is implanted in the breasts of the Indonesian people and it is that which I have tried to dig up again, and have put forward as an offering to you. . . . If you, especially the undergraduates, are still clinging to, and being borne along the democracy made in England, or democracy made in France, or democracy made in America, or democracy made in Russia, you will become a nation of copyists!

Sukarno contended that the Malay peninsula was populated by Malay peoples who had once been part of the traditional greater Indonesian empires of Sailendra and Srivijaya and had only been separated from Indonesia as a result of colonial policies (see the box on p. 1173).

Sukarno's contention had some historical validity, in that the political separation of Malaya from the Indonesian archipelago was in effect the result of a bargain between the British and the Dutch after the Napoleonic Wars. But it made little sense to the people of the resource-rich Malay peninsula, who saw no advantage in the creation of a Greater Indonesia dominated by the charismatic but demagogic Sukarno, who might be inclined to redistribute their wealth to the poorer Indonesian islands. In the end, Indonesia dropped its claim after Sukarno's fall from power in the mid-1960s. The territorial disputes between Cambodia and its neighbors, however, have not yet been resolved.

ASEAN and the Issue of Regional Integration

The reunification of Vietnam under Communist rule in 1975 (see Chapter 27) had an immediate impact on the region. By the end of the year, both Laos and Cambodia had Communist governments. In Cambodia, a brutal revolutionary regime under the leadership of the Khmer Rouge (Red Khmer) dictator Pol Pot carried out the massacre of more than one million Cambodians. But the Communist triumph in Indochina did not lead to the falling dominoes that many U.S. policymakers had feared. One reason was that the political and economic situation within the region had gradually stabilized during the 1960s and 1970s. In Indonesia, Sukarno, who had begun to cooperate with the PKI in order to limit the influence of the army, was forced from office in 1967 and replaced by a military government under General Suharto (b. 1921). The new government made no pretensions of

An Indonesian's View of Sukarno

In the early 1960s, Sukarno launched a campaign called *konfrontasi* (confrontation) to destroy the new nation of Malaysia and integrate the Malay peninsula into a Greater Indonesia. The campaign aroused suspicion throughout the region and was abandoned by his successor, General Suharto. In the following poem, an ordinary Indonesian, employed as a clerk in a hotel in Jakarta, expresses his opinion of Sukarno's grandiose plans.

My Wife, the Faceless Men, and Me

My wife crouches by the fire
Her fan flickering;
She is cooking a little fish for my dinner.
My wife is very beautiful—
Beneath her clothing she is like a goddess.
When we have eaten
She will lie beside me
And we will make love.

On the other side of the city,
At his desk,
A secretary of state is writing a speech

For his minister. Tomorrow it will be on the front page
Of every newspaper (by order);
Foreign correspondents will send it round the world;
It will be on the radio.

In his speech the minister will say,
"We, the People,
Will resist Imperialism to the last drop of Indonesian blood.
Ever onward, no retreat."
Tell me, please, who are these faceless men
Who speak for me,
Not knowing my name, calling me "The People,"
Spilling my blood for me?

Who will save me from them,
The statesmen,
The public officials, and security men?
Supposing I am the last Indonesian,
Lying with my wife
Who has a body like a goddess:
Do they think I will want to get up and resist Imperialism?
They should ask me first.

reverting to democratic rule, but it restored good relations with the West and sought foreign investment to repair the country's ravaged economy. Meanwhile, other countries in the region, such as Malaysia, Thailand, and the island state of Singapore, were experiencing relative political stability and rapid economic growth. Singapore had been included in the new state of Malaysia in 1962, but ethnic tensions between the Chinese who were the majority on Singapore and the dominant Malays on the peninsula led it to declare itself an independent republic in 1965.

With political stability and improving economies came increasing mutual cooperation in the form of a new regional organization known as the Association for the Southeast Asian Nations (ASEAN). Composed of Indonesia, Malaysia, Thailand, Singapore, and the Philippines, at first ASEAN concentrated on cooperative social and economic endeavors, but after the end of the Vietnam War, it began to seek a greater degree of political and military cohesion to resist further Communist encroachment in the region. When renewed territorial and ethnic rivalry between the Communist governments in Vietnam and Cambodia led the Vietnamese to invade Cambodia and install a pro-Hanoi regime in December 1978, ASEAN cooperated with other states in supporting non-Communist resistance forces, which eventually forced Vietnam to withdraw its troops. By the end of the decade, negotiations to resolve the dispute had begun, and in 1991 a temporary coalition government of the opposing groups was formed in Phnom Penh. But mutual suspicion has made cooperation difficult to achieve, and Khmer Rouge guerrillas remain a threat in rural areas.

Today, Southeast Asia is one of the most stable and prosperous areas in Asia. While some countries in the region, notably Burma (now called Myanmar), the Indochinese states, and the Philippines, continue to face

♦ **Portrait of Sukarno.** Sukarno was the leader of the anti-colonialist movement in the Dutch East Indies. After independence was achieved in 1950, he served as the president of the new Republic of Indonesia. A charismatic speaker, Sukarno was initially highly popular, but the failure of many of his grandiose projects and his flirtation with the Indonesian Communist Party eventually led to his downfall.

serious political and economic difficulties, most of the members of ASEAN have entered a stage of steady economic growth. Singapore is often classed with South Korea, Taiwan, and Hong Kong as the "newly industrializing countries" (sometimes called the "little tigers"), and both Malaysia and Thailand have been identified as potential future members of the club (see Chapter 32). Whether Myanmar, the Indochinese states, and the Philippines will be able to overcome their internal problems remains to be seen.

Although Vietnam is still ruled by its Communist Party, Hanoi has begun to cooperate with nearby states in

foreign affairs and was recently accepted into ASEAN, which expects further expansion before the end of the decade. Perhaps the main current source of concern for government leaders in the region is the chronic dispute over ownership of the Spratly and Paracel Islands in the South China Sea. Most of the states in the area have staked claims to one or more of the islands, which are reportedly located over large oil reserves, but it is Beijing's insistence that both island groups are historically Chinese that has made a compromise settlement difficult.

Problems of National Development

A generation ago, many Western social scientists assumed that Southeast Asia would inevitably pass through a predetermined process of political and economic evolution from traditional preindustrial societies to modern societies on the Western capitalist democratic model. They thought the transitional period would be difficult, but believed Western advice and technological assistance could make it easier.

As we have seen, many Southeast Asian political leaders generally accepted this assessment. New political systems incorporating Western-style institutions were established, and governments spoke bravely of a new era of growth and material prosperity. By the end of the first decade of independence, however, it was apparent that they had been overoptimistic. Fragile experiments in Western-style democracy came to an end, ethnic and ideological tensions rose to the surface, and deep-rooted economic problems set back plans for rapid economic growth.

One problem was that independence had not brought material prosperity or ended economic inequality and the domination of the local economies by foreign interests. Underdevelopment was not automatically solved by the end of colonial rule, even though foreign domination had been one of its causes. Most economies in the region were still characterized by tiny industrial sectors based on light industry and the processing of raw materials for export, backward agricultural sectors, and burgeoning populations; they lacked technology, educational resources and capital investment, and leaders trained in developmental skills. It is not surprising, then, that independence did not immediately bring rapid economic growth and an improvement in the standard of living.

The presence of widespread ethnic, linguistic, cultural, and economic differences also made the transition difficult. In Burma, for example, one-third of the population was composed of a variety of ethnic groups not directly related to the majority Burmese population. Many of them resented the efforts of the devout Buddhist prime minister U Nu (b. 1907) to impose his unique combination of Marxist and Theravada Buddhist values on the entire population. Some ethnic groups allied with the local Burmese Communist Party to launch a rebellion against the government.

Ethnic differences also caused problems in Malaya. The majority Malays—most of whom were farmers—feared economic and political domination by the local Chinese minority, who were much more active and experienced in industry and commerce. When the British controlled the area, colonial officials had kept the two communities apart, while recognizing the suzerain political power of the local Malay sultanates. With independence, however, many Malays feared that Chinese economic dominance would intensify and extend into politics. Malay fears were vocally expressed in 1970 in a provocative book by Mahathir Bin Mohamad (currently Malaysia's prime minister). Mohamad cited numerous cases of discrimination in the employment of Malays by Chinese or other non-Malays and concluded that "from these inequalities of opportunity spring other inequalities, such as the miserable houses of the Malays compared to the houses of the non-Malays, the poor health of the Malays against the vigor of the non-Malays, the high death and infant mortality rates of the Malays compared to non-Malays, the lack of savings and capital of the Malays when compared to non-Malays."[11]

In 1961, the Federation of Malaya, whose ruling party, the United Malays National Organization (UMNO), was dominated by Malays, had integrated former British possessions on the island of Borneo into a new Union of Malaysia in a patent move to increase the non-Chinese proportion of the country's population. Similar reasons dictated the expulsion of the island of Singapore three years later. Yet periodic conflicts persisted as the Malaysian government adopted a program to guarantee the Malay peoples control over politics and a larger role in the economy. In 1969, tensions between Malays and Chinese erupted into violent confrontations on the streets of Malaysian cities.

In some cases, the tensions were economic or regional rather than ethnic. In Indonesia, for example, many urban intellectuals, supported by poor rice farmers on the inner islands of Java and southern Sumatra, advocated a socialist approach that would limit Western investment and equalize income among the Indonesian people. Prosperous planters and merchants on the outer island of Sumatra, on the other hand, preferred more free enterprise and a good relationship with the West, their primary market for exports. Such tensions contributed to the collapse of Indonesian democracy and the institution of Sukarno's experiment with Guided Democracy in 1959.

Some of these problems are common to developing societies everywhere and were experienced by many European countries during the early stages of industrialization. Many Southeast Asians, however, experienced

♦ **Holocaust in Cambodia.** When the Khmer Rouge seized power in Cambodia in April 1975, they immediately emptied the capital of Phnom Penh and systematically began to eliminate opposition elements throughout the country. Thousands were tortured in the famous Tuol Sleng prison and then marched out to the countryside where they were massacred. Their bodies were thrown into massive pits. The succeeding government disinterred the remains, which are now displayed at an outdoor museum on the site.

◆ **Tradition and Modernity in Malaysia.** Few countries in Southeast Asia have tried harder to achieve modernization without destroying their cultural heritage than Malaysia. In this photograph, modern skyscrapers tower over a mosque in the downtown section of the capital of Kuala Lumpur. The inner courtyard provides shelter from the heat of the tropical sun.

lingering doubts about whether Western-style democracy and materialistic culture were relevant to their region. They questioned whether Western secular institutions and values were appropriate in societies that traditionally ascribed a charismatic or semireligious character to their leaders (in Burma, for example, the ruler was viewed by his subjects as an incipient Buddha-to-be). Similar doubts were expressed about the introduction of capitalism into Southeast Asian societies. In Burma, Prime Minister U Nu said that Marxist ideas of economic equality were more appropriate to a Buddhist society than the capitalist search for profit and launched what he called a "Burmese Way to Socialism."

In the initial enthusiasm after independence, many Southeast Asian political leaders submerged their doubts as they tried to imitate the West. But as disillusion set in, some began to search for a more eclectic approach that would combine native and foreign elements. When Sukarno in Indonesia abrogated the Constitution of 1950 and turned to Guided Democracy, he described the new system as a return to native traditions. Guided Democracy, he asserted,

> is the genuine reflection of the identity of the Indonesian nation, who since ancient times based their system of government on *musjawarah* [deliberation] and *mufakat* [consensus] with the leadership of one central authority in the hands of a "sesepuh"—an elder—who did not dictate, but led, and protected. Indonesian democracy since ancient times has been Guided Democracy, and this is characteristic of all original democracies in Asia.[12]

That *sesepuh*, of course, would be Sukarno himself.

The main opposition to Sukarno and his plans came from the army and conservative Muslims. Both resented Sukarno's increasing reliance on the PKI, and the Muslims were upset by his refusal to consider a state based on Islamic principles. One of the so-called five principles (*pantja sila*) that Sukarno had popularized as the basic goals of the Republic of Indonesia was religious freedom. As a representative of the Muslim community stated in 1957, the heroes and patriots of the Indonesian revolution sacrificed their lives not only for independence but "for one idealism, for one ideal inspired by the goal and purpose of their lives: to devote themselves to God, praise be to Him the Most High, by upholding His Word and by expecting merely His grace. They fought to place Islam in the life of our society and state. They fought to establish the Sovereignty and the Law of Islam. . . ."[13]

The combined opposition of the army and the orthodox Muslims proved too much for Sukarno to surmount. But the military government that replaced him also found it difficult to placate Muslim demands for an Islamic state. As in Pakistan, pressure for the strict application of Islamic law continues in Indonesia despite efforts by the government to repress it. In a few areas, including western Sumatra, militant Muslims have taken up arms against the state.

Indonesia was not the only country in the region to abandon democratic institutions for centralized power. In Burma and Thailand, the military seized control from civilian governments in the interests of law and order. Both promised to return the government to civilian authorities but failed to do so. In the Philippines, President Ferdinand Marcos (1917–1989) discarded democratic restraints and established his centralized control over a system called the "New Order." In Vietnam, both north and south were ruled by authoritarian governments, although they were based on widely differing ideological principles. In North Vietnam, Ho Chi Minh's Communist Party adopted the Marxist concept of the dictatorship of the proletariat. In the south, Ngo Dinh Diem and his successors paid lip service to the Western democratic model, but ruled by authoritarian means.

In recent years, many Southeast Asian societies have shown signs of evolving toward more democratic forms. One example is the Philippines, where the Marcos regime was overthrown by a massive public uprising in 1986 and replaced by a democratically elected government under President Corazon Aquino (b. 1933), the widow of a popular politician who had been assassinated under mysterious circumstances a few years earlier. Malaysia is also a practicing democracy, although tensions persist between Malays and Chinese as well as between secular and orthodox Muslims. Even the military governments in Thailand and Indonesia have found it expedient to hold national elections with multiparty candidates to prevent political unrest.

The results have been mixed. In the spring and summer of 1996, violent protests by students demanding increased freedoms and by Muslims demanding a larger role for Islam in society prompted the Suharto government in Indonesia to arrest many dissidents and warn against a revival of the Communist Party. One of the leaders of the student movement was a daughter of onetime president Sukarno. In Thailand, where widespread corruption has poisoned the political system, aspiring candidates can purchase the votes not just of individuals, but of families and entire polling districts.

Even in Vietnam, where the Communist Party refused to surrender its claim to total power, the trend in recent years has been toward a greater popular role in the governing process. Elections for the unicameral parliament are more open than in the past, and local authorities lobby effectively in Hanoi for the interests of their constituents. As in neighboring China, however, the government is suspicious of Western forms of democracy and represses all forms of criticism that are aimed at the party's guiding role over society and the state (see the box on pp. 1178 and 1179).

The trend toward more representative systems of government, however halting and imperfect, is due in part to increasing affluence and the growth of an affluent and educated middle class. Although Indonesia, Burma, and the three Indochinese states are still overwhelmingly agrarian, Malaysia and Thailand are undergoing relatively rapid economic development, and tiny Singapore with its educated and industrious workforce has become a leading exporter of manufactured goods and a major oil refining center for oil-producing nations throughout the region. Malaysia has benefited from exports of rubber, tin, and palm oil, Thailand from tourism and a major U.S. military presence during the Vietnam War, and Singapore from strong leadership and the absence of an impoverished hinterland. Indonesia, although still hindered by a large urban and rural proletariat, has vast economic resources and may be able to enter the transitional stage to an advanced industrial society. Yet here, too, traditional

◆ **The Freedom Monument in Jakarta.** President Sukarno ordered the erection of a massive monument to freedom (*Merdeka*) in downtown Jakarta. At the base of the obelisk is a museum portraying the key events in the Indonesian struggle for independence from the Dutch. Many Indonesians have criticized Sukarno for spending precious funds on a monument, while the country's many social and economic needs were neglected.

inhibitions often hamper efforts to foster the entrepreneurial spirit. According to an Indonesian author, "some years back, Indonesian shopkeepers in Jakarta . . . unblushingly protested to the government about 'unfair practices' by a Chinese shopkeeper, who tried to boost his

☙ Whose Human Rights? ❧

In 1995, twenty years after the end of the Vietnam War, the United States and Vietnam finally agreed to exchange ambassadors. Yet many issues continue to cloud the relationship, including an accounting of U.S. soldiers missing in action during the conflict and U.S. concerns about Vietnamese violations of human rights. In this passage, vice foreign minister Tran Quang Co argues that developing countries like Vietnam should not be held to the same standard as the advanced countries of the West. His complaint echoes the feelings of many other Asians, who resent preaching on human rights from countries whose record during the colonial era was hardly unblemished.

Tran Quang Co, Comments on Human Rights

In the best of all worlds, human rights would become a field for cooperation rather than a battleground of confrontation. But for this to happen, it is important to keep in mind that such rights are a product of human evolution and as such evolve with time, being neither absolute nor immutable. It is therefore strange that some of those who advocate human rights as a cornerstone of international relations pay so little regard to differences in stages of socioeconomic development— and the ensuing differences in the perception of im-

peratives and the setting of national priorities. A starving country, for example, will be far more concerned with feeding its people rather than the forms and methods of democracy.

I hasten to add that my intention here is not to fall into the over-simplistic, quasi-mechanical argument that the higher the level of socio-economic development, the higher too the level of human rights. All I wish to stress is that socio-economic development provides objective conditions and possibilities for better implementation of human rights, both individual and collective.

The point is that human rights is an aggregate product that calls for a balanced, holistic approach. History shows that economic rights have always been as important as, if not more than, civil and political rights. During the 1980s, we have had our own experience of this with the "boat people" problem. Facing hard economic conditions after decades of war, thousands of Vietnamese chose illegal immigration in hopes of finding a better material life abroad. But because of political motivation, some countries have interpreted this as an exodus of political refugees. It is blatantly clear that this is not at all the truth. In-

---

sales by giving away prizes (including motorbikes) to people who came to buy at his store. When the government-owned enterprises lost money, the first reaction was always to increase the price of their services. No attempt was made to look into their own inefficiency and mismanagement."[14]

Economic growth will undoubtedly lead to political and social changes. Yet the nations of the region likely will continue to avoid a crude imitation of Western models of development. All show a distinct preference for strong centralized leadership and the fostering of community spirit rather than Western individualism. Prime Minister Lee Kuan-yew, long-time leader of Singapore, for example, has rejected the Western liberal democratic and individualist model. He has persistently urged his people to follow the more communitarian Japanese model and to rely on their inherited Confucian traditions to foster community spirit, a work ethic, and high moral fiber. The authoritarianism inherent in Lee's interpretation of these values has aroused criticism in the West and even within Singapore itself. But for the most part, Singaporeans ap-

pear willing to accept the bargain as the necessary price for political stability and economic prosperity.

Lee Kuan-yew's cue has been taken up by other leaders in the region. Malaysian prime minister Mahathir Bin Mohammad is a prominent critic of the Western tendency to sermonize to Asians about the virtues of democracy and human rights. In a recent book entitled *The Asia That Can Say No*, coauthored with Shintaro Ishihara (see Chapter 32), Mahathir urged his Asian readers to resist U.S. efforts to promote American values, warning that the United States was trying to hold back economic growth in the region for its own benefit. He even questioned the value of the U.S. security shield and argued that Japan should step in to fill the gap.

Daily Life: Town and Country in Contemporary Southeast Asia

Like much of the non-Western world, most Southeast Asian countries today can still be classified as dual societies. Their modern cities resemble those in the West

deed, the success of our economic reform has halted this sad phenomenon.

It should also be clear that human rights cannot be summed up merely as individual rights. Human rights also encompass the collective rights of communities and nations to self-determination; the right to sovereign use of national natural resources, the right to development, the right to equality of status among nations.

To some in the developed North, these collective rights might appear somewhat abstract and remote. But to nations that have recently emerged from colonial bondage and are struggling to develop in an unfavourable and still unfair international environment, there is nothing remote about these aspirations at all. One is tempted to think sometimes that the reason affluent nations speak so little of self-determination, sovereignty and equality is that in their everyday lives as rich and powerful nations they take these rights for granted. In other words, they call the shots.

More interesting still is that the same rights and rules so often invoked for judging relations between governments and their people are by no means followed when it comes to relations between states. If democracy is indeed a worthy goal for regulating relations within a society, for example, should it not also be followed among nations? It seems somehow strange to us that the heightened attention that certain quarters display over a few specific cases of what they consider to be human-rights violations in our country often goes together with a blithe indifference for the hundreds of thousands of Vietnamese whose human rights were abridged in many different ways during the war and from whose consequences they continue to suffer today.

To put it another way, we all need to remember that human rights will ever be a complex and sensitive issue, if only because by its nature it touches at the core of each society's scale of values and way of life. Certainly all states must strive to improve the human rights for their people, and they are accountable both to their own peoples and the world community at large. What we find disquieting is the growing practice in bilateral dealings of pushing limited areas of concern without regard for our values, often going into details and aspects so specific that it raises the question of national sovereignty. At the international level, diversity no longer is hailed as a virtue.

---

while the villages in the countryside often appear little changed from precolonial days. The distinction between town and country in modern Southeast Asia has been eloquently expressed by the Thai author Phya Anuman Rajadhon in *Life and Ritual in Old Siam*. The cities, he writes (almost certainly referring to Bangkok),

> are crowded with thronging humans. There is a deafening din of people and of cars almost all the time. One cannot see anything at a distance, for buildings and shops and houses intervene almost everywhere. The atmosphere is hot and oppressive and impure; one breathes with difficulty. Foul and rotten odors assail the nose frequently. Some places are disgustingly dirty and cluttered.

What a sharp contrast to life in the country:

> Not too far out from the city, one sees great vacant space as far as the eye can reach; clumps of trees rise at regular intervals. In the extreme distance one sees the treetops looking as if placed in orderly rows. The sky is clear to the distant horizon. . . . At long intervals one sees a few people in the distance. The air one breathes feels pure and fresh. This is the conditions of the meadows and fields outside of town.[15]

No one who has traveled in contemporary Southeast Asia can fail to be affected by the difference between the peaceful rural scenes of palm trees and rice paddies stretching as far as the eye can see and the congested and polluted atmosphere of the region's modern cities. In Bangkok, Manila, and Jakarta, broad boulevards lined with shiny white and silver skyscrapers alternate with muddy lanes passing through neighborhoods packed with wooden shacks topped by thatch or rusty tin roofs. Soft drink cans and coconut shells are scattered along the roadways, and there is a pervasive smell of urine, rotting fruit, and frying meat.

Nevertheless, in recent decades millions of Southeast Asians have fled from the peaceful rice fields to the urban slums. To many Southeast Asians, especially the young, the village represents boredom and poverty, while the city represents excitement and opportunity. Although most urban jobs are menial, such as selling cheap clothing or fruit at a roadside stall or driving a pedicab or (for the fortunate) a taxicab, the earnings are better than they can get in their villages. A few urban migrants become even more affluent, and their success inspires others to come to the cities.

In recent years, a number of manufacturing companies in the advanced countries have taken advantage of these conditions to establish factories in Indonesia and other states in the region. The practice has provoked criticism in the United States, where labor groups and human rights activists charge that workers in such factories—mostly young women—are underpaid and forced to labor in substandard conditions. Indeed, daily wages are often under U.S. $2.50 a day, while fires and other accidents have taken the lives of workers in a few celebrated cases. For many of the employees, however, the job represents an opportunity. "Thanks to God, it's enough money for me," said one young woman at a Nike factory in Serang. She says she saves more than half of her salary and sends it back to her family. Her father is a schoolteacher.[16]

These urban migrants change not only their physical surroundings but their attitudes and values as well. Many experience feelings of deracination, or a sense of being uprooted from their family and village. Sometimes the move leads to a decline in traditional beliefs. Surveys suggest, for example, that belief in the existence of nature and ancestral spirits tends to decline among the urban populations of Southeast Asia, although it has not disappeared. Even major religions like Buddhism and Islam sometimes suffer from the secular focus of urban living.

In Thailand, Buddhism has recently come under heavy pressure from the rising influence of materialism. While temple schools still provide a ladder of upward mobility for thousands of rural youths whose families cannot afford the cost of a public education, the behavior of Buddhist monks—many of whom chafe under their vows of chastity and fasting—has aroused deep concern among many observers. In one highly publicized recent case, a handsome young monk, whose popular appeal is reminiscent of that of television evangelists in the United States, was involved in a sex scandal with some of his female followers. The case aroused a major controversy in part because the church leaders had relied on the monk's charismatic personality to help raise funds for Buddhist causes.

The increasingly secular attitudes in Thailand and other Southeast Asian societies have also been linked to the rising incidence of drugs, pornography, and crime throughout the region. Family values appear to be eroding, and surveys indicate that many parents spend less than fifteen minutes a day with their preschool children, as compared with an average of about forty-five minutes in the United States. Care for the elderly has also suffered. As one observer complained: "Times have changed. Just 10 years ago, people used to live under the same roof and work in nearby fields. Today, people work in the city or in factories. Either they have moved away entirely or don't spend as much time at home."[17] Some countries have attempted to reverse such trends. In Malaysia, an Islamic revival among ethnic Malays has led to a greater acceptance of a traditional Muslim code of behavior.

Perhaps the greatest changes in lifestyle have taken place within the middle class and the small but influential financial and professional elites. Western values, tastes, and customs have deeply penetrated the lives of the affluent urban minority throughout Southeast Asia. A taste for Western films, novels, food, and alcohol and the conspicuous consumption of luxury goods like expensive automobiles, clothing, and household appliances have become common among the wealthy throughout the region. Most speak English or another Western language, and many have been educated abroad.

The urban elites have not lost their cultural roots entirely, however. Buddhist, Muslim, and even Confucian beliefs remain strong, even in cosmopolitan cities like Bangkok, Jakarta, and Singapore. According to unconfirmed reports, when new buildings are erected, local shamans are consulted to avoid irritating the nature spirits in the earth. As the Indonesian intellectual and journalist Mochtar Lubis observed, "deep in the subconscious of the Indonesian—even in that of someone who is Western-educated and has attended a university in Europe or America—is a belief in mystical, supernatural powers, in spirits that possess the power to aid and hurt man."[18] According to Lubis, Sukarno himself believed in supernatural powers and carried a sacred kris (dagger) as a charm to ward off evil spirits. At the same time, Lubis points out, Sukarno took no chances and rode in a bulletproof car built in the United States.

This preference for the traditional also shows up in lifestyle. Native dress, or at least an eclectic blend of Asian and Western dress like the leisure suit, is still common. Traditional music, art, theater, and dance remain popular, although Western rock music has become fashionable among the young, and Indonesian filmmakers complain that Western films are beginning to dominate the market. Southeast Asian novels and short stories, although often Western in form, still focus on local problems or political issues. Sometimes, as in Indonesia, books and plays carry an implicit political message, as authors express their discontent with the current political leader. The most vocal critic of the Suharto regime is the writer Pramoedya Toer (b. 1925). His four-volume masterpiece, *The Buru Quartet,* traces the rise, triumph and betrayal of Indonesian nationalism. Like many other writers in the Third World today, his novels cry out against tyranny and injustice. In July 1996, he was detained by police following anti-government riots in Jakarta.

Western influence is less readily apparent among the less affluent urban dwellers. Yet their lifestyles are changing as well, stimulated by widespread access to television (including, in many countries, old American television programs like *Dallas*, *Kojak*, and *All in the Family*) and the rapid expansion of the educational system. Indeed, the spread of literacy is one of the most impressive aspects of the social changes taking place in Southeast Asia. The literacy rate is well above 80 percent in Singapore,

◆ **The Route to Freedom.** The Hmong, a mountain people of Laos, assisted Royal Lao and U.S. forces in resisting a Communist takeover of their country during the Vietnam War. After the end of the conflict, many fled from Laos as a result of persecution by the new revolutionary regime. The tapestry below, woven by a Hmong refugee living in the United States, illustrates their flight from Laos en route to a new life.

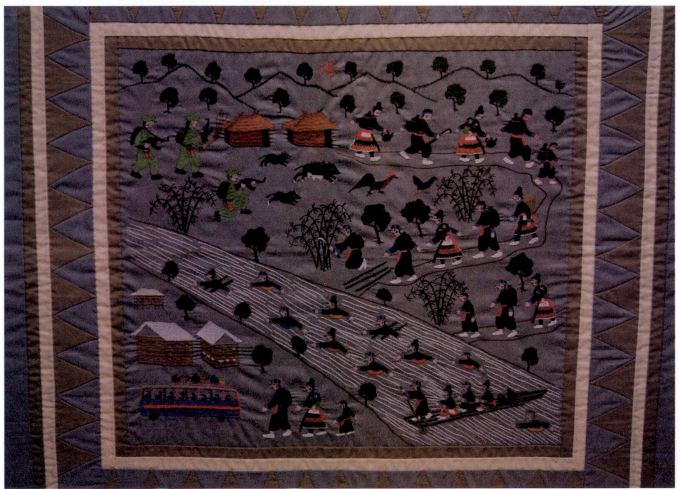

Thailand, and the Philippines and is over 75 percent even in such predominantly rural societies as Myanmar and Indonesia.

This superficially Westernized way of life is less prevalent in the three states of Indochina. Isolated from much of the capitalist world since the end of the Vietnam War in 1975, the cities of Vietnam, Laos, and Cambodia lack the visible evidence of Western influence—the skyscrapers, expensive automobiles, and traffic jams and pollution found elsewhere in the region. Physically, Hanoi in North Vietnam still looks much as it did sixty years ago before World War II. Automobiles remain scarce, and most residents travel by bicycle or motor bus. Yet even such cities as Hanoi and Phnom Penh are not beyond the reach of the all-pervasive influence of Western culture. Coca-Cola, fashionable sneakers, and sweatshirts (or at least a facsimile thereof) are for sale in the shops, and a concert featuring the music of the Beatles or the Rolling Stones gathers immense crowds of adolescents.

The integration of Southeast Asia into the emerging world culture is less advanced, of course, in rural areas, where little has changed since precolonial days. Most peasants still live in traditional housing and adjust their lives to the annual harvest cycle. Travel is by cart or bicycle or on foot. Telephones are rare—one for every fifty people in Thailand and for nearly two hundred in Indonesia. Only rarely does the average rural Southeast Asian visit the major cities. Yet through the spread of electricity, radio and television (although relatively few peasants can as yet afford to buy their own set), and newspapers, changes are coming to the countryside as well.

The increasing inroads made by Western culture have caused anxiety in some countries. In Malaysia, for example, fundamentalist Muslims criticize the prevalence of pornography, hedonism, drugs, and alcohol in Western culture and have tried to limit their presence in their own country. Signs stating "Dada means death" (death to drugs) are a graphic illustration of what happens to drug pushers, whether native or foreign. The Malaysian government has attempted to limit the number of U.S. entertainment programs shown on local television stations and has replaced them with shows on traditional themes.

Neighboring countries have adopted similar measures. Pornography, long hair, and even chewing gum have long been forbidden in Singapore. In Myanmar, where the military government has been suspicious of all foreigners, until recently tourists were allowed to remain inside the country for only seven days and were not permitted to walk unescorted on the streets of the capital Rangoon. Even in easygoing Thailand, concern has been expressed

that Christian missionaries have been undermining the Buddhist character of Thai society. A more immediate problem, however, is the rapid spread of AIDS, a consequence of the Thai government's tolerance of widespread prostitution as a means of encouraging tourism.

One of the most significant changes that has taken place in Southeast Asia in recent decades involves the role of women in society. In general, women in Southeast Asia have historically faced fewer restrictions on their activities and enjoyed a higher status than women elsewhere in Asia. Nevertheless, they were not the equal of men in every respect. In Vietnam, Confucian precepts imported from China limited women's legal rights and occupational opportunities. In Buddhist and Muslim societies, women ranked lower on the social scale than men and generally did not play an active role in religious ritual. But women did not suffer from the extreme policies of seclusion, social degradation, and even physical mutilation such as the foot-binding practiced in many other societies in precolonial times. In that sense, it is clear that the relatively egalitarian traditions of early Southeast Asian societies moderated the rigid sexual discrimination practiced in other Confucian and Muslim societies.

The advent of colonial rule brought some minor improvements to the status of women in Southeast Asia. With the opening of government-supported public schools, females for the first time began to be educated alongside males. Colonial rule also opened up new career opportunities for women. The vast majority of women remained in the home or in the rice fields, but some found jobs as maids or cooks in the homes of the wealthy or worked in the factories in the growing colonial cities. Daughters of elite families occasionally even went abroad for higher education.

But perhaps the most striking effect of the colonial period was the arousing of women's consciousness. In the 1910s, for example, a magazine specifically for women appeared in French Indochina. While it tended to concentrate on woman's role as a wife, mother, and homemaker, its very existence focused attention on the fact that women were expected to become educated and to play an active role in modern society. In the 1920s, the publication of a second magazine, called *Women's News*, revealed the attitudinal changes that had taken place in a few short years. Articles in *Women's News* reflected the growing demand for equality in status, education, and occupation that was occurring in many Western countries. The magazine catered to the small but vocal elites in Hanoi and Saigon, and its advertisements were similar to those in magazines aimed at the sophisticated and the affluent in Europe and the United States.

Such direct attacks on traditions of sexual inequality were somewhat less common elsewhere in Southeast Asia, because outside Vietnam rigid Confucian social ethics were found only in local Chinese communities and women in general were less restricted than in Vietnam. In the Dutch East Indies, women benefited from the modernist movement among many Western-educated Muslims, which attempted to reconcile traditional fundamentalist beliefs with contemporary Western notions of social and sexual equality. Women were not cloistered from males as in many other Islamic societies, and young women were sometimes permitted to attend the religious schools set up by modernist elements to introduce young Indonesians to Muslim teachings. In some cases, they even attended coeducational classes.

With independence, the trend toward liberating Southeast Asian women continued. Virtually all of the constitutions adopted by the newly independent states granted women full legal and political rights with men, including the right to work. In some respects, that promise has been fulfilled. In countries throughout the region, women have increased opportunities for education and have entered new careers previously reserved for men. Social restrictions on female behavior and activities have been substantially reduced, if not entirely eliminated. Women have become more active in politics, and in 1986 Corazon Aquino became the first woman to be elected president of a country in Southeast Asia. The wife of her predecessor, Imelda Marcos, had been influential in Filipino politics in her own right.

Yet women are not truly equal to men in any country in Southeast Asia. Sometimes the distinction is simply a matter of custom. In Thailand, women are not permitted to become monks. In Vietnam, women are legally equal to men, yet no woman has served on the Communist Party's ruling Politburo. In Thailand, Malaysia, and Indonesia, women rarely hold senior positions in government service or in the boardrooms of major corporations. Similar restrictions apply in Myanmar, although Aung San Huu Kyi, the leading figure in the democratic opposition movement, is the daughter of one of the heroes of the country's struggle for liberation.

Sometimes, too, women's rights have been undermined by a social or religious backlash. The revival of Islamic fundamentalism stemming from the Iranian Revolution has had an especially strong impact in Malaysia, where Malay women are expected to cover their bodies and wear the traditional Muslim headdress. Women who dress in skimpy bathing suits at the beach have sometimes been criticized or even physically attacked by conservative Muslims. A local consumer group argues that Barbie dolls give a warped idea of female beauty and attractiveness and has called for a ban on their sale. Even in non-Muslim countries, women are still expected to behave demurely and to exercise discretion in all contacts with the opposite sex. Yet the signs of change are everywhere. In predominantly Muslim Indonesia, talk radio programs provide advice to their listeners on how to gain greater sexual satisfaction from their marriage.

Conclusion

In a half century of independence, the nations of South and Southeast Asia have changed in many ways. Much of the legacy of the colonial era has been erased, and the countries in both regions are embarked on their own indigenous road to the future. Yet the differences between the two regions are striking. While most South Asian societies continue to suffer from serious problems of political conflict and economic underdevelopment, Southeast Asia has shrugged off the Cold War tensions surrounding the Vietnam War, and there are promising signs of political stability and pluralism throughout the region.

To be sure, this bright prognosis must be qualified. Myanmar remains isolated from trends elsewhere in the region and appears mired in a state of chronic underdevelopment and brutal military rule. The three states of Indochina remain potentially unstable and have not yet been integrated into the region as a whole. All three are among the poorest nations of Asia, and the political situation in Cambodia remains especially perilous.

All things considered, however, the situation in Southeast Asia is more promising today than would have appeared possible a generation ago. The nations of Southeast Asia appear capable of coordinating their efforts to erase the internal divisions and conflicts that have brought so much tragedy to the peoples of the region for centuries. The situation in the South Asian subcontinent, however, remains one of serious concern. Communal tensions are on the rise in India and Sri Lanka, while political instability appears endemic in Pakistan.

Whatever the case, the peoples of both regions are now in control of their own destiny, while many reject the old assumption that modernity, Asian-style, must simply be a warmed-over version of the Western model.

CHAPTER NOTES

1. The quotation is from the document on p. 1153.
2. Quoted in Larry Collins and Dominique Lapierre, *Freedom at Midnight* (New York, 1975), p. 252.
3. Stephen Hay, ed., *Sources of Indian Tradition*, vol. 2 (New York, 1988), p. 386.
4. Ayub Khan, *Friends, Not Masters: A Political Autobiography* (Lahore, 1967), cited in ibid., 2:399–400.
5. *New York Times*, April 26, 1996.
6. Letter to Narandas Gandhi, May 20, 1944, reproduced in Martin Green, ed., *Gandhi in India: In His Own Words* (Hanover, N.H., 1987), p. 309.
7. Kusum Nair, *Blossoms in the Dust: The Human Factor in Indian Development* (New York, 1961), p. 76.
8. Jan Myrdal, *Asian Drama: An Inquiry into the Poverty of Nations*, abridged version (New York, 1971), p. 345.
9. *New York Times*, February 6, 1991.
10. Ibid., May 2, 1996.
11. Mahathir Bin Mohamad, *The Malay Dilemma* (Kuala Lumpur, 1970), p. 94.
12. Quoted in Harry J. Benda and John A. Larkin, eds., *The World of Southeast Asia: Selected Historical Readings* (New York, 1967), p. 250. The Indonesian word *musjawarah* was adopted from the Arabic word *mashwara*, which carries the connotation of "consultation."
13. Ibid., p. 252.
14. Mochtar Lubis, "Mysticism in Indonesian Politics," in Robert O. Tilman, ed., *Man, State, and Society in Contemporary Southeast Asia* (New York, 1969), p. 185.
15. Benda and Larkin, *The World of Southeast Asia*, pp. 289–90.
16. *New York Times*, July 28, 1996.
17. *Far Eastern Economic Review*, August 1, 1996.
18. Lubis, "Mysticism in Indonesian Politics," p. 180.

SUGGESTED READINGS

For a recent survey of contemporary Indian history, see S. Wolpert, *A New History of India*, rev. ed. (New York, 1989). V. S. Naipaul, *India: A Wounded Civilization* (New York, 1977) is a provocative study of independent India from a friendly but sometimes critical perspective. Also see P. Brass, *The New Cambridge History of India: The Politics of Independence* (Cambridge, 1990) and C. Baxter, *Bangladesh: From a Nation to a State* (Boulder, Colo., 1997).

On the period surrounding independence, see the dramatic account by L. Collins and D. Lapierre, *Freedom at Midnight* (New York, 1975). On Nehru's government, see D. Norman, ed., *Nehru: The First Sixty Years*, 2 vols. (London, 1965). For insight into Nehru's character, see S. Gandhi, ed., *Two Alone, Two Together: Letters between Indira Gandhi and Jawaharlal Nehru, 1940–1964* (London, 1992).

The life and career of Indira Gandhi have been well chronicled. For two recent biographies, see T. Ali, *An Indian Dynasty: The Story of the Nehru-Gandhi Family* (New York, 1985) and K. Bhatia, *Indira: A Biography of Prime Minister Gandhi* (New York, 1974.)

Social issues are examined in a number of recent studies. For an overview, see K. Bhatia, *The Ordeal of Nationhood: A Social Study of India since Independence, 1947–1970* (New York, 1971). See also J. M. Freeman, *Untouchable: An Indian Life History* (Stanford, Calif., 1979); R. G. Revankar, *The Indian Constitution: A Case Study of Backward Classes* (Rutherford, N.J., 1971); and W. and C. Wiser, *Behind Mud Walls, 1930–1960*, rev. ed. (New York, 1984). On Indian literature, see D. Ray and A. Singh, eds., *India: An Anthology of Contemporary Writing* (Athens, Ohio, 1983). See also S. Mann and K. Lalita, eds., *Women Writing in India*, vol. 2 (New York, 1993). Novels mentioned in the text include A. Desai, *Cry, the Peacock* (New Delhi, 1980) and S. Rushdie, *Midnight's Children* (Harmondsworth, 1980).

There are a number of standard surveys of the history of modern Southeast Asia. Unfortunately, many of them are now out-of-date because of the changes that have taken place in the region since the end of the Vietnam War. For an introduction with a strong emphasis on recent events, see D. R. SarDesai, *Southeast Asia: Past and Present*, 2d ed. (Boulder, Colo., 1989). For a more scholarly approach, see D. J. Steinberg, ed., *In Search of Southeast Asia*, 2d ed. (New York, 1985).

The best way to approach modern Southeast Asia is through individual country studies. On Burma, see J. Silverstein, *Burmese Politics: The Dilemma of National Unity* (New Brunswick, N.J., 1980). On Thailand, see D. Wyatt, *Thailand* (New Haven, Conn., 1982). On the Philippines, the best overall survey is D. J. Steinberg, *The Philippines: A Singular and a Plural Place* (Boulder, Colo., 1994). On Malaya and Singapore, see K. von Vorys, *Democracy without Consensus* (Princeton, N.J., 1975) and C. M. Turnbull, *A History of Singapore, 1819–1975* (Kuala Lumpur, 1977). For insight into the problem of racial tension in Malaysia, see M. bin Mohamad, *The Malay Dilemma* (Kuala Lumpur, 1970).

There is a rich selection of materials on modern Indonesia. On the Sukarno era, see J. Legge, *Sukarno* (New York, 1972) and H. Jones, *Indonesia: The Possible Dream* (New York, 1971). On the Suharto era and its origins, see H. Crouch, *The Army in Indonesian Politics* (Ithaca, N.Y., 1978) and M. Vatikiotis, *Indonesian Politics under Suharto* (London, 1993).

Most of the literature on Indochina in the last two decades has dealt with the Vietnam War and the related conflicts in Laos and Cambodia. For an excellent overall history, see S. Karnow, *Vietnam: A History* (New York, 1983), a companion volume for the PBS series on the war. F. Fitzgerald's *Fire in the Lake* (New York, 1970) won a Pulitzer Prize for its discussion of the reasons for the strength of the Viet Cong. On the brutal reign of the Khmer Rouge in Cambodia, see F. Ponchaud, *Cambodia Year Zero* (New York, 1977). On conditions in Vietnam since the end of the war, see R. Shaplen, *Bitter Victory* (New York, 1986), a study by a veteran journalist.

CHAPTER
32

Toward the Pacific Century: Japan and the Little Tigers

In August of 1945, Japan was in ruins, its cities destroyed, its vast Asian empire in ashes, its land occupied by a foreign army. A decade earlier, Japanese leaders had proclaimed their national path to development as a model for other Asian nations to follow. A few years later, they had attempted to construct their vast Greater East Asia Co-prosperity Sphere under Japanese tutelage. The result had been a bloody war and ultimate defeat.

Half a century later, Japan has emerged as the second greatest industrial power in the world, democratic in form and content and a source of stability throughout the region. Japan's achievement has spawned a number of Asian imitators. Known as the "little tigers," the four industrializing societies of Taiwan, Hong Kong, Singapore, and South Korea have achieved considerable success by following the path originally charted by Japan. Along with Japan, they have become economic powerhouses and rank among the world's top seventeen trading nations. Other nations in Asia have taken note and are now adopting the Japanese formula. It is no wonder that observers are talking about the coming of the "Pacific Century."

The astounding recent success of some countries in East and Southeast Asia has prompted some commentators in the region to declare that the global balance of power has shifted and is now to be found in the lands of the Pacific rather than in Europe or the United States. Western critics retort that Asia's achievement has taken place at great cost, as authoritarian governments

1945	1955	1965	1975	1985	1995

End of World War II in the Pacific

U.S. occupation of Japan

Liberal Democrats
defeated in Japan

United States–Japan security treaty

Economic recession in Japan

Period of
Korean War

Syngman Rhee overthrown
in South Korea

Chung Hee Park
assassinated

Students riot at
Kwangju in South Korea

United States–
Republic of China
security treaty

Independence of
Republic of Singapore

First free general elections on Taiwan

Hong Kong
returned
to China

Chinese naval maneuvers in Taiwan Strait

in the region have trampled on human rights and denied citizens the freedom to fulfill their own destiny. To Chan Heng Chee, currently Singapore's ambassador to the United States, this debate is not "a clash of civilizations leading inevitably to war." It is a temporary phase that she hopes "will promote better appreciation and understanding on all sides so that we might all learn to appreciate, and perhaps benefit from, what is best in the other."[1]

The Allied Occupation

For five years after the end of the war in the Pacific, Japan was governed by an Allied administration under the command of U.S. General Douglas MacArthur. The occupation regime, which consisted of a Far Eastern Commission in Washington, D.C., and a four-power Allied Council in Tokyo, was dominated by the United States, although the country was technically administered by a new Japanese government. As commander of the occupation administration, MacArthur was responsible for demilitarizing Japanese society, destroying the Japanese war machine, trying Japanese civilian and military officials charged with war crimes, and laying the foundations of postwar Japanese society.

During the war, senior U.S. officials had discussed whether to insist on the abdication of the emperor as the symbol of Japanese imperial expansion. During the

◆ **General MacArthur and Emperor Hirohito.** After the end of World War II, U.S. General Douglas MacArthur was appointed supreme commander of the Allied powers. In that capacity, he directed U.S. policy during the occupation from 1945 to 1950. Here MacArthur stands side by side with Emperor Hirohito of Japan. Note the cultural and attitudinal differences of the two leaders expressed by their contrasting body language.

≥ The Emperor Is Not Divine ≤

At the close of World War II, the United States agreed that Japan could retain the emperor, but only on condition that he renounce his divinity. When the governments of Great Britain and the Soviet Union advocated that Hirohito be tried as a war criminal, General Douglas MacArthur, the supreme commander of Allied occupation forces in Japan, argued that the emperor had a greater grasp of democratic principles than most other Japanese and that his presence was vital to the success of Allied occupation policy. That recommendation was upheld. On New Year's Day, 1946, the emperor issued a rescript denying his divinity. To many Japanese of the era, however, he remained a divine figure.

Hirohito, Rescript on Divinity

In greeting the New Year, we recall to mind that the Emperor Meiji proclaimed as the basis of our national policy the five clauses of the Charter at the beginning of the Meiji era. . . .

The proclamation is evident in its significance and high in its ideals. We wish to make this oath anew and restore the country to stand on its own feet again. We have to reaffirm the principles embodied in the Charter and proceed unflinchingly toward elimination of misguided practices of the past; and keeping in close touch with the desires of the people, we will construct a new Japan through thoroughly being pacific, the officials and the people alike obtaining rich culture and advancing the standard of living of the people.

The devastation of the war inflicted upon our cities, the miseries of the destitute, the stagnation of trade, shortage of food and the great and growing number of the unemployed are indeed heart-rending, but if the nation is firmly united in its resolve to face the present ordeal and to see civilization consistently in peace, a bright future will undoubtedly be ours, not only for our country but for the whole of humanity.

Love of the family and love of country are especially strong in this country. With more of this devotion should we now work toward love of mankind.

We feel deeply concerned to note that consequent upon the protracted war ending in our defeat our people are liable to grow restless and to fall into the slough of despond. Radical tendencies in excess are gradually spreading and the sense of morality tends to lose its hold on the people with the result that there are signs of confusion of thoughts.

We stand by the people and we wish always to share with them in their moment of joys and sorrows. The ties between us and our people have always stood upon mutual trust and affection. They do not depend upon mere legends and myths. They are not predicated on the false conception that the Emperor is divine and that the Japanese people are superior to other races and fated to rule the world.

Our Government should make every effort to alleviate their trials and tribulations. At the same time, we trust that the people will rise to the occasion and will strive courageously for the solution of their outstanding difficulties and for the development of industry and culture. Acting upon a consciousness of solidarity and of mutual aid and broad tolerance in their civil life, they will prove themselves worthy of their best tradition. By their supreme endeavors in that direction they will be able to render their substantial contribution to the welfare and advancement of mankind.

The resolution for the year should be made at the beginning of the year. We expect our people to join us in all exertions looking to accomplishment of this great undertaking with an indomitable spirit.

---

summer of 1945, the United States rejected a Japanese request to guarantee that the position of the emperor would be retained in any future peace settlement and reiterated its demand for unconditional surrender. After the war, however, the United States agreed to the retention of the emperor after he agreed publicly to renounce his divinity (see the box above). Although many historians have suggested that Emperor Hirohito opposed the war policy of his senior advisers, some recent studies have contended that he fully supported it.

Under MacArthur's firm tutelage, Japanese society was remodeled along Western lines. The centerpiece of occupation policy was the promulgation of a new constitution to replace the Meiji Constitution of 1889. The new charter, which was drafted by U.S. planners and imposed on the Japanese despite their objections to some of its provisions, was designed to transform Japan into a peaceful and pluralistic society that would no longer be capable of waging offensive war. The constitution specifically renounced war as a national policy, and Japan unilaterally agreed to maintain armed forces only sufficient for self-defense. Perhaps most importantly, the constitution established a parliamentary form of government based on a bicameral legislature, an independent judiciary, and a universal franchise; it also reduced the power of the emperor and guaranteed human rights.

But more than a written constitution was needed to demilitarize Japan and place it on a new course. Like the Meiji leaders in the late nineteenth century, occupation administrators wished to transform Japanese social institutions and hoped their policies would be accepted by the Japanese people as readily as those of the Meiji period had been. The Meiji reforms, however, had been crafted to reflect native traditions and had set Japan on a path quite different from that of the modern West. Some Japanese observers believed that a fundamental reversal of trends begun with the Meiji Restoration would be needed before Japan would be ready to adopt the Western capitalist, democratic model.

One of the sturdy pillars of Japanese militarism had been the giant business cartels, known as *zaibatsu*. Allied policy was designed to break up the *zaibatsu* into smaller units in the belief that corporate concentration, in Japan as in the United States, not only hindered competition but was inherently undemocratic and conducive to political authoritarianism. Occupation planners also intended to promote the formation of independent labor unions, to lessen the power of the state over the economy, and to provide a mouthpiece for downtrodden Japanese workers. Economic inequality in rural areas was to be reduced by a comprehensive land reform program that would turn the land over to the tillers. Finally, the educational system was to be remodeled along U.S. lines, so that it would turn out independent individuals rather than automatons subject to manipulation by the state.

The Allied program was an ambitious and even audacious plan to remake Japanese society and has been justly praised for its clear-sighted vision and altruistic motives. Parts of the program, such as the constitution, the land reform program, and the educational system, succeeded brilliantly. But as other concerns began to intervene, changes or compromises were made that were not always successful. In particular, with the rise of Cold War sentiment in the United States in the late 1940s, the goal of decentralizing the Japanese economy gave way to the desire to make Japan a key partner in the effort to defend East Asia against international communism. Convinced of the need to promote economic recovery in Japan, U.S. policymakers began to show more tolerance for the *zaibatsu*. Concerned at growing radicalism within the new labor movement, where left-wing elements were gaining

strength, U.S. occupation authorities placed less emphasis on the independence of the labor unions.

Cold War concerns also affected U.S. foreign relations with Japan. On September 8, 1951, the United States and other former belligerent nations signed a peace treaty restoring Japanese independence. In turn, Japan renounced any claim to such former colonies or territories as Taiwan (which had been returned to the Republic of China), Korea (which, after a period of joint Soviet and U.S. occupation, had become two independent states), and southern Sakhalin and the Kurile Islands (which had been ceded to the Soviet Union). The Soviet Union refused to sign the treaty on the grounds that it had not been permitted to play an active role in the occupation. On the same day, the Japanese and Americans signed a defensive alliance and agreed that the United States could maintain military bases on the Japanese islands. Japan was now formally independent, but in a new dependency relationship with the United States.

The Japanese Miracle: The Transformation of Society in Modern Japan

By the early 1950s, then, Japan had regained at least partial control over its own destiny. Although it was linked closely to the United States through the new security treaty and the new U.S.-drafted constitution, Japan was now essentially free to move out on its own. As the world would soon discover, the Japanese adapted quickly to the new conditions. From a semifeudal society with autocratic leanings, Japan has progressed into one of the most stable and advanced democracies in the world today. It has risen from the ashes of total destruction in 1945 to become the second largest and in many ways the most advanced economy in the world.

Japan's achievements in the area of human services are especially noteworthy. Its record on health is impressive, even though it has one-third more people per doctor than in the United States. Life expectancy is high, and the infant mortality rate is only five per thousand, the lowest in the world. The literacy rate is almost 100 percent, and a significantly higher proportion of the population graduates from high school than in most advanced nations of the West. Crime rates are low (on an average day, according to a recent statistic, 4,584 crimes are committed in Japan compared to 93,474 in the United States), and although Japan suffered badly from environmental pollution during the 1950s and 1960s, it has moved rapidly to improve its urban environments. Despite its near-total lack of domestic sources of oil, Japan today is less dependent upon oil imports than is the oil-rich United States.

Japan appears equally blessed in the area of foreign affairs. Under the umbrella of U.S. nuclear protection, Japan has been able to avoid conflicts with foreign countries and has adhered to its constitutional restriction of staying out of foreign wars. Though linked to the United States through the 1951 security treaty, Japan has carried out an increasingly independent foreign policy in recent years and has succeeded in maintaining amicable relations with virtually all nations. Its only serious dispute is with Russia, which has consistently refused Japan's request for the return of four islands in the Kurile chain near the northern Japanese island of Hokkaido.

In recent years, Japan's rapid emergence as an economic giant has often been described as the "Japanese miracle." Whether or not this description is justified, Japan has made a dramatic recovery from the war. Although the "miracle" is often described as beginning after the war as a result of the Allied reforms—a chronology that ascribes most of the credit to U.S. postwar policies—in fact, as we have seen, Japanese economic growth began much earlier with the Meiji reforms, which helped to transform Japan from an autocratic society based on semifeudal institutions into an advanced capitalist democracy. The seeds of the Japanese miracle were sown in the Meiji period, or even in the late Tokugawa era, well over a hundred years ago.

Moreover, although we tend to think of Japanese achievements primarily in economic terms, a modern

Map 32.1   Modern Japan.

economic sector can only be developed where changes are taking place in politics, social institutions, culture, and human values as well. It is in these areas where the Allied occupation may have had its most salutary effects. To fully understand modern Japan, then, we must examine not just the economy but the multifaceted changes that have occurred in recent decades throughout Japanese society.

Politics and Government

The Allied occupation administrators started with the conviction that Japanese expansionism was directly linked to the institutional and ideological foundations of the Meiji Constitution. Accordingly, they set out to change Japanese politics into something closer to the pluralistic approach used in most Western nations. The concepts of universal suffrage, governmental accountability, and a balance of power among the executive, legislative, and judicial branches that were embodied in the Constitution of 1947 have held firm, and Japan today is a stable and mature democratic society with a literate and politically active electorate and a government that actively seeks to meet the needs of its citizens.

Yet a number of characteristics of the current Japanese political system reflect the tenacity of the traditional political culture. Although Japan had a multiparty system with two major parties, the Liberal Democrats and the Socialists, in practice there was a "government party" and a permanent opposition—the Liberal Democrats were not voted out of office for thirty years. The ruling Liberal Democratic Party included several factions, but disputes were usually based on personalities rather than substantive issues. Many of the leading Liberal Democrats controlled factions on a patron-client basis, and decisions on key issues such as who should assume the prime ministership were decided by a modern equivalent of the *genro* oligarchs. That tradition changed suddenly in 1993, when the "ruling" Liberal Democrats failed to win a majority of seats in parliamentary elections. Mirohiro Hosokawa, the leader of one of several newly created parties in the Japanese political spectrum, was elected prime minister. He promised to launch a number of reforms to clean up the political system. The new coalition government quickly split into feuding factions, however, and in 1995 the Liberal Democratic Party returned to power under a cabinet led by Prime Minister Ryutaro Hashimoto. Hashimoto promised to carry out a series of reforms to make the government more efficient and less prone to corruption.

One of the problems is that the current system continues the centralizing tendencies of the Meiji period. The government is organized on a unitary rather than a federal basis; the local administrative units, called prefectures, have few of the powers of states in the United States. Moreover, the central government plays an active and sometimes intrusive role in various aspects of the economy, mediating management-labor disputes, establishing price and wage policies, and subsidizing vital industries and enterprises producing goods for export. This government intervention in the economy has traditionally been widely accepted and is often cited as a key reason for the efficiency of Japanese industry and the emergence of the country as an industrial giant. The Japanese call this process *nemawashi*, or "root-binding," a term that "originally comes from gardening, where it designates the careful untangling and binding of each of the roots of the tree before it is moved." The government plays an active role in resolving major issues and consults all relevant groups before a decision is reached. If the decision works to the disadvantage of any group, "it is understood that they will be given special consideration now or in the future." Thus, the roots of the disadvantaged group are bound and "do not impede the effective moving of the tree."[2]

In recent years, the tradition of active government involvement in the economy has increasingly come under fire. Japanese business, which previously sought government protection from goods imported from abroad, now argues that deregulation is needed to enable Japanese firms to innovate and keep up with the competition. Such reforms, however, are likely to be resisted by powerful government ministries in Tokyo.

Another problem that has shaken Japanese self-confidence in recent years has been corruption in government. A number of senior politicians, including two recent prime ministers, have been forced to resign because of serious questions about improper financial dealings with business associates. Concern over political corruption was undoubtedly a major factor in the defeat suffered by the Liberal Democrats in the summer of 1993.

Japan is also experiencing a rise in nationalist sentiment and growing demands for a more assertive stance toward the United States (see the box on p. 1192). Although the Japanese government has generally resisted such demands, some officials share these attitudes and quietly applaud Malaysian prime minister Mahathir Mohamad when he calls on Japan to play a larger role in Asian affairs.

Last, but certainly not least, minorities like the *eta* (now known as Burakumin) and Korean residents in

Americans: Look in the Mirror!

Shintaro Ishiwara, a contemporary writer and movie director, is one of many Japanese who have become exasperated at the tendency of the United States to blame Japan for U.S. problems. In a recent book, Shintaro bluntly informed his readers that the problems of the United States are of its own making. Needless to say, when published in an English translation, the book caused a stir in the United States.

Shintaro Ishiwara, *The Japan That Can Say No*

I realize that these are very trying times for Americans. Until very recently, the United States was the unrivaled military and economic leader of the free world. Now, suddenly, Japan seems to have usurped that economic power. Americans from all walks of life are upset, frustrated, and worried about their country.

Most of America's woes are self-made, but some prefer to blame Japan, saying that our market is closed to U.S.-made products and we are an unfair trader. Those who cannot take stock of themselves—whether an individual, company, or nation—face an uncertain future. I want to believe that the United States, with its enormous underlying strength, will pull itself together and come roaring back. Yet there are many worrisome signs.

In October 1989, *Newsweek* reported that most Americans viewed Japan as a greater threat than the Soviet Union. The word "threat" might be appropriate if Americans had attempted to put their house in order. Instead, Congress looks to Japan for a scapegoat, uses high-handed tactics, and tries to push us around. To confuse a hypothetical military foe with an economic competitor and stick a ridiculous label like "threat" on us shows how dangerously confused the United States is. It would be fairer and more productive if Americans stopped the arm-twisting and sanctions and got their country back into shape.

Japan can help by compromise and cooperation, but the outcome depends primarily on American efforts.

Let's be candid. America's problem is not Japan's economic strength but its own industrial weakness. As many senior Japanese executives have pointed out, the fundamental cause is the endemic shortsightedness in U.S. boardrooms. Some uninformed Americans make long lists of the evils of Japanese-style management and demand corrective action. Of course, there are impediments to free trade in Japan, but our businessmen are always ready to make reasonable adjustments. Before pointing the finger at Tokyo and Osaka, Americans should deal first with the host of problems in their own backyard.

A Japanese friend of mine established his own company and built it into a medium-sized corporation with a U.S. subsidiary. He is convinced that the complete separation of capital and management in the United States hurts business.

In Japan, companies are either family owned and managed or there is a psychological solidarity between the shareholders and management. In the United States, professional managers run the company for the stockholders, who often become adversarial if dividends slide. What are the consequences of these different arrangements?

Managers who pursue immediate profits miss out on large midterm (ten-year) gains. But U.S. institutional investors do not care where a company will be a decade from now. They are only interested in getting a quick, high return on their capital. If earnings fall off a bit, the big boys unload the stock before its value drops.

I hope the United States is not too proud to roll up its sleeves and do whatever is necessary to revive its manufacturing industry and economy. Then, America's enormous potential in high-technology fields will bloom and contribute to the next era. U.S. attacks on Japan's trade practices and demands for reforms are not a black-and-white issue; some points are valid and others are not. One thing, however, is certain: American critics should take a cold shower and calm down.

Japan continue to be subjected to legal and social discrimination. In recent years, official sources have been reluctant to divulge growing evidence that thousands of Korean women were conscripted to serve as prostitutes (euphemistically, "comfort women") for Japanese soldiers during the war, and many Koreans living in Japan contend that such prejudicial attitudes continue to exist.

Representatives of the Korean women have demanded both financial compensation and a formal letter of apology from the Japanese government for the treatment they received during the Pacific War.

The issue of Japan's behavior during World War II has been especially sensitive. A U.S. political scientist teaching for a year at Kobe University reports that many of his students said they had learned about Pearl Harbor, the invasion of China, and the massacre of Chinese civilians in Nanjing "from my uncle, from my grandfather, from TV, from books, from family talk," but not from their classes. Several students told him that they knew of teachers who had been disciplined for teaching about the war. Asked why such things were not taught in school, they always answered, "Because the Government, or the Education Ministry, does not want us to know."[3]

There is ample evidence that such is the case. Critics at home and abroad, for example, have charged that textbooks printed under the guidance of the Ministry of Education do not adequately discuss the crimes committed by the Japanese government and armed forces during World War II. Other Asian governments have been particularly incensed at Tokyo's failure to accept responsibility for such behavior and have demanded a formal apology. The current government of Prime Minister Hashimoto has responded with a statement that expresses remorse, but only in the context of the aggressive actions of all colonial powers during the imperialist era. In the view of many Japanese, the actions of their government during the Pacific War were a form of self-defense. Elsewhere in the region, however, fear of a potential revival of Japanese militarism is still strong.

Still, such problems are minuscule compared to the impressive achievements realized by Japan since the dark days at the end of World War II. The nation's postwar leaders dedicated themselves to realizing Japan's national aspirations within a democratic and pluralistic framework. Although the current fragility of the party system raises questions about future trends in Japanese politics, few countries today possess a political system as stable and respective of human values as that of Japan.

The Economy

Nowhere are the changes in postwar Japan so visible as in the economic sector, where Japan has developed into a major industrial and technological power in the space of a century, surpassing such advanced Western societies as Germany, France, and Great Britain. Here, indeed, is the Japanese miracle in its most concrete manifestation.

The process began a century ago in the single-minded determination of the Meiji modernizers to create a "rich country and strong state" (*fukoku kyohei*). Their initial motive was to guarantee Japan's survival against Western imperialism, but this defensive urge evolved into a desire to excel and, during the years before World War II, to dominate. That desire led to the war in the Pacific and, in the eyes of some, still contributes to Japan's problems with its trading partners in the world today.

As we have seen, the officials of the Allied occupation identified the Meiji economic system with centralized power and the rise of Japanese militarism. Accordingly, MacArthur's planners set out to break up the *zaibatsu* and decentralize Japanese industry and commerce. But with the rise of Cold War tensions, the policy was scaled back in the late 1940s, and only the nineteen largest conglomerates were affected. In any event, the new antimonopoly law did not hinder the formation of looser ties between Japanese companies, and as a result, a new type of informal relationship, sometimes called the *keiretsu* or "interlocking arrangement," began to take shape after World War II. Through such arrangements among suppliers, wholesalers, retailers, and financial institutions, the *zaibatsu* system was reconstituted under a new name.

The occupation administration had more success with its program to reform the agricultural system. Half of the population still lived on farms, and half of all farmers were still tenants. Under a stringent land reform program in the late 1940s, all lands owned by absentee landlords and all cultivated landholdings over an established maximum were sold on easy credit terms to the tenants. The maximum size of an individual farm was set at 7.5 acres, while an additional 2.5 acres could be leased to tenants. The reform program created a strong class of yeoman farmers, and tenants declined to about 10 percent of the rural population.

During the last forty years, Japan has re-created the stunning results of the Meiji era. At the end of the Allied occupation in 1950, the Japanese gross national product was about one-third that of Great Britain or France. Today, it is larger than both put together and well over half that of the United States. Japan is the greatest exporting nation in the world, and its per capita income equals or surpasses that of most advanced Western states. In terms of education, mortality rates, and health care, the quality of life in Japan is superior to that in the United States or the advanced nations of Western Europe.

By the mid-1980s, the economic challenge presented by Japan had begun to arouse increasing concern in both official and private circles in Europe and the United States. Explanations for the phenomenon tended to fall into two major categories. Some commentators pointed to cultural factors. The Japanese are naturally group-oriented and find it easy to cooperate with one another. Traditionally hardworking and frugal, they are more inclined to save than to consume, a trait that boosts the savings rate and labor productivity. The Japanese are family-oriented and therefore spend less on welfare for the elderly, who normally live with their children. Like all Confucian societies, the Japanese value education, and consequently the labor force is highly skilled. Finally, Japan is

◆ On the Assembly Line. Automation is sometimes cited as one of the key reasons for the vaunted efficiency of the Japanese industrial machine. Mechanical robots, as shown above, perform tasks in Japan that elsewhere are performed by human beings. In recent years, however, some Japanese companies have discovered that robots are less adaptive to the need for rapid change and innovation on the assembly line than are their human counterparts.

a homogeneous society, in which people share common values and respond in similar ways to the challenges of the modern world.

Others cited more practical reasons for Japanese success. Paradoxically, Japan benefited from the total destruction of its industrial base during World War II and does not face the problem of antiquated plants that plagues many industries in the United States. Under the terms of its constitution and the security treaty with the United States, Japan spends less than 1 percent of its gross national product on national defense, whereas the United States spends more than 5 percent. Labor productivity is high, not simply because the Japanese are hard workers (according to statistics, Japanese workers spend a substantially longer period of time at their job than do workers in other advanced societies), but be-

cause corporations reward innovation and maintain good management-labor relations. Consequently, employee mobility and the number of days lost to labor stoppages are minimized (on an average day, according to one estimate, 603 Japanese workers are on strike compared to 11,956 Americans). Just as it did before World War II, the Japanese government promotes business interests rather than hindering them. Finally, some charge that Japan uses unfair trade practices, subsidizing exports through the Ministry of International Trade and Industry (MITI), dumping goods at prices below cost to break into a foreign market, maintaining an artificially low standard of living at home to encourage exports, and unduly restricting imports from other countries.

The truth in this case is probably a little of both. Undoubtedly, Japan has benefited from its privileged position beneath the U.S. nuclear umbrella as well as from its ability to operate in a free trade environment that provides both export markets and access to Western technology. The Japanese have also taken a number of practical steps to improve their competitive position in the world and the effectiveness of their economic system at home.

Yet many of these steps were possible precisely because of the cultural factors described here. The concept of "root-binding" and the tradition of loyalty to the firm, for example, derive from the communal tradition in Japanese society. The concept of sacrificing one's personal interests to those of the state, though not necessarily rooted in the traditional period, was certainly fostered by the *genro* oligarchy during the Meiji era.

In recent years, the concern that Japan might overtake the United States and reduce it to a second-rank economic power has abated somewhat. One reason is the increasingly competitive position of U.S. firms in the global marketplace. But another is the economic downturn the Japanese economy has experienced in the 1990s, when it has encountered some of the problems that have afflicted the United States in the recent era, as well as others that may be the consequence of factors unique to Japan. In the first place, a rise in the value of the yen has hurt exports and burst the bubble of investment by Japanese banks that had taken place under the umbrella of government protection. With declining exports and a domestic market that is much smaller than the U.S. market, the Japanese economy has been mired in a long-term recession.

These economic difficulties have placed heavy pressure on some of the vaunted features of the Japanese economy. The tradition of lifetime employment created a bloated white-collar workforce and has made downsizing difficult. Today, job security is on the decline, and increasing numbers of workers are being laid off. Unfortunately, many of those who suffer the worst are women, who lack seniority and continue to face various forms of discrimination in the workplace. A positive consequence is that job satisfaction is beginning to take precedence over security in the minds of many Japanese workers, while salaries are beginning to reflect performance more than time on the job.

A final factor is that slowly but inexorably the Japanese market is beginning to open up to international competition. Foreign auto makers are winning a growing share of the Japanese market, while the government—concerned at the prospect of growing food shortages—has committed itself to facilitating the importation of rice from abroad. The latter move was especially sensitive, given the almost sacred role that rice farming holds in the Japanese mind-set.

A Society in Transition

Although the Meiji Restoration resulted in significant changes in Japanese customs and attitudes, the essentially hierarchical character of traditional society persisted. Japanese farmers, miners, and factory workers were ruthlessly exploited to provide the sinews of state power, while the male-oriented character of pre-Meiji Japan remained substantially unchanged.

Allied planners during the occupation set out to change social characteristics that they believed had contributed to Japanese aggressiveness before and during World War II. The new educational system removed all references to filial piety, patriotism, and loyalty to the emperor, while emphasizing the individualistic values of Western civilization. The new constitution and a revised civil code attempted to achieve true sexual equality by removing remaining legal restrictions on women's rights to obtain a divorce, hold a job, or change their domicile. Women were guaranteed the right to vote and were encouraged to enter politics.

Such efforts to remake Japanese behavior through legislation were only partially successful. During the last forty years, Japan has unquestionably become a more individualistic and egalitarian society. Freedom of choice in marriage and occupation is taken for granted, and social mobility, though not so extensive as in the United States, has increased considerably beyond prewar levels. Although Allied occupation policy established the legal framework for these developments, the primary credit undoubtedly can be assigned to the evolution of Japan into an urbanized and technologically advanced industrial society.

At the same time, many of the distinctive characteristics of traditional Japanese society have persisted into the present day, although in somewhat altered form. The emphasis on loyalty to the group and community relationships, for example, known in Japanese as *amae*, is reflected in the strength of corporate loyalties in contemporary Japan. Although competition among enterprises in a particular industry is often quite vigorous, social cohesiveness among both management and labor personnel is exceptionally strong within each individual corporation, although, as we have noted, this attitude has eroded somewhat in recent years.

One possible product of this cohesiveness may be the relatively egalitarian character of Japanese society in terms of income. A chief executive officer in Japan receives on average seventeen times the salary of the average worker versus eighty-five times in the United States. The disparity between wealth and poverty is also generally less in Japan than in most European countries and certainly less than in the United States. In Japan, the poorest 20 percent of the population possesses about 9 percent of the wealth, while the richest 20 percent owns 37 percent. In the United States, the poorest 20 percent possesses only 4 percent of the wealth, while the richest 20 percent owns 46 percent.[4]

Emphasis on the work ethic also remains strong. The tradition of hard work is implanted at a young age within the educational system. The Japanese school year runs for 240 days a year compared to 180 days in the United States, and work assignments outside class tend to be more extensive (according to one source, a Japanese student averages about five hours of homework per day). Competition for acceptance into universities is intense, and many young Japanese take cram courses to prepare for the "examination hell" that lies ahead. The results are impressive: the literacy rate in Japanese schools is almost 100 percent, and Japanese schoolchildren consistently earn higher scores on achievement tests than children in other advanced countries.

At the same time, this devotion to success has often been accompanied by harsh discipline from teachers and what Americans might consider an oppressive sense of conformity (see the box on p. 1196). To give one example, the Japanese professional tennis player Kimiko Date played tennis with her right hand at the insistence of her father, even though she was naturally left-handed. As a child, she made no protest, "because I thought everybody played that way." In school, bullying of nonconforming students by their peers has become endemic and arouses serious concern among educators and political leaders alike. As one Japanese writer who specializes in educational matters has observed:

❧ Growing Up in Japan ❧

Japanese schoolchildren are exposed to a much more regimented environment than U.S. children experience. Most Japanese schoolchildren, for example, wear black and white uniforms to school. These regulations are examples of rules adopted by middle school systems in various parts of Japan. The Ministry of Education in Tokyo concluded that these regulations were excessive, but they are probably typical.

School Regulations: Japanese Style

1. Boys' hair should not touch the eyebrows, the ears, or the top of the collar.
2. No one should have a permanent wave, or dye his or her hair. Girls should not wear ribbons or accessories in their hair. Hair dryers should not be used.
3. School uniform skirts should be ____ centimeters above the ground, no more and no less (differs by school and region).
4. Keep your uniform clean and pressed at all times. Girls' middy blouses should have two buttons on the back collar. Boys' pant cuffs should be of the prescribed width. No more than 12 eyelets should be on shoes. The number of buttons on a shirt and tucks in a shirt are also prescribed.
5. Wear your school badge at all times. It should be positioned exactly.
6. Going to school in the morning, wear your book bag strap on the right shoulder; in the afternoon on the way home, wear it on the left shoulder. Your book case thickness, filled and unfilled, is also prescribed.
7. Girls should wear only regulation white underpants of 100% cotton.
8. When you raise your hand to be called on, your arm should extend forward and up at the angle prescribed in your handbook.
9. Your own route to and from school is marked in your student rule handbook; carefully observe which side of each street you are to use on the way to and from school.
10. After school you are to go directly home, unless your parent has written a note permitting you to go to another location. Permission will not be granted by the school unless this other location is a suitable one. You must not go to coffee shops. You must be home by ____ o'clock.
11. It is not permitted to drive or ride a motorcycle, or to have a license to drive one.
12. Before and after school, no matter where you are, you represent our school, so you should behave in ways we can all be proud of.

Many Japanese incorrectly believe that our education has been a success because there aren't as many dropouts or drug abuse cases as in the United States. But in fact Japanese schools are akin to prisons ruled by fear, where kids must constantly be looking around to make sure they're behaving exactly like everyone else.[5]

Some young Japanese find suicide the only escape from the pressures emanating from society, school, and family. Parental pride often becomes a factor, with "education mothers" pressuring their children to work hard and succeed for the honor of the family. Ironically, once the student is accepted into college, the amount of work assigned tends to decrease, since graduates of the best universities are virtually guaranteed lucrative employment offers. Nevertheless, the early training instills an attitude of deference to group interests that persists throughout life. Some outside observers, however, believe such practices can have a detrimental effect on individual initiative.

The tension between the Japanese way and the foreign approach is especially noticeable in Japanese baseball, where major league teams frequently hire U.S. players to play on their teams. One American noted the case of Tatsunori Hara, one of the best Japanese players in the league. "He had so many different people telling him what to do," remarked Warren Cromartie, a teammate, "it's a wonder he could still swing the bat. They turned him into a robot, instead of just letting him play naturally and expressing his natural talent."[6] To Hara's Japanese coach, however, conformity was the key to teamwork, and teamwork in Japan is the road to success.

By all accounts, independent thinking is on the increase in Japan. In some cases, it leads to antisocial behavior, such as crime or membership in a teenage gang. Usually, it is expressed in more indirect ways, such as the recent fashion among young people of dyeing their hair brown (known in Japanese as "tea hair"). Because the practice is banned in many schools and generally frowned upon by the older generation (one police chief dumped a pitcher of beer on a student with brown hair whom he noticed in a bar), many young Japanese dye their hair as a gesture of independence and a means of gaining acceptance among their peers. When seeking employment or getting married, however, they return their hair to its natural color.

One of the more tenacious legacies of the past is sexual inequality, for the subordinate position of women in Japanese society has not been entirely eliminated (see the box on p. 1198). Although women are now legally protected against discrimination in employment, very few have reached senior levels in business, education, or politics where, in the words of one Western scholar, they remain "acutely disadvantaged." Ironically, in a recent survey of business executives in Japan, a majority declared that women were smarter than men. Women now comprise nearly 50 percent of the workforce, but most are in retail or service occupations, and their average salary is only about half that of males. There is a feminist movement in Japan, but it has none of the vigor and mass support of its counterpart in the United States. Most women in Japan consider being a homemaker the ideal position; only 15 percent of the women surveyed by a poll taken during the 1980s wanted a full-time job.[7]

In the home, however, a Japanese woman has considerable responsibility. She is expected to be a "good wife and wise mother" and has the primary responsibility for managing the family finances and raising the children. Japanese husbands carry little of the workload around the house, spending an average of nine minutes a day on housework compared to twenty-six minutes for American husbands. At the same time, Japanese divorce rates are well below those of the United States, while only 1.4 million elderly Japanese (undoubtedly, most of them women) live alone compared to 8.6 million in the United States.

Japan's welfare system also differs profoundly from its Western counterparts. Applicants are required to seek assistance first from their own families, and the physically able are ineligible for government aid. As a result, less than 1 percent of the population receives welfare benefits, as compared with more than 10 percent who receive some form of assistance in the United States. Some observers attribute the difference to several factors, including a low level of drug addiction and illegitimacy in Japan, as well as the importance of the work ethic and family responsibility.

No one is more conscious of Japanese distinctiveness than are the Japanese themselves. While the old Meiji concept of *kokutai* (national polity) has been officially disavowed, the feeling that Japan is a unique and indeed a superior culture survives. Both the self-confidence that comes from Japan's economic achievements and the sense of ethnic and cultural homogeneity that is a product of Japanese history contribute to this sense of uniqueness. The Japanese are proud of what they have achieved and are convinced that it is a direct product of their hard work, community spirit, and common sense of destiny.

Whether the unique character of modern Japan will endure is unclear. As noted earlier, there are already indications of a growing tendency toward hedonism and individualism among Japanese youth. Older Japanese frequently complain that the younger generation lacks their sense of loyalty and willingness to sacrifice. Some have also discerned signs that the concept of loyalty to one's employer is beginning to erode among Japanese youth. Some observers have predicted that with increasing affluence Japan will become more like the industrialized societies in the West. Nevertheless, Japan is unlikely to evolve into a carbon copy of the United States. Not only is Japan a much more homogeneous society, but its small size and dearth of natural resources encourage a strong work ethic and a sense of togetherness that have long since begun to dissipate in American society.

Religion and Culture

The sense of racial and cultural pride that characterizes contemporary Japan is rather different from Japanese attitudes at the beginning of the Meiji era. When Japan was opened to the West in the nineteenth century, many Japanese became convinced of the superiority of foreign ideas and institutions and were especially interested in Western religion and culture. Although Christian converts were few, numbering less than 1 percent of the population, the influence of Christianity was out of proportion to the size of the community. Many intellectuals during the Meiji era were impressed by the emotional commitment shown by missionaries in Japan and viewed Christianity as a contemporary version of Confucianism.

Today, Japan includes almost 1.5 million Christians along with 93 million Buddhists and 111 million who follow Shintoism; these figures are large because they include the many Japanese who believe in both Buddhism and Shintoism. Shintoism has not been identified with reverence for the emperor and the state since the occupation period. As in the West, increasing urbanization has led to a decline in the practice of organized religion

An Era of Women

Although a considerable amount of serious scholarship on Japanese women has been written in the past few years, little has been translated into foreign languages. This is hardly surprising, since for every Japanese book translated into English, the Japanese publish thirty-five to forty titles from the United States and Europe in their own language. One recent collection of essays by Japanese women labels the current period "The Era of Women," thus implying that Japanese women are breaking out of their traditional feudal role and choosing new values and venues. In the introduction to the book, Kumiko Fujimura-Fanselow, a professor of education and women's studies at a leading Japanese university, provides an overview of the status of Japanese women today.

The Status of Japanese Women

Recent advances in the area of politics, employment, education, and culture as well as marriage and family are cited in support of this notion of the era of women. On the cultural front an impressive number of women writers have appeared in recent years, and an increasing number of them have become recipients of prestigious literary awards. On the political front is the growing presence of female politicians, exemplified most prominently by the appointment of Doi Takako as leader of Japan's largest opposition party, the Socialist Party, in 1986, as well as the successful election of a record high of twenty-two female candidates in the 1989 election for the House of Councilors of the National Diet. Women have increasingly become visible in local politics also: female representation in local (prefectural, municipal, town, and village) assemblies grew from 1 percent in 1976 to 3.3 percent in 1992, and the first female mayor was elected (in Ashiya) in 1991. A quick glance at educational statistics reveals a higher percentage of female as compared to male high school graduates entering colleges and universities—46 versus 41 percent in 1994. The overwhelming majority of female college and university graduates, over 80 percent, are taking up employment and doing so in a wider range of fields than in the past. Better education and the availability of more job opportunities have increasingly made it possible for women to look upon marriage as an option rather than a prescribed lifestyle. Data indicate that college-educated women are choosing to continue working and to postpone marriage. A report released by the Management and Coordination Agency in July 1992 showed that 56.2 percent of women aged twenty-five to twenty-nine with at least a bachelor's degree were unmarried in 1990, up 15.7 percentage points from 1980, and the work force rate for women aged twenty-five to twenty-nine gained 7.1 percentage points to 61.2 percent.

Looking specifically at developments on the employment front, we can point to the passage of the Equal Employment Opportunity Law (EEOL) in 1985, which, among other things, opened up the previously all-male career track within Japanese companies to university-educated women, and also the Child Care Leave Law of 1991, which requires companies to grant unpaid leave to either parent until the child reaches the age of one. We see signs of women shedding traditional stereotypes and going into a variety of traditionally male occupations and professions. For example, in the years since the first female news co-announcer appeared on NHK (Japan's government-sponsored television network) in 1979, female newscasters have become a presence on nearly all news programs.

A dramatic development has been the advancement by married women, including those with children, into the labor force. Even in the cases of those who choose not to work outside the home, very few remain content to be housewives exclusively. Instead, they seek a life outside the home through a variety of activities, including study at privately run "culture centers," which offer courses in everything from foreign languages, literature, and law to traditional arts, handicrafts, cooking, and sports. Others take up classes offered at local government facilities or at one of the more than a hundred women's centers that have been established throughout Japan, some of which help housewives acquire skills for reentering the job market. Housewives have also become enthusiastically involved in a variety of community-related activities, including volunteer work, establishment of consumer cooperatives, efforts to protect the environment, political movements, peace movements, and campaigns against political corruption. Whereas not so long ago married women were expected to stay at home most of the time, today we typically see groups of middle-aged women playing tennis or swimming together, going shopping, eating out, and traveling and sightseeing both within and outside the country.

although evangelical sects have proliferated in recent years. In all likelihood, their members, like those belonging to similar sects elsewhere, are seeking spiritual underpinnings in an increasingly secular and complex world. The largest and best-known sect is the Soka Gakkai, a lay Buddhist organization that has attracted millions of followers and formed its own political party called the Komeito. Its conservative message and religious leanings remind some observers of similar parties in other parts of the world.

As we have seen, Western literature, art, and music also had a major impact on Japanese society. Western influence led to the rapid decline of traditional forms of drama and poetry and the growth in popularity of the prose novel. After the Japanese defeat in World War II, many of the writers who had been active before the war resurfaced, but now their writing reflected their demoralization, echoing the spiritual vacuum of the times. Labeled "apure" from the French "apres-guerre" (postwar), these disillusioned authors were attracted to existentialism, and some turned to hedonism and nihilism. This "lost generation" described its anguish with piercing despair; several committed suicide. For them, defeat was compounded by fear of the Americanization of postwar Japan.

One of the best examples of this attitude was the novelist Yukio Mishima (1925–1970), who led a crusade to stem the tide of what he described as America's "universal and uniform 'coca-colonization'" of the world in general and Japan in particular.[8] In *Confessions of a Mask*, written in 1949, Mishima described the awakening of a young man to his own homosexuality. His later novels, *The Thirst for Love* and *The Temple of the Golden Pavilion*, were riveting narratives about disturbed characters. Mishima's ritual suicide in 1970 was the subject of widespread speculation and transformed him into a cult figure.

One of Japan's most serious-minded contemporary authors is Kenzaburo Oe (b. 1935). His work, which was rewarded with a Nobel Prize for literature in 1994, presents Japan's ongoing quest for modern identity and purpose. His characters reflect the spiritual anguish precipitated by the collapse of the imperial Japanese tradition and the subsequent adoption of Western culture, a trend that, according to Oe, has culminated in unabashed materialism, cultural decline, and a moral void. Yet, unlike Mishima, he does not seek to reinstate the imperial traditions of the past, but rather to regain spiritual meaning by retrieving the sense of communality and innocence found in rural Japan (see the box on p. 1201).

One of Oe's most famous novels is *A Personal Matter* (1964), in which the author recounts in fictionalized

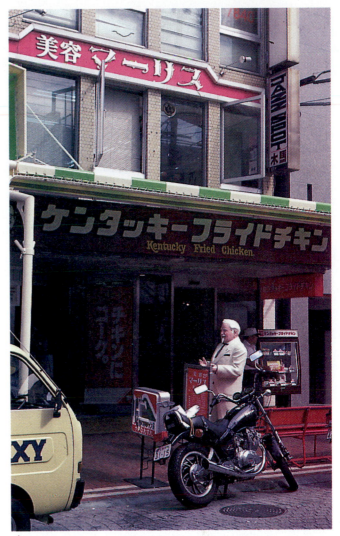

◆ **KFC in Japan.** Although Japan has been widely criticized for its reluctance to import goods from other countries, the Japanese people display a strong interest in many aspects of Western culture. Items of American culture, including Mickey Mouse, fashionable sneakers, and Kentucky Fried Chicken, are especially prized. This outlet, complete with a statue of Colonel Sanders, is on a downtown street in Kobe.

form how his own experience in raising a brain-damaged son led him from despair to a final sense of transcendent humanism. In *Teach Us to Outgrow Our Madness*, a collection of four novellas, Oe describes the fascination of Japanese children when they first saw a black American soldier held in captivity at the end of World War II. At first, the children view him as an intimidating oddity, but eventually they accept him as a human being and admire his powerful body and sense of joy in being alive.

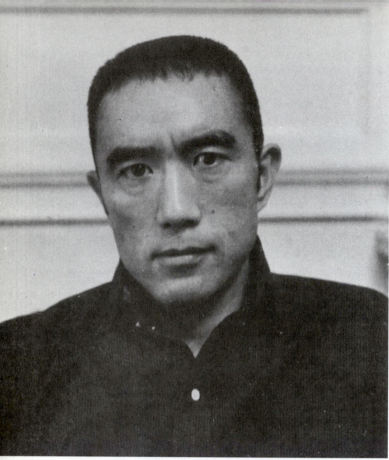

◆ **Yukio Mishima.** Postwar Japan gave rise to a "lost generation" of authors who, disillusioned and demoralized after the defeat, echoed the spiritual vacuum of the times. For some, the humiliation was compounded by what they perceived as the Americanization of Japan. This attitude is perhaps best exemplified by the writings of Yukio Mishima, who made it his crusade to restore the strengths of traditional Japan and stem the tide of U.S. "coca-colonization." His ritual suicide in 1970 transformed him into a cult figure.

Haruki Murakami, one of Japan's most popular authors today, was one of the first to discard the introspective and somber style of the earlier postwar period and speak a more contemporary language. *A Wild Sheep Chase*, published in 1982, is an excellent example of his gripping yet humorous writing.

Since the 1970s, increasing affluence and a high literacy rate have contributed to a massive quantity of publications ranging from popular potboilers to first-rate fiction. In 1975, for example, Japan already produced twice as much fiction as the United States, a trend that has continued into the 1990s. Much of this new literature deals with the common concerns of all the affluent industrialized nations, including the effects of urbanization, advanced technology, and mass consumption.

One recent phenomenon is the so-called industrial novel, which seeks to lay bare the vicious infighting and pressure tactics that characterize Japanese business today. In the novel *Keiretsu*, Ikko Shimizu describes the abortive efforts of the owner of Taisei Lighting, a headlight supplier, to cope with the pressure imposed by one of his main customers, the giant affiliate Tokyo Motors. Another popular genre is the "art-manga" or cartoon. Michio Hisauchi presents serious subjects, such as Japanese soldiers marooned after the war on an island in the South Pacific, in *Japan's Junglest Day*, a full-length novel in comic book form with cartoon characters posing philosophical questions.

The theater has gone through a similar process of growth, and some traditional forms, like *kabuki* drama, have survived by adopting new subject matter. Japanese drama has sometimes been a showcase for radical political views, which has limited its popular appeal and led to official efforts to suppress it before World War II. A new type of play influenced by the Theater of the Absurd of Samuel Beckett and Eugene Ionesco and reflecting the search for personal and national identity became popular in the 1960s.

As we have already observed in previous chapters, there were many women writers during early Japanese history. With the rise of the samurai class, however, works by women vanished until the Meiji Restoration, when a few courageous women wrote of their struggle for self-fulfillment in a male-dominated society. Japanese literary critics, who were invariably men, accepted "female" literature as long as it dealt exclusively with what they viewed as appropriately "female" subjects, such as the "mysteries" of the female psyche and motherhood. Even today Japan has separate literary awards for men and women, and women are not considered capable of abstract or objective writing. Nevertheless, many contemporary women authors are daring to broach "male" subjects and are producing works of considerable merit.

Other aspects of Japanese culture have also been influenced by Western ideas, although without the intense preoccupation with synthesis that is evident in literature. Japanese artists had begun to be influenced by Western art prior to the Meiji period, a process that accelerated in the late nineteenth and early twentieth centuries, when Impressionists, Cubists, and Surrealists, among others, jockeyed for preeminence. Western music is highly popular in Japan, and scores of Japanese classical musicians have succeeded in the West. Even rap music has gained a foothold among Japanese youth, although without the association with sex, drugs, and violence that it has in

The Ambiguity of Being Japanese

Kenzaburo Oe is one of Japan's most prestigious contemporary authors. Admired for their riveting style and unbridled imagination, Oe's novels often portray anguished protagonists who appear paralyzed by despair. A key theme in his writings is Japan's post–World War II quest to restore its sense of identity and purpose. In his speech accepting the 1994 Nobel Prize for literature, Oe spoke movingly of Japan's current position, caught between the ideologies of East and West. In this excerpt from the speech, note the author's pain in coming to terms with the recent history of his nation and the atrocities committed by Japanese soldiers during World War II.

Kenzaburo Oe, Japan, the Ambiguous, and Myself

After a hundred and twenty years of modernization since the opening up of the country, contemporary Japan is split between two opposite poles of ambiguity. This ambiguity, which is so powerful and penetrating that it divides both the state and its people, and affects me as a writer like a deep-felt scar, is evident in various ways. The modernization of Japan was oriented toward learning from and imitating the West, yet the country is situated in Asia and has firmly maintained its traditional culture. The ambiguous orientation of Japan drove the country into the position of an invader in Asia, and resulted in its isolation from other Asian nations not only politically but also socially and culturally. And even in the West, to which its culture was supposedly quite open, it has long remained inscrutable or only partially understood.

In the history of modern Japanese literature, the writers most sincere in their awareness of a mission were the "postwar school" of writers who came onto the literary scene deeply wounded by the catastrophe of war yet full of hope for a rebirth. They tried with great pain to make up for the atrocities committed by Japanese military forces in Asia, as well as to bridge the profound gaps that existed not only between the developed nations of the West and Japan but also between African and Latin American countries and Japan. Only by doing so did they think that they could seek with some humility reconciliation with the rest of the world. It has always been my aspiration to cling to the very end of the line of that literary tradition inherited from those writers.

The present nation of Japan and its people cannot but be ambivalent. The Second World War came right in the middle of the process of modernization, a war that was brought about by the very aberration of that process itself. Defeat in this conflict fifty years ago created an opportunity for Japan, as the aggressor, to attempt a rebirth out of the great misery and suffering that the "postwar school" of writers depicted in their work. The moral props for a nation aspiring to this goal were the idea of democracy and the determination never to wage a war again—a resolve adopted not by innocent people but people stained by their own history of territorial invasion.

---

the United States. Although some of the lyrics betray an attitude of modest revolt against the uptight world of Japanese society, most lack any such connotations, as in, for example, the rap song "Street Life":

> Now's the time to hip hop,
> Everybody's crazy about rap,
> Hey, hey, you all, listen up,
> Listen to my rap and cheer up.

As one singer remarked, "We've been very fortunate, and we don't want to bother our Moms and Dads. So we don't sing songs that would disturb parents."[9]

No longer are Japanese authors seeking to revive the old Japan of the tea ceremony and falling plum blossoms.

Raised in the crowded cities of postwar Japan, soaking up movies and television, rock music and jeans, Coca Cola and McDonalds, many contemporary Japanese authors speak the universal language of today's world.

Many English words have entered the Japanese vocabulary, although with Japanese pronunciations. Corporate downsizing is known as *kosutu daun* (cost down), while a student who cuts class is engaging in *esukeepu* (escape). Even rice, the very symbol of Japanese uniqueness, is sometimes known as *raisu* when sold in a restaurant. Yet even as the Japanese enter the global marketplace, they retain ties to their own traditions. Business executives sometimes use traditional Daoist forms of physical and mental training to reduce the stress inherent in their jobs, while others retreat to a Zen monastery to learn to focus their willpower as a means of besting a competitor.

There are some signs that under the surface, the tensions between traditional and modern are exacting a price. As novelists like Yukio Mishima and Kenzaburo Oe feared, the growing focus on material possessions and the decline of traditional religious beliefs have left a spiritual void that cannot but undermine the sense of community and purpose that has motivated the country since the Meiji era. Some young people have reacted to the emptiness of their lives by joining religious cults such as Aum Shinri Kyo, which came to world attention in 1995 when members of the organization, inspired by their leader Asahara Shoko, carried out a poison gas attack on the Tokyo subway that killed several people. Such incidents serve as a warning that Japan is not immune to the social ills that currently plague many Western countries.

South Korea: A Peninsula Divided

While the world was focused on the economic miracle occurring on the Japanese islands, another miracle of sorts was taking place across the Sea of Japan on the Asian mainland. In 1953, the Korean peninsula was exhausted from three years of bitter fraternal war, a conflict that took the lives of an estimated four million Koreans on both sides of the 38th parallel and turned as many as one-quarter of the population into refugees. Although a cease-fire had been signed at Panmunjom in July 1953, it was a fragile peace and left two heavily armed and mutually hostile countries facing each other suspiciously.

North of the truce line was the People's Republic of Korea (PRK), a police state under the dictatorial rule of the Communist leader Kim Il-sung (1912–1994). To the south was the Republic of Korea under the equally autocratic President Syngman Rhee (1875–1965), a fierce anti-Communist who had led the resistance to the northern invasion and now placed his country under U.S. military protection. But U.S. troops could not protect Syngman Rhee from his own people, many of whom resented his reliance on the political power of the wealthy landlord class. After several years of harsh rule, marked by government corruption, fraudulent elections, and police brutality, demonstrations broke out in the capital city of Seoul in the spring of 1960 and forced him into retirement.

The Rhee era was followed by a brief period of multiparty democratic government, but in 1961 a coup d'etat placed General Chung Hee Park (1917–1979) in power. The new regime promulgated a new constitution, and in 1963 Park was elected president of a civilian government. He also set out to foster the recovery of the economy from decades of foreign occupation and civil war. Adopting the nineteenth-century Japanese slogan "rich country and strong state," Park built up a strong military while relying on U.S. and later Japanese assistance to help build a strong manufacturing base in what had been a predominantly agricultural society (in 1961, about 40 percent of the gross national product came from agriculture). Because the private sector had been relatively weak under Japanese rule, the government played an active role in the process, creating a superministry called the Economic Planning Board that instituted a series of five-year plans. These plans targeted specific industries for development, promoted exports, and funded infrastructure development. Under a land reform program, large landowners were required to sell all their farmland above 7.4 acres to their tenants at low prices.

The program was a solid success. Benefiting from the Confucian principles of thrift, respect for education, and hard work (during the 1960s and 1970s, Korean workers spent an average of sixty hours a week at their jobs), as well as from Japanese capital and technology, Korea gradually emerged as a major industrial power in East Asia. The growth rate of the economy rose from less than 5 percent annually in the 1950s to an average of over 9 percent under Chung Hee Park. The key areas selected for industrial development were chemicals, textiles, and shipbuilding. By the 1980s, Korea was moving aggressively into automobiles. The largest corporations, such as Samsung, Daewoo, and Hyundai, were transformed into massive conglomerates called *chaebol*, the Korean equivalent of the *zaibatsu* of prewar Japan, although they were more recent in origin and were still under their original ownership. Taking advantage of relatively low wages and a stunningly high rate of saving, Korean businesses began to compete actively with the Japanese for export markets in Asia and throughout the world. The Japanese became concerned about their "hungry spirit" and began refusing to share technology with the South Koreans.[10] Per capita income also increased dramatically, rising from under $90 (in U.S. dollars) annually in 1960 to $1,560 (twice that of Communist North Korea) twenty years later.

But like many other countries in the region, South Korea was slow to develop democratic principles. Although his government functioned with the trappings of democracy, Park continued to rule by autocratic means and suppressed all forms of dissidence. Opposition began to develop under the leadership of the charismatic figure Kim Dae Jung. His power base was in the relatively impoverished rural districts in southwestern Korea, where the government's land reforms had had only minimal success in raising living standards.

In 1979, Chung Hee Park was assassinated. Once again, a brief interregnum of democratic rule ensued, but in 1980 a new military government under General Chun Doo Hwan seized power. The new regime was as authoritarian as its predecessors, but opposition to autocratic rule had now spread from the ranks of college and high school students, who had led the early resistance, to much of the urban population. Protests against government policies became increasingly frequent. In 1987, massive demonstrations drove government troops out of the southern city of Kwangju, but the troops returned in force and killed an estimated two thousand of the demonstrators.

Under increasing pressure from the United States to moderate the oppressive character of his rule, Chun promised national elections in 1987 but then reversed his decision. Amidst growing protests, the regime steadily lost credibility, and in 1989 elections were finally held. There were three candidates, the government nominee Roh Tae Woo and two opposition figures, Democratic Party leader Kim Dae Jung and his rival Kim Young Sam. With the opposition candidates splitting the antigovernment vote, Roh Tae Woo won the election with less than 40 percent of the vote.

The election results discouraged many Koreans, while the violent character of the student protests alienated many moderates. Nevertheless, new elections in 1992 brought Kim Young Sam to the presidency. Kim selected several women for his cabinet and promised that he would make Korea "a freer and more mature democracy." In the meantime, representatives of South Korea had made tentative contacts with the Communist regime in North Korea on possible steps toward the eventual reunification of the peninsula.

During the mid-1990s, Kim Young Sam attempted to crack down on the rising influence of the giant *chaebols,* which were accused of giving massive bribes in return for favors from government officials. Ex-presidents Chun Doo Hwan and Roh Tae Woo were tried and convicted of using the office to enrich themselves and their families. But the problems of South Korea were more serious than the endemic corruption. A growing trade deficit, combined with a declining growth rate, led to an increase in both unemployment and bankruptcies. Ironically, a second problem resulted from the economic collapse of Seoul's bitter rival, the PRK. Under the rule of Kim Il-sung's son Kim Jong Il, the North Korean economy was in a free fall, raising the specter of an outflow of refugees that could swamp neighboring countries. To relieve the immediate effects of a food shortage, the Communist government in Pyongyang relaxed its restrictions on private farming, while Seoul agreed to provide food aid to alleviate the famine.

◆ **Melding Past and Present in South Korea.** South Korea has made a greater effort to preserve aspects of traditional culture than most of its neighbors in East Asia. Here an architect has tried to soften the impact of modernization by camouflaging a gas station in Seoul with a traditional Korean tile roof.

Taiwan: The Other China

South Korea is not the only rising industrial power trying to imitate the success of the Japanese in East Asia. To the south on the island of Taiwan, the Republic of China is beginning to do the same.

After retreating to Taiwan after their defeat by the Communists, Chiang Kai-shek and his followers established a capital at Taipei and set out to build a strong and prosperous nation based on Chinese traditions and the principles of Sun Yat-sen. The government, which continued to refer to itself as the Republic of China (ROC), contended that it remained the legitimate representative of the Chinese people and that it would eventually return in triumph to the mainland.

In some ways, the Nationalists had much more success on Taiwan than they had achieved on the mainland. In the relatively secure environment provided by a security treaty with the United States, signed in 1954, and the comforting presence of the U.S. Seventh Fleet in the Taiwan Strait, the ROC was able to concentrate on economic growth without worrying about a Communist invasion. The regime possessed a number of advantages that it had not enjoyed in Nanjing. Fifty years of efficient Japanese rule had left behind a relatively modern economic infrastructure and an educated populace, although the island had absorbed considerable damage during World War II and much of its agricultural produce had been exported to Japan at low prices. With only a small population to deal with (about seven million in 1945), the ROC could make good use of foreign assistance and the efforts of its own energetic people to build a modern industrialized society.

The government moved rapidly to create a solid agricultural base. A land reform program, more effectively designed and implemented than the one introduced in the early 1930s on the mainland, led to the reduction of rents, while landholdings over three acres were purchased by the government and resold to the tenants at reasonable prices. As in Meiji Japan, the previous owners were compensated by government bonds. The results were gratifying: food production doubled over the next generation and began to make up a substantial proportion of exports.

In the meantime, the government strongly encouraged the development of local manufacturing and commerce. By the 1970s, along with Japan and South Korea, Taiwan was one of the most dynamic industrial economies in East Asia. The agricultural proportion of the gross national product declined from 36 percent in 1952 to only 9 percent thirty years later. At first, the in-

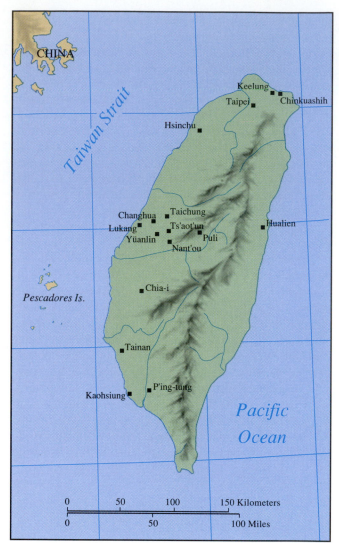

✤ Map 32.2 Modern Taiwan.

dustrial and commercial sector was composed of relatively small firms engaged in exporting textiles and food products, but the 1960s saw a shift to heavy industry, including shipbuilding, steel, petrochemicals, and machinery, and a growing emphasis on exports. The government played a major role in the process, targeting strategic industries for support and investing in infrastructure. Several of the so-called ten major construction projects in the 1970s involved improvements in transportation and communications, such as a new international airport, harbor development, and a freeway linking the north and the south. At the same time, as in Japan, the government stressed the importance of private enterprise and encouraged foreign investment and a high rate of internal savings. During the 1960s and 1970s, industrial growth averaged well over 10 percent annually, while the value of exports reached nearly 50 percent of the gross national product. By the mid-1980s, over three-quarters of the population lived in urban areas.

In contrast to the People's Republic of China (PRC) on the mainland, the ROC actively maintained Chinese tradition, promoting respect for Confucius and the ethical principles of the past, such as hard work, frugality, and filial piety. While there was some corruption in the government and the private sector, income differentials between the wealthy and the poor were generally less than elsewhere in the region, and the overall standard of living of the population increased substantially. Health and sanitation improved, literacy rates were quite high, and an active family planning program reduced the rate of population growth. Nevertheless, the total population on the island increased to about 20 million in the mid-1980s.

In one respect, however, Chiang Kai-shek had not changed; increasing prosperity did not lead to the democratization of the political process. The Nationalists continued to rule by emergency decree and refused to permit the formation of opposition political parties on the ground that the danger of invasion from the mainland had not subsided. Propaganda material from the PRC was rigorously prohibited, and dissident activities (promoting either rapprochement with the mainland or the establishment of an independent Republic of Taiwan) were ruthlessly suppressed. Although representatives to the provincial government of the province of Taiwan were chosen in local elections, the central government (technically representing the entire population of China) was dominated by mainlanders who had fled to the island with Chiang Kai-shek in 1949.

Some friction developed between the mainlanders, who numbered about two million, and the native Taiwanese; except for a few aboriginal peoples in the mountains, most of the natives were ethnic Chinese whose ancestors had emigrated to the island during the Qing dynasty. While the mainlanders were dominant in government and the professions, the native Taiwanese were prominent in commerce. Mainlanders tended to view the local population with a measure of condescension, and at least in the early years, intermarriage between members of the two groups was rare. Many Taiwanese remembered with anger the events of March 1947, when Nationalist troops had killed hundreds of Taiwanese demonstrators in Taipei. More than a thousand leading members of the local Taiwanese community were arrested and killed in the subsequent repression. By the 1980s, however, these fissures in Taiwanese society had begun to diminish; by that time, an ever-higher proportion of the population

CHRONOLOGY

Japan and the Little Tigers Since World War II

End of World War II in the Pacific	August 1945
Chiang Kai-shek retreats to Taiwan	1949
End of U.S. occupation of Japan	1950
Beginning of Korean War	June 1950
Truce at Panmunjom ends Korean War	July 1953
United States–Republic of China security treaty	1954
Syngman Rhee overthrown in South Korea	1960
Rise to power of Chung Hee Park in South Korea	1961
Independence of Republic of Singapore	1965
Death of Chiang Kai-shek	1975
Chung Hee Park assassinated	1979
End of United States–Republic of China security treaty	1979
Students riot at Kwangju in South Korea	1987
First free general elections on Taiwan	1992
Election of Kim Young Sam as president in South Korea	1992
Return of Hong Kong to mainland control	1996

had been born on the island and identified themselves as Taiwanese (see the box on p. 1207).

During the 1980s, the ROC slowly began to evolve toward a more representative form of government, a process that was facilitated by the death of Chiang Kai-shek in 1975. Chiang Ching-kuo, his son and successor, was less concerned about the danger from the mainland and more tolerant of free expression. On his death, he was succeeded as president by Lee Teng-hui, a native Taiwanese. By the end of the 1980s, democratization was underway, including elections and the formation of legal opposition parties. A national election in 1992 resulted in a bare majority for the Nationalists over strong opposition from the Democratic Progressive Party. But political liberalization had its dangers; some leading

Democratic Progressives began to agitate for an independent Republic of Taiwan, a possibility that aroused concern within the Nationalist government in Taipei and frenzied hostility in the PRC. When a presidential election in early 1996 aroused a political debate over the issue, Beijing responded by holding naval maneuvers in the Taiwan Strait. After his reelection, President Lee calmed the waters by making conciliatory remarks directed toward the mainland, but the fundamental issue of the future of the island remains unresolved.

Whether Taiwan will become an independent state or be united with the mainland is impossible to predict. Certainly, the outcome depends in good measure on developments in the PRC. During his visit to China in 1972, President Richard Nixon said that this was a question for the Chinese people to decide (see Chapter 27). In 1979, President Jimmy Carter abrogated the mutual security treaty between the United States and the ROC that had been in force since 1954 and switched U.S. diplomatic recognition from the Republic of China to the PRC. But the United States continues to provide defensive military assistance to the Taiwanese armed forces and has made it clear that it supports self-determination for the people of Taiwan and that it expects the final resolution of the Chinese civil war to be by peaceful means. In the meantime, economic and cultural contacts between Taiwan and the mainland are steadily increasing, although the Taiwanese have shown no inclination to accept the PRC's offer of "one country, two systems," under which the ROC would accept the PRC as the legitimate government of China in return for autonomous control over the affairs of Taiwan.

Singapore and Hong Kong: The Littlest Tigers

The smallest, but by no means the least successful, of the "little tigers" are Singapore and Hong Kong. Both are essentially city-states with large populations densely packed into small territories. Singapore, once a British crown colony and briefly a part of the state of Malaysia, is now an independent state. Hong Kong was a British colony but returned to the control of the PRC on the mainland in 1997. Both have emerged as industrial powerhouses with standards of living well above the level of their neighbors.

The success of Singapore must be ascribed in good measure to the will and energy of its political leaders. When it became independent in August 1965, Singapore was in a state of transition. Its longtime position as an entrepôt for trade between the Indian Ocean and the South China Sea was declining in importance. With only 618 square miles of territory, much of it marshland and tropical jungle, Singapore had little to offer but the frugality and industriousness of its predominantly overseas Chinese population. But a recent history of political radicalism, fostered by the rise of influential labor unions, had frightened away foreign investors.

Within a decade, Singapore's role and reputation had dramatically changed. Under the leadership of Prime Minister Lee Kuan-yew (b. 1923), once the firebrand leader of the radical People's Action Party, the government encouraged the growth of an attractive business climate while engaging in massive public works projects to

◆ **The Chiang Kai-shek Memorial in Taipei.** While the Chinese government on the mainland attempted to destroy all vestiges of traditional culture, the Republic of China on Taiwan sought to preserve the cultural heritage as a link between past and present. This policy is graphically displayed in the mausoleum for Chiang Kai-shek in downtown Taipei, shown in this photograph. The mausoleum, with its massive entrance gate, not only glorifies the nation's leader, but recalls the grandeur of old China.

❧ Beautiful Island, Beautiful Literature ❧

In the period immediately following the end of the Chinese civil war, Taiwanese literature, fueled by the humiliation at the hands of the Communists, expressed a deep nostalgia for the mainland. By the 1960s, however, some Taiwanese authors had begun to turn to Western literature for models, while others found inspiration in the Taiwanese countryside. Known as the "nativists," the latter not only began to dominate the literary scene but also turned to politics. Some authors dared to criticize the repressive conditions under the Nationalist government and attempted to arouse the Taiwanese people's consciousness of their own cultural identity. One example is the novelist and short story writer Song Zelai (b. 1952). In this excerpt, Song attacks the inauthenticity of those Taiwanese writers who either ape Western authors or hark back to a distant Chinese imperial past.

Song Zelai on Taiwanese Literature

More than once have I seen an intellectual of my generation. . . . Having chanced to hear about some Western writer in the bookstalls, or by word of mouth, he'd get some crazy idea that he'd penetrated the writer's soul, then look upon him as a kindred spirit and become his disciple. He'd swallow the author's words whole like a date, pit and all, without any critical or skeptical reflection. Then he'd publish an article brimming with high expectations and self-confidence, referring to himself as "Taiwan's Joyce" or "Taiwan's Lawrence," and patterning himself after the one or the other in every thought and gesture. How absurd! When it gets to the point of looking askance at all literature but that of their idol, these literati not only view Taiwan literature with disdain, they oppose the works of the ancient sages and philosophers in toto. In their insular and impoverished mental lives, there is no literary history and no writers, not even any living people; there is nothing at all but an exaggerated view of the "self."

There is another type of irresponsible writer who doesn't really understand or put into practice the essentials of Chinese culture, and who doesn't seek to understand China's present situation, either. His mind is totally wrapped up in the Tang-Song epoch. Ask him what it is in the Tang-Song epoch that so obsesses him, and he'll say something like "Along riverbanks of willow blow morning breezes under a waning moon." China is thus transformed into a fairy-tale princess for him to pursue. Perhaps he will boast that he is a rich young bravo, a footloose traveler who leaves a trail of flowers behind him. This sort of talk is sheer nonsense, first-class tommyrot. . . . In food and dress, he is as affluent as any man about town, yet he paints and composes poems in the Chinese style, proclaiming loudly that he is a descendant of the dragon, a son of China, and interminably shouting out its name in woe. Sometimes I wonder if he's still living in the same world as we are. . . .

My brothers, enough of your slogans; if your hearts are ill at ease, try going down to the fields with the peasants. If your spirit cannot tear itself away from the Tang-Song epoch, try going into business. If you are a captive of Joyce, please come out of the labyrinth and return to your parents' side. Then you will enjoy a fulfilling life and be able to see Taiwan, a beautiful island with a beautiful literature. Both you and your readers will be the beneficiaries.

As I have said repeatedly, I only hope that the people of this land will treasure instead of denigrate themselves. When we reach a happy medium between self-effacement and arrogance and are grateful for our happy lot, then may we count our blessings.

---

feed, house, and educate its two million citizens. The major components of success have been shipbuilding, oil refineries, tourism, electronics, and finance—the city-state has become the banking hub of the entire region.

Like the other little tigers, Singapore has relied on a combination of government planning, entrepreneurial spirit, export promotion, high productivity, and an exceptionally high rate of saving to achieve industrial growth rates of nearly 10 percent annually over the last two decades. Unlike some other industrializing countries in the region, it has encouraged the presence of multinational corporations to provide much needed capital and technological input. Population growth has been controlled by a stringent family planning program, and literacy rates are among the highest in Asia.

As in the other little tigers, an authoritarian political system has guaranteed a stable environment for economic growth. Until his recent retirement, Lee Kuan-yew and his People's Action Party dominated Singaporean politics, and opposition elements were intimidated into silence or arrested. The prime minister openly declared that the Western model of pluralist democracy was not appropriate for Singapore and lauded the Meiji model of centralized development. Confucian values of thrift, hard work, and obedience to authority have been promoted as the ideology of the state. The government has had a passion for cleanliness and at one time even undertook a campaign to persuade its citizens to flush the public urinals. In June 1989, the local *Straits Times*, a mouthpiece of the government, published a photograph of a man walking sheepishly from a row of urinals. The caption read "Caught without a flush: Mr. Amar Mohamed leaving the Lucky Plaza [a local shopping center] toilet without flushing the urinal."[11]

But economic success is beginning to undermine the authoritarian foundations of the system, as a more sophisticated citizenry begins to demand more political freedoms and an end to governmental paternalism. Lee Kuan-yew's successor Goh Chok Tong has promised a "kinder, gentler" Singapore, and political restrictions on individual behavior are gradually being relaxed. There is reason for optimism that a more pluralistic political system will gradually emerge.

The future of Hong Kong is not so clear-cut. As in Singapore, sensible government policies and the hard work of its people have enabled Hong Kong to thrive. At first, the prosperity of the colony depended on the plentiful supply of cheap labor. Inundated with refugees from the mainland during the 1950s and 1960s, the population of Hong Kong burgeoned to over six million. Many of them were willing to work for starvation wages in sweatshops producing textiles, simple appliances, and toys for the export market. More recently, Hong Kong has benefited from increased tourism, manufacturing, and the growing economic prosperity of neighboring Guangdong province, the most prosperous region of the PRC. In one respect, Hong Kong has differed from the other societies discussed in this chapter, in that it has relied on an unbridled free market system rather than active state intervention in the economy. At the same time, by allocating substantial funds for transportation, sanitation, education, and public housing, the government has created favorable conditions for economic development.

Unlike the other little tigers, Hong Kong remained under colonial rule. Until recently, British authorities did little to foster democratic institutions or practices, and most residents of the colony cared more about economic survival than political freedoms. In 1983, in talks between representatives of Great Britain and the PRC, the Chinese leaders made it clear they were determined that Hong Kong should return to mainland authority in 1997, when the British ninety-nine-year lease over the New Territories, the foodbasket of the colony of Hong Kong, ran out. The British agreed on condition that satisfactory arrangements could be made for the welfare of the population. The Chinese promised that for fifty years, the people of Hong Kong would live under a capitalist system and be essentially

◆ **Old and New in Singapore.** The city-state of Singapore is one of the most modern societies in all Asia and is sometimes referred to as the "showcase of tomorrow." Some Singaporeans regret that so much of the past has been destroyed in the process. In this photograph, skyscrapers tower above traditional sampans in the Singapore River; the buildings stand on the site where Stamford Raffles first landed on the island in 1819.

self-governing. Recent statements by Chinese leaders, however, have raised questions about the degree of autonomy Hong Kong will receive under Chinese rule, which began at the end of June 1997 (see the box on p. 1210).

On the Margins of Asia: Postwar Australia and New Zealand

From a geographical point of view, Australia and New Zealand are not part of Asia, and throughout their short history, both countries have identified culturally and politically with the West, rather than with their Asian neighbors. Their political institutions and values are derived from Europe, while in form and content their economies resemble those of the advanced countries of the world rather than the preindustrial societies of much of Southeast Asia. Both are currently members of the British Commonwealth and of the U.S.-led ANZUS alliance (Australia, New Zealand, and the United States), which serves to shield them from political turmoil elsewhere in the region.

Yet trends in recent years have been drawing both states—especially Australia—closer to Asia. In the first place, immigration from East and Southeast Asia has increased rapidly. More than half of the current immigrants to Australia come from East Asia, and by early in the next century, about 7 percent of the population of about 18 million people will be of Asian descent. In New Zealand, residents of Asian descent represent only about 3 percent of the population of 3.5 million, but about 12 percent of the population are Maoris, Polynesian peoples who settled on the islands about a thousand years ago. Secondly, trade relations with Asia are increasing rapidly. About 60 percent of Australia's export markets today are in East Asia, and the region is the source of about half of its imports. Asian trade with New Zealand is also on the increase.

In the meantime, the links that bind both countries to Great Britain and the United States have been loosening. Ties with London became increasingly distant after Great Britain decided to join the European Community in the early 1970s. Today elements in both countries are urging withdrawal from the British Commonwealth at the end of the century, although the outcome is far from certain. Security ties with the United States remain important, but many Australians opposed their government's decision to cooperate with Washington during the Vietnam War, and the government today is seeking to establish closer political and military ties with the ASEAN

◆ **A Junk in Hong Kong Harbor.** Hong Kong, like Singapore, has become one of the most modern cities in the world. The island of Victoria, shown here in the background, groans under the weight of thousands of gleaming skyscrapers. Yet signs of the past still coexist with the present, as this picture of a traditional Chinese junk demonstrates.

alliance. Further removed from Asia both physically and psychologically, New Zealand assigns less importance to its security treaty with the United States and has been vocally critical of U.S. nuclear politics in the region.

Whether Australia and New Zealand will ever become an integral part of the Asia-Pacific region is uncertain. Cultural differences stemming from the European origins of the majority of the population in both countries hinder mutual understanding on both sides of the divide, and many ASEAN leaders express reluctance to accept the two countries as full members of the alliance. But economic and geographic realities can be a powerful force, and should the Pacific region continue on its current course toward economic prosperity and political stability, the role of Australia and New Zealand will assume greater significance.

Conclusion

What explains the striking ability of the four little tigers to follow the Japanese example and transform themselves into export-oriented societies capable of competing with

⋙ *Return to the Motherland* ⋘

After lengthy negotiations, in December 1984 China and Great Britain agreed that on July 1, 1997, Hong Kong would return to Chinese sovereignty. Key sections of the agreement are included here. In succeeding years, authorities of the two countries held further negotiations. Some of the discussions raised questions in the minds of residents of Hong Kong as to whether their individual liberties would indeed be respected after the colony's return to China.

The Joint Declaration on Hong Kong

The Hong Kong Special Administrative Region will be directly under the authority of the Central People's Government of the People's Republic of China. The Hong Kong Special Administrative Region will enjoy a high degree of autonomy, except in foreign and defense affairs which are the responsibility of the Central People's Government.

The Hong Kong Special Administrative Region will be vested with executive, legislative, and independent judicial power, including that of final adjudication. The laws currently in force in Hong Kong will remain basically unchanged.

The Government of the Hong Kong Special Administrative Region will be composed of local inhabitants. The chief executive will be appointed by the Central People's Government on the basis of the results of elections or consultations to be held locally. Principal officials will be nominated by the chief executive of the Hong Kong Special Administrative Region for appointment by the Central People's Government. . . .

The current social and economic systems in Hong Kong will remain unchanged, and so will the lifestyle. Rights and freedoms, including those of the person, of speech, of the press, of assembly, of association, of travel, of movement, of correspondence, of strike, of choice of occupation, of academic research, and of religious belief will be ensured by law. . . . Private property, ownership of enterprises, legitimate right of inheritance and foreign investment will be protected by law. . . .

the advanced nations of the West? The debate is reminiscent of the argument about the reasons for Japan's success. Some point to the traditional character traits of Confucian societies, such as thrift, a work ethic, respect for education, and obedience to authority. A recent poll of Asian executives found that more than 80 percent believed that Asian values differed from those of the West, and most added that these values had contributed significantly to the region's recent success. Others place more emphasis on deliberate steps taken by government and economic leaders to meet the political, economic, and social challenges faced by their societies.

There seems no reason to doubt that cultural factors connected to East Asian social traditions have contributed to the economic success of these societies. Certainly, habits such as frugality, industriousness, and subordination of individual desires all played a role in the ability of their governments to concentrate on the collective interest. As one U.S. scholar of Asian descent has recently noted:

In their outward appearance these East Asian *nouveaux riches* are Westernized. Yet behind this facade the people of these countries pursue a way of life that remains essentially Oriental. They prefer to eat Oriental food, observe lunar-calendar-based national festivities, place the family in the center of their social and economic relationships, practice ancestor worship, emphasize frugality in life, maintain a strong devotion to education, and accept Confucianism as the essence of their common culture.[12]

Political elites in these countries have been highly conscious of these factors and willing to use them for national purposes. Prime Minister Lee Kuan-yew of Singapore deliberately fostered the inculcation of such ideals among the citizens of his small nation and lamented the decline of Confucian values among the young. In South Korea, Chung Hee Park noted the connection between economic development and the collective values of traditional East Asian societies:

Just as a home is a small collective body, so the state is a large community. . . . One who does not maintain a wholesome family order cannot be expected to show strong devotion to his state. A society that puts the national interest above the interests of the individual develops faster than one which does not.[13]

The importance of specifically Confucian values, however, should not be overemphasized as a factor in what authors Roy Hofheinz and Kent E. Calder call the "Eastasia Edge." In the first place, until recently mainland China did not share in the economic success of its neighbors despite a long tradition of espousing Confucian values. In fact, some historians in recent years have maintained that it was precisely those Confucian values that hindered China's early response to the challenge of the West.

Moreover, while such traits as frugality and hard work undoubtedly played a significant role in the economic development of East Asian societies, they are not necessarily a direct product of the Confucian tradition. In Japan, for example, indigenous traditions probably had a greater effect on behavior and attitudes than Confucian teachings, and in societies with a majority Chinese population, it was often precisely those groups least influenced by Confucian doctrine—such as merchant groups in South China—that have most actively participated in the economic revolution of the late twentieth century. Thus, the determining factor is not so much Confucianism per se as the common emphasis on family values, self-sacrifice, and hard work that characterizes societies throughout the region.

As this and the preceding chapter have shown, without active encouragement by political elites, such traditions cannot be effectively harnessed for the good of society as a whole. The creative talents of the Chinese people were not efficiently utilized under Mao Zedong or in the little tigers while they were under European or Japanese colonial rule (although Japanese colonialism did lead to the creation of an infrastructure more conducive to later development than was the case in European colonies). Only when a "modernizing elite" took charge and began to place a high priority on economic development were the stunning advances of recent decades achieved. Rural poverty was reduced if not eliminated by stringent land reform and population control programs. Profit incentives and foreign investment were encouraged, while the development of export markets received high priority.

There was, of course, another common factor in the successes achieved by Japan and its emulators. All the little tigers received substantial inputs of capital and technology from the advanced nations of the West—Taiwan and South Korea from the United States, and Hong Kong and Singapore from Britain. Japan relied to a greater degree on its own efforts, but received a significant advantage by being placed under the U.S. security umbrella and guaranteed access to markets and sources of raw materials in a region dominated by U.S. naval power.

Western observers are keenly aware that economic advancement in the region has often been achieved at the cost of political freedom and sometimes individual human rights. Government repression of opposition is common throughout East Asia except in Japan. As many

♦ **The Aesthetics of Food in China.** In many countries of East Asia, the aesthetic presentation of food is as important as the taste. In this roadside stall in downtown Taipei, the vendor has attractively presented a variety of delectable foods for the prospective buyer.

point out, the rights of national minorities and women are often still limited in comparison with the advanced countries of the West. Until recently, women in South Korea had no right to inheritance or the legal custody of their children in case of divorce.

Many commentators in the region take vigorous exception to such criticism. In a recent article, Singapore's Minister of Foreign Affairs S. Jayakumar has argued that pluralistic political systems could be "very dangerous and destabilizing" in the heterogeneous societies that currently exist in the region. Moreover, he maintains that the central role of the government has been a key factor in the economic success achieved by many Asian countries in recent years.[14] Others go even further and declare that the current task of Western countries in East Asia is not to lecture, but to learn (see the box on p. 1213). Only thus can the Western countries hope to create the disciplined and cohesive social order that now prevails in most East Asian societies.

Western observers may have a point in asserting that in much of Asia political and social development has not kept pace with economic growth, at least by the standards of Western societies. But it should be kept in mind that progress in human rights was equally slow in Europe and North America and even now often fails to match expectations. A rising standard of living, increased social mobility, and a changing regional environment brought about by the end of the Cold War should go far to enhance political freedoms and promote social justice in the countries bordering the Pacific.

◆ **You Can Take it With You!**
While wealthy Chinese in traditional China buried clay models of personal possessions to accompany the departed to the next world, ordinary people burned paper effigies, which were transported to the afterlife by means of the rising smoke. This custom survives in many Chinese communities today, as this photograph taken in modern-day Singapore demonstrates. Some merchants make their living by manufacturing such popular paper objects as television sets, elegant furniture, and even Mercedes automobiles.

To Those Living in Glass Houses

*K*ishore Mahbubani is permanent secretary in the Ministry of Foreign Affairs in Singapore. Previously, he served as his country's ambassador to the United Nations. In this article, adapted from a piece in the Washington Quarterly, the author advises his audience to stop lecturing Asian societies on the issue of human rights and focus attention instead on problems in the United States. In his view, today the countries of the West have much to learn from their counterparts in East Asia. This viewpoint is shared by many other observers, political leaders, and foreign affairs specialists in the region.

Kishore Mahbubani, "Go East, Young Man"

For the last century or more, in the passage of ideas across the Pacific, the flow has fundamentally been one way. Poverty-stricken and backward Asian societies have looked to the United States for leadership. Not surprisingly, a deeply ingrained belief has settled in the American mind that the U.S. mission in East Asia is to teach, not to learn. The time may have come for this mind-set to change.

In a major reversal of a pattern lasting centuries, many Western societies, including the U.S., are doing some major things fundamentally wrong while a growing number of East Asian societies are doing the same things right. The results are most evident in the economic sphere. In purchasing power parity terms, East Asia's gross domestic product is already larger than that of either the U.S. or European community. Such economic prosperity, contrary to American belief, results not just from free-market arrangements but also from the right social and political choices. Although many East Asian societies have assumed some of the trappings of the West, they have also kept major social and cultural elements intact—elements that may explain their growing global competitiveness.

In most Asian eyes, the evidence of real social decay in the U.S. is clear and palpable. Since 1960, the U.S. population has grown by 41%. In the same period, there has been a 560% increase in violent crimes, a 419% increase in illegitimate births, a 400% increase in divorce rates, a 300% increase in children living in single-parent homes, a more than 200% increase in teenage suicide rates, and a drop of almost 80 points in Scholastic Aptitude Test scores. A clear American paradox is that a society that places such a high premium on freedom has effectively reduced the physical freedom of most Americans, especially those who live in large cities. They live in heavily fortified homes, think twice before taking an evening stroll around their neighborhoods, and feel increasingly threatened by random violence when they are outside.

To any Asian, it is obvious that the breakdown of the family and social order in the U.S. owes itself to a mindless ideology that maintains that the freedom of a small number of individuals who are known to pose a threat to society (criminals, terrorists, street gang members, drug dealers) should not be constrained (for example, through detention without trial), even if to do so would enhance the freedom of the majority. In short, principle takes precedence over people's well-being. This belief is purely and simply a gross violation of common sense. But it is the logical end-product of a society that worships the notion of freedom as religiously as Hindus worship their sacred cows. Both must be kept absolutely unfettered, even when they obviously create great social discomfort. . . .

My hope is that Americans will come to visit East Asia in greater numbers. When they do, they will come to realize that their society has swung much too much in one direction: liberating the individual while imprisoning society. The relatively strong and stable family and social institutions of East Asia will appear more appealing. And as Americans experience the freedom of walking on city streets in Asia, they may begin to understand that freedom can also result from greater social order and discipline. Perhaps the best advice to give to a young American is: "Go East, Young Man."

CHAPTER NOTES

1. Quoted in *Far Eastern Economic Review*, November 24, 1994.
2. Ezra F. Vogel, *Japan as Number One: Lessons for America* (Cambridge, Mass., 1979), p. 94.
3. Bernard K. Gordon, "Japan's Universities," *Far Eastern Economic Review*, January 14, 1993.
4. These figures are from Tom Heymann, *On an Average Day in Japan* (New York, 1992), pp. 152–56.
5. *New York Times*, January 30, 1993.
6. Robert Whiting, *You Gotta Have Wa* (New York, 1990). The comment by Kimiko Date is in the *New York Times*, November 19, 1996.
7. Janet Hunter, *The Emergence of Modern Japan: An Introductory History since 1853* (London, 1989), p. 152.
8. Yukio Mishima and Geoffrey Bownas, eds., *New Writing in Japan* (Harmondsworth, 1972), p. 16.
9. *New York Times*, January 29, 1996.
10. Ezra F. Vogel, *The Four Little Dragons: The Spread of Industrialization in East Asia* (Cambridge, Mass., 1991), p. 57.
11. Stan Seser, "A Reporter at Large," *The New Yorker*, January 13, 1992, p. 44.
12. Quoted in Hung-chao Tai, ed., *Confucianism and Economic Development: An Oriental Alternative?* (Washington, D.C., 1989), p. 2.
13. Ibid., p. 17, citing Roderick MacFarquhar, "The Post-Confucian Challenge," *The Economist*, February 9, 1980.
14. *Far Eastern Economic Review*, May 30, 1996.

SUGGESTED READINGS

The number of books in English on modern Japan has increased in virtually direct proportion to Japan's rise as a major industrial power. Though many deal with economic and financial issues and cater to the business world, increased attention is also being paid to political, social, and cultural issues. A number of standard treatments of the postwar period are available. Perhaps best known is J. K. Fairbank, E. O. Reischauer, and A. M. Craig, *East Asia: Tradition and Transformation* (Boston, 1976). For a more culture-oriented approach, see C. Schirokauer, *Modern China and Japan: A Brief History* (New York, 1982). For a more contemporary view, see R. Buckley, *Japan Today* (Cambridge, 1985). P. Duus, ed., *The Cambridge History of Japan*, vol. 6 (Cambridge, 1988) contains a number of interesting scholarly articles on twentieth-century issues, although most of them deal with the prewar period. For a topical approach with strong emphasis on economic and social matters, J. E. Hunter, *The Emergence of Modern Japan: An Introductory History since 1853* (London, 1989) is excellent.

Relatively little has been written on Japanese politics and government. A recent treatment is J. A. A. Stockwin, *Japan: Divided Politics in a Growth Economy* (London, 1982). For an extensive analysis of Japan's adjustment to the Allied occupation, see H. Fukui, "Postwar Politics, 1945–1973," in volume 6 of *The Cambridge History of Japan*. Political dissent and its consequences are dealt with in N. Fields, *In the Realm of the Dying Emperor* (New York, 1991).

Japanese social issues have often been examined from an economic perspective as foreign observers try to discover the reasons for the nation's economic success. C. Nakane, *Japanese Society* (Harmondsworth, 1979) provides a scholarly treatment, while R. J. Hendry, *Understanding Japanese Society* (Beckenham, 1987) is more accessible. For a more local treatment, see R. P. Dore, *Shinohata: A Portrait of a Japanese Village* (New York, 1978) and T. C. Bestor, *Neighborhood Tokyo* (Stanford, Calif., 1989). T. Heymann, *On an Average Day in Japan* (New York, 1992) provides an interesting statistical comparison of Japanese and American society. On the role of women in modern Japan, see D. Robins-Mowry, *The Hidden Sun: Women of Modern Japan* (Boulder, Colo., 1983) and N. Bornoff, *Pink Samurai: Love, Marriage and Sex in Contemporary Japan* (New York, 1991).

Books attempting to explain Japanese economic success have become a growth industry. The classic account is E. F. Vogel, *Japan as Number One: Lessons for America* (Cambridge, Mass., 1979). For a provocative response pointing to signs of Japanese weakness, see J. Woronoff, *Japan as—Anything but—Number One* (Armonk, N.Y., 1991). C. Johnson, *MITI and the Japanese Miracle* (Stanford, Calif., 1982) provides an excellent analysis of the role of government in promoting Japanese economic interests. For the costs of Japanese economic success on society, stressing its effects on group solidarity and the agricultural sector, see R. J. Smith, *Kurusu: The Price of Progress in a Japanese Village* (Stanford, Calif., 1978). Y. Saisho, *Women Executives in Japan* (Tokyo, 1981) discusses women who are trying to find the key to economic success in Japanese business.

On Japanese literature after World War II, see H. Hibbett, ed., *Modern Japanese Literature: An Anthology of Fiction, Film, and Other Writings since 1945* (New York, 1977). For a stimulating discussion of the issue from a theoretical bent, see M. Ueda, *Modern Japanese Writers and the Nature of Literature* (Stanford, Calif., 1976). Short story writing is chronicled in I. Morris, ed., *Modern Japanese Stories: An Anthology* (Rutland, Vermont, 1962); Y. Mishima and G. Bownas, eds., *New Writing in Japan* (Harmondsworth, 1972); and A. Birnbaum, *Monkey Brain Sushi: New Tastes in Japanese Fiction* (Tokyo, 1991). On Japanese women authors, see N. M. Lippit and K. I. Selden, eds., *Stories by Contemporary Japanese Women Writers* (New York, 1982).

On the four little tigers and their economic development, see E. F. Vogel, *The Four Little Dragons: The Spread of Industrialization in East Asia* (Cambridge, Mass., 1991); J. W. Morley, ed., *Driven by Growth: Political Change in the Asia-Pacific Region* (Armonk, N.Y., 1992); and J. Woronoff, *Asia's Miracle Economies* (New York, 1986). For an interesting collection of articles on the role of Confucian ideology in promoting economic growth, see Hung-chao Tai, ed., *Confucianism and Economic Development* (Washington, D.C., 1989). For individual treatments of the little tigers, see Hak-kyu Sohn, *Authoritarianism and Opposition in South Korea* (London, 1989); D. F. Simon, *Taiwan: Beyond the Economic Miracle* (Armonk, N.Y., 1992); C. M. Turnbull, *A History of Singapore, 1819–1975* (Oxford, 1977); and K. Rafferty, *City on the Rocks: Hong Kong's Uncertain Future* (London, 1991).

REFLECTION

Toward a Global Civilization?
The World since 1945

As World War II came to an end, the survivors of that bloody struggle could afford to face the future with at least a measure of cautious optimism. With the death of Adolf Hitler in his bunker in Berlin, there were reasons to hope that the bitter rivalry that had marked relations among the Western powers would finally be put to an end, and that the wartime alliance of the United States, Great Britain, and the Soviet Union could be maintained into the postwar era. In the meantime, the peoples of Asia and Africa saw the end of the war as a gratifying sign that the colonial system would soon come to an end and bring about a new era of political stability and economic development on a global scale.

With the perspective of half a century, we can see that these hopes have been only partly realized. In the decades following the war, the capitalist nations managed to recover from the extended economic depression that had contributed to the start of World War II and advanced to a level of economic prosperity never before seen throughout world history. The bloody conflicts that had erupted among European nations during the first half of the twentieth century came to an end, and Germany and Japan were fully integrated into the world community.

At the same time, the prospects for a stable, peaceful world and an end to balance of power politics were hampered by the emergence of the grueling and sometimes tense ideological struggle between the socialist and capitalist camps, a competition headed by the only remaining great powers, the Soviet Union and the United States. While the two superpowers were able to avoid an open nuclear confrontation, the postwar world was divided into two heavily armed camps in a balance of terror that on one occasion—the Cuban Missile Crisis—brought the world briefly to the brink of nuclear holocaust.

Once again, Europe became divided into hostile camps as the Cold War rivalry between the United States and the Soviet Union forced the European nations to become dependent upon one or the other of the superpowers. The creation of two mutually antagonistic military alliances—NATO in 1949 and the Warsaw Pact in 1955—confirmed the new division of Europe, while a di-

vided Germany—and a divided Berlin—remained its most visible symbols. Repeated crises over the status of Berlin only intensified the fears in both camps.

In the midst of this rivalry, the Western European states, with the assistance of the United States, made a remarkable economic recovery and reached new levels of prosperity. In Eastern Europe, Soviet domination, both politically and economically, seemed so complete that many doubted it could ever be undone. Soviet military intervention, as in Hungary in 1956 and Czechoslovakia in 1968, reminded the Soviet satellites of their real condition. But communism had always been a foreign ideology to many Eastern Europeans and had never developed deep roots. When a new Soviet leader—Mikhail Gorbachev—indicated that his government would no longer pursue military intervention, Eastern European states acted quickly at the end of the 1980s to establish their freedom and adopt new economic structures based on Western models. Although many Europeans rejoiced over the possibility of creating a new, undivided Europe, the ethnic hatreds and tensions that had plagued these nations before World War II reemerged and threatened to divide Europeans once again.

Outside the West, the peoples of Africa and Asia had their own reasons for optimism as World War II came to a close. In the Atlantic Charter, issued after a meeting near the coast of Newfoundland in August 1941, Franklin Roosevelt and Winston Churchill had set forth a joint declaration of their peace aims calling for the self-determination of all peoples and self-government and sovereign rights for all nations that had been deprived of them. Although Churchill later disavowed the assumption that he had meant these conditions to apply to colonial areas, Roosevelt on frequent occasions voiced his own intention to promote the end of colonial domination throughout the world.

In the end, that optimism was at least partly justified. Although some colonial powers were reluctant to divest themselves of their colonies, World War II had severely undermined the stability of the colonial order, and by the end of the 1940s, most colonies in Asia had received their independence. Africa followed a decade or two later. In a few instances—notably in Algeria, Indonesia, and Vietnam—the transition to independence was a violent one, but for the most part, it was realized by peaceful means.

Broadly speaking, the leaders of these newly liberated countries set forth three goals at the outset of independence. They wanted to throw off the shackles of Western economic domination and ensure material prosperity for all of their citizens. They wanted to introduce new political institutions that would enhance the right of self-determination of their peoples. And they wanted to develop a sense of nationhood within the population and establish secure territorial boundaries. It was a measure of their optimism that the governments of most of the newly liberated countries opted to follow a capitalist or a moderately socialist path toward economic development. Only in a few cases—China and Vietnam were the most notable examples—did revolutionary leaders opt for the Communist mode of development.

Regardless of the path they chose, however, most governments in Africa and Asia did not achieve their ambitious economic goals. Virtually all of them remained economically dependent upon the advanced industrial nations or, in the case of those who chose to follow the socialist model of development, were forced to rely on the Soviet Union. Some faced severe problems of urban and rural poverty.

What had happened to tarnish the bright dream of economic affluence? During the late 1950s and early 1960s, one school of thought was dominant among scholars and government officials in the United States. Known as modernization theory, this school took the view that the problems faced by the newly independent countries were a consequence of the difficult transition from a traditional agrarian to a modern industrial society. Modernization theorists were convinced that the countries of Asia, Africa, and Latin America were destined to follow the path of the West toward the creation of modern industrial societies, but would need time as well as substantial amounts of economic and technological assistance to complete the journey. In their view, it was the duty of the United States and other capitalist nations to provide such assistance, while encouraging the leaders of these states to follow the path already adopted by the West. Some countries going through this difficult period were especially vulnerable to Communist-led insurgent movements. In such cases, it was in the interests of the United States and its allies to intervene, with military power if necessary, to hasten the transition and put the country on the path of self-sustaining growth.

Beginning in the 1960s, modernization theory began to come under attack from a new generation of younger scholars, many of whom had reached maturity during the Vietnam War and had growing doubts about the roots of the problem and the efficacy of the modernization approach. In their view, the responsibility for continued economic underdevelopment in the developing world lay not with the countries themselves, but with their continued domination by the ex-colonial powers. In this view, known as dependency theory, the countries of Asia, Africa, and Latin America were the victims of the international marketplace, which charged high prices for the manufactured goods of the West while dooming pre-industrial countries to low prices for their own raw material exports. Efforts by such countries to build up their own industrial sectors and move into the stage of self-sustaining growth were hampered by foreign control—through European- and American-owned corporations—over many of their resources. To end this "neocolonial" relationship, the dependency theory advocates argued, developing societies should reduce their economic ties with the West and practice a policy of economic self-reliance, thereby taking control over their own destinies.

Both of these approaches, of course, were directly linked to the ideological divisions of the Cold War period and suffered from the weaknesses of their political bias. Although modernization theorists were certainly correct in pointing out some of the key factors that were involved in economic development and showing that in some instances traditional attitudes and practices were incompatible with economic change, they were too quick to see the Western developmental model as the only relevant one and ignored the fact that traditional customs and practices were not necessarily always incompatible with nation building. They also too readily identified economic development in the developing world with the interests of the United States and its allies.

By the same token, the advocates of dependency theory alluded correctly to the unfair and often disadvantageous relationship that continued to exist between the ex-colonies and the industrialized nations of the world and the impact that this relationship had on the efforts of developing countries to overcome their economic difficulties. But they often explained away many of the mistakes made by the leaders of developing countries while assigning all of the blame for their plight to the evil and self-serving practices of the industrialized world. At the same time, the dependency theorists' recommendation for a policy of self-reliance was not only naive but sometimes disastrous.

In recent years, the differences between these two schools of thought have declined, as their advocates have attempted to respond to criticism of the perceived weaknesses in their theories. Although the two approaches still have some methodological and ideological differences, there is a growing consensus that there are different roads to development and that the international marketplace can have both beneficial and harmful effects. At the same time, a new school of developmental theory, known as the world systems approach, has attempted to place recent developments within the broad context of world history. According to world systems theory, the global economy that has emerged among previously autonomous states is now beginning to develop serious internal contradictions and may be in the process of transformation.

A second area of concern for the leaders of African and Asian countries after World War II was to create a new political culture responsive to the needs of their citizens. For the most part, they accepted the concept of democracy as the defining theme of that culture. Within a decade, however, democratic systems throughout the developing world were replaced by military dictatorships or one-party governments that redefined the concept of democracy to fit their own preferences. Some Western observers criticized the new leaders for their autocratic tendencies while others attempted to explain that after traditional forms of authority were replaced, it would take time to lay the basis for pluralistic political systems. In the interval, a strong government party under the leadership of a single charismatic individual could mobilize the population to seek common goals. Whatever the case, it was clear that many political leaders in both regions, and Western observers as well, had underestimated the difficulties in building democratic political institutions in developing societies.

The problem of establishing a common national identity has in some ways been the most daunting of all the challenges facing the new nations of Asia and Africa. Many of these new states were a composite of a wide variety of ethnic, religious, and linguistic groups who found it difficult to agree on common symbols of nationalism. Problems of establishing an official language and delineating territorial boundaries left over from the colonial era created difficulties in many countries. In some cases, these problems were exacerbated by political and economic change. The introduction of the concept of democracy sharpened the desire of individual groups to have a separate identity within a larger nation, while economic development often favored some at the expense of others.

The introduction of Western cultural values and customs has also had a destabilizing effect in many areas. Although such ideas are welcomed by some groups, they are firmly resisted by others. Where Western influence has the effect of undermining traditional customs and religious beliefs, it provokes violent hostility and sparks tension and even conflict within individual societies. To some, Western customs and values represent the wave of the future and are welcomed as a sign of progress. To others, they are destructive of indigenous traditions and a barrier to the growth of a genuine national identity based on history and culture.

From the 1950s to the 1970s, the political and economic difficulties experienced by many developing nations in Asia, Africa, and Latin America led to chronic instability in a number of countries and transformed the developing world into a major theater of Cold War confrontation. During the 1980s, however, a number of new factors entered the equation and shifted the focus away from ideological competition. China's shift to a more accommodating policy toward the West removed fears of more wars of national liberation supported by Beijing. At the same time, the Communist victory in Vietnam led not to falling dominoes throughout Southeast Asia but to a bitter war between the two erstwhile Communist allies, Vietnam and China. It was clear that national interests and historic rivalries often took precedence over ideological agreement.

In the meantime, the growing success of the "little tigers" and the poor economic performance of socialist regimes led a number of developing countries to reduce government regulations and adopt a free market approach to economic development. Still, the role of government leadership in hindering or promoting economic growth should not be ignored. The situation in China is an obvious case in point. While Communist policies may have been beneficial in rectifying economic inequities and focusing attention on building up the infrastructure in the 1950s, the policies adopted during the Great Leap Forward and the Cultural Revolution had disastrous economic effects. Since the late 1970s, China has realized massive progress with a combination of centralized party leadership and economic policies emphasizing innovation and the interplay of free market forces. By some measures, China today has the third largest economy in the world.

Similarly, there have been tantalizing signs in recent years of a revival of interest in the democratic model in various parts of Asia, Africa, and Latin America. Free elections have been held recently in South Korea, Taiwan, and the Philippines, while similar developments have taken place in a number of African countries. Nevertheless, it is clear that in many areas, democratic institutions are quite fragile, and experiments in democratic pluralism have failed in a number of areas. Many political leaders in Asia and Africa are convinced that Western traditions of individualism and unbridled freedom of the press can be destabilizing and destructive of other national objectives. A good case in point is China, where official tolerance of free expression led ultimately to the demonstrations in Tiananmen Square and the bloody crackdown that brought them to an end. Many still do not believe that democracy and economic development go hand in hand. During the 1990s, some Asian leaders like Malaysian prime minister Mahathir Mohamad have become openly critical of the Western tendency to place individual freedom over community responsibility and to lecture Asian countries about their record on human rights.

Nevertheless, social and political attitudes are changing rapidly in many Asian countries, as new economic circumstances have led to a more secular worldview, a decline in traditional hierarchical relations, and a more open attitude toward sexual practices. In part, these changes have been a consequence of the influence of Western music, movies, and television. But they are also a product of the growth of an affluent middle class in many societies of Asia and Africa. This middle class is often strongly influenced by Western ways, and its sons and daughters ape the behavior, dress, and lifestyles of their counterparts in Europe and North America. When Reebok sneakers are worn and coveted in Lagos and Nairobi, Bombay and Islamabad, Beijing and Hanoi, it is clear that, for good or ill, the impact of modern Western civilization has been universalized.

Does this mean that the industrial nations of the West have triumphed and have remade the rest of the world in their own image? Some observers, like the U.S. scholar Francis Fukuyama, argue that capitalism and the Western concept of liberal democracy have vanquished all of their rivals and will ultimately be applied universally throughout the globe. In fact, however, it is much too early to reach such conclusions. It is true that virtually the entire world has now been transformed as the result of the Industrial Revolution that began in Western Europe at the end of the eighteenth century. Countries throughout the world today are not only linked to the economic marketplace put in place by the Western industrialized nations, but are also adopting political and social institutions and values originally introduced from Europe or the United States.

But such institutions have been severely modified to meet local conditions and traditions, and in East Asia today, some governments are effectively using such indige-nous traditions as community spirit, the propensity to save, and government interventionism not only to imitate, but to surpass the performance of Western countries. It is no empty phrase to speak of the coming era as the Pacific Century, proving that capitalism is by no means a Western monopoly.

It should also be kept in mind that the global economy today is highly dependent upon the continued economic prosperity of the industrialized countries. A global economic turndown, or even the persistence of the economic stagnation of the early 1990s, could put a serious dent in the pace of economic development in many parts of the world. That in turn could lead to serious political instability and a crisis in the global economy.

Whatever happens to the current economic situation, it has clearly taken on a truly global character. In fact, today we live not only in a world economy, but in a world society, where an economic downturn in the United States can create stagnant conditions in Europe and Asia, where a revolution in Iran can cause a rise in the price of oil in the United States and a change in social behavior in Malaysia and Indonesia, and where the collapse of an empire in Russia can send shockwaves as far as Hanoi and Havana, Cuba.

One consequence of this process of interdependence is a growing recognition of the common danger posed by environmental pollution. There is nothing new about human beings causing damage to their natural surroundings. It may first have occurred when Neolithic peoples began to practice slash-and-burn agriculture or when excessive hunting thinned out the herds of bison and caribou in the New World. Today, however, environmental problems have taken on a global character—the effects of global warming and the destruction of the ozone layer will not be limited to a single region. Some people in the West point to overpopulation in the developing countries and the high rate of destruction of the rain forest in developing areas such as Brazil and Malaysia. Observers from Asia or Africa are likely to retort that most of the damage is done by industrial pollution and that the advanced Western countries on a per capita basis use up much more than their share of world resources.

The fact that environmental damage is a common concern suggests the growing need for cooperation and coordination of efforts on a global scale. Such cooperation, however, has often been hindered by political, ethnic, and religious disputes. India, Pakistan, and Bangladesh have squabbled over the use of the waters of the Ganges and Indus Rivers, as have Israel and its neighbors over the scarce water resources of the Middle East. Pollution of the Rhine River by factories along its banks provokes angry disputes among European nations, while the United States and Canada have argued about the effects of acid rain on Canadian forests.

The collapse of the Soviet Union and its satellite system between 1989 and 1991 seemed to provide an enormous boost to the potential for international cooperation on global issues and led to optimistic predictions that the end of the Cold War would bring about what Francis Fukuyama called the "end of history," when political conflicts would be replaced by peaceful economic competition. So far, however, the collapse of the Soviet empire has had almost the opposite effect, as the disintegration of the Soviet Union has led to the emergence of several squabbling new nations and a general atmosphere of conflict and tension throughout much of Eastern Europe. The rise of nationalist sentiment among various ethnic and religious groups in Eastern Europe is, of course, a direct consequence of the collapse of a system that in its own way resembled the transnational empires of the Romanovs, the Habsburgs, and the Ottomans. But the phenomenon is worldwide and growing in importance, and can be seen as a natural consequence of the rising thirst for group identity in a vast and rapidly changing world. Shared culture is our defense against the impersonal world around us.

Even as the world becomes more global in culture and interdependent in its mutual relations, centrifugal forces are at work attempting to redefine the political, cultural, and ethnic ways in which it is divided. Such efforts are often disruptive and can sometimes work against measures to enhance our human destiny. But they also represent an integral part of human character and human history and cannot be suppressed in the relentless drive to create a world society. In a recent book entitled *The Clash of Civilizations and the Remaking of the World Order*, the political scientist Samuel P. Huntington has suggested that the post–Cold War era, far from marking the "end of history" and the triumph of the Western idea, will be characterized by increased global fragmentation and a "clash of civilizations" based on ethnic, cultural, or religious distinctions. According to Huntington, cultural identity has replaced shared ideology as the dominant force in world affairs. As a result, he argues, the coming decades may see an emerging world dominated by disputing cultural blocs in East Asia, Western Europe and the United States, Eurasia, and the Middle East, with the societies in each region coalescing around common cultural features against perceived threats from rival forces elsewhere around the globe. The dream of a universal order dominated by Western values, he concludes, is a fantasy.

In the confusing conditions at the end of the twentieth century, Huntington's thesis may serve as a corrective to the tendency of many observers in Europe and the United States to see Western civilization as the zenith and final resting place of human achievement. But in dividing the world into competing cultural blocs, he has seriously underestimated the centrifugal forces that exist within each region, as well as the transformative effect of the Industrial Revolution and the emerging global informational network. There are already encouraging signs that as the common dangers posed by environmental damage, overpopulation, and scarcity of resources become even more apparent, societies around the world will find ample reason to turn their attention from cultural differences to the demands of global interdependence. As the world faces a new century, its greatest challenge may be to reconcile the drive for individual and group identity with the common needs of the human community.

Index

Document Credits

CHAPTER 26

CHAPTER 27

CHAPTER 28

Map Credits

The authors wish to acknowledge their use of the following books as reference in preparing the maps listed here:

Map 14.2 Geoffrey Barraclough, ed., *Times Atlas of World History*, (Maplewood, N. J.: Hammond, Inc. 1978), p. 160.

Map 16.3 Geoffrey Barraclough, ed., *Times Atlas of World History*, (Maplewood, N. J.: Hammond, Inc. 1978), p. 173.

Map 17.1 Jonathan Spence, *The Search for Modern China*, (New York: W. W. Norton, 1990), p. 19.

Map 17.2 Conrad Schirokauer, *A Brief History of Chinese and Japanese Civilizations, 2d ed.*, (San Diego: Harcourt Brace Jovanovich, 1989), p. 330.

Map 17.3 John K. Fairbank, Edwin O. Reischauer, and Albert M. Craig, *East Asia: Tradition and Tranformation*, (Boston: Houghton Mifflin, 1973), pp. 402–403.

Map 18.1 *Atlas of World History*, (New York: Harper & Row Publishers, 1987), p. 187.

Map 22.4 Geoffrey Barraclough, ed., *Times Atlas of World History*, (Maplewood, N. J.: Hammond, Inc. 1978), p. 235.

Map 23.1 John K. Fairbank, Edwin O. Reischauer, and Albert M. Craig, *East Asia: Tradition and Tranformation*, (Boston: Houghton Mifflin, 1973), pp. 451.

Map 23.4 Geoffrey Barraclough, ed., *Times Atlas of World History*, (Maplewood, N. J.: Hammond, Inc. 1978), p. 243.

Photo Credits

CHAPTER 14

484 North Wind Picture Archives **487** Jomard, "Les Monuments de la Geographie" Paris, 1862, Photo courtesy of the New York Public Library **488** Courtesy of William J. Duiker **489** North Wind Picture Archives **491** North Wind Picture Archives **493** Courtesy of William J. Duiker **496** Courtesy of William J. Duiker **501** Historical Society of Pennsylvania **506** Courtesy of William J. Duiker **510** Courtesy of William J. Duiker **517** Courtesy of William J. Duiker **519** Courtesy of William J. Duiker

CHAPTER 15

530 The National Galleries of Scotland, by permission of Earl of Rosebery **533** Staatliche Museen Preussischer Kulturbesitz, Kupferstichkabinett, Berlin (West), Photo: Jorg P. Anders **536** Alte Pinakothek, Munich **537** Bibliotheque Publique et Universitaire, Geneva **543** Scala/Art Resource, NY **547** Kunsthistorisches Museum, Vienna **552** Hyacinthe Rigaud, Louise XIV, Musée du Louvre, © Photo R.M.N. **553** Giraudon/Art Resource, NY **557** Russian School, *Czar Peter the Great*, Rijksmuseum, Amsterdam **558** The National Galleries of Scotland, by permission of Earl of Rosebery **562** *Laocoon*, El Greco, National Gallery of Art, Washington, Samuel H. Kress Collection **563** Peter Paul Rubens, *The Landing of Marie de Medicis at Marseilles*, Musée du Louvre, © Photo R.M.N. **564** Nicholas Poussin, *Landscape with the Burial of a Phocian* , Musée du Louvre, © Photo R.M.N.

CHAPTER 16

570 Courtesy of the Board of Trustees of the Victoria and Albert Museum **575** MS Fr.9087, f.207, Bibliotheque Nationale, Paris; photo © Sonia Halliday Photographs **577** Courtesy of the Topkapi Sarayi Musezi, Istanbul **580** Giraudon/Art Resource, NY **582** Don Smetzer/Tony Stone Images **587** George Holton/Photo Researchers, Inc. **589** Reza-ye Abbasi, *Two Lovers*, 1630, The Metropolitan Museum of Art, Francis M. Weld Fund 1950(50.164) **591** Courtesy of the Board of Trustees of the Victoria and Albert Museum **597** SEF/Art Resource, NY **599** Tony Stone Images **601** Werner Forman/ Art Resource, NY

CHAPTER 17

606 Collection Musée Guimet, Paris, Photo © Michael Holford, London **609** Werner Forman/Art Resource, NY **610** Courtesy of Claire L. Duiker **616** National Palace Museum, Taipei, Taiwan, Republic of China **619** © British Museum **626** Dean Conger/National Geographic Image Collection **627** Werner Forman/Art Resource, NY Kuroda Nagamasa, Kuroda Collection, Japan **630** Collection Musée Guimet, Paris, Photo © Michael Holford, London **633** Courtesy of William J. Duiker **638** Torii Kiyotada, Japanese, act. c.1720–1750, *Naka-no-cho Street of the Yoshiwara*, wood block print, c. 1740, Clarence Buckingham Collection, 1939.2152, Photograph © 1993, The Art Institute of Chicago **642** Courtesy of William J. Duiker

CHAPTER 18

646 Giraudon/Art Resource, NY **649, *left*** Courtesy of the Lilly Library, Indiana University, Bloomington, Indiana **649, *right*** Courtesy of the Lilly Library, Indiana University, Bloomington, Indiana **651** Bibliotheca Nazionale Centrale, Firenze **656** Dumesnil, *Queen Christina of Sweden with Descartes*, Musée du Louvre, © Photo R.M.N. **660** Giraudon/Art Resource, NY **662** Mary Evans Picture Library **669** Giraudon/Art Resource, NY **670** Antoine Watteau, *The Pilgrimage to Cythera*, Musée du Louvre, © Photo R.M.N. **671** Courtesy of James R. Spencer **675** Nathaniel Hone, *John Wesley*, ca. 1766, by Courtesy of the National Portrait Gallery, London

CHAPTER 19

680 Benjamin West, *The Death of General Wolfe*, Transfer from the Canadian War Memorial, 1921, Gift of the second Duke of Westminster **684** Joseph Vernet, *Port of Dieppe*, Depot du Louvre au Musée de la Marine, © Photo R.M.N. **686** Giovanni Michele Graneri, *Market in Piazza San Carlo*, 1752, Museo Civico di Torino **690** Benjamin West, *The Death of General Wolfe*, Transfer from the Canadian War Memorial, 1921, Gift of the second Duke of Westminster **696** The Granger Collection, NY **698** John Trumbull, *The Declaration of Independence, 4 July 1776*, Yale University Art Gallery, Trumbull Collection **704** Scala/Art Resource, NY **707** Anonymous, *Fall of the Bastille*, (Detail) Musée National des Chateau de Versailles, © Photo R.M.N. **711** Giraudon/Art Resource, NY **713** Giraudon/Art Resource, NY **716** Louis David, *Sacre de l'empereur* (detail), Musée du Louvre, © Photo R.M.N.

CHAPTER 20

722 Lecomte, *Battle in the rue de Rohan*, 1830, Giraudon/Art Resource, NY **725** Mansell Collection, London **731** © Ann Ronan at Image Se-

CHAPTER 21

CHAPTER 22

CHAPTER 23

CHAPTER 24

CHAPTER 25

CHAPTER 26

CHAPTER 27

CHAPTER 28

CHAPTER 29

CHAPTER 30

Magnum Photos **1122** Courtesy of William J. Duiker **1125** © M. Courtney-Clarke **1129** UPI/Corbis-Bettmann **1134** Courtesy of William J. Duiker **1140** Courtesy of William J. Duiker **1141** Courtesy of William J. Duiker **1142** UPI/Corbis-Bettmann

CHAPTER 31

1148 Courtesy of William J. Duiker **1154** UPI/Corbis-Bettmann **1160** Courtesy of William J. Duiker **1161** Courtesy of William J. Duiker **1162** Courtesy of William J. Duiker **1168** Courtesy of William J. Duiker **1174** AP/Wide World Photos **1175** Courtesy of

William J. Duiker **1176** © John Elk/Stock Boston **1177** Courtesy of William J. Duiker **1181** Courtesy of Charles and Shirley Cross

CHAPTER 32

1186 Courtesy of William J. Duiker **1187** UPI/Corbis-Bettmann **1194** Reuters/Susumu Takahashi/Archive Photos **1199** Courtesy of William J. Duiker **1200** Courtesy of William J. Duiker **1203** Courtesy of William J. Duiker **1206** Courtesy of William J. Duiker **1208** Courtesy of William J. Duiker **1209** Courtesy of William J. Duiker **1211** Courtesy of William J. Duiker **1212** Courtesy of William J. Duiker